The Virgin BOOKS
Guide to British Universities 2012

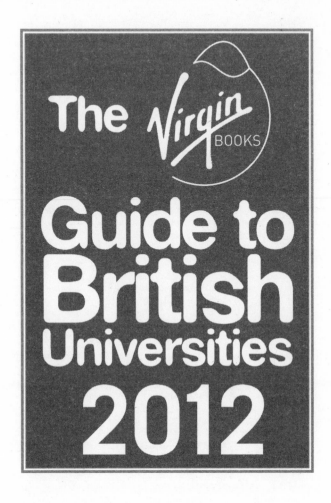

The Virgin BOOKS
Guide to British Universities 2012

Piers Dudgeon

2 4 6 8 10 9 7 5 3 1

Published in 2011 by Virgin Books, an imprint of Ebury Publishing
A Random House Group Company

Copyright © Piers Dudgeon 2011

Piers Dudgeon has asserted his right under the Copyright, Designs
and Patents Act 1988 to be identified as the author of this work

The Random House Group Limited Reg. No. 954009

Addresses for companies within the Random House Group can be found at
www.randomhouse.co.uk

A CIP catalogue record for this book is available from the British Library

The Random House Group Limited supports The Forest Stewardship Council [FSC], the leading
international forest certification organisation. All our titles that are printed on Greenpeace-approved FSC-
certified paper carry the FSC logo. Our paper procurement policy can be found at
www.randomhouse.co.uk/environment

Use has been made of first-degree qualifiers entering employment (2008/9).
Copyright © Higher Education Statistics Agency Limited, 2010.
Reproduced by permission of the Higher Education Statistics Agency Limited.

Design & Technical Consultant
Jonathan Horner, www.web-first.co.uk

Printed and bound in Great Britain by
CPI Mackays, Chatham, Kent, ME5 8TD

ISBN 9780 7535 40039

REVIEWS

'An exhaustive tome that complements the hard sell of individual prospectuses with information they won't provide. The research base is truly impressive' *Student World*

'Glistening with success – a worthy contender for the best all-purpose buy for the aspiring undergraduate' *Yorkshire Post*

'This is a very impressive piece of work... a serious and honest picture of student life at each major higher education establishment in the UK... VAG looks set to take over as the nation's favourite antidote to the occasional excesses of the higher education marketing professionals' *Careers Adviser*

'The guide offers racy but reliable profiles that focus as much on the way of life as academic considerations' *Daily Telegraph*

'The value of this book lies in the info-crammed pages on universities, starting with Aberdeen and ending with York' *The London Evening Standard*

'The book offers an unofficial prospectus for students - written by students!' *Daily Mirror*

'It gives an entertaining, fact-filled, warts-and-all account of university life...well-researched information' *Mail on Sunday*

'The book gives vital information' *Bristol Evening Post*

'The "bible" of student life... Packed full of facts and information' *Eastern Daily Press*

'Just the thing to make a truly informed choice' *Dundee Sunday Post*

WHAT STUDENTS (AND PARENTS) SAY

'This is by far the best guide to what it is like to actually live at university and the practicalities of studying there which goes beyond league tables'

'Very helpful guide...different to all the others. It puts emphasis on what the students themselves think about the universities rather than just looking at league tables. This book was really useful for me as a prospective university student'

'What really distinguishes it from other guides is its varied sources of information, including from many of the students themselves. Obviously being independent, it is valuably impartial and unlike the majority of guides it does not dwell on league tables and the grandeur of Oxbridge for too long'

'*The Virgin Guide* was recommended to me by a friend whose daughter had used it to great effect the previous year. It was the best present I could have bought for my daughter who was in a real muddle about which universities to apply for and what course to go for. This guide stands out for its no-nonsense, honest and well-researched information. I really liked the way it was laid out so you could dip in and dip out and didn't feel swamped by it. The opening chapter on how to write the personal statement was practical too. My daughter liked the "what's it really like" views of current students as it made the whole overwhelming process seem a lot more human and manageable. Excellent'

'This is the most user friendly, relevant and truthful guide to university applications as far as I am concerned. I have three sons, one through uni, one at uni and the other coming up to applications time and all have said how valuable and accurate the book was'

'This is what all soon-to-be-students really want to know'

'A "must have" for all potential Uni students (and their parents). Written in a clear and entertaining style that will not put off teenagers'

CONTENTS

UK UNIVERSITIES

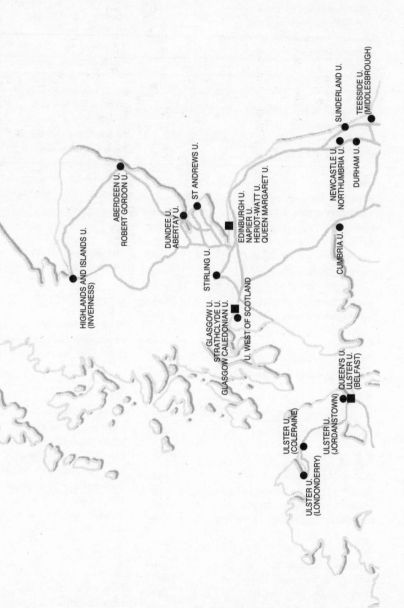

HIGHLANDS AND ISLANDS U.
(INVERNESS)

ABERDEEN U.
ROBERT GORDON U.

DUNDEE U.
ABERTAY U.

ST ANDREWS U.

STIRLING U.

GLASGOW U.
STRATHCLYDE U.
GLASGOW CALEDONIAN U.

U. WEST OF SCOTLAND

EDINBURGH U.
NAPIER U.
HERIOT-WATT U.
QUEEN MARGARET U.

SUNDERLAND U.

TEESSIDE U.
(MIDDLESBROUGH)

NEWCASTLE U.
NORTHUMBRIA U.

DURHAM U.

CUMBRIA U.

QUEEN'S U.
ULSTER U.
(BELFAST)

ULSTER U.
(COLERAINE)

ULSTER U.
(JORDANSTOWN)

ULSTER U.
(LONDONDERRY)

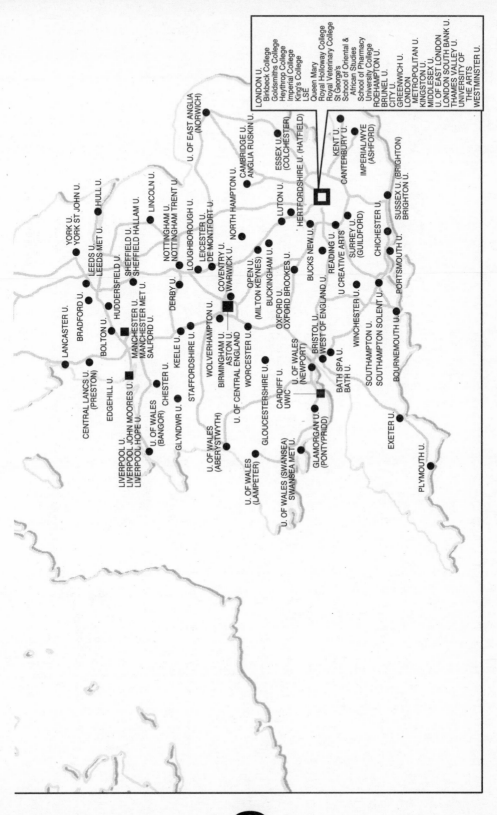

LONDON U.
Birkbeck College
Goldsmiths College
Heythrop College
Imperial College
King's College
LSE
Queen Mary
Royal Holloway College
Royal Veterinary College
St George's
School of Oriental &
    African Studies
School of Pharmacy
University College
ROEHAMPTON U.
BRUNEL U.
CITY U.
GREENWICH U.
LONDON
METROPOLITAN U.
KINGSTON U.
MIDDLESEX U.
U. OF EAST LONDON
LONDON SOUTH BANK U.
THAMES VALLEY U.
UNIVERSITY OF
    THE ARTS
WESTMINSTER U.

INTRODUCTION

CHOOSING A UNIVERSITY

Going to University is an experience for which there simply is no substitute. It is an opportunity (if you choose wisely) to travel far and wide intellectually, emotionally and socially, learning much about the world and even more about yourself. It is a chance to meet people unlike any that you will have met in your own little world of school and home, people who will stretch you and challenge your views, a process that will enable you to grow to a position of real autonomy and independence.

Unfortunately, 'choosing wisely' isn't as simple a matter as at first it may seem. The university marketing machines, well oiled and sometimes a bit slippery, make it harder than it needs to be. Then there is the sheer folly to which applicants are prone.

For example, when Prince William went up to St Andrews in 2002, there was a 45% increase in applications, boosted mainly by girls who fancied their chances as Queen (including of course Kate Middleton). Some of them may have read in the *Virgin Guide* the little known statistic that more romances develop at St Andrews into marriage than at any other university. The latest evidence that it is true is before our eyes even as the 2012 edition of the *Guide* is published.

Arguably, chasing a Prince is only a folly if you lose. There are other, more common and mundane follies, like going to a particular university 'because your friends are'. I don't know how many pupils there are at your school, but the university you will be going to could be more than thirty times the size of it. I defy you to imagine how big that is. It is unusual for school friends still to be best buddies after the first year, even after the first term. The university situation simply does not support so parochial an approach to life.

Some parents fear their children will choose a university on the basis of where the liveliest social scene is. Years ago, when we first published the *Guide*, students in their thousands opted for Manchester because of the **Hacienda** club, or went to Liverpool on account of the legendary *Cream @* **Nation**. We were dubbed 'the Alternative Guide' because we told them where the best student scene was. Elegant, Establishment organisations jumped on the bandwagon. In 1999, believe it or not, the Adam Smith Institute actually polled students as to which university was best for booze, drugs and sex, right down to the number of times a student might be expected to indulge in any of these in a day. Researchers discovered what every student knows, that you have to head North to have the best time. I remember announcing the results of this survey to the sixth form of a public school on the East coast of Yorkshire at 9.30 one Monday morning. The headmaster, who was sat in the front row, went whiter and whiter as the seconds ticked by.

So greatly have times changed that few today, saddled with the spectre of £20k+ student debt, would consider choosing a university on the basis that it is the best place to get laid. Yet, even given the spectre of such a debt, which becomes yours on graduation, many will cede their right to choose to their parents. This may be the most possessive generation of parents there has ever been. Universities are tired of seeing them, often instead of their children, on Open Day, tired of fielding calls from them, as if they don't know that their child is one of 30,000.

UCAS is partly to blame. In 2008 UCAS allowed students to appoint another adult to act as their 'agent', and inevitably parents took over. It is the inability of parents to let go, to allow children their independence that will inhibit their success in the end. It starts with choosing a university and goes further. I know a mother who has her children send their essays home from university for re-writing and cannot see how this undermines their self-esteem.

If you choose a university because there is a Prince in view, or because your friends are going there, or your parents rate it, or indeed because it's less than 100 miles away from home, or principally for any second or third-tier reason, you may of course be lucky. But you will increase your chances of success and happiness if you begin by making the choice your own and grasping the first principle of application, which is that there is no overall best university, there is no second best, or third, or fourth best university, but there may be one or two universities that would be very good for your present and future happiness.

Realising this suggests a different starting point altogethr, a bit of self-analysis.

> *The first principle of choosing a university is to take on board that there is no overall best university, but there may be a very good one for you.*

1. **What subject do you yourself want to study?**

Not, what subject do your parents want you to study, but what do *you* want. Says Misham Bhana at Edinburgh: 'Don't do Medicine unless you're sure you definitely want to be a doctor. It sounds obvious, but there's a lot of clinical work and if you don't enjoy talking to patients you'll probably hate it.' The essence of Medicine is not being good at A level chemistry, for which as a GP you will have little use, or wanting the security of £100k+ on the NHS. It is that you are that rare altruistic sort of person who really cares.

> *You would be amazed how many unhappy students are doing courses because their friends are, or their parents wanted them to.*

Aneesa Patel, Aberdeen: 'Make sure your subject is the one you want to do. You would be amazed how many unhappy students are doing courses because their friends are, or their parents wanted them to.'

2. **What are your predicted grades?** Of the universities that offer a degree in your chosen subject, which ones will even look at you? We heard the other day from a head of sixthform that in the current round, universities are for the first time making pupils offers that exceed their A level predictions, and that there is a general trend upwards in the level required in conditional offers - several A* offers, more 4 grade offers, and a typical standard of AAA rather than AAB/ABB virtually across the board; pupils predicted less than BBB are unlikely to be centre picture. Many offers have gone up mid-cycle, so that even Brian Heap's meticulous and essential *University Degree Course Offers*, cannot be expected to keep up with them. It is as well, therefore, to rely for points requirements on UCAS and the university web sites.

With a chosen subject and a collection of universities that offer it within your band of predicted grades, you should by now have a

> *In the current round, universities are for the first time making pupils offers that exceed their A level predictions, and there is a general trend upwards in the level required.*

dozen possibilities. The next question is the most important of all.

3. **Which course to study and why?** I cannot over-state how significant this question is. There is a subtle and vital difference between a subject and a course. A course is how a particular department of a particular university delivers your chosen subject. One course in history may concentrate on imparting research skills rather than history itself. One degree in animation may be more artistic than scientific than another. You may be all pumped up that your predicted grades will be sufficient to get you into Cambridge to read Music, and as yet not know that the music degree at Cambridge may be anything but what you want, being cerebral and not performance orientated, because Cambridge takes it for granted that students are accomplished performers before they arrive.

Go to www.ucas.com/students/coursesearch. Enter the subject of your choice and one by one look at the courses each of the universities you have listed are offering. Make a list of the interesting-looking ones. Then go to the web site of the appropriate department of each university and read a detailed exposition of them. University web sites may be Googled. Many are in the form www.[universityname].ac.uk.

Ask yourself how the course deals with your subject? Is it actually of interest to you?

The question may then arise as to whether you should be considering a joint or combined course rather than a single subject degree? What is the difference between a joint or combined course? Where lies the benefit of either?

A cross-faculty joint or combined degree may have distinct advantages. Looking at a subject from a different point of view - a science subject from a humanities point of view, for example - can be very effective. It may raise issues, for example ethical issues in this case, that otherwise would not have been dealt with on a purely scientific basis. Joint courses can enrich your study in all sorts of ways. At Queen Mary's College, London, you can study History alone, or you can conjoin it with Comparative Literature or German Literature, or politics, an opportunity to make connections and dig far deeper into the whole culture of an era. These kind of courses are a rich cultural resource, well suited to a career in publishing or investment banking, where breadth of knowledge pays dividends.

Take another seriously good university, the University of London's School of Oriental &

African Studies (known as SOAS), which offers students an opportunity unique in this country to study law and social sciences, languages and cultures, arts and humanities focused exclusively on Asia and the Middle East, areas at the centre of current world affairs. In the legendary bar at SOAS you are more likely to meet an intellectual adventurer just back from three months in the jungles of South East Asia than Tracey from Essex wondering whether her BA in Media Studies will get her an internship at Sky. It is an incredible place and an amazing curriculum. Employers are attracted by the unique combination of skills, knowledge and cultural experience acquired from the SOAS programmes. Many build careers as human rights lawyers, politicians, journalists, diplomats and ambassadors, or take jobs in the civil service, business and finance, or in arts and cultural institutions. How might the courses you are considering affect your future?

We were the first Guide to go into the minutiae of real graduate jobs and no one dives deeper into this pool than we do today. But look now at the web site of the Institute, Society or professional Association related to the subject of the courses you are considering. What does the Institute of Psychology say about studying psychology at this university rather than that one? Many universities offer courses in Forensic Science, but which ones are actually accredited by the Forensic Science Society? Go to www.forensic-science-society.org.uk and see. The answer is Lincoln, Portsmouth, Strathclyde, Bristol West of England, Wolverhampton, Robert Gordon, Glamorgan, Kent, Teesside, Nottingham Trent, Huddersfield, Derby, De Montfort, Abertay.

And what about Law? Did you know that Northumbria is the only university in the country to offer would-be solicitors and barristers exemption from the Legal Practice Course in its 4-year MLaw? Contact www.lawsociety.co.uk and see. If you can't find what you want on site, email them. You never know where that email may lead.

You are by now on the hunt, beginning to enjoy the whole process, and there are many other layers to peel away. What extra-curricular aspects of the universities you are considering recommend the course you might study with them over others? Sometimes what goes on outside the lecture theatre turns out to be just as relevant to a student's future as what goes on in it.

This was certainly true for Nick Coupe, a Londoner who chose to read English and Theatre at Leeds over his other choices because of the extra-curricular theatre scene there, which is vibrant. In his first year Nick was given the money by the Student Union at Leeds to put on *The Changeling* by Thomas Middleton, playing to 300 people over the inside of a week.

'I'm involved with Theatre Groupd, which is a Student Union society and they take proposals from students of all years, first to third years can propose to direct a play and then they give you funding. and the venue to put it on and the support that you need.

'For me the Leeds Union is massive, seriously into everything it does - really high quality student paper, student radio, student TV and you can get involved really easily. One of my friends who has only been here the same time as me is already President of LSTV.'

Nick is serious about what he wants to do. Since Year 1 he has been working in the holidays for a theatrical agent in London. He approached the agent off his own bat. He knows it's no good bleating about not getting a job as a graduate. He knows he will get a job. He doesn't worry about things like that, because he is passionate about what he is doing.

Sometimes what goes on beyond the lecture theatre turns out to be more relevant to your future than what goes on in it.

Getting an internship - Nick's was paid, but few are - is important. Some accountancy companies are now no longer even considering applications from graduates who have not worked for them as interns, as work experience in the holidays or as part of their course.

Quality of the extra-curricular scene is what made for true value for Nick Coupe. It was why he chose Leeds. Last year he represented the University at the finals of the Student Drama Festival in Scarborough. He is on his way.

Now go further; ask yourself how well are the courses actually *taught* at the universities you are considering? We at the *Guide* visit universities and look at the latest assessments and inspection reports of the courses that are open to you. We also ask students actually there how it is. How cutting edge is the research in the department you fancy? You want to go somewhere where the lecturers are writing the latest books on your subject, somewhere with a worldwide reputation. *The Virgin Guide* will tell you.

Again, what level of interest in your studies will you find from these research crazed experts?

Oxford is among the best for research reputation but also one of the few universities in the world that bases its teaching on the tutorial system. Tutorials are very small group teaching, maybe one, two, or three students plus a tutor. They will take place at least once a week for an hour in each subject studied, an incredible amount of individual attention and teaching from international experts in your chosen field.

What's it like elsewhere? The *Guide* looks at what students say about the helpfulness and interest lecturers show and what size tutorial groups you can expect. At Leeds the scene varies terrifically from dept to dept. In English the teaching staff will know you by name, say hello to you if you see them out and about. You can just pop into someone's office and have an informal chat about essays, rather than having to make an appointment and know exactly what you want to say and have ten minutes. In History you may barely know your lecturers' names.

To see how satisfied students are overall with the course you are considering, go to www.unistats.com/ which gives you a student rating of the teaching of each subject at each university, a poll undertaken by the Higher Education Funding Council on behalf of the Government. It also shows you how many graduates of the department you will be in actually found real graduate jobs after six months of leaving.

Thus far, your researches should have delivered say 5 to 7 universities that offer courses that you are happy with and are within your band of points. Now, widen your perspective to the university itself.

4. **How do the universities themselves actually fit with what you want?** You are going to whittle your list down further by considering secondary and tertiary level criteria. How significant these criteria actually are will depend on your own needs, taste and style. It may be that you rank one or more of them as primary criteria, that's up to you.

Let's start by looking at the actual place. Go to the Map on page 8 of the *Guide* and find out where your universities are. Are you certain that you know where you will actually be based? Depending on the particular course you choose, you may read for a Durham University degree in Psychology in Durham city or many miles to the south at

Durham's Stockton-on-Tees campus, which is an entirely different experience. You may be planning to read Drama at Hull University, a good idea, but will you be at the Scarborough or the Hull campus? Finally, use the 'Getting There' sections of the entries in the Guide: time and distance from home by rail and road may be an issue. How significant is that information to you?

Consider the location, the setting and the architecture. Do you want a campus or a civic university, one like Nottingham that is all together on a green-field site on the edge of town or one that inhabits the town, with all the facilities and amenities of the town, like Bristol? Are you happiest with classical or modern architecture, concrete Essex or the feel of the Bailey colleges in Durham? Do you want a college-based system like Durham, Lancaster and Oxbridge?

> *Follow the Virgin Guide and construct your own 'this is what I want' pathway.*

Now is the time to go to as many Open Days as you can. Ask questions, especially of students that will be part of Open Day. Open day dates are published on web sites. We have included in the *Guide* as many as were fixed at time of going to press. Look at the *Guide* too for info on accommodation, and at the university web sites for how the halls look.

See, too, how good your choices are for sport, if that is of importance to you: read our reviews and go to www.bucs.org.uk, the site of British University and College Sport. How do the universities you are considering perform at inter-university arts and media festivals and in other extra-curricular areas. What is the nightlife like on campus and in the city?

By now and after a series of Open Day attendances you will have settled on your ultimate UCAS-Top 5, and have a sense of a 'first choice' and an 'acceptable fallback' - your UCAS-Two, according to your own set of priorities.

But then you are really only at the starting line. For like it or not, the better universities are highly selective. They may yet not let you in. There is also the question of discrimination on account of social and economic factors, your postcode, your class, your school (whether State or Independent). There is no point in bothering about what is beyond your control, but this highlights the fact that universities *are* selective and you will need to do everything in your power to appeal to the ones you would be happy to attend, your UCAS 5.

WHAT UNIVERSITIES WANT

The Personal Statement

That the top universities do discriminate, that they are selective, is clear. They discriminate by means of points requirements, by assessment of an individual's UCAS personal statement, by an applicant's school references and by means of interview. For the last decade, Government has seemed to find discrimination unacceptable, and has insisted on all universities 'widening participation', giving each university a benchmark, more or less a quota, of how many candidates from social classes 4 to 7 they should take.

Universities have responded by setting up expensive and time-consuming Access initiatives, and their success at roping in applicants from all but the lowest socio-economic level has been closely monitored. We include the results of this monitoring along with what the draw is from state and public schools under 'Equality of Opportunity' in the 'University/ Student Profile' box at the start of each university entry, because it gives an idea of the student mix.

> *Interview is not the norm; personal statements are in place of the interview, which once upon a time everyone had to undertake.*
> *But what do universities want?*

The percentage of 'social class 4-7 intake' is what marks a university's success (or lack of it) in the Government's plans for widening participation. Social classes 4 to 7 are the lowest other than 'long-term unemployed' or 'never worked', though why their children don't get a look in is not clear.

Classes 4 to 7 are marked down officially as 'small employers and own account workers', 'lower supervisory and technical occupations', 'semi-routine occupations', and 'routine occupations'. It is the children of these classes that the Government want to protect from discrimination by our top universities.

Today, a great deal of the PR for universities in the second and third divisions is that they attract high percentages of these classes, while the first division universities don't. Meanwhile the first division universities do their damnedest to sift through and pick from the brave souls in classes 4 to 7 who turn up at their Access events, so that they won't be penalised financially by the Government for failing to meet their quotas.

The emphasis of offers to such applicants naturally shifts from grades or points, because classes 4 to 7 don't have a lot of them. Sadly, the Government fails to address the reason for this, which is that they have been educated at schools which the Government itself has failed to do anything with.

The emphasis in the selective process has been to shift to something else, therefore, and it is interesting that very often this 'something else' is similar to what the top universities use to decide who to take of their most academically minded applicants, those with straight A*s.

Implicit, is the notion that there is something other than academic ability which can be harnessed and turned to good effect both in the world of academia (in higher education exams in particular) and in life.

So, we thought that this year that we would ask universities what that something is, 'What do you look for in applicants beyond grades, tests and references?' so that you can think about it and use it to construct your all-important personal statement.

I have heard parents and teachers question that the personal statement is all-important. In the *Times*, Christopher Lote, admissions tutor to the Faculty of Medicine at the University of Birmingham, was quoted as saying that the personal statement 'is not worth the paper it is written on and disadvantages the honest applicant... If personal statements were personal, we'd have no problems. But they are not. We have no idea who writes them.'

The faculty apparently uses students' personal statements to quiz students in interview, but not to select them for interview in the first place. On the other hand, Jake Duffin, undergraduate admissions officer for Law at Queen Mary, University of London, has said that even a student whose grades are below the entry requirements may be offered a place if they have submitted a 'very interesting or well-written statement'.

I began my research by asking universities ahead of a talk I was giving to sixth-form careers advisers, 'What value does the personal statement hold for your admissions tutors?'

The University of Warwick's director of

admissions said that tutors 'read every single personal statement and they play an important role in the decisions we make'.

Said LSE: 'The competition to get in to LSE is fierce. Each year, the School receives 19,000 undergraduate applications for 1,200 places. Therefore, predicted or actual grades do not guarantee admission. When reviewing the applications, LSE places strong emphasis on the personal statement. The personal statement must be well written, containing no spelling or grammatical mistakes, and focus 75 per cent of the content on the subject area of study.'

Exeter: 'We consider your achieved academic performance in level 2 and 3 qualifications (GCSEs, A and AS Levels, and their equivalents), your predicted performance in future examinations, your personal statement, your reference, any additional statement supplied by your school or college regarding any special personal or extenuating circumstances which may impact, or have impacted on your studies. Alongside these factors, we may also take into account the educational context in which your academic achievements have been gained.'

The Head of Recruitment, International and Outreach Office at the University of East Anglia, wasted no time in responding: 'I realise your talk is not solely about personal statements but generally this is the section where the student gets to sell themselves.' I was then offered UEA's power point presentation, which 'is designed to get them thinking about what to write and what to include.'

In our opinion it would be a foolish applicant who failed to take the UCAS personal statement seriously. Interview is not the norm; personal statements are in place of the interview which once upon a time everyone had to undertake. So, what do universities want?

Oxford said: '1. Evidence that you are able to think independently; 2. Self-motivation and enthusiasm for your subject; 3. Willingness to engage with new ideas, beyond the scope of your school or college syllabus, and that you are committed to your subject(s).'

Goldsmiths: '1. Evidence of an understanding of the nature of academic study including the demands for independent research, changing patterns of thinking, meeting new experiences; 2. An ability to work and communicate effectively in groups; 3. Also to work alone, demonstrating self motivation and organization; 4. An ability to communicate effectively in written and oral form. 5. Evidence of commitment to four years of full-time study within the field.'

Nottingham: '1. Engagement and understanding of the subject area. 2. Relevant work experience and/or independent reading outside of the school curriculum. 3. Awareness of the qualities and skills required to undertake a degree.'

Royal Holloway was meticulous in its response: 'As a general guide, your personal statement should include: What interests you in your chosen subject area? If you've studied the subject before, was there are a particular area that grabbed your interest? If you've not studied the subject before, what is it that has made you want to try something new?

> *'Don't just tell us what you've read or done - tell us what you found interesting about it and how it has developed your knowledge and interest in your chosen subject.'*

'Remember: if you're applying to study a combined degree, you should make a connection between the different subjects.

'What reading, research or extra work have you done into your subject area? Don't just tell us what you've read or done - tell us what you found interesting about it and how it has developed your knowledge and interest in your chosen subject.

'What skills and personal qualities do you have? Don't just tell us what they are - tell us how you've developed these skills and how they fit to your chosen course or career - you may be a good communicator or work well with others through being involved in a sports team. How will these abilities develop in your chosen course?

'Do you have a particular career you would like to go into after study? If so, how could this degree help you get there?

'You should remember that, although parts of the personal statement should be subject specific, they should not just feature general information about a subject, or be like a mini essay about that subject. As the admissions tutor already knows about their subject area, they are interested in learning something about you - so make your personal statement personal!'

A seasoned sixthform careers teacher, who has sat in on the interview panel for applicants to read

Medicine at UCL, says: 'One of the key criteria on which applicants for medicine are judged is the evidence they can provide to show that they have a commitment to caring for people.'

He advises to seek voluntary work in a hospice, a care home, or hospital; to work in school with younger/educationally weaker students; and to work for charity. But it will not be enough simply to do these things and list them. Universities want to know how you responded to these experiences. That will tell whether you are indeed the caring person you say you are, or whether in fact you are going into this profession for reasons centred more on yourself, that you think it would be rewarding, financially or otherwise. Anyone who has watched *The Apprentice* will know just how stupid the apprentices sound when they tell Lord Sugar how good they are at something and show in their work that they are not good at it at all. A caring side is not a difficult thing to show, if you have one, but those who do not will definitely be rumbled. It has to be genuine. So, work from the inside out.

Queen's Belfast points out that 'actual requirements vary depending on the nature of the degree programme, but in all cases, evidence of independent study skills are important and for vocational courses evidence of motivation and commitment together with a knowledge of what the chosen career entails, should be demonstrated in the personal statement.'

Bournemouth suggested that if, for example, you are a prospective student aiming for a place in TV Production, you should be able to show that you have been 'following and analysing production techniques or current narratives in programme-making'.

Lincoln made a similar point about applying to read Architecture. You 'should have a sketch-book or an album of photos of visits to cities, buildings and interiors. Perhaps have recorded stages of construction on a building site, show you are able to take the initiative to develop interests of your own outside of architecture. Journalism applicants should be prepared to talk to the interviewer, discussing their work, points of interest and their creative ideas.' If you want to study a vocational course, can you 'display an understanding of the role of the professional?'

What is clear is that university is no longer something that just *happens* off A levels. Admissions tutors want a 'well rounded' student who can provide evidence of their enthusiasm for the subject and course they have chosen to study, evidence of reading around their subject, a readiness and willingness to learn and an understanding of how the chosen course will help you meet your personal ambitions, someone who is capable of making the most of the potentially enormously rich experience that is before them. How serious are you?

> '*What skills and personal qualities do you have? Don't just tell us what they are, tell us how you've developed these skills and how they fit to your chosen course or career.*'

Do's and Don'ts on the Personal Statement

1 Mention responsibility with examples of duties undertaken.
2 Be reflective - explain why.
3 Mention authors/writers and artists when talking about specific research and background reading.
4 Spell check and read through with teachers and parents.
5 Be clear and concise - admissions tutors don't have time to read between the lines.
6 Be enthusiastic about the course.

DON'T

1 Mention a specific institution unless applying only to one.
2 Talk about your A level course syllabus in detail.
3 Plagiarise - UCAS now have a filter and will know.
4 Lie or exaggerate.
5 Try to be a comedian or be over-confident about achievements.

Some Useful Web Sites

www.ucas.com/students/coursesearch/
www.ukcoursefinder.com
www.gmc-uk.org/education/index.asp
www.unistats.com
www.qaa.ac.uk/reviews/reports/instIndex.asp
www.nus.org.uk/Students-Unions/

www.bucs.org.uk : uni sports site
www.thestudentroom.co.uk/
www.studentfinancewales.co.uk (Wales)
www.studentfinance.direct.gov.uk (England)
www.delni.gov.uk/studentfinance (N. Ireland)
www.saas.gov.uk (Scotland)
www.yougo.co.uk

OXFORD AND CAMBRIDGE

In many people's minds Oxford and Cambridge are the pinnacle of achievement. I talked about this with Tim Morrison, a careers master responsible for getting around 40% of his sixth form into Oxbridge each year. Tim was educated at a State day school in Essex and read Classics at St John's Cambridge from 1999 to 2002. I wanted him to tell me what was involved in studying at Oxbridge and how to overcome the ultimate application hurdle.

I had my own thoughts, some of which I delivered to Tim fairly provocatively: 'It seems to me that if you sit for Oxbridge you are sitting for a completely different experience than is on offer at any other university. They will expect you to rise to the challenge of one-to-one with dons who are working at the coal face of their subject, writing books about it. One can imagine that few of these suffer fools gladly, which is presumably why one hears about horrendous interview experiences where the don humiliates the applicant.

'Then, once you're there, there's no time to do anything but work. The terms are shorter and the work load is far greater than at any other university. If you are reading English you are going to have to read umpteen books and write a 3,000 word essay every week at a level that will engage one of the finest brains in Britain. Question, does this make for one-dimensional graduates? Answer, it makes for academically-minded graduates. If there is a limitation we should be clear to our readers what it is.

'The other thing that makes me wary is that Oxbridge graduates never tire of telling you where they studied. Old school tie, jobs galore. There is absolutely no doubt about the nepotism. Oxbridge graduates are the choice of Oxbridge graduate employers in virtually any sphere you care to mention – from publishing to politics, from theatre to media, from industry to the civil service. Yet, even so, I know that it is not true that overall Oxford and Cambridge have the best graduate job figures.

'The picture one gets from the statistics is that Oxbridge graduates are less prepared for the world of work than many from other universities, and that they make up for it with a certain overweening confidence derived from the myth. One suspects that is because there is simply no possibility of developing in the way that other undergraduates may. Both Oxford and Cambridge unions, who look after the extra-curricular development of their stu-

dents, had very low ratings in the recent *Times Higher* Student Experience Survey...'

Tim was already back in the lap of his *alma mater*, and later put down his thoughts in the following piece:

Punting downriver, sipping champagne and discussing Wittgenstein, before waltzing into a top city job... Oxbridge exerts a powerful pull on the imagination, but the reality needs to be considered carefully before applying.

There is no doubting the advantages that the two universities offer. The surroundings are stunning: people travel across the world simply to visit a place that you could be calling home. Their degrees are also hugely respected by employers, and will open any number of doors after you leave. Perhaps most importantly, both are home to some of the finest minds in the world, who will push you to your limits, and will help you to discover enormous amounts about the subject that interests you most. That said the hugely competitive and academically-pressured nature of the universities will not suit everyone, and some may find the whole experience all too one-dimensional.

WHY DOES EVERYONE TREAT OXBRIDGE' SO DIFFERENTLY?

It is partly their amazing history and reputation that accounts for why Oxford and Cambridge are treated slightly separately from other top universities, but there is more to it than that. Not only do the two universities contain some of the world leaders in their fields, they also expect these top minds to teach undergraduates in very small groups (often one-on-one). For this reason they take a different approach to admissions from most other universities. First, they have a commitment to interview a huge proportion of applicants in all subjects, in order to discover who they want to spend the next three or four years working with. Second, there is the college system. The colleges are separate, self-contained institutions, and it is to one of these, rather than the universities themselves, that you will apply. The colleges usually have somewhere for undergraduates to live and eat, as well as their own bar, chapel and library. Often, particularly in arts subjects, much of the teaching is done here too, though lectures are given at a central faculty.

SHOULD I APPLY?

Before thinking about whether you have a chance

of getting in you should think about whether it will suit you. The surroundings and quality of teaching are of course outstanding, and the teacher:student ratios are amazing. Often you will be taught in a group of one or two, meaning you get the close attention of one of the top minds in your field for at least an hour a week, and develop close relationships with the people who teach you. Although this can be intimidating at first, most people ultimately relish the opportunity. If you prefer to go about your work in quiet anonymity, however, you may wish to think carefully about whether it is for you.

OTHER COMMON CONCERNS

They are small, boring towns. There is an element of truth in this and, especially because of the small college-based nature of life, they can feel rather claustrophobic at times. There are a huge number of sports teams, societies etc. so there is always something to do, but if it is top clubbing you are after, look elsewhere.

They are full of posh public school boys. This is largely untrue. Admissions tutors just want the best people to teach, and choose the best people in the country (and indeed the world), with no prejudice whatsoever. There are a few of these kinds of characters around, and they tend to be rather high-profile, but you will find people from all sorts of backgrounds at all of the colleges.

I won't be clever enough. It is true that academic standards are high, and you will be asked to work very hard indeed. It can also be tough getting used to the fact that you are no longer the cleverest person around. Not everyone is a genius, however. They are just bright and enthusiastic people who are keen to learn.

The workload is huge. This is undoubtedly the case. In arts subjects in particular, the difference between what is expected at Oxbridge compared to other universities can be huge. Every week you will be expected to read a number of books and articles and produce at least one essay of between 2,000-3,000 words. This means that work has to be a priority for most of the time that you are there (which, incidentally, is only about half the year — there are two eight week terms, one four week term and exams for a few weeks). You are not allowed to get a job during term time, and taking on big extra-curricular commitments is very difficult indeed.

What do I do next? The incredibly focused nature of life at the two universities means that you do not really have as much time as you might like to plan your career. An Oxbridge degree may well be the best thing to put on a CV, but that is not to say that it offers the best preparation for the world of work.

WILL I GET IN?

The applicant:place ratio is relatively encouraging, particularly in some subjects, but the quality of candidates you are up against is generally very high indeed. There are no hard and fast rules about exactly how they will assess your application, but the following are important:

1. *A strong academic track record.* They will of course take your circumstances and education into account, but will nonetheless expect you to have performed very well, particularly in subjects relevant to the one you are applying for.

2. *Genuine enthusiasm for the subject.* This needs more than simply asserting how passionate you are about it — you need to prove it by reading around areas of interest, doing relevant work experience and so on. You can convey this both in your personal statement and at interview.

3. *Potential to develop further.* This is difficult to assess, but they want to know whether you will flourish when you are really pushed academically. This is the main reason for interviewing you.

HOW DO I CHOOSE A COLLEGE?

It can seem impossible choosing between colleges. There are a few factors that are important, but you should not get too worried about it — the significant minority of applicants who fail to get into the college of their choice end up perfectly happy. Some things you might like to weigh up include:

1. *Big or small* — do you like the idea of a small college, where you get to know everyone in your year, or somewhere bigger and more diverse?

2. *Location* — some of the colleges are in peaceful surroundings a little way out of town, others are very central and convenient for lectures, shops etc.

3. *Old or new* — while some of the older colleges are prettier from the outside, and more prestigious, their newer counterparts are often purpose-built and therefore more pleasant to live in.

4. *Your subject* — it is worth trying to find out how many teachers of your subject there are at the college (the answer is sometimes zero) and roughly how many undergraduates they take each year for it.

There are league tables published (known as the Tompkins Table at Cambridge, and the Norrington Table at Oxford) of the undergraduate results, which may be of interest, but these reflect overall achievement — it could well be, for example, that everyone doing your subject got a First, but the average score at that college was low because of other results.

The number of applicants per subject at each college is also published in the prospectuses. Some candidates therefore apply to one where fewest people applied, in the hope that this will improve their chances. There is not really much point in this, since:

i.   The numbers vary hugely every year.
ii. The colleges communicate with each other, so that those with too many good candidates send them over to those with too few.

WHAT IS THE INTERVIEW LIKE?

Your personal statement, school/college reference, and public exam results will all be taken into account, and if these are of a good enough standard you will usually be called for interview. The two universities are beginning to take measures to cut down the proportion of candidates they interview, however. At Cambridge this can take the form of excluding you on the basis of your AS scores (if you apply to Cambridge you will have to declare your scores in a separate form, whether or not they have been mentioned in your reference).

Applicants to Oxford are often asked to sit a pre-test (usually at your school/college in October or November). Generally those who come in the bottom quarter are then told that they will not be interviewed. You can get information about pre-tests and practice papers from the university website, but largely speaking they are designed to be general tests of ability, that do not rely too heavily on specific knowledge or revision. You may wish to practise to ensure you understand how they work, and roughly how much time to spend on each question. As far as is possible, however, they are designed to be revision-proof: dons do not want to know who is the best-prepared candidate, but who is the best at understanding, assimilating and using new information, or getting immediately to the heart of an argument. Although they are looking for potential, they will want to see that you already have the ability to think and write clearly about difficult topics.

If you get over these hurdles you will then have an interview, usually in early December. There are a number of myths and anecdotes about Oxbridge interviews (dons standing on their heads, rugby balls thrown at you, etc.) but they are much more standardised and professional in reality. They are predictable in that they will usually ask you about your current A-level work, as well as interests mentioned in your personal statement. They will of course push you beyond what you are comfortable with, introducing concepts and ideas that are new to you and forcing you to justify every statement that you make. This can be an uncomfortable and very challenging experience, but also an exhilarating one: to discuss your favourite subject with some of the most knowledgeable and sharpest minds in the field should be something that excites you.

They will not expect you to understand everything, but they want to see how quickly you pick things up and how well you can apply them to what you already know. This will vary hugely from subject to subject (a new poem in English, a new topic in Maths, an unknown skull in Biology), but the principles do not vary: are you interested in, and capable of quickly picking up, ideas about the subject. You may well be asked to take some sort of written test in addition to just discussing things at interview — they will usually warn you about this in advance.

This may seem rather daunting, but the extra time that they put into choosing the right people for the course pays dividends: Oxbridge has comfortably the lowest drop-out rate of any university (just 1.2% against a national average of 9%).

There are lots of good reasons for applying to Oxbridge, and it is an amazing experience, but you need to go into it with your eyes open. Do not apply just because you have done well at school so far, and your teachers think you should, or your parents like the idea of it, often for their own reasons. The courses that Oxford and Cambridge offer are sometimes quite different from those at other universities, and the style of teaching and lifestyle are more intense than anywhere else. Equally, if you do think it will suit you, ignore silly prejudices and cliches and go for it. It is a unique opportunity to work closely with great minds, and push yourself to your academic limits. Anyone who really loves a subject will surely jump at that chance.

Tim Morrison, March 2011

NEW TEST FOR ADMISSION

Clearly, the view that the A Level system is the gold standard does not add up if it is not delivering to University the kind of student that the selective universities want, and they are having to resort to tests of their own.

The National Admissions Tests are long with us. And now there's the Cambridge Pre-U, a new test that is being accepted with and even in place of A levels. See www.cie.org.uk/qualifications/academic/upp ersec/preu.

Cambridge University explains: 'Teachers tell us they want to be able to prepare learners for higher education more effectively with exciting syllabuses that are stimulating to teach.

'Universities tell us they want learners who are equipped to benefit from a higher education experience, which calls for an independent and self-directed style of learning. This is why we have developed Cambridge Pre-U as a coherent curriculum underpinned by a core set of educational principles. It offers genuinely interesting syllabuses which learners can study in any combination to gain the Cambridge Pre-U Diploma, or on an individual subject basis.'

You can study towards the full Cambridge Pre-U Diploma or you can study certain Principal Subjects within the qualification alongside A Levels. A number of schools are getting excited about it, and there's no doubt it is a very interesting development.

The pre-U is an entrance to university exam which scores because it encourages pupils to lock into a particular subject of their choice and exercise precisely the skills that universities want applicants to have when they arrive.

The Cambridge Pre-U involves initiative and independent work and that most important thing of reading around a subject. It is already part of the UCAS tariff (see www.ucas.com/students/ucas_tariff/tarifftables/), but some schools are still unsure what universities other than Cambridge think about it. So, we asked them.

Do universities take the Cambridge Pre-U into serious consideration? One or two hadn't heard of it. Kent, Nottingham Trent, Winchester and Glasgow Caledonian said simply, 'No,' they didn't take it into consideration. Central Lancashire accepts it, but like Glyndwr and Wolverhampton they hadn't yet had an applicant present it. Hertfordshire said that if presented it might be taken into consideration, but they hadn't come across it yet.

The rest, far in the majority, welcomed it and intend to formulate offers on an equivalent basis with existing level 3 qualifications, some with the caveat that its value may vary depending on which Principal Subjects were chosen.

Sheffield considers it for entry 'to all of our undergraduate degree courses. We require a minimum of three Pre-U Principal Subjects and will consider a mix of A-level and Pre-U subjects, provided at least three subjects overall are offered.

For Southampton University, Grade D3 at the pre-U is simply equivalent to an 'A' at A level; M2 to a 'B', M3 to a 'C'. The Cambridge Pre-U looks set to become a popular alternative to A levels.

The National tests, meanwhile, are well established. What are they? Who are they for?

UKCAT is the UK Clinical Aptitude Test used in the selection process by a consortium of medical and dental schools. See www.ukcat.ac.uk. BMAT, the BioMedical Admissions Test, is another test for entry to medical, veterinary and related courses. See www.bmat.org.uk. GAMSAT is the Graduate Medical School Admission Test. See www.gamsat.uk.org. HPAT is required to read certain medical courses at Ulster. Medical and dentistry schools require different tests: see web sites.

LNAT is the National Admissions Test for Law. See www.lnat.ac.uk/ or www. kaptest.co.uk for an online practice test.

HAT is the History Aptitude Test required by Oxford; MML the Modern and Mediaeval Languages Test required by Cambridge. STEP is a clutch of Sixth Term Examination Papers required to read Mathematics at Cambridge and Warwick. See www.maths.cam. ELAT is required by Oxford to read English. TSA (Cambridge) is a Thinking Skills Assessment required by Cambridge for computer science, natural science, engineering and economics: tsa.ucles.org.uk/index. html.

TSA (Oxford) is equired by Oxford to read PPE, Economics & Management, or experimental psychology. TSA UCL is University College London's requirement to read European social & political studies.

With UK tuition fees ready to soar as high as £9,000 a year, going to a university abroad has become a realistic option.

There are thousands of courses delivered in English in Europe and more than 20,000 applicants chose to take this route last year.

Often you will find a simpler application process and a cheaper and very good product. Earlier this year I spoke at an international school in Brussels and was struck by the sixth-formers' mature outlook. They were thinking about applying to universities all over the world. It made me feel just how insular we are in Britain.

Holland is an increasingly popular choice, Maastricht University in particular. Have a look at the Studielink portal - Holland's UCAS. You can expect to pay around a sixth of the fees you will pay at most British universities in 2012.

Then, there is America.

Consultants have been over here in strength for some time, recruiting, particularly from the best of our State schools, where they expect to be able to recruit from families on more modest incomes. American universities are on the face of it expensive, but there are good deals on offer to applicants whose family income is below $60,000.

A commercial organisation called Naviance is especially active in this area. It produces a product called *Family Connection*, which allows for College search, application, and to be able to see the progress of the application as the student fills it in. There is also Scholarship information.

I heard about it from Chris Conway, sixth-form careers teacher at Shrewsbury School, who had just returned from a fact-finding trip to America and he agreed to share what he had learned with this year's Guide.

UNIVERSITY IN
THE UNITED STATES

America - the Land of the Free, is not the phrase that comes to mind when thinking about the option of crossing the Atlantic to go to university. Costs (including tuition and room and board) can vary from as low as $15,000 per year (for the standard four year course) at a small state university to around $45,000 per year at top Ivy League institutions. It is also true that most institutions do not offer financial assistance to international students.

However, getting beyond this daunting barrier, some loopholes appear. Sports scholarships do exist, and can be extremely generous (they can cover all fees). Of course they are skewed towards American sports, but nevertheless, students who are stars at: athletics, golf, rowing, squash, soccer and tennis - to give a few examples, could look realistically towards such funding.

There are also some institutions which offer financial support to students on academic grounds, and indeed a handful of universities choose on a 'needs blind' basis i.e. the ability to pay does not affect their selection (for international students there are Harvard, Princeton, Yale, Dartmouth, Cornell, MIT and Amherst). This means that such universities have to be wealthy enough to cover any fee costs - which can be up to 100%. As tuition fees rise at UK universities, all this needs to be looked at carefully, and when making the comparison remember to include living costs at UK institutions!

This all begs the question of why should one consider an American university education. At the heart of the answer lies the fact that Americans do value education, finance it well, and as a result a great deal of what is on offer is very good. Amongst the nearly 4,000 US universities and colleges, standards clearly vary.

However, the *Times Higher Magazine's* World Rankings put 7 US institutions in the top ten universities, and 28 in the top 50. It is important to realise that the quality stretches far beyond the customary image of Harvard and the Ivy League. The Ivy League by the way is actually a descriptive term for an athletic conference made of eight private institutions of higher education in the Northeastern United States, comprising the universities of: Brown, Columbia, Cornell, Dartmouth, Harvard, Pennsylvania, Princeton and Yale.

The traditional hallmark of the American model is that of the 'Liberal Arts' education. In this, generally the first two years are aimed at providing a broad education from the humanities through to sciences. In the final two years, a degree of specialisation occurs with students typically spending around 50% of their time on the major subject in the end. There are variations on this theme with some colleges (e.g. Brown) allowing much wider student choice than others. By the way Americans will use ìCollegeî where we use ìUniversityî, but they have essentially the same meaning.

This holistic view of the academic offering by US Colleges is mirrored in general by the way they value students and select them. They want students who are 'roundedì' and who will contribute outside a particular subject, and indeed outside the straight academic world. They have their own distinctive characteristics, and they are looking to recruit students who will 'fit' their own particular template.

The starting point of any application is to offer some academic credibility, and apart from good GCSEs (and AS and A-levels if their results are already known), it is a requirement to take either the SAT or ACT tests - run by competing companies.

The SAT is the most common and are administered by The College Board (www.collegeboard.com). Their website gives the dates of the tests, the location of centres in the UK, and all the information that is needed - including being the point of application for any tests.

Be aware that there are two types of test: the SAT itself (essentially reasoning based around Reading, Writing and Maths) and Subject tests. All universities require the SAT and some require a number (usually 1 or 2) of Subject Tests. Each university will have their own score threshold on these tests, and these can be found from their websites.

Key issues are:

* The tests are designed by Americans for Americans, and the language and style is different to most UK exams. Specific coaching for these tests and/or practice at past questions can be very productive. It is worth making the assumption that taking the tests twice will lead to improved scores.

* The SAT itself is long (about three and a half hours testing plus registration) and all tests occur on a Saturday and start early. Registration begins around 7.45 a.m.

* All test dates have a registration deadline, and centres get booked up early.

* Not all subjects studied at A-level are accommodated in the subject tests, and some e.g. American History are clearly aimed at Americans.

On top of the tests, applicants have to write an Admissions Essay to be submitted with their application to each university. There is no equivalent body to UCAS in America, each university is applied to separately, and each will require an Admissions Essay which will enable them to select students who they think will 'match' with their institution.

As you can see the process is complex and different to the UK experience. Help is available from The Fulbright Commission (www.fulbright.co.uk)

and it may even be worth investing in the advice of expert consultants to assist with the process. It is certainly worth attending Fulbright's College Day in September, which is held in London, and allows prospective students to talk to representatives from many US universities as well as meet consultants. There are also many books which can give valuable information about the colleges including: *Rugg's Recommendations on the Colleges*, the *Fiske Guide to Colleges*, *The Best 373 Colleges*, and *Colleges that Change Lives* - which can be easily Googled.

When considering a US education, one aspect which should not be ignored, is that of employment after graduating. Unless you are an American citizen or marry one, it is unlikely that employment in America will be possible beyond a limited internship period. Thus it is worth bearing in mind that that the majority of UK employers will be aware of relatively few US universities.

The notion of going to university across the pond is a big decision to take. The quality and variety of Higher Education offered is not in question, but the process is time-consuming and demands a great deal of individual effort and research.

There are books and league tables (e.g. http://colleges.usnews.rankingsandreviews.com/best-colleges/rankings/national-universities) that give information - but remember that any rankings are only useful if you understand the criteria used to establish the order. On top of this, it is a very different cultural experience to being an undergraduate in the UK: drinking alcohol under the age of 21 is illegal; football has a different meaning; the concept of student debt is no surprise to American students - that has been their expectation for generations - and of course it is simply a long way from home.

However, the nature of the education offered does produce well-rounded graduates - which many UK employers value and claim that UK universities are not producing.

If the American experience is pursued, the following practical points may be worth noting:

It is always prudent to take the SAT and SAT Subjects Tests twice: students generally show a marked score improvement, especially if they have undertaken a substantial course of SAT revision in the interim.

Students must leave time to assemble American university application references, etc.

Factoring in AS-level commitments, an application timeline might look like this:

Year 12: 1. From entry to Year start seriously considering American universities. 2. Christmas Term: undertake programme of SAT revision. 3.

Late January: sit SAT Reasoning Test for the first time. 4. Early June: sit SAT II Subjects Tests for the first time.

Year 13: 1. Compile application materials. 2. October: re-sit SAT, if necessary. 3. November: re-sit SAT II Subjects Tests, if necessary. 4. Mid-November: file early application(s). 5. Mid-December: finalise and submit regular applications (ultimate deadline usually January 1st).

It is clear that the American university experience is becoming more attractive to British sixth-formers. Recent data from the Fulbright Commission shows that a record 8,861 UK students studied in the US in 2009-10, a 2% rise from 2008-9. With our Higher Education system currently undergoing dramatic changes in style and cost, it surely makes sense to investigate one which is already proven to be delivering high quality.

Chris Conway, March 2011

NO PANIC CLEARING

WHAT IS CLEARING?

Clearing is the way that UCAS, the central clearing agency matches the places on degree courses which remain to be filled after exams results are out and conditional offers are confirmed, or withdrawn.

It is generally thought to be a service for those who have failed to get the required points to take up a conditional offer, but it may as well be an occasion to 'up' your choice because you have done better than expected (this is called 'Adjustment'; get instructions about how to do this on the UCAS site).

So, Clearing happens after the exam results are out. It operates between mid-July and September. You will receive instructions from UCAS whether or not you will need to use the system, unless of course you have moved house and not told UCAS (an astonishingly common occurrence).

On the day, at UCAS head office in Cheltenham, just across the road from the famous racecourse where many a punter has lost out by following a spirited hunch rather than taking a rational decision, 100-odd 'advisers', who have been trained for months to promote reason over emotion, man telephones for 12 hours a day and take thousands of calls from applicants, many of whom are in a serious state of arousal. The role of the team is not only to advise but to counsel the more emotional callers. A sense of panic attends Clearing partly because of the number of candidates chasing places and the sense that the best courses may well go in the early hours and days.

Last year, on the first morning I was interviewed for three hours by a whole succession of BBC local radio programmes. The emotional atmosphere was tangible after it was announced that 187,625 applicants were chasing Clearing places, compared to 140,908 the previous year. No doubt it will be the same or worse this year, but the important thing is to keep cool and follow a plan.

'The key to Clearing,' says an experienced sixth-form careers teacher, 'is to have done a little research in advance - call it Plan B - and then move quickly, if necessary, on results day.'

What to do

Don't panic. Check Track, which you will know all about from your careers teacher, and if you have achieved less than the grades on offer be sure that you have indeed been rejected. As another teacher advises, 'Do NOT assume that if you do not meet the grades that you will be automatically rejected. They may well still take you. Find out.' If Track is still saying 'Conditional' get on the phone, but NOT to UCAS, to the University admissions tutor. UCAS list the numbers for you to call.

How you handle the admissions tutor is hugely important. Look upon it as an opportunity. 'Prepare your conversation well, and sell yourself. Remember the tutor wants to talk to you, not to your parents or the school.' Have your module marks and a piece of paper and pen handy.

The tutor wants to fill the place with the kind of person who has the skills and motivation you will have imparted on your personal statement and who is capable of handling this conversation. That you have the guts to make this call is part of the deal. So, prove it.

If you have performed well in modules that are especially relevant to the course you are after, make the point strongly. If you are not impressive then he will not be interested.

If in the end he won't take you on that course, ask whether there are any associated courses that you might consider. Say why you chose this university over others. Show that you have gone about the application professionally, that you are motivated to do so. Remember they want students who won't be swelling the drop-out stats next year.

If he says there may be other courses, but he

can't say at that time because he is waiting for responses to offers made to other applicants, ask when you should call back. Be keen. Don't let him off the hook. Take notes of what is said, including the tutor's name and what you or he agrees to do, and most important take a note of any email address or telephone number he gives you.

If unsuccessful, before consulting Clearing vacancies online at UCAS, consider telephoning any universities that made you an offer earlier which you declined. But don't compromise your position by settling for any course, or you WILL be a drop-out statistic with a nasty debt to pay back.

There are also other options. Consider having a bad paper re-marked. Ask your teachers about the advisability of this. Consider re-sits.

'I always tell our lot,' says a careers teacher, 'that if they are in that position, unless they are desperate to go to uni this autumn, better to apply again next year, when there's the whole range of courses available to them again. They can then use this "surprise" gap year as a real opportunity to do something new and different - gain some useful experience that will help them develop and add something to their CV.'

There may in your case be good reason to want to start University in a particular year, such as fees hikes and the like. But the key is not to compromise your principles of application which we set out above, in 'Choosing a University'.

Treat the Clearing vacancies online as you would your original course search. Then, expect to be on the phone for hours. Expect it to be hard to get through. But do it yourself. No one can do this for you. University is about doing things for yourself.

SOURCES FOR STATISTICS

SOURCES FOR STATISTICS

Information and figures used in the editorial boxes and drawn upon in the text entries of *The Virgin Guide* come from various sources: student populations and analyses from the university admission offices, the Higher Education Statistic Agency (HESA) and UCAS. Social demography and drop-out rates come from HESA, accommodation costs, etc. from the accommodation offices of the universities, research statistics from the Research Assessment Exercise (RAE) 2008 (see http://submissions.rae.ac.uk/results/) and *Times Higher Education*, teaching assessments from the Quality Assurance Agency (QAA) — see www.qaa.ac.uk — and from the universities.

The phrase 'Social Class 4-7' in the 'University/ Student Profile' boxes refers to 'NS-SEC classes 4,5,6 & 7'.

Where asterisk stars - ★★★ - occur in the boxes, the range is 1 to 5 - ★ to ★★★★★ - (poor to very good) with 3 stars the average.

Average points requirement for entry, overall student satisfaction rates, and the percentage of students into real graduate jobs at each university, are drawn from the national student survey undertaken by the Higher Education Funding Council for England (HEFCE) — see www. unistats.com/.

Student views and ratings come from students themselves, but our ratings for helpful/interested staff, tuition in small groups, good social life and good student union are informed by the ground-breaking national Student Experience Survey carried out by Opionpanel for the *Times Higher Education* magazine, which also compiles the World' Top 200 Universities league table

As ever at *The Virgin Guide* the most telling information is our students' views, but second to it is HESA's incredibly useful draw-down on the universities' own research into where everyone who gets a job after leaving university actually ends up.

I would like to thank all parties for their help and co-operation.

Swelling the student journalistic cohort this year are Tom Wordie, Stephen Craige, Alexander Blake, Nick Davies, Jack Lewis, Christopher Cox, , Christopher Jamieson, Alex Taylor, Will Gastrell, Rory Vokes-Dudgeon, Rosie Legg, Jess Horsell, Tristan Wike, Emma Stirling, Rondal Lancelyn, Linley Portsmouth, Charlie Callaghan, Alexander Gitting, Alisdair Hinton and Corrie-Anne Rounding. Many thanks to them. Students at university who would like to write for the next edition should email me at janthony78@ymail.com.

Piers Dudgeon, April 2011

POINTS TARIFF FOR ENTRY

A full account of the UCAS points tarrif is given on the UCAS website: www.ucas.com/students/ucas_tariff/tarifftables/.

For the IB, you have to study six subjects, three to a high level, three to a standard level. A pass earns you 4 marks. If you pass six subjects you amass 24 marks, which UCAS have made equivalent to 260 points in the tariff.

A LEVEL POINTS TARIFF

A Level Grades	A level Points
A*	140
A	120
B	100
C	80
D	60
E	40

AS Level Grades	AS Level Points
A	60
B	50
C	40
D	30
E	20

INTERNATIONAL BACCALAUREATE

IB Diploma Marks	IB Points
24	260
25	282
26	304
27	326
28	348
29	370
30	392
31	413
32	435
33	457
34	479
35	501
36	523
37	545
38	567
39	589
40	611
41	632
42	654
43	676
44	698
45	720

BEST DEAL LEAGUE TABLES

The tables opposite, through to page 30, show the Higher Education Funding Council (HEFCE)'s Student Survey results for selected subjects. Only universities which can show 60%+ leavers in real graduate-type jobs after six months of graduation are included (50%+ in the cases of Creative Arts, History, English, Geography, Philosophy, Politics and Psychology, as students of these are among the least easy to place in graduate employment). There are noticably fewer universities getting even 50% of graduates in English and History into real graduate jobs this year.

That a university has not been included may be for reasons other than poor graduate employment figures, however, simply perhaps that not enough data was submitted to HEFCE.

Those who did declare fully and have graduate employment figures over these threshholds, have been listed, and can be compared in terms of entry requirements, job expectation, and student satisfaction for the subjects listed. Once again, among the unsung heroes are Lancaster and SOAS. Huddersfield and Northumbria also make regular appearances, and the rise of Lincoln and Staffordshire in particular is clear.

Three columns of figures tell you: 1. how many UCAS points were accepted; 2. what percentage of students that got in found real graduate jobs at the end; and 3. how satisfied these students were that the course was interesting and was taught well.

ABBREVIATIONS
ND = No data available
Uni Arts = University of the Arts
KCL = King's College London
Liverpool JM = Liverpool John Moores University
LSE = London School of Economics
SOAS = School of Oriental & African Studies
UCL = University College London
Bristol UWE = West of England, Bristol

Architecture/Building/Planning

	A Level Points Accepted	Real Graduate Jobs	Student Satisfaction
Aberdeen	368	65%	61%
Anglia Ruskin	275	75%	69%
Bath	480	100%	91%
Birmingham City	280	75%	55%
Brighton	380	85%	71%
Bristol UWE	280	80%	90%
Cambridge	500	85%	ND
Cardiff	480	90%	91%
Central Lancashire	265	85%	66%
Coventry	260	60%	67%
De Montfort	240	70%	54%
Derby	200	60%	75%
East London	200	80%	80%
Edinburgh	422	70%	67%
Edinburgh Napier	282	60%	66%
Glamorgan	215	75%	55%
Glasgow Caledonian	ND	67%	79%
Glyndwr	ND	75%	53%
Greenwich	260	80%	81%
Heriot-Watt	360	65%	71%
Huddersfield	230	60%	83%
Kent	340	85%	73%
Kingston	310	79%	80%
Leeds Metropolitan	300	65%	45%
Lincoln	260	65%	89%
Liverpool	440	70%	74%
Liverpool John Moores	270	70%	79%
London Metropolitan	230	85%	69%
London South Bank	220	75%	79%
Loughborough	300	75%	84%
Manchester	435	70%	70%
Manchester Met	320	84%	88%
Newcastle	420	85%	48%
Northumbria	340	70%	93%
Nottingham	415	70%	86%
Nottingham Trent	270	74%	70%
Oxford Brookes	380	75%	88%
Plymouth	360	75%	78%
Portsmouth	320	69%	82%
Queen's	380	80%	76%
Reading	340	84%	75%
Salford	280	75%	69%
Sheffield	480	86%	86%
Sheffield Hallam	325	70%	86%
Strathclyde (Naval)	353	85%	70%
Ulster	280	65%	85%
UCL	460	90%	ND
Uni Wales Cardiff	235	70%	70%
Westminster	340	80%	79%

Biology

	A Level Points Accepted	Real Graduate Jobs	Student Satisfaction
Bath	470	80%	90%
Bolton	140	75%	71%
Bradford	260	65%	84%
Cambridge	560	77%	90%
Central Lancashire	270	60%	69%
Durham	460	70%	79%
Edinburgh	436	65%	93%
Glasgow Caledonian	ND	55%	85%
Heriot-Watt	300	60%	91%
Imperial College	450	70%	90%
Lancaster	390	60%	89%
Leicester	390	60%	94%
Manchester	435	70%	88%
Middlesex	160	73%	72%
Northumbria	280	65%	77%
Nottingham	370	60%	90%
Nottingham Trent	180	65%	96%
Oxford	480	75%	97%
Portsmouth	260	65%	90%
Reading	340	65%	88%
Royal Holloway	310	60%	89%
Sheffield	450	60%	98%
Sheffield Hallam	240	60%	82%
Southampton	385	65%	96%
St Andrews	430	70%	88%
Sussex	380	60%	96%
Uni Wales Cardiff	240	80%	86%
Warwick	440	65%	88%
Westminster	220	60%	79%
Wolverhampton	260	60%	65%
York	410	60%	94%

Business Studies

	A Level Points Accepted	Real Graduate Jobs	Student Satisfaction
Aberdeen	360	60%	75%
the Arts, London	230	62%	41%
Aston	390	77%	83%
Bath	440	86%	92%
Birmingham	390	66%	83%
Bournemouth	320	60%	80%
Bristol	420	90%	88%
Cardiff	380	71%	91%
Central Lancashire	260	60%	89%
Chester	240	65%	82%
City	410	75%	91%
Coventry	220	60%	88%
Durham	400	75%	88%
Edinburgh	412	69%	82%
Edinburgh Napier	276	68%	89%
Exeter	380	65%	82%

	A Level Points Accepted	Real Graduate Jobs	Student Satisfaction		A Level Points Accepted	Real Graduate Jobs	Student Satisfaction
Glasgow	402	70%	85%	Dundee	360	80%	81%
Gloucestershire	230	75%	80%	Durham	380	90%	67%
Harper Adams	240	85%	91%	East Anglia	300	75%	91%
Heriot-Watt	360	75%	95%	Edinburgh	456	85%	90%
Huddersfield	210	65%	63%	Edinburgh Napier	274	69%	ND
Hull	270	60%	86%	Essex	280	80%	85%
Imperial College	460	75%	ND	Exeter	330	80%	79%
KCL	420	80%	80%	Glasgow	360	85%	96%
Lancaster	410	86%	90%	Gloucestershire	240	70%	67%
Leeds	410	76%	81%	Glyndwr	ND	65%	87%
Leicester	310	70%	76%	Goldsmiths	150	60%	67%
Lincoln	260	62%	91%	Heriot-Watt	300	60%	74%
Liverpool	380	63%	86%	Huddersfield	250	82%	67%
Manchester	400	64%	86%	Hull	200	90%	89%
Manchester Met	240	61%	71%	Imperial College	480	100%	88%
Newcastle	360	90%	87%	Kent	300	86%	82%
Northumbria	300	71%	78%	KCL	360	80%	77%
Nottingham	400	84%	85%	Lancaster	360	76%	75%
Nottingham Trent	260	69%	75%	Leeds	360	80%	81%
Plymouth	260	65%	75%	Lincoln	260	60%	74%
Reading	370	70%	80%	Liverpool	340	70%	94%
Robert Gordon	314	77%	88%	Loughborough	310	85%	89%
Royal Agricultural	260	60%	91%	Manchester	380	90%	81%
Staffordshire	190	61%	81%	Newcastle	310	85%	89%
Strathclyde	417	60%	91%	Northumbria	240	81%	77%
Sunderland	210	60%	81%	Nottingham	360	80%	86%
Surrey	ND	75%	78%	Nottingham Trent	220	73%	67%
Warwick	450	80%	87%	Oxford	540	95%	90%
				Oxford Brookes	220	80%	85%

Computer Science

				Plymouth	240	82%	63%
Aberdeen	336	90%	88%	Queen's Belfast	320	70%	89%
Abertay Dundee	313	73%	ND	Queen Mary	260	70%	85%
Aberystwyth	260	90%	96%	Reading	330	90%	82%
Aston	300	78%	80%	Robert Gordon	288	80%	85%
Bath	430	100%	84%	Salford	220	65%	63%
Bedfordshire	120	65%	61%	Sheffield	400	95%	89%
Birmingham	380	75%	92%	Southampton	420	75%	92%
Birmingham City	160	70%	57%	Southampton Solent	180	70%	75%
Bournemouth	230	81%	75%	Staffordshire	240	78%	80%
Bradford	200	52%	61%	Strathclyde	372	65%	81%
Brighton	260	70%	69%	Surrey	360	80%	78%
Bristol	460	95%	90%	Sussex	300	85%	94%
Bristol UWE	220	68%	64%	Swansea	310	75%	81%
Cambridge	550	95%	91%	Swansea Met	155	70%	70%
Canterbury	140	60%	76%	Teesside	240	73%	82%
Cardiff	350	65%	80%	UCL	400	90%	ND
Chester	240	65%	80%	Warwick	470	93%	78%
Coventry	220	70%	61%	York	420	90%	91%
Derby	210	65%	74%				

Creative Arts, Art & Design

	A Level Points Accepted	Real Graduate Jobs	Student Satisfaction
Uni Arts, London	300	61%	63%
Bangor	300	55%	85%
Bournemouth	280	71%	88%
Bristol UWE	240	52%	77%
Brunel	350	74%	85%
Buckinghamshire New	160	57%	61%
Central Lancashire	230	55%	79%
Chester	250	55%	60%
Dundee	336	52%	68%
East London	180	58%	56%
Edinburgh Napier	294	65%	53%
Essex	330	65%	90%
Uni Creative Arts	220	53%	66%
Glasgow School Art	370	67%	66%
Glyndwr	230	55%	72%
Greenwich	210	60%	65%
Heriot-Watt	360	74%	77%
Hertfordshire	240	50%	69%
Huddersfield	260	62%	75%
Kent	310	68%	59%
Kingston	280	61%	81%
Lancaster	370	55%	85%
Leeds	390	51%	53%
Lincoln	270	55%	83%
London Met	240	50%	44%
London South Bank	200	55%	63%
Manchester Met	240	51%	68%
Middlesex	140	53%	72%
Newcastle	380	70%	85%
Northumbria	300	62%	68%
Nottingham Trent	310	61%	72%
Oxford	470	80%	91%
Reading	320	75%	70%
Sheffield Hallam	300	54%	59%
Sunderland	180	50%	76%
Teesside	290	50%	73%
Uni Wales Carmarthen	290	55%	71%
Newport	250	51%	56%
West London	ND	55%	57%
Westminster	240	60%	73%

Dentistry

	A Level Points Accepted	Real Graduate Jobs	Student Satisfaction
Aberdeen	490	100%	93%
Birmingham	470	100%	85%
Bristol	420	100%	95%
Cardiff	440	100%	97%
Dundee	506	100%	90%
Exeter	460	100%	94%
Glasgow	488	100%	96%
KCL	460	100%	86%
Leeds	420	100%	91%
Liverpool	480	100%	81%
Manchester	440	100%	84%
Newcastle	460	100%	92%
Plymouth	470	100%	84%
Queen's Belfast	450	100%	96%
Queen Mary	440	100%	77%
Sheffield	470	100%	93%

Economics

	A Level Points Accepted	Real Graduate Jobs	Student Satisfaction
Anglia Ruskin	220	60%	60%
Bath	480	85%	74%
Birmingham	400	70%	90%
Birmingham City	225	70%	67%
Bristol	460	84%	88%
Bristol UWE	260	60%	79%
Cambridge	540	95%	ND
Cardiff	390	65%	81%
Central Lancashire	220	70%	78%
Coventry	260	65%	84%
Cumbria	220	68%	59%
Derby	220	60%	74%
Durham	510	83%	86%
Edinburgh	440	90%	93%
Exeter	410	74%	92%
Glasgow	440	85%	89%
Hull	260	70%	87%
Kent	300	65%	93%
Lancaster	410	80%	87%
Leeds	430	70%	82%
Leicester	340	75%	84%
Liverpool	380	70%	84%
LSE	540	95%	83%
Loughborough	390	60%	85%
Manchester	420	65%	77%
Newcastle	400	85%	93%
Nottingham	480	82%	90%
Oxford	540	89%	89%
Oxford Brookes	300	70%	98%
Robert Gordon	300	74%	97%
Royal Holloway	380	65%	84%
SOAS	420	80%	79%
Sheffield Hallam	260	69%	75%
Southampton	420	60%	80%
Staffordshire	230	76%	76%
St Andrews	486	85%	88%
Stirling	330	75%	84%
Strathclyde	429	60%	93%
Surrey	360	70%	92%

	A Level Points Accepted	Real Graduate Jobs	Student Satisfaction
Sussex	360	70%	88%
Newport	200	75%	75%
UCL	480	90%	ND
Uni Wales Cardiff	220	65%	80%
Warwick	510	92%	83%
York	450	70%	79%

English

	A Level Points Accepted	Real Graduate Jobs	Student Satisfaction
Bristol	460	55%	75%
Cambridge	500	63%	93%
Durham	510	65%	97%
Huddersfield	310	50%	81%
KCL	440	65%	78%
Lancaster	400	58%	95%
Leeds	440	51%	90%
Leicester	380	55%	93%
Newcastle	430	56%	93%
Nottingham	440	66%	84%
Oxford	520	83%	ND
Queen Mary	370	57%	95%
Royal Holloway	410	55%	82%
Staffordshire	230	65%	91%
St Andrews	470	65%	87%
Sussex	400	66%	95%
UCL	480	60%	91%
Warwick	460	65%	96%
Westminster	240	55%	75%
York	470	65%	83%

Finance & Accounting

	A Level Points Accepted	Real Graduate Jobs	Student Satisfaction
Aberdeen	332	60%	70%
Aberystwyth	260	60%	97%
Birmingham	390	60%	89%
Brighton	240	65%	85%
Bristol	420	85%	89%
Cardiff	400	67%	92%
City	410	79%	92%
Dundee	340	60%	93%
Durham	400	85%	79%
Edinburgh	430	85%	87%
Exeter	410	80%	87%
Glasgow	468	95%	95%
Heriot-Watt	340	65%	86%
Huddersfield	260	70%	84%
Hull	260	60%	92%
Lancaster	400	85%	89%
Leeds	430	75%	83%
Lincoln	240	70%	97%
Liverpool	390	65%	76%

	A Level Points Accepted	Real Graduate Jobs	Student Satisfaction
LSE	480	91%	78%
Loughborough	400	89%	94%
Manchester	440	70%	76%
Newcastle	410	84%	91%
Northumbria	300	80%	82%
Nottingham	400	85%	84%
Oxford Brookes	310	65%	93%
Queen's Belfast	400	63%	83%
Reading	380	90%	85%
Robert Gordon	345	100%	96%
Sheffield	360	65%	85%
Sheffield Hallam	260	65%	87%
Staffordshire	180	75%	84%
Stirling	348	65%	94%
Strathclyde	458	80%	97%
Warwick	470	85%	94%

Geography

	A Level Points Accepted	Real Graduate Jobs	Student Satisfaction
Aberdeen	358	55%	92%
Birmingham	380	58%	90%
Bournemouth	240	60%	65%
Bristol	470	70%	75%
Cambridge	520	75%	98%
Chester	280	50%	90%
Coventry	270	50%	91%
Durham	460	90%	88%
East Anglia	390	60%	95%
Edinburgh	440	60%	98%
Exeter	390	60%	89%
Hertfordshire	240	70%	80%
Hull	290	60%	93%
KCL	380	65%	82%
Lancaster	400	65%	94%
Leeds	420	56%	88%
Leicester	330	55%	92%
LSE	470	95%	78%
Manchester	400	65%	75%
Newcastle	360	60%	87%
Nottingham	420	80%	90%
Oxford	490	75%	92%
Reading	60	57%	88%
Sheffield	400	65%	86%
Southampton	400	52%	87%
Staffordshire	240	60%	95%
St Andrews	420	70%	92%
Stirling	305	50%	85%
Sussex	350	65%	95%
UCL	420	55%	90%
York	365	55%	94%

	A Level Points Accepted	Real Graduate Jobs	Student Satisfaction		A Level Points Accepted	Real Graduate Jobs	Student Satisfaction
History				**Law**			
Bristol	440	63%	80%	Aberdeen	416	65%	95%
Cambridge	520	68%	93%	Birmingham	420	75%	83%
Courtauld Inst.	430	60%	83%	Bristol	460	65%	81%
Durham	500	70%	98%	Cambridge	540	65%	ND
Huddersfield	260	55%	95%	City	350	65%	63%
KCL	470	55%	96%	Durham	500	65%	93%
Leeds	420	52%	92%	East Anglia	390	60%	88%
Lincoln	265	50%	90%	Exeter	410	65%	91%
LSE	460	80%	69%	Huddersfield	300	65%	71%
Manchester	390	51%	79%	KCL	460	65%	89%
Newcastle	410	56%	89%	Lancaster	420	70%	95%
Nottingham	410	60%	89%	LSE	480	60%	ND
Oxford	500	75%	94%	Manchester	450	60%	79%
Queen Mary	360	50%	88%	Northumbria	340	78%	94%
SOAS	350	50%	89%	Oxford	530	80%	95%
St Andrews	460	65%	95%	Reading	380	75%	96%
Sussex	370	65%	92%	Robert Gordon	336	70%	87%
UCL	440	65%	89%	Surrey	360	55%	69%
				Sussex	370	70%	94%
Languages				UCL	480	65%	94%
Aston	390	60%	90%	Westminster	300	66%	67%
Bath	440	71%	93%				
Birmingham	380	61%	88%	**Management**			
Bristol	430	70%	88%	Aberdeen	376	65%	80%
Bristol UWE	260	65%	70%	Bournemouth	290	70%	77%
Cambridge	540	68%	95%	Bristol UWE	260	60%	71%
Chester	240	60%	88%	Cambridge	ND	85%	ND
Durham	480	73%	88%	Central Lancashire	270	65%	92%
Edinburgh	460	64%	83%	City	425	75%	94%
Essex	320	60%	88%	De Montfort	200	60%	95%
Glasgow	420	62%	89%	Edinburgh Napier	276	60%	ND
Heriot-Watt	376	75%	93%	Essex	280	60%	77%
Hull	300	60%	92%	Exeter	390	75%	92%
KCL	460	60%	81%	Glasgow	408	65%	87%
Lancaster	400	70%	67%	Gloucestershire	230	65%	68%
Leeds	410	60%	90%	Greenwich	200	60%	92%
Manchester	400	65%	84%	Heriot-Watt	360	70%	94%
Newcastle	410	62%	84%	Hertfordshire	210	75%	92%
Northumbria	280	80%	99%	Huddersfield	270	65%	63%
Nottingham	400	60%	81%	Keele	270	65%	82%
Oxford	520	74%	96%	KCL	420	80%	80%
SOAS	390	68%	83%	Leeds	410	75%	82%
Sheffield	410	65%	85%	Leicester	310	70%	76%
Staffordshire	230	65%	91%	Lincoln	250	75%	90%
St Andrews	440	70%	91%	LSE	460	85%	74%
Sussex	360	70%	78%	Loughborough	400	75%	93%
UCL	445	70%	92%	Manchester	420	80%	78%
Warwick	430	62%	92%	Manchester Met	220	60%	62%
				Newcastle	370	70%	62%

	A Level Points Accepted	Real Graduate Jobs	Student Satisfaction		A Level Points Accepted	Real Graduate Jobs	Student Satisfaction
Nottingham	400	84%	85%	Bristol	462	100%	68%
Oxford	520	90%	ND	Cambridge	580	100%	92%
Oxford Brookes	320	64%	86%	Cardiff	460	100%	58%
Plymouth	210	65%	58%	Dundee	500	100%	94%
Reading	390	95%	80%	East Anglia	440	100%	87%
Sheffield	380	68%	80%	Edinburgh	540	100%	92%
Sheffield Hallam	280	80%	71%	Exeter	460	100%	94%
Surrey	360	64%	74%	Glasgow	508	100%	64%
Sussex	335	75%	82%	Hull York	500	100%	87%
Warwick	460	90%	90%	Imperial College	520	100%	91%
Westminster	255	85%	62%	Keele	440	100%	62%
				KCL	480	100%	85%

Mathematics

				Leeds	480	100%	85%
Bath	500	85%	85%	Leicester	473	100%	90%
Birmingham	420	57%	92%	Liverpool	490	100%	66%
Bristol	520	76%	82%	Manchester	480	100%	67%
Cambridge	570	92%	ND	Newcastle	480	100%	97%
Cardiff	420	60%	88%	Nottingham	490	100%	89%
Durham	540	83%	84%	Oxford	540	100%	96%
East Anglia	410	65%	94%	Plymouth	470	100%	84%
Edinburgh	446	60%	82%	Queen's Belfast	480	99%	86%
Glasgow	414	60%	87%	Queen Mary	450	100%	77%
Heriot-Watt	400	65%	94%	Sheffield	480	100%	89%
Hertfordshire	220	40%	91%	Southampton	440	100%	83%
Imperial College	540	95%	ND	St George's	440	100%	89%
KCL	440	65%	88%	St Andrews	510	ND	97%
Lancaster	430	70%	92%	UCL	480	100%	91%
Leeds	430	68%	82%	Warwick	ND	100%	85%
Liverpool	400	60%	82%				
LSE	540	95%	83%	**Philosophy**			
Loughborough	390	60%	93%	Aberdeen	324	60%	92%
Manchester	450	66%	86%	Bristol	480	70%	86%
Newcastle	410	64%	87%	Cambridge	540	65%	96%
Nottingham	460	68%	90%	Durham	450	65%	91%
Oxford	550	93%	ND	Edinburgh	450	55%	81%
Queen Mary	300	60%	82%	Glasgow	410	55%	96%
Royal Holloway	365	65%	94%	Heythrop	350	50%	80%
Sheffield	400	60%	90%	Keele	280	50%	82%
Sheffield Hallam	260	60%	100%	KCL	445	65%	91%
St Andrews	520	75%	95%	Lancaster	360	60%	88%
Sussex	360	80%	87%	LSE	520	80%	84%
UCL	490	75%	86%	Newcastle	340	60%	88%
Warwick	540	75%	89%	Oxford	540	81%	94%
York	440	60%	90%	Royal Holloway	380	55%	92%
				Sheffield	430	55%	94%

Medicine

				Sussex	380	65%	96%
Aberdeen	490	100%	93%	UCL	480	65%	88%
Birmingham	500	99%	83%	Warwick	460	55%	82%
Brighton & Sussex	480	100%	85%	York	430	55%	85%

Physical Science

	A Level Points Accepted	Real Graduate Jobs	Student Satisfaction
Aberdeen	343	60%	85%
Bath	420	68%	89%
Bradford	190	60%	81%
Brighton	260	60%	85%
Bristol	460	61%	87%
Cambridge	573	77%	90%
Durham	520	83%	90%
East Anglia	300	60%	87%
Exeter	380	60%	87%
Heriot-Watt	318	70%	86%
Huddersfield	200	80%	86%
Hull	260	75%	94%
Imperial College	510	77%	81%
Lancaster	380	70%	100%
Leicester	340	70%	95%
Liverpool	390	66%	89%
Loughborough	300	65%	97%
Manchester	410	60%	93%
Manchester Met	220	60%	73%
Newcastle	350	75%	86%
Northumbria	290	60%	85%
Nottingham	400	77%	92%
Oxford	540	83%	90%
Plymouth	220	61%	87%
Queen's Belfast	390	60%	100%
Robert Gordon	352	65%	79%
Royal Holloway	340	70%	93%
Sheffield	390	65%	92%
Southampton	400	63%	94%
Staffordshire	220	60%	94%
St Andrews	480	75%	96%
Strathclyde	365	60%	95%
Surrey	320	65%	83%
Sussex	370	80%	97%
UCL	430	61%	89%
Warwick	460	68%	89%
York	420	65%	91%

Politics

	A Level Points Accepted	Real Graduate Jobs	Student Satisfaction
Aston	350	65%	89%
Bath	440	85%	87%
Birmingham	390	52%	87%
Birmingham City	240	51%	81%
Bradford	300	65%	95%
Bristol	420	74%	86%
Brunel	290	55%	88%
Cambridge	480	75%	95%
Durham	460	80%	88%
Edinburgh	428	65%	76%

	A Level Points Accepted	Real Graduate Jobs	Student Satisfaction
Essex	330	50%	95%
Exeter	410	55%	95%
Glasgow	420	55%	91%
Goldsmiths College	290	50%	81%
Hull	330	60%	87%
Keele	290	50%	90%
Kent	290	50%	86%
KCL	420	70%	84%
Lancaster	370	55%	84%
Leeds	390	74%	87%
Leicester	340	65%	96%
Liverpool JM	240	50%	78%
LSE	470	80%	82%
Loughborough	320	67%	86%
Manchester	410	60%	72%
Newcastle	380	65%	92%
Northumbria	280	60%	76%
Nottingham	410	69%	88%
Oxford	520	80%	93%
Queen Mary	360	50%	88%
Royal Holloway	350	50%	90%
SOAS	410	70%	79%
Sheffield	440	70%	96%
Southampton	390	50%	83%
St Andrews	464	80%	94%
Surrey	320	60%	80%
Sussex	360	65%	86%
Swansea	290	50%	75%
Warwick	470	70%	90%
Westminster	230	60%	72%
York	460	70%	76%

Psychology

	A Level Points Accepted	Real Graduate Jobs	Student Satisfaction
Bath	480	65%	70%
Bournemouth	270	60%	84%
Bradford	240	50%	84%
Bristol	440	50%	89%
Cambridge	480	75%	95%
Central Lancashire	290	56%	91%
Chester	280	53%	85%
Derby	230	50%	76%
Dundee	330	50%	91%
Durham	420	51%	81%
Exeter	420	50%	86%
Glasgow	400	67%	93%
Huddersfield	260	50%	88%
Kent	360	53%	97%
Lancaster	400	56%	83%
Leicester	370	56%	82%
Middlesex	200	65%	69%

	A Level Points Accepted	Real Graduate Jobs	Student Satisfaction
Newcastle	420	59%	81%
Northumbria	330	56%	87%
Nottingham	420	58%	84%
Oxford	480	80%	93%
Roehampton	220	66%	74%
Sheffield	400	70%	79%
Staffordshire	240	50%	90%
Surrey	390	60%	87%
Sussex	380	66%	97%
UCL	490	70%	90%
Warwick	430	50%	91%
Westminster	260	59%	74%

Veterinary Sciences

	A Level Points Accepted	Real Graduate Jobs	Student Satisfaction
Bristol	460	96%	90%
Cambridge	540	90%	91%
Edinburgh	484	96%	84%
Glasgow	480	100%	95%
Harper Adams	280	78%	88%
Liverpool	495	97%	94%
Royal Vet College	440	98%	80%

UNIVERSITY OF ABERDEEN

The University of Aberdeen
Regent Walk
Aberdeen AB24 3FX

TEL   01224 272090/91
FAX   01224 272576
EMAIL sras@abdn.ac.uk
WEB www.abdn.ac.uk

Aberdeen University Students' Association
The Hub
Old Aberdeen AB24 3TU

TEL 01224 272965
FAX 01224 272977
EMAIL ausa@aberdeen.ac.uk
WEB www.ausa.org.uk

VIRGIN VIEW

*T*he University of Aberdeen has maintained a place in the Times Higher Magazine's *World's Top 200*, appearing 22nd among the British contingent. So popular is it with Americans that it is one of only two British universities (the other is St Andrews) to appear in The Fiske Guide to Colleges, the No. 1 university guide in America. Fiske says, 'The University has a distinctly medieval aura.'

Aberdeen is indeed the oldest university outside Oxbridge, its Chair of Medicine was the first established in the English-speaking world, and King's College Aberdeen was founded in 1495.

As one of four ancient universities in Scotland, the teaching is traditional, seminars, tutorials, etc, and some of the lecture rooms full of traditional character (and draughts).

Ideologically, they are adamant that the 'industrialisation' of higher education - the current obsession with student employability and how universities contribute to the national economy, will not deter the higher purpose of traditional liberal learning or the role of humanities and social sciences in siciety. It's the idea that university might just be about something other than getting a job to stoke the economy.

There's a consistently high student satisfaction rate - 89% gave the teaching their vote in the latest HEFCE survey, but in a Times Higher Education *survey they have voted their Student Union, or*

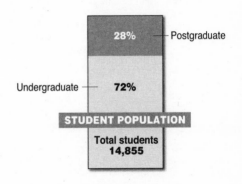

Association, the worst in the UK.

Students Kevin Walsh and Alan Tanner source the roots of dissent in long-term disillusion and bitter experience. 'Nobody is quite sure why Aberdeen students don't seem to care for who represents them [in the union], but we might suggest that the fact that the representation does not always seem to produce tangible results is a factor in this unfortunate trend.' So, nothing new there then.

This has no effect on students' social life and extra-curricular fun and games, which they give a 4-star rating.

FEES, BURSARIES

If you are a Scottish-domiciled first degree student you are eligible for you tution fees to be covered by

UNIVERSITY/STUDENT PROFILE	
University since	**1495**
Situation/style	**Civic**
Student population	**14855**
Total undergraduates	**10760**
Mature	**38%**
International	**23%**
Male/female ratio	**45:55**
Equality of opportunity:	
state school intake	**80%**
social class 4-7 intake	**26%**
drop-out rate	**7%**

the Scottish Government. Sassernachs pay £1,820. There are entrance scholarships worth £1,000 p.a., allocated on the basis of financial need or academic merit. Also sports scholarships and awards made to talented musicians. See www.abdn.ac.uk/undergraduate/finance.php and www.abdn.ac.uk/undergraduate/scholarships.php

CAMPUS

Aberdeen is on the North East coast of Scotland, pretty much final step on the way to the Arctic (a couple of farms and the odd island notwithstanding). Easily reachable, if you've a bit of time on your hands, Aberdeen provides a safe haven for those trying to get as far away as possible from parents, and the rest of civilisation.

The Granite City, as it is accurately called, harbours a bit of a cosmopolitan atmosphere (there's some docks) and a very long beach. The climate is raw, as are the people, but when the sun shines, everything warms up and it's actually a beautiful city.

The city itself is framed around Union Street, with the main university campus about a mile (and a lung-busting hill) north of the centre. This is King's College campus, the oldest part of the university, located in the imaginatively entitled Old Aberdeen. Most students study here, among Gothic towers, cloisters, and cobbled streets.

> *'Aberdeen has a good reputation, without the stigma of being an Oxbridge wannabe, like St Andrews or Edinburgh... The climate is raw, as are the people, but when the sun shines, everything warms up and it's a beautiful city.'*

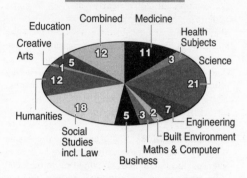

SUBJECT AREAS (%)

Education — Combined 12 — Medicine 11 — Health Subjects — Science 3 — Science 21 — Engineering 7 — Built Environment 2 — Maths & Computer 3 — Business 5 — Social Studies incl. Law 18 — Humanities 12 — Creative Arts 1 — 5

There are other campuses: one in town which is not used anymore, except to keep dead bodies for first year medics to play about with, the hospital, where they keep the live bodies for the rest of the medics to play about with, the Hilton campus for Education, complete with its own halls of residence, and the new Foresterhill campus, where the medics study 25 mins from King's College.

STUDENT PROFILE

There's a highish count of public school types (20%), but the successful completion of the Summer School for Access guarantees a place on most of the uni's degree courses. Writes Rob Littlejohn, 'The students come in eight distinct groups: Aberdonians, who talk smugly about pubs in other parts of town and watch quietly as we get lost; Country Teuchters (pronounced 'choochters' - there you know some local dialect already), very similar to Aberdonians, but without the urban sophistication; Edinburgh Public Schoolers, a feature of most Scottish unis with better English accents than most of those south of the border and more money than sense; Other Scots - Scotland has a greater tradition of staying at home to study and we do get some Edinburghers keen to distance themselves from a public school education, Glaswegians pining for home, sectarianism and annoying accents, and Dundonians just happy to be somewhere else. There's also the Huge Bands of Others - Northern Irish, random English, and other foreign students.'

ACADEMIA & JOBS

Eighty-nine per cent of Aberdeen's teaching was

TEACHING SURVEY AT A GLANCE

Avg. UCAS points accepted	**369**
Acceptance rate	**17%**
Overall satisfaction rate	**89%**
Helpful/interested staff	★★★★
Small tuition groups	★★★
Students into graduate jobs	**72%**

Teaching most popular with undergraduates :
Anatomy, Physiology, Pathology, Anthropology, Biology, Civil and Chemical Engineering, Computer, English (100%), Languages, Geography, History, Iberian Studies (100%), Law, Medicine, Dentistry, Pharmacology, Philosophy, Theology, Physics, Politics, Psychology, Sociology, Sports Science, Zoology.

Teaching least popular with undergraduates:
Architecture, Building, Planning (62%).

adjudged either Excellent or Highly Satisfactory in the assessments, and in the most recent examination in 2008 nearly 90% of research undertaken was recognised to be of international quality, with eleven subjects ranked amongst the top 25% in the UK: Health Services Research; Biological Sciences; Agriculture and Food Science; Pure Mathematics; General Engineering (including mining); Town and Country Planning; Anthropology; French; English Language and Literature; Theology, Divinity and Religious Studies; and History.

There are three 'Colleges': Arts and Social Sciences; Life Sciences & Medicine; and Physical Sciences, through which are taught more than 600 undergraduate degrees and 140+ masters degrees.

For the Medicine degree, AAB is required in 3 A levels, taken at the first sitting: Chemistry plus one of Maths, Biology or Physics. Most other subjects are acceptable for the third subject. The UK Clinical Aptitude Test (UKCAT) is also required.

Industrial placements combined with strong relationships with industry, major research centres and other leading international universities help ensure that courses are relevant to the requirements of the modern world and professional graduate jobs do certainly follow - 76% of graduates have them within six months of graduation. Mainly they become doctors or find themselves in social work, in the education sector (notably primary), in government administration, accountancy, banking, or in the retail sector or mining (especially gas and oil), and a lot go on to become lawyers, for Law is, along with Medicine, Divinity, and Engineering, one of the pillars of the Aberdeen establishment.

A new £57-million library opens next year.

SOCIAL SCENE

They've taken away all the student nightclubs and bars they used to have on campus. But September 2006 saw completion of **The Hub**, 'a one-stop shop for all your needs'. The Machar Bar is a long, thin wooden-floored pub with no music and no pool table; just copper drinking jugs, a dartboard and bags of room.

The Students Union, or Association, funds 100+ clubs and societies, counting sports ranging from football and karate to boxing and underwater hockey, and masses of cultural societies including a particularly busy University Music Programme - orchestra, choral society, chapel choir or concert band. The weekly student paper - free and run by students - is *Gaudie*.

Beyond campus, in the lanes around Belmont Street, trendy vodka bars, lively drinking dens and

RESEARCH EXCELLENCE		

% of Aberdeen's research that is
4* *(World-class) or* **3*** *(Internationally rated):*

	4*	3*
Hospital Based Clinical Med.	15%	60%
Epidemiology, Public Health	10%	50%
Health Services Research	25%	55%
Primary Care	25%	40%
Biological Sciences	15%	40%
Pre-clinical. Human Biological	5%	35%
Agriculture, Vet, Food Science	20%	35%
Earth Systems, Enviro. Sci.	10%	50%
Chemistry	5%	35%
Pure Mathematics	20%	45%
Computer Science	20%	50%
General Eng., Mineral, Mining	20%	35%
Town and Country Planning	20%	40%
Geography	10%	40%
Economics and Econometrics	20%	45%
Business and Management	10%	30%
Law	5%	30%
Politics	5%	20%
Sociology	15%	40%
Anthropology	30%	25%
Psychology	5%	45%
Education	5%	20%
Sports-Related Studies	5%	25%
French	20%	35%
German, Dutch, Scandinavian	0%	25%
Iberian and Latin American	10%	35%
Celtic Studies	0%	15%
English Language and Lit.	30%	35%
Philosophy	0%	25%
Theology	15%	65%
History	30%	30%
History of Art, Architec., Design	20%	35%
Music	5%	45%

student-friendly clubs sit alongside courtyards ideal for a summertime beer. Writes a Union wallah: 'The city boasts a huge variety of venues ranging from trendy clubs to old-world pubs full of atmosphere and everything in between.' The cavernous Tunnels is the city's live-music nucleus. The **Lemon Tree** and other venues also stage well-known performers. Aberdeen's oldest pub is **Ma Cameron's**, where they've been quenching student thirsts since 1789, and next to King's College the **Bobbin** is big on sports screens, pool tables and pulsing music, the student pub.

SPORT The £28-million Aberdeen Sports Village was completed in August 2009 in partnership with Aberdeen City Council and Sportscotland. There's a full-size indoor football pitch and running straight with throwing and jumping areas, a large

WHAT IT'S REALLY LIKE

UNIVERSITY:

Social Life	★★★★
Societies	★★★★
Student Union services	★
Politics	**Internal**
Sport	**58 clubs**
National team position	**31st**
Sport facilities	★★★★★
Arts opportunities	**Drama, music exc.; film good; dance, art poor**
Student newspaper	**Gaudie**
Student radio	**Aberdeen Student Radio - NSR**
Bar	**Off-campus bar**
Union ents	**Guarded promise**
Union societies	**70+**
Most active society	**MedSoc**
Parking	**Some**

CITY:

Entertainment	★★★★
Scene	**Intoxicating**
Town/gown relations	**Good**
Risk of violence	**Low**
Cost of living	**Average**
Student concessions	**Average**
Survival + 2 nights out	**£60 pw**
Part-time work campus/town	**Good/excellent**

The centre is base for the Sports Union's 58 affiliated clubs and Intra Mural sports programme: www.abdn.ac.uk/ sportandexercise/performance.

PILLOW TALK

Halls of Residence, on-campus or nearby, offer traditional single study bedrooms or self-catering flats. These and university-administered property in the city have trained wardens in residence. In 2008, 520 new en-suite bedrooms were opened at Hillhead Halls: www.abdn.ac.uk/accommodation. All students are entitled to park in designated student parking areas.

GETTING THERE

☞ By road: from south, A92 and ring road where

ACCOMMODATION

Student rating	★
Guarantee to freshers	**100%**
Style	**Halls, flats**
Security guard	**All**
Shared rooms	**Some halls**
Internet access	**All**
Self-catered	**Most**
En suite	**Some**
Approx price range pw	**£72-£198.45**
City rent pw	**£65-£140**

games hall, squash courts, fitness suite and performance gym, exercise studios, sports science facilities and dining and conference areas. Plans for phases two and three include additional grass and artificial surfaces, and an Olympic-sized pool.

you'll pick up signs; from north, A96 or the A92.
☞ By rail: Edinburgh, 2:30; Dundee, 1:15; Newcastle, 4:50; London King's Cross, 7:00.
☞ By air: Aberdeen International Airport.
☞ By coach: London, 11.30; Birmingham, 12.35.

UNIVERSITY OF ABERTAY DUNDEE

The University of Abertay Dundee
Bell Street
Dundee DD1 1HG

TEL 01382 308000
FAX 01382 308298
EMAIL sro@abertay.ac.uk
WEB www.abertay.ac.uk

Abertay Dundee Students' Association
1-3 Bell Street
Dundee DD1 1HG

TEL 01382 308950
FAX 01382 308326
EMAIL president@abertayunion.cac.uk
WEB www.abertaystudents.com/

VIRGIN VIEW

*L*ocated on a modern campus in the centre of Dundee, Abertay, formerly the Dundee Institute of Technology, resists the Higher Education Funding Council's interest in the opinion of its small, 4,000-strong body of students as to what goes on, boldly and

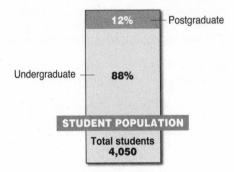

STUDENT POPULATION

Total students
4,050

Undergraduate — 88%

12% — Postgraduate

STUDENT PROFILE

Around 73% of students are from Scotland, 6% from Ireland, 4% from England and Wales, and 17% from overseas. Altogether, around 70 nationalities are represented. There's a 36% take from the lowest four socio-economic groups and 3% from 'low-participation neighbourhoods'.

ACADEMIA & JOBS

Abertay has four academic schools: Computing, the Dundee Business School, Science & Engineering, and Social & Health Sciences. At the core of its provision is the International Centre for Computing and Virtual Entertainment (IC-CAVE). A defining mark of Abertay is that it was the first

possibly wisely electing not to be part of the National Student Survey.

There is, in fact, a high local intake and sizeable mature and overseas student population, and a good and often idiosyncratic reputation for its courses in Computing, Business and Sport.

Its record for student employment is traditionally high, but a mere 56% have real graduate jobs six months after graduation, in spite of massive graduate employment projects. Nevertheless, students like it here. The drop-out rate is 7% and falling.

FEES, BURSARIES

Non-Scottish UK student fees are £1,820. If you are a Scottish-domiciled first degree student you are eligible for your tuition fees to be covered by the Scottish Government. There's no reason to go short if you come here. Sporty types scramble for the Abertay Elite Athletes Development Programme. Academic types go for the Young Student's Bursary, or various Opportunity Bursaries, Career Development Loans, and named funds, trusts and bursaries, like the Robert Reid Fund for students from poor backgrounds. There's also a Disabled Students' Allowance, various Overseas Scholarships, and HE Discretionary Funds for students with kids or other dependents.

UNIVERSITY/STUDENT PROFILE	
University since	**1994**
Situation/style	**Civic**
Student population	**4050**
Total undergraduates	**3560**
Mature	**39%**
International	**23%**
Male/female ratio	**50:50**
Equality of opportunity:	
state school intake	**98%**
social class 4-7 intake	**38%**
drop-out rate	**7%**

university to offer Computer Games Technology as a degree. An Abertay student, David Jones, created the legendary Lemmings and Grand Theft Auto. It is now the only UK University with official accreditation for both computer games technology and computer arts. Skillset is the sector skills council for the creative industry. Abertay now has 4 out of the 10 sccreditations awarded by Skillset throughout the UK.

In March 2010, a team of Abertay students won two BAFTAs in one night. The Butterflyers, five computer games programmers and artists, picked

SUBJECT AREAS (%)

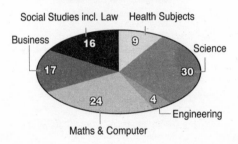

Social Studies incl. Law   Health Subjects
Business
Science
Engineering
Maths & Computer

16 9 30 4 24 17

TEACHING SURVEY AT A GLANCE	
Avg. UCAS points accepted	**270**
Acceptance rate	**35%**
Overall satisfaction rate	**76%**
Helpful/interested staff	★★★★
Small tuition groups	★★★
Students into graduate jobs	**56%**

Subjects most popular with undergraduates:
Computer Arts, Games Technology, Earth Systems & Environmental Technology, General & Mineral Engineering, Law, Psychology.

RESEARCH EXCELLENCE

% of Abertay's research that is
4* (World-class) or 3* (Internationally rated):

	4*	3*
Allied Health Studies	0%	10%
Earth Systems, Enviro. Sci.	10%	35%
General Eng.. Minera, Mining	5%	20%
Business and Management	0%	15%
Law	0%	20%
Psychology	0%	15%

up the Ones to Watch Award at the BAFTA Videogames Awards in London, and the Best New Game Award at the BAFTA Scotland New Talent Awards in Glasgow. The Butterflyers were one of three winning teams in last year's Dare to be Digital competition, organised and promoted by Abertay University. Dare to be Digital pits teams from all over the world against each other in an intense, highly competitive 10-week race to produce a fully functioning prototype computer game that is then judged by industry experts and voted for by the public in a special showcase event at the Edinburgh Fringe Festival.

The modelling and visualisation technologies that underpin computer games are already feeding through into a range of new disciplines at Abertay, such as environmental modelling and prediction, anti-cancer drug treatment methodologies, policing techniques, urban planning, critical systems infrastructure and many other exciting new areas, involving psychologists, biologists, software engineers, computer scientists and business experts working together.

Employment-wise, they have Embreonix, Scotland's first graduate enterprise centre dedicated to helping students set up their own business, and a £5 million investment for Games IP, the UK's first dedicated prototyping centre for the computer games industry, which aims to create 400 new jobs and build the skills for 300 others, as well as help create 30 new businesses and provide support for more than 80 existing small companies. Grants of £25k are available.

As befits Scotland's top 'new' university for environmental research, the Centre for the Environment is a £4-million research and knowledge transfer centre, designed to provide small and medium-sized companies with expert help in devising more environmentally-friendly products, services and processes.

Sports trainers and coaches also flow out of Abertay in number, and there's a new sports science laboratory for their BSc Sport Coaching &

Development and Sport, Health & Exercise, and a new degree last year: MBA Sports Development.

Other popular employment areas are banking, local government, higher education, law, hospitals and the community. Nurses (SEN, SRN, RGN, etc) are a prominent feature, and there's a new MSc Sexual & Reproductive Health degree.

In the Law provision, Abertay are European LLB Specialists, but also consider their BSc Forensic Sciences degree and BSc Forensic Psychobiology. Bestselling crime writer Ian Rankin opened a gruesome scene-of-the-crime-house here. 2009 saw the official opening of a 'Scenes of Crime' bank, first of its kind on Scotland.

There's a good reputation, too, for placing graduates from their BSc Civil Engineering and Dip HE Civil Engineering Studies, and although there are no dedicated BSc degrees in Quantity Surveying there's a strong current of graduates finding employment in this area, too.

Watch out, too, for their Human Resource Management provision, another department which makes a solid showing in the job figures

WHAT IT'S REALLY LIKE

UNIVERSITY:

Social Life	★★★
Societies	★★
Student Union services	★★★★
Politics	**Activity low**
Sport	**29 clubs**
National teamposition	**99th**
Sport facilities	★
Arts	**Dance, music, film average; art, drama poor**
Student magazine	**None**
Nightclub	**Basement**
Bars	**Bar One, Sportsbar, Rooftop garden**
Union ents	**Wednesdays, Playground; Fridays, Slinky**
Union societies	**35**
Most popular society	**Role-Playing**
Parking	**None**

CITY:

Entertainment	★★★★
Scene	**Pubs, good live**
Town/gown relations	**Average**
Risk of violence	**Low**
Cost of living	**Average**
Student concessions	**Good**
Survival + 2 nights out	**£60 pw**
Part-time work campus/town	**Excellent/average**

SOCIAL SCENE

STUDENTS' ASSOCIATION Local intake it may be, but now they have a £6 million Student Centre, which opened its doors to students for the first time in Spring 2005, and was later opened again, officially, by Midge Ure. It contains a nightclub, coffee shop, two bars, and the Hannah Maclure Centre, which has a cinema, art gallery and rooftop terrace. In Spring 2011 they won the Best Bar None competition against stiff opposition throughout Scotland. Daytime obsessions are more or less satisfied this year by thirty-five clubs and societies (mainly sport).

SPORT The Elite Athlete Development Programme has supported more than 30 international athletes in the last three years, including two world champions and five British champions. There's a good variety of sports/pursuits at the recreational level, with intra-mural activities, club sports, a gym and a £500,000 sports science laboratory, but for the rest students must make do with free access to local Astroturf pitches, pools and stadia. There's also golf and the Glenshee Ski Slopes not far away.

ACCOMMODATION	
Guarantee to freshers	**100%**
Style	**Halls, flats**
Security guard	**Campus**
Shared rooms	**None**
Internet access	**All**
Self-catered	**All**
En suite	**Some**
Avg. price range pw	**£45-£127**
City rent pw	**£60**

PILLOW TALK
Brand new for freshers, a purpose built residence with 500 bedspaces 5 mins from the University.

GETTING THERE
☛ By road: M90, M85, A85, A972.
☛ By rail: Newcastle, 3:00; London Euston, 6:00.
☛ By air: Dundee Airport for internal flights; Edinburgh International Airport is an hour away.
☛ By coach: London, 10:05; Newcastle, 6:05.

UNIVERSITY OF WALES, ABERYSTWYTH

The University of Wales, Aberystwyth
Aberystwyth
Ceredigion SY23 2AX

TEL 01970 622021
FAX 01970 627410
EMAIL ug-admissions@aber.ac.uk
WEB www.aber.ac.uk

Aberystwyth Guild of Students
Aberystwyth
Ceredigion SY23 3DX

TEL 01970 621700
FAX 01970 621701
EMAIL union@aber.ac.uk
WEB www.aberguild.co.uk

VIRGIN VIEW

*T*he University of Aberystwyth's location makes it a top choice for many applicants. 'Think Wales; think west; think coast,' write Pete Liggins and Kate Glanville. 'It is then slap bang in the middle, a lovely seaside town whose two main industries are tourists in the summer and students in the closed season.'

Its academic strengths are in niche areas such as countryside management, tourism, international politics, Welsh/Celtic studies, Irish, geography and earth sciences, equine science, marine & freshwater biology, information & library studies, theatre, film and TV (there's a £3.5-million centre for these).

The uni certainly has its specialities; its very Welshness can seem daunting to some,

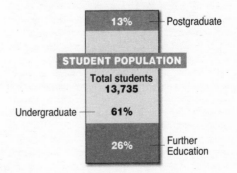

STUDENT POPULATION

Total students
13,735

Postgraduate 13%
Undergraduate 61%
Further Education 26%

UNIVERSITY/STUDENT PROFILE

University since	**1872**
Situation/style	**Campus**
Student population	**13735**
Total undergraduates	**8385**
Mature	**35%**
International	**14%**
Male/female ratio	**45:55**
Equality of opportunity:	
state school intake	**94%**
social class 4-7 intake	**34%**
drop-out rate	**6%**

but it isn't long before you realise that what makes Aber a good bet is the way it delivers every aspect of student services right through academia and into the social side of the Students' Guild, whatever your expectations.

Students love it. An incredible 92% of them gave it a thumbs-up in the nationwide survey, and the drop-out rate is low (6%). In particular they like the interest shown in them by teaching staff and the small size tuition groups. Yet oddly, Aber always seems to show a poor graduate employment rate, 55% in real graduate jobs after six months. Perhaps they just can't drag themselves off the beach until winter sets in.

FEES, BURSARIES

UK & EU Fees for 2011-12, £3,375. National Welsh entrant grants aside, there are bursaries available to UK and EU students, on a sliding scale according to family income. Any student may apply for one of the Excellence Bursaries to reward academic achievment in specific subjects prior to gaining entry to the uni. These can be worth as much as £3,334 over a 5-year course; £2,000 for the more usual 3-year and £1,400 for a 2-year Foundation course. There are also 50 Entrance scholarships worth up to £1,200 p.a. and some 250 Merit Awards of up to £1,000 p.a. These require you to sit exams in two named subjects - there are 39 to choose from. Then there are £400 discounts on the first year's accommodation fee, music bursaries worth £400 a year, and care leaver bursaries worth between £1,000 and £1,800 a year for students under 24 years of age, who have spent a period of time in care prior to their 16th birthday. www.aber.ac.uk/en/scholarships/aber-bursaries.

CAMPUS

Most of the university, including the main Students' Guild building, is contained within the Penglais campus, set on a hill above beautiful Cardigan Bay. But there is another campus at Llanbadarn, less than a mile away and home to the Department of Information and Library Studies, the College of Further Education and the Institute of Rural Studies. The sites are linked by a common telephone system, and there's a good bus service (if you're too lazy to walk).

STUDENT PROFILE

The student body is diverse. There are plenty of English here, though homage is paid to the Welsh hosts by their own countrymen, and the Students' Guild, or Yr Undeb as it translates in Welsh, plays a key role in supporting the native lingo: 'The unwritten rule is that you should accept anyone's right to speak in Welsh and not get paranoid that they are talking about you if you can't understand.' Relatively few public school types (6%).

ACADEMIA & JOBS

The best teaching, say students, is in Accounting and Sports Science, both had 100% class approval. Biology and Geography followed up with 98%.

There is great strength in the Institute of Geography & Earth Sciences, where you'll find Earth Planetary & Space Science, Environmental Earth Science (and with Education), Geography (there's a well-trod pathway for cartographers), and Water Sciences (see also the Marine Biology degrees). They took 'Excellent' in the assessments.

New recently was the Institute of Biological, Environmental and Rural Sciences, which brings together staff from the Institutes of Rural Sciences and Biological Sciences. It is set to play a major role in a £27-million initiative launched by the Biotechnology and Biological Sciences Research Council to develop clean, green and sustainable fuels. The aim is to provide the science to underpin and develop the important and emerging

> *'Think Wales, think west, think coast. It's a lovely seaside town, whose two main industries are tourists in the summer and students in the closed season. The unwritten rule is to accept anyone's right to speak Welsh and not to get paranoid when they do that they're talking about you.'*

UK sustainable bioenergy sector - and to replace the petrol in cars with fuels derived from plants.

In the area of another strength - Politics - Aber has a history, which goes back to the 1960s when there were things called ideals hard fought for on campus. Now, there's a £5 million HQ for the world-renowned Department of International Politics. For graduates today, all this opens up a sound route into the Defence industry.

In-depth strength in Drama/Dance/Performing Arts produces Arts administrators, managers, and stage managers in number.

There is a good administrative reputation all round, it seems, with managers and administrators of one sort or another heading Aber's graduate employment list. Would-be museum archivists, curators, librarians should look with respect at their BA Museum & Gallery Studies and BA Information & Library Studies. The latter can be combined with American Studies, Art History,

SUBJECT AREAS (%)

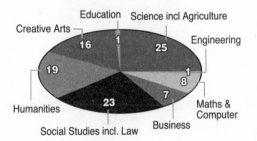

- Education 1
- Science incl Agriculture 25
- Creative Arts 16
- Engineering 1
- 8
- 19
- 7
- Humanities 23
- Maths & Computer
- Social Studies incl. Law
- Business

Drama, Fine Art, languages, Film & TV, etc, and their Museum & Gallery Studies joins the same joint honours scheme. The whole mind set in this area favours research jobs in media (publishing is especially strong) and government.

Look, too, at the computer provision - software engineers dominate the employment figures. Courses include Artificial Intelligence and Robotics, Computer Graphics Vision and Games, Mobile and Wearable Computing.

Sports Science is among the most popular departments and it has just been included in the London Olympics Organising Committee Pre-Games Camp Training Guide, as a training centre for elite athletes in mountain biking.

Note their specialist LLB Human Rights and European Law and Business & Commercial Law degrees. Law students can qualify now in Aber without needing to proceed to Law College, and the Law Dept allows non-Law graduates to take a 2/3-year full-time/part-time Senior Status law degree.

TEACHING SURVEY AT A GLANCE

Avg. UCAS points accepted	**280**
Acceptance rate	**27%**
Overall satisfaction rate	**92%**
Helpful/interested staff	★★★★
Small tuition groups	★★★★
Students into graduate jobs	**55%**

Teaching most popular with undergraduates:
Accounting (100%), Agriculture, Animal Science, Biological Sciences (98%), Celtic Studies, Computer, Drama, Economics, English, Finance, Geology, Geography (98%), Law, Journalism, Maths, Politics, Sports Science (100%).

SOCIAL SCENE

The best times in Aber are had on those sun-shimmering days when there are half a dozen beach fire parties to chill out at. With students making up half the town's population, if you are out day or night then you are bound to bump into someone you like, or would sooner forget.

Students' Guild Llanbadarn has **Y Gwyllt - The Outback** bar, and entertainment facilities, discos and a pool room. Back at base camp, in the Penglais Guild building, there's **Bar 9** and the Joint, a nightclub, with **Cwrt Mawr Bar** the halls pub on this campus. Sadly, this isolated coastal resort is not a draw for big name bands, but 'live' is definitely part of the ents menu.

Guild facilities also include dance, art and

RESEARCH EXCELLENCE

% of Aberystwyth's research that is
4* *(World-class) or* **3*** *(Internationally rated):*

	4*	3*
Agriculture, Vet., Food Science	10%	35%
Physics	5%	15%
Pure Mathematics	5%	35%
Computer Science	25%	45%
Geography	20%	45%
Business and Management	5%	25%
Library and Infor. Mgt	10%	40%
Law	5%	30%
Politics	40%	25%
Sports-Related Studies	0%	15%
European Studies	20%	15%
Celtic Studies	25%	40%
English Language and Lit.	10%	30%
History	10%	35%
History of Art, Architec., Design	5%	20%
Drama, Dance, etc	30%	30%

WHAT IT'S REALLY LIKE

UNIVERSITY:

Social Life	★★★★
Societies	★★★★
Student Union services	★★★★
Politics	**Traditionally very strong**
Sport	**Consistent**
National team position	**62nd**
Sport facilities	★★★★
Arts opportunities	**Good Arts Centre**
Student magazine	**The Courier Yr Utgom**
Student radio	**Bay Radio**
Nightclub	**The Joint**
Bars	**Bar 9, Cwrt Mawr, Outback**
Union ents	**Comedy, cheese, clubnights beach parties**
Union societies	**40**
Parking	**Good**

TOWN:

Entertainment	★★
Scene	**Scenic seaside**
Town/gown relations	**Good**
Risk of violence	**Low**
Cost of living	**Average**
Student concessions	**Poor**
Survival + 2 nights out	**£60 pw**
Part-time work campus/town	**Good**

ACCOMMODATION

Student rating	★★★★
Guarantee to freshers	**100%**
Style	**Halls, flats**
Security guard	**All**
Internet access	**All**
Self-catered	**Some flats, no halls**
En suite	**No halls, some flats**
Approx price range pw	**£70-£103.50**
City rent pw	**£60-£75**

and there is orienteering, mountain-biking, rambling, sub-aqua and hang-gliding too.

TOWN There's a one-screen cinema, where films tend to be shown around two to three weeks after their actual release date. The flick makes up for this by being cheap, friendly and licensed - so you can have a pint while watching the film - and the programme sports some of the cheapest and best local advertising you will ever have the pleasure to view. The cinema's ethos seems to sum up the whole town; everything is more laid back here: the sun shines and things slow down; it's life without the big city stresses.

Aber is also blessed with a number of pubs, described by one student as 'beyond definition; every taste should be catered for somewhere. There is something of a worrying trend, however, towards refitting and furbishing with an emphasis

drama workshop spaces, an art cinema, studio theatre and art gallery.

Student media is pre-eminent with *The Courier* (*Yr Utgorn* - www.thecourier.org.uk/), *Ur Ytgorn* - Welsh language magazine, and Bay Radio.

Traditionally, political activity is high compared to many, with, typically, active Welsh Language campaigning, and international human rights, and peace and justice issues to the fore.

The Guild also offers a range of courses to develop employment skills.

SPORT It's a big thing at Aber, American Football being among their areas of excellence. There are fifty acres of pitches and specialist facilities for water sports, including a boat house, an indoor swimming pool, two sports halls, an all-weather floodlit sports pitch, squash courts and indoor facilities for football, badminton, basketball, hockey and tennis.

Cardigan Bay and nearby Snowdonia offer windsurfing and skiing opportunities respectively,

on American tack, for each of these is a true local - one in particular won't serve a pint of Guinness in less than five minutes.'

Safety is not an issue in Aberystwyth.

PILLOW TALK

Penbryn and Pantycelyn only are catered. Cost ranges from a twin room space in Cwrt Mawr, close to all campus amenities, to a single room in catered Pantycelyn (designated as 'mixed Welsh' hall to keep the lingo native, the latter, like all so-called catered, includes a pre-paid meal ticket sufficient for at least one meal a day.

GETTING THERE

☞ By road: A484 from north or south; A44 from the east.

☞ By rail: London Euston, 5 hours. Chart your route carefully or you'll end up on a slow local line through the mid-Wales countryside.

☞ By coach: London, 7:00; Newcastle, 11:00.

ANGLIA RUSKIN UNIVERSITY

Anglia Ruskin University
East Road
Cambridge CB1 1PT

TEL 0845 271 3333
FAX 01245 251789
EMAIL answers@anglia.ac.uk
WEB www.anglia.ac.uk

Anglia Ruskin Students' Union
East Road
Cambridge CB1 1PT

TEL 01603 593272
EMAIL info@angliastudent.com
WEB www.angliastudent.com

VIRGIN VIEW

*A*nglia Ruskin is based in Cambridge city centre and in Chelmsford, Essex. The university comes out of Cambridgeshire College of Arts and Technology and the Essex Institute of Higher Education, which merged in 1989 to form Anglia Higher Education College. In 1991, this became Anglia Polytechnic, and Anglia Polytechnic University the following year. Its re-branding as Anglia Ruskin occurred a decade later.

In its student population it is very much a 'new' university. All but 3% are state school educated, and 39% are drawn from socio-economic classes 4-7. There is a high acceptance rate of applicants, an effort to institute manageable, decent size tuition groups, and students rate staff interest fairly highly.

They are looking for around 240 points at A level and/or evidence of enthusiasm for the subject area, an ability to research, and for transferable skills and work experience.

At the end there is a good 'real graduate job' rate - in the first six months after graduation: 72%, boosted in particular by the primary teacher, nursing, midwifery, allied health professions (Radiography), and social work provisions. Ninety-two per cent of the Faculty of Health & Social Care leavers and 96% of the Initial Teacher Training leavers are soon in employment.

Open Day are to be held on 7 May 2011, 8 October 2011, 19 November 2011, 11 February 2012, and 28 April 2012.

CAMPUSES

The flagship campus is in Cambridge, which is just now undergoinh a redevelopment programme of its library, lecture theatres and teaching facilities, and the creation of a new business school and

UNIVERSITY/STUDENT PROFILE	
University since	**1992**
Situation/style	**City/town campuses**
Student population	**19830**
Total undergraduates	**17615**
Mature	**67%**
International	**13%**
Male/female ratio	**33:67**
Equality of opportunity:	
state school intake	**97%**
social class 4-7 intake	**39%**
drop-out rate	**12%**

meeting places, all scheduled for completion by the autumn.

The Rivermead Chelmsford campus is home to the School of Education and the Ashcroft International Business School, and the much-vaunted Postgraduate Medical Institute, which now partners twenty NHS and private healthcare organisations and works closely with UCL Partners, Queen Mary University of London, Cambridge and Yale universities.

FEES, BURSARIES

UK & EU Fees 2011-12: £3,375 p.a. The university offers an Aspire scholarship award of £500 a year. See www.anglia.ac.uk/aspire. Also: www.anglia.ac.uk/sports_scholarships and www.anglia.ac.uk/studentfinance.

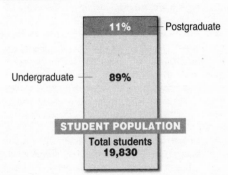

Postgraduate 11%

Undergraduate 89%

STUDENT POPULATION
Total students
19,830

TEACHING SURVEY AT A GLANCE

Avg. UCAS points accepted	**240**
Acceptance rate	**22%**
Overall satisfaction rate	**71%**
Helpful/interested staff	★★★
Small tuition groups	★★
Students into graduate jobs	**72%**

Teaching most popular with undergraduates:
Biology, Building, English, History, Archaeology,
Languages, Ophthalmics and other subjects allied
to Medicine (94%), Psychology, Sociology,

Teaching least popular with undergraduates:
Accounting (35%), Film (38%).

STUDENT PROFILE

There's an eclectic mix of arty types, nurses, laddish engineers and teachers. This is a modern university. Many local and mature students come here for Anglia's tickets into industry. Many are part-time, sponsored by employers.

Writes Jill Walker. 'We have lots of mature students, who make everyone work harder 'cos they are the only ones to do the reading. Lots of students are local. Cambridge is far more international than Chelmsford.'

ACADEMIA & JOBS

There are five faculties: Ashcroft International Business School; Arts, Law & Social Sciences; Education; Health & Social Care; and Science & Technology.

An Employer Mentoring Scheme is designed to support second-year undergraduates in thinking about, and planning for, the transition from study to work. Each student is matched with a mentor from their chosen career field, who volunteers time to provide skills-building, support and encouragement. Degree courses are designed to be vocational and relevant with an emphasis on practical skills. Many are developed with employers and accredited by professional bodies.

The Ashcroft International Business School has a course with Barclays Bank Plc. Students are work-based, sponsored and salaried for all three years of the course. The Department of Vision and Hearing Sciences, which delivers a Foundation Degree in Ophthalmic Dispensing, finds graduates work with retail opticians such as Specsavers, Boots and Vision Express. The Biomedical Science and Applied Biomedical Science courses are accredited by the Institute of Biomedical Science, the former offering lab placements funded by the Eastern Region Strategic Health Authority. Students are paid a bursary of up to £6,000 and laboratories

£7,000 to cover training costs.

All students can take modules in Spanish, Italian, French, German, Japanese, Chinese and Russian - no matter what subject they are studying, and there is special support for students returning to learning after first careers, and for students with dyslexia or specific learning difficulties.

Less well publicised is the heartening, in-depth academic expertise among lecturers revealed in the latest survey of research undertaken at British universities, which looks at work cited world-wide in academic papers. In particular, Anglia has a good record at world and international levels in History, Psychology, English Language and Literature, Social Work, and Social Policy & Administration.

Training teachers is one of its core commitments, health is another defining strength.

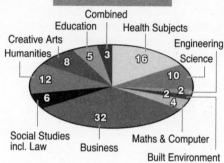

SUBJECT AREAS (%)

Combined — Education — Health Subjects — Engineering — Science — Creative Arts — Humanities — 8 — 5 — 3 — 16 — 10 — 12 — 2 — 2 — 6 — 4 — 32 — Social Studies incl. Law — Business — Maths & Computer — Built Environment

Look at their Pharmacy, Genetics, Health & Social Care degrees. In nursing, they offer Adult, Child, Learning Disabilities and Mental Health degrees, and BSc Midwifery. Interesting, too, is the Vet Nursing degree delivered by the College of West Anglia. In Forensic Science they are one of the

RESEARCH EXCELLENCE

% of Anglia Ruskin's research that is
4* (World-class) or 3* (Internationally rated):

	4*	3*
Geography and Enviro. Studies	**5%**	**15%**
Health	**5%**	**10%**
Social Work, Policy & Admin	**5%**	**25%**
Psychology	**5%**	**40%**
European Studies	**0%**	**20%**
English Lang. and Lit.	**15%**	**45%**
History	**20%**	**40%**
Art and Design	**5%**	**25%**
Music	**5%**	**10%**

nation's leaders and there is a Forensic Science laboratory, complete with scene of crime workshops.

Their long-term reputation for art and design was one of the points of excellence acknowledged in the research assessment. They offer Illustration as an integral part of the graphics course.

Look, also, at the programme of drama degrees, which sets the scene at the Mumford Theatre on Cambridge campus, and at a range of new degrees in the area of Performing Arts.

The Music Technology degrees are a productive employment niche. Again, there's much activity in publishing and journalism.

Another significant graduate employment area is opened up by the Sports Science degree. Anglia is among the biggest producers of physical training instructors in Education, and they are designated a University Centre of Cricketing Excellence

SOCIAL SCENE

The Students' Union on Cambridge campus has music, arts and language laboratory facilities, and a bar and nightclub (**Academy**). At Chelmsford it's the Tindal building, again with bar/venue (**SU Bar**) and restaurant.

Ents - Cambridge: *Flirt* club night on a Friday (cheesy tunes/disco); on Wednesday the union becomes pre-club venue (**Rev's**) for night out in the city, usually Sidney Street club known variously as **Life/22/The Place**; then there are open mic nights/comedy on a Tuesday. Sunday night has a quiz. They have also showcased up and coming bands. Other student popular Cambridge clubs include **Cindies** (actually called **Ballare**) and **Kambar** (Cambridge's alternative scene, Indie Fri/Sat). But listen, this is not London, Manchester, Leeds, Newcastle. Nor is it Chelmsford either, where it's club & society night Monday; *Skint* (cheap drinks) Wednesday. something like karaoke, poker, bingo Thursday, and *That Friday Feeling*, cheap cocktails and wine to end the week.

Student radio station CUR 1350 took Bronze at this year's National Student Radio Awards. It is shared with Cambridge University.

SPORT There are tennis courts and a multigym on the Cambridge campus, and 100 metres away the Kelsey Kerridge Sports Centre with gym and nearby swimming pool. Half a mile north of the campus there are three football pitches, a rugby pitch and a cricket square. Rowing crews rack their eights at Cambridge Uni's Emmanuel College Boat House. There's also a sports centre at Chelmsford.

PILLOW TALK

No official guarantee, but in reality they can accommodate 95% freshers at Chelmsford and 90% at Cambridge. At Chelmsford there's a student village with en-suite rooms in flats of 3-6. At Cambridge there are en-suite and older style hallsand uni-owned and leased houses.

WHAT IT'S REALLY LIKE	
UNIVERSITY:	
Social Life	★
Societies	★
Student Union services	★
Politics	**Cambridge: interest high; Chelmsford low**
Sport	**26 clubs**
National team position	**104th**
Sport facilities	★
Arts opportunities	**Drama, music exc; dance good; film, art average**
Student magazine	**The Apex**
Student radio	**CUR 1350**
National Radio Awards	**Bronze (2010)**
Bar venues	**The Academy, SU Bar**
Union ents	**Clubnite *Flirt* + tie-up with town**
Union societies	**35**
Parking	**None Cambridge; limited Chelmsford.**

ACCOMMODATION	
Student rating	★
Guarantee to freshers	**90-95%**
Style	**Halls, flats**
Security guard	**For some**
Shared rooms	**Some halls**
Internet access	**All**
Self-catered	**All**
En suite	**Some (most flats)**
Approx price pw	**£71-£126**
Cambridge city pw	**£75-£130**
Chekmsford town pw	**£72-£110**

GETTING THERE - Cambridge

☛ By road (from London): M25/J27, M11/J11, A10. From west or east: A45. From northwest: A604. From Stansted Airport: M11.

☛ By train: London's Liverpool Street, under the hour; Nottingham, 2:30; Sheffield, Birmingham New Street, 3:00.

☛ By coach: London, 1:50; Birmingham, 2:45; Leeds, 5:00; Bristol, 5:30.

GETTING THERE - Chelmsford

☛ By road: A12, A130 or A414.

☛ By rail: London Liverpool Street, 35 mins.

☛ By air: 10 miles from the M25 and access to Stansted Airport and Heathrow.

☛ By coach: London, 1:40; Norwich, 5:00.

ASTON UNIVERSITY, BIRMINGHAM

Aston University, Birmingham
Aston Triangle
Birmingham B4 7ET

TEL 0121 204 3000
FAX 0121 333 6350
EMAIL ugenquiries@aston.ac.uk
WEB www.aston.ac.uk

Aston Students' Guild
The Triangle
Birmingham B4 7ES

TEL 0121 204 4855
FAX 0121 333 4218
EMAIL guild.president@aston.ac.uk
WEB www.astonguild.org.uk

VIRGIN VIEW

*A*ston University, Birmingham, is a small university slap bang in the eye of the urban vortex, yet sheltered from any of the city's urban excesses in an attractive, green-field campus bowl - a crisp and tasty morsel in Birmingham's tangled spaghetti junction. As a student said of its particular locus, 'The dual carriageway acts as a kind of natural barrier. You go under the flyover and suddenly, wow! It's Birmingham.'

Aston stands for business, science, health, and European studies. The worlds of work and academia are at no point distinct - 70% or more undergrads take sandwich courses, i.e. a year's placement in industry as part of the degree course. 70% gained firsts and upper second class degrees in 2009 and 2010, and from 2012 they are offering all students the chance to learn a language alongside or as part of their degree - French, German, Spanish, Arabic, or Mandarin.

As a result there is a perennially high employment rate. Some 79% find a graduate level job in their discipline within six months, and with an overall student thumbs-up to the experience here of 75% and a drop-out rate of no more than 6%, it is clearly a good and enjoyable deal, and in many ways quite its own sort of experience.

FEES, BURSARIES

UK & EU Fees, 2011-12: £3,375 (£1,680 for placement year, but placement bursaries available, see www.aston.ac.uk/fees). Aston bursaries of up

UNIVERSITY/STUDENT PROFILE	
University since	**1966**
Situation/style	**City campus**
Student population	**10490**
Total undergraduates	**7760**
Mature	**23%**
International	**30%**
Male/female ratio	**51:49**
Equality of opportunity:	
state school intake	**91%**
social class 4-7 intake	**37%**
drop-out rate	**6%**

to £500 available to students with family incomes of less than £25,000. Awards of £1,000 for all students on placement. Additional £500 for students on year abroad or unpaid placements. Sports scholarships worth £500 p.a. are available.

For update visit www.aston.ac.uk/fees.

CAMPUS

Aston is well defined, straightforward, scientific. You get what you see at The Triangle. The clean lines of this modern, high-rise, plate-glass, green-

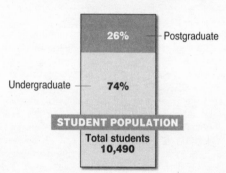

26% — Postgraduate

Undergraduate — 74%

STUDENT POPULATION
Total students
10,490

field Birmingham city campus (complete with artificial lake) brook no idle intent. Twenty-four hour CCTV and well-trained, friendly security staff are everywhere. Campus is also part of a recognised police beat and enjoys close relations with the local force for advice on prevention etc. Crime is extremely low. This is a determinedly close-knit community. No car parking for freshers.

STUDENT PROFILE

More than a third of intake is from social classes 4-7 and public school kids are thin on the ground.

Expect to find suits in the business section, and earnest, professional techies behind the superb lighting and sound systems in the Guild Hall, as they prepare for some serious Aston student nights.

There is a fresh-faced authenticity about the place. Aston is the only university where someone like me will be met by union and university executives around the same table. There are no divides, rather there is exuberance about their open, genuinely caring attitude, a contra-current to the traditional angst-ridden, existential flow of undergraduate life, and in an odd sort of way quite sweet and disarming. See what you think, sign up for Open Day: 21 June and 20 September, 2011.

One hundred and fifty volunteers elect to become Aston aunties and welcome freshers on the basis that Auntie knows best. Every year they have different slogans, like 'We are family!' or 'The cream of Brum.' For Fresher's Week they do city tours, campus tours, supermarket trips (?!), cultural crawls, canal cruises, fun things like go-karting and paintballing, an Alton Towers trip, and the departments all have other things organised, visits to the newly refurbished library for example.

Said one union bod: 'We had a classic quote yesterday from a student whose parents had just left: 'Oh, I haven't even been here for twelve hours yet and I feel at home already.'

If I'd heard this anywhere else I wouldn't have believed it, but at Aston what you see is what you get. You can thrust, you can parry, but 'you won't

TEACHING SURVEY AT A GLANCE	
Avg. UCAS points accepted	**360**
Acceptance rate	**14%**
Overall satisfaction rate	**83%**
Helpful/interested staff	★★★
Small tuition groups	★
Students into graduate jobs	**79%**

Teaching most popular with undergraduates:
Biology, Business, Chemistry, Chemical Engineering, Computer, Electronic & Electrical Eng. (100%), English, Languages, Maths & Statistics, Ophthalmics (95%), Pharmacy, Politics, Psychology, Sociology.

Teaching least popular with undergraduates:
Audiology (31%).

hear a thing against Aston from us,' they say.

ACADEMIA & JOBS

In-depth expertise lies in Business, Health, Engineering, and European Studies. Students praise the teaching of Biology, Business,

RESEARCH EXCELLENCE		
% of Aston's research that is		
4* (World-class) or 3* (Internationally rated):		
	4*	3*
Allied Health Studies	15%	35%
General Eng., Mineral, Mining	10%	25%
Business and Mgt Studies	15%	45%
European Studies	5%	15%

Chemistry, Chemical Engineering, Computer, Electronic & Electrical Eng. (100% thumbs-up)), English, Languages, Maths & Statistics, Ophthalmics (95%), Pharmacy, Politics, Psychology, Sociology, but are less suree about Audiology. Also, one has to say that in spite of the care taken of students outside the lecture hall, Aston students do not rate staff highly for their helpfulness or interest in them, and small-group tutorials are thin on the ground. Aston were rated 77th and 92nd nationally in these matters by their students.

Broadly, Aston consists of three faculties: Life & Health Sciences; Engineering & Applied Science (Civil Engineering, Chemical Eng. and Applied Chemistry, Mechanical & Electrical Eng., Electronic and Applied Physics, Computer Science and Applied Maths); and Management Languages & European Studies. The latter includes the Aston

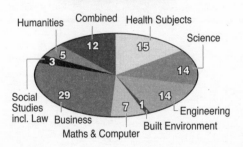

SUBJECT AREAS (%)

Humanities 5, Combined 12, Health Subjects 15, Science 14, Engineering 14, Built Environment 1, Maths & Computer 7, Business 29, Social Studies incl. Law 3

Business School and School of Languages and European Studies.

The Business School is one of the largest in Europe and one of only a handful in the world to have triple accreditation from the major European (EQUIS), American (AACSB) and MBA bench-marks of quality for business education. Aston had two finalists in two years in the BBC Surallan Sugar show. Alex Wotherspoon (2008) and Kate Walsh (2009) came 3rd and 2nd respectively out of 20,000.

Business-related courses tackle the behavioural side of enterprise, such as Organisational Studies, Human Psychology and Psychology with Management.

New this year is Law with Management LLB, a qualifying Law degree with a management focus and a placement year (3-year option also available). Law society accreditation has now been confirmed and the degree leads to the award of an LLB degree. Note also the new Finance BSc degree - a 4-year sandwich programme

Aston is now one of only 4 UK Universities where more than 50% of students take sandwich or year abroad programmes. Most placements are paid (£16k is average and it can be a lot more).

Full marks too to Pharmacy and its business and management courses, while Biological Sciences, Optometry, French, German, and Psychology were not far behind.

Ophthalmics and pharmacy dominate the graduate employment stats at Aston, more than 20% of students getting their first jobs in dispensing chemists, hospitals or opticians. If you have your eyes tested in England there's a good chance that it will be an Aston graduate doing it. Then of course the graduates of the business school buff up the employment figures in areas such as banking and all kinds of middle-man monetary activities, while a few get into accountancy.

Aston is heavy on workload, extremely well resourced and geared to top-class employment by means of industry contact, study-abroad programmes, language combinations and sandwich courses. Your friends, like you, are probably up for a four-year term, at the end of which a job is more or less unavoidable.

The University tells us: 'Over 200 companies and organisations visit us each year to promote to and recruit our graduates.'

A word too about the potential of their electronic engineering and computer provision. For

WHAT IT'S REALLY LIKE	
UNIVERSITY:	
Social Life	★★★
Societies	★★★
Student Union services	★★
Politics	**Interest low**
Sport	**35 clubs**
National team position	**84th**
Sport facilities	★★★
Arts opportunities	**Dance, music excellent; drama good**
Student newspaper	**Aston Times**
Bars	**B4 Bar**
Union ents	**In limbo**
Union societies	**30**
Most popular societiy	**Fusion (dance music), Islamic**
Parking	**No**
CITY:	
Entertainment	★★★★★
Scene	**Excellent**
Town/gown relations	**Average**
Risk of violence	**Average**
Cost of living	**High**
Student concessions	**Excellent**
Survival + 2 nights out	**£120 pw**
Part-time work campus/town	**Good/Excellent**

would-be software engineers on the smaller-uni ticket, there are two key unis, Essex and Aston. See in particular their Engineering and Applied Science degree: Professional Engineering MEng - 4 years in Electronic Engineering with Integrated placement year. So, students graduate with an MEng and professional experience in 4 years rather than the usual 5.

SOCIAL SCENE

STUDENTS' GUILD The no-nonsense efficiency of this uni far from cripples any desire for after-work pleasure, either at the Students' Guild or a walk away in the centre of Brum itself, but of late there has been a tempering of high spirits in the Guild with the university taking the reins and less of a club scene than there might be. Still, the facilities have been spruced up and are in place, the **Blue Room** and the **Base** being for lounge lizards with an appetite for a Subway sandwich, the **Loft** being split into four areas and offering more sofas, an IT suite, with

> *'Aston is mainly for science, engineering and business. It is very defined, very straightforward, very scientific. You get what you see at The Triangle, and students do seem to enjoy themselves.'*

'hot-desk' tables for internet access, and a well furnished suite to practice presentation skills. If this all sounds a bit tame, there is at least the newly refurbished **B4 Bar**, a venue the stewardship of which has just been handed back to the Guild. So, let's see what they make of it.

The Astonbury 12-hour Festival is a major post-exam highlight: 3,000 visitors, 2 stages, 10 bands (including Zane Lowe, Guru Josh, Nick Grimshaw, Chipmunk and the Futureheads) stalls and fairground rides - over 12 hours in June. www.astonbury.com. So, the Guild can deliver.

SPORT Aston came 84th in the BUCS sports competitive rankings, not bad for a small university. There's a gym - now 75 stations, an all-weather pitch and additional facilities at the Outdoor Sports Centre 6 miles from campus - 40 acres of pitches, floodlighting, pavilion and all weather facilities. On campus there are two sports centres - **Grade II listed Woodcock to be refurbished during 2011,** and **Gem Sports Hall**. It is sport for everyone, rather than club level; 'relaxed' is the word used, although the options are varied enough to include American Football, korfball and other alternative sports.

TOWN See *Student Birmingham.*

PILLOW TALK
Self-catering flats and houses, all on campus within 2 mins walk of each other and 5 mins from other campus facilities. Upgrade of all student

ACCOMMODATION	
Student rating	★★
Guarantee to freshers	**100%**
Style	**Flats**
Security guard	**Police beat**
Shared rooms	**None**
Internet access	**All**
Self-catered	**All**
En suite	**85%**
Approx price range pw	**£72-£125**
City rent pw	**£50-£130**

accommodation to award-winning standard of Lakeside Residences occurred during 2010-11. 85% of accommodation at Aston is en suite. They guarantee to find all freshers flats who hold Aston as CF/UF choice and apply for accommodation before the end of July. No guarantee for clearing and insurance students.

1,350 new, fully networked en-suite rooms opened in 2010 , green technologies to the fore, and the usual internet/data/digital connections, access and security features.

GETTING THERE
☞ By road: M6/J6, A38M 3rd exit, then first exit at Lancaster Circus roundabout.
☞ By rail: Bristol Parkway, Sheffield, 1:30; Euston, 1:40. New Street 12 mins' walk from campus.
☞ By air: Birmingham International Airport.
☞ By coach: London, 2:40; Bristol, 2:00.

UNIVERSITY OF WALES, BANGOR

University of Wales, Bangor
Gwynedd LL57 2DG

TEL 01248 382016/7
FAX 01248 370451
EMAIL admissions@bangor.ac.uk
WEB www.bangor.ac.uk

Bangor Students' Union
Gwynedd LL57 2TH

TEL 01248 388011
FAX 01248 388020
EMAIL undeb@undeb.bangor.ac.uk
WEB www.undeb.bangor.ac.uk

VIRGIN VIEW

Setting the whole deal in context for a semi-final of University Challenge, Jeremy Paxman described the natural environs of Bangor, which is in North Wales just across the Menai Strait from the Isle of Anglesey, as 'one of the most beautiful locations of any British university, between the beaches of

Anglesey and the mountains of Snowdonia.' It is also well-equipped for students interested in sport - especially those involving the great outdoors, and we shouldn't be surprised to find an 86% student satisfaction rating.

In fact, the university puts this down to having 'one of the largest Peer Guiding Schemes of any university, with second and third year students involved in mentoring

UNIVERSITY/STUDENT PROFILE

University since	**1884**
Situation/style	**Rural bliss**
Student population	**17745**
Total undergraduates	**8800**
Mature	**45%**
International	**14%**
Male/female ratio	**39:61**
Equality of opportunity:	
state school intake	**95%**
social class 4-7 intake	**34%**
drop-out rate	**6%**

new students to help them settle in'. It won them 6th place nationally in the 2010 Times Higher *student poll on the matter of 'helpful/interested staff'.*

But it isn't only this. Besides the beauty and the great outdoors and the staff interest, there is a friendliness within the relatively small caucus of undergraduates that really does characterise the place as special. Look at them on Facebook; follow them on Twitter: www.facebook.com/pages/Bangor-University/17264864578?v=wall and http://twitter.com/BangorUni.

Bangor started life on 18 October, 1884, in an old coaching inn, a promising beginning, particularly as half the student intake was female, which was swimming against the tide in those days. There are now more women than men (61:39).

Not overly demanding at entry (around 280 points should see you in), it has risen to be one of the most popular universities. Open day dates in 2011 are 2 July, 15 and 29 October.

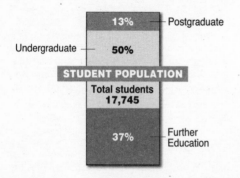

FEES, BURSARIES

UK & EU fees 2011-12: £3,375 for non-Welsh students. Bursary and scholarship awards: There is a range of bursaries and scholarships worth over £2M available to those starting at Bangor in 2011. Bangor Bursaries up to £500 a year if household income is below £35,000. Start-up Bursaries of £1,000 are available to those entering the University from care. Welsh-medium study Bursaries of £250 a year are available to those who choose to study more than 40 credits a year through the medium of Welsh. 40 Merit Scholarships are worth up to £3,000 to those who excel in the annual Entrance Scholarship examinations. 14 Excellence Scholarships of up to £5,000 each are available in several subject areas. Sports Scholarships are worth up to £2,000 per year: www.bangor.ac.uk/studentfinance. They also offer International Entrance Scholarships of 10% off the first year's tuition fees: www.bangor.ac.uk/international/future/ scholarship _ug.php.

CAMPUS

Bangor itself is a small, town-size community that manages not to protest at the regular incursion of a student population which more than doubles the local population at the start of each term. While not exactly a campus university, all the buildings, with the exception of the School of Ocean Sciences, which is a few miles from the Menai Bridge, are within walking distance of one another.

It is cheap, safe, and, writes Becki Thurston, 'being on the north coast of Wales, Bangor has gobsmacking views of Snowdonia, up which you can climb, walk and cycle, or at which you can just look; and what with the mountains as a climbing frame and the west coast giving decent surf, you can't help but notice all the fit bods around.'

STUDENT PROFILE

There is a sizeable Welsh population, largely female, and a number of mature students. Precious few come from public school (5%), indeed many inhabit areas new to the idea of sending to university.

It is friendly, but cutting-edge cool it is not. If you come to Bangor, you'll likely be sporty, interested in outward bound perhaps, maybe a classical music lover (there is an international reputation for music here). This is no place for the club loon. As Becki Thurston put it, 'you'll probably find more night life in a tramp's vest.'

The International Welfare Unit assists and advises, and orientation days are arranged to help international students get acclimatised to the country. The ELCOS (English Language Courses for Overseas Students) Unit provides instruction for those whose language skills need polishing. There's also an organisation (called 'Shekina') which offers help to wives and husbands of students and organises a range of activities, including English language courses.

ACADEMIA & JOBS

At 63% the students into real graduate jobs after six months is not high. The subject area at Bangor most productive of graduate jobs is Biological Sciences. The biggest employment area is the hospital health sector owing to the number of nursing students here: adult, child, learning disability and mental health nurses. After Biological Sciences, languages graduates do best in employment, flooding the education, publishing and many other sectors.

The academic structure delivers six 'colleges', each a federation of schools.

The College of Arts & Humanities schools are English, Welsh, History & Welsh History, Linguistics & English Language, Modern Languages, Music, Theology & Religious Studies, NIECI (National Institute for Excellence in the Creative Industries), ELCOS (English Language Centre for Overseas Students), and WISCA (Welsh Institute for Social and Cultural Affairs).

'OK, so you'll probably find more night life in a tramp's vest, but before you run away, think! That top bit of totty in your lecture, halls, launderette, is likely to be in the same club as you!'

The College of Business, Social Sciences & Law has the Bangor Business School and schools of Law and Social Sciences.

The College of Education & Lifelong Learning has schools of Education and Lifelong Learning.

The College of Natural Sciences incorporates schools of The Environment & Natural Resources, encompassing Geography and Regional Studies, the schools of Biological Sciences and Ocean Sciences, the Welsh Institute of Natural Resources, encompassing the CAZS - The Natural Resources and the BioComposites Centre.

The College of Physical & Applied Sciences incorporates the schools of Chemistry, Electronics, and Computer Science. Finally, the College of Health & Behavioural Sciences.

The College of Health & Behavioural Sciences has the schools of Healthcare Sciences, Psychology, Sport, and Health & Exercise Sciences, and no less than The Institute of Medical & Social Care Research. The North West Cancer Research Fund Institute at the School of Biological Sciences conducts fundamental research into the causes of cancer.

Note that Social Work has just been cut from the degree programme. New courses this year include Medical Sciences BMedSci, Medical Education BMedSci (Intercalated), Exercise, Behaviour Change and Disease BSc (Intercalated), Exercise Physiology BSc (Intercalated), Sport Science BSc (Intercalated).

In research, psychology and music in particular a fifth to a quarter of their work has been adjudged world class, and more or less half of the research in these areas gained a 3-star international rating.

TEACHING SURVEY AT A GLANCE

Avg. UCAS points accepted	**280**
Acceptance rate	**14%**
Overall satisfaction rate	**86%**
Helpful/interested staff	★★★★★
Small tuition groups	★★★
Students into graduate jobs	**63%**

Teaching most popular with undergraduates:
Education and Teacher Training (100%), Business, Celtic Studies (100%), Chemistry, Computer, Creative Arts, Languages, Finance and Accounting, History, Linguistics, Physical Science, Psychology, Sociology, Theology, Zoology.

Teaching least popular with undergraduates:
Social Work (59%).

SUBJECT AREAS (%)

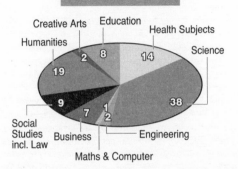

Creative Arts — 2
Education — 8
Health Subjects — 14
Science — 38
Humanities — 19
Social Studies incl. Law — 9
Business — 7
Engineering — 1
Maths & Computer — 2

The same is true of the Agriculture, Environmental, Celtic Studies, and Accounting & Finance provisions.

A £10 million Business and Management Centre houses Bangor's School for Business and Regional Development, which is now numbered among the better taught in the University.

There is an employment niche for museum archivists, curators, and librarians. They come from across the academic board - from Humanities, Languages, Biological Sciences, and Law. Look also at the Information Technology degrees.

There's also a preponderance of translators sufficient to make the Language Department a highflyer in this area nationally.

Another notable feature of the academic provision generally is that it favours students with disabilities - there are study support centres which house CCTVs, scanners and braille embossers. They also have induction loops and infra-red transmission equipment to help those with hearing difficulties. A Dyslexia Unit is internationally renowned.

RESEARCH EXCELLENCE

% of Bangor's research that is
4* *(World-class)* or **3*** *(Internationally rated):*

	4*	3*
Health Services Research	5%	20%
Biological Sciences	5%	20%
Agriculture, Vet., Food	5%	40%
Earth Systems and Enviro.	10%	50%
Chemistry	10%	35%
Computer Science	15%	35%
Electrical and Electronic Eng.	30%	40%
Accounting and Finance	15%	50%
Social Work,l Policy & Admin.	5%	25%
Psychology	20%	45%
Education	10%	20%
Sports-Related Studies	10%	25%
European Studies	5%	20%
Celtic Studies	10%	45%
English Language and Lit.	15%	30%
Linguistics	5%	30%
Theology	5%	25%
History	15%	35%
Music	25%	45%

WHAT IT'S REALLY LIKE

UNIVERSITY:	
Social Life	★★★
Societies	★★★★★
Student Union services	★★★
Politics	**Good**
Sport	**Good**
National team position	**70th**
Sport facilities	★★★
Arts opportunities	**OK**
Student newspaper	**Seren, Y ddraenen**
Student radio	**Storm FM**
Nightclub	**Amser/Time**
Bars	**Main/Prif Far, Jock's Bar**
Union ents	**Live acts, DJs, comedy**
Union societies	**Masses**
Most active societies	**Mountain walking, Football, Community Action**
Parking	**Good**
TOWN:	
Entertainment	★★
Scene	**Scenic, fun**
Town/gown relations	**Average-poor**
Risk of violence	**Low**
Cost of living	**Low**
Student concessions	**OK**
Survival + 2 nights out	**£40-£50 pw**
Part-time work campus/town	**Good**

SOCIAL SCENE

STUDENTS' UNION 'OK, so you'll probably find more night life in a tramp's vest, but would you really want to live *there?*' asks Beki. 'Bangor isn't exactly overrun with nightclubs, but before you run away, think! That top bit of totty in your lecture, halls, launderette, is like to be in the same club as you!'

Adding to possibilities of random rendezvous, they have recently made a £1-million investment in the Student Union. There's a 1,000-capacity, award-winning **Amser/Time** nightclub (open to the public and students at a discount) and two bars: the 390-capacity **Main (Prif Far)** and the 100-capacity basement bar, **Jock's**. Prices are very low.

Both social life and extra-curricular activity score big at Bangor. There are masses of student societies - Community Action (student volunteers) is probably the most popular, mountain walking and football close behind.

There's a Welsh-language student magazine called *Y ddraenen* and an English newspaper, *Seren*.

Political activity is high. The drama soc, Rostra, is very popular.

The uni has its own professional chamber ensemble and student symphony orchestra, chamber choir, opera group, chamber ensembles and concert band.

SPORT Rock climbing, paragliding, mountain biking, canoeing, sailing, and surfing are available as well as the usual team sports - rugby, hockey

ACCOMMODATION

Student rating	★★★★★
Guarantee to freshers	**100%**
Style	**Halls, flats**
Security guard	**All**
Shared rooms	**None**
Internet access	**All**
Self-catered	**All**
En suite	**All flats, not in hall**
Approx price range pw	**£66-£88**
Town rent pw	**£65-£70**

and football. Women's Rugby is traditionally strong. 1,500+ participate weekly in sporting activities. You will benefit from a Lottery-sourced, £4.5 million extension to the sports hall. There's great emphasis on sport, thanks to the Sports Science and PE courses. Outward-bound activities, such as mountaineering, are especially popular, as are rowing, sailing and canoeing. This is a small uni and so makes a poor showing in national team competitions, but it does its own thing with flair.

Town 'As far as towns go, we ain't no Liverpool or Birmingham,' says Becki Thurston, 'but that doesn't mean we're pants and boring. Although it's designated a city, it's diddy. The bonus is that we take over. There's nowhere doesn't feel like home. Wherever you go, wherever you are, you'll bump into someone you know. Trouble is, people know who you snogged last night, even before you've sobered up enough to realise!'

A positive advantage of Bangor's size is that competition between pubs etc. is strong. So prices are low. Besides pubs - Irish, **Wether-spoons**, **Fat Cat** and late-night pub/clubs **Joot and Joop**, you'll find café bars, restaurants (Spanish, Italian, Greek, Chinese, Indian), and two more nightclubs - **Octagon** and **Bliss**.

For arts lovers the city offers a varied mix of classical concerts; there are regular visits from the BBC National Orchestra for Wales, other orchestras from afar, and from the Centre for Creative & Performing Arts.

PILLOW TALK

A vast sum has recently been spent upgrading the main student accommodation site, hence the 5-star rating from students (box above). You get a view over the Menai Straits at Arfon for a mere £70 a week in 2010. Neuadd JMJ (1 and 2) are exclusively for Welsh speakers/scholars. Some halls have car parking spaces.

GETTING THERE

☛ By road: A5, A55, A487; 90 minutes from M56.
☛ By rail: London Euston, 4:00; Birmingham New Street, 3:00; Manchester Oxford Road, 2:30; Liverpool Lime Street, 2:15.
☛ By coach: London, 8:00; Leeds, 6:15.

UNIVERSITY OF BATH

The University of Bath
Claverton Down
Bath BA2 7AY

TEL 01225 383019
FAX 01225 386366
EMAIL admissions@bath.ac.uk
WEB www.bath.ac.uk

Bath Students' Union
Claverton Down
Bath BA2 7AY

TEL 01225 386612
EMAIL sabbs@bath.co.uk
WEB www.bathstudent.com/

VIRGIN VIEW

*B*ath is a small, happy science and business-based university with a huge, world-wide reputation built on its sandwich course provision, excellence in sport, and streamlined curriculum.

It is first choice for many capable of Oxbridge, although in fact its ratings in the Times Higher's *Student Experience Survey* for lecturers' helpfulness and interest, and individual tutorial attention, are a good deal lower than at Oxbridge. But much may depend on which subject you choose to study here and overall student satisfaction with the teaching at Bath - 86% - is very good, while

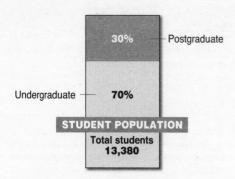

30% — Postgraduate

Undergraduate — 70%

STUDENT POPULATION
Total students
13,380

84% getting real graduate jobs within 6 months of leaving justifies the average ask at A level of 440 points. A tiny 3% drop out.

The complete absence of an Arts provision at Bath has an interesting effect, as Tom Alderwick notes: 'I guess science people here feel less restricted artistically than at a uni where the Drama Society is dominated by students who are studying the subject. We are not really worried about that at Bath, which is probably a plus. I don't know personally how good the arts societies are, but I know people enjoy going along.'

Like so many at Bath, Tom's thing is

UNIVERSITY/STUDENT PROFILE	
University since	**1966**
Situation/style	**City campus**
Student population	**13380**
Total undergraduates	**9305**
Mature	**28%**
International	**28%**
Male/female ratio	**54:46**
Equality of opportunity:	
state school intake	**77%**
social class 4-7 intake	**20%**
drop-out rate	**3%**

sport. 'It stems from the reputation... Bath is one of the top four sports unis, often higher.'

It is a centre for International Sport, and the amazing facilities are used by many professional clubs. 'Bath rugby club use the gym up there at the Sports Training Village, and when there are events like the World Cup or Olympics, people come in and train.'

CAMPUS

The self-contained campus is situated 2 miles south-east of the city, at the top of Bathwick Hill. It is one of the safest campus in the UK and has a national police security award to prove it. Being apart from the urban action is not considered a problem. No on-campus parking, but bright orange buses run regularly until 3 a.m., and are cheap (ten-trip and longer season tickets are available).

Writes fresher Tristan Wike: 'When you first arrive in Bath I guess the most imposing fact about the location of the university is the whopping great hill that leads up to the University! Some may see a rather larger obstacle for a drunken stumble back to halls from town, others a cracking fitness training opportunity. Others, like myself, may see it as both! In all seriousness don't let this phase you as there are regular buses from the university around every 5 minutes give or take... Then, from the university campus it only takes about 5 minutes to be down in the bath tub. The town has a great student feel about it and whenever you're down there it is tricky to avoid meeting other students like yourself!

'The campus itself is small, making it easy for students to roll out of bed 5 minutes before lectures and still make it! The architecture of the campus is overall pretty good! The parade area which is a straight enclosed area where all the main lecture theatres are as well as the library (which should have been more floors but they didn't take into account the weight of the books....idiots) may seem a bit of a concrete jungle but as soon as you step off it there are huge areas of grass to sit and chill with your mates after (or during) lecture time.'

FEES, BURSARIES

UK & EU Fees, 2011-12: £3,375 p.a. Bursaries of up to £1,200 are available for students with a family income of £50,000 or less, on a sliding scale. Other merit- and subject-based awards are also available: chemistry, chemical engineering, modern languages and European studies. Then there are the sports scholarships

STUDENT PROFILE

'The people that go to Bath,' says Tristan Wike. 'You can't really get a feel for this from a prospectus. If I'm brutally honest there is quite a large portion of what are known as Rah. However, there are a lot of other people if this isn't your particular style. These range from 'intense study geeks', who will not speak to you ever, though they do seem to talk to others, so perhaps it's just me. Then you get the 'sport types', where the education is almost a bi-product. These can be recognised by the blue and yellow 'team Bath' clothing donned daily. Finally, you get the in-between-ers who like their work, their social, their sport. So the message is, if you are thinking about applying to Bath, don't worry about not fitting in everyone does!'

ACADEMIA & JOBS

Bath concentrates on seven areas - Sciences, Social Sciences (Economics, Politics, Psychology, Social Policy, Social Work, Sociology), Engineering, Pharmacy & Pharmacology, Business, Languages, and Sport.

The programmes are modular, consisting of self-contained units taught and assessed on a semester basis. The academic year is divided into two semesters.

Tom Wordie reads International Management with a Modern Language. 'I'm really happy with the course,' he says. It's meant to be one of the best places to do it in the country. Tutorials are very useful, but a bit more guidance with coursework, assignments and exams wouldn't have gone amiss.'

'The course that I am currently studying is biology,' writes Tristan. 'I went from a spoon-fed private school to a lot of individually driven work. If you don't do it, it doesn't get done and you will lose out. Less advice, more facts. At Bath, most of the lectures are done by Power Point presentation in large comfortable lecture theatres, which are definitely comfy enough to fall asleep in. The lecturers are a bit odd and a few boring, but on the whole if you like your subject you will like them. On the Biology course there is a lot of tutor-to-tutee contact. I have tutorials with 3 other students once a week and I get set various essays and research to do alongside the course. Nothing too strenuous, but don't miss practicals, which are long but very tricky to catch up on, which does not put you in good stead with the lecturer! The library is central to the uni, with a large number of computers and areas for loud and quiet, and group and individual, study. There are also lots of books ... but that's expected. The library system for taking out and renewing books is simple, the late fees quite reasonable.'

Says Tom Alderwick, who is studying Politics and Economics: 'The main reason I chose Bath is because of the sandwich degree. Over half the students here do sandwich courses.' The benefits are clear, as Tom demonstrated when we asked what kind of placement a Politics and Economics under-graduate might expect: 'In my department you can either go for a political or a business placement. There's one offered by the House of Commons and the House of Lords, and there are quite a few in Brussels, political lobbying or doing

something with the EU. Big accountancy firms offer work and some people go into banking. I've just recently sorted mine out. I have a year working for American Express. I'll be working in Victoria, in London, getting paid a salary of £18,000.

'American Express held first round interviews here on campus and then we went to the offices in London for further interview, and we had to give a presentation and have lunch. So yes, it's quite competitive.

'My house mate is doing Management with

TEACHING SURVEY AT A GLANCE

Avg. UCAS points accepted	**440**
Acceptance rate	**15%**
Overall satisfaction rate	**86%**
Helpful/interested staff	★★★
Small tuition groups	★★
Students into graduate jobs	**84%**

Teaching most popular with undergraduates:
Accounting, Aerospace Engineering, Architecture, Biology, Business, Chemistry, Civil Engineering, Engineering & Technology., Finance, Languages (Iberian Studies, 100%), Maths, Molecular Biology, Pharmacy, Physics, Politics, Sports Science.

Teaching least popular with undergraduates:
Social Work (55%).

RESEARCH EXCELLENCE

% of Bath's research that is
4* *(World-class)* or **3*** *(Internationally rated):*

	4*	3*
Pharmacy	20%	40%
Biological Sciences	10%	40%
Chemistry	5%	55%
Physics	20%	50%
Pure Mathematics	25%	35%
Applied Mathematics	20%	50%
Statistics	20%	40%
Computer Science	25%	50%
Electrical and Electronic Eng.	25%	35%
Chemical Engineering	10%	45%
Mech., Aero., Manufac. Eng.	10%	45%
Architecture/Built Environment	25%	45%
Business and Mgt Studies	30%	40%
Social Work, Policy & Admin.	35%	40%
Development Studies	15%	30%
Education	15%	30%
Sports-Related Studies	15%	20%
European Studies	10%	35%

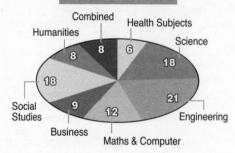

SUBJECT AREAS (%)

- Combined 8
- Humanities 8
- Health Subjects 6
- Science 18
- Engineering 21
- Maths & Computer 12
- Business 9
- Social Studies 18

French and he has just sorted his placement to work in Paris, for Barclays. My other house mate, she does Spanish, so for six months she is going to a university in Argentina and then for the next six months she is going to go to Spain, to a job there.'

Students with disabilities and learning difficulties now have free access to state-of-the-art laptops that cater specifically for their learning needs. The Assistive Technologies Initiative enables students to use laptops containing software that can do everything from translating speech into written text, to helping people 'map' their thoughts and ideas.

The high 86% statistic of graduates into real graduate jobs after six months favours banking and accountancy, aircraft manufacture, the construction industry, architecture and engineering design, government, secondary and higher education, hospital and social work, pharmaceuticals, sport, public administration, and personnel.

Vectura, a company established by academics at the uni, is among the top four university spin-off companies in the UK. Now, a new Student Enterprise Centre, based in the Student Union, with two dedicated business support professionals, gives students free access to the training, support and resources they need to turn their business ideas into reality.

STUDENT SCENE

STUDENTS' UNION Here's Tristan's assessment of Bath through a fresher's eyes: 'Every single rumour I'd heard about Freshers Week was a realised fact during my first week at Bath. When around 40 people in my block rang the door bell and asked if they could come in, all with their own beverages, I knew the week was going to go well. Freshers Week consists of ploughing into **Founder's Hall** after an intense pre-lash. Then dancing, or for me just shouting lots and jumping up and down all night, before getting cheesy chips and trying to find your way back to your halls. So yer get ready

for funnels and in the words of super bad "rock out with your cocks' out". Actually, don't. One of my friends did and you get quite a lot of anger from large men in orange jackets. These blokes don't like you having people on your shoulders either, just a word of warning.

'After Freshers, if you are still up for partying there are 3 nights on campus in **Elements**, the campus club, despite the fact it is very small. It *is* small, but if you get a group of mates there and you have had a few, you can make a cracking night of it! *Score* on Wednesday night was the best for me. This was after heavy hockey socials, following a hard day on the pitch. My team, the hockey team, would treck on up to campus to *Score* on a Wednesday and fill the dance floor for hours of dancing until the lights came on. There's also *Comeplay* on a Saturday, which is probably most popular.'

Elements, the Student Union nightclub, is reckoned to be the largest venue in Bath . **Plug** bar is more day to day, recently expanded by the removal of a staircase, comfortable and typical - pool tables, live sports etc, plus a few events like Acoustic nights, quizzes, etc.

There are 82 societies and more than 50 sports

WHAT IT'S REALLY LIKE	
UNIVERSITY:	
Social Life	★★★
Societies	★★★
Student Union services	★★★
Politics	**Union active**
Sport	**52 clubs**
National team position	**4th**
Sport facilities	★★★★★
Arts opportunities	**Good**
Student newspaper	**BathImpact**
Student radio	**URB**
Student Radio Awards	**2 Gold in 2010**
Student TV	**CTV**
Nightclub	**Elements**
Bars	**Plug**
Union ents	**Cheesy**
Union societies	**82**
Parking	**None**
CITY:	
Entertainment	★★★
Scene	**Average clubs, good pubs**
Town/gown relations	**Good**
Risk of violence	**Low**
Cost of living	**High**
Student concessions	**Good**
Survival + 2 nights out	**£80 pw**
Part-time work campus/town	**Excellent/good**

clubs, so plenty to do. BUST is the drama society, BUSMS the musicals society. Very popular and with few arts bods around, unlikely sorts get a go. There are also student bands and orchestras. Behind it all is BTS - Backstage Technical Services. All events are crewed by BTS, from the bands that appear in **Elements** to the summer ball, and productions by BUST and BUSMS.

Media-wise, there's a weekly newspaper, *BathImpact*, a very impressive radio station, URB, which won two Golds in the National Student Radio Awards last year, and a TV station, CTV, with monitors installed in the Plug bar. Politics brings societies for the three main parties, and the popular Debating Soc., into action.

> *'I dare say that after four years I will think, if I never hear another cheesy song again it will be too soon.'*

The Union won a Silver Award in the Sound Impact Awards (National Ethical and Environmental recognition for students' unions) in 2009. A new Arts Complex is planned for later this year.

Town Writes Tristan: 'Bath is probably one of the safest places you'll ever go to.' But this comes at a price. Katie Mellors: 'I came to Bath from a large Northern city with a good nightlife, and I must admit it took a while to adjust to all that's worth going to in Bath. They only play cheese here, and I dare say that after four years I will think, if I never hear another cheesy song again it will be too soon. But for now I am loving every minute of the social side to my degree. The clubs in town have cheap drinks and are safe. The main town night for students is on a Monday. You know almost everyone in the club and have such a laugh that you will not forget a single night out, either on campus or off.'

Adds Tom: 'Student societies arrange socials, get buses to go to Bristol. The Economics Society arranges a bus and takes every one there and brings them home about 3 a.m.' Bristol is certainly far more sophisticated a scene for those with a nose for cool. It's 15 mins away by train.

Sport There are fantastic sports facilities on campus, ranging from an Olympic size swimming pool, 8-lane athletics track, squash, badminton and tennis courts. Bath is the venue to host the Paralympics GB team's preparation camps for London 2012. Numerous other Olympic athletes use the training facilities. Right on campus there's a generous range of team pitches and no facility is more than a stroll away. The £35-million sports village has a floodlit running track; 50-metre and 25-metre pools; a 4-court tennis hall; 16 hard tennis courts; 2 synthetic grass pitches; a shooting range; sports hall; squash courts; a performance testing lab; weight training rooms; a physio centre.

Tristan warns: 'Sport is huge, but if you aren't a national player at any sport it is quite a large chunk out of your loan to join for the year.'

PILLOW TALK

There's a 4-year, £110-million campus refurb in progress, including halls. Says Tristan: 'Norwood is the worst hall really, right above the SU, so pretty noisy most nights. John Wood is off-campus, which means having to get the bus up every day. Then there's Westwood, second cheapest after Norwood. Not gonna lie, it does have a kind of prison feel. But once you make a room your own, then it's OK. Westwood is where some of the wildest pre-lashes happen, so if you're up for a good time Westwood is crackalackin! Eastwood is the next up, made up of small houses pretty much. These are nice rooms with communal showers and toilets, but definitely bearable and barely a step down form the next expensive accommodation, which are Solsbury and Marlborough. These flats have en-suite bathrooms

ACCOMMODATION	
Student rating	★★★★★
Guarantee to freshers	**100%**
Style	**Halls**
Security guard	**Campus 24/7**
Shared rooms	**None**
Internet access	**All**
Self-catered	**All**
En suite	**Some**
Approx price range pw	**£83-£135**
City rent pw	**£75-£95**

(wet rooms really). A thing with these - you have to clean them yourself, whereas in Eastwood, where the accommodation is not much worse, they get their bathrooms cleaned and bog roll re-filled by cleaners. Woodland is the most posh. Double beds, en-suite baths and the Ugg boots to match.'

GETTING THERE

☛ By road: M4/J18, A46.
☛ By rail: London Paddington or Southampton, 1:30; Birmingham, 2:15; Cardiff, 1:50.
☛ By air: Bristol Airport.
☛ By coach: London, Birmingham, 3:15.

BATH SPA UNIVERSITY

Bath Spa University
Newton St Loe
Bath BA2 9BN

TEL 01225 875875
FAX 01225 875444
EMAIL enquiries@bathspa.ac.uk
WEB www.bathspa.ac.uk

Bath Spa University Students' Union
Newton St Loe
Bath BA2 9BN

TEL 01225 875588
FAX 01225 876151
EMAIL www.bathspsu.co.uk
WEB www.bathspasu.co.uk

VIRGIN VIEW

*B*ath Spa, a University College since 1999 and a uni since 2005, came out of Bath Academy of Art, Bath College of Education and Newton Park College, the last two being teacher training colleges.

There are four faculties, Applied Sciences, Art and Music, Education and Human Sciences, and Humanities, on two campuses: Sion Hill and Newton Park.

Its defining character seems at first sight to be traditional arts - creative writing, drama, dance, film, fine art, music, design, etc., but there is a clever mix with humanities, appropriate not only to its continuing drive to educate teachers, but also to the responsibility Bath Spa feels to the practical matter of paid work for its budding artists.

A joint honours provision attaches

'I arrived a timid, not-sure-why-I-was-leaving-home type of person... if you have a shell to come out of, you'll discard it within weeks of coming here.'

Business, Management and Cultural courses to Performance Arts, for example, so that when you look at where graduates end up, besides the cream going into artistic creative work, there is a graduate force not just surviving but building a career base in specialist retail and design activities, publishing, printing, government administration, and community and cultural work. Far and away their most employable students choose Creative Arts & Design courses as a main focus. Education, History, Languages follow, and only then those principally studying Business courses.

The teaching most highly rated by the students is in Music and history.

Another terrific recommendation is the low drop-out rate (6%), and according to the Times Higher's *Student Survey*, 86% of students are satisfied with what goes down at Bath Spa.

FEES, BURSARIES

UK & EU Fees 2011-12 £3,375 p.a. Bursaries for students in receipt of HE Maintenance grant. See www.bathspa.ac.uk/services/student-services/current-students/your-money/bsu-bursary-faqs.asp.

CAMPUSES

In 2010 the Uni was awarded Gold accreditation under the EcoCampus national environmental scheme. Newton Park is 4 miles west of the city in a landscaped saucer of Duchy of Cornwall countryside, an original Capability Brown design, with a Georgian manor house at its administrative hub and a cash dispenser, recently installed by the

UNIVERSITY/STUDENT PROFILE	
University since	**2005**
Situation/style	**City campus**
Student population	**8160**
Total undergraduates	**5370**
Mature	**47%**
International	**3%**
Male/female ratio	**29:71**
Equality of opportunity:	
state school intake	**95%**
social class 4-7 intake	**35%**
drop-out rate	**6%**

Students' Union. There are half hourly and late-night buses to and from town. Campus includes a Students' Union, library and ICT suites, a Performing Arts arena with a 214-seat theatre, , a refectory, and a Creative Writing Centre housed in a 14th-century Gatehouse, renovated in collaboration with English Heritage. Now, in 2010, there are proposals for a major redevelopment of academic facilities, residences and amenities.

Sion Hill (the Art and Design campus) is within walking distance of the city centre on the north side. It comprises a large modern building and the Georgian crescent Somerset Place, set in attractive grounds. A £3.5m scheme has provided new specialist workshops, art studios, library, refectory, etc.

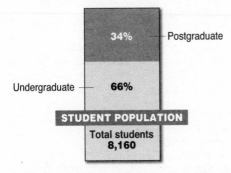

STUDENT POPULATION
Total students
8,160

STUDENT PROFILE

It is a small, quiet, supportive community, appealing particularly to females (71% of undergrads) and mature undergraduate entrants (47%) One student told of its 'friendly, warming atmosphere.' She admitted, 'I arrived a timid, not-sure-why-I-was-leaving-home type of person... if you have a shell to come out of, you'll discard it within weeks of coming here.'

It is far from being some sort of specialist dumping ground for sensitive souls, however. Bath Spa comes out high in league table of new unis.

ACADEMIA & JOBS

Bath Spa University is a Centre for Excellence in Teaching and Learning for creative subjects, with particularly good resources and facilities. A new structure of schools was announced in 2010: Art & Design; Education; Humanities & Cultural Industries; Music & Performing Arts; Science, Society & Management.

There is a mix of seminars, lectures and workshops, also practical sessions in science subjects and performance-based subjects (music, performing arts, dance). Courses are modular in structure offering flexibility so that students can

TEACHING SURVEY AT A GLANCE

Avg. UCAS points accepted	**280**
Acceptance rate	**16%**
Overall satisfaction rate	**86%**
Helpful/interested staff	★★★★
Small tuition groups	★★
Students into graduate jobs	**61%**

Teaching most popular with undergraduates:
Business, English, Fine Art, History, Archaeology, Music (98%), Geography, Psychology.

Teaching least popular with undergraduates:
Design Studies (69%).

build up a programme of study to suit their particular interests and career aspirations. Full-time students take 120 credits each year (some core, some optional) from modules worth either 20 or 40 credits. Students have 12 hours formal contact time in Year 1. There is a 4-star rating for staff interest in students and decent-size tutorials.

The Minerva virtual learning environment (using 'Blackboard' VLE software) allows students to access online teaching materials, and provides a range of other functions including announcements from tutors, online discussion groups, an email tool, and other aids to communication.

By far the majority of the 30-odd per cent of Bath Spa graduates who find employment in Education do so as primary school teachers, some specialist music teachers among them, for music is another vital string to their bow.

At Newton Park, an academic interest in music is given a performance dimension at the **Michael Tippett Centre**, a 250-seater auditorium. But music technology is one of the fastest growing career opportunities.

Graduates are entering the recording industry,

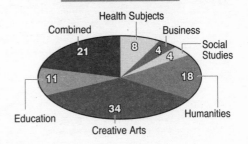

SUBJECT AREAS (%)

RESEARCH EXCELLENCE

% of Bath Spa's research that is
4* (World-class) or 3* (Internationally rated):

	4*	3*
Biological Sciences	**0%**	**0%**
Geography and Enviro. Studies	**0%**	**15%**
Psychology	**0%**	**5%**
Education	**0%**	**15%**
English Language and Lit.	**5%**	**25%**
Theology	**0%**	**10%**
History	**5%**	**40%**
Art and Design	**5%**	**15%**
Media	**10%**	**10%**
Music	**10%**	**20%**

new media (web audio, sound design, game audio, VR), the broadcasting industry (composing for TV, film, radio, etc) and the music technology industry (product development, software design).

Bath Spa's relevant degree is the BA Creative Music Technology, and now new Foundation Degrees, many run in conjunction with partner FE colleges (eg Broadcast Media, Popular Music, Music Production) are available.

There are excellent facilities and well-used industry links. The degree is part of an impressive department, which includes a Foundation and BA degree in Commercial Music - performance and songwriting are key elements (students played their first live gig in January 2002) - a BA (Hons) Music and a BA Performing Arts.

Specialist facilities have been built for students of creative arts subjects as part of the Artswork project (Bath Spa's a Centre for Excellence in Teaching and Learning): MusicLab, DesignLab, BroadcastLab, FashionLab, PerformanceLab and PublishingLab.

Coupled with the development on the 'entrepreneurial third year', students develop essential skills in business planning, project management and enterprise start-up.

All this sets the tone of the Bath Spa 'real world' approach throughout the curriculum, whether in arts courses or food, nutrition and health, from which graduates carve out careers in the food industry and the hotel and restaurant trade, and also in counselling, in hospital and in all sorts of human health activities.

New degree courses include Contemporary Circus and Physical Performance, Creative Media Practice, Further Education Management, Musical Theatre, and Professional Musicianship.

SOCIAL SCENE

New refectory, delicatessen, SU bar, lounge, shop and offices, as Bath Spa tooled up for life as a university: *Flirt!* on Wednesday, Friday and Saturday could be indie, metal, whatever - good nights, plus good jazz and live bands.

Said the SU: 'The campus estate is absolutely beautiful. Bath and Bristol are just a bus ride away. Small numbers create a real community aspect and a sense of belonging.

'The new SU is amazing - chill out in the afternoon over coffee and bacon sandwiches or get your groove on in the evening on one of the biggest dance floors and largest capacity clubs in Bath.'

PILLOW TALK

Seventy per cent of first year students can be accommodated in university accommodation, in self-catering halls located on or near campus. Off-site blocks between Newton campus and the city (both on a good bus route) are Waterside Court and Charlton Court. The off-site option for Sion Hill campers is Bankside House, although they too can opt for Waterside and Charlton Courts. Private rented houses are reserved for the unlucky 30% who don't make the cut. All accommodation is self-catered. Most have a security guard. Internet access assured. No car parking.

WHAT IT'S REALLY LIKE

UNIVERSITY:	
Social Life	★★
Societies	★★
Student Union	★★
Politics	**No**
Sport - national position	**133rd**
Sport facilities	★
Arts opportunities	**Excellent**
Student magazine	**H20**
Bar/venue	**SU bar and lounge**
Union ents	**Cheese, jazz, live**
Union societies	**25**
Most active society	**LGBT**
Parking	**None**
CITY:	
Entertainment	★★★
Scene	**Average clubs, good pubs**
Town/gown relations	**Good**
Risk of violence	**Low**
Cost of living	**High**
Student concessions	**Good**
Survival + 2 nights out	**£80 pw**
Part-time work campus/town	**Average/good**

GETTING THERE

☞ By road Newton Park: from London and east: M4/J18, A46, A4, A39 to Wells, turn left after 200 yards into Newton Park Estate. By road Sion Hill: M4/J18, A46, A420, first left to Hamswell, at second give-way take a right and second right into Landsdown Crescent, over crossroads, first right to Sion Hill on your right.

☞ By rail: London Paddington or Southampton, 1:30; Birmingham, 2:15; Cardiff, 1:50.

☞ By air: Bristol Airport.

ACCOMMODATION	
Student rating	★★
Guarantee to freshers	**90%**
Style	**Halls, flats**
Security guard	**Most**
Shared rooms	**Some halls**
Internet access	**All**
Self-catered	**All**
En suite	**Some**
Approx price range pw	**£79-£135**
City rent pw	**£73-£80**

UNIVERSITY OF BEDFORDSHIRE

The University of Bedfordshire
Park Square Campus,
Luton LU1 3JU

TEL 01582 743500/489326 (international)
FAX 01582 489323
EMAIL go via www.beds.ac.uk/ask
WEB www.beds.ac.uk

University of Bedfordshire Students' Union
Europa House
Luton LU1 3HZ

TEL 01582 743265
FAX 01582 457187
EMAIL [firstname.surname]@beds.ac.uk
WEB www.ubsu.ac.uk

VIRGIN VIEW

*W*hen De Montfort University's Faculty of Education, Bedford campus, merged with Luton University in 2006 it gave birth to the University of Bedfordshire, and for the first time the county had its very own Centre of Higher Education.

Applications to the University have soared to 16,800 over the last three years. That's an increase of 110%. Now there are almost five applicants competing for every place.

As part of their ongoing investment programme, a new £34m Campus Centre was built on the Luton campus, opening in September 2010. Now, it acts as a base for a whole range of social spaces and student services, including entertainments, the Careers and Employment Service, and SiD - the Student Information Desk.

Some 76% of Bedfordshire's students like what is going on, according to the Times Higher National Student Survey. But no-one in the administration is running away with the idea that they have arrived at the

summit. 'Support,' they say, 'is one of our core values,' although students rate staff interest in them tenth lowest in the country.

But hey, the drop-out rate is dropping, and students are getting jobs - the same percentage who declared themselves satisfied with what is going down overall, and that is what this university is ultimately all about.

CAMPUS

Park Square is the main campus in the centre of Luton. It is home to a £5.5-million Media Arts Centre, a £7.8-million Learning Resources Centre,

UNIVERSITY/STUDENT PROFILE	
University since	**2006**
Situation/style	**Town campus**
Student population	**17280**
Total undergraduates	**13240**
Mature	**58%**
International	**32%**
Male/female ratio	**38:62**
Equality of opportunity:	
state school intake	**99%**
social class 4-7 intake	**45%**
drop-out rate	**10%**

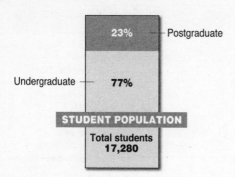

STUDENT POPULATION

Total students
17,280

undergraduates part-timers. There is a 62% female population (largely nurses and primary school teachers and secondary PE with QTS), and 56% are 'mature'.

ACADEMIA & JOBS

In 2009 they were awarded top marks - a 'confidence' rating in their academic standards from the Government's Quality Assurance Agency.

They operate through six faculties: Business, Design & Technology, Health Care & Social Studies, Humanities, Management, Science & Computing, and Education. They are one of the largest providers of Initial Teacher Training in the UK. The School of Physical Education & Sport Sciences has 100 years teaching experience and a tradition of top marks at inspection.

Nursing is a large section of what the uni is about, and popular specialist routes are Dental Nursing, Mental Health Nursing, and Midwifery, which sit alongside other degrees like Health Science, Health Psychology, and BSc Psychology.

The top career areas for graduates are primary and secondary education, nursing, fashion retail, social work, medical practice activities.

For many others, 'Media and sport are the big attractions,' as one student put it. They are indeed excellent providers to the radio/TV sector, and advertising, publishing, film and publishing take from Beds. in quantity. There is excellent job strength too in sports and fitness clubs.

Finally, there are jobs aplenty for graphic artists, designers and Illustrators, who follow their BA Graphic Design, Interior Design, and similar degrees.

There's a high level of involvement from prospective employers and professional bodies in most of their degrees - whether to provide accreditation, a skills framework or work

and the aforesaid new Student Centre. On line too is £40m worth of new accommodation, on track to be completed in 2012.

Open Days at Luton Campus this year are: 19 March,16 April 2011, 9 July, 15 October, 29 October (Business, Media Arts, Computing and Biomedical Science courses only), 27 November.

Bedford Campus is 20 miles away, 20 minutes on foot from Bedford town centre. Originally, this was the local sports college. As De Montfort's Bedford campus it was spread across two sites - Landsdowne (Humanities) and Polehill (Sport and Education - the bit that is now Beds). There was an exceptional sense of community. It was a thriving, self-sufficient set-up, one we picked out as a model for larger institutions. And they were proud. They'd been national finalists in women's rugby at Twickenham, won the women's football, and were the first men's hockey finalists.

Sixty million pounds has since been invested in new facilities - £20 million on student halls of residence, £8 million on a Physical Education and Sport Science Centre, and £6 million on a new Campus Centre, with a £4.5-million 280-seat theatre, studio, gallery and Fairtrade restaurant.

Open Days at Bedford Campus this year are: 9 July, 17 September (Sport courses only),15 October 2011, 29 October 2011 (Education courses only), 26 November.

FEES, BURSARIES

UK & EU Fees, 2011-12 £3,375 p.a. Every new UK/EU undergraduate student starting a full-time course in the 2011-12 academic year will be offered a bursary of £337 per year. There are also many academic, sport and other bursaries and scholarships, including £15,000 for Graduate of the Year! Go to www.beds.ac.uk/money for the works.

STUDENT PROFILE

The student body is almost exclusively State School educated, with 45% coming from the traditional working classes and 34% of

---

TEACHING SURVEY AT A GLANCE

Avg. UCAS points accepted	**190**
Acceptance rate	**22%**
Overall satisfaction rate	**76%**
Helpful/interested staff	★★★
Small tuition groups	★★
Students into graduate jobs	**76%**

Teaching most popular with undergraduates:
Sociology, Social Policy & Anthropology, Complementary Medicine, Psychology, Social Work, Film.

Teaching least popular with undergraduates:
Media Studies (62%), Comuter Science (61%).

experience opportunities. Accreditation from professional bodies includes: the British Psychological Society, the General Social Care Council, Qualified Teacher Status, Chartered Management Institute, Association of Chartered Certified Accountants, Institute of Biomedical Scientists, Institute of Electrical and Electronic Engineering, the Institute of Engineering and Technology, and the British Computer Society

Art and Design students study 'Experiential Learning' and 'Professional Practice' units as part of their course, and all students are encouraged to participate in the Flux Competition, a whole raft of enterprise and employability challenges crammed into less than 36 hours, designed by Working Knowledge Group to bridge the gap between academia and the world of work.

SOCIAL SCENE

STUDENTS' UNION/LUTON   **The main SU bar is located on the mezzanine floor of the new Campus Centre and is open 8 a.m. to 11 p.m.** Ents currently include The Comedy Lounge and Invasion (house, techno, dance). On Saturday, it appears, everyone goes home or to the **Hat Factory** for live bands. The brain-damaging effects of such revelry can be put to the test at the regular *Quiz Nights*, and students with bright ideas can also put the facilities to their own use if they can convince the powers that be that enough people will attend.

Undisputed highlight of the year is the *May Ball*, which attracts thousands of the Luton faithful. The gowned and tuxedoed masses arrive in such numbers that the event is one of the country's largest. The likes of Prodigy, Tim Westwood, Jeremy Healy, Dodgy, Space and the Bootleg Beatles have rocked their world, while casinos, funfairs and top nosh add to the experience.

Most active societies, of which there are 26 in all, include Islamic, Darts, Christian Union, Creative Writing. Media-wise, there's *The Blend* newspaper and UBSTV. Students can benefit from the Radio LaB and the TV LaB, designed to gain hands-on experience of presenting and producing their own shows.

Town/Luton 'Luton is a brilliant in-between town,' said Becky Hill. 'We have access to London in less than an hour, and Milton Keynes is brilliant for shopping.' If this sounds a bit of a back-handed compliment, it is. Luton is not a place you'd go out of your way to spend time in. But there are pubs galore and a handful of clubs.

'Most popular club is **Liquid**. Bars - **The Park**, **Riley's** for pool, **The Galaxy Centre** - with arcades, bowling, cinema - **Hat Factory** (theatre, UBSU Saturday band nights), and **Vauxhall Recreational**

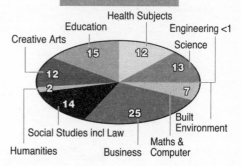

SUBJECT AREAS (%)

Creative Arts 12 · Education 15 · Health Subjects 12 · Engineering <1 · Science 13 · Built Environment 7 · Maths & Computer · Business 25 · Social Studies incl Law 14 · Humanities 2

Centre for sports and gym access.'

STUDENTS' UNION/BEDFORD The £14-million redevelopment brings a new Campus Centre with a 300-seat auditorium, in addition to sport facilities and accommodation. Bedford students spend a lot of their time at the union bar. Town club **Oxygen** and **Bar Soviet** are the official UBSU partners here. Wednesday nights are the stuff of legend. The official student night is Monday at **Oxygen**. It's **Esquires** for live bands like Guilly Mots and Electric Soft Parade, and the Corn Exchange for theatre, dance and orchestra. Bedford also traditionally has Freshers, Christmas and Summer balls.

Bedord town is a place for pubs and bars (more than clubs). **The Forresters** (traditional), **Pilgrims Progress** (excellent value with decent food), the **Bull Nosed Bat**, **The Bedford Lounge** (with dance floor), the **Litton Tree**, **The Rose** (pop venue with dance floor), **Venom** for r&b, **New York, New York** (bit cheesy). Late licensing to 2 or 3 a.m. is the thing. There are off-campus club nights at places like **Nexus**, and what was **Limehaus** is now a cool venue called **The Pad** - dance nights, big names, small but intimate. Nightclubs big with students are **Oxygen** (4 floors, masses of rooms, **Bar Soviet** (the student

RESEARCH EXCELLENCE

% of Bedfordshire's research that is
4* *(World-class)* or **3*** *(Internationally rated):*

	4*	3*
Earth Systems, Enviro. Sci.	5%	10%
Computer Science	0%	30%
Business and Mgt Studies	0%	15%
Social Work, Policy & Admin.	5%	45%
Sports-Related Studies	5%	15%
English Language and Lit.	15%	25%
Media	10%	40%

WHAT IT'S REALLY LIKE

UNIVERSITY:	
Social Life	★
Societies	★
Student Union services	★★
Politics	No
Sport	33 clubs
National team position	66th
Sport facilities	★★
Arts opportunities	Good drama; average art
Student newspaper	The Blend
Student TV	UBSTV
Bars	Mezzanine Bar, Bar Soviet
Union ents	Sportsnight, themed nights, town clubnights
Union societies	26
Most popular society	Islamic (Luton), Dance (Beds)
Parking	Limited
TOWN:	
Entertainment	★★★
Scene	Pubs, clubs
Town/gown relations	Poor
Risk of violence	Average
Cost of living	Average
Student concessions	Good
Survival + 2 nights out	£32 pw
Part-time work campus/town	Average/good

ACCOMMODATION

Student rating	★★
Guarantee to freshers	95%
Style	Halls, flats
Security guard	All
Shared rooms	Some
Internet access	All
Self-catered	All
En suite	Some Luton, most Bedford
Approx price range pw	£80-£139
Town rent pw	£60-£100

Championships give the spread. The annual Rugby Sevens is as famous as it is notorious.

PILLOW TALK

In Luton, the Student Village lies within staggering distance of the Union, town centre and lecture halls, and offers secure accommodation to 1,600 students in eleven separate halls, single-sex and mixed flats, each with shared kitchen, laundry facilities, and bathroom. Several flats are designed for students with disabilities. With around 25% of students living in uni-managed accommodation close by, the town centre feel almost like a campus.

The new £40m accommodation referred to above is on track to be completed in 2012, and will offer 850 fully furnished, state-of-the-art study bedrooms - complete with en-suite facilities and high-speed internet. The new halls will also house a gym and social spaces, all just a stone's throw away from campus.

Twenty million pounds has been invested in accommodation at the Bedford campus. Liberty Park now has upwards of 500 new, en-suite rooms.

GETTING THERE
☞ By road: M1/J10t.
☞ By rail: King's Cross, 40 mins; Nottingham, 1:45; Oxford, 2:15; Birmingham New Street, 2:30.
☞ By air: London Luton Airport.
☞ By coach: London, 1:15; Manchester, 5-6:00.

affiliated bar with themed nights), **Time Out** (small & funky, open till 5 a.m.) **Esquires** is a live music venue with a reputation for hosting new bands - even Cold Play and Oasis - before their time. **Corn Exchange** is a live venue for theatre, music and comedy.

SPORT The £8-million Physical Education and Sport Science Centre is set to train athletes for the 2012 Olympics at Bedford, so you'll be awed by the facilities. They feature regularly in the national student finals. Besides football, rugby and hockey, gongs in Mountain Biking and White Water Kayak

BIRKBECK COLLEGE, LONDON

Birkbeck College
University of London
Malet Street
London WC1E 7HX

TEL 020 7631 6000
    020 7631 6316 (course enquiries)
FAX 020 7631 6270
EMAIL admissions@admin.bbk.ac.uk
WEB www.bbk.ac.uk

Learn as you earn – Birkbeck College, founded in 1823 by Dr George Birkbeck as the London Mechanics' Institution, became a college of London University in 1920.

It is part of a secluded campus precinct shared with the School of Oriental & African Studies (see entry), UCL (including SSEES, the School of Slavonic & Eastern European Studies, once a bastion for Cold War spies) and the University of London Union (ULU), it provides part-time degrees for study in the evening, after the working day.

Undergraduates are mostly mature students who, provided they shine at interview, shouldn't worry too much if they don't have high grade A levels (or even any A levels).

But don't run away with the idea that this is a mickey mouse college. Only 29 British universities make it into the *Times Higher Magazine's* World Top 200, and Birkbeck is among them at No. 23 (152 overall). The box below speaks for the College's immense world-class research reputation, and the teaching by experts is personal.

On the fourth floor of the main building, the newly refurbished **George Birkbeck** bar has a pool table and Sky digital channels on a large screen. Students and lecturers come out of evening lectures and dive straight into the bar. The Union organises regular end-of-term discos, has a strong welfare arm and organises various societies and sports clubs, many of which have stood the test of time.

Five faculties organise nineteen academic

RESEARCH EXCELLENCE

% of Birkbeck's research that is
4* *(World-class) or* **3*** *(Internationally rated):*

	4*%	3*%
Biological Sciences	15%	40%
Earth Systems/Enviro. Sci.	25%	55%
Computer Sci.and Informatics	15%	50%
Electrical and Electronic Eng.	10%	50%
Economics and Econometrics	20%	50%
Business and Mgt Studies	10%	40%
Law	15%	45%
Politics/International Studies	10%	35%
Sociology	5%	40%
Psychology	25%	45%
French	5%	15%
German, Dutch, Scandinavian	5%	30%
Iberian and Latin American	20%	40%
English Language and Lit.	35%	25%
Linguistics.	5%	15%
Philosophy	25%	35%
History	35%	35%
History of Art, Architec. Design	20%	55%

COLLEGE PROFILE

College of London Uni since	**1920**
Situation/style	**City site**
Student population	**18285**
Undergraduates	**14645**

departments. They are the **School of Arts**: English & Humanities; European Cultures & Languages; History of Art & Screen Media; Media & Cultural Studies; Iberian & Latin American Studies; Birkbeck Language Unit. **School of Business, Economics and Informatics**: Computer Science & Information Systems; Economics, Mathematics & Statistics; Management; Organisational Psychology. **School of Law**. **School of Science**: Biological Sciences; Earth & Planetary Sciences; Psychological Sciences. **School of Social Sciences, History & Philosophy**: Applied Linguistics & Communication; Geography, Environment & Development Studies; History, Classics & Archaeology; Philosophy; Politics; Psychosocial Studies; Social Policy & Education.

Says Andrea Ward: 'It's impossible to classify Birkbeck undergraduates other than that they are people who *want* to study. The range is vast: foreigners, locals; old, young; conservative, liberal; nerds, jocks; alcoholics, teetotals; suits, overalls. This makes Birkbeck an interesting place to be. Most students have full-time jobs/careers and many have families, so time is a Birkbeck student's most valuable asset.

'Still, we find time for study weekends in the country and 'how-to' days (how to make notes, how to write exams). These sessions are invaluable and provide an opportunity to meet students on different courses and discover they are having just as hard a time as you are.

'And then, of course, there is the bar. The buzz at the bar is a mix of civilised debate, heated argument, and, probably most of the time, sleazy gossip.. Our lecturers and tutors often come with us (indeed, many a time they are the ones who instigate the bar sessions).

'Coming to college after spending a few years in the "real world" makes a big difference to the learning experience. The first year is particularly tough. But make it through and you're likely to stay the distance. In the end, Birkbeck becomes a way of life. And it is a good one.'

GETTING THERE

☞ Euston Square (Circle, Hammersmith & City and Metropolitan); Warren Street (Victoria, Northern); Russell Square (Piccadilly).

STUDENT BIRMINGHAM – THE CITY

Birmingham has shaken off its grey image to incredible effect in the last decade. Developments right across Britain's second city total hundreds of millions of pounds. Improved social and shopping facilities carry the bonus of better graduate job prospects and mean that whatever you're after from your student career, Birmingham can probably supply.

The most dramatic recent development has to have been Birmingham's **Bull Ring Centre**. There's been a market here at least since 1154, when Peter de Birmingham, a local landowner, obtained a Royal Charter for a cattle and food market. In 1964 a new concrete-smothered mixed market of indoor shops and outdoor stalls was built, a design unintegrated with the city that proved to be locked into its time and of questionable practical form. In 2000 it was reduced to a hole in the ground, and then recently it opened anew in spectacular form to public applause. The big name designers and retailers, like **Selfridges**, have flocked their in droves, and Birmingham Retail has been resurrected, the time the whole operation took to complete giving the rest of Brum's shopping world a chance to flourish, with such as **Mailbox** offering us a chance to drool at **Harvey Nichs**, Armani, DKNY, etc, even if many students will stick to the pedestrianised areas around New Street and the Pallasades, where every high street store you could want is juxtaposed with designer off-cut stores and street markets.

CAFES, PUBS, CLUBS

Aston students report, 'There are so many places to go, and so much to do that you will always be spoilt for choice... Spend an evening in a canal-side café, pub or restaurant, take a trip to the cinema, theatre or ballet or laugh the night away at the **Glee Comedy Club**. The Broad Street, Brindley Place/Mailbox area is particularly popular with our students and has lots of places to eat and drink beside the canals, for example **The Works**, **Flares** (2 floors of cheese), **Hard Rock Café**, **Bar Epernay** (rotating piano), **Fifty Two Degrees North**, the pricier **Zinc** and Aussie-themes **Walkabout** (amongst many others). Rumour has it that there are 100 pubs and bars within a one-mile radius of the Aston University Campus – **The Square Peg** (Wetherspoons), **Bar Med**, **Chambers**, **Sack of Potatoes** (facing Aston Uni), **Gosta Green** (It's A Scream), the stylish **RSVP Bar**...the list is endless. Numerous pre-clubbers like **Poppy Red**, **Ipanema**, **The Living Room**,

and **SoBar** are also open late, as you would expect from a real entertainment city like Birmingham. The bars, cafés and clubs at **The Arcadian Centre** (near the Chinese Quarter) are also popular with students.

Birmingham is bursting with clubs playing anything from dance, house, drum 'n' bass and jungle, to hard rock, 70s, 80s, lounge, soul, jazz and garage. **The Que Club** (one of the largest clubs in the UK) alas is no more, but clubs like **The Sanctuary**, **The Medicine Bar**, **Bakers**, new club **Air** (home to Godskitchen), **The Works** and **Bobby Brown's** play host to top DJs and attract clubbing aficionados from across the UK in their coachloads.

LIVE

The recently opened **Birmingham Academy** is the best local venue – it's one of the essential stops on any band's UK tour, its reputation boosted far and wide in 2001 by Radio 1's hosting most of its One Live in Birmingham events there.

The **Wolverhampton Civic**, just a short train ride away, is still seen as a main Midland live venue, and the **NEC** is equally popular with bands of U2 or S Club proportions. In the smaller venues expect massively varying music styles and quality. **Ronnie Scott's** offers more than just jazz, whilst the **Fiddle and Bone** is a pub with a plethora of acts for free – from tribute bands to student musos through to Beethoven. Further into the backstreets you'll find a glut of pubs with fascinating (but sometimes frightening) live acts.

COMEDY, THEATRE, ARTS

Judging by the success of venues like the **Glee Club**, the new rock 'n' roll this may be. The venue attracts the best comic newcomers and the established talents of Eddie Izzard and Harry Hill – all for under a fiver if you go on a student night.

At the newly-revamped **Hippodrome** or **Alexandra Theatre** can be seen an array of Lloydesque and other West End shows, as well as the magnificent Welsh National Opera.

In the **Symphony Hall**, the renowned City of Birmingham Symphony Orchestra resides, playing host also to hundreds of international performers and offering a huge variety of classical music all year round.

For smaller fry the **Midlands Arts Centre**, or **MAC** as it is known, nestles comfortably on the edge of Cannon Hill Park near the University of Birmingham. With its combination of theatre, exhibitions, cinema and a damn fine bar it offers excellent choice and value. **The Electric Cinema**, showing arthouse, world and classic cinema in a charming setting, is the place to go if you want to see something different, although if it's Hollywood blockbusters you're after the **Odeon**, **UGC** and **Starcity** complexes offer about six billion different films, allegedly on twice as many screens.

For theatre **The Rep** in town has come in for a great deal of well-deserved praise lately with their showcase for new work, **The Door**, and also show fantastic productions in their main theatre. Stratford-upon-Avon is but a short train ride away, but watch out for the RSC's value for money student trips to productions there. For community productions (usually) as good as the professionals, check out the **Crescent Theatre**, offering Shakespeare and other productions.

For art you are spoilt in Brum, **The Barber Institute** on the University of Birmingham's campus is astounding. For more modern exhibitions head for **Ikon** or **The Angle** galleries.

Crucially all these places offer heavy discounts for students. Life with a 10% discount is what being a student is all about.

UNIVERSITY OF BIRMINGHAM

The University of Birmingham
Edgbaston
Birmingham B15 2TT

TEL 0121 414 3344
FAX 0121 414 7159
EMAIL admissions@bham.ac.uk
WEB www.bham.ac.uk

Birmingham Guild of Students
Edgbaston Park Road
Birmingham B15 2TU

TEL 0121 251 2300
FAX 0121 251 2301
EMAIL info@guild.bham.ac.uk
WEB www.guildofstudents.com/

VIRGIN VIEW

*B*irmingham is the original 'red-brick' uni, with all that that entails beyond its masonry - none of the snobbery attached to Oxbridge and for many second only to it, though some from the softer south may recoil at the city itself. 'My first impression,' said Sorrel from the Garden of Kent, 'was that it didn't look to me to be very nice. I mean at home it's all countryside and really, really quiet and pretty, and then Birmingham is completely the opposite, especially where students live in their second and third years [Selly Oak].'

Nevertheless, she gave her approval of the campus itself, which is away from the urban hubbub: 'I think it is a very impressive campus. You know, it's all sort of red brick, old buildings. But then you have also really modern buildings, the sports science facilities have been recently built.'

Sorrel is studying Sport. 'And right in the centre of the campus by the main library there is a nice sort of green area with lots of

UNIVERSITY/STUDENT PROFILE	
University since	**1900**
Situation/style	**Campus**
Student population	**29185**
Total undergraduates	**18495**
Mature	**34%**
International	**19%**
Male/female ratio	**45:55**
Equality of opportunity:	
state school intake	**81%**
social class 4-7 intake	**23%**
drop-out rate	**4%**

benches where you can sit and work on the grass, so it's quite communal.'

So much for the aesthetics. Birmingham was positioned 145th in the World Top 200 Universities, published by the Times Higher, 21st among the 29 British universities placed. It is a popular first choice and for the top flight candidate, a useful back-up.

In the last research assessment of universities, it achieved an impressive list of 4- and 3-star results - world class and *international renown - across the board, from Epidemiology to English (see our Research Excellence box below).*

Chipping away at the coal-face of a subject by way of research is not teaching it, but when asked, students gave the lecturers plaudits for hands-on help and interest.

The medics and nurses dominate the employment stats, but whatever you study, as a Birmingham graduate you have a 79% chance of getting a graduate-level job within six months of leaving.

Overall, 86% of students said they were satisfied with the Birmingham experience. There is a 6% drop-out rate.

CAMPUS

The self-contained campus lies a couple of miles south of the city in leafy Edgbaston. Parking is not encouraged.

FEES, BURSARIES

UK & EU Fees, 2011-12: £3,375 p.a. Bursaries for all students whose family income is £36,170 or less. Students from low-income backgrounds who achieve a minimum of AAB at A level, more than 34 points in the IB, or DDD in BTEC, will get more. There are five music scholarships each year.

STUDENT PROFILE

There's a high (19%) public school intake, though not as high as Oxbridge, Bristol, Durham. Says Sorrel: 'I'd say the student population is quite diverse. You have got people from all different races, and then you have got quite a few private school people, but also you have state school people. There is definitely a good mix.'

Southerners think that Brum is north enough, but not too far north. Northerners, bored with Manchester and Leeds, see it as the next best city without London's expense. Thanks to strong overseas links there's also a large international

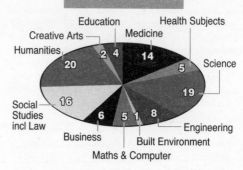

SUBJECT AREAS (%)

- Education
- Health Subjects
- Creative Arts
- Medicine
- Humanities — 20
- 2, 4, 14
- Science — 5
- 19
- Social Studies incl Law — 16
- 6, 5, 1, 8
- Engineering
- Business
- Built Environment
- Maths & Computer

community. The gist is that there are loads of people with interests sympathetic to yours at Birmingham, and you'll meet them through lectures, accommodation or socialising.

TEACHING SURVEY AT A GLANCE

Avg. UCAS points accepted	**400**
Acceptance rate	**13%**
Overall satisfaction rate	**86%**
Helpful/interested staff	★★★★
Small tuition groups	★★★
Students into graduate jobs	**79%**

Teaching most popular with undergraduates:
Accounting, African & Middle Eastern Studies, American & Australasian Studies, Anatomy, Physiology, Pathology, Biology, Chemical Engineering, Chemistry, Computer, Creative Arts, Dentistry, Economics, Education, Languages, Geology, Germand & Scandinavian Studies, Geography, Materials & Minerals Technology, Maths, Medical Science & Pharmacy, Subjects allied to Medicine, Music, Nursing, Physics, Planning (100%), Politics, Social Policy, Sociology, Sports Science, Technology, Theology.

Teaching least popular with undergraduates:
Social Work (71%), Media Studies (72%).

In an effort to ease the plight of disabled students, the uni has an action plan to adapt and re-design facilities and access points, to increase disability staffing, expand the equipment pool, assistive technology in libraries, availability of specialist software, more support workers, etc.

For international students, there's now a 'Welcome Week' induction programme before the start of term, and three full-time Student Advisers and free lessons in English during term time.

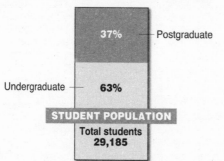

- 37% — Postgraduate
- Undergraduate — 63%

STUDENT POPULATION

Total students
29,185

ACADEMIA & JOBS

Involvement with the world of work is an aspect of a number of courses, and the proximity of important industries and businesses, as well as artistic nuclei, is key to the academic provision. Even the Arts School non-vocational courses give special attention not just to what is studied, but how. Skills such as organisation, analysis, presentation, communication and problem-solving are to the fore.

The degree in Medicine is the 4/5-year MBCgB. There's a Black Country strategy in partnership with hospital trusts in Wolverhampton, Dudley, Sandwell and Walsall. 340 - 360 Tariff points (i.e. minimum AAB grades) normally achieved in Year 13 from three A levels or equivalent normally including two GCE science A levels - Chemistry and one of Biology, Maths, Physics. Biology at a minimum of AS is compulsory. For dentists, it's the 5-year BDS; entry ABB-AAB.

Birmingham is one of the few unis offering non-Law graduates a 2-year full-time or 3-year part-time Senior Status Law Degree. All candidates must sit the National Admissions Test for Law (LNAT).

It is not necessary to take a degree to become a qualified accountant any more than it is to become a solicitor, but Birmingham is the big graduate provider in this sector, with Warwick and Durham not far behind. At the Business School A level requirements are high, and conceptual, analytical, ICT and problem-solving skills are to the fore, as are communication/discursive skills and the ability to work on one's own. Birmingham also lead in getting graduates jobs as tax experts and consultants. For a job in banking, look at the BSc Money, Banking & Finance plus one year (well spent) to combine with French, German, Italian, Portuguese or Spanish.

Note this language interest; it's characteristic of all kinds of courses at Birmingham. The department is also high in the pecking order for graduates wanting jobs as interpreters, and leads many into the area of human resource management.

Would-be electrical, electronic and telecommunications engineers note that full marks in the old teaching assessments, high praise in the National Student Survey and a good reputation for research put the department high on any discerning applicant's list. And there's a Business Management orientation available for most of what's on offer.

Music is another niche area. An amazing 50% of their Music research is world-class (4 star), 35% of international stature (3 star). A new music

RESEARCH EXCELLENCE		
% of Birmingham's research that is **4*** *(World-class)* or **3*** *(Internationally rated):*		
	4*	*3*%*
Cardiovascular Medicine	5%	35%
Cancer Studies	15%	65%
Infection and Immunology	10%	40%
Other Clinical Subjects	20%	55%
Epidemiology/Public Health	10%	50%
Health Services Research	15%	50%
Primary Care	35%	30%
Psych., Neurosci, Clin. Psychol.	5%	20%
Dentistry	10%	50%
Biological Sciences	10%	40%
Earth Systems/Enviro. Sci.	15%	50%
Chemistry	10%	50%
Physics	20%	40%
Pure Mathematics	15%	40%
Applied Mathematics	10%	35%
Computer Sci.and Informatics	30%	45%
Electrical and Electronic Eng.	10%	50%
Chemical Engineering	20%	45%
Civil Engineering	10%	55%
Mech., Aero., Manufac. Eng.	20%	50%
Metallurgy and Materials	15%	60%
Town and Country Planning	10%	40%
Geog. and Enviro. Studies	15%	40%
Archaeology	10%	40%
Economics and Econometrics	15%	50%
Business and Mgt Studies	20%	35%
Law	15%	45%
Politics/International Studies	5%	40%
Social Work, Policy & Admin.	15%	45%
Sociology	5%	25%
Development Studies	10%	25%
Psychology	25%	55%
Education	10%	35%
Sports-Related Studies	25%	35%
American Studies	20%	25%
Middle East and Afric. Studies	20%	40%
European Studies	20%	25%
French	10%	35%
German, Dutch, Scandinavian	15%	45%
Italian	15%	35%
Iberian and Latin American	5%	45%
English Language and Lit.	25%	35%
Classics, Ancient History, etc.	20%	30%
Philosophy	5%	40%
Theology	15%	45%
History	20%	40%
History of Art, Architec. Design	30%	40%
Drama, Dance, Perform. Arts	15%	50%
Music	50%	35%

auditorium with considerable rehearsal space is in prospect as we write. There's a Centre for Early Music Performance & Research, excellent rehearsal facilities and a brilliant Electro-Acoustic Music Studio, which is worth exploring in detail on the web. Five different degree routes are offered.

They are also up there with the best in Psychology and Sport, both of which enjoy 25% 4-star and 35% 3-star ratings. The sport degrees are Sport & Exercise Sciences; Sport, Physical Education & Coaching Science, Sports Science & Materials Technology. Says sporty Sorrel: 'I really liked the sound of the course at Birmingham. Also, I do athletics and cross country and the coach for athletics at Birmingham is the Great Britain coach. He invited me to go and train with them and the athletes showed me around the uni. I decided that for my running it would be really good. I want ultimately to become a PE teacher.'

The specialist Applied Golf Management Studies assumes a handicap on entry of 4.4 or less (women 6.4). Coaching is a key element and you'll be expected to take up a summer placement in the community. Not a bad way to spend three years. You might consider their very strong student media as compatible in career terms.

SOCIAL SCENE

GUILD OF STUDENTS The main source of non-academic entertainment on campus is the Student Union. By day they offer numerous eateries and bars, the largest one being **Joe's,** which is just now being relocated and will be given a new name.

There's the chance to join one of over 150 societies, and a huge range of student services (legal advice, local info from the ARC (Advice & Representa-tion Centre - currently in refurb.), part-time job info at the Job Zone, etc).

Media-wise Birmingham has *Redbrick* newspaper, Burn FM (radio) and G:TV, but it isn't anything like as award-winning as once it was, and graduates no longer find their way into media jobs as often through the set-up.

Some freshers prefer the hall bars to the Guild, before moving on to one of the city-centre clubs and bars. Students living in neighbouring Selly Oak or Harbourne frequent the many local student pubs and balti houses in those areas, as well as the most popular city club nights.

Guild nights are a bit unimaginative. Typically, there's Curryoke Thursdays (karaoke for free curry for 2), theme party nights on Friday (*Bad Taste, Tequila Night, 999 Emergency Services*, etc), and *Fab 'n' Fresh* at **The Underground** on Saturday. **The Underground** is legendary. There's also **Deb Hall**, which is used for debating and musical and theatre productions, as well as nightclub events.

Said one student: 'Birmingham isn't just about getting rat-arsed and going for a closing-time curry,

WHAT IT'S REALLY LIKE	
UNIVERSITY:	
Social Life	★★★★★
Societies	★★★★
Student Union services	★★★★
Politics	**Activity high**
Sport	**Key; 43 clubs**
National team position	**3rd**
Sport facilities	★★★★
Arts opportunities	**Film excellent; drama, dance, music, art good**
Student newspaper	**Redbrick**
Student radio	**Burn FM**
Student TV	**G:TV**
Nightclub	**The Underground, Deb Hall**
Bars	**Joe's (for now)**
Union ents	**Theme nights, comedy, live bands**
Union societies	**150+**
Most active society	**Rock Soc**
Parking	**Poor**
CITY:	
Entertainment	★★★★★
Scene	**Excellent**
Town/gown relations	**Average**
Risk of violence	**High**
Cost of living	**High**
Student concessions	**Excellent**
Survival + 2 nights out	**£80 pw**
Part-time work campus/town	**Average/excellent**

but more students do that than spend their time in an art gallery.' Representative? On campus, artistic input is high. Across drama, dance, music and art, extra-curricular societies are very active. The Film Society is excellent. There's a chamber orchestra, an orchestra of 100 and a choir of 220. For art there's **The Barber Institute** - founded in 1932 it incorporates both Fine Art and Music departments and has been described as 'one of the finest small picture galleries in the world'. There's also a musical theatre group which nurtures, milks and dispenses talent that abounds among students. If you're into theatre, Birmingham is one of the places to be. There's a Guild group and a Drama Dept group in the uni's **Studio Theatre**; students perform all over the city (often before taking their productions to the Edinburgh Fringe), and there's a student humour night at the **Glee Club** in town.

If you find yourself dipping into the overdraft it's easy to find a job at the Guild, where students are given decent wages for bar work, security, marketing, and other jobs. Alternatively, businesses around the city always want flexible, enthusiastic part-timers. Most of them advertise in the Guild's Job Zone.

SPORT Birmingham came 3rd nationwide in university sports last year. Only Loughborough and Leeds Met did better. **The Munrow Sports Centre's** mission statement 'to enhance the sporting experience of the university by providing opportunities at all levels' sums up the sporting situation. For the casual athlete the Active Lifestyles Programme offers weekly courses in martial arts, swimming, aerobics and team games.

> *'Birmingham isn't just about getting rat-arsed and going for a closing-time curry, but more students do that than spend their time in an art gallery.'*

The Athletic Union is made up of 40+ sports clubs, each with a qualified coach. Clubs exist also at inter-departmental and inter-hall levels. Interests are more than catered for by the 25m pool, two gyms, a climbing wall and full-size running track, as well as two floodlit, synthetic pitches, physiotherapy and sports science support, and a Fitness Services Unit for all levels.

Off-campus, 5 miles from home, there are seventy acres of pitches served by coaches and minibuses, and by Lake Coniston in Cumbria, 170 miles away, they have a Centre for Outdoor Pursuits (watersports, mountaineering, mountain biking, etc).

TOWN Says Sorrel: 'Birmingham is obviously known for good night life, so anyone here has a good social experience at university. The clubs are all on Broad Street. You quite often get bar crawls, and you can do that on the one street. Students from the Food College, Birmingham City University, and Aston University all tend to go to the same bars and clubs and integrate with one another.' The city does have less desirable areas (name a city that doesn't) but the average student has little contact with them, and if you're sensible about sticking in groups after dark and not flashing your cash you shouldn't have any problems. As in all student areas there are complaints from disgruntled locals about kick-out time noise and student mess, but the Guild liaises with residents and police to keep the peace.

PILLOW TALK

'Halls are dotted all over the place,' says Sorrel. 'They are all reasonably close. I was in one called Tennis Courts which was about a ten minute walk onto campus, and the majority of them are about ten minutes away, but there are some in the city centre. One I went to - IQ5 - was really modern and nice, but you have to get a bus or train in. It's just behind Broad Street, so really close to the bars and clubs. For the first year definitely it's better to be close to campus, I would say.'

Which hall is most likely to appeal to a public school type? 'I would say Shackleton. Tennis Courts and Shackleton are quite close to each other.' However, there is also the ultra posh Jarratt Hall, boasting 620 en-suite bedrooms. Also new hall Mason opened in 2008, accommodating 804 students in single en-suite rooms, plus 36 self-contained apartments.

The main area is the Vale, a beautiful grassy bit set around a lake which houses catered and self-catered halls, and the Hub Centre with two bars, eating areas, welfare and committee rooms. Other self-catered halls are either adjacent to the main campus or a bus journey away (The Beeches and Hunter Court). Limited car parking at Pritchatts & Vale villages. Apply on arrival.

ACCOMMODATION	
Student rating	★★★★
Guarantee to freshers	**95%**
Style	**Halls, flats**
Security guard	**CCTV, Security Centre, police.**
Shared rooms	**Some**
Internet access	**All**
Self-catered	**Most**
En suite	**Some**
Approx price range pw	**£77.50-£233**
City rent pw	**£50-£70**

GETTING THERE

☛ By road: A38. Avoid entry through suburbia from the M40; instead use M42/J1, A38.

☛ By rail: London Euston, 1:40; Bristol Parkway or Sheffield, 1:30; Liverpool Lime Street, Manchester Piccadilly,1:40; Leeds, 2:15. Frequent trains from New Street to University Station.

☛ By air: Birmingham Airport.

☛ By coach: London, 2:40; Bristol, 2:00; Manchester, 2:30.

BIRMINGHAM CITY UNIVERSITY

Birmingham City University
Franchise Street
Perry Barr
Birmingham B42 2SU

TEL 0121 331 5595
FAX 0121 331 7994
EMAIL choices@bcu.ac.uk
WEB www.bcu.ac.uk

Birmingham City Students' Union
The Union Building
Perry Barr
Birmingham B42 2SU

TEL 0121 331 6801
FAX 0121 331 6802
EMAIL students.union@bcu.ac.uk
WEB www.birminghamcitysu.com

VIRGIN VIEW

UNIVERSITY/STUDENT PROFILE	
University since	**1992**
Situation/style	**Civic**
Student population	**24850**
Total undergraduates	**20630**
Mature	**55%**
International	**9%**
Male/female ratio	**49:61**
Equality of opportunity:	
state school intake	**97%**
social class 4-7 intake	**45%**
drop-out rate	**11%**

*B*irmingham City University, as the old Central England University and even older Birmingham Polytechnic is now called, is a huge, urban conglomeration of sites, incorporating Business, Engineering & Technology, Built Environment, Law & Social Sciences, Computing, Health, the Birmingham Institute of Art & Design, the Acting School, and two little gems a Jewellery School and the Birmingham Conservatoire.

Student Union officers have always told us, 'We're a really friendly university, whichever campus you study on and wherever you live,' and this is undoubtedly true. But the main campus, Perry Barr, where they do the whole cheesy student thing, is not the centre of the universe for everyone at BCU.

If you are studying music at the world-renowned Conservatoire, for example, you tend to avoid Perry Barr like the plague, and have your own very good time doing so.

Says recent graduate Tim Wilkinson: 'The thing is split up into so many different colleges, all quite far apart. A lot of the places I know of, but have never ventured anywhere near. Nor would I. We all have our own section.'

When you go to an Open Day you hear about 'the different Student Union clubs and stuff, but the trouble is that most of them are to do with Perry Barr.' The SU sabbaticals do a great job putting up posters at the various satellite campuses about what's happening at HQ, but it does little to bring the whole student body together.

So, what you have at BCU is a federation, and the character of the place is not about to change - £150 million has been allocated to the building of yet another city centre campus, in the Eastside district of Birmingham.

As a result, statistics which treat BCU as a single, unified item, may not be accurate for your campus.

At the Conservatoire, percussionist Tim had an amazing 40 hours of 1-on-1 tuition in a year. His girlfriend Katie, who was a pianist, got 35 hours with one tutor 1-on-1 and 5 hours with another. It is a very personal scene at the Conservatoire.

'You build up personal relationships with the teachers, they are happy for you to go and find them at any time, they know who you are, they know what you are doing.'

In fact, across the whole university, students turned in an average 3-star rating for interest and helpfulness of staff. But it is probably important, if you are considering applying to BCU, to research the particular subject and college campus to which you are applying, as if it was quite distinct from the rest.

FEES, BURSARIES

UK & EU Fees for 2011-12: £3,375. Students in lower income brackets will be eligible for grants for living costs, also bursaries are available to anyone receiving a full or partial maintenance grant. See www.bcu.ac.uk/prospective/finance.

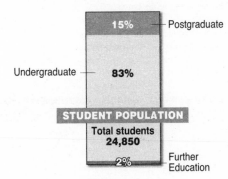

Postgraduate **15%**

Undergraduate **83%**

STUDENT POPULATION

Total students 24,850

2% Further Education

STUDENT PROFILE

As diverse as its campus sites, but with the emphasis clearly on work-purpose and real-world living. Many are mature, many local and many from overseas, and UCE far exceed their Government benchmarks for recruiting from under-represented groups in higher education.

CAMPUS SITES & FACULTIES

A CCTV system covers each site. 150 cameras are constantly monitored and the system is key to supporting the work of a 70-strong security team to ensure a safe environment in which to study.

PERRY BARR Main campus. Location: north of city; approach via M6/M5 Junction 7 and A34 Walsall Road. Access to city: 15 minutes by bus plus rail link to Birmingham New Street. Accommodation: two halls for 850 students - the Coppice and Oscott Gardens (en suite); both self-catering. Bars: **Bar 42**, pub/food in daytime, nightclub/venue in the evening. Faculties: Business School; Education; Law, Humanities, Development & Society; and Health. The Department of Media and Communication, part of the Birmingham Institute of Art & Design (BIAD) is also here.

A new campus specifically for BIAD is planned.

The Business School (www.business.uce.ac.uk Galton Building, Perry Barr Campus) provides single and joint programmes to over 4,000 students in such as Accountancy, Advertising, Business, Business Law, Business Psychology Computing, Economics, Finance, ICT Internet Systems, Human Resources, Management, Marketing, Multimedia, Network Technology, Software Engineering and Public Relations.

The Faculty of Education (www.ed.uce.ac.uk Attwood Building, Perry Barr Campus) proides both primary and secondary and operates in the multi-ethnic context of the West Midlands. The students who join its initial teacher training courses are also from diverse backgrounds.

The Faculty of Law, Humanities, Development & Society (www.lhds.uce.ac.uk Perry Barr Campus) might as well be called the School of Diversity. It delivers academic and vocational programmes in Construction, Criminal Justice, English, Housing, Law, Planning, Property, Psychology and Sociology; there is something for almost everyone.

There is a real practical bent. Law students may spend a summer in America, working on death row cases. The School of Law also boasts a 'highly commended' Legal Practice Course, and all law students can make use of a mock courtroom. Meanwhile, criminal justice students experience real prison visits.

At the National Academy of Writing, published authors, Jim Crace, Melvin Bragg, Jilly Cooper, Ian Rankin, Philip Pullman have been involved.

In the School of Property, Construction and Planning, professional accreditation is available for

TEACHING SURVEY AT A GLANCE

Avg. UCAS points accepted	**240**
Acceptance rate	**18%**
Overall satisfaction rate	**73%**
Helpful/interested staff	**★★★**
Small tuition groups	**★**
Students into graduate jobs	**80%**

Teaching most popular with undergraduates:
Drama, Mechanical, Production & Manufacturing Engineering, Nursing, Sociology, Social Policy & Anthropology.

Teaching least popular with undergraduates:
Social Work (49%).

all would-be surveyors, town planners and construction managers. And so on.

The Faculty of Health (www.health.uce.ac.uk Westbourne and Perry Barr Campuses) attracts over 7,000 full and part-time students each year. They have partnerships with NHS Trusts and health and social care providers, and are the largest provider of qualified staff to the NHS and Social Services in the region. All undergraduate courses include practice placements.

In employment terms, BCU accounts for a large number of non-hospital nurses (adult, child,

RESEARCH EXCELLENCE

% of Birmingham Citys research that is
4* *(World-class)* or **3*** *(Internationally rated):*

	4*	3*
Town & Country Plannig	10%	15%
Business & Management	5%	20%
Art & Design	30%	30%
Social Work,I Policy & Admin.	5%	15%
Education	5%	20%
English	5%	15%
Music	15%	25%

disabilities and mental health) and senior hospital nurses (SRN, RGN), also for 12% of graduate midwives with their 3-year BSc (Hons) Midwifery. Other certainties in this sector are BSc (Hons) Diagnostic Radiography and BSc (Hons) Radiotherapy. Then there's a particular niche - BSc (Hons) Speech & Language Therapy.

MILLENNIUM POINT Location (Curzon Street, Birmingham B4 7XG) on the east side of the city centre, well served by buses, public car parks and New Street, Snow Hill and Moor Street railway stations. Faculties: a £114-million building housing tourist attractions, commercial and retail businesses, and UCE's Faculties: Technology Innovation Centre (tic) and Birmingham School of Acting (BSA).

Technology Innovation Centre (www.tic.ac.uk , Millennium Point) Tic is a key faculty of the university, offering a wide range of interactive media, ICT, design technology and advanced engineering courses.

Birmingham School of Acting (www.bssd.ac.uk,

> '*The thing is split up into so many different colleges. A lot I know of, but have never ventured near. Nor would I. We all have our own section.*'

Millennium Point) merged with BCU in 2005. Formerly Birmingham School of Speech and Drama, it was founded in 1936. The main focus is acting. There's a BA (Hons) Acting and a one-year Graduate Diploma for postgraduate students. A Musical Theatre course is planned for September 2007. The School's courses are accredited by the National Council for Drama Training.

WESTBOURNE Location: south city suburb of Edgbaston, on Westbourne Road, accessed via M5/J3, A456 or M5/J4, AA38. Regular, cheap and late-night bus service to and from city centre. Faculty: Health. There's been a major £25 million redevelopment of this campus including new classrooms, a suite of clinical skills facilities, lecture theatres, a Students Union complex - including a new shop, a coffee bar, a bar (The Lounge), and Student Activities centre. Accommodation: one hall - 245 single study-bedrooms and 34 shared (two bedrooms and joint study); self-catering.

GOSTA GREEN Birmingham Institute of Art and Design (BIAD) is one of the largest faculties of art, design and media education in the United Kingdom. Here you'll find Fashion, Textiles & 3-Dimensional Design and the Department of Visual Communication. But BIAD's Dept of Media and Communication is based at Perry Barr. At Gosta Green you'll also cop the School of Theoretical and Historical Studies. Students have access to adjacent Aston Uni union facilities.

Location: adjacent to Aston Uni campus, edge of city centre; accessed via M6/J6, A38M. Ignoring the signs to Aston Uni, leave the A38M at third exit and take the first exit at Lancaster Circus r/about.

BOURNVILLE CENTRE FOR VISUAL ARTS Location: 4 miles to the south of the city on the Bournville Village Trust, an urban village, built by the Cadbury family over a century ago. Two listed buildings, refurbished to the tune of £6 million.

THE ART DEPARTMENT Grade I listed Venetian Gothic property on Margaret Street, centrally sited.

THE JEWELLERY SCHOOL Recent refurbishment makes this the smartest, coolest site within BCU; also state-of-the-art workshops and technology. Location: Vittoria Street in the city centre - the

SUBJECT AREAS (%)

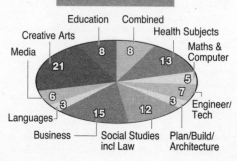

Education 8
Combined 8
Creative Arts
Health Subjects
Media
Maths & Computer 13
21
5
7
3
Engineer/ Tech
6
3
15
12
Languages
Business
Social Studies incl Law
Plan/Build/ Architecture

famous old Jewellery Quarter, a walk from Birmingham New Street.

THE BIRMINGHAM CONSERVATOIRE This is the purpose-built Conservatoire, a little gem, a lively, creative environment, one of our best music colleges, it has been going in one form or another since 1859. Based in the heart of the city centre only a few minutes' walk from Symphony Hall, the Conservatoire has some of the finest performing and teaching facilities of its kind in the country, including the recently refurbished 520-seat Adrian Boult Hall, 150-seat Recital Hall customised for performance with live electronics, four recording studios and a specialised music library, recently rebuilt from the ground up, with around 95,000 individual scores and parts and 10,000 sound recordings. There's both a BMus (Hons) and a specialised BMus (Hons) Jazz. The Conservatoire also works in collaboration with the Technology Innovation Centre to provide a BSc (Hons) course in Music Technology; with South Birmingham College to provide an HND in Popular Music; and with BIAD to provide a new MA in Digital Arts in Performance.

Location: Close to the Birmingham Rep Theatre and ICC & Symphony Hall, it is sited on a traffic island (Paradise Circus) a few minutes walk from Birmingham New Street station. It offers more of a challenge by car. From M6 South or North-West leave at J6 and follow the A38(M) and signs to 'City centre, Bromsgrove, (A38)', over a flyover and through Queensway tunnel (signposted 'Broms-grove and Queen Elizabeth Hospital'). Leave tunnel left but stay in right-hand lane of exit road. No parking for you on Paradise Island. Unload and move on or seek car park close by: after exit for A456 (Broad Street), take left into Cambridge Street.

ACADEMIA & JOBS

The teaching most popular with students is in Drama, Mechanical, Production & Manufacturing Engineering, Nursing, Sociology, Social Policy & Anthropology. The least popular teaching occurs perenially in Social Work.

Overall, student satisfaction is an unexciting 73%, but 80% get real graduate jobs within six months of graduating. Generally, there is emplkoyability skills training built in and many of the courses involve employers in design and often delivery, with more than 120 course recognised by professional bosies.

Of course, the employment figures are boosted substantially by those studying Nursing and Radiotherapy degrees, and those being prepared as primary level teachers. But generally there are more getting jobs in that toughest of markets,

WHAT IT'S REALLY LIKE	
UNIVERSITY:	
Social Life	★
Societies	★
Student Union services	★
Politics	**Luke warm**
Sport	**24 clubs**
National team position	**109th**
Sport facilities	★
Arts opportunities	**Good**
Student magazine	**Spaghetti**
Student radio	**SCRatch**
Student TV	**Tiger tv**
Venue	**Bar 42**
Bars	**Bar 42, ibar, Village Inn, Lounge, Pavilion, Conservatoire**
Union ents	**Very popular**
Union societies	**30**
Parking	**OK**
CITY:	
Entertainment	★★★★★
Scene	**Excellent**
Town/gown relations	**Average**
Risk of violence	**Average**
Cost of living	**Average**
Student concessions	**Excellent**
Survival + 2 nights out	**£80 pw**
Part-time work campus/town	**Good/excellent**

artistic creation, than there are in 'beverage serving activities'. Actors and musicians are of course among those who make a good showing in the artistic sector. A number of graduates in Computing become software consultants. Otherwise, the various faculties boost employment figures in particular in personnel, it seems, in miscellaneous business and management activities, in the hotel and restaurant trade, in building and civil engineering, banking, the Law, accounting, and the occasional niche area, like the rag trade, where dedicated degrees (Fashion, Textiles) point the way.

SOCIAL SCENE

Union HQ is **Bar 42** on Perry Barr Campus, where there's a well-planned programme for all the satellite campuses. Says Tim: 'It's really cheesy, sixties, seventies, eighties music. We do get told about these nights. Someone from the Students Union will come to the Conservatoire, put posters up so you know about them, but that's more than you ever want to know about them.'

ibar is the student bar at the prestigious Millennium Point. Then there's **the Lounge** at Westbourne Campus, and there's a small bar at the

Conservatoire. In addition, there's the **Village Inn** at Hamstead halls (see *Pillow Talk*), and the **Pavilion** out at Moor Lane Sports Centre. Parties and events are held every term in the Village Inn and ibar. Come Wednesday, *Sports Night*, it's off to the **Oceana** nightclub in town.

TOWN Says Tim: 'Broad Street is the place to go out in town, because it's just lined with every different type of café and bar. There are even casinos, which is where most student loans end up. There is everything to do there, but because so many students do go there, you will often find on Friday and Saturday nights the more discerning students avoid it.'

The cooler brigade make their own music. 'Come Friday/Saturday night, when people from Perry Barr flock in, we and other students that live nearby, go elsewhere.

'Because Broad Street is so close we can go out there any night of the week, me and a couple of friends we will often find a place on Broad Street right by the canal, like **Pitcher and Piano** or the **Handmade Burger Company**. There is a big jazz section at the Conservatoire. Pretty much everyone has a group of friends that are in a jazz band. There is a place right at the bottom of Broad Street, the **Yardbird** (named after the Yardbirds), and every night they do different things, but Thursday they do live jazz, and most of the time that is the Conservatoire's night out. It's not very big, it can hold maybe 200 people, and that's the best place to go. Because basically you know everyone playing, it's all students playing there. But the biggest reason we go there is that we don't get Birmingham University or Birmingham City University students going there.'

Bohemia rules, and Tim and his friends are also to be found in the **Rag Market**: 'I will often go there to buy meat, it's so much cheaper than Tesco's. We bought half a goat for £15 earlier this year! And me and my flatmates cooked it up and made goat curries, I mean £15 for half a goat. So the rag markets are like what the Bullring used to be.'

Back at Perry Barr thirty student societies are now up and running. Student magazine is *Spaghetti Junction*. SCRatch Radio is the community radio station, and there's student TV too. Student Community Action (SCA), the Union volunteering project, passes on key skills that employers are always asking for, as well as making a real difference to the local community. A so-called LEAP campaign currently promotes sport for local children. Drama, Cheerleading, RAG (Raising and Giving) and ACS (Afro Caribbean Society) are highly active socs. Politically the Union has shown its teeth in campaigns like 'Sentenced to debt', against Top-Up fees, and in a Housing Accreditation Scheme to improve housing standards in the city.

SPORT The Union runs the massive Moor Lane Sports Centre, with extensive conference and banqueting and partying facilities attached, playing host, too, to the annual Frisbee tournaments. A new £7-million sport centre - comprising a sports hall and eighty-station fitness suite - is due to open at main campus Perry Barr later this year.

ACCOMMODATION

Student rating	★
Guarantee to freshers	**100%**
Style	**Halls, flats**
Security guard	**All**
Shared rooms	**None**
Internet access	**All**
Self-catered	**All**
En suite	**No halls, some flats**
Approx price range pw	**£77-£106**
City rent pw	**£77-£100**

PILLOW TALK

Hamstead Campus is a 16-acre residential campus 2 miles from the Perry Barr Campus, with good bus services between the two and to city centre. They guarantee a place in halls for all freshers.

There is other accommodation (see www.bcu.ac.uk/accommodation/), the newest, swishest is to be had at Jennens Court in Jennens Road, Birmingham - 3, 4, 5 and 6-bedroom flats with lounge and kitchen area and en-suite bedrooms, plus laundry, parking spaces and bike racks.

All accommodation is self-catered, and has internet and security.

GETTING THERE

☞ By road: M1, M5, M6 and M40 all give ready access to the city. See also campus notes.
☞ By rail: Bristol Parkway or Sheffield, 1:30; London Euston, 1:40; Liverpool, 2:00; Leeds, 3:00.
☞ By air: Birmingham International Airport.
☞ By coach: London, 2:40; Bristol, 2:00.

UNIVERSITY OF BOLTON

The University of Bolton
Deane Road
Bolton BL3 5AB

TEL 01204 903903
FAX 01204 399074
EMAIL enquiries@bolton.ac.uk
WEB www.bolton.ac.uk

University of Bolton Students' Union
Deane Road
Bolton BL3 5AB

TEL 01204 900850
FAX 01204 900860
EMAIL BISU@Bolton.ac.uk
WEB www.bolton.ac.uk

VIRGIN VIEW

In the beginning, in 1982, the old Bolton Institute was formed out of the Bolton Institute of Technology and Bolton College of Education (Technical). Subsequently, Bolton College of Art became part of the picture too. They have had the distinction of being able to award their own degrees for some time, but in January 2005 they achieved university status.

Student satisfaction is fair at 78%, but they have a drop-rate of just under 20%, which suggests they are still finding their feet.

CAMPUS

In June 2005 they opened The Design Studio on Deane Campus, a £6-million remodelling of Deane Tower that has completely transformed the face of the campus. New corporate hospitality facilities adjoin it, including lecture theatre, boardroom and breakout rooms - the Deane Suite. This kicked off an extensive, phased landscaping and refurbishment programme.

Last September they opened the £2.5 million Social Learning Zone at the heart of campus (see Social Scene below), next to the library.

Not content with this, they also opened a £1-

UNIVERSITY/STUDENT PROFILE	
University since	**2004**
Situation/style	**Town campus**
Student population	**8955**
Total undergraduates	**6785**
Mature	**71%**
International	**10%**
Male/female ratio	**49:51**
Equality of opportunity:	
state school intake	**99%**
social class 4-7 intake	**52%**
drop-out rate	**20%**

million campus in United Arab Emirate known as Ras Al Khaimah campus, just 45 minutes from Dubai for around 150 students initially, to increase to around 700 in five years.

It offers undergraduate and postgraduate courses in Built Environment, Engineering, Business, IT and Art & Design. Bolton students can study at Ras Al Khaimah for part of their course.

FEES, BURSARIES

UK & EU Fees for 2011-12, £3,375 p.a. The Vice Chancellor's Award, worth up to £15,000, is made annually to three academically-gifted full-time UK undergraduate students, irrespective of financial means. The Excellence Scholarship, worth £500 p.a. is awarded to all full-time UK undergraduate students who have successfully accumulated a minimum of 300 UCAS points at A2-level or equivalent. The Care-Leavers Scholarship, worth £1,000 p.a. is awarded to full-time UK undergraduate students who have been in local authority care, foster care or looked after by relatives other than parents. Finally, two other awards are available: the MOD Enhanced Learning Credits Scheme and the Access to Learning Fund.

STUDENT PROFILE

Among undergraduates there is a large mature population (71%) and 45% are part-timers. There are many too who come from local families new to

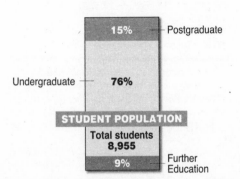

15% — Postgraduate
Undergraduate — 76%
STUDENT POPULATION
Total students
8,955
9% — Further Education

the idea of university, and there is a large overseas presence. The diversity is impressive, and loyalty among students who go on YouTube canvassing for the university is also impressive.

ACADEMIA & JOBS

Departments are Art & Design, Built Environment, Business Studies, Business Logistics & Info Systems, Computing, Cultural & Creative Studies (from English to Media, from Arts in the Community to stage and screen), Education, Engineering & Design, Health & Social Studies, Management, Product Design & Development, Psychology & Life Sciences, Sport, Leisure & Tourism Management.

They emphasise that they specialise in degree courses tailored to meet employer needs, that many are taught by professionals with industry experience, but the percentage employed with real graduate jobs is only 65%, as against 94% at the neighbouring Bolton College (Vocational Training and Further Education).

Single largest area of graduate employment here is 'human health (including social work) and hospital activities'. Go for the biomedical sciences,

biological sciences, community health, social studies, youth work and counselling degrees. Then it's 'public administration activities', fed by social studies, biological sciences, architecture and building degrees (including quantity surveying).

A new foundation degree in Offender Services, just launched, is the first of its kind in the UK. The programme is designed as a practical course aimed at people working in offender services and associated fields, or those considering a career in the sector.

Also, the uni has signed a partnership agreement with the BBC TV, ahead of the Corporation's move to Salford in 2011, to 'open up pathways into employment' in the media industry for students, and to develop new talent.

In addition to the £6m Design Studio, two floors of adjacent state-of-the-art teaching space and a new Product Design Studio, costing £3.5m,

RESEARCH EXCELLENCE

% of Bolton's research that is
4* (World-class) or 3* (Internationally rated):

	4*	3*
General Eng., Mineral, Mining	10%	15%
Architec., Built Environment	10%	30%
Business and Management	0%	10%
Social Work, Policy & Admin.	5%	40%
Psychology	0%	5%
Education	0%	15%
English Language and Lit.	0%	10%
Philosophy	0%	55%
Art and Design	0%	0%

opened in September 2006.

There is a flexible approach to entry. Typically, 200 points will see you in.

SOCIAL SCENE

STUDENT UNION As well as new Students' Union offices and the stylish **Loft** bar, the **Social Learning Zone** (known as the **SLZ**) incorporates a laid-back student meeting area, which at night is converted into a venue for gigs, club nights and other student functions.

Ents-wise it's a quiz on Monday, pool and big screen footie on Tuesday. Mid-week Wednesday is Student Night at **McCauleys** ('Bolton's student friendly nightclub') after drinks warm-up at the **Venue Café Bar**. Thursday is open mic night and Friday live local bands.

Societies-wise it is again fairly undeveloped as yet: Christian Union, Students with Disabilities, Islamic Soc, Afro Caribbean Soc and Motorsports

SUBJECT AREAS (%)

Health Subjects
Creative Arts — Education — Engineering Science
Humanities **14** **1** **7** **15**
8 **8**
6 **5**
Social Studies incl Law **15** **21**
Business Maths & Computer Built Environment

WHAT IT'S REALLY LIKE	
UNIVERSITY:	
Social Life	★★
Societies	★
Student Union services	★
Politics	**Little interest**
Sport	**13 clubs**
National team position	**136th**
Sport facilities	★
Arts opportunities	**Few**
Student newspaper	**Student Direct**
Student Radio	**Bolton Radio**
Nightclub/bar	**The Venue**
Union ents	**Live, and light ents progr. + tie-ups with clubs in town**
Union clubs/societies	**5**
Parking	**Available**
TOWN:	
Entertainment	★★
Scene	**Clubs, pubs**
Town/gown relations	**Good**
Risk of violence	**Average**
Cost of living	**Low**
Student concessions	**Good**
Survival + 2 nights out	**£60 pw**
Part-time work campus/town	**Average**

(Bolton are strong in automobile engineering and product design and offer degrees in Motor Vehicle & Transport.)

There's a newspaper, *Student Direct*, masterminded by Manchester University, and a radio station has just launched: Bolton Radio. Other than that, it's the annual 3-Legged Fancy Dress race

SPORT Building work has started on a joint venture with Bolton Council and NHS Bolton to build a £30-million health and fitness centre, which will include a 25m swimming pool, fitness suites and studios, rehabilitation, clinical and laboratory facilities. There will also be a gym and sports complex, in addition to the urgent care, diagnostics and treatment centre, managed by the NHS.

The Uni is nationally competitive in men's basketball, women's basketball, men's football, women's football, men's hockey, netball, men's rugby union, men's cricket, men's water polo, but in the national league ithese weren't enough to lift

them the bottom rung. They languished last, at 106th, in 2009. Compatible sports rehab., coaching, development and management degrees will help. The annual sports ball and award ceremony is already a high point of the social calendar.

TOWN Bolton's proximity to Manchester and to the Pennine Moors makes for a nice balance. A couple of nights of Mancunian debauchery, followed by a soul-searching chill on the wilderness of Tufton moor might be just the thing if you ever manage to tear yourself away from campus. Bolton itself offers a handful of clubs, but McCauley's is fave.

There's a cinema complex, the ground-breaking **Octagon Theatre** (modern interpre-tations of Shakespeare and equally at home with Alan Bennett) and live music venue **Albert Halls**, which includes comedy, jazz, classical music. Buit it's nearby Manchester for the high life.

PILLOW TALK

There are two halls, self-catering, with security guard and car parking. The Hollins comprises two blocks with flats servicing six to nine, the Orlando Village is eight blocks, each with eight six-bedroom flats plus a common room. Both are close to the town centre. All freshers get a place. Rooms cost £65.00 per week. All are let on a 38-week contract. You pay £50 per year extra to have internet access

ACCOMMODATION	
Guarantee to freshers	**100%**
Style	**Flats**
Security guard	**All**
Shared rooms	**All**
Internet access	**Extra £50**
Self-catered	**All**
En suite	**None**
Approx price range pw	**£67.50**
Town rent pw	**£60**

in your bedroom. Competition in town costs about £40 per week. Car parking at Orlando Halls and Hollins Halls, free but in demand.

GETTING THERE
☞ By road: M61/J3, A666 for Chadwick; M61/J5, A58 for Deane. Good map on web site.
☞ By coach: London, 5-7:00; Liverpool 2:00.
☞ By rail: Manchester frequent.
☞ By air: Manchester Airport 30 mins.

BOURNEMOUTH UNIVERSITY

Bournemouth University
Talbot Campus
Fern Barrow
Poole
Dorset BH12 5BB

TEL 08456 501501
    01202 961916
FAX 01202 962736
EMAIL skBUenquiries@bournemouth.ac.uk
WEB www.bournemouth.ac.uk

Bournemouth Students' Union
Talbot Campus
Fern Barrow
Poole
Dorset BH12 5BB

TEL 01202 965774
FAX 01202 535990
EMAIL subu@bournemouth.ac.uk
WEB www.subu.org.uk

VIRGIN VIEW

*B*ournemouth *is a seaside resort with a spectacular reputation for night life. It is also a university which has cut out some highly individual niches in its undergraduate programme, and built a reputation for getting students real graduate jobs in places (especially media), which others fail to reach.*

In December 2008 inspectors from the Quality Assurance Agency descended and commended Bournemouth for its Peer Assisted Learning Scheme, its development opportunities for student mentors, the additional support it provides for first year students, and generally the roles the teaching staff play in liaison, advice and support across the University. This was also recognised in the recent National Student Survey, enough for us to accord the University a 3-star rating for the student centred nature of the teaching.

For a university known principally for its teaching rather it did well in the last research assessment. Indeed, Bournemouth was the fourth most improved UK university in terms of research quality, which suggests increasing depth in the academic provision.

Fifteen per cent of research going on in Art & Design and Media was adjudged world class, and 55% and 35% respectively of international significance. Architecture and Nursing did well too, with 10% world class and 25% and 30% respectively of international significance. Business and Computing also came through with distinction. The only dog was Law, which achieved nothing in the two top classes.

There's a great time to be had on and off

UNIVERSITY/STUDENT PROFILE	
University since	**1992**
Situation/style	**Campus**
Student population	**17965**
Total undergraduates	**15635**
Mature	**44%**
International	**12%**
Male/female ratio	**40:60**
Equality of opportunity:	
state school intake	**95%**
social class 4-7 intake	**33%**
drop-out rate	**7%**

campus at Bournemouth, but student satisfaction is 77%, which seems a bit ungrateful.

Open Day dates in 2011 are 8 June, 9 September, 15 October, and 22 October.

CAMPUSES

Talbot (2 miles from the town centre) is the main campus; the other, Lansdowne Campus, is near the town centre and is home to the School of Health & Social Care and a centre for postgraduate study for the Business School. There's a no-parking rule within a mile. Students are also discouraged from bringing cars on to Talbot, though many do. There's a free bus service between campuses and halls.

FEES, BURSARIES

UK & EU Fees, 2011-12: £3,375 There's a means tested non-repayable cash bursary, also sport scholarships, music scholarships, an Academic Achievement scholarship for three Grade A's at A Level or an average of three Distinctions at BTEC National Diploma or equivalent, and the Endemol scholarships for third year TV Production students of minority ethnic origin (Black and Asian), which involve placement with a professional mentor from the industry in addition to financial support.

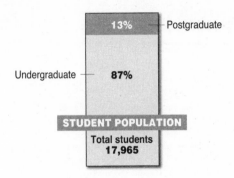

STUDENT POPULATION

Postgraduate 13%

Undergraduate 87%

Total students
17,965

Finally, Citizenship scholarships are offered to students who can demonstrate that they have contributed significantly to community-related projects outside formal education or work.

Further information on all scholarships available to BU students can be found at: http://www.bournemouth.ac.uk/futurestudents/undergraduate/funding/scholarships.html. Info regarding tuition fees for international students: www.bournemouth.ac.uk/futurestudents/undergraduate/funding/tuition_fees.html.

STUDENT PROFILE

The main campus is very studenty and unpretentious. This may be a career-orientated student body, but there's a relaxed scene both in the Union and in town. Only 5% of students come here from public school. There are 44% mature students and 12% from overseas.

ACADEMIA & JOBS

There are six academic schools: Applied Sciences; Business; Design, Engineering & Computing; Health & Social Care; Media; and Tourism.

Health (including Paramedic Science, Physiotherapy, Occupational Therapy) dominates the graduate employment figures, but big too are Government administration, banking, management consultancy, retail, computer, PR, accounting, engineering, sport, defence, broadcasting and other media, advertising, film, travel and hotel... And so it goes on. Bournemouth has degrees for all these and more, and their graduates get jobs.

Close working relationships with business and industry shapes their courses and fuels research and consultancy interests. Forty-week professional placements are integral to their four-year undergraduate programmes.

Embedded in many courses are units that provide real world experience and academic credit. For example, students taking Retail Management form groups and follow a brief from a leading retailer as part of a consultancy exercise, which results in the top team receiving a prize and many

of the ideas generated by the team being taken on by the company concerned. Advertising & Marketing students undertake a similar exercise.

Typically, the uni's Advertising and Marketing Communications degree is twinned with an agency through the Institute of Practitioners in Advertising. Six months work experience is part of it. As a result, a disproportionate number of Bournemouth graduates become advertising account executives with major agencies, or execs in publishing companies, public relations consultancies, research consultancies or in the marketing departments of other large companies.

They are also specialists in commercial & business law, and have degrees combining Law & Taxation and Accounting & Taxation. You can also take the Common Professional Examination (CPE)

TEACHING SURVEY AT A GLANCE	
Avg. UCAS points accepted	**300**
Acceptance rate	**15%**
Overall satisfaction rate	**77%**
Helpful/interested staff	★★★
Small tuition groups	★
Students into graduate jobs	**74%**

Teaching most popular with undergraduates:
Accounting, Complementary Medicine, Creative Arts & Design, Journalism (91%), Sports Science.

Teaching least popular with undergraduates:
Social Work (61%), Geography (65%), Law (66%).

here, which you'll need if you want to become a solicitor and don't have a law degree.

Of the many art colleges and universities with Animation degrees, few have as fruitful a line into film as Bournemouth, who host the National Centre for Computer Animation. Recently BU graduate Andy Lockley, one of a team of four at

SUBJECT AREAS (%)

Creative Arts
Humanities
Health Subjects
Engineering
Science
Social Studies incl Law 22
Creative Arts 3
Humanities 9
Health Subjects 13
Engineering Science 12
3
3
Business 35
Maths & Computer

RESEARCH EXCELLENCE

% of Bournemouth's research that is
4* *(World-class)* or **3*** *(Internationally rated):*

	4*	3*
Clinical Subjects	0%	20%
Nursing and Midwifery	10%	30%
Computer Science	5%	30%
General Eng., Mineral, Mining	5%	35%
Geography & Environment	10%	35%
Archaeology	10%	25%
Business and Management	5%	25%
Law	0%	0%
Art and Design	15%	55%
Media	15%	35%

the company Double Negative, collected the 2011 Oscar and BAFTA for Best Visual Effects for their work on the film *Inception*. Current BU student Sam Shetabi (TV Production) won the inaugural BBC Blast/BAFTA youth Screen Skills Award in 2010. Graduate Jessie Versluys (TV Production 2001) won last year's British Academy's prestigious BreakThrough Talent Award. Recently the Media School unveiled a state-of-the-art Motion Capture facility. 'MoCap' tracks and records the movement of a human subject or object as computerised motion data so that three-dimensional images can be animated with realistic motion in real time - animating characters in computer games, film or TV. Look at their animation degrees. The Wallisdown Campus of The Arts Institute at Bournemouth, which is now a university sector institution, is adjacent.

Meanwhile, Bournemouth's BA Hons Television Production offers practising TV producers, writers and technicians as your teachers. Great resources and top employment track record.

Activities are backed by good student media, *Nerve Magazine*, Nerve TV an award winner in the 2009 RTS TV Awards), and BiRST Radio: they took Silver in this year's Student Radio Awards. Look especially at Scriptwriting for Film & TV. Those not making it straight into scriptwriting find work as script readers, editors, agents, production assistants, researchers, etc, or write for radio, magazines, corporate videos, even computer games. Recent figures showed that 18 out of 23 traceable graduates were in permanent employment. There is also a strong Creative Writing degree.

In sport, golf is a speciality. Student golfer Andy Shakespear returned from the 2008 world university golf championships with two bronze medals, while Caroline Atkins from Bournemouth's Sport & Recreation team flew the flag during the recent England ladies cricket tour of Australia and New Zealand.

SOCIAL SCENE

STUDENTS' UNION 'I know what you're thinking. Bournemouth? Surely not,' writes Aidan Godley. 'Isn't that where all the shops are fitted with bicoal windows so the old people can see inside? Well, that's only half the story. The half you don't hear about is the one that, per square foot, has more clubs and facilities for the younger generation than London's West End. The Student Union has its own nightclub in town, The Old Fire Station!'

SU nightclub, The Old Fire Station (**TOFS** for short) is the envy of many a Student Union up and down the country. Staple fare is *Dubnium*, south coast leaders in soundsystem culture, upfront dubstep, reggae, jungle, and drum&bass. *Beat Redemption*: DJs, VJs, live bands, a mash-up of

WHAT IT'S REALLY LIKE

UNIVERSITY:	
Social Life	★★★
Societies	★★
Student Union services	★★★
Politics	**Little interest**
Sport	**Competitive**
National team position	**33rd**
Sport facilities	★★
Arts opportunities	**Available**
Student magazine	**Nerve**
Student newspaper	**Student Press**
Student radio	**BiRST FM**
National Radio Awards	**Silver, 2010**
Student TV	**Nerve TV**
TV awards	**Winner 2009**
Nightclub	**The Old Fire Station**
Bars	**Dylans, D2**
Union ents	**Lollipop, Comedy Nation, Milk, Beach Break Live.**
Union clubs & societies	**72**
Parking	**Limited Talbot; none Lansdowne**
TOWN:	
Entertainment	★★★★
Scene	**Beach, shopping, night life vibrant**
Town/gown relations	**Good**
Risk of violence	**Average**
Cost of living	**High**
Student concessions	**Good**
Survival + 2 nights out	**£80 pw**
Part-time work campus/town	**Good**

emerging and established talent. The legendary Friday night out *Lollipop*, with more r'n'b and cheese than you can shake a stick at. Popular too are the funky theme nights (new this year is jungle themed *Hall Wars*), and *Comedy Nation*. *Milk* is Indie, rock and retro pop on Tuesdays. Balls are frequent and memorable - Freshers, Christmas, Valentine's, Sport - and the Summer ball, the *creme de le creme* of the entertainment calendar in a large field just outside town - more like a festival than a ball. **TOFS** and **O2 Academy** also offer consistent live fare. And of course *Beach Break Live* is the nation's only student festival, held in mid-June next to a 6-mile sandy beach with 20k students swarming.

> '*Bournemouth, per square foot, has more clubs and facilities for the younger generation than London's West End.*'

Talbot Campus is home to **Dylan's Bar**, with very cheap menu - pizza, burgers and healthier options like baked potatoes and omelettes. Evening entertainment includes quizzes, DJ's and live gigs. **D2** is a more relaxed sports bar where football is screened on the large projector screen.

Both on-campus bars are open seven days a week during term time.

What else is it good for? Well, media of course - they copped a Silver at the last National Student Radio Awards, and there's the usual clubs and societies, from diving to computer gaming, poetry to horse riding and music: the orchestra and choir take some rhythmic beating.

There are also volunteering opportunities in which to get involved throughout the year with MAD days, Community Champions, etc.

SPORT The men's football and golf teams both reached the finals of the national student championships (BUCS) in 2010 and remain in contention at time of going to press. Proximity to the sea encourages windsurfing, sailing, paragliding, jet skiing, etc. The reigning men's BUCS surf champion and the current indoor 60m athletics champion are both Bournemouth students. The uni provides full-time instructors and facilities for a wide range of other sports, and there has been a huge improvement in their national placing recently (33rd last year). A sports hall includes squash courts and multigym. Cricketers play at the county-standard ground, Dean Park.

TOWN Dropped in the middle, where four roads meet, we found wall-to-wall pleasure, whatever your bent. There's no shortage of things to spend money on, and part-time opportunities for work are legion. It is an extraordinary place, a born-again English seaside resort, and if bar and club life proves too much, there's always the beach.

PILLOW TALK

Accommodation is guaranteed for first years. Places in the student village on Talbot (3 to 7-bed en suite houses), and in Hurn House (single study bedroom with sink in central Bournemouth), Cranborne House (single en-suite study bedroom 5 mins from Hurn House; subsidised uni bus) and new Purbeck House (single, en-suite study bedrooms close to Cranborne House) are limited to 250, 152, 497 and 518 respectively. Rooms in Talbot are en suite. Abbotsbury House in Pokesdown, close to Bournemouth Hospital is the new residence (4-6 bed flats) for nurses. Newish are the 308-bed Corfe House in Poole and a further 150 beds at Okeford House in Winton. 400-bed Lyme Regis House halls at Lansdowne campus opened in 2009. Another halls near Lansdowne, a 299-bedroom development is to open in September 2011. All halls have good security and internet access. As in most seaside

ACCOMMODATION	
Student rating	**★★★**
Guarantee to freshers	**95%**
Style	**Halls, flats**
Security guard	**All halls, some flats**
Shared rooms	**None**
Internet access	**All**
Self-catered	**All**
En suite	**Many**
Approx price range pw	**£74-£91**
City rent pw	**£80-£110**

resorts, town accommodation is plentiful and good.

GETTING THERE

☞ By road: M3/M27/A31/ A338, The Wessex Way; at second r/about follow uni signs to Talbot. From west A35 then A3049 (Wallisdown Road). For Bournemouth campus, leave A338 at St Paul's r/about (Travel Interchange junction) on to St Paul's road and find a car park.

☞ By rail: London Waterloo, 1:45; Bristol, 2:30; Manchester, 5:37.

☞ By coach: London, 2:15; Bristol, 3:10.

UNIVERSITY OF BRADFORD

The University of Bradford
Richmond Road
Bradford BD7 1DP

TEL 01274 232323
FAX 01274 235585
EMAIL course-enquiries@bradford.ac.uk
WEB www.bradford.ac.uk

Bradford University Union
The Communal Building
Bradford BD7 1DP

TEL 01274 233300
FAX 01274 235530
EMAIL ubu@bradford.ac.uk
WEB www.ubuonline.co.uk/

VIRGIN VIEW

A university since 1966, Bradford came out of the local Technical College, which was itself spawned by the textile industry in the 1860s. Today the connection between higher education and the workplace remains key. Their slogan is 'Making Knowledge Work' and they have erected a 5-metre high, bronze sculpture to celebrate it. Sandwich courses are Bradford's stock in trade.

UNIVERSITY/STUDENT PROFILE	
University since	**1966**
Situation/style	**City campus**
Student population	**12740**
Total undergraduates	**9485**
Mature	**48%**
International	**26%**
Male/female ratio	**48:52**
Equality of opportunity:	
state school intake	**94%**
social class 4-7 intake	**53%**
drop-out rate	**13%**

Departments undertaken most high-powered, world-renowned research are Archaeology, Politics, Pharmacy, Nursing and Midwifery, Social Work, and Mechanical, Aeronautical, and Manufacturing Engineering.

But it is the graduate employment picture that identifies most clearly the academic character of Bradford students. Making Knowledge Work is not just about helping you into employment - although that is one of the University's strengths. It means making your knowledge and skills work for the benefit of the world beyond university, and making what you learn here work for you on a personal level as well.

Of course, Bradford is not London, nor is it Milton Keynes, nor yet is it Leeds. In fact, Bradford may challenge the Southerner's picture of what he would like the North to be, but what it does offer all its undergraduates, and always has done, is a very studenty, close-knit, pub-based, curry-central experience, uninhibited by issues of wealth and class.

To many a Bradford student, the Southerner's picture of the acceptable face of the North, namely Leeds (because of its premier-league nightclubs and Harvey Nichs)

appears rather expensive and, well, just a tad outre. Bradford students can easily partake of Leeds, as the city is just a few moments down the road, but few do.

New students in 2011 and 2012 will be among the first to benefit from an £84m campus investment in accommodation (The Green, see Pillow Talk) and brand new Student Central (see Social Scene).

It is not demanding at entry. For this university, published standard offers are only a guide. Factors other than academic achievement will be taken into account, such as evidence of relevant experience, skills and aptitude when considering individual applicants.

See the University's own social networking site: http://www.brad.ac. uk/developme/; or Wild West Yorkshire - a videozine created by students - http://www. wildwestyorkshire.com/. Their Alumni Facebook page is http://www.facebook. com/Bradfordalumni. The Students Union Facebook page is http://www.facebook. com/ubuonline0910. Finally, you can find them on You Tube: http://www.youtube. com/UniversityOfBradford.

Alternatively, if you're in the area on July 2, 2011, pop in to Open Day.

CAMPUS

The main campus, a 10-minute stroll from town, is compact and bounded by roads on all four sides. All teaching, except for Business Studies, is carried out on site, and there are many halls of residence on and nearby it.

FEES, BURSARIES

UK & EU Fees, 2011-12: £3,375. The University offers a range of scholarships and bursaries. See www.bradford.ac.uk/undergraduate

STUDENT PROFILE

They have an open access policy, and the intake from the lower socio-economic classes (4-7) is well over their government benchmark. Fifty-three per cent come from the social classes 4-7. For many university is a first time experience for the family. Only 6% public school kids apply successfully.

There is a particular welcome to overseas students and careful monitoring of all processes of integration. Most undergrads are scientists and techies, but life isn't predictable.

ACADEMIA & JOBS

Broad study areas at Bradford are Archaeological Sciences, Chemical and Forensic Sciences, Computing & Informatics, Design & Technology, Engineering, Geography & Environmental Sciences, Health Studies, Humanities, ICT, Law, Life Sciences, Management and Business, Media Studies, Psychology, Social Sciences.

Far and away the largest employment sector entered into by Bradford graduates is health. Many go to work in hospitals, some into the community as social workers and counsellors, while yet others go on to occupy themselves in specialist retail, the dispensing of spectacles, pharmaceuticals, and other medical goods.

TEACHING SURVEY AT A GLANCE

Avg. UCAS points accepted	**250**
Acceptance rate	**24%**
Overall satisfaction rate	**83%**
Helpful/interested staff	★★★★
Small tuition groups	★
Students into graduate jobs	**79%**

Teaching most popular with undergraduates:
Accounting, Anatomy, Physiology & Pathology (94%), Business (93%), Chemistry, Civil, Chemical Engineering, Geographical Studies, History, Management, Medical Technology, Ophthalmics (96%), Pharmacology, Physical Geography (96%), Politics (95%).

Teaching least popular with undergraduates:
Computer Science (61%).

After these come Bradford's bankers and the like, what is known today as 'monetary intermediation', graduates in Economics, Accountancy & Finance, and Business

SUBJECT AREAS (%)

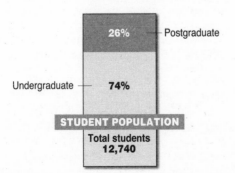

Humanities — Combined 13 — Health Subjects 34 — Science 6 — Engineering 12 — Maths & Computer 6 — Business 10 — Social Studies incl Law 18 — 1

Computing. And at length those quite different creatures who succumb to the lure of museum, library, and other archival and cultural activities, including, no doubt, some of those well-taught archaeologists. Many graduates also take up teaching posts in higher and secondary education.

The courses listed here had a success rate of over 90% into professional level employment: Pharmacy (4 and 5 year programme), Radiography - both 100% employment. Nursing Degree (99%), Nursing Advanced Diploma (96%), Occupational Therapy (94%), Optometry(94%).

This picture from 2009 graduates shows consistency with data going back over a seven year period at Bradford. These courses are

STUDENT POPULATION

Postgraduate 26%
Undergraduate 74%

Total students 12,740

RESEARCH EXCELLENCE

% of Bradford's research that is
4* *(World-class)* or **3*** *(Internationally rated):*

	4*	3*
Nursing and Midwifery	10%	25%
Medical Bioscience	5%	35%
Optometry	5%	35%
Pharmacy	15%	40%
Computer Science	5%	40%
Electrical and Electronic Eng.	0%	10%
Civil Engineering	5%	50%
Mech., Aero., Manufac. Eng.	10%	30%
Archaeology	20%	30%
Business and Management	15%	30%
Politics	15%	35%
Social Work, Policy & Admin.	10%	40%
Development Studies	5%	25%
History	5%	20%
Media	5%	15%

applied programmes with integrated work experience which is validated by professional bodies. But a number of other programmes have opportunities to gain experience through sandwich placements. Overall, 15% of Bradford students are on sandwich courses, while a wide range of other courses have embedded academic modules related to career evelopment.

The Bradford graduate employment map is also studded with systems analysts, software engineers, computer/IT consultants and programmers. Look at the Computing and Cybernetics faculties.

There is also a fine track record in film through its BSc Computer Animation & Special Effects degree, and the BSc Animatronics is especially interesting in that it teaches technology and skills to create, sculpt and animate motorised puppets - the 'live' monster that you see in movies.

Look, too, at another niche area - their Electrical and Electronic Engineering, Mobile Communications and Telecommunications degrees. Again, the Automotive Design Technology and Integrated Industrial Design (Eco Design, Sports Technology, etc) degrees make them leaders in careers for design and development engineers.

Other key strands take us further into the ethos of the place, Bradford's famed Department of Peace Studies (studied from the standpoints of ethics, psychology, sociology, history), and such as International Relations & Security Studies and Conflict Resolution.

SOCIAL SCENE

Student Central is the new name for the Students' Union building. The sometime Communal Building has been gutted, pulled apart and turned into a fantastic 21st Century hive for swarming students.

It is student central because it connects to the library, clubs, bars, a shop, the Students' Union, student radio RamAir, study and social space, a lecture theatre and much more.

Sports Bar is the main bar with TV screens. Then there's **Central Bar**, **Amp Bar** (connected to the amphitheatre area outside), two club venues (one for the legendary *FND*, *Friday Night Disco*), and of course equally legendary **Escape Club** - 100 capacity club for student-led nights.

Student media is now Ram Air 1350 and monthly newspaper *The Bradford Student*, sequel to *Scrapie* (remember *Scrapie*? - I've been doing this too long!), and Bradford Student Cinema, which will make a film of whatever you want for your sport or society? All you gotta do is fill in a form.

There's no Arts faculty at Bradford, but they have three of the most pulsating Arts venues to be found. Theatre in the Mill is home to the Theatre Group, which puts on a show (student or pro) every week and has the cheapest bar (Scaff Bar) in the uni. The Tasmin Little Music Centre does similar stuff for a student jazz ensemble, choral society, chamber choir and three orchestras, and an amazing series of Music for Lunch at the Alhambra Studio in Great Horton Road. Then there's Gallery II for art.

> *'The single most redeeming feature about "Bratford" (learn to prononce the "t") is how far your money goes.'*

Student cinema happens three times a week - Art movies and the latest blockbusters, many only a few months after general release, all for a couple of quid. Showings are in Great Hall (capacity 1,300).

Among some fifty societies, Twirl Soc and Amnesty are the most popular. Amnesty International is of course the foremost organisation in defence of human rights. Twirl Soc, you may be intrigued to discover is about twirling, throwing, juggling anything that spins in a circle of motion. Politics spins left, activity average - war, racism, recycling.

SPORT There are 35 sports clubs - women's volleyball is a particular strength. An on-campus sports centre has a 25m swimming pool, sauna suite, solarium, Nautilus fitness suite, etc. There are squash courts and a dozen or so pitches for cricket, football and rugby, plus 9,000 square metres of artificial turf sand-grass for 5-a-sides, netball, and hockey. One site is behind the halls, the other 4 miles from campus, where the pavilion has a bar. In the city the Bradford Bulls rule.

CITY Very inexpensive. Music and theatre are a big part of what Bradford is about - local bands and drama groups brighten local venues such as **The Priestley**, **Delius**, **St George's Hall**, **Love Apple**.

You may have heard there's also a large multi-cultural population, bringing with it a fantastic mix of art, culture and food. Bradford is of course curry central. Students have curry locals; staff and dishes become firm friends. Writes Andi: 'Bradford can be a fun place to live and study and there's always something to do, even if it means visiting the beautiful countryside. Yorkshire folk have got it right when they call it God's own country. Come to Bradford and tell them Andi sent you.'

PILLOW TALK

The Green is opening Sept 2011 - the University's new eco-friendly student village. Buildings are arranged as a small village, with rooms available in apartments or townhouses. Every building there meets the highest standards of sustainability, meaning it costs very little to heat and light, and it makes the most of natural resources like solar power and rainwater.

ACCOMMODATION	
Student rating	★★
Guarantee to freshers	**100%**
Style	**Halls**
Security guard	**Some**
Shared rooms	**Some**
Internet access	**Most**
Self-catered	**All**
En suite	**Some**
Approx price range pw	**£53.50-£94**
City rent pw	**£43**

Most halls are on the main campus or a short five-minute walk away. Most have free Broadband access. Generally security is good. Some halls have wardens. There's no sharing. All rooms are single study-bedrooms. Residence agreements are for 42 weeks (September to July) and therefore include the Christmas and Easter vacations. You may be able to stay over summer too if life's that tedious.

WHAT IT'S REALLY LIKE	
UNIVERSITY:	
Social Life	★★
Societies	★★
Student Union services	★★★
Politics	**Left-wing**
Sport	**35 clubs**
National team position	**89th**
Sport facilities	★★★★
Arts opportunities	**Excellent; art avg**
Student magazine	**Bradford Student**
Student radio	**RamAir 1350**
Nightclub	**Escape**
Bars	**Sports, Central, Amp**
Union ents	**FND + live**
Union societies	**85**
Parking	**On-street only**
CITY:	
Entertainment	★★★
Scene	**Curry central**
Town/gown relations	**OK**
Risk of violence	**Average**
Cost of living	**Low**
Student concessions	**Excellent**
Survival + 2 nights out	**£40 pw**
Part-time work campus/town	**Good**

University and Bradford halls are on campus in close proximity to the Library, Sports Centre, Students' Union, teaching areas, social areas and events.

They are organised into self-contained flats of 6 or 8 bedrooms, with a shared kitchen and dining area and bathroom facility.

Arkwright Hall is just over the road, with deluxe and standard en-suite rooms split into flats of 3, 4 and 5 bedrooms with shared kitchen and living accommodation.

Halls on Laisteridge Lane are 5 minutes' walk away, closer to the School of Health Studies and include the recently refurbished Dennis Bellamy hall - each floor has 21 rooms split into flats of 7 with a shared kitchen/dining area in each flat. Trinity B & C Halls are also on this site.

GETTING THERE

☛ By road: M62 and M606 connect with national motorway network; from north, A629/A650; from northeast, A1 or A19, then A59, A658.
☛ By rail: London King's Cross, Birmingham, 3:00; Edinburgh, 4:00; Manchester, 1:00.
☛ By air: Leeds/Bradford Airport.☛ By coach: London, 4:30; Manchester, 1-2:30.

STUDENT BRIGHTON - THE CITY

It's often been said there is something a little bit cheeky about Brighton & Hove. Made popular by the flamboyant Prince Regent, Brighton has a reputation for naughtiness and frivolity. What you will find is a welcoming city full of diversity and tolerance, perhaps the most cosmopolitan place in the UK. It's multitude of clubs, shops, restaurants and vast range of entertainment make Brighton and Hove the 'city by the sea' that really does have everything for everyone, so it's no wonder so many students never leave and settle for good. For a visual taste of brighton and surrounds, see www.visitbrighton.com; www.visiteastbourne.com and www.visit1066country.com/.

NIGHTLIFE
The town has a huge array of clubs and pubs. The place to be for students on a Wednesday seems to be **Oceana** - *Fuzzy Logic* on Wednesdays - where students dance the night away fuelled by the cut price drinks.

Students head for the seafront clubs, including **The Beach** (classic soul to 90s indie) and **Concorde2**, live bands, club nights, home of the famous *Big Beat Boutique*. If it's drum & bass you're after, lesbian and gay clubs, reggae or salsa, you won't be disappointed; check local listings for info. If trash is your thing go to **Dynamite Boogaloo** and revel in cheesy and camp disco 'toons' and be astounded by the almighty Dolly Rocket and Boogaloo Stu's outrageous live cabaret.

Midweek madness continues with the Latino feel and many participate in the carnival-style nights. You could be forgiven for thinking that no one works in Brighton, as week-night events are often as packed as the big weekend events.

EATS
Brighton boasts cuisine from almost every country in the world. Entire streets, like Preston Street on the Brighton/Hove border are devoted to gastronomic indulgence, there are late-night and 24-hour restaurants, shops and supermarkets for the night owls. There are over 400 restaurants including Cordon Bleu, English, French, Indian, Mexican, freshly caught fish (and chips), Japanese, Thai, tapas, Greek, Spanish, Lebanese, Egyptian, American, Cajun, greasy spoon, vegetarian, places with beautiful views of the sea, sushi and take-away. The numerous Italian eateries situated in the **Lanes** are locked in a price war, each bending over backwards to offer pizzas and pastas at amazingly cheap prices, making it possible to have a filling meal and a pint for under a fiver in a decent restaurant.

It is said that there are nearly as many pubs in Brighton & Hove as there are days in the year, they range from sophisticated late-night-cocktail-bars, high street pub chains to small independent owned drinking dens.

Do head for the student friendly **Ali-Cats** which is good for cocktails and shows free early evening movies. **Mrs Fitzherbert's** offers a cosy drink regular and acoustic nights. For THE student pub experience seek out **The Druid's** where the insatiable landlord Chippy offers students a warm welcome, great food and regular drinks promotions to make everyone feel at home.

SHOPS
With the best shopping south of the capital, there are more than 700 independently owned shops to browse. For designer clobber and antiques The **Laines** will suit any wannabe David Dickinson, but the prices will not be 'cheap as chips'. The North Laine is the bohemian centre of the town: with feel-good veggie cafés, bars, great second hand emporiums and a mishmash of fabric and clothes shops there is not much you can't get your mitts on in this district. Kemp Town boasts a flea market, a second hand book shop and is home to Brighton's own Lesbian and Gay quarter, with bars, clubs and shops to attract the Pink Pound. Big name stores can be found under one roof at **Churchill Square**, and the **Marina** has designer outlet stores in addition to a gigantic Asda, bowling alley, cinema, casino and other attractions.

STREET/BEACH LIFE
Whether it is the middle of winter and you want to blow away the cobwebs, or top up the tan in the summer you will find the beach is a welcome respite from the hub bub of city life. Boasting two piers, the famous west pier now open again after the huge fire a few years back, you can visit fortune tellers, play the penny falls, buy more rock than you can shake a stick at and kiss me quick, squeeze me slow to your heart's content.

Highlights of the many events include the month-long **Brighton Festival** held in May, both revellers and locals flock to the beach and streets to enjoy the food, drink, juggling, samba band processions, free film shows on huge screens, firework displays and annual events like the **Pride Parade** and the **Winter Solstice** 'Burning of the Clocks' extravaganzas mean you are never short of something to do. There is also talk of **Fatboy Slim** holding another of his legendary beach parties.

ARTS

All over the city, self-expression is the way. Brighton Uni's **Grand Parade Gallery** and the **Brighton Art Gallery** in Pavilion Gardens feature regular innovative ever changing exhibitions.

Innovative, contemporary art is also displayed in a multitude of cafés, bars and often in the street. There are many live venues, which again cater to all tastes. The **Dome** concert hall has hosted diverse artists including the London Philharmonic, Beverly Knight and Air.

In terms of comedy, theatre and film, Brighton is incredibly spoilt. **The Paramount Comedy Festival** comes to town in October bringing big name talent like Jo Brand, Bill Bailey and Johnny Vegas. The **Komedia Cabaret** bar has two different productions simultaneously each night with deals for students. **The Dome**, **Theatre Royal** and the **Brighton Centre** get the big-name touring artists in addition to the snooker championships. **The Gardner Arts Centre** on the University of Sussex campus plays host to art, film, theatre, comedy and music, and is nationally acclaimed. If it all gets too much you can always nip to the flicks, The **Odeon** is the most student-friendly offering discounts; the **UGC** is part of the **Marina** multiplex, and the **Duke of York's** the only cinema with legs (no it's true they are hanging off the roof!), a Brighton treasure and the oldest purpose-built cinema in Britain shows art-house and classic films.

It is almost as if Brighton was made for students; you cannot ask for a better place to be.

Harvey Atkinson

UNIVERSITY OF BRIGHTON

The University of Brighton
Mithras House
Lewes Road
Brighton BN2 4AT

TEL 01273 644644
FAX 01273 642607
EMAIL admissions@brighton.ac.uk
WEB www.brighton.ac.uk

Brighton Students' Union
Steam House
Pelham Crescent
Brighton BN2 4AF

TEL 01273 642896
FAX 01273 694060
EMAIL S.U.President@brighton.ac.uk
WEB www.ubsu.net/

VIRGIN VIEW

*T*he *University of Brighton can trace its roots back to 1877, when the School of Art opened on Grand Parade, opposite the Royal Pavilion. Since then, Brighton town has been re-born as a city, inevitable consequence of its long-term reputation as London-by-the-sea. It is an energetic, laid-back, imaginative, vibrant, artistic, commercial, alternative, innovative, refreshing coastal cocktail, and its very own university evinces some of these elements too, especially the Faculty of Arts & Architecture.*

The cream of the art world strut their stuff on Grand Parade, while the business suits, techies and teachers, doctors and sporty types do their thing out of town, variously at the Moulsecoomb, Falmer, and Eastbourne campuses.

Made popular by the flamboyant Prince Regent, Brighton has a reputation for

UNIVERSITY/STUDENT PROFILE	
University since	**1992**
Situation/style	**Seaside campuses**
Student population	**20975**
Total undergraduates	**16850**
Mature	**49%**
International	**13%**
Male/female ratio	**37:63**
Equality of opportunity:	
state school intake	**93%**
social class 4-7 intake	**30%**
drop-out rate	**9%**

naughtiness and frivolity, but there are many different sides to the city, from the seafront to the North Laine area (the hub), to that self-contained little bit of it, Kemptown, redolent of Graham Greene's Brighton Rock, where the village within the town, the real Brighton still lies closest to the surface.

The university operates a flexible admissions policy. It welcomes applications from students with qualifications and experience outside the traditional A-level route. Relevant experience may be regarded as equivalent to formal qualifications. If you are living, studying or working in Sussex you may be guaranteed an offer or at least an interview for certain subjects, providing you have certain essential qualificaitions.

See www.sussexlearningnetwork.org.uk/sussexroutes. If you are studying in Sussex, visit www.progressionaccord.org.uk.

CAMPUS

Brighton University spreads through central Brighton and into the surrounding areas of Moulsecoomb, Falmer and off to the east along the coast from Brighton, Eastbourne. For Moulsecoomb go north up the Lewes Road from the arts campus on Grand Parade - (rail and bus links are good, parking is not). Grand Parade is the old art college and Moulsecoomb the old technical college, while

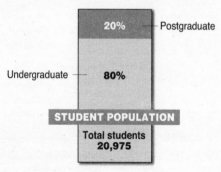

the Falmer site was once Brighton's teacher training college and still offers teacher training today.

Along the coast to the west lies University Centre Hastings (UCH), which opened in September 2003 to widen access still further to Brighton University degrees. UCH sees itself as playing an important role in the regeneration of Hastings, which is just as well, as for a long time it was a haven for heroin addicts.

Whatever you do, find out which campus you're bound for and visit

> *'Made popular by the flamboyant Prince Regent, Brighton has a reputation for naughtiness and frivolity, but also as an innovative, imaginative, artistic coastal culture. There are many different sides to Brighton, from the North Laine area to Kemptown, where true Brighton still lies closest to the surface.'*

it; they are all very different. Dates for open days in 2011 follow:

Brighton: Grand Parade campus

Open day 2 November for photography, moving image and sound arts (including film and screen studies); 9 November for fashion and textile design, craft; 16 November for fine art, performance and visual art, photography. 23 November for graphic design and illustration; 30 November for humanities, history of art and design.

Brighton: Moulsecoomb campus

Open day 8 October for accounting, business, economics, finance, law, architecture, computing, mathematics, construction, built environment, engineering, geography, geology, environment, media, life sciences, pharmacy.

Brighton: Falmer campus

Open day 15 October for education, teaching, health, nursing, midwifery, humanities, literature, language, media, social sciences, psychology.

Eastbourne: Darley Road campus

Open day 1 October for health professions, midwifery, hospitality, retail, travel, tourism.

Eastbourne: Chelsea School

Open day 22 October for sport and exercise.

Hastings campus

Open day 29 October for for broadcast media; 12 November for applied social science, business, computing, education, history, media studies and joint honours.

FEES, BURSARIES

UK & EU Fees, 2011-12: £3,375. Bursaries, worth between are made to all eligible home and EU students. See www. brighton.ac.uk/money.

Two hundred Academic scholarships are awarded at the end of years 1 and 2, and year 3 of four-year courses, as well as years 1 to 4 of Brighton & Sussex Medical School degrees.

There are Elite Athletes scholarships and others for 'talented sports performers' and disabled athletes.

Finally, 75 International Scholarships are awarded to

outstanding degree applicants.

STUDENT PROFILE

Brighton attracts students from over 140 countries. There is no typical Brighton student. It is all very disparate: 49% are mature, almost a third are working class, and only 7% are from public school.

Cutting-edge artists may appear the most visible in town, but, given the dominance too of bread-head businessmen and shimmering-with-health sporty types looking for lung space, they're far from representative of the student corpus.

ACADEMIA & JOBS

Students graduate from courses that include medicine, architecture, business, pharmacy, education, engineering, fashion design and paramedic practice. Research areas include sustainability, ageing, diabetes, gun crime and social inclusion. The University of Brighton pioneered the UK's first degrees in podiatry and sports journalism. They refer to themselves as 'a leading professional and applied university'.

Five faculties: Arts and Architecture; Education

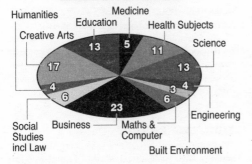

SUBJECT AREAS (%)

- Humanities
- Education
- Medicine
- Health Subjects
- Creative Arts
- Science
- Social Studies incl Law
- Business
- Maths & Computer
- Engineering
- Built Environment

13, 5, 11, 17, 13, 4, 6, 3, 4, 23, 6

and Sport; Health; Management and Info. Sciences; Science and Eng. See Campus above for detail and where you'll be studying.

Their strength in Art and Design has been recognised in the award of national teaching centres in design and creativity. But there's also its reputation in areas such as sport and tourism-hospitality, and in teacher education training. Health-related subjects, including Medicine, have also grown strongly in reputation. See www.bsms.ac.uk

Successes in fashion and textiles are both local and international and include employment with DKNY, Calvin Klein, Versace, Dolce & Gabbana, Valentino, Givenchy, Alexander McQueen, Hussein Chalayan and Julien MacDonald.

Graphic artists, designers, illustrators,

TEACHING SURVEY AT A GLANCE

Avg. UCAS points accepted	**270**
Acceptance rate	**17%**
Overall satisfaction rate	**79%**
Helpful/interested staff	★★★
Small tuition groups	★★
Students into graduate jobs	**71%**

Teaching most popular with undergraduates:
Anatomy, Physiology & Pathology (97%), Building, Chemistry, Engineering & Technology, Finance & Accounting, History, Information Services (95%), Maths, Mechanical, Production & Manufacturing Engineering, Mechanically-based Engineering, Philosophy (100%), Physical Geography & Environmental Science, Physical Science, Sociology, Medicine.

Teaching least popular with undergraduates:
Performing Arts (65%), Music (62%).

sculptors, ceramists and set designers also thrive. Thirty-five per cent of research in Art & Design is world-class, and 30% of international significance.

In terms of sheer number of graduates who get jobs, medicine, and subjects allied to it (nursing, midwifery and health professions), provide for the most, then business, then creative arts & design, then education, secondary and primary.

But beyond this too, all academic study is linked closely to professional practice and focused on the application of learning. Career planning agreements are entered into with every student.

RESEARCH EXCELLENCE

% of Brighton's research that is
4* *(World-class)* or **3*** *(Internationally rated):*

	4*	3*
Clinical Subjects	5%	30%
Biomedical Sciences	10%	25%
Allied Health Professions	0%	15%
Earth Systems, Environment	0%	40%
Physics	0%	45%
Applied Mathematics	0%	15%
Computer Science	15%	40%
Mech., Aero., Manufac. Eng.	5%	65%
Business and Management	20%	25%
Library and Infor. Management	10%	30%
Social Work, Policy & Admin.	0%	35%
Education	10%	25%
Sports-Related Studies	10%	25%
European Studies	0%	10%
Art and Design	35%	30%
Media	5%	30%

WHAT IT'S REALLY LIKE

UNIVERSITY:

Social Life	★★
Societies	★★
Student Union	★
Politics	**Average; student issues, anti-war**
Sport	**Competitive out at Eastbourne**
National team position	**34th**
Sport facilities	★★
Arts opportunities	**Drama/Dance OK**
Student newspaper	**The Verse**
Guardian Media Awards	**Best Photographer**
Student Radio	**Burst**
Union venue	**None**
Union ents	**Fuzzy Logic @ Oceana in town**
Union societies	**50+**
Parking	**Not good**
TOWN:	
Entertainment	★★★★★
Scene	**Exceptional**
Town/gown relations	**OK**
Risk of violence	**Low**
Cost of living	**High**
Student concessions	**Good**
Survival + 2 nights out	**£100 pw**
Part-time work campus/town	**Average/excellent**

Most courses offer placements and work experience opportunities. Many are accredited by professional bodies, so that students are work-ready immediately after graduation. And ready to help is a network of 60,000 active alumni worldwide. Last year 2500 students attended careers fairs, seminars, and employability skills Programmes. Brighton is about putting graduates into work.

SOCIAL SCENE

STUDENTS' UNION The sad truth is that ents at Brighton Student Union have been flattened by a series of mishaps. First they had the **Basement**, a seriously good club/venue that was commandeered by the uni administration. Then they took over **Akademia**, a café bar and theatre on Manchester Street, which again was prised from them. Now they eat their heart out at a clubnight on Wednesday nights at **Oceana, the official night out being** *Fuzzy Logic* **on Wednesdays**. As a fresher you might find yourself at a series of events at the large yellow **Gladstone** pub on Lewes Road, or being shuttle-bussed to **Audio** nightclub, or to **Brighton Pier** for fun and games. You'll have a fine time, though going out on the town can be expensive. Many of the jobs in Brighton are service sector based, so the wages reflect this, but there are opportunities for students to work in call centres and for local businesses where the rates of pay can be well above the minimum wage.

The Union claims 50+ societies and 70+ sports clubs, but it is impossible to pull the student scene together with so many outposts and such diversity.

At University Centre Hastings they have a radio control room, a small voice booth and large studio area. Students can access the latest technology to develop their broadcasting skills, be they budding presenter or producer.

PILLOW TALK

Accommodation for freshers is guaranteed only to international students, students under 18, BSMS students, or students with disabilities.

It's all self-catered, mainly halls but also uni-leased houses/flats. They claim to be the cheapest in the south of England.

Largest halls are Varley, midway between the Falmer and Moulsecoomb campuses. No parking, but free shuttle to Falmer. Halls on Falmer campus include 162 en-suite rooms.

Eastbourne has Welkins Halls, the multi-million pound complex accommodating 354, groups of six rooms, en suite, sharing dining and kitchen areas.

Robert Tressell halls of residence in Hastings opened a couple of years ago. If you don't opt for these, do yourself a favour anyway and read Socialist legend Robert Tressell's classic *Ragged Trousered Philanthropists*, a book to remind us all of what out-and-out consumerists we have all become.

GETTING THERE

To Brighton

☞ By air: Gatwick and Heathrow Airports.
☞ By road: M23 (past Gatwick), A23 to Brighton, A27 eastbound for Falmer, right turn (south on B2123) for Moulsecoomb. From east or west, A27.

ACCOMMODATION

Student rating	★★
Guarantee to freshers	**67%**
Style	**Halls, flats**
Security guard	**All**
Shared rooms	**None**
Internet access	**Most**
Self-catered	**All**
En suite	**Some**
Approx price range pw	**£80-£148**
City rent pw	**£75-£95**

To Eastbourne
☛ By road: A27 and signs south on to A22.
☛ By rail: London Victoria, 1:10. Change at

Brighton for Moulscoomb and Falmer (8 mins).
☛ By coach: London, 1:50.

● ●

UNIVERSITY OF BRISTOL

The University of Bristol
Senate House
Tyndall Avenue
Bristol BS8 1TH

TEL 0117 928 9000
FAX 0117 925 1424
EMAIL ug-admissions@bristol.ac.uk
WEB www.bristol.ac.uk

Bristol Students' Union
Queens Road
Clifton
Bristol BS8 1LN

TEL 0117 954 5800
FAX 0117 954 5817
EMAIL communications-ubu@bristol.ac.uk
WEB www.ubu.org.uk/

VAG VIEW

*B*ristol University is a major player, once considered to be the choice of privilege, but now, rather confusingly, it operates an 'Access to Bristol' policy, which is gradually beginning to persuade applicants from hitherto under-represented groups to apply, so much so that today it is the turn of the privately educated to complain that they are the ones being discriminated against.

The Access to Bristol scheme is a programme of events designed to encourage academically motivated pupils from schools and colleges identified by the Recruitment Office to apply to the university, and they encourage such applications with special bursaries. Visit www.bristol.ac.uk/accesstobristolbursary.

As a student at Bristol, whatever your intended area of study and whatever your background, you can expect the content of your programme to be directly informed by internationally-recognised research, and also to have regular contact with the researchers who are leading this work.

Equally, you can expect employers to be more interested in you than in graduates from most universities. The Graduate Market 2011 report by High Fliers ranked Bristol as the seventh most targeted UK university by the largest number of top employers in 2010-2011.

Besides all this, in Bristol there is a

strong sense of community. The University is small enough to feel warm and friendly and big enough and broad enough to stretch you and create an impressive network for your future.

And Bristol itself is a great city. Students become part of it so much that many choose to stay. Over a fifth find work in Bristol and make the city their home.

So what do they want from you for all this, if you happen not to be one that falls into the Access net?

Admissions tutors tell us they look closely at what you say about your personal interests, career aspirations and intellectual motivation in the personal statement. They will scrutinise your examination record and the report provided by your academic referee, and weigh up your post-school and out-of-school experiences and breadth of interests, 'as well as, and in some cases in place of,

UNIVERSITY/STUDENT PROFILE	
University since	**1909**
Situation/style	**Civic**
Student population	**21720**
Total undergraduates	**15210**
Mature	**31%**
International	**19%**
Male/female ratio	**47:53**
Equality of opportunity:	
state school intake	**60%**
social class 4-7 intake	**14%**
drop-out rate	**3%**

your examination results'. This amounts to a huge sea change since we first published the Guide.

Open days in 2011 fall on 30 June and 21 September: 9.30am - 4pm.

CAMPUS

Writes Alex Taylor: 'Bristol is situated on the West coast of England, across the channel from Wales. This inevitably means wet and rainy winters but just wait till the summer season hits the West coast. The 450 acres of Greenland around the university precinct and Stoke Bishop campus [residential halls] is wonderful.

'The University Precinct is in a beautifully old area of Bristol called Clifton, which is about a 20-minute walk to the main shopping centre of town.'

University buildings in Clifton, such as the Gothic Wills Memorial Building and the 18th-century Royal Fort House, epitomise the historic past of the city. The row of Victorian houses which form the Arts department is also a pretty place to spend your undergraduate days.

FEES, BURSARIES

UK & EU Fees, 2011-12: £3,375 p.a. For up-to-date information about 2012 fees, see www.bristol. ac.uk/undergraduate/2012/moneymatters.

For 2011-12 there's a bursary for students in receipt of full HE Maintenance Grant and for those whose household income is £50,020 or less. Local students, defined as living in the BA or BS postal code at the time of their UCAS application, will also be eligible for the Local 'Top-up' bursary. There's also an Access Bursary for students from particular schools and colleges.

In addition, Vice-Chancellor's Scholarships are awarded to students with exceptional musical, dramatic or sporting talent. See www.bristol.ac.uk/ studentfunding/home_ug/burs_schols/vc_schol.ht mlFinally, there are one-year scholarships under the Eliahou Dangoor Scheme, see www.bristol. ac.uk/studentfunding/dangoor_ schol.html.

STUDENT PROFILE

For years Northerners have thought of Bristol as 'a Southern poof's university,' as one student put it. The undergraduate body of two universities far to the North, Durham and Edinburgh, is similar proportionally in terms of public school intake, and both have been criticised by students in the past for the boorish behaviour of said kids, indeed mainly from the South, whom they refer to as 'chavs with money'. I put this to Hannah, a second year undergraduate at Bristol reading Maths, and asked her whether it was true of Bristol.

'Well definitely there are quite a few groups of you know, that sort of public school... actually not so much public school but loads of middle class "private" school students from London. There are so many people here from London and it is a bit sickening sometimes.'

Hannah is herself from London, where she attended a Roman Catholic day school. 'I have talked to a couple of friends at Durham, and they said basically everyone is from public school, or really posh sort of people. I think at Bristol you get more the street-wise student, it's much more kind of "alternative". There are lots of different types obviously, but these are the sort of people who would apply to a place like Bristol, where there's so much stuff going on, a really busy city and so many different music genres, a place which isn't just made up of students like Durham is.'

Hannah seemed to be saying that the Bristol student is 'intelligent cool', rather than 'boorish Rah'. As at Oxbridge, there is also the sense that Bristol wants students who can hack the greater workload. 'I think you do have to do a lot of work if you want to get a good degree and there are some very hard-working people at Bristol.'

But there is a difference. Writes Alex Taylor from North Yorkshire: 'Bristol is full of party animals waiting for the clock to strike 11p.m., so if your one of those boozed up grimy clubbers there's a social group for you. And even if you

---

TEACHING SURVEY AT A GLANCE

Avg. UCAS points accepted	**440**
Acceptance rate	**10%**
Overall satisfaction rate	**84%**
Helpful/interested staff	**★★★★**
Small tuition groups	**★★**
Students into graduate jobs	**79%**

Teaching most popular with undergraduates:
Accounting, Aerospace Engineering, Anatomy, Physiology & Pathology, Animal Science, Biology and related Sciences, Business, Chemistry, Classics, Computer, Dentistry, Economics, Electronic & Elec. Eng., Finance, French Studies, General Engineering, German & Scandinavian Studies, Iberian Studies, Italian Studies, Mechanical, Production & Manufacturing Engineering, Microbiology, Molecular Biology, Music (100%), Pharmacy, Philosophy, Physical Geography, Physical Science, Politics, Psychology, Veterinary Science, Zoology.

Teaching least popular with undergraduates:
Archaeology, Medicine (68%), Drama (52%).

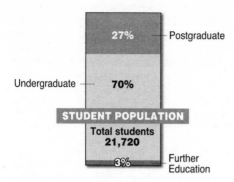

STUDENT POPULATION
Total students
21,720

just fancy a quiet drink with a few intellectual friends to discuss the day's lectures there are plenty of places to do that too.'

ACADEMIA & JOBS

What about the teaching staff at Bristol? Did Maths student Hannah find them available when she needed to consult them? Do they have an interest in teaching, or are students a necessary evil in a research dominated environment?

'Goos question. I think for Mathematics lecturers it's quite hard, because they are not generally really people! For some of them (and this is a bit of a generalisation), some of them would be more interested in their own work. But we have had a few lecturers who have been really, really good and really easy to access. It was much easier in first year because we had tutorials then and we don't now.'

In the *Times Higher's* National Student Survey Bristol is noted for its helpful/interested staff, but less so for small-size tutorials. In her first year Hannah had tutorials of four or five people at least twice a week. Why did they stop?

'I don't actually know. Maybe because they are too difficult to organise, because you are allowed to choose different modules in the second year, so everyone is doing a whole range of different things, whereas in first year everyone does the same one subject.'

I ask what modules Hannah is taking and it emerges that she has chosen subjects wholly unconnected with Maths.

'Well, actually this year I'm doing an open unit in Social Anthropology, so I have been using the library quite a bit, which I don't need to do for Maths, and I'm doing French as well.'

What made her choose these?

'Oh well, that was because I found Maths really full on. I just wanted to try some different things.'

Doing these three subjects, which involve quite different modes of learning, Hannah discovered made her much more interested in all of them. It freshened her thinking about Maths. In particular, Social Anthropology involves a great deal of reading in the library, Maths none. And French cleanses her mind in another way.

One can begin to see why Hannah was accepted at Bristol. There is interest in what she is doing and self-awareness of how her mind works. She also finds time to be ladies team Captain of the Bristol University sailing team, a sport in which Bristol University excels.

Writes Laura Cattell: 'Bristol is cutting edge for Medicine and Veterinary Science, the uni is a Mecca for the Science and Technology subjects. However, there are over 34 subjects on offer, and over 20% study Humanities or Languages. The Arts and Social Sciences library is a bit dark and dingy, but there are plenty of good faculty libraries, and excellent access to online journals and resources. The IT provision is good, staff are very helpful and range from the old-fashioned tweedy types to more dynamic younger ones.'

Ruth Naughton Doe: 'Courses at Bristol vary. Sciences, Medical Sciences, Social Sciences and Law seem to provoke good reviews from the students I talk to, but the Arts Faculty does not. There have also been many debates about lack of contact time [with lecturers, tutors], most Arts students having only 6-10 hours a week. Talk to a student before choosing Bristol to do an Arts Degree.'

A new £2-million Multimedia Centre for the Faculty of Arts was completed in July 2009. The two-storey extension greatly enhances modern language teaching facilities and provides access to live European media.

Writes Ancient History undergraduate Alex Taylor: 'The Teaching is absolutely flawless, the lecturers really try to interact with the students and don't make it seem like they have better things to be doing, which we all know they do. On my

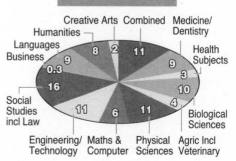

SUBJECT AREAS (%)

course, which is relatively small, there are about 5 students to every one lecturer and my personal tutor only sees about 9 other students, so everything is very personal and you get to work closely with your lecturers and tutors.

What I like most about the teaching is we do various activities in groups. This really allows you to interact and learn from other, perhaps more intelligent, students. It also takes the pressure off having to learn everything yourself. You research one particular topic and then learn the rest in discussion with the class.

'The library system is again flawless. You have your normal loans for used books, which is 2 weeks, and then you have a month for books which people don't use which is most of the books in the 4 vast libraries.'

For the 5/6-year Medicine degree (MB, ChB), you'll need to be able to tell them what you expect from a career as a doctor, that you are aware of the levels of commitment and challenge, and what you in particular have to offer.

Candidates are encouraged to offer four subjects at AS, three being taken to full A level. Chemistry required at A level for course A100, plus one other science subject. AAB grades required at A level. Links are strong with special clinical academies in Bristol, Bath, Cheltenham, Gloucester, Taunton, Swindon, where in years 3-5 you'll spend half your time.

The Dental School swept the boards at the 2010 Dental Defence Union Educational Awards, winning the Dental Teacher of the Year award and Dental Care Professional Teacher of the Year award. For would-be dentists, it's the 5/6-year BDS. The 6-year course allows entry with 2 non-science subjects. For vets, there's the 5-year BVSc. Candidates must sit the Biomedical Admissions Test (BMAT). Also a 3-year Veterinary Pathogenesis and a 4-year Vet Nursing & Practice Administration. Teaching was rated satisfactory by 87% of students.

As elsewhere, Bristol has discarded a number of courses for 2011 and 2012 entry, so be sure to consult the web site. One new pearl is BSc Management, a high-quality management education whether you see your future career in the private, public business or not-for-profit sectors.

SOCIAL SCENE

STUDENTS' UNION The one sour note is sung about the Union. In the *Times Higher Education's* Student Experience Survey it came 108th nationally this year. This may be a bit unfair. Ruth writes: 'The Student's Union is housed in one of the ugliest buildings in Bristol and far from where most students spend time, but it is very lively.'

There have been persistent rumours about plans to relocate it, and we can announce now that

RESEARCH EXCELLENCE

% of Bristol's research that is
4* (World-class) or 3* (Internationally rated):

	4*	3*
Cardiovascular Medicine	10%	45%
Infection and Immunology	5%	45%
Other Clinical Subjects	5%	55%
Epidemiology, Public Health	35%	35%
Health Services Research	20%	60%
Primary Care	25%	45%
Psychiatry, Neuroscience, and Clinical Psychology	5%	55%
Dentistry	20%	40%
Biological Sciences	10%	40%
Biochemistry	20%	45%
Pre-clinica/Human Bio. Sci.	15%	40%
Agriculture, Vet., Food Sci.	0%	40%
Earth Systems, Environment	25%	50%
Chemistry	25%	50%
Physics	20%	35%
Pure Mathematics	30%	40%
Applied Mathematics	25%	45%
Statistics	25%	45%
Computer Science	30%	40%
Electrical and Electronic Eng.	10%	55%
Civil Engineering	25%	55%
Mechanical Engineering	20%	60%
Aerospace Engineering	25%	55%
Geography and Environment	30%	40%
Archaeology	15%	35%
Economics and Econometrics	30%	55%
Accounting and Finance	10%	45%
Business and Management	0%	30%
Law	15%	40%
Politics	10%	30%
Social Work, Policy & Admin.	20%	40%
Sociology	10%	40%
Psychology	10%	50%
Education	25%	35%
Sports-Related Studies	20%	35%
Russian, Slavonic, East Euro.	15%	45%
French	5%	30%
German, Dutch, Scandinavian	15%	35%
Italian	20%	35%
Iberian and Latin American	10%	20%
English Language and Lit.	20%	50%
Classics, Ancient History, etc.	20%	35%
Philosophy	30%	35%
Theology	15%	30%
History	15%	40%
History of Art, Architec., Design	15%	30%
Drama, Dance, etc.	45%	30%
Music	10%	75%

ceremonies, and **Café Zuma** serves hot and cold meals throughout the day.

Says Hannah: 'Not many people go out in the actual Union. It has got a reputation for being really rubbish, but actually there are loads of really cheap gigs that play there which are amazing, like kind of alternative indie bands which normally if you went to see in London would be three or four times the price.'

Alex Taylor cuts to the chase: 'Being at a city University means that the night-life is not centred around the Student Union, and so the Union doesn't seem to do much at first glance. But in fact, it offers hundreds of societies and clubs to join and organises various balls. The Fresher's Ball, for example, was great fun... However, putting the seeming let down of the Student Union aside, the actual night-life in Bristol is among the best. It's night-life like you've never experienced before and you do have to get used to it. But I, for one, can't imagine having as good a time in, say, Newcastle as I do in Bristol. This is because Bristol is the home of dub-step and drum&bass, and so the clubbing is very grimy and urban, while if you still prefer mainstream music there is **Panache** on a Monday, **Syndicate** on a Friday and **Joe Publics** on a Wednesday. In fact there is a mainstream night on every night of the week, but the clubs I prefer to visit are more into the dubstep scene, one in particular is **Dojo's**. While it looks small and not very grand, the atmosphere once the early hours of the morning kick in is immense and I would fully recommend giving the heart of Bristol clubbing a chance. After all, you can dance to mainstream music anywhere you go!

'As for the pubs and bars, among the dozens down Whiteladies Road (the road from the halls of residence at Stoke Bishop) on the way to the farthest clubs, there is a bar-style for everyone.'

in the summer of 2011 there is to be 'a significant redevelopment', the first tremors of which may be felt in a new ground-floor **Bar 100**, complete with smoking terrace, sofas, pool tables, Sky sports, the focus for bar quizzes, sports events, pool comps, karaoke, and the likes of Burns Night and resident DJ nights.

The Epi upstairs is for the time being at least still in existence, but mainly for bookings. There's also **Mandela/AR2** for small gigs and as a bar for larger gigs in the adjacent **Anson Rooms**, which features such as The Vaccines (came 3rd in BBC's Sound of 2011, The Kills (alternative rock duo), Drive By Truckers (alternative country), and man of the moment, songwriters and producer Jamie Woon. The **Avon Gorge** room is for large society events and awards

'It's night-life like you've never experienced before. I can't imagine having as good a time in, say, Newcastle. Bristol is the home of dub-step and drum&bass, the clubbing is grimy and urban.'

The Union is also noted for its many societies and RAG, which raises over £100,000 each year. Among the most active are Debating, Ballroom Dancing, UBFS (University of Bristol Film-MakingSociety), Dance soc, BUMS (Bristol University Music Society), STA (Stage Technicians Association), and International Affairs. The Drama Society utilises two theatres: the 200-seater Winston Theatre, and the smaller Lady Windsor Studio Theatre. *Epigram* is the student newspaper, student radio BURST.

SAFETY 'At night the Downs can be a little sketchy,' writes Alex, 'and there have been rapes and knifings in the past (not half as bad as Nottingham though). Never walk back alone after dark and stick to the pavement rather than wondering across the grass.'

COST OF LIVING 'More expensive than some University towns, but if you know where to go it is very cheap indeed. In first year I'm in catered halls and I would say about 70 quid a week is sufficient to live off, save 40 quid for two nights out and the other 30 on food and pre-lash drinks and whatever else you may need.'

SPORT 'Bristol has a fantastic reputation. It has the University gym [the Indoor Centre on Tyndall Avenue, which includes an indoor running track] for a friendly game of squash or a yoga class or just weight lifting or keeping fit. The more professional athletes head down to the Coombe Dingal complex, which offers multiple sports pitches, from astro to indoor tennis courts. Access to all of this, obligatory membership of the Athletics Union, etc will set you back around £450. I know it sounds a little steep, but for what you get out of it, it's reasonable.'

PILLOW TALK

Writes Laura: 'Most first year students get allocated a place in halls which means a choice of two locations: Stoke Bishop and Clifton. Stoke Bishop is about 40 mins from the University precinct, while Clifton halls are in one of the nicest parts of the city and just a 15 minute walk away.'

ACCOMMODATION	
Student rating	★★★★
Guarantee to freshers	**91%**
Style	**Halls, flats**
Security guard	**Some**
Shared rooms	**Some**
Internet access	**All**
Self-catered	**Some halls, most flats**
En suite	**Some**
Approx price range pw	**£61-£166**
City rent pw	**£60-£85**

Writes Alex: 'With the Downs 2 minutes walk away football, rugby, kite surfing, ultimate frisbee all become a part of life up at Stoke Bishop. On top of that Badock Hall offers the wildest parties.'

There is new city centre, self-catered accommodation this year for 121 students at 33 Colston Street.

Ratio of parking spaces varies from 1:3 to 1:29, although some residences have no parking.

GETTING THERE

☞ By road: M4/J19, M32 or M5/J17 and follow signs to the zoo (an elephant).
☞ By rail: London Paddington or Birmingham New Street, 1:30; Nottingham, 3:00.
☞ By air: Bristol Airport.
☞ By coach: Birmingham, 2:00; London, 2:20.

BRISTOL, UNIVERSITY OF THE WEST OF ENGLAND

Bristol, University of the West of England
Frenchay Campus
Coldharbour Lane
Bristol BS16 1QY

TEL 0117 32 83333
FAX 0117 32 82341
EMAIL admissions@uwe.ac.uk
WEB www.uwe.ac.uk

UWE Students' Union
Frenchay Campus
Coldharbour Lane
Bristol BS16 1QY

TEL 0117 32 82577
FAX 0117 32 82986
EMAIL union@uwe.ac.uk
WEB www.uwesu.net

VIRGIN VIEW

*U*niversity of the West of England, or UWE as it is known, sees itself as a 'new' university, which is understood to mean 'positive, forward-looking, a real value

university'.

UWE attracts a distinctive breed of student quite different to that of its neighbour. Forty per cent come from within a 40-mile radius, 47% are mature. The result is that many have a mature real-world outlook on

UNIVERSITY/STUDENT PROFILE	
University since	**1992**
Situation/style	**Campus/ city sites**
Student population	**31645**
Total undergraduates	**25360**
Mature	**47%**
International	**9%**
Male/female ratio	**43:57**
Equality of opportunity:	
state school intake	**89%**
social class 4-7 intake	**35%**
drop-out rate	**9%**

what they want to do and spread that ethos, which drives the university's strategy.

Frenchay, the main campus sited in the north of Bristol, is the hub, nestling in Silicon Gorge, with Hewlett Packard and Aardman's, the makers of Wallace and Grommit, on their doorstep, along with the NHS, organisations that characterise three of the university's academic concentrations - computer, film, and subjects allied to Medicine.

There is more. Environment Agency and Airbus are on hand, as is BBC TV's natural history base in Bristol.

UWE has over 1,000 partnerships with employers like these, including formal relationships with the BBC and Hewlett Packard, which ensure the curriculum is up to minute and internships. Lecturers tend to be practitioners, straddling academia and the real world of work. The ethos is practical. Health and social care hopefuls will find themselves in a real hospital, even on Open Day. Their future employment is on the schedule even before Day One. Industry designs the courses, refreshes the curriculum, assesses the students' work - student projects in Built Environment are considered locally by real architectural companies. Getting a job at the end is simply another step in a 3-4-year process as inevitable as the one before. Seventy-two per cent get graduate level jobs within six months.

Yet the vocational element is not at the expense of academia, as is shown by the rise of the Philosophy Department, which, only a short while ago, was a mere History and Politics adjunct. Says Charlotte, a newish graduate: 'It's only recently that they have become their own little department, but it's a really good course. I have got nothing but good things to say about it.'

This development is in fact astute vocationally too. Industry is waking up to the fact that philosophy graduates think creatively and productively about problems, whatever they may be, problems in the research laboratory and on the shop floor. All of a sudden employers are actively seeking philosophy graduates to work for their companies.

So, UWE is in the forefront right now, in the National Student Survey enjoying three stars for helpful/interested staff.

It welcomes applications from those who do not have typical entry requirements but can provide evidence of personal, professional and educational experience which indicate their ability to meet the demands of their course.

What are they looking for? A clear reason for course choice, enthusiasm for your chosen subject, and an ability to communicate. Remember that when drawing up your personal statement or sitting an interview.

Open Days are scheduled for 1 and 15 Oct, 2011, and 19 Nov 2011 (Bower Ashton campus only) and 4 Feb and 3 March, 2012.

FEES, BURSARIES

UK & EU Fees, 2011-12: £3,375 p.a. There's an income-assessed Bursary for students in receipt of the full HE Maintenance Grant. Other awards include an Access Bursary for undergraduates who have completed a recognised Access course, and a Care Leavers Bursary for full-time undergraduates who have been in local authority care. See

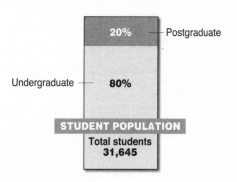

Postgraduate 20%

Undergraduate 80%

STUDENT POPULATION
Total students
31,645

TEACHING SURVEY AT A GLANCE

Avg. UCAS points accepted	**260**
Acceptance rate	**21%**
Overall satisfaction rate	**80%**
Helpful/interested staff	**★★★**
Small tuition groups	**★**
Students into graduate jobs	**72%**

Teaching most popular with undergraduates:
Education, Teacher Training, Accounting, Architecture, Biology, Drama, English, Finance, Fine Art, Forensic Science, Law, Media, Maths, Philosophy, Physical Geography & Environmental Science (95%), Physical Science, Planning, Politics, Psychology, Tourism.

Teaching least popular with undergraduates:
Computer Science (64%), Film (65%).

www.uwe.ac.uk/money/bursary.shtml. UWE also offers more than £100,000 worth of scholarships for international students each year. See www.uwe.ac.uk/international/scholProg.shtml.

STUDENT PROFILE

The student body is a good mix, despite the high number who come from the locality. Eleven per cent come from public schools (higher than to most 1992 universities), and they mix happily with the 35% who come from socio-economic groups officially designated as social class 4-7.

> *'People come here from all levels for the niche courses that UWE is good at, and for the city of Bristol. It long ago shed its new university image.'*

CAMPUS

There are three campuses in Bristol now, plus regional centre Gloucester concentrating on nursing. Only Bower Ashton, which houses the Faculty of Creative Arts, is in the south of Bristol. The main campus at Frenchay, close to Bristol Parkway station, but 4 miles out of the city centre, has the main body of students and includes Student Services, which brings together the various non-academic services. Faculty of Health is based at Glenside.

FRENCHAY (address above) Location: north of the city, near Bristol Parkway Station. Faculties: Business and Law, Creative Arts, Humanities and Education, Environment and Technology, Health and Life Sciences. Library has recent £6.5 million extension. Campus security is good.

CCTV and this is one of the only campuses to have its own bobby.

BOWER ASHTON Kennel Lodge Road, off Clanage Road, Bower Ashton, Bristol BS3 2JU; Tel: 0117 32 84716. Location: south of river, west but in easy reach of city centre. Faculty: Creative Arts. £4 million going into a complete redevelopment strategy, the first students to benefit going in this year. Ents facilities: opening hours short in Bower's Bar, but good, buzzy atmosphere.

GLENSIDE Blackberry Hill, Stapleton, Bristol BS16 1DD. Tel: 0117 32 88534. Location: northeast of city centre, good bus service to city action. Faculty: Health & Life Sciences. Accommodation: purpose-built, self-catering. Learning resources: library. Sport facilities: space for aerobics, etc. Ents facilities: Union bar, good restaurant, not far from Frenchay.

THE HARTPURY CAMPUS Hartpury House, Gloucester GL19 3BE. Tel: 01452 702132. www.hartpury.ac.uk/. An Associate Faculty since 1997, the college comprises 200 hectares of countryside, with woodlands, farm, lake and equine centre. Animal Science, etc. Students bring their own horses. Oh, and premiere division Gloucester Rugby Club train there.

ACADEMIA & JOBS

Faculties have merged into four: Business and Law; Creative Arts, Humanities and Education; Environment and Technology; and Health and Life Sciences.

SUBJECT AREAS (%)

RESEARCH EXCELLENCE

% of UWE"s research that is
4* *(World-class)* or **3*** *(Internationally rated):*

	4*	3*
Nursing and Midwifery	5%	35%
Allied Health Professions	15%	50%
Agriculture, Veterinary, Food	5%	40%
Applied Mathematics	0%	10%
Computer Science	10%	35%
Engineering,Mineral, Mining	10%	45%
Architecture, Built Environment	5%	40%
Town and Country Planning	5%	45%
Geography and Environmental	0%	20%
Accounting and Finance	10%	30%
Business and Management	0%	30%
Law	5%	15%
Politics	0%	15%
Social Work, Social Policy	0%	25%
Sociology	0%	15%
Education	5%	10%
English	5%	25%
Linguistics	10%	35%
History	5%	35%
Art and Design	10%	50%
Communication, Media Studies	15%	45%

The main employment sectors accounting for graduate jobs at UWE are: health, education (enormous numbers into primary schools), tourism (from Business, Biological Sciences, and Design), administration of economic and social policy (a steady stream via Social, Economic & Political Studies departments, Business Administration, and such as BSc Public Health), specialist retail (fashion in particular), architectural, engineering and technical consultancy, banking, insurance and accountancy, social work, computing, sports activities, the creative arts.

Nursing is a big feature and the range of degrees is wide: Health & Community Practice, Learning Disabilities, Adult Nursing, Care of the Older Person, Cancer Care, Emergency Care, Critical Care, Palliative Care, Mental Health, Children's, etc. Check campus situation, many are at Glenside in Bristol, but Adult and Mental are also available at the Gloucestershire site, where there are also Learning Disabilities and Children's Nursing degrees. Physiotherapy, Occupational Therapy and Radiotherapy score in this sector too. This year there is a new BSc (Hons) Healthcare Science (Life Science).

A popular development has been Veterinary Nursing Science, and Veterinary Practice Management.

UWE's top-rated Business School bring students into jobs in retail, business and management consultancy, human resource management, and the transport industry in particular, and there's a range of dedicated Accountancy degrees with interesting add-ons. In the insurance/pension sector, UWE is a particular force, as they are for would-be investment analysts.

Principal employment strengths in computing include the computer games sector, and systems analysts. Randal Lancelyn, who read Robotics, found the course 'really good', though queried the relevance of some of the first year modules and questioned the parsimonious use of the BRL in the Du Pont building, shown off and then put away for post-grads. Look closely at course structure, and ask questions at Open Day.

In Law, they are specialists in European and commercial & business law. They also offer a Legal Practice Course (LPC), essential step to becoming a solicitor, and are one of only eight unis where the BPTCC (Bar Professional Training Course, essential to becoming a barrister) may be

WHAT IT'S REALLY LIKE

UNIVERSITY:	
Social Life	★★★
Societies	★★★
Student Union	★★★
Politics	**Average**
Sport	**Strong**
National team position	**36th**
Sport facilities	★★★
Arts	**Drama very good**
Student newspaper	**Western Eye**
Magazine supplement	**Westworld**
Student Radio	**Hub**
Nightclub/venue	**Red**
Central campus bar	**Escape**
Other campus bars	**Glenside, Bower**
Union ents	**Clubnights, live**
Union societies	**41**
Most active societies	**Drama, Dance, Comet Cheerleaders**
Parking	**None on campus**
CITY:	
Entertainment	★★★★★
Scene	**Full on waterfront and fringe**
Town/gown relations	**Good**
Risk of violence	**Average-high**
Cost of living	**High**
Student concessions	**Good**
Survival + 2 nights out	**£70-£100 pw**
Part-time work campus/town	**Good/Excellent**

undertaken. Bristol University Law students take their law practice and bar vocational courses here. There is a mock court on campus. Always this practical, real-world emphasis. There is also a car crash scene for forensic science students.

Millions have been spent on new studios, suites and facilities for Creative Arts students at the Bower Ashton campus, widely known for its fashion, and of course the Animation courses, source of the outflow into the film industry. Peter Lord, one of the producers of Aardman, teaches there. Sixty UWE students appeared in the list of credits for Chicken Run.

SOCIAL SCENE

STUDENTS' UNION **Escape** on Frenchay is the main bar. Free wifi, jukebox, pool, TV, and music on plasma screens. There's also **Red** - café culture by day, and another main venue for club nights, bands,

ACCOMMODATION	
Guarantee to freshers	**Apply early**
Style	**Flats, houses**
Security guard	**Some**
Shared rooms	**None**
Internet access	**Most**
Self-catered	**All**
En suite	**50%**
Approx price range pw	**£91-£132.50**
City rent pw	**£60-£85**

etc. - 3 a.m. closing on Monday (for Lock-In, resident DJ, classic hits), and Friday's *Flirt*, the UK's No. 1 student night.

Glenside is the perfect place for a pint before a big night out, and Bower's bar is uniquely the students own.

The media set-up is good. There's *Western Eye* (newspaper) with *Westworld* (magazine) its arts supplement, and Hub (the radio station). They also have a very active Drama society, and there seems to

be good synchronisity with the Old Vic, TV companies and film units that prey on Bristol, with dramsoc students being regularly invited onto casts.

The musicals scene is famed. Ian Henderson's your man, lecturer in Music Theatre, Vocal Tutor and Musicals' Producer. Ian.Henderson @uwe.ac.uk.

SPORT Massive rivalry with Bristol University, a Varsity match (rugby), a boat race (the biggest outside Oxbridge), and the sports centre at Frenchay really is all that it's cracked up to be, with an eight badminton court sports hall, aerobics studio, large fitness room with masses of machinery, and two glass back squash courts. There are 43 clubs - everything from sky diving to American football - and they came 36th nationally last year.

PILLOW TALK

First-year students are guaranteed accommodation in University approved accommodation provided requirements threy apply before 1 July. International students are offered accommodation where possible. Contact: accommodation@ uwe.ac.uk.

All the beds at Frenchay (1,932 of them for first years) will have been snapped up by May, so if you want a part of the new student village, get in quick. Security is superb. Besides CCTV, you have to unlock four doors before you get to your en-suite, broad-banded room, six of which make up a flat. The rest of student accommodation is in the city, including harbourside city centre accommodation.

There is no student parking on campus.

GETTING THERE

☛ By road to Frenchay, Glenside, St Matthias: M4/J19, M32, A4174; or M5/J16, A38, A4174; Bower Ashton, M5/J19, A369.
☛ By rail: London Paddington, Birmingham New Street, 1:30; Nottingham, 3:00.
☛ By air: Bristol Airport.
☛ By coach: Birmingham, 2:00; London, 2:20.

BRUNEL UNIVERSITY

Brunel University
Uxbridge
Middlesex UB8 3PH

TEL 01895 265265
FAX 01895 203102
EMAIL course.enquiries@brunel.ac.uk
WEB www.brunel.ac.uk

Union of Brunel Students
Uxbridge
Middlesex UB8 3PH

TEL 01895 269269
FAX 01895 462300
EMAIL su.president@brunel.ac.uk
WEB www.brunelstudents.com

VIRGIN VIEW

*B*runel, known as the University of West London until recently when Thames Valley University took the nickname as its own new name, is based close to the M25, M40 and M4 confluence. Heathrow Airport is just around the corner. Students are fifty minutes by tube and thirty minutes by overland train from central London.

Out of a 19th-century, technical background, Brunel established itself in the late 1960s as a science/technology/ engineering uni, which was 'all well and good if you had long oily hair, wore AC/DC T-shirts and had the personality of a walnut,' recalls Satiyesh Manoharajah. However, things have been a-changing these past few years. The Social Sciences, Arts and Media faculties have greatly expanded, bringing an influx of generally more exciting students and, indeed, women!

There is now an almost equal male/female ratio, but while there are a few arty types, 'the general mix is still of engineering, computing and sporty types,' according to Ollie Wright.

The change is more noticeable perhaps in what students are studying. Drama, Media, Music, Social Work are now on the curriculum. But one thing that certainly hasn't changed is the preponderance of sandwich courses - paid placements in the world of work incorporated into many of the courses, from Aviation Engineering to Psychology & Anthropology, from Business & Management to Biomedical Sciences.

Brunel was a pioneer of the sandwich course. You may take a one-year block (for a 'thick-sandwich' course) or in some cases two six-month periods (for a 'thin-sandwich' course). Many students subsequently gain employment with their placement companies.

Careers advice and opportunities are co-ordinated by the Placement and Careers Centre. With an extensive careers library and interactive online service, a major autumn careers fair, regular workshops, employer presentations and subject-specific 'Careers Uncovered' events, students make

UNIVERSITY/STUDENT PROFILE	
University since	**1966**
Situation/style	**Suburban campuses**
Student population	**15090**
Total undergraduates	**10830**
Mature	**33%**
International	**23%**
Male/female ratio	**52:48**
Equality of opportunity:	
state school intake	**96%**
social class 4-7 intake	**38%**
drop-out rate	**8%**

informed decisions from their first year onwards. Local, national and international recruiters target Brunel and there are typically over 1,000 employers advertising with them at any one time.

Employment is constantly on their minds, now more than ever, for while success in the employment league tables goes back decades, right now the league tables don't favour them so much. Last year only 67% got graduate type jobs six months after they graduated, according to Government statistics.

Students are taking the responsibility for their future on their own shoulders. Their Entrepreneurship Society is the fastest growing student-led group at Brunel.

A more positive word for their excellent campus accommodation, rated 5 stars by their students and good on every count, 8th best in Britain. A word too for the sport here, which is Top 20 level nationally, another tradition that goes way back, to Brunel University College, which was the Loughborough of its day, its song the Borough Blazer (after the college's original name, taken from its position on Borough Road).

Today, around 300 points will get you in. What are they looking for besides in the personal statement? 'A commitment to the area of academic study, particularly in an applicant's personal statement. A specific interest in certain degree courses, where an applicant has undertaken work experience because of this, including mature applicants. Applicants who have researched the degree

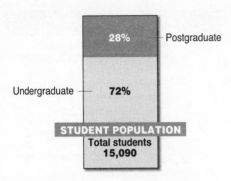

Postgraduate — 28%

Undergraduate — 72%

STUDENT POPULATION
Total students
15,090

course, its content and the entry criteria thoroughly.'

Open days, 2011: 17 and 24 June, 9, 14 and 16 September. All subject-specific; pre-booking is recommended.

CAMPUSES
Everything is now centred on the Uxbridge campus. Packed with bizarre, grey, concrete buildings, it has undergone a huge facelift in recent years, the main excitement being created by a £6.5-million outdoor sports complex, a £7-million indoor athletics facility, and a £9-million Health Services and Social Care Building.

Says Olly Wright: 'The library building, called the Bannerman Centre, the refurbished pubs and club, Indoor Athletics Centre and four new halls have made big changes to the landscape.'

FEES, BURSARIES
UK and EU Fees, 2011-12: £3,375 p.a. There are bursaries for students in receipt of full HE

TEACHING SURVEY AT A GLANCE

Avg. UCAS points accepted	**300**
Acceptance rate	**17%**
Overall satisfaction rate	**75%**
Helpful/interested staff	**★★★**
Small tuition groups	**★**
Students into graduate jobs	**67%**

Teaching most popular with undergraduates:
Aerospace Engineering, Anatomy, Physiology & Pathology (98%), Biology, Design Studies, Electronic & Electrical Engineering, History (100%), Politics, Sociology.

Teaching least popular with undergraduates:
Drama (51%), Social Work (41%).

Maintenance Grant, see www.brunel.ac.uk/ugstudy/finance/support/brunel. Awards are also available for elite performance athletes (e-mail sports-scholarships@brunel.ac.uk for further details).

There are academic and music scholarships too. See www.brunel.ac.uk/ugstudy/finance/support/brunel. For musicians, auditions are held at the beginning of each academic year (see www.brunel.ac.uk/about/pubfac/artscentre/awards).

Awards are also available to students from low socio-economic background. See www.brunel. ac. uk/ugstudy/finance/support/brunel.

STUDENT PROFILE
There is a 96% state school take, and 38% of undergraduates are drawn from among the four lowest socio-economic classes (4, 5, 6 & 7). International students account for 23% of total. The International Pathway Centre facilitates entry with an appropriate orientation strategy, language preparation, and support.

ACADEMIA & JOBS
Brunel provides degree courses in Design, Systems, Electronic, Computing and Mechanical Engineering, Education, Health and Social Work, the Humanities, Social Studies, the Creative and Performing Arts, and Sports Science. Sandwich placements and strong links with industry and business are to the fore.

The teaching most popular with undergraduates is in Aerospace Engineering, Anatomy, Physiology & Pathology (98%), Biology, Design Studies, Electronic & Electrical Engineering, History (100%), Politics, and Sociology. Least popular is the teaching of Drama and Social Work.

Health and Social Work courses are a prominent part of what is being delivered. Near enough 20% of Brunel graduates take jobs in health and social work. The Biomedical Science degrees (Genetics, Human Health, Immunology), and courses like Occupational Therapy and Physiotherapy, account for this. Many also go into the manufacture of pharmaceuticals and medicinal chemicals. While others become social workers in spite of the unpopular teaching, and there's a fair drift into the community from graduates of the Youth and Community degree.

But Business is productive of more jobs overall. A host of degrees in Business & Management, Business Economics, Economics & Finance, Finance & Accounting and Financial Computing pave the way for large numbers of graduates into banking, accountancy, etc.

Engineering fares well, but all those sexy Aerospace, Aviation and Motorsport degrees, along with the more traditional Civil and Mechanical Engineering degrees, lead in relatively small number into engineering jobs (around 3%), or merely to boosting the figures of graduates finding work in software consultancy and Engineering Design Consultancy from the Computer division.

Brunel's graduates of Computer and Electronic Systems, and Games Design find work in some 50 job categories in the Higher Education Statistics Agency's graduate employment record, and account for around 10% of Brunel's graduate jobs overall.

Arts are also to the fore in the curriculum - from English to Film/TV Studies, from Drama to Creative Writing. The novelist, Fay Weldon, teaches creative writing here. Brunel is also up among the best for turning out actors, rivalling specialist colleges. Their Performing Arts Department, which includes the Rambert School of Ballet & Contemporary Dance, is a centre for Film & Television Studies as well as for Drama and Music.

The Antonin Artaud building, a venue to support the teaching and research in performing

RESEARCH EXCELLENCE

% of Brunel's research that is
4* (World-class) or 3* (Internationally rated):

	4*	3*
Health Services Research	15%	50%
Allied Health Professions	10%	15%
Environmental Sciences	10%	30%
Applied Mathematics	5%	55%
Statistics	15%	35%
General Eng., Mineral & Mining	5%	45%
Mechanical, Aeronautical, Manufacturing Eng.	10%	40%
Geography	5%	20%
Economics and Econometrics	10%	50%
Business and Management	10%	35%
Library, Info. Management	20%	30%
Law	5%	45%
Politics	5%	20%
Social Work, Social Policy	5%	30%
Sociology	10%	40%
Anthropology	20%	30%
Psychology	5%	30%
Education	5%	10%
Sports-Related Studies	15%	20%
English	15%	30%
Art and Design	0%	35%
Drama, Dance, Performing Arts	15%	25%
Communication, Media Studies	10%	25%
Music	15%	30%

SUBJECT AREAS (%)

Creative Arts 10, Education 1, Health Subjects 7, Science/Engineering 14, Humanities 12, Social Studies incl Law 13, Business 19, Maths & Computer 12, 12

arts, was opened by director and playwright Steven Berkoff not so long ago. Graduates find work in the film industry, in radio and television, and in the creative arts. But the number that do is relatively small.

The line into radio and TV is clearer via their Broadcast Media and Communications & Media degrees. Publishing is also a popular sector.

In the Law Department they are specialists in Business & Commercial Law. Other social sciences show strong emphasis on Politics, Sociology, and Social anthropology. Psychology has a good reputation here, both for world-class research and

teaching. Graduates spread into a host of different areas with the skills and knowledge they accrue. Labour recruitment and personnel, and the Civil Service, are strong areas, fed by a number of different departments.

Brunel are among the leaders in finding jobs for graduates in Sport. Today athletes, team players and would-be officials revere their modern Sports Science degrees - Coaching, Administration and Development, Fitness, PE, and Technology. They make their mark in the National University Championships too, coming 18th last year.

STUDENT SCENE

The Students Union has undergone a huge refurbishments of its bars, nightclub and food hall, and there are new shops, a balcony café and central atrium.

'The nightclub is the **Academy**,' writes Olly. 'No extra space has been gained, which would have been useful as some nights it does fill up and some are turned away. The new design is better than before, there's lots of stainless steel creating more light and space-age feel. It is open seven days a

WHAT IT'S REALLY LIKE

UNIVERSITY:	
Social Life	★★★
Societies	★★★
Student Union services	★★★★
Politics	**Average Student issues**
Sport	**Good**
National team position	**18th**
Sport facilities	★★★★★
Arts opportunities	**Excellent drama, film; good art, dance, music**
Student magazine	**LeNurb**
Student radio	**Radio Brunel**
Nightclub	**Academy**
Bars	**Loco's Bar**
Union ents	**Good clubnites & live bands**
Union societies	**120**
Campus fresher parking	**None for freshers**

CITY:	
Entertainment	★★★★★
Scene	**Cheesy local club, good pubs, cinema. Mainly London beckons**
Town/gown relations	**Good**
Risk of violence	**Average**
Cost of living	**High**
Student concessions	**Good**
Survival + 2 nights out	**£100 pw**
Part-time work campus/town	**Average/Excellnt**

of Battle of the Bands.

'One night the Union hired out a couple of poker tables, a blackjack table, a roulette wheel and some croupiers and put on a *Casino Night*, which was free and no real money was gambled, but still fun nonetheless.

'The bar is **Loco's** and has also been refurbished, with all new leather sofas, chairs and tables, a no-smoking section, many plasmas covering the walls, three pool tables, a table football table, two fruit machines and a couple of monopoly machines. For a uni bar, the drinks are expensive, but compared to London prices they are cheap. Again, Loco's is not open to townies and there is security on the doors from 7pm. They also have a typical pub food menu until 7pm.

'Another pub on campus - **Bishops Bar** - is not run by the Union, and generally the drink prices are lower. This is the place to go to watch football, while Loco's generally shows rugby. Bishops has also been newly refurbished and they are still in the process of finishing the balcony.

'The local London students certainly do desert the uni at weekends, and their exit is noticeable by Friday afternoon when all the car parks are empty, apart from one or two lonely cars. But there is still a good amount of students around and the Academy is certainly never lacking people on a Friday night.'

Pronto is the number one fast food outlet on campus.

The Arts Centre is the platform for musical concerts throughout the year. Student groups include The Brunel Singers, an orchestra, guitar, brass, wind and string groups; all are professionally trained and music bursaries are awarded annually. Classes in photography and various visual art forms are given on a weekly basis by visiting professionals. There are several drama groups.

week from 9 or 10 pm till 2am, apart from Sunday when it shuts at 12.30am, but not to townies, as all entrants are checked against Brunel photographic identification on the door. Students may bring guests as long as they are students and have signed in at the student union reception.'

The Academy has seen Westwood, Trevor Nelson, Hed Kandi and Pendulum, and their urban scene attracts some of the best talent in London, but there is an incredible choice of nights, in just one month they had: *Base Night, ACS Traffic Light Party, Global, Flirt!, Brassie, Blackout* (student switch off, the most fun you'll have with the lights out), *Funk Off, Plan B, Indicate* (yeh, indie night). Also live gigs and whole season

> *'The tradition of sport goes back through the mists of time to Brunel University College, the Loughborough of its day, its song the Borough Blazer still heard on campus today.'*

SPORT Fourteen million pounds has been invested in a world-class sports complex, which includes an indoor athletics and netball centre, an outdoor athletics arena and floodlit turf, and all-weather pitches and courts. The gym and free-weights room have also been refurbished. Hurricanes Superleague netball are based here, and UK Athletics use it as a training faculty for elite athletes.

'Many of the students are doing sport science and related subjects,' says Olly. They are indeed one of the top unis for sport, coming 18th overall last year, up from 21st the previous. You can dabble, satisfy curiosity or take up fanatically more or less what you want to at Brunel.

Town 'Mmm...the lovely town of Uxbridge... There are two shopping centres, The Chimes and The Pavilions, containing all the shops one could ever need. There is even an Odeon on the top floor of Chimes. Uxbridge also has a few nice student-happy pubs, like the **Hog's Head**, the **Zanzi Bar**, the **Metropolitan**. There's also a nightclub, **Royale's**, not recommended, plays cheesy pop and there is a guaranteed fight at 3am when everyone leaves, the only positive being the cheap drinks.

'Generally, the locals must be used to living with students as there is peace between us. There are many takeaways - if you go a day without a menu coming under your room door in halls then there is something wrong - four pizza houses, a few Indians and Chinese.'

PILLOW TALK

Their accommodation has been transformed in recent years. In 2008, they completed a £250-million campus redevelopment pro-gramme, which saw the refurbishment of existing halls and the construction of the Isambard Complex. See

ACCOMMODATION	
Student rating	★★★★★
Guarantee to freshers	**100%**
Style	**Halls, flats**
Security guard	**Some**
Shared rooms	**None**
Internet access	**All**
Self-catered	**All**
En suite	**84%**
Approx price range pw	**£86.52-£110.25**
City rent pw	**£75-£100**

www.brunel.ac.uk/life/accommodation.

All bedrooms (halls and flats) have internet and are self-catering; all but 3 halls (Chepstow, Clifton, Saltash) are en-suite.

If you live in a halls of residence, or within 2 miles of the University, you will not be allowed to bring a car onto campus.

GETTING THERE

☛ By Underground: **Uxbridge** – Metropolitan line and Piccadilly during peak hours. Then bus, U3 or U5.

UNIVERSITY OF BUCKINGHAM

The University of Buckingham
Hunter Street
Buckingham MK18 1EG

TEL 01280 820313
FAX 01280 822245
EMAIL Go via:
www.buckingham.ac.uk/admissions/fees

Students' Union
The University of Buckingham
Hunter Street
Buckingham MK18 1EG

TEL 01280 822522
FAX 01280 812791
EMAIL student.union@buckingham.ac.uk
WEB www.buckingham.ac.uk/life/social/su/

VIRGIN VIEW

*N*ame *a university which engenders greater student satisfaction than Cambridge, achieves 9% more graduate-level jobs for its students, six months after graduation, as Cambridge, and requires of its applicants less than half the A level points.*

The answer is Buckingham, Britain's only independent university. They have one member of staff for every eight or nine

UNIVERSITY/STUDENT PROFILE	
University since	**1976**
Situation/style	**Town campus**
Student population	**1060**
Total undergraduates	**740**
Mature	**57%**
International	**60%**
Male/female ratio	**53:47**
Equality of opportunity:	
state school intake	**87%**
social class 4-7 intake	**No data**
drop-out rate	**10%**

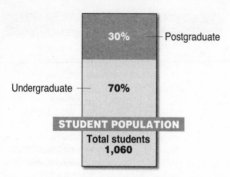

STUDENT POPULATION
Total students
1,060

Postgraduate 30%

Undergraduate 70%

STUDENT PROFILE

More than half the undergrads are mature and 60% come from overseas. 'Each student mixes with 79 other different nationalities,' they say, and since there are only 740-odd Buckingham undergraduates in total, that is quite a mix. The male/female split is 53/47; 87% are state school educated, but few are low down the socio-economic scale or resident in so-called 'low-participation neighbourhoods'.

ACADEMIA & JOBS

Buckingham has specialised in two-year degrees since its inception thirty-one years ago. The degrees operate on a four-term per year basis. What elsewhere is a long summer holiday is at Buckingham a term of teaching.

New in 2008 was the Medical School. Currently only a postgraduate degree is on offer, a two-year MD in Clinical Medicine which attracts overseas medical graduates who find it difficult to secure junior doctor posts as a result of recent Government restrictions. An undergraduate degree is mooted. Still under construction, it will be a 4-year course for students coming from any discipline. The course will be fully GMC accredited and lead to a Foundation Year post within the UK National Health Service.

Other departments include Accounting, Business, Economics, English Language Studies (EFL), English Literature, Financial Services, History, History of Art, Information Systems, International Hotel Management, International Studies, Law, Marketing, Politics and Psychology. Also available, and paired with English are degrees in Multimedia Journalism and Media Communications. They say that for A level candidates they ask for three passes, but combinations of A and/or AS levels are also considered.

Recent additions to the subjects on offer include a BA in Art History & Heritage Management with a term at the British Institute in Florence; BSc in

students, while the average is one to every seventeen or eighteen. What's more, the norm is tutorial groups of no more than six.

They see their unique value in terms of the learning environment, staff accessibility, and their superb graduate employment figures.

What they are looking for in applicants is motivation to complete in two years what others do in three, evidence of enthusiasm for the subject, extra curricular activities that support maturity and commitment.

Campus facilities have improved considerably in recent years and a new six acre site has recently been acquired for expansion.

CAMPUS

The three sites - Hunter Street, 8-acre Verney Park and the more recently developed Chandos Road complex, are walking distance apart and within the town boundaries.

FEES, BURSARIES

2011-12: Total fees for UK undergraduates taking the two-year degree are now £17,880, and there are discounts for payment in advance. Overseas students pay £29,520 and there is a range of scholarships for both home and overseas candidates. Bear in mind, there are 4 terms per year and 2 years for most undergraduate courses. The logic is as follows. The time it takes to complete a degree at Buckingham is eight terms, the duration of which is two years. So, you end up paying less, especially in living expenses, than you would at other universities.

Scholarships, grants and loans are available. Students are eligible for the same Student Finance England support as those of State-supported unis.

TEACHING SURVEY AT A GLANCE	
Avg. UCAS points accepted	**310**
Acceptance rate	**24%**
Overall satisfaction rate	**95%**
Helpful/interested staff	★★★★★
Small tuition groups	★★★★
Students into graduate jobs	**95%**

Teaching most popular with undergraduates:
Accounting, Business, Economics (99%), English, Languages, Law, Politics (100%), Psychology.

Business Enterprise and an MSc in International Financial Services. Masters programmes in Security and Intelligence Studies, (in Buckingham) Biography, Military History and Decorative Arts are now taught in London.

As this is an independent institution, it is not obliged to be assessed by the Quality Assurance Agency for Higher Education. However, in November 2003 it submitted voluntarily to an Institutional Audit by the QAA and was awarded a judgement of Broad Confidence in the quality of its programmes and the academic standards of its awards.

Areas of particular strength - Buckingham's Law and Business Schools are very popular and highly regarded. 2006 saw the introduction of the Bachelors in Business Enterprise, which offers students the chance to set up their own business as part of the degree. The Aylesbury Vale Enterprise Hub also opened in 2006 and offers advice and space to start up businesses in the Vale, incorporating a hatchery space for entrepreneurs who are at the 'pre-start' stage of their business plan.

Other recent degrees include an MA in Global Affairs, BA degrees in Business Enterprise, Journalism with English Literature, Journalism with Communication Studies, Journalism with International Studies, and a BSc in Economics with Business Journalism.

A majority of graduate jobs come out of the Business courses; then Law; then (in the publishing, education, and business sectors) Languages.

The opportunity to study with students from so many different countries sets students up well to work abroad after they graduate. There is an excellent alumni network. Graduates' close contact with fellow graduates offers unique mentoring for their future careers.

There are libraries at each site, a language centre and a networked IT set-up (a computer suite at Verney Park is accessible 24/7). There's a trained teacher of the dyslexic, who works with students from the minute they arrive. Degree courses are very concentrated, however. The intensity of the academic experience leaves little time or desire for the worst excesses of student fun and games.

SOCIAL SCENE

STUDENTS' UNION At one-tenth of the average size of a British university, Buckingham provides a cosy enough environment. The Union, located in the **Tanlaw Mill** on the Hunter Street site (refectory and George's Bar, pool tables, video games, lounge with Satellite TV), organises discos on Fridays and a Graduation Ball. Then there's the **Franciscan Building** (Verney Park) for private-

WHAT IT'S REALLY LIKE	
UNIVERSITY:	
Social Life	★
Societies	★
Student Union	★
Politics	**Internal**
Sport	**Local & BUSA**
Arts opportunities	**Few**
Student magazine	**Cygnet**
Union ents	**Functions, films, discos, balls**
Union venue	**Tanlaw Mill**
Union Societies	**11, mainly cultural**
Parking	**Available**
TOWN:	
Entertainment	★★
Scene	**Trad pubs**
Risk of violence	**Low**
Student concessions	**Some**
Cost of living	**Average**
Survival + 2 nights out	**£50-£80 pw**
Part-time work campus/town	**Poor/Excellent**

hire cellar parties. There are currently eleven societies, mainly cultural or departmental, quite a few organised trips and a series of concerts and lectures.

The most active student society is Bahamian. There's a magazine called Cygnet, and in November 2005, a cinema opened on campus. Films are shown over the weekend, and often one mid-week showing. For escape, there are various restaurants and traditional country pubs in Buckingham, or Milton Keynes (14 miles), Oxford (23 miles), London (58 miles). Bring a car.

SPORT Four all-weather tennis courts, one all-weather five-a-side pitch, a swimming pool, gym complex and sports field; other playing fields a mile away. There are riding schools in the vicinity. The uni teams are mainly locally competitive. Matches played against alumni and staff are also regular features. There is a campus fitness programme - aerobics classes, martial arts - and a well-equipped fitness centre. They are currently raising funds to build a Sports Hall.

PILLOW TALK

Guaranteed first-year, self-catered accommodation from converted cottages to mixed halls of residence at Hunter Street and Verney Park, or shared flats at Hunter Street. Security is tight on campus. All bedrooms have internet access.

GETTING THERE

☛ By road: M40/J9 from the south, then A41, A421. Also A422, A421. A413 from the north.
☛ By rail: Buckingham has no station, the nearest are at Bicester and Milton Keynes. London Euston, 1:00; Birmingham New Street, 1:20.
☛ By air: Heathrow or Gatwick.
☛ By coach: London, 1:20.

ACCOMMODATION	
Guarantee to freshers	**100%**
Style	**Halls, flats, houses**
Security guard	**Security**
Shared rooms	**None**
Internet access	**All**
Self-catered	**All**
En suite	**Some**
Approx price range per week	**£81-£141**
Town rent per week	**£90+**

BUCKINGHAMSHIRE NEW UNIVERSITY

Buckinghamshire New University
Queen Alexandra Road
High Wycombe HP11 2JZ

TEL 0800 0565 660
    01494 522141 (switchboard)
FAX 01494 605023
EMAIL advice@bucks.ac.uk
WEB www.bucks.ac.uk

Bucks Students' Union
High Wycombe
Buckinghamshire HP11 2JZ

TEL 01494 610600
FAX 01494 556195
EMAIL union@bucks.ac.uk
WEB www.buckingham.ac.uk/life/social/su/

VIRGIN VIEW

*B*uckinghamshire New University can trace its history back to a School of Science and Art founded in 1893 and to Buckinghamshire College of Higher Education, formed in 1975 out of High Wycombe College of Technology and Art and Newland Park College of Education.

From 1992 Brunel University validated the College's degrees. Then, in 1999, four years after it had been given powers to award its own degrees, it was confirmed by the Privy Council as Buckinghamshire Chilterns University College. Finally, in October 2007, it gained university title and another new name.

Last year it had the highest percentage increase in applications of a UK university for its full-time undergraduate honours degree courses, and saw a 54% increase as at the UCAS deadline of 22 January 2010, placing it in the Top 10 universities for percentage increases in applications. This year, according to statistics released by UCAS in early 2011,

their applications increased enough to put them in the Top 15 in the UK.

They put this down partly to the commitment they have made to the student experience through a student support package they call 'the Big Deal' which includes a £500 cash bursary paid to all fulltime UK and EU students, except those on Nursing programmes, plus additional faculty-based support and free access to all gigs and club nights, a deal which led to nomination

UNIVERSITY/STUDENT PROFILE	
University since	**2007**
Situation/style	**Campus sites**
Student population	**9570**
Total undergraduates	**8765**
Mature	**61%**
International	**15%**
Male/female ratio	**44:56**
Equality of opportunity:	
state school intake	**97%**
social class 4-7 intake	**40%**
drop-out rate	**10%**

in 2009 for a Times Higher *award.*

This is an unashamedly 'new' university, unfolding on a wave of PR directed at students, whom they perceive as consumers in the modern fashion.

The National Student Survey shows that students themselves regard the best teaching to be in fact in Law, Computer Science, Psychology, and Social Work, and some of the worst in Marketing. Perhaps the practitioners should become the teachers.

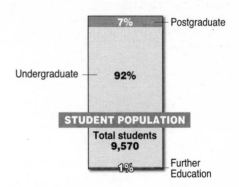

Postgraduate 7%

Undergraduate 92%

STUDENT POPULATION
Total students
9,570

1%

Further Education

FEES, BURSARIES

UK and EU Fees, 2011-12: £3,375 p.a. No academic scholarships. There's a sports bursary for students competing at county level or above. Overseas students with an IELTS score of over 6.5 get a discount on fees, and a discount is offered for fees paid in advance.

CAMPUS

The Gateway hub of the new university is located on Alexander Road in the centre of **High Wycombe**. Gateway offers a range of new facilities, including an events hall, gym, dance and drama studios, music and video production suites, a high-tech learning resources centre and meeting rooms, a mix of facilities for the whole student body, which encourages interaction between students from a variety of disciplines. Nursing courses are delivered at another location: 106 Oxford Road in **Uxbridge**.

OPEN DAYS

High Wycombe Open Days, *2011 (11am - 4pm)*: 2 April, 15 June, 1 and 29 October, 16 November. *2012 (11am - 4pm)*: 22 February, 28 April, 13 June.

Nursing - Uxbridge Campus Open Days, *2011 (11am - 2pm)*: 14 May, 25 June, 20 August, 15 October, 3 December. *2011 (6pm - 8pm)*: 22 June, 12 October, 30 November. *2012 (11am - 2pm)*: 14 January, 21 April, 23 June. *2012 (6pm - 8pm)*: 18 April, 20 June.

Mechanical Engineering Design Open Days *2011 (5pm - 7pm)*: 14 March, 11 April, 16 May, 13 June, 4 and 18 July, 15 August, 12 and 26 September.

STUDENT PROFILE

The University has prioritised those with limited or no family background in higher education, young people and mature learners from low participation neighbourhoods, applicants with specific difficulties. They are not hidebound by a points at A level hurdle. Mature students, in particular, may be considered by virtue of their experience alone.

Result is that there is a large mature population (61%) and most students are local. Ninety-seven per cent are state school educated, and more than a third come from social classes 4-7. The drop-out rate of 10% is well within the Government benchmark for Bucks New, so they must be getting it right.

ACADEMIA & JOBS

Their courses are geared to the world of work; many are accredited by professional bodies and the majority are either unique or only found in a handful of other universities in the UK. Employability skills development is embedded in the curricula. Students benefit from longstanding partnerships with industry, business, the professions, sporting bodies and the public sector

There has been a complete reorganisation of departments into three faculties. Creativity & Culture produces around a third of the graduate jobs at Bucks New. It is the umbrella for four schools: Arts & Media (Creative Writing, Drama, English, Film, Journalism, etc.), Design & Craft (Art & Design, Ceramics & Glass, Furniture, Jewellery, Product Design, Spatial Design), Visual & Communication Arts (Advertising, Graphic Arts, Animation, Fine Art, Textiles), and Music, Entertainment & Moving Image (Music Management and Production, TV & Film).

Advertising degree graduates pour out of the Design school. Others find work as graphic artists, designers and illustrators, in media & government research, and textiles.

Also, they are sector leaders in furniture design. High Wycombe has been associated with the craft for more than a century and Bucks New delivers the largest range of furniture design programmes in the world. They just launched the National School of Furniture, a partnership between higher and further education and businesses and associations to offer benefits to students and industry alike.

There is also a Jewellery degree, which brings graduates into the Fashion industry and has a new degree this year: 3D Contemporary Crafts and Products: Jewellery, Metal, Glass, Ceramics.

Media degrees, which include Film & TV Production, Radio Production, Journalism, Sports & Events Broadcasting, Music Management, Production, etc. Evidence of degrees leading to jobs in the radio and television industry is strong, and

RESEARCH EXCELLENCE

% of Bucks's research that is
4* *(World-class)* or 3* *(Internationally rated)*:

	4*	3*
Allied Health Professions	**0%**	**10%**
Business and Management	**0%**	**20%**
Sports-Related Studies	**0%**	**5%**
Art and Design	**5%**	**25%**

TEACHING SURVEY AT A GLANCE

Avg. UCAS points accepted	**180**
Acceptance rate	**22%**
Overall satisfaction rate	**69%**
Helpful/interested staff	**No data**
Small tuition groups	**No data**
Students into graduate jobs	**68%**

Teaching most popular with undergraduates:
Law (90%), Computer Science,
Psychology, Social Work.

Teaching least popular with undergraduates:
Marketing (49%), Languages (41%).

there is a visible presence in the publishing industry too.

The Enterprise & Innovation faculty delivers Business & Management, Computing & Advanced Technologies, and Sport, Leisure & Travel. All are important elements in their graduate employment portfolio. There's an interesting niche in Air Transport & Pilot Training - two degrees that yield around 3% of their graduate employment provision.

Finally, Society & Health delivers Nursing, Community Health & Social Care, which looks after around 11% of the graduate employment

SUBJECT AREAS (%)

Medicine 1
Creative Arts
Health Subjects 3
Engineering 12
Humanities 36
Science
Social Studies incl Law 1
15
Business 17
<1
6
Built Environment <1
Maths & Computer 9

provision), and Human Sciences & Law. They are specialists in commercial and business law, and have a strong employment track record with their police degrees.

SOCIAL SCENE

STUDENTS' UNION includes **The Venue**, a 1,100 capacity club and bar (**The White Room** and **The Lounge**) at the centre of the High Wycombe campus. It incorporates plasma screens, pool tables, free internet and a café service during the day, and won a Best Bar None award for the most improved Student Union venue in the UK, as well as a bronze at the Sound Environmental Impact Awards.

Uxbridge students get **Pulse**, a café and eaterie run by the Union, and can share Brunel Uni's main bar **Loco's** and nightclub, the **Academy** (see Brunel entry).

There's a handful of societies, but no great pretence at this stage of extra-curricular clout, except that Bucks Television is a brand new webTV site for development by students. It was nominated for a *Times Higher Education* award last year in the 'Outstanding ICT initiative' category.

TOWN High Wycombe has the shopping monster **Eden Complex**, which opened in 2008 and includes otherwise sparse parking spaces. The town has a lively enough collection of clubs (1,000-capacity **Pure** and smaller bar clubs **Obsession**, **Litton Tree** and **The Garden**). A fair assortment of other bars, eateries, cafés and pubs complete the scene. Arts-wise, there's a big name theatre, **The Swan**, a twelve-screen multiplex in Eden and six-screen **Empire**, plus the **Town Hall** for comedy.

Uxbridge has **The Chimes** and **The Mall** for shopping, a clutch of good value restaurants, including some good Indians and hot, hot, hot **Sukanya Thai**. **Liquid & Envy** in the High Street is the town's club. Otherwise there are the expected bars and pubs and **Odeon** cinema.

SPORT The new Sports & Fitness Centre includes gym, human performance lab accredited by the

ACCOMMODATION	
Guarantee to freshers	**70%**
Style	**Halls, flats**
Security guard	**Some**
Shared rooms	**Some**
Internet access	**Most**
Self-catered	**All**
En suite	**Some**
Approx price range pw	**£81.97-£129.85**
City rent pw	**£55-£90**

PILLOW TALK

There are two halls at High Wycombe - Brook Street and John North Halls, with self-catering accommodation for 500. No-one coming to the uni from within a 25 mile radius gets a look in. As part of their ambitious redevelopment plans for the town, they are building new accommodation at Hughenden Road - en-suite student rooms with communal facilities, rooms for disabled students and larger rooms for mature students. The first phase of this (234 student rooms) opened last year.

GETTING THERE

☞ By road to High Wycombe: M40/J4, A4010.
☞ By rail to High Wycombe: London Marylebone, 35 mins.

British Association of Sport and Exercise Sciences, treatment room, and dance studio. In addition, the strong partnerships with London Wasps (rugby union premiership) and Wycombe Wanderers (football league 1) who train on Uni territory, are a meaningful additional point of interest, not to say inspiration to those in the know.

UNIVERSITY OF CAMBRIDGE

Cambridge Admissions Office
The University of Cambridge
Kellet Lodge
Tennis Court Road
Cambridge CB2 1QJ

TEL 01223 333308
FAX 01223 746868
Email admissions@cam.ac.uk
WEB www.cam.ac.uk/admissions/undergraduate/

Cambridge University Students' Union
11/12 Trumpington Street
Cambridge CB2 1QA

TEL 01223 356454/333313
FAX 01223 323244
EMAIL info@cusu.cam.ac.uk
WEB cusu.cam.ac.uk

VIRGIN VIEW

*T*he University of Cambridge, stands at No. 6 in the latest Times Higher Education *table of the Top 200 Universities Worldwide, and at No. 1 among British Universities.*

It began life early in the 13th century, more than 100 years after Oxford. Its colleges have always been self-governing, with their own property and income, and tradition continues to be an important dimension of the Cambridge experience.

The only question for many is how on earth to get in. The points ask is of course astronomical. But that isn't the problem. The problem is that many meet the academic requirement and are still not accepted. So,

UNIVERSITY/STUDENT PROFILE	
University since	**1209**
Situation/style	**City collegiate**
Student population	**22820**
Total undergraduates	**15725**
Mature	**36%**
International	**24%**
Male/female ratio	**48:52**
Equality of opportunity:	
state school intake	**59%**
social class 4-7 intake	**13%**
drop-out rate	**1%**

we thought we'd ask them what they look for beyond grades, tests, references, etc. This is what they said: 'We treat and assess everyone individually and look at - and for -

different things in different people for different courses. However, in general Admissions Tutors are looking for the students they believe have the most academic potential, are best suited to the course in question, and who will most benefit from what we have to offer, whatever their background.

'In particular we are looking for students who are passionate about the subject they have applied for, and have demonstrated that interest outside the set curriculum.

'We also look for an indication of a student's ability to think critically and independently, a willingness to argue logically with the capacity to keep an open mind to new ideas too. Self-discipline, motivation and commitment are all important.'

Cambridge Open Days in 2011 are to be held on 7 and 8 July. For Department and College Open Days see www.cam.ac.uk/opendays/.

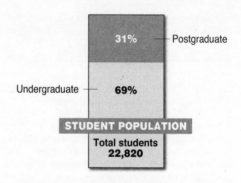

STUDENT PROFILE

'If you're thinking of applying to Cambridge: congratulations!' writes Caroline Muspratt, a student of Modern & Medieval languages at Christ's. 'Why do I say that? Because even to consider applying, you must be a straight-A student, from a private school, with a white, middle-class background and parents who earn nearly £100k a year. Right?

'Wrong! It's a common misconception that state school students, ethnic minorities, poor people, etc, don't get in. None of this matters. It won't affect your application, it won't change the friends you make, the societies you join, or the grades you get. I'm from a state school, I have working-class parents, and I'm the first person in my family ever to go to university. And yes, there are people here who went to Eton and have spent their whole lives being groomed for Cambridge, but students are students and the public-state divide is little more than a media fabrication.'

Katie Lydon went to school at Bolton comprehensive and is 'more than fulfilled,' and quite unable to identify the typical Cambridge student or dominant group, only the caricature: 'Cliques grow up around sports, drama and other activities, as well as drinking societies and simple

'I'm from a state school, I have working-class parents, and I'm the first person in my family ever to go to university. And yes, there are people here who went to Eton.'

friendship groups. Although there is the odd example of the elitist stereotype, they are in the minority.'

FEES, BURSARIES

UK & EU Fees, 2011-12: £3,375 p.a. Bursary for students in receipt of full Maintenance Grant falls under the Cambridge Bursary Scheme (www.cam.ac.uk/cambridgebursary/). Sport awards include their Talented Athlete Scholarship Scheme (www.sport.cam.ac.uk/bursaries-and-scholarships/index.html). Individual colleges offer financial support, which may include scholarships and prizes for academic achievement. For music awards (choral, organ and instrumental awards), see www.cam.ac.uk/admissions/undergraduate/musicawards/.

ACADEMIA & JOBS

All Cambridge undergraduates study for the BA degree, whether they are reading an arts or science subject. There are three graduate colleges not profiled below, which do take the odd bod for undergraduate studies if they have already done a degree elsewhere or are over 21 at entry. These are: Hughes Hall, CB1 2EW. Tel 01223 334 897, WEB www.hughes.cam.ac.uk; St Edmund's CB3 0BN. Tel 01223 336 086, WEB www.st-edmunds.cam.ac.uk; and Wolfson CB3 9BB. Tel 01223 335 918. WEB www.wolfson.cam.ac.uk.

'The work ethic is very strong throughout the university,' warns Caroline. 'You'll be expected to study hard, and to achieve a lot in a short time... it can initially be intimidating, and I wasn't the only one who spent the first few weeks convinced that the interviewers had made a mistake. After a few alcohol-aided evenings out with other freshers, you realise that you are on a level pegging with most of them.

'Teaching is done through supervisions and lectures. Supervisions are given by fellows or research students to one or two students. It's a very intensive way of learning, and the short teaching term (eight weeks) means that there isn't much let up. This can take its toll, especially in the stressful summer exam term. Libraries are excellent, but...it can be difficult to get hold of books when the entire year is doing the same paper.'

The most popular single employment sector for Cambridge graduates is health. The leading Medicine degree is the 5/6-year MB, BChir. Chemistry is required among 3 A levels, and at least one further A level and one AS level (preferably two A levels) in two of Biology, Maths and Physics. You will also have to sit the Biomedical Admissions Test (BMAT) test (see bmat.org.uk). The test is being used to assess scientific aptitude, not fitness to practise medicine (which will continue to be assessed in interview) and focuses on scientific abilities relevant to the study of medicine.

The MB, BChir involves heavy science-based pre-clinical in first two years, core subject study (Anatomy through to Psychology) the speciality. A number of graduates go into full-time laboratory research. For those who don't there's the chance to do the PRHO at top Addenbrooke's Hospital.

The veterinary degree is a 6-year MB and not available at Peterhouse or King's colleges.

Law is another key Cambridge profession. All candidates for the degree must sit the National Admissions Test (LNAT). Non-Law graduates may apply for a 2-year Senior Status Law degree here.

However, neither Medicine nor Law degrees

yield the most graduate jobs. At Cambridge, that distinction goes to degrees in Languages. Singly, Languages produce more than 17% of graduate jobs among Cambridge graduates. The degrees favour work in education, publishing, secondary education, management consultancy, museum and archival work, public administration, higher education, social work, TV and broadcasting, advertising, etc., etc. Languages are a good bet.

Another little nugget, possibly more widely known, is that from student activity in drama come the new generations of directors, producers and theatre managers (there being no vocational drama degree at Cambridge University). Arts administrators and managers are also legion from this source.

SOCIAL SCENE

STUDENTS' UNION 'Fresher's Week is organised by college JCRs (Junior Common Rooms), involving pub crawls and ents,' writes Katie. 'What I found especially encouraging was the willingness of the different year groups to mingle, and the fact that you are assigned ìcollege parentsî in different years to help you settle in.'

The Cambridge Union boasts more than 400 student societies for the few with time on their hands. Drama Society is big on tours to America and Europe every year, and a high number of productions go to the Edinburgh festival.

Media-wise, the student papers, Varsity and Cambridge Student, and radio station CUR are award-winning. Most recently, in 2009, students took five gongs at the *Guardian* Awards: Journalist, Reporter, Sports Writer and Columnist of the Year.

There is no central nightclub, but CUSU run popular student nights at local clubs and live acts or many and various.

SUBJECT AREAS (%)

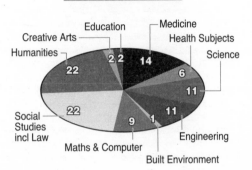

Education — Medicine
Creative Arts — Health Subjects
Humanities — Science
2 2 14
22
6
11
Social Studies incl Law — 22
9 1 11
Engineering
Maths & Computer
Built Environment

SPORT 'Sports facilities are abundant,' writes Katie, 'but vary between colleges. If sport is your thing, check out the college facilities, where exactly the playing fields and so on are before you apply. All have, or share, a boathouse and operate a novice rower training programme, which can be a really good way of getting to know people if you can hack the early mornings.

TOWN 'If you're looking for somewhere with 24-hour opportunity, forget Cambridge; take a 45-minute train ride to London,' Katie advises.

'Club fare in town ranges from cheesy and sweaty through the slightly nicer, smaller, more chilled and alternative. You will find that there is a student night every week night.

'What the city lacks in clubs, it makes up for in pubs. There are dozens in the town centre.' Says Stephen Craiger: 'I'm a pub man myself. Clubs are avoided Fri/Sat (town comes out) - aggressive all round. Town/gown divide is very much present.'

What does it all cost?

'Cambridge is a relatively cheap city,' writes Caroline. 'If you're trying to work out a budget, allow about £80 per week for food, going out two nights a week, and all the other bits and pieces you'll need. Everything in Cambridge is within walking distance (unless you're at Girton).'

PILLOW TALK

'Amazing!' says Stephen Craiger. 'En suite, spacious, nice view. Better than I expected.'

Students at Cambridge are provided with College accommodation. Sometimes this is in the main College grounds, alternatively it can be in a purpose-built block outside the main College or a College-owned house. The style of accommodation varies a lot but most students will have a room of their own. Some accommodation has en suite facilities where as others has shared WC and bath/shower facilities. Students have access to the College cafeteria as well as self-catering facilities and most rooms have Internet access. Colleges also have Porters' Lodges staffed 24 hours a day.

Students are provided with accommodation for three years of undergraduate courses and in many cases a fourth year as well. Room rents are subsidised by the colleges and they are increasing, but you can currently expect to pay from about £70 to £130. Every college has a normal canteen and a Formal Hall, where you'll pay around £11 or £12 (more for guests), but for this you get a three-course meal with coffee, served by waiting staff as you sit on long, candlelit tables. Grace is said in Latin and vast quantities of wine and port are consumed.

GETTING THERE

☞ By road: M25/J27, M11/J11, A10. From west or east, A45. From northwest, A604.

☞ By rail: London's Liverpool Street, under the hour; Nottingham, 2:30; Birmingham, 3:00.

☞ By air: Stansted Airport, M11.

☞ By coach: London, 1:50; Birmingham, 2:45; Leeds, 5:00; Bristol, 5:30.

COLLEGE CAMEOS
by Katie Lydon

CHRIST'S
Cambridge CB2 3BU
Tel 01223 334 953
WEB www.chrlsts.cam.ac.uk

Founded in 1448, Christ's is a beautiful college situated in its own extensive grounds in the centre of town. It has a strong academic reputation, regularly tops the Tompkins Table, and there's a strong atmosphere of study. Library access is 24-hour access and computer facilities, including room connections, are available. Christ's also makes 'easy offers' to around a third of its intake.

The balance of north/south and state/independent school students is relatively good, with 49% of the 2000/01 intake coming from the state sector. Women are under represented, but not drastically.

Uniquely, there are two bars, though one closes at 8.30pm. The ents committee puts on around four themed nights a term, and there is a formidable biennial May Ball. The JCR publish an alternative prospectus (see web site).

The college sporting reputation has become good and the drama society, CADS, is well known and respected across the university. The college has a squash court and boathouse - sports pitches are twenty minutes away - and use of its own theatre; there is a cinema that puts on both recent releases and classic films.

Writes Christ's Caroline Muspratt of the accommodation: 'The rooms are generally very good apart from the 'typewriter', a horrible building at the back of Christ's. You may be lucky enough to get an en-suite bathroom; otherwise you can be sharing with anything from three to twelve people. The kitchens are usually very small and ill-equipped: the college wants to encourage everyone to eat in Hall. Upper Hall opens for breakfast, lunch and dinner, and the food ranges from excellent to mediocre. Formal Hall, which starts later in the evening, is particularly good: you can book in guests, and the three-course meal is served in a medieval dining hall.'

CHURCHILL

Cambridge CB3 ODS
TEL 01223 336 202
WEB www.chu.cam.ac.uk

Churchill was founded in 1960. The distance (five-minute cycle) from town is more than compensated for by the extensive grounds, proximity to sports facilities and the relaxation of being off the tourist trail. Academically it is strong and dominant in Computing, Natural Sciences and Engineering

The state school presence is high, and men are the dominant sex, though Churchill was the first all-male college to admit women (1972). While very different from and less photographed than its older, town centre counterparts, Churchill's modern architecture is Grade I listed and popular for its functionality.

College ents are regular and popular with students throughout the university, as is its huge bar. All rooms have network and phone connections, and there are extensive sports facilities on site.

CLARE

Cambridge CB2 1TL
Tel 01223 333 246
WEB www.clare.cam.ac.uk

Founded in 1326, Clare is the second oldest college. It occupies extensive grounds that begin in a town-centre huddle of other colleges, and stretch to straddle the River Cam across to the University Library and arts faculties. It is friendly, academically successful and is continually over-subscribed. Students are quite evenly divided between the arts and sciences. English and Engineering applicants are encouraged to take a gap year.

Clare choir is famed in Cambridge and throughout the country, and Clare is also home to some of the best alternative ents in the university. Its hugely popular cellar based venue hosts regular live band sessions ranging from jazz to drum 'n' bass, attracting names such as the James Taylor Quartet. Its May Ball is renowned and tickets sought after.

The drama and art societies are particularly good, and Clare sports teams, especially rugby and hockey (men's and women's) and boat club are strong.

Accommodation is usually very good, with most first years living together in the same court, many in en-suite bathrooms. In later years there is

RESEARCH EXCELLENCE

% of Cambridge's research that is
4* *(World-class) or* **3*** *(Internationally rated):*

	4*	3*
Cardiovascular Medicine	35%	50%
Cancer Studies	35%	45%
Infection and Immunology	35%	45%
Hospital Clinical Subjects	35%	45%
Laboratory Clinical Subjects	45%	40%
Epidemiology, Public Health	40%	45%
Primary Care	20%	45%
Psychiatry, Neuroscience, & Clinical Psychology	40%	40%
Biological Sciences	20%	40%
Agriculture, Veterinary, Food	5%	40%
Environmental Sciences	40%	50%
Chemistry	40%	40%
Physics	25%	40%
Pure Mathematics	30%	45%
Applied Mathematics	30%	45%
Statistics	30%	45%
Computer Science	45%	45%
General Eng., Mineral, Mining	45%	45%
Chemical Engineering	30%	55%
Metallurgy and Materials	40%	55%
Architecture, Built Environment	30%	50%
Town and Country Planning	30%	45%
Geography	30%	40%
Archaeology	30%	30%
Economics and Econometrics	30%	45%
Business and Management	35%	40%
Law	25%	35%
Politics	20%	30%
Sociology	20%	35%
Social Anthropology	35%	35%
Biological Anthropology	35%	25%
Psychology	35%	50%
Education	30%	35%
Middle Eastern/African Studies	35%	40%
Asian Studies	15%	35%
East European Languages	25%	30%
French	20%	35%
German, Dutch, Scandinavian	25%	30%
Italian	45%	35%
Iberian and Latin American	30%	40%
Celtic Studies	45%	30%
English	40%	25%
Linguistics	20%	30%
Classics, etc	45%	25%
Philosophy	35%	30%
Philosophy of Science	25%	40%
Philosophy	35%	25%
Theology	40%	25%
History	40%	25%
History of Art	10%	50%
Music	45%	40%

WHAT IT'S REALLY LIKE	
UNIVERSITY:	
Social Life	★★★★
Societies	★★★★★
Student Union services	★★
Politics	**Active**
Sport	**Huge**
National team position	**14th**
Sport facilities	★★
Arts opportunities	**Drama/dance excellent, rest good**
Student magazine	**Inprint, May Anthologies, etc**
Student newspaper	**Varsity, Cambridge Student**
Guardian Awards 2009	**5 awards**
Student radio	**CUR**
National Radio Awards	**Bronze, 2010**
Student TV	**CUTE**
Nightclub	**None**
Union ents	**College JCRs**
Bars	**All colleges**
Union societies	**400+**
Parking	**Buy a bike**
CITY:	
Entertainment	★★★
Scene	**Cheesy clubs, great pubs**
Town/gown relations	**Average-poor**
Risk of violence	**Low**
Cost of living	**Average**
Student concessions	**Good**
Survival + 2 nights out	**£80 pw**
Part-time work campus/town	**Not permitted**

the opportunity to move out to the large houses that constitute Clare Colony, a short walk along the river.

CORPUS CHRISTI
Cambridge CB2 1RH
Tel 01223 338 056
WEB www.corpus.cam.ac.uk
Founded in 1352, Corpus is situated right in the centre of Cambridge, opposite Kings (popular myth claims that Corpus actually owns Kings' land and that the lease is soon to expire, to the amusement of the inhabitants of the smaller college). Small but friendly, Corpus' architecture is as pretty as that of its bigger neighbours, but the college is better than most at protecting its students from the constant tourist invasion that can be a liability of a central college.

Corpus places a strong emphasis on academic

pursuits, and presents an incentive to achievement in the form of its controversial academic room ballot. Strengths are mainly in the arts, especially History and English, but it is also strong in Engineering.

Traditionally enthusiasm is the only pre-requisite here for sport, and the college offers a wide range of facilities, including on-site squash and a strong boat club. There's an annual sports 'Challenge' with Corpus Christi, Oxford.

The JCR is active and the bar a central feature, though its opening hours are variable. The film society puts on a regular mix of classic and new titles, and the drama society (The Fletcher Players) is well known and has links with the intimate, adjacent venue, **The Playroom**.

DOWNING
Cambridge CB2 1DQ
Tel 01223 334 826
WEB www.dow.cam.ac.uk
Downing is one of the newer town centre colleges, founded in 1800 just off Cambridge's main shopping street, close to the science, architecture and engineering faculties (the Sidgwick arts site is a little further). Once through the gates one finds an array of unusual neo-classical architecture and large, open, green spaces. It's a peaceful retreat, brilliant in summer. The atmosphere is friendly and lively, politically neutral and relaxed.

Academically, Downing is always in the Top 10; all subjects are well represented; Law and Medicine are particular strengths. The library is well stocked and pleasant, with an especially good law section. The JCR organises a good Freshers' Week; bar, common room and TV room are excellent. Termly events usually attract big name DJs and are popular across the university. They are perennially successful in sports; particular strengths are rowing, rugby and athletics. There are network connections in all rooms.

EMMANUEL (EMMA)
Cambridge CB2 3AP
TEL 01223 334 290
WEB www.emma.cam.ac.uk
Emma is a relaxed, open college founded in 1584 in the centre of town, opposite the arts cinema and the largest pub in the country. Emma students come from a wide range of backgrounds. It offers scholarships and hardship funds; financial status should never be a barrier to entry.

Emma is also outstanding academically, consistently featuring among the top five colleges. Arts are a particular strength, and it is often the most popular choice for English applicants.

The bar runs weekly funk and cheese events and is the best and most popular in Cambridge. Sport is strong, especially women's rowing and football. There's a squash court and an outdoor swimming pool. The municipal (and indoor) pool is close by, as are most of the shops and both cinemas. Drama and film societies are prominent, and a May Ball happens every other year.

Most rooms have network connections; unusually, Emma offers a free, weekly laundry service.

FITZWILLIAM (FITZ)

Cambridge CB3 0DG
TEL 01223 332 057
WEB www.fitz.cam.ac.uk

Founded in 1969, Fitz is one of the newest colleges in the university, occupying modern, spacious, award-winning buildings - the oldest date from 1963, very different from the classical architecture elsewhere but regarded as functional and user-oriented in a way older colleges often aren't.

Being a five-minute bike ride away from the town centre in open, generally quiet grounds, students have a reputation for being relaxed and sociable. The college is good academically, comes about mid-Tompkins Table, but is not as frenzied as some. A high proportion of its intake comes from state schools.

Tradition isn't as prominent as in other colleges, though there is just enough to remind you that you are at Cambridge. The bar is well-loved and is the centre of social activity, and what are widely thought of as some of the best ents in Cambridge are put on twice a term.

Sport, especially football, is strong, and the college has its own squash court and gym.

GIRTON

Cambridge CB3 0JG
TEL 01223 338 972
WEB www.girton.cam.ac.uk

Girton was founded as a women's college in 1869, began to admit men in 1979, and now the latter slightly outnumber the former. It sits on a beautiful 50-acre site a couple of miles out of the city centre and, uniquely, has its own student car park. Architecturally impressive and undisturbed by tourist invasion, the distance encourages a close-knit community and strong collegiate atmosphere; there's a 24-hour garage across the road for bits and pieces, and Girton village isn't far.

Girton isn't the most academic of colleges, the atmosphere is unpressured and relaxed. The **Cellar Bar** is the social focus and ents venue. The formal hall food is famed across the university for

ACCOMMODATION	
Student rating	★★★★★
Guarantee to freshers	**100%**
Style	**College, hall or house**
Security guard	**Porter's Lodge**
Shared rooms	**None**
Internet access	**Most**
Self-catered	**Plus college**
En suite	**Some**
Approx price range pw	**£70-£130**
City rent pw	**£70-£120**

its quality, so much so that the boat clubs and drinking societies of other colleges strive to get themselves invited for dinner. Sport is popular at Girton, and facilities include an on-site indoor heated swimming pool. The boat club is popular and does well.

Students initially live in college, then move out to nearby houses or Wolfson Court - much more central, near the University Library and Sidgwick site.

GONVILLE & CAIUS

Cambridge CB2 1TA
TEL 01223 332 447
WEB www.cai.cam.ac.uk

Founded as Gonville in 1348, 'Caius' (pronounced 'Keys') was added to the name in 1558. It occupies a convenient city centre site, but tourist traffic is less than might be expected as it sits between Trinity's famous Great court and King's Chapel.

Caius is academically strong, always in the top half of the Tompkins Table, and its particular strengths are in Economics, Law, History and Medicine. The always accessible library is excellent, as are the computer rooms, and most student rooms are connected. Drama and music are popular, and Caius Films has become a prominent presenter of varied movies, drawing a cross-collegiate audience.

Sport is taken fairly seriously, with the boat club very successful. Squash, netball, football, hockey and racquet facilities are within a few minutes walk of college and served by a licensed pavilion.

Uniquely its students are compelled to buy forty-five dinner tickets per term at around £4 each. While this may seem a little expensive, the result is a stronger college atmosphere.

The college can accommodate all undergraduates well, though again, quite expensively.

HOMERTON

Hills Rd, Cambridge CB2 2PH
TEL 01223 507 252
WEB www.homerton.cam.ac.uk

Homerton was founded in 1695 as a College of Education and moved to its present site in 1894. It still specialises in Education, but offers other subjects too, including Archaeology and Anthropology, Computing Science, Economics, Engineering, English, Geography, History, History of Art, Land Economy, Music, Natural Sciences, Oriental Studies, Philosophy, Social & Political Sciences, and Theology & Religious Studies.

Situated a bit out of the town centre, close to the railway station, Homerton tends to cultivate a fairly close community. There is a relatively high proportion of mature students, and women outnumber men. They recruit mainly from state schools, though students are drawn from all backgrounds.

Participation in university activities, such as journalism, drama and politics, is strong. Facilities are excellent - Homerton's on-site sound and dance studios are the rehearsal venue for many university productions. It also boasts its own gym, squash court and sports field. Men's rugby and women's rowing are both strong.

Students initially live in college, but there is the opportunity to move out into houses scattered around the town in later years.

JESUS

Cambridge CB5 8BL
TEL 01223 339 495
WEB www.jesus.cam.ac.uk

Jesus was founded in 1496 and, 'greener' and more open than some of its neighbours, overlooks the common and river from its spacious grounds, five minutes from the city centre.

Academically Jesus is relatively strong, and takes its students from a variety of backgrounds. The JCR bar is a popular social hub, but ents are few because of lack of room. Music and drama are strong, and the college offers exhibitions to organ and choral scholars.

Sport is very strong, and the college's location means that all of its facilities, which include pitches for soccer, American football, cricket, rugby and hockey, and squash and tennis courts, are on site. The boat club is a short walk across the common.

Accommodation for all undergraduates is in college or houses across the street - some of the latter have been recently refurbished and a new on-site block of en-suite accommodation opened.

KING'S

Cambridge CB2 1ST
TEL 01223 331 417
WEB www.kings.cam.ac.uk

Founded in 1441, King's and its famous chapel are most popularly representative of Cambridge. Its public perception, however, as the epitome of prestige and tradition, contrasts sharply with the reality. It takes over 80% of its students from the state sector and is reputedly obsessed with being politically correct. Its students aren't required to wear gowns at formal dinners or elsewhere - in fact, there are no formal arrangements for meals.

King's fame attracts more tourists than any other college, but most come only to visit the chapel, and careful controls ensure that this doesn't impinge on study too much.

Academically King's is average, but its students are the most diverse bunch in the university. The atmosphere is relaxed and while students work hard, they make time for other activities - university drama, politics and journalism all feature high numbers of King's students.

Ents, based in their Cellar, are among the best in Cambridge, with queues forming long before the tickets for their famous termly Mingle events go on sale. The choir is of course world famous, making several recordings a year, and choral and organ scholarships are offered. Sport isn't a King's strength, perhaps something to do with the fact that its rowers wear purple lycra?

LUCY CAVENDISH

Cambridge CB3 0BU
TEL 01223 330 280
WEB www.lucy-cav.cam.ac.uk

Lucy Cavendish was founded in 1965 as a college for mature women. It is placed in a pretty cul-de-sac behind St John's, five minutes from the city centre.

Academically, Medicine, Law and Veterinary Science are strong. Sport isn't a particular strength, although the first Lucy Cavendish rowing crew hit the river a couple of years ago. Having had to start at the bottom, its reputation has yet to rise to the surface. The college has its own gym and access to squash and badminton courts. There's a summer ball after the festivities of May Week have died down and its own students are still around.

A recently built block of rooms with en-suite facilities has increased the on-site accommodation available to students.

MAGDALENE

Cambridge CB3 0AG
TEL 01223 332 135
WEB www.magd.cam.ac.uk

Magdalene (pronounced 'Maudlin'), founded in 1542, straddles Bridge Street, alongside the river on the north side of the city. Its grounds meet those of St John's and allegedly trespass on its land, which why students of the former refer to Magdalene students as their 'villagers'.

You'll hear that there is an overwhelming public school presence, and that tradition is paramount, with a nightly, formal candlelit dinner. But Magdalene students claim no atmosphere of elitism or arrogance. Most regard the dinner (non-compulsory) as a pleasant social occasion rather than an imposed tradition.

Academically not outstanding, but its students participate widely in university sport, drama and journalism, and have recently had a heavy involvement with the Cambridge Union.

Facilities are good - the college shares playing fields with St John's - and it has its own Eton Fives court. Most impressive facility is its music room, with grand piano, two harpsichords and an organ. The bar and other social facilities are good, and well complemented by the adjacent **Pickerel Inn**.

NEW HALL

Huntingdon Rd, CB3 0DF
TEL 01223 762 229

Ten minutes walk from the city centre, Murray Edwards was founded as New Hall in 1954 to increase access to Cambridge for women. It is still a women-only college, but Ros Smith (a New Hall graduate) and Steve Edwards have given the college two transforming gifts, an endowment of £30 million and a new name.

Indisputably, many Murray Edwards students are pooled here as second choice, but many others chose to be there, and the two 'groups' cohere to form a pleasant and sociable community.

Academically the college is continually close to the bottom of the Tompkins Table. Particular strengths are Medicine, Physics and Economics. The college hosts the largest contemporary exhibition of women's art in permanent residence.

Its futuristic **Dome** houses a famed rising kitchen, applauded when it appears at meal times, and is generally thought of as one of the best ent venues in the university, hosting large events with big-name DJs - including the respected termly Vibrate - and yes, men are allowed in. No May ball, but a garden party is held.

Sports facilities are good, including tennis, squash and netball courts, and the college is close to playing fields. Murray Edwards rowers are feared by other colleges' women crews.

College accommodation is available to all undergraduates.

NEWNHAM

Cambridge CB3 9DF
TEL 01223 335 783
WEB www.newn.cam.ac.uk

Newnham, founded in 1871 as an all-women college, continues to admit female students only, and, like Murray Edwards, is anything but insular - guests of both sexes are welcome around the clock...as long as they are accompanied.

The college is situated close to the river and Sidgwick arts site, in attractive grounds with extensive gardens (where, uniquely, you may walk on the grass). Students are from a mix of backgrounds, though predominantly state school. Unspectacular academically, Newnham's strengths are in the arts.

Sport facilities include cricket, hockey, lacrosse, football and rugby pitches, a croquet lawn and tennis courts. Newnham's is the oldest women's boat club in England. Newnham students are also heavily involved in life outside college, particularly in drama and journalism.

PEMBROKE

Cambridge CB2 1RF
TEL 01223 338 154
WEB www.pem.cam.ac.uk

Pembroke was founded in 1347 and enjoys the benefits of a central location without the hassle of being on the tourist trail. It has pretty gardens, hidden from the roads by high walls.

Academically strong, computer facilities are good, and student rooms are mostly connected to the network. Pembroke also has busy dramatic, musical and journalistic interests. The Pembroke Players and the musical society are known across the university, and the college has its own newspaper, Pembroke Street. They also have a popular bar and regular ents, a sports ground and boat club, and enjoy high-level participation and reasonable success in rowing, rugby, football, netball and hockey.

Accommodation is good and either in college or nearby houses; a new block has just been completed.

PETERHOUSE

Cambridge CB2 1RD
TEL 01223 338 223
WEB www.pet.cam.ac.uk

Peterhouse is the oldest and smallest college in Cambridge. Founded in 1284, the buildings are attractive and close to Pembroke and the engineering and science faculties.

Reputed to be more stringent than most in its interviewing and admissions procedures, Peterhouse has particular strengths in Classics, English, History, Law, Engineering, Maths, Medicine and Natural Sciences. Its stereotype - oft denied - is that of a staunchly right-wing, public-school environment. Men outnumber women significantly, but allegations of a sexist culture appear unfounded as girls from other colleges choose to join Peterhouse choir and other activities. (the college has its own theatre). Sports are actively pursued, particularly rugby, football and rowing. The college also has its own magazine and many of its students are involved in university newspaper journalism.

QUEENS'

Cambridge CB3 9ET
TEL 01223 335 540
WEB www.quns.cam.ac.uk

Founded in 1448, in pleasant grounds straddling the river, and close to most faculties, Queens' is open, pleasant, and students say the most people-based college in Cambridge. Certainly its students come from staggeringly different backgrounds. Around the top of the academic league tables, strengths are in natural sciences, medicine, engineering, languages and law.

Facilities are fantastic, including a hall that hosts some of the biggest ents in Cambridge (such as the famed cheesy Jingles); it doubles as theatre or sporting venue. The entertainment schedule is the envy of the university, and there is a huge May Ball every other year. The drama society puts on some of the most innovative and controversial plays in Cambridge, there's a thriving gossip magazine, the film society provides a college cinema two nights a week, and the sporting ethos, while placing emphasis on enjoyment, embraces success at university level (there are squash courts and playing fields). Yet, Queen's still manages to remain a genuinely friendly, relaxing, unpretentious, but inspiring place to be.

College can accommodate all students, and all rooms are connected to the internet.

ROBINSON

Cambridge CB3 9AN
TEL 01223 339 143
WEB www.robinson.cam.ac.uk

Robinson is the newest Cambridge college, founded in 1979 and based in red-brick buildings behind the University Library and arts faculties, next to the uni rugby ground - slightly out of town (five-minute cycle), but close to sports facilities. Its 'new' status means tradition is kept to a minimum.

Here, Cambridge stereotypes are despised and disproved.

Academically average, the emphasis is on personal freedoms and development. Robinson draws the majority of its intake from state schools; the atmosphere between staff and students is very open and respectful, with meetings open to everyone.

Ents are well attended and include karaoke and music nights featuring anything from cheese to jazz. The JCR publishes its own alternative prospectus - check the web site.

Accommodation is comfortable, functional and available to all undergraduates.

ST CATHERINE'S (CATZ)

Cambridge CB2 1RL
TEL 01223 338 319
WEB www.caths.cam.ac.uk

Catz is a small college on the main street, along from King's, almost opposite Corpus Christi, and within ten minutes' walk of the main arts, science and engineering faculties. Founded in 1473, its relatively small size makes for an inclusive community. There's a good social mix, though women are a minority (usually around 40%).

It has a tradition of academic excellence. Strengths are in Natural Sciences, Geography and Medicine. The library is new and well stocked.

Even though its ents are generally poor, Catz has a good social tradition: Freshers' Week is legendary, recently the bar and common room have been refurbished, and its formal dinners are popular and over-subscribed.

Music and drama are strong, and Catz has its own 150-capacity theatre in the Octagon buildings. The literary Shirley society is the best known in Cambridge. Sport is strong, notably rugby and athletics.

The boathouse is a short cycle away, and facilities are generally good - there's an Astroturf pitch, courts for racquet sports, and pitches for field sports. Swimming is a Catz strength, and though it doesn't have its own pool, the excellent, new town facility is close.

Students live initially in college, moving out to the Octagon colony of flats near the Sidgwick site in the second year.

ST JOHN'S

Cambridge CB2 1TP
TEL 01223 338 703
WEB www.joh.cam.ac.uk

St John's was founded in 1511 in the centre of Cambridge, next to its long-standing rival, Trinity. It is the second largest college in Cambridge and so is able to house all its undergraduates.

Architecturally impressive, its buildings chart varied and increasingly modern styles, culminating in the listed Cripps Building, seen as ugly by some, but functional and popular accommodation for first years.

Academically, John's is very strong (fourth in the tables for the last couple of years, and generally in the top five) and boasts an impressive and very well-stocked new library. Its beautiful Old Library houses many ancient manuscripts. Computing facilities are excellent, with two main computer rooms and terminals scattered around the library and in the JCR. All student rooms in college have internet connections. Book grants are automatic; travel grants and hardship loans are generous.

St John's choir is respected globally, the college chapel providing a beautiful setting, and the jazz Society is famed across the university. Drama - the Lady Margaret Players - is a great tradition, the freshers' play a big draw, and they have their own venue in the **School of Pythagoras**, apparently the oldest university building in the country. The film society operates twice a week, and there are disco clubnights three times a term in the underground **Boiler Room**, noted for its drum 'n' bass, hip hop and cabaret. Sport is strong, especially rugby, football and the famous Lady Margaret Boat Club. There are extensive pitches at the back of college and a new boathouse just down the river. There are also squash, badminton, tennis and netball facilities. Finally, John's formal hall is arguably the best (and best value for money), and tickets for their May Ball are among the most sought after.

SELWYN

Cambridge CB3 9DQ
TEL 01223 335 896
WEB www.sel.cam.ac.uk

Selwyn was founded in 1882 and sits in pleasant grounds close to the Sidgwick site of arts faculties. The college's proximity to green fields and 15 mins distance from the bustle of the city centre gives it an atmosphere less claustrophobic than most.

Not noted for its academic reputation, though usually in the top half of the Tompkins Table, Selwyn's strengths include engineering, history and natural sciences.

There is an even mix between arts and science students and between men and women, and students come from a wide variety of backgrounds.

Facilities are good - the library is satisfactory. For arts students, faculty libraries are on the doorstep and can be equally accessible. Most student rooms are connected to the internet, and communal computer facilities are good.

Drama (The Mitre Players) have their own venue in the **Diamond**, and the music and film societies are also active.

Sport is not a major strength, except rowing, where in recent years Selwyn has become a force. The bar is popular, and there are several student run ents. The impressive May Ball is biennial.

All undergraduates can be accommodated either in college or in nearby houses.

SIDNEY SUSSEX

Cambridge CB2 3HU
TEL 01223 338 872
WEB www.sid.cam.ac.uk

Sidney was founded in 1596 on what is known to today's students as 'Sainsbury's Street'. The modern world beyond the gates may be extremely busy, but once inside you'll find architecture dating back 400 years and a relaxed and unpressured atmosphere.

Accommodating a balance of arts and science students, with an even ratio of women to men, Sidney isn't the most academic of colleges, although it is currently pushing its way up the Tompkins Table.

The bar is good and run by students, with a sound system better than that of most other college bars, pool table and table football. The frequent ents are well attended

College food has allegedly improved since it was voted second worst in Cambridge in 1993. Sport isn't strong. A sports ground, a short cycle away, is shared with Christ's; the boathouse is close.

Students are accommodated either in college or in nearby houses.

TRINITY

Cambridge CB2 1TQ
TEL 01223 338 422
WEB www.trin.cam.ac.uk

Founded in 1546, Trinity is the largest college in Cambridge. Situated centrally with beautiful views onto the river and the Backs and next to St John's, Trinity is its (friendly) rival in almost everything.

The college architecture is much admired, notably the Wren Library and Great Court, whose 'run' was made famous in Chariots of Fire (though actually filmed at Eton).

There is an impressive academic record - they are rarely out of the top four or five in the Tompkins Table - particularly in sciences. Contrary to popular belief, it recruits a significant majority from the state sector; women are, however, poorly represented (around 40%).

As befits the richest college in Cambridge, facilities are excellent, the library well stocked and computer facilities first class. Book grants are available to all students, room rents are among the lowest in the uni (although rooms have varying facilities, due to the age of the buildings, all are comfortable).

Ents aren't particularly notable, but the bar is well used, if a bit small. Extra-curricular activities are fervently pursued, and sport is strong. The boat club has recently listed several impressive victories, facilities are superb and nearby.

TRINITY HALL (Tit Hall)

Cambridge CB2 1TJ
TEL 01223 332 535
WEB www.trinhall.cam.ac.uk
Trinity Hall was founded in 1350 and nestles in pretty riverside grounds next to Trinity, its bigger and richer rival.
There is a popular myth about Trinity porters

phoning their Tit Hall counterparts to ask them to turn the music down at some gig - the reply came that Trinity Hall was 'there first' and so would do as it pleased. This anecdote sums up the atmosphere - it's a close, strong community that refuses to be overshadowed by its neighbours simply because of its size. There's a good mix of students and of men and women.

Tit Hall is, according to the Tompkins Table, academically average, but its traditional strength is Law. The new library, overhanging the river, is well stocked, if a little noisy in the summer, when it's a feature on guided punt tours.

Bar and JCR are lively and ents often referred to as the best. They face tough competition from King's, but are enjoyed for their individual style, the quality that best represents Tit Hall's students.

Sport and sporting facilities are good, and drama and music societies active.

CANTERBURY CHRIST CHURCH UNIVERSITY

Canterbury Christ Church University
Rochester House
Canterbury
Kent CT1 1UT

TEL 01227 782900
FAX 01227 470442
EMAIL admissions@canterbury.ac.uk
WEB www.canterbury.ac.uk

Canterbury Christ Church Students' Union
Canterbury
Kent CT1 1QU

TEL 01227 782817
FAX 01227 458287
EMAIL ccsu@canterbury.ac.uk
WEB www.ccsu.co.uk

VIRGIN VIEW

*B*efore Canterbury Christ Church achieved university status in 2005 it excelled for a decade as a university college, awarding its own degrees. Founded by the Church of England in 1962 (and currently boasting the Archbishop of Canterbury as Chancellor), it is located in modern buildings on part of St Augustine's Abbey (built in AD 597) and at various other sites in Kent.

It began as a teacher training college, and is now one of the largest teacher training centres in the UK, but the diversity of its programmes is reflected in the unique profiles of each of its campuses, from Commercial Music and Policing at

Broadstairs, Health and Education at Medway, Leadership and Management at its Salomons Campus, to Performing Arts at University Centre Folkestone.

UNIVERSITY/STUDENT PROFILE	
University since	**2005**
Situation/style	**City campus**
Student population	**16755**
Total undergraduates	**12620**
Mature	**61%**
International	**8%**
Male/female ratio	**30:70**
Equality of opportunity:	
state school intake	**97%**
social class 4-7 intake	**40%**
drop-out rate	**9%**

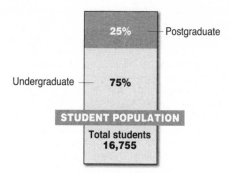

Postgraduate — 25%

Undergraduate — 75%

STUDENT POPULATION

**Total students
16,755**

Canterbury Christ Church partners in the Universities at Medway Students' Association (UMSA) - see the Kent entry); **University Centre Folkestone** (Glassworks, Mill Bay, Folkestone, CT20 1JG; 01303 251071. This lies in the heart of the creative quarter, the oldest part of this lively seaside town**, and was** developed with the University of Greenwich, with higher education facilities for the Performing Arts, Business and IT, and Fine Art with Digital Media. Finally, **Salomans Campus at Tunbridge Wells is set in beautiful landscaped grounds in the heart of the garden of England** and is for postgraduate study.

Canterbury, the main campus in the heart of the city, offers an extensive range of subjects across all five faculties and is supported by an award-winning library and new Sports Centre (opened in 2009).

Overall there was a high level of student satisfaction (81%) in the national survey.

Open days in 2011 are to be held on 18 June and 8 October in Canterbury, 11 June and 1 October (Folkestone), 2 July and 1 October (Broadstairs).

CAMPUS

Canterbury is a good place to be, small and friendly, if not exactly jumping with action. It is just big enough to hold a cathedral, some run of the mill shops and a fair range of pubs - and on first visit you might wonder that there's room for two degree-awarding institutions. The more widely known of these is the University of Kent (UKC), a traditional campus university situated up what has become known to the thousands of UKC students who trundle up and down it daily as Mount Everest. Canterbury Christ Church's campus is situated on the east side of the city on a World Heritage site, which has been a centre of scholarly pursuit and the arts for over 1,400 years, has close historical and constitutional links to the Anglican Church and is indelibly associated with the origins of English Christianity, culture and language, which makes this year's new degree programme in Church Music thoroughly appropriate.

There are other campuses, too: nearby **Broadstairs Campus** (Northwood Road, Broadstairs, CT10 2WA, close to the blue flag award winning beaches of Kent; 01843 609120) - business, computing, digital media, education, health, commercial music, performing arts, policing); **Medway Campus** (30 Pembroke Copurt, ME4 4UF, the historic Chatham Maritime site and picturesque port; 01634 890800) - education, health and policing: Greenwich and Kent universities are, with

TEACHING SURVEY AT A GLANCE	
Avg. UCAS points accepted	**240**
Acceptance rate	**21%**
Overall satisfaction rate	**81%**
Helpful/interested staff	**★★★★**
Small tuition groups	**★★**
Students into graduate jobs	**78%**

Teaching most popular with undergraduates:
American & Australasian Studies (100%), Biology & related sciences, English, Geographical Studies (97%), History, Human & Social Geography (97%), Languages, Music, Sociology, Social Policy & Anthropology, Theology.

Teaching least popular with undergraduates:
Film, Creative Arts & Design (64%), Media Studies (61%).

On campus, student parking is only available at Broadstairs, Medway or Salomons Campuses.

FEES, BURSARIES

UK & EU Fees, 2011-12: £3,375 p.a. Bursaries worth £900 and £560 are available to students on the

SUBJECT AREAS (%)

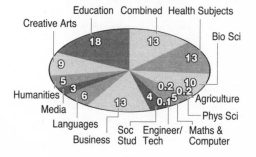

Education Combined Health Subjects
Creative Arts
Bio Sci
18   13
13
9
5
10
Humanities   3   6   0.2   0.2
Media   13   4   0.15   0.2   Agriculture
Phys Sci
Languages
Business   Soc   Engineer/   Maths &
Stud   Tech   Computer

RESEARCH EXCELLENCE

% of Canterbury's research that is
4* (World-class) or **3*** (Internationally rated):

	4*	3*
Allied Health Professions	0%	5%
Education	10%	25%
Sports-Related Studies	0%	20%
English	0%	20%
Theology	0%	20%
History	0%	30%
Music	10%	20%

usual means-test basis. There are also Music scholarships of £100-£300 and scholarships totaling £4,000 have recently been awarded to talented drummers under a scheme set up by former Clash drummer, Nicky 'Topper' Headon. In addition, scholarships are offered across a range of sports. (www.canterbury.ac.uk/sportscholarships/available-scholarships.asp)

STUDENT PROFILE

Canterbury lead the way with their policy to encourage students into higher education who would only a few years ago not have considered it. There is a 40% intake from social classes 4-7 and 62% of undergraduates are mature. There is a 'Progression Accord' scheme with around 20 Schools and Academies in the Kent and Medway area to spread the word at that level too. Generally, there's a preponderance of local, new-to-uni families entering the uni, but as a gateway to the rest of the UK and the continent, there is also a thriving European and international student population of more than 1,300 souls, representing cultures from across the world. Indeed, the very scattered nature of Canterbury's student body defies any attempt at a more searching analysis than that. From spring 2011, through the Partnerships and Widening Participation office, they will be offering a range of subjects through 'Gateway'. A student who successfully completes the short course, including an assignment, will be given 20 UCAS equivalent points, which they may use to support their entry onto one of the programmes at the University.

ACADEMIA & JOBS

There are now five faculties: Arts & Humanities, Business & Management, Education, Health & Social Care, and Social & Applied Sciences. For the latter, with their education and development in Clinical Psychology and Clinical Reporting, they are considered one of the best in the country. See Campus above for subject allocation over the campuses.

The flagship Library and Student Services Centre, Augustine House, was opened in Canterbury in September 2009, providing a single point of access for all student facing services and state-of-the-art library resources. In addition, the Drill Hall Library at Medway provides 90,000 items, 400 computers and 250 study spaces for Canterbury, and students from Greenwich and Kent universities who share the site.

Notably, Canterbury continues to be the largest centre of higher education in Kent for the public services - notably teacher training, nursing, policing, health and social care. Its Department of Media has a strong reputation within the industry and close links with major media companies and corporations.

Broadstairs Campus is a designated Apple and Adobe Accredited Training Centre. Students are able to take additional professional qualifications that are certified by these companies alongside their studies, enhancing their employability after graduation.

At Folkestone, performing arts students play an active part in local street festivals and arts programmes, giving valuable first-hand experience with all aspects of performance production.

WHAT IT'S REALLY LIKE

COLLEGE:	
Social Life	★★
Societies	★★
Student Union	★★
Politics	**Left of Centre**
Sport	**Sport-for-all**
Sport facilities	★★
National team position	**79th**
Arts opportunities	**Excellent**
Student newspaper	**Unified**
Student radio	**CSR**
Student television	**Christ Church TV**
2010 Radio Awards	**Gold & Bronze**
Union ents	**Theme nights**
Live venue capacity	**450**
Union societies	**17**
Parking	**Very poor**
CITY:	
Entertainment	★★★
Scene	**Touristy, historic, very studenty; pubs OK**
Town/gown relations	**Good**
Risk of violence	**Average**
Cost of living	**High**
Student concessions	**Adequate**
Survival + 2 nights out	**£80 pw**
Part-time work campus/town	**Average/Good**

The university works extensively with industry and business via academic programmes, consultancy, and funded projects, notably with the NHS, TDA, local councils, Kent Police, Kent Fire & Rescue Service, Learning & Teaching Scotland, Teach First, Children's Workforce Development Council and the London Borough of Newham.

The largest area of employment is Education - many students end up as teachers, most in the Primary sector, but also in Secondary and Higher sectors. Most come to this from the Faculty of Education of course, but sizeable numbers enter from Social Studies, Creative Arts (such as Music, Art, Performing arts), and Biological Sciences.

Courses in subjects allied to Medicine produce virtually the same number of jobs. The newly expanded Medway campus provides health programmes in nursing, radiography, occupational therapy and operating department practice, as well as education programmes in childhood and early years studies. Students can study a range of Foundation Degrees and Postgraduate programmes in health, including Midwifery, and Speech & Language Therapy, and postgraduate programmes in Education. It also offers research opportunities in health topics.

The newly formed Business & Management faculty adds graduate jobs in retail, insurance, accounting and bookkeeping to the picture. While Creative Arts, which incorporates the very popular Music and Performing Arts programmes, almost matches business for jobs and is served by an £8-million Music Centre with a 350-seat concert auditorium, a suite of fully equipped rehearsal and practice rooms, and flexible space that can be used to provide additional areas for teaching and workshops. The BBC has a recording studio based at the University.

The Uni is a significant provider also in other niche areas, such as sport, and advertising.

STUDENT SCENE

Building work has begun on a new accommodation and student centre close to the Canterbury Campus in St George's Place. This is due to open in 2012. The existing Students Union building will be remodelled for music students' use as rehearsal rooms etc.

Meanwhile, from its base in North Holmes Road, CCSU provides a network of more than 500 student representatives, and manages over 50 sports clubs and societies, from the Circus Society to the Entrepreneurial Society and from the Fencing Club to the Lacrosse Clubs, with over 1,000 weekly active members.

Toxic is Canterbury's No. 1 student night, but they go out for that, to city nigthclub **Chill**. It occurs on a Monday when the natives won't be so restless.

ACCOMMODATION	
Student rating	★★
Guarantee to freshers	**1505 available**
Style	**Halls, flats**
Security guard	**Campus**
Shared rooms	**No data**
Internet access	**No data**
Self-catered	**All flats, no halls**
En suite	**Some**
Approx price range pw	**£78.50-£156**
City rent pw	**£73-£160**

Otherwise, in the SU it's classic anthems and old school cheese: quizzes, promotions, giveaways, fancy dress nights - *Pimps & Hookers* - parties, balls. Wednesday is Sports Fed night, where all the teams get horrifically drunk. Thursday is *Frame 25*, student cinema, which shows recent movies on a weekly basis.

There are balls all year round - Freshers', Halloween, Graduation, Christmas - the climax being the Summer Ball with fairground and bands.

Ents at Medway are held at **Coopers**, the bar at the heart of it all - same fare, theme nights, etc. At Broadstairs, it's **Horizons Bar**.

The media provision at HQ in Canterbury had been a bit pathetic, given the focus on media in the curriculum, but now they have *Unified*, a monthly newspaper, CSR, a radio station that broadcasts on 97.4FM and won Gold and Bronze in the 2010 National Student Radio Awards, and CCTV, which broadcasts ton the web - www.ccsu.co.uk - and on SUB screens in the Canterbury SU.

TOWN Writes Dominic Conway: 'Nice big cathedral, old cobbled streets, strong whiff of history in the air and a two hour walk to the beach. That is Canterbury. To accommodate the evident wealth of students there are two clubs (plus some secret ones) and plenty of good bars. Most pubs have music, a dj, or jukebox. **The Penny Theatre** in Northgate has good atmosphere, good music. If you keep your ear to the ground local groups will put on authentic unpretentious rock shows and Whitstable on the coast hides a number of world class musicians playing jazz, blues, and Turkish folk music that will content even the most selective muso. There is also a wide variety of shops and supermarkets to take your pick from. The toughest thing is avoiding the temptation to spend money in one of the many restaurants and café bars that line the streets. Apart from that everything is very simple and easy to find. If you come here you will have everything really: countryside and seaside, but still be near to London.'

SPORT A £5-million pounds sports centre opened recently, with eight badminton courts, a fitness centre and studio. They have 20 acres of sports fields with four football pitches, four tennis courts, and lacrosse and rugby pitches.

PILLOW TALK

A new student centre with 204 single, en-suite bedrooms and 10 three-bedroom family houses around a landscaped outdoor area, complete with an SU café bar, internet café and office space will be opened in 2012 and be managed with wardens and 24-hour security.

Meanwhile, it's the usual catered halls and self-catered flats (some en suite), and self-catered houses. On the Canterbury Campus main site, Davidson, Lang and Temple are en suite, Fynden and Thorne are single rooms with washbasins and catered, but rent quoted does not include meals. Canterbury-based self-catered residences at College Court and Holmes Court are 2 mins from campus. Lanfranc and Oaten Hill are farther, but the latter is a refurbished oast house and much in demand. Newest is the Parham Road Student Village, a 10-min walk from campus, with houses and flats for 3 to 7 students and a new block this year, Amandos Court. Finally, there's Pin Hill, 15 mins away from campus, 5 halls, Ramsey, Coggan, Runcie and Carey (all very episcopal) and Benson House (40 en-suite rooms). Broadstairs and Chatham cmpuses both have self-catered residences.

GETTING THERE

☛ By road: M2 and A2 connect Canterbury to London and beyond.
☛ By coach: London Victoria, 1 hour 45 mins.
☛ By rail: two or three times an hour from London Victoria, Charing Cross and Waterloo East stations. The fast service takes 1 hour 20 mins.

STUDENT CARDIFF - THE CITY

Cardiff is one of the best places to study in Britain. As well as three universities, it has well-situated, cheap housing, lively nights out, friendly people, great shops and hundreds of miles of countryside just a little to the north. And, if there's one thing Cardiff has in its bag of tricks that almost all others in the UK haven't, it is its status as a capital. As a result, a medium-sized city with a similar population to Coventry is loaded with amenities, arts venues, stadia, beautiful civic parks, a world-class research university and everything else you, a naive 18-year-old from the backwoods of some distant shire, could want. And cos it's so small, most of it is easily walkable - result.

SHOPPING

If you ignore the Victorian splendour that marks out many of Cardiff's city centre shops and focus on the dull plastic high street facades of Queen Street you could be in Newcastle, Manchester or any city in the UK. But, if you're willing to wander a bit Cardiff has some of the best shops in the UK. From **Spillers** in the Hayes (Britain's oldest record shop don'tcha know), to **Madame Fromage**, a wondrous land of cheeses and continental meats, in the Castle Arcade.

As any Cardiffian with an ounce of sense will tell you, it's the **Arcades** that house most of Cardiff's best stores. The narrow alleys that splinter various city centre streets are filled with secondhand book shops, vintage and designer clothes stores, cafés and shoe shops. You could live here for years and still discover shops you're sure you've never seen before.

Away from the fun of the arcades, the recently completed **St David's 2** in the Hayes is the place to blow your novelty-sized loan cheque.

FILMS

The best cinema in Cardiff is **Chapter Arts** in deepest, darkest Canton. Canton's actually a lovely part of the city, but it's a good 20-minute walk from the city centre, so 90% of students won't bother with it. You should; this converted school-turned arts complex has one of the best bars in the city and shows films that wouldn't get near a multiplex.

More conventionally there is the huge, and dependable, **Cineworld** megaplex which has 3 floors of screens, 2 bars, and means to sate any culinary desires you have, as long as they involve hot dogs and gulp-sized colas. Ditto **Vue**, which is lodged in some godawful leisure complex glued onto the **Millennium Stadium**. There's a big **UCI** down in the Bay too. So Cardiff, if you're one for the motion pictures, is super.

SPORT

Cardiff Bay - the International Sports Village now offers an ice rink, a 50m swimming pool as well as the first on-demand white water rafting and canoe centre in the UK. There are also plans for a real-snow ski dome and sports arena. The Village will also be home to new casinos, hotels, restaurants and a new 400ft viewing tower that will offer views across South Wales and the Bristol Channel.

ARTS

Cardiff's capital status means it gets more arts money pumped into it than a Tracey Emin cash machine exhibit. With too many art galleries to mention, it's probably best you stop by the **National Museum and Art Gallery** (which is free) and let them point you in the direction of other galleries in the city.

The New Theatre is a good stop for standard touring fare and the occasional big budget local show but the city is also home to smaller local theatres like the **Sherman** on Senghennydd Road, which put on shows by local companies as well as small tours and comedy.

Ah, stand-up, a great place for you to show-off that new found campus wit in front of a crowd of literally hundreds with a heckle or too. The Sherman and New Theatre have tonnes of comedy shows throughout the year, but your best bet is **St David's Hall**, which has recently been host to student favourites like Dylan Moran, The Mighty Boosh and Paul Merton. There's also the weekly stand-up show in the students' union as well as **The Glee Club** in the Bay which is host to many a promising chortle merchant.

EATING OUT

Although it has no Michelin stars, Cardiff has many a restaurant for you and your friends to go and have one of those big group meals where one person inevitably doesn't pay and everyone else has to stick an extra quid in. The new Brewery Quarter off St Mary's Street is home to **La Tasca**, **Nando's**, **Hard Rock Café** and many others. It's as safe a bet to take your society chums as it is your parents on a rare visit.

Of course there are plenty of smaller, independent eateries; enough curry houses to smelt you tastebuds (try **Chillis** on Whitchurch Road), enough pub grub to feed a league's worth of hungry rugby players (try the Sunday roast at the **Blackweir** on North Road) and vegetarian options to suit the most hardened carrot muncher (**The Greenhouse** on Woodville Road, for example).

The Bay also offers everything from **Pizza Express** to Turkish to **Harry Ramsden's**. You can stuff yourself before trekking around the fancy new Welsh parliament building or visiting Roald Dahl's old gaff, the **Norwegian Church**.

PUBS

There are, thank goodness, enough pubs to sooth the insistent needs of every kind of student. There are rowdy discount card pubs like the **Woodville** (Cathays Terrace) and the **George** (Macintosh Place), small slightly-traditional, but not quite, pubs like the **Pen & Wig** and **Rummer Tavern**, a smorgasbord of **Wetherspoons**, as well as a few choice, if pricey, city centre watering holes like **Floyds**.

St Mary's Street is the natural home of all the pile 'em high, sell 'em cheap pubs that cause Cardiff to resemble Baghdad on a weekend night. If that's your kind of thing then you'll be thrilled, but if not take the time to explore bars out of the city centre like **Bar En-Route** on Cathays Terrace, the aforementioned Chapter Arts bar and plenty more pubs that aren't full of people dressed for a round of pub golf. Suffice to say, if one of your key aims in exploring higher academia is to consume vault-loads of booze, then Cardiff will service you as well as anywhere.

CLUBS AND LIVE VENUES

Thanks to having venues of almost every size, Cardiff is one of Britain's best cities to catch a gig. Whether it's the noisy and new at **Barfly** and **Clwb Ifor Bach** (or **Welsh Club** as it will quickly become known), the mid-sized rock of the students' union (recent gigs include Bloc Party, Kaiser Chiefs, Panic! At The Disco) or the pomp of the **Cardiff International Arena**, you'll be well catered for. St David's Hall is mainly a classical venue but occasionally hosts the likes of Morrissey. **The Point** at the Bay is a converted church that is probably the city's best small venue, local heroes Super Furry Animals and Stereophonics have played warm-ups there in the not-so-distant past.

If sweaty rock music isn't your thing, and frankly there are better things to do on a Friday night than get your shoes stamped on by Strokes fans in Barfly, you won't struggle to find somewhere to spend your dimes.

All the plastic chain nightclubs are here, **Liquid**, **Jumpin' Jaks**; you name it... But if you check out the likes of super-trendy **Soda**, where Wales's golden couple Charlotte Church and Gavin Henson are regulars, and which is so trendy it doesn't have a sign on the door, you can have a night as good as any in Britain.

Keep an eye out for monthly nights by LAmerica and Cool House which switch residences around the city.

Will Dean

CARDIFF UNIVERSITY

Cardiff University
Cardiff CF10 3AT

TEL 029 2087 4455
FAX 029 2087 4457
EMAIL enquiry@cardiff.ac.uk
WEB www.cardiff.ac.uk

Cardiff Students' Union
Cardiff CF1 3QN

TEL 029 2078 1400
FAX 029 2078 1407
EMAIL studentsunion@cf.ac.uk
WEB www.cardiffstudents.com

VIRGIN VIEW

Cardiff is a tip-top uni academically, with a 4-star rating for staff interest in its students and an average entry requirement (390 points) not as demanding as some.

It is also hugely popular with its students (86% were polled satisfied), and they run a breathlessly active extra-curricular scene.

But, as Lisa Andrews writes, 'You have applied to a number of unis, but the choice has come down to a place at Cardiff or a place at an English university. Which do you go for?'

Wise up. Yoiu should be more concerned whether they want you. What they look for in the personal statement is a sense of the background to an applicant's declared interest in a subject, and what they have read about it. Also any employment, work experience, placement, or voluntary work, connected to it, and the applicant's careers aspirations and long term aims.

Recommended sites include www.visit

> **'So your choice has finally come down to a place at Cardiff or a place at an English university. Which do you go for? Cardiff's all rain, rugby and sheep, right? Wrong.'**

UNIVERSITY/STUDENT PROFILE	
University since	**1883**
Situation/style	**Civic**
Student population	**30010**
Total undergraduates	**20330**
Mature	**38%**
International	**17%**
Male/female ratio	**42:58**
Equality of opportunity:	
state school intake	**85%**
social class 4-7 intake	**23%**
drop-out rate	**5%**

cardiff.com, www.cardiff.ac.uk/stay connected/ (for facebook, twitter and flickr) and www.cardiffstudents.com. Open Days are 9 September 2011 and 25 April 2012.

CAMPUS

Cardiff is a campus in the city, an academic precinct, separate and yet part of the city. A short walk from the classical lines of the main university buildings brings you to the fastest growing capital in Europe. Yet, when you go there what you notice is its compactness and accessibility, its clean lines and the way they have maintained a sense of wide open space. Writes Charlie Callaghan: 'Everything is within walking distance. Cardiff is a pretty small city, though it has more than adequate shops, nightlife and the Millennium Stadium. It is also well connected to the rest of the country by train.'

FEES, BURSARIES

UK & EU Fees, 2011-12: £3,375 p.a. Welsh students get a grant from the Welsh Assembly Government. UK/EU students who are awarded NHS-funded places for Dental Therapy/Hygiene, Nursing, Occupational Therapy, Physiotherapy, Radiography, will be paid by the NHS, who may also pay

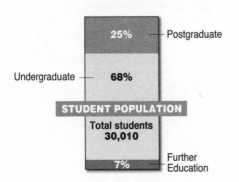

25% — Postgraduate

Undergraduate — 68%

STUDENT POPULATION

Total students 30,010

7% — Further Education

tuition fees for medical and dental students from the fifth year of study. Each Cardiff University Scholarship is worth £3,000. In order to obtain a scholarship you need to achieve grades AAA at A-level (or alternative qualification equivalent) and satisfy all aspects of your offer. In addition, you must have accepted the offer of a place to study from Cardiff on a firm basis by 31st July. Tuition Fees: www.studentfinancewales.co.uk. Bursaries and Scholarships: www.cardiff.ac.uk/scholarships. Sport - www.cf.ac.uk/sport/performance/bursary

STUDENT PROFILE

Writes Lisa Andrews: 'Okay, so if you opt to study at Cardiff, chances are that 9 times out of 10 you'll get soaked on the way to lectures and spend the next hour dripping puddles in your pew. And on match days, it's hard to avoid the Welsh rugby spirit, if only because your quiet local is heaving with red-shirted fans. But with 20,000 undergraduates of 100 nationalities, Cardiff is nothing if not culturally diverse.' The statistics support Lisa's case. This is not a Welsh university, it is a world-class university in Wales, and it's a well-balanced picture, public and state school, rich and poor.

Charlie Callaghan confirms the diversity. 'There are people from all backgrounds and countries. There is no particular dominant group; you get to experience many different people. I have been living with two Pakistani boys this year. Wherever you come from, you will fit in here.'

ACADEMIA & JOBS

Cardiff is part of the flagship GO Wales programme providing work experience placement opportunities during term-time and vacations. Other opportunities to develop employability skills include the Student Enterprise Unit, Student Development Unit, Jobshop and the Student Volunteering Programme.

When one looks at Cardiff's graduate employment figures, it is clear that well over 30% of graduates find work in the health industry (doctors, dentists, nurses, social workers, therapists, radiographers, etc).

Besides degrees in medicine and dentistry, important elements of Cardiff's presence in the health industry are its biologists and pharmacists, occupational therapists and ophthalmic opticians. There's a £20-million teaching facility for the School of Optometry and Vision Sciences, and now the Cochrane Building is a brand new building offering facilities for all five healthcare schools on what is know as the Heath Park Campus.

Another impressive element of graduate employment lies in the Civil Service and

TEACHING SURVEY AT A GLANCE

Avg. UCAS points accepted	**390**
Acceptance rate	**15%**
Overall satisfaction rate	**86%**
Helpful/interested staff	★★★★
Small tuition groups	★★
Students into graduate jobs	**77%**

Teaching most popular with undergraduates:
Education, Accounting, Anatomy, Physiology & Pathology, Architecture, Biology & related sciences, Business, Celtic Studies, Chemistry, Civil Engineering, Engineering & Technology, Languages, Finance, French Studies, Geology, History, Law, Maths, Mechanical Engineering, Medical Technology, Molecular Biology, Music, Ophthalmics, Media, Social Studies, Pharmacy (99%), Philosophy, Physical Geography & Environmental Science, Physics & Astronomy, Planning, Politics, Psychology, Social Policy, Sociology, Theology, Zoology.

Teaching least popular with undergraduates:
Italian Studies (62%), Medicine (58%).

government administration, where Social Studies (Politics, Economics, etc), the Town & City Planning degrees, and Languages, and Historical & Philosophical Studies play their part.

Cardiff is also strong in Architecture, Engineering Design, Construction and Civil Engineering.

Another strength is in Banking and Accountancy. There is a whole host of international courses in Accounting, Economics, and Business Administration, and the Business Management Human Resources degree yields excellent job figures in the industry. The

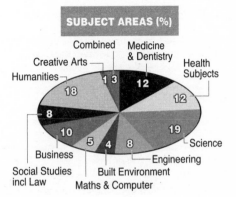

SUBJECT AREAS (%)

Combined 3, Medicine & Dentistry 12, Health Subjects 12, Creative Arts 1, Humanities 18, Science 19, Engineering 8, Built Environment 4, Maths & Computer 5, Social Studies incl Law 10, Business 8

RESEARCH EXCELLENCE

% of Cardiff's research that is
4* *(World-class) or* **3*** *(Internationally rated):*

	4*	3*
Cardiovascular Medicine	5%	35%
Cancer Studies	10%	55%
Infection and Immunology	10%	40%
Hospital Clinical Subjects	0%	25%
Primary Care	5%	60%
Psychiatry, Neuroscience, & Clinical Psychology	20%	60%
Dentistry	15%	50%
Nursing and Midwifery	15%	30%
Allied Health Professions	20%	35%
Pharmacy	15%	40%
Biological Sciences	15%	40%
Environmental Sciences	15%	55%
Chemistry	10%	50%
Physics	5%	45%
Pure Mathematics	5%	35%
Computer Science	20%	50%
Electrical and Electronic Eng.	10%	40%
Civil Engineering	25%	65%
Mechanical, Aeronautical & Manufacturing Engineering	20%	45%
Architecture/Built Environment	20%	45%
Town and Country Planning	30%	35%
Archaeology	15%	40%
Business and Management	35%	35%
Law	25%	35%
Sociology	25%	30%
Psychology	25%	45%
European Studies	15%	30%
Celtic Studies	15%	40%
English	35%	25%
Philosophy	5%	25%
Theology	5%	30%
History	10%	35%
Media	45%	30%
Music	15%	55%

curriculum makes more than a few tax experts and consultants too.

Defence is another key graduate employment area, and recruits from a wide range of subjects.

Their Computer Science degrees feed graduates into software consultancy in particular, Media and Languages into Radio and TV in particular, though by far the most Language students from Cardiff end up in the Civil Service, and in publishing, specialist retail, the hotel and restaurant trade, personnel, higher education, and work in our diverse British communities.

In Journalism they have one of a handful of industry-respected postgrad degrees that many careers advisers will recommend you take before you begin the search for full-time employment. Meanwhile, their BA Journalism, Film and Broadcasting degrees are good enough to make them an attractive proposition in journalism anyway. Student media helps. They have a newspaper, magazine, radio and TV stations, see Social Scene below.

There's also a fair smattering of graduates going into artistic literary areas, again from the Languages Department and Historical & Philosophical Studies, a department which also creates a steady flow of graduates to archival work in libraries and museums.

In Law Cardiff is one of eight institutions where the Bar Vocational Course (BVC) may be undertaken (essential for barristers). Also, non-Law graduates may opt for a 2-year full-time or 3-year part-time Senior Status Law degree here. There's also a strong line into the Police from Languages, Biological Sciences and Business depts.

In research Cardiff is world-renowned in Psychiatry, Neuroscience & Clinical Psychology, Computer Science, Engineering, Planning, Law, Sociology, Psychology, and especially in English. Many other Cardiff departments achieved 4-star ratings, but in these, world-class research is being undertaken between 20% and 35% of the time.

The College of Medicine campus has a 920-bed hospital. The 5/6-year MB BCh degree combines academic study well with clinical and communication skills. There's even a pre-med Foundation for Arts A level candidates or those with one Science and Arts. A-Levels must include two science GCE A level subjects out of Chemistry, Biology, Physics and Maths (one being Chemistry or Biology at grade A.) Chemistry or Biology required at AS. If applicants offer two or more Maths subjects at AS or A level, only one will count towards meeting the conditions of an offer. General Studies is not acceptable at AS or A level, nor is Critical Thinking acceptable at A level. You will be required to sit for UKCAT.

SOCIAL SCENE

STUDENTS' UNION The union is a top-class venue under continual enhancement. The **Taf bar** has recently been extended and changed from olde worlde style to a stylish modern design. Evenings there inevitably lead to nights in **Solus**, the union's 1,800-capacity, custom-built nightclub with an immense dance floor and state-of-the-art sound and lighting systems. With an eclectic music policy crossing the spectrum from dub-step to cheese, few would dispute that Solus offers some of Cardiff city's best nights out.

Then there's **Great Hall**, a major concert hall with top-line acts. The adjoining all-day café-bar used to transform itself into **Seren Las**, an intimate club by night. It still has a stage area, but is now called **CF10** and acts much the same after hours - as a chill-out room during club and gig nights, as well as being a popular haunt for club and society ents.

The Union, which has had an amazing facelift recently - a 3-phase programme costing some £6 million - is not just popular for its bargain booze and carefree clubbing. Writes Lisa. 'Besides the regular 6-night ents programme, it is home to 60 sports

ACCOMMODATION

Student rating	★★★★
Guarantee to freshers	**100%**
Style	**Halls, flats**
Security guard	**All**
Shared rooms	**Some**
Internet access	**All**
Self-catered	**Most**
En suite	**Most**
Approx price range pw	**£65-£91**
City rent pw	**£55+**

WHAT IT'S REALLY LIKE

UNIVERSITY:

Social Life	★★★★★
Societies	★★★★
Student Union services	★★★★★
Politics	**Activity high**
Sport	**60 clubs**
National team position	**15th**
Sport facilities	★★★
Arts opportunities	**Excellent**
Student newspaper	**Gair Rhydd**
Student radio	**XPress Radio**
Student Radio	**CUTV**
Student magazine	**Quench**
Guardian 2008 Awards	**Mag. of the Year**
Nightclub	**Solus**
Live venue	**Great Hall**
Bars	**Taf, CF10**
Union ents	**6 nights a week**
Union societies	**150**
Parking	**Adequate**

CITY:

Entertainment	★★★★
Scene	**Buzzing**
Town/gown relations	**OK**
Risk of violence	**Low**
Cost of living	**Low**
Student concessions	**Excellent**
Survival + 2 nights out	**£80 pw**
Part-time work campus/town	**Excellent**

clubs and 150 societies. High on the list are the Film Society, Act One, for drama, LGB, the lesbian/gay group, SHAG, sexual health awareness group, etc. There's the aforesaid student newspaper, *Gair Rhydd* and Xpress Radio, both award-winning in past years, and the magazine *Quench*, and now CUTV. Finally, Act One, the drama soc is especially popular, putting on productions at the **Sherman Theatre** next door.

It's everybody to their own: 'Outside of lectures, I usually go into town, as the clubs are better than in the Union. Also, I participate in Model United Nations, the highlight being the Harvard Conference,' writes Charlie Callaghan. 'And I volunteer for an organisation aiding refugees and help organise a hip hop night at a bar in town.'

SPORT All traditional sports are catered for and the uni is a major contender in the BUSA leagues - overall 15th nationally in team sports last year. The Talybont Sports Centre has a £2 million multi-purpose sports hall and there are 33 acres of pitches. Olympic Football will take place at the Millennium Stadium during the 2012 games. The University has been selected to be a training venue for the squads.

PILLOW TALK

Talybont is en suite, own bar, comprehensive sports facilities, and next to a 24-hour Tesco. Writes Charlie: 'It's the largest, very good accommodation, very sociable atmosphere, but 20 mins from uni.

The lazy should avoid University Hall, a good half-hour away and the free bus service isn't so free - Uni Hall rent is a few hundred pounds extra to subsidise it. All other halls are a walk away. Newest to their portfolio is Allensbank, likewise en-suite. All residences come with internet access and security.

GETTING THERE
☛ By road: M4/J32, A470 signposted Cardiff or M4/J29, A48(M)/A48 and A470 signposted City.
☛ By rail: London Paddington, 2:30.
☛ By air: Cardiff airport for USA and inland.
☛ By coach: London, 3:00; Manchester, 5:40.

UNIVERSITY OF CENTRAL LANCASHIRE

University of Central Lancashire
Preston
Lancs PR1 2HE

TEL 01772 201201
FAX 01772 894939
EMAIL enquiries@uclan.ac.uk
WEB www.uclan.ac.uk

Central Lancashire Students' Union
Fylde Road
Preston PR1 2TQ

TEL 01772 893000
FAX 01772 894970
EMAIL suinformation@uclan.ac.uk
WEB www.uclansu.co.uk

VIRGIN VIEW

*T*he University traces its origins back to
1828, when Preston Institution for the
Diffusion of Knowledge was founded.
Growth in student numbers makes it one of
the largest universities in the country, with
some 30,000 students in total and around
25,000 undergraduates.

They are known as a caring university.
'The i' is a one-stop-shop (info centre), a first
point of contact for such as financial
support, council tax enquires, international
student guidance, to NUS card distribution,
accommodation and disabled student advice.

A fourth-year health student, confined in
a wheelchair since infancy, went out of her
way to praise its accessibility to the disabled,
the helpfulness of staff, and for the chance
they gave her of the 'few wild years' she had
enjoyed there.

Wild indeed, for UCLan's approach to the
social side of things is legendary. More than
a decade ago the nightclub was hailed by
media critics as diverse as The Observer
and DJ Magazine as, 'Best student dance
club in the UK,' and 'One of the Top 30 clubs
in the country,' respectively.

Ultimately, however, the uni is a modern
university dedicated to getting graduates jobs,
and recruiting from social groups new to the
idea of going to university. One result of its
open access policy has been a wild drop-out
rate.

UCLan offers courses specifically
designed to ease students back into education
(51% are mature), aimed at those motivated
to learn and participate in higher education,
but who may not have had the opportunity
to follow a traditional academic route.

Special 'Accreditation of Prior Learning'
is offered to students who may have
sufficient past experience or alternative
qualifications. See www.uclan.ac.uk/apl for
more details. Visit www.uclan.ac.uk/
opendays to find out the date of the next
open day. Or get into UCLan via facebook or
twitter: www.facebook.com/official.uclan,
www.twitter.com/UCLanfor.

UNIVERSITY/STUDENT PROFILE	
University since	**1992**
Situation/style	**Civic**
Student population	**28130**
Total undergraduates	**24595**
Mature	**51%**
International	**14%**
Male/female ratio	**43:57**
Equality of opportunity:	
state school intake	**98%**
social class 4-7 intake	**44%**
drop-out rate	**17%**

CAMPUSES

The main campus is in Preston. Over £120 million
has recently been invested in new buildings and
facilities, including a second campus which opened
at Burnley, and soom two more at West Lakes and
Llangollen.

Burnley Campus (Princess Way,Burnley,BB12
0EQ; 01282 733400) brings hgher education to the
town for the first time. On offer are degrees in Art,
Design and Fashion (including Music and
Performance); Business; Community Leadership;
Computing, Engineering and Science; Education;
Health & Social Care; Languages; Law, Policing; and
Sport. There's a Sports Centre, two food outlets and
a Students' Union Resource Centre.

FEES, BURSARIES

UK & EU Fees, 2011-12: £3,375 p.a. Generous
maintenance grants are currently available for
students whose household incomes are below a

certain amount. These do not have to be paid back. www.uclan.ac.uk/fees.

Scholarships are reviewed on an annual basis. View www.uclan.ac.uk/information/prospective _students/fees_and_finance/scholarships_bursarie s.php.

All UCLan students who continue on to postgraduate study at UCLan will be eligible for 20% off the cost of their postgraduate tuition fees.

STUDENT PROFILE

None of the Radley/Eton brigade are to be found here. UCLan is a 1992 'new' university recruiting a large number of undergraduates from the state sector (98%) and from social groups who haven't traditionally benefited from a university education'. No-one cares a damn either way.

ACADEMIA & JOBS

Schools of study are: Art, Design and Performance; Lancashire Business School; Forensic and Investigative Sciences; Built and Natural Environment; Languages and International Studies; Computing, Engineering and Physical Sciences; Pharmacy and Biomedical Sciences; Education and Social Sciences; Lancashire Law School; Social Work; Psychology; Health; Dentistry (postgraduate only); Sport, Tourism and the Outdoors; Journalism, Media and Communication.

They are adjudged world-class for research for such as, Physics, Architecture (Surveying also part of the degree provision), Archaeology, Business, Social Work, Psychology (Neuropsychology and Neurosciences degrees as well), Linguistics (this got the highest praise), History, and Media.

In the undergraduate provision Media is also a traditional strength. , as is Sport: they have more graduates going into the sports industry than any other university bar Cardiff UWIC. The Sports Journalism BA (Hons) course has become the first undergraduate sports journalism degree in the UK to receive full accreditation from the Broadcast Journalism Training Council (BJTC). A new £17 million state-of-the-art indoor sports centre is currently being built on campus, due to open in Spring 2011.

But what do students think? In the National Survey, 83% were satisfied with the teaching particularly in Education, Business Studies, Communications & Information Studies (94%), Drama, Engineering & Technology, English Studies, Forensic & Archaeological Science, Historical & Philosophical Studies, Journalism, Law, Management, Maths & Statistics (99%), Mechanical Engineering, Physical Geography & Environmental Science (96%), Physical Science, Psychology, Publicity Studies (95%), Social Policy,

TEACHING SURVEY AT A GLANCE	
Avg. UCAS points accepted	**260**
Acceptance rate	**23%**
Overall satisfaction rate	**83%**
Helpful/interested staff	★★★
Small tuition groups	★★
Students into graduate jobs	**75%**

Teaching most popular with undergraduates:
Education, Business Studies, Communications & Information Studies (94%), Drama, Engineering & Technology, English Studies, Forensic & Archaeological Science, Historical & Philosophical Studies, Journalism, Law, Management, Maths & Statistics (99%), Mechanical Engineering, Physical Geography & Environmental Science (96%), Physical Science, Psychology, Publicity Studies (95%), Social Policy, Sociology, Sports Science.

Teaching least popular with undergraduates:
Architecture, Building & Planning (66%)

Sociology, Sports Science.

Of all the faculties, Arts is where the jobs come thickest and fastest, particularly in the area of fashion, both in design work and in retail. Expectations are that the Fashion Entrepreneurship degree helps. UCLan is renowned for helping graduates start their own businesses. The results of the HEBCIS report rank UCLan top in the North West and second nationally for the volume of graduate start-up businesses it supports in the Business Incubation Unit, which totalled 126 last year. But there is a huge variety of disiplines in the faculty: Fine Art, Ceramics, Acting, Music (Practice, Production, Theatre), Creative & Cultural Industries, Advertising, as well as Asian Fashion, Creative Fashion Knit, and Fashion Promotion: all carefully aimed at making their graduates busy in the world of work.

The Lancashire Business School comes next,

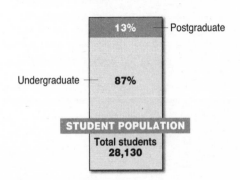

13% — Postgraduate

Undergraduate — **87%**

STUDENT POPULATION
Total students
28,130

RESEARCH EXCELLENCE

% of Central Lancashire's research that is
4* *(World-class) or* **3*** *(Internationally rated):*

	4*	3*
Nursing and Midwifery	10%	40%
Allied Health Professions	10%	10%
Physics	5%	35%
General Eng., Mineral, Mining	0%	30%
Architecture/Built Environment	5%	35%
Archaeology	5%	15%
Business and Management	5%	25%
Law	0%	15%
Politics	0%	5%
Social Work, Policy & Admin.	10%	30%
Psychology	5%	15%
Education	0%	5%
English	0%	20%
Linguistics	15%	25%
History	10%	25%
Art and Design	0%	15%
Media Studies	15%	20%

SUBJECT AREAS (%)

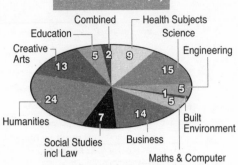

again putting graduates into retail in specialist stores, but also into many other areas.

Nursing (including Mental Health), Midwifery, Health Informatics, Paramedic Practices, Deaf Studies, Human Biology, Acupuncture, etc., then account for 11% of graduate jobs.

The well-known Journalism and other Media degrees, such as Media Production and TV Production, account for about 5% of graduate jobs, in publishing (mostly), television of course, advertising, and a whole host of other sectors.

The sport degrees that score so well are of a wide variety, including Coaching, Development, Management, PR, Technology, Therapy, and degrees with names like Adventure Sports Coaching and Strength & Conditioning.

> *'The University isn't just about Bounce Heaven and Goodgreef or nites by BPZ. Some select their university for academic ideals, and Central Lancashire does great things in this field too.'*

Finally, quirkily, note their Astrophysics degrees and that UCLan is the only UK institution that will be collaborating closely with NASA and its international partners in the launch of a new solar observing satellite named the Solar Dynamics Observatory (SDO).

SOCIAL SCENE

STUDENTS' UNION Step into the award-winning, £6.5-million Student Union building. Enjoy all that the new £15.3 media Centre promises. In these two areas - hedonism and media - UCLan have always reigned supreme.

Source is the Student Union bar in the centre of campus. **53 Degrees** is the venue and club, Brook Street, Preston, the home for clubbing in Lancashire. The building has a 1,500 capacity venue on the ground floor and a more intimate 400 capacity club upstairs. Downstairs is the main venue. Bands that have played here include Ian Brown, The Streets, Dizzee Rascal, Klaxons, Gossip, Super Furry Animals, Happy Mondays, The Coral, The Buzzcocks, The Futureheads, Gomez, The Stranglers, Just Jack, Calvin Harris, Starsailor, Reverend & the Makers, to name a few. Upstairs has featured hotly tipped acts like The Twang, Little Man Tate, The View, Jack Penate, Maximo Park, Hard Fi, The Hoosiers, The Rascals, Maccabees, Team Waterpolo, Iglu & Hartly and many more. But there are fantastic clubnights too, like *Bounce Heaven* and *Goodgreef*, nights by BPZ, Self Help, Back to Bowlers, Hardcore Sensation, Dubstep featuring Stenchman, as well as weekly club night *Promo*.

Rescuing you from *Okey Dokey Karaoke* quiz nights, toga parties, *Aftershock Frenzy*, and compelling comedy from Silky and the like, is Thursday's *Premo*, the place to be (drinks £1 each) before the big night out, *Promo*, at 53 Degrees. Friday is *Crash @* Source, wheeling and dealing as the prices of drinks rise and fall throughout the night - 'if the Crash happens you can be quids in for your favourite drink!'. Saturday is *The Mash Up*, a mix of pop, indie, retro, '90s, dance and r'n'b tunes.

Yet bigger news is *The Worx* - 'everything old

WHAT IT'S REALLY LIKE

UNIVERSITY:

Social Life	★★★
Societies	★★★
Student Union services	★★★★★
Politics	**Interest low**
Sport	**Competitive**
National team position	**37th**
Sport facilities	★★★
Arts	**Drama, dance, film, music, all good, art excellent**
Student newspaper	**Pluto**
Student radio station	**Frequency 1350**
Student television	**PSTV**
Nightclub	**53 Degrees**
Bars	**Source**
Union ents	**Massive**
Union societies	**33**
Parking	**Adequate**

CITY:

Entertainment	★★★
Scene	**Good clubs, excellent pubs**
Town/gown relations	**Good**
Risk of violence	**Low**
Cost of living	**Average**
Student concessions	**Good**
Survival + 2 nights out	**£50 pw**
Part-time work campus/town	**Good/average**

benefit of students to the local economy, and are very accommodating - loads of student discounts, tons of shops, a range of restaurants and two large-screen cinemas mean that there's always something to do when the workload lessens. Staff in venues all over town are always friendly.'

SPORT Thirty clubs (counting Cheerleading). They came 37th position nationally with their teams. A £12-million outdoor multi-sport complex is sited two miles from campus. **The Preston Sports Arena** has 8-lane athletics track, 5 grass pitches, 2 floodlit all-weather, 4 floodlit netball and tennis courts, 1.5 km cycling circuit, 7 floodlit training grids, plus 18-station fitness suite. There's also the on-campus, recently refurbished **Foster Sports Centre** for badminton, tennis, basketball, volleyball, soccer, fencing, martial arts, etc. And a new £17-million

ACCOMMODATION

Student rating	★★★★
Guarantee to freshers	**100%**
Style	**Halls, flats**
Security guard	**All**
Shared rooms	**Some**
Internet access	**All halls, some flats**
Self-catered	**All**
En suite	**Some**
Approx price range pw	**£45-£81**
Town rent pw	**£40-£65**

skool to suit all needs, acid, hardcore, Italian, piano and uplifting anthems'. Coming soon are *Pendulum* live at 53 Degrees, and when the *Radar Tour* takes to the road in the summer, the NME's annual showcase of new sounds.

There's also *Stand and Deliver Comedy Club*, Lancashire's largest comedy club fortnightly on Fridays, with such as Dave Spikey, Alan Carr, Ross Noble and Phoenix Nights star, Justin Moorhouse.

There are 31 student societies. Student media currently includes Frequency Radio, Preston Student Television (PSTV), and of course *Pluto*, the award-winning student newspaper that's been around for more than 25 years.

TOWN 'With something like 40- 50 pubs within 5 mins walk of the university,' writes Neil Doughty, 'there's always somewhere to hide away out of the rain. With 20,000+ students making up a sixth of the in-term residents of Preston, the locals are well aware of the

state-of-the-art indoor sports centre is currently being built on campus, due to open in 2011.

PILLOW TALK

They guarantee to assist all freshers to find accommodation either in uni-owned halls and houses or privately owned ones. None of the uni residences are catered, there's a top-up smartcard that students can use to pay for their meals at refectories around campus. Leighton Hall, a private hall with 350 en-suite rooms and studios, opened recently. Get on to it quick.

GETTING THERE

☛ By road: travelling south, M6 (J32/M55), exit 1 (A6); travelling north, M6/J31, A59.
☛ By rail: London, 3:00; Manchester Oxford Road, 50 mins; Lancaster, 23 mins.
☛ By coach: London, 5:15; Liverpool, 1:00.

UNIVERSITY OF CHESTER

The University of Chester
Parkgate Road
Chester CH1 4BJ

TEL 01244 511000
FAX 01244 511300
EMAIL enquiries@chester.ac.uk
WEB www.chester.ac.uk

Chester Students' Union
University of Chester
Chester
Cheshire CH1 4BJ

TEL 01244 513399
FAX 01224 392866
EMAIL csupres@chester.ac.uk
WEB www.chestersu.ac.uk

VIRGIN VIEW

Established by William Gladstone in 1839 as the first teacher-training college in the country with a Church of England foundation, Chester University comes out of Chester College, which became University College Chester in 1996, before being granted full university status in 2005.

Chester is a Roman town in the north west of England, with a picturesque centre, a thriving tourism industry and a lowish cost of living.

The university's curriculum has expanded beyond teaching education into Health Care, Applied Sciences, Humanities, Social Sciences, Performance Arts & Media, and Business & Management.

In the 2011 Times Higher Education's Student Experience Survey, they came 43rd nationally overall, but 8th for helpful and interested staff, a feature which is already telling in the class of degree being awarded.

Open Days in 2011 fall on 11 June and 1 October (Chester Campus); 8 October (Warrington and Riverside campuses).

CAMPUS

The uni is now a three-campus beast. **Chester Campus** is a 32-acre site, 5 mins walk from the city centre, and has undergone a variety of developments over the last 18 months. New facilities include a high-tech fitness suite, a modern School of Health and Social Care building, a large state-of-the art multi-purpose building featuring a brasserie, computer suite, conference facilities and high specification teaching areas. Next to campus is a newly built block of self-catered apartments, offering en-suite rooms.

Warrington Campus is set on a 35-acre site a short bus ride away and has recently benefited from general improvements and refurbishments,

UNIVERSITY/STUDENT PROFILE	
University since	**2005**
Situation/style	**City campus**
Student population	**13485**
Undergraduates	**10270**
Mature	**53%**
International	**3%**
Male/female ratio	**29:71**
Equality of opportunity:	
state school intake	**98%**
social class 4-7 intake	**40%**
drop-out rate	**11%**

including a modern dining area, new facilities within the Department of Media and a brand new Students' Union building. There is also a new Lifelong Learning Centre, incorporating new learning resources (libraries etc), learning support services and CITS (computer management/support etc), together with a café, lounge area and seminar rooms. A site has also been cleared for a new £2.9 million Business Management and IT Centre.

An impressive reputation has been built at Warrington Campus with production courses and links to a range of media organisations including the BBC and Granada Television. In addition, Business, Computer Science, Media, and Sport & Exercise Sciences are all at least part-based at Warrington.

During the summer of 2010 they purchased and renovated Riverside campus from the local council, as new home of the faculties of Health and Social Care and Education and Children's Services. It's a 25 minute walk from the main Chester campus.

There's no student parking for students, but a comprehensive train and bus service lies within close walking distance of the main campus, and cycling is actively encouraged by the University.

FEES, BURSARIES

UK & EU Fees, 2011-12: £3,375 p.a. There is a University of Chester Bursary for students in receipt of full HE Maintenance grant. Two-thirds of the student body receive it. There's also the Chester

Sports Scholarship Scheme, sport being a defining element of student life at Chester. See www.chester.ac.uk/undergraduate/moneymatters.html.

STUDENT PROFILE

The stats tell us that there is a high number of undergraduates (36%) from backgrounds not traditionally associated with going to university, and many are mature (i.e. over-21 at registration). Very few, only 3%, come here from the independent school sector. It is also a largely female undergraduate population, once described by the uni as an 'overwhelming majority', but if you're a bloke you may find you'll be able to cope.

Says Alastair Coles: 'If you are considering coming to Chester, you are most likely white, Northern, female, not the sort of person who got two As and a B at A level, and probably sporty.'

The lean to female is down to the numbers studying Nursing, Midwifery and Education - Primary.

Finally, very few of Chester's undergraduates come from outside the EU. It is a notably local scene. When it was a mere university college, this was just as true, but always notably a tight, compact

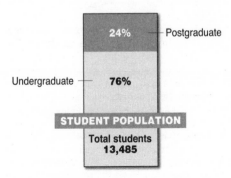

Postgraduate 24%

Undergraduate 76%

STUDENT POPULATION

Total students
13,485

unit, with a friendly and relaxed atmosphere. This is unlikely to change.

ACADEMIA & JOBS

The uni has been re-organised into seven schools of study: Applied & Health Sciences; Business, Management & Law, Arts & Media, Education, Health & Social Care, and Social Sciences.

Departments are Biological Sciences, Business, Computer, Education, English, Fine Art, Geography, Health & Social Care, History and Archaeology, Law, Leadership & Management, Maths, Media, Modern Languages, Performing Arts, Psychology, Social & Communication Studies, Sport and Exercise Sciences, Theology & Religious Studies, Work Related Studies.

In the recent countrywide survey of Britain's

TEACHING SURVEY AT A GLANCE

Avg. UCAS points accepted	**260**
Acceptance rate	**14%**
Overall satisfaction rate	**78%**
Helpful/interested staff	★★★★★
Small tuition groups	★★★
Students into graduate jobs	**78%**

Teaching most popular with undergraduates:
Animal Science, Archaeology (96%), English (96%), European Languages, Geographical Studies, History, Iberian Studies (96%), Imaginative Writing, Maths, Psychology, Social Work, Sports Science, Theology.

Teaching least popular with undergraduates:
Media Studies (58%), Education (59%).

research provision, Chester managed four subjects in the world-class category. History did best, with 15% of its research accorded world-class status, and 30% of international significance. The others were Performing Arts, English, and Sport.

Teaching most popular with undergraduates is in Animal Science, Archaeology (96% gave the thumbs-up), English (again 96%), European Languages, Geographical Studies, History, Iberian Studies (96%), Imaginative Writing, Maths, Psychology, Social Work, Sports Science, Theology.

Most students will undertake the Work Based Learning (WBL) module in Level 5 (Year 2) of their degree programme, which involves spending 5 weeks working for an organisation followed by submission of a reflective report.

Law is a relatively new part of the curriculum, offered both as single and combined honours. The department has close links with the Chester Centre of the College of Law, where LPC and Graduate

RESEARCH EXCELLENCE

% of Chester's research that is
4* *(World-class)* or **3*** *(Internationally rated):*

	4*	3*
Allied Health Professions	0%	15%
Applied Mathematics	0%	15%
Geography & Enviro. Studies	0%	10%
Social Work,l Policy & Admin.	0%	15%
Sports-Related Studies	5%	20%
English	5%	15%
Theology	0%	30%
History	15%	30%
Art and Design	0%	5%
Drama, Dance, Performing Arts	5%	25%

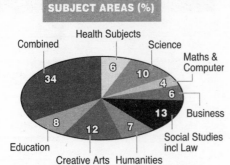

SUBJECT AREAS (%)

Health Subjects
Combined — Science
Maths & Computer
34
6 — 10 — 4
6
13 — Business
8 — 12 — 7
Education — Social Studies incl Law
Creative Arts — Humanities

Awards. There's no student paper at the moment, just a termly one put out by the university. But they promise a new one called *The Source* before long.

SPORT Sport is of obsessive extra-curricular interest on the Chester campus, and there are constantly evolving facilities to support it, including a refurbished all-weather hockey pitch, a 25m pool, a fitness suite and sports hall - all part of a £5-million development.

Chester is one of 90 educational establishments across the country delivering sporting services to a variety of Talented Athlete Scholarship Scheme (TASS) athletes. The Uni came 74th nationally in the BUSA team sports last year.

TOWN Moving away from the campus into Chester itself, you'll find one of the prettiest historic city centres in the country. A big plus is that in comparison to most, it is also relatively cheap. Popular student haunts are the Odeon cinema, the Gateway Theatre, and over sixty pubs, most within walking distance.

PILLOW TALK

There is a variety of accommodation available to freshers: halls, flats, houses, on-campus, off-campus,

Diplomas can be studied for - the College of Law is the largest legal training and education establishment in Europe.

The School of Health and Social Care is the major provider of pre-registration nursing and midwifery education across Cheshire and the Wirral. It also offers a wide range of undergraduate and postgraduate programmes for other health care professionals.

SOCIAL SCENE

STUDENTS UNION There are two Union centres, one for each campus. The new bar at Warrington (Wazza) is **Fu Bar** (was Scholars). It hosts live bands and *T.P.I. Wednesday* (beach party time, grass skirts at the ready, with DJ Paul Webber, 8pm-1am); also games and quiz nights, and there's a re-launch of classic alternative night, *Deckheadz*. There's also *Padgates* club night on Saturday.

At the Chester campus there is a fractious history attached to the fun and games. Some years ago the so-called Small Hall venue had to be closed down. It was so popular that massive queues would form outside, and it fell victim to noise-pollution protestors. These problems still characterise student life on campus, judging by the SU's 'Shhh' campaign to highlight problems caused to neighbours.

Still, students have now moved into a new phase with the opening of a £2-million, purpose-built Student Union building. **CH1** is th stylish bar, close to all the halls and next to the canteen. *SU Friday* is the imaginatively titled cheese night of the week. Then there's *Cruise* (Mondays), *Fusion* (drum 'n bass fused with dubstep), *Dead Beat* (Indie), and *Acoustic Lounge* brings live music in on a Saturday.

Society activity is as busy as you want to make it, though don't expect radical politics. Arts are well provided for, especially music and drama, with both the Drama Department and Society putting on frequent productions. There's a radio station, The Cat, based on Warrington campus. It scooped a silver gong at the 2010 National Student Radio

WHAT IT'S REALLY LIKE	
UNIVERSITY:	
Social Life	★★★
Societies	★★
Student Union services	★★★★
Politics	**Little interest**
Sport	**Key**
National team position	**74th**
Sport facilities	★★★
Arts opportunities	**Music, drama excellent**
Student newspaper	**None**
Student Radio	**The Cat**
National Radio Awards	**Silver, 2010**
Bars	**CH1, Fu Bar**
Union ents	**Cheesy**
Union clubs & societies	**70+**
Parking	**Adequate**
CITY:	
Entertainment	★★★
Scene	**Pubs cheesy, clubs OK**
Town/gown relations	**There's a history**
Risk of violence	**None**
Cost of living	**Average to low**
Student concessions	**Good**
Survival + 2 nights out	**£90 pw**
Part-time work campus/town	**Good/excellent**

etc, but look in particular at a modern, high-specification, block of self-catered flats for freshers, completed three years ago. It's situated directly opposite the Chester campus.

Internet access is not available in many of the rooms. Hall security goes no further than normal campus security.

GETTING THERE

☛ By road: the uni is situated at the junction of the A540 and Cheyney Road.

☛ By rail: London Euston, 2:45; Sheffield, 2:25; Birmingham New Street, 1:45; Liverpool Lime Street, 40 mins; Manchester Oxford Road, 1:00.

☛ By coach: London, 6:00; Sheffield, 3:00.

ACCOMMODATION	
Student rating	★★
Guarantee to freshers	**No**
Style	**Halls, flats**
Security guard	**None**
Shared rooms	**Some halls**
Internet access	**Most**
Self-catered	**Some**
En suite	**Some**
Approx price range pw	**£60-£132**
Town rent pw	**£50-£90**

UNIVERSITY OF CHICHESTER

The University of Chichester
College Lane
Chichester PO19 4PE

TEL 01243 816002
EMAIL admissions@chi.ac.uk
WEB www.chiuni.ac.uk

Chichester University Students' Union
Bishop Otter Campus
Chichester PO19 6PE

TEL 01243 816390
EMAIL c.woodwood@chi.ac.uk
WEB www.chisu.org

VIRGIN VIEW

Situated between the South Downs and the sea at Chichester and at nearby Bognor Regis, Chichester University was once known as the West Sussex Institute of Higher Education, then as Chichester College of Higher Education. A decade ago it became University College Chichester and gained the power to award its own degrees. Forty-two per cent of its graduates go into Education, and Sports Science is the popular specialisation, but more recently they have built a reputation in the schools of Visual and Performing Arts, and Cultural Studies. Nor are performing arts students solely becoming teachers, but into arts entertainment as performers as often as administrators.

Chichester became a fully fledged university in 2005 and had a clear vote of confidence from its students in the last National Student Survey - 83% declared themselves satisfied with what they are up to. Then, in the 2011 Times Higher Magazine's Student Experience Survey, their students voted their lecturers into 9th

UNIVERSITY/STUDENT PROFILE	
University since	**2005**
Situation/style	**Coastal sites**
Student population	**5010**
Undergraduates	**3890**
Mature	**43%**
International	**4%**
Male/female ratio	**34:66**
Equality of opportunity:	
state school intake	**97%**
social class 4-7 intake	**35%**
drop-out rate	**7%**

nationally for their helpfulness and interest.

CAMPUSES

The Bishop Otter Campus, in name at least, takes us back to 1839 when Bishop Otter College was founded by the Church of England as a teacher training establishment. There is, today, a striking modern chapel in the campus grounds, which lie within this walled cathedral city, widely known for its annual Festival of Music and Arts.

The less imaginatively named Bognor Regis Campus is located five miles away. Bognor is, as she sounds, a seaside resort long in the dying.

Bishop Otter is the bigger of the two campuses, though Bognor has most of the

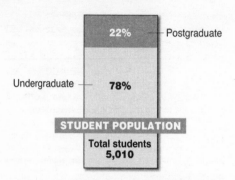

STUDENT POPULATION

22% — Postgraduate

Undergraduate — **78%**

Total students
5,010

Teacher Training provision. The campuses are far enough apart to cause something of a psychological split, and the Student Union has been preoccupied with getting the bus service between the two improved.

FEES, BURSARIES

UK & EU Fees, 2010-11: £3,375 p.a. There are bursaries for students receiving the Maintenance Grant on a sliding scale, according to income. There's also the 'Talented Sports Performer' Bursary Scheme, which makes annual payments to outstanding sports persons.

STUDENT PROFILE

Lots of students are local, mature, and from neighbourhoods and socio-economic groups with little hope of going to university until a few years ago, when places like Chichester rose to the fore. There is a strong female presence, great sporting prowess, and a sense that no lack of family experience of going to university is going to hold

TEACHING SURVEY AT A GLANCE

Avg. UCAS points accepted	**270**
Acceptance rate	**20%**
Overall satisfaction rate	**83%**
Helpful/interested staff	★★★★★
Small tuition groups	★★★
Students into graduate jobs	**66%**

Teaching most popular with undergraduates:
Education, Computer Science, Drama, English Studies (96%), History & Philosophical Studies (96%), History (100%), Imaginative Writing (97%), Media Studies, Teacher Training, Sports Science.

Teaching least popular with undergraduates:
Dance (63%).

them back in any way.

ACADEMIA & JOBS

There are six schools: Teacher Education; Physical Education; Sport, Exercise & Health Science; Cultural Studies; Visual & Performing Arts; and Social Studies.

Undergraduates may study for single honours, joint or major/minor programmes, or BA (QTS). Degrees include a range of Business degrees, Dance, Creative Writing, Music, Fine Art, Events Management, Human Resource Management, Media, Sport, and Social Work - all of which, along with the Teaching, find expression in the graduate employment picture, while a range of Theology degrees maintain continuity with the college's Church of England past.

Sixty-eight per cent of graduates get graduate-

RESEARCH EXCELLENCE

% of Chichester's research that is
4* (World-class) or 3* (Internationally rated):

	4*	3*
Sports-Related Studies	**5%**	**15%**
English	**0%**	**25%**
Theology	**0%**	**15%**
History	**0%**	**30%**
Drama, Dance, Performing Arts	**0%**	**40%**

style jobs within six months of graduation, 61% of these in education, principally as primary and secondary school teachers, in community and counselling activities, in sport, specialist retail, the restaurant industry, and public administration.

Teaching most popular with undergraduates is in Education, Biological Sciences, Computer Science, Dance, Drama, English Studies, History & Philosophical Studies, History, Imaginative Writing, Teacher Training, Sports Science.

Beyond lectures, there is a strong tradition in jazz and classical music, and student music society performances and workshops (the college and Chichester Cathedral are regular venues).

Dance (ballet, jazz and tap) is supported by the Studio, and, like music and art, involves public performance/exhibition at both student and professional level.

There's a Learning Resources Centre at Bishop Otter - a library (200,000 items), a media and computer facility, and art gallery. A similar centre at Bognor Regis has recently been refurbished.

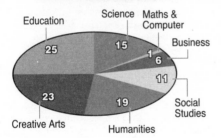

SUBJECT AREAS (%)

Education 25
Science 15
Maths & Computer 1
Business 6
Social Studies 11
Humanities 19
Creative Arts 23

Graduation, Christmas and Summer.

There are alternative music societies, arts societies, a role-playing games, society even an English literature appreciation society. Oh, and an LGB (gay) Society flourishes, regularly holding events on campus and in a gay pub in the town. 'There's been a big growth,' says a bod at the union, which, for a moment, sounded a tad alarming.

Level of political activity has recently been impressively high, with a focus on Drink Awareness, Anti-Bullying, Mental Health Awareness, and a campaign for better inter-site transport and washing facilities.

SOCIAL SCENE

STUDENT UNION A new Union building opened at Chichester campus recently, with a 650 capacity **ZeeBar**. At Bognor, it's **The Mack**. The majority of students are local, so weekends are not that big, but ents are impressive for so small a clientele, and as cheesy as you like. *Big Wednesday* is Sports Night in Chichester, while down in Bognor it's *The Alternative* (live music and DJ's). There were also Comedy Nights, and 4 balls a year - Freshers,

SPORT Sport is key; last year their teams came 66th nationally, which is good for a uni of less than 5,000. There are 13 sports clubs, all, except netball, with both men's and women's teams.

PILLOW TALK

There is catered accommodation in halls at both sites, and higher capacity and en suite at Bognor. New self-catering halls of residence opened at the Chichester Campus in September 2006, with 124

WHAT IT'S REALLY LIKE	
UNIVERSITY:	
Social Life	★★
Societies	★★
Student Union services	★★★★
Politics	**Active**
Sport	**Key**
National team position	**66th**
Sport facilities	★★★★
Arts opportunities	**Music, dance, drama excellent**
Student newspaper	**The Clash**
Nightclub	**ZeeBar**
Bars	**ZeeBar, The Mack**
Union ents	**Cheesy. 6 nights, not Saturday**
Union societies	**7**
Most popular society	**Business & Management Soc**
Parking	**Poor**
CITY:	
Entertainment	★★
Scene	**Arts good**
Town/gown relations	**Good**
Risk of violence	**Average**
Cost of living	**Low**
Student concessions	**Average**
Survival + 2 nights out	**£70 pw**
Part-time work campus/town	**Good/**

ACCOMMODATION	
Student rating	★★★
Guarantee to freshers	**100%**
Style	**Halls**
Security guard	**Campus**
Shared rooms	**Some**
Internet access	**All**
Self-catered	**Some**
En suite	**Most**
Approx price range pw	**£91-£155.05**
Town rent pw	**£75**

en-suite rooms with communal kitchens and lounges.

They have also acquired 93 extra shared facility rooms close to the university, bringing total accommodation provided to 675 students. This allows them to guarantee accommodation to all freshers. Remaining accommodation is allocated on a 'first come, first served' basis.

GETTING THERE

☛ By road: to Bishop Otter campus, A286 from the north. From east and west it's the A27. The road between Chichester and Bognor is the A259.
☛ By rail: London Victoria, 0:45; Birmingham, 4:00.
☛ Frequent trains from Gatwick Airport.
☛ By coach: London, 4:40; Birmingham, 6:00.

CITY UNIVERSITY

City University
Northampton Square
London EC1V OHB

TEL 020 7040 5060
FAX 020 7040 8995
EMAIL enquiries@city.ac.uk
WEB www.city.ac.uk

City University Students' Union
Northampton Square
London EC1V 0HB

TEL 020 7040 5600
FAX 020 7040 5601
EMAIL studentunion@city.ac.uk
WEB www.citysu.com

VIRGIN VIEW

City received its Royal Charter in 1966. The university is, as its name suggests, very much at the hub of life in the City of London and occupies a singular place in the world of higher education. It has a fine reputation in professional education, and staff pride themselves on close contact with professional institutions, business and industry. Many of the programmes are accredited by professional bodies.

But the social scene is hopeless. Go to City and you go to London and attend a university during the day as you might a job. Campus life is on hold.

In the Times Higher's *Student Experience Survey they came 110th nationally. But this is not some also-ran institution, it is a top-line university - 86% of graduates get professional jobs within 6 months of graduating. As the University itself says, their 'value added' is graduate employment, London location, and a first-class learning environment.*

The University's commitment to academic excellence is backed by the highest quality support and facilities. High-tech equipment, coupled with online learning resource Moodle, form an integrated learning environment that combines virtual and physical learning spaces to support the University's educational activities.

Between 2011 and 2012 works will provide a new lecture theatre and more seminar rooms, refurbished Library facilities and new and reconfigured office accommodation. But no commune or fun palace.

That's City for you.

CAMPUS

City Uni inhabits the famed City of London, but is only fifteen minutes from the West End, a dawdle from Islington, with its theatres, cinemas,

UNIVERSITY/STUDENT PROFILE	
University since	**1966**
Situation/style	**City sites**
Student population	**21725**
Undergraduates	**14680**
Mature	**63%**
International	**25%**
Male/female ratio	**44:56**
Equality of opportunity:	
state school intake	**93%**
lower classes intake	**41%**
drop-out rate	**13%**

fashionable restaurants, trendy bars, clubs and traditional pubs, and a short way (in the opposite direction) from Clerkenwell, once-artisan London and now a fashionable area for cool, young, City-mile workers.

The main university buildings form part of Northampton Square. Main library, lecture theatres and Students' Union are here. The Department of Arts Policy and Management are nearby in the Barbican Centre. The Dept. of Radiography and

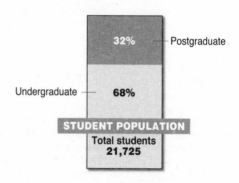

halls of residence are also within walking distance. The St Bartholomew School of Nursing is some way away in West Smithfield and Whitechapel in the East End. The Business School now occupies new premises in the heart of the city (see Academia below).

'City University is located within walking distance of no less than four tube stations (Barbican, Angel, Farringdon, Old Street), but strangely very few people can ever find it!' writes Catherine Teare. 'Tasteful, grassy Northampton Square, which supports a sizeable bandstand and water trough, has been the site for many an adventure for students - a place to chill in summer and the bandstand a place to shelter when raining. The men's rugby team used to use it for their initiation ceremonies - something about running round it in the buff!'

FEES, BURSARIES
UK & EU Fees 2011-12: generally £3,375 p.a., but the University charges tuition fees which vary between programmes, as well as between UK/EU and other students. There are bursaries for students in receipt of full HE Maintenance Grant, and school-based scholarships in specific subjects. For further details on fees and funding, visit www.city.ac.uk/study.

STUDENT PROFILE
Full-time, first-degree undergraduates, 38% of whom are mature and 10% from overseas, make up only 68% of the student body. Many students are part-timers and there is a large number of postgraduate students.

Says Catherine: 'City University is like nowhere else. The mixture of cultures and personalities makes it one of the most diverse university communities in London.'

Few arrive from public school (7% of undergraduate entrants).

ACADEMIA & JOBS
Taught courses are offered in Arts (Journalism, Cultural Policy and Management, Music and Languages), Business, Engineering and Mathematical Sciences, Community and Health Sciences, Informatics, Law and Social Sciences.

Great emphasis is placed on links with industry and the professions - Journalism, Law, Banking. However, its showing in the *Times Higher Education* magazine's Student Experience survey was very low for small-size tutorial groups.

Within each of their seven Schools academics conduct world leading research, often collaborating across Schools through their seven Interdisciplinary Centres. These Centres bring together leading academics in different fields to address the complex

TEACHING SURVEY AT A GLANCE	
Avg. UCAS points accepted	**340**
Acceptance rate	**12%**
Overall satisfaction rate	**80%**
Helpful/interested staff	★★
Small tuition groups	★
Students into graduate jobs	**86%**

Teaching most popular with undergraduates:
Aural & Oral Sciences (100%), Business Studies, Civil Engineering, Finance, Journalism, Management Studies, Mathematics & Statistics, Mechanical Production & Manufacturing Eng.

Teaching least popular with undergraduates:
Law (63%).

problems of today's communities the world over.

Still, a number of City graduates go into banking, financial activities, accountancy, or business. The Cass Business School is a £50-million building which provides, so they say, 'a state-of-the-art resource for management education in the 21st Century'.

There are dedicated degrees in Actuarial Science. Half the staff in the Actuarial Science & Statistics Department are Fellows of the Institute of Actuaries. There's a high 'ask' at A level, but a 4-year degree with a first-year Foundation course looks inviting, as does a study abroad option.

The health provision is massive. They have a School of Nursing (including degrees in Mental Nursing, and Midwifery), and there is a strategic link with University of London Queen Mary's School of Medicine & Dentistry (see entry), boosted by a recent £10-million investment.

Now there's a new School of Allied Health Professions, which brings together Optometry & Visual Science, Language & Communication Science (speech therapy), Radiography (the Saad

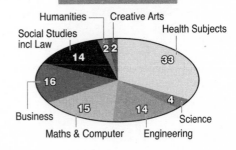

SUBJECT AREAS (%)

Humanities — Creative Arts
Social Studies incl Law
Health Subjects 33
2 2
14
16
15 14 4
Business Science
Maths & Computer Engineering

Centre for Radiography Clinical Skills Education is the new teaching facility), Health Management, and Food Policy (postgrad. only).

Seventeen per cent of graduates go on to work in hospitals, 24% altogether into some sort of health occupation, many also becoming dispensing opticians, for which there is the dedicated 2-year Foundation in Dispensing Optics, and then the BSc Optometry.

There are two BSc Radiography degrees, Diagnostic and Therapeutic, also well-trod pathways into employment. See, too, the dedicated BSc route into Speech and Language Therapy, another certainty in terms of employment.

Law graduates (who will have been particularly well schooled in performance skills) have, in City's Inns of Court School of Law, one of the few institutions validated to run LPCs (Legal Practice Course), essential for solicitors.

The passage from graduate to barrister is smooth, as The Inns of Court School of Law is also one of the few places where you can study for the Bar Vocational Course (BVC). There's also a LLB Law & Property Valuation alongside a degree in Real Estate Finance & Investment.

Location favours would-be journalists, too - you are in the very heart of British media, and you will be lectured by practitioners. City journalism launched Kate Adie, First Lady of Conflict. The portfolio of degrees espouses the idea of combining journalistic skills with a particular subject area.

They get their graduates jobs aplenty in this area, and in publishing and advertising.

Note, too, City's renowned postgraduate journo provision: International Journalism Diploma/MA is practically orientated with a focus on both print and broadcast - very hands on, very productive employment-wise. There is also a PhD for mid-career practitioners.

City is also traditionally strong in engineering and computing.

The library has just undergone a £2.3 million overhaul.

SOCIAL SCENE

STUDENTS' UNION The *Times Higher* Student Experience Survey reveals a poor Student Union, poor social life, poor welfare support and poor accommodation. However, the renowned Journalism course provides welcome support to the extra-mural media side of life. The monthly glossy *Massive* has been replaced by *City Offline*, which keeps students well informed of forthcoming events and current hot topics. The radio station (Divercity) and TV station (SUBtv)

have gone, and the web site is down.

The Student Union has tried to give a stable base for the disparate and scattered student body, but frankly, other than the sound community life in one of the halls, student life at City has been on a seemingly unstoppable dive into oblivion for quite a few years. You should be aware that you are not joining a student scene that you'd find at some other London universities.

RESEARCH EXCELLENCE

% of City's research that is
4* (World-class) or 3* (Internationally rated):

	4*	3*
Health Services Research	0%	5%
Nursing and Midwifery	30%	40%
Allied Health Professions:		
Language and Communication	10%	30%
Optometry and Visual Science	10%	20%
Applied Mathematics	5%	15%
Computer Science	15%	40%
General Eng., Mineral, Mining	10%	35%
Economics and Econometrics	10%	45%
Business and Management	15%	40%
Library and Infor. Management	15%	50%
Law	5%	30%
Social Work,I Policy & Admin.	20%	45%
Sociology	15%	30%
Psychology	5%	45%
Art and Design	5%	40%
Music	30%	35%

In an attempt to halt the slide they recently spent £1.5 million on the facilities. There's a new venue, **Ten^2**, named after its address, 10 Northampton Square, and dear old **Saddlers Bar** has been given a new lease of life and now fills one entire floor of the main building, providing space for 160 diners during the day, an HD multi-screen TV system, air-hockey table, table football and pool tables. Students may book it for up to 400 people. There's a sophisticated multi-zone sound and lighting system, but it is rarely used. How about employing an ents manager, having a good time, and making some money?

Weekends are a washout and although Wednesdays are Student Club and Society Night, the whole scene frankly needs a bit of inspiration.

'Does City have a campus life? Yes and No,' writes Catherine. 'As City is located in central

> *'City University is like nowhere else. Does it have a campus life? Yes and No. As City is located in central London it affords a wild social life.'*

WHAT IT'S REALLY LIKE

UNIVERSITY:

Social Life	★
Societies	★
Student Union services	★
Politics	**Avoided**
Sport	**Unfocused**
National team position	**117th**
Sport facilities	**Average**
Arts opportunities	**Some**
Student magazine	**City Offline**
Nightclub	**Ten^2**
Bars	**Saddlers**
Union ents	**Limited**
Union societies	**50**
Most popular society	**Law, Islamic**
Parking	**Non-existent**

CITY:

Entertainment	★★★★★
Scene	**Excellent local pubs, clubs, arts**
Town/gown relations	**Good**
Risk of violence	**High**
Cost of living	**High**
Student concessions	**Good**
Survival + 2 nights out	**£110 pw**
Part-time work campus/town	**Excellent**

ACCOMMODATION

Student rating	★
Guarantee to freshers	**Apply early**
Style	**Halls, flats**
Internet access	**All**
Self-catered	**All**
En suite	**Some**
Approx price range pw	**£170-£267**
City rent pw	**£110-£400**

London it affords a wild social life. Students use a number of sites dotted around London, which makes it hard for us to feel like we belong.' The union is, in effect, closed to ents.

As for societies, there is little to shout about either. There have also been some effective student campaigns on Racism, Women's Safety and Islamophobia, and they raised £1k for Comic Relief.

In 2007 a Student Centre opened at Northampton Square where students can go for help and advice on a wide range of topics including housing, financial support, visa and immigration advice, fee payments, course registration and graduation enquiries.

TOWN Location is all. Never was that more true - you'll be 5 mins walk from the attractions of Angel, Old Street, Shoreditch, Hoxton and Farringdon, and just a short bus ride from the West End.

If you walk north towards Angel you come to Upper Street, which must have the most bars and restaurants in any one area of London after the West End. There is something for everyone, cheap and expensive. It has a friendly, safe atmosphere and a 24-hour Sainsbury's on Thursday to Saturday.

If you walk west down Roseberry Avenue, you come to Exmouth Market and its surrounding area. This offers pretty much the same as Upper Street, but on a smaller scale. Exmouth Market has some of the best sandwich shops in London and, especially in the summer, a really welcoming atmosphere.

Camden is a mere 10-minute tube ride away, while the West End is twenty minutes on the bus. Many clubs offer discounts to students with an NUS card, but you must make sure you go on the right night. The nearest places to shop are Holloway Road, Oxford Street and Camden.'

SPORT Interest may be high but levels and facilities are not impressive, and now they no longer have Sports Night at Saddlers. There are pitches in Walthamstow; a small rowing club is based, of course, on the Thames; the Saddler's Sports Centre, with badminton, football, netball, tennis, aerobics and yoga and a good martial arts programme, a couple of squash courts; and some Islington facilities are popular nearby.

PILLOW TALK

All applicants over 18 living outside Greater London who firmly accept an offer and submit an accommodation application form by 15 May are guaranteed a place in halls. Finsbury & Heyworth, lhave communal showers, toilets and kitchens, a launderette, recreation room and vending machine. Liberty Court is run by a private landlord: 3 to 5 study bedrooms with shared kitchen and bathroom. Liberty Court is undergoing a full internal refurbishment through summer 2010.

No car parking available. Cycle storage available at all Halls of Residence

'Popular private housing student areas,' reports Catherine, 'include Hackney, Stoke Newington and Shoreditch.' Cycle storage is available at all halls.

GETTING THERE

☛ All sites are well served by buses.
☛ Nearest Underground stations to main sites: Angel (Northern line), Farringdon and Barbican (Hammersmith & City, Metropolitan and Circle).
☛ For the School of Nursing, it's either District or Metropolitan, depending on the station you choose. All is accessible from City.

COVENTRY UNIVERSITY

Coventry University
Priory Street
Coventry CV1 5FB

TEL 024 7688 7688
FAX 024 7615 2223
EMAIL studentenquiries@coventry.ac.uk
WEB www.coventry.ac.uk

Coventry University Students' Union
Priory Street
Coventry CV1 5FJ

TEL 024 7679 5200
FAX 024 7655 5239
EMAIL suexec@coventry.ac.uk
WEB www.cusu.org

VIRGIN VIEW

*A*fter devastating bombing during the
Second World War, Coventry rose from
the ashes to become a major industrial force.
Elements of what later became the university
evolved during this time, and in 1970 the
Coventry College of Art merged with
Lanchester College of Technology and Rugby
College of Engineering Technology to form
Lanchester Polytechnic. In 1987 the name
was changed to Coventry Polytechnic. Then,
in 1992, the poly became a university.

There was a 79% student satisfaction
rate in the Higher Education Funding
Council's latest National Student Survey, and
69% find real graduate jobs within six
months of graduating from the university.

Open days in 2011 are 18 June, 21
September, 8 October, 22 October.

CAMPUS

The modern precinct campus is directly opposite
the bombed-out ruins of the original cathedral.
Looking around the ecclesiastical shell is a
thought-provoking experience. Students from Cov
were sketching it at the time we visited. Especially
memorable is a sculpture of reconciliation (two
figures embrace to express forgiveness for the
Luftwaffe's devastation of Coventry) created by
Josefina de Vasconcellos and, as it happens, given
by Richard Branson. An identical sculpture stands
in the Peace Garden at Hiroshima, Japan.

FEES, BURSARIES

UK & EU fees 2011-12: £3,375 p.a. A bursary of £329
is available to all eligible undergraduates who
qualify for a full or partial grant. A range of
academic (£1,000) and sports scholarships (£1,500
and £3,000) is also available.

UNIVERSITY/STUDENT PROFILE	
University since	**1992**
Situation/style	**City campus**
Student population	**20230**
Undergraduates	**16045**
Mature	**46%**
International	**21%**
Male/female ratio	**52:48**
Equality of opportunity:	
state school intake	**97%**
social class 4-7 intake	**42%**
drop-out rate	**9%**

STUDENT PROFILE

There is a large mature student population, bent
on vocational training. Many undergrads come via
the state sector from the locality, but also a lot
from overseas. A third of first degree undergrads
are part-timers. The uni has been diligent in its
open access policy, giving many families their first
taste of a university education.

We think of the university speciailising in all
those traditionally male degrees, Automative and
Aerospace Engineering and Design, Civil
Engineering, Motorsport, Motorcycle, and
Powertrain Engineering, Building, and those odd
little apparently masculine niches associated with

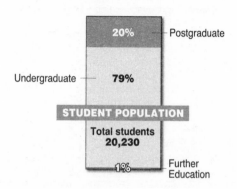

Postgraduate — 20%

Undergraduate — 79%

STUDENT POPULATION
**Total students
20,230**

1% — Further Education

this university, Disaster Management, and Natural Hazards. But the balance between male and femal students is almost equal.

ACADEMIA & JOBS

The University has significantly reduced its course provision this year, but introduced a few new courses which have a particularly keeen focus on employment and allow for an international experience through partnerships with other universities across the world and through the use of modern technologies that allow overseas collaborations without ever leaving your home lecture theatre. These are: Aerospace Electronics, Analytical Chemistry & Forensic Science, and Music Production for Online Industries.

There are three faculties: Health & Life Sciences; Business, Environment & Society; Engineering & Computing, and two schools: Lifelong Learning and Art & Design.

Think of Coventry and one thinks of engineering, but the largest single graduate employment sector is not engineering at all, it is health and social work - around 30% go into these areas from degrees like Physiotherapy, Nursing (Adult and Mental Health), Dietetics, Midwifery, Occupational Therapy, Paramedic Science, Operating Department Practice, and Biomedical Science degrees, all dovetailing into community degrees in Social Work, Welfare, and Youth Work.

Motor vehicle manufacturing and associated trading account for about 4% of graduate output

TEACHING SURVEY AT A GLANCE	
Avg. UCAS points accepted	**260**
Acceptance rate	**23%**
Overall satisfaction rate	**79%**
Helpful/interested staff	★★★
Small tuition groups	★★
Students into graduate jobs	**69%**

Teaching most popular with undergraduates:
Anatomy, Physiology & Pathology, Biology & related sciences, Dance (95%), Fine Art, History Human & Social Geography (100%), Management Studies, Mechanical, Production & Manufacturing Engineering, Medical Science & Pharmacy (97%), Nutrition, Physical Geography & Environmental Science, Psychology.

Teaching least popular with undergraduates:
Journalism (50%), Drama (36%)..

only, however significant a relative contribution that may be nationwide, for Coventry are among the leaders and this city is the home of car manufacture, and the car industry is central to its calling, with degrees in 3D Design Representation, Automotive Design, and Automotive Design & Illustration, as well as the range of BEng hons. Racing car designers and team managers note: the degrees in Motorsports Engineering are not demanding at entry.

Design also favours graphic artists, designers and illustrators (often the advertising industry or journalism as destination). BSc Architectural Design Technology favours the would-be town planner, while jobs in the construction industry are very much available to Cov's Built Environment graduates - Building, Surveying and Quantity Surveying.

Would-be solicitors will observe that Coventry are European, commercial and business Law specialists, and non-Law graduates may opt for a 2-year, or 3-year part-time, Senior Status Law degree here. There are also degrees in Forensic Science.

Computer and Games Technology degrees translate into jobs in software consultancy and supply. If you have an adventurous streak and purposeful outlook, rifle through their Disaster Management degrees and the one in Natural Hazards. This is a genuine niche.

The Careers Service continues to offer support to all students beyond graduation, by email, phone or by coming in to see the careers team. Employability workshops and individual guidance are also available.

RESEARCH EXCELLENCE		
% of Coventry's research that is 4* (World-class) or 3* (Internationally rated):		
	4*	3*
Allied Health Professions	5%	5%
Applied Mathematics	0%	20%
Computer Science	5%	20%
Electrical and Electronic Eng.	5%	45%
Mechanical, Aeronautical & Manufacturing Engineering	0%	25%
Metallurgy and Materials	0%	20%
Town and Country Planning	0%	20%
Business and Management	0%	20%
Library and Info. Management	5%	35%
Law	0%	5%
Politics	5%	5%
Social Work,l Policy & Admin.	5%	20%
Psychology	0%	0%
Education	0%	20%
Sports-Related Studies	0%	15%
Art and Design	5%	55%

SUBJECT AREAS (%)

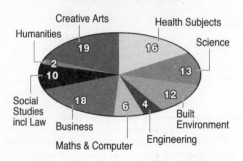

Creative Arts — 19
Humanities — 2
Health Subjects — 16
Science — 13
Built Environment — 12
Engineering — 4
Maths & Computer — 6
Business — 18
Social Studies incl Law — 10

Currently they are in the process of significantly reducing their course provision and introducing new courses with a greater focus on employability, so look carefully at the departmental listings. One new course is Music Production for Online Industries, the only course in Europe that teaches you the technology and techniques involved in online production and distribution.

SOCIAL SCENE

STUDENT UNION **The Hub**, opening in September 2011, is the new central venue for all student related activity, housing a music venue, restaurants and shops as well as plenty of study spaces including a roof terrace for working on collaborative projects.

They had a referendum for the name of the new venue and **Square One** was the clear winner with 52% of the votes.

The student centre offers a 'one-stop' service. Students can get help on a range of issues including finance, registry, accommodation, international office, recruitment and admissions and student services.

Until next year the campus will as usual be a hive of activity revolving around the café/bar, **Revolution**, located on the top floor of the Union building in Priory Street and known for its hot chocolate. It serves breakfast through to late-night munchies and screens all the top sporting fixtures. There's also a Premier convenience store, a café called **Coffee**, a computer cluster, hairdresser's and the Union's main offices.

Artie and indie types will be found in the

> *'They have deliberately gone for the vocational - that was their background. We have students for whom Coventry is exactly right.'*

WHAT IT'S REALLY LIKE

UNIVERSITY:

Social Life	★★★
Societies	★★
Student Union services	★★
Politics	**Internal**
Sport	**Competitive**
National team position	**73rd**
Sport facilities	★★★★
Arts opportunities	**Film, art exc.; dance, music popular; drama improving**
Student newspaper	**Source**
Student radio	**Source FM**
Student TV	**Source TV**
Venue	**Studio 54**
Bar	**Square One**
Union ents	**Busy**
Union clubs/societies	**50**
Parking	**Poor**

CITY:

Entertainment	★★
Scene	**Clubs 'n pubs**
Town/gown relations	**Nothing special**
Risk of violence	**Variable**
Cost of living	**Low**
Student concessions	**OK**
Survival + 2 nights out	**£70 pw**
Part-time work campus/town	**Average/Good**

Golden Cross and **Fads** cafeteria in the art block. Language and engineering students will be found in the library. Sporting people will be found at the Union bar or slumped in the corner somewhere. International students seem to be everywhere.

Much of uni social life is dominated by societies, which are particularly sporty, though the sometime award-winning media, *Source* newspaper, radio and TV station, appeal too. Most societies have their local haunts: the **Hope and Anchor** is frequented by 'The Lanch' Rugby Union team, for example. Sporting societies often organise theme-night fund-raising events - *Man 'O' Man, The Full Monty, Slave Trade*, etc. - and these are high on the student social calendar.

What was once **The Planet** on the corner of Cox Street - a revolution in its day - is now **Studio 54**. Here you get Skint on Tuesdays, 8pm-12am, or

Blok Party. Room 1:Dubstep, Electro, Hip-Hop & Mashup. Room 2: Funky House. On Wednesday it's WKD Wednesdays, the official Vodka Kiss @ Platinum pre-bar. The week ends with SOP Fridays, 7pm until late, and that's all at FiftyFour. It's but a short walk from campus.

SPORT The uni muscled its way to 73rd in the overall BUCS ratings for team sports last year. They've had their Olympic swimmers and pumped-up boxing champs. **The Sports Centre** is campus central, with fitness suite, injury clinic, 4-court and 2-court halls and dance studio. Thirty-seven acres of uni playing fields are at Westward Heath, 4 miles away, and cater for rugby, soccer, hockey and cricket. There's also a 9-hole golf course.

TOWN The compact city centre has a much-loved traditional indoor market. The £33-million **Sky**

ACCOMMODATION	
Student rating	★★
Guarantee to freshers	**85%**
Style	**Halls, flats**
Security guard	**Some**
Shared rooms	**Some flats**
Internet access	**All**
Self-catered	**Some**
En suite	**Some**
Approx price range pw	**£92-£122**
City rent pw	**£60-£110**

Dome complex houses a multi-screen cinema, bars and café bars, two nightclubs, restaurants, and there is a 4,000-seat arena, a popular concert venue that doubles as an ice rink.

The **Herbert Art Gallery** and **Museum** and **Belgrade Theatre** provide the cultural dimension. Sport is, however, the thing, with the £60-million **Coventry Arena** no longer a dream. The **City**

Sports Centre has an Olympic-sized swimming pool.

Cost of living is quite low, and there are lots of student discounts. Wednesday nights is student night at **Lava Ignite**. Other city nightclubs include **Jumpin Jacks**, **Coventry Kasbah**, and **Colisseum**. There's also **Escape Coventry**, a bar and mini venue. See also the Student Union at nearby Warwick University.

Otherwise, 'Most pubs in Cov are of the Rat, Parrot and Firkin ilk,' says Andrew Losowsky, 'but **The Golden Cross** and **The Hand and Heart** are worth a look for something different.'

PILLOW TALK
'Priory Hall is the largest of the student residences over 600 rooms,' writes Jennifer Johnston. 'It is dominated by lads who haven't yet discovered how to open a tin of beans. Singer Hall is organised into flats and is self-catered. Caradoc Hall is a tower block of self-contained flats and is just out of the city centre. There are lots of suitable student houses in the Stoke, Earlsdon and Radford areas of the city, with good low rents.'

New-ish accommodation includes university-owned Sherbourne House and Lynden House and non-university Liberty Park and Trinity Point. Raglan House was completed for occupation in September 2007 - self-catered, en-suite cluster flats.

Car parking is available in selected properties.

GETTING THERE
☞ By road: from London M1/J17, M45, A45, signs for City Centre. From the south, M40/J15, A46, signs for City Centre. From the southwest, M5, M42/J6, A45. From Northwest, M6/J2, City Centre signs. From north, M1/J21, M69, City Centre.
☞ By rail: London Euston, 80 mins; Manchester Piccadilly, 2:30; Nottingham, 1:45; Bristol, 2:30.
☞ By air: Birmingham Airport.
☞ By coach: London, 1:20; Leeds, 4:00.

UNIVERSITY FOR THE CREATIVE ARTS

University for The Creative Arts
Farnham
Surrey GU9 7DS

TEL 01252 892696
FAX 01252 892624
EMAIL admissions@ucreative.ac.uk
WEB www.ucreative.ac.uk

University for the Creative Arts Students' Union
Farnham
Surrey GU9 7DS

TEL 01252 710263
FAX 01252 713591
EMAIL rhayes@ucreative.ac.uk
WEB www.uccasu.com/

UNIVERSITY/STUDENT PROFILE

University since	**2007**
Situation/style	**Confederacy**
Student population	**7585**
Total undergraduates	**5070**
Mature	**25%**
International	**12%**
Male/female ratio	**35:65**
Equality of opportunity:	
state school intake	**97%**
social class 4-7 intake	**36%**
drop-out rate	**11%**

VIRGIN VIEW

*I*n 1987 three Kentish art colleges - Canterbury, Maidstone and Medway - merged , and the result, known as KIAD, became the third largest higher education Art & Design college in the UK. Alone among such colleges, they had a School of Architecture. Kent University awarded their degrees, and proximity to Europe, a large overseas student population, and strong links abroad gave them an international flavour. They also had accommodation. But even the three of them together were a small unit (2,000 odd), and when the work was done, the scene for students was not exactly overpowering.

Then in 2005 they met the Surrey Institute of Art & Design, a like-minded of higher education organisation, founded in 1969 with a 16-acre campus in leafy Farnham, Surrey, and a small site in Epsom.

The Institute was also small - around 2,500 undergraduates - youthfully minded, a groovy set-up with a fast-track reputation for getting graduates jobs in interesting artistic and media areas, in subject specific degrees - from producers and theatre managers to graphic artists, from advertising account executives to animators, from fashion journalists to interior designers, from clothing & textile designers to photographers, from TV & film cameramen to archivists and librarians. But could it face the future alone?

It was about then that KIAD spent millions on new Fine Art studios, art gallery, library, computer suites and a 90-seat lecture theatre, making the Canterbury campus in particular an even more attractice proposition. And so the merger was mooted, the knot was tied, and they took the title of University soon after.

Together, in spite of their scattered base, they cut an impressive figure in the higher education world of Art and Design. Five per cent of their research was recently adjudged world-class, 5% of it of international significance.

In the old Surrey Institute the real-world spirit was amazing, their principal aim to get their students into work, and this is part of the mix too. High on the agenda are integrating processes and disciplines in the courses which need to be second nature in an artist's work. They put the onus on students on certain courses to 'produce' their own projects, find sponsors for film work, for example, organise their own work placements.

UCA is constantly involved with the industries and agencies on which their students' livelihoods will depend.

But this is a dicey area work-wise and only 57% of graduates can expect to be in work within six months of graduation, around 15% in clothing retail, 9% into some sort of specialised design activity, just over 3% into architectural jobs.

Photography, publishing, creative arts entertainment and artistic creation take more than 8%. Then there's advertising, TV and film, arts facility work (about 5%), and education, PR, etc.

It's all tailor-made work to what they have been studying, an impressive real-world creative set-up that works.

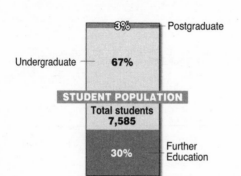

STUDENT POPULATION
Total students 7,585
Postgraduate 3%
Undergraduate 67%
Further Education 30%

TEACHING SURVEY AT A GLANCE

Avg. UCAS points accepted	**240**
Acceptance rate	**19%**
Overall satisfaction rate	**64%**
Helpful/interested staff	★★
Small tuition groups	★★
Students into graduate jobs	**57%**

Teaching most popular with undergraduates:
Architecture (81%).

Teaching least popular with undergraduates:
Fine Art (54%).

FEES, BURSARIES

UK & EU Fees, 2011-12: £3,375 p.a. Minimum Standard Bursaries for students in receipt of the full Maintenance Grant. Creative Scholarships are awarded to up to 160 students in each year group (£1,000 p.a.). Only students from households with a family income of under £40,000 may apply.

STUDENT PROFILE

Twenty-one per cent of entrants are mature students and two-thirds are female. Artistic types predominate obviously. There's a fairly low intake from beyond the EU, but there are enough EU students from beyond the English Channel for them to run a pre-Session course in English at the Canterbury campus.

CAMPUS

CANTERBURY CAMPUS New Dover Road, Canterbury Kent CT1 3AN. Tel: 01227 817302. Undergraduate courses - Foundation Degree in Architectural Technology. BA (Hons) degrees in Architecture ARB/RIBA Part 1, Architectural Technology, Fine Art, Interior Architecture & Design, plus a pre-Session course in English for the Creative Arts.

Accommodation: Ian Dury House is a nine-flat en-suite development situated on campus; each flat houses six students. No parking. Rent a little over £90 per week. If you want to create a little space between yourself and campus at the end of the day, go for Hotham Court, a new, 107-room block of en-suite and shared facilities in flats of two, four, five and six single study bedrooms about half an hour away rent depends on whether you get an en-suit apartment, but in any case it's also around the £90 mark. You'll be in good company, for not only is Hotham Court close to another UCA block of four flats, Riverdale House, but it's in amongst Canterbury Christ Church student village All Riverdale is en-suite. Rent's the better side of £90.

EPSOM CAMPUS Ashley Road, Epsom, Surrey KT18 5BE. Tel: 01372 728811. Undergraduate courses - BA (Hons) degrees in Fashion, Fashion Journalism, Fashion Management & Marketing, Fashion Promotion & Imaging, Graphic Design, Graphic Design: New Media, Music Journalism.

Accommodation: Woodcote Side is a block of twelve flats, 2 to 6 beds per flat, situated about a mile from campus. Pretty basic, but you can expect to pay upwards of £90 a room, depending on size. Room size, that is.

Alternatively it's Worple Road on campus - three blocks of flats into which they squeeze 54 students. But here you get en-suite and there are flats with wheelchair access. Rent is just over £90 per week.

FARNHAM CAMPUS Falkner Road, Farnham, Surrey GU9 7DS. Tel: 01252 722441. Undergraduate courses - Foundation degrees in Creative Advertising Production, Hand Embroidery (delivered by the RSN at Hampton Court), and Music Video Production. BA (Hons) degrees in Advertising & Brand Communication, Animation, Arts & Business Management, Arts & Media, Computer Games Arts, Digital Film & Screen Arts, Film Production, Fine Art, Graphic Communication, Graphic Storytelling & Comic Art, Interior Architecture & Design, Journalism, Leisure Journalism, Motoring Journalism, Photography, Product Design Sustainable Futures, Sports Journalism, Textiles for Fashion & Interiors, Three Dimensional Design (Ceramics, Glass, or Metalwork & Jewellery).

Accommodation: Main Hall is situated on campus and was built for the purpose of accommodating students in 1976, so don't expect ultra modern tic-tac.

There are seven flats with four or five beds in each flat, including some 'same gender' twin bedrooms.

Twenty years newer is the campus village - 343 students occupy single bedrooms, each with its own washbasin. Each house or flat accommodates up to 8 students. Some have en-suite bedrooms, and some wheelchair access. Rent varies - around £70-£90 per week.

RESEARCH EXCELLENCE

% of UCC's research that is
4* *(World-class)* or 3* *(Internationally rated):*

	4*	3*
Art & Design.	**5%**	**25%**

MAIDSTONE CAMPUS Oakwood Park, Maidstone, Kent ME16 8AG. Tel: 01622 620000. Undergraduate courses - Foundation degrees in Broadcast Media and Graphic Media. BA (Hons) degrees in Animation Arts, Broadcast Media, Graphic Design: Visual Communications, Graphic Media, Illustration, Photography & Media Arts, Photography & Video, Printmaking, Video Arts Production.

Accommodation In Maidstone it's Westree Court - 134 study bedrooms arranged in flats of 4, 6 and 7 persons less than a mile from campus. Students have their own rooms with en-suite shower, toilet and wash-basin. Rent is about £90 per week.

ROCHESTER CAMPUS Fort Pitt, Rochester, Kent ME1 1DZ. Tel: 01634 888702. Undergraduate courses - Foundation Degree in Art & Design: Creative & Technical Practice. BA (Hons) degrees in Art & Design: Creative & Technical Practice, Applied Arts, CG Arts & Animation, Contemporary Jewellery, Contemporary Photographic Practice, Creative Arts for Theatre & Film, Design, Branding & Marketing, Fashion Atelier, Fashion Design, Fashion Management, Fashion Promotion, Fashion Textiles, Modelmaking, Product Design, Silversmithing, Goldsmithing & Jewellery, Style Futures.

Accommodation The Doust Way student flats are about five minutes from campus, close to the river - 214 rooms mostly arranged in flats of six. Students have their own room with an en-suite shower, toilet and wash basin. Rent £90+ per week.

SOCIAL SCENE

There are bars at all the campuses, and as they say, 'You can be sure of a creative angle on the action.' Freshers' Week, Graduation Ball. For a fledgling university what more could you want than artistes teaching you to break dance, or pulling you in to a bit of life drawing, before getting down to some serious poker? You can do all these things in societies - also Cinema, Drama, Musicians, Tech Crew, and more - yes the old LGBT is here and Salsa, and an international club for the Greeks and Turks. There's even a student magazine and eleven sports clubs, including, of course, Capoeri, Snow Sports, and Yoga.

In the old Surrey Institute they always had a good time at the pubs in leafy Epsom, trips to the Brixton Academy, or to clubs in Guildford, or Kingston - the **Works** may no longer be trading, but it's not all **Oceana** at Kingston: **Bar-Eivissa** becomes **Studio 48** on Friday and Saturday night, then there's gay club **Escape**, alternative basement club **Bacchus** offers everything from indie and punk to hip hop and house. Poised they are in Surrey - on the edge - and in Epsom itself there's the 400-seater **Playhouse** (plays, films, alternative comedy, jazz).

In Canterbury, you're spoiled for fun. Pubs and clubs keep two universities satisfied already, and there's the **Venue** and **Lighthouse** at Kent Uni, and the Canterbury Christ Church University's *Toxic* Monday night at city nightclub **Chill**.

GETTING THERE

☛ By road: Rochester: M20/J4, A228. Maidstone: M20/J6, A229. Canterbury: from the west, M2, A2; from the south, A28 or A2; from the east, A257; from the northeast, A28; from northwest, the A290.
☛ By rail: London to Canterbury, 90 mins; to Maidstone, under the hour; Rochester, 40 mins.

UNIVERSITY OF CUMBRIA

The University of Cumbria
Fusehill Street
Carlisle
Cumbria CA1 2HH

TEL 01228 616234
FAX 01228 616235
WEB www.cumbria.ac.uk

University of Cumbria Students' Union
Lancaster
Lancashire LA1 3JD

TEL: 01524 65827
FAX 01524 841924
EMAIL info@su.ucsm.ac.uk
WEB thestudentunion.org,uk/

The University of Cumbria was formed officially on 1st August 2007 from an amalgamation of St Martin's College, *Cumbria Institute of the Arts, and the Cumbrian campuses of the University of Central Lancashire. It is a courageous*

UNIVERSITY/STUDENT PROFILE

University since	**2007**
Situation/style	**Confederacy**
Student population	**13105**
Total undergraduates	**10415**
Mature	**56%**
International	**3%**
Male/female ratio	**26:74**
Equality of opportunity:	
state school intake	**98%**
social class 4-7 intake	**45%**
drop-out rate	**11%**

attempt to put higher education on a sound footing in one of our most beautiful, but relatively lightly populated, counties. HQ is in Carlisle.

CAMPUS

The University has campuses in Carlisle, Penrith, Ambleside and Lancaster and a specialist teacher-education centre in London. The uni also has strong links and close partnership with four Further Education Colleges in Cumbria (Lakes Colleges, Furness College, Carlisle College and Kendal College).

ST MARTIN'S COLLEGE

St Martin's is a teacher training college with a Church of England foundation (1964), but it is also the base for a number of courses leading to employment in health and the caring professions - nursing, midwifery, occupational therapy, radiography - in the Church, in the worlds of art, design and imaging science, in drama, dance, music, in media, in business and in the sports and leisure industries. Degrees have been awarded by nearby Lancaster Uni since 1967.

The main St Martin's campus is a mile or so from the central shopping area of Lancaster, and offers teacher training, primary and secondary, and degrees in business, sport, arts, humanities, social sciences, health (including nursing). There are also smaller campuses in Ambleside (Lake District) and Carlisle, and Health/ Nursing training centres at Whitehaven and Barrow-in-Furness. Ambleside specialises in Early Years QTS, 3 and 5-11, with drama and PE among the options, and three degrees in Adventure Recreation Mgt and Outdoor Studies. Carlisle is also for Early Years QTS, but with music and religion among the options, and various degrees in social sciences, health (including nursing, radiography,

occupational therapy and physiotherapy), and business and info technology. Finally, in Tower Hamlets, London, there's a centre for teacher training, primary years.

CUMBRIA INSTITUTE OF ARTS

Located on 3 sites in Carlisle, the main green-field campus overlooking Rickerby Park and the River Eden - paradise indeed - Cumbria is a cracking college academically, with teaching assessment scores of 21 out of 24 for Art & Design and 19 for Communication & Media. It is also well resourced with electronic and media production facilities and a £4.5-million development incorporating a new

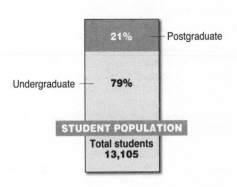

STUDENT POPULATION
Total students
13,105

Postgraduate — 21%
Undergraduate — 79%

library, theatre and dance studio, and improved teaching accommodation. Courses focus on creative writing, drama, dance, film, journalism, and fine art and design.

CENTRAL LANCASHIRE UNIVERSITY CAMPUSES

The old Cumbrian campuses of Central Lancashire University (UCLan) are at Newton Rigg (Penrith)

TEACHING SURVEY AT A GLANCE

Avg. UCAS points accepted	**260**
Acceptance rate	**28%**
Overall satisfaction rate	**70%**
Helpful/interested staff	★★★
Small tuition groups	★★
Students into graduate jobs	**78%**

Teaching most popular with undergraduates:
Anatomy, Physiology & Pathology, Drama, English Studies, Fine Art, Nursing, Subjects allied to Medicine, Performing Arts.

Teaching least popular with undergraduates:
Education (47%), Design Studies (46%).

RESEARCH EXCELLENCE

% of Cumbria's research that is
4* (World-class) or **3*** (Internationally rated):

	4*	3*
Education	0%	5%
English	0%	10%
Theology	5%	10%
History	0%	20%
Art and Design	0%	10%

and Carlisle. Newton Rigg has 250 hectares at the head of the Eden Valley, where a faculty of Land-Based Studies had been quietly doing its thing as Newton Rigg Agric College until, in 1998, UCLan took it over. UCLan's Carlisle campus used to be part of Northumbria University, which ran great courses - business, computing, travel, tourism, etc - at generous entry rates, for which many an applicant put his name down before realising to his horror that he wasn't going to be based in Newcastle. It has been well shepherded by UCLan since then and as the Cumbria Business School boasts 'a significant number of international students from a wide variety of countries, including China Nigeria and the USA'.

FEES, BURSARIES

UK & EU Fees, 2011-12: £3,375. There are grants, scholarships, teaching bursaries to accompany the Government Maintenance grant (if your parents' earnings are low enough). For students on NHS-funded full-time courses, fees paid are by the strategic health authority. Extra allowances are available for older students and students with dependants. There is also a range of support people studying part-time.

ACADEMIA

The uni has four faculties. Arts, Design & Media will enjoy a £6 million redevelopment programme. Education is delivered across 3 campuses (Lancaster, Ambleside and Carlisle) and at 2 sites in London (Tower Hamlets and Greenwich). Health, Medical Science & Social Care offer training as a nurse (adult, child, learning disabilities or mental health branches), midwife, occupational therapist, physiotherapist, radiographer or social worker. And there's a degree in Child, Young Person and Family Studies.

Meanwhile, Lancaster University is leading the way in a collaboration with UCLan, Cumbria and Liverpool universities, and the University Hospitals of Morecambe Bay Trust in recruiting teaching and research staff to meet the terms of a government decision to allow 50 extra places a year for Liverpool medical students to be based full time at the Lancaster campus.

Finally, there is a Faculty of Science & Natural Resources.

Student satisfaction with the teaching in the Higher Education Funding Council's National Student Survey was, at 70%, not high, but the figure of 78% students into graduate-level jobs within six months of graduation is not so bad.

The teaching most popular with undergraduates is in Geographical Studies (besides Geography, there's Forestry & Woodland Science), Social Studies (including Youth and Community degrees), Social Work, Initial Teacher Training, and Education (which comes in a whole host of joint honours degrees - Art & Design, Childhood Education, English, History, Maths, PE, RS, Science, etc.).

Least popular are the media and journalism degrees and Biological Sciences (including some of the Sports degrees), where only around half the class gave the thumbs up. However, in 2009 two students from the BA Multimedia, Design & Digital Animation course were nominated for a National Royal Television Award.

STUDENT UNION

In Carlisle, the **Calva Bar** is open daily from 10.30a.m. to 11 p.m., and stages live bands, hypnotists, comedians and theme nights. In Ambleside, the Overdraught Bar is central to student social life. Regular theme nights and music genre nights make up the programme. There's a 280 capacity and the bar is open seven days a week from 7pm. The **JCR** is the social heart of Lancaster and offers a programme that dovetails with **Liquid**, a local club with student nights on Monday and Wednesday. In the JCR, it's 'quality music and pound-a-pint night' on Monday, and *Music Corner* - a live band showcase on Tuesday. *Wild and Wacky* Wednesdays is the pre-Liquid party night. Then there's *Thursday Night Lite* - chilled night - and *Bar FTSE* on a Friday. On

ACCOMMODATION

Guarantee to freshers	**98%**
Style	**Halls**
Security guard	**Halls**
Shared rooms	**Ambleside**
Internet access	**Planned**
Self-catered	**Some**
En suite	**Many**
Approx price range pw	**£50-£80**
Town rent pw	**£45-£60**

Saturday, it's *Chillout* in the JCR, and the *BIG Quiz* on Sunday.

PILLOW TALK

They offer only 1,200 rooms across the various campuses, so apply early. Internet access is 'planned' but not yet delivered. Some rooms in Ambleside are twins, though many elsewhere are a modern enough conception to be en-suite even.

Town accommodation is plentiful, and the uni office will help you get something. There are 'house hunting help days, where you can meet other students, receive guidance from a buddy (a second or third-year student), view accommodation and question prospective landlords.'

DE MONTFORT UNIVERSITY

De Montfort University
The Gateway
Leicester LE1 9BH

De Montfort Students' Union
Mill Lane
Leicester LE2 7DR

TEL 0116 255 1551
FAX 0116 257 7533
EMAIL enquiry@dmu.ac.uk
WEB www.dmu.ac.uk

TEL 0116 255 5576
FAX 0116 257 6309
EMAIL dsureception@dmu.ac.uk
WEB www.mydsu.com

VIRGIN VIEW

*L*eicester's De Montfort University (DMU) has emerged from a period of shrinkage, when it ceded some eight sites or campuses to Lincoln and Bedfordshire universities, to build, if not the new Jerusalem, new Centres of Excellence, the material expression of a new order.

The principles on which they are moving forward seem sound. They have designed the new order with the learning environment principally in mind and the curriculum with graduate employment to the fore, and they have decided that the future will be ever so much easier if their students take responsibility for themselves in a spirit of entrepreneurship.

DMU students on sandwich courses can now chose to start their own businesses instead of taking work placements with established employers. As a result, graduates of the university now lead the region in starting businesses and are in the Top 20 of self-starters in the UK. Each year DMU graduates are responsible for more than 100 business start ups.

The principle also inspires DMU's Student Union, which has become a limited

UNIVERSITY/STUDENT PROFILE	
University since	**1992**
Situation/style	**City campus**
Student population	**21585**
Total undergrads	**17090**
Mature	**45%**
International	**9%**
Male/female ratio	**43:57**
Equality of opportunity:	
state school intake	**98%**
social class 4-7 intake	**42%**
drop-out rate	**10%**

company and Institute of Leadership and Management, bent on spreading the word to other Unions. They have already trained sabbatical officers, ex-students who are taking a year out to run their Student Unions, at ten universities up and down Britain.

Meanwhile, massive modern buildings have sprung up on campus to celebrate the new emerging DMU order - a Performance Arts Centre of Excellence building, an award-winning £9-million Campus Centre, a suite of Creative Technology Studios, and the £35 million Business and Law building, which is opening this Autumn.

In the same period, 43% of its research activities across nineteen subject areas have been rated world-class or internationally significant. Some subjects, like English, Civil Engineering, Business, Nursing & Midwifery, Drama, Dance & Performing Arts, Media Studies, and Music have knocked the competition into a cocked hat.

Success in this area does not mean that DMU lecturers are becoming research boffins for whom students are a necessary evil.

For the Higher Education Funding Council's national survey shows that 82% of students are satisfied with the teaching they receive, and their lecturers earn three

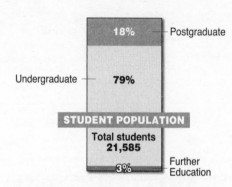

STUDENT POPULATION

18% Postgraduate
Undergraduate 79%
Total students 21,585
3% Further Education

TEACHING SURVEY AT A GLANCE

Avg. UCAS points accepted	**220**
Acceptance rate	**17%**
Overall satisfaction rate	**82%**
Helpful/interested staff	★★★
Small tuition groups	★★
Students into graduate jobs	**65%**

Teaching most popular with undergraduates:
Accounting, Aural/Oral Sciences, Business Studies, Drama, Education, English, Finance, Fine Art, History, Human Resource Management (100%), Journalism, Law, Management Studies, Marketing, Nursing, Psychology.

Teaching least popular with undergraduates:
Architecture (54%).

---

stars for helpfulness and interest.

The Student Union has always been in the forefront when it comes to extra-curricular societies and pleasure zones. They still are, but now they are listening to a new voice among their students calling for space in the Union building not to celebrate the pound-a-pint ethos, but for a 'Nasa', a 'non-alcoholic social area'. The tide is turning. DMU's Nasa is the most used area in the Union.

To all this they welcome applications from UK and international students with a wide range of qualifications and experience. Visit dmu.ac.uk/ug for details of current entry and admissions criteria. Contact your chosen faculty admissions team in the DMU

Enquiry Centre to discuss your particular circumstances - tel: 08459 45 46 47 or email: enquiry@dmu.ac.uk.

What are they looking for? 'A genuine understanding of the subject/career field you are applying to, a focused application with evidence of extra curricula efforts to pursue your interest/career, and a passion and enthusiasm for your chosen subject.'

Open days in 2011 are on 2 July, 8 October and 22 October.

FEES, BURSARIES

UK & EU Fees 2011-12: £3,375 p.a. Bursary of £350 for students with household incomes £30k or less. The Academic Scholarship (value, £1,000) is available for freshers with 340 UCAS points from three A Levels or equivalent. The Access Scholarship (value, £1,000) is for mature applicants with an Access to Higher Education Qualification. There is also a Care Leavers Bursary (£1,000) for any student being cared for by a local authority at time of application. Finally, the Estranged Student Bursary (£1,000) is for students identified as being 'estranged' by Student Finance England. See

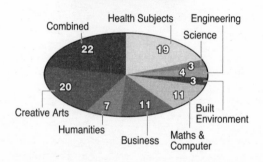

SUBJECT AREAS (%)

Combined 22
Health Subjects 19
Engineering
Science 4
3
3
Built Environment 11
Maths & Computer 11
Business 7
Humanities
Creative Arts 20

www.dmy.ac.uk for further details.

STUDENT PROFILE

There's a 45% mature undergraduate entrant population and an open-access policy that brings in many who might not have gone to uni a few years ago - 42% from social classes 4-7.

ACADEMIA & JOBS

Faculties are Art & Design; Business & Law; Technology (new name for Computer & Engineering); Health & Life Sciences; and Humanities.

Art & Design produces most jobs last time, 22% of the total. Specialist design jobs and retail in particular. Fashion is a key area - Clothing with Design, Contour Fashion (the only degree in the world to specialise in lingerie, bodywear, swimwear, performance sportswear, 'structured' eveningwear and bridalwear, established in 1947 at the request of the corset industry), Fashion Design, Textile Design etc. Students visit underwear manufacturers throughout Europe and Asia, after Hong Kong businessman Andrew Sia set up the Ace Style Institute at the university.

Design altogether is strong - Product Design, Interior Design, Design Crafts/Management/ Innovation/Products. The Architecture degrees keep architectural consultancy a perennially important graduate job destination for DMU students.

Next in number come graduate jobs in the heath industry. There's a host of degrees - Biomedical Science, Dental Technology, Medical Science, Pharmacy, Health Studies, Social Work, Nursing, and Midwifery, which has moved to the city campus so that all of DMU's provision will be based on one campus from September 2011.

Then come the bankers and businessmen and teachers and computer programmers. This last is a particular thing at DMU right now. You can develop, test and evaluate the latest 3D gaming in the new Games Development Studios. Kitted out with powerful gaming computers, RealD 3D technology, HD projection and the latest consoles and portable games devices, the studios provide the latest facilities for the gaming industry. They're equipped with Alienware and Dell XPS machines and have Xbox 360, Nintendo Wii and Playstation 3 consoles ready with game developer software. There is also a Valve Café software

> *'One of the most fab things about Leicester is its location right in the centre of the country. No matter how much you want to get away from home initially, it is mentally and financially beneficial if home is not 100 miles away.'*

licence which enables students to use classic Valve games such as Half Life, Counter Strike and Unreal Tournament and a range of game development tools such as the Valve Hammer editor.

But let's get back to the principles on which the whole deal at DMU moves forward: 1. sound learning environments - not only the games studios but the mock courtroom, the pharmacy practice suites and the dance studios, the award-winning Demon FM radio station and the £8 million sports centre, opening in 2012, designed by the architects who built the Olympic Aquatic Centre for London 2012.

2. courses with built-in employability: placements characterise many of them. More than one-third of students who undertake a placement year go on to secure employment with the company, and a survey by Hobsons revealed that 70% of employers who offer work placements take on at least one of the students when they graduate. In fact, many employers admit they offer work placements as a way of finding good future staff. Incredibly, DMU claim that their graduates earn

RESEARCH EXCELLENCE

% of De Montfort's research that is
4* (World-class) or 3* (Internationally rated):

	4*	3*
Nursing and Midwifery	10%	20%
Allied Health Professions	5%	20%
Pharmacy	5%	40%
Computer Science	10%	35%
Electrical and Electronic Eng.	5%	30%
General Eng., Mineral, Mining	5%	45%
Civil Engineering	25%	45%
Mechanical, Aeronautical & Manufacturing Engineering	5%	45%
Architecture/Built Environment	15%	50%
Business and Management	10%	25%
Law	0%	20%
Politics	5%	15%
Social Work,l Policy & Admin.	5%	25%
English	40%	20%
History	0%	45%
Art and Design	5%	40%
Drama, Dance, Performing Arts	20%	30%
Media Studies	25%	35%
Music	15%	40%

an average salary of £24,000 six months after completing their course. Here is a graduate of BSc (Hons) Radio Production on £75,000 p.a. There is a graduate of BA (Hons) Drama Studies on £23,250. Why? Because, they say, students are work-ready when they leave here.

SOCIAL SCENE

STUDENTS' UNION The Campus Centre building has restaurants and a bar, the Students' Union administration, a dance theatre and performing arts studios. The venue is called **Level 1** - DJ booth, laser lighting, amazing effects: 'We now have comfy leather sofas and funky chairs,' they say, 'a quadrant of bars, more drinking stations on your nights out.' On the first Friday of every month it is now home to the legendary *Brighton Beach*, first launched in 1996 to celebrate the best guitar music, music ranging from 60s soul and pop to classic indie, northern soul, Britpop and psychedelia.

Regular ents nights are a mix of activities from comedy to film previews, from karaoke to live gigs.

WHAT IT'S REALLY LIKE	
UNIVERSITY:	
Social Life	★★★
Societies	★★
Student Union services	★★★
Politics	**Active**
Sport	**30 clubs**
National team position	**94th**
Sport facilities	★★
Arts opportunities	**Theatre, music & film good**
Student newspaper	**Demon**
Student radio	**Demon FM**
Student TV	**Demon TV**
Nightclub	**Level 1**
Bars	**Bars 1 to 4**
Union ents	**7 days a week**
Union societies	**30**
Most popular society	**Chinese Soc, Hindu Soc**
Parking	**Limited. Some halls**
CITY/TOWN:	
Leicester Nightlife	★★★★★
City scene	**Top town - clubs, pubs, curries**
Town/gown relations	**OK**
Risk of violence	**Average**
Cost of living	**Average**
Student concessions	**Good**
Survival + 2 nights out	**£50-£80 pw**
Part-time work campus/town	**Good/Excellent**

ACCOMMODATION	
Student rating	★★★
Guarantee to freshers	**100%**
Style	**Flats**
Security guard	**Some**
Shared rooms	**None**
Internet access	**All**
Self-catered	**Most**
En suite	**Most**
Approx price range pw	**£85-£159**
City rent pw	**£35-£165**

Monday is Students and Societies Night, where any club or society puts on ents and enhances their resources. Tuesday is *Quiz Night*. Wednesday is *Univibe*, a year-old night of r&b flava musik, ranging from desi beats, ragga, bhangra to hip hop. Thursday is *Kinky*, a 21st-century disco night. Friday is *Death at the Stairs*, an indie/rock night. Saturday is *The Big Bad Cheese* - two rooms, one r&b, the other cheesy tunes.

Besides all this they have a lot of local independent bands, DJ sets and the like. Among the many societies there is a great reputation for media. Radio station Demon Fm has won awards for many years and built up a huge reputation within the industry. This term it has been awarded a community licence, which means transmission 24/7. There's also Demon TV and the *Demon* newspaper of course. In the old days they were always up among the annual media awards, nut not recently.

TOWN See *Student Leicester entry*. Leicester's Phoenix Square opened in November 2009. The development includes the £1m DMU **Cube**, an interactive digital art gallery, cinemas and café bar.

SPORT Hitherto there's been an emphasis on fun rather than serious competition at the John Sandford Sports Centre, and perhaps that will never change, but there is something new in the wings. Work is about to start on a sports and leisure complex to include a 25 metre swimming pool, eight courts for racket sports and five-a-side football, a fully equipped gym, fitness studios for yoga, pilates and aerobics, a climbing wall and a café. It will open in 2012.

PILLOW TALK

Most accommodation is in cluster flats with 4-6 students sharing. Other units 7-10 share. All accommodation has internet access. 1,800 of rooms for freshers have been built in the last two years. Limited parking at some halls.

GETTING THERE

- Leicester by road: M1/J21 or M6 then M69.
- By rail: London St Pancras, 75 mins.
- By air: Birmingham International Airport or East Midlands International Airport.

UNIVERSITY OF DERBY

University of Derby
Kedleston Road
Derby DE22 1GB

TEL 01332 590500
EMAIL askadmissions@derby.ac.uk
WEB www.derby.ac.uk

Derby University Students' Union
Kedleston Road
Derby DE22 1GB

TEL 01332 591507
FAX 01332 348846
EMAIL info@udsu.co.uk
WEB www.udsu-co.uk/

VIRGIN VIEW

The University of Derby is situated at the southern edge of the Peak District, 10 miles west of Nottingham. It has been a diffuse conglomeration of as many as twelve sites scattered across the city, but is now much more clearly concentrated at the main Kedleston Road Campus and the relatively new Buxton Campus 50 minutes away.

In the Higher Education National Student Survey, overall satisfaction with the university was 79%, and in the most recent analysis, although most of its graduates entered employment, the instance of real graduate-level jobs six months after leaving is 61%.

There was student approval of the teaching in a number of areas, specifically in Education, Accounting, Biology & related Sciences, English Studies, History, Teacher

UNIVERSITY/STUDENT PROFILE	
University since	**1992**
Situation/style	**City campus**
Student population	**22725**
Undergraduates	**14130**
Mature	**56%**
International	**10%**
Male/female ratio	**43:57**
Equality of opportunity:	
state school intake	**97%**
social class 4-7 intake	**38%**
drop-out rate	**12%**

Training, Languages, Law, Marketing, Music, Subjects Allied to Medicine, Performing Arts and Physical Geography.

Generally, there is evidence to suggest that the lecturers at Derby are very helpful and interested in their students.

*As for life outside the lecture hall, Derby undergraduates have always had a good time, and now, besides a vibrant city scene, they have at Kedleston Road a new Union bar and venue, the **Academy**, conceived by their own Architectural Design students.*

*There is also a Student Union out at Buxton, the second campus, with the **Boiler House** and the **Hub** serving the students' every need.*

Open Days in 2011: 19 March , 11 June 2011, 3 September, 8 October, 29 October, 26 November. In 2012: 4 February, 17 March.

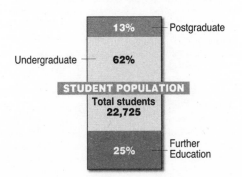

Postgraduate 13%
Undergraduate 62%

STUDENT POPULATION
Total students
22,725

Further Education 25%

CAMPUS

The main site at Kedleston Road is 10 minutes walk from the city centre. Buxton Campus became part of the scene after the merger of High Peak College with the university. From there they deliver both further and higher education. The idea is that you can move through the various levels within the university, from NVQs and BTECs, to Foundation Degrees and Higher Level qualifications.

There is also a presence at Markeaton Street in Derby, where most of the Arts, Design and Technology courses are taught, and at Britannia Mill they have the School of Social Care and Therapeutic Practice. Finally, 35 minutes away to the north, in Chesterfield, there's a campus for nurses and other healthcare professionals.

You can apply for a permit to park your car on

TEACHING SURVEY AT A GLANCE

Avg. UCAS points accepted	**220**
Acceptance rate	**18%**
Overall satisfaction rate	**79%**
Helpful/interested staff	★★★
Small tuition groups	★★
Students into graduate jobs	**61%**

Teaching most popular with undergraduates:
Education, Accounting, Biology & related Sciences, English Studies, History, Teacher Training, Languages, Law, Marketing, Music, Subjects Allied to Medicine, Performing Arts, Physical Geography.

Teaching least popular with undergraduates:
Architecture, Building & Planning (57%).

site. Cost p.a. is £220. Frequent shuttle bus services run between Derby sites and into the city centre.

FEES, BURSARIES

UK & EU Fees, 2011-12: £3,375 p.a. for full time bachelors degrees, foundation degrees and HNDs. There's a bursary for students who have studied full time at one of their partner schools or colleges (£200), and one if you're paying £3,375 tuition fees out of a household income below £36,592. They expect over two thirds of their students to qualify for some support.

STUDENT PROFILE

Derby is at the forefront of the 'new university' revolution, which released higher education to the masses in 1992, when so many of the old

RESEARCH EXCELLENCE

% of Derby's research that is
4* *(World-class)* or **3*** *(Internationally rated)*:

	4*	3*
Biological Sciences	**0%**	**15%**
Psychology	**0%**	**10%**
Art and Design	**5%**	**20%**
Media Studies	**25%**	**15%**

polytechnics were redefined as universities. Its open access policy has attracted a very large mature undergraduate population (56%). There are also many part-timers and many from traditional working-class families (38%), and from postcode areas which have never before supplied to the university sector. Inevitably this has also resulted in a high drop-out rate (12%).

ACADEMIA & JOBS

Derby's courses are focused on helping you to improve your career prospects. There are close links with employers, placement opportunities, competitions, such as The Entrepreneur and Business Quest, to help you develop your business and enterprise skills. The idea is to tailor your degree to match your career aspirations. Many courses are accredited by professional bodies, and you can accrue professional qualifications while working towards some degrees.

Their schools are Art, Design & Technology; Business, Computing & Law; Education, Health & Sciences; and the further and higher education provision out at Buxton.

This last is a joint honours curriculum delivering such as Hospitality, Spa Therapies (Buxton is a spa town), Public Services Management, Public Relations, the Culinary Arts, Sports, Travel &

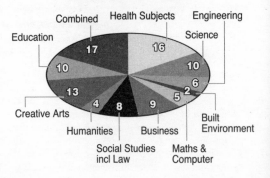

SUBJECT AREAS (%)

Tourism, Events Management, Countryside Management, etc. The main academic aspiration is to make teachers and healers out of its students. Education (principally Primary School) and Health (mainly hospital work) together account for more than a quarter of Derby's graduate employment.

The Health degrees include Nursing, Healing Arts, Diagnostic Radiography, and Occupational Therapy. On Chesterfield Campus there's a fully-functioning Clinical Skills Suite with hospital beds, drug trolleys, hoist and other medical equipment, and SimMan, an electronically programmed robot, simulates ailments for treatment by the student nurses. The BSc in Occupational Therapy is recognised by the College of Occupational Health and the Health Professions Council.

One curriculum niche evident in their graduate employment figures - they send a sizeable cohort each year into aircraft manufacture. Design is productive of jobs in other areas too, notably Architecture Design, and Creative Design Practices, where advertising is a popular destination for many.

This in-depth expertise in design was recognised in the latest nationwide assessment of research, in which 25% of their research was adjudged either world-class or internationally significant.

The other success in research is Media, where 25% of its work was accorded world class status and 15% of international significance. Look at the Broadcast Media, Film & TV, and sound production provision. There are jobs in radio, television, and film for the best graduates each year. About the same number find work from the artistic/creative degrees, Theatre Arts, Dance, and Creative Writing. They just acquired **Derby Theatre**, securing this important cultural asset for the city and providing performing arts students with a choice learning environment.

On the business side, BA Human Resource Management is to be recommended, and there are well-trod pathways into catering and tourism, transport planning and distribution, sales management, etc.

SOCIAL SCENE

STUDENTS' UNION The new facility at Kedleston Road is the **Academy Bar** - two levels and decking outside which looks out over Markeaton Park.

They've had live acts here - We Are Scientists, Scouting for Girls - but mainly it's themed nights at **Level 2**, like the recent Union Blue, or use is made of the 40-foot screen for *Popcorn* - 'an afternoon of the greatest movies ever made'. T are pre-party games and activities all afternoon on a Wednesday,

WHAT IT'S REALLY LIKE	
UNIVERSITY:	
Social Life	★★★
Societies	★★
Student Union services	★★★
Politics	**Interested, but 'non-engaging'**
Sport	**29 clubs.**
National team position	**98th**
Sport facilities	★★
Arts opportunities	**Drama OK**
Student magazine	**Dusted**
Student radio	**DRS**
Nightclub	**Level 2**
Bars	**Academy Boiler House**
Union ents	**Rock, hiphop, cheese & big balls**
Union societies	**29**
Most active societies	**D:One, LGBT**
Parking	**Permits £220 p.a.**
CITY:	
Entertainment	★★★
Scene	**Small, friendly, pub rock/indie**
Town/gown relations	**Good**
Risk of violence	**Low**
Cost of living	**Average**
Student concessions	**Good**
Survival + 2 nights out	**£70 pw**
Part-time work campus/town	**Excellent**

leading to the big night at **Zanzibar** in town - *Spank* (10pm till 3). Tuesday tends to be spent at the First Floor in **Rockhouse**, also in town - 'the official rock night of Derby SU' - two rooms of rock, all the classics, metal, nu-metal, industrial, punk, ska. Society nights are also popularly organised at **Walkabout**. There are somewhat lighter musical goings-on at the **Boiler House** at Buxton, but they all come together in the May Ball, a five stage affair at Kedleston Road, live acts on the Main Stage, *Godskitchen* @ the **Academy**, indie and acoustic stages, and the *Silent Arena* (headphone disco, the new rave). The ball runs from 9pm till 6 am, but there are three pre-bars - **Varsity**, **Barracuda**, and **Sun Lounge** in town, and an *After-Party* at **Zanzibar** from 6am. Then there's Graduation Ball and the Awards Dinners. There's a theory that Derby isn't a 56% mature student

> *'Derby undergraduates have always had a good time, and now, besides the city scene at venues like the Rockhouse and Zanzibar, they have a new Union bar and venue.'*

population, they're just amazingly tired.

The Source is the Independent Student Advice Centre at Kedleston Road. It's the Hub at Buxton. They have a student magazine - *Dusted*, a radio station - DRS, which sponsors various party and/or comedy nights, 15 societies, including one - International - at Buxton, and 29 sports clubs (9 at Buxton), including American Football, Basketball, and Dodgeball.

Students tend to be 'slightly non engaging' when it comes to NUS campaigns, 'but we are working on that!'

SPORT Not a serious contender on the national stage. On-site facilities include a gymnasium and pitches. They have just invested £750,000 in a floodlit all weather pitch.

TOWN Derby is nicely poised between 'friendly town' and 'sprawling metropolis'. Says Asam Rashid: 'There are many student-friendly bars in Derby that are safe, fun and not so expensive.' Besides the clubs, mentioned above, there's a large variety of pubs, and the **Derby Playhouse** (with which the SU secure good discounts) three cinemas, two of which are multiplexes and require a short trip by taxi. The third is in the town centre and dispenses arthouse fare.

ACCOMMODATION	
Student rating	★★★
Guarantee to freshers	**100%**
Style	**Halls**
Self-catered	**All**
En suite	**Some**
Approx price range pw	**£81-£102**
City rent pw	**£65-£140**

PILLOW TALK

Halls with flats, lodges, and houses are of a good standard at various locations around the city; none is catered; 50% are en suite (all rooms at Peak Court are en suite). All the halls are wired up so you can subscribe to telephone and free internet use. Freshers are guaranteed accommodation if their applications are received by August 31.

GETTING THERE

☞ By road: Kedleston Road campus is just off the A38, the main southwest/northeast thoroughfare which goes south to Exeter and meets the M1 at Junction 28. M1/J25 for access from the east, A6 from the southeast (Loughborough way).

☞ By rail: rail links with Derby are easy. London is two hours away.

☞ By coach: London, 3:15.

UNIVERSITY OF DUNDEE

The University of Dundee
Nethergate
Dundee DD1 4HN

Dundee Students' Association
Airlie Place
Dundee DD1 4HP

TEL 01382 383838
FAX 01382 388150
EMAIL contactus@dundee.ac.uk
WEB www.dundee.ac.uk

TEL 01382 386060
FAX 01382 227124
EMAIL dusa@dundee.ac.uk
WEB www.dusa.co.uk

VIRGIN VIEW

*F*ounded in 1883 as University College Dundee, seven years later it became part of St Andrews University and remained so until it gained independence in 1967.

Today, Dundee is a traditional, premier-league university, but unusually relaxed and friendly. It has a history, but isn't steeped in it. Nor does it feel bound by tradition to repeat itself.

Generally, however, teaching is in the traditional, tutorial-based mould: lecturers are rated 4 stars for interest in students, and 3 stars for size of tuition groups. The uni came 5th nationally in the Times Higher Student Experience Survey *last year.*

Long before it was fashionable, support was undertaken here in an online environment, with 24/7 internet-based access to resources, timetables, lecture enhancements, assessments, assignment submission, discussion boards and collaborative working opportunities.

They claim to have been the first university in Scotland to engage with an online Personal Development Planning programme, which acts to ensure that a student's academic education occurs in concert with their personal and career development. Students create portfolios to illustrate their personal development, and these are being utilised for external appraisal such as for job applications. The results are there to see - 87% student satisfaction and an 80% graduate job rating after six months.

The University has a strong focus on 'the professions' with many degrees accredited by relevant professional bodies. It is No. 1 in the UK for student satisfaction in anatomy and physiology, environmental science, geography, pharmacology and planning. What's more, the University is officially quoted (HESA) as having the highest graduate starting salaries in Scotland and 6th in the UK, with an average first job salary of £24,299.

How do you get in? They take each applicant's individual circumstances and potential into account when assessing their application. In the personal statement they are looking for a clear sense of an applicant's motivation for studying a particular course, relevant work experience, and achievements both in and out of school. So, no surprises there then. You get the feeling that it's be a good idea to dig a little deeper into the very special culture that is Dundee before writing that statement.

A time-lapse video (www.dundee.ac.uk/admissions/video) was launched to enable just that, and Open Day visits in 2011 are as follows: Main Visit Days - 31 August 2011 and 1 October; Medicine, Nursing & Midwifery -22 June and 31 August; Art and Design - 1 and 2 November. You might also dip into the experience of their own student bloggers - www.dundee.ac.uk/admissions/tada/what_the y_say.htm.

CAMPUS

'Dundee lies on the East Coast of Northern Scotland, a couple of hours away from Glasgow,

UNIVERSITY/STUDENT PROFILE	
University since	**1967**
Situation/style	**City campus**
Student population	**15615**
Total undergraduates	**10550**
Mature	**52%**
International	**13%**
Male/female ratio	**40:60**
Equality of opportunity:	
state school intake	**91%**
social class 4-7 intake	**25%**
drop-out rate	**8%**

Edinburgh and Aberdeen,' writes Sameen Farouk. 'Next door is St. Andrews. Dundee is one of a handful of genuine get-away-from-it-all universities. The scenery up here is breathtaking.

'The main campus, with compact teaching facilities, IT centre, the main libraries, the art college, sports facilities, the union, the dental hospital, John Smith Bookshop, Bonar Hall, the famous Wellcome Trust building (all within 5 mins walk of each other), is located on the edge of the town centre. It is safe, clean and increasingly accessible to the disabled community.

'The medical campus is located in the town's main hospital, Ninewells. Other sites, the nursing college (Kirkaldy in Fife, 35 miles from Dundee) and Northern College - the Faculty of Education & Social Work (Gardyne Road) are a little further out.'

'Without being steeped in outmoded tradition, the university retains a strong self-image, and the students form a very real community around the central core of campus.'

FEES, BURSARIES

UK & EU Fees p.a., 2011-12: £1,820 (£2,895 for Medicine). If you are a Scottish-domiciled, first degree student you are eligible for your tution fees

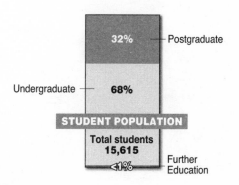

to be covered by the Scottish Government. There are scholarships based on musical or sporting ability, and for applicants to medicine and dentistry. Visit www.dundee.ac.uk/prospectus/bursaries for more details.

STUDENT PROFILE

'Without being steeped in outmoded tradition,' writes Hannah Hamilton, 'the university retains a strong self-image, and the students form a very real community around the central core of campus.'

Dundee attracts students from all walks of life and from all areas. The inevitable scattering of public school types joins a healthy dose of students from Ireland and a very strong international community.

'Dundee could never be criticised for being a quaint English retreat,' agrees Sameen. 'The university recruits internationally and has strong Arab, Chinese, Malaysian, Korean and Hispanic communities. There is also a substantial South-Asian population. The local communities are also targeted keenly, and there is a growing population of mature students.'

Once among the elite in the context of the Government's as pirations to level the socio-economic playing field in Higher Education, Dundee meets its Government benchmark for student intake from the four lower classes, but this is no ex-poly ,asquerading as a 'new' university, bent on matching course to job.

It is a university for the professions: medicine, dentistry, nursing, architecture, finance, and the law. Dundee sends more graduates into the professions than any other university in Scotland,

TEACHING SURVEY AT A GLANCE	
Avg. UCAS points accepted	**353**
Acceptance rate	**16%**
Overall satisfaction rate	**87%**
Helpful/interested staff	★★★★
Small tuition groups	★★★
Students into graduate jobs	**80%**

Teaching most popular with undergraduates:
Education, Teacher Training, Accounting, Anatomy, Physiology & Pathology, Architecture, Biology, Business & Administrative Studies, Dentistry, English, European Languages (100%), Finance, Geography (Physical, 100%), History, Law, Maths, Medical Science & Pharmacy (100%), Medicine, Nursing, Subjects Allied to Medicine, Creative Arts & Design, Pharmacy, Philosophy, Politics, Psychology, Zoology (100%).

Teaching least popular with undergraduates:
Business (60%).

and it is well balanced socially, classless, with its eye on other things. Just as soon as you think you have sussed Dundee, all certainties are thrown to the wind. For example, Africa's biggest hip-hop stars just graduated from the University, touted as 'the only MCee with an MSc', whatever that means. Naetochukwu Chikwe, better known to the 3 million who bought his first record as Naeto C, attained a Masters in Energy Studies last year.

> *'I suppose, if you are a Scot, and you want to study medicine, Edinburgh would have to be high on the list, but people have had very good experiences of Dundee.'*

ACADEMIA & JOBS

Besides the College of Art & Design, Architecture, Engineering & Physical Science; College of Arts & Social Sciences; College of Life Sciences; College of Medicine, Dentistry and Nursing, there's a new School of Business and School of the Environment this year, bringing together complimentary areas.

'I suppose, if you are a Scot, and you want to study medicine,' said a sixth-form careers mistress, 'Edinburgh would have to be high on the list, but people have had very good experiences of Dundee.' For post-medics it was just rated the best place to work in Europe.

The requirement for sassenachs is for three A levels to include Chemistry and one other science. You will also sit UKCAT. The degree is the 5/6-year MBChB. Integrated med school and hospital. Course problem/ community-based, i.e. clinical

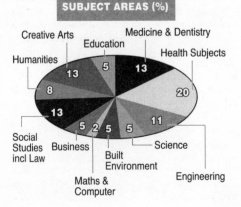

SUBJECT AREAS (%)

Creative Arts — 13
Education — 5
Medicine & Dentistry — 13
Health Subjects — 20
Humanities — 8
Social Studies incl Law — 13
Business — 5
Maths & Computer — 2
Built Environment — 5
Science — 5
Engineering — 11

experience from Year 1. For dentists it's the 5/6-year BDS.

Medical and biosciences degrees here are key and the undergraduate curriculum in life sciences has just been reviewed and improved to emphasise practical skills including labs, fieldwork and problem solving with common core modules shared in Levels 1 and 2.

The University has various schemes to help graduates less likely than medics to get a job, a Skills Award endorsed by the CBI which recognises job skills learned at university, a Career Planning Module is worth credits at Level 2, and Internship Module, which is basically a placement with an outside company, and there's the Enterprise Gym, where you learn to flex business enterprise muscle with high-powered practitioners.

Some 40% of all Dundee graduates find work in health and social work. Around 70% of these in hospitals. Many others become teachers, almost half of them in Primary Education. The first cohort of secondary school teachers graduated in 2005 on a course which allows distance learning and part-time study.

Architectural Consultancy is another popular end game. The department merits a world-class tag for only 5% of its research work, whereas its sister department, Civil Engineering, was adjudged world-class for 15% and internationally significant in 70%, which is very high.

Art & Design also demands attention - 35% of its research is world-class, 20% internationally significant. Textile Design (the city's industrial heritage) was always rated highly in the old teaching assessments. Companies like Nike and Calvin Kline queue up to employ Dundee graduates. Bang in the middle of the city's cultural quarter with its pubs, clubs and gallery shops, the Art/Design College, through its reputation in the fashion and design industries, provides a global dimension to what has been called 'Dundee-chic'.

Dundee Contemporary Arts is a multi-million-pound centre for visual arts with the university's Visual Research Centre at its hub, an art laboratory equipped with cutting edge facilities for producing design prototypes, videos, prints, artists' books, etc. Jobs for graduates in this area are diverse, from graphic designers and illustrators to printers, publishing production managers, set designers and jewellery designer-makers, as well as artistic creation of course. With a nice cross-faculty touch, the University offers the world's first and only degree course in Forensic and Medical Art (MSc Forensic & Medical Art).

This is typical of Dundee. Other niche areas include an MSc Islamic Accounting & Finance programme in the School of Business and a

RESEARCH EXCELLENCE

% of Dundee's research that is
4* (World-class) or 3* (Internationally rated):

	4*	3*
Laboratory Clinical Subjects	5%	60%
Primary Care Clinical Subjects	5%	40%
Dentistry	10%	40%
Nursing and Midwifery	10%	40%
Biological Sciences	25%	40%
Applied Mathematics	10%	35%
Computer Science	15%	50%
General Eng., Mineral, Mining	5%	30%
Civil Engineering	15%	70%
Architecture/Built Environment	5%	35%
Geography	15%	45%
Economics and Econometrics	5%	40%
Accounting and Finance	5%	35%
Law	5%	45%
Politics	10%	20%
Social Work, Policy & Admin.	5%	30%
Psychology	5%	30%
Education	5%	15%
English	10%	35%
Philosophy	10%	35%
History	15%	50%
Art and Design	35%	20%

postgraduate MSc in Business Intelligence. Meanwhile, the cross-faculty principle, one that appeals to employers and coal-face researchers alike, is again tapped by the School of the Environment, which brings together staff from a number of disciplines to benefit Architecture, Environmental Science, Geography and Town and Regional Planning students.

In Law, they are internationally rated for research, European law specialists and offer both Scots and English Law. Non-Law graduates may take a 2-year full-time or 3-year part-time Senior Status Law degree here. Now a new International Water Law Research Institute is to open, it's the first of its kind in the world, and is set to train future leaders to arbitrate water conflicts.

SOCIAL SCENE

STUDENTS' ASSOCIATION The SA was rated 1st in Scotland and 4th in the UK in the 'Good Student Union' category of the Times Higher's Student Experience Survey this year. There are 2 nightclubs: **Mono** (900 capacity), Dundee's largest nightclub which often plays host to big acts such as Groove Armada, Biffy Clyro, and Dundee's own 'The View', and **Floor 5** (350 capacity). The 2 bars are **Air** (cool, relaxed café bar during the day; bar and live music/comedy venue at night) and **The**

Liar (best venue to watch televised sport in Dundee), plus a huge games room with pool tables, games machines, and a **Food on 4** catering outlet. Ents offer *Skint* in Mono on Tuesday and Saturday. Mono also has regular club nights with top Radio 1 DJs like Vic Galloway and Trevor Nelson, and special event theme nights and society fundraisers.

There are some 50 societies, most active being Lip Theatre, Islamic Society, DARE (Development and research expeditions) People and Planet. The SRC and many societies push campaigns on global warming, nuclear disarmament, etc.'

The Magdalen is the student magazine, then there's Discover Radio and DUSA TV. Arts students recently starred alongside Hollywood star Brian Cox, television presenter Lorraine Kelly and Dundee chart-toppers The View in 'Skint', DUSA TV's student-made soap opera.

SPORTise (Institute of Sport and Exercise) has a wide range of high class facilities, a 400 metre-square gym, 2 exercise studios, 3 glass-backed, competition standard squash courts, a strength

ACCOMMODATION	
Student rating	★★★★★
Guarantee to freshers	**100%**
Style	**Flats**
Security guard	**Most**
Shared rooms	**None**
Internet access	**Most**
Self-catered	**All**
En suite	**Most**
Approx price range pw	**£96-£112**
City rent pw	**£60**

performance centre, a dance/indoor cycling studio, a 25m swimming pool with sauna, 4 newly resurfaced, floodlit, all-weather tennis courts and 2 large indoor sports halls.

There is a Regional Strength Performance Centre and laboratories for sports science, performance assessment and research activities.

The Institute was accredited in 2008 by the London 2012 Olympic Organising Committee as an official Pre-Games Training Camp venue.

TOWN Dundee, which already ranks among the world's most intelligent cities for its scientific expertise, has been voted Scotland's sexiest city by the *Scotland on Sunday* newspaper. 'For many years Dundee has seemed to play second fiddle to Aberdeen, Glasgow and Edinburgh,' writes Michael Sheldon. 'However, if you scratch the surface of the City of the 3 J's (Jute, Jam and Journalism) you will find one of Scotland's most progressive and desirable cities.

'Tired tourist touts will tell you that it is the birthplace of *The Beano* and *The Dandy*, home to the RRS Discovery (made famous by Scott of the Antarctic), and to the Mills Observatory (the only full-time public observatory in the UK). And then direct you to the Verdant Works Museum, where the history of Dundee's textile industry is documented and non-Dundonians learn what "an ingin ene inna" means!' But this city is not stuck in the past. Recently, it has reinvented itself.

'Two unis - Abertay and Dundee - means two modern centres of entertainment. There are also three cinemas at Camperdown, Douglas and in the DCA, an Ice rink, loads of Parks and Coffee Shops.'

The Perth Road and West Port areas are best for pubs, with establishments such as **The Speedwell Bar**, with a huge selection of whiskies, the **Art Bar** and **Tally's**. Club-wise, there's **Fat Sam's**, open seven days a week, **Underground**, which is not so much a club as a bar open till 2.30 a.m., and for something different, **The Reading Rooms**. 'The

WHAT IT'S REALLY LIKE	
UNIVERSITY:	
Social Life	★★★★★
Societies	★★★★
Student Union services	★★★★★
Politics	**Society-based**
Sport	**45 clubs**
National team position	**43rd**
Sport facilities	★★★★★
Arts opportunities	**Music, film, art excellent; drama good; dance avg**
Student magazine	**Magdalen**
Student radio	**Discover Radio**
Student television	**DUSA TV**
Nightclubs	**Mono, Floor 5**
Bars	**Air, The Liar**
Union ents	**Full on**
Union societies	**50**
Most popular	**Lip Theatre, Islamic Society, DARE**
Parking	**Poor**
CITY:	
Entertainment	★★★★
Scene	**Scotland's sexiest**
Town/gown relations	**Average**
Risk of violence	**Low**
Cost of living	**Low**
Student concessions	**Good**
Survival + 2 nights out	**£80 pw**
Part-time work campus/town	**Excellent/Good**

new meets the old close to the university in **The Cultural Quarter**, where lie the **Dundee Rep Theatre**, the multi-million-pound **Dundee Contemporary Arts Centre**, **The Sensations Science Centre**, a hands-on science museum for the big kid inside you. All this and the city's multiple-floor shopping centres, **The Wellgate** and **The Overgate**.'

PILLOW TALK

There are five residence sites, each comprising between 30 and 90 self contained flats, all single rooms Four sites offer en-suite facilities. Not all would agree that halls were the best option: 'Personally, I found hall a bit of an expensive option.,' says Sameen.

However, over 1,000 new en-suite rooms opened in 2006, relatively expensive (see Accommodation box), but very nice.

Student parking is not allowed unless you've got a crying need.

GETTING THERE

☛ By road: M90, M85, A85, A972.
☛ By rail: Newcastle, 3:00; London Euston, 6:00.
☛ By air: Dundee Airport for internal flights; Edinburgh International Airport is an hour away.
☛ By coach: London, 10:05; Birmingham, 10:05; Newcastle, 6:05.

● ●

UNIVERSITY OF DURHAM

The University of Durham
Old Shire Hall
Old Elvet
Durham DH1 3HP

TEL 0191 334 2000
FAX 0191 334 6055

EMAIL admissions@durham.ac.uk
WEB www.dur.ac.uk

Durham Students' Union
Dunelm House
New Elvet
Durham DH1 3AN

TEL 0191 334 1777
FAX 0191 334 1778

EMAIL student.uniont@durham.ac.uk
WEB www.durham21.co.uk

VIRGIN VIEW

*F*ounded in 1832, Durham is, like Oxford and Cambridge, a collegiate university, although unlike Oxbridge its colleges are purely residential. Academically, it is faculty based. It offers all the advantages of the best of British universities and is demanding at entry, shamelessly going after Oxbridge rejects, delaying its selection until after those two more ancient universities have taken their pick. But it combines this policy with another, designed to net applicants from elsewhere, particularly from non-traditional higher education heartlands, 'low participation' neighbourhoods and social classes. We know a sixth former who got in to Durham with one AS level and a GNVQ.

But the thing about Durham is that the students really enjoy the experience. Durham

students benefit from a campus the beauty of which will never leave you; from the wide range of extra-curricular activities - over 90% of their students participate through a student union society; from belonging to one of a supportive college community that adds

UNIVERSITY/STUDENT PROFILE	
University since	**1832**
Situation/style	**City collegiate**
Student population	**16845**
Undergraduates	**11370**
Mature	**21%**
International	**21%**
Male/female ratio	**49:51**
Equality of opportunity:	
state school intake	**59%**
social class 4-7 intake	**17%**
drop-out rate	**3%**

a sense of identity and security early on and inspires great loyalties; and from Durham's research led teaching, close interaction with staff at the cutting edge of their chosen discipline.

The happy result of their strategy is that 87% of undergraduates registered their satisfaction in the national survey, and whenever we have interviewed Durham students, whether from state schools and poorer neighbourhoods or from more privileged backgrounds, the response has been equally positive. Unspurprisingly, its 3% drop-out rate is among the lowest in the country.

So what do they expect of you in return? Money certainly. Durham was one of the first to declare fees in 2012 at £9,000. But how can you be sure to get an offer, given the crazy competition for places? 'Multiple factors are taken into account (1) A-Level (or equivalent) grades; (2) GCSE (or equivalent) grades; (3) the personal statement; (4) the reference; (5) the development of study skills; (6) motivation for the degree programme applied for; (7) independence of thought and working; (8) skills derived from non-academic extra-curricular activities such as engagement in sport, the arts or voluntary and community work; and (9) contextual consideration of merit and potential.'

So now you know. Get writing that

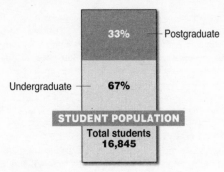

STUDENT POPULATION
Total students
16,845

personal statement. Durham City pre-application Open Days: Monday 27th June 2011 and Saturday 2nd July 2011. Queen's Campus pre-application Open Days: Friday 17th June 2011, Friday 24th June 2011 and Friday 16th September 2011.

CAMPUS

Durham is a small, stunningly beautiful city, 16 miles south of Newcastle. The nucleus of the medieval city, where the five Bailey colleges and the Arts and Social Sciences Departments are located, is formed by a bend of the River Wear around a rocky peninsular, dominated by the 11th-century cathedral and castle. Sixty million pounds has now been invested in a new student services building, library extension, Law School, refurbishment of the Bailey and Palace Green and catering facilities across the university. It provides a 'one-stop-shop', bringing together all the uni's student services hitherto dotted around the City.

Queen's Campus, Stockton, lies south down the A1(M), on the banks of the River Tees. There are two colleges, John Snow and George Stephenson. The campus is at the heart of a planned £300-million investment in the surrounding North Shore area.

FEES, BURSARIES

UK & EU Fees, 2011-12: £3,375 p.a. Fees for 2012-13 will be £9,000. In 2011-12 there are Sport, Music and the Arts Scholarships worth £2,000 each per year. www.durham.ac.uk/undergraduate/finance/vc_sc holarships; Academic Excellence scholarships worth £2,000 twww.durham.ac.uk/undergraduate/finance/afford/vc-excellence; the Durham Grant Scheme: £1,000 per year guaranteed to full-time undergraduate students in receipt of the maximum Maintenance Grant or Special Support Grant www.durham.ac.uk/undergraduate/finance/dgs.

STUDENT PROFILE

Writes Alex Pharaoh: 'I came to Durham from a grammar school in North Yorkshire, aware that it

---

TEACHING SURVEY AT A GLANCE

Avg. UCAS points accepted	**460**
Acceptance rate	**15%**
Overall satisfaction rate	**87%**
Helpful/interested staff	★★★★
Small tuition groups	★★★
Students into graduate jobs	**81%**

Teaching most popular with undergraduates:
Education (100%), Anthropology, Archaeology, Business Studies, Chemistry, Classics, Economics, English, European Languages, Geology, History (98%), Human & Social Geography, Law, Molecular Biology, Linguistics, Subjects allied to Medicine, Philosophy, Physical Geography, Physics & Astronomy, Politics, Sociology, Theology (97%).

Teaching least popular with undergraduates:
Computer Science (67%).

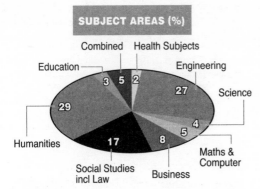

SUBJECT AREAS (%)

- Combined — 5
- Health Subjects — 2
- Education — 3
- Engineering — 27
- Science
- Humanities — 29
- Social Studies incl Law — 17
- Business — 8
- Maths & Computer — 5, 4

They have first-class links with the major firms. There's a dedicated degree and Foundation degree. Defence is another strength in employment, taking graduates largely through Modern Languages, Physical Sciences, and Social Studies.

Physics, Physics with Astronomy, etc, are very strong. In the Institute of Computational Cosmology there's a £1.4-million supercomputer capable of making ten billion calculations a second and 'recreating the entire evolution of the universe'.

Many graduates of Modern Languages, Social Studies, Physical Sciences, and History & Philosophy find work in the Civil Service, and a mass of Durham graduates get jobs in human resources and recruitment through Modern Languages, Biological Sciences, and Social Studies.

Subjects within Social Studies and Modern Languages account for 33% of all the employment provision at Durham.

had a reputation of being a haven for public schoolers and Oxbridge rejects, and, yes, a lot of people here do fall into one of these categories.'

Says recent graduate Martha Wright: 'I feel it's really mixed. My friendship group was very varied. We had a Harrow boy, but also state school people like me, so we didn't really notice the difference that much. We had friends from Newcastle, Reading, Scotland, London, Yorkshire. You have got your central bar in College, and all the events that happen in College, and you tend to meet people from all the years there.'

ACADEMIA & JOBS

Teaching strengths, often backed by research strengths (see Research Excellence box), lies in Education, Anthropology, Archaeology, Business Studies, Chemistry, Classics, Economics, English, European Languages, Geology, History, Human & Social Geography, Law, Molecular Biology, Linguistics, Subjects allied to Medicine, Philosophy, Physical Geography, Physics & Astronomy, Politics, Sociology, and Theology. Durham students rated the teaching of Education more highly than students at any other university. In fact, they were unanimous in 2010.

There is a medical faculty, shared with neighbours Newcastle, but it is primarily aimed at mature students, with a special Pre-med programme for applicants without the necessary scientific background for Stage 1 entry. The course (MBBS) has two years at Stockton before transfer to Newcastle, where in years 3, 4 and 5, students will be assigned a regional clinical unit. Required subjects include Chemistry and/or Biology at AS or A level. If only one of Biology and/or Chemistry is offered at A or AS level, the other should be offered at GCSE grade A (or Dual Award Science grade A). You must also sit UKCAT.

This is a uni with great contacts in the City. In Accountancy they are one of the big three providers, along with Nottingham and Warwick.

RESEARCH EXCELLENCE

% of Durham's research that is
4* *(World-class)* or **3*** *(Internationally rated):*

	4*	3*
Biological Sciences	10%	40%
Environmental Sciences	15%	55%
Chemistry	20%	45%
Physics	20%	40%
Pure Mathematics	20%	40%
Applied Mathematics	15%	60%
Statistics	5%	45%
Computer Science	20%	45%
General Eng., Mineral, Mining	10%	50%
Geography	30%	40%
Archaeology	35%	40%
Business and Management	15%	40%
Law	30%	35%
Politics	15%	35%
Social Work, Policy & Admin.	15%	45%
Anthropology	20%	35%
Psychology	15%	45%
Education	20%	35%
Middle Eastern, African	20%	45%
East European Languages	5%	35%
French	15%	35%
German, Dutch, Scandinavian	20%	40%
Italian	5%	20%
Iberian and Latin American	20%	45%
English	30%	30%
Classics, etc.	25%	40%
Philosophy	15%	40%
Theology	40%	25%
History	20%	40%
Music	30%	30%

DURHAM COLLEGES

Each college has its own distinct identity. The system promotes great loyalties and sporting rivalries. The Durham college stereotype is described in the rivalry between the so-called Bailey colleges (John's, Chad's, Cuth's, University - known as Castle - and Hatfield), situated in the Bailey area of the medieval city, and the Hill colleges (Trev's, Van Mildert, Mary's, Collingwood, Grey's and Aiden's), situated southwest of the Bailey.

Graduate Sophie Vokes-Dudgeon urges: 'Pick your college carefully. Within a couple of days you'll have learned your college songs and rituals, and feel a strange affiliation with this set of buildings, which will manifest itself loudly on many a river bank or touch line throughout your life as a Durham student. The stereotypical image we have is of Rahs on the Bailey and Plebs on the Hill. And then there's St Hild & St Bede, the biggest college, a minute or two further out, perhaps with a more diverse mix than some of the others. Don't go entirely by the stereotypes though; be sure to visit and talk to students.

'The Hill colleges are more like a campus, all a drunken stagger from one another. Next to the Science site, computers and library too, but what you gain in convenience you lack in history and surroundings. The Bailey colleges are also near enough for a bar crawl, and the cobbled streets and cathedral backdrop make it far more aesthetically pleasing. Chad's and John's bars are barely big enough to swing a cat, however, and you may be more likely to stumble upon Evensong than a pint of lager in St John's. Hild Bede bar resembles an airport lounge.

'Colleges also differ in facilities. Hild Bede has a newish multigym, an abundance of tennis courts, squash courts, gyms, and beautiful if basic accommodation. Castle, on the other hand, offers third years the chance to live in a castle, while Collingwood gives you en-suite shower rooms and kettles. The choice is yours!'

'Trevs is very representative of the whole student body,' writes Eleanor. 'It is also friendly and has strong college spirit. There are loads of social events, two balls a year and one of the larger, and more tasteful bars. We are fairly standard when compared to other colleges. Our accommodation is decent, not as nice as Collingwood, however. Bailey accommodation tends to be the worst, as it is the oldest and they also room some students far from the main building, Cuth's is worst for this. Hill Colleges have purpose built accommodation blocks. John's is very religious, Van Mildert is good for music opportunities, Cuth's is famed for having a bar with proper opening hours!'

Says Alex: 'My college, Collingwood, is known as one of the best. We have the most modern accommodation, more en-suite rooms, more IT networked rooms, less room sharing, better central facilities, such as bar and gym, and allegedly, better food than others. We are one of the newest colleges, and have less tradition than those on the Bailey, which can be seen as a good or bad thing. We have a great social calendar - bar theme nights, "megaformal" dinners, bops, trips, sporting events and the legendary Summer Ball.'

From October, 2006, applicants have been able to opt for a new Durham-based college, the first for more than 30 years, named after the Northumberland-born writer, pioneer of women's education and social reformer, Josephine Butler. The 400 rooms are en suite and self-catering - 6 to a flat - on the southern edge of the city, close to the Science Site and main University Library. Special student rate buses are frequent. There's a bar, a launderette, an IT Suite, a music practice room, a large hall, a variety of smaller rooms available for events, and special provision for the disabled, especially students with special dietary requirements. Flats are available from October to June, including the Christmas and Easter vacations.'

Down at Stockton, John Snow (which has nothing to do with the inestimable TV news journalist - he went to Liverpool for a while) and George Stephenson Colleges look quite inviting in the prospectus pictures, but they are going to have to do something to liven things up a bit, which is why we're going to spend some time on them. Like many, Lawrence Mantini, an Oxbridge wannabe, found himself there when his public exams didn't quite go the way he planned. He put what seemed to us, a brave face on his lot:

'It's kind of like your own little community. You see everyone because you are living so close to one another. There are about six different halls [within John Snow], three floors and each floor is split into three different flats: six rooms share a kitchen. My whole floor knows one another, so we just go from side to side really. After the first year they encourage you to go out and find a house, which I have got to do in the next couple of weeks. It tends to either be Thornaby or Stockton. It's not the prettiest town, but it has everything you need, and the water is very nice, you get the rowers coming by and everything. Thornaby and Stockton have kind of merged into one, as far as I can tell.

> *'Pick your college carefully. Within a couple of days you'll have learned your college songs and rituals, and feel a strange affiliation with this set of buildings, which will manifest itself loudly on many a river bank or touch line throughout your life as a Durham student.'*

'John Snow is about ten minutes away from the actual teaching base and then Stephenson is right next door to it. Pub-wise there are one or two places that are student friendly, Weatherspoon-type places. It's one of the downsides, I guess. There is only one student night in Stockton, it's good but it can get repetitive going to the same place every Monday night.'

'There's the **Arc**,' I suggest.

'I've been there once or twice. They show a constant round of drama productions and comedians and stuff. I actually tried to go, but it was sold out. It's a nice looking place. I think there is a small cinema.'

'So, what does a student do at Stockton Campus?'

'There's the college bar. It's a waterside bar and it's a really nice, modern, big kind of bar. They show sports there and have events there, all different drinks and food. John Snow and Stephenson share that bar. It's quite a highlight of the whole campus. Otherwise, I'm either doing my assignments or I go into town quite a lot, but apart from that there is not a whole lot to do to be honest.

'There is opportunity to do sport. I just haven't taken it up. John Snow have their own boat club and they have got a wide range of sports clubs, they use the water well, and there are the university teams at Durham, which is a half an hour bus ride away. The bus is free if you have your campus card. Mainly people go to Durham for sporting things and on Friday nights there is a student night.'

[In fact, a new multi-million pounds Sports Centre just opened, offering an outstanding fitness experience. Includes a fully equipped fitness suite, and impressive rang of state-of-the-art facilities and a variety of exercise classes.]

'What kind of people are students at Stockton?'

'There is a fair amount of mature students on my course, I'd say. On my floor I'm the only Londoner, but apparently there are quite a lot. There are not that many Northern people here, it's more Midlands and Southern, I would say. I applied for main Durham campus, but because of my grades they offered me a course here. It's not as pretty as Durham, but I'm happy to be here, yeah.'

'Where else did you apply?'

'I applied to Oxford, Warwick, York and Bristol.'

'There is no doubt that the [Applied Psychology] course at Stockton is a very good one,' we say.

'Yeah, I would highly recommend it. Tonight I'm going to go up to Durham to the student night there.'

SOCIAL SCENE

STUDENTS' UNION The social scene in Durham is better. The SU building and main bar, **Kingsgate**, have had a facelift, and **Pitstop**, a shop, has opened at the entrance to the building. Kingsgate is the union bar with balcony overlooking the river. Food is served in the nearby **Riverside Café** until 11 pm (waitress service). Venues remain **Vane Tempest Hall** and the **Margot Fonteyn**

ACCOMMODATION	
Student rating	★★★★★
Guarantee to freshers	**96%**
Style	**Halls, flats**
Security guard	**All**
Shared rooms	**Some halls**
Internet access	**All**
Self-catered	**Some halls, all flats**
En suite	**Some halls, most flats**
Approx price range pw	**£122-£154**
City rent pw	**£50-£100**

Ballroom, though everyone knows it all simply as **'the DSU'**, the Durham Student Union.

Martha put me neatly in the picture: 'On a Friday all of it is open, like different rooms for different music. So you have got *Planet of Sound* downstairs in the big hall, and there's a cheese room for *Twisted*, which on Saturday makes way for drum and base. And *Revolver's* on Saturday, which is indie.

'On a Wednesday most people go to **Loveshack** in town. That's the new nightclub, it's really good. It's got a VW Van inside as a sofa. Yeah, Loveshack's best on a Wednesday, when all the sports teams generally go out.

'The Student Union is probably best on a Tuesday, when there's a one-off night for *Twisted*. There is so much competition at the moment with all the clubs trying to promote themselves. Loveshack is about £3 entry, the most you will ever pay to get in anywhere in Durham is about £5.50 for *Planet of Sound*. Also every college has a Social Committee and every club will contact the Social Chair, like me for Aiden's. They offer you deals all the time. I think lots of the Bailey colleges get free entry for **Klute**, but it's all up to your Social Chair where you are going to get free entry.

'Then there's the **Loft**. I think Loft is more used when a college rents it out for a night. It isn't the best, but it's still quite good. **Studio** is probably better than Loft now. Studio has two floors of different music and every night they have a different night going.

'The **Reform** is good, that's the pre-club place opposite Studio. I don't go to **Chase**. I'm not really sure what sort of people go to Chase. I think it might be quite expensive. **Fishtank** is a little alternative, it's a house that has been renovated into a club and they do alternative nights. There is quite a big alternative scene, and they do *Dove Step* as well. Like it's really big in London, *Dove Step*, and drum 'n' bass, and Fishtank put on all the alternative things that maybe Durham doesn't promote as such. That is just round the corner from the Viaduct [landmark on the Durham scene], usually free entry unless it's a big night. Then **Fabio's** does jazz, and you can eat there and then go upstairs to a little bar, quite pricey but really nice - quite a classy night always.'

Martha aligned herself to the Alternative Society, the bohemian alternative to what goes on up the Bailey, an unthinkable prospect at Durham only a few years ago: Among other societies, student media is first class, with *Palatinate* and Purple FM proving to be a worthy claw sharpener for the real thing. There is also *The Grove*, a twice termly poetry magazine. The Union is active on welfare (Advice Centre, Nightline, etc) and DUCK is the charities kommittee, which raises more than half a million each year. In student politics, Labour, Conservative and Lib Dem socs are all active, as well as People & Planet and Fight Racism, Fight Imperialism. The Union has an active policy of independence from all political parties. Green Corner is the very active environmental group. Others of their 124 societes include Pagan Witches, Bellydancers, Medieval Warmongerers and the Chemistry Society.

TOWN/GOWN When term begins, students herd in and outnumber locals. In the past it has proved to be a recipe for disaster. Writes Eleanor: 'Locals are generally friendly, and students are normally safe. Weekends are more dangerous, however, as country locals invade and they are more inclined to indulge in the favourite sport of student bashing.' Says Alex, 'There is some tension. Trouble is easily avoided if you shun the pink shirt/ bodywarmer/scarf, and don't talk in a loud southern accent on your mobile phone at 3 am, drunk, in the middle of the road, wearing a DJ.' They have a university security patrol that goes round the city every night. They also have a night-bus which picks up all around town and drops off at all the colleges.

SPORT Durham is very sporty, they came 6th last year, and the beautiful river is a temptress to hundreds of novice rowers. Academic concessions for sporty types are apparent, though not admitted. High standards are encouraged by inter-college rivalry, Castle vrs Hatfield (rugby), Castle vrs Hild Bede (rowing). College rowing crews are often better than other university crews. Sixty acres of fields are maintained to first-class standard. New facilities include an indoor rowing tank, fencing stiles, squash courts, an extended and resurfaced sports hall, increased strength and conditioning provision and a performance analysis suite.

GETTING THERE

- ☛ By road: A1/J6. Well served by coaches.
- ☛ By rail: King's Cross, 3:00; Edinburgh, 1:00.
- ☛ By air: Newcastle, Teesside Airports (25m).
- ☛ By coach: London, 5:30; Birmingham, 4:00.

UNIVERSITY OF EAST ANGLIA

The University of East Anglia
Earlham Road
Norwich NR4 7TJ

TEL 01603 456161
FAX 01603 458553
EMAIL admissions@uea.ac.uk
WEB www.uea.ac.uk

Union of University of East Anglia Students
Union House
Norwich NR4 7TJ

TEL 01603 593272
FAX 01603 250144
EMAIL su.comms@uea.ac.uk
WEB www.ueastudent.com

VIRGIN VIEW

Set apart in rural Norfolk, and yet only 15 minutes by road from the centre of Norwich, East Anglia University (UEA) was founded in 1964 and reaches out to the world with innovation and flair.

It is among the best on virtually any grounds you care to mention, and perhaps because it is so cut off from the world, the student body seems more reflective, more worldly wise perhaps than most.

In the Government's National Student Survey, 90% of them said they were satisfied with what they get. UEA is an exceptional student experience. They came 3rd nationally in the Times Higher's Student Experience Survey 2011. The campus and the student union have been winning awards for far longer than 1997 when this Guide started up. Their strength academically lies both in research - 90% of their provision is of an international standard, 50% world rocking - and in teaching: lecturers get 4 stars for their helpfulness and interest in students, and 3 for small size tuition groups.

If there is a niggle it is that you are there on campus with everything you need and much of what you want, but no means of getting off it. It's miles from anywhere, other than Norwich. Perhaps that's the reason why an ungrateful 7% do not see the whole experience through to the end.

Still, it's highly competitive to get in; 2011 applications were up 17% on 2010 entry, so

UNIVERSITY/STUDENT PROFILE	
University since	**1964**
Situation/style	**Campus**
Student population	**15290**
Undergraduates	**12210**
Mature	**39%**
International	**18%**
Male/female ratio	**41:59**
Equality of opportunity:	
state school intake	**89%**
social class 4-7 intake	**29%**
drop-out rate	**7%**

what are they after other than grades and points?

The Head of Student Recruitment at the University was emphatic: 'Generally the personal statement is the section where the student gets to sell themselves.' So, what do they want to glean there? '1. Academic interest in the subject for which you have applied. 2. Personal interest and extra-curricular activities.'

Open Days in 2011 are 1 and 2 July, and 1 October. If you want to mug up beforehand, they've got an iPad Prospectus App. Launched in Jan 2011 the new service is free of charge. A version for the iPhone is also in the pipeline.

CAMPUS

The campus, built on a 320-acre, sometime golf course, has won awards for its architecture - Denys Lasdun's ziggurats (glass-fronted buildings, tiered upwards like garden terraces after the ancient

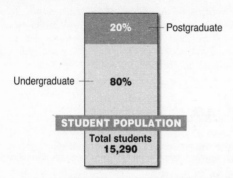

STUDENT POPULATION

Postgraduate 20%

Undergraduate 80%

Total students
15,290

performance: www.uea.ac.uk/sixthform/finance /UEA+Bursaries; and www.uea. ac.uk/sixthform/ finance/UEA+Scholarships.

STUDENT PROFILE

UEA has a well-balanced student population for a pukka uni, with an 89/11 split between state and public school types (way above its Government benchmark), 29% from the lower socio-economic classes and 11% from postcodes new to the idea of going to university. There is a fair-sized mature intake (39%) and 41/59 boys/girls, owing to the nursing degrees.

tiered mounds of Babylonia) continue to amaze. It revolves around the Square, a student rendezvous, transformed into an open-air disco at the end of the academic year. But, as student Daniel Trelfer declares, self-containment isn't to everyone's taste:

'Everything you need is on campus, but while some people are happy to live for twelve weeks inside a square quarter mile, others go insane and have to run to town to feel free again.' Yet even that is no solution, for 'the campus and the city of Norwich are strangely similar in that both are somewhere in the wilderness miles from anywhere. The fact that the nearest town is 45 mins away by train, and even then it's only Ipswich, gives you some idea of how remote Norwich is. If you drive there you will see nothing but flat lands, tractors and trees for the last half hour of your journey.'

FEES, BURSARIES

UK & EU Fees, 2011-12: £3,375 for all full-time undergraduate programmes except Physiotherapy, Occupational Therapy, Speech and Language Therapy, Nursing and Midwifery, which will continue to be covered by the NHS Student Grants Unit. Sliding-scale bursaries etween £300 and £600 for students in receipt of HE Maintenance Grant, dependent on parental income, and for those leaving care. There are awards for sport and music, and a range of scholarships for academic

TEACHING SURVEY AT A GLANCE	
Avg. UCAS points accepted	**360**
Acceptance rate	**16%**
Overall satisfaction rate	**90%**
Helpful/interested staff	**★★★★**
Small tuition groups	**★★★**
Students into graduate jobs	**74%**

Teaching most popular with undergraduates:
Accounting, Anatomy, Physiology & Pathology (100%), Aural/Oral Sciences, Biological Sciences, Film & Photography, Computer, Drama,Economics, English, Finance & Accounting, French Studies, Geology, History, History & Archaeology, Human & Social Geography, Law, Maths, Media (100%), Medicine, Languages, Microbiology, Molecular Biology, Music, Nursing, Ocean Sciences, Subjects allied to Medicine, Pharmacy, Philosophy, Physical Geography, Physical Science, Politics, Psychology, Social Studies, Sociology (100%), Social Policy & Anthropology.

Teaching least popular with undergraduates:
Imaginative Writing (79%).

SUBJECT AREAS (%)

Education — 21
Creative Arts
Humanities — 30
Medicine — 7
Health Subjects
Science — 15
16
Social Studies incl Law — 15
Business — 7
Maths & Computer — 7

ACADEMIA & JOBS

UEA is made up of 23 academic departments known as Schools of Study, which are grouped into the Faculties of Arts & Humanities, Social Sciences, Science and Medicine & Health Sciences.

Graduate employment poses a few question marks. Seventy-four per cent get real graduate-level jobs within six months of leaving, which is OK, but not top of the tree. An awful lot more get pretty average sorts of jobs to begin with, which is often the case with unis that specialise in humanities and languages (one thinks of St Andrews). Graduates have to start somewhere, and many who start as clerks find success in the end. UEA has itself conducted surveys that show this.

Possibly uniquely, Language graduates find it easier to get jobs than graduates of any department other than Health and Social Studies. They are wanted by employers across the board, account for 11% of UEA's graduate job output. This years sees a number of interesting degrees in Japanese.

Far and away the most jobs for UEA graduates are, however, found in the health industry. Physiotherapy is particularly productive and directs attention to an expanding aspect of UEA's curriculum - Midwifery, Nursing (Adult, Children, Learning Disability, Mental Health), Operating Department Practice, Occupational Therapy, Physiotherapy, Biochemistry, Biomedicine, Pharmacy,

> 'The LCR has been voted the best student venue in the country by the music industry's Live! magazine. Each year more than 50 live bands grace its stage; gigs are sold out months in advance.'

Pharmaceutical Chemistry, and of course the programme in Medicine. The MBBS Medicine with a Foundation Year was recently introduced to widen participation in Medicine from under-represented groups. Theory and practice is integrated throughout in the 5-year MB BS, and clinical experience is yours from the outset, thanks to extensive collaboration with close-to-campus Norfolk & Norwich University Hospital. They consider a wide range of qualifications, but you must have a background in to at least A Level equivalent, three subjects including Biology/Human Biology, plus additional grade B in a fourth subject to AS level.

Community youth workers and social workers also come out of here in abundance. Naturally they come through Social Sciences (from the dedicated Social Work degrees), from Biological Sciences, but also via Languages.

UEA also enjoys particular success in the literary firmament. There are twice-yearly literary festivals, a writer in residence, and it is here that Sir Malcolm Bradbury years ago set the literary firmament alight with his creative writing school, out of which came Ian McEwan and Kazuo Ishiguro, among others. There is also a fine reputation for the 4-year American Studies, which scored full marks in the old assessments. Campus is home to the Arthur Miller Centre for American Studies. Arts graduates are given a ringing endorsement by UEA's MA in creative entrepreneurship, which supports artists, writers and musicians in practical business skills.

Another clue to UEA's academic identity is its concern for the environment. They pride themselves on being at the forefront of green awareness and this year there is a whole raft of new degrees in Climate Science. The climatic research unit is a world authority of course, and the uni is home to the Tyndall Centre for Climate Change Research. The Jackson Institute, with the largest environmental research programme in the UK, has also set up here, and there's a new Institute for Connective Environmental Research - an attempt to bring together science, industry, politics, business to make real steps forward in the area of environmentalism.

Finally, they are European and American law specialists. All candidates must sit the National Admissions Test for Law (LNAT).

RESEARCH EXCELLENCE

% of UEA's research that is
4* (World-class) or 3* (Internationally rated):

	4*	3*
Epidemiology, Public Health	5%	40%
Health Services Research	5%	40%
Nursing and Midwifery	10%	30%
Allied Health Professions	0%	15%
Pharmacy	15%	40%
Biological Sciences	10%	40%
Environmental Sciences	25%	45%
Chemistry	5%	50%
Pure Mathematics	15%	45%
Applied Mathematics	5%	40%
Computer Science	20%	45%
Economics and Econometrics	15%	50%
Business and Management	10%	35%
Law	5%	35%
Politics	10%	15%
Social Work, Policy, Admin.	10%	45%
Development Studies	25%	35%
Psychology	0%	15%
Education	15%	35%
American Studies	20%	30%
English	20%	45%
Philosophy	5%	30%
History	20%	40%
History of Art	50%	20%
Media Studies	50%	40%
Music	0%	40%

ACCOMMODATION

Student rating	★★★★★
Guarantee to freshers	**100%**
Style	**Flats**
Security guard	**Campus-wide**
Shared rooms	**Some**
Internet access	**All**
Self-catered	**All**
En suite	**Most**
Approx price range pw	**£52.15-£155.26**
City rent pw	**£50-£80**

SOCIAL SCENE

STUDENTS' UNION The **LCR** (Lower Common Room) has been voted the best student venue in the country by the music industry's *Live!* magazine. Each year more than 50 live bands grace its stage; gigs are sold out months in advance. Union bars feature **The Union Pub** - all-day opening, pool tables, table footie, arcade machines, jukebox and large screen TV. Then there's **The Union Bar (Blue Bar)**, **The Hive** (redeveloped a few years ago, creating a light, more spacious environment), and **The Grads Bar**. Live in the Hive includes (free) local bands, as well as karaoke, quizzes, games and comedy shows. Besides the LCR, the uni has its own venue in Norwich - **The Waterfront**. There are 3 bars and 2 rooms of music.

They are a 5-star uni for extra-curricular, with 70 societies and 40 sports clubs. It is a highly developed student culture and has to be because campus is so cut off. Politics is a scene. The 3-weekly Union Council meeting is a passionate event.

Gays get a good deal: LBG is among the most active societies, and Rock Gospel Choir. **The Studio** is the UEA theatre, drama a top-rated course. Their TV station is Nexus, radio Livewire. *Concrete* is the newspaper, which often wins national awards. There is a track record for graduate careers in radio/TV and publishing, and top ratings for teaching in media/communications.

SPORT Good, though not top notch, they came 60th in the national league last year. Great facilities. The purpose-built Sportspark includes a 50-metre pool, athletics track, 7-a-side soccer pitches, an Olympic Gymnastic centre, indoor arena, squash and tennis courts, a climbing wall, a fitness centre, dance studios and 40 acres of playing fields and pitches.

TOWN Apparently, Norwich has a pub for every day of the year. It also has the **Theatre Royal** (touring companies, RSC, National), **The Maddermarket**, a smaller, amateur but vibrant venue. The bohemian **King of Hearts** rules for music, art, jazz, literature readings, and **The Norwich Arts Centre** for live music, from rock and jazz to chamber music, exhibitions, dance workshops and comedy - David Baddiel, Frank Skinner, Lee & Herring and The Fast Show's Simon Day all played here. There are four cinemas in Norwich: the Odeon, Vue, Hollywood, and Cinema City (arthouse).

PILLOW TALK

Accommodation (highly rated by students, see box above) is guaranteed to all first years who live over 12 miles from UEA. Students live in their own study bedrooms within 8-12 person flats. There are standard and en-suite rooms on campus, in the adjoining university village, and in the city centre.

GETTING THERE

☛ By road: A11(M), A47.
☛ By rail: London Liverpool Street, 2:00; Birmingham New Street, 4:00; Sheffield, 3:50.
☛ By air: Norwich Airport.
☛ By coach: London, 2:50; Birmingham, 6:00.

WHAT IT'S REALLY LIKE

UNIVERSITY:	
Social Life	★★★★★
Societies	★★★★★
Student Union services	★★★★
Politics	**Active**
Sport	**40 clubs, but not obsessional**
National team position	**60th**
Sport facilities	★★★★★
Arts opportunities	**Excellent**
Student newspaper	**Concrete**
Student radio	**Livewire 1350**
Student TV	**Nexus**
Nightclub	**LCR, Waterfront**
Bars	**Union Pub, etc.**
Union ents	**Massive**
Union societies	**70**
Most popular society	**Rock Gospel Choir**
Parking	**Very tight**
CITY:	
Entertainment	★★★
Scene	**OK pubs, clubs**
Town/gown relations	**Average**
Risk of violence	**Low**
Cost of living	**Average**
Survival + 2 nights out	**£70 pw**
Part-time work campus/town	**Good/excellent**

UNIVERSITY OF EAST LONDON

The University of East London
Docklands Campus
4-6 University Way
London E16 2RD

TEL 020 8223 2835
FAX 020 8223 2978
EMAIL admiss@uel.ac.uk
WEB www.uel.ac.uk

The University of East London Students' Union
Docklands Campus
4-6 University Way
London E16 2RD

TEL 020 8223 7025
FAX 020 8223 7508
EMAIL students.union@uel.ac.uk
WEB www.uelsu.ac.uk

VIRGIN VIEW

In UEL we have the former East London Polytechnic, now University of the People in London's East End, traditionally the soul culture of the Metropolis, which has for the past 250 years taken into itself a diverse immigrant population.

Today, it is as lively an evolutionary culture as it ever was, and the Uni is an integral part of it. UEL's stated mission is 'to provide the highest possible quality of education in order to meet...' not the needs of the country or Europe or the world, but '...the needs of individuals and of the communities and enterprises in our region.'

Its mission is no less ambitious for its narrow demographic focus, for in many ways UEL has its doors more widely open to the real world than most of its competitors, what with its high intake from beleaguered communities, its low entry requirements and, against all odds, a fierce determination to hang on to its students for the full term of their courses and equip them for a world that many off to Bristol and Durham universities can barely imagine.

Following a full-scale institutional audit by the Quality Assurance Agency in 2005, UEL was praised for its culture of equality and diversity, its equitable approach and support for its part-time staff and students, the effectiveness of its staff development, and the integration into the curriculum of skills development for students, particularly through the Skillzone programme (see Academia below).

UNIVERSITY/STUDENT PROFILE	
University since	**1992**
Situation/style	**City sites**
Student population	**26315**
Undergraduates	**19520**
Mature	**70%**
International	**18%**
Male/female ratio	**44:56**
Equality of opportunity:	
state school intake	**98%**
social class 4-7 intake	**47%**
drop-out rate	**10%**

Clearly they are doing something right. The Queen opened the newish Business School and Knowledge Dock Centre on the waterfront of the Royal Albert Dock. The event followed the successful completion of a £110-million investment and development programme, which saw an overhaul at Stratford campus, too.

It's only when polls like the Times Higher Education 'Student Experience' Survey come along that UEL just does not do itself justice. It was second to bottom last time, but in a very real sense there is no fair comparison with most other universities on most counts.

When it comes to research expertise staff acquit themselves well. In the first national assessment of the research performance of our universities for seven years, UEL leapt from one plaudit in 2001 to 78% of its research submission being rated as at least of 'internationally recognised' quality, with a significant percentage rated world-class in terms of originality, significance and rigour. The uni jumped 28 places to be placed among the Top 3 post-1992 universities in London for research, and in the Top 10 post-1992 universities in the UK. What it needed, as we said last year, was for the staff to show an interest in their students. They were rated worst in the country for this a year ago, but now they get three stars for helpfulness and interest, which is surely fundamental in a uni like UEL. The student satisfaction rate rose too.

It's still of course a cool place to be. Tinchy Stryder took a degree in digital arts and moving image here recently and found the lecturers passionate about what they were doing.

CAMPUSES

DOCKLANDS CAMPUS 4-6 University Way, London E16 2RD. Located on the waterfront of the Royal Albert Dock, it serves 7,000 students focused on the new economy, cultural and creative industries. The Architecture and Visual Arts facility was completed in 2003, and a new Business School and Enterprise Centre opened in 2007. Here, too, are the School of Computing and Technology, the Learning Resource Centre and Knowledge Dock, a restaurant, bar and cafés, and a Student Union development. Also accommodation of course; see Pillow Talk below.

STRATFORD CAMPUS Romford Road, London E15 4LZ. Tel 020 8223 3000. Close to the London 2012 Olympic Park, the Stratford campus is now expanding rapidly. A new Centre for Clinical Education in Podiatry, Physiotherapy and Sports Science - areas of significance in their graduate

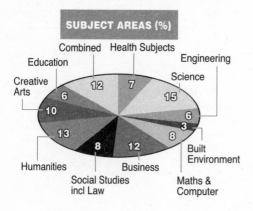

SUBJECT AREAS (%)

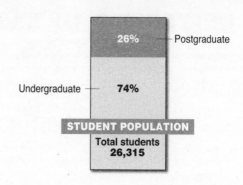

STUDENT POPULATION
Total students
26,315

employment profile - was opened last year by HRH the Duchess of Cornwall. A new £16-million Cass School of Education and a Conference and Computing Centre with landscaped gardens will open this year.

As at Docklands, there are brand new Student Union facilities here, and work is now being undertaken on new buildings for the Schools of Law and Education.

FEES, BURSARIES

UK & EU Fees, 2011-12: £3,375. There are bursaries for students in receipt of full HE Maintenance grant, a Progress Bursary to all who complete the first semester and progress to a second, and 200 Achievement scholarships to first-year students for sport, academic excellence, citizenship, and voluntary work. See www.uel.ac.uk/studentlife/moneymatters/bursaries.htm.

STUDENT PROFILE

UEL have large ethnic, overseas (18%), and mature student populations (70% of the latter), and welcomes many from the lower socio-economic orders and those neighbourhoods where people have never thought about university for themselves before. There is a friendly, laid-back feel to the place. Students are getting on, and will do provided they're not bound fast by politically correct red tape, as some feel they are.

ACADEMIA & JOBS

The uni's Skillzone is a learning support and employment service. They know their way around the forms.

Today, the Knowledge Dock (formerly the Thames Gateway Technology Centre) works with over 2,000 companies and entrepreneurs across the region. It provides a range of business services, training, consultancy, and funded programmes including the DTI flagship Knowledge Transfer

Partnerships and the Shell Technology Enterprise Programme, for which it was named best new agency. UEL invests among the highest per student for library and learning resources. It is also a leader in disability and dyslexia support. Facilities include a regional Access Centre offering dyslexia screening and tutoring, technology training, exam support and an RNIB Resource Centre for blind and visually impaired students on physiotherapy programmes.

At UEL, look for degrees in Biological Sciences (including Psychology), in Creative Arts & Design (Culture, Art, Dance, Music), in subjects allied to Medicine (Physiotherapy is a major career field), in Social Studies (a high percentage of graduates find employment as social workers, probation officers or community youth workers), Education, Computer, Sport. More graduate jobs come to UEL in the area of health and social work, community and counselling than anywhere else. Then it's teaching, and a whole lot of students doing Engineering, Computer Science, Business, etc. get jobs in the motor trade.

Media (including Journalism), Art & Design, Performing Arts, Sociology and Social Work all contributed to their success in the recent research assessment exercise.

For their Cultural Studies series (courses like Third World Development) and their Playwork series, as well as in degrees like Dance: Urban Practice and the Early Childhood Studies series, UEL proclaims its distinctive identity, which feeds into the artistic endeavour in such courses as

> *'UEL is diverse, but there's a friendly, laid-back feel to the place. It's cool enough for Tinchy Stryder, and students are getting on, and more would do if someone put the whole thing together.'*

Community Arts, Music (theory and production), Psychosocial Studies and in their brand of Journalism. For these courses they want students from diverse social, intellectual, and cultural backgrounds, and they find a number of them on their doorstep.

'The course,' said one student of a BA (Hons) Cultural Studies degree, who went on to edit Sky Magazine, 'gives fuel to things you're already thinking about and puts them in context.'

There's respect for their psychologists, who deal with real issues of the community in which they live and work. UEL's School of Psychology dropped only one point in the old teaching assessments and is now one of the leading schools in Britain for undergraduate and professional diploma programmes. They run a range of postgraduate programmes in partnership with Relate, the Psychosynthesis and Education Trust, and the Tavistock Clinic (the UK's leading centre for post-graduate training in mental health).

In 2003, they brought together the Schools of Architecture and Art & Design to form the School of Architecture and the Visual Arts, located in a new 6,000 sq m purpose-designed studio building at Docklands. UEL is rated highly for the teaching of architecture, and there's a strong pathway into the profession. They are one of a few Schools to be awarded unconditional validation by the Royal Institute of British Architects (RIBA) and the Architects Registration Board (ARB).

TEACHING SURVEY AT A GLANCE

Avg. UCAS points accepted	**160**
Acceptance rate	**27%**
Overall satisfaction rate	**76%**
Helpful/interested staff	★★★
Small tuition groups	★
Students into graduate jobs	**61%**

Teaching most popular with undergraduates:
Accounting, Civil Engineering, Engineering & Technology, English Studies, Finance, Law, Social Work, Social Studies, Sociology, Social Policy & Anthropology.

Teaching least popular with undergraduates:
Film & Photography (31%).

RESEARCH EXCELLENCE

% of UEL's research that is
4* *(World-class)* or **3*** *(Internationally rated):*

	4*	3*
Allied Health Professions	10%	20%
Law	5%	30%
Social Work, Policy & Admin.	0%	35%
Sociology	10%	30%
Psychology	0%	20%
Education	5%	20%
Art and Design	10%	30%
Drama, Dance, Performing Arts	5%	30%
Media Studies	20%	60%

SOCIAL SCENE

Political awareness is the most notable aspect at student level, and it can be deadening when it lacks a sense of the community to which students belong. So completely bereft of community spirit has UEL student union been in recent years that finally they wheeled in the National Union of Students to tell them where they were going wrong. Out of a series of focus groups came a mind-blowing document that shows how dull the Union has been, plus 30 recommendations. There are signs that something might now be moving

reggae, old school, cheese, pop, rock n roll, triphop, hip hop and dub - comedy nights, cabaret, live bands, video nights and the odd society 'do'. One-offs include Spring Ball, Valentine Bash, Diwali Rave, Hallowe'en Night, Christmas Rave.

A lot of bar activity/events were laid on by students through cultural societies, like *Reggae Nite with DJ Freestyle*, *Wheel of 4 Tunes*, *Good Friday Society Nite*, *Calender (sic) Club Nite*, DJ's r&b, hiphop, catwalk, samba band.

Years ago UEL was one of a handful of universities capable of organising a decent sit-in,

ACCOMMODATION	
Student rating	★
Guarantee to freshers	**100%**
Style	**Halls, flats**
Security guard	**All**
Shared rooms	**Some halls**
Internet access	**All**
Self-catered	**Most**
En suite	**Some**
Approx price range pw	**£102-£140**
City rent pw	**£100-£140**

forward, but they are like the tremors of a man coming out of a very deep coma. .

The UEL community is amazingly rich culturally. The potential is great. They have seventeen odd societies listed, most of them rooted in a particular religion or nationality, but what has been missing from view is any sense of the whole community. It is incredible that the university administration has done so little.

The NUS report shows that students at UEL require a deeper level of support from their unon - any support! But in particular representation over issues they care about, and socially. All trust has been lost. 'Students identified with the University and in some cases the Union,' reads the report, 'However, they felt there was no obvious community to connect to... There was still a perception that the union was not trusted by the univerity and in turn, students were less likely to trust the union.'

> **'Students identified with the University and in some cases the Union, but they felt there was no obvious community to connect to...'**

What a waste! There was a time, before they lavished millions on UEL, when the union hosted a culturally rich ents programme, including dedicated and *Mixed Flavour* discos - indie, soul, swing, '70s/'80s, jungle, hip hop, ragga, bhangra,

WHAT IT'S REALLY LIKE	
UNIVERSITY:	
Social Life	★
Societies	★
Student Union services	★
Politics	**Potentiall strong**
Sport	**Relaxed, 8 clubs**
National team position	**124th**
Sport facilities	★
Arts opportunities	**Potentially lively**
Student magazine	**Refuel**
Bars	**Each campus**
Union ents	**Disorganised**
Most popular society	**Islamic**
Parking	**Poor**
CITY:	
Entertainment	★★★★★
Scene	**Local clubs 'n uptown flavours**
Town/gown relations	**Poor**
Risk of violence	**Random**
Cost of living	**High**
Student concessions	**OK**
Survival + 2 nights out	**£80 pw**
Part-time work campus/town	**OK**

getting together with Goldsmiths to do a *Rough Guide to Occupation*. Now, it's like dead. Student media still breathes life into magazine, *Re:fuel*, and that's about it.

What happens now is that students get together under their own steam. You'll hear of a group that likes to watch and talk about anime or manga. You'll catch a whisper about a pool of photographers and filmmakers who want others to join them to document events through one year. But there's no union effort to bring it all together, no inspiration, no representation.

Town 'Well it's London, so all bets are off,' said our informant. 'Cost of living is high, general things (food etc) are fairly priced compared to other places. It's the social side of things that costs so much. Start saving now. Risk of violence is, surprisingly random. Arguably, people would say London is prone to greater violence. But really it's all quite random. You'll need about £80 to live on if you want to go out at least two nights. Chance of part-time employment is high. Both within the Students' Union and wider a-field.'

PILLOW TALK

Allocation priority is given to students with special needs, and then to students entering their first year at the university from outside the local area.

A number of rooms are reserved for applicants whose normal place of residence is outside the UK.

On-campus residences are at Docklands campus, either Circular Halls (West), facing west along the dockside, single rooms in flats, or Student Village (East): this is the waterfront Student Village opened spring 2007 with single rooms or studio flats, café-bar, shops, SU facilities.

GETTING THERE

☛ **Stratford** by Underground, Central Line; closest overland rail station is Maryland (connect London Liverpool Street).
☛ **Barking** by Underground, City & Hammersmith and District lines; Goodmayes overland station.
☛ **Docklands** via the Docklands Light Railway.

EDGE HILL UNIVERSITY

Edge Hill University
St Helens Road
Ormskirk
Lancashire L39 4QP

TEL 01695 657000 (course information)
    01695 579997
FAX 01695 584355
EMAIL study@edgehill.ac.uk
WEB www.edgehill.ac.uk

Edge Hill University Students' Union
St Helens Road
Ormskirk
Lancashire L39 4QP

TEL 01695 575457
FAX 01695 577904
EMAIL enquiries@edgehill.ac.uk
WEB www.edgehill.ac.uk

VIRGIN VIEW

*E*dge Hill was founded in 1885 as the UK's first non-denominational teacher training college for women. Initially based in the Edge Hill district of Liverpool, the College moved 12 miles to the north, to Ormskirk, in 1933. In 1960 it became co-ed, and diversified into health in 1968. In the 1970s it became a partner college of Lancaster University and in time offered a broad range of degree courses.

In 1980 it took into itself Chorley College of Education and in 1993 the Sefton School of Health Studies. Thirteen years later the college achieved university status. Edge Hill has always been an unusually slick set-up, whose boss used to call himself a Chief Executive and who always had a team of marketing and communications executives

UNIVERSITY/STUDENT PROFILE	
University since	**2006**
Situation/style	**Town campus**
Student population	**24340**
Undergraduates	**13605**
Mature	**66%**
International	**1%**
Male/female ratio	**24:76**
Equality of opportunity:	
state school intake	**99%**
social class 4-7 intake	**45%**
drop-out rate	**12%**

following close behind.

It has embarked upon an ambitious building programme. Recently a £14-million Faculty of Health building, which is also a facility for Online Teaching, opened. Last year, an £8-million Business School opened its doors, a facility that includes a mock court room for Law and Criminology students.

Teaching is good here. In the National Student Survey, 83% of their students gave the thumbs-up to their teachers. In the Times Higher's *Student Experience Survey they were praised for their supportive and interested staff. A new htudent Hub, home to Student Union activity, is set to open in September. Things are on the rise. 'Getting off at Edge Hill', the last stop before the tunnel into Lime Street on the Manchester–Liverpool line, Britain's first, is a sexy Scouse reference to pulling out on time before climax. But with the drop-out rate falling, those pulling out of Edge Hill University today are getting fewer.*

Open Days in 2011 (all 10am - 3pm) are: 18 June, 20 and 25 August, 8 October, 19 November. Also, 16 June, 2012.

CAMPUS

Writes Peter Cooper: 'The campus is about 10 minutes walk from the centre of Ormskirk, a small market town. If you like a small community where you are likely to get to know everyone then this is a good campus. It is a relatively safe place and although it may not have all the facilities of a larger university, it compensates with its friendly atmosphere. Liverpoool, Preston, and even Manchester, are readily accessible.'

The main Ormskirk campus consists of 75 landscaped acres, with lake, theatres and sports centre. In addition, they have campuses at Aintree and Chorley. The Faculty of Health is based at the former, which is known as University Hospital Aintree, and the Faculty of Education's continuing professional development (CPD) work is located at the latter, known as Woodlands Campus.

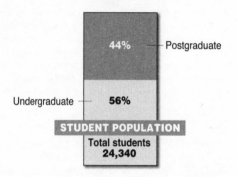

TEACHING SURVEY AT A GLANCE	
Avg. UCAS points accepted	**240**
Acceptance rate	**22%**
Overall satisfaction rate	**83%**
Helpful/interested staff	★★★★
Small tuition groups	★★★
Students into graduate jobs	**74%**

Teaching most popular with undergraduates:
Business, Dance, English Studies, Geographical Studies, History (97%), Imaginative Writing, Languages, Law, Nursing, Physical Geography and Environmental Science (100%), Psychology, Subjects Allied to Medicine.

Teaching least popular with undergraduates:
Media Studies (58%), Computer Science (52%).

In addition, there are uni sites in Liverpool, Silkhouse Court where a part-time BSc (Hons) in Information Systems is studied, and in Manchester, Shrewsbury, Winsford (Cheshire) and the Wirral.

FEES, BURSARIES

UK & EU Fees, 2010-11: £3,375 Entrance scholarships in Creative Arts, Performing Arts, Sport and Volunteering, worth £2,000 over three years. High Achievers scholarship for students who earn 360 UCAS points, worth £1,000 in their first year. £500 per annum for a student whose family annual income is less than £25,000. £750 per annum for care leavers.

STUDENT PROFILE

Edge Hill easily surpasses its Government benchmarks for encouraging under-represented socio-economic groups into higher education. Virtually all their undergrads come from state schools, 39% from the four lowest socio-economic classes and a quarter from so-called 'low participation neighbourhoods'. There is also a large local and mature student population and, mainly on account of the Nursing provision, numbers of women greatly exceed those of men. None of these stats give a feel of the place, however, which is lively enough. When, a few years ago the college was taken to court by a neighbour for the regular early hours clamour of students enjoying themselves, the judge commented, 'It's like Brideshead Revisited meets St Trinians, isn't it?', as the prosecution itemised the complainants' 5-year 'noise diary'.

ACADEMIA & JOBS

There are three faculties: Education; Health; and

44% — Postgraduate

Undergraduate — **56%**

STUDENT POPULATION
Total students
24,340

Humanities, Management, Social & Applied Sciences, (within which fall the Business School, English Language and Literature, Creative Writing and Film Studies, History, Law and Criminology, Media, Natural, Geographical and Applied Sciences, Performing Arts, Social and Psychological Sciences, Sport and Physical Activity.

The Faculty of Education is one of the largest providers of ITT in the UK, covering a range of subjects at Early Years, Primary, Key Stage 2/3 and Secondary level. The Business School offers Accountancy, Business, Computing, Management and Web Development. The Performing Arts department offers Drama, Dance, Visual Theatre, Music and Theatre Design. The Department of Sport and Physical Activity offers Physical Education, Coaching, Sports Science, Sports Psychology and Sports Therapy, and benefit from 25 acres of sports facilities

The Edge Hill University Employability Programme is endorsed by the ILM and is a module for 2nd year Arts and Sciences students.

Around 45% of all graduates become primary or secondary teachers or go into hospital work of some sort. Other defining areas are social work, community & counselling activities, regional & local government administration, and recreational, cultural & sporting activities in the community. These destinations point us to the core courses at Edge Hill.

The community health destinations of Edge Hill graduates - hospital and beyond - arise from their degrees in Nursing, Midwifery, Operating Department Practice, Assisting Professional Practice, Child & Youth Studies, Counselling, Social Work, Playwork, Working with Families & Communities/with Vulnerable Adults, Complementary Medicine, Women's Health, Nutritional Health, and so on.

The sports degrees also take graduates into

RESEARCH EXCELLENCE		
% of Edge Hill's research that is 4* (World-class) or 3* (Internationally rated):		
	4*	3*
Nursing and Midwifery	5%	25%
Geography	0%	5%
Social Work, Policy & Admin.	0%	15%
Education	0%	5%
English	0%	20%
History	10%	15%

recreational jobs in the community, while jobs in local and regional government administration come principally from the degrees in Biological Sciences, but also from Creative Arts, Languages, Law, and Business.

They boast that they are one of only fourteen institutions to have National Council for the Training of Journalists accreditation for the undergraduate Journalism programme.

SOCIAL SCENE

Ten years ago a student described Edge Hill to us as 'a small, friendly community that caters for the basics'. Now, it is less small, but just as friendly, and there is a great deal more on campus than the college bar and dining room.

Shortly, a new Student Hub, home to Student Union activity, will open. Meanwhile, the **Venue** is the place for live music, dance nights, themed discos, sports nights, resident and visiting DJs, quizzes, pool, video games, and big screen TV. **Sages** is the original 1930s dining room, but that has now been joined by the **Terraced Café**, **The Diner** (fast food), **Grinders** (coffee bar), and **Water's Edge** (restaurant with cyber café). Still not satisfied students opt for club-loon outings to Manchester, Liverpool and Preston, or slip into Ormskirk, heaven forbid, and sample **The Styles** or **Disraeli** bars.

With some 50 societies on offer, the extra-curricular scene is better here than in many a more mature university. **The Rose Theatre** and **Studio Theatre** on campus are used for student theatre and music events, and by visiting companies - more than 100 films, theatre and musical performances are staged every year. Community Action has 150 volunteers.

And then there are the sports clubs.

SPORT Which brings us to Sporting Edge. There is a sports crazy element at Edge Hill, and the facilities are good, thanks to a £1.9-million Lottery Grant

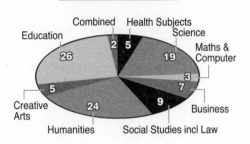

SUBJECT AREAS (%)

Education 26, Combined 2, Health Subjects 5, Science 19, Maths & Computer 3, Business 7, Social Studies incl Law 9, Humanities 24, Creative Arts 5

and additional funds made available to afford the £3.9 million it all cost - a 4-court hall, a fitness suite, squash court, 7 floodlit tennis courts, 4 soccer pitches, 2 rugby pitches, 5 netball pitches, a 5-lane athletics track and an 8-lane straight, a cricket square, gymnasium, swimming pool, synthetic hockey pitch and 5-a-side area. On top of this there's the **Wilson Centre** - specialist labs to measure sporting performance.

Some of these facilities are used by Premiership football squads and professional rugby league sides.

Finally, a fully-equipped dance studio with sprung floor hosts a varied programme of exercise classes, including aerobics, yoga and pilates.

ACCOMMODATION	
Student rating	★★
Guarantee to freshers	**75%**
Style	**Halls, flats**
Security guard	**All**
Shared rooms	**None**
Internet access	**All**
Self-catered	**Most halls, all flats**
En suite	**Some halls, most flats**
Approx price range pw	**£56-£97**
Town rent pw	**£60-£70**

PILLOW TALK

Thirty-one halls of residence provide over 1,000 rooms on campus. Lectures, shops and the library are all within easy reach. Half of them are catered, a fifth en suite. Rooms are allocated on a first come first served basis, although priority will be given to students with disabilities, care-leavers, and/or to those who live outside a 10-mile radius. New self-catered, en-suite accommodation at

Founders Court at Ormskirk campus opened last year. Chancellors Court under construction.

GETTING THERE

☛ By road: M6/J26, M58/J3, A570 to Southport. The uni is 2 miles along on the right.
☛ By rail: Northern Line Merseyrail train connections from Liverpool Central and Preston Stations. Alight at Ormskirk, not Edge Hill.

STUDENT EDINBURGH - THE CITY

Edinburgh has a worldwide reputation for being one of the most interesting and exciting places to live and study. It is a city of contradictions. On the one hand it is an ancient city, with dramatic architecture and a rich cultural history. On the other hand it is a cosmopolitan capital and a critical financial and political centre. It is also a 24-hour city with an eclectic range of bars and clubs to suit any taste. Edinburgh, with consummate ease, combines ancient with modern, and work with play, making it one of the most vibrant and exciting cities in Europe.

CITY SCAPE

Edinburgh is centred round the beautiful castle that heads up the tourist filled Royal Mile complete with ancient cobbled streets and historical landmarks aplenty. The city is compact making it easy to get around simply by walking, although if you do get tired feet, the extensive bus network is ready and waiting. The town is essentially split into two with the ancient splendour of Old town, which houses the University, and the Georgian New Town separated by the stunning Princes Street gardens. Pay a visit in the festive season and

you will find an outdoor ice rink and huge Christmas market. This is also the site of the famed Edinburgh Hogmanay party that leads the world in celebrating the New Year.

COFFEE CULTURE

Edinburgh is typified by its coffee culture. You are never more than 5 minutes away from a good coffee and a comfy seat. Many of the best can be found around George Square, conveniently close to Edinburgh's central campus. **Assembly** and **Negociants** on Teviot place provide good lunches and tasty cocktails. The **Human Be-In** offers chic upmarket surroundings whilst the American style diner, **Favorit**, offers good food at good prices until early in the morning. **Bean Scene** on South Clerk Street offers a comfy haven away from the hustle and bustle. It also boasts its own record label of up and coming talent, and regular live performances from its artists. For those of you who are star struck, the **Elephant House** is famed as J.K.Rowling's favourite coffee spot. It is where she wrote some of *Harry Potter*. It, and its smaller cousin, **Elephant and Bagels**, offer excellent food and friendly original decor. Those of you with a serious addiction to chocolate won't be disappointed with the range available in Edinburgh. **Plaisir du Chocolat** on the Royal Mile offers the best hot chocolate money can buy, but it will cost you a small fortune. **Chocolate Soup** in Hanover Square offers fabulous hot chocolates in a huge variety of flavours, served in the biggest cups known to man.

SILVER SCREEN

The city excels in cinemas. At the **Cameo** in Tollcross there's thematic music before the credits roll and the pleasure of enjoying a pint in its enticingly comfortable seats. **The Cameo** features a range of unusual films that you won't find at the big chain cinemas. It isn't arthouse cinema, but it is a break from the one-dimensional Hollywood blockbusters. **The Filmhouse** serves the more arty audience, excelling at foreign films. For Hollywood, head to the **UGC Multiplex** at Fountainpark or **Vue** cinema at the top of Leith Walk.

The city also holds an annual International Film Festival in August. The uni's Film Society offers membership at a bargain price of £15 and gets you entry to a massive range of great films throughout the academic year.

SPOTLIGHTS

Due mainly to the Edinburgh festival, the city has an excess of theatres. **The Playhouse** at the top of Leith Walk hosts all the major touring musicals. There are often generous student discounts. **The Lyceum** offers Shakespeare or post-modern avant-garde. The world famous **Traverse**, nestling nearby amongst high-class eateries, dishes up excellent experimental Scottish drama as well as having one of the hippest bars in Edinburgh. If you're into more mainstream theatre or opera, head to the **King's Theatre** or **Festival Theatre**. Then there's the only student-run pro theatre in the UK, **Bedlam** on Bristo Place. Regular favourites are the Improverts, who run a 'whose line it is anyway' style show, and perform every Friday in term time.

Edinburgh is also steeped in comedy grandeur due to the famed festival, but the laughs don't stop there: comedy continues all year round. Edinburgh University Students' Association hold one of the most famous venues, the **Pleasance**, which plays hosts to the Comedy Network every fortnight. Everyone, from Harry Hill to Frank Skinner, has played here on their way to fame. So, there is plenty of, 'I saw them before they were famous' boasting potential. **The Stand**, in York Place, is the city's only purpose-built comedy venue. It serves up good food and a great ambience in a cosy basement. **Jongleurs** comedy club in the **Omni Centre** is another venue. Although the comedy is

average, there are usually good deals on the door.

RETAIL RELIEF

If you fancy some retail therapy, head down to Princes Street, which houses nearly all the major high street brands. If you fancy really splashing out, then George Street has all the fine boutiques, stuffed with luxury goods aplenty.

If retro is the requirement, **Armstrongs** and **The Rusty Zip** deliver the goods, while **Flip** on South Bridge is good for flares, cords and comedy seventies gear. For the ultimate in budget retailing, check out the numerous charity shops on Nicholson Street. Skaterkids are well-serviced in Edinburgh, with both **Cult Clothing** and **Odd One Out** especially popular with the baggy-trousered contingent.

For music, head to Cockburn Street, home to the capital's Number 1 music shops, **Fopp** and **Avalanche**, both of which are infinitely better value than their mainstream Princes Street rivals.

Edinburgh has the largest collection of second-hand book stores in the world. So, for all you book worms, there are plenty of places to spend your days. **Till's** on Buccleuch Street, **Armchair Books** at West Port, **McFeely's** on Buccleuch Street and **MacNaughtons** at Gayfield Place are but a few of the delights in store for you.

PUB IT

Like so much of Edinburgh the key word is variety. Edinburgh's pubs and bars have the benefit of staying open until 1am every night. If a pint in a traditional pub is your aim, head to the **Blind Poet** or the **Pear Tree**. The latter boasts an impressive beer garden and many a late night can be spent clutching a pint in the cold Scottish air. If you are looking for a cheap pint then try one of the Scream pubs such as the **Tron** or **The Crags**, conveniently located next to the main Student Union halls. If you are looking for something a little more fancy then head over to New Town and enjoy the delights of **Prive Council** or **Beluga** on Chambers Street.

Both offer upmarket chic surroundings and not unreasonable prices. The Royal Mile offers a plethora of bars, but often more expensive. Head to the Cowgate where you will find a virtual tunnel of bars. Of particular note is **Bannermans**, which holds live music nights for unsigned bands nearly every night of the week.

IN THE CLUB

Edinburgh has more clubs per head than anywhere else in Britain – fact. This means that you have a massive choice of venues and a huge variety of styles to choose from. For those looking for a traditional chart club night out then **City**, with its excellent lighting and sound, **Faith**, with its impressive décor and **Why Not?**, with its clean crisp image are all favourites. For the more chic amongst you, head to **Opal Lounge** or **Po Na Na** for stylish surroundings and swanky drinks. Beware the price tag that comes with the venue! Goth and Rock are catered for by **Opium** on the Cowgate and **Citrus** on Lothian Road. **Honeycomb** puts on an awesome funk night on Tuesdays, and the unique design of the club, with its literal honeycomb structure, is worth seeing anyway. **Bongo Club** offers the best hip hop and reggae in town. **Liquid Rooms** offers an excellent venue and a huge variety of nights, although it can be pricey. **Ego** on Picardy Place offers nights tailor made for gay clubbers, especially Tuesdays. With two floors of music, dirt cheap drink, and a young crowd this is an excellent night out. **CC Blooms** is the only permanent Gay Club with **Planet Out** and **Habana** providing the best of the bar scene.

Venues chop and change their nights each week, so for complete up-to-date listings pick up a copy of *The List*.

Iain Walters

UNIVERSITY OF EDINBURGH

The University of Edinburgh
57 George Square
Edinburgh EH8 9JU

TEL 0131 650 4360
FAX 0131 651 1236
EMAIL sra.enquiries@ed.ac.uk
WEB www.ed.ac.uk

Edinburgh University Student Association
Student Centre House
5/2 Bristo Square
Edinburgh EH8 9AL

TEL 0131 650 2656
FAX 0131 668 4177
EMAIL eusa.enquiry@eusa.ed.ac.uk
WEB www.eusa.ed.ac.uk

VIRGIN VIEW

If you are looking at parents' perceptions, it's Oxbridge then Durham and Bristol, and Edinburgh is the Scottish equivalent. Edinburgh, they know, is the place to be.

An Edinburgh degree is a very good degree to have. It is still considered to be part of a Scottish person's birthright.

In fact, there have been mutterings south of the border that Scots get more than their fair share of places, even that sassenachs are, in some cases, the victims of discrimination.

Putting this to the university is met with straight speaking. They use 'varying methods' in the selection of undergraduate students. For some subjects the number of applications they receive 'broadly equates to the number of offers we are able to make. This means that if you achieve, or are predicted to achieve, the minimum entry requirements, and you have a good personal statement, demonstrating an interest in your subject, and a supportive academic reference, you have a very good chance of being made an offer of admission.'

For other subject areas, the number of

UNIVERSITY/STUDENT PROFILE	
University since	**1583**
Situation/style	**Civic**
Student population	**24525**
Undergraduates	**17285**
Mature	**26%**
International	**23%**
Male/female ratio	**44:56**
Equality of opportunity:	
state school intake	**71%**
social class 4-7 intake	**19%**
drop-out rates	**4%**

applications they receive 'outweighs the number of offers we are able to make. Applications which meet the minimum entry requirements progress to a selection process in which each application received by the specified deadline is given full and equal consideration by at least two professional admissions staff.

'At the heart of the University's admissions principles are commitments to fair admissions and to widening access. The University aims to ensure that suitably

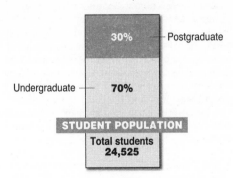

30% — Postgraduate

Undergraduate — **70%**

STUDENT POPULATION

Total students 24,525

qualified students who demonstrate academic potential are encouraged to apply to the University, regardless of the school or college they have attended, where they live or their social and cultural background. Competition for places at Edinburgh is greater than ever: in 2010 there were, on average, 14 applications per place.'

There is a continual, rolling strategy of improvement and expansion to the fabric of the university. New this year is a £4.5-million extension to the Centre for Sport, a 3-storey development providing 1,900 sqm of space was launched by HRH Prince Philip Duke of Edinburgh last August.

Open Days for 2011 are: 17 June, 5 and 24 September.

CAMPUS

'The University is primarily divided into two main campuses, two miles apart,' writes James Lumsden. 'George Square (with its central city location) for Arts & Social Science, and KB (King's Buildings) for Science and Engineering. Recently, the university has spent wads of cash reinventing KB into somewhere that you no longer want to leave before you arrive. The result reminds some of a cross-channel ferry.

'George Square, meanwhile, has its own brand of ugliness, in the shape of Appleton and David Hume towers. For a beautiful city that's known as "the Athens of the North", Edinburgh University seems to have done its damnedest to flout convention.'

Actually, it is impossible not to be impressed by the gothic beauty of the University Precinct, as you walk up to it from the railway station for the first time, high above the city. One thinks of Scott and Robert Louis Stevenson, and not a little of 'The Strange Case of Dr Jekyll and Mr Hyde', which is all as it should be, for Stevenson was an undergraduate

here. He founded the student newspaper in 1887.

The city is a treasure-trove of cultural and recreational opportunities. Most students thrive on Edinburgh life, even though the cost of living can make it difficult to do it justice. Some scientists complain of isolation, although there is a regular bus link with the main university area around George Square.

The old Moray House Institute of Education is the uni's Faculty of Education. Founded in 1835, there are two sites, Holyrood in the heart of the Old Town, adjacent to the university's central premises and, 6 miles away on the northwest edge of the city, a campus hitherto known as the Scottish Centre for Physical Education and home to PE, Leisure Studies and Applied Sports Science. The sporting facilities put Edinburgh in the Top 10 for sports trainers and coaches.

FEES, BURSARIES

UK & EU Fees. The tuition fee level for session 2011-2012 will be £1,820, or, for Medicine, £2,895. Scottish and non-UK EU students studying in Scotland can apply to have their tuition fees paid by the Scottish Government through the Students Awards Agency for Scotland (SAAS). Students from England, Wales & Northern Ireland, although liable to pay their tuition fee up-front, can apply to Student Finance England, Wales or Northern Ireland as appropriate for fee, grant and loan support and will be entitled to the same level of government support as they would if they were

TEACHING SURVEY AT A GLANCE	
Avg. UCAS points accepted	**440**
Acceptance rate	**8%**
Overall satisfaction rate	**86%**
Helpful/interested staff	★★★★
Small tuition groups	★★★
Students into graduate jobs	**77%**

Teaching most popular with undergraduates:
Accounting, Archaeology (100%), Biology & related subjects, Chemical Engineering, Chemistry, Computer Science, Creative Arts & Design, Economics, Electronic & Electrical Eng., Engineering & Technology, English, Geology, Human & Social Geography, Law, Medicine, Music, Nursing, Physical Geography, Physics & Astronomy, Psychology, Sociology (100%), Social Policy & Anthropology, Sports Science, Subjects allied to Medicine, Theology.

Teaching least popular with undergraduates:
Social Work (40%).

studying at home.

Over 180 Access Bursaries will be awarded to UK students from schools or colleges in the UK who are experiencing financial difficulties in taking up their place: £1,000: The Access Bursary Application Deadline is 1 April 2010.

Up to 90 Accommodation Bursaries of £1,000 will also be offered on the basis of significant financial need. The Accommodation Bursary Application Deadline is 1 April 2010. www.ed.ac. uk/schools-departments/student-funding/undergraduate/uk-eu/bursaries.

STUDENT PROFILE

'Often represented by a myopic media as a toffs' university,' writes James Lumsden, 'the true diversity of student and university life at Edinburgh goes misrepresented; there are more than 20,000 students from a wide variety of backgrounds and circumstances.'

Nevertheless, in the modern context, the uni does have its share of rahs. Jamie Scattergood: 'I was fully aware of the public school contingent etc., but there is a huge, huge public school contingent here, and the Radley, Eton boys are very insular. When I first got here, the best way to integrate socially, I thought, is to join the rugby team. There is a boy from Radley... just because we are not from Radley or Eton he's quite hostile. I would say there are about 40 or 50 people here like that. But in general it is pretty easy to make friends, people seem to be very friendly. I don't like the fact that the rugby club is so cliquey, so literally people won't socialise outside the club. I'm not playing rugby next year, put it like that. Recently I have made a conscious effort to meet more people and already I have met 20/30 really good people. Also, my advice would be, don't come to Edinburgh with a friend. Make new ones...'

In fact, the University has recently been awarded the Frank Buttle Trust Quality Mark for Care Leavers in Higher Education. You get this for encouraging children in care to apply. Wonder what the Radley-Eton brigade made of that.

ACADEMIA & JOBS

The Scottish degree structure differs significantly from those in the rest of the UK. The fourth year leads to a breadth and depth of study much sought-after by employers. However, Jamie questions whether it is as heavy a workload as it might be.

'I'm doing Economics and Politics. Very happy with the course. It is pretty much as expected. I think the organisation is pretty good. Certain things take a bit of time. I don't think the relationship between the lecturers and students is that brilliant, but it works. It's not put on a plate for

you, but in general it's pretty good. You get some lecturers who are brilliant. Quite a few in the Politics classes are American and they are really passionate about Politics. The tutorial size is about 12, it ranges between 10 and 20. The library is huge, absolutely huge, and you can't really expect them to stock 100 of each book, so I think in general they are pretty good. But the thing that I found quite frustrating, and I know this may sound silly, but I'm so *un-busy* at the moment. I'm doing a lot of extra-curricular stuff just to keep myself

RESEARCH EXCELLENCE

% of Edinburgh's research that is
4* *(World-class)* or **3*** *(Internationally rated):*

	4*	3*
Hospital Clinical Subjects	40%	40%
Psychiatry, Neuroscience & Clinical Psychology	10%	55%
Biological Sciences	15%	45%
Agriculture, Veterinary, Food	20%	35%
Environmental Sciences	15%	55%
Chemistry	30%	40%
Physics	20%	45%
Pure Mathematics	25%	45%
Applied Mathematics	15%	50%
Statistics	10%	35%
Computer Science	35%	50%
General Eng., Mineral & Mining	15%	40%
Architecture/ Built Environment	25%	45%
Geography	20%	35%
Economics and Econometrics	25%	45%
Business and Management	10%	40%
Law	30%	25%
Politics	10%	45%
Social Work, Policy & Admin.	30%	35%
Sociology	30%	25%
Anthropology	25%	35%
Psychology	15%	45%
Education	15%	30%
Middle Eastern, African	25%	45%
Asian Studies	10%	25%
East European Languages	5%	35%
French	10%	45%
German, Dutch, Scandinavian	25%	25%
Italian	0%	25%
Iberian and Latin American	15%	35%
Celtic Studies	20%	30%
English	40%	30%
Linguistics	30%	30%
Classics etc.	10%	35%
Philosophy	20%	45%
Theology	30%	30%
History	25%	35%
History of Art	15%	45%
Music	20%	45%

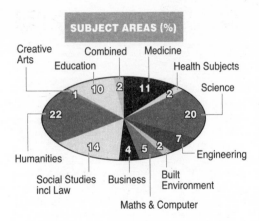

SUBJECT AREAS (%)

Creative Arts — 1
Education — 10
Combined — 2
Medicine — 11
Health Subjects — 2
Science — 20
Engineering — 7
Built Environment — 2
Maths & Computer — 5
Business — 4
Social Studies incl Law — 14
Humanities — 22

busy. What I'm trying to say is that Edinburgh should *up* its entry standards. All I did last term was two essays. Do you see where I'm coming from? It's quite frustrating.'

At least Jamie's teachers are well informed. Almost two thirds of the work submitted for the last Research Assessment Exercise was rated as world-leading or internationally excellent, the highest proportion in Scotland. The university's entry was among the largest in the UK and produced strong results across the board. The College of Medicine and Veterinary Medicine was the star performer, with all of the work in hospital-based clinical subjects rated at the international level and 40 per cent at the highest grade. Informatics, linguistics and English literature also produced outstanding results.

Students say the best taught subjects are Accounting, Archaeology (100%), Biology & related subjects, Chemical Engineering, Chemistry, Computer Science, Creative Arts & Design, Economics, Electronic & Electrical Eng., Engineering & Technology, English, Geology, Human & Social Geography, Law, Medicine, Music, Nursing, Physical Geography, Physics & Astronomy, Psychology, Sociology (100%), Social Policy & Anthropology, Sports Science, Subjects allied to Medicine, Theology. These subjects all received 85% or greater positive response from the students polled.

The degree in Medicine is a 5/6-year MB ChB. They promise 'early clinical contact' and deliver it in Year 1, together with case-based learning tutorials using problem-based learning methods.

> **'I was fully aware of the public school contingent etc., but there is a huge, huge public school contingent here, and the Radley, Eton boys are very insular.'**

You will need three A levels and one AS in four subjects. Non-science VCE AS and A levels may replace non-science GCE AS and A levels. Only one Maths will be considered. Chemistry plus Maths or Physics or Biology at A Level and Biology at least at AS.

The veterinary provision actually scored better than Medicine at the teaching assessments. New this year are two landmark buildings which will house a new Vet School and the Rosslin Institute out at Easter Bush, Roslin, Midlothian, the development worth some £80 million.

Graduate jobs are not a problem for Edinburgh graduates. Health and education are the two single largest destination sectors, and jobs also proliferate in community & counselling activities, banking, accounting, the hotel/restaurant trade, veterinary, the Civil Service, personnel, publishing, software consultancy & supply, retail, management, museum/library/archive, engineering design, sport, architecture, advertising, media, Defence, and much else besides.

On the curriculum, Languages, Historical & Philosophical Studies, Social Studies, and Biological Sciences are especially strong in graduate job placement for students at Edinburgh.

SOCIAL SCENE

One hears that Edinburgh is an expensive place to enjoy four years. Jamie agrees: 'I think the comment about needing money to enjoy yourself at Edinburgh is pretty much true. I spend £60-£80 a week. It depends on the week. In Freshers Week I spent £500, but I suppose I could survive with £20-£25.' He might in Pollock Halls, where most freshers live, as it's catered.

The Pleasance has the **Cabaret Bar** (capacity 175), which hosts parties, discos, live bands, acoustic nights, theatre/dance/comedy. For society nights they can provide djs, sound and lighting technicians. **The Theatre** on the first floor is the principal performance space in the Pleasance, and the **Highland Room**, with lino floor and mirrored wall, is used for dance classes, meetings, rehearsals (capacity 70). Tea, coffee, buffets can be supplied. The **Ochil Room** is another space much-used for classes and meetings, and there are nine other, slightly smaller rooms available too.

Teviot Union, the oldest, purpose-built Students' Union building in the country, has 5 levels of possible entertainment. The **Under-**

ACCOMMODATION	
Student rating	★★★
Guarantee to freshers	**100%**
Style	**Halls, flats**
Security guard	**All halls.** **some flats**
Shared rooms	**Some**
Internet access	**All**
Self-catered	**All flats,** **no halls**
En suite	**Most halls,** **no flats**
Approx price range pw	**£56.42-£226.24**
City rent pw	**£60-£85**

ground is a great little club (capacity 410) and theatre venue, most commonly used for club nights, band nights, discos and parties. The **Terrace Bar** is a split level affair. The **Mezannine** can seat 300 for dinner, and is another club night, band night, disco or party venue. Then there's the **Debating Hall**, sounds a bit stodgy, but no stranger to the odd ceilidh. Capacity depends on the event, for discos it's 400. The **Loft Bar** boasts a roof terrace. The **Balcony Room** is a small bar perched at the top of one of Teviot's gothic turrets.

For night-time pleasure it's **The Potterow**, 1,200 capacity, regularly reached on weekends. The newly refurbished **Bristo Lounge** has its own bar and is ideal for acoustic gigs or informal parties.

Down at King's Buildings, there's a £3.4 million student facility for the 7,000 science and engineering campus - catering and bar facilities, a games room, squash courts, a multi-gym, a sports hall and advisory and welfare services. KB get quizzes, pool comps and film nights by way of ents.

Meanwhile the University Theatre Company draws crowds for its many productions at **Bedlam Theatre**, the site of Bristo Bedlam, where 'the mad, manic and mental' were once locked away. Now Bedlam's the UK's only student-run theatre.

Holly Crane, who threw herself into extra-curricular media when she was up had a hugely positive view of this aspect of the university: 'I know everyone is supposed to fall in love with their university, but Edinburgh just makes it so easy,' she writes. 'It's the ideal advert for higher education: a place where you learn not only facts and formulae from your academic studies, but also about what you can do, what you want to do - and what you don't want to do - with the rest of your life.'

Holly was sensitive to 'a discernible buzz about the university, a condensed feeling of potential, and energy. This is partly due to the city itself: there's just enough of the "ivory tower" atmosphere

to leave you inspired but not oppressed by your impending academia. But it's also to do with the type of students. With many doing four-year (or longer) degrees, there is, if not more time, then more reason, to get up off your arse and do something a bit different.'

There is opportunity aplenty to do so - loads of clubs and societies centred on the Pleasance, the most popular being Film Soc, The *Edinburgh Student* (newspaper) took Critic of the Year at the *Guardian* Media Awards in 2009. There's also a mag. called *Nomad*, a radio station, Fresh Air fm, and Nightline (welfare). *Edinburgh Student* is Britain's third biggest student newspaper, with a weekly circulation of 12,000 copies distributed to all the universities and higher education colleges around Edinburgh. They took two gongs at the National Student Drama Awards in 2010.

SPORT The university is pre-eminent in sport, came 5th in the UK last year. Besides its twenty-five acres of playing fields and residential centre on

WHAT IT'S REALLY LIKE	
UNIVERSITY:	
Social Life	★★★★★
Societies	★★★★
Student Union services	★★★★
Politics	**Active**
Sport	**Key**
National team position	**5th**
Sport facilities	★★★★★
Arts opportunities	**Good**
NSDF (Drama) Awards	**Two, 2010**
Student magazine	**Hype**
Student newspaper	**Edinburgh Student**
Guardian Awards 2009	**Critic of Year**
Student radio	**Fresh Air FM**
Nightclub	**Potterow**
Bars	**Sportsman's, Teviot, The Pleasance**
Union ents	**Cheese, comedy, Indie**
Union societies	**200**
Most popular societies	**Amnesty**
Parking	**Poor**
CITY:	
Entertainment	★★★★★
Scene	**Seething**
Town/gown relations	**Good**
Risk of violence	**Low**
Cost of living	**High**
Student concessions	**Excellent**
Survival + 2 nights out	**£150+ pw**
Part-time work campus/town	**Good/excellent**

Loch Tay, there's a sports centre with conditioning gymnasia, a fitness and sports injury centre, and a wide range of team and individual activities. Says Jamie: 'The gym is amazing. Recently I was on a bench press next to the South African rugby team! They were all using our gym, it was surreal!'

TOWN 'When you do step out, the city offers everything,' writes James Lumsden. 'There are enough bars and pubs to see you from this life into the next, and plenty of theatres, cinemas, clubs, and 'cultural stuff' to stop at, en-route. See **Student Edinburgh** above.

PILLOW TALK

Freshers from outside Edinburgh are guaranteed a place in uni accommodation provided they apply by September 1, and that UCAS has guaranteed their place at Edinburgh by that date. There's a mix of traditional full board halls, student houses, and flats. Main accommodation for first years is Pollock Halls, a complex of houses, together with a bar, shop and dining rooms, which take around 2,000 first years. All rooms are single, but, if you pay extra, you can upgrade to a double bed and en-suiteshower. Most people go for full board; breakfast and supper in the week and three meals at the weekend. However, each house has a kitchen area where you can test out your culinary talents (toast). Another residential area is Robertson's Close which consists of self-catering flats. There are also uni-run student houses.

Says Jamie: 'Pollock Halls is where freshers begin. The one I'm in is typical of halls, about 50/60 years old. I didn't get very lucky, but it's en-suite. The Chancellors Court holds about 700 people and the rooms are like 3-star hotel rooms. They are currently making new accommodation for more people at Pollock. Unfortunately my window is right by the construction site. I think I'm going to get compensation for that.'

The new hall is John Burnett House, opened last year. Fresher car parking is severely limited.

GETTING THERE

☞ By road: M90 or M9 or A1 or M8.
☞ By rail: London King's Cross, 4:30; Glasgow Central, 50 mins; Newcastle, 1:30.
☞ By air: Edinburgh Airport.
☞ By coach: Glasgow, 1:10; London, 9:10; Birmingham, 8:10; Newcastle, 3:10.

EDINBURGH NAPIER UNIVERSITY

Edinburgh Napier University
Craiglockhart Campus
Edinburgh EH14 1DJ

TEL 08452 60 60 60
FAX 0131 455 6464
EMAIL info@napier.ac.uk
WEB www.napier.ac.uk

Edinburgh Napier Students' Association
12 Merchiston Place
Edinburgh EH10 4NR

TEL 0131 229 8791
FAX 0131 228 3462
EMAIL nsa@napier.ac.uk
WEB www.napierstudents.com

VIRGIN VIEW

In 2009, Napier University changed its name to Edinburgh Napier University, thereby rushing up the alphabetical order in the Guide, and, more purposefully in its pursuit of student applicants at home and abroad, clarifying and capitalising on its location in Scotland's beautiful capital city.

Napier has always had a good reputation for getting graduates jobs. In 2008 the Higher Education Statistics Agency (HESA) named it Scotland's No. 1 university for employability,

UNIVERSITY/STUDENT PROFILE	
University since	**1992**
Situation/style	**Civic**
Student population	**13645**
Undergraduates	**11455**
Mature	**57%**
International	**24%**
Male/female ratio	**46:54**
Equality of opportunity:	
state school intake	**94%**
social class 4-7 intake	**35%**
drop-out rate	**16%**

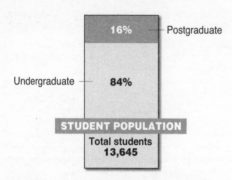

16% — Postgraduate

Undergraduate — 84%

STUDENT POPULATION
Total students
13,645

what Napier does have is an excellent rapport between lecturers and students (we give this a 4-star rating). The teaching is good here. The lecturers are helpful and interested in their students. It is reckoned to be one of the top universities in the UK for 'Value Added', measuring admission qualifications against honours results.

What might be possible if they got the extra-mural side together too?

CAMPUS

Long-term policy is to have one campus per faculty with state-of-the-art facilities, student accomm- odation and a proper Student Association presence. The first step was completed with the opening of the **Craiglockhart** Campus, home to the Business School. Now this year they have

with 97.5% of its graduates in employment or further study within six months of graduating. The Higher Education Founding Council calculate real graduate jobs as 76% currently.

Its difficulty has always been that it is a bit split up, with no central focus. A lack of facilities was another criticism by its students in the national poll. There has been no one place where Napierites congregate, and very little going on outside the lecture theatre to amuse or interest its students.

Napier has been like a day college that closes down after lectures. Whether this is partly down to there being a large mature undergrad. population (57%) and a high number of locals is not clear, but being without much of a social or extra-curriciular scene will surely have done little to encourage a younger crew, or stem the drop-out rate, which is 16%.

Now they are at least moving in a positive direction by rationalising the split-campus format, and when the Times Higher Education *managed to find a way in to ask questions of their undergraduates for the Student Experience Survey, it fell clear that*

TEACHING SURVEY AT A GLANCE	
Avg. UCAS points accepted	**286**
Acceptance rate	**20%**
Overall satisfaction rate	**80%**
Helpful/interested staff	★★★★
Small tuition groups	★★
Students into graduate jobs	**76%**

Teaching most popular with undergraduates:
Accounting, Biology & related sciences, Business Studies, Finance, Law (100%), Nursing, Psychology, Sociology, Sports Science.

Teaching least popular with undergraduates:
Journalism (59%), Design Studies (53%).

redeveloped the **Sighthill** campus for the Faculty of Health, Life & Social Sciences. It includes a 5-storey learning resource centre, 25 specialised teaching rooms including clinical skills laboratories, an environmental chamber and biomechanics laboratory, a crime scene scenario room, three IT-enabled lecture theatres and seminar rooms as well as integrated sports facilities. In addition, a clinical skills suite is equipped with advanced technology to meet the demands of the healthcare sector now and in the future and will lead the way in Scotland for cross-sector clinical skills education. Just as significantly, a new gym and Sports Centre with 1,200m2 sports hall opened at the Sighthill Campus in January 2011. The new facilities significantly enhance the services available to students, staff and people from the local community.There are now plans to refurbish the campus at **Merchiston**, where the Faculty of Engineering, Computing &

SUBJECT AREAS (%)

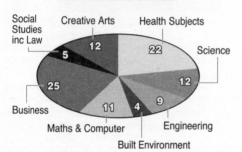

Social Studies inc Law — 5
Creative Arts — 12
Health Subjects — 22
Science — 12
Business — 25
Maths & Computer — 11
Built Environment — 4
Engineering — 9

Creative Industries is based, and to include 'a social learning space'. It won't stop there, for there are, in addition, half a dozen other sites spread out mostly through the south and west of Edinburgh.

Open Days 2011 25 August (Craiglockhart); 1 October, 10am - 3pm (Merchiston, Craiglockhart and Sighthill Campuses)

FEES, BURSARIES

UK & EU Fees, 2011-12: In line with other Scottish higher education institutions, it's £1,820 p.a. for non-Scottish dwellers. There are bursaries based on financial hardship, company sponsored scholarships, and scholarships based on academic excellence. A Student Grant Initiative is open to all students who wish to carry out a project that will either enhance their studies at Edinburgh Napier, or provide them with a good personal development opportunity (£1,000 per project). The RUK Bursary is for ex-Scotland UK students who would have been eligible for a national minimum had they studied at a university in the rest of the UK.

STUDENT PROFILE

The student profile shows a fairly typical 'new' demography: 57% mature, 94% state school intake, 35% from working class homes; most are locally based. Edinburgh Napier has developed through building effective partnerships with colleges. The development of approximately 2000 college

RESEARCH EXCELLENCE		
% of Napier's research that is **4*** *(World-class) or* **3*** *(Internationally rated):*		
	4*	*3**
Nursing and Midwifery	5%	35%
Health Professions	5%	5%
Environmental Sciences	0%	20%
Computer Science	0%	20%
Civil Engineering	5%	25%
Built Environment	5%	30%
Business/ Management	0%	15%
Information Management	10%	50%
Law	0%	5%
Sociology	0%	10%
Psychology	0%	5%
English	5%	15%
Art and Design	0%	25%
Music	0%	5%

'articulation routes' have enabled students to use their college qualifications to gain direct entry into year two or three of the University. Widening participation is high on the university's list of priorities.

ACADEMIA & JOBS

There are 3 faculties: Business; Engineering, Computing & Creative Industries; and Health, Life & Social Science.

In the old days, health was the big graduate employment destination, swelled by Nursing, which is now off the curriculum. There are other dimensions to the provision, however, including Biomedical Sciences, Immunology & Toxicology, Applied Nutrition, Social Sciences with Health, Complementary Medicine, Herbal Medicine, and the well designed Vet Nursing top-up/BSc (Hons).

The uni is known for business, too, and recently they got together with Paris-based business school IPAG to offer an MSc in International Marketing and Tourism. Languages, Marketing and Tourism are features of other Business degrees, as is Hospitality Management, and all are rich seams in Napier's graduate employment field. They also have dedicated degrees in Accounting and a good reputation for jobs in banking and finance.

Architecture sits alongside courses in Building and Quantity Surveying, Built Environment, Construction & Project Management, and again, all these are strong areas of graduate employment, as is Civil Engineering, which teams up with Transport Engineering and sits alongside Transport

WHAT IT'S REALLY LIKE	
COLLEGE:	
Social Life	★★
Societies	★★
Student Union services	★
Politics	**Interest low**
Sport	**21 clubs**
National team position	**56th**
Sport facilities	★
Arts opportunities	**Average**
Student mag/news	**Veritas**
Bars	**Union Bar**
Union ents	**DJs**
Union societies	**11**
Most popular society	**Drama**
Parking	**Poor**
CITY:	
Entertainment	★★★★★
Scene	**Seething**
Town/gown relations	**Good**
Risk of violence	**Average**
Cost of living	**High**
Student concessions	**Excellent**
Survival + 2 nights out	**£100+ pw**
Part-time work campus/town	**Poor/excellent**

Management, and Civil & Timber Engineering, which finds a cosy niche forestry as a career path - the whole picture is one of academia and jobs dovetailing neatly, the one into the other.

Computer Science is a major contributor to their employment figures, as are degrees in Sport

ACCOMMODATION	
Student rating	★
Guarantee to freshers	**60%**
Style	**Flats**
Security guard	**Some**
Shared rooms	**None**
Internet access	**All**
Self-catered	**All**
En suite	**None**
Approx price range pw	**£95-£96**
City rent pw	**£60**

(almost 20% of total jobs), Publishing, Advertising, all dedicated degrees proven for employability over time. Now they also have a series of 'Customised' degrees, which allow you to get involved in the game of curriculum design they play so well. You can pic 'n' mix from virtually any subject area you care to choose.

Most of Edinburgh Napier's courses include a work placement, and the close relationship with industry and commerce helps to produce consistently good graduate employment figures. But Napier's success in the job market isn't just down to curriculum design. 'Confident Futures' is its programme of personal development available to all students and designed to promote confidence, improve self-awareness, so to enhance their employability.

SOCIAL SCENE

The **Union Bar**, 12 Merchiston Place, is round the corner from Merchiston Campus. Sports night is on Wednesday, sponsored by **Cool It** Events. **Open Mic** nights feature every other Thursday. Friday is **Cocktails Night**. And that's about it. There are 11 student societies on offer and 21 sports clubs. Their teams came 56th nationally last year, which is a massive year on gain. There is a student newspaper, **Veritas**, and the most active student society is the Drama Club. Recent political campaigns of interest have included Student Retention, Access to Top Quality Sports Facilities and the Student Experience, which has resulted in a new Fitness Suite at Craiglockart campus. There are also great links with Meadowbank Sports Centre, all of which has resulted in the great team performance nationally.

PILLOW TALK

Uni accommodation in apartment develop-ments in the city centre is guaranteed to freshers coming 'outwith a 30-mile radius of Edinburgh'. There is no catered accommodation. Four-person flats have one shared bathroom; five-person flats have two shared bathrooms. Developments are all centrally located, modern, purpose built student accommodation, all within easy access of Napier's campuses.

Says a student: 'Napier provides housing for over 1,000 students, it's quite expensive but is quickly snapped up. For safe student living, private sector, consider Tollcross, Gorgie/Dalry, Marchmont and Bruntsfield.'

A new 725-bed hall is planned in the city centre for summer 2013.

GETTING THERE

☛ By road: from north, M90; from Stirling, M9; from Newcastle, A1; from Glasgow, M8.

☛ By rail: London King's Cross, 4:30. Glasgow Central, 50 mins; Newcastle, 1:30.

☛ By coach: Glasgow, 1:10; London, 9:10.

UNIVERSITY OF ESSEX

The University of Essex
Wivenhoe Park
Colchester
Essex CO4 3SQ

TEL 01206 873333
FAX 01206 873598
EMAI admit@essex.ac.uk
WEB www.essex.ac.ok

Essex Students' Union
Wivenhoe Park
Colchester
Essex CO4 3SQ

TEL 01206 863211
FAX 01206 870915
EMAIL su@essex.ac.uk
WEB www.essexstudent.com

VIRGIN VIEW

*E*ssex University is based in Wivenhoe Park, Colchester. It was launched around the same time as York, Sussex and Warwick in the mid-1960s. Yet, after it had briefly marked its card as main seat of student revolution, it disappeared from public consciousness, partly one suspects because it will never win any prizes for beauty. It is a grey, drab institution, made almost entirely of concrete.

It is, however, the UK's leading university in social sciences, with politics and sociology ranked first, economics third and linguistics fourth nationally. In fact the most recent assessment of the research provision of all UK universities placed it in the UK Top 10 in 8 of its 14 submitted subject areas.

There are other good reasons for applying, the extra-curricular sport, ents and student media among them. Essex is also, of course, convenient for London.

Essex graduates go on to a wide range of carees, taking leading roles in business, law, human rights, teaching, government, the media, journalism, publishing, voluntary agencies and research.

They have strong relationships with employers such as BT, Grant Thornton and Santander, but more than this their student body is happy. In the latest Higher Education Funding Council poll, 88% of Essex students expressing satisfaction with what they are up to here academically.

They are committed to widening access, but are clear that they are looking for highly motivated students, and that the personal statement is key. They want evidence somehow or other of skills in 'critical thinking, analysis, problem solving and communication'.

Open Days in 2011 (Colchester Campus): 18 June, 17 September, 22 October. Southend Campus: 24 September.

CAMPUS

The campus comprises 200 acres of landscaped parkland, 2 miles from the centre of Colchester, capital of Roman Britain and now commuter and

UNIVERSITY/STUDENT PROFILE	
University since	**1965**
Situation/style	**Town campus**
Student population	**12295**
Undergraduates	**9555**
Mature	**37%**
International	**32%**
Male/female ratio	**46:54**
Equality of opportunity:	
state school intake	**96%**
social class 4-7 intake	**39%**
drop-out rate	**9%**

garrison town, and a regional centre for commerce, light industry and high technology. It is an hour away from London by train.

Perhaps a subliminal need for aesthetic redemption has drawn them to the coast. For, as of 2007, Essex has been up and running with Southend-on-Sea, about 40 miles south of Colchester, on Elmer Approach, Southend-on-Sea, Essex SS1 1LW. Tel: 01702 328200. The plan has been hatching since further education college South East Essex's move to a new £52 million building there two years ago. Essex are taking over the old Odeon cinema and teaming up with SEEC for everything from library to student sport facilities.

Since 2000 the famous drama school, East 15 in Loughton, has also been part of Essex University. East 15 has been providing professional training in theatre, film, TV, radio and related fields for more than 45 years. The School has a campus in Loughton, on the borders of East London, and shares Essex's new campus in Southend-on-Sea.

A while ago Essex launched a £250-million capital investment plan to build a new student centre and additional library, to be completed by the end of 2013, and a computing, teaching and learning space for the Colchester Campus, now complete, and a range of student services and facilities. A £400,000 refurbishment of the Student

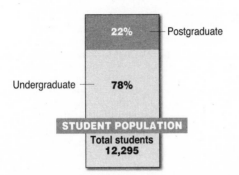

22% — Postgraduate

Undergraduate — 78%

STUDENT POPULATION
Total students
12,295

Union bar has this year been delivered. The Southend Campus has benefited from new student accommodation and the Acting School from new studio and performance facilities.

FEES, BURSARIES

UK & EU Fees, 2011-12: £3,375 p.a. Fees for 2012-13 will be £9,000. In 2011-12 there's a bursary of £700 for students with a household income of up to and including £25,000. There are awards in Maths, Computer Science, Electronic Engineering, and Sport, and East 15 scholarships and bursaries, and degrees related to Science, Technology, Engineering (the Eliahou Dangoor 'STEM' scheme). www.essex.ac.uk/studentfinance/ug/university_support

STUDENT PROFILE

Nick Margerrison writes: 'People come to Essex from every conceivable part of the known world. This provides you with a unique opportunity to get to know a wide variety of different cultures.'

Mixed socially, economically and nationally (they draw from 130 countries), the student body at Essex is a third overseas, a third mature, and a third from what used to be called the skilled working class. But it is very much traditional in that it is mainly full-time, undergraduate, and, as Nick says, 'small and friendly.'

ACADEMIA & JOBS

In Colchester there are five Schools - Social Sciences, Law (Essex are European Law and Human Rights specialists), Maths & Computer Sciences, Science & Engineering, and Comparative Studies (Humanities, but with a cross-cultural, international approach). Everything is international here, with modern languages a big feature whatever you're up to. This year also sees the number of courses offered as International Exchange or Study Abroad options extended significantly.

The new Southend-on-Sea campus has the School of Entrepreneurship and Business, which delivers BSc programmes in Business and Service Industry Management, International Enterprise and Business Development, Marketing and Innovation, New Technology and Digital Enterprise Management, and New Venture Creation and Enterprise Management.

Then there's the School of Health & Human Sciences, which delivers BSc programmes in Nursing, Health & Human Sciences, and Social Psychology & Sociology, and BA programmes in Health Studies and Health Studies & Sociology.

Finally, the drama school East 15 has BA programmes there in Acting and Stage Combat, Physical Theatre, World Performance, and

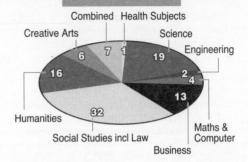

SUBJECT AREAS (%)

Community Theatre. The Loughton campus delivers East 15 degrees in BA programmes in Acting, Acting & Contemporary Theatre, and Community Theatre.

The first year is thrown open to a study of four or five courses to enable you to investigate your chosen subject from a variety of points of view. This might involve studying Sociology from an Economics point of view, History from a Psychology pov. Then in the second year you move forward to a single or joint honours degree with deeper understanding.

The Frontrunner programme is a student placement scheme available across all three campuses involving more than 30 departments with Frontrunners Plus offering students the chance to move onto a higher level of responsibility. All schools, departments and centres integrate employability skills into their courses. 'The Big E' initiative, complete with its own awards, offers business workshops with national business

RESEARCH EXCELLENCE		
% of Essex's research that is *4* (World-class)* or *3* (Internationally rated)*:		
	4*	3*
Biological Sciences	5%	35%
Computer	15%	50%
Electrical/Electronic Eng.	20%	40%
Economics	40%	55%
Accounting and Finance	10%	45%
Law	5%	45%
Politics	45%	30%
Sociology	35%	25%
Psychology	10%	45%
English	10%	45%
Linguistics	25%	35%
Philosophy	20%	55%
History	35%	35%
History of Art	25%	50%

TEACHING SURVEY AT A GLANCE

Avg. UCAS points accepted	**300**
Acceptance rate	**19%**
Overall satisfaction rate	**88%**
Helpful/interested staff	★★★★
Small tuition groups	★★★
Students into graduate jobs	**64%**

Teaching most popular with undergraduates:
Accounting, American & Australasian Studies, Biology & related sciences, Comparative Literary Studies, Computer Science, Creative Arts & Design, Drama, Economics, Electronic & Electrical Engineering, Engineering & Technology, English, History, Archaeology, Law, Linguistics, Maths, Languages, Philosophy (100%), Politics, Psychology, Sociology, Social Policy, Anthropology, Subjects Allied to Medicine, Sports Science.

WHAT IT'S REALLY LIKE

UNIVERSITY:	
Social Life	★★★★
Societies	★★★
Student Union services	★★★★
Politics	**Activity high**
Sport	**43 clubs**
National team position	**39th**
Sport facilities	★★★
Arts opportunities	**Good**
Student newspaper	**The Rabbit**
Student radio	**Red Radio**
Student TV station	**SX:TV**
Nightclub	**Sub Zero**
Bars	**SU, Level 2, Mondo, Top Bar**
Union ents	**Full on**
Union clubs/societies	**120**
Parking	**No parking if you live on campus**
CITY:	
Entertainment	★★★
Scene	**Clubs 'n pubs**
Town/gown relations	**Average**
Risk of violence	**Low**
Cost of living	**Low**
Student concessions	**Adequate**
Survival + 2 nights out	**£70 pw**
Part-time work campus/town	**Excellent/good**

leaders, the business Boot Camp and Essex Apprentice scheme.

SOCIAL SCENE

STUDENTS' UNION The Union nightclub is **Sub Zero**, refurbished recently at a huge cost; capacity 1,200, fully DDA compliant, draft products, luxurious seating areas and dancing stage. Sub Zero capped an impressive first year by winning the Smirnoff BEDA award for 'best student club in the country'. Watch out for big name events on Saturday nights, I mean huge, special one-off events like Dreadzone plus the New Town Kings, leading local Ska band...

Smaller is **Level 2**, an intimate 300-capacity venue that hosts regular week night events, such as *Vibez*, International night, Sports Fed, Alternative night, many a society night, and even Tango classes on Thursdays. Lords of Level 2 include Trevor Nelson, Masterstepz, Mista Jam and Shortee Blitz. Then there's **Mondo** next door - pizza joint by day and a 250-capacity venue, which can run in conjunction with Level 2 to form a 550-capacity club, by night.

Then there's laid-back **Top Bar** - juke box, real ale, big screen sports, and the option of ordering hot food from Sizzlers next door. And **SU Bar**, of course, the main, pub-type bar, with a full programme of footy and curry, karaoke nights, mini Flirt!, SU Bar disco, and the *Sunday Pub Quiz*.

In addition they tot up 120 societies and 43 sports clubs, a student newspaper called *The*

> *'Sub Zero capped an impressive first year by winning the Smirnoff BEDA award for best student club in the country.'*

Rabbit, SX:TV and Red Radio. Winner of last year's Society of the Year Award was the Law Soc, but very popular are Islamic Soc, Indie Soc, RnB Soc, Human Rights Soc, all of which run regular events for their members and the rest of campus.

The V-team is the University's volunteering organisation, run by the Student Union, working in a local school, being a sport coach, getting stuck in with some conservation work. It's an opportunity to make a difference to people and the community and have some fun. Enrichment through extra-curricular activities is increasingly a main principle of the Essex ethos.

TOWN 'Colchester suffers from its relative proximity to other major venues in attracting big names in entertainment,' writes Stephen Peters. 'Some occasionally grace us with their presence, but for the real stars get on the train to Cambridge or London. New talent can be seen at the local **Arts Centre**. But if you like a drink, Colchester and its environs can provide.

ACCOMMODATION

Student rating	★★★★
Guarantee to freshers	**100%**
Style	**Flats**
Security guard	**On campus**
Shared rooms	**None**
Internet access	**All**
Self-catered	**All**
En suite	**Most**
Approx price range pw	
Colchester	**£64-£104**
Southend	**£109-£125**
City rent pw	**£65**

'Most tolerate students as long as you don't share your dinner with their toilet floor. *The Wivenhoe Run* is infamous, and has to be experienced if you reckon you can down a few. But Colchester is a garrison town. Students, squaddies and alcohol are a volatile mix. Most of the time, though, you wouldn't know they are there. Find out where not to go in town when you get here (most notably the squaddie pubs).

'The nightclubs are pretty useless. Stick to the university nightclub, and only venture to town clubs for student nights.

'Local transport links are average. Buses are frequent and not too expensive. Have the right change though, or the bus drivers, notoriously miserable, get a bit shirty. Trains to London are quick and reasonably reliable. And if you have a bit of money to spend, Lakeside and Bluewater are just down the road.'

SPORT The Student Union website has run a poll as to how many applicants chose Essex for its sport facilities. There's a hall with six badminton courts, fitness room, sauna, sun-bed, squash courts, table tennis, climbing wall, plus a sportsturf pitch, floodlit tennis courts, three cricket pitches (one artificial wicket) plus nets, Squirrel Run circuit, 18-hole disc/frisbee-golf, grass and synthetic pitches, and a watersports centre. There are coaching courses in badminton, pilates, squash and tennis, and a relatively new Master's degree in Sports Science (Fitness and Health) is a sign of uni commitment.

City clubs offer sailing, windsurfing, canoeing.

PILLOW TALK

More new rooms have recently been built on campus for first years. More than half of students live in uni accommodation. Tesco is within walking distance of campus, so shopping is easy.

Accommodation ranges from flats for 13 to 16 in the famous Towers (tower blocks) to smaller, en-suite flats for six people - South Courts, Houses and University Quays have smaller flats containing 4 to 8 rooms, all of which have en suite facilities.

All accommodation is networked, so you can use your computer to access the internet and uni network from your rooms free of charge. It has become an essential for all uni accommodation. Each room also has a telephone at Essex, which provides free use of the internal telephone system.

Brand new University Square (single study rooms, cluster kitchens) opens in September at the Southend Campus:. Students at the Loughton Campus live in house shares.

GETTING THERE

☞ By road: A12. Well served by coach services.
☞ By rail: London Liverpool Street, 1:00, every half-hour; Birmingham New Street, 3:30; Sheffield, 4:00. Ten-minute taxi run to campus.
☞ By coach: London, 2:10; Norwich, 6:15.

UNIVERSITY OF EXETER

The University of Exeter
Northcote House
The Queen's Drive
Exeter EX4 4QJ

TEL 0844 6200012 (UK callers)
 + 44(0)1392 723044 (ex-UK callers)
FAX 01392 263857
EMAIL ug-ad@exeter.ac.uk
WEB www.exeter.ac.uk/undergraduate

The Students' Guild
Exeter University
Devonshire House
Exeter EX4 4PZ

TEL 01392 263536
FAX 01392 263376
EMAIL info@guild.ex.ac.uk
WEB www.exeterguild.org

VIRGIN VIEW

*E*xeter lies in South Devon, at the end of the
M5 motorway. The main campus is
beautifully set on a hill 15 minutes walk from
the centre of the cathedral city, which itself lies
close to the sea on one side and the wild open
spaces of Dartmoor on the other.

It became a university in 1955 out of the
University College of the South West, first
established in 1922. Before that it was the
School of Art (est. 1855). In the 1970s Exeter
took St Luke's College of Education into the
fold, and by the time Margaret Thatcher ruled
the waves in the 1980s, it had a reputation as
something of a haven for the green wellie
brigade: the Students' Guild's web site address
used to be gosh.exeter.ac.uk.

More recently, Exeter has divested itself of
all caricature, and in 2010 and 2011 its Student
Guild won National Student Union of the Year,
even though its own students rate it only 23rd
in the country. At the same time it slipped
seven places in the Times Higher *Student
Experience Survey* to 18th place, and its quest
for real graduate level jobs for its students
achieved only 71% success after six months of
graduation, which does not ultimately put it
among the high flyers.

Exeter is, however, listed in the World Top
200 Universities compiled (again the Times
Higher). It sits in the 184th slot, last of a
paltry 29 British Unis to make the cut.

Many have it down as a first choice
nonetheless, and if you go to its beautiful
Streatham campus in the month of June,
when the rhodos are in bloom you will fall in
love with it. Open Days in 2011 are - Exeter
campuses: 14 June, 17 September. Cornwall
Campus: 18 June, 1 October.

CAMPUS

'The university is very easy to fall in love with,'
writes Jo Moorhouse. 'It has one of the most
beautiful campuses in the country, in one of the
most beautiful counties in Britain.'

'Students at Exeter have the best of both
worlds;' writes Julie Moore, 'a cathedral city with
the countryside right on the doorstep.

'Being near the beach makes the surfing society
a popular choice, and with Newquay just down the
road the summer terms are filled with weekend
trips and beach parties.

'Many people, myself included, made Exeter
their first choice uni after one tour of the campus.
A lush green settlement dotted with ponds and
famous sculptures, campus has a relaxed
atmosphere with some perfect spots for chilling out
with friends in the sun. Everything is within
walking distance, which means if you have a
lecture at 9am you can get up ten minutes before
and still make it. There is no shortage of shops,
cafés and bars, and you have no real need to leave.

'The only thing they forget to tell you is that
flat roads are a rare luxury in Exeter, and some of
the student halls are at the bottom of Cardiac hill,
and definitely not advised for anyone with a heart

UNIVERSITY/STUDENT PROFILE	
University since	**1955**
Situation/style	**Campus**
Student population	**16195**
Undergraduates	**11485**
Mature	**25%**
International	**20%**
Male/female ratio	**47:53**
Equality of opportunity:	
state school intake	**71%**
social class 4-7 intake	**21%**
drop-out rate	**2%**

condition! The other side is that you do get used to
it, but tend to laugh less at the ongoing joke about
"the Exeter thighs".

ST LUKE'S CAMPUS The schools of Education, Sport
and Health Sciences and the Peninsula Medical
School are based at St Luke's Campus, about a mile
away from the main Streatham Campus. A regular
bus service operates between the two.

THE CORNWALL CAMPUS is the £100-million campus

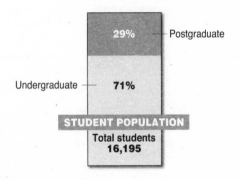

29% — Postgraduate

Undergraduate — 71%

STUDENT POPULATION

Total students
16,195

at Tremough, a 70-acre estate deep in Cornwall overlooking the Fal estuary. Since 2004 Exeter's dominion over the South West has been celebrated in the Combined Universities of Cornwall, a collaborative partnership with the University of Plymouth and the Peninsula Medical School, Falmouth College of Arts, the Open University in the South West, the College of St Mark & St John near Plymouth, and Cornwall's Further Education colleges - Cornwall College, Truro College and Penwith College.

The campus offers the very latest in academic, research and residential facilities. The Fal is one of the most beautiful aspects of nature in all England and worth the trip on its own.

FEES, BURSARIES

UK & EU Fees, 2011-12: £3,375 p.a. Fees for 2012-13 will be £9,000. In 2011-12 there is a sliding scale bursary up to £1,500 for students in receipt of the full HE Maintenance Grant. There are also 30 + Sports Scholarships each year, including a tailored scholarship of up to £2,000, music and other subject specific cholarships: www.exeter.ac.uk/scholarships/undergraduate and www.exeter.ac.uk/scholarships/international.

STUDENT PROFILE

For some time now Exeter has made a concerted effort to diversify its student population. The most recent national statistics show that participation of state schools is around 73%, a figure that has risen by about 4% in seven years. The take from lower socio-economic orders is some 17%, and from neighbourhoods altogether new to the idea of university, 4%. The number of international students applying is also certainly rising. But this massaging of the student population figures in the name of equality of opportunity, which is such an obsession of succeeding Governments, and a job which would be far better done by schools than

TEACHING SURVEY AT A GLANCE	
Avg. UCAS points accepted	**400**
Acceptance rate	**14%**
Overall satisfaction rate	**90%**
Helpful/interested staff	**★★★★**
Small tuition groups	**★★★**
Students into graduate jobs	**71%**

Teaching most popular with undergraduates:
Accounting (98%), African & Modern Middle Eastern Studies, Archaeology, Biology, Cinematics & Film, Classics (100%), Drama (98%), Economics, Engineering & Technology, English, Euro Languages, Finance, French Studies, General Engineering, Geology, German & Scandinavian Studies, History, Human & Social Geography, Law, Management, Maths, Medicine, Dentistry, Physical Geography, Physics, Politics, Psychology, Sociology, Sports Science, Theology (100%).

universities, has made little noticeable difference to campus.

ACADEMIA & JOBS

Last year academia was restructured into 5 colleges and 1 school: College of Social Sciences & International Studies; College of Humanities; College of Engineering, Maths & Physical Sciences; College of Life & Environmental Sciences; the University of Exeter Business School; and the Peninsula College of Medicine and Dentistry.

The Peninsula College is of course Exeter's collaboration with Plymouth University and the NHS in Devon and Cornwall, the NHS hand ensuring a strong clinical element in course design. The BM, BS degree focuses on the biological mechanisms that produce disease and its social impact. It looks very hands-on. First undergraduate intake occurred in 2002, half in Exeter (at St Luke's), half in Plymouth. Both unis already had successful postgraduate medical schools. Students work initially with patients in Plymouth and Exeter, then in Truro in Cornwall, finally up with the hillbillies above Dartmoor.

In September 2007 the first dental students joined the Medics. The Dentistry course, operating on sites in Plymouth, Truro and Exeter, is a 4-year Graduate Entry Hon BDS. The programme is designed for those with a good honours degree in a biomedically related or health care professional subject, or with relevant experience of working as a health care professional. The Graduate Medical Schools Admissions Test (GAMSAT) will be required.

Languages are more than three times

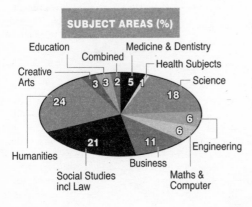

SUBJECT AREAS (%)

Education
Combined
Creative Arts
3 3 2 5 1
24
21
11
18
6
6
Humanities
Social Studies incl Law
Business
Maths & Computer
Engineering
Science
Health Subjects
Medicine & Dentistry

productive of real graduate jobs at Exeter than Medicine and Dentistry - education, publishing, business and management, the hotel/restaurant industry, the Civil Service are some of the many employment areas. Then comes Biological Sciences, which looks after a further 15% of jobs (notably in primary/secondary education, hospital work, accountancy and tax consultancy, public admin., personnel, advertising, defence, etc).

Social Studies produces around 14% of the job total, Economics graduates stealing most of the jobs, in accountancy and consultancy, and then others in personnel and public admin.

Engineering & Technology and Architecture establish the vital construction and architectural consultancy dimension; business leads into the field of insurance, among much else; computer science into software consultancy and supply; and there is a media and information technology influence, which further strengthens the muscle Exeter flexes in the publishing industry. .

Another string is a speciality in things Arabic. 'It has had a lot of inward investment from that direction,' we were told. 'It is very good on Middle Eastern languages, there's a large teaching/library facility on that side.' Arab & Islamic Studies continues to be a growth area at Exeter with rising undergrad. and postgrad. numbers and an expanding range of courses, including the introduction of Kurdish and Persian options.

'I did politics and there was quite a cross-over with Arab/Islamic, history of the Middle East, Middle East politics, etc,' said a graduate Guild officer, 'and the resource [the Institute of Arabic & Islamic Studies] is really good: letters, firsthand evidence... A lot of people don't realise that you don't have to know Arabic to study there. With the building of the institute - fantastic building! - we have got the largest Arabic Library and Middle East resource outside the Middle East and America. That may seem a bit random, here in Exeter, but the fact is that we are in the forefront on this thing, and it has a knock-on effect.'

In Law, there's an international Grade 5 for research, and they are European law specialists with LLB French Maitrise/German Magister as well as Law with European Study/International Study.

At the Cornwall Campus they have an Environment and Sustainability Institute to tackle climate change and sustainability by bringing together researchers across science, engineering

RESEARCH EXCELLENCE		
% of Exeter's research that is 4* (World-class) or 3* (Internationally rated):		
	4*	3*
Hospital Clinical Subjects	5%	60%
Health Services	5%	45%
Biological Sciences	10%	40%
Physics	15%	45%
Pure Mathematics	10%	45%
Applied Maths	10%	50%
Computer Science	15%	50%
General Engineering	10%	45%
Minging, Minerals	5%	30%
Geography	20%	40%
Archaeology	15%	50%
Economics	20%	55%
Accounting	10%	45%
Business/Management	15%	45%
Law	10%	35%
Politics	20%	35%
Sociology	20%	35%
Psychology	15%	40%
Education	20%	40%
Sports	10%	25%
Middle Eastern/African	15%	25%
East European Languages	5%	55%
French	15%	35%
German	15%	40%
Italian	10%	25%
Iberian/Latin American	15%	30%
English	45%	20%
Classics	30%	30%
Theology	10%	40%
History	20%	40%
Performing Arts	35%	40%

and technology, the arts and humanities and the social sciences. This enlightened cross-faculty approach will also forge new BA and BSc degrees and modules.

> *'The university is very easy to fall in love with. It has one of the most beautiful campuses in the country, in one of the most beautiful counties in Britain.'*

The Forum is an exciting development at the heart of the Streatham Campus, creating an inspirational mix of outside and inside space that will deliver a new Student Services Centre, a refurbished library, new technology-rich learning spaces, a 400-seat lecture theatre, a new University reception and retail and catering outlets. The project is due for completion in December 2011.

An Innovation Centre provides start-up homes for small businesses, usually hi-tech. Funding is available in the region. Careers advice is given by alumni through the 'Expert' scheme, on how to get into hard-to-enter sectors like media, and non-profit organisations (charities).

Finally, the Exeter Award is an achievement award designed to enhance students' employ-ability by providing them with official recognition and evidence for future employers of extra-curricular activities that they've undertaken while at Exeter. In its first year, nearly 3,000 students signed up for the award in Exeter and Cornwall. Students can also go on to complete the Exeter Leaders Award which focuses on leadership and outstanding achievement. www.exeter.ac.uk/exeteraward.

Perhaps driven by the relatively low 'real graduate job' percentage mentioned above, the University has upped its expenditure in this area considerably, creating a £48 million hub for the new Division for Employability and Graduate Development. The division's Career Zone provides help at each stage of career planning and job hunting. Placements are available in sectors as diverse as management, museums and mining, and they are bringing to bear on this issue the experience of a worldwide network of past graduates. There are of course also the 'milk round' Careers Fairs (four a year), attended by around 200 companies.

STUDENT SCENE

THE STUDENTS' GUILD The Students' Guild Union watering holes are **The Ram**, **The Long Lounge**, **The Lemmy** nightclub. 'In the summer of 2005,' they say, 'the surrounding rooms of The Lemon Grove/Cornwall House were refurbished at a cost of £1.25 million to include state of the art sound (Funktion One) and lighting systems (as used in Ibiza clubs), a DJ booth to go with them and a state of the art air conditioning system amongst various cosmetic and structural fixes.

On quieter evenings there are open mic nights (Tuesdays or Wednesdays) and a **Cash-giveaway** quiz (every Sunday). It's also home to Big Screen Sport, with two projectors and a host of plasma screens. But the Lemmy is one of the main live venues in the South West and comes alive Friday and Saturday. 'Last year you could have seen the Kooks supporting the Subways in the Lemmy while Rooster were headlining in the Great Hall. Previous bands have included Blur, Radiohead, Coral, Muse and Keane.'

The gigs are usually public events, but the weekend 'Lemmy' is student only. Entscard holders get free admission.

Then they have the university orchestra and choral society, in the Great Hall. There's also a

WHAT IT'S REALLY LIKE	
UNIVERSITY:	
Social Life	★★★★
Societies	★★★★
Student Union services	★★★★
Politics	**Student issues**
Sport	**Key**
National team position	**10th**
Sport facilities	★★★★
Arts opportunities	**Excellent, esp. theatre**
Student newspaper	**Exeposé**
Student radio	**Xpression fm**
Radio Awards 2009	**Silver**
Student TV	**XTV**
Nightclub	**The Lemmy**
Bars	**Ram, Long Lounge**
Union ents	**Lemmy disco + live acts**
Union societies	**105**
Parking	**No parking**
CITY:	
Entertainment	★★★
Scene	**Good pubs; average clubs**
Town/gown relations	**Average**
Risk of violence	**Low**
Cost of living	**Average**
Student concessions	**Good**
Survival + 2 nights out	**£80 pw**
Part-time work campus/town	**Average/good**

tradition of musicals in the Northcote Theatre, the part-'pro' campus theatre. Footlights, Exeter Theatre Company and the Gilbert & Sullivan Society perform there, and the Exeter University Symphony Orchestra puts on termly concerts.

There is massive interest in media here. 'The weekly newspaper (*Exepose*), recently 'Publication of the Year' following the *Guardian* Media Awards, the TV station (XTV, winner of two national awards in 2008) and student radio (Xpression fm - 2 Silvers in the 2008 nationals and 1 in 2009) have brought countless Exeter undergraduates into the business.

Someone reels off a list: 'Nick Baker, the wildlife presenter, Emma B from Radio 1, Thom Yorke of Radiohead who was a D, Isobel Lang, the weather presenter, people on the production side, like Paul Jackson who produced Red Dwarf - he came back to do a creative writing thing with the students in English, Stewart Purvis, chief exec of ITN.'

Around 400 freshers attend the Welcome to the Media event in freshers weeks. Those who stick with it are subjected to a period of training by the

Exepose student media team.

Sport Their £8-million facilities definitely get the thumbs up from students. New indoor tennis facilities to LTA standards opened in 2004. Said Julie: 'This uni is full of sports fanatics, excellent opportunities to join very competitive teams - it's all a very serious business. Also so many surfing, windsurfing and beach bum type societies to join.'

All major team games are well represented, also martial arts, watersports (rowing, canoeing, sailing - six Lark dinghies on the Exe Estuary) and ultimate frisbee. On-campus facilities include sports hall (basketball, netball, volleyball, tennis - there's a new LTA standard indoor/outdoor tennis centre - badminton, indoor cricket net), a climbing wall and traversing wall, rooms for fencing, martial arts, weights, etc. Pitches include 2 all-weather pitches, large grass pitch with nets area, and there are sixty off-campus acres of playing fields nearby.

Town 'There are certain pubs that you shouldn't really go into,' warns Juliet Oaks, 'and during Freshers Week the Students' Guild does advise you which to avoid. Also, although Exeter is a city, it is in the West Country: clubbing is not exactly the best.

However, there is at least one student night at a club every night of the week. Entry before 10:30 is usually free or very cheap. Some of the clubs distribute tickets beforehand and these are definitely worth getting. A night out can cost around £40 if you push the boat out.

'For shopping there's enough diversity for anyone, from skaters to Goths.'

PILLOW TALK

Wide choice of good catered and self-catered accommodation. The majority of freshers take the catered option, but 250 self-catering rooms are reserved for them too.

ACCOMMODATION	
Tudent rating	**★★★★**
Guarantee to freshers	**100%**
Style	**Halls, flats**
Security guard	**All**
Shared rooms	**Some halls**
Internet access	**All**
Self-catered	**Halls none, flats all**
En suite	**Some**
Approx price range pw	**£77.63-£187.11**
City rent pw	**£60-£120**

All the accommodation is either on campus or close by. There are en-suite rooms at ground level in the newer halls and flats suitable for disabled students, as well as some specially adapted rooms in the older residences.

With the exception of a small number of rooms in the older residences, study bedrooms have a high-speed connection to the University data network, which can be used for e-mail and Internet access. There is a modest fixed charge for this facility.

Two new self-catered residences opened in 2008 and 2009 in the city. £150 million is being spent on continuing upgrades to on-campus accommodation and the building of new residences at our Cornwall Campus.

See www.exeter.ac.uk/accommodation. No parking either at Streatham or St Luke's campuses.

GETTING THERE

☞ By road: M5/J30.
☞ By rail: London Paddington, 2:30; Birmingham, 3:00; Plymouth, 1:15.
☞ By air: Exeter Airport is 15 mins from campus.
☞ By coach: London, 4:00; Birmingham, 4:30.

UNIVERSITY OF GLAMORGAN

The University of Glamorgan
Pontypridd
Mid Glamorgan CF37 1DL

TEL 08456 434030
FAX 01443 654050

EMAIL enquiries@glam.ac.uk
WEB www.glam.ac.uk

Glamorgan Students' Union
Pontypridd
Mid-Glamorgan CF37 1UF

TEL 01443 483500
FAX 01443 483501

EMAIL rdavies3@hotmail.com
WEB www.glamsu.com

VIRGIN VIEW

Glamorgan University lies at Treforest in the Taff Valley, South Wales, a sometime coal mining village off the M4, not pretty but there are stunning views over the valley, a friendly atmosphere, and it's only 25 minutes from Cardiff's dens of iniquity by road (or you can go by train from the railway station near campus - trains run every 20 minutes).

But let's not leave before we have arrived. 'Living up here is nice,' writes Fiona Owen. 'It's nice to belong to a close-knit community. The area is scenic and there are lots of places to go for lovely walks with your friends or your new squeeze.'

There's even the odd lecture. Glamorgan lecturers get 3 out of 5 stars for helpful interest in their students, which is good, and 3 for size of tuition groups, meaning they're smallish. In the Government's National Student Survey 79% of Glamorgan's students gave the university their approval, and that's bearing in mind, also according to Government statistics, that only 57% will get real graduate-style jobs when they leave.

A sense that this will be the case might be thought to lie behind the decision of 17% of them to drop out before graduation. Not many student retention rates are as poor.

Yet, as January 2010 dawned, so UCAS declared that Glamorgan had attracted 12% more applicants than the previous year, which itself had been a bit of a record. The 2009 increase followed an impressive result in the national assessment of university research, where more than 70% of their research activity had been assessed as being

UNIVERSITY/STUDENT PROFILE	
University since.	**1992**
Situation/style	**Rural campus**
Student population	**25770**
Undergraduates	**17635**
Mature	**53%**
International	**22%**
Male/female ratio	**50:50**
Equality of opportunity:	
state school intake	**98%**
social class 4-7 intake	**39%**
drop-out rate	**17%**

of a quality recognised internationally for its 'originality, significance and rigour'.

Now, the uni has been splashing out £130 million on facilities across campus, including a new Student Union and accommodation. The new Union is an amazing transfrmation (see Social Scene below) and is not reflected in the earlier poor student star ratings in our 'What It's Really Like' box.

CAMPUS

Main campus is a couple of miles from the market town of Pontypridd. Another campus for the Creative Industries, ATRiuM, is in the heart of the city centre. The £35-million development brings together subjects like Animation, Film, TV and Radio, Design, Drama, Music Technology and Culture & Society.

FEES, BURSARIES

UK & EU Fees, 2011-12: £3,375 p.a. Students from Wales and the EU are eligible for a non-means tested grant from the Welsh Assembly Government towards the cost of tuition fees, and there's a sliding scale Welsh National Bursary available to UK students according to household incomes. In addition, STEM scholarships worth £4,500 are available to students of Science, Technology, Engineering or Maths, and a Vice Chancellor's Award of £2,500 for exceptional students who demonstrate significant personal achievement. Also, there's a Sports Scholarship for athletes who are competing at national and international level. See http://money.glam.ac.uk/.

STUDENT PROFILE

The student body is largely local, and in higher education speak, 'non-traditional'. Fifty-three per cent are over 21 at inception, 39% from the lowest socio-economic orders.

Once on board, there's genuine warmth:

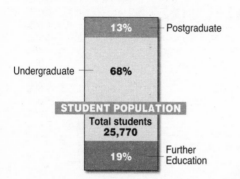

Postgraduate 13%

Undergraduate 68%

STUDENT POPULATION
Total students
25,770

Further Education 19%

'Glamorgan University is small enough to generate real warmth and a sense of close-knit community, but large enough for you to be inconspicuous when that's what you want/need,' writes Beth Smith.

ACADEMIA & JOBS

Glamorgan's results in the National Research Assessment were indeed a considerable improvement on those of the previous assessment, where they had no world-class research at all. On this occasion, part of the research in sixteen subjects was found to be either world-class or of international significance. In Nursing & Midwifery, Computer Science, Engineering, Built Environment, Business, Sport, English, History, Performing Arts, and Media between 5% and 15% of the research was world-class. English came out best, with 15% of its provision world-class and 30% of international significance.

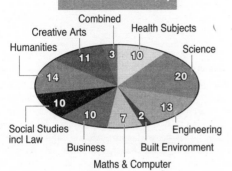

SUBJECT AREAS (%)

Combined — 3
Creative Arts — 11
Humanities — 14
Health Subjects — 10
Science — 20
Engineering — 13
Built Environment — 2
Business — 7
Maths & Computer — 10
Social Studies incl Law — 10

When it came to the students' turn to comment on the teaching, as opposed to the research, provision, they found the best classes are in Accounting, Combined programme, English Studies, Finance, Geographical Studies (98%), Historical & Philosophical Studies, History, Imaginative Writing (97%), Languages, Law, Marketing, Maths, Nursing, Physical Geography & Environmental Science, Sociology, Social Policy & Anthropology, Sports Science, and Subjects allied to Medicine.

The sheer number of midwifery and nursing degrees (Adult, Child, Mental Health, and Learning Disabilities) means that they dominate the graduate employment picture. Also contributing are degrees such as Chiropractic, Health Sciences, and Care Practice. Glamorgan's Chiropractic course is accredited by both the General Chiropractic Council and the European Council on Chiropractic Education.

There are other useful occupational niches, like social work, community counselling, where

degrees like Applied Psychology and the other social sciences come to play; and police work (the Forensic degrees and also Police Sciences - there's even a student society!). The degree in Substance Misuse couldn't be more carefully aimed.

Next most productive of jobs is Creative Arts & Design, with 13% of the graduate corpus going into arts, entertainment and recreation and education,

RESEARCH EXCELLENCE

% of Glamorgan's research that is
4* *(World-class) or* **3*** *(Internationally rated):*

	4*	3*
Nursing/Midwifery	10%	25%
Allied Health	0%	0%
Biological Sciences	0%	10%
Applied Mathematics	0%	20%
Computer Science	5%	35%
General Engineering	5%	55%
Built Environment	10%	40%
Business/Management	5%	10%
Law	0%	15%
Social Work	5%	40%
Psychology	0%	10%
Education	0%	20%
Sports	5%	15%
English	15%	25%
History	10%	40%
Performing Arts	5%	25%
Media Studies	10%	20%

and designers finding work in fields as disparate as the motor trade and information/ communication: PR and marketing companies.

Then came Engineering & Technology, with about the same share of jobs and most finding them in public administration and defence, thereafter in manufacturing, education, scientific and technical professions, PR, and the building trade.

> *'If you're a disco queen and demand that you put your spangly dancing trousers on at least a couple of times a week, the union has a formidable entertainment schedule to tease and tantalise you.'*

The third most productive area is Business. The School is the largest in Wales and launches a new suite of modules this year in BA (Hons) Business Management,

SOCIAL SCENE

STUDENTS' UNION The new Union has gone down a treat, masses of glass everywhere and all amazingly new. If you're a disco queen and demand that you put your spangly dancing trousers on at least a couple of times a week, the union has always been a venue with a formidable entertainment schedule to tease and tantalise. But now the design and technical specification is beyond all their dreams.

The Basement (650 capacity) and Cables Bar are the venues: live music, alternative nights, house nights, drum 'n' bass, international parties, plus all the chees you can handle.

Then there's the Randy Dragon Inn for the traditional pub experience and decent English breakfasts for just £3.

As ever, there's an active student media set-up, the student magazine, *TAG*, and Tequila Radio - a 7 days a week online station, child of the award-winning GTFM of yesteryear. It's a newish radio society spawned by the School of Cultural & Creative Industries (Cardiff campus). Other societies include the popular Chiropractic and Lesbian, Gay & Bi-sexual, Hellenic, Police Sciences and Christian Encounter - an eclectic mix - there's the uni concert band and big band, and a 40-member mixed choir. Something for everyone, you might say, but students will be students, as Stephen Harley observes: 'There are only three things that dominate every student's life: money, alcohol and sex. But if you come to Glamorgan there is a fourth thing, the mountain on which they built the university. Whenever you go down the hill from the halls of residence you should do as much as possible while you're at the bottom. The first time you go out for the evening and forget your wallet will, I promise you, be the last. Also important to note, the nightlife in Treforest is... well it isn't. There is a handful of good pubs which have the expected student buzz and the ents at Shafts make up for the short hours.'

Sport A major part of university life, in particular rugby, though in recent years, students in karate, football, hockey and basketball have also gone on to gain success at national and international level. Facilities are of a professional standard. There's a **Sports Centre** with six badminton courts, climbing wall, all indoor sports, but no swimming pool. There's a smaller hall for keep-fit, table tennis, martial arts, fencing, plus four squash courts (one glass-backed), two conditioning rooms, sauna/solarium suite, and 30 acres of floodlit pitches - football, rugby and hockey, plus trim trail, cricket pitch, archery - and one of the UK's only FIFA approved 3 'G' rubber crumb pitches. Nearby you'll find swimming pools, golf courses, running tracks, and the Brecon Beacons for horse riding, canoeing, mountaineering, hang gliding, walking. Also sailing and windsurfing.

PILLOW TALK
Students at Cardiff Campus occupy new, privately owned halls of residence located opposite the campus. The majority of halls on the Treforest campus is reserved for first year students.; 476 new en-suite rooms will open there this year.

The uni also lets houses close by, and a meal voucher service is available. New rules allow students to stay over Christmas and Easter vacs at no extra cost. Many students live in private rented accommodation locally; others in Cardiff.

GETTING THERE
☛ By road: M4/J32, A470. Exit Llantrisant, A473.
☛ By rail: London Paddington, 2:45; Birmingham, 2:15; York, 5:00.
☛ By air: Cardiff Airport.
☛ By coach: London, 4:00; Birmingham, 3:40; Bournemouth, 6:00.

STUDENT GLASGOW - THE CITY

'Glasgow - the only place in the world where you can get a free fish supper at 9 in the morning just by picking it out of the hands of a drunk who's passed out in the street the night before.' So said Rab C Nesbitt of his beloved home town, but - while there are still pockets of the city where the claim probably holds true, he neglects to mention the hundreds of other factors that make Glasgow one of the country's most popular student destinations.

Though not the capital, Glasgow is regarded by many as the only proper city in Scotland. Edinburgh may have the Parliament, Aberdeen has the oil, Dundee... is also a city, apparently, but Glasgow is where the fun is to be had. This is where the clubs, the shopping, the music venues, the theatres, Europe's (formerly the world's) tallest cinema building are. Sure, it may rain more than in any other city in Europe, but Glasgow's famous sense of humour more than makes up for that. Perhaps that's why the city now hosts Europe's largest annual comedy festival, and is the home of Scottish TV and media.

With relatively cheap rents and centrally located universities and colleges, Glasgow seems purpose-built for student living. Would-be applicants may be put off by perceived crime rates, but according to local police violent incidents are increasingly rare, and students are generally unlikely to fall victim.

In recent years the city has been changing at an incredible pace. Formerly downtrodden areas are undergoing regeneration, in keeping with a city aiming to be at the forefront of the modern Europe, while the historic sites of the old town - including one of the oldest universities in the world - are preserved as a link to the past.

Of course, should you ever find a reason to leave the city - perhaps, after the inevitable excesses of freshers' week, you just want to go and die in a field somewhere - picturesque Loch Lomond is only half an hour away.

Just remember to at least attempt to get a degree while you're here.

CITY SCENE
Glasgow, like most of Scotland, is known for its drinking, patter and scenery and it doesn't disappoint. In town, *Viper Mondays* is always a good night. **Viper** is not the largest club, but the drinks are cheap and the place is always packed. The other two clubs I would recommend are **O'Couture** on Sauchiehall Street on a Wednesday, where most of the sports clubs end up. Then on a Thurssday there is *Jellybaby* in **ABC**. **Bamboo** is great on a Wednesday and Sunday and has music to suit most people on different dance floors. **ABC O2** arena is another place I would recommend. Although a little more expensive it does show some

good live music such as Cee Lo Green and other acts. To be honest, I would recommend most of the clubs in Glasgow. Drinks are generally cheap and fun is always to be had somewhere.

ARTS & ENTERTAINMENT

Glasgow's arts scene is unparalleled outside of London, with a mind-boggling array of theatres, galleries, cinemas and concert halls.

Many of the 14 major theatres offer student tickets for a fiver, bringing a night at the shows within almost any budget. All tastes are catered for - those seeking cutting-edge writing and performance need look no further than the **Arches** or the **Tramway**, more traditional fare is on offer at the **Citizens'** in the Gorbals, and shameless panto-afficionados should check out the **Kings**, or perhaps seek psychiatric advice.

Opera, ballet and classical performances can be found at the **Theatre Royal**, and the **Glasgow Film Theatre** showcases a variety of independent and classic films, complementing the blockbusters at the massive **Cineworld** complex.

The **Kelvingrove Art Gallery and Museum** has a wonderfully eclectic mix of exhibits, and the **Centre for Contemporary Arts** showcases the latest in design and concept art, while **The** Hunterian is for Modern Art.

SPORT

Home to both of Scotland's football teams, Glasgow affords the unique opportunity to witness the Irish troubles re-enacted weekly on the pitch, though the sectarian clashes which have marred the city's sporting reputation have, receded in recent years. Rugby fans are still within an hour of Murrayfield by train, and those interested in more minority sports should be well served by some excellent university clubs.

PUBS

Glasgow has a thriving pub scene. Some of the lowest drinks prices in the country have cost students many a degree. Central to the life of any West End dwelling student will be Byres Road and the more upmarket Ashton Lane - try **Nude** or **Radio** , or **Jinty McGinty's** for a pint. Those in the city centre may prefer **The State** off Sauchiehall Street or **O'Neills'** mock-Irish charm or the classy appeal of **Royal Exchange Square**, while the **Pot Still's** world-class range of whiskies makes it well worth the trip from any part of town.

Rory Vokes-Dudgeon

UNIVERSITY OF GLASGOW

The University of Glasgow
University Avenue
Glasgow G12 8QQ

TEL 0141 330 6062
FAX 0141 330 2961
EMAIL ugenquiries@gla.ac.uk
WEB www.gla.ac.uk

Glasgow University SRC
University Avenue
Glasgow G12 8QQ

GUU: 0141 339 8697
QMU: 0141 339 9784
EMAIL enquiries@src.gla.ac.uk
WEB www.src.gla.ac.uk

VIRGIN VIEW

*G*lasgow University was founded in 1451. *It started life on the east side in the heart of the medieval city, close to the Cathedral, which was itself built only 250 or so years earlier. It moved to Gilmorehill on the more fashionable west side in 1870, where today it takes breath over beautiful Kelvingrove Park, just north of the Clyde.*

The QS World University Rankings places the University of Glasgow in the Top 100 Universities in the world. It is one of

UNIVERSITY/STUDENT PROFILE	
University since	**1451**
Situation/style	**City Campus**
Student population	**24240**
Undergraduates	**19010**
Mature	**38%**
International	**13%**
Male/female ratio	**42:58**
Equality of opportunity:	
state school intake	**87%**
social class 4-7 intake	**25%**
drop-out rate	**8%**

only 3 Scottish institutions in the Top 100. In the Times Higher's *Top 200* it is 18th of only 29 British universities present, ahead of Sheffield, Dundee, Newcastle, Leeds, East Anglia, Nottingham and Exeter. In the same highly regarded magazine's Student Experience Survey they came 7th in the UK. In the British Government's Student Survey it commanded 90% satisfaction from its students for the second year running.

The 5-star social life and extra-curricular society menu is carried from campus into a city whose pub, club and arts scene has been the envy of those in the know for longer than most of your parents can remember.

What do they want from you?

For applicants to undergraduate degrees in the Arts, Social Sciences, Science and Engineering, admission is based on the outcome of grades/points.

For applicants to Dentistry, Education, Medicine, Nursing and Veterinary Medicine, the selection process will normally involve entry requirements other than grades alone and is likely to involve personal statements, commitment to the chosen course, involvement in extra-curricular activities and work experience.

Applicants considered for adjusted offers of entry may live in an area of deprivation; may have attended a secondary school with a low progression record to Higher Education, or apply from an adult Access course. They may have spent time in care; or they may be the first in their family to attend university.

Open Days in 2011 are on 16 June and 7 September. They also host four afternoon visits throughout the year. See www.glasgow. ac.uk/about/visit/opendays/afternoonvisit/

CAMPUS GLASGOW

Writes Rory, a second year student of Psychology and Biology: 'The university is situated in Glasgow's West End, generally known as one of the nicer parts of the city. To Buchannan Street, the main shopping area, it's a 20-minute walk, or if you have some spare change a £4 taxi.

'The university buildings are within a 5-minute walk of each other. Architecturally, it is amazing. It was considered as a location for the Harry Potter films, but the university turned down the offer, concerned about disturbance to uni life.

TEACHING SURVEY AT A GLANCE	
Avg. UCAS points accepted	**414**
Acceptance rate	**15%**
Overall satisfaction rate	**90%**
Helpful/interested staff	★★★★
Small tuition groups	★★★★
Students into graduate jobs	**75%**

Teaching most popular with undergraduates:
Accounting, Anatomy, Physiology & Pathology, Archaeology, Biology & related sciences, Business Studies, Film & Photography, Comparative Literary Studies, Computer Science, Creative Arts & Design, Dentistry, Drama, Economics, Electronic & Electrical Engineering (100%), Engineering & Technology, English, Euro Languages, Finance, French Studies, Genetics (100%), Geology, History, History & Archaeology, Human & Social Geography (100%), Teacher Training, Law, Management, Maths, Mechanical, Production & Manufacturing Engineering, Microbiology (100%), Molecular Biology, Nursing (100%), Pharmacy, Philosophy, Physical Geography, Physics, Astronomy, Politics, Psychology, Social Policy, Anthropology, Social Studies, Sociology, Anthropology, Sports Science, Subjects allied to Medicine, Theology, Vet Science, Zoology.

Teaching least popular with undergraduates:
Iberian Studies (64%), Medicine (64%).

'When I found out I was going to come here I was apprehensive to say the least. All that people kept saying to me was that I was going to get stabbed. In fact, I have not heard of any problems of this sort. The only problem is when students venture beyond the West End into town and get into a state where they are obviously vulnerable to attack. Even then I have only heard of a couple of guys who lost their phones.'

St Andrew's College is the Faculty of Education, based since summer 2002 on Glasgow Caledonian Uni's old campus on Park Drive, where the West End starts. The Vet school and outdoor sports facilities are located at Garscube, by the sports fields, 4 miles away. To the south, in Dumfries, is Crichton campus, which offers innovative study programmes to a mixture of full-time and part-time students.

FEES, BURSARIES

Scottish and EU-domiciled students studying full-time are entitled to free tuition. Fees for non-Scotttish UK domiciled: £1,820 p.a. (£2,895 p.a. for Medicine). Awards include 50 undergraduate

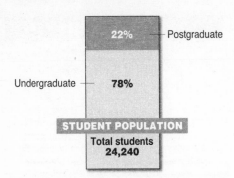

STUDENT POPULATION

Total students
24,240

22% — Postgraduate

Undergraduate — **78%**

Talent Scholarships, which provide successful applicants with £1,000 per year of the degree programme studied, and 50 International Excellence Scholarships, which offer £3,000 per year of study to talented international applicants. www.glasgow.ac.uk/scholarships/

STUDENT PROFILE

You'll not find the Rah brigade here that you'll find at Edinburgh. There are no social divisions, no self-consciousness, just a natural sense of community.

ACADEMIA & JOBS

In the past year the University has been restructured, moving from 9 Faculties to 4 Colleges: Arts, Social Sciences, Science and Engineering, and Medicine, Veterinary Medicine and Life Sciences.

Continues Rory: 'What's great about Glasgow is that you take 3 subjects in first year, so you are not necessarily kept on a course you don't like. This is not the case if you choose Medicine or Vet Science, but it is for most standard courses, such as Biology, Psychology, Business, Economics, etc. The lectures are 50 minutes long and all lecture notes are available online. Lecture theatres are large and generally comfy, so, be warned, it can be easy to fall asleep in a 9 o'clock lecture.'

Seventy-five per cent of their academic staff contribute research the majority of which is rated world leading or internationally excellent.

But graduate employability is a priority. Glasgow's Careers Service has links to more than 4,500 employers and close contacts with the major graduate recruiters in the public, private and non-governmental sectors.

Initiatives to prepare undergraduates for the world of work include the University's Club 21 Business Partnership Programme, which has

> *'Our main piece of advice is, if you come, be prepared to fall in love with it: the buildings, the union, the atmosphere and, most of all, the people.'*

connections with more than 120 employers at a local, national and international level. Students can apply for between 8 and 12 weeks' paid summer work experience in an area relevant to their degree programme and/or skills. Some of the placements even attract a scholarship of £1,000.

Skills for Work networking events run four times a year, and offer students the chance to meet and chat with employers working in the areas of: charities, engineering, science and financial services. And the University is one of three higher education institutions piloting the Aiming University Learning at Work Programme, which enables students studying subjects such as maths, history, physics, psychology, business and bioscience to take part in work experience as part of their degree.

The graduate class of 2008, a typical crop, produced 271 primary teachers, 214 hospital doctors, 161 secondary school teachers, 91 engineers, 68 veterinary surgeons, 35 accountants, 29 teachers of English as a foreign language, 29 software developers, 22 university lecturers, 15 biological and life scientists, 1 professional footballer. They took up employment in 32 countries around the world, with the most popular destinations being Australia, France, Spain and USA.

ART SCHOOL

Close to, associated with, but separate from the uni is the nearby Art School, the main building of which was designed by the city's most famous artist-designer, Charles Rennie Mackintosh (1868-1928), the leader of the famous 'group of four', who

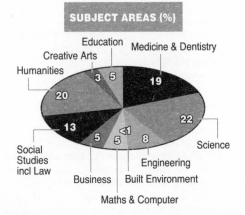

SUBJECT AREAS (%)

Education
Medicine & Dentistry
Creative Arts
Humanities
3
5
19
20
22
13
5
<1
8
Science
Social Studies incl Law
Engineering
Business
Built Environment
Maths & Computer

studied here. It is world class. We asked two students, Emma Stirling and Corrie-Anne Rounding, what it's all about today.

'On my first day, doing Jewellery, my tutor told me that if I got through the term without totally changing the way I see and think about things, he would have failed. Even after a short amount of time there, you find yourself noticing things you would never have taken notice of before.

'With 9 courses and between 16 and 80 students on each course (the smallest being jewellery, the largest architecture) the School of Art is intimate and friendly. There is roughly 1 lecturer for every 10 people, with an extra 15 lecturing in Historical and Critical Studies (a first-year course requirement and not as boring as it may sound). The lecturers mostly leave you to do your own thing, unless you ask for help, checking in on you at critical points to ensure you're on the right track.

'Because the school is fairly small and most courses require students to attend 9.30-to-5, it is very sociable, with events (such as cake-eating and hoola-hoop contests) organised to fill the time when you feel like a bit of a break from work.

'The atmosphere in the studios is really good as well, whether you feel like working, gossiping or just a bit of a skive'.

SOCIAL SCENE

Alone among universities Glasgow has two Student Unions delivering second-to-none ents menus, and a third body, a Student Council, overseeing the vital area of extra-mural activities.

Glasgow University Union (GUU) was founded in 1885. It has 6 bars: the **Beer Bar** (traditional, with the names of the campus's fastest drinkers immortalised round the bar), **Altitude**, **Deep 6** (pseudo-trendy basement music bar - live bands, karaoke, juke box - open till 2am Fridays, half price cocktails, etc.), the **Playing Fields**, **Balcony Bar**, nightclub, the **Hive (see below)**.

Then there is Queen Margaret's Union (QMU), which operates out of **Jim's Bar** (one of the main bars on campus), the **Games Room** (6 pool tables, masses of gaming machines and sofas), the bottle bar and **Qudos**, the 1,100 capacity nightclub.

Writes Rory: 'Glasgow, like most of Scotland, is known for its drinking, patter and scenery and it doesn't disappoint. The two unions are great for a night out, but I would defiantly recommend the **Hive** on a Thursday night. This is home of the *Pint of fun*, which has ended a few people's nights in its time. QMU is known for such nights as *Cheesy Pop Fridays*, not my cup of tea, but I have heard it can be a quality night'. See Glasgow City for the scene in town.

Say Emma and Corrie-Anne of the Art School

scene: 'The student union, **The Vic**, is usually

RESEARCH EXCELLENCE

% of Glasgow's research that is
4* *(World-class) or* **3*** *(Internationally rated):*

	4*	3*
Cardiovascular Medicine	15%	50%
Cancer Studies	25%	50%
Infection & Immunology	5%	65%
Clinical Subjects	10%	25%
Epidemiology	10%	45%
Psychiatry%	0%	25%
Dentistry	15%	45%
Allied Health	15%	45%
Biological Sciences	15%	40%
Veterinary	5%	50%
Environmental Sciences	5%	50%
Chemistry	10%	60%
Physics	20%	40%
Pure Mathematics	15%	40%
Applied Mathematics	10%	40%
Statistics	15%	35%
Computer Science	30%	50%
Electrical/Electronic Eng.	20%	45%
Civil Engineering	15%	40%
Aeronautical Engineering	10%	35%
Marine Engineering	10%	45%
Town/Country Planning	15%	45%
Geography	10%	40%
Archaeology	10%	40%
Economics	25%	50%
Accounting	10%	35%
Business	10%	45%
Information Management	25%	30%
Law	15%	40%
Politics	15%	30%
Social Work	5%	35%
Sociology	10%	30%
Psychology	20%	40%
Education	10%	20%
European Studies	5%	35%
East European Languages	0%	5%
French	15%	30%
German	10%	25%
Italian	0%	40%
Iberian/Latin American	5%	25%
Celtic Studies	10%	50%
English	35%	35%
Classics	10%	15%
Philosophy	5%	50%
Theology	10%	35%
History	25%	35%
History of Art	45%	40%
Performing Arts	40%	45%
Music	35%	30%

WHAT IT'S REALLY LIKE

UNIVERSITY:

Social Life	★★★★★
Societies	★★★★★
Student Union services	★★★★★
Politics	**Activity average Student issues**
Sport	**45 clubs**
National team position	**30th**
Sport facilities	★★★★★
Arts opportunities	**Drama, music, art exc; dance good; film average**
Student newspaper	**GU Guardian**
Student magazine	**GUM, Qmunicate, GUUi**
Student radio	**SubCity Radio**
Student TV	**G.U.S.T.**
Nightclubs	**Qudos, Hive**
Bars	**6-bar GU, 3-bar QMU**
Union ents	**Cheesy Pop**
Union societies	**120**
Parking	**All halls**

CITY:

Entertainment	★★★★★
Scene	**Vigorous**
Town/gown relations	**Good**
Risk of violence	**High**
Cost of living	**OK**
Student concessions	**Poor**
Survival + 2 nights out	**£70-£80 pw**
Part-time work campus/town	**Poor/good**

fact, the only certain cuts as we went to press are MA Czech, MA Polish, MA Slavonic & East European Studies, BSc Environmental Chemistry, and BTechs Technology & Environment. But there could be more in May, and building up to all this has been a student occupation of the Hetherington Building, and at one stage for a short time the Senate itself, marches galore and one allegedly unseemly face-up between the protesters and members of the rugby club after a night at the Hive.

Mention must be made of the lively journalistic scene: Subcity Radio the SRC-run *Guardian* (newspaper), the *Glasgow University Magazine* (*GUM*, oldest student magazine in Scotland), the two Union publications, *GUUi* and *Qmunicate*, and GUST (oldest student TV station in the UK).

SPORT Excellent facilities, including a 25m pool, steam room and sauna, two activity halls with sprung flooring, basketball, volleyball, five-a-side soccer; a fitness and conditioning area, fully equipped. A one year gym membership is only £40. Writes Rory: 'Sport in Glasgow is an important part of student life. There are the obvious rugby, hockey, football, swimming teams, to the more obscure, American football, shinty and caving. I joined the Glasgow University Rugby Club (GURFC) and it has definitely improved my enjoyment of university. When I was researching Glasgow as a sixth-former I was told it did not have a rugby club. In fact, it had been disbanded for a year and a half due to the team's antics off the field. As a rugby club they play hard, both on and off the field, with trips to Newcastle, Dublin and a

pretty good on a Thursday night, although dubstep, which is what you get, is not to everyone's taste. Art school students socialise with the other three unis, particularly Glasgow University, as we share half of our halls with them. Any creative event is usually well received, and everyone says they have been to more fancy dress parties here than in their whole life, from *Tranny Night* to *Pensioner Party*. There's always something on, from exhibitions (along with free booze) to fashion shows to studio parties, for the Glasgow art students' philosophy is 'work hard, play hard. Our main piece of advice is, if you come, be prepared to fall in love with it: the buildings, the union, the atmosphere and, most of all, the people.'

Back at the uni, the Students Representative Council (SRC) administers 120 student societies, supports volunteers and class reps and is the official voice of the students on campus, constantly running Environment & Sustainability campaigns and recently up in arms about the course cuts. In

ACCOMMODATION

Student rating	★★★
Guarantee to freshers	**100%**
Style	**Halls, flats**
Security guard	**Present**
Shared rooms	**Most**
Internet access	**All**
Self-catered	**Most**
En suite	**Some**
Approx price range pw	**£75-£147**
City rent pw	**£75-£110**

scheduled tour for next year. It is now one of the larger associations and puts out 2 strong teams. I would definitely recommend joining a sports club most are open to beginners.'

PILLOW TALK

'Halls can be as close as a 10-minute walk, or as far

as a 30-minute walk away. Kelvinhaugh Street halls are closest to uni and nice, for halls. Across the road are Caincross halls, mostly shared: about 4 rooms to a kitchen. The Murano Street Village is full of flats for 5-8 people, but it's at least a 20-minute walk to the nearest club and a 25-minute walk from uni. The other two self-catered halls are Queen Margaret, very nice but expensive and located far from uni. Behind these are the cheapest halls, Winton, very quiet, but not nice. Wolfson are catered halls, far away from uni, but a free bus service to and fro during the day.'

Get your application in by August 22, or like Rory you'll end up sharing in Kelvinhaugh.

GETTING THERE
☞ By road: M8/J19 or J18. Good coach services.
☞ By rail: Edinburgh, 50 mins; London King's Cross, 5:00. Main campus Underground Station is Hillhead.
☞ By air: Glasgow Airport.
☞ By coach: London, 8:20; Birmingham, 6:20; Newcastle, 4:20.

GLASGOW CALEDONIAN UNIVERSITY

Glasgow Caledonian University
70 Cowcaddens Road
Glasgow G4 0PB

TEL 0141 331 3000
FAX 0141 331 3005
EMAIL studentenquiries@gcu.ac.uk
WEB www.gcu.ac.uk

Glasgow Caledonian Students' Association
70 Cowcaddens Road
Glasgow G4 0BA

TEL 0141 331 3886
FAX 0141 353 0029
EMAIL student.association@
glasgow.caledonian.ac.uk
WEB www.caledonianstudent.com

UNIVERSITY/STUDENT PROFILE	
University since	**1992**
Situation/style	**City campus**
Student population	**18410**
Undergraduates	**15135**
Mature	**52%**
International	**11%**
Male/female ratio	**40:60**
Equality of opportunity:	
state school intake	**97%**
social class 4-7 intake	**37%**
drop-out rate	**11%**

Lenin was pin-up boy in the shipyards. Glasgow Caledonian takes no noticeable political line, but it is a university of the people.

Founded in 1971, it took title in 1992, along with all the nation's polytechnics. Since then they have centralised operations on one site instead of five, opened new accommodation, a Sports Centre, a £17-million Health building and a Learning Centre called the Saltire Centre. Their promise of a new Student Union building has also been fulfilled.

VIRGIN VIEW

*G*lasgow Caledonian is located on the east side of the city on Cowcaddens Road, opposite the Bus Station and close to Buchanan Street shopping mall and George Square, where famously the military once met a strike of 80,000 as if it were a Bolshevik uprising, with troops, tanks, a howitzer, and machine gun nests around the city centre.

Things have changed since 1919, when

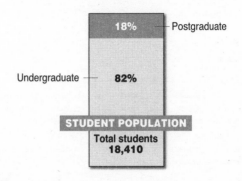

18% — Postgraduate

Undergraduate — 82%

STUDENT POPULATION
Total students
18,410

TEACHING SURVEY AT A GLANCE

Avg. UCAS points accepted	**324**
Acceptance rate	**15%**
Overall satisfaction rate	**83%**
Helpful/interested staff	★★★
Small tuition groups	★★
Students into graduate jobs	**70%**

Teaching most popular with undergraduates:
Accounting, Anatomy, Physiology & Pathology, Biology & related sciences, Complementary Medicine, Finance, Forensic & Archaeological Science, Law, Medical Science & Pharmacy, Medical Technology, Ophthalmics, Other Subjects Allied to Medicine, Social Work, Sociology.

Teaching least popular with undergraduates:
Design Studies (61%), Technology (60%).

It is a real-world institution, with a large student body. Added value lies in cultural diversity and 'internationalisation', in social mission and close links with industry and the public sector.

Glasgow Caledonian University is committed to wide access to higher educatin; 50% of its students are the first in their families to go to university. There are, however, strict academic guidelines to be met to gain entry. Its commitment to widening access is exemplified by its award-winning Caledonian Club, which works with children from nursery throughout their school years to raise educational aspirations and build life skills.

Open Day in 2011 is 7 September.

CAMPUS

City campus is part of an amazing concentration of some 50,000 students. Close to Caley are Strathclyde University, the College of Building and Printing, the College of Food & Technology, and the College of Commerce are in the vicinity.

FEES, BURSARIES

Fees for English, Welsh and Northern Irish approx. £1,820 p.a. EU Fees: none to pay. Look out for the £5,000 p.a. Magnus Magnusson Awards, the £3,600 p.a. Moffat Scholarships, the £1,000 p.a. Masterton Undergraduate Bursaries in Civil Engineering, and the sports bursaries programme. See www. gcal.ac.uk/arc/bursary.html and www.moffat centre.com/scholarships/index.html and www. gcal.ac.uk/giving/magnusscholarship.html.

STUDENT PROFILE

'Most of Caley's recruits,' writes Rachel Richardson, 'are home-based students looking for a more vocational course.' Statistically, 49% of

RESEARCH EXCELLENCE

% of Glasgow Cal's research that is
4* *(World-class)* or **3*** *(Internationally rated):*

	4*	3*
Vision Sciences	5%	25%
Allied Health Professions	15%	45%
Applied Mathematics	5%	5%
Computer Science	0%	15%
General Engineering	0%	20%
Buikt Environment	15%	45%
Accounting/Finance	0%	15%
Business/Management	0%	25%
Law	0%	15%
Sociology	5%	5%
Psychology	0%	10%
Education	0%	25%
History	10%	25%
Media Studies	10%	15%

undergraduates are mature. Many are local, but the university is putting that right with a convincing appeal beyond the EU. It took first place in the *Times Higher Education* Awards in 2008 for Outstanding Support for Overseas Students, and for the third time in a row, it was rated Scotland's best international student experience in the International Student Barometer survey, carried out by independent research specialists' i-graduate.org.

Its home contingent is all but 2% state school educated; 35% come from the lower socio-economic bracket, 4% from neighbourhoods which

SUBJECT AREAS (%)

- Humanities — 6
- Combined — 3
- Social Studies incl Law — 1
- Health Subjects — 28
- Science — 10
- Engineering — 7
- Built Environment — 6
- Maths & Computer — 9
- Business — 30

until recently, we are told, never dreamt of taking a degree. Caley has been awarded the Frank Buttle Trust quality mark for support to students who come to university from public care.

ACADEMIA & JOBS

The university's six schools are this year diminishing to three: The School of Health & Life Sciences; The School of Engineering, Computing and the Environment; and The School of Business, Law and Social Sciences.

The School of Health & Life Sciences is one of the biggest nursing education providers in Scotland. In the recent assessment of the nation's research provision, Glasgow Caledonian was ranked first in Scotland in subjects allied to Medicine and second in Built Environment. In the UK at large it figured in the Top 10 and Top 20 respectively in these areas for research.

These are its great strengths. Thirty-six per cent of graduate jobs come out of degrees in subjects related to Medicine (Nursing, Operation Depart-ment Practice, Occupational Therapy, Physio-therapy, Podiatry, Radiation Oncology Science, Biomedicine, Diagnostic Imaging Science, Food Bioscience, Human Biology, Nutrition Dietetics).

They are one of the biggest nursing education providers in Scotland. One in five nurses and healthcare professionals educated in Scotland are educated at GCU. Besides the Nursing, principal wage earners on the curriculum are Optometry and Ophthalmic Dispensing. The Department of Vision Sciences is the only such teaching establishment in Scotland.

In addition, the fields of construction and finance are particularly strong. Its range of Built Environment programmes is considered the best in Scotland.

Other niche areas include Risk Management. They are the only UK university to offer a degree. In addition, the university's journalism courses were recently rated the best in Scotland by the

WHAT IT'S REALLY LIKE	
UNIVERSITY:	
Social Life	★
Societies	★★
Student Union services	★
Politics	**Activity low**
Sport	**On the rise.**
National team position	**77th**
Sport facilities	★★★
Arts opportunities	**Slim**
Student magazine	**The Edit**
Student radio	**Radio Caley**
Venue	**The Bedsit**
Bars	**Hanover**
Union ents	**Quiz, Caleyoke.**
Union ocieties	**34**
Parking	**Poor**
CITY:	
Entertainment	★★★★★
Scene	**Cool**
Town/gown relations	**Good**
Risk of violence	**Average**
Cost of living	**Average**
Student concessions	**Good**
Survival + 2 nights out	**£70 pw**
Part-time work campus/town	**Good.**

National Council for the Training of Journalists.

SOCIAL SCENE

STUDENT ASSOCIATION The trouble has been that Caledonian has not been very active extra-murally. The large mature, local and part-time population is suggested as the reason for the relatively low level of action. The challenge is that after nightfall and at weekends the place is deserted, while in the day, the bars can be full to overflowing. The latest *Times Higher Education* Student Experience Survey put the university last in Britain in the Student Union category.

The Hanover Students Union Bar is, as if you would never guess, the Student Union bar in the North Hanover Street Building. Typical fare - pub quizzes, *Superstar Karaoke*, comedians.

Media-wise *The Edit* is the student magazine, and Radio Caley is their brand new radio station, launched in February 2009.

Then there's **the Hub**, info and resource centre for sports clubs and societies, 35 at the last count. Students use the Hub to organise student activities for socs like Alpha for Students, Amnesty International, Chinese Students Association, Christian Union, Music Soc, Muslim Soc, GT Events, Hellenic Society, International Students, Lesbian, Gay, Bisexual Society, SSOS. There are now 27 societies, many more than there were.

ACCOMMODATION	
Student rating	★
Guarantee to freshers	**No guarantee**
Style	**Halls, flats**
Security guard	**All**
Shared rooms	**Some**
Internet access	**All**
Self-catered	**All**
En suite	**Most**
Approx price range pw	**£86.46-£96.21**
City rent pw	**£75-£110**

Finally, **Arc** gives access to health and fitness services and facilities, including a gym, a place to relax and de-stress at a yoga or t'ai chi class, to work out, play badminton or book in for a therapeutic massage session. See also Student Glasgow.

Sport Investment in sport facilities has been rewarded with some success in the national BUCS league. They have zipped up from the depths to take 77th position.

There are 26 sports clubs: American football, rugby, soccer (male and female), athletics catered for alongside such as snowboarding, hillwalking and table tennis. It's the Bearsden dry ski slopes for GCU Club Ski and the real white stuff for weekends in semester two.

The Hillwalking and Mountaineering Club is the largest - weekends away in Glen Coe.

PILLOW TALK
For lucky first years, it's Caledonian Court, adjacent to campus, 6-8 bedroom flats. Freshers are not guaranteed accommodation, but priority criteria include: aged under 19 by September in the year of entry, distance from family home, special needs.

GETTING THERE
☞ By road: M8/J19 or J18. Good coach services.
☞ By rail: 50 minutes Edinburgh, 5 hours London.
☞ By Underground: Cowcaddens and Buchanan Street Stations are nearby.
☞ By air: Glasgow Airport.

UNIVERSITY OF GLOUCESTERSHIRE

The University of Gloucestershire
Park Campus
Cheltenham
Gloucestershire GL50 2RH

TEL 0844 801 0001
FAX 01242 543334
EMAIL marketing@glos.ac.uk
WEB www.glos.ac.uk

Gloucestershire Uni Students' Union
PO Box 220
The Park
Cheltenham GL50 2RH

TEL 01242 714360
FAX 01242 261381
EMAIL union@glos.ac.uk
WEB www.yourstudentsunion.com

VIRGIN VIEW

*G*loucestershire University was born out of Cheltenham & Gloucester College of Higher Education in 2001, following a merger between the College of St Paul and St Mary and the higher education section of Gloucestershire College of Arts and Technology. No need to ask where it is based.

It fared so-so at the hands of its students in the 2010 National Survey: 78% are happy with what they do, 68% get real graduate jobs within six months of leaving.

But when asked by the Times Higher Education *magazine about their lecturers, the students were much more positive. There is clearly a good rapport. This is a teaching university, where personal help and interest in you will be an important part of the deal.*

So no surprise then that the current drop-out rate is a relatively tame 7%.

UNIVERSITY/STUDENT PROFILE	
University since	**2001**
Situation/style	**Campus**
Student population	**9635**
Undergraduates	**7025**
Mature	**43%**
International	**7%**
Male/female ratio	**41:59**
Equality of opportunity:	
state school intake	**95%**
social class 4-7 intake	**36%**
drop-out rate	**7%**

CAMPUS
There are three sites in Cheltenham. Park Campus is the main site, then there's Francis Close Hall (FCH) and Pittville. When you turn up at Park,

don't confuse it with the nearby Gloscat, monstrous further education establishment in crying need of a facelift. No, this is the one up the road that copped the dosh. The main campus is leafy, white, with everything (halls, bars, lecture theatres) close to hand and spanking new it seems, though many of the buildings must have been here for some time. It was once a botanic garden.

The newer £15-million Oxstalls Campus has opened in the nearby city of Gloucester. It was part of their remit that they would open up there. It is being used by the schools of Sport and Nursing, but will be developed and the subject base widened. There's a Student Union building, halls of residence for completion this year, a refectory and astroturf, a sports science building and learning resources centre. .

FEES & BURSARIES

UK & EU Fees 2011-12: £3,375 p.a. Relief on a sliding scale for those meeting the conditions of the Higher Education Maintenance Grant. Students qualifying for a full grant are eligible for a bursary. A one-off payment of £500 is available for students who attain 3 A grades at A level. Students from partner colleges are eligible for a payment of £1,200. Applications to the Sports Scholarship Scheme are open to all undergraduates, on arrival at the University of Gloucestershire. Successful candidates receive a £500 bursary along with support services.

STUDENT PROFILE

Broadly, Pittville attracts interesting/arty-types, Park be-suited-&-booted business management-types. Like Oxford Brookes, and unusual in a new-uni demography, there was once a lean to independent school types. Now, on the Government's say-so, the intake of the lower socio-economic orders has risen to 36%, and they take a fair whack from so-called low-participation neighbourhoods, while public school types have dwindled to 5%. Despite big changes, students talk of the 'really great sense of community', unusual for a multi-campus institute.

ACADEMIA & JOBS

First degree subjects fall under 3 faculty heads: Arts & Education (split between Park and Pittville), Business & Social Studies (Park), Environment & Leisure (FCH and Oxstalls). The programmes (BA/BSc Hons) are modular and very broad based. There is a choice of single, joint or major/minor courses, each of them composed of more than twenty modules with often less than clear synergy between subjects.

Hundreds of main subject combinations are

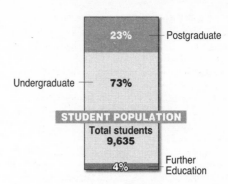

STUDENT POPULATION
Postgraduate 23%
Undergraduate 73%
Further Education 4%
Total students 9,635

offered, from which you will build your course. It can be quite daunting.

In the latest national assessment of all our universities, Gloucestershire's research provision was found to be world-class in 5% of four subjects subjects submitted - Planning, English, History, and Art & Design, and in 10% of Education.

Subjects which 85% or more of the class say are best taught are Education, Film & Photography, Finance, Accounting and Social Work.

Students are least happy with the teaching in Sociology, Communications & Information Studies, where only 55% and 57% of the class gave the thumbs up respectively.

Subjects most productive of graduate jobs are Business (18%), Education (18%), Biological Sciences (including Sport) (16%), Creative Arts & Design (13%), Media (7%), Social Studies (7%), Computer Science (6%).

The Business degrees earmark their students for particular employment areas - marketing, human resources, etc., but 7% of them end up in the hotel and restaurant business, the largest single sector among business jobs, which suggests that the Hospitality Management degree has muscle, and there's a niche in sport through the Business

---

TEACHING SURVEY AT A GLANCE

Avg. UCAS points accepted	**240**
Acceptance rate	**23%**
Overall satisfaction rate	**78%**
Helpful/interested staff	★★★★
Small tuition groups	★★★
Students into graduate jobs	**68%**

Teaching most popular with undergraduates:
Education, Film & Photography, Finance, Accounting, Social Work.

Teaching least popular with undergraduates:
Sociology (55%), Communications & Information Studies (57%), Journalism, Psychology (61%), Management Studies (62%).

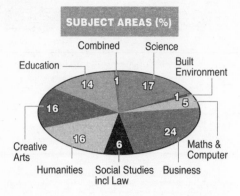

SUBJECT AREAS (%)

- Combined — 1
- Science — 17
- Built Environment — 1
- Education — 14
- Creative Arts — 16
- Humanities — 16
- Social Studies incl Law — 6
- Business — 24
- Maths & Computer — 5

church colleges, and that Lord Carey, former Archbishop of Canterbury, is University Chairman.

For graduates seeking work in the creative arts or media, there are well-directed named degrees in Advertising, Film Management/Production, Radio Production, TV Production, Broadcast Journalism, Publishing (Books and Magazines), also Photojournalism. But the figure above of 7% into media is misleading, only a handful of graduates actually made it into TV or radio jobs and paper journalism not at all. It has to be said, the research provision for Journalism didn't attract the assessors much and its teaching appealed to a mere 61% of the class.

SOCIAL SCENE

'Cheltenham & Gloucester is a fab, mad, lovely place,' I was told and didn't find much to contradict it. There are four bars, one on each campus. A workmanlike ents programme makes good use of the large, airy **Park Bar**, in Cheltenham, with stage and seriously provocative sound and lighting systems.

There's karaoke, fun and games type drink promo nights, Bingo, various balls (the Summer Ball sells upwards of 7,000 tickets, then there's Christmas Ball, Freshers Ball, Graduation Ball).

Management & Sports Development/Sport & Exercise Science degrees.

Among those studying Education, well over half become primary school teachers. Again, sport is a favourite alternative destination, as is community work, government administration, and the ubiquitous hotel and restaurant trade.

Of those studying Biological Sciences, which includes the many Sports Science degrees, 10% get jobs in the sports industry, but many more go the teaching route, or into the hotel/restaurant industry. Some find work as sports gurus in the community, youth work, etc, but Glos graduates who find work in the community as carers tend to progress through Social Studies/Sciences. There is a whole range of degrees, like School, Youth & Community Work, Youth Work, Social Work, and the BSc Psychology. Other degrees, Applied Theology, Children & Family Work & Practical Theology, for example, remind us that Glos was fathered by two

RESEARCH EXCELLENCE

% of Gloucestershire's research that is
4* *(World-class) or* **3*** *(Internationally rated):*

	4*	3*
Planning	5%	35%
Geography	0%	15%
Business/Management	0%	10%
Social Work	0%	10%
Psychology	0%	10%
Education	10%	15%
Sports	0%	10%
English	5%	30%
Theology	0%	40%
History	5%	20%
Art and Design	5%	5%
Media Studies	0%	0%

WHAT IT'S REALLY LIKE

UNIVERSITY:

Social Life	★★★★
Societies	★★★
Student Union Services	★★★
Politics	**Interest low**
Student Union	**Good**
Sport	**Very competitive**
National team position	**40th**
Arts opportunities	**OK, film good**
Student newspaper	**Space**
Student Radio	**Tone Radio**
Nightclub	**Sub:Mission @ Park**
Bars	**Park, Pittville, FCH and Oxstalls**
Union ents	**Cheesy + huge Balls**
Union societies	**70**
Parking	**No parking**
TOWN:	
Entertainment	★★★
Scene	**OK clubs, pubs, good shopping**
Risk of violence	**Average**
Cost of living	**High**
Student concessions	**Excellent**
Survival + 2 nights out	**£70-£80 pw**
Part-time work campus/town	**Good**

Also some local live bands do their thing. Sports bar, **Oxtalls**, at the Gloucester campus is big on match days, of course.

It is fair to point out, however, that the emphasis is on club-nights in town with the local SU bar providing a kind of pre-club, and at weekends it's quiet. The big student night is Wednesday's *Blue & Blue* at **MooMoo** in Cheltenham, a mix of electro and dubstep, with chart and indie downstairs.

There is a sense of the society scene maturing. *Space* is the excellent fortnightly newspaper, Tone Radio the student radio station, and they were runners-up for a *Guardian*/Sky News Broadcaster of the Year Award in 2008. The Film Society is also active. PDS (The Pittville Degree Show Society) puts on charity fund raisers throughout the year. The Art Society delivers fine shows at the end of each year in Pittville.

SPORT They do well in the BUSA leagues (40th nationally last year). It's their big thing. There is a swimming pool, sports hall, pitches (known as The Folley), a fitness suite, and at Oxstalls a sports science lab and astro turf pitch.

TOWN Cheltenham itself has fantastic shops (classy, unique and your high street shops too), some good pubs, the Arts Centre and a few clubs. 'Gold Cup Week brings the Irish to town and loadsa money,' a student confides, 'a great week for all the girls to go out. You get plied with drink after drink. This week is RAG week, just the best week of the academic calendar!! Tons of fun and misbehaviour, being on a float, driven in front of crowds of people, drunk in charge of a water pistol by 9am, expecting a lot of "cheek" from the rugby boys. And all for charity!.' Is it always so...baby doll? we wonder. 'Well, Christmas carols in FCH chapel are always a laugh...specially with all that mulled wine in you.'

ACCOMMODATION	
Guarantee to freshers	**75%**
Style	**Halls, flats**
Security guard	**All**
Shared rooms	**Some**
Internet access	**All**
Self-catered	**Most**
En suite	**Most**
Approx price range pw	**£71-£105**
City rent pw	**£55-£67**

PILLOW TALK

Apply early for the luxurious-looking, mixed, self-catered or half-board halls at Park. Priority goes to first years and overseas students. New halls in Gloucester and 100-room Regency Halls in central Cheltenham opened in September 2006.

GETTING THERE

☛ By road: M5/J11 or M40/A40 or M4/J15, A419. Good coach service.

☛ By rail: Bristol Parkway, 45 mins; Birmingham, 1.00; London Paddington, 2:30.

☛ By coach: London, 2:35; Birmingham, 1:10.

GLYNDWR UNIVERSITY

Glyndwr University
Plas Coch
Mold Road
Wrexham LL11 2AW

TEL 01978 293439
FAX 01978 290008
EMAIL sid@glyndwr.ac.uk
WEB www.glyndwr.ac.uk

Glyndwr Students' Guild
Plas Coch
Mold Road
Wrexham LL11 2AW

TEL 01978 293226
FAX 01978 293227
EMAIL guildbar@newi.ac.uk
WEB www.newi.ac.uk

VIRGIN VIEW

Glyndwr is a new university, located on the north western side of Wrexham in North East Wales.

Wrexham is on the borders of Wales and England within easy motoring of Chester and Liverpool.

We know Glyndwr of old at the Virgin Guide, before the founding of so many new universities precluded from coverage the anomalous Further Education colleges that also offer degree courses. Now, NEWI, as it was called then, has made it into the upper echelon. NEWI stood for the North East Wales Institute. It was a small college of the University of Wales, founded in 1975, of about 4,200 souls, very much part of the local community, which has a sound artistic tradition. Theatre Clwyd, at nearby Mold, for example, is a draw to top-flight theatre and opera companies, and the International Eisteddfod is held at Llangollen.

Now, Glyndwr is the name of a legend, a Welsh warrior chieftain with a touch of magic at his fingers.

Owain Glyndwr, anglicised by Shakespeare as Owen Glendower, was the man behind the Welsh Revolt against Henry IV of England. When it was put down, he disappeared. Never captured or tempted by Royal Pardons, nor ever betrayed, Glyndwr was last seen in 1412. His final years a mystery, he passed into Welsh myth.

The name is an excellent choice for the University, so long as they're not counting on tempting too many English across the border.

They run a tight ship at Glyndwr and thoroughly deserve the chance to develop as a university. It is all before them.

They are proud to have one of the highest intakes of students from non-traditional backgrounds and those claiming Disabled Student Allowance. Applications are encouraged from all walks of life. Motivation and commitment are considered as important as academic requirements.

Individual support they claim is high, but we cannot compare it yet to other universities, as Glyndwr is not part of the Times Higher Student Experience Survey or other surveys. Mingle with them on http://glyndwruni. edublogs.org/; www.facebook.com/ glyndwruni; www.twitter.com/glyndwruni; and www.youtube.com/glyndwruniversity. Open Days: 4 June and 20 August 2011.

One certain plus is that there is a low cost of living in this neck of the woods.

CAMPUS

There are two main sites within five minutes' walk of each other. Plas Coch is headquarters. It may be found along the Mold Road, between Wrexham's Racecourse football ground and a retail park containing a supermarket, a multi-screen cinema, and

UNIVERSITY/STUDENT PROFILE	
University since	**2008**
Situation/style	**Campus**
Student population	**7730**
Undergraduates	**6815**
Mature	**67%**
International	**37%**
Male/female ratio	**51:49**
Equality of opportunity:	
state school intake	**99%**
social class 4-7 intake	**54%**
drop-out rate	**11%**

a number of restaurants and other shops. Plas Coch houses most of the programmes. Techniquest Glyndwr, the Science Discovery Centre, is based here, as is William Aston Hall, the key venue in Wrexham for concerts and live entertainment. The 900-seat hall stages plays and concerts - classical and pop/rock, and has a bar. The BBC National Orchestra of Wales plays here, and it has also attracted the likes of Billy Bragg, and Buddy Holly's Winter Dance Party 2009.

Also on site are a number of excellent places to eat and drink, including the **Scholar's Rest** refectory and three coffee shops. The Glyndwr University Student Village is situated at the northern edge of the site, a short distance from the library, supermarkets and the Students' Guild.

The **Terry Hands Theatre** also opened here in 2006, following a £130,000 investment in NEWI's Theatre and Performance facilities. It is named after one of three who founded the famous Liverpool Everyman Theatre in 1964, and is now the Director of **Clwyd Theatre Cymru**.

The second site, the North Wales School of Art & Design, is 10 minutes' walk away in Regent Street, in the centre of town.

There are also plans to develop facilities for land-based education on the site of the Welsh College of Horticulture, in Northop, Flintshire.

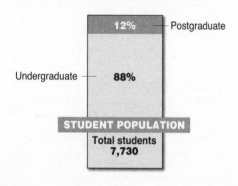

Postgraduate 12%

Undergraduate 88%

STUDENT POPULATION

Total students 7,730

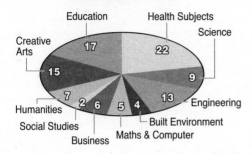

SUBJECT AREAS (%)

Education 17
Health Subjects 22
Science 9
Creative Arts 15
Engineering 13
Humanities 7
Social Studies 2
Business 6
Maths & Computer 5
Built Environment 4
(2, 6, 5, 4, 13)

FEES, BURSARIES

UK & EU Fees, 2011-12: £3,375 p.a. Welsh students receive a Welsh Assembly Government fee remission grant. In addition, the Glyndwr University bursary (up to £500) is available to those in receipt of the full HE Maintenance Grant, the exact amount awarded dependent on family income. They also offer the Gifted Athletes Scholarship and the Care Leavers Scholarship, for those once in Care.

STUDENT PROFILE

As expected, many of the students come from the locality at this stage, but there is a large cohort from overseas too (37%); 67% are mature, 62% part-timers, almost all state school educated, more than 50% are working class. Their local college has turned into a university, and suddenly they are transformed.

ACADEMIA & JOBS

In 2010 a reshaping of the internal structure saw the replacement of seven academic schools with a

TEACHING SURVEY AT A GLANCE

Avg. UCAS points accepted	**200**
Acceptance rate	**46%**
Overall satisfaction rate	**74%**
Helpful/interested staff	**No data**
Small tuition groups	**No data**
Students into graduate jobs	**78%**

Teaching most popular with undergraduates:
Education (97%), Biological Sciences, Computer Science, English (97%), Sports Science (98%).

Teaching least popular with undergraduates:
Social Work, Social Studies (50%), Film (43%).

School for Undergraduate Studies and a Graduate School. These commission academic programmes from two new University Institutes: the Institute for Arts, Science and Technology and Institute for Health, Medical Sciences and Society.

Niche areas in the curriculum gear them towards the creative industries, including computer game development, creative media computing, broadcasting and journalism, sound and broadcasting and radio production and communication.

Land-based degrees include equestrian psychology and animal studies. All undergraduate and postgraduate engineering programmes offered are accredited by at least one of the industry's three major professional bodies, the Institution of Mechanical Engineers, the Royal Aeronautical Society and the Institution of Engineering and Technology (IET).

A £5m Creative Industries Centre features TV, radio and online production facilities and brings together different disciplines associated with the creative industries, including art and design, computing and engineering. It will also be the new

RESEARCH EXCELLENCE

% of Glyndwr's research that is
4* *(World-class)* or **3*** *(Internationally rated):*

	4*	3*
Nursing & Midwifery	**0%**	**25%**
Computer Science	**5%**	**35%**
Metallurgy & Materials	**5%**	**30%**
Social Work	**0%**	**20%**
Education	**0%**	**5%**
Art & Design	**0%**	**5%**

home of BBC Cymru Wales in north east Wales.

A new £3-m Performing Arts and Conference Centre opened in 2009. Facilities include a 180-seat theatre and advanced AV equipment.

SOCIAL SCENE

STUDENTS UNION The new Students' Guild offers the usual ents, discos, quizzes in the bar. The main eaterie is the **Scholar's Rest**. Other outlets at Plas Coch include **Fellows Café Bar**, **Chapters Retail & Café Bar** (an 'essentials' shop), and **Café Darganfod**.

SPORT There is a Sports Centre at the heart of the main campus. It is one of North Wales' premier sporting venues. They have two floodlit artificial pitches, one a water-based international hockey pitch, the other sand-based for football. Adjacent is a Human Performance Laboratory. Other facilities include a 1,000 sqm wooden sprung floor, a dance studio, fitness suite, sun shower and spectator facilities. They run classes for such as yoga, pilates, kick boxing and step., and the centre supports the main teams: hockey, football and basketball.

PILLOW TALK

Priority is given to finding accommodation for 1st

ACCOMMODATION	
Guarantee to freshers	**80%**
Style	**Halls, flats**
Security guard	**24-hour**
Shared rooms	**Some**
Internet access	**Most**
Self-catered	**All**
En suite	**Some**
Approx price range pw	**£62-£145**
City rent pw	**£60-£120**

year students until there are no more rooms left - 600 rooms are available at the university. Wrexham Village is a brand new £40 million Student Housing complex which is next to The Racecourse football ground, home of Wrexham FC. Phase 2 in construction, to be completed by September 2011. The accommodation is a two minute walk from Glyndwr's Wrexham campus and includes 117 single en-suite rooms. CCTV coverage of the site and laundry facilities.

There's also a range of University-managed accommodation in Wrexham.

Car parking for freshers is limited and under review.

GETTING THERE
☞ By road: A483.
☞ By rail: Birmingham, 2:12; Cardiff, 3:40; Manchester, 1:30.
☞By coach: Birmingham, 3:20.

GOLDSMITHS COLLEGE, LONDON

University of London Goldsmiths College
New Cross
London SE14 6NW

TEL 020 7078 5300
FAX 020 7919 7509
EMAIL admissions@gold.ac.uk
WEB www.goldsmiths.ac.uk

Goldsmiths Students' Union
Dixon Road
London SE14 6NW

TEL 020 8692 1406
FAX 020 8694 9789
EMAIL gcsu@gold.ac.uk
WEB www.goldsmithssu.org

VIRGIN VIEW

*G*oldsmiths is a college of the University of London, famous for its postmodern art department, ents programme, and for the active commitment of its students to fairness and justice. It is located in south-east London, and has been listed as 'cool brand leader' (as has MTV) by the Brand Council.

'Ours is one of the most exciting colleges in the country,' I was told. 'It is unpretentious [Oh, right], set in London and neatly poised between a bad-ass ents programme and radical action. We have one of the most politically active Students' Unions in the country.'

The University the diversity of students and staff as defining. 'Students can learn from the differing perspectives here.'

Then there's their creative and innovative

UNIVERSITY/STUDENT PROFILE	
College of London Uni since	**1904**
Situation/style	**Campus**
Student population	**7815**
Undergraduates	**5500**
Mature	**50%**
International	**18%**
Male/female ratio	**34:66**
Equality of opportunity:	
state school intake	**90%**
social class 4-7 intake	**32%**
drop-out rate	**11%**

approach to teaching. At Goldsmiths they encourage students to challenge and overcome preconceived boundaries. There is a strong emphasis on interdisciplinarity, and departments work together to offer differing perspectives on subject areas.

Goldsmiths is committed to life-long learning, and half its students are classified as mature (over 21 for undergraduate study). Mature students may not necessarily be required to meet the same formal academic qualifications as other applicants (although for some programmes such as PGCEs, entry requirements are in part determined by external bodies). Applicants are considered on their individual merits, not only their academic background. Any relevant work or life experience which you can demonstrate will be taken into account when considering you for a place.

They are looking for evidence of active engagement with the chosen discipline. That means reading, travel, voluntary work, paid work in a relevant field, and an understanding of the relevance of it all to your long term goals; they want to know about work experience, voluntary activity; they want to detect an ability to work and communicate effectively in a group, to work alone demonstrating self-motivation and organisation, an ability to communicate effectively in written and oral form, including confidence in written English and the ability to read and understand complex texts, a commitment to full-time study within the field, an understanding of the nature of academic study including the demands for independent research, changing patterns of thinking, meeting new experiences. An ability to face and overcome personal challenges. It's hard to see what's left to teach you.

Open Days in 2011 are: 25 June, 10am-2pm, and 9 November, 12noon-5pm.

CAMPUS

South East London location, close to the centre of things, but with lots of local hidden gems.

At Goldsmiths almost everything is together on one site, so there's a strong campus feel to life here: they are big enough to offer some good facilities, but not so big that things seem impersonal and unfriendly. That's the university line, anyway.

'So, you want to know about Goldsmiths?' said

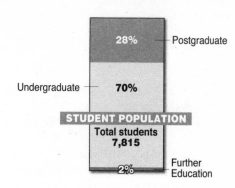

STUDENT POPULATION
Total students
7,815

- Postgraduate 28%
- Undergraduate 70%
- Further Education 2%

Siobhan Daly. 'Well, don't come here looking for the architectural splendours of Oxbridge or the serenity of Durham. This is south-east London: bold, brash and full of embodiments of Delboy Trotter. One of my friends cried when she arrived, saying that it looked more like Grange Hill than a university.'

Writes Laura Cattell: "'Oh brave New Cross that has such people in it..." Just a bleak 7-minute train ride from London Bridge will deliver you to New Cross. Although not one of the best parts of London, estate agent rhetoric is beginning to convince some that this is "an up-and-coming urban area". I wouldn't go that far, but plans are indeed underway to build a Health and Culture Centre in New Cross.

'Cost of living is cheaper than in many parts of the capital and Campus is open, safe and welcoming. The buildings aren't outstanding, but the students are and this former Arts College has a great, friendly atmosphere.

Goldsmith's is one of the most local universities in London, in that it really encourages local people

> *'Well, don't come here looking for the architectural splendours of Oxbridge or the serenity of Durham. This is south-east London.'*

TEACHING SURVEY AT A GLANCE	
Avg. UCAS points accepted	**300**
Acceptance rate	**14%**
Overall satisfaction rate	**81%**
Helpful/interested staff	★★★
Small tuition groups	★
Students into graduate jobs	**74%**

Teaching most popular with undergraduates:
Anthropology, Design Studies, English, Languages, Social Work.

Teaching least popular with undergraduates:
Teacher Training (64%).

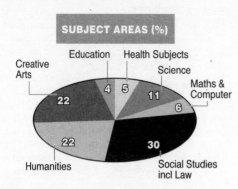

SUBJECT AREAS (%)

Education — 4
Health Subjects Science — 5
Creative Arts — 22
Maths & Computer — 11
— 6
Humanities — 22
Social Studies incl Law — 30

to enrol and ahas good links with the community.'

FEES, BURSARIES

UK & EU Fees 2011-12: £3,375. A Goldsmiths Bursary worth up to £1,000 p.a. is available to students from low household income backgrounds. See www.goldsmiths.ac.uk/ug/costs/funding/uk/bursaries.

There's also a series of scholarships awarded for academic achievement/potential. The Mayor's New Cross Award is worth £11,395 and available if you studied at a secondary school/college in Lewisham.

Ten Excellence Scholarships (£500) are awarded to others who excel at A Level.

Up to 33 scholarships (£1,000) are available under the Eliahou Dangoor scheme to students with strong academic ability in computing. Eligible programmes are: BSc Computer Science; BSc

Computing & Information Systems; BSc Creative Computing. Goldsmiths claims that their Computing department is one of the leading departments in Europe for creative computing. It has attracted over £5million over recent years.

Visit www.goldsmiths.ac.uk/ug/costs/funding/uk/scholarships and check with your admitting department for additional funding opportunities.

STUDENT PROFILE

You don't need me to say this. Damian 'pickled-cows' Hirst, Placebo, Julian Clary and Blur all strutted their stuff here. 'This doesn't, however, mean that you have to conform to the general "I'm-finding-myself" principle of dressing,' Siobhan reassures. 'Just do whatever you want; be yourself. If you are a heterosexual man, you'll love it here. If you are a homosexual woman, you'll also love it here. Goldsmiths is 66% women. The competition is hot!

'That said,' writes Laura, 'students here are a diverse crowd - masses of international students [18%], mature students [50%], "non-traditional" students [32%] - its widening participation scheme is one of the best in the country.'

ACADEMIA & JOBS

Forty-five per cent of their research work in Media is world-class, 35% of international significance. In Music, it's 30%/40%; Sociology, 35%/35%; Computer, 20%/40%; Anthropology, 25%/30%; Art, 35%/20%, and so on. Right through Design, Psychology and History of Art the results were world-class and far better than outsiders expected, given their showing in the last assessment seven years ago. The Sociology Department was placed joint top in the country in the national assessment.

But then along came the *Times Higher Education* magazine and put some salient questions to Goldsmiths' students and discovered that the one-to-one communication between lecturer and student is not always as generous as the students would like. We give them 3 stars out of a maximum 5 for interest in students, based on the survey's findings, but for small group tuition they achieve only 1 star.

Three years ago Laura wrote of the excellent results Goldsmiths attained in the old teaching inspections, but added: 'Personal tutors often leave a little to be desired,' anticipating that matters would improve with the creation of a Peer Assisted Learning scheme. They have improved, but the small tutorial group is still a dream.

Spoonfed you are not. Goldsmiths is unusual, individualistic, even a tad eccentric, and to an extent it is up to the individual to find his or her way into its culture. There is no change without

RESEARCH EXCELLENCE		
% of Goldsmith's research that is *4* (World-class) or 3* (Internationally rated):*		
	4*	*3**
Health Professions	0%	0%
Computer Science	20%	40%
Politics	10%	20%
Social Work	10%	25%
Sociology	35%	25%
Anthropology	25%	30%
Psychology	10%	40%
Education	10%	20%
English	15%	50%
History	10%	20%
Art	35%	20%
Design	20%	35%
History of Art	20%	30%
Performing Arts	20%	45%
Media Studies	45%	35%
Music	30%	40%

WHAT IT'S REALLY LIKE

COLLEGE:	
Social Life	★★
Societies	★★
Student Union services	★★
Politics	**Anarchy**
Sport	**Fun**
National team position	**126th**
Sport facilities	★
Arts opportunities	**Excellent film, theatre**
Student magazine	**Smiths**
Student radio	**Wired**
Club venue + bar	**The Stretch**
Bar & café	**The Green Room**
Union ents	**OK disco**
Union societies	**21**
Most popular societies	**Respect**
Parking	**Limited, street**
CITY:	
Entertainment	★★★★★
Scene	**Wild, expensive, but locally not**
Town/gown relations	**OK**
Risk of violence	**Average -high**
Cost of living	**High**
Student concessions	**Good**
Survival + 2 nights out	**£100 pw**
Part-time work campus/town	**Excellent**

pain. It is not Goldsmiths' place to pamper or coddle. That's not only true of Goldsmiths, but of Oxford and Cambridge too and reveals the weakness of 'flat playing field surveys', the rigour of which can sometimes iron out what is interesting in such as the lecturer-student relationship.

Says the uni: 'Our distinctive approach to learning encourages students to explore ideas that challenge and push preconceived boundaries, meaning that they are stretched intellectually and creatively to investigate fresh new ways of thinking.

'Goldsmiths is all about the freedom to experiment, to think differently, to be an individual. That's why our list of former students includes names like Antony Gormley, Julian Clary, Damien Hirst, Mary Quant, Bridget Riley, Vivienne Westwood, Graham Coxon, Malcolm McLaren. We bring creative and unconventional approaches to our subjects, but everything we do is based on the highest academic standards of teaching and research.'

At the end of it all, however, it is all too easy to lose sight of the fact that Goldsmiths, the hip college of London Uni with its cutting-edge, cool appeal, gives most of its graduates to primary school education.

SOCIAL SCENE

STUDENTS UNION Their building is called Tiananmen, **The Stretch** is the bar/club venue - Roni Size, Goldie, Athlete have visited. 'Our Students' Union may be a concrete monstrosity, but there's a fab nightlife hidden inside and rather outstanding alcohol prices,' writes Siobhan.

Writes Laura: 'The Student Union shuts down at the weekend, which is a bit of a shocker, but it does make up for it in the week by putting on plenty of cheap nights such as [legendary] *Club Sandwich* - pop/dance/indie/r&b on Wednesday, *Goldsmiths Introducing* (new talent) on Thursday; also bingo, *Superquiz* and karaoke.' Tuesday is Film or Comedy Club. They are 'for hire' Friday through Sunday.

Student societies range from Respect to Capoeira. In politics, anarchy rules. Students love to campaign here, religious awareness and equality being of particular importance. There's also a strong culture of altruism. They piloted a prison visiting scheme, and were nominated for a National Student Volunteering Award.

Student magazine *Smiths* regularly features in the national student media awards. In the summer a new Media and Communications building opens. Modern technological and purpose-built accommodation and equipment, a large lecture theatre, meeting spaces and a café with outside seating are among the treats.

ACCOMMODATION

Student rating	★★
Guarantee to freshers	**80%**
Style	**Halls, flats**
Security guard	**Most**
Shared rooms	**None**
Internet access	**Most**
Self-catered	**All**
En suite	**Most**
Approx price range pw	**£91.50-£202**
City rent pw	**£82-£120**

Generally, however, there's a fairly uneventful picture of Goldsmith's Student Union and the extra-curricular opportunity on campus.

TOWN Writes Laura: 'The local pubs are great - not a pretentious wine bar in sight. **New Cross Inn** is worth a try as is the **Amersham Arms** - particularly on a Monday when you can enjoy top comedy for just a few pounds.

'Cinema is good; nearest is Peckham Multiplex or **Greenwich Picturehouse/Odeon Theatre** - in general a good arts scene locally, and very close to London's theatreland.

'Night clubs average/good, but the local Venue is pretty awful.

'There are several cheap ethnic restaurants. If you're fed up with New Cross and Deptford then Greenwich is a 10-minute bus ride away - lovely with plenty of great restaurants and trendy bars. Best ones are the Gipsy Moth or the Spaniard.'

Sport Not sporty, but there's a new fitness centre (**Club Pulse**). Around £25 or so a month gets you use of gym, all exercise classes for free, but no swimming pool. 'They have a good women's football team and their basketball team aren't bad either,' says Laura. 'Playing fields, as on most University of London campuses, are pretty far away, but they do exist.'

PILLOW TALK

They have 1,000 places within walking distance of the campus, flats, houses, and purpose-built residences. Otherwise it's London. Writes Laura: 'Goldsmiths seems to own all the streets around campus, so students pour out of every corner, though they merge pretty well with the locals. 'Areas such as Brockley, New Cross, Deptford and parts of Peckham are popular with students. Lewisham can be pretty awful in parts, so look carefully. Greenwich and Blackheath are the best and safest parts, but reflect this in the rental prices.'

GETTING THERE

☛ By road: at the junction of A2 and A20.
☛ By rail: New Cross Gate or New Cross Underground and overland.

UNIVERSITY OF GREENWICH

The University of Greenwich
Old Royal Naval College
London SE10 9LS

TEL 020 8331 9000 (course enquiries)
    020 8331 8000 (switchboard)
FAX 020 8331 8145
EMAIL courseinfo@gre.ac.uk
WEB www.greenwich.ac.uk

Students' Union University of Greenwich
Cooper Building
Greenwich SE10 9JH

TEL 020 8331 7629
FAX 020 8331 7628
EMAIL J,Chan@greenwich.co.uk
WEB www.suug.co.uk/

VIRGIN VIEW

A university since 1992, Greenwich came out of Woolwich Polytechnic, Avery Hill College of Higher Education, Dartford College of Education, and Garnett College. Ten years later Dartford and Woolwich were closed and it concentrated its resources at three campuses, its flagship the £50-million headquarters at Greenwich Maritime Campus, the old Naval College on the south bank of the Thames opposite the Isle of Dogs, a setting described by the London Evening Standard *as 'one of the grandest of any university in the world'. It is regularly used as a film or TV location, last year for* The Duchess, Young Victoria, Wolf Man, Dorian Gray, Sherlock Holmes *and* Little Dorrit.

What students dislike most about Greenwich University is the disparate nature of the place, the lack of community and dearth of student activity. The Student

UNIVERSITY/STUDENT PROFILE	
University since	**1992**
Situation/style	**City sites**
Student population	**26120**
Undergraduates	**20550**
Mature	**59%**
International	**25%**
Male/female ratio	**48:52**
Equality of opportunity:	
state school intake	**98%**
social class 4-7 intake	**56%**
drop-out rate	**15%**

Union has been poor. It came off very badly in the 2011 Times Higher Education's *Student Experience survey, which may be why 15% of students don't stay the course.*

On the up-side, 84% of them think well of the teaching. There's a strong study ethic on most campuses, in spite of the fact that student to staff ratios in tutorial groups are hardly beneficial.

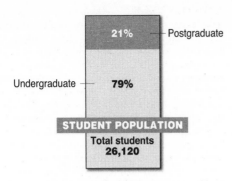

STUDENT POPULATION

21% — Postgraduate

Undergraduate — 79%

Total students 26,120

FEES, BURSARIES

UK & EU Fees, 2011-12: £3,375 p.a. There is a Mature Student Bursary and the Greenwich Partnership Bursary. There are cash scholarships for UCAS point scores and scholarships for sport and music. www2.gre.ac.uk/study/finance/undergraduate/bursaries.

STUDENT PROFILE

Students vary from campus to campus, but what many have in common is a passion for technical and vocational courses.

Medway and Avery Hill have a high proportion of mature and live-at-home students. But across all campuses Greenwich is a safe haven for international students . The university provides immigration info concerning visas, working and health, and academic assistance: English classes, study skills, personal tutors and social events geared to integrate into the British and uni communities.

Statistics show that 59% of Greenwich's students are mature (as a result there are good childcare facilities), 56% are drawn from the lower socioeconomic orders.

It is in every sense very much a 'new' university, taking higher education out of its privileged past into the community, and with a large, 34% part-times population.

CAMPUSES

GREENWICH CAMPUS has Humanities, Business, Law, Computing, Maritime Studies, and Maths. Designed by Christopher Wren in the 17th century, the building is now a UNESCO World Heritage site. It is regularly used as a location for films and TV. In the last year for the *King's Speech*, *Pirates of the Caribbean: Stranger Tides*, *Sherlock Holmes 2*, and *Iron Lady*. In February 2011 five Oscars were given to films shot on campus - the King's Speech and Wolfman.

Some 2012 Olympic events will be held next door, e.g. the Equestrian events and at the nearby 02 (North Greenwich Arena), gymnastics, trampoline and basketball.

Only a 20-minute train ride finds you in central London, but Greenwich is a lovely part of the city so you may just find yourself content to stay there.

There's a library, computing facilities of course, some postgrad. accommodation, conference centre and the Greenwich Maritime Institute (a research/ postgrad. teaching facility).

There's also **Bar Latitude** and an excellent party atmosphere, by all accounts, but light on ents. Drinks promos, pool competition nights, karaoke, comedy. Greatly enhanced campus catering facilities opened in March 2007.

Nearby there are a number of pubs, among them **The Gipsy Moth**, **The Spaniard**, and a cheesy club called **The North Pole**). There are also bars, restaurants and takeaways, and downriver is the **02 Arena**, which last year was the world's best attended music venue.

Nearby Deptford has a great market on Wednesdays and Fridays. Cost of living is reasonable for a London university, particularly in areas surrounding Avery Hill and Medway (see below). Greenwich is definitely the pricier of the three, but worth it.

AVERY HILL Bexley Road, Eltham, London SE9 2PQ, and Every Hill Road, Eltham, London SE9 2HB. It delivers Health & Social Care, Social Sciences, Education, Architecture, Landscape, and Construction. A £14-million building project features a multi-purpose sports hall, a 220-seat lecture theatre and 4 clinical skills laboratories, which replicate real NHS wards.

Close by is the not so lovely New Eltham, but connections to London are good. Waterloo is just 30 mins away by train. The campus is pleasant - 86 acres of parkland - but a little quiet and with, for some time, a dwindling Student Union, reflective perhaps of the student demographic: mature or live-at-home.

However, new catering and fitness facilities

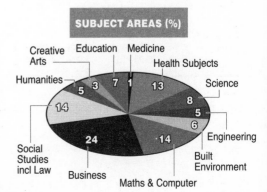

SUBJECT AREAS (%)

Creative Arts — 3
Education — 7
Medicine — 1
Humanities — 5
Health Subjects — 13
Science — 8
Engineering — 5
14 — Built Environment
Social Studies incl Law — 24
Business — 14
Maths & Computer — 6
14

TEACHING SURVEY AT A GLANCE

Avg. UCAS points accepted	**220**
Acceptance rate	**20%**
Overall satisfaction rate	**84%**
Helpful/interested staff	★★★
Small tuition groups	★
Students into graduate jobs	**74%**

Teaching most popular with undergraduates:
Biology & related sciences, Drama, English, History & Archaeology, Human Resource Management, Languages, Marketing, Law, Maths & Statistics (100%), Molecular Biology, Nursing, Pharmacy (100%), Philosophy (98%), Politics, Sports Science, Theology (98%).

Teaching least popular with undergraduates:
Design Studies (65%), Finance (64%).

have recently been established, following a £3m project to remodel the **Dome**, the student night-club, part of the village complex that also includes accommodation. This is still the liveliest SU venue at the uni. It can hold 1,000 punters. There's also an

RESEARCH EXCELLENCE

% of Glreenwich's research that is
4* (World-class) or 3* (Internationally rated):

	4*	3*
Nursing/Midwifery	**5%**	**25%**
Pharmacy	**5%**	**20%**
Horticulture, Animal Science	**5%**	**25%**
Statistics/Operational Research	**0%**	**40%**
Computer Science	**0%**	**20%**
General Engineering	**0%**	**20%**
Civil Engineering	**5%**	**30%**
Mechanical, Aeronautical, Manufacturing Engineering	**30%**	**40%**
Architecture/Building	**10%**	**30%**
Business/Management	**5%**	**15%**
Law	**0%**	**5%**
Politics	**0%**	**0%**
Development Studies	**0%**	**25%**
Psychology	**0%**	**15%**
Education	**5%**	**5%**
English	**0%**	**25%**
Linguistics	**0%**	**20%**
History	**10%**	**25%**
Media Studies	**0%**	**10%**

upgraded café, dining area and a relaxed social space, with Wi-Fi access throughout. A new gym offers modern fitness facilities, showers and changing rooms at the heart of campus.

MEDWAY Pembroke, Chatham Maritime, Kent ME4 4AW. Has Engineering, Science, Pharmacy, Nursing, some Business, and incorporates the Natural Resources Institute. There's a sports hall with badminton and basketball courts and a weights room. A new library, converted from a naval drill hall and shared with the University of Kent, cost £15 million and has 370 PC study spaces, 400 open study spaces, more than 157,000 books and pamphlets, and 2.7 miles of shelves. Computer equipment and the latest software are available on an open access basis, so you can log in and connect to the resources you need.

There's a friendly traditional pub-style bar, **Coopers**, with adjacent nightclub, **Purple** - DJs and regular ents. Medway students get dual membership of Greenwich SU and the Universities at Medway Students' Association - Kent and Canterbury Christ Church universities (see entries).

Over all the campuses, student balls are best: Fresher's Ball, Football Dinner and Dance, Christmas Dizzy, Valentine's Ball, and the biggest, the May, or Summer, Ball. The location changes each year. Rag Week tends to precede it, in the nick of time bringing the student body together in slave auctions and fancy dress parades to raise money for charity.

There's a range of societies on offer, many indicative of the diverse student body: Afro-Caribbean, Chinese, Cypriot, Hellenic, Malaysian, Mauritian, Nigerian, to name but a few.

ACADEMIA & JOBS

Greenwich is a university of vocational courses, led in their design by the needs of the workplace.

The schools, or faculties, are Architecture & Construction; Business; Chemical & Life Sciences; Computing & Mathematical Sciences; Education & Training; Engineering; Health; Humanities; NRI (Earth & Environmental Sciences); Social Sciences & Law (Social Science subjects).

You may be interested to know that at the sharp end of things, far away from the student bar, their work on controlling the tsetse fly in Africa was just named as one of the ten most important discoveries made in a UK university over the last ten years.

Meanwhile, Nursing, Pharmacy, Food Science, Engineering, Architec-ture, Construction, Business, and History were all found to be world-class in the nalast national research assessment exercise. These are areas where the teaching is drawing on a deep

WHAT IT'S REALLY LIKE	
UNIVERSITY:	
Social Life	★
Societies	★
Studebt Union	★
Campus scene	**Ents-focused, disparate**
Politics	**Interest low**
Sport	**Small interest**
National team position	**110th**
Sport facilities	★
Arts opportunities	**Interest low**
Student magazine	**Sarky Cutt**
Nightclubs	**Dome, Purple**
Bars	**Bar Latitude, Coopers, Sports Bar**
Union ents	**Good club nights & comedy**
Union societies	**19**
Most popular society	**Gaelic**
Parking	**Greenwich none; Avery/Medway permits**
CITY:	
Entertainment	★★★★★
City scene	**Go to London**
Town/gown relations	**Average-good**
Risk of violence	**Avery Hill worst**
Cost of living	**Invariably average**
Student concessions	**Locally not much**
Survival + 2 nights out	**£80-£100 pw**
Part-time work campus/town	**Good/Average**

ACCOMMODATION	
Student rating	★
Guarantee to freshers	**100%**
Style	**Flats**
Security guard	**Most**
Shared rooms	**None**
Internet access	**All**
Self-catered	**All**
En suite	**Most**
Approx price range pw	**£87-£167**
City rent pw	**£65-£120**

provision then accounts for 10% of employment, principally again in retail, and of course software consultancy and supply. But it is health and social work that dominate the figures, the province of both Avery Hill and Medway: Biomedical Science, numerous Health degrees, Medical Sciences, Nursing, Midwifery, Osteopathy, Paramedic Science, Pharmaceutical Science, Social Work, Counselling, and so on.

Environmental health is another popular employment destination, engineered by such ast Environmental Sciences, Human Nutrition and a BSc in Public Health, which may be extended to include industrial placement.

Disabled and dyslexic students benefit from a dedicated Resource Centre here at Greenwich.

SPORT Most sporting life goes on at Avery Hill (see Campus entry above). Football, rugby, hockey, netball, American football, basketball, cricket, and tennis are played at inter-university and inter-southeast club standard, and the boat club trains to a very high standard.

PILLOW TALK
Greenwich accommodation is 10-15 minutes walk from campus: new Cutty Sark and plush McMillan Student Village en-suite residences. Binnie Court and Devonport House are nice and cheaper. Avery Hill village, set in parkland, 20 mins walk from Eltham High Street has flats and maisonettes, some en suite. Medway halls are shared en-suite flats. Parking: OK for loading/unloading on arrival at Greenwich halls; none at Avery Hill; there are limited permits at Medway.

GETTING THERE
☞ By road from M25, join A2 (J2) and follow signs to Woolwich Ferry, thence Greenwich.
☞ By rail to main Greenwich site: trains to Greenwich or Maze Hill overland stations, or Docklands Light Railway from Bank.
☞ By coach: Bristol, 2:20; Birmingham, 2:40; Newcastle, 6:05; Manchester, 4:35.

well of knowledge. Notably, 30% of research work in Mechanical and Manufacturing Engineering was world-class and 40% of international significance. The figures were 10% and 40% respectively for Architecture and Construction. Both are identifying areas of the curriculum. The Medway School of Engineering offers a wide range of programmes that includes mechanical, manufacturing, electrical and electronic, computer and communications engineering and engineering design. The Avery Hill schools of Architecture and Construction account for 9% of graduate employment. Planning permission is currently being sought to build a new School of Architecture & Construction, together with a Library, at Stockwell Street in the heart of Greenwich town centre.

Seventy-four per cent of students have graduate level employment within six months of leaving. For Greenwich Business graduates optimum employment areas are retail, banking, personnel, accounting and insurance, with dedicated degrees for some of these. Next comes Education, mainly primary school teaching. The Computer Science

HERIOT-WATT UNIVERSITY

Heriot-Watt University
Riccarton Campus
Edinburgh EH14 4AS

TEL 0131 451 3451
FAX 0131 451 3630
EMAIL admissions@hw.ac.uk
WEB www.hw.ac.uk

Heriot-Watt Students' Association
Riccarton Campus
Edinburgh EH14 4AS

TEL 0131 451 5333
FAX 0131 451 5344
EMAIL admissions@hw.ac.uk
WEB www.hwusa.org

VIRGIN VIEW

*B*ased in Edinburgh, Heriot-Watt is a research-led, technological university, high on academic, industrial and business collaboration; many of its courses are accredited by professional bodies, and relevant to employers' needs.

It is small but achieves big results, a university strong on teaching, with lecturers praised for their help and interest in their students and hot on research - they moved up nine places in the last national research assessment. In-depth strength resides in Mathematics, Petroleum Engineering, Physics, Computer Science, Business & Management, the Built Environment, and Art & Design (notably in Fashion).

There is also a very good social life here, and there's a decent Student Union, with a reputation for environmental campaigning.

At the end of it all, 74% of graduates find real graduate jobs within six months of leaving, and no suprise that some 87% of them are satisfied with the whole deal, although against the run of things, this year some 9% failed to finish.

CAMPUS

The main campus at Riccarton, 6.5 miles southwest of Edinburgh city centre, is an attractive 380-acre campus in a huddle with a number of independent research companies. Smart modern buildings are set in pleasant grounds, with trees, playing fields, an attractive artificial loch, squirrels, ducks and swans.

'The sense of seclusion at leafy Riccarton campus definitely aids study,' writes Richard Biggs, 'and has given rise to a community spirit that doesn't exist at inner city universities. However, the LRT buses that run to and from campus tend to be erratic - not fun in winter.'

UNIVERSITY/STUDENT PROFILE	
University since	**1966**
Situation/style	**City campus**
Student population	**10430**
Undergraduates	**5785**
Mature	**44%**
International	**33%**
Male/female ratio	**64:36**
Equality of opportunity:	
state school intake	**90%**
social class 4-7 intake	**30%**
drop-out rate	**9%**

Since the merger with The Scottish College of Textiles, Heriot-Watt has also had a Scottish Borders campus. Situated in a small town in the Scottish Borders called Galashiels, Gala, as the campus is known), is only 33 miles/90 minutes by bus from Edinburgh, but unfortunately (if you are in a hurry) some two and a half hours by train, which detours via Berwick-upon-Tweed.

Further, the International Centre for Island Technology, part of the Institute of Petroleum Engineering, sustains a third campus, in Stromness, Orkney. There is also a campus in Dubai.

FEES, BURSARIES

Fees for English, Welsh and Northern Irish areapprox. £1,820 p.a., but the uni offers a number of scholarships. See www.scholarships.hw.ac.uk/. There are

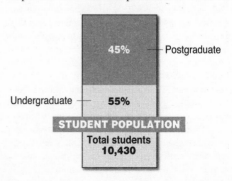

45% — Postgraduate

Undergraduate — 55%

STUDENT POPULATION
**Total students
10,430**

also sports scholarships, funded jointly by the university, the Alumni Fund, the Royal & Ancient Golf Club of St Andrews, and the Scottish Physical Recreation Fund. See www.hw.ac.uk/sports/sports-scholarships.htm.

STUDENT PROFILE

'Though entry requirements can now be fairly steep, they throw a wide net for applicants, and claim a dogged policy of targeting 'pupils from schools where applications to university are low, students who have no family background or cultural experience of higher education and mature students with no formal qualifications who maybe want a second chance to enter university via an access course.'

They are, they say, committed to equal opportunities for all and go out of their way to pull in a diverse mix of student.

In the past they have been named as one of the elite universities who show that open access can be made to work by focusing on ability and potential, rather than on points scores at Scottish Highers or A level.

However, the fact remains that on average successful applicants to study at Heriot Watt actually attain 350 points, and while state school intake runs at 90%, intake from lower socio-economic groups (30%), and low-participation neighbourhoods (5%) is not that special, though either equal to or surpassing Heriot's Government benchmarks.

International students meanwhile make up 33% of the student body, which is large, and a new International Study Centre opened in 2008 to help prepare these undergraduates.

Recruitment overseas is definitely a focus here, and there are many foreign exchange students, the study of languages and a year abroad being a special feature of many of Heriot's courses.

ACADEMIA & JOBS

The schools are Engineering and Physical Sciences; Life Sciences; Built Environment; Mathematical & Computer Sciences; Management & Languages; and Textiles & Design.

Students rate the teaching highest (85% or more approval of the class) in Biology & related sciences, Building, Business, Chemical Engineering (100%), Chemistry, Civil Engineering, Economics (100%), Finance & Accounting, Languages, Law, Management, Maths, Mechanical, Production & Manufacturing Engineering, Linguistics, Physical Science, Psychology, Social Studies (100%).

Planning - Urban, Rural & Regional finds least of the class enthusiastic (54%), but nevertheless accounts for 8% of graduate employment, a good deal less than at one time. The degree is

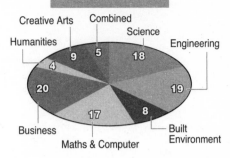

SUBJECT AREAS (%)

Creative Arts — 9
Combined — 5
Science — 18
Engineering — 19
Humanities — 4
Business — 20
Maths & Computer — 17
Built Environment — 8

Architectural Engineering, which may be taken as BEng or BSc, and there's Structural Engineering & Architectural Design (BEng and MEng).

Engineering is the second strongest graduate employment area, and a healthier 13% of these find work in architectural and engineering activities. There are also Engineering/Technology degrees that take a good number into gas and oil extraction.

Meanwhile, a quarter of all success Heriot job-hunters come off a Business course and find work in banks, accountancy, management, and personnel. You'll find degrees dedicated to these. They also find their way from Business into the Civil Service, who also smile on Heriot's Language graduates, though they like their Computer, Planning & Housing, and Maths graduates too.

But more of Heriot's mathematicians find jobs in insurance and pension funding than anything else, also accounting, financial consultancy, security broking and fund management. There are dedi-

TEACHING SURVEY AT A GLANCE	
Avg. UCAS points accepted	**350**
Acceptance rate	**15%**
Overall satisfaction rate	**87%**
Helpful/interested staff	★★★
Small tuition groups	★★★
Students into graduate jobs	**74%**

Teaching most popular with undergraduates:
Biology & related sciences, Building, Business, Chemical Engineering (100%), Chemistry, Civil Engineering, Economics (100%), Finance & Accounting, Languages, Law, Management, Maths, Mechanical, Production & Manufacturing Engineering, Linguistics, Physical Science, Psychology, Social Studies (100%).

Teaching least popular with undergraduates:
Planning - Urban, Rural & Regional (54%).

RESEARCH EXCELLENCE

% of Heriot-Watt's research that is
4* (World-class) or 3* (Internationally rated):

	4*	3*
Food Science	5%	35%
Environmental Sciences	0%	25%
Chemistry	10%	40%
Physics	15%	40%
Pure Mathematics	25%	45%
Applied Mathematics	15%	50%
Statistics	10%	35%
Computer Science	15%	45%
General Engineering	10%	45%
General Eng./Petroleum	20%	45%
Chemical Engineering	10%	35%
Civil Engineering	5%	50%
Architecture & Building	10%	50%
Planning	20%	30%
Business/Management	10%	35%
Psychology	0%	5%
Sports Studies	10%	15%
European Studies	10%	20%
Art and Design	15%	35%

cated degrees in Actuarial Science, and other niches in other disciplines, for example in brewing and distilling (there's a dedicated BSc), in photonics, and in translating and interpreting - the popular Heriot linguists again.

'Modern languages are an outstanding strength,' one sixthform adviser confirmed, and certainly their employment figures for translators and interpreters are good. 'You can walk straight out of Heriot-Watt into a job in the EC.' Also, for foreign students, the School of Management and Languages now offers a range of language support classes (MA Foreign Languages and TESOL). Equally, there is also a big foreign exchange programme - all students can choose to study abroad at some point during their course.

> *'There is a community spirit that doesn't exist at inner city universities. Modern languages are an outstanding strength. You can walk straight into a job in the EC.'*

Creative Arts account for 15% of graduate output now, 40% of whom go into fashion retail or design. Heriot graduates of dedicated degrees in Fashion, Textiles and related areas, including Management, Marketing and Promotion are much in demand.

The uni merged with the Scottish College of Textiles in 1999. There's collaboration with industry and business in the design of the courses. They offer the employment-oriented BA Fashion Design for Industry and BSc Clothing Design & Manufacture or Textiles & Fashion Design Management.

It has been in partnership with George Davies of 'Next', 'George at Asda' and the 'per una' collection for Marks & Spencer. They have the George Davies Centre for Retail Excellence, and run in-company projects and master classes with other leading retailers. The first postgrad. course in International Fashion Marketing began here five years ago.

Heriot's strength is in the close relationship it has with industry, business and national support networks. In cahoots with the Scottish Institute for Enterprise they deliver an enterprise-training programme, bringing entrepreneurial skills to science and engineering from the first year of studies.

SOCIAL SCENE

STUDENTS' ASSOCIATION The Union on Edinburgh campus is a lively, campaigning body. In fact it won 'NUS Campaign of the Year' at the national student awards in 2008/9, its constant refrain an environmental one, again applauded in 2009 when it was presented with a Bronze award at the Sound Environmental Impact Awards.

The Union has three main venues: **Geordies** (bar) - the Heriot-Watt local with hustlers pool area: 3 pool tables and arcades, big screen and plasma screens, and home to the ever-popular and entertaining Monday night pub quiz. Then there's **Liberty's**, a café-bar with free wireless internet access, and Zero° nightclub (capacity 450). Its stage is also used for live music and *Comedy Club*.

Friday is *JAM* in **Zero°**: pop, chart, cheese and legendary student anthems; also *Night Train* in Liberty's: diverse range of 'quality music'. Every other Tuesday is *Comedy Club*: 'Well-established laughter session offering a changing line-up of some of the best local comics around. A bargain at only £3,' says The List. Saturday is *Lounge* in Liberty's - 'chillout to the sound of DJ's playing an eclectic mix of cool tunes" says the Student Association. 'Crayons to play with too!' Thursday in Zero° brings live music and, 'Often attracts Scotland's hottest band talent.' - *The List*. Thursday is *Traffic*, a crossroads of indie and alternative tunes. Every other Sunday in Zero°, alternating with *Your Turn* (open mic night) in Liberty's is *Have you got the S-Factor?*

See also Student Edinburgh.

Down at Gala, they are also getting some sort of scene together. There are newish Union premises,

WHAT IT'S REALLY LIKE

UNIVERSITY:

Social Life	★★★
Societies	★★★
Student Union services	★★★
Politics	**Environment Student debt**
Sport	**30 clubs, hockey strong**
National team position	**50th**
Sport facilities	★★★★
Arts opportunities	**Music, film good; dance, art average, drama poor**
Student newspaper	**Watts On**
Nightclub	**Zero°**
Bars	**Geordies, Liberty's**
Union ents	**JAM (cheese) heads big ents**
Union Societies	**30**
Most popular societies	**Poker Society**
Parking	**Poor**

CITY:

Entertainment	★★★★★
Scene	**Seething**
Town/gown relations	**Good**
Risk of violence	**Low**
Cost of living	**High**
Student concessions	**Excellent**
Survival + 2 nights out	**£60-£85 pw**
Part-time work campus/city	**Excellent**

ACCOMMODATION

Student rating	★★
Guarantee to freshers	**100%**
Style	**Halls, flats**
Security guard	**None; campus patrols**
Shared rooms	**None**
Internet access	**Edinburgh campus only**
Self-catered	**Most halls, all flats**
En suite	**Most halls, no flats**
Approx price range pw	**£64-£100**
City rent pw	**£60-£85**

large swimming pool, ice rink and the Meadowbank Stadium. Half the city is made of parks and open spaces .

PILLOW TALK

In Edinburgh it's catered and self-catered study bedrooms and self-catered flats. Midlothian, Linlithglow, Pentland House are the catered halls. You get a weekly allowance of more than £50 to spend at campus food outlets. Rents £64.13-£75.02 per week. Self-catered is available at Leonard Horner Hall: 4-6 rooms per kitchen. Rent £82.18 p.w. En-suite self-catered is offered at Robert Bryson, George Burnett, Robin Smith and Lord Home halls, again 4-6 rooms per kitchen. Rent £98.98 p.w. Finally, there are self-catered flats in a house called Ettrick: 4-5 bedrooms, £69.12-£82.12 p.w. Each Hall of Residence has a warden to help students settle in and sort out any problems. There are patrols by Security Patrol Officers at night. These Officers can be called by students.

At Scottish Borders there are self-catered rooms and flats in halls on campus, and flats in the town centre. Rents per week: £76.20-£100.

GETTING THERE
☛ By road: A71 or A70; if the latter, turn off at Currie on to Riccarton Mains Road.
☛ By rail: London King's Cross, 4:30; Glasgow Central, 50 mins; Newcastle, 1:30.
☛ By air: nearby Edinburgh Airport for inland and international flights.
☛ By coach: Glasgow, 1:10; London, 9:10; Birmingham, 8:10; Newcastle, 3:10.
☛ To Gala, A7 south from Edinburgh.

a full ents programme, a musician-in-residence and lashings of sponsorship from North Sea oil, which has led to COMA - not a state of unconsciousness due to inebriation, but the name for a network of groups available for gigs.

SPORT The Edinburgh campus boasts the impressive National Squash Centre, but also has a number of large playing fields (five football, two rugby, one cricket), a floodlit training area, jogging track, three tennis courts, three sports halls, climbing wall, two multigyms, golf driving nets, weights and fitness rooms and indoor sports courts. Membership is spilt into Gold, Silver and Bronze tariffs (year, academic year and term), ranging from around £25. The Heart of Midlothian Football Academy opened recently and includes pro-quality facilities and floodlit and indoor synthetic pitches. The city of Edinburgh has many golf courses, a

UNIVERSITY OF HERTFORDSHIRE

The University of Hertfordshire
College Lane
Hatfield
Hertfordshire AL10 9AB

TEL 01707 281269
FAX 01707 286040
EMAIL a.a.bruno@herts.ac.uk
WEB www.herts.ac.uk

Hertfordshire Students' Union
College Lane
Hatfield
Hertfordshire AL10 9AB

TEL 01707 285000
FAX 01707 286150
EMAIL uhsu@herts.ac.uk
WEB uhsu.herts.co.uk

VIRGIN VIEW

*H*ertfordshire University is among the most impressive of the 1992 unis in rate of growth and learning resources. It has brilliant modern facilities, in particular for sport, home at one time or another for both Saracens from the RFU Premiership and Arsenal ladies. Yet the Student Experience is a bit disappointing. The exhaustive, national Times Higher Education *Student Experience Survey* shows deep disatisfaction in terms of social life and extra-curricular activities.

However, there's no doubt they offer a good deal academically. Students praised the helpfulness and interest of lecturers and the quality of facilities, especially the library and of course the sports facilities.

The University says of itself that it is in 'the vanguard of a new type of emerging university'. Hertfordshire is 'business-like and business-facing'. Perhaps it needs to be a bit human too.

But, meanwhile, its integrated approach to research and teaching and close contact with industry and with the capital city, strengthened by a strategically advantageous location (on the A1, minutes from the M25 and M1, and within striking distance of four airports: Luton, Stansted, Heathrow and Gatwick), got it an 81% student satisfaction for teaching and graduate employment at the Government's national student survey. And this is being done with a student population which is diverse, very much a 'new' university demography, more than 20% of them part-time.

The evidence is that Herts is working with its student base well, and interestingly, for all its business and scientific weighting, some of the most popular teaching is in Imaginative Writing. That may bode well.

UNIVERSITY PROFILE	
University since	**1992**
Situation/style	**Suburban campuses**
Student population	**25195**
Undergraduates	**19840**
Mature	**42%**
International	**18%**
Male/female ratio	**44:56**
Equality of opportunity:	
state school intake	**98%**
social class 4-7 intake	**41%**
drop-out rate	**9%**

CAMPUSES

The uni is based at Hatfield. The main site comprises the original campus and the new de Havilland Campus, half a mile away, the two made one by cycleways, footpaths and shuttle buses.

DE HAVILLAND The £120-million campus houses the Business School and schools of Education and Humanitiesre, and this year the Law school joins them from its old site in St Albans. There's a learning resources centre, a £15-million sports centre open to the public - its 3-year membership target met in the first month - an amazing 60-seater auditorium and student residences.

COLLEGE LANE At the original College Lane campus the doors were opened for the first time last year on the **Forum** - a new student venue. The Forum is a joint venture between the University of Hertfordshire and the Students' Union.

It is designed to accommodate student needs not only for a social scene, but quiet areas for study and reflection, a nursery, a convenience store, and a multi-storey car park. Central to the student experience, it will cover 8,000 square metres and include an auditorium for live gigs and club nights, a balcony bar, style bar, refurbished student bar, mini

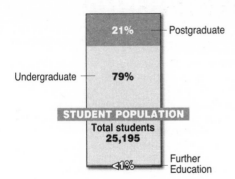

STUDENT POPULATION
Total students
25,195

- Postgraduate **21%**
- Undergraduate **79%**
- Further Education **<1%**

ACADEMIA & JOBS

They describe themselves as the UK's leading 'business-facing University', by which they mean they work closely with leaders from industry and the professions to shape every course and ensure worthwhile work placements. They have their own business support organisation called Hertfordshire Business Link, where more than 50 advisers are constantly on the phone to companies, creating opportunities for student placements and jobs.

Students say that the best taught subjects are Anatomy, Physiology & Pathology, Biology & related sciences, Economics, Electronic & Electrical Engineering, Euro Languages, History, Human Resource Management, Imaginative Writing, Initial Teacher Training, Law, Management, Maths, Medical Technology, Molecular Biology, Music, Subjects Allied to Medicine, Pharmacy, Physics & Astronomy (100% gave this the thumbs-up), and Psychology.

The subject areas most productive of jobs are Business (21%), Subjects allied to Medicine (15% - Nursing, Pharmacy, Physiotherapy, Radiography, Paramedic Science, etc.), Creative Arts & Design (again 15%). Then comes Biological Sciences (including Sport), Social Studies, Education, Computer, Engineering, Law and Languages.

Jobs galore take graduates from Aerospace Engineering into the aircraft industry and defence. Similarly, Computer Science graduates pour into software consultantcy and the like.

Art & Design is a special focus, one made keener in 2005 with the launch of a School of Film,

club, a restaurant, a coffee bar and a convenience store.

Currently among student societies are the radio station, Crush, and the *Horizon* newspaper. The most active of 17 student societies are Christian Union, Drama and Alternative Music.

TOWN There's a 9-screen **UCI** in the Galleria Centre, and a pub that offers cut-price drinks. The union make merry with a student night at **Pub2Club**, but generally the nightlife is poor. London beckons.

> *Herts places a high priority on research that is applied and used to develop leading-edge programmes for students. This integration of the research and teaching provisions is key, and carries with it the approval of industry.*

FEES, BURSARIES

UK & EU Fees, 2011-12: £3,375 p.a. There's a bursary of £1,000 for those in receipt of the full HE Maintenance Grant. In addition there are two types of Chancellor's Scholarship: the Chancellor's Entrepreneurial and Excellence Scholarship, worth £2,500 a year and the Chancellor's Gifted and Talented Scholarship, worth £2,000 a year. Science and Engineering Scholarships (worth up to £3,000 over 3-4 years) are also available on certain science and engineering degrees for achievers of 300 UCAS points. Finally, they offer 135 externally funded scholarships, sponsored by companies such as Tesco and T-Mobile. See www.herts.ac.uk/courses/fees-bursaries-scholarships/.

STUDENT PROFILE

There is a very large student body of just under 24,000, 98% of which is drawn from the state sector, and 41% from the lower socio-economic groups. Twenty-one per cent are local part-timers, 42% are mature, and they welcome over 5,200 international students from 130 different countries. There are in fact more than 99 cultures represented on campus.

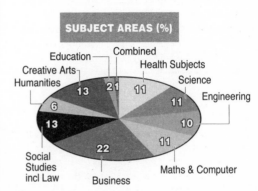

SUBJECT AREAS (%)

- Education — 21
- Combined — (Combined)
- Creative Arts / Humanities — 13
- Health Subjects — 11
- Science — 11
- Engineering — 11
- Maths & Computer — 11
- Business — 22
- Social Studies incl Law — 13
- 6
- 10

TEACHING SURVEY AT A GLANCE

Avg. UCAS points accepted	**240**
Acceptance rate	**16%**
Overall satisfaction rate	**81%**
Helpful/interested staff	★★★
Small tuition groups	★★
Students into graduate jobs	**68%**

Teaching most popular with undergraduates:
Anatomy, Physiology & Pathology, Biology &
related sciences, Economics Electronic &
Electrical Engineering, Euro Languages,
History, Human Resource Management,
Imaginative Writing, Initial Teacher Training, Law,
Management, Maths, Medical Technology,
Molecular Biology, Music, Subjects Allied to
Medicine, Pharmacy, Physics & Astronomy
(100%), Psychology.

Teaching least popular with undergraduates:
Social Work (69%), Design Studies (68%),
Mechanical Engineering,
Computer Science (67%).

Music and New Media. Two years later a £10-million Media Centre opened at College Lane, housing the latest technology for the teaching of music, animation, film, television and multi-media.

On the one hand Creative Arts at Herts means what you might expect it to mean: Fashion, Fine Art, Graphic Design, Interior & Spatial Design, Photography. On the other, it means Industrial Design, Product Design, and, uniquely, Model Design & Model Effects.

This last - Model Design & Model Effects - may be unique in the UK. You can spend up to half the second year working in industry with companies such as Artem, Asylum Models & Effects, Hothouse Models & Effects, Machine Shop Special Effects and internationally renowned companies such as Seymour Powell design consultants, the architects Foster and Partners and the Richard Rogers Partnership.' At Herts, Creative Arts is industry, the distinction between Art and Technology, Art and Science, has all but disappeared. All the visiting lecturers are professionals currently working in the Film & TV industry.

The award-winning Learning Resources Centre at College Lane and its twin at adjacent de Havilland are open 24/7. Both make use of a computer system, StudyNET, their 'Managed Learning Environment', a personalised academic workspace for students on which appears information relevant to programmes of study.

Recently opened on College Lane is an Innovation Centre to provide incubation resources to spin out new companies, and an Automotive Centre, to bring together academia and industry.

STUDENT UNION

We found a good deal less to complain about than the students in the *Times Higher* survey. I mean, Florence and the Machines for the Summer Ball is surely worth more than a 1 star rating!

Stuff goes on at **Style Bar**, **Elehouse**, the **Attic** or **Auditorium**. The latter plays host to Propaganda's famous indie nights, electro house, dubstep and nu-disc, as well as tribute bands like Antarctic Monkeys, *Flirt!* and chart and commercial dance. At the Attic you'll see the likes of teen trie Twenty Twenty or hard rock F-Alt, while at Elehouse there are theme nights, Rock 'n' Roll Bingo and Quiz Night.

Culturally Herts is no slouch either, with its annual Mayfest music and arts gathering. Music includes such as Brixton-based hip hop colllective Throwdown, folk, and classical (the de Havilland Philharmonic), drama at the Auditorium, film, dance, and comedy.

Student media includes *Universe*, a free newspaper, Union TV, and Crush Radio.

SPORT There are 17 degrees offered in Sport, and jobs in Sport account for a healthy proportion of graduate jobs. They came 48th nationally in the BUCS inter-university team league last year. Base is the big new, £15-million sports complex, a 12-court sports hall, 3 artificial turf and 4 grass pitches, squash courts, a cricket hall and an aerobics studio, an 8-lane swimming pool, indoor cricket nets,

RESEARCH EXCELLENCE

% of Hertfordshire's research that is
4* *(World-class)* or **3*** *(Internationally rated):*

	4*	3*
Nursing/Midwifery	**25%**	**30%**
Pharmacy	**5%**	**30%**
Physics	**15%**	**40%**
Computer Science	**10%**	**45%**
General Engineering	**15%**	**35%**
Business/Management	**5%**	**30%**
Social Work	**0%**	**15%**
Psychology	**5%**	**25%**
Education	**0%**	**20%**
English	**10%**	**35%**
Philosophy	**0%**	**35%**
History	**25%**	**45%**
Art & Design	**10%**	**50%**
Music	**5%**	**10%**

WHAT IT'S REALLY LIKE

UNIVERSITY:	
Social Life	★★
Societies	★★
Student Union services	★★★
Politics	Average: Fees
Sport	29 clubs
National team position	48th
Sport facilities	★★★★★
Arts opportunities	Good
Student newspaper	Universe
Student TV	Union TV
Student radio	Crush Radio
Bars	Elehouse, Style
Venues	Auditorium, Attic
Union societies	17
Parking	College Lane only
CITY:	
Entertainment	★★
Scene	London beckons
Town/gown relations	Average
Risk of violence	Low
Cost of living	High
Student concessions locally	OK
Survival + 2 nights out	£70 pw
Part-time work campus/town	Excellent/poor

ACCOMMODATION

Student rating	★★★
Guarantee to freshers	100%
Style	Halls, flats
Security guard	All
Shared rooms	Some halls
Internet access	All
Self-catered	All
En suite	Some flats
Approx price range pw	£63-£105
Town rent pw	£62-£90

PILLOW TALK

Halls are self-catering: 1,600 at the de Havilland campus (11-room, en-suite flats), all with broadband internet access and refrigerator.

There are 1,400 new rooms on the College Lane campus (flats, houses and traditional halls), the houses located in the Roberts Way student Village, which are shared between 8 people, communal bath/shower facilities, 6 single rooms in each house and 1 double room, shared kitchen/diner and internet access in all rooms.

The Student Union runs a letting agency for private lets, a professionally run, student-friendly service.

GETTING THERE

☞ **Hatfield** by road: A1(M)/J3. By rail: London King's Cross, 22 mins.
☞ By coach: London, 1:00.

and a 100-station fitness suite.

Saracens rugby club and Arsenal ladies football club use the facilities and they are punting for 2012 Olympic training status.

HEYTHROP COLLEGE, UNIVERSITY OF LONDON

Heythrop College
Kensington Square
London W8 5NI

TEL 020 7795 6600
FAX 020 7795 4200
EMAIL enquiries@heythrop.ac.uk
WEB www.heythrop.ac.uk

Heythrop College Students' Union
Kensington Square
London W8 5HQ

TEL 020 7795 6600
FAX 020 795 4200
EMAIL enquiries@heythrop.ac.uk

VIRGIN VIEW

*H*eythrop is an independent college within the University of London specialising in Theology and Philosophy and with a refreshingly evolutionary concept of higher education. For their inspiration they turn to the Swiss psychologist Jean Piaget, noted for his revolutionary work on the cognitive functions of children. Piaget wrote that 'the principal goal of education is to create people who are capable of doing new things, not simply of repeating what other generations have done... The second goal of education is to form minds which can be critical, can verify, and not accept everything they are offered.' Trawling through all that the higher educational establishments of this country can offer, such a breathtakingly simple statement seems almost unutterably bold. Their teaching is the traditional university method of tutorials and small-group seminars. They possess one of the finest collections of theological and philosophical literature anywhere to be found, their 250,000 volumes available to every one of their students without queue.

Since Easter 2009, they have their own hall of residence on site for 100 students. Otherwise, go to www.halls.london.ac.uk or www.housing.lon.ac.uk.

COLLEGE PROFILE	
College of London Uni since	**1971**
Total student population	**895**
Full-time undergraduates	**430**
- mature	**60%**
- overseas	**12%**
- male/female	**58/42**
Avg. UCAS points accepted	**340**
Acceptance rate	**34%**
Overall satisfaction rate	**77%**
Students into graduate jobs	**73%**
ACCOMMODATION:	
Availability to freshers	**100%**
Style	**Uni Lon. Halls**
Approx cost per night.	**£17.15-£60.00**
City rent p.w.	**£110**

STUDENT SCENE

'Ideally situated in the centre of Kensington, Heythrop projects an atmosphere of elegance and solemnity, but this really is the most friendly of colleges,' writes Clare Barker, 'quite impressive given the great diversity among Heythrop students. A huge number are either mature undergraduates or postgrads; then there's the diversity of religions and interests, and the proximity of **Lamda** – its drama students share one of our common rooms and make more unorthodox the already bizarre crowd milling around the corridors... And then there are the nuns. Campus is owned by nuns – and they keep rabbits. The nuns (and their rabbits) are very amiable and don't seem at all fazed at having leery students sharing their home. However, their presence leads to Heythrop having a prevailing feeling of a religious institution – strange, considering the vast number of philosophy students who are not diplomatic in the expression of their beliefs.'

GETTING THERE

☛ High Street Kensington tube station.

UNIVERSITY OF HUDDERSFIELD

University of Huddersfield
Queensgate
Huddersfield HD1 3DH

TEL 01484 422288
FAX 01484 472765
EMAIL prospectus@hud.ac.uk
WEB www.hud.ac.uk

Huddersfield Students' Union
Queensgate
Huddersfield HD1 3DH

TEL 01484 538156
FAX 01484 432333
EMAIL: students.union@hud.ac.uk
WEB www.huddersfieldstudent.com/

VIRGIN VIEW

*H*uddersfield University traces its history back to the Young Men's Mental Improvement Society, founded in 1841. It was awarded university status in 1992 after two other incarnations, first as a technical college then as a polytechnic. Today it has a city-centre campus (Queensgate), Holly Bank campus, 2 miles to the north, and Storthes Hall, 4 miles to the south-east.

Huddersfield town, just 20 miles south west of Leeds, is an unusual mix. Its roots in the Industrial Revolution are not in doubt, but it is also known far and wide for its annual poetry festival, with the Albert pub as artistic font; folk and jazz are equally present. Sometime Heritage minister Stephen Dorrell once famously remarked that Huddersfield was the Paris of the North. One can't pretend this didn't raise a few eyebrows, but he did have a point of sorts. The uni and the town are of a similar weave.

There is this traditional, industrial, people-culture, but the academic spectrum is wide and its character modern. When you hear that it has the largest Music Department of any UK university, and that in the recent research assessment exercise it was announced that 20% of the department's research is world-class and 55% of international significance, you begin to wonder what other gems are lurking.

Now, with new Drama and Media facilities, it is also developing a strong Performing Arts, Broadcast and Humanities cluster of degrees, aided by the high profile of the University's Chancellor, X-Men and Star Trek: The Next Generation star, Patrick Stewart, who drops by to give drama workshops.

In the recent National Government Student Survey, 79% of students gave their approval to the teaching and on real graduate-employment was 80% after 6 months of leaving, which is exceptional. There is heavy emphasis on work placement and future employability throughout all schools and courses. A third of the students in all subjects take sandwich courses, one of the highest proportions in Britain. Over 1,500 employers support learning on campus, and this latest Unistats ranking means that Huddersfield lies 16th out of all UK universities for getting students into real graduate-level jobs.

Open Days on main campus in 2011 will be held on 15 June, 17 September, 26 and 27 October. And already they want to play - the all-new iHud is a program that enables applicants to request a prospectus and set up a personal web page which you can update whenever you log in.

CAMPUS

Storthes Hall campus is set in 350 acres of parkland 4 miles away from the main campus and connected to it by a subsidised bus service.

'I can't remember a more depressing view,' wrote student Tim Wild, a film-maker who came up to Huddersfield from Brighton as an undergraduate, about the initial culture shock.

'Most people only have the vaguest idea where the bloody place is, so I'll attempt to clear up the confusion. Smack bang in the middle - three hours away from London by car, and about three thousand light years away in attitude. That's why this place is special - they really couldn't give a toss whether you're from Taunton or Timbuktu, as long

UNIVERSITY/STUDENT PROFILE	
University since	**1992**
Situation/style	**Town campus**
Student population	**21590**
Undergraduates	**17735**
Mature	**54%**
International	**7%**
Male/female ratio	**44:56**
Equality of opportunity:	
state school intake	**98%**
social class 4-7 intake	**44%**
drop-out rate	**13%**

as you can hold your ale and laugh at yourself.

'If it's glamour and sophistication you're after, then stay away, because you'll only spoil it for the rest of us. I won't pretend it's paradise, but that's part of the appeal, in an odd way. Because it's the middle of nowhere, there are no cliques, no elite to try and be part of. It's just cold and grey and everyone here's in it together. Like the blitz, without the Germans.'

The university has recently also opened up centres in Oldham (where Open Days will be held in 2011 on 16 February, 22 June, 22 August and 14 September) and Barnsley (17 February, 16 June, 23 August, 19 October) to encourage participation in Higher Education in both towns.

FEES, BURSARIES

UK & EU Fees, 2011-12: £3,375. There's £500 a year for eligible students with a household income of less than £25,000.

STUDENT PROFILE

Huddersfield is deeply committed to widening participation in Higher Education. Around a third of students are part-timers and 54% mature. Intake from classes and neighbourhoods not traditionally represented at university are 44% and 16% respectively. As Tim Wild suggests above, social climbers

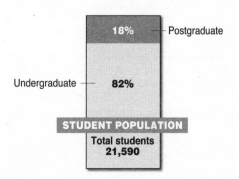

18% — Postgraduate

Undergraduate — 82%

STUDENT POPULATION

Total students 21,590

TEACHING SURVEY AT A GLANCE

Avg. UCAS points accepted	**250**
Acceptance rate	**21%**
Overall satisfaction rate	**79%**
Helpful/interested staff	★★★★
Small tuition groups	★★★
Students into graduate jobs	**80%**

Teaching most popular with undergraduates:
Education, Anatomy, Physiology & Pathology (100%), Biology & related Sciences, Chemistry, Complementary Medicine, Drama, Finance, History, Initial Teacher Training, Marketing, Medical Science & Pharmacy (100%), Nursing, Physical Science, Psychology, Tourism, Transport.

Teaching least popular with undergraduates:
Journalism, Sports Science (58%), Mechanically-based Engineering, Mechanical, Production & Manufacturing Engineering (59%).

need not apply.

ACADEMIA & JOBS

Huddersfield offers a wide range of innovative courses, from music production to fashion design and from engineering to computer games design. Many place a strong emphasis on placement years.

> *Huddersfield University traces its history back to the Young Men's Mental Improvement Society, founded in 1841. Now its Chancellor is X-Men and Star Trek film star Patrick Stewart, who drops by to give drama workshops.*

The academic schools are Human and Health Sciences, Applied Sciences (Transport & Logistics, Chemical and Biological Sciences, Geographical and Environmental Sciences), Computing and Maths, Design Technology (Textiles, Architecture), Education, Engineering, Business, Music and Humanities.

Generally, the lecturers are extremely helpful and interested in their students, and tuition groups are well sized for the purpose. The subjects that provide most graduate employment are the Creative Arts, Business, subjects allied to Medicine, Biological Sciences, then Engineering, Education, Computer, and Social Studies.

A new £17 million Business School is now open and over the next 18 months the university plans to invest some £58 million in facilities.

There is a £14-million 'flagship' Creative Arts building at the entrance to the main campus, home to students studying music and music technology, fashion, creative imaging, multimedia, and busi-ness design awareness.

It is seldom that the Creative Arts cause such a storm - the faculty accounts for 23% of all jobs.

Behind it are degrees like Architecture and Interior Design (a 4 to 5-year BA/BSC), the foundation for 6 more in a similar vein, and Product Design, Transport Design, Digital Arts Practice, Digital Film and Visual Effect, and 5 Music Technology degrees (an area that got full marks at inspection), and of course the Fashion and Textiles courses: Fashion & Textile Buying/Managing/Retailing, 6 Fashion Design degrees, and Fashion Media & Promotion.

Students wanting to become fashion, clothing and textile designers should look no further. As befits a uni in the heart of the old woollen/textile industry, this is where it's at. There's high energy and superb employment results in this niche area at Huddersfield.

Graduate nurses and teachers enjoy 100% graduate employment, which is good but not so surprising. What is, is that of the University's core subject areas 19 are in the upper half of graduate employment statistics nationally.

In Business, the Huddersfield Business Generator has created over 80 start-up businesses, and now a BA in Enterprise Development is launched with input from TV 'Dragon'Theo Paphitis, offering practical help and advice in setting up a business. They tell us that Business Masters graduates from Huddersfield earn at least £8,000 p.a. more than their peers at other institutions, with an average starting salary of over £38,000.

They are among the giants for the catering

SUBJECT AREAS (%)

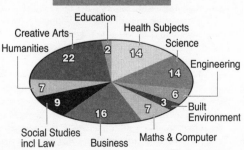

Creative Arts, Humanities — 22
Education — 2
Health Subjects — 14
Science
Engineering — 14
Built Environment — 6
Maths & Computer — 3
— 7
Business — 16
Social Studies incl Law — 9
7

RESEARCH EXCELLENCE

% of Huddersfield's research that is
4* *(World-class)* or **3*** *(Internationally rated):*

	4*	3*
Chemistry	0%	25%
Computer Science	5%	20%
General Engineering	5%	30%
Accounting/Finance	0%	30%
Politics	0%	0%
Social Work	10%	35%
Sociology	0%	25%
Education	5%	10%
English	5%	15%
History	5%	40%
Media Studies	0%	0%
Music	20%	55%

industry with dedicated degrees in Hospitality Management mixed to your taste with Tourism & Leisure.

Transport and Logistics is perhaps the best-kept niche-secret of all. On the BA in Enterprise Development you are mentored to start your own business as part of the course.

Heavy emphasis on work placement throughout all schools and courses gives Huddersfield 16th place out of all UK universities for graduates into graduate-level jobs.

Finally, they are commercial & business law specialists.

SOCIAL SCENE

STUDENTS' UNION There is a new £4-million Student Union building, the current one having been converted to studio space for drama and media. There are both alcoholic and non-alcoholic social areas, space for bands performing and administrative areas for student societies.

The **Venue** is the multi purpose bar, which plays host to a variety of events including club and band nights. UHSU has two regularly scheduled club nights: Friday night is *Grrrr*, an indie, rock and metal night; Saturday night plays host to *Quids In*, with drinks offers and a 'party' DJ playing disco, pop and some dance music. There are also one-off DJ events, like recently Hed Kandi played.

Student media has the newspaper *Huddersfield Student*, Ultra FM student radio. Generally students are pretty apathetic, however, and rate their union, their social life and the extra-curricular opportunities low. The SU occasionally attempts to get the student body into a more political frame of mind, but politics rarely run beyond campus concerns. They also had a *Give It A Go* programme to gal-

vanise more interest in societies. Islamic Soc is one of a few that zing.

SPORT Facilities are not extensive. There's a sports hall on campus, with a newish fitness centre and playing areas elsewhere, which provide for football, rugby (league and union), hockey, cricket and tennis. There is also a new Astroturf pitch and two new top-quality soccer pitches. Students have a discount at an Olympic standard sports centre with swimming pool in town. Rugby League players enjoy a sponsorship arrangement with Huddersfield Giants

PILLOW TALK

The uni no longer owns any accommodation, but recommends as its preferred and approved accommodation, the Storthes Hall Park Student Village and Ashenhurst Houses. These are privately-owned and operated by Ubrique Investments Limited trading as 'digs'. See www.campusdigs.com for further information.

Other hall-type accommodation and private shared houses are available around the town with rents from around £70 per week. City rents range between £40 and £90.

WHAT IT'S REALLY LIKE

UNIVERSITY:	
Social Life	★★★
Societies	★
Student Union services	★★★
Politics	**Interest low**
Sport	**Regional force**
National sporting position	**114th**
Sport facilities	★
Arts opportunities	**Music, film; art, drama**
Student newspaper	**Huddersfield Student**
Student radio	**Ultra FM**
Nightclub & bar	**Venue**
Union ents	**2 club nights and DJ events**
Union societies	**38**
Parking	**Non-existent**
TOWN:	
Entertainment	★★★
Scene	**Pubs, music, poetry, drama**
Town/gown relations	**Good**
Risk of violence	**Low**
Cost of living	**Average**
Student concessions	**Good**
Survival + 2 nights out	**£50 pw**
Part-time work campus/town	**Good**

ACCOMMODATION

Student rating	★★
Guarantee to freshers	**None**
Style	**Halls/flats**
Security guard	**24 Hour**
Shared rooms	**Some**
Internet access	**All**
Self-catered	**All**
En suite	**All**
Approx price range pw	**£69-£94**
City rent pw	**£40-£90**

Limited parking, with permit, is available at all halls of residence. Limited parking on campus for students with disabilities.

GETTING THERE
☞ By road: M62/J24, M1/J38-40.
☞ By rail: London via Wakefield, 3:30; Liverpool Lime Street, 1:45
☞ By air: Leeds/Bradford, Manchester Airports.
☞ By coach: London, 5:00; Leeds, 1:10.

UNIVERSITY OF HULL

The University of Hull
Cottingham Road
Kingston upon Hull HU6 7RX

TEL 0870 126 2000 (prospectus)
    01482 466100 (admissions)
FAX 01482 442290
EMAIL admissions@hull.ac.uk
WEB www.hull.ac.uk

Hull University Union
University House
Cottingham Road
Hull HU6 7RX

TEL 01482 445361
FAX 01482 466280
EMAIL [initial.name]t@hull.ac.uk
WEB www.hullstudent.com

VIRGIN VIEW

*H*ull city's most famous literary son, the late poet and librarian Philip Larkin, described the city of Kingston upon Hull as 'in the world, yet sufficiently on the edge of it to have a different resonance.'

For centuries it was cut off from the rest of the country to the south by the Humber, to the north by the glorious, wide open Yorkshire Wolds (now home to David Hockney), and to the west by a large expanse of nothing. Then all the way from Liverpool on the opposite coast came the M62, meeting on its way the A1(M)), and suddenly Hull became part of the rest of the world, though as student Adam Ford told us, 'You'd be surprised at the number of people in Liverpool who still think that the M62 stops in Leeds.'

The essence of Hull is that it is distinct, not just because it has its own telephone system and white phone boxes, 'It is distinct culturally,' a sixthform careers master said to me in hushed tones. He teaches just an hour away and still he can't find his way into it; he sends pupils to Newcastle (two hours to the north), to York (an

UNIVERSITY/STUDENT PROFILE

University since	**1954**
Situation/style	**Campus**
Student population	**22370**
Undergraduates	**19045**
Mature	**49%**
International	**14%**
Male/female ratio	**43:57**
Equality of opportunity:	
state school intake	**95%**
social class 4-7 intake	**36%**
drop-out rate	**8%**

hour to the west), to Sunderland, to Teesside, but rarely, if ever apparently, to Hull.

The point, then, is that in its insularity, Hull has developed this 'unique resonance'. For the same reason, it is a cheap place to live, more than 2% below the national average: you can buy a three-bedroom house there for what it costs to send a child to public school for two years; parents do and sell it when their darling leaves. But perhaps more important than all this is that academically the University of Hull is very strong, with high scores in teaching assessments, the Queen's Anniversary Prize for

Social Work and Social Policy, a first class reputation for arts & social sciences - politics and languages especially - for health, for science and for business. The joint Hull York medical school is the jewel in the crown.

Finally, the campus is a friendly and creative place to be, and there's a great Students' Union - in the Times Higher *Student Survey its Union came 7th best in the country this year. Drop-outs are 8%, which given the Uni's generous access policy, is a triumph.*

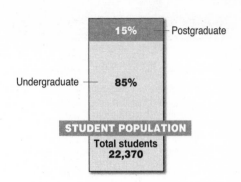

Postgraduate **15%**

Undergraduate **85%**

STUDENT POPULATION

Total students 22,370

CAMPUS

'The university is situated on Cottingham Road, about half an hour's walk, or a fifteen minute bus ride, from the city centre,' writes Albertina Lloyd. 'Cottingham Road connects Beverly Road and Newland Avenue, and you will come to know these three roads very well - Newland Avenue for shops (one claimed to sell "everything but the girl" and gave the band their name) and cafés, Cottingham Road for takeaways and Beverly Road for pubs. So, all that a student needs is situated within a short distance of the campus itself.'

'Hull prides itself on being one of the friendliest campuses in the country,' notes Danny Blackburn. 'It is a genuinely warm and welcoming environment, in which everyone feels as if they belong. The bars, corridors and lecture theatres all emanate a tremendous feeling of one-ness; it is apparent from day one.'

Now, Hull has expanded into the old and neighbouring Lincoln & Humberside Uni campus, locating Health Education there and the new Hull-York Medical School.

There is, too, Hull's Scarborough Campus, 40 miles north up the coast, which is known for Drama, and is indeed the seat of the National Student Drama Festival (NSDF), its patron Sir Alan Ayckbourn, whose plays are always premiered in the town's Stephen Joseph Theatre.

FEES, BURSARIES

UK & EU Fees, 2010-11: £3,375 p.a. If in receipt of HE Maintenance grant there's a bursary on a sliding scale. For Sir Brynmor Jones/Ferens Scholarships for Academic Excellence, see www.hull. ac.uk/money.

STUDENT PROFILE

Writes Jez Horsell: 'The University of Hull near the village of Cottingham is full of students who are not fabulously wealthy or of Einstein intelligence, but who combine with a wide variety of students from a mix of social and economic backgrounds to create a down to earth set with a work-hard-play-

hard attitude. Whether you are from the North or the South there is a place for you at Hull University.'

The uni has always been seen as one of the 'access elite', in that it enjoys a pukka academic reputation, but has been able to bring in a number of undergrads from poorer areas/classes.

Currently 32% fall into this category, and 18% come from families new to the whole idea of going to university. Hull developed its policy by making conditional offers to 16-year-olds and running clubs for 11 and 12-year-olds.

ACADEMIA & JOBS

Eighty five per cent or more students rate the teaching at Hull in Accounting, American & Australasian Studies, Biology & related sciences, Business, Chemistry, Computer Science, Drama, Economics, Engineering & Technology, English Studies, Languages, Finance, French Studies (100%), History, Archaeology, Human & Social Geography, Iberian Studies, Imaginative Writing, Law, Management, Marketing, Mechanical, Production & Manufacturing Engineering, Mechanically-based Eng., Molecular Biology, Music, Performing Arts, Physical Geography, Philosophy, Physical Science, Physics & Astronomy, Politics, Psychology, Sociology, Sports

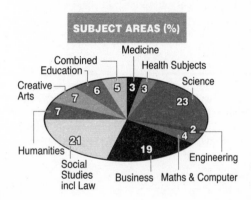

SUBJECT AREAS (%)

Medicine

Combined Education

Creative Arts

Health Subjects

Science

6 5 3 3

7

23

7

2

4

21

19

Humanities

Social Studies incl Law

Business

Maths & Computer

Engineering

TEACHING SURVEY AT A GLANCE

Avg. UCAS points accepted **280**
Acceptance rate **26%**
Overall satisfaction rate **87%**
Helpful/interested staff ★★★★
Small tuition groups ★★★
Students into graduate jobs **70%**

Teaching most popular with undergraduates:
Accounting, American & Australasian Studies,
Biology & related sciences, Business, Chemistry,
Computer Science, Drama, Economics,
Engineering & Technology, English Studies,
Languages, Finance, French Studies (100%),
History, Archaeology, Human & Social Geography,
Iberian Studies, Imaginative Writing, Law,
Management, Marketing, Mechanical, Production
& Manufacturing Engineering, Mechanically-based
Eng., Molecular Biology, Music, Performing Arts,
Physical Geography, Philosophy, Physical
Science, Physics & Astronomy, Politics,
Psychology, Sociology, Sports Science,
Medicine and subjects allied to it.

Teaching least popular with undergraduates:
Teacher Training (67%).

and gauge which lecturers are the best and switch to those modules. The library has tonnes of resources for every course and there is the Student Advice Service in the library to help you on anything from essay structure to presentation giving.'

The Politics Department is well known for its Westminster-Hull Internship Programme established by Professor the Lord Norton of Louth, who teaches at Hull, whereby students have the unique opportunity to work on a placement with high-profile MPs. As a result, a high number of Hull graduates are working in Westminster.

The recent success in the research assessment of English reminds one of the distinguished array of poets that the University has either educated or employed, men such as Philip Larkin, Andrew Motion and Roger McGough. Kinship between English and Drama draws us to another great strength of the curriculum. There are currently five Theatre degrees and eleven Drama degrees at Hull. Playwright Alan Plater opened the Anthony Minghella Drama Studio on campus in memory of the former Hull student and lecturer who went on to become an acclaimed film director.

Small surprise then that Hull students win so many awards regularly at the National Student Drama Festival - 6 in 2010.

Business makes a notably large contribution to graduate jobs, particularly in accountancy and the hotel and restaurant industry. There are numerous dedicated degrees in both.

Biological Sciences makes almost as big an impact, with jobs in hospitals for students of such as Human Biology and Biology with Molecular Sciences, and other Biology degrees taking their students into secondary education in number, while degrees in Sport, Psychology and Social Work, play their part in creating jobs in the community. 'Social Work, community and counselling activities' are in fact the third largest employment category for Hull graduates.

Science, Medicine and subjects allied to it.

The results of the nationwide assessment of the research provision across all our universities suggests in Hull's case that there's an in-depth knowledge bank to be drawn on in fifteen subjects, in particular health subjects like Biomedical Science, Nursing, and Operation Department Practice,

> *'One of the friendliest campuses in the country. All my lecturers operate an open door policy, and are never too busy to help out. Many of them use the all-important currency of humour in lectures.'*

20% of which were adjudged 4 star, world-class. Geography & Environmental Studies, History, and Drama were also up there, and Politics, Social Work, and English too. Substantial amounts of the research in these subjects (between 25% and 40%) were also assessed as internationally significant.

Writes Jez: 'I study history at Hull and it was a great choice. Although a couple of the modules are a bit dry and lack lustre the rest are well taught. The new Ebridge system has been brought in for the whole of the University and makes all the material for your course available online to print out and this has been invaluable. The standard of lecturer varies as they all have their own methods of teaching, some embracing technology whilst others have not. My advice is speak to some of the second years

The degree in Medicine at the Hull York Medical School is a 5-year BMBS (Bachelor of Medicine, Bachelor of Surgery). You may be based at either Hull or York Uni campuses (it's a dual effort, both follow the same curriculum). Hull has a decade's experience in Medicine through its Postgrad. Medical School, while York's Biosciences and Health departments have long been top rated for teaching and research. Small-group clinical contact from Year 1. Equal emphasis on physical, psy-

RESEARCH EXCELLENCE

% of Hull's research that is
4* *(World-class)* or 3* *(Internationally rated):*

	4*	3*
Health Professions	20%	40%
Biological Sciences	5%	10%
Chemistry	5%	45%
General Engineering	0%	40%
Geography	15%	40%
Business/Management	5%	40%
Law	5%	40%
Politics	10%	25%
Social Work	10%	30%
Psychology	5%	30%
Education	5%	20%
Sports Studies	0%	10%
English	10%	45%
Philosophy	5%	30%
History	15%	50%
Performing Arts	15%	30%
Music	5%	35%

chological and social aspects. A low student-teacher ratio promised. You will need AABb at A-level (to include A Level Biology at grade A, and also A Level Chemistry - may tie the second grade A to Chemistry - applicants should check the website). They do not accept General Studies at A2 or AS or Critical Thinking at A-Level. You will need to sit for UKCAT. Caring experience and interpersonal skills will be a significant separator.

Education is another big subject here, though Initial Teacher Training got a poor 67% OK from the class. Primary school teachers account for 65% of graduate jobs in Hull's Education provision.

Generally the teaching is good. 'All of my lecturers operate an open door policy, and are never too busy to help you out,' writes Joe Whinam. 'Many use the all-important currency of humour in lectures. **The Brynmor Jones Library** is absolutely huge, and I have never had problems getting a book from there. Seven floors packed full of books, great views, quiet work places and gorgeous exchange students. The computer network is surprisingly reliable and allows you to access your private account from any computer off campus, as well as course information, lecture notes, e-mail and all the programs you'd ever need.'

Finally, there is a good reputation for Law - they are European law specialists (French, German) with a 4* rating for research. There's also a good line into the police. Note the BA Criminology, Criminology with Psychology, and Criminology with Law. There's also Social Policy &

Criminology and now Citizenship & Social Justice, and an intriguing bunch of Chemistry with Forensic Science & Toxicology degrees.

SOCIAL SCENE

STUDENTS' UNION 'Hull Union offers so much that you actually needn't venture off campus for a good night out,' writes Laura French. 'You'll hear third years tell how the newly refurbished bar, **The Sanctuary** is not as good as the **Rez**' (the old bar in the union). Just ignore them, a change is as good as a rest. Another bar, the **John McCarthy**, and a full-sized club, **Asylum**. Asylum is great fun; you will grow to love it, and its predictable soundtrack (mostly 80s/90s cheese and current pop). They have different nights on every night, but the most popular are the Athletic Union (AU) nights on a Wednesday. Buy your tickets in advance.'

Writes Jez: 'Lecturers have been known to deliberately not timetable lectures on Thursday morning due to the popularity of Wednesday nights in Asylum, particularly with the AU students. The Union puts on two great nights, one being Tower on Wednesdays and the other being Brassick on a Saturday.

'University campus is not the only place to go for nights out, however. On Mondays the best place to go is **Piper** on Newland Avenue which is a hot spot for Hull University Students. Or if you fancy a big night out **The Sugar Mill**. Tuesday nights is time for the city centre (safety, 8/10) and the night called *Revolver*, a mini pub crawl from **Barracuda** to **Mission** and on. Thursday nights are great if you go to **Welly** or to **Pozition** nightclub.

'At weekends the town clubs are not student focused and can be quite expensive. On Fridays you can go to either Piper or the event *Shinobi* at Welly. On Saturdays it is back to Asylum, The Sugar Mill, Pozition and Welly.

'But it's not just nights out that make for a good social life. There are many pubs that students use, first years tend to gather at the **Cross Keys** or **Hallgate Tavern**; second and third years favour a selection of cafes and pubs around Beverly Road and Newland Avenue like the **Haworth**, **Wetherspoons**, **Fusion** and the **Gardener's Arms** and cafés like **Planet Coffee**.'

Writes Laura: 'Newland Avenue and Princes Avenue provide everything from greengrocers to convenience stores to café bars. They are slightly bohemian in feel, and, being in Hull, are much cheaper than their equivalents in other cities.'

The on-campus **Gulbenkian Theatre** is the focus of the student drama scene, mentioned in *Academia* above. There is a newspaper, *Hullfire*, and a student radio station, Jam 1575, which took

the usual Rugby Union Men and Women's, Netball, Hockey, Lacrosse and a whole host of others, like Roller Hockey. There is a one-off Athletic Union £40 charge to join, to pay for insurance and general upkeep. It doesn't matter what standard of play you are, you can join any club you want, even if you have never played before!

PILLOW TALK

Not before time, the uni has spent £16 million on refurbishments to halls over the last few years. Needler (£81.97-£84.98 p.w.), The Lawns (£93.73-£110.60), Ferens (£78.96-£84.98) and Thwaite (£111.65-126.63) are in the village of Cottingham, a couple of miles from campus, great for pubs (karaoke at the Hallgate, a winner), takeaways and shops. Regular buses run. Lawns is absolutely huge, has its own bar and police station. Thwaite is a posh version of Needler, but it is out of the way of everyone else. There is also Taylor Court flats (£88.83 p.w.), 8 bedrooms per flat. Students houses come in around £52.36 to £71.68.

In Scarborough, Cayley Hall has 6 modern blocks, all rooms en suite and catered, for £126.14 p.w. You can opt for a managed student house, where self-catered rooms, exclusive of bills, can be as low as £54.04 p.w.

Writes Jez: 'Many students do go home or to visit friends at weekends but the majority stay, study and go partying. Cost of living is not high. Most students are able to survive on £50-80 per week for food, booze, travel and a night out or two.'

GETTING THERE
☛ By road: M62, A63, A1079, B1233.
☛ By rail: Leeds, 1:00; Manchester, 2:15; London King's Cross, 4:30; Birmingham New Street, 3:00.
☛ By air: Humberside, Leeds/Bradford Airports.
☛ By coach: London, 5:10; Manchester, 3-4:00.

Bronze at the 2009 Radio Awards. The Techincal Committee is a parallel organisation heavily into sound and lighting systems and gets its performance kicks at the Friday and Saturday discos.

Politically the union is 'largely left wing and campaigns are well supported,' says Peter Bainbridge, 'like Third World First, Animal Rights, Amnesty International, and there's a particularly active Women's Committee and Lesbian and Gay Society. 'Though the locals aren't the most tolerant,' says Peter, 'there are gay-friendly places.'

Town Hull has undergone a major facelift in the form of the **St Stephen's Development**, a £200 million project at the heart of the city. There's a retail centre, a state-of-the-art transport interchange, a hotel, modern residences and a new home for the legendary **Hull Truck Theatre**.

Hull's Old Town has a fine Museum Quarter.

Sport Writes Jez: 'There are over 43 clubs in AU,

IMPERIAL COLLEGE LONDON

Imperial College
South Kensington
London SW7 2AZ

TEL 020 7594 8001
FAX 020 7594 8004
EMAIL admissions@imperial.ac.uk
WEB www.imperial.ac.uk

Imperial College Union
Prince Consort Road
London SW7 2BB

TEL 020 7594 8060
FAX 020 7594 8065
WEB www.imperialcollegeunion.org

VIRGIN VIEW

*T*he *Imperial College of Science, Technology and Medicine is based principally in South Kensington, London. Formerly a constituent college of the University of London, Imperial became independent of the University in July 2007, on the 100th anniversary of its founding.*

Mergers have formed its character since the beginning, where, in 1907, it arose out of the marriage of the prestigious Royal College of Science, the Royal School of Mines and the City & Guilds College. The RCS gave Imperial pure Science, the RSM gave it Mining (and related fields, such as Geology) and the City & Guilds College, Engineering. Mergers with three London teaching hospitals leave it with a massive medical provision.

In the poll of polls, the Top 200 Universities in the World, Imperial took ninth place this year, Cambridge and Oxford the only UK universities ahead of it.

However, in the 2010 Times Higher Education Magazine's *Student Experience poll of students, it came 62nd in the UK alone. It is informative to note on what grounds. Imperial scored worst on the following counts: social life, community atmosphere, student union, student welfare, staff relationships, prices of bar fare and amenities, small group tuition, and fair workload.*

Nevertheless, Imperial has one of the lowest drop-out rates in the country (3%), which suggests that feeling wanted

UNIVERSITY/STUDENT PROFILE	
School of London Uni since	**1908**
Situation/style	**City campus**
Student population	**14150**
Undergraduates	**8580**
Mature	**21%**
International	**38%**
Male/female ratio	**64:36**
Equality of opportunity:	
state school intake	**62%**
social class 4-7 intake	**19%**
drop-out rate	**4%**

isn't the highest priority for its students. And no doubt their disappointment will be assuaged when they are among the 89% who get top graduate jobs at the end of their stay.

CAMPUSES

'The main campus is situated in South Kensington, Zone 1, Central London,' writes Saurabh Pandya. 'We are right next to the Victoria & Albert, Science and Natural History museums (and are granted free access to them). Travel is easy, the nearest tube is a ten-minute walk away. Generally, it is a low crime area, well lit and pretty safe for students, especially as the uni, the union and most uni

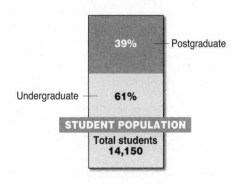

Undergraduate — **61%**

39% — Postgraduate

STUDENT POPULATION
Total students
14,150

STUDENT PROFILE

There is a sense of privilege in the air. They take around the same number of public school kids as Durham - only this lot are quieter. Another factor is the gender imbalance 64% male, though it seems even worse. Writes Saurabh: 'The male:female ratio here is about 100:1. Blokes have practically no chance of getting a woman, ever, and consequently Imperial is the sexual frustration capital of Britain!'

Sarah Playforth agrees, but feels for the girls: 'What you pull is not guaranteed to be human, but the good thing about the student body is that the college's international reputation leads to a large cultural diversity and you can make friends from all over the world.' It does indeed, 38% of undergraduates were international students at the last count. There's also a large mature student population - 21%.

ACADEMIA & JOBS

Students say the best teaching is to be had in Aerospace Engineering, Biology, Civil Engineering, Computer, Electronic & Electical Engineering, Materials & Minerals Engineering, Mechanical, Production & Manufacturing Engineering, Medicine, Physics & Astronomy, Technology. All these attracted thumbs up from 85% of the class or more. Even the least well taught - Molecular Biology, Biophysics & Biochemistry - found favour with 72%.

'The work is hard, let's get that straight from the outset,' writes Saurabh. 'Most successful applicants have AAA or higher at A-level, and so a high standard will be expected of you.'

accommodation are all within 5 mins of each other.'

Says Sarah Playforth, 'This has got to be the best situated college in london, probably in England and perhaps even in the world. If you come from a small town like I do, you'll be blown away by it.

'Now, the negative. If daddy doesn't own half the oil fields in Texas you are likely to hit a major financial crisis if you eat out at anywhere other than McDonalds. Yes, central London is an extremely expensive place. By the time you graduate you'll probably have acquired an overdraft equivalent to the annual budget of a small country.'

FEES, BURSARIES

UK & EU Fees, 2011-12: £3,375 p.a. All students in receipt of the full Government HE Maintenance Grant will receive a student support bursary up to a maximum of four years. There's also an award at the midpoint in a year for those in receipt of a partial HE Maintenance Grant.

> *'This has got to be the best situated college, probably in England, perhaps even in the world. If you come from a small town like I do, you'll be blown away by it. Now, the negative. If Daddy doesn't own half the oil fields in Texas you are likely to hit a major financial crisis.'*

Among scholarships are awards for students from financially disadvantaged backgrounds, premium scholarships offered from the Student Opportunities Fund, City & Guild scholarships, a Grocers' Company Queen's Golden Jubilee Scholarship, and so on... There are loads of them, and the biggest test is to find them on the Imperial web site. So, let us help: www3.imperial.ac.uk/registry/studentfinancialsupport/ugscholarships.

The ask is becoming ever more demanding, which is why there is surprise when the college gets marked sown by its students for lack of small-size tuition groups. But facilities are good.

'The library occupies five floors and is shared with the Science Museum. It is pretty comprehensive, and as you would expect at a science and technology uni, the computing facilities are also first rate. There are plenty of PCs, and these are upgraded every eighteen months. Staff tend to be leading figures in their field, and regardless of subject you will get a world class education by coming here.'

The Medicine degree in this, the largest med. school in the country, is a 6-year MB BS.

There's a special route in via a foundation year at Thames Valley Uni. Otherwise, the requirement is three A levels and a high grade in a fourth subject at AS level. AS levels must include Biology and Chemistry and A levels must include two sciences, at least one of which must be Biology or Chemistry. General Studies is excluded and Maths cannot be offered with Further or Applied Maths as two individual subjects. BMAT is also required. All learning is in a clinical context. Traditional, but with special emphasis on communication skills.

SUBJECT AREAS (%)

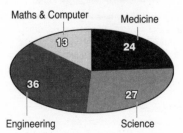

Maths & Computer 13
Medicine 24
Engineering 36
Science 27

law, and information technology.

Imperial graduates become doctors, bankers, accountants, higher education lecturers, software consultants, engineering design consultants, manufacturers (especially of aircraft), or they go and work in Defence, or for a construction company. Jobs in oil extraction, mining, etc, also proliferate. Getting an authentic graduate job for an Imperial graduate is hard to avoid, 89% of them had one last time within six months of leaving.

SOCIAL SCENE

STUDENTS' UNION Imperial is great at isolating itself and perhaps at alienating itself as well. It has left London University and it has left the National Union of Students. Students will barely notice the latter. ICU cards are accepted at most places in London, but they might miss the University of London Union (ULU) card, which is also widely recognised and allows use of some great facilities.

Imperial's facilities feature **FiveSixEight**, the Union's new bar in Beit Quad, known for its real ale and collection of pewter tankards in memory of various Union big-wigs and sporting heroes no-one has been there long enough to remember. Then there's the Union bar, small, intimate, except on Wednesdays when it gives itself to the uproar of post-match Wednesday club-nights for the sports crowd. The Beit Quad bars are in the ground floor of the Union building. Then there's the Charing Cross Hospital bar, the Reynolds Bar, located behind the hospital, which is on Fulham Palace Road, SW6, and which does, besides much worse, a regular Wednesday Sports Night and a Friday Bop Night.

New this year is new nightclub **Metric**, a venue for students to launch their own society or club nights - stage, dancefloor and dj booth central to the design, with an LED acrylic wall for far-out visuals. There's also an as yet un-named bar and café here.

Another attraction is the cinema - 'the biggest student cinema in the country and the sixth biggest screen in London. It shows films much later than elsewhere but only go if you think the film is worth getting a sore bum for,' says our reporter.

The number of student societies at Imperial is pretty overwhelming - 235 includes everything from Chess to E-commerce, to Rugby to Juggling, and a large number of overseas clubs too. And just because they are a techno-based uni, it doesn't mean they don't have any arty clubs - Opera, Drama, Art, Dance, etc., are all very active.

Film is rated excellent by students. Media, too, is very active both from a techno and literary pov. There's the student newspaper, *Felix*, and IC radio, which picked up a bronze gong at the 2010 National Student Radio Awards, and STOIC, the TV arm; also the arts newsletter - *Phoenix*, and the science mag. -

includes a 25m swimming pool, four squash courts, a gym, a 25m rifle range, a training studio, sauna, steam room and poolside spa bath. Nearby there are tennis and netball courts, and a weights room. The 60-acre pitches are at Harlington, near Heathrow. Facilities include a floodlit multi-purpose surface and a pavilion with bar. There are a further 15 acres at Teddington (four pitches and a cricket square), 22 acres at Cobham, the boathouse at Putney and a sailing club at Welsh Harp Reservoir in North West London. In addition, its site at Charing Cross Hospital has a 25m swimming pool and squash.

PILLOW TALK

You are guaranteed a place in either Imperial College or London University intercollegiate accommodation for the first year of study. Imperial accommodation is self-catering. 'If you are lucky,' writes London-based Saurabh, 'you'll get into one of the halls right next to campus, and you can spend all year perfecting your "get up at 8:55 and be in time for 9:00 lecture" technique. These are the Southside, Northside, Eastside and Beit halls. If you are especially lucky, you will be placed in Beit Hall, which has Ikea-style kitchens and every amenity you could possibly want. There are other halls in Evelyn Gardens (15 minutes from campus) or Pembridge Gardens (40 minutes, or 20 by tube).'

Prices are not low, unless you opt for 2 or even

I, Science. *Felix* still glows from Best Journalist and Newspaper of the Year awards bestowed on it by the *Guardian* only a couple of years ago. Meanwhile, *I, Science* was runner-up for Magazine of the Year, and one 'Angry Geek' for Columnist of the Year. Plans are afoot for a special edition sports magazine.

SPORT Besides national competition in the uni leagues, where Imperial came 17th last year, they excel in the London University league. But in rowing - the big thing at ICS - you're talking international levels. The boathouse is at Putney bridge.

A sports centre, Ethos, recently opened at the South Kensington campus - a 70-station fitness gym, 25m deck-level swimming pool, a sauna/steam room and spa, a five-badminton-court sports hall, a state-of-the-art climbing wall, exercise studio, and a sports injury unit.

Another at Prince's Gardens (Exhibition Road)

3 to a room (see box). While for single de-luxe you could pay more than £227 p.w. So, dig oil.

GETTING THERE

☞ By Underground: South Kensington (Circle, District and Piccadilly lines).

UNIVERSITY OF KEELE

The University of Keele
Keele
Staffordshire ST5 5BG

TEL 01782 734005/733994 (admissions)
    01782 732000 (switchboard)
EMAIL undergraduate@keele.ac.uk
WEB www.keele.ac.uk

Keele Students' Union
Keele
Staffs ST5 5BJ

TEL 01782 733700
FAX 01782 712671
EMAIL sta15@kusu.keele.ac.uk
WEB www.kusu.net

VIRGIN VIEW

*K*eele University is situated in Staffordshire, in an area known as the Potteries, whose most famous literary son, Arnold Bennett (Clayhanger, Anne of the Five Towns) couldn't get away fast enough, though to be fair he had been under pressure from his father to settle down and become a solicitor, and the place did later inspire him to write.

The Uni was founded in 1949 with a coherent educational philosophy to provide a broadly based undergraduate education, in sharp contrast to the (then) heavy emphasis on the high specialised single honours degree.

This strategy is today visible still in the dual honours degree, which Keele pioneered and which offers a rare opportunity to cut across traditional faculty lines. Ninety per cent of Keele's students opt for this type of degree. Employers, Keele believes, are looking for people who can appreciate the wider context in which they work.

Nearly all undergraduates, irrespective of the subject combination they are studying, have the opportunity to spend a semester at one of the uni's partner institutions in North America (American Studies modules encourage this), Australia, South Africa or Europe. Keele has been awarded the European Quality Label for mobility. Bennett would have liked that.

Students are passionate about this uni, almost as if they are part of a cult rather than a campus commune - 89% of them made their feelings known in the recent National Student Survey.

The University does not operate a system of standard offers. Some students with non-traditional qualifications will be invited for interview, depending upon their recent study experience. Candidates out of formal education for more than three years and not qualified to A-level or BTEC standard, may yet qualify for entry to the Foundation Year programmes [01782 734478 p.w.haycock@ acad.keele.ac.uk].

UNIVERSITY/STUDENT PROFILE	
University since	**1962**
Situation/style	**Rural campus**
Student population	**10365**
Undergraduates	**8430**
Mature	**47%**
International	**10%**
Male/female ratio	**39:61**
Equality of opportunity:	
state school intake	**92%**
social class 4-7 intake	**34%**
drop-out rate	**6%**

In particular, they welcome applicants whose studies cross traditional boundaries e.g. science/arts combinations.

Open Days in 2011: 19 June, 21 August, 15 October, 16 October.

CAMPUS

Keele was the first completely new university after the Second World War, and the prototype of the green-field campus university. Today the majority of academic activities are still located on campus, with the exception of parts of the Faculty of Health, which are located on the nearby hospital site.

Campus is a 617-acre country estate with lakes and woodland, just north of the A525 and west of Newcastle-upon-Lyme. Write Mark Holtz and Gareth Belfield: 'Keele University's self-contained campus is a stone's throw from Stoke-on-Trent, a

TEACHING SURVEY AT A GLANCE

Avg. UCAS points accepted	**300**
Acceptance rate	**14%**
Overall satisfaction rate	**89%**
Helpful/interested staff	★★★★
Small tuition groups	★★★
Students into graduate jobs	**74%**

Teaching most popular with undergraduates:
Education, American & Australasian Studies,
Anatomy, Physiology & Pathology, Biology,
Chemistry, Computer, English, Finance &
Accounting, Forensic & Archaeological Science,
Geology, History, Human Resource Management,
Human & Social Geography, Languages, Law,
Maths, Media Studies, Molecular Biology, Nursing,
Pharmacy, Physical Geography & Environmental
Science, Politics, Psychology, Social Policy, Social
Studies, Sociology.

constant worry for those students without protective headgear. In theory, the university is set within tiny Keele village, but the campus has grown over such a large area that saying it is part of Keele village is akin to saying that London is part of Westminster. The campus is on a hill top and is so exposed you expect a policeman to come along and arrest it for indecency. Nearby Newcastle-under-Lyme, Hanley (Stoke) and Crewe can be reached by the bus service called (joyfully) PMT. Trainwise, Manchester is only 30 minutes away, as is Birmingham. London direct can be done in around two hours. The M6 is within earshot of the campus, and sounds like the sea if you are drunk enough.'

Keele is planning an ambitious project to transform the heart of the campus with seating areas, an events plaza, significant pedestrianisation and new signs.

FEES, BURSARIES

UK & EU Fees, 2011-12: £3,375 p.a. They have a bursary, up to £800 a year, for full-time undergraduates not receiving NHS funding but in receipt of a

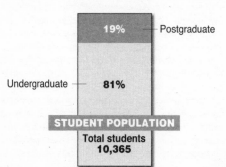

full maintenance grant. The Keele Scholarship (£1,000) is awarded for three A grades at A level or equivalent, if family income is below £40,000. See www.keele.ac.uk/studentfunding/undergraduatebursaries/.

The KeeleLink Award (£500 p.a.) is for students from schools and colleges in the KeeleLink partnership. There's a programme worth £300 for athletes who compete nationally or internationally. The Study Abroad Bursary (£500) and Care Leaver Bursary, for students who have been in care, complete the picture. Email bursaries@keele.ac.uk or call 01782 734240.

STUDENT PROFILE

Write Mark and Gareth: 'Take a generous measure of "traditional" students, two heaped tablespoons of mature, nursing, international and local students, heavily season with postgraduates, add a dash of complete weirdoes and you have the recipe for the most diverse and interesting con-

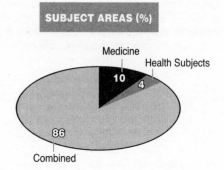

coction of a university anywhere in the world. It's impossible not to fit in at Keele, with over half the students living together on campus, you're never really in danger of running out of people to borrow sugar from.' Female students abound (61% of undergrads), as do mature students (47%). Parttimers (more than a third) also influence the mix.

A Welcome Web has been designed to support students to settle in: www.keele.ac.uk/depts/aa/class/welcome/

ACADEMIA & JOBS

While the Dual Honours degree breaks down barriers in the curriculum, Keele's International Strategy educates students to become 'Global Graduates'. A third of first years at Keele are studying a language or a related cultural module. Nearly all students can study abroad at one of 50 partner universities for a semester.

Students say that the teaching is best in American & Australasian Studies, Anatomy,

Physiology & Pathology, Biology, Chemistry, Computer, Education, English, Finance & Accounting, Forensic & Archaeological Science, Geology, History, Human Resource Management, Human & Social Geography, Languages, Law, Maths, Media Studies, Molecular Biology, Nursing,

RESEARCH EXCELLENCE		
% of Keele's research that is **4*** (World-class) or **3*** (Internationally rated):		
	4*	**3***
Clinical Subjects	0%	15%
Primary Care Clinical	15%	25%
Physics	5%	35%
Applied Mathematics	15%	45%
General Engineering	10%	40%
Business/Management	10%	35%
Law	10%	40%
Politics	10%	20%
Social Work	15%	50%
Psychology	0%	25%
Russian	15%	20%
English	10%	40%
History	20%	35%
Music	20%	45%

Pharmacy, Physical Geography & Environmental Science, Politics, Psychology, Social Policy, Social Studies and Sociology.

Keele lecturers get 4 out of 5 stars from their students for help and interest in them and 3 for decent sized tuition groups.

In recent years Keele has been successful in establishing programmes in undergraduate medicine and pharmacy.

The Medicine degree is a 5-year MBChB or 4-year fast track programme with direct entry to Year 2. There is, in addition, Medicine with Health Foundation Year, designed to provide an entry to Medicine for those without the conventional science A-level subjects normally required for direct entry. Continuation after the Foundation Year is subject to achieving specified grades.

Normal requirements to read Medicine at Keele are 2 Sciences at A level, one of which must be Chemistry or Biology plus one other rigorous subject. (Chemistry must be taken at AS Level.) Sciences not offered at A/AS Level must be offered at GCSE. You will also be required to sit the UKCAT test.

> *'Locals refer to you as "duck" if they like you. If they don't like you they'll just try to run over you.'*

The School of Medicine is on three sites: on the main campus, at the University Hospital of North Staffordshire 3 miles away, and at Keele's Associate Teaching Hospital at the Shrewsbury and Telford Hospitals in Shropshire.

Students of subjects allied to Medicine find more graduate jobs than any. Human biologists, medicinal chemists and pharmacists flock to hospitals from keele, as do nurses and midwives, pharmacists, physiotherapists and the like. These degrees (and one working with the visually impaired) now account for around 20% of the total graduate jobs at Keele. As a result of 'virtual patient' technology developed by the School of Pharmacy, which opened in 2006, students learn partly by communicating with a 'patient' and at the end of the session the 'patient' gives feedback to the student about their performance.

Social Studies graduates come next - 16% of the jobs come from this area of the curriculum. It takes them into the community and local government, specialising in such as social security, counselling, law and order... Degrees such as Psychology, Law, or even Marketing with Social Science, Social Work, Politics, all count here.

A new School of Sociology and Criminology came into existence in August 2008, delivering two Dual Honours principal programmes in these subjects. A School of Public Policy and Professional Practice has now also been established, focusing on public policy and professional concerns in education, health, social care and the voluntary sector.

A new Keele Business School is focused on high quality professional undergraduate and pre-experience PGT programmes and a development of CPD programmes, including a part-time MBA. Banking and accounting are major destinations, with dedicated degrees also taking large numbers into recruitment/personnel (the Human Resources degrees).

Green issues have also been rising up the university's agenda. A degree in Environment and Sustainability was introduced in 2009 and all undergraduates can take a module in either. Keele Connect provides a company with a graduate for 12 weeks to work on an environmental project.

Law is also worth a particular mention. Part of the multi-subject curriculum, but also a single honours subject. If you want to work as a solicitor and you already have a degree in another subject, you can take the Common Professional Examination (CPE) here.

ACCOMMODATION

Student rating	★★★
Guarantee to freshers	70%
Style	Halls, flats
Security guard	Halls, not flats
Shared rooms	None
Internet access	Halls only
Self-catered	All
En suite	Some halls
Approx price range pw	£68-£115
Town rent pw	£40-£80

WHAT IT'S REALLY LIKE

UNIVERSITY:	
Social Life	★★★
Campus scene	★★★
Student Union services	★★★★
Politics	Average
Sport	Not impressive
National teamposition	72nd
Sport facilities	★★★
Arts opportunities	Excellent
Student newspaper	Concourse
Nightclub	K2
Bars	Sam's Bar, Ballroom, Lounge
Union ents	Cheesy + live
Union societies	80
Most popular society	Drama
Parking	Not if in halls
TOWN:	
Entertainment	★★
Local (Stoke) scene	Pubs/clubs
Town/gown relations	OK
Risk of violence	Average
Cost of living	Below average
Student concessions	Average
Survival + 2 nights out	£50 pw
Part-time work campus/town	OK/poor

STUDENT SCENE

STUDENTS UNION Sam's Bar opens up to the Ballroom to take around 1,100 on big live act nights. In the good old days the Rolling Stones used to use the KUSU building as a rehearsal room and even now, on a still winter's night, faint echoes can be heard of the Eurythmics, UB40, Oasis and a young Jarvis Cocker, who graced the stage. More recent visitors were Fun Lovin' Criminals, Idlewild, Mis-Teeq, Liberty X, Atomic Kitten, Toploader, Reef, The Pet Shop Boys, Levellers, The Proclaimers.

The Lounge is - surprise - a lounge bar. K2, formerly The Club, is now KUSU's 'premier Entertainment Venue'. With a top-specification PA & lighting system, it features a permanent 6m x 4m stage. Here, on a Monday is pop, chart & dance with resident DJ Chris; alternate Tuesdays is Comedy Club - Mark Lamarr, Peter Kay, Ed Byrne, Paul Tonkinson, Adam Bloom, Richard Morton and more. On other Tuesdays you might have Stella Screen - box office smashes before general release. Wednesdays - whole building is R-wind (retro - 80s, 90s) and indie/alternative from resident DJ The Rich. They also do fancy dress nights and, in The Lounge, Quiz and Cocktail evenings and Sunday karaoke competitions.

The extra-curricular scene is very lively. Student radio, the sometime award-winning KUBE, is particularly active at the moment. It won Best Internet Only station at the European Radio Awards. Six months later they won the gold award for online radio at the international Radio Awards in New York. Finally, Keele has a history of political turbulence, but you wouldn't notice now.

SPORT It is a sport for all philosophy, which aims to ensure there are no barriers to participation. Facilities include a gym, sports hall, floodlit synthetic pitch, 50 acres of grass pitches, tennis courts, fitness centre, squash courts, etc.

TOWN 'Aaarghh! Keele, the Potteries, where the main industry is not so much in decline, as plummeting down a precipice of bankruptcy. Locals refer to you as "duck" if they like you. If they don't like you they'll just try to run over you.'

PILLOW TALK

£3.2m has been spent improving student halls of residence, including completing 'the student social space initiative'. Each Hall of Residence now has a dedicated non-alcohol social area where students can gather. Money well spent? It's what the students said they wanted and they got it.

There are 5 halls on campus. No shared rooms now. Some have been adapted for students with disabilities. All are self-catering, but an optional meal plan provides breakfast and an evening meal.

No parking permits for freshers in halls.

GETTING THERE

☛ By road: from the north M6/J16, A500, A531, right on to A525, right through Keele village; from south, M6/J15, A5182, left on to A53, right at Whitmore following signs.
☛ By rail: good service more or less everywhere, London 1:30 to Stoke-on-Trent station, then taxi.
☛ By coach: London, 4:00.

THE UNIVERSITY OF KENT

The University of Kent at Canterbury
The Registry
Canterbury CT2 7NZ

TEL 01227 764200
FAX 01227 827077
EMAIL informatio@kent.ac.uk
WEB www.kent.ac.uk

Kent University Students' Union
The University
Canterbury CT2 7NW

TEL 01227 824200
FAX 01227 824204
EMAIL union@kent.ac.uk
WEB www.kentunion.co.uk

VIRGIN VIEW

The University of Kent is a friendly, cosmopolitan university with very friendly campuses in Canterbury and Medway.

Value added at Kent is its International focus. The University offers a wide range of placement and study options abroad and has strong international links and partnerships with many prestigious universities, a position strengthened by postgraduate centres in Brussels and Paris.

It also offers a study-abroad scholarship, and the thought behind this principle gains expression too in the cultural diversity seen across Kent's campuses: around a fifth of Kent students come from countries outside the UK.

Where there is competition for a place, Kent says, they are looking for 'a well rounded student who provides evidence of their enthusiasm for the subject and course, evidence of reading around their subject, a readiness and willingness to learn and an understanding of how the chosen course will help them meet their personal ambitions. These qualities may be demonstrated in the Personal Statement or at interview.'

Open Days, 2011: Medway campus, 25 June; Canterbury campus, 9 July.

CAMPUS

Canterbury Campus is situated on a hill overlooking the famous Cathedral, about a mile from the city centre and seven miles from the beach at Whitstable. Everything you need is within walking distance: accommodation, the library, the sports centre, banks, shops, a theatre, bars and cafés, and a purpose-built club, all surrounded by green open spaces, courtyards, ponds and woodland.

Says Laura Budd: 'I like Canterbury because it is not too big and not too wild and you are not too

UNIVERSITY/STUDENT PROFILE	
University since	**1965**
Situation/style	**City campus**
Student population	**18295**
Undergraduates	**15640**
Mature	**31%**
International	**18%**
Male/female ratio	**46:54**
Equality of opportunity:	
state school intake	**93%**
social class 4-7 intake	**29%**
drop-out rate	**7%**

far away from the coast - Whitstable, Herne Bay and Dover. I was hoping to go to Exeter University and there was a lot of disappointment when I got my results and didn't quite make it. But I have always liked Canterbury ever since I first came, especially with the Cathedral. It's just a really friendly place to be. When we first had a look round it, me and my parents - we missed the Open Day and it was a self guided tour - people were coming up to us: "Oh, are you OK? Do you need to know where to go?" You know, really approachable.'

Dominic Conway: 'If you come to this Uni you will have everything really: countryside and seaside, but still be near to London; and entertainment and nightlife, but still have a calm working environment. For the more hardcore among you it may seem a little too relaxed, but with the facilities and

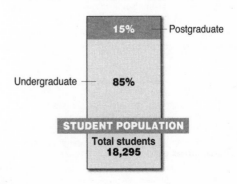

Postgraduate 15%

Undergraduate 85%

STUDENT POPULATION
Total students
18,295

the high teaching standards you should definitely get a good education, and if you don't have enough fun, it's more likely to be your fault than theirs.'

Medway Campus (Chatham Maritime, Kent ME4 4AG. Tel: 0800 975 3777) The Medway region is famous for its cultural and naval heritage. Today, the naval base at Chatham Maritime, HMS Pembroke, has been redeveloped as part of a £120-million partnership between the universities of Kent, Canterbury Christ Church, Greenwich, and Mid-Kent College, the 'Universities at Medway'.

The shared site, within walking distance of the River Medway, is made up of refurbished Grade II listed buildings and modern architecture.

Facilities include the new Medway School of Pharmacy, studios and rehearsal rooms for Music Technology and Audi Design programmes, an industry-standard newsroom for the Journalism programme, treatment rooms and a performance testing laboratory for Sport Studies students, and a £10-million library, the Drill Hall Library, at 184 metres in length and with 2.7 miles of shelving, reportedly the longest library in Europe.

Students like Medway. Daniel Hawkins wrote that 'When I first visited , I knew straight away that this was the place for me.' And there's no doubt that the location and facilities, with all the participants continuing to plough in resources as we write, will make it work for many. But it is important to visit

whichever campus you choose and be aware that Medway is not Canterbury, and vice versa. They are 30 miles apart and quite different experiences.

FEES, BURSARIES

UK & EU Fees: £3,375 p.a. If in receipt of HE Maintenance grant there's a bursary (up to £1,000). There are bursaries too for applicants proceeding from less privileged backgrounds, and scholarships for sport (£250-£5,000), music (also up to £5,000) and academic achievement (£1,000). See also their

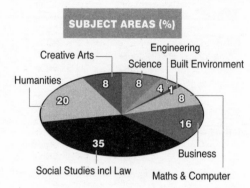

SUBJECT AREAS (%)

Creative Arts — 8
Engineering
Science | Built Environment — 8 4 1
Humanities — 20
8
16
35
Business
Social Studies incl Law
Maths & Computer

Study Abroad awards (£2,000) and Disabled Student bursaries: www.kent.ac.uk.funding. There are 44 Partner Schools and Colleges Scholarships worth £1,000 a year each.

STUDENT PROFILE

Intake from poorer socio-economic groups (29%) and neighbourhoods beyond the traditional university heartlands has risen consistently over the last few years, in line with government policy. There is also a large percentage of mature students (31%) and 18% this time from outside the UK.

Of Kent's reputation as 'the UK's European university', student of French Laura Budd, who had just returned from the Continent said: 'You do get a lot of students from Europe. Some of them come over for a few months and some come over for their whole degree. There are three options for my year out. You can go to a French university and study, you can be a language assistant and teach in schools, or you can do a work placement. I want to be a primary school teacher, so I'm going to France to teach.'

Catherine Robertson goes so far as to suggest that the reason why 'many British people haven't even heard of UKC is the uni's dedication to attracting overseas students,' but concludes 'what you will find is a friendly student body, and lecturers and tutors who pursue their own work as energetically as they do yours.'

TEACHING SURVEY AT A GLANCE

Avg. UCAS points accepted	**310**
Acceptance rate	**21%**
Overall satisfaction rate	**87%**
Helpful/interested staff	★★★★
Small tuition groups	★★
Students into graduate jobs	**56%**

Teaching most popular with undergraduates:
Accounting, American & Australasian Studies, Archaeology, Biology & related sciences, Business, Chemistry, Classics, Comparative Literary Studies, Economics, Electronic & Electrical Engineering (100%), Engineering & Technology (100%), English, Languages, Forensic & Archaeological Science, French Studies, History, Archaeology, Iberian Studies, Law, Management, Maths, Molecular Biology (100%), Physical Science, Physics & Astronomy, Politics, Psychology, Social Policy, Sociology, Pharmacy, Theology.

Teaching least popular with undergraduates:
Art & Design (59%), Design Studies (57%).

RESEARCH EXCELLENCE

% of Kent's research that is
4* (World-class) or 3* (Internationally rated):

	4*	3*
Psychiatry	10%	20%
Biological Sciences	5%	30%
Environmental Sciences	5%	50%
Physics	0%	30%
Pure Mathematics	0%	35%
Applied Mathematics	10%	35%
Statistics	20%	45%
Computer Science	15%	50%
Electrical/Electronic Eng.	15%	25%
Metallurgy and Materials	25%	55%
Economics	15%	60%
Business/Management	10%	45%
Law	30%	35%
Politics	0%	35%
Social Work	30%	40%
Anthropology	20%	30%
Psychology	10%	30%
French	15%	35%
German	5%	15%
Iberian	5%	20%
English	30%	35%
Classics	5%	5%
Philosophy	10%	25%
Theology	10%	30%
History	35%	35%
Performing Arts	35%	35%

ACADEMIA & JOBS

Ninety-seven per cent of staff work in departments delivering world-class research, according to the last research assessment. At Kent you are taught by research-active experts, but who are also interested in their students, according to what the students themselves said in the latest *Times Higher* Student Experience Survey.

The best teaching, they say, is in Accounting, American & Australasian Studies, Archaeology, Biology & related sciences, Business, Chemistry, Classics, Comparative Literary Studies, Economics, Electronic & Electrical Engineering (100% of the class gave this the thumbs-up), Engineering & Technology (also 100%), English, Languages, Forensic & Archaeological Science, French Studies, History, Archaeology, Iberian Studies, Law, Management, Maths, Molecular

> *'Nice big cathedral, old cobbled streets, strong whiff of history, a two hour walk to the beach - that's Canterbury. It's just a really friendly place to be.'*

Biology (100%), Physical Science, Physics & Astronomy, Politics, Psychology, Social Policy, Sociology, Pharmacy, and Theology. Only Art and Design failed to enthuse.

Kent's commitment to the assimilation of European culture goes far and wide in the curriculum, but it is not just about learning to speak a language. Says Laura: 'My department isn't just French, it's one of six in the faculty of Humanities called the School of European Cultural Languages, and includes nine subjects. It's also Philosophy, Religious Studies, Classics, Archaeology and Comparative Literature. French is just a section of that department.'

There are other clear strengths. Drama was both a success at the research assessments and focus for student and professional theatre companies at the campus-based Gulbenkian Theatre.

In social sciences Kent is also pre-eminent, with Social Policy, Economics, Anthropology and Psychology rated world-class for research.

If you want to set up your own business, iyou can opt to take the CB612 Enterprise module to that end. The Canterbury Innovation Centre opened in 2009.

SOCIAL SCENE

STUDENTS' UNION Canterbury campus: 'Each of the colleges has its own bar: **Origins Bar & Bistro** in Darwin, (famous for its fajitas and party atmosphere) **Mungo's** in Eliot (refurbished in 2008, excellent desserts) **K-Bar** in Keynes (decked area outside, comfy seats inside, good pizza), and **Rutherford Bar** in Rutherford (live music and a great open mic night). The student village, Park Wood has its own bar, **Woody's** (good pub grub, drinks promos and loads of events).

As well as the bars, there's the **Gulbenkian Café** and the **Library Café**; great for grabbing a quick coffee and a sandwich. For more substantial fare, go to **Dolche Vita** in Keynes (fusion dishes, salads and sandwiches), **Rutherford Dining Hall** (new menu every day including vegetarian dishes and an large salad bar) or **Bag it & Go** in Rutherford (made to order sandwiches and light meals). There's also the new **Sports Pavilion Café**, and cafés in Sports Centre and Woolf College.

the Canterbury campus nightclub was completely refurbished and now offers two floors of state-of-the-art design, sound and lighting systems. A new live entertainments venue, The Attic, was

ACCOMMODATION

Student rating	★★★★★
Guaranteed if apply by July 31	100%
Style	Halls, houses, flats, village
Security guard	All
Shared rooms	Some
Internet access	100%
Self-catered	Some
En suite	Some
Approx price range pw	£83-£137
City rent pw	£65-£100

WHAT IT'S REALLY LIKE

UNIVERSITY:	
Social Life	★★★
Societies	★★★★
Student Union services	★★★★
Politics	Student issues
Sport	35 clubs
National sporting position	41st
Sport facilities	★★★★
Arts opportunities	Film, drama exc, music art good
Student magazine	UMM
Student newspaper	inQuire
Student radio	CSRfm
Nightclub	The Attic
Bars	Everywhere
Union ents	Good
Union societies	80
Parking	None
CITY:	
Entertainment	★★★
Scene	Touristy, historic, v. good pubs
Town/gown relations	Good
Risk of violence	Average
Cost of living	Average
Student concessions	Adequate
Survival + 2 nights out	£80 pw
Part-time work campus/town	Good

also introduced. It has a stage, increased capacity and is open 6 nights a week offering jazz, comedy, live bands (student, local and mainstream) and theme nights. Kent Union also hosts the annual Summerball. Past acts include Florence and the Machine (2010), Pendulum (2010) Dizzee Rascal (2009) and Pigeon Detectives (2009).

Now there's to be a new music performance centre. While music is not on the curriculum, hundreds of students, staff and the local community take part in a wide range of musical activities. As well as concerts on campus, there are opportunities to perform in other venues, including Canterbury Cathedral and on tour abroad. Each summer, the Uni holds its annual ArtsFest, attracting thousands.

Writes Dominic Conway: 'The ever growing list of societies means that any student will feel well catered for. The Gulbenkian Theatre hosts some remarkable shows, the manager is in close communication with the Drama department and is very well informed on the acts that students want to see. Its stage is open to comedy and music, as well as some bright lights in the world of modern theatre.'

Kent has its own radio station, CSRfm. It's not just a university radio station; its focus is on the entire Canterbury community, and it's an opportunity to gain hands-on experience working in radio, from presenting, news reading or promoting the station in the local community. There's also a student newspaper, inQuire, also available online.

Continues Dominic: 'If campus gets too much, Canterbury is just a 20 minute walk away. Nice big cathedral, old cobbled streets, strong whiff of history in the air and the locals never seem to mind or complain about the amount of students!'

There's a brand new club, **Chill**, with booths available for hire. They have regular celebrity guests/DJ's and host a weekly student night. **The Works**, near to Canterbury East station, is a popular student haunt and features three floors of the very best in old school classics and party, commercial R&B/Hip Hop and dance. They host two stu-

dent nights a week and offer plenty of promotional deals. **Studio 41** is an old favourite, with its 'Girls and Boys' night on Saturdays, unmissable theme nights and regular appearances by Invicta FM DJs. Among the bars try the **Old Brewery**, **Alberry's** and the **Cuban** (fab cocktails). Late licences mean there's always somewhere to party in Canterbury.

UMSA/MEDWAY CAMPUS The scene here is run by the Universities at Medway Students' Association (UMSA). There's a campus shop, Advice Centre, Jobshop and a wide range of student activities including over 17 sports teams, 27 societies and a student magazine (UMM).

Coopers is the campus pub, with comfy sofas, widescreen TVs, a Nintendo Wii, an X-box, and a pool room. You'll get open mic nights and theme nights, plus a late licence.

Then there's the **Gulbenkian Café** in the Rochester building and the **Venue Café** in the Pilkington Building for light lunches or main meals, or just to grab a coffee or relax between lectures.

Off campus, the Medway towns have great pubs and clubs. For live music, there's the **Blue's Rock Café** at Gillingham Football Club and the

Tap'n'Tin, a unique venue that has attracted many up and coming artists as well as more established performers, including Pete Doherty, The Bees and The View. Dedicated clubbers are only half an hour away from some of Kent's best venues, and there's a free bus service to and from campus.

SPORT/CANTERBURY Facilities include a cardio/fitness suite, dance studio, two multi-use sports halls, playing fields, 3G football and Astro pitches, tennis courts and a new £2.5-million sports pavilion, completed in July 2009.

Students can also join the Sports Federation, run by Kent Union, who run over 35 different clubs, anything from American Football to Ski and Snowboarding. The facilities will be used as a pre-games training camp for London 2012, as has Medway (below).

SPORT/MEDWAY Sports include rugby, football, tennis, netball, mixed hockey, athletics, snow sports and rowing. The campus Sports Hall and Fitness Suite has a fully equipped weights and cardio room. The Universities at Medway Boat Race is a major fixture.

There's also loads of things to do off campus, including golf, climbing, sailing, go-karting and athletics. Kent students get discounted rates at Medway Park, a new £11-million centre of excellence which has an 8-lane athletics track, gym, 25m pool, judo centre and a 12-court sports hall.

PILLOW TALK

A lot of money has recently gone into accommodation, so the standard is high.

Canterbury: first years must apply by July 31. College accommodation (Becket Court, Rutherford, Eliot or Keynes) is on a room and breakfast basis, or you can get an allowance towards an evening meal. You'll also have access to a kitchenette, which has a kettle, microwave and small fridge. Most self-catered accommodation (Tyler Court, Darwin College, Darwin Houses and Park Wood student village) is in a house or flat with kitchen. The accommodation is all within a few minutes walk of central campus, and there's a great sense of community.

Medway: first years are offered brand new accommodation at Liberty Quays, which is on the waterfront, a 10-min. walk from campus. All the rooms are en-suite and have large, shared kitchen facilities. There's also a laundry and common rooms, plus a Tesco Express, Domino's and Subway.

GETTING THERE

Canterbury

☛ By road: from west, M25, M2, M20, A2, south and south east, A28, A249,M20, M2, A2; east, A257; north, M25, M2, A2. Sat nav: CT2 7NP.

☛ By rail: London Victoria (85 mins), Charing Cross or Waterloo East (90 mins), St Pancras high speed service to Canterbury West (60 mins), Eurostar from Paris, Brussels or Lille (2 hours).

☛ By air: Heathrow, Stansted and Gatwick

☛ By coach: London Victoria, 1 hour 45 mins.

Medway

☛ By road: from west, north, and east; M25, A2; south and south east; M2, A278, A2, A289. Sat nav: ME4 4AG.

☛ By rail: London Victoria (85 mins), Charing Cross (55 mins) St Pancras high speed service to Ebbsfleet International (20 mins), and Eurostar from Paris, Brussels or Lille (2 hours)

☛ By air: Heathrow, Stansted and Gatwick.

☛ By coach: London Victoria (1 hour 15 mins)

KING'S COLLEGE, LONDON

King's College, London
Waterloo Bridge House
London SE1 8WA

TEL 020 7836 5454
FAX 020 7836 1799
EMAIL enquiries@kcl.ac.uk
WEB www.kcl.ac.uk

King's College Students' Union
Surrey Street
London WC2R 2NS

TEL 020 7836 7132
FAX 020 7379 9833
EMAIL president@kclsu.org
WEB www.kclsu.org/

VIRGIN VIEW

*K*ing's College London (KCL) is one of London University's oldest and most prestigious colleges, founded by George IV in 1829 and one of the federal university's original colleges in 1836. In the course of its history it has developed through many mergers, most recently, in the summer of 1998, with

UNIVERSITY/STUDENT PROFILE	
College of London Uni since	**1836**
Situation/style	**Civic**
Student population	**22275**
Undergraduates	**14155**
Mature	**45%**
International	**22%**
Male/female ratio	**39:61**
Equality of opportunity:	
state school intake	**73%**
social class 4-7 intake	**25%**
drop-out rate	**4%**

United Medical & Dental Schools of Guy's Hospital (where medical teaching began in the 1720s) & St Thomas's (where medicine has been taught since the 16th century). The full name for the medical school is King's College London Medical School at Guy's, King's College and St Thomas's Hospital.

KCL stands at No. 77 in the Times Higher's *2010 table of the world's Top 200 universities (seventh highest among UK universities), and in the most recent assessment of the research provision of all UK universities, 60% of its research activity was deemed world-class or internationally excellent. In total 91% of research activity entered was rated of international significance.*

But it is, above all, a health orientated university. There are six Medical Research Centres at KCL, more than any other UK institution. Over 30% of its graduates become doctors or dentists, and only a few less than that graduate in subjects allied to medicine and find work in hospitals, or become pharmacists, or civil servants in the health area.

There is also a strong presence of KCL graduates in banking and accounting, and in all areas of the civil service, and the media, especially in publishing, advertising, radio and television.

Its scholars in Ancient History and Classical Studies, and graduates of the Information Management and Language degrees run our museums, libraries and other national archival institutions.

KCL's students are intensely loyal, 86% came out in overall support of the teaching in the National Student Survey last year and

87% of these found graduate jobs within six months of leaving. Not finishing a course here is rare: the drop-out rate is a tidy 4%.

Word on the ground is that KCL succeeds not in spite of, but because of its location in the Capital: 'Want to live and work smack in the centre of London?' write Ben Jones and Chris Wilding. 'Want high frequency bus and tube links with a 30% discount? You got it. Clubs? Pubs? Venues? Theatres? Museums? Galleries? Shops? Yeah, got them too. In fact, by nestling snugly and unassumingly within the heart of the capital, KCL appears to its students a seventh heaven.' But, as with all London colleges, at a price.

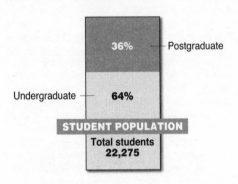

Postgraduate 36%

Undergraduate 64%

STUDENT POPULATION
Total students
22,275

CAMPUSES

There are now five campuses, four of which cluster around the Thames, close to the centre of town. With the Students' Union **Macadam** building at its core, the **Strand campus** lies on the north bank, close to Covent Garden. Here are the schools of Humanities, Law and Physical Sciences. Just over the river across Waterloo Bridge is the newer **Waterloo Campus**, incorporating Education, Management, Health & Life Sciences, Nursing & Midwifery and the Stamford Street apartments with the basement gym, K4.

Three bridges to the east lies **Guy's campus**. Students of Medicine and Dentistry enjoy a new SU building with bar, swimming pool, ballroom, shop and welfare centre, as well as accommodation.

Then there's **St Thomas's campus** (Continuing Medical & Dental teaching), which looks across the river to the Houses of Parliament; and **Denmark Hill campus**, the south of the Oval base for clinical teaching at King's College Hospital and the Dental Institute, and home to the Institute of Psychiatry.

FEES, BURSARIES

UK & EU Fees, 2011-12: £3,375 p.a. For all new full-time, home undergraduates, there's a bursary of between £100 and £1,350 awarded on a sliding scale, according to level of maintenance grant. Forty scholarships of £1,800 go to students who at the end of the year are adjudged to have excelled on their programme of study and contributed to the student life of department, school or college.

STUDENT PROFILE

Both King's and University College London, the mother of all London University colleges, have a high public school intake, UCL's being higher than King's. There is, at King's, what one student described as a 'friendly competitiveness' with UCL. I have heard a KCL student refer to UCL students as 'godless scum', while UCL routinely call KCL 'the Strand Poly'. In apparent contravention of this public school profile, the uni has been digging

TEACHING SURVEY AT A GLANCE

Avg. UCAS points accepted	**410**
Acceptance rate	**11%**
Overall satisfaction rate	**86%**
Helpful/interested staff	★★★
Small tuition groups	★★
Students into graduate jobs	**87%**

Teaching most popular with undergraduates:
Anatomy, Physiology & Pathology, Biology and related sciences, Classics, Dentistry, History, Archaeology, Iberian studies, Law, Media, Communications, Maths, Medicine, Molecular Biology, Nutrition, Pharmacology, Philosophy, Physics & Astronomy, Theology and Religious studies..

Teaching least popular with undergraduates:
German & Scandinavian Studies (53%).

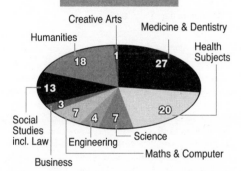

SUBJECT AREAS (%)

Creative Arts — 1
Medicine & Dentistry — 27
Health Subjects — 20
Humanities — 18
Social Studies incl. Law — 13
Business — 3
Engineering — 7
Science — 4, 7
Maths & Computer

Students say that the best teaching at KCL is in Anatomy, Physiology & Pathology, Biology and related sciences, Classics, Dentistry, History, Archaeology, Iberian studies, Law, Media, Communications, Maths, Medicine, Molecular Biology, Nutrition, Pharmacology, Philosophy, Physics & Astronomy, and Theology. All these were approved by 85% or more of the class.

The degree in Medicine is the 5-year MBBS. There is full integration of medical science and clinical teaching, plus a wide range of special study modules. Fifth year includes an opportunity to study abroad. For entry there's a special Graduate/Professional programme for mature students.

Chemistry and Biology must be included in your portfolio of exam results, one at A level and the other at least AS-level. UKCAT is also required.

The fifth-year study abroad option in Medicine (and Dentistry, as it happens, destinations range from the United States to Papua New Guinea) is symptomatic of many courses at KCL, which has exchange programmes with some of the most prestigious universities in 15 countries across Asia, Australia, Europe and North America. Some exchange programmes are a compulsory part of the curriculum, while others are not. All can be counted towards the degree. Each department has an academic adviser who will guide you through

around and found quite a healthy percentage of applicants from less traditional classes and neighbourhoods - 25% of their undergraduates now come from the lower socio-economic orders. There is also a 45% mature population, which they are encouraging in particular in their medical faculty, and part-timers make up 20% of the cohort.

ACADEMIA & JOBS

There's something wonderfully traditional about KCL's 'AKC', the course unique to the college and awarded since 1835. It provides lectures on aspects of ethics, philosophy and theology, Biblical studies and Christian doctrine, and can be taken by everyone.

> *'Music is as strong as medicine and can be found in harmony with applied computing; war studies combines with theology, and there's an international centre for prison studies within the Law School.'*

RESEARCH EXCELLENCE

% of KCL's research that is
4* *(World-class) or* **3*** *(Internationally rated):*

	4*	3*
Cardiovascular Medicine	20%	60%
Cancer Studies	5%	50%
Infection/Immunology	15%	55%
Hospital Clinical Subjects	25%	50%
Lab. Clinical Subjects	5%	30%
Health Services	10%	40%
Neuroscience	15%	40%
Dentistry	30%	40%
Applied Biomedical Sciences	5%	30%
Nutritional Sciences	30%	35%
Pharmacy	15%	40%
Biological Sciences	20%	45%
Human Biological Sciences	20%	35%
Physics	10%	40%
Pure Mathematics	20%	50%
Applied Mathematics	15%	50%
Computer Science	15%	45%
Electrical/Electronic Eng.	5%	35%
Mechanical, Aero., Manufacturing Eng.	10%	35%
Geography/Environment	20%	50%
Business/Management	30%	40%
Information Management	35%	30%
Law	15%	35%
Politics	15%	30%
Education	30%	35%
American Studies	15%	35%
French	25%	40%
German	25%	35%
Portuguese	30%	35%
Spanish	20%	45%
English	15%	55%
Classics Studies	30%	35%
Philosophy	35%	40%
Theology	10%	55%
History	25%	35%
Performing Arts	40%	45%
Music	45%	40%

come thick and fast in other areas of Health, such as pathology, pharmacy, nursing, physiotherapy and more jobs in hospitals for graduates in Biochemistry, Biomedical Sciences, Human Sciences, and Physiology. Thereafter, Languages lead to banking, publishing and museum-archival work, and Social Studies (Politics - including the trail-blazing War Studies, and Economics) lead to recruitment into Defence, banking, and the civil service.

Behind all the science lies excellence also in subjects like Philosophy, Theology and the 4-year BMus, a collaboration with The Royal Academy of Music, which combines intellectual and practical approaches.

If you are accepted at King's you will be joining a community of future professionals, achievers and influencers who share your links with the College. When you graduate, your connections with the College and its alumni - former students of the College - can, if you want, be with you for life, whether for business, pleasure or continued learning. At graduation you automatically become a member of the Alumni Association: a worldwide network tof 120,000.

STUDENT SCENE

In keeping with many student unions' apparent assumption that they can educate the masses by naming bars after prominent politicians, the showpiece attraction of King's Strand campus is its airy venue, **Tutu's**. Blessed with a stage, bar, café, dance floor and spectacular views of the South Bank, this offers an in-house retreat for the college's loose-livered and free of fancy. A bust of the venue's namesake presides with piously disapproving glare over a feast of comedy nights, discos, live acts and all the other student malarkey.

Fave nights are *Truffle Shuffle* (80s fancy dress), *The Final Fuse* (urban conflagration of r&b, Bhangra, hip hop, and UK garage), Friday night's legendary *Phase* (party classics), and Saturday's *After Skool Klub. Quest* is new this year, a club night you choose the tracks to. **The Waterfront**, acts as

the exchange process.

Thoroughly compatible with this is KCl's encouragement of students to take a Language module in their course. Almost all students may take modules at the Modern Language Centre, which again count towards the final degree. They include more than 20 languages, ranging from Arabic to Urdu, Bengali, Catalan, Hebrew, Hindi, Japanese, Mandarin, Panjabi, Turkish and all the traditional European languages.

After Medicine and Dentistry, graduate jobs

ACCOMMODATION

Student rating	★★
Guarantee to freshers	**1333 places**
Style	**Halls, flats**
Security guard	**Some**
Shared rooms	**Some**
Internet access	**Some**
Self-catered	**Some**
En suite	**Some**
Approx price range pw	**£71.19-£144.41**
City rent pw	**£110+**

WHAT IT'S REALLY LIKE

UNIVERSITY:	
Social Life	★★★
Societies	★★
Student Union services	★★★★
Politics	**Average: student issues**
Sport	**44 clubs**
National team position	**58th**
Sport facilities	★★
Arts opportunities	**Good**
Student newspaper	**Roar**
Guardian Media Awards	**Digital Journalist of Year**
Nightclub	**Tutu's**
Bars	**The Waterfront, Guy's Bar**
Union ents	**Phase, Truffle Shuffle, After Skool, Quest**
Union societies	**94**
Parking	**None**
CITY:	
Entertainment	★★★★★
Scene	**Wild, expensive**
Town/gown relations	**Average-good**
Risk of violence	**London v. high**
Cost of living	**High**
Student concessions	**Abundant**
Survival + 2 nights out	**£150 pw**
Part-time work campus/town	**Excellent**

reporting, though in 2010 it was undergraduate Will Benton who was voted the Digital Journalist of the Year Award. Then there's *The Notebook*, a creative writing magazine, and *Satyrica*, the Classics Department paper. And of course KCL Radio, the student radio station. All in all, the Union keeps its flock busy - but with the bright lights of the West End topping the list of countless distractions, it will only ever deter a relatively small proportion of its students from finding ways to get deeper in debt.

SPORT There are four sports grounds in Surrey and south London, rifle ranges at the Strand, the aforesaid K4 fitness club, a swimming pool and gym at Guy's, and highly successful boat and sub-aqua clubs. Nationally, KCL's teams came 58th last year.

PILLOW TALK

They have 1,333 places in traditional halls, 1,321 in self-catering apartments, 175 in Liberty Living residencies and 660 in the University of London Intercollegiate halls. See www.kcl.ac.uk/accomm.

They guarantee halls for full-time undergraduates who apply on time (June 30) and whose home address is outside the M25.

All residences are within London Travel Zones 1 or 2, and close to one or more of the campuses.

Rents in London start from approx £100 p.w. to however much you are willing to pay plus bills on top.

All students are strongly advised not to bring cars with them. A resident with a disability who requires parking at halls should make a written request to the Residence Manager in advance.

GETTING THERE

☞ **Strand campus**: Temple (District Line, Circle), Aldwych (Piccadilly), Holborn (Piccadilly, Central). **Waterloo campus**: Waterloo/Waterloo East overland; Waterloo Underground (Bakerloo, Northern). **Guy's campus**: (Northern) and overland. **St Thomas's campus**: as Waterloo or Westminster (Circle, District, Northern, Bakerloo). **Denmark Hill campus**: Denmark Hill overland.

a perfectly pleasant preamble and afterparty to its big brother, **Tutu**, upstairs.

TGuy's Bar looks after the medics at their London Bridge campus.

Clubs and societies are legion, with salsa, debating and the King's Players (theatre), popular choices. A further popular activity (although one without its own notice board) was reported by irreverent and controversial student tabloid, Roar. 'Basement Boys Use Bogs for Buggering' ran the headline. Roar, incidentally, is regularly nominated by the *Guardian* in its annual student awards for its

KINGSTON UNIVERSITY

Kingston University
40-46 Surbiton Road
Kingston upon Thames KT1 2HX

TEL 020 8547 7053
FAX 020 8547 7080
EMAIL admissions-info@kingston.ac.uk
WEB www.kingston.ac.uk

Kingston Students' Union
Penrhyn Road
Kingston upon Thames: KT1 2EE

TEL 020 8517 2868
FAX 020 8547 8862
EMAIL studentsunion@kingston.ac.uk
WEB www.kusu.co.uk

UNIVERSITY/STUDENT PROFILE

University since	**1992**
Situation/style	**London sites**
Student population	**25930**
Undergraduates	**19535**
Mature	**43%**
International	**18%**
Male/female ratio	**47:53**
Equality of opportunity:	
state school intake	**97%**
social class 4-7 intake	**41%**
drop-out rate	**10%**

VIRGIN VIEW

*K*ingston is in Surrey, off the A3, London's outflow to the south west. Whatever they tell you about it being the oldest Royal borough, the place where Saxon kings were crowned (the Coronation stone lies in the Guildhall - King's Stone, geddit?), it is, in the cold light of reality, a shopping centre/housewife's paradise, a lace-curtained, wife-swapping suburbia 25 mins from central London by train.

Shoppers come from miles to the mall, the market and the endless chain-shops, while its pubs and clubs attract streams of youthful revellers and the sometime Kingston Poly delivers higher education to its many thousands of students.

We're talking vocational at the University, 'even those courses that don't on the surface appear to be vocational,' says the marketing department. 'The transferable skills that students gain while they're here make them very employable.' Students say that London being only 15 minutes away facilitates the career process further.

In the Higher Education Funding Council's National Student Survey (2009) 79% of Kingston's students expressed themselves satisfied with the deal on offer here. In the Times Higher's more recent Student Experience Survey there was less enthusiasm about the size of tuition groups, but a general murmur in support of the helpfulness and interest of the teaching staff. And while their lecturers are not among the leaders in the field of research, last year, in the first research assessment since 2001, 96% of the work submitted was rated as being of at least national significance, and there was evidence of a fair measure of world-class research going on in Nursing, Business, English, History of Art, Architecture and Design.

The undergraduate population is fluid and challenging. There are around 2,500

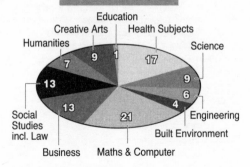

SUBJECT AREAS (%)

Education — 1
Creative Arts — 9
Health Subjects — 17
Humanities — 7
Science — 9
Social Studies incl. Law — 13
Engineering — 6
Business — 13
Built Environment — 4
Maths & Computer — 21

part-timers, 43% mature students and not far short of 41% from the lowest socio-economic groups, yet Kingston gets 70% of them real graduate jobs within six months of leaving, and keeps all but 10% of them until the end of the course.

CAMPUS SITES

The uni is based at four campuses near the A3, London's south-west outflow - Penrhyn Road, Kingston Hill, Knights Park and Roehampton Vale. Current plans include a £20 million, 6-storey teaching building and landscaped courtyard at the main Penrhyn Road campus, and extensions to library and teaching facilities at Kingston Hill and Roehampton Vale.

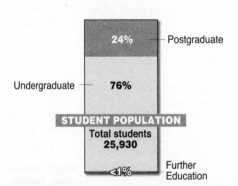

Postgraduate — 24%
Undergraduate — 76%

STUDENT POPULATION
Total students
25,930

Further Education — <1%

PENRHYN ROAD Kingston upon Thames, KT1 2EE. Tel (all sites): 020 8547 2000. Faculties: Science and some Technology.

KINGSTON HILL Kingston upon Thames, KT2 7LB. Faculties: Business, Education, Music, Law, Social Work, and Healthcare Sciences.

KNIGHTS PARK Kingston upon Thames, KT1 2QJ. Faculties: Art & Design, Architecture, Quantity Surveying, Estate Mgt.

ROEHAMPTON VALE Kingston upon Thames, KT1 2EE. Faculties: Mechanical, Aeronautical and Production Engineering.

FEES, BURSARIES

UK & EU Fees 2011-12: £3,375 p.a. Bursaries of between £300 and £1,000 awarded to HE Maintenance grant holders.

STUDENT PROFILE

They attract a mix of customer, from engineers to trendy artists, from nurses to would-be lawyers and City types, most notably a mature undergraduate body. Generally it's a 'new' university audience at Kingston. Writes Paul Stephen: 'It's an easy place to make friends, and the best time to start is freshers week. Although the events aren't really up to much, due to the limited space, the Students' Union makes a real effort to welcome you.

RESEARCH EXCELLENCE		
% of Kingston's research that is		
4* *(World-class)* or **3*** *(Internationally rated):*		
	4*	3*
Nursing and Midwifery	15%	30%
Health Professions	5%	20%
Computer Science	5%	30%
General Engineering	5%	20%
Town/Country Planning	0%	10%
Geography/Environment	5%	25%
Economics	5%	15%
Business/Management	10%	35%
Law	0%	10%
Psychology	0%	20%
Education	0%	25%
European Studies	5%	15%
English	10%	30%
History	5%	25%
Art and Design	0%	30%
History of Art	10%	40%
Performing Arts	5%	30%
Music	0%	10%

TEACHING SURVEY AT A GLANCE	
Avg. UCAS points accepted	**230**
Acceptance rate	**17%**
Overall satisfaction rate	**80%**
Helpful/interested staff	★★★
Small tuition groups	★
Students into graduate jobs	**70%**

Teaching most popular with undergraduates: Biology & related sciences, Communications, Dance, Drama, English, Teacher Training, Journalism, Languages, Mathematics and Statistics, Medical Science & Pharmacy, Molecular Biology, Nursing, Pharmacology.

Teaching least popular with undergraduates: Music (55%), Planning (52%).

Freshers' angels work round the clock to show you around, introduce you to others and generally force you to have a good time. Each year it's different, but last year's Freshers Ball featured ice-skating, Laserquest and mechanical surfing. My freshers week was awesome, and I made some friends then that I still hang out with now.'

There's a special welcome programme for the many international students they attract: a course, 'Understanding Britain', an international scholarship programme worth up to £300 per year; and fun events, parties and trips.

ACADEMIA & JOBS

The University's Faculty of Health and Social Care Sciences offers courses in nursing, midwifery, radiography, physiotherapy, social work, paramedic science, biomedical sciences and continuing professional development, and is one of the significant graduate employment areas at Kingston.

Supporting this area of health are a number of new facilities and projects. For pharmacist undergraduates a practice laboratory opened in 2009, and radiotherapy students are among the first in the country to learn their clinical skills in a simulated cancer treatment room. There is also a new academic partnership with the Royal Marsden School of Cancer Nursing and St George's, University of London (see entry), with courses, research and other opportunities for students studying to be cancer care professionals. Meanwhile, a number of research projects at the Centre for Paramedic Science position Kingston at the forefront of paramedic education.

Other areas of Academic strength include architecture, aeronautical engineering, forensic

WHAT IT'S REALLY LIKE

UNIVERSITY:

Social Life	★★
Societies	★★
Student Union services	★★
Politics	**Student issues**
Sport	**Competitive**
National team position	**71st**
Sport facilities	★
Arts opportunities	**Drama, music, film, art good; dance poor**
Student magazine	**Fresh**
Student newspaper	**The River Mouth**
Guardian Media Awards	**Publication of Year**
Bars	**Space, Hannafords, Knights Park**
Union ents	**Eclectic**
Union societies & clubs	**73**
Most popular society	**Islamic/Afro-Caribbean**
Smoking policy	**Gannets, Hannafords OK**
Parking	**Adequate**
CITY:	
Entertainment	★★★★
Local scene	**Club scene OK**
Town/gown relations	**Average**
Risk of violence	**Low**
Cost of living	**Very high**
Student concessions	**Average**
Survival + 2 nights out	**£80 pw**
Part-time work campus/town	**Excellent**

science, geography, geology, illustration and animation, fashion, law, mathematics, and social sciences and surveying.

Student engineers flock to Kingston to study BEng Civil, Aeronautical, Mechanical, Electronic, Automotive, Motorcycling and Motorsport degrees., and there is a BSc(Hons) Automotive Design taught jointly with Kingston's talented design department. There are jobs aplenty for Kingston graduates notably in engineering design, and in air transport, Defence, construction, and the manufacture of motor vehicles and aircraft.

In Building and Planning there are also real jobs in quantity in architectural consultancy and engineering, in the construction industry, in estate agency, property development and town planning, though this is an area of the teaching that got few plaudits from students in the last national survey undertaken by HEFCE on behalf of the Government. Planning, and Music,

as it happens were the two classes that attracted fewest votes from their students, and perhaps not coincidentally they were among the weakest subjects submitted to the National Research Assessment programme (see our Teaching and research Excellence boxes).

The leading edge for graduate employment is with Creative Arts & Design (which produces 18% of graduate jobs at Kingston). Besides Fine Art they offer Graphic Design, Illustration, Interior Design, Product & Furniture Design, and Fashion. The BA Hons Fashion produces the second largest number of graduates into the industry. Meanwhile, the BA Interior Design scores highly on the employment graph, producing the fifth largest number of graduates into the industry. And a new BSc(Hons) Product Design Engineering combines traditional art and design modules with those offered by engineering-based programmes.

Of Business graduates, which is the second best for jobs out of here, most go into accounting, retail, especially fashion, banking and finance, etc.

There is a mass of computing courses, games programming, graphics and digital image, cyber security, as well as 'with business'. Many graduates go into software engineering, telecommunications, and all sorts of other areas with their computing skills, clothing retail again - they must have their connections! As well as banking, public administration, etc.

Among social studies graduates there is a niche for probation officers in the BA Criminal Justice Studies, which includes a diploma in Social Work. There's also BA Social Welfare Studies and various Psychology and Sociology combinations. Finally, they are European law specialists, and if you do not have a Law degree, but want to become a solicitor, you can take the Common Professional Examination (CPE) here.

In addition to getting 70% into real graduate jobs within six months of leaving last time, Kingston has been awarded a grant from the Economic Challenge Investment Fund, enough to support over 1,000 unemployed graduates through current challenging economic times at a graduate jobseeker boot-camp.

They offer students the opportunity to build their own prospectus on www.kingston.ac. uk/personalised-prospectus/. You tick boxes to indicate where you are based (local, national, international) and the courses of intereste. The University then sends a tailor-made programme.

Kingston is markedly vocational. Sandwich courses aboud, as do employment-enhancing language schemes for non-language undergraduate, a Teaching & Learning Support scheme, which supplies individually or group-designed study skills programmes, EFL courses for overseas students and a 'peer assisted' learning scheme for first years.

SOCIAL SCENE

STUDENTS' UNION Writes Paul Stephen: 'The Students' Union runs 3 bars on different campuses. **The Space**, based at the Penrhyn Road campus, was refurbished recently, giving it a café bar vibe with the addition of comfy leather sofas, a juice bar and "fair trade" coffee and tea. There is also a Subway sandwich counter. It's a good place to chill after lectures or to have a game of pool, but can easily be arranged for pre-club nights or live music. There are three pool tables, 5 plasma TVs, a big screen and quiz machine.

'Then there's **Hannaford's** on the Kingston Hill campus. From the outside it's just an old bomb shelter, but inside it's a fairly modern bar, with Subway again. Seeing as it sits right next to the halls of residence on Kingston Hill, Hannaford's has the vibe of a "local", with regular quiz and pool nights. The bar has also hosted comedy, guest dj and live band nights.

'Finally, there's **Knights Park Bar** on the artsy Knights Park campus, next door to Middle Mill Halls. The bar has a patio, which sits on the side of the Hogsmill River, making it the perfect place for a beer on a sunny day. The small bar has a bohemian feel and offers a variety of ents. Three Saturdays a month it is home to Dickfest - unsigned bands and artists. The fourth hosts Preflex, a straight-friendly gay night - cheesy pop, sparkly house and glam indie. Non stop erotic dancing features every other Friday - sleazy electronica, post punk, punk, quality old school indie, dodgy cover versions and Johnny Cash! For the hard-core drinkers among you, ask the bar staff about Drunk Thursdays.

'The Afro-Caribbean society and the Islamic society are the busiest on campus, but there are many more, ranging from People and Planet to Circus skills societies.'

In 2010 Kingston won the coveted Publication oif the Year award from the *Guardian* for its newspaper, *The River*, actually put together by the department of Journalism, not the Union. They also have another publication, *Mouth*. But the Union has a magazine called *Fresh*. There are promises too for a student radio station.

TOWN 'In town there is something on offer every night of the week. **Oceana** is Kingston's superclub - 5 bars and 2 nightclubs. Then there's **The Works**, home to R&B, hip hop and garage until the recent arrival of New *Slang* - Thursday's indie and alter-

ACCOMMODATION	
Student rating	★★
Guarantee to freshers	**None**
Style	**Halls, flats**
Security guard	**All**
Shared rooms	**None**
Internet access	**All**
Self-catered	**All**
En suite	**Most**
Approx price range pw	**£96-£120.25**
City rent pw	**£100+**

native club night, with signed bands and guest DJs. **McCluskey's** is on the river bank and offers cheap drinks and cheesy tunes.

Bacchus is an alternative basement club playing everything from indie and punk to hip hop and house. **Bar Eivissa** is also worth a visit on a Monday or Wednesday, the atmosphere is always good. And gay friendly club **Reflex** was the inspiration for Preflex at Knights Park.'

SPORT 2010 saw the opening of the £2.65m Tolworth Court sports pavilion and upgraded sports ground. The 55-acre site boasts a 2-story pavilion with 14 changing rooms, a first-aid room and a large social area. New cricket squares and improved facilities have also been added to the site's 14 football pitches, two rugby pitches, and a floodlit, multi-use, hard-court area for netball, tennis and five-a-side football. Kingston runs an Elite Athlete scheme to encourage students to compete at top levels in their sport. There's also rowing on the Thames.

PILLOW TALK

First years have the 'comfort' of halls. If you live in hall at Kingston, you'll have a single room in a flat shared with other students. You'll share the kitchen with between 2 and 9 others. Kingston Hill campus has on-site, en-suite facilities. There are 4 other residential sites including Middle Mill Hall, self-catering flats opposite Knights Park Campus. Most are now en suite. Rooms are also available in a newly built, privately owned, student halls development in central Kingston, which have been leased by the uni's Accommodation Services.

GETTING THERE

☞ By road: M1/J6a, M25/J13, A30, signs to A308 (Kingston). From London: A3 to Robin Hood Roundabout, then A308.
☞ By rail: frequent trains from London Waterloo to Kingston. No Underground this far out, but well served by buses.
☞ By air: Heathrow.

UNIVERSITY OF LANCASTER

University of Lancaster
Lancaster LA1 4YW

TEL 01524 65201
EMAIL ugadmissions@lancaster.ac.uk
WEB www.lancs.ac.uk

Lancaster Students' Union
Slaidburn House
Lancaster LA1 4YA

TEL 01524 593765
FAX 01524 846732
WEB www.lusu.co.uk

VIRGIN VIEW

*L*ancaster University, founded in 1964, is far away from the Lancashire industrial towns of popular imagination. It sits to the north of the county, sandwiched between the sea and the Forest of Bowland, a huge fell space, open and giving life to myriad becks. Lancaster itself is a city certainly, but it is small and has cobbled streets and well-maintained historic buildings.

A well-thought-out curriculum, a good chance of ending up with a first or upper second, consistently good teaching assessments, a recent £50-million capital expenditure on resources (art gallery, libraries, union, music buildings, halls, etc.), good ents (they own their own nightclub in town), an active media, drama and sporting traditions, and a beautiful 250-acre, landscaped campus within sight of the Lakes - all this contributes to Lancaster remaining a special kind of choice. It is also one of the safest campuses in Britain, and a well established collegiate system provides close-knit communities within the whole campus community.

Students love it here - 87% of them said so in the latest Government Student Survey, and the drop-out rate, at 5%, is low. Open Days, 2011: 24 August and 17 September.

UNIVERSITY/STUDENT PROFILE	
University since	**1964**
Situation/style	**Rural collegiate campus**
Student population	**12695**
Undergraduates	**9430**
Mature	**30%**
International	**22%**
Male/female ratio	**46:54**
Equality of opportunity:	
state school intake	**92%**
social class 4-7 intake	**26%**
drop-out rate	**5%**

CAMPUS

'The university has a beautiful countryside location at Bailrigg, on the outskirts of Lancaster,' writes Lis Maree. 'It is 3 miles from Lancaster city centre and set in acres of landscaped woods and parkland. On a clear day the view can extend as far as the Lakeland fells. Lancaster is just 10 minutes away by bus, a friendly, bustling place which has all the amenities of a larger city, while retaining the unique charm of its antiquity.'

COLLEGE LIFE

The essential element of the Lancaster experience is the collegiate system. Virtually everything is done with or for your college

Writes Lisa: 'The colleges of the university are a very distinctive feature of campus life. Even staff are members, many of them active in collegiate life. The colleges vary considerably in atmosphere and size, but each is a busy centre of social, recreational and educational activity. All on-campus accommodation is located within college, which makes it easy to get to know people and quickly to gain a sense of belonging in this kind of supportive community.'

You might think, with campus being a small, all-encompassing 'city' miles from anywhere, it could get a bit claustrophobic in time, but that is not the experience of students. By your second year you will probably be ready to break out, but the urge is satisfied by leaving your college residence rather than the uni as a whole. For in your second

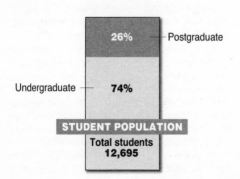

26% — Postgraduate

Undergraduate — 74%

STUDENT POPULATION
Total students
12,695

year renting accommodation in town is actively encouraged, while continuing allegiance to your college is ensured by both sporting and course activities.

The result of this very successful organic experiment is that when you ask students what it's like at Lancaster University, the words that crop up time and again are 'friendly', 'relaxed', 'unintimidating'. In fact, I can't imagine that Lancaster's system of 'personal advisers' - a 1:5 staff to student welfare and educational advice service, has much to do.

FEES, BURSARIES

UK & EU Fees 2011-12: £3,375. A bursary of £1,000 per annum will be payable to new UK students, where SLC assessed income below £34,000. A scholarship of £1,000 will be payable in year one to new students making the University firm UCAS choice and achieving the specified scholarship grades.

STUDENT PROFILE

'The best thing about the uni is the warm, friendly atmosphere created by the students in their somewhat wind-chilled and rainy environment. The student body comprises a wide cross-section of people, including large percentages of privately educated and overseas students.'

They were among the UK's 'access elite' in the matter of taking classes of student new to the idea of university, and although others have now overtaken them, they do have the perfect access policy that cuts through the political correctness and ignorance that habitually surrounds the ideal: 'The University aims to admit those students who are likely to meet the demands of their chosen programme of study and succeed in it. Evidence of aptitude (such as previous and anticipated examination results, professional qualifications, and other evidence of academic ability or potential) and suitability for their chosen programme are the primary criteria for selection. Special consideration may be given to applicants who cannot meet the published requirements due to mitigating educational or personal circumstances.'

ACADEMIA & JOBS

There has been some inpired rationalisation recently. They now have a Department of Politics, Philosophy and Religion (PPR) - formed in 2010,

RESEARCH EXCELLENCE		
% of Lancaster's research that is 4* (World-class) or 3* (Internationally rated):		
	4*	3*
Health Professions	20%	40%
Environmental Sciences	15%	55%
Physics	25%	45%
Pure Mathematics	10%	40%
Statistics	15%	45%
Computer Science	25%	55%
Electrical/Electronic Eng.	10%	45%
General Engineering	10%	40%
Business/Management	25%	50%
Law	5%	40%
Politics	5%	15%
Social Work	20%	40%
Sociology	35%	25%
Psychology	10%	30%
Education	15%	30%
European Studies	5%	30%
English	20%	40%
Linguistics	20%	25%
Philosophy	10%	30%
Theology	15%	40%
History	15%	40%
Art and Design	25%	55%

'Set in acres of landscaped woods and parkland, on a clear day the view can extend as far as the Lakeland fells.'

merging the old Departments of Politics and International Relations, Philosophy, and Religious Studies. Each of these had an excellent reputation for teaching and research within their specific disciplines. The new department not only allows researchers and students to continue to engage in subject-specific teaching, learning and research, but also to engage with a range of topics and problems of great contemporary importance that benefit from an *interdisciplinary* approach. For example: problems of religion and conflict, diplomacy, terrorism, health, well-being and human rights.

All 22 subjects submitted by Lancaster to the last Research Assessment were found to have produced world-class research. Physics came top nationwide. Computer Science and Art & Design were both 80% world-class (4 star) and internationally excellent (3 star). Business and Management and Environmental Science were similarly rated 75% and 70% respectively.

Lancaster's Management School is ranked in the top 5 in the UK and entrepreneurship is embedded in the culture. There are visiting inspi-

TEACHING SURVEY AT A GLANCE

Avg. UCAS points accepted	**390**
Acceptance rate	**22%**
Overall satisfaction rate	**87%**
Helpful/interested staff	★★★★
Small tuition groups	★★★
Students into graduate jobs	**73%**

Teaching most popular with undergraduates:
Accounting, Biology, Business Studies, Economics, English studies, Finance and Accounting, Fine Art, German & Scandinavian Studies, History, Human and Social Geography, Law, Linguistics (100%), Marketing, Maths, Mechanical, Production & Manufacturing Eng., Molecular Biology, Biophysics & Biochemistry, Philosophy, Physical Geography & Environmental Science, Physical Science (100%), Physics & Astronomy (100%), Sociology, Social Policy & Anthropology, Theology.

Teaching least popular with undergraduates:
Music (64%), Iberian Studies (63%), French Studies (61%), Drama (59%), Social Work (50%).

rational speakers, support for business ideas and start-ups, student placements and a rolling programme of entrepreneurship workshops.

They also have a large Arts, Humanities, Social Sciences faculty, with strengths across the board, including creative and performing arts, and there are smaller science, technology and medical faculties with many top rated departments, including Maths, Physics, Engineering and Environmental Science.

Then there's the medical provision in the newly established School of Health and Medicine, traditionally a big graduate job provider. New developments include a research centre specialising in Bipolar disorder and a new Centre for Organisational Health and Wellbeing. Admission to a 5-year MBChB is husbanded and managed jointly with Liverpool University, although you'll study at Lancaster.

Chasing graduate jobs, the Careers Service, which has 4,000 employers on its books, gets together with the Students Union and academic faculties in the Lancaster Award, which recognises the extra-curricular achievements that make so many of the 73% who get real graduate jobs within 6 months of leaving employable. They expect over 500 students to graduate with the Award in 2012. It is what graduate recruiters have wanted of universities for a long time.

Want a sure bet for graduate employment? Go for the unique Ernst & Young Degree, BSc (Hons) in Accounting, Auditing and Finance. It offers a four-year sandwich programme and a certain job at the end.

Generally at Lancaster the system is that your first year is a kind of taster year. They've woken up to the fact that a number of students study subjects at degree level that they haven't studied at school. In Part One (your first year) you take three subjects. One of these has to be what you intend to major in, but the other two can be completely off the wall. If you registered to do Politics, but, after a first year studying Politics, Law and Computing (for instance), you decide that you really should have applied to do Law all along, then so long as you get the required marks in your first year exams, transfer between departments is easy. This flexible programme in Part One is very popular.

Finally, there's a first-class exchange scheme with many Lancaster students attending European and US institutions during their degree. Clearly, languages are a strength here. Note, too, that in Law they are European specialists.

SOCIAL SCENE

'Each of the colleges has its own JCR (Junior Common Room), complete with bar and pool table,' reports Lisa. 'Many universities have only one union bar and the nine we have on campus provide perfect venues for bar crawls that last all night long.

'At the end of the academic year each college has its own entertainment event, affectionately named the extrav, which usually results in farcically ridiculous antics and the presence of Chesney Hawkes or Abba and Elvis tribute bands.'

A poll puts **Pendle Bar** in first place in a college league of bars, followed closely by **Grizedale** (Shite disco on Friday) and **Lonsdale.** most colleges organise subsidised fortnightly trips to clubs - Liverpool and Manchester are just over an hour away.

Sugar House is the union nightclub in town. It opens on Thursday, Friday and Saturday for indie, alternative to r&b, hip hop and also cheesy pop, and on other nights for live ents - bands, comedy, etc. - this year the Thrills, Fun Loving Criminals and the Dream Team.

The high-scoring Drama Department (full marks on inspection) empowers a studio theatre and the on-campus **Nuffield Theatre**, used for both student and 'pro' touring companies. A newly opened £10m building provides performance space for the Lancaster Institute for Contemporary Arts.

The Lancaster Theatre Group is the most active society. Media-wise they are full strength with newspaper *SCAN*, radio station Bailrigg FM (BFM as it is known) and the student web site. All

WHAT IT'S REALLY LIKE

UNIVERSITY:	
Social Life	★★★★
Societies	★★★★
Student Union services	★★★★
Politics	**Active, not Left: fees, welfare**
Sport	**31 clubs**
National team position	**46th**
Sport facilities	★★
Arts opportunities	**Art, drama, music, film good; dance poor**
Student newspaper	**SCAN**
Student radio	**Bailrigg FM**
Nightclub	**Sugar House**
Bars	**College bars**
Union ents	**Indy/Alternative, r&b, hip hop, cheesy pop, live and comedy**
Union societies	**65**
Most popular society	**Theatre group**
Parking	**Strictly limited**
TOWN:	
Entertainment	★★★
Scene	**Excellent pubs, main uni club**
Town/gown relations	**Good**
Risk of violence	**Low**
Cost of living	**Average**
Student concessions	**Average**
Survival + 2 nights out	**£70 pw**
Part-time work campus/town	**Poor/average**

ACCOMMODATION

Student rating	★★★★★
Guarantee to freshers	**100%**
Style	**Halls, flats**
Security guard	**All**
Shared rooms	**Some**
Internet access	**All**
Self-catered	**All**
En suite	**Most**
Approx price range pw	**£73.85-£146.37**
Town rent pw	**£72-£98**

have been award-winning in the national student competitions over the last few years.

'There is a huge variety of societies,' writes Lisa. 'including alternative music, taekwando, photography, kickboxing, floorball, debating and juggling.

'If politics is your passion, the union is one of the most pro-active at the moment, campaigning for just about everything from abortions to AIDS. The Film Society is the largest society, and very popular are Bailrigg fm and the newspaper, *Scan.*'

SPORT A new £20m sports centre is due to open in the summer of 2011. Inter-college rivalries mean that if you enjoy sport, but aren't good enough to play at inter-university level, you will certainly be good enough to play at college level. A very high proportion of students enjoy competitive team sport, even those that aren't that good, but the place really comes alive at Roses - Lancaster vrs York Uni, a huge weekend of sport and socials.

TOWN 'The social life at Lancaster should not be underestimated,' writes Guy McEvoy. 'Lancaster town itself has been transformed over the past five years by massive investment from the major brewers. Trendy pubs are now displacing the traditional Northern watering hole in the centre of town (though these can still be found on the edges if that is your thing). The union-run Sugar House remains the most popular club.'

Writes Lisa: 'If you are on a very tight budget I would suggest drinking in the college bars before going out into Lancaster and then clubbing dry.

'Student friendly pubs include **The Merchants**, **The Firkin**, **The Walkabout**, **Paddy Mulligan's**, **The Waterwitch** and **Blob Shop**. Recommended nightclubs are Sugar House, of course, and **Liquid**, **The Carleton** (host to Chesney Hawkes in the past), **Elemental**, and **Tokyo Joe's** in Preston.

PILLOW TALK

Lncaster won the National Housing Survey's Best University Halls Award in 2010. All campus accommodation is located within undergraduate colleges, and most of it is very new: 4,400 new campus rooms have been delivered since 2003. The majority are en-suite, but there are some rooms with shared facilities. There are also brand new Eco-residences, townhouses for 12 students, with a living room, and a shower room for each 2 students.

GETTING THERE

☞ By road: M6/J34, A683 or M6/J33, A6.
☞ By rail: London Euston, 3:30; Newcastle, 3:00; Sheffield, 2:30; Leeds, 2:30; Manchester, 1:30.
☞ By coach: London, 5:50; Leeds, 3:55.

STUDENT LEEDS - THE CITY

Leeds is one of the most prosperous cities in Europe, conveniently placed in the middle of the country, where two main motorways, the M1 and the M62, intersect. It has an international airport and the busiest train station outside London. Says Londoner Nick Coupe: 'Leeds is sort of the right size for me. It is just a really nice varied city, which is what I was looking for. I feel it can be whatever you want it to be. There are libraries and benches and quiet little bookshops where you can just go in and keep yourself to yourself, but equally there are these massive clubs and huge shopping areas. One of the things when it came to making an application was that Leeds has a really good night life.'

CULTURE

Leeds is the clubbing capital of the North, but has a fantastic variety on offer, from the **West Yorkshire Playhouse** (Sir Ian McKellan, Ben Elton and Irvine Welsh have all premiered productions here) to **Opera North** to **Back 2 Basics** and **Speed Queen**, with the main nocturnal student activities being based in three areas of the city, Headingley, the Union and the City Centre. There is, too, a fantastic gay scene, it is home to some of the best urban music nights and altogether it is truly multicultural

For art truly on the cheap, there are many free galleries, some of which showcase student work. The best of these are **The Henry Moore Institute** and **The Leeds Art Gallery,** which stand next to each other in town. A quick mention must be given to **The Royal Armouries** which was given to Leeds ahead of London.

FILM

In the age of the futuristic multiplex the best thing about film in Leeds is that the cosy independent cinema has survived. Like most places everything is student friendly price-wise, but real value and satisfaction can be found in the cinemas dotted around studentland and cost a few pounds a pop.

The **Hyde Park Picture House** is eighty-five years old and the height of cool. Cult and independent films, as well as the occasional blockbuster, can be found here, and its location slap bang in the in the middle of Hyde Park ensures that it's a student favourite. Headingley has two lovely cinemas – **The Cottage Road** and **Lounge** – both quite plush and with a lovely retro feel to them. Finally **ABC** in town plays the latest that Hollywood has to offer for prices that seem to be stuck in 1987.

PUBS

A must in these parts is completing the fabled Otley Run, involving a drink in every establishment from **Boddington Hall**, four miles north of campus, to Leeds Met's **Met Bar** on the outskirts of the city centre – four miles, twenty-odd pubs and a lot of drinking. All these pubs are geared towards students and the best remain the same year in, year out. **The Original Oak** and **The Skyrack** in central Headingley are pretty much the busiest pubs in the world. No space to move, but forever popular – go on your own and you'll soon bump into someone you know. Also cheap and cheerful 24/7 are the union bars: at Leeds Uni, it's **The Old Bar** (rumoured to be the longest in Europe) and now **Stylus** (1000 capacity), and down the road, the aforementioned **Met Bar**.

CLUBS

Whatever you're looking for is here. **Oceana**, **Gatecrasher**, **Mint**, **Rios**, **Mezz**, you'll find your particular pleasure before too long.

If you're into largin' it at every opportunity then **The Afterdark** in Morley is without doubt the best techno club north of London, with a galaxy of stars playing. Deeply fashionable and just off Leeds University campus is **The Faversham**, a pub in the week but a club on Thursday to Saturday with a crowd that is there to be seen. Situated in Call Lane, the redlight district, **The Fruit Cupboard** hosts the best R&B night in the city and is great for chilling out. Finally, no sampling of Leeds clubland can go by without mentioning the renowned hard house night *Speed Queen, now a memory on a facebook appreciation society, though you may find different.* There are many, many gems, many, many facets to explore before you'll find yourself. Events details can be found in the weekly edition of *Leeds Student*, the newspaper for all students in Leeds.

SHOPPING

Leeds is often called the 'Knightsbridge of the North', but many up here think that Knightsbridge is the 'Briggate of the South'. In fact, from charity shops to **Harvey Nichols** your budget can be catered for. The main areas are in town and the best is **The Victoria Quarter**. Under a stained glass arcade independent and designer labels compete for your loan, but be prepared to spend. **The Corn Exchange** is another big hall much along the same lines, and for value, range and sheer presence the huge, Victorian, covered Kirkgate market is a joy to behold. If strapped for cash go to Hyde Park Corner and Headingley.

Karl Mountsfield

UNIVERSITY OF LEEDS

The University of Leeds
Leeds LS2 9JT

TEL 0113 343 2336
FAX 0113 343 2665
EMAIL study@leeds.ac.uk
WEB www.leeds.ac.uk

Leeds University Union
PO Box 157
Leeds LS1 1UH

TEL 0113 380 1234
FAX 0113 380 1205
EMAIL comms@luu.leeds.ac.uk
WEB www.luuonline.com

VIRGIN VIEW

*L*eeds is England's second city for the legal
profession and banking, and the
University, founded in 1904, is a massive
place - there are more than 32,000 students -
and the culture runs rich and deep, so that
graduate leavers are reflective of society as a
whole - artistic, scientific, creative, the top
50% going into health, finance and banking,
education, and the civil service, community
work and artistic and literary creation,
business, management and advertising,
architecture and engineering, software and
media (especially radio, TV, and publishing).
The buzz that you get when you drop into
the Union is this in pupation.

'What Leeds Uni has to offer, which I
doubt anywhere else could match,' observed
a recent graduate, 'is the students themselves.
There's a real atmosphere about the place.
You can do whatever you want. You can
really get involved at Leeds. And students do.
You don't come to a place like Leeds if you're
an introvert.'

'The Union is never inactive. There is
something on almost 24/7,' writes Zoe. They
have so many student societies that they split
them into 10 groups just so you can absorb
what's on offer: Faith & Culture,
Departmental, General Interest, Martial Arts
& Dance, Media, Outdoor Activities,
Performance, Political & Campaigning,
Sports, and Volunteering.

But there is a downside. 'Student life in
Leeds can lack the close-knit community feel
of a smaller uni. It can also be a somewhat
overwhelming experience. Can be overwhelming because there is so much going on
you don't know what to get involved in, especially in Fresher's week... People are everywhere... and you have to accept the good
with the bad. It can sometimes be quite
cliquey in societies and halls...'

In the 2010 QS World University
Rankings, the University rose 14 places to
number 85, but they are not letting that stop
them recuiting far and wide.

'Access to Leeds' is an alternative
admissions scheme designed to help students
whose personal circumstances may affect
their ability to achieve the exam grades
Leeds asks. It's open to you if you meet two
or more of the following criteria and have
the potential to succeed: you are first generation of immediate family to apply to higher
education; you attend a school which
achieved less than 45% five GCSE passes at
grade A* to C (including English and Maths)
in 2010; your only option is to attend a local
university; your studies were disrupted; you
grew up in care; you live in a geographical
area with low levels of progression into higher education.

But what do they want at the competitive end? What do they want from you? A
well written, informative personal statement
is key. They want evidence of enthusiasm
for and of reading around the subject, and
an awareness of how your chosen subject

UNIVERSITY/STUDENT PROFILE	
University since	**1904**
Situation/style	**City campus**
Student population	**32370**
Undergraduates	**23695**
Mature	**25%**
International	**18%**
Male/female ratio	**41:59**
Equality of opportunity:	
state school intake	**75%**
social class 4-7 intake	**22%**
drop-out rate	**5%**

fits with your long-term aims. See www.leeds.ac.uk/A2L for more. Open Days, 2011: 24 and 25 June, 8 October.

CAMPUS

The campus is a mix of differing architectural styles, ranging from neo-gothic to '70s concrete to modern glass and steel, situated just to the north of the city centre before you get to the bulk of student housing areas.

Everything's within easy walking distance, and 'it's relatively safe,' writes Londoner Amy Shuckburgh. 'On the whole it doesn't have an intimidating feel to it. The same precautions should be taken as in any city: it is inadvisable to walk around late at night on your own; use taxis if possible; union night bus services are provided for girls along all routes, both girls and boys are strongly advised not to walk through Hyde Park at night.'

The union has an arrangement with a taxi service - any student can travel free on production of their union card, which is then presented by the driver to the union for payment. The union settles with the student later.

FEES, BURSARIES

UK & EU Fees, 2011-12: £3,375 p.a. Around one in four students will receive the Leeds Bursary of up to £1,540. It is awarded to undergraduates with a family income of £36,600 or less. Scholarships of up to £3,000 are also awarded, based on financial need and academic excellence. Find out more at www.leeds.ac.uk/info/2012/your_finances.

STUDENT PROFILE

'There is a left-wing, anti-Capitalist stance at Leeds,' says Jude Corrigan. 'It is very prevalent here.' Nothing wrong with that, except that when you look at the student body, you see anything but true socialist flesh and bones on it. Compare it with neighbouring Leeds Met. Leeds has one of the lowest intakes from the state school sector (73% as against Met's 93%). Numbers of students from the four lowest socio-economic classes are likewise minimal (22% against Met's 37%). The only minority group stat that exceeds the Met's is international students. Leeds has 18% from overseas, the Met 8%. The point is however that Leeds Uni is anything but working-class, and when you look at its student politics closely you have a kind of Champagne socialism, undergraduates with gusto born of privilege playing pretentiously at real life, and leaving the socialist playground as soon as they get their well-paid professional jobs. I asked Nick Coupe how he found it.

'You can categorise people quite easily here. The most popular newspaper by a long way is the *Guardian*. Then there's what they call the Devonshire type - Devonshire are the halls of residence where you get the public school, very very Abercrombie and Fitch kind of people. But they are not typical Leeds. I remember a protest here when I first came when some anti-war students took over one of the university buildingsto protest against what Israel was doing in Gaza. There's a lot of things like that where the students demand that the University should be affiliated with Gaza, but at the same time there are also jokes going around about the authorities in the Middle East sitting up and saying, "Oh wait, Leeds University!! We'd better get out!" You do sometimes feel that people are being overly political and overly campaigning, you know, for the sake of it. But our Union is very very

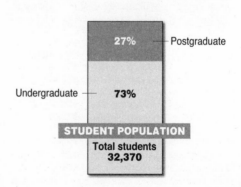

Postgraduate — 27%

Undergraduate — 73%

STUDENT POPULATION
Total students
32,370

RESEARCH EXCELLENCE

% of Leeds' research that is
4* *(World-class)* or **3*** *(Internationally rated):*

	4*	3*
Cardiovascular Medicine	5%	40%
Cancer Studies	15%	65%
Hospital Clinical Subjects	5%	25%
Epidemiology	10%	50%
Health Services	20%	40%
Dentistry	20%	40%
Nursing/Midwifery	25%	35%
Biological Sciences	15%	45%
Food Science	20%	35%
Environmental Sciences	15%	55%
Chemistry	20%	50%
Physics	15%	35%
Pure Mathematics	10%	45%
Applied Mathematics	15%	40%
Statistics	25%	40%
Computer Science	25%	55%
Electrical/Electronic Eng.	30%	50%
General Engineering	20%	60%
Civil Engineering	10%	45%
Mechanical, Aero., Manufac. Eng.	20%	55%
Town/Country Planning	20%	45%
Geography/Environment	25%	45%
Business/Management	20%	50%
Law	15%	40%
Politics	5%	10%
Social Work	35%	30%
Psychology	10%	40%
Education	20%	40%
Sports	10%	20%
Asian Studies	5%	40%
Russian	5%	10%
French	15%	40%
German	25%	25%
Italian	25%	50%
Iberian	20%	40%
English	35%	30%
Linguistics	5%	45%
Classics	5%	25%
Philosophy	20%	45%
Theology	15%	30%
History	15%	50%
Art and Design	15%	40%
History of Art	25%	20%
Performing Arts	20%	50%
Media Studies	15%	35%
Music	20%	45%

have free Yorkshire Water dispensers dotted all around the Union building.

Perhaps the answer is, don't be held in thrall by those in control here; 9 times out of 10 they are not who they think they are (or give you the impression they are). Opt for Leeds, but do your own thing and demand the money from the Union to allow you to do it in whatever type of society you choose to set up, even if it doesn't agree with their politics. Leeds is not a place to follow dumbly behind anyone.

ACADEMIA & JOBS

In the recent Research Assessment, Leeds rose from 26th to 14th place nationally, with research from all 46 subjects submitted world-class to some extent, and 80% of the research in Cancer, Computer, Electrical & Electronic and General Engineering, Minerals & Mining being either world-class or internationally excellent.

Researchers don't always make good teachers. But overall Leeds merit 4 stars for helpful, interested staff, and where small tuition groups are feasible, as in English & Drama, which Nick is studying and which also did well at the research assessments (60% world-class and internationally excellent), and which moved into a £5-million performance complex at the heart of the Leeds campus in the summer of 2007:

'I personally really really enjoy my course. I was quite nervous, I applied for English at five universities and English & Theatre at Leeds. I came for the interview and the Open Day and sort of fell in love with it and decided this was definitely what I wanted to be doing. The first year is quite rigid, you study what you are told to study, but when you get into second year you can really choose what you want to be studying and how. I am doing modules on Harold Pinter at the moment which is what I'm really interested in, so it's great that I can be studying the stuff I'm reading in my spare time as well. I've had a very different experience to all my friends because there are only 25 people on my course in my year, so all the lecturers and all the teaching staff know you by name, or say hello to you if you see them out and about, which is something. One of my friends does history and he barely knows his lecturers' names. I think it's a great system here that you can just pop into someone's office and have an informal chat about essays rather than having to make an appointment and know exactly what you want to say and have ten minutes. You genuinely can go and have a cup of tea and a chat about the module which I would have thought was quite unusual.'

The new Performance Centre includes a 180-seat theatre, the Alec Clegg studio theatre, a dance

student dominated so I guess that is a good thing.'

Recently students here voted overwhelmingly to stop selling bottled water in the Union shops due to its negative environmental impact - they now

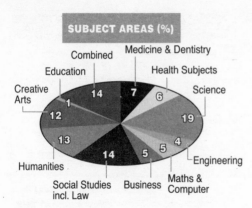

SUBJECT AREAS (%)

Combined · Medicine & Dentistry · Education · Health Subjects · Creative Arts · Science · Humanities · Engineering · Social Studies incl. Law · Business · Maths & Computer

14 · 7 · 6 · 1 · 19 · 12 · 13 · 4 · 14 · 5 · 5

Most students get the chance to spend a semester or academic year abroad, no matter what they are studying. You can choose from over 200 institutions - from Spain to Singapore. 'One reason we recommend Leeds is that you can do exotic languages, Arabic,' said a sixth-form teacher. They are high placed in a league of graduate interpreters and translators, but languages find graduates a whole range of careers, in advertising, market research, media & government research, publicity, PR, government administration and the Civil Service, and it seems more likely than not that a graduate of Leeds will leave with a language or cultural studies course in tow.

The Leeds degree in Medicine is a 5-year MB ChB with its 3-phase focus on the fundamentals of clinical practice, clinical practice in context, professional competence. Communication skills, ethics, health & prevention of disease, community-based medicine, medical info & management are recurring themes. There's also Dentistry, and a nursing provision (child, adult, and midwifery), Midwifery, and BSc Radiography - Diagnostic.

In England's Second City for Finance, Economics also holds much appeal, and there are more budding barristers than it is wise to shake a stick at. They are, too, a contender wherever media is mentioned. Again it's the joint hons programme, with languages to the fore, that appeals. Look also at BA Broadcast Journalism or BA Broadcasting.

studio, and all the facilities associated with a public licensed venue, but the point that Nick made about lecturer interest was what struck a chord with fresher Susan Green: 'What's best about this uni is the very approachable lecturers. There's always someone around to help out.'

Other features of the learning environment is that they have some of the best IT facilities in the country and a student library with around 2.8 million items, one of the finest in the country. As well as the books you need for your studies, you can also access over 33,000 online journals from home, halls or anywhere else. Collections of outstanding national and international importance include English Literature, Russian Archive, Cookery, Romany, and the Liddle Collection (a First World War archive. You can use these any time you want.

The Arts Faculty joint honours courses distinguish the curriculum. The range of these two-main-subjects programmes is wide and challenging, with Chinese, Japanese and Arabic joining the language provision, while Economics, Accounting, the Law and Politics provide some of the overt vocational elements against a rich worldwide cultural backdrop of Russian, Jewish, Roman and other civilisations. It is a heady mix. Leeds prides itself in offering some 375 of these, involving 58 subjects taught across 32 departments. First-year students divide their time equally between three subjects: the two named subjects and a third or 'elective' subject. Thereafter, they concentrate on two of the three. Employers take a keen interest in graduates with two named subjects from Leeds.

There's particular mention, too, of languages.

> *'For me the Student Union is massive, a massive, massive Union, really high quality student paper, student radio, student TV that you can get involved with really easily.'*

Generally, Leeds students benefit from a whole raft of supplementary and interactive learning material. VLE (Virtual Learning Environment) gives access to study materials plus wikis, blogs, podcasts and discussion boards.

SOCIAL SCENE

Leeds was NUS Student' Union of the year (2009/10) and the UK's only Gold Accredited Union. But it's not all glitter.

'For me,' says Nick, 'the Student Union is massive, a massive, massive Union, really high quality student paper, student radio, student TV that you can get involved with really easily. One of my friends who has only been here the same amount of time as me, is already Vice President of LSTV, so although it is massive you can still get very heavily involved in something.'

The Union ents are good too. A £4.8m extension added 40% more shopping and meeting space for students and gave the city a new music venue. The nightclub is called **Stylus** (capacity 1,000), which is adjacent to **Pulse** (capacity 290; has been done out really nicely; in general the Union doesn't get too shabby before they refurbish). And newest venue is **Mine**, with a capacity of 450 and offering different events every week. There are then two bars jointly known as **The Terrace** (complete with sun-terrace and disabled access), **Old Bar,** a traditional pub really, down in the basement, which has been fuelling students since 1939. That leaves the **Riley Smith Hall** (capacity 600) to host productions from the students' performing societies and **The Refectory** (capacity 2,000) as the biggest venue in Leeds, which has hosted more of the world's biggest bands than we'd care to mention.

But there is power on tap too. 'At Leeds we are very strongly two separate institutions, the university and the union. Everybody knows that. But there's mutual respect. Community issues, drug and alcohol policy, things like that we work together on, but politically we like to be independent.'

There's an award-winning track record in media. The radio station is LSR, the weekly student newspaper, *Leeds Student*, a magazine called *Lippy* (women's welfare magazine) and Leeds Review (a new interdisciplinary arts society; they publish an arts journal which provides a platform for students to circulate their work), and TV station LSTV. Then there are the arts, and fund-raising, sport and Community Action societies. Over 2,000 students volunteer in the local community.

'For drama, we've got **The Raven Theatre**. It seats a couple of hundred. The Theatre Group does three or four plays a term. The really big shows, musicals - *Grease, The Whizz, Hair* - are in The Riley Smith Hall.

'There's modern dance (they run jazz, tap, contemporary lessons), there's ballroom and salsa every Wednesday in the Refectory, which is packed out. You can barely move in there.

'The Symphony Orchestra and Symphonia and the chorals are all involved in the Leeds concert season, and then there's dance big bands - they've been on tour, had a CD out, played gigs in the city.

'The Film Society is very big, and the Film Making Society has really taken off. For art we've got the Henry Moore Institute and the galleries and the gallery exhibition in the Parkinson Court.'

SPORT 'The rivalry between the two unis is friendly and good-humoured,' writes Zoe Perkins. 'Once a year it comes to a head in the Varsity Sports Day where respective teams compete at some 20 different sports for the Varsity Cup. The Met always wins. Leeds are always sore losers.'

The Edge, a new £14-million campus fitness centre and 25m, 8-lane pool opened in 2010. There are two sports halls, one large enough to take 1,500

WHAT IT'S REALLY LIKE	
UNIVERSITY:	
Social Life	★★★★★
Societies	★★★★★
Student Union services	★★★★★
Politics	**Campaigning**
Sport	**34 clubs**
National team position	**16th**
Sport facilities	★★★
Arts opportunities	**Excellent**
NSDF (drama) Awards	**3 in 2010**
Student magazine	**Lippy**
Student newspaper	**Leeds Student**
2009 Guardian Awards	**Newspaper of Year**
Student radio	**LSR FM**
2010 Radio Awards	**1 Gold, 5 Silver, 3 Bronze**
Student TV	**LSTV**
Nightclubs	**Stylus, Pulse, Mine**
Bars	**Terrace, Old Bar**
Union ents	**Funky house & chart, drum & bass/old skool, r&b**
Union societies	**210**
Parking	**Off-campus halls**
CITY:	
Entertainment	★★★★★
Scene	**Wild**
Town/gown relations	**Average**
Risk of violence	**Average**
Cost of living	**High**
Student concessions	**Abundant**
Survival + 2 nights out	**£120 pw**
Part-time work campus/town	**Good/average**

spectators. Playing fields are 5 miles from campus; there are also cricket squares, a floodlit synthetic pitch and 6 floodlit tennis courts. There's rowing in Leeds and York, sailing on nearby lakes and reservoirs, hiking, climbing, canoeing and caving in the Yorkshire Dales. Students use the city's international swimming pool, and golf courses in the area.

PILLOW TALK

There is a range of accommodation and a choice of location - on campus, close to the city centre, or around the popular student area of Headingley. There are five catered residences and many more self-catering halls, from modern multi-storey blocks on large sites to converted Victorian town houses and everything in between. 24-hour security, a Residence Watch service and comprehensive welfare provision help students feel safe. You can park at most off campus accommodation.

Says Nick: 'Accommodation is quite a tricky

one because there are many different types. I was in Bodington Halls, which is half an hour's drive from campus really, but when you get there, there are thousands of people and it's a really great atmosphere. The main issue is proximity to campus, apart from... Devonshires are quite separate. Devonshire Halls is in Hyde Park, about a 15 minute walk, but there is a Devonshire type of person and it's sort of renowned. All the other halls compete against Devonshire and turn their nose up at the Devonshire types, because they are very Abercrombie and Fitch.'

GETTING THERE
☞ By road: M62/J39, M1; or M62/J27, M621; or A1, A58; or A65, A650.
☞ By rail: Newcastle, 1:45; London Euston, 2:30; Birmingham New Street, 2:20.
☞ By air: Leeds/Bradford Airport.
☞ By coach: London, 4:00; Edinburgh, 6:00.

LEEDS METROPOLITAN UNIVERSITY

Leeds Metropolitan University
Calverley Street
Leeds LS1 3HE

TEL 0113 812 0000
FAX 0113 283 3129
EMAIL course-enquiries@leedsmet.ac.uk
WEB www.lmu.ac.uk

Leeds Met Students' Union
Calverley Street
Leeds LS1 3HE

TEL 0113 209 8400
FAX 0113 234 2973
EMAIL [initial.name]@leedsmet.ac.uk
WEB www.leedsmetsu.co.uk

VIRGIN VIEW

Not long ago Leeds Met had a reputation for sport and little else, which was a pity because it had started out in 1992 as a torch bearer for new universities and was described in the Guide *by student Rebecca O'Neill as having something for everyone. We said: 'Leeds Met has a clear sense of what it is about, is refreshingly uncomplicated and shows results. Its students also seem to have a good time. It really is as simple as that.'*

The 'results' were jobs. Leeds Met was and is 'a centre for applied learning,' as another student put it. But then for a while some of its lecturers felt more like salesmen for the Vice Chancellor's pet sports projects than teachers. It lost its way.

That is now history. The VC is long gone. Ironically now, they seem to be better at sport than ever, in No. 2 position, nudging Loughborough in their perennial dominance, and with a rather interesting niche in race walking which could just come to fruition in 2012. But more interestingly they have also shot ten places up the student satisfaction scale in the Times Higher's *annual poll, where they praise their lecturers for being helpful and interested in them and for decent size tuition groups, hitting a better-than-average 3 star score in all academic matters and coming 19th in the country for the standard of the library. And, of course, this is Leeds; the social life here is very good.*

Postgraduate 15%
Undergraduate 85%

STUDENT POPULATION
Total students
27,800

UNIVERSITY/STUDENT PROFILE

University since	**1992**
Situation/style	**City sites**
Student population	**27800**
Undergraduates	**23660**
Mature	**40%**
International	**8%**
Male/female ratio	**48:52**
Equality of opportunity:	
state school intake	**93%**
social class 4-7 intake	**37%**
drop-out rate	**10%**

TEACHING SURVEY AT A GLANCE

Avg. UCAS points accepted	**250**
Acceptance rate	**17%**
Overall satisfaction rate	**77%**
Helpful/interested staff	★★★
Small tuition groups	★★★
Students into graduate jobs	**63%**

Teaching most popular with undergraduates:
Education, Accounting, Anatomy, Physiology &
Pathology (100%), Aural & Oral Sciences,
Computer Science, Finance, Human & Social
Geography, Landscape Design, Nursing, Nutrition,
Other Subjects Allied to Medicine, Social Work.

Teaching least popular with undergraduates:
Management (48%), Architecture (45%).

CAMPUS

The so-called Civic Quarter campus is in the heart of Leeds. Headingley campus is 3 miles away in 100 acres of parkland (Beckett Park).

The cultures of the two sites differ as to the type of student. Sports, business and computing students colour Headingley, while City has a lot more arts, health sciences and engineering. 'Students who play sport go out there;' said a student. 'Students who want the library and the big ents come down here.'

The Rose Bowl is the hub of Civic Quarter. It contains lecture theatres, Helpzone and a student refectory. The library is in the Leslie Silver building, is open 24/7. Other buildings include the Electric Press, Old Broadcasting Place, Old School Board and Hepworth Point.

In contrast, Headingley Campus has vast green spaces and world-class sports facilities. Many of the buildings look out onto the grassy expanse of the Acre. There's a shop, post office, refectory, 24/7 library, Students Union and accommodation.

No student car parking at Civic Quarter and limited pay-and-display spaces at our Headingley Campus.

FEES, BURSARIES

UK & EU Fees 2011-12: £3,375 p.a. They offer a package for international students that can fund 50% or 100% of tuition fees. There are also Commonwealth Shared Scholarships for students from developing Commonwealth countries in MSc Public Health and MSc Responsible Tourism Management. The Carnegie Sports Scolarships are well enough known, but don't think you'll get one just because you have reached a junior or senior world-class performance level. Competition for these is fierce. See www.leedsmet.ac.uk/internat/ scholarships_fees.htm.

STUDENT PROFILE

'The demographics are quite different to Leeds University,' says student Kate Denby. 'A large proportion of students at our Leeds site are part-time. They'll come from the Yorkshire area, maybe do evening courses. The full-timers, who come from all over, tend to be more the mature type of student, people who have been out in the world. There are also lots of international students, many of whom come on exchange. It's a more cosmopolitan atmosphere than in Leeds University.'

There's also a low public school showing and a number come from the lower socio-economic groups, and from neighbourhoods that until recently, when the Government began to push for their inclusion, never considered university as an option.

ACADEMIA & JOBS

There are six faculties. The Carnegie Faculty of Sport & Education is self-explanatory. Arts & Society includes Architecture, Landscape & Design; Contemporary Art & Graphic Design; Building & Quantity Surveying, Architectural

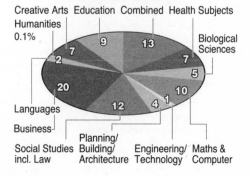

SUBJECT AREAS (%)

Creative Arts, Education, Combined, Health Subjects, Humanities 0.1%, Biological Sciences, Languages, Business, Social Studies incl. Law, Planning/Building/Architecture, Engineering/Technology, Maths & Computer

RESEARCH EXCELLENCE

% of Leeds Met's research that is
4* *(World-class)* or **3*** *(Internationally rated):*

	4*	3*
Allied Health Professions	0%	10%
Business/Management	0%	20%
Information Management	10%	35%
Education	0%	20%
Sports	15%	25%
Art and Design	5%	10%
Media Studies	15%	40%

Technology; Cultural Studies; Film, TV & Performing Arts; Social Sciences; Civil Engineering; Construction; Project Management; Planning, Human Geography & Housing; Youth & Community Studies. Business and Law incorporates all that you might expect, including Accounting & Financial Services. While Innovation North has Creative Technology, Music, Computing & IT. Then, there's the Faculty of Health, and lastly the Leslie Silver International Faculty, including Tourism Management, Hospitality Management & Retailing, Events Management, Applied Global Ethics, and the School of Languages.

For best and worst teaching, see box above.

In the *Times Higher Education* Student Experience Survey in 2009 students criticised their lecturers for lack of help and interest in them, but now the tide has turned and once again we see the centre of applied learning in full flow. Said Kate. 'I'm doing a degree in Public Relations. It's hands on. What you generally find is a lot of students go on placement. They might have a year's placement or a day each week placement. I have no lectures on a Thursday and go into a company and work one day a week. You can do that sort of thing off your own bat or you can get placements via the placements office. People who come here have a goal.'

The reality is that the single largest employment sector for Leeds Met graduates is health. Nursing and degrees in Biomedical Science, Osteopathy, Physiotherapy, Health care Sciences, Dietetics and the like find 6% of these, but Business graduates are also strong into the health industry, as are Biological Sciences graduates of course and Social Studies. Altogether they account for 16% of graduate jobs here.

Primary, secondary tertiary and higher educa-

> '**This is a centre for applied learning. I'm doing a degree in Public Relations. It's hands on. People who come here have a goal.**'

tion is another very strong sector, fed mainly by Education and Biological Sciences (includes Sport).

Retail, especially sports clothing, is another strong sector, principally for Business graduates, Law, architecture, specialised design, accounting, advertising and market research are other niches, fed by dedicated degrees. The hotel and restaurant industry seems to respect the Hospitality degrees.

Kate seems to have got it right: 'People who come here have a goal.' It would be a good idea to ask the department you are intersted in where the cohort of graduates last year ended up. They will have the information.

SOCIAL SCENE

'LMU's **Met Bar** is a huge area, a whole floor of the building which includes an enormous bar, café and the **Stage Venue**. Legendary acts that have graced The Stage (1,100 capacity) include Nirvana, Bob Marley and the Wailers and The Buzzcocks, as well as modern day legends such as Elbow, Julian Casablancas and Glasvegas. Popular club night FUEL, the best in punk, rock, metal, emo and alternative party jams here every Friday.

Monday is *mezz pre-party*, at Met Bar **Mezz** in town playing house, indie and funk. *Sports Wednesdays* is the preferred place to kick off your night after games, again before heading to town. Kicking off on the 1st Friday of each month is *Lyrically Justified*, an open mic night. Saturdays are all about *Quids Inn*, its simple, £1 entry and £1 drinks with our resident DJ. Kirkstall Bar is the Students' Union's Bar at the heart of Kirkstall Brewery Halls. Monday play your own toons - hike your i-pod to the bar, Thursday Karaoke, Friday drinks offers. Sunday quizz..

'Anyone who's anyone plays Leeds Met. Leeds Uni is better at things political,' is the considered student opinion. 'Ents is a totally professional area,' Kate Denby says. 'Everyone who works there is a paid professional, although we do have two students who work part-time for us in an events capacity, qualified to do lighting for example. We generally do 9 events a week across all three venues, so there's a lot to organise.'

The students now have their own television channel, MET TV, which transmits entertainment, music, comedy, and Met Air is the re-named student radio station, while *Leeds On* is the university's student-run, student-governed and student-written newspaper. The complete reappraisal of student media, which has been managed in the background

WHAT IT'S REALLY LIKE	
UNIVERSITY:	
Social Life	★★★★
Societies	★★
Student Union services	★★
Politics	**Student issues**
Sport	**50 clubs. Sport dominates**
National team position	**2nd**
Sport facilities	★★★★
Arts opportunities	**Very little. Dance good**
Student newspaper	**Leeds On**
Student radio	**Met Air**
Student television	**Met TV**
Venues	**The Stage**
Bars	**The Met, Kirstall Brewery**
Union ents	**Mixed and Mezz**
Union societies	**20**
Parking	**Poor**
CITY:	
Entertainment	★★★★★
Scene	**Wild**
Town/gown relations	**Average**
Risk of violence	**Average**
Cost of living	**High**
Student concessions	**Abundant**
Survival + 2 nights out	**£90 pw**
Part-time work campus/town	**Good/aveage**

technology to analyse team play.

A Leeds Met Sports, Health and Fitness Membership costs just £100 for students. It has to be the deal of all time.

PILLOW TALK

The £17-million residential development, Kirkstall Brewery, has 2 squash courts, a weight training and fitness centre, a two-floor bar complex (capacity around 1,000), regular weekly and one-off events, laundry and shop. Carnegie Village is a development of high quality purpose-built student flats on Headingley campus. There are also townhouses for 9-12 and a small number of en-suites and studio flats. Both Kirkstall and Carnegie are for Headingley campus students.

Closer to Civic Quarter campus are Liberty Park flats (4-6 students, 14 mins walk from campus), 1 Mill Street (a 10-storey block of flats: 4-6, 23 mins walk), Opal One Two in the thick of stu-

ACCOMMODATION	
Student rating	★★★★
Guarantee to freshers	**65%**
Style	**Halls, flats**
Security guard	**Campus**
Shared rooms	**Some**
Internet access	**Most**
Self-catered	**All**
En suite	**Some**
Approx price range pw	**£90-£145**
City rent pw	**£65**

by the University, is all part of the Big Change at Leeds Met. Bodes well.

SPORT Sports facilities at Headingley include Regional Gymnastics and Tennis Centres, squash courts, a 21m pool, an athletics track, floodlit synthetic turf pitches, a dance studio and fitness suite. Students enjoy the world-class facilities at the Carnegie Stand at Headingley Carnegie Stadium. The ground floor is home to a Helpzone and the **Carnegie Café** where you can rub shoulders with champions. There are coaching facilities, developed to allow players and students to use modern

dentsville on Burley Road (16 mins). There are more, but not enough, so apply early.

GETTING THERE

☛ By road: M1, A1 or M62. Good coach services.
☛ By rail: Newcastle, 1:45; London Euston, 2:30; Birmingham New Street, 2:20.
☛ By air: Leeds/Bradford Airport.
☛ By coach: London, 4:00; Edinburgh, 6:00; Bristol, 5:45.

STUDENT LEICESTER – THE CITY

The city is still sometimes unfairly seen as having little more to it than Walkers Crisps and its most famous son, Gary Linekar, but its profile is always on the up, be it through its football and rugby teams, Comedy Festival (nationally acclaimed comedians attract a 20,000+ audience), curries or

nightclubs.

Leicester is compact enough to retain a strong community atmosphere, modern enough to combine this with what you want from a city, and there is always something going on.

Coming to university in a city like Leicester

after growing up in a quaint market town could have been daunting, but for me, it was incredibly exciting.

To Londoners coming north perhaps Leicester doesn't sound very glamorous, but you will soon discover behind the grey seventies buildings and run-down knitwear factories that this is a friendly and vibrant city with many hidden gems.

There are of course flaws, the biggest has to be the great big ring road around the city centre that can defeat even the most experienced navigator.

First, being a student in Leicester is great, because there are so many of us about. In term time, students make up a tenth of the population. Consequently there are always offers in bars and shops hungry for their disposable income.

Leicester is also a multicultural city and many different languages are spoken here. 'Diversity' is the buzz word here and on the whole it works very well. It's also the UK's first environmental city, with tons of bike routes and parks dotted about.

My favourite place in Leicester is Bradgate Park. Unfortunately I didn't discover this gem until my final year, so you will be one step ahead. The park is breathtaking and the perfect place to chill out, away from deadlines and other stresses.

Another reason why Leicester is so good for students is its aforesaid compactness. It is easy to cross on foot and both universities are within walking distance of the city centre, train and bus stations, which means you don't spend a fortune on bus fares or petrol. My halls of residence were within stumbling distance of the union bar and I could wake up 10 minutes before a lecture.

My other favourite place is the Narborough Road. This long road near De Montfort University defines being a student. Everything a student could possibly need is all on one road - taxis, kebab shops, a library, convenience stores, charity shops, internet cafés, trendy bars and banks. It's bustling, vibrant and loud, and I love it!

NIGHT LIFE

The nightlife in Leicester is excellent and varied.

As well as the big clubs such as **Liquid** and **Zanzibar**, it has a variety of smaller late night clubs for those who like to party until the early hours. There are also lots of alternative clubs, many with student nights such as **Mosh**, **Fan Club** and **Leicester Square**. The West End, close to De Montfort University, is an area filled with trendy cafés and cool bars. And of course both student unions are popular venues with legendary night *Brighton Beach* rumoured to be back at de Montfort (DMU).

ART CULTURE

Leicester City Council is investing heavily in the arts and creating a cultural quarter with a new theatre and art-house cinema. Currently, cultural needs are catered for by various galleries, museums and theatres throughout the city. Leicester also hosts one of the UK's largest comedy festivals each February. This hugely successful festival started as a student project at DMU.

There are other festivals throughout the year, including the Summer Sundae - Leicester's answer to Glastonbury, the lively Afro-Caribbean festival and many religious festivals. It also hosts the largest Diwali celebration outside of India and it's really worth heading down to; as well as a whole area lit up with decorations and pretty lights there is also a magnificent fireworks display.

SHOPPING

The city has all the usual high street stores. Most important for students is the recent addition of a huge **Primark**. For those who want something unique, check out the **Leicester Lanes**. They aren't the equal of Brighton's Lanes, but they are filled with boutiques and independent shops, and are perfect for picking up something different.

There are big supermarkets close to both universities, but for bargains there is no better place then the Leicester market, the largest covered market in Europe.

Nikki Slawson

UNIVERSITY OF LEICESTER

The University of Leicester
Mayors Walk
University Road
Leicester LE1 7RH

TEL 0116 252 2674
EMAIL study@le.ac.uk
WEB www.le.ac.uk

Leicester Students' Union
Percy Gee Building
University Road
Leicester LE1 7RH

TEL 0116 223 1203
FAX 0116 223 1112
EMAIL su-services@le.ac.uk
WEB www.leicesterstudent.org

VIRGIN VIEW

Year on year, Leicester University has been among the most popular universities in the UK. In 2010 89% per cent of its students expressed themselves satisfied in the annual Government poll, which is very high. Indeed, Leicester has been in the top 10 for student satisfaction every year since the National Student Survey began in 2005.

However, in the more broad-ranging Times Higher *Student Experience Survey* this year they slipped seven places to 20th and dropped out of the magazine's World Top 200 altogether.

Last year we raised an eyebrow when Leicester slipped 30 places in the BUCS team sports national league. This year their teams recovered, but students gave their sports facilities their lowest rating but one, the lowest going to the University's connections with industry, which some would regard as more worrying for students' futures, although heavens above 80% of their graduates get real graduate jobs within 6 months of leaving, which again is high.

Steadying the boat are helpful lecturers who are clearly attentive and interested in their students - the students themselves are the first to admit this - and cutting edge research which provides a stimulating and exciting well of knowledge on which lecturers draw.

Also putting a smile on students' faces is a £16m revamp of the Students Union building, Percy Gee, which was completed in 2010, and features the Leicester O2 Academy as live venue and nightclub.

So, why did the students mark their Union down into 29th place in the Times Higher *survey in its re-vamp year? Maybe they're spoilt brats. Certainly there is little respect for history. For here, when today's students were barely born and the house scene was in its infancy the legendary* High Spirits *club-night, first given breath in Percy Gee, travelled to Es Paradis in Ibiza, to the Queen Club in Paris and the Venue in Jersey. There must have been some energy around in those days.

Besides the cracking Union there is Leicester 'student city'. Two universities

UNIVERSITY/STUDENT PROFILE	
University since	**1957**
Situation/style	**City campus**
Student population	**16505**
Undergraduates	**10110**
Mature	**43%**
International	**19%**
Male/female ratio	**47:53**
Equality of opportunity:	
state school intake	**89%**
social class 4-7 intake	**26%**
drop-out rate	**6%**

means that 12% of the city's population are students. As well as great shopping and a buzzing nightlife, Leicester is full of cultural highlights, including the largest Diwali celebration outside India, Britain's longest running comedy festival and the 3-day Summer Sundae Big Weekender music festival.

Open Days in 2011 are: 11 June (Medicine only), 1 and 27 July, 24 September and 8 October.

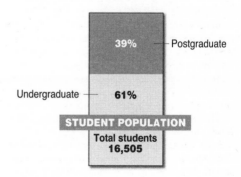

39% — Postgraduate

Undergraduate — **61%**

STUDENT POPULATION
Total students
16,505

CAMPUS

'The main university campus is situated close to the city centre and within walking distance of all university halls of residence,' writes Christina McGear. 'But, unlike many inner city universities, everything you need is situated on campus including banks, restaurants, cafés, shops, the university library and union. This means that you never have far to walk between lectures.'

FEES, BURSARIES

UK & EU Fees 2011-12: £3,375. There's a Special Support Grant for those on a full or partial HE Maintenance Grant. At least one bursary per term is awarded by the Sports Association to assist student sportsmen and women to pursue their chosen sport. Through the Eliahou Dangoor Scholarship

TEACHING SURVEY AT A GLANCE

Avg. UCAS points accepted	**360**
Acceptance rate	**14%**
Overall satisfaction rate	**89%**
Helpful/interested staff	★★★★
Small tuition groups	★★★
Students into graduate jobs	**80%**

Teaching most popular with undergraduates:
American & Australasian Studies, Anatomy, Physiology & Pathology, Archaeology, Biology, Chemistry, Engineering & Technology, English, French Studies, Genetics, Geology, History, Human & Social Geography, Law, Maths, Mechanical, Production &Manufacturing Engineering, Medical Science & Pharmacy, Medicine, European Languages, Molecular Biology, Physical Geography & Environmental Science, Physical Science, Physics & Astronomy, Politics, Social Policy.

RESEARCH EXCELLENCE

% of Leicester's research that is
4* *(World-class) or* **3*** *(Internationally rated):*

	4*	3*
Cardiovascular Medicine	**10%**	**45%**
Cancer Studies	**5%**	**50%**
Infection/Immunology	**5%**	**25%**
Hospital Clinical Subjects	**5%**	**25%**
Epidemiology	**10%**	**50%**
Biological Sciences	**10%**	**35%**
Environmental Sciences	**10%**	**55%**
Chemistry	**5%**	**35%**
Physics	**15%**	**40%**
Pure Mathematics	**10%**	**40%**
Applied Mathematics	**5%**	**40%**
Computer Science	**20%**	**45%**
General Engineering	**15%**	**30%**
Geography/Environment	**10%**	**30%**
Archaeology	**25%**	**40%**
Economics	**20%**	**50%**
Business/Management	**15%**	**40%**
Law	**5%**	**35%**
Politics	**5%**	**10%**
Criminology	**5%**	**30%**
Social Work	**5%**	**20%**
Sociology	**10%**	**20%**
Psychology	**5%**	**10%**
Education	**5%**	**25%**
French	**0%**	**25%**
Italian	**10%**	**15%**
Iberian	**5%**	**45%**
English	**15%**	**45%**
History	**20%**	**30%**
History of Art	**10%**	**30%**
Media/Communication	**5%**	**55%**
Museum Studies	**65%**	**30%**

Scheme they award entrance scholarships of £1,000 to straight A, UK-resident students in Science, Technology, Engineering and Mathematics.

STUDENT PROFILE

Student type? They'll tell you many are from the southeast - which is true, with a number from independent schools, good, white middle-class kids. But Government stats released as we go to press show that Leicester is the most socially inclusive of Britain's top-15 universities, with 89% of intake being from state schools or colleges, exceeding its benchmark by 5.7 percentage points, and over a quarter of entrants coming from lower socio-economic groups, again exceeding its quota. Truth is, Leicester has always been convenient to a wide cross-section of UK journeymen because of its position in the middle of the country. Basically, the population is well-balanced class-wise, race-wise (they come here from more than 100 countries), age-wise and sex-wise, and everyone has a good time, even if sometimes there's the odd pout.

ACADEMIA & JOBS

On assessment 65% of Leicester's research work was found to be world-class (the top category) and 30% internationally significant. There are five teaching faculties - Arts, Law, Medicine, Science, Social Sciences. Top teaching assessments are in Economics, Sport, Psychology, Physics, Politics, History of Art, Maths, and Biosciences. They are widely targeted by employers. An on-line database keeps all students up to date with the latest job vacancies

The Faculty of Medicine would be a jewel in anyone's crown, and was one of three medical

SUBJECT AREAS (%)

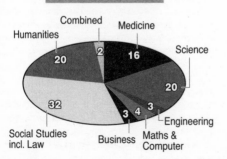

Combined — Medicine
Humanities — Science
Humanities 20
2
16
Science
20
32
3 4 3
Engineering
Social Studies incl. Law — Business — Maths & Computer

schools given the go-ahead to form joint schools with other universities. Leicester's partner is Warwick. Part of the deal is a fast track medical degree for biological sciences graduates.

The 4/5-year MB ChB is in fact the backbone in terms of graduate employment: 23% of Leicester graduates leave the department for work in hospitals. You'll need four AS levels, including Biology and Chemistry, three of them, including Chemistry, continued to A level. If candidates take 2 Maths A levels, only one will count towards an offer. UKCAT is also required.

The uni also has a world-class record in genetics - it was here that genetic fingerprinting was first developed. The career pathways of biological science graduates from Leicester are various, but in a given year 15% or so become biochemists, medical scientists, biological scientists or biochemists. Another strength is Pharmacology. BSc Psychology with Cognitive Neuroscience is new this year.

There is also a particular reputation in the field of physics and astronomy. They have the largest uni-based space research centre in Europe. The Beagle 2 Mars Probe, the UK's first mission to another planet, had its Operation Control Centre at Leicester. There is a Space Research and Multi-disciplinary Modelling Centre.

They send lots into the civil service, defence and public administration generally from social studies, history and philosophy, languages and law, and even medicine. And there's a big showing in banking and the like from their economics department. Secondary school teachers get started here in number too, from languages and history and philosophy, biological and physical sciences.

Finally, there's an interesting Law provision; they are specialists in French law. Explore the difference between English & French Law (LLB/ Maitrise) and Law with French Law and Language. The latter is of 4-year duration.

SOCIAL SCENE

You will take possession of a thoroughly re-vamped Student Union building. The **O2 Academy** is where the action takes place in a 1,450 capacity live-music and club venue catering for the biggest live acts on the touring circuitl.

The ARC is the upper floor of the Percy Gee building, the home of all the societies within the University of Leicester.

The Scholar, home of the Late Lounge, is a

WHAT IT'S REALLY LIKE	
UNIVERSITY:	
Social Life	★★★
Societies	★★★★
Student Union services	★★★
Politics	**Involved**
Sport	**30 clubs**
National team position	**85th**
Sport facilities	★★★
Arts opportunities	**All excellent**
Student newspaper	**Ripple**
Student radio	**LUSH FM**
Student TV	**LUST**
Nightclub	**Element**
Bars	**Redfearn**
Venue	**Venue**
Union ents	**Red Leicester, Madfer it, Brighton Beach**
Union societies	**100**
Parking	**Very limited**
CITY:	
Leicester Nightlife	★★★★★
City scene	**Top town - clubs, pubs, curries**
Town/gown relations	**OK**
Risk of violence	**Average**
Cost of living	**Average**
Student concessions	**Good**
Survival + 2 nights out	**£70 pw**
Part-time work campus/town	**Excellent**

relaxed and laidback place to grab food, a drink, meet up with friends and watch Live Sport.

There are around 100 societies and endless sports clubs (30), the former divided into academic, campaigning, performance, recreational, religious and cultural) to join.

'When the house scene was in its infancy the Student Union's High Spirits club-night travelled to Es Paradis in Ibiza, to the Queen Club in Paris and the Venue in Jersey.'

Leicester University Theatre (LUT) is one of the largest and most active societies; the theatre has become recognised throughout the Midlands as a breeding ground for young talent, with many members finding employment after graduation. There's a good campaigning arm and lively media - *Ripple* is the newspaper, Lush FM the radio station. LUST, the TV, all always contenders for student media awards when they come round.

SPORT is big, though local competition is traditionally with Nottingham rather than international-level Loughborough, and more recently with De

ACCOMMODATION

Student rating	★★★★
Guarantee to freshers	100%
Style	Halls, flats
Security guard	Some
Shared rooms	Some
Internet access	Some
Self-catered	Some
En suite	Some
Approx price range pa	£74.20-£165.60
City rent pw	£55

Montfort University. There's a sports hall, Greenhouse 1, on campus. The Greenhouse 2 is a 160 square metre facility stuffed full of the latest treadmills, steppers, bikes and resistance equipment. Rugby, lacrosse and football pitches are at Stoughton Road, east of campus, close to Manor Road Sports Centre.

PILLOW TALK

'All halls are within walking distance,' writes Christine, 'and are served regularly by the number 80 bus. Beaumont Hall in Oadby is one of the most attractive, set amongst beautiful botanical gardens.'John Foster Hall is the newest, with high quality en-suite rooms, together with a number of older converted buildings offering self-catered accommodation. The university will support any student wishing to live in private accommodation. See www.le.ac.uk/accommodation for details.

GETTING THERE

☞ By road: M1/J21 or J22. Good coach services.
☞ By rail: London St Pancras, 1:20; Manchester Piccadilly, 1:30; Sheffield, 1:30; Birmingham New Street, 1:00; Nottingham, 0:30.
☞ By air: Bus from Birmingham International and East Midlands International Airports.
☞ By coach: London, 2:30; Leeds, 3:00; Cardiff, 4:10.

UNIVERSITY OF LINCOLN

The University of Lincoln
Brayford Pool
Lincoln LN6 7TS

TEL 01522 886644
FAX 01522 886880
EMAIL enquiries@lincoln.ac.uk
WEB www.lincoln.ac.uk

Lincoln Students' Union
Brayford Pool
Lincoln LN6 7TS

TEL 01522 886006
FAX 01522 882088
EMAIL (see website)
WEB www.lincoln.ac.uk

VIRGIN VIEW

*L*incoln University has arrived. No-one can remember Humberside University or the fact that Hull was once its main base; and the bandwagon still keeps rolling on.

The university has invested over £100 million in its Brayford Pool campus in the heart of Lincoln - new library, performing arts centre, a media and technology enterprise centre - and now they have converted a former railway engine shed into a £6-million student union that looks set to make the Lincoln experience complete. **The Engine Shed**, as it is called, is, with a capacity of 1,500, one of the biggest concert venues in the East Midlands, and all extra-curricular student activities will be focused here too.

In the National Student Survey 82% of students gave their approval, which keeps it in the top 25%; and there is a drop-out rate of only 8%, way below the Government benchmark and for a 'new' university encouraging indeed.

Everything the safe and student-friendly city of Lincoln has to offer is within walking distance of the campus. The Sports and Recreation Centre offers some of the best facilities available anywhere, including a

UNIVERSITY/STUDENT PROFILE

University since	1992
Situation/style	City campus
Student population	13830
Undergraduates	10000
Mature	37%
International	8%
Male/female ratio	44:56
Equality of opportunity:	
state school intake	98%
social class 4-7 intake	41%
drop-out rate	8%

gym, squash courts, dance studio, football pitches and basketball courts.

What's more, the university welcomes applications from students who may not have the required academic qualifications. You'll need to be able to demonstrate 'work experience or learning that is relevant, current and appropriate'.

Open Days in 2011: 11 May, 7 July, 1 and 29 October, 12 and 26 November. In 2012: 18 January (1 to 5pm), also 9 May and 11 July, 2012. There are 'informal tours' on the third Wednesday of each month.

CAMPUS

Brayford Pool Campus is on the riverside in this picturesque cathedral city. It's pretty impressive, although, reports Paula McManus, 'sometimes it feels more like an airport or shopping centre than a university: security guards are constantly on patrol to stop any damage being done to this sparkling new building.' How can they win!

Holbeach Campus is non-residential and home to a £3.5-million food packaging and processing training factory for food sector employees. The National Centre for Food Manufacturing opened in March 2009, and the new academic year will see new BSc(Hons) degrees in Food Manufacture and Agriculture & Environmental Management, created in response to national food security concerns and to build on Lincoln's long-established expertise in food manufacturing and agriculture.

The agriculture and equine provision is at the 1,000-acre **Riseholme Park Campus**, near Lincoln, while **Lincoln's Art & Design School, with a history of 150 years,** is situated within walking distance of the cathedral.

FEES, BURSARIES

UK & EU Fees, 2011-12: £3,375. Bursary of £500 for students in receipt of the full maintenance grant. Sports Bursary of up to £1,000 for students who perform at a national or international level, or have the potential to do so. Siemens plc is sponsoring 12 University of Lincoln Engineering students in 2011. The package consists of full tuition fees payment, plus contributions towards living costs for the duration of the course. 180 scholarships of £2,000 are available to new, self-financing international (i.e. non-EU) students starting in September 2011. Alongside this a series of Special Criteria Scholarships is also available for 2011 entry international students. It includes a Faculty Champion Prize of £3,000 and the Vice Chancellor's Prize of £1,200. The Blackburn Bursary worth £1,500 is

TEACHING SURVEY AT A GLANCE	
Avg. UCAS points accepted	**260**
Acceptance rate	**26%**
Overall satisfaction rate	**82%**
Helpful/interested staff	★★★★
Small tuition groups	★★★
Students into graduate jobs	**63%**

Teaching most popular with undergraduates:
Accounting, Architecture, Business, Complementary Medicine (100%), English, Finance, Fine Art, History, Languages, Law, Management, Marketing, Subjects Allied to Medicine, Sociology, Social Policy & Anthropology, Sports Science, Tourism.

Teaching least popular with undergraduates:
Nursing (58%).

open to UK undergraduates previously in local authority care. Also, nursing and social work students may be eligible for national bursary schemes.

STUDENT PROFILE

Recruitment has been successful among social groups to non-traditional applicants. More than a third of undergraduate entrants come from the middle to lower end of the social spectrum and from new-to-uni social groups. Many are mature students; few arrive from the public school sector.

ACADEMIA & JOBS

The Lincoln Business School, the Lincoln School of Architecture and the Institute of Medical Sciences were launched as recently as 2003, yet they are now heavily subscribed, firm fixtures. They were joined by the School of Journalism in 2004, and the School of Performing Arts and Lincoln School of Engineering, the first dedicated school of engineering to be created in the UK for more than 20 years, followed.

In the Government's National Student Survey,

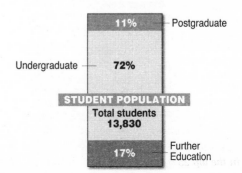

Postgraduate 11%
Undergraduate 72%
STUDENT POPULATION
Total students 13,830
Further Education 17%

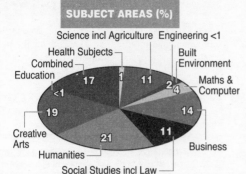

SUBJECT AREAS (%)

Science incl Agriculture
Engineering <1
Health Subjects
Built Environment
Combined
Education 17 1 11 2 4 Maths & Computer
<1
19 14
Creative Arts
21 11
Humanities Business
Social Studies incl Law

Engineering moves into a new purpose built home in the centre of the Brayford campus.

The last research assessment suggests that at Lincoln in-depth strength may be found in Communication, Culture & Media, and in Computer Science.

New graduate employment initiatives include an Employer Mentoring Scheme, an opportunity to work with a professional on a one to one basis; a Graduate Internship Programme where 100 recent graduates are placed with local companies for a period of between 3-6 months, and The Lincoln Award, a joint project with the Student Union, providing official recognition and evidence of employability related activities.

In Computer, it's Games, Information Systems, and here, in amongst these degrees, one begins to see why Creative Arts & Design supplies most of the graduate jobs - around a fifth of graduate jobs flow from a close brotherhood with Computer in the Design Department: degrees in Animation, Games Design, Architecture, Design for TV and Film, Interactive Design, as well as the more traditional Fine Art, Graphic Design, Illustration, Interior Design, and the specially employment friendly Fashion and Exhibition Design provision.

Language and cultural experience is an integral part of the whole academic recipe. 25% of first degree students take a language as part of their course and 15% spend time abroad.

In the health faculty, Lincoln have teamed up with Nottingham to offer a certificate in Health Science to students from poor or deprived backgrounds who want to go on to study medicine at one of the best medical schools in the country, with a bursary that gets you going.

Prospective animal health technicians should also be aware that Lincoln lead in this field since taking on De Montfort's agric. Operation. Note the degree in Bio-Veterinary Science.

They also offer a track for probation officers through their Criminology degrees, which ties up interestingly with anything from Psychology to Journalism and Forensic Science.

There is a series of five sports degrees (a new £2m Human Performance Centre is home to these), while Lincoln's Holbeach campus of the National Centre for Food Manufacturing is the source of important degrees in this area.

2010, 10 of its courses ranked in the top 10 nationally. The Accounting programmes ranked number one in the UK for the second year, while Tourism and Marketing ranked second and Business Studies and Management programmes each ranked fifth. Arts programmes also performed well with Fine Art ranked 2nd nationally and Design 6th. Lincoln's Sociology and Journalism courses both ranked in the top 10 at 7th and 8th respectively.

Lincoln has carved out a strong niche in Media Production and Journalism and has well established links to the BBC. The Social Work programme also has graduate prospects. Conservation & Restoration and Design for Exhibition & Museums is another niche area with employment prospects.

The Siemens connection (see *Fees, Bursaries*) has created a number of new degrees in Engineering and this year the School of

SOCIAL SCENE

STUDENTS' UNION **The Engine Shed** is the 1,500-capacity night club and live music venue. Within are a main room for live music and club events and 3 bars - the **Tower**, **Sport Bar** and **Pod Bar**. Regular club/disco nights include Wednesday night's *Fever Pitch* (the official Athletic Union club

RESEARCH EXCELLENCE

% of Lincoln's research that is
4* *(World-class)* or **3*** *(Internationally rated):*

	4*	3*
Health Professions	0%	10%
Agriculture	5%	5%
Computer Science	15%	35%
Architecture	5%	30%
Business/Management	0%	20%
Law	0%	10%
Politics	5%	15%
Social Work	5%	30%
Psychology	5%	20%
Education	5%	30%
History	0%	40%
Art and Design	5%	10%
Performing Arts	5%	15%
Media Studies	15%	55%

WHAT IT'S REALLY LIKE

UNIVERSITY:

Social Life	★★★
Societies	★★★
Student Union services	★★★
Politics	**Student issues**
Sport	**Good, 12 clubs**
National team position	**61st**
Sport facilities	★★★
Arts opportunities	**Film OK**
Student magazine	**Bullet**
Student newspaper	**The Linc**
Student radio	**Siren**
Venue	**Engine Sheds**
Bars	**Tower, Sport, Pod**
Union ents	**Cheese**
Union societies	**62**
Most active society	**International, Equine, Drama**
Parking	**None**

CITY:

Entertainment	★★★
Scene	**Good pubs; average clubs**
Town/gown relations	**Average**
Risk of violence	**Low**
Cost of living	**Average**
Student concessions	**Average**
Survival + 2 nights out	**£50 pw**
Part-time work campus/town	**Average/good**

ACCOMMODATION

Student rating	★★★★
Guarantee to freshers	**100%**
Style	**Halls, flats**
Security guard	**All**
Shared rooms	**Some**
Internet access	**All**
Self-catered	**Most**
En suite	**Most**
Approx price range pw	**£97-£110**
City rent pw	**£57-£115**

Team,' they tell us, 'is made up predominantly of International players from Germany and Sweden.'

TOWN Think of the city of Lincoln, doesn't it remind you of Canterbury or York, both highly successful olde worlde cathedral seats of learning? To fresher Caroline Stocks, when she first set eyes on it, the place seemed promising if rather sedate: 'It's easy to see why so many pensioners flock to Lincoln during the summer, or why the annual Derby-and-Joan Christmas outing is to the town's festive market. There's the majestic cathedral and ancient castle, which sit on a hill overlooking the town, with its tiny old shops on cobbled streets. There are the visitors who stroll along the castle ramparts before taking a look at the 19th-century prison museum. There's the Brayford Pool, where swans paddle lazily, pausing only to let pleasure boats or brightly painted barges pass. And overlooking this pool...there are the university buildings...very modern.

The campus and all the bars/clubs are right in the middle of the city, based round the Waterfront - you won't use a taxi while in Lincoln, everything is central. In November 2011 a major digital arts festival will attract artists from all over the world.

PILLOW TALK

They offer only 39% of freshers university accommodation, but there are approximately 3,000 rooms in high-quality purpose-built private student residences just off campus, and they'll sort this out with you. Private developments near campus include The Junxion (569), Brayford Court (86), Brayford Quays (330), Hayes Wharf (224), and The Pavilions (2,200).

GETTING THERE

☞ By road: from north, A15; northwest, A57, A46 Lincoln by-pass.
☞ By rail: King's Cross, 2:00; Nottingham, 1:00.
☞ By coach: London, 4:10.

night), featuring a range of DJ's and regular themed events and guest appearances, like Ralf Little, Outhere Brothers and Roy Walker. *Saturday Essential* is the funky weekend club night. Live bands this year have included The Zutons, Ocean Colour Scene, Embrace, The Babyshamles, Dirty Pretty Things and the Kings of Leon.

The building is also home to the SU and a shop, and will soon house a job shop, activities centre and book shop. They claim to have 62 societies up and running, and 12 sports clubs, some with up to 70 members.

The student mag. is *Bullet Magazine*, newspaper *The Linc*, student radio station Siren Radio. Among the most active student societies are ACS, International Students, Equine, and Drama.

SPORT There's a sports centre with pitches and a gym. Five years ago a student could say, 'We are not major contenders yet against other universities.' Not so now. They have good sports teams for their size, coming 61st out of well over 100 nationally. Golf and football are specialities and badminton, volleyball and rugby made their way commendably in the direction of finals. 'Our Volleyball

STUDENT LIVERPOOL – THE CITY

Visitors to Liverpool are constantly amazed by the rich tapestry of theatres, concert halls, museums, galleries, bars, shops and restaurants which the city centre has to offer. Liverpool also offers an abundance of parks and gardens, including Sefton Park with its beautifully restored Palm House. A short ferry journey across the Mersey will take you to the more rural surroundings of the Wirral.

The city celebrated its 800th Birthday in 2007 and became European Capital of Culture in 2008 with the special theme of *Performance* to highlight iys cultural and sporting achievements. As the birthplace of The Beatles, Liverpool is renowned for its musical talents. The *Mathew Street Festival*, *Liverpool Summer Pops* and *Creamfields* are some of the annual music events which take place around the city, with The Royal Liverpool Philharmonic Orchestra providing classical music performances throughout the year.

All three universities played their part in this, as did cultural institutions like the **Playhouse** and **Everyman** theatres, **The Tate** and **Bluecoat** art galleries, the 4th Liverpool Biennial, The Royal Liverpool Philharmonic Society, FACT, the **European Opera Centre** and numerous smaller galleries and theatre companies, several of which are run by Liverpool graduates.

The city's thriving alternative student scene is clustered around three main epicentres: the city centre, Lark Lane and Penny Lane/Smithdown Road. Here's a whistle-stop guide to some of the hidden gems.

STAR PUB

Despite being part of the *It's a Scream* chain of pubs, the **Brookhouse** (Smithdown Road) is one of Liverpool's most popular student pubs, due to its proximity to the centre of student population. **Kelly's**, again on Smithdown, is a regular haunt for second and third years. **The Caledonia** on Catherine Street is always good for a few pints. Most decent nights have a pre-party here. **The Pilgrim** in Pilgrim Street offers cheap beer and passable Sunday lunch fare. It's quiet, safe and pleasant – a good place to chill the morning after the night before. Lark Lane's **Albert Hotel** is a busy, smoky student local with a friendly atmosphere and good draught beers.

STAR BAR

L'agos (or Lago's) is by far the star bar. Trendy decor, wonderfully cheap drinks, soulful music and a good mix of students and locals. **The Magnet** on Hardman Street co-exists with a restaurant, club

and a vintage clothing shop. The food not always the best but the atmosphere is always brilliant, and the club is home to some very popular nights. **Hannah's Bar** on Hardman Street has an unpretentious atmosphere, live music or DJs most evenings and good looking bar staff. Fleet Street's **Rocomodo's** (**Modo's**) is suave and modern. It serves posh cocktails at decent prices, is often filled with beautiful people and opens until 2. Also in Fleet Street, is **Baa Bar**, which serves £1 cocktails called 'shooters' and is a common first stop on nights out in the city centre. **The Penny Lane Wine Bar** is friendly and small, with a good summer beer garden.

STAR EATERY

The new **Bluu Bar**, often with big queues (only a good thing?) has really tasty food, with a laid back atmosphere, leather sofas, perfect for a swish lunch.

The Everyman Bistro on Hope Street is attached to the famous theatre set up by graduates of the Liverpool Uni in the 1960s. At moderate prices the food is healthy, well presented and often veggie friendly. The adjacent bar was one of the first places in Liverpool to stock the legendary spirit absinthe – scourge of the Romantics and very trendy. **The Tavern Company** on Smithdown Road is a superb Mexican restaurant loved by students and parents alike. **Maranto's** (Lark Lane) is a large restaurant with a huge bar serving good, moderately priced international cuisine. More expensive is nearby **Viva**, but well worth it as a treat (or when the parents are in town). Best take-away in Liverpool is Smithdown Road's little-known **Pizza Parlour** – authentic pizzas at decent prices, with wine or Italian beer to drink at the counter while your order is prepared.

CLUBS

If it's clubbing you want then Liverpool is the place to come. **Cool Seel Street club The Masque was** started by 3 students 6 years ago and is intensely popular, full of beautiful people and attracts the biggest DJs around. It has won *Mixmag's* Club of the Year award.

Cream @ **Nation**? A distant memory... Today, **Nation** hosts the raucously fabulous student night *Medication* on a Wednesday (probably what it's most well known for now), as well as the drum 'n' bass fest *X*.

But the people behind Cream are back in a lounge bar/restaurant, **Baby Cream**, at Albert Dock.

At the other end of the spectrum is Tuesday night **The Blue Angel** (108 Seel Street) - 'even Johnny Vegas could pull here,' says Itchy. **The Raz,** as it is affectionately known, is Liverpool's cheesiest student dive, but alumni look back with tender memories - 'Best chat up line from a very pissed Welshman:' says Lotty. "I saw you coming down the stairs and I thought you were a vision of loveliness" - I did snog him and my mate snogged him the week after! Happy days...' Others can't imagine why you don't go looking for somethiung finer, like **Le Bateau** on Duke Street, known for its indie.

Look, too, at **L2** (The Lomax) for live and alternative dance nights, **Krazy Horse** for indie and hard rock, **Cavern Club** for Beatles nostalgia. Another outstanding club is the gay friendly **Garlands** (Eberle Street), also a winner of *Mixmag's Club of the Year Award*. Temporarily, **The State** is home to Garland's nights. Meanwhile, Monday's student night is *Double Vision* at **The Guild of Students**, Saturday's is *Time Tunnel* (city centre).

SHOPS

The one shop students couldn't live without is **WRC** (West World Retail Corp.) on Bold Street. For labels and good trainers for boys and girls visit **Open** (city centre) and **Drome** women (sorry lads). Hardman Street's **Bulletproof** is a good retailer of pretty much passé '70s clothing; it sells clothes by weight. Slater Street's **Liverpool Palace** and School Lane's **Quiggins** are *pot pourris* of student goods and services - from tatooists to African art. The University of Liverpool's *Monday Market* taps the same market for books, wall hangings and plants, but some stallholders provide products as diverse as PCs and collector's items.

THEATRE & MOUTH ART

The Everyman, Hope Street, is one of the most student-friendly venues around, is known for giving local writers a break, and has started the careers of several big-name Liverpudlian actors, like Pete Postlethwaite and Julie Walters. The more 'street level' **Unity Theatre** nearby does work-shops and alternative theatre experiences. Currently, Hanover Street's **Neptune** is a cosy venue favoured by touring shows and comedy acts. **The Egg Café** (Newington, top floor) has bags of atmosphere and features open floor slots for local poets. **The Everyman Bistro** hosts the Dead Good Poets Society, a collective of performance poets, twice a month.

FILM, MUSIC & COMEDY

The new **FACT** centre - a gateway to the city's **Ropewalks** development, which is regenerating a sadly neglected area of the city - is an arts complex showing a wide range of films from quality blockbusters to the most obscure Eastern European cinema as well as media exhibitions and art installations. There are a few good chain cinemas on London Road, Switch Island and Edge Lane. **The Philharmonic**, Hope Street, shows classic films on its unique raising screen, with traditional organist.

Probably the two best venues for live music are **Liverpool Academy** at the University and **The Picket** (Hardman Street). The former has three venues with the largest having a 2,000+ capacity and has played host to many big names including Coldplay, Groove Armada, The Hives, Faithless. **The Picket** is famed for showcasing loads of local bands, but at present is under threat of closure.

The Rawhide Comedy Club at **Blue Bar** (the Docks) specialise in the field - essential to book ahead. With the **Everyman** they stage mainly established comedians. Sniggers Comedy at the Guild of Students hosts some decent comedians.

VISUAL ART

The Tate Gallery on Albert Dock has 3 floors featuring major touring exhibitions. **The Walker Gallery** (William Brown Street) offers traditional fare. Liverpool Uni has a small gallery by Abercromby Square. **The Open Eye** (Wood Street) exhibits touring photographic shows. Seek out also a plethora of little-known galleries, and the **Bluecoat of course**.

Anne Fuell

UNIVERSITY OF LIVERPOOL

The University of Liverpool
Foundation Building
765 Brownlow Hill
Liverpool L69 7ZX

TEL 0151 794 2000
FAX 0151 794 6502
EMAIL ugrecruitment@liv.ac.uk
WEB www.liv.ac.uk

Liverpool Guild of Students (LGOS)
PO Box 187
160 Mount Pleasant
Liverpool L69 7BR

TEL 0151 794 6868
FAX 0151 794 4174
EMAIL thebase@liv.ac.uk
WEB www.lgos.org/

VIRGIN VIEW

*E*stablished in 1881, Liverpool is the original redbrick university, a great big bustling traditional university, which far from feeling a need to keep up with the times seems somehow to absorb modern exigencies and move at its own pace.

Liverpool is a well-balanced university. They meet their Government benchmarks for widening participation There are rising applications year on year, low-ish average points requirement for a top uni, and a total of 53% of research staff were ranked in the highest categories of 4* (world-leading) and 3* (internationally excellent) in the latest Research Assessment Exercise.

Less good showing last year in the Times Higher's *Student Experience Survey*, but this was a grouse at the accommodation in the main, which it will someday be a gargantuian ask to remedy. Lecturers this year were marked high enough for their levels of interest in their students, and overall 85% of students there are satisfied with the teaching. What's more, there are very few drop-outs (5%).

The University is also expanding to everyone's benefit. It has established a joint venture university in Suzhou, China, with Xi'an Jiaotong University. An exchange programme at the institution - Xi'an Jiaotong-Liverpool University (XJTLU) - is enabling Liverpool-based students to undertake work experience at Suzhou Industrial Park (SIP), which is home to 76 Fortune 500 companies. From September 2011, students studying Electrical Engineering and Electronics,

UNIVERSITY/STUDENT PROFILE	
University since	**1661**
Situation/style	**City campus**
Student population	**19950**
Undergraduates	**16400**
Mature	**34%**
International	**15%**
Male/female ratio	**45:53**
Equality of opportunity:	
state school intake	**85%**
social class 4-7 intake	**25%**
drop-out rate	**5%**

Computer Science and Maths will have the opportunity to spend a year of their programme studying at XJTLU.

Open Days at Liverpool in 2011 will be held on 24 and 25 June, and 1 October.

CAMPUS

The campus Precinct is a few mins walk from the centre of this city, famous for football, the Beatles and the Mersey ferry. With Liverpool Uni, John Moores, and Liverpool Hope, not to mention nearby Edge Hill Uni and the possibility of a university on the Wirral, this same city is now, also, one of the major centres of higher education in Britain.

FEES, BURSARIES

UK & EU Fees, 2011-121: £3,375 p.a. The Liverpool Bursary scheme awards on a sliding scale to those who are eligible for the HE Maintenance Grant. The Opportunity and Achievement Scholarship, worth £4,000 to support students with a household income of less than £20,817, is another aimed at relieving hardship. A full list of our bursaries and scholarships for students starting in 2011 is available in the accompanying document or on our website via the link below: www.liv.ac.uk/study/undergraduate/money/future/scholarships-bursaries-2009.htm

STUDENT PROFILE

It is interesting that long before Government quotas existed Liverpool was running access courses for, and offering bursaries and access funds to, students without traditional academic qualifications. It is in the nature of the ethos of Liverpool to do so. Today, the university is popular with state and public school kids alike, and students from a whole range of backgrounds, including many from abroad. The perennially low drop-out rate (5%) shows that everyone is having a good time.

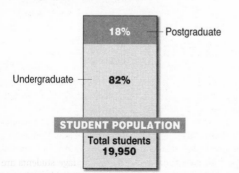

18% — Postgraduate

Undergraduate — 82%

STUDENT POPULATION
Total students
19,950

TEACHING SURVEY AT A GLANCE

Avg. UCAS points accepted	**390**
Acceptance rate	**14%**
Overall satisfaction rate	**84%**
Helpful/interested staff	★★★★
Small tuition groups	★★★
Students into graduate jobs	**69%**

Teaching most popular with undergraduates:
Anatomy, Physiology & Pathology, Animal Science, Archaeology, Biology & related sciences, Business, Celtic Studies, Chemistry, Classics, Computer, English, History, Languages, Mechanical, Production & Manufacturing Engineering, Molecular Biology, Nursing (100%), Pharmacology, Toxicology & Pharmacy (100%), Philosophy, Physical Geography & Environmental Science, Physical Science, Physics & Astronomy, Planning, Politics, Sociology, Social Policy & Anthropology, Vet Sciences, Zoology.

ACADEMIA & JOBS

See the box above for a list of subjects best taught here.

In the last research assessment, Architecture was among the very best performers - 75% of the work was adjudged either world-class or internationally excellent, an achievement shared by Computer Science, with Chemistry and history 70% and with 5% of their provision world-class.

When it comes to graduate employment, 69% only of graduates had proper graduate-level jobs within six months of leaving last time. About a fifth of these come in the shape of hospital work for those on the medicine and dentistry course and other subjects allied to medicine. Thereafter, graduates mainly of social studies and history and philosophy find work in economic and social policy administration. Graduates in architecture and

RESEARCH EXCELLENCE

% of Liverpool's research that is
4* *(World-class) or* **3*** *(Internationally rated):*

	4*	3*
Cancer Studies	10%	30%
Infection/ Immunology	20%	45%
Clinical Subjects	5%	55%
Health Services	10%	45%
Dentistry	10%	30%
Health Professions	10%	30%
Biological Sciences	10%	30%
Human Biol. Sciences	10%	45%
Veterinary	5%	40%
Environmental Sciences	15%	60%
Chemistry	20%	50%
Physics	20%	35%
Pure Mathematics	10%	35%
Applied Mathematics	15%	45%
Statistics	0%	35%
Computer Science	30%	45%
Electrical/Electronic Eng.	15%	40%
Civil Engineering	5%	45%
Mechanical, Aero., & Manufacturing Eng.	15%	45%
Metallurgy and Materials	35%	35%
Architecture	30%	45%
Town/Country Planning	10%	40%
Geography Environment	10%	45%
Archaeology	25%	40%
Business/Management	10%	40%
Law	10%	45%
Politics	0%	15%
Sociology	5%	25%
Psychology	5%	25%
American Studies	15%	20%
European Studies	20%	20%
French	15%	25%
German	10%	35%
Iberian	15%	35%
English	30%	35%
Classics	10%	40%
Philosophy	0%	25%
History	35%	35%
Music	10%	50%

SUBJECT AREAS (%)

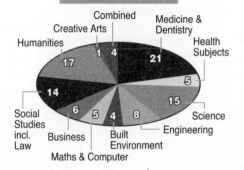

Combined 1
Creative Arts 4
Medicine & Dentistry 21
Humanities 17
Health Subjects 5
Social Studies incl. Law 14
Business 6
Maths & Computer 5
Built Environment 4
Science 8
Engineering 15

building and planning and engineering are the next largest sector finding jobs in the sector to which their courses dedicated them. There are other specist groups, such as the veterinaries who are equally well fitted to their vocations, and of course many business, economics and law students find their way readily into banking and other financial services. There are niches. Advertising and publishing are two and language students are in demand wherever you look. Reliable pathways into the Civil Service are Law and languages. They are European specialists in Law.

Faculties include Arts, Engineering, Law, Medicine & Dentistry, Science, Social & Environmental Studies, and Veterinary Science. The Medicine degree is a 4/5-year MC ChB with the simplest of requirements - Biology, Chemistry plus one other subject, and B in a fourth AS subject. Clinical skills are introduced in Year 1. Graduates with a 2:1 in an approved biomedical discipline or health/social care profession may also apply. The course focuses particularly on the ability to use and apply information in the clinical setting.

Dentists have the 5-year BDS, and vets meanwhile opt the 5-year BVSc, which requires relevant work experience. There are healthy employment

> *The Students' Guild has four live music venues which go by the name of* Liverpool Academy. *This is the biggest capacity venue in the city. Annually, they run in excess of 180 live music events.*

stats, too, for the degrees in radiography, physiotherapy and occupational therapy. £1m has been invested in a virtual environment for Radiotherapy training, the most comprehensive practical experience available to radiotherapy students in the UK.

Environmental Sciences has taken delivery of a custom-built coastal research catamaran with lab and study areas. Twelve lucky students can join the four crew members at any one time. It is being used to sample all aspects of marine ecosystems.

SOCIAL SCENE

STUDENTS' GUILD The Guild and the night life have good ratings in the Student Experience Survey, and in September 2011, the Guild building will undergo a £9-million refurbishment. Right now it has four live music venues which go by the name of **Liverpool Academy**, the biggest capacity venue in the city. Annually, they run in excess of 180 live music events. Right now they have billed Chase and Status, Kate Nash, The Unthanks, MagnumNights of the Living Fred (Right Said Fred and guests) and a whole lot more, including tribute bands The Carpet Crawlers (Genesis), The Clone Roses and The Rising (Bruce Springsteen). They have two weekly club nights, called *Time Tunnel* (Saturday) and *Double Vision* (Monday) and the capacity for these is 2,600. In total, the Guild has nine bars, of which, **The Gilmore**, **The Liver Bar** and the **Saro Wiwa** are open throughout the day.

The student online newspaper, *LSMedia*, has become a virtual passage into the media. If that's your thing, get involved. ICON is the radio station; GuildTV the word in student television.

As elsewhere, there are all kinds of societies with which to get involved - 90 at the last count and 45 sports clubs. Among the former, the most popular are Islamic Soc, Drama, RockSoc, and LUST - that's Liverpool Uni Show Troupe.

The Guild runs LUSTI (Liverpool Uni Student Training Initiative) to train students in communication, assertiveness, time and stress management, meeting skills etc.

PULSE is a new job-centre service to help students find part-time jobs with local employers during term and more full-time during the vacations.

SPORT The Sports Centre - extended in 2004 - includes swimming pool, squash courts, weight training, indoor cricket nets, climbing wall, sun

WHAT IT'S REALLY LIKE

UNIVERSITY:	
Social Life	★★★★
Societies	★★★★
Student Union services	★★★
Politics	**Activity high: student issues**
Sport	**Strong**
National team position	**32nd**
Sport facilities	★★★★
Arts opportunities	**Excellent**
Student newspaper	**LSMedia**
Student radio	**ICON**
Student television	**GuildTV**
Nightclub venue	**Academy**
Bars	**9 bars, Gilmore, Liver Bar, Saro Wiwa...**
Union ents	**Time Tunnel, Double Vision, major live gigs**
Union societies	**90**
Most popular societies	**Islamic**
Parking	**Limited**
CITY:	
Entertainment	★★★★★
City scene	**Fab**
Town/gown relations	**Good**
Risk of violence	**Average**
Cost of living	**Low**
Student concessions	**Excellent**
Survival + 2 nights out	**£70 pw**
Part-time work campus/town	**Good/Excellent**

beds, facilities for aerobics, dance, trampolining. There's a hall at the gym for judo, fencing, archery, four additional squash courts, rifle and pistol range and a weights room. The main sports ground, near the halls, includes two floodlit artificial turf pitches for hockey, field sports, five rugby and six soccer pitches, four tennis courts, a lacrosse pitch, two cricket squares and two artificial wickets, bar and cafeteria. Two other grounds add a further six soccer pitches, and there's a base for climbing, walking, canoeing and field studies in Snowdonia, which accommodates eighteen.

TOWN See Student Liverpool.

PILLOW TALK

Students are frankly dissatisfied with halls. But all is not lost. In September 2012 a £45 million Eco project will produce 700 en-suite study bedrooms on its city centre campus. The scheme, with low energy heating and cooling system, rainwater harvesting, low energy lighting and solar thermal water heating, will include shops and a 250-seat restaurant. The residences are planned to open in September 2012.

Most first years dwell in massive catered halls (Greenbank or Carnatic) 3 miles out. All freshers who apply by August 31 are guaranteed a place. See *At A Glance* box for prices. If you're expecting luxury

ACCOMMODATION	
Student rating	★★
Guarantee to freshers	**100%**
Style	**Halls**
Security guard	**All**
Shared rooms	**None**
Internet access	**All**
Self-catered	**Some**
En suite	**Some**
Approx price range pw	**£81.20-£111.30**
City rent pw	**£45-£120**

accommodation you'll be sorely disappointed, though the community spirit which grows up in halls like Rankin on the Carnatic site stand you in great stead. They have bars and ents, and are linked to uni and city centre by a regular bus service.

Car parking at the Halls of Residence is limited and is charged at £10 per term.

GETTING THERE

☞ By road: M6/J21a, M62, A5080, A5047. Well served by National Express coaches.
☞ By rail: Manchester, 40 mins; Sheffield, 1:45; Leeds, Birmingham, 2:00; London King's Cross, 3:00.
☞ Liverpool airports for inland/Ireland flights.
☞ By coach: London, 5:00; Manchester, 50 mins.

LIVERPOOL HOPE UNIVERSITY

Liverpool Hope University
Hope Park
Liverpool L16 9JD

TEL 0151 291 3295
FAX 0151 291 2050
EMAIL admission@hope.ac.uk
WEB www.hope.ac.uk

Liverpool Hope Students' Union
Derwent House
Merseyside L16 9LA

TEL 0151 291 3651
FAX 0151 2913535
EMAIL union@hope.ac.uk
WEB www.hopesus.co.uk/

VIRGIN VIEW

For years they offered degrees in a variety of subjects, all of them awarded by Liverpool University. In those days, the Pro-rector's introduction - 'Hope is a great virtue with both sacred and secular connotations,' - sounded a bit like a sermon, and we should not be surprised, for Liverpool Hope, once the Liverpool Institute, has its roots in an ecumenical amalgamation of two colleges with religious foundations - St Katherine's,

an Anglican foundation, and Notre Dame, its Roman Catholic neighbour - a union championed years ago by the then Bishop of Liverpool - the cricketing David Sheppard. In 2005, when Hope became a university, its first Vice-Chancellor, Professor Gerald John Pillay, was fittingly a theologian.

Liverpool Hope offered Liverpool University course elements, such as Theology and Religious Studies, which it lacked. At the same time, Liverpool offered Hope top-notch facilities for its Sport, Recreation & Physical

UNIVERSITY/STUDENT PROFILE

University since	**2005**
Situation/style	**Civic**
Student population	**6980**
Total undergraduates	**5570**
Mature	**43%**
International	**8%**
Male/female ratio	**29:71**
Equality of opportunity:	
state school intake	**98%**
social class 4-7 intake	**46%**
drop-out rate	**8%**

Education courses, which are still part of the syllabus today. It was a good marriage - made in heaven you might say.

But Hope was always bound to come good in its own right in these days of 'widening participation' because at the heart of its mission is a determination to make higher education more widely available, not for political correctness, but because it is an implicit in its ethos, and always has been. It was doing 'access' already - for real.

Springing from its religious roots is a determination to provide for 'those who have hitherto not had the most distinguished or easy path to academic honours.' Foundation courses prepare students without the required grades to study a degree course. Lecturers go out into the community and preach, sorry teach, those who for one reason or another can't take up a place at Hope. They called it their 'Reach Out' degree route long before Blair's Labour called it 'out-reach'. At Everton, a £15.5-million development was set up to house Hope's community-education strategy. More recently, they

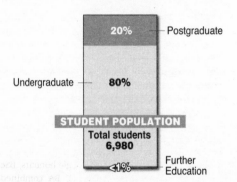

Undergraduate — **80%**

20% — Postgraduate

STUDENT POPULATION

Total students
6,980

<1% — Further Education

developed what they call a Network of Hope, a partnership with communities further afield that would otherwise not have had such a provision. It is now possible for students to undertake full- and part-time degree level study in Hope courses at colleges within the bounds of their local communities.

Characteristic of the Hope community ethos is Urban Hope, a wholly owned subsidiary company of Liverpool Hope University with expertise in the areas of widening access. It raised millions in the deprived Kensington area of the city, built the award-winning Life Bank building, which accommodates a 62-place nursery, the local Sure Start project and a primary care trust, as well as accommodating courses for the local community college. Urban Hope is has developed a 'community campus' nearby, which includes a £1.6-million Sports Centre.

Hope is running with a strong current in this vibrant, ever evolving city, and it was rewarded first with university college status and then university status because it is running with it rather well. In the National Student Survey, undertaken by the Higher Education Funding Council, 79% of Hope students declared themselves satisfied.

CAMPUS

With such an eternally optimistic agenda, how disappointing that its name comes from its location, **Hope Park**, Childwall, some 3 miles from the centre of Liverpool, the original buildings of the two constituent colleges forming the basis of a campus none too exhilarating architecturally. This is the centre of operations, however, and where you'll find the student union HQ.

The Creative Campus, Hope at Everton, a few miles away, has two Grade II Listed buildings, a hall of residence offering self-catering en-suite accommodation for 188 students and the refurbished St Francis Xavier's Church, which is now well-established as one of the most important arts venues on Merseyside.

Here, students study Creative & Performing Arts subjects, Fine Art & Design, Film Studies, Dance, Drama & Theatre Studies and Music. Wholly appropriately, they share with the European Opera Centre, the Music Space Trust and The Cornerstone Gallery, with its continuous exhibition of professional art. Playwrights, artists and musicians, including Visiting Professors Willy

Russell and John Godber, Alan Bleasdale, Julian Lloyd Webber, Joanna McGregor and ex-Beatle Stuart Sutcliffe complete the scene.

The Reach Out Community Forum ties up with such as the Everton Development Trust, the Rotunda Community Arts Centre, local churches and secondary schools. The Hope Community Youth Theatre is based here, and The Royal Liverpool Philharmonic Orchestra, the 10:10 Ensemble and youth and community choirs all practise here.

FEES, BURSARIES

UK & EU Fees, 2011-12: £3,375 p.a. Bursaries are available on a sliding scale according to parental income. Academic scholarships worth £2,000 and £1,000 p.a. are awarded to high scorers at A level and £500 to applicants from Hope's partner schools and colleges. See www.hope.ac.uk/studentfunds/pages/2007-08/eng/scholarship.htm

STUDENT PROFILE

Around 34% of undergraduates are mature, 70% of them are female, which is apt, because its constituent colleges were both women's colleges; 27% are part time, 98% are from the state sector and 41% from the lower socio-economic classes and 14% from 'low-participation' neighbourhoods. Also, most, of course, are local. Beyond statistics, there is a spirit about the place - a relaxed, focused, community spirit - which is Hope's own, although campus can be a bit lonely at weekends. The drop-out rate - just below 12% do not complete the course - is above the Government benchmark.

ACADEMIA

Students say the best teaching is in History & Philosophy, Theology & Religious Studies, Social Studies, Sociology, Subjects allied to Medicine, Computer Science, Business Studies, Psychology, Law, Education Studies, Business & Administrative Studies, and Drama.

SUBJECT AREAS (%)

Business
Maths & Computer
Social Studies incl Law
Humanities
11   10
7
9
55
17   Creative Arts
Combined
Education

TEACHING SURVEY AT A GLANCE

Avg. UCAS points accepted	**260**
Acceptance rate	**20%**
Overall satisfaction rate	**76%**
Helpful/interested staff	**No data**
Small tuition groups	**No data**
Students into graduate jobs	**64%**

Teaching most popular with undergraduates:
Geographical Studies (100%), History, Teacher Training, Philosophy, Theology & Religious Studies, Physical Geography & Environmental Science (100%), Social Work, Theology.

Teaching least popular with undergraduates:
Dance (49%).

The least popular teaching were Sports Science and Performing Arts - Dance, Drama & Theatre Studies, music, which suggests the core areas are the thing and they don't quite get the modernising add-ons quite right. Interesting that the same is true at Lampeter. Even so, these two subjects satisfied more than two-thirds of the class.

Generally, this is a teaching, not a research

RESEARCH EXCELLENCE

% of Liverpool Hope's research that is
4* (World-class) or 3* (Internationally rated):

	4*	3*
Computer Science	0%	20%
Politics	0%	0%
Social Work	5%	0%
Psychology	0%	5%
Education	0%	20%
English	0%	10%
Theology	5%	15%
Performing Arts	0%	0%
Music	0%	30%

institution. Its showing in the recent nationwide research assessment was dire. They came fourth from bottom. Out of nine subjects submitted only 5% of two of them - Social Work and Theology - was rated world-class. But that was probably because they were getting on with them out there in the street rather than pouring over books and papers.

Subjects at Liverpool Hope are grouped into four Deaneries: Arts & Humanities, Education, Business & Computing, and Sciences & Social Sciences. All of the undergraduate programmes are modular. There are BA and BSc single honours, BSc combined honours (major/minor), BA combined honours (major/minor), and equal weight combined honours for both BA and BSc subjects. There are also a load of 1-year Certificates in HE, the BA with QTS teacher training degrees, and a BDes (Design), the first year of which can be studied on the Isle of Man. Students are stimulated by the content and sympathetic delivery of the programme, and produce some imaginative work in response.

Theology is, of course, still on offer and scored 23 points at the teaching assessments and a Grade 4 at the research assessments. Business, however, scored full marks at the assessments and features in the BA single honours and widely throughout the 450 combination courses offered. There is also an apparently improbable course called Gaming Technology, which has in fact nothing to do with gambling, but computer games technology.

Teacher Training focuses on primary teaching - English Lang./Lit., Art/Design, Geography, History, Information Technology, Maths, Music, Special Needs, Sport Studies, Religion - and a series of Advanced Study of Early Years is part of the BA Hons combined course strategy.

Among social sciences, Psychology and Sociology both had good teaching assessments on inspection and are popular, and clearly their Childhood & Youth Studies, Social Work, Special Needs and Pastoral Leadership programmes are central to Hope's ethos. Sports Studies and Sports Development are add-ons to all kinds of subjects in the curriculum, which looks a bit odd. For true sport students they are available as single honours as Sport Psychology, Sport Studies, or Sport & Health Studies. There's an air-conditioned fitness suite, equipped with cardiovascular and resistance equipment.

The £5.3 million Sheppard-Worlock Library houses 250,000 books, many PCs and 500 study places. There is an on-site nursery that provides for children younger than two years, and the employment future prospects of both its many mature and more youthful students are encouraged by elective modules in languages and IT, and by modules which take students out into the workplace and community, both in the UK and overseas.

There's a 64% chance of real graduate employment for Hope graduates within six months of leaving.

SOCIAL SCENE

Student Union The two student bars are D2 (with video wall) on the ground floor of the Union, and the lounge-style **Derwent Bar** upstairs.

There is also a Union presence (and bar) at Everton. Ents are traditional fare - bands (of the tribute variety), comedians (Jack Dee and Lee Evans have played here), karaoke, jazz nights, and

WHAT IT'S REALLY LIKE

UNIVERSITY:	
Social Life	★★
Societies	★
Student Union services	★
Politics	**Caring**
Sport	**Easy going**
National team position	**118th**
Sport facilities	★★
Arts opportunities	**Excellent**
Bars	**D2, Derwent**
Union ents	**DJs, cheese, karaoke, quiz**
Union societies	**45**
Parking	**Adequate**
CITY:	
Entertainment	★★★★★
City scene	**Fab**
Town/gown relations	**Good**
Risk of violence	**Average**
Cost of living	**Low**
Student concessions	**Excellent**
Survival + 2 nights out	**£80 pw**
Part-time work campus/town	**Good/Excellent**

a multitude of society thrashes. Tuesday takes students out to **The Blue Angel** in town (108 Seel Street) - 'even Johnny Vegas could pull here,' says Itchy. **The Raz**, as it is affectionately known, is Liverpool's cheesiest student dive, but alumni look back with tender memories - 'Best chat up line from a very pissed Welshman:' says Lotty. '"I saw you coming down the stairs and I thought you were a vision of loveliness" - I did snog him and my mate snogged him the week after! Happy days...'

Regular DJ Welsh Dave of the Derwent grooms Hope students for such antics. Wednesday is sports or societies night. 'It's always a popular night in D2 with each team coming up with a weekly theme to get ya involved.' On Friday comes 'The WORLD Famous all day party. Music and fun throughout

ACCOMMODATION

Student rating	★★★
Guarantee to freshers	**100%**
Style	**Halls, flats**
Security guard	**24-hr security**
Shared rooms	**Some**
Internet access	**All**
Self-catered	**All**
En suite	**Some**
Approx price range pw	**£74-£98**
City rent pw	**£45-£120**

the day in the Derwent bar from 12 with Karaoke and DJ's starting at 6. Getting you warmed up and in the mood for our Flagship night Reload, starting at 9.' It's DJ Welsh Dave again plus up and coming DJ's eager to fill his shoes. Saturday most people have gone home and it's live football and rugby on the screens. Then it's the Sunday Night Social - quiz, bingo, sing-a-long, 'with great acts every week'.

There are plenty of societies and an opportunity to be part of the team that produces the award-winning Liverpool Student newspaper that serves all 3 Liverpool universities.

SPORT Hope Park Sports is managed by Healthworks, an outside firm. Facilities include a multi-purpose sports hall for 5-a-side football, badminton, basketball and tennis, volleyball, netball and hockey. There's access to football and rugby pitches and squash courts and the new fitness suite mentioned under Academia above. They have recently installed a floodlit, all-weather Astroturf pitch for hockey, tennis, football; and there's a gym, exercise classes and coaching courses for the whole gamut of abilities and levels of fitness.

Among a handful of unusual clubs is Kick Boxing, and the Mountaineering club is worth a mention not least because of Plas Caerdeon, Hope's Outdoor Education Centre. This old manor house in 18 acres of woodland overlooking the glorious Mawddach Estuary (Snowdonia) hosts field and study trips, but it's also a bolt hole for music students on Composition weekend, Drama students for rehearsals and anybody for simpler regenerative pleasures. There is good accommodation.

PILLOW TALK

There are nine Halls of Residence at the main Hope Park campus. About three miles lies Aigburth Park, a satellite accommodation campus also for students who study at Hope Park. Free shuttle buses are provided. The common room has a large TV screen with DVD and SKY, plus vending machines and games tables. Finally, there's Gerard Manley Hopkins Hall (188 en-suite study rooms) adjacent to the Creative and Performing Arts Centre in Everton.

GETTING THERE

☛ By road: easy access M62 (east/west), which connects with M6 (north/south) at Junction 21a.
☛ Well served by National Express coaches.
☛ By rail: Manchester, 0:40; Sheffield, 1:45; Leeds or Birmingham, 2:00; London Kings Cross, 3:00.
☛ Speke Airport 5 miles away.

LIVERPOOL JOHN MOORES UNIVERSITY

Liverpool John Moores University
Roscoe Court
4 Rodney Street
Liverpool L1 2TZ

TEL 0151 231 5090
FAX 0151 231 3462
EMAIL courses@ljmu.ac.uk
WEB www.ljmu.ac.uk

Liverpool John Moores Students' Union
The Haigh Building
Maryland Street
Liverpool L1 9DE

TEL 0151 231 4900
FAX 0151 231 4931
EMAIL studentsunion@livjm.ac.uk
WEB www.l-s-u.com

VIRGIN VIEW

*L*iverpool *John Moores (LJMU) is Liverpool's metropolitan university, in a spiritual sense more part of the city than the Liverpool University. Half its students come from Merseyside, and the university's roots run deep into the city's industrial history.*

Origins go back to 1823 as the Liverpool Mechanics' and Apprentices' Library. As poly, the institution brought together the City Colleges of Art and Design and Building,

Commerce, and the Regional College of Technology, the City of Liverpool College of Higher Education, the IM Marsh College of Physical Education, the FL Calder College of Home Economics and the Liverpool College of Nursing and Midwifery - all of which give a good clue to the uni's academic profile today.

Finally, LJMU owes its name and ethos to one of the city's most famous entrepreneurs. Sir John Moores CBE (1896-1993) built Littlewoods - the football pools organisation - from scratch. 'Sir John's business success was built upon his

UNIVERSITY/STUDENT PROFILE

University since	**1992**
Situation/style	**Civic**
Student population	**25995**
Undergraduates	**21070**
Mature	**40%**
International	**12%**
Male/female ratio	**46:54**
Equality of opportunity:	
state school intake	**95%**
social class 4-7 intake	**41%**
drop-out rate	**12%**

philosophy of the equality of opportunity for all,' the uni says. 'This fundamental belief...is a reflection of the university's commitment to higher education, to access, to flexibility and to participation.' Most of all, perhaps, it gives the clue to the underlying ethos - applied learning - they are very hot, across the board, on how what is learned and imbued here can be applied on graduation in the world of work.

CAMPUS

LJMU is roughly three main sites: Mount Pleasant and Byrom Street/Henry Cotton campuses, which are in the centre of town, and IM Marsh, home to the Faculty of Education, Community & Leisure, which is based in Aigburth in South Liverpool.

Each has lecture theatres, seminar rooms, laboratories, editing suites, individual study and computer rooms, as well as union bars, shops and sports facilities. Everything is in and around the city, accessible to public transport and in easy reach of the city centre and halls of residence.

Writes Emma Hardy: 'LJMU buildings are scattered across the city, many are impressive. The School of Media, Critical and Creative Arts, where I study, is one of the most impressive buildings in Liverpool. Located next to the Anglican Cathedral, the views from it are spectacular and the facilities are exemplary. The main library is a great glass structure of imposing stature and, like much of the rest of the university, likely to take your breath away when you first see it. But there are some grim high rise blocks too. Prospective students do well to bear in mind that what they see on Open Day are the best bits.'

FEES, BURSARIES

UK & EU Fees, 2011-12: £3,375 p.a. Students with a household income less than £25,000 qualify for a bursary. The Vice Chancellor's Award is awarded for academic - a maximum of six (£10,000 p.a.) awards are made each year. Dream Plan Achieve Scholarships (£1,000) are awarded to applicants with 360 UCAS points in three subjects. Achievers Awards - scholarships of £1,000 p.a. - are available to students who can show particular commitment,

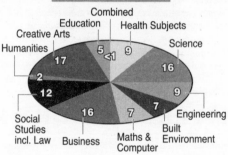

SUBJECT AREAS (%)

Combined • Education • Creative Arts • Health Subjects • Humanities 17 • Science • 5 • <1 • 9 • 16 • 2 • 12 • 9 • 16 • 7 • 7 • Engineering • Social Studies incl. Law • Business • Maths & Computer • Built Environment

determination and achievement in areas such as the arts, sports, citizenship or volunteering. Sports Scholarships are also up for grabs.

STUDENT PROFILE

Not far short of half of LJMU students come from Merseyside, 31% are part-timers. Two thirds are eligible for a LJMU bursary, indicating they come from lower income households, as are over 65% of LJMU's scholarship winners. Students are recruited from around 106 countries and 11% are classified as a having a Black and Minority Ethnic background. There is also a high percentage of disabled (many dyslexic) students because they run a rigorous support programme.

Generally, LJMU's problem has not been getting students so much as hanging on to them: their drop-out runs at around 12%, quite high, though only a fraction above their Government benchmark.

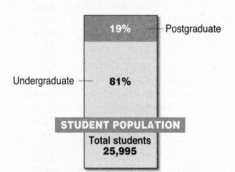

Postgraduate — 19%

Undergraduate — 81%

STUDENT POPULATION

Total students 25,995

Asked to give us a profile from the ground, Emma concluded, 'Despite the huge diversity in matters of taste and style, your LJMU student is a mellow person, out to enjoy their time at university. The general atmosphere is far from snobbish, and with such a wide range of people studying here, friends are not hard to find, no matter what your age, or what your interests.'

Also, Liverpool is a great place to be, fun, and imaginatively anarchistic, a personality that brings all the LJMU students together.

ACADEMIA & JOBS

Writes Emma: 'LJMU is big on student feedback. Tutors are approachable and changes do get made. Questionnaires regarding each and every module taught are distributed to students and the uni does listen to complaints. The emphasis is on making the experience as enjoyable as possible.'

LJMU has three modern Learning Resource Centres, two of which are open 24/7. A virtual learning environment, Blackboard, links students to assignments, lecture notes, useful internet sites and other multimedia resources. Over 2,000 workstations are available in the LRCs and student open-access facilities. 100% of student rooms are wired for internet access.

Generally, there's a vocational bias, they're strong on sandwich courses and have good contacts with industry - professional associations offer direct employment routes, for example, in pharmacy, surveying and engineering. And now they've established a business club for graduates called NEXUS, through which you'll be able to network and tap into uni-based expertise and resources. You also get lots of hands-on help in landing a job: a 'Ready for Work' programme is held weekly throughout the year - free, short, practical sessions and workshops designed to improve employability and prepare you for the first graduate job. All students are encouraged to develop skills and abilities like analysing and problem solving, team working and communicating, planning and organising, showing initiative, reasoning, and computing: 70% get real graduate jobs within six months of graduating.

They have six faculties: Business and Law; Education, Community & Leisure; Media, Arts & Social Science; Health & Applied Social Sciences; Science; and Technology & Environment.

Students in 2010 voted that the best teaching is in Accounting, American & Australasian Studies, Communications & Information Studies, English Studies, Geographical Studies, History, Imaginative Writing, Journalism, Marketing, Pharmacology, Toxicology & Pharmacy, Physical Geography and Environmental Science, Sociology, and Zoology.

Biological Sciences produce the most jobs, then Arts & Design, Business, subjects allied to Medicine, Social Studies, Education, Architecture, Building & Planning, Engineering & Technology, Computer Science, and Media.

A £24-million Art and Design Academy and a £22.5-million life sciences building opened recently, the latter including an 70-metre indoor running track and labs for testing cardio-vascular ability, motor skills and bio-mechanics functions.

Sports Science is a big deal here. In the last

research assessment 50% of their work was either world-class or internationally excellent. See Science & Football, Sports Development & PE, Exercise Science, Sports Science/Technology, and Outdoor Education with PE.

Education is a defining provision - secondary and primary. There are also ESOL and TESOL courses - English for non-English speakers and courses for teachers of same.

In Art & Design, look for Creative Writing, Dance, Drama, Fashion, Fine Art, Graphic Arts & Interior Design, but also Creative Arts & Social Science, making the link to the Social Studies strengths. The degrees in Social Work and Applied Psychology keep LJMU in the top echelon of graduate providers in community work and counselling.

Drama students and local community groups make use of Black Box Theatre Company, Momentum Theatre Company, Liverpool Youth Service and Unity Theatre following a £200,000 refurbishment of the LJMU's Joe H Makin Drama Centre. Arts links to Media through Interactive Media Design, and Computer & Electronics via the Digital Broadcast degree. Radio & TV broadcasters and sound recordists love this uni, in particular their BSc Broadcast Technology. There's a Granada TV partnership status and great tie-ups with Sky TV. Look, too, at BA Hons Journalism, which includes practical TV Journalism (there's also International Journalism) and Media Professional Studies for TV production, business and management enterprise, info technology and media theory. The latter is run in partnership with Mersey Television (Brookside and Hollyoaks producer, Phil Redmond, is their Honorary Professor).

The uni's nursing and midwifery students now benefit from 'SimMan' - a high-tech 'universal patient simulator' mannequin, which is part of the new Clinical Practice Suite, developed in partnership with the Cheshire and Merseyside Strategic Health Authority: 6 rooms designed to function like real hospital wards. This is part of a strong health provision, including Paramedic Practice, Medicinal Biochemistry, Analytical/Medicinal Chemistry. Another related area is Food & Nutrition, and Biosciences. See also BSc Nutrition, and Public Health. There's a good employment track record, too, for prospective chemists and those planning a career in Pharmaceutical Manufacture.

Students are requested to identify any disabilities including Dyslexia as early as possible, so as to take advantage of JMU's rigorous support programme.

Animal health technicians, carers, nurses are trained here too. LJMU leaves the vet degrees to Liverpool Uni and positions itself instead with the likes of BSc Animal Behaviour and Zoology.

The Architecture and Property Management degrees (see also the Real Estate Management and BSc Quantity Surveying) are another great graduate employment focus. The in-depth knowledge bank evident from their 60% world-class and internationally excellent ratings at the research assessment.

In Law, they deliver the Legal Practice Course required for becoming a solicitor. There's a 'mock' courtroom to give law degree and legal practice students the chance to gain intensive trial practice. And, as is so often the case in a city university with Criminology, Forensic Science and Social Psychology degrees and a strong Sport provision, jobs come easy with the police.

SOCIAL SCENE

STUDENTS' UNION As a prospective student, bear in mind that it is up to you to make the most of your time at LJMU. This means finding out about what is going on and getting involved in what interests you. Radio stations, newspapers, clubs, societies and events need student support and make a return with interest through the character and abilities they impart.

The Union (LSU) has various clubs and societies. Most of its organised activities take place in the main LSU building, the **Haigh**. Facilities include **Drift Café** - a place to relax with its fair-trade hot drinks, cakes and smoothies. There's free wi-fi and PC access. **Scholars** is the traditional student pub, with pool tables, jukeboxes and TVs. It serves quality bar food. and the official warm-up event to *Medication*, Liverpool's legendary student night every Wednesday at **Nation**. There are 3 rooms, r'n'b, dance & trance, and pop, cheese & soft rock.

The Engine Room serves lunch during the day and transforms into a nightclub at night. The ents menu is not quite what it was in the old days, but there's plenty of variety: see calendar to download on www.l-s-u.com.

Students gather at Scream, just behind the University, and besides Scholars and Nation (for Medication), favourite club haunts are '**Bumper**, **Mood**, **Koco**, **Baabaa**, **Bamboo**, the **Pilgrim**, oh yeh and especially **Krazy Horse**.' Check 'em out. These kids are never wrong.

ACCOMMODATION	
Student rating	★★
Guarantee to freshers	**100%**
Style	**Flats**
Security guard	**All**
Shared rooms	**None**
Internet access	**All**
Self-catered	**All**
En suite	**Most**
Approx price range pw	**£70-£127**
City rent pw	**£45-£125**

WHAT IT'S REALLY LIKE	
UNIVERSITY:	
Social Life	★★★
Societies	★
Student Union services	★★
Politics	**Active: safety, sex, housing**
Sport	**19 clubs**
National team position	**64th**
Sport facilities	★★
Arts opportunities	**Music excellent; drama, dance, film, art good**
Student newspaper	**Looprevil**
Student radio	**Looprevil Radio**
Nightclub Bar	**Scholars**
Union ents	**Pre-Med**
Union societies	**Some**
Most popular societies	**Afro-Carribean, Christian Union**
Parking	**Poor**
CITY:	
Entertainment	★★★★★
City scene	**Fab**
Town/gown relations	**Good**
Risk of violence	**Average**
Cost of living	**Low**
Student concessions	**Excellent**
Survival + 2 nights out	**£70 pw**
Part-time work campus/town	**Good/Excellent**

Shout used to be the media - newspaper and radio, often award-winning. Now it's Looprevil - that's Liverpool spelled backwards - the other side of Liverpool is what you get, geddit? There's The *Looprevil Press* (newspaper) and Looprevil Radio.

Situated in the Haigh is UNITEMP, LJMU's own employment agency. It does offer some exclusive Unitemp related jobs, but doesn't beat getting the local newspaper, visiting the job centre, or simply asking around for vacancies.

SPORT Sport is highly competitive. They came 64th in the BUCS teams league last year. The facilities include a swimming pool, all weather hockey and football pitches, fully equipped gym, dance studios, and climbing walls. Most facilities are based at LJMU's IM Marsh Campus, 3 miles from the city centre. LJMU's proudest boast is its Base Fitness Centre, well equipped and professionally staffed. There's a student sports pass for free/reduced price access to facilities - badminton courts, swimming pools, squash courts, athletics tracks.

PILLOW TALK

All freshers are guaranteed a place in city-centre halls: individual study bedrooms within shared flats alongside other LJMU students. Most rooms now also have private en-suite bathrooms. All accommodation is self-catering.

Victoria Hall is central, en suite and with broadband connections, good security (£92-£98 p.w.). Prospect Point is close to popular London

Road shopping area - flats with 5/6 bedrooms each (£92.50). Nearby is Opal Court with gym and pool (£102+ p.w.). North Western Hall is massive, hard by Lime Street Station, right in the centre of things, (£69-£76). Marybone is modern, City Campus, only £72.50. For de-luxe it'll be around £127 p.w.

GETTING THERE

☛ By road: M62, M6/J21a. Well served by coach.
☛ By rail: Manchester, 40 mins; Sheffield, 1:45; Leeds, Birmingham, 2:00; London King's Cross, 3:00.
☛ Liverpool airports for inland/Ireland flights.
☛ By coach: London, 5:00; Manchester, 50 mins.

STUDENT LONDON - THE CITY

Two sites you should have if you are coming to London to live as a student, the University of London Halls site: www.halls.london.ac.uk/student/Default.aspx and the private housing unit of the University of London Housing Services: http://housing.london.ac.uk/cms/.

Another thing, London is an expensive place to live unless you bury your embarrassment at being labelled a 'bake bean loving, beer-swilling creature of the night' and learn to flash your student card.

With a population of over seven million, London is one of the most diverse cities in the world – 30% of residents were born outside England. Greater London not only covers a lot of multicultural ground, but also physical, as it spans 1584 square kilometres. That space is filled with so many interests and attractions that you could not visit them all in one lifetime; London plays host to more than 200 carnivals and festivals annually. With its mixture of historical landmarks and modern masterpieces, London is a great place to learn, and not just in the lecture theatre.

THEATRE

On an average day in London you will be able to watch one of 76 plays, 33 musicals, 19 operas or 16 dance performances. If you were to go to one a day starting on the first of January, you wouldn't be finished until the end of May. The West End is one of the UK's biggest attractions: the choice of plays and shows is superb, but you often end up paying more up there. **The National Theatre** (Southbank, Embankment tube, +44 (0)20 7452 3000) and **The Globe Theatre** (21 New Globe Walk, Mansion House tube, +44 (0)20 7902 1400) are two of the most popular repertory companies. Playing less commercial performances, they often have the best offerings. The NT is subsidised. Otherwise there are countless fringe theatres showing allsorts for allsorts.

TKTS is the place to go for theatre on a budget. As the only official half price and discounted theatre ticket operation in London, they offer tickets on the day of the performance only, and have no phone number, so you have to visit. They are based in both Leicester Square and Canary Wharf DLR Station. Many theatres offer student tickets with proof of ID, otherwise it can be worth waiting at the venue box office for returns or standby tickets before the performance.

DANCE

Whether you're up for a class or just sitting back and watching somebody else shake their thang, London is a great place for dance.

The Barbican Centre (Silk Street, +44 (0)20 7638 4141, Barbican tube) is Europe's largest arts venue and a key member of the dance scene, especially the unconventional. Students get half price tickets in advance for all Wednesday evenings. **The London Coliseum** (St Martin's Lane, +44 (0)20 7836 0111, Leicester Square tube) is home to the English National Opera and is the London base of the English National Ballet. Standby tickets are available to students. There are many more major venues including **The Place**, Riverside Studios, Royal Opera House and Sadler's Wells.

To get involved yourself, there are classes of many different styles held in many venues. **Dance**

Attic (Old Fulham Baths, 368 North End Road, +44 (0)20 7610 2055, Fulham Broadway tube) costs £50 a year for students to join, you then just pay per class. **Pineapple Dance Studios** (7 Langley Street, +44 (0)20 7836 4004, Covent Garden Tube) costs £70 a year, that's half price for students. For full Dance listings visit www.londondance.com.

COMEDY

A comedy club is a great choice for an evening out in London. There are dozens of great venues scattered around, but here are a few of the more student friendly offerings.

Backyard Comedy Club, 231 Cambridge Heath Road, +44 (0)20 7739 3122, Bethnal Green tube. This converted factory is now a club owned by comedian Lee Hurst, who quite often acts as host. There is also a restaurant and disco after the show for anyone wanting a full night out.

Chuckle Club, London School of Economics, Houghton Street, +44 (0)20 7476 1672, Holborn tube. For less than a tenner you can see a host of comedians, including household names. Being a student union bar the drinks are all fairly cheap.

The Cosmic Comedy Club, 177 Fulham Palace Road, Hammersmith tube. This club is free to get in. You just have to pay what you think it was worth afterwards. Also, every week the BBC makes comedy programmes for radio. It's free, so anyone can go along. Call BBC Radio Theatre +44 (0)20 8576 1227.

CLUBS AND VENUES

London has around 15% of all the clubs in Britain. That means that you are never lost for a place to go for a spot of late night drinking. The biggest clubbing nights are still Friday and Saturday, but any day is a good day. Some of the bigger names include **Fabric** and **Ministry of Sound**, but there are hundreds of other venues catering for every taste. **www.londonnet.co.uk** has a great clubs section where you can select which day of the week you want to go out, or which style of music, and see complete listings. For free entrance into 25 London nightclubs, including **Café de Paris** and **Elysium**, become a Circle Club member, for just a £20 admin fee. It gives you free admission during the week and half price at weekends, and you can also purchase 2-4-1 drinks vouchers in advance. Visit **www.circleclubcard.com** for full details.

CINEMA

London has almost 500 cinema screens and a choice of over 100 films showing at any time. Leicester Square is the centre for cinema in London. Every year it hosts numerous star-studded premieres on the many huge screens. But it isn't particularly student friendly with rather expensive ticket prices, making London's independent cinemas the better option. The **Prince Charles Cinema** (7 Leicester Place, Leicester Square tube) is one such place. *Feel-good Fridays* cost just £1 and the most non-members have to pay for a regular performance is £4. Annual Membership is just £7.50. For a search that allows you to find a cinema by a particular postcode, tube location or where a certain film is showing visit www.viewlondon.co.uk. Alternatively most of the chain cinemas in Greater London offer student prices. **UGC** offers an unlimited monthly card for £13.99. Orange mobile customers can text FILM to 241 on Wednesdays and receive a code allowing them two tickets for the price of one.

ART

In London there are around 50 exhibitions open to the public each day. 17 national museums and galleries, as well as many other smaller, local galleries, allow free entrance. These include the **British Museum**, **National Gallery**, **Tate Modern** and **V&A Museum**. London exhibits countless works or all kinds, both permanent and temporary collections. For a list of all the contemporary exhibitions London has to offer at any time, visit www.newexhibitions.com. For more details about all the major London galleries go to www.londontourist.org/art.

MUSIC

There are 9 major concert halls in London – **Barbican** (where they often hold free events), **Purcell Room**, **Royal Albert Hall**, **Royal Festival Hall**, **Royal Opera House**, **Queen Elizabeth Hall**, **St John's Smith Square**, **Wembley Arena** and **Wigmore Hall** - as well as 47 major rock and pop venues, including **Astoria**, **Barfly**, **Brixton Academy**, **Forum and Garage**. From ultra-trendy to cheesy and trashy, international superstars to local legends, you will find whatever type of music you are after in London, and all of your favourite musicians will have played here, or will play here at some time. www.bbc.co.uk/music/whatson has regularly updated information covering all kinds of music. For the cheapest tickets go direct to the venue box office and avoid those booking fees, but for the best tickets visit www.gigsandtours.com or www.ticketmaster.co.uk.

SHOPPING

Camden is a great place to shop. The cheap goods and cosmopolitan atmosphere make it a unique experience. You can find just about anything there and can easily spend a day wandering the many shops and stalls. The market is open seven days a week and the nearest tube station is Camden Town. Covent Garden market offers more specialist goods with many arts and crafts. This historic setting is full of street entertainers and is easily accessed from a number of tube stations including Covent Garden and Leicester Square. **Portobello Road**, in the trendy Notting Hill area , is also worth a mention (open on Saturdays). Then there' **Oxford Street** (**Selfridges**), Knightsbridge (**Harrods**), Regents Street. Most High Street stores offer a student discount, just remember, always flash your student ID, and don't be afraid to ask.

Paul Stephen

LONDON METROPOLITAN UNIVERSITY

London Metropolitan University
31 Jewry Street
London EC3N 2EY

TEL 020 133 4200
  020 7753 3272 (Campus North)
EMAIL admissions@londonmet.ac.uk
WEB www.londonmet.ac.uk

London Metropolitan Students' Union
2 Goulston Street
London E1 7TP

TEL 020 7320 2769
FAX 020 7320 3201
EMAIL d.everett@uni.ac.uk
WEB www.londonmetsu.org.uk

VIRGIN VIEW

*L*ondon Metropolitan University was formed in 2002 by the merger of North London and London Guildhall universities. 'The new university is one of the biggest in the UK,' wrote John Shaw at the time. He was on the future strategy task group. With '13 main sites, grouped into two campuses (London North and London City),' it was Shaw's job to identify the two unis' very different histories and cultures and direct the

UNIVERSITY/STUDENT PROFILE

University since	**1992**
Situation/style	**Civic**
Student population	**26380**
Undergraduates	**19505**
Mature	**64%**
International	**22%**
Male/female ratio	**44:56**
Equality of opportunity:	
state school intake	**97%**
social class 4-7 intake	**58%**
drop-out rate	**15%**

way forward.

It was not an easy commission. First there was the geographical problem. North London University, the old London Poly which took University title in 1992, was based in the Holloway Road, London Guildhall, one of the largest providers of part-time professional courses (mainly Business, but also Law, Psychology, Musical Instrument Technology and Art & Design)in the country was located in the East End of London.

Really the only way they came together was in the uniquely diverse character of their students.

London Guildhall boasted a handful of celebrity singers, Alison Moyet and Sonya from Echobelly, an MP (Kate Hoey), a pants-stroking comedian (Vic Reeves) and Margaret Thatcher's errant son, Mark. Said student Stuart Harkness of the main body: 'The resilience of the university stemmed largely from its streetwise clientele, devoid of opulent silver spoons and armed with a left wing, if slightly lethargic, political bias. They'll stand at the bar, or at the odd demo, but in general

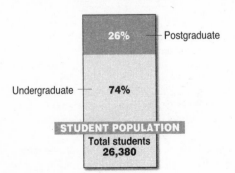

| Postgraduate | 26% |
| Undergraduate | 74% |

STUDENT POPULATION

Total students
26,380

the attitude is more down to earth than a rattlesnake's belly in a wagon wheel rut.'

Then there was the North London equivalent, soon to be suitor. The nearest they came to celebrity was having as the centrepiece of their theatre an organ that was once played by William Lloyd Webber, father of 'cello-playing Julian and musical impresario Andrew. As North London University from 1992 its students studied Business, but also Environment & Social Studies, Humanities, Education, Science, Computing, and Engineering. Sounds good, but it was all a bit of an uphill struggle. What the university was up against was what it called in 1995-6, 'the general difficulties faced by all graduates in gaining employment and University of North London graduates in particular. Reasons for this include the preponderance of mature students and a general misunderstanding of the quality and type of education provided here.'

The problem they had was that employers were not taking their graduates seriously. So they set about teaching their students to look at themselves closely, to analyse themselves, build up a picture of their strengths and weaknesses, and to develop personal skills, communication skills, and what they called in those days 'personal transferable skills.' When we spoke to student Maureen Okolo, however, it was far from clear that she had taken on board what the university intended by these personal transferable skills: 'UNL is in the right place for a great big, delicious slice of London's night life. Step outside and find yourself in the infamous Holloway Road... Uni life is great, if you like that sort of thing. Just expect constant rounds of socialising with chic, retro, funky, cool, funny individuals from all walks of life.'

I sometimes think back to those days and wonder whether Mr Shaw might have done better had he met Stuart Harkness and Maureen Okolo and really empathised with them before he set about the massive PR operation that still today markets London Metropolitan University as 'one of the foremost providers of undergraduate, postgraduate, professional and vocational education and training in Britain.'

Clearly, it is not. But it is a people's university with masses of potential if only if it was managed from the bottom up rather than the top down, as indeed North London Poly used to be - a great place, with easy relations between lecturers and students, everyone part of the same scene, not teaching personality traits but encouraging their students simply to be. Then it wouldn't find itself in the pickle it did last year when recently it was ordered by the Higher Education Funding Council to investigate itself after allegations that one of its departments had leant on students to mark up its teaching so to improve its ratings in the National Student Survey.

Survey results, league tables, 'facts and figures' are the stock in trade of the top-down PR operation which simply doesn't suit certain higher education institutions. Why straightjacket its efforts in this way? Let them instead get on with what they are good at, or were good at before this union took place.

Only 67% of London met students are satisfied with the teaching, and the Times Higher *Student Experience Survey* has them languishing second to last. Then there's the student drop-out rate, 15%. The stats make poor reading. But not quite all of them. London Met finished 42nd in the BUCS sports team league table of all universities last time, out of 146 places. Why don't they shout about that a bit?

All teams play under the London Mets brand, a brand which, the Uni hopes, will gleam with success in the University sector and National Leagues. Let's bring it to fever pitch.

CAMPUS SCENE

It is an unusual set-up for a uni, with its umpteen sites, academic and residential in E1, E2, E9, E14, EC3, and N7.

CITY CAMPUS has the 12 sites in the City and the East End, which is a racially diverse area with, in particular, a thriving Bangladeshi community giving the cultural flavour to the eating and shopping delights of Brick Lane. The campus's main Moorgate site is built on what used to the most infamous insane asylum in England, the Bethlem Royal Hospital.

WHAT IT'S REALLY LIKE	
UNIVERSITY:	
Social Life	★
Societies	★
Student Union services	★
Politics	**Internal**
Sport	**Competitive**
National team position	**42nd**
Sport facilities	★
Arts	**Available**
Student magazine	**VerveZine**
Student radio	**Metsu Radio**
Nightclub venues/bars	**Sub Bar, Sub Club (Aldgate), Rocket (Holloway Road)**
Union ents	**Big Fish, etc.**
Most active society	**Islamic Soc**
Parking	**Non-existent**
CITY:	
Entertainment	★★★★★
Scene	**Wild, expensive**
Town/gown relations	**Average-good**
Risk of violence	**'Average'**
Cost of living	**Very high**
Student concessions	**Locally adequate**
Survival + 2 nights out	**£100 pw**
Part-time work campus/town	**Good/excellent**

CAMPUS NORTH comprises a collection of sites around the Holloway Road, a student-friendly area packed with takeaways, cafés, restaurants and shops.

So there we have it. Chapel Market and Camden Lock meet Aldgate, Petticoat Lane and Spitalfields.

FEES, BURSARIES

UK & EU Fees, 2011-12: £3,375. If in receipt of full HE Maintenance grant there's a bursary of £1,000; if in receipt of partial grant, bursaries are on a sliding scale as to parental income. They also have

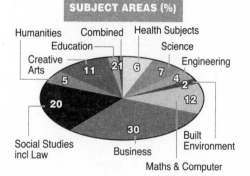

SUBJECT AREAS (%)

Humanities — 11
Combined — 21
Health Subjects — 6
Education
Science — 7
Creative Arts — 5
Engineering — 4
— 2
— 12
Social Studies incl Law — 20
Business — 30
Built Environment
Maths & Computer

TEACHING SURVEY AT A GLANCE

Avg. UCAS points accepted	**190**
Acceptance rate	**16%**
Overall satisfaction rate	**67%**
Helpful/interested staff	★★
Small tuition groups	★
Students into graduate jobs	**60%**

Teaching most popular with undergraduates:
Mathematical Sciences, Maths & Statistics,
Medical Science & Pharmacy, Pharmacology,
Toxicology & Pharmacy,
Subjects Allied to Medicine.

Teaching least popular with undergraduates:
Languages (55%), Fine Art (54%), Film &
Tourism (47%), Film & Photography (43%).

scholarships. See www.londonmet.ac.uk/scholar-ships

STUDENT PROFILE

A high proportion originate from London and the surrounding Southeast, but the melting pot is fuelled by those from farther afield, nearly 8,000 international students from 155 countries. The cosmopolitan flavour makes London Met a truly multi-cultural university. 'Multiple faiths are therefore evident and well catered for with prayer rooms at various university sites, a chaplaincy and numerous students' union-funded cultural societies, including Christian, Islamic, Muslim, Afro-Caribbean, to name but a few. All seem to respect each others' practices under the umbrella of LGU brotherhood.'

They run their own offices in China, India, Pakistan and Bangladesh, and provide a three-day orientation course for international students each September. There is also a successful peer support scheme, involving language support, a buddy system and subject area support. But all that aside, what we have is a cultural recipe with flavour, which is also what we have at Campus North, whose undergraduate body is to a large extent drawn from the local, notably ethnic population.

SOCIAL SCENE

Students Union London Met's **Rocket** has a fascinating history, worth a book of its own. It has been around since the inception of the North London Poly itself. It began as the Great Hall when the first students arrived in 1896. Some of their concerts were actually conducted by Proms inventor Sir Henry Wood. Since then it became a proscenium arch theatre, the arch picked up for a song from the old **Marlborough Theatre** down the road opposite the **Nag's Head**, after which it was used as a cinema, where William Lloyd Webber played the organ... And so the tale goes on. Today, the Rocket Complex, as it is known, is a meeting place of some style, cool enough for like-minded City students, used to their ground-floor **Hub Bar** in Goulston Street (where one of Jack the Ripper's victims was found) to get up and out, and go along.

Certainly the Rocket's entertainment list looks suitably enticing.

'The award-winning venue the Rocket Complex comprises a nightclub, live music venue (with the latest turbo sound floodlight system), 2 licensed bars, external courtyard, pool and games room, coffee bar and shop,' chirps a union wallah. 'The weekly events programme includes *The Big Fish* ("the best student night in London" - *Time Out*), *Pint Sized Comedy Club* and regular events showcasing music and culture from around the globe. Headliners include... Trevor Nelson, Jools Holland, Punjabi Hit Squad, Asian Dub Foundation, Kele le Roc, Ms Dynamite, Artful Dodger, Timmi Magic, DJ Hanif, DJ Luck + MC Neat, Jah Shaka, Latina Max + London's largest Brazilian Carnival.'

Sounds more enterprising than the ents down in City campus's **Hub** - *Bar Footsie* to *One Ton Quiz*, *Big Fish* again and, right now, the *Easter Eggstravaganza*. More up to the minute perhaps is the **Met Lounge**, also at Goulston Street, a smoke - and alcohol-free social space - wireless internet, newspapers, refreshments: it's the coming thing.

There's a new student magazine launched in December 2008, *VerveZine*, and a new radio station launched jointly by the Radio Soc and the Union - was to be called Verve Radio, but going out as Metsu Radio. There are internal media and arts awards aplenty and excellent departments in these areas. There is also political activity (and a tradition of that). Islamic Soc is the most active society.

SPORT The Mets are seriously good, 42nd 1st year, 28th and 25th two years previously. The rugby team plays at Saracens ground. The Peter May Centre, Walthamstow, is home to such as cricket, football and hockey. The Arsenal stadium is right behind the old North London Uni buildings. Pitches, courts, sports halls, all the usual requirements are to a high standard. A new Sports Centre on North Campus has large sports hall and a fitness gym with a wide range of cardiovascular equipment and fixed weight machines, plus a free weights area. At Whitechapel High Street on City Campus there's a fitness gym with a range of cardiovascular equipment and fixed weight machines, plus a range of dumbbells.

The men's and women's tennis teams and men's table tennis have won European Universities titles over the last two seasons; the women's and men's basketball team are both playing in the top division of the English Basketball League.

ACADEMIA & JOBS

Business (there is a particular strength in Accounting) and Architecture are clearly strengths. It is quite clear from the 2008 assessment of the nation's research provision that London Met has in-depth expertise in Maths, Architecture, Social Work, Social Policy etc., Education, American Studies, and Media - 10% to 15% of all these subjects were considered world-class. Social Work came out best with 50% of the provision either world-class or internationally excellent.

Around a third of Campus North students graduate in business subjects and there is a dominant but well thought-out joint degree series. Down at City around a third of students graduate in a very similar joint vocational degree system and more than a quarter graduate in business subjects. Some joint courses require travel to both campuses.

Then we have another important area - health, with degrees such as Herbal Herbal Medicine Science alongside Pharmaceutical Science and Pharmacology, and Biomedical Sciences, a programme that scores particularly strongly in the employment table. There is also a notable lean at North towards the therapeutic care side, with degrees in Social Work and BSc Psychology (Applied) & Health Studies.

Still on the professional front, look to either campus for LLB Law. While City are commercial & business law specialists, North have LLB (Social Justice).

Another string to North's bow is sport, while a defining niche at City, for which they scored a near perfect score at the teaching assessments, is Fine Art,

RESEARCH EXCELLENCE

% of London Met's research that is
4* (World-class) or 3* (Internationally rated):

	4*	3*
Health Professions	5%	25%
Human Biological	0%	5%
Food Science	0%	5%
Pure Mathematics	10%	25%
Statistics	5%	20%
Computer Science	0%	10%
Metallurgy and Materials	0%	0%
Architecturet	15%	25%
Town/Country Planning	5%	30%
Economics	0%	35%
Business/Management	0%	15%
Law	0%	10%
Politics	5%	15%
Social Work	10%	40%
Psychology	0%	10%
Education	10%	40%
American Studies	10%	15%
European Studies	5%	30%
Art and Design	0%	10%
Performing Arts	0%	25%
Media Studies	15%	25%

ing a reputation for artistic excellence, with well-respected jewellery-making and furniture departments, and many student-led initiatives leading to national awards.'

Jewellery design/making may be a small, specialist field, but City hits the spot employment-wise.

Furniture design and manufacture is another area of supreme confidence. North's response is with the BA Interior Architecture & Design, and a range of Architecture which achieves a sound employment record in architectural consultancy and construction.

PILLOW TALK

Students have access to over 1,300 rooms in halls, each situated close to either the London City or London North campuses. Accommodation is guaranteed for all first years who live more than 25 miles away and who accept a conditional or unconditional offer of a course and return their halls application by the 8th August.

ACCOMMODATION

Student rating	★
Guarantee to freshers	**35%**
Style	**Halls, flats**
Security guard	**Secure**
Shared rooms	**Some**
Internet access	**Most**
Self-catered	**Most**
En suite	**None**
Approx price range pw	**£72-£240**
City rent pw	**£110+**

GETTING THERE

☞ By Underground to City Campus: Aldgate (Metropolitan and Circle lines), Aldgate East (District and Hammersmith & City).
☞ By Underground to Campus North: Holloway Road (Piccadilly Line).

Design, Silversmithing, and Jewellery, including Fashion Jewellery, appropriate to the traditional strength of this area of London in the art and craft movement. Writes Sam Hall: 'The university is gain-

LONDON SCHOOL OF ECONOMICS & POLITICAL SCIENCE

The London School of Economics
& Political Science
Houghton Street
London WC2A 2AE

TEL 020 7955 6613
FAX 020 7955 6001
Email stu.rec@lse.ac.uk
WEB www.lse.ac.uk

LSE Students' Union
East Building
Houghton Street
London WC2A 2AE

TEL 020 7955 7158
FAX 020 7955 6789
EMAIL su.comms@lse.ac.uk
WEB www.lsesu.com

VIRGIN VIEW

*T*he London School of Economics &
Political Science (LSE) is part of the
University of London. It has the highest percentage of world-leading research of any university in the country, topping or coming
close to the top of a number of rankings of
research excellence.

LSE has produced 35 world leaders and
heads of state and 16 Nobel Prize Winners. It
is as secure as the British Establishment,
with which, despite the school's history of
'60s student revolt - ex-LSE student Mick
Jagger, Grosvenor Square, the Vietnam War
and all, it is indeed synonymous.

LSE goes hand in hand with Westminster
and Whitehall, with the City and with the
legal and the media sub-strata too. In fact,
its geographical position ensures it closer
contact with all departments of the
Establishment than either Oxford or
Cambridge. It is fundamental to its identity,
for the vibrant and cosmopolitan capital city
is an ideal setting for undergraduates to
study real world issues, which is what you

UNIVERSITY/SCHOOL PROFILE	
University since	**1900**
Situation/style	**City campus**
Student population	**9575**
Undergraduates	**4250**
Mature	**27%**
International	**68%**
Male/female ratio	**47:53**
Equality of opportunity:	
state school intake	**71%**
social class 4-7 intake	**19%**
drop-out rate	**5%**

will be doing here, and with almost half LSE
undergraduates from overseas, there is a
unique opportunity to study contemporary
issues with people from all parts of the
world. It encourages students to question
their own assumptions and beliefs and think
broadly about the issues shaping society.

One of the perks is the continuous drift of
influential speakers visiting, academics,
Nobel prize winners such as Amartya Sen,
state leaders such as David Cameron, and
business leaders such as James Caan.

If there is a problem with LSE it is that
the lecturers seem to find students something
of a necessary evil. In the 'helpful/interested'
category of the Times Higher *Student
Experience Survey 2010*, they scored low in
this area. In case you hadn't noticed, there
are more postgraduates than undergraduates
at LSE. You will not be all they are thinking
about.

However, 89% of you will get proper
graduate jobs within six months of leaving,
and not any job but one with probably the
highest starting salary in the UK - an aver-

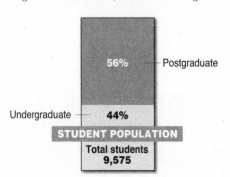

56% — Postgraduate

Undergraduate — **44%**

STUDENT POPULATION

**Total students
9,575**

age starting salary of £29,756 a year.

The competition to get in to LSE is fierce. Each year, the School receives 19,000 under-graduate applications for 1,200 places. Therefore, predicted or actual grades do not guarantee admission. When reviewing the applications, they place strong emphasis on the personal statement - 'It must be well written, containing no spelling or grammatical mistakes, and focus 75 per cent of the content on the subject area of study,' they say.

2011 Undergraduate Open Days are to be held on 30 March and 29 June.

TEACHING SURVEY AT A GLANCE	
Avg. UCAS points accepted	**480**
Acceptance rate	**7%**
Overall satisfaction rate	**80%**
Helpful/interested staff	★★★
Small tuition groups	★
Students into graduate jobs	**89%**

Teaching most popular with undergraduates:
Sociology.

Teaching least popular with undergraduates:
History (69%).

CAMPUS

'The LSE is the filling in a sandwich,' writes Dominique Fyfe, a student from America. 'On one side (the capital's financial and legal district) the air is serious and the suits Armani, and the FT-reading societal stress-set is on the go until long after the sun is down.

On the other, west of Kingsway (hitherto the dividing line, a road where all those who cannot drive test their inabilities), lie the expensive, funky, multi-purpose Covent Garden and London's the-atreland and Soho, haven for sex addicts and non-traditionalists, and the book lovers' paradise of Charing Cross Road.'

To translate, LSE is situated between Kingsway and the Strand, at the heart of London culture and the legal establishment, and not far from the City or Westminster either. It is a campus crowded with buildings, the so-called Old Building being on the site of the small hall, where it all began and from which it has steadily expanded into buildings close by - the East Building, Clare Market, St Clement, St Philips, Clement House, all built on land which is among the most expensive per square foot in the world.

FEES, BURSARIES

UK & EU Fees, 2011-12: £3,375. The LSE Bursary is available for students from low-income back-grounds (from England and Wales) and is worth up to £7,500 over a three-year programme. The LSE Discretionary Bursary is available for new LSE stu-dents who face exceptional needs. The value of the award may vary according to need. Each year they awards a number of scholarships to UK, EU and overseas students. Visit lse.ac.uk/financialSupport

STUDENT PROFILE

Their take from the state school sector is 71% and from the lower socio-economic classes 19%, which is healthy for a university up there with Oxbridge.

But Nick Davies, an ex-public schoolboy reading Politics & Philosophy, makes the really significant point: 'LSE students are around 70% from overseas. Personalities are generally liberal within the department, but still leave room for other opinion. There is a good mix of personalities.'

'Interesting conversation is one thing you will not find a lack of at the LSE,' writes Dominique. 'The students here think critically in the classroom but also have a point of view in friendly discussion outside. Many are highly driven, always ready for an intellectual challenge and very competitive. However, not all are so intense; some don't even find the library until summer exams!

'Naturally, most of the students you will meet here are reading for a degree in Economics, but what makes the school a fascinating place is that there are so many studying other subjects, like anthropology, finance, social psychology and phi-losophy, and you learn from everybody.

'The LSE is a breeding ground for global nomads. In between lectures, the Houghton Street hub of LSE activity overflows with student repre-sentatives of all races of our world. Languages you will begin to learn in this global microcosm are Indian, French, Italian, Spanish, Russian, German,

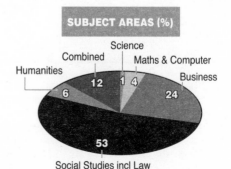

SUBJECT AREAS (%)

Science
Combined
Humanities
Maths & Computer
Business
12
1 4
6
24
53
Social Studies incl Law

RESEARCH EXCELLENCE

% of LSE's research that is
4* *(World-class) or* **3*** *(Internationally rated):*

	4*	3*
Pure Mathematics	5%	40%
Statistics	15%	40%
Geography Environment	20%	50%
Economics	60%	35%
Business/Management	30%	40%
Law	45%	30%
Politics	30%	30%
Social Worn	50%	30%
Sociology	20%	25%
Anthropology	40%	25%
European Studies	20%	45%
Philosophy	35%	30%
History	35%	30%
Media Studies	45%	30%

not to mention English of course. Not only do these students of all cultures bring their traditions but they also bring the trendy, money-sucking, modern fashions, but don't worry if your wardrobe didn't appear in the latest issue of *Cosmo* or *GQ*; nobody really cares whether its Oxfam or Armani.'

ACADEMIA & JOBS

Writes Dominique, 'Lectures and classes are well enough taught. In fact I find myself wanting to go to them - a truly novel experience for me! Don't be surprised if the reading list for a class is more like a library's inventory record! The lectures are monologues, but the classes are interactive and "cosy" in size (maximum fifteen students). Essays are written for classes but not always formally assessed or given a definitive deadline, which can make procrastination seem dangerously attractive.'

The LSE library, the British Library of Political and Economic Science, founded in 1896, contains one million volumes, 28,000 journals (10,000 on current sub.), numerous specialist manuscripts - all totalling some three million items. Even so, it is not immune from student criticism: 'LSE's library is overwhelming and quite frankly I would not go there if I didn't have to. The process is as follows: when you reach the library half of the books you are looking for are not there and if they are, there is only one copy of the main text for

> *'The LSE is a breeding ground for global nomads. In between lectures, the Houghton Street hub of LSE activity overflows with student representatives of all races of our world.'*

about twenty to forty-plus students and are titled as set texts, which means that they can only be borrowed for twenty-four hours. Return it twenty-four hours too late and the librarians grow the devil's tail and horns and collect a large amount of your own precious money! If that seems a tough sentence, it is and is meant to be.'

A Language Centre specialises in creating courses targeted to the particular needs of students and offers EAP, French, German, Italian, Japanese, Russian, Spanish, Arabic, Chinese, Portuguese, Norwegian, Basque, Turkish. Sixty-five per cent of the European Studies research provision was designated world-class or of international significance.

LSE students work in banking and other financial services, local and national government, business and management consultancy, charities, professional services firms and the media. See lse.ac.uk/graduateDestinations.

A course called LSE100 marks you out as a success from the start. Launched in 2009-10, it introduces all freshers to the fundamentals of thinking as a social scientist, by exploring real problems and real questions, drawing on a range of disciplines across the social sciences. It helps produce a distinctive LSE graduate with skills that cut across narrow subject areas.

SOCIAL SCENE

STUDENTS' UNION **The Three Tuns**, **Underground Bar**, **Quad** and shop are all newly refurbished. 'Many students drift in the direction of the pub, The Three Tuns,' says Dominique, 'which has a "cool" atmosphere. The drinks are cheap, the company is friendly and the music plays at a level that doesn't reach eardrum-damaging decibels.'

Frankly, ignore the *Times Higher* Student Experience Survey, which suggests social life, societies and student union virtually don't exist at LSE (wnd which translate into one or two stars in our 'What it's really like' ratings. We have described the special tenor of the community at Houghton Street, but there is masses that is good that is going. We can only assume that the student body is so detatched from the bureaucracy of the exercise that few particip[ated.

'The Students Union offers a wide range of societies at the Freshers' Fair. The Socialism Society and other political groups will attack in a desperate attempt to sway you, but other societies adopt a less obtrusive approach. There are plenty of opportuni-

Exilo; *Afta Skool* (indie) is a Saturday clubnight at Quad. They can get 1,000 bodies in to the 3-room club, made up of the Tuns, the Quad, with its sofa-strewn mezzanine, and the smaller venue, the Underground. There are also student nights at selected sites in London's clubland.

Town See *London Student City*.

Sport In the basement of the Old Building there's a training room and multi-gym. The school also has its own sports grounds in South London. There are also netball, tennis courts and four large swimming pools within two miles of Houghton Street. The University of London Union has facilities for squash, basketball, rowing and swimming. LSE cricketers may use the indoor facilities at Lords. LSE sports teams came 54th nationally last year in the national team league.

ties to get involved, be it through the arts, politics, radio, religion (most religions and denominations are observed), business, or cultural groups. Sports teams exist, but I can give you little information about them, as I am motivationally challenged as regards any kind of physical activity.'

LSE claims the only weekly Students Union General Meeting in the country. More than 200 students regularly attend to hold union officers to account and to debate campus level, national and international issues. 'Those who get involved in the SU are usually left-wing,' says one who does; 'those who focus on careers are right-wing. Occasionally there are clashes.'

Excellent media: magazine *Script*, newspaper *Beaver*, radio station PuLSE, TV LooSE TV. They won Writer of the Year at the 2009 *Guardian* Awards.

LSE also has its own dedicated ents manager and the Friday night clubnight, *Crush*, is one of the most popular student nights in London every Friday. Other regular ents are *Mind the Gap*, and for LGBT students - gays - there's a gay salsa night,

PILLOW TALK

All first year students are guaranteed a place in LSE or London University accommodation - basically halls and one block of self-catering flats. 'Residence halls are cheap and easy,' writes Dominique, 'but in my opinion the London University intercollegiate option is preferable. You will find the quality of food to be not much better than that of pig slop, but living next door to two vets, across the hall from a nurse, next door to a musician, down the hall from an opera singer, and one floor above a physiotherapist could only happen in an intercollegiate hall (see Introduction). This option definitely widens your social circle. Rooms are basic with a small single bed (not much room for two if you have big plans), a desk and a wardrobe.'

GETTING THERE

☛ Holborn (Piccadilly, Central lines), Temple (District, Circle lines), Charing Cross (Jubilee, Northern, Bakerloo lines).

LONDON SOUTH BANK UNIVERSITY

London South Bank University
103 Borough Road
London SE1 0AA

TEL 020 7815 7815
FAX 020 7815 8273
EMAIL enquiry@lsbu.ac.uk
WEB www.lsbu.ac.uk

London South Bank Students' Union
Keyworth Street
London SE1 6NG

TEL 020 7815 6060
FAX 020 7815 6061
EMAIL hoggm@lsbu.ac.uk
WEB www.londonsouthbanksu.com

VIRGIN VIEW

*L*ondon South Bank University was once South Bank Poly, and still the majority of students come from the locality, which includes a rich tapestry of ethnic groups. Much of it is clustered around a triangle formed by Borough Road, London Road and Southwark Bridge Road, just south of the Thames at Elephant and Castle.

The university projects you into the big city, where the streets are paved with whatever you want them to be paved with. You come to London South Bank University (LSBU), you come to London...for a bit of gritty realism.

CAMPUS

The good thing about the location is that it allows easy access to more attractive elements, such as the South Bank arts complex, the Tate Modern, Globe Theatre and the London Eye. The West End is only three stops away on the Underground, Whitechapel and the East End is equally accessible, and the nearby Thames is once again a main artery of the Capital.

Writes Laura Cattell: 'LSBU is on London's cultural doorstep - The National Theatre, The Globe, and the British Film Institute are a walk away from

UNIVERSITY/STUDENT PROFILE	
University since	**1992**
Situation/style	**City sites**
Student population	**24280**
Undergraduates	**18165**
Mature	**73%**
International	**13%**
Male/female ratio	**43:57**
Equality of opportunity:	
state school intake	**99%**
social class 4-7 intake	**49%**
drop-out rate	**16%**

the main campus. The City of London lies just over the river with the Houses of Parliament and Westminster Abbey is close by.'

'Location - prime,' agrees Lola Brown. 'Situated in zones 1/2, the main campus is indeed ideally located on the uber trendy South Bank, but Elephant & Castle itself is a bit of a hole, though it is improving rapidly with some major urban regeneration happening. It has its own tube station (Bakerloo & Northern lines).'

The learning resources (including a library) and the Students Union is currently on Keyworth Street, where two years ago the brand new 9-storey Keyworth Centre opened. There are yet two other sites further away - the Faculty of Health & Social Care at Harold Wood Hospital (Romford) and Whipps Cross Hospital (Leytonstone) - a situation rather optimistically 'solved' by calling these two distinct sites the Redwood Campus.

FEES, BURSARIES

UK & EU Fees, 2011-12: £3,375 p.a. See www.lsbu.ac.uk/fees for the latest info. There are bursaries and scholarships for sport and academic prowess, and support for ethnics.

STUDENT PROFILE

Seventy-three per cent of undergraduates are mature, some 49% are part-timers, almost a third come from the London Borough of Southwark,

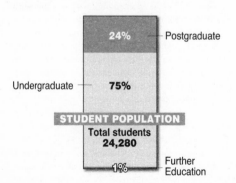

24% — Postgraduate

Undergraduate — 75%

STUDENT POPULATION
Total students
24,280

1% — Further Education

over half from ethnic minorities, and 13% are from overseas (from more than 120 different countries). In socio-economic terms, 49% come from the lower classes 4-7, and many are the first generation from their family to go to university.

'A real cross section!' exclaims Lola. 'Freshers here are not generally middle-class white kids, though there are a fair few of those too.'

In the context of the demography the loss of 16% as drop-outs is not surprising.

ACADEMIA & JOBS

Students say the best teaching is in Accounting and Biological Sciences. Generally, engineering gets the thumbs down: Engineering & Technology (54% of the class only said OK), Mechanically-based Engineering (46%), Mechanical, Production and Manufacturing Engineering (44%).

The criticism is a shame because Engineering was among the highlights of LSBU's submission at the national research assessment - 60% of the research work LSBU does in Engineering was graded either world-class or internationally excellent. So, the in-depth knowledge is there, it's the teaching, it appears, that isn't. And yet, that is not the case according to their students.

In the *Times Higher Magazine's* Student Experience Survey 2011 London South Bank's students marked the University down not on the quality of staff or how helpful or interested the lecturers are in them, nor on the quality of the courses. What they said was lacking was any sort of community atmosphere or social life or extra-curricular activities. Facilities and campus environment were also criticised, and as the the Student Union it was dissed almost completely. These sort of problems eat away every day at the culture of a university.

The graduate employment graph shows that far and away the most graduate jobs at London South Bank go to students of subjects related to

Medicine at LSBU - students of Nursing (children's as well as adult), Operating Department Practice, Theatre Practice, Therapeutic Radiography, Applied Science, Bioscience, Biochemistry, etc. These account for a third of all the jobs going on graduation from LSBU. Social Studies degrees are

RESEARCH EXCELLENCE

% of London South Bank's research that is
4* *(World-class) or* **3*** *(Internationally rated):*

	4*	3*
Nursing/Midwifery	**5%**	**30%**
Computer Science/	**5%**	**25%**
General Engineering/	**5%**	**55%**
Business/Management	**5%**	**15%**
Information Management	**0%**	**15%**
Social Work	**15%**	**45%**
Psychology	**0%**	**20%**
Sports	**5%**	**20%**
Media Studies	**15%**	**25%**

also productive in this area of employment and showed up best in the research assessment, with 15% of South Bank's research world-class and 45% internationally excellent.

Employment in architecture, construction, planning is also a pretty good cert, from the Architecture and Built Environment degrees obvious, and Building Services Engineering, Quantity Surveying and the like.

Generally, the portfolio of degrees is markedly vocational. There's a taste of the workplace about everything on offer.

Besides Built Environment, Engineering, Design & Technology, and Health & Social Care, faculties include Business & Management (by far

SUBJECT AREAS (%)

Creative Arts — 4
Education — 1
Combined — 7
Health Subjects — 10
Science —
Engineering — 8
— 14
Built Environment — 12
Maths & Computer — 5
Business — 24
Social Studies incl Law — 8
Humanities — 7

WHAT IT'S REALLY LIKE

UNIVERSITY:

Social Life	★
Societies	★
Student Union services	★
Politics	**Student issues, activity low**
Sport	**10 clubs**
National team position	**90th**
Sport facilities	★★
Arts opportunities	**Good; art poor**
Student newspaper	**LDN Press**
Student radio	**Rare FM**
Bar	**Rigg Bar**
Union ents	**Occasional**
Union societies	**7**
Most popular societies	**Afrikan, Islamic, Forensic Science**
Smoking policy	**Union, halls OK**
Parking	**Poor**

CITY:

Entertainment	★★★★★
Scene	**Excellent**
Town/gown relations	**Average**
Risk of violence	**'Average'**
Cost of living	**Very high**
Student concessions	**Excellent**
Survival + 2 nights out	**£100 pw**
Part-time work campus/town	**Average/excellent**

ACCOMMODATION

Student rating	★
Guarantee to freshers	**75%**
Style	**Flats**
Security guard	**All**
Shared rooms	**None**
Internet access	**All**
Self-catered	**All**
En suite	**Most**
Approx price range pw	**£99-£122**
City rent pw	**£100+**

on the tube to get to Oxford Circus so the whole of London is your oyster. Elephant is not, however, the nicest of areas, but keep your wits about you and everything's cool.'

On campus **The Rigg Bar** is at the heart of what the Union has to offer. At night it doubles as a club. Friday is the zenith of ambition, with live music and DJs at the heart of it, but nothing else at the weekend.

But hold everything. The Student Union is temporarily situated on Thomas Doyle Street. And perhaps the current dearth of atmosphere picked up by its students (see Academia) has something to do with that. A new building is scheduled to open in 2012, when maybe things will begin to take a turn for the better.

the largest), Computing, Science, Humanities & Social Science.

The course programme is modular in structure. There are decent learning resources, a centre has 400 Pentium PCs with Internet facility and allows access to a CD-ROM network.

In addition, there are four libraries, one at each of the four sites, with a total of 300,000 books. The teaching picture is very good., while asking grades are low.

Business offers a less than certain employment pathway - some 17% of jobs are accounted for by Business graduates, but a large number enter employment as general administrators, sales assistants, and accounts and wages clerks.

SOCIAL LIFE

'It's London, innit,' exclaims Lola. 'Anything, anytime, whatever you like to do. The South Bank itself has a buzzing vibe every night and there are some fantastic restaurants in the Elephant. We're close to both the **Old Vic**, Shakespeare's **Globe** theatre and the famous **South Bank Arts Complex**, **National Theatre** and **Royal Festival Hall**, which'll inject you with culture. There's the **IMAX** cinema and it takes only about five minutes

A social life can be sourced through sports clubs & societies. They say that there are 22, societies including LGBT and Socialist Worker Student Society. The most active is tabled as Arts & Media, whioch has recently produced a new student newspaper, *LDN Press*.

But the sense one has is the same as at East London University. Things in the extra-curricular scene have been let go, and they need someone to pull the whole student thing back together again.

There is a grand tradition of cultural societies, such as the Afrikaan society with its club night, Black Pepper. Islamic is also big - there are prayer rooms for Islamic students. Maybe that is the place to start. Organisation is what is required. 'Politically,' writes Lola, 'we're verging on the left wing, but the most political thing to happen is an occasional guest speaker or a meeting.'

SPORT There was a spectacular enhancement of the fortunes of LSB's Athletic union a few years ago when they finished 49th in the national leagues, but they were 90th last time out. They created an Academy of Sport, Physical Activity & Wellbeing, so that the indoor sports facilities on the main campus include a 40+ station fitness suite, weights room, sports hall and injury clinic. Its main indoor facilities are on the Southwark campus. The sports ground is a 21-acre site at Turney Road, Dulwich, with pavilion and bar.

Sports range from traditional (rugby, netball) to Jitsu and Whu Shu Kwan, and the Academy runs a 'Revitalise' class programme, offering a mixture of exercise and relaxation classes including yoga, Pilates, aerobics and circuits.

PILLOW TALK

LSBU has 1,400 single study bedrooms located across 4 residential buildings, both standard and en-suite. All are within a 10-minute walk of the main Southwark campus, are self-catered basis and located within self-contained flats. Flats accommodate between 2 and 9 residents. Every bedroom is equipped with a 'pay as you talk' telephone and internet access. See more at www.lsbu.ac.uk/halls.

GETTING THERE

☛ By Underground: Elephant and Castle (Bakerloo and Northern Lines) or mainline Waterloo station.

LOUGHBOROUGH UNIVERSITY

Loughborough University
Ashby Road
Loughborough
Leicestershire LE11 3TU

TEL 01509 223522
FAX 01509 223905
EMAIL admissions@lboro.ac.uk
WEB www.lboro.ac.uk

Loughborough Students' Union
Ashby Road
Loughborough
Leicestershire LE11 3TT

TEL 01509 635000
FAX 01509 635003
EMAIL union@lborosu.org.uk
WEB www.lufbra.net

VIRGIN VIEW

*L*oughborough has been voted the best student experience in the Times Higher Magazine's national poll for the fifth year running. It is used to coming top. It has dominated university sport for far longer.

When people think of Loughborough, which has been a university since 1966, they think of its sport, for it is the best by such a long way that some of its teams can't find decent opposition on the university circuit and turn to professional clubs to sharpen their teeth on. Then, perhaps older people think of its engineering capability, for it came out of Loughborough Technical Institute.

Surprise then that the weekly student magazine, Label, received a letter from a reader complaining that coverage favoured the arts at the expense of sport. Surprise too that the official uni line is: 'Contrary to popular belief, sport does not pervade everything at Loughborough - couch potatoes are also welcome, and there are plenty of non-sporting activities for students to get involved in.' Surprise, again, that alongside aeronautical

UNIVERSITY/STUDENT PROFILE	
University since	**1966**
Situation/style	**Campus**
Student population	**17165**
Undergraduates	**12120**
Mature	**18%**
International	**19%**
Male/female ratio	**63:37**
Equality of opportunity:	
state school intake	**83%**
social class 4-7 intake	**23%**
drop-out rate	**2%**

and electronic and electrical manufacturing, and sport, and defence, and the construction industry, we find artistic/literary, film/video and publishing as categories of graduate employment in which Lboro students excel.

The uni is now pre-eminent in social science, in English, in library & information management - these have been adjudged research areas of renown. Meanwhile, psychology, drama and art & design are among its top teaching subjects at inspection, and the student media is making waves in national competitions.

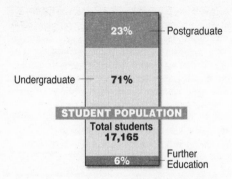

STUDENT POPULATION
Total students
17,165

- 23% Postgraduate
- Undergraduate 71%
- 6% Further Education

Technology Park on the edge of the campus, making it one of the biggest campus universities in the UK, with a total area of 410 acres. The new space is used to enhance its research portfolio and links with industry.

FEES, BURSARIES

UK & EU Fees, 2011-12: £3,375. There are bursaries for students in receipt of the HE Maintenance Grant, there's a bursary on a sliding scale according to income (bursaries@lboro.ac.uk) and scholarships for top sports performers (sports-scholars@lboro. ac.uk, and over 100 'year of entry' scholarships for overseas students (international-office@lboro. ac.uk, and a Care Leavers Bursary up to the value of £750. See www.lboro.ac.uk/admin/ar/funding/ ug/ukeu/bursaries/index.htm.

STUDENT PROFILE

'A typical Lboro student,' Vicky writes, 'is one who enthuses about sport and thrives on competition, and appears to be a walking advert for sportswear companies. There are students who are not like this, but they make less noise and therefore attract less attention. Sport at Lboro is impossible to ignore. This enthusiasm is not a bad thing, but if you don't share a love of sport it can become a tad irritating.'

There is a high-ish public school intake relative to most other universities, and a relatively low take from the lower socio-economic groups and 'low-participation' neighbourhoods. But none of this is very relevant. Students like it here, the drop-out rate (2%) is very low.low.

Loughborough also has strong environmental credentials. It is one of the partners in the Government's £1 billion national Energy Technologies Institute (ETI), which will help accelerate the UK's transition to a low-carbon economy. The headquarters of the ETI are now based on campus.

But to put its sport into perspective, 80 past and present Loughborough students competed across 6 sports in the 2010 Commonwealth Games and won 44 medals. If the University had been a country it would have contributed to as many medals as South Africa and finished 8th highest in the table. The campus has been chosen as the training camp for Team Japan and Team GB for 2012.

Open Days, 2011: 30 June, 21 and 22 September.

> **They have been No.1 in the Student Experience Survey for 5 years, but:**
> **'Sport at Lboro is impossible to ignore. This enthusiasm is not a bad thing, but if you don't share a love of sport it can become a tad irritating.'**

ACADEMIA & JOBS

Many of Loughborough's degrees are available with

CAMPUS

Loughborough is a campus university situated just off the M1 at Junction 23. 'It is one of the largest campuses in Europe,' writes Vicky Cook, 'and conforms to the stereotype of a leafy, green, self-contained campus. This has its advantages, everything is located within walking distance from halls (though the free campus bus is worth remembering on rainy days). There are bars, restaurants (although nothing gourmet) and three food shops to buy overpriced essentials when a walk into town is too great an effort. And, should campus and small market town become too claustrophobic, Leicester and Nottingham are mercifully close.

The uni recently acquired the Holywell

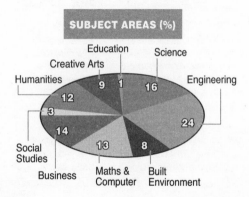

SUBJECT AREAS (%)

- Education 9
- Science 1
- Creative Arts
- Humanities 12
- Engineering 16
- 3
- 14
- 24
- Social Studies 13
- 8
- Business
- Maths & Computer
- Built Environment

a sandwich (placement) option, allowing students to gain real-life working experience, a paid salary and valuable employer contacts.

In the research assessment they came 28th nationwide and 85% of Design and Technology was found to be world-class or internationally excellent. New this year is Design Ergonomics a 3-year/4-year full-time sandwich BSc (Hons) in which people are seen as the primary driver for the design process. Loughborough are one of the biggest providers of year-long placement (sandwich) courses in the UK, with over 60% of their undergraduate courses available with this option. Five years ago they were awarded over £4 million in recognition of their excellent in linking industry and employers with engineering teaching and learning.

In Architecture and Built Environment, 75% of research was adjudged world or at least international class; in Aeronautical Engineering it was 70%. For prospective aeronautical engineers it has got to be a preferred choice.

Automobile engineers are similarly well placed careers-wise by Loughborough's degrees, as are civil, mechanical and construction engineering graduates. Twenty-two per cent of jobs come out of the Engineering & Technology degrees

TEACHING SURVEY AT A GLANCE

Avg. UCAS points accepted	**360**
Acceptance rate	**15%**
Overall satisfaction rate	**89%**
Helpful/interested staff	★★★★
Small tuition groups	★★★
Students into graduate jobs	**70%**

Teaching most popular with undergraduates:
Accounting, Aerospace Engineering, Anatomy, Physiology & Pathology, Building, Chemistry (99%), Civil Engineering, Computer Science, Design Studies, Drama, Economics, Electronic & Electrical Engineering, English, Finance, Human & Social Geography, Info. Services, Languages, Management Studies, Materials & Minerals Technology, Physical Geography & Environmental Science, Physical Science, Physics & Astronomy, Politics, Psychology, Sports Science.

Teaching least popular with undergraduates:
Fine Art (67%).

Many graduates become software engineers and consultants out of their Computer Systems and Software Engineering orientations. They are up there with Brunel as the largest suppliers to the sector. They come also through Maths.

If you are a sassy sixthformer thinking of maths at Loughborough you could do worse than get hold of their new mobile phone app, developed to boost maths skills. The app, which contains hundred of formulae and graphs relevant to the Pure Maths AS and A2 syllabi, is the first free-of-charge A-level maths revision resource. It is available through all major app stores.

Though known for engineering, business and built environment, the uni is pre-eminent in Art & Design, and in Social Sciences. For a few years now the sometime largely female Art College down the road has been making a welcome impact on the largely male engineering/techno-based population, both socially and academically. A strength in textiles was awarded full marks at the teaching assessments, and these degrees and the Graphic and Communication degrees are telling too in the graduate employment figures.

In Social Sciences, the influences are the Economics degrees - with Accountancy, Geography, Politics, Social Policy, and Sociology, as well as all the single honours degrees in those subjects and in Psychology. The message from the Economics Department is that if you want to read Economics at Loughborough, *reading* is what you must be prepared to do.

Aspiring bankers/merchant bankers come

RESEARCH EXCELLENCE

% of Looughborough's research that is
4* *(World-class) or* **3*** *(Internationally rated):*

	4*	3*
Public Health	0%	15%
Chemistry	0%	25%
Physics	15%	35%
Pure Mathematics	10%	45%
Applied Mathematics	10%	40%
Computer Science/	15%	40%
Electrical/Electronic Eng.	15%	45%
Civil Engineering	15%	50%
Mechanical, Aero.,	20%	50%
Manufacturing Eng.		
Architecture	25%	50%
Geography Environment	10%	40%
Economics	5%	40%
Business/Management	15%	45%
Information Management	15%	40%
Sociology	25%	20%
Education	5%	15%
Sports	25%	35%
European Studies	10%	30%
English	10%	40%
Art and Design	5%	30%
Design and Technology	55%	30%

through Business Economics & Finance and, at Management Sciences, as well as the Economics, Languages and Computer areas.

Loughborough's Business School has the cornerstone 4-year sandwich degree, BSc (Hons) International Business, but they have an eye for business in every aspect of the curriculum, from engineering to fashion.

SOCIAL SCENE

STUDENTS' UNION The union club has much to offer, currently Tuesday is *Stupid Tuesday* (party tunes), Thursday is *Universal Thursday* (international flavour) and sometimes a pub quiz.

Mid-week is *Hey Ewe* after all the sports matches have been played (and usually won!) in the afternoon. Says Jennie Byass: 'We all meet up with our sports or social clubs for an hour or so for some social drinking, and then proceed onto Fusion, where the key theme to the night is cheesy music and lots of dancing. *Midnight Madness* happens between half 11 and half 12 at which time all drinks are only one pound!

'JC's is the sports bar, where everyone goes to celebrate victories. **Cognito** - bar - flashing dance floor, what more can I say? Live acts here have included Girls Aloud for the Freshers Ball, DJ Spoony, and Navi, a Michael Jackson impersonator, amazing!'

We asked an anonymous student about that hour's drinking on match night. 'There are certain rituals and traditions which we here in Loughborough have developed and institutionalised over the years,' I was told: 'The rugby shirt worn with jeans, AV's, collars up, Hey Ewe mayhem on a Wednesday evening, drinking games and of course Nasty...the Lufbra drink...' This latter, though increasingly at risk to the almighty Red Bull/voddie alternative (decried by purists as expensive and injurious to health), remains the people's choice.

Then Friday is *FND* (Friday Night Disco) - LSU's premier night out: 3 rooms of music, including just now FF Audition, a battle of the bands audition night - win the chance to play the Freefest on May 4. Saturday is *Pulse* (r&b). And through it all are scattered live bands - *Make Noise: Battle of the Bands 2009*, and such as Official Secrets Act, The Young Knives, and appropriately, Athletic.

There are 40 societies, the more traditional such as the International Students' Association and the LGBT Association, while quirkier ones, like the Hot Air Balloon club, the Breakdancing club and the circus society, Fever, show the possibilities. The Media Centre houses the 24/7 student radio station (LCR), which won Gold at the National Awards this year, the student magazine offices (*Label*) and a

TV/video editing suite. LSUTV wins awards practically every year. The 'talk' studio and production studio (drum booth, guitar booth) beyond leave you in no doubt that these students have not been overcharged at £1.4 million. Sound, vision, print, web, all of it together on a single floor and serviced by student engineers who know their stuff.

The SU also has a student advice centre and employment exchange, and adjacent nursery with subsidised places for students' children.

SPORT Lboro teams beat everyone every year. Supportive of the effort is a huge investment in facilities on campus, including a 'super-gym' strength and conditioning centre, high-performance indoor and outdoor athletics centres and an Olympic-size swimming pool.

Says Jennie: 'The only problem that comes with such a high standard of facilities is the limited

WHAT IT'S REALLY LIKE	
UNIVERSITY:	
Social Life	★★★★★
Societies	★★★★★
Student Union services	★★★★★
Politics	**Light**
Sport	**Simply the best**
National team position	**Always No. 1**
	53 clubs
Sport facilities	★★★★★
Arts opportunities	**Surprisingly good**
NSDF (Drama) Award	**Lighting, 2010**
Student magazine	**Label**
Student radio	**LCR**
2010 Radio Awards	**Silver award**
Student TV	**LSUTV**
Nightclub	**Fusion + bar upstairs**
Bars	**JC's, Cognito**
Union ents	**FND (disco), Hey Ewe (cheese), Envy (r&b) + live**
Union societies	**40**
Most popular society	**International**
Parking	**No 1st years**
TOWN:	
Entertainment	★★
Scene	**Market town, good pubs**
Town/gown relations	**Good**
Risk of violence	**Average**
Cost of living	**Average**
Student concessions	**Excellent**
Survival + 2 nights out	**£70pw**
Part-time work campus/town	**Good/average**

times non-elite athletes can use them. The focus here is undoubtedly on the elite athlete, and I've found it quite hard coming here after being towards the top standard of sports back home to being right at the bottom of the pile here.'

Sports scholarships are available only to elite athletes. To be eligible you will have excelled at least at junior international level or equivalent and have fulfilled the normal academic requirements for undergraduate entry. The benefits are financial support each year, first class coaching, access to extensive training and competition facilities, sports medicine and sports science support, and a life skills programme.

Town Loughborough is a small market town, pleasant, with all the basic shops you need, and plenty to offer, including a greater sense of security when compared to the majority of the big cities. But it is quite a different proposition to the other cities of sport, such as Manchester or Sheffield...

PILLOW TALK

In 2008/09, the University added 1,500 rooms to campus accommodation. A new student village is a mix of 4- and 5- storey buildings, arranged around a courtyard, and has a combination of self-catering facilities and flexible dining packages for the nearby restaurant and social centre.

Last year there was some major refurbishment and upgrade undertaken of existing catered accommodation.

Says Jennie: 'I am in catered accommodation and my hall is situated in the heart of the student village, with food, washing rooms and leisure facilities all with in about a minute's walk. Some people

ACCOMMODATION	
Student rating	★★★★★
Guarantee to freshers	**100%**
Style	**Halls, flats**
Security guard	**All**
Shared rooms	**Some**
Internet access	**All**
Self-catered	**Some**
En suite	**Most**
Approx price range pw	**£115-£153.85**
Town rent pw	**£40-£130**

are not so fortunate and I have seen some of the halls which could certainly do with some attention.'

Accommodation in town is more expensive, because of the utility bills, but it is quieter, less claustrophobic and less intrusive as you choose who you live with. All hall rooms are computer networked and carry phone sockets. There's something to suit every pocket, 'and the sense of loyalty and community spirit in these halls is of an intensity usually reserved for centuries-old universities.'

First year undergraduate students living in halls will not in normal circumstances be issued with a parking permit.

GETTING THERE

☞ By road: M1/J23, A512.
☞ By rail: London St Pancras, 1:45; Birmingham New Street, 1:30; Sheffield, 1:30; Nottingham, 0:20; Leicester, 0:15.
☞ By air: East Midlands Airport close by.
☞ By coach: London, 2:45; Exeter, 6:50; Newcastle, 8:10; Manchester, 4:30.

STUDENT MANCHESTER – THE CITY

Writes fun-loving Alexandra Negri Not unlike London, Manchester is a city that never sleeps. Whatever day of the week or time of night, there is always somewhere to go, whether it is in the centre of town or the 'fields of fallow' - Fallowfield is the area of student residences at the furthest end of the Oxford Road corridor.

Oxford Road is of course student central. It sees tens of thousands of students pacing up and down it each day, whether it's to go to the various libraries, the lecture theatres, eateries, the infamous **Academy** (where the supremely tacky, yet unmissable *Torremolinos* is held every year), or the ridiculously cheap student bars (favourites including **Kro 1 & 2**, **The Footage**, **Sku Bar** and the

Student Union of course.

The social scene in Manchester is endless and there is definitely something for everyone's taste and these are just a few suggestions and popular attractions.

Fallowfield is the perfect place to start for student nightlife. If you find yourself so far-flung and are not looking to venture far from your squalor, it's a passable destination for cheesy nights, stick-to-the-floor dance halls and cheap drinks. **Robo's** (popular on a Tuesday night), **Queen of Hearts** and the **Orange Grove** are a few of the famous haunts for students, all of which have their particular qualities; Robo's is a *Scream* bar, so with a yellow card you can gain even cheaper cheap drinks, and Queen of Hearts and Orange Grove are both pub-based, showing sports, serving pub grub and furnished with the odd pool table.

For first years, or those still clinging on to their youth, there is the infamous *Bop* held at **Owen's Park** every Friday. Don't be put off by the thousands that turn up hoping to be one of the lucky ones to enter the youth club come school gym. Turn up early, 10pm-ish, and either drink your wait away, or get legless inside for a tenner on Kermit's spunk, cheeky vimto's, snakebites or whatever other exotic tipple takes your fancy.

If you're feeling like breaking free of Fallowfield, then all the way down Oxford Road, right into the centre of town are places worthy of a visit. First hit the aptly named Curry Mile, either to start the night, or to satisfy the after-hours munchies - most curry house, kebab shops and pizzerias are open until the early hours.

If it is just a cheap meal you are after, then Rusholme is the place, as many restaurants here do BYOB (bring your own booze). Be careful though, because of the Muslim culture some restaurants do not allow alcohol at *All!!*

Through Rusholme and onto Oxford Road takes us past **Revolution**, **Space**, **Dry** and **Font**, a few other watering holes worth a visit.

Before you know it, you're in town and across the border between 'night out on a tenner', and tenner a drink'!! For the more hard-up students do not fear, there are still many establishments that cater for the tightest wallet.

If it's the clean cut, well chiselled, Cologne-smelling ladies man that takes your fancy then **42's** is definitely NOT the place for you. Long haired, scruffy t-shirt, skinny jeaned Indie boys fly the flag for 42's. Probably my, along with another 50% of the student population's, favourite place to be on a Thursday night. It's hot, it's sweaty, it's smoky, it's cheap, it's indie rock and roll, to quote one of the more frequently played artist there. Other Indie nights include **5th Avenue**, and **The Venue**.

The famous **Sankies** is host to some, if not all, the world's most famous DJ's, and after a recent re-vamp, promises to be worthwhile to those of you who do not fight shy of a good rave. Be sure to check the listings, as nights do vary, and in the summer, be prepared to stay til the break of dawn. Their boat parties, the 'Smugglers Run', down the Irwell (yes the Irwell!) are a real summer treat!

Or for the more elite who prefer to spend your student loan sipping Champers and gazing at footballers, try the bars on Deansgate, **Panacea** and **Coco Rooms**.

Northern Quarter has an eclectic mix of bars from live jazz and open mic nights at **Matt and Phred's** to soul and funk at **Bluu** bar and burlesque nights at **Mint Lounge** and the newly opened **Birdcage**. It is also home to the highly acclaimed **Affleck's Palace**, an eccentric shop where one can find anything from vintage classic to the best fancy dress.

Like most cities Manchester does have areas with a bad reputation, but in general, it's a safe city if you find yourself having to walk home, kebab in hand with not a penny to your name. For those in 4-inch stilettos I recommend a taxi. There are always black cabs around, and it will cost you around £7 to get back to Fallowfield, depending.

After a night out in the **Printworks** which holds **Tiger Tiger**, **Pure** and **Opus**, as well as one of the only 24 bars, a **Weatherspoons**, which I don't recommend, there is a late night bus service that stops right outside. An eventful ride home is usually guaranteed for those who prefer this mode of transport in the early hours.

Canal St., the home of 'pride' is defiantly worth a visit for some fantastic restaurants, happy hour deals, varied bars, and overall friendly fun, and sometimes bizarre service!

For the more refined there are two main theatres in Manchester, **The Palace Theatre** and **The Opera House**, which see many major productions. There are also a number of art galleries and exhibitions around town, a favourite of mine being in the **URBIS**, which recently displayed an exhibition on Graffiti Art and hosted the infamous 'Little Black Dress' design competition. **G-mex** is one of the larger exhibition centres which holds events like the ideal home show and career fairs.

THEATRE

Writes Elka Malhotra **The Royal Exchange Theatre** offers 2 stages (one in the round) and a combination of modern and traditional plays (all at student discounts). Situated in a rather nice area right in the city centre, it's also a good place to pop in for a cuppa during the day. **The Palace Theatre** in Oxford Road is designed for more family-friendly showings, they offer a good mix of shows and fairly big names. **The Contact Theatre** caters more to the student market and has occasional art exhibits as well as writing, DJ and drama workshops. **The Contact** also features the **Café Deluxe**, which makes hearty sandwiches and a mean cup of coffee. **The Green Room** is another avant-garde venue which, like **The Contact**, boasts its own nightclub nights, a small theatre and a small café-bar. **The Lowry** is also worth a mention here. Although a little more out-of-the-way than its rivals, it offers the largest stage outside of London, with Ferrari-designed seating! On a more low-key note, **The Library Theatre** offers a range of events from jazz to comedy, and traditional plays.

CINEMAS

Going to the cinema in Manchester costs about £4 pretty much everywhere. **The Filmworks** is by far the most popular, and despite seeming a little like an airport, boasts a ridiculous number of screens, some of which show IMAX 3D movies as well as arthouse and mainstream films. **The Odeon** is the city centre's only mainstream cinema, a quieter venue. In his days as Manchester United's captain, Eric Cantona used to get his French film 'fix' at the **Cornerhouse**, the best place for arthouse, foreign and small budget films. It also features a small but interesting art gallery and what is arguably the first modern-style bar in Manchester. Opened in 1985 it has an arty clientele and Belgium beers.

There is also the **AMC** situated in the Great Northern building on Deansgate, which usually shows all the latest releases. Although quite a way to travel out of the city and relatively expensive, **The UCI** at The Trafford Centre is also a nice little cinema complex (the outer facia has Islamic pillars beside the centre's themed food court).

COMEDY

Manchester knows how to have a laugh and **The Comedy Store**, situated on Deansgate Locks is definitely the best for doing that. *The Best In Stand-Up* on Friday and Saturday provide a fantastic night out and offer great student concessions, just make sure you buy tickets in advance the night is known to sell out. **The Frog and Bucket** is another popular comedy venue, although different in style, less slick and more traditional in its humour. They offer open mic nights on Mondays. **The Buzz** is possibly the longest running venue and has featured many a great, such as Jack Dee. **The Dancehouse Theatre** is also known to host occasional comedy nights, as is **The Contact**, known for its up-and-coming, very modern acts). Other popular comedy venues include **Bar Risa** and **Jongleurs**.

SHOPPING ON A LOAN

Affleck's Palace alone features more interesting little stalls than you can shake an oversized stick at, and is quite a Manc institution. A maze of a place it offers piercings, tattoos, t-shirts, CDs, vintage clothing, condoms, fancy dress, fetish wear and the ever popular rainbow-coloured hair extensions. **The Coliseum** is similar, situated behind **Affleck's**, on a smaller scale and with more of a gothic twist. **The Arndale Market** is handy for picking up cheap, fresh food as well as clothes, shoes and practical jokes – all fairly cheap.

The Student Market in the Academy sells bikes, clothes, hippie items, discount CDs and a variety of other stuff and is a favourite haunt on a Tuesday lunchtime. **The Trafford Centre** is the second biggest shopping centre in England and has literally miles of shops, but it's so big that your funky new purchases will probably have gone out of fashion by the time you leave.

Most chain shops can be found in the city centre. Student discounts are ubiquitous. A little more up market are **Harvey Nichols** and **Selfridges**, as well as the King Street area of the city centre which also features **DKNY**, **Max Mara** and **Hermes**.

UNIVERSITY OF MANCHESTER

The University of Manchester
Oxford Road
Manchester M13 9PL

TEL 0161 275 2077
FAX 0161 275 2106
EMAIL admissions@manchester.ac.uk
WEB www.manchester.ac.uk

Manchester Students' Union
Oxford Road
Manchester M13 9PR

TEL 0161 275 2930
FAX 0161 275 2936
E: communications@umsu.manchester.ac.uk
WEB www.umsu.manchester.ac.uk

VIRGIN VIEW

*W*hat they offer is a reputable learning experience rooted in a rich educational heritage, boosted by cutting-edge research and innovation - all at the heart of one of the world's most vibrant cities.

The last research assessment ranked

Manchester third behind only Oxford and Cambridge in terms of Research Power, with 65% of its activity judged to be world-class or internationally excellent.

Their 'bold agenda', they say, is to make the University one of the top 25 universities in the world by 2015. It is a knotty ambition with which to grapple as the various world tables

UNIVERSITY/STUDENT/PROFILE	
University since	**1903**
Situation/style	**City campus**
Student population	**38190**
Undergraduates	**27645**
Mature	**29%**
International	**23%**
Male/female ratio	**47:53**
Equality of opportunity:	
state school intake	**79%**
social class 4-7 intake	**25%**
drop-out rate	**5%**

vary in terms of criteria. In the Shanghai Jiao-Tong University (SJTU) rankings, Manchester sits at 44th in the world. In the Times Higher's version they are 87th. In the QS Top 500 they are almost at their desired position already: they sit at 30th.

Manchester is cool and energetic in a way students from too many other universities don't even begin to understand. If you don't believe me, forget Open Day, go to Oxford Road as the whole mighty monster awakens at the start of termnext academic year, and feel the vibes. Students gave it a 5-star rating for social life in the Student Experience Survey. Not surprised.

It is now one unit with the old Institute of Science & Technology (UMIST, as it was called) up the road. The Manchester Business School, just off Oxford Road, is in the vicinity too. In this feverishly studenty neck of the woods they are joined also by another Oxford Road university, Manchester Met, and with the Royal Northern School of Music. It must be the largest conglomeration of students anywhere in the world.

The whole area is, to all intents, campus.

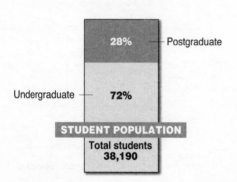

Undergraduate — **72%**

28% — Postgraduate

STUDENT POPULATION
Total students
38,190

Unable at first to take it all in, but aware that something special is going down, you, the wise fresher, will resist throwing him/herself frantically into the fray, as they encourage you to do at lesser universities until you wake up to the carnage, vomiting in the street. Nor will you retreat into your shell intimidated, as scores of them do at places like Imperial. You will imbibe, certainly, take it all in, but then consider how best it can serve you, and focus your mind on your own thing. For Manchester is a place for individuals, brilliant kids who like to do their own thing, in drama, in media, in whatever is their thing, and if you are ready it will release you to do the same.

Manchester focuses the mind of the individual adventurer wonderfully.

2011 open days are being held on 17 June, 18 June and 8 October.

CAMPUS

North Campus (the old UMIST campus) and South Campus (the original Manchester Uni campus) are both on Oxford Road, a few minutes apart. The Wilmslow/Oxford Road runs through the centre of campus, linking it at the top end with Manchester Metropolitan University, and at the bottom end with the most populous areas of student residences - Rusholme, Fallowfield, etc. The whole street is campus, but it is also city. City and university are absolutely inseparable, not least because they share the same vibe. It is an active, buzzing scene, a place some parents dread their children choosing.me parents dread their children choosing.

'The sheer size can be enough to make even the most adventurous of newcomers feel like catching the first train home,' writes Nicola Chapman. 'That is until you realise everyone is in the same position.'

FEES, BURSARIES

UK & EU Fees, 2011-12: £3,375. If in receipt of full HE Maintenance grant there's a bursary. Scholarship-wise, there's the Talented Athlete Scholarship Scheme, The Manchester Advantage Scholarship, The Manchester Success Scholarship, The President's Award, and there are music scholarships, and accommodation bursaries. See it all on www.manchester.ac.uk/undergraduate/funding/.

STUDENT PROFILE

In general, they're an intelligent, resourceful, lively crew, not afraid or too lazy to lay themselves on the line and apply themselves, and not averse to letting their hair down either. Alexandra Negri: 'For anyone going to a) a city as big as Manchester, b) leaving the tlc of your family, and c) being thrown into a world of slightly smelly, converse wearing, hard-up students, can be a bit daunting. However, the first days if not weeks could be the best you will ever imagine.'

The demographic picture is intriguing - 20% mature students, 23% from outside the EU, 21% public school, and 25% from the lower socio-economic orders.

'Uni really opens your eyes to different social groups, cultures and religions and this is especially the case in Manchester, where they have one of the biggest international student bases in the UK. Do not be put off by this, because you get to met even more weird, wacky and wonderful people than you ever hoped.'

ACADEMIA & JOBS

Students rate the teaching best in Anatomy, Physiology & Pathology, Anthropology, Aural & Oral Sciences, Biology, Business Studies, Chemistry, Classics, Electronic & Electrical Engineering, Geology, Italian Studies (where 100% of the class gives the thumbs-up), Maths & Statistics, Molecular Biology, Music, Nursing, Other Subjects Allied to Medicine Pharmacology, Toxicology & Pharmacy, Physical Science, Physics & Astronomy, Theology, Tourism, and Zoology. Teaching they say is worst in Design Studies (58% only go for it), Mechanical, Production & Manufacturing Engineering (55%), and African & Modern Middle Eastern Studies (53%).

Medicine passes muster with only 67% of the class. In fact Manchester students consider teaching staff in general as only averagely interested in them and helpful. Research has taken over from teaching in some quarters. The University has said publicly that they are addressing the problem.

The research is, however, very good, which means that you will have highly informed teachers, men and women working at the coal-face of your subject even if they care less about you than their research.

At the recent national assessment of the research provision of our research institutions they came 8th nationally (6th if you only count universities). Of course, manchester is where Ernest, First Baron Rutherford did the work which led to the splitting of the atom, and where the computer was invented, so there is some precedent.

There are 4 Faculties: Engineering & Physical Sciences; Humanities; Life Sciences; Medical & Human Sciences.

Medical subjects dominate the graduate employer stats. A quarter of all jobs go to graduates in medicine or subjects allied to it, in spite of what the students say about the teaching. They have

created Europe's premier biomedical campus here, a series of linked scientific and hospital facilities on Oxford Road.

In the 5/6-year MBChB critical faculties and communication skills are to the fore, as is constructing a methodology of self-education. You will need a combination of Chemistry, plus one of Biology, Physics, Maths, plus a further rigorous academic subject at A level. Sciences not taken at AS/A level must be high graded at GCSE. Equally acceptable are three sciences, or two sciences plus one other rigorous subject. You must also take UKCAT.

Among other degree subjects in this employment bonanza are Nursing, Midwifery, Optometry,

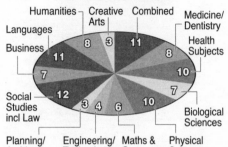

SUBJECT AREAS (%)

Humanities — Creative Arts — Combined — Medicine/Dentistry
Languages — Health Subjects
Business — 8 — 3 — 11 — 8
11 — 10
7 — 7
Social Studies incl Law — 12 — 3 — 4 — 6 — 10 — Biological Sciences
Planning/Architecture — Engineering/Technology — Maths & Computer — Physical Sciences

RESEARCH EXCELLENCE

RESEARCH EXCELLENCE

4* *(World-class)* or **3*** *(Internationally rated):*

	4*	3*
Cardiovascular Medicine	15%	60%
Cancer Studies	30%	60%
Hospital Clinical	10%	60%
Laboratory Clinical	5%	45%
Epidemiology	15%	45%
Community Clinical	40%	40%
Clinical Psychology	5%	45%
Dentistry	30%	45%
Nursing/Midwifery	50%	35%
Health Professions	20%	30%
Pharmacy	30%	40%
Biological Sciences	25%	40%
Human Biol. Sciences	20%	45%
Environmental Sciences	20%	50%
Chemistry	20%	45%
Physics	20%	35%
Pure Mathematics	20%	40%
Applied Mathematics	25%	35%
Statistics	20%	35%
Computer Science	30%	55%
Electrical/Electronic Eng.	25%	45%
General Engineering	20%	50%
Chemical Engineering	25%	60%
Metallurgy and Materials	20%	60%
Town/Country Planning	20%	40%
Geography Environment	15%	50%
Archaeology	15%	45%
Economics	25%	55%
Business/Management	25%	40%
Law	10%	40%
Politics	20%	30%
Social Work	15%	30%
Sociology	40%	20%
Anthropology	20%	30%
Development Studies	25%	40%
Psychology	10%	35%
Education	20%	35%
Middle Eastern/African	15%	45%
Asian Studies	10%	25%
Russian	35%	35%
French	15%	35%
German	20%	35%
Italian	20%	35%
Iberian	30%	45%
English	30%	45%
Linguistics	10%	45%
Classics	25%	30%
Philosophy	10%	35%
Theology	25%	40%
History	20%	40%
History of Art	40%	40%
Performing Arts	45%	40%
Music	50%	35%

Oral Health Science, Biochemistry, Biomedical Materials Science, Biotechnology, Cell Biology, Genetics, and Physiology.

In Social Studies, which accounts for 11% of graduate employment, jobs abound more in the political and economic arenas than in community work: the civil service, accountancy, banking and financial activities, recruitment and personnel, and only then social work/community counselling. A few more accountants come out of the Manchester Business School. 'The teaching standard at the Business School is high,' writes Alexandra. 'You will get the grades you deserve as long as you take courses you are interested in and are prepared to put the work in. Saying that a few slip-ups may be kindly overlooked in the haze of first year, and in general teachers are helpful and approachable if you are struggling. The workload is substantial but not great. You may find you have more lecture hours than fellow students on other courses. However, there will be less reading or coursework as a result. The Business School has its own library and computer clusters on hand, but you are still free to use any of the other resources around campus. The usual rush in the first weeks to secure text books from the library always occurs and it always seems to be the exchange students who get there first. Do not fear, either the books will be available at other libraries or you can purchase all set textbooks at Blackwell's located in the Precinct. Manchester Business School has a real sense of community because it is set aside from the rest of campus.'

Within Education, both adult and higher sectors are particularly well served. By far the most popular route into them is via the joint hons Languages, from which there's also a Top 10 provision of translators and interpreters. Note the Chinese and Japanese provision.

Architecture, town planning and property development are all rich employment seams out of Manchester. There's BA Architecture, but also an interesting series of MEng Structural Engineering & Architecture.

There is a good reputation for both English and Drama, the latter ably expressed extra-muraly.

Finally, Man Uni are European law specialists.

SOCIAL SCENE

STUDENTS' UNION It is an unadventurous soul who appears at the foot of MUSU's steps and resists propulsion inside - bodies hurry purposefully like ants, drawn irredeemably by the sights and sounds of the **Solem Bar**. 'Swedish sauna meets trendy metal,' sour-pussed someone, but actually it's a cosy place to hang out, and perhaps shoot some pool on the tables. It's open most nights till 11.

Up the road, is the old UMIST's **Harry's Bar** - Barnes Wallis Building, North Campus, perfect place to chill after lectures again, like Solem, there's pool, screens and surround sound. Nest door is **Paddy's Lounge**.

On the first floor is of the Steve Biko Building is **Biko's Café**, where there are PCs with free internet and email access. The menu consists of healthy breakfast options and 'healthy choice' salad bar.

'Next door to the Union, South Campus, is the **Academy**, a 1,200-capacity live band venue,' Leonie Kenyon tells us, 'It pulls itself round in time for the Student Market

> *'The sheer size of Manchester and its University can be enough to make even the most adventurous feel like catching the first train home. That is until you realise everyone is in the same position.'*

during the day, a prime spot for posters, bikes, CDs, clothes and hippy items, a favourite haunt of students especially at lunchtime when the homemade chocolate cakes are rather popular! Another union nightclub is the **Cellar**, which features Horny on Friday, and plays a mixture of pop and cheese. On weekday afternoons it is also used as a café.'

Pangaea happens twice a year, a student-run, student-only, twelve-room mega event with a variety of headliners, genres and surprises, everything from Psi-trance to Mad Hatters and hopefully something a little weird. Meanwhile, students galvanise themselves into national prominence with their drama and media. Manchester's *Student Direct* is the city's No. 1 weekly student newspaper. With a readership of over 50,000, it serves the universities of Manchester, Salford and Bolton, and in the 2009 *Guardian* Awards it picked up 'Travel Writer of the Year'. Fuse FM (radio) and MSTV complete the picture. No surprise the uni is high in the employment league for editors, publishing and the like. In the area of drama, the uni is a major force, the annual springtime student festival still reigns supreme. They won an award in the 2010 National Student Drama Festival, a Gold award in the National Student Radio competition, and two runner-up gongs in the *Guardian* Media Awards: Publication of the Year (*Student Direct*) and Reporter of the Year - that was student Girish Gupta.

SPORT The teams came 9th this year and last in the national uni team ratings last year. Facilities include a boat house on the Bridgewater Canal, Yacht Club at Pennington Flash, Leigh, 18 miles west of the city. Pitches (31 acres) for rugby, soccer, hockey, lacrosse, cricket, netball, are close to the student village at Fallowfield, also tennis courts, all-weather, artificial grass areas and pavilion. In Fallowfield, too, is the Armitage Centre with sports hall and squash courts close by. A further 90 acres lie ten miles south, below the M63, at Wythenshawe sports ground.

On campus itself is the McDougal Centre, which has a swimming pool, indoor games hall, gym, squash and fives courts, an outside five-a-side court, rifle range, climbing wall, bowls carpets, sauna and solarium. The new Commonwealth Games swimming pool is open to students. There are bursaries, two offered by the exclusive XXI, an elite sports club founded in 1932.

WHAT IT'S REALLY LIKE

UNIVERSITY:	
Social Life	★★★★★
Societies	★★★★
Student Union services	★★★
Politics	**Less active than once were**
Sport	**Key**
National team position	**9th**
Sport facilities	★★★★
Arts opportunities	**Excellent; high profile drama, dance, film**
NSDF (Drama) Awards	**1 in 2010**
Student newspaper	**Student Direct**
2010 *Guardian* Awards	**R-up Publication of the Year**
Student radio	**Fuse FM**
National Radio Awards	**Gold in 2010**
Student TV	**MUSTV**
Nightclub and venues	**Cellar, Academy 1,2 & 3**
Bars	**Solem, Harry's, Paddy's Lounge**
Union ents	**Club Tropicana, Pangaea**
Union societies	**200**
Parking	**Not encouraged**
CITY:	
Entertainment	★★★★★
City scene	**Legendary**
Town/gown relations	**Average-poor**
Risk of violence	**High**
Cost of living	**Average**
Student concessions	**Good**
Survival + 2 nights out	**£90 pw**
Part-time work campus/town	**Average/good**

PILLOW TALK

All freshers are guaranteed a place in halls and flats. New last year was All Saints View, close to the University, just off Grosvenor Street, 19 high-quality one-bedroom flats.

The most populous areas of student residences - Rusholme, Fallowfield, etc - are at the bottom end of the Oxford Road corridor. Writes Leonie: 'Under the railway line and through Rusholme's Curry Mile - which, as the name would suggest, is full of curry houses and interesting Eastern-style shops. Although located next to the infamous Moss Side, it's quite safe.

'Fallowfield is the ideal place to live as it is secure, lively, and features some very nice little houses. The student halls range from very nice to eyesore, and are backed by the university-owned Armitage Sports Centre, which offers student discounts on a range of sporty activities.'

Withington is a little quieter, a little more expensive, and that little bit further away from uni and the town centre, but has a good variety of pubs, shops and coffee shops. Similarly Didsbury (home of the 'Didsbury Dozen' series of pubs - a pub crawl classic) has a good deal to offer, but is more expensive than the wholly studenty Fallowfield area.

Victoria Park is seen as the posh alternative, probably because most of its halls are large, leafy, Victorian buildings. It lies between Fallowfield and the main campus - approximately 15 minutes walk from the main university buildings.

ACCOMMODATION	
Student rating	★★★★
Guarantee to freshers	**100%**
Style	**Halls, flats**
Security guard	**24-hr security**
Shared rooms	**None**
Internet access	**All**
Self-catered	**Some**
En suite	**Some**
Approx price range pw	**£75-£140**
City rent pw	**£55-£75**

There are also private halls of residence in the city centre Student Village, popular with students at Manchester Met since it is right on their doorstep. Victoria Hall is another privately owned student residence near the city centre.'

It is not done for freshers to bring cars.

GETTING THERE

☛ By road: M63/J10, A34.
☛ By rail: London Euston, 2:30; Leeds, 1:45; Liverpool Lime Street, 0:50.
☛ By air: Manchester Airport for international and inland flights.
☛ By coach: London, 4:35; Bristol, 5:00; Newcastle, 5:00.

MANCHESTER METROPOLITAN UNIVERSITY

The Manchester Metropolitan University
All Saints
Manchester M15 6BH

TEL 0161 247 2000

EMAIL enquiries@mmu.ac.uk
WEB www.mmu.ac.uk

Manchester Met Students' Union
99 Oxford Road
Manchester M1 7EL

TEL 0161 247 1162
FAX 0161 247 6314

EMAIL mmsu@mmu.ac.uk
WEB www.mmunion.co.uk

VIRGIN VIEW

*M*MU is one of the largest universities in Britain. Value subsists in some 700 courses, many of which are designed to include industry placements and exchange programmes with international universities. But many pick it for its reputation as a party-till-you-die university. When you visit, they do not disappoint:

'Everyone gets very focused on what's going here, which is massive,' confessed one student. Its bars are always heaving and there's a great social scene, especially if you're gay. It has been voted by Diva *magazine 'the best place in the country to be a gay student', ahead of London and Brighton. With a high female to male ratio (59:41), the lesbian end of LGBT (Lesbian, gay, bisexual and transgender soci-*

UNIVERSITY/STUDENT PROFILE

University since	**1992**
Situation/style	**Campus**
Student population	**34515**
Total undergraduates	**27720**
Mature	**37%**
International	**9%**
Male/female ratio	**41:59**
Equality of opportunity:	
state school intake	**96%**
social class 4-7 intake	**39%**
drop-out rate	**12%**

ety) rules. Again, this city has what you want in abundance if gay is your thing - especially in Canal Street, the gay village of Manchester, just a short walk from MMU.

'It's true, we still have a really strong gay scene within the Union.' You won't need to be told about Manchester's Mardi Gras, an unforgettable weekend of parades and parties. But the hub - day in, day out - is the Village: late licensing, all-night cafés and a huge choice of venues, all within walking distance of one another and MU and MMU.

CAMPUS

Writes Anna Sargent: 'The University has various sites, all, excluding the Crewe and Alsager sites, are near the city centre. All Saints is the central site, containing the main Student Union building and university facilities. It is on Oxford Road, possibly the most heavily student populated and polluted road in Britain. Crewe and Alsager are a bit out on a limb.'

TEACHING SURVEY AT A GLANCE

Avg. UCAS points accepted	**250**
Acceptance rate	**18%**
Overall satisfaction rate	**75%**
Helpful/interested staff	**★★★**
Small tuition groups	**★**
Students into graduate jobs	**67%**

Teaching most popular with undergraduates:
Architecture, Building & Planning, English, English-based Studies, Human & Social Geography, Medical Technology, Philosophy, Physical Geography & Environmental Science, Politics.

Teaching least popular with undergraduates:
Tourism (58%),Media Studies (57%), Art (54%).

Crewe and Alsager are towns in Cheshire about 6 miles apart, some 35 miles south of Manchester, their semi-rural campus environments a million miles away in spirit from heaving Oxford Road. Do not expect to have much to do with Manchester if you live, and your course is taught, out there.

'There's not a lot of contact with Crewe & Alsager,' our student guide admitted. 'They always say there is, but in practice there's not. They have their own set-up down there. They're very sports and drama orientated. I think you still get some who enrol and are quite surprised that it's not just down the road and you can't always get up here on a Saturday night! I understand quite a few drop out over that.'

Now they are investing £154m in a new campus, Birley Fields, at Hulme, just south of manchester city centre, where they plan to relocate the Faculties of Education and Health, complete with student residences, car parking and facilities for community use.

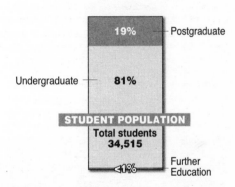

Undergraduate — **81%**
19% — Postgraduate

STUDENT POPULATION
Total students
34,515

<1% — Further Education

FEES, BURSARIES

UK & EU Fees, 2011-12: £3,375. If in receipt of the HE Maintenance grant there's a sliding scale bursary according to your means.

STUDENT PROFILE

Writes Anna: 'There's a friendly feeling about Manchester Met, but it suits the sort of person who likes to get involved, rather than wander anonymously around a large institution.'

Thirty-seven per cent of undergraduates are mature and nearly 4,000 are part-time. Only around 4% hail from public school. Far greater are those from the lower socio-economic reaches.

Bruce McVean sees only advantage in this. 'MMU is perceived to be the more dynamic university because it is not as staid as Manchester University.' Bruce was an engineering student at Manchester Uni and, seeking a course change to Geography, was turned down by Manchester and accepted by MMU. 'But I now know people doing

Geography at Manchester and there's not a lot of difference between the two departments. When students are actually here, I don't think they perceive much difference between the two establishments.'

ACADEMIA & JOBS

The modular courses have a practical emphasis, tracing a clear vocational line to jobs in industry, where their employment rate is good.

Some 700 courses are offered from within Art & Design; Community Studies, Law & Education; Food, Clothing & Hospitality Management; Humanities & Social Science; Management & Business; Science & Engineering.

At Alsager there's a range of sports science subjects, plus the departments of Humanities & Applied Social Studies (Sociology scored an excellent 21 on inspection) and the Modular Office, which looks after all inter-departmental modular mixes. At Crewe, the Business & Management Department sits alongside the Department of Environmental & Leisure Studies with its own stream, woodland and conservation habitats. Other than that, there is the School of Education (PGCEs and Primary and Secondary degrees).

By far the greatest number of jobs come out of

> 'It's true, we still have a really strong gay scene. Gays won't need to be told about Manchester's Mardi Gras... but the hub – day in, day out – is the Village: late licensing, all-night cafés and a huge choice of venues.'

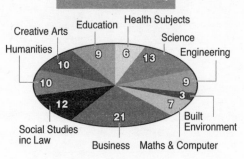

SUBJECT AREAS (%)

Creative Arts — Education — Health Subjects — Science — Engineering — Humanities — Social Studies inc Law — Business — Maths & Computer — Built Environment

9, 6, 13, 10, 9, 10, 3, 12, 7, 21

Business (note their Hospitality Management and Human Resource Management degrees in particular. Then it's Education, Art & Design (including Fashion, Textiles, Furniture, Advertising, Design & Art Direction, Graphics, Illustration, Animation, and Landscape Architecture). There is a sound track record, too, in Architecture, which can be combined with Structures, Construction, Environmental Studies, or with Humanities. Biological Sciences is a big provider, and of course includes Sport, the speciality of the out-of-town campuses. But there is also a massive presence jobs-wise in Education (50% Primary, then Secondary, Higher, and Adult), subjects allied to Health (Nursing, Dental Technology, Speech Therapy/Pathology and the like), Social Studies, which supplies graduates principally to community counselling and local & regional government), and Computer (software consultancy & supply, banks, and telecommunications).

SOCIAL SCENE

STUDENTS' UNION There are of course many collaborations between Manchester Uni and Manchester Met, the unions being but a walk apart on Oxford Road, but there are also marked differences between the two.

There is activity within student societies at Manchester Met - 70 all told, but, as one student said to me, 'Politics is a dirty word... We don't have a very political union. We have political groups - Socialist Workers and so on, but that whole scene is more active at Manchester University. It's a lot more that our Union here provides a service, it's more of a social and representational thing.

RESEARCH EXCELLENCE		
% of Manchester Met's research that is 4* (World-class) or 3* (Internationally rated):		
	4*	3*
Health Professions	5%	15%
Biomedical Sciences	5%	30%
Environmental Sciences	5%	40%
Computer Science	5%	30%
General Engineering	0%	35%
Metallurgy and Materials	0%	30%
Economics	0%	10%
Business/Management	5%	30%
Information Management	0%	20%
Social Work	5%	15%
Sociology	5%	30%
Education	20%	35%
European Studies	0%	20%
English	15%	20%
Philosophy	5%	35%
Art and Design	10%	35%
Performing Arts	5%	25%

The student magazine is *Pulp*. Last year undergraduate writer James Harker was awarded Writer of the Year in the *Guardian* Media Awards. There's also student radio - MMU Radio is the newest student radio station, broadcasting over the internet 24 hours a day, 7 days a week - and somewhere in MMU they are tinkering with TV, because they got nominated in the 2009 RTS Student TV Awards.

Main watering holes at union headquarters id **The Met** bar, open 7 nights a week on All Saints Campus, Oxford Road. *Rock Kitchen* is the weekly rock bash @ The Met. Room 1 is rock, metal, classic, dance; room 2, punk, emo, hardcore, ska, and anthems, hosted by DJs Stevie B, Adam, the Rock-It-Crew, and Boxer. Plus specials like *Sex Lies and R&B*, and *Skool Disco* - 'free sweets, soggy school dinners and prizes for the best fancy dress', and live acts. Friday is *Double Vision* (party toons) - 2 floors of 'utter madness' - in the main room, commercial dance and chart stompers from past to present, plus r&b, soul and jazz upstairs and hip hop treats and laid back beats in the back room. All culminates in the Summer Ball at the Palace Hotel, Manchester.

Down in Crewe + Alsager there is a Union presence, and bars, shops, clubs and societies at both campuses, and even a nightclub at Crewe. It is not Manchester, so don't come here if that's what you're after, but there are bus nights to city clubs and

WHAT IT'S REALLY LIKE

UNIVERSITY:	
Social Life	★★★
Societies	★★
Student Union services	★★
Politics	**Low interest**
Sport	**Well equipped**
National team position	**63rd**
Sport facilities	★★
Arts opportunities	**Music, film excellent; rest good**
Student newspaper	**Student Direct**
Student magazine	**Pulp**
Guardian Media Awards	**Writer of 2010**
Student radio	**MMU Radio**
Nightclub	**K2**
Bars	**MancUnion**
Union ents	**Double Vision**
Union societies	**70**
Parking	**Poor**
CITY:	
Entertainment	★★★★★
City scene	**Legendary**
Town/gown relations	**Average-poor**
Risk of violence	**High**
Cost of living	**Average**
Student concessions	**Good**
Survival + 2 nights out	**£90 pw**
Part-time work campus/town	**Average/good**

ACCOMMODATION

Student rating	★★
Guarantee to freshers	**54%**
Style	**Halls, flats**
Security guard	**Some**
Shared rooms	**Some**
Internet access	**All**
Self-catered	**Some**
En suite	**Most**
Approx price range pw	**£77-£142**
Rent pw	**£55-£75**

among a handful of societies may be found.

Alsager has an **Arts Centre** with a resident theatre company. There are two theatres (the **Axis Theatre** seating 500), a dance studio and an art gallery.

SPORT

The Aquatics Centre at Manchester campus is a £30m swimming pool complex: 2 Olympic-standard main pools. The Sugden Sports Centre features a refurbished 100-station fitness suite with state-of-the-art resistance and cadiovascular training machines as well as two 8-court sports halls. The Didsbury Sports Centre consists of a 5-court sports hall, fitness gym and exercise studio. High-spec

engineering and science labs too.

A new sports centre is now open on the Crewe campus: 8-court sports hall, 50-station fitness gym, and 3G artificial turf pitch as well as sports injury clinic. It's home base for the Exercise & Sports Science Department. They also have 32 acres of pitches for football, cricket, rugby union and league, and there's a full size, floodlit, artificial turf pitch available on the Alsager site.

PILLOW TALK

Eight halls in Manchester, four in Cheshire. They are good for the first year , but are not cheap and it is fairly difficult to get your first choice.

In Manchester, the halls at All Saints have the best location; those at Didsbury require a considerable bus journey.

GETTING THERE

☞ By road: Manchester, M63/J10, A34. Coach services good. Crewe/Alsager, M6/J16.
☞ By rail to Manchester: London Euston, 2:30; Leeds, 1:45; Liverpool Lime Street, 0:50.
☞ By air: Manchester Airport.
☞ By coach: London, 4:35; Bristol, 5:00; Newcastle, 5:00.

MIDDLESEX UNIVERSITY

Middlesex University
Trent Park
London N14 4YZ

TEL 020 8411 5000
FAX 020 8362 5649
EMAIL admissions@mdx.ac.uk
WEB www.mdx.ac.uk

Middlesex University Students' Union
Trent Park
London N14 4YZ

TEL 020 8411 6450
FAX 020 8440 5944
EMAIL [[initial.name]@mdx.ac.uk
WEB www.musu.mdx.ac.uk

VIRGIN VIEW

*L*ondon's strength derives from its unique mix of cultures, as does Middlesex's, so they say. The capital's 9 million residents speak some 300 languages. Middlesex's student body includes students from all over the world.

There are many impressive elements in Middlesex's strategy, not least their Able Centre, a disability support centre with recording studios turning out audio texts for blind students, a dyslexia support co-ordinator and a sign language bureau, which has appealed to thousands beyond campus too. But there is a huge locally based and mature student population and it would be a mistake to believe that this uni picks you up and takes you out of life in quite the same way as a traditional campus university like Nottingham, Kent or Sussex.

Most people who come to Middlesex are not that bothered that the extra-curricular scene at the Students' Union is second rate, or that much of what is on offer has been taken out of the hands of the students, but it may be that this is what ultimately will be important to the student. The drop-out rate is

UNIVERSITY/STUDENT PROFILE	
University since	**1992**
Situation/style	**Campus/city sites**
Student population	**21350**
Total undergraduates	**16450**
Mature	**50%**
International	**23%**
Male/female ratio	**41:59**
Equality of opportunity:	
state school intake	**99%**
social class 4-7 intake	**48%**
drop-out rate	**11%**

certainly high, but within the Government benchmark for the University.

CAMPUS

Getting to grips with this university has been like wrestling with a family of octopuses, so many tentacles are there reaching out across north London and beyond. At one time there were some 18 sites and campuses, but today they are based at 2 or 3 main campus sites, and offer 4 schools of study.

The School of Arts & Education is based at the Trent Park/Cat Hill campus. they concentrating their energies on 2 or 3 main-campus sites, pulling the whole operation together in a £100-million strategy. Trent Park Bramley Road, London N14 4YZ, is set in 900 acres of woodlands and meadows. Cockfosters or Oakwood tubes (Piccadilly line). Performing Arts, IT, Cultural Studies, Education Product Design & Engineering, Biological Science. For Cat Hill, Barnet, Herts EN4 8H, go to Cockfosters (Piccadilly line).

The Business School, the School of Health and Social Sciences and the old School of Computing Science (now re-named the School of Engineering and Information (EIS) and incorporating new Engineering courses) are based at the Hendon campus in North West London. Students in some

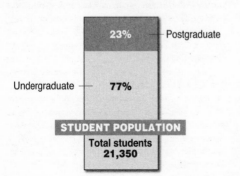

Postgraduate 23%

Undergraduate 77%

STUDENT POPULATION
Total students
21,350

TEACHING SURVEY AT A GLANCE

Avg. UCAS points accepted	**160**
Acceptance rate	**17%**
Overall satisfaction rate	**78%**
Helpful/interested staff	★★
Small tuition groups	★
Students into graduate jobs	**71%**

Teaching most popular with undergraduates:
Accounting, Dance, Drama, Teacher Training,
Maths & Statistics, Social Work.

Teaching least popular with undergraduates:
Animal Science (55%), Education Studies, Film &
Photography (57%).

health areas also study at the Archway campus, well placed for local hospitals and health care providers.

For Hendon, The Burroughs, London NW4 4BT, go to Hendon Central (Northern line). A new £17-million learning resource centre opened here recently.

FEES, BURSARIES

UK & EU Fees, 2011-12: £3,375. For those eligible for the HE Maintenance Grant there's also the Middlesex Bursary (see www.mdx.ac.uk/study/und ergrad/ugfees/bursaries.asp). Further awards include the Future Gold Scholarship, the Chancellor's Scholarships for sport and academic achievement, and awards to applicants for Academic Excellence. See www.mdx.ac.uk/study/undergrad/ugfees/scholarships.

STUDENT PROFILE

Middlesex is a large university and has anything but a traditional university clientele. Many undergraduates are mature, many come from new-to-uni social groups. There is also a large number of part-timers among non-degree (HND) undergraduates.

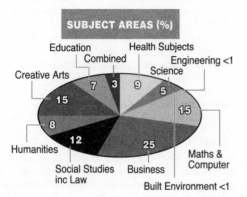

SUBJECT AREAS (%)

Education — Combined 3 — Health Subjects 9 — Engineering <1 — Science 5 — Creative Arts 7 — 15 — Maths & Computer 15 — Humanities 8 — 12 — Business 25 — Social Studies inc Law — Built Environment <1

Where numbers have escalated since 1995 is in overseas recruitment. They have won awards for attracting students in from Europe and further afield. Language support is an essential requirement - there's a series of courses incorporating a Foundation year for non-EU international students. Coping with the high drop-out rate that their open-doors policy has helped create is clearly the thought behind the £1,000 bursaries for applicants with 300 points at entry, mentioned in Fees, Bursaries above.

ACADEMIA & JOBS

In the last national assessment of the research provision of our universities, Middlesex showed commendable world-class work in Performing Arts,

RESEARCH EXCELLENCE

% of Middlesex's research that is
4* *(World-class)* or **3*** *(Internationally rated):*

	4*	3*
Nursing/Midwifery	**5%**	**30%**
/Health Professions/	**5%**	**25%**
Computer Science/	**10%**	**25%**
Geography Environment	**5%**	**35%**
Business/Management	**5%**	**25%**
Law	**0%**	**15%**
Social Work	**5%**	**45%**
Psychology	**0%**	**10%**
English	**5%**	**30%**
Philosophy	**20%**	**45%**
Art and Design	**5%**	**20%**
History of Art,Architecture	**15%**	**40%**
Performing Arts	**20%**	**35%**
Media Studies	**0%**	**45%**

History of Art, Architecture & Design, and Philosophy. There hadn't been an assessment for seven years, and on the last occasion these last were top of the tree too. So, expect to find deep seams of knowledge in these departments. Look carefully at Philosophy at Middlesex, which came first among post-1992 universities and ahead of Durham, Warwick and Edinburgh, and also gets a strong rating from students for its teaching. On the History of Art, Architecture & Design front, be aware of the Interior Art & Design degrees.

In the annual Government student survey, students at Middlesex found the teaching best in Accounting, Dance, Drama, Teacher Training, Maths & Statistics, and Social Work.The teaching was least good in Animal Science, Education Studies, Film & Photography.

Full-time courses are made up of 4 year-long

WHAT IT'S REALLY LIKE

UNIVERSITY:	
Social Life	★
Societies	★
Student Union services	★★
Politics	**Active**
Sport	**Competitive**
National team position	**80th**
Sport facilities	★★
Arts opportunities	**Excellent**
Student magazine	**MUD: Middlesex Union Direct**
Nightclub	**Enfield forum**
Bars	**1 on each campus**
Union ents	**Not a lot**
Union societies	**30**
Parking	**Poor**
CITY:	
Entertainment	★★★★★
City scene	**Wild, expensive**
Town/gown relations	**Average-good**
Risk of violence	**Average**
Cost of living	**Very high**
Student concessions	**Good**
Survival + 2 nights out	**£100 pw**
Part-time work locally	**Fair**

modules, each worth 30 credits. A student needs to amass 120 credits in each year before progressing onto the next, and 360 in total to be awarded an honours degree. Examinations for each module take place at the end of the year. There is continual assessment, and coursework also contributes to the overall assessment result.

The 4 academic schools are Arts & Education, Computing Science, Health & Social Sciences, and Business.

Business certainly pumps out most graduates into jobs, with accountancy and banking high on the list. Middlesex have plenty of Management degrees too, with such as Marketing, Business, Info Systems, and International-style biases, and their joint hons programme allows Management combinations in a whole host of areas. Sales managers proliferate in the end, most of them with an Art & Design bias - textiles, knitwear, jewellery, fashion providing the focus.

Art & Design is the next big job provider, with a massive 38% of their output actually becoming creative artists, rather than having to take second choice occupations.

Jobs for graduates in Art & Design proliferate for graphic artists, designers and illustrators, and elsewhere there's a dedicated BSc Computing Science Graphics & Games which puts them up

there in the Top 10 for computer game design. Back in the arts area, among Fine Art, Fashion (also Knitwear and Textiles), Product Design, and Jewellery, the latter stands out as a good niche.

As for Performing Arts, musicians, composers, and would-be music industry managers are all well served here, and those interested in Dance and Drama. Be aware of the Jazz speciality in Music at Middlesex. For actors, directors, producers there are two BA degrees: Drama & Theatre Studies and Technical Theatre Arts.

Journalism, Publishing and TV Production also have dedicated degrees. Plans are afoot at Hendon for a new building for Art, Design and Media programmes.

Health is another strong area jobs-wise - Nursing, Pre-Registration Midwifery, and Veterinary Nursing, a joint course with the Royal Veterinary College (the best in the field). See, too, the Herbal Medicine and Traditional Chinese Medicine and Acupuncture, where Middlesex was a pioneer. The BSc Vet Nursing leads to the RCVS Vet Nursing Certificate.

There's also a strong line in psychotherapists at the graduate job bank. Look at the Social Sciences with Communication & Language Studies and the BSc Psychology, which carries British Psychological Society accreditation.

Finally, there is a discernable pattern of careers in environmental health and a whole range of Health & Policy Studies degrees in the BSc joint degree series, also Occupational Health & Safety and BSc Environmental Health.

They are also commercial and business law specialists, a subject that carries some useful management and other tie-ups.

SOCIAL SCENE

STUDENTS' UNION Shame, the bars and ents are now run by a private contractor (Scolarest); competitive sport directly by the university. This is no way to encourage a strong student culture.

The four bars - Enfield, Tottenham, Trent Park and Cat Hill - provide drinks promos and ents during the week, but they close at weekends. There's a Freshers' Ball, of course, and some tell of a Middlesex extravaganza, a 36-hour festival in the summer at Trent Park, and there's a student magazine called MUD - Middlesex Union Direct.

SPORT Gym facilities exist on all campuses. Sport is an area of continual investment, and students are OK at it (teams came 80th nationally). Recent large projects include a £2.5m state-of-the-art gym, the Real Tennis Centre at Hendon, and two artificial hockey pitches at Trent Park. Students have access to uni swimming pools, indoor and outdoor, foot-

ACCOMMODATION	
Student rating	★
Guarantee to freshers	**75%**
Style	**Halls, flats**
Security guard	**All**
Shared rooms	**None**
Internet access	**All**
Self-catered	**All**
En suite	**Most**
Approx price range pw	**£94-£120**
City rent pw	**£110+**

ball and rugby pitches and a golf club.

PILLOW TALK

All halls are self-catering. Student union facilities and local supermarkets suffice. All students have a shared kitchen too. Most halls have been built over the past 6 years; all are within easy reach of their respective campuses. A security officer is on sight from 5pm to 9am Monday to Friday and all weekend. There's also an interactive website (studentpad) with details of private houses/flats to rent and also rooms within family homes.

STUDENT NEWCASTLE - THE CITY

The Toon is at the cutting edge of student life. Offering the very best in entertainment, its lively and vibrant atmosphere, progressive and diverse character make it an essential stop for any fun lovin' student. Ranked as the 7th best party city in the world, Newcastle is also heading up the field in all things cultural. Along with Gateshead, its neighbour on the Tyne, recent years have witnessed a massive boom for Newcastle Arts - the **Baltic Centre for Contemporary Art**, a 4- storey converted flour mill which houses numerous temporary exhibitions, and the **Sage Music Centre** on Newcastle's very own south bank.

NIGHTLIFE

Geordie attitude turns on the old adage, 'work hard, play hard', and be it the legendary **Bigg Market**, the swanky watering holes of the Quayside or the cosmopolitan bars of Jesmond's Osborne Road and the area around Central Station, there is opportunity for everyone to play as hard as they like, often at a price most students can afford.

When it comes to clubbing and live acts, both universities are up there with the best in live entertainment. The Darkness, Coldplay, Kosheen, Shed 7, Elbow, Starsailor, Mark Owen and Jools Holland are just a few of the big name acts to have played . **The Telewest Arena** attracts all the major national tours, from Justin Timberlake, Beyonce and Blue to Stereophonics and Craig David, while the **City Hall** has it's own share of the stars, the likes of Norah Jones and Travis The only downside is that our location means a lot of small tours do not visit. Don't expect to see everyone.

If you want to sample musical delights a little closer to home there are also smaller more inti-

mate live venues such as **The Cluny** and **The Head of Steam** which showcase the cream of Newcastle's homegrown musical talent.

The city's club scene has rocketed to success in recent years with the launch of numerous highly acclaimed club events. Writes Katie Ashworth: 'When it comes to clubs, I generally go to alternative clubs and pubs, as opposed to ones that would play dance music. For indie buffs, I would recommend: **The Cooperidge** on a Monday, **The Cluny**, *Stone Love* @ **Digital** on Thursdays, **The Forth** generally every night, **The Global** on gig nights, **The Head of Steam**, **The Hancock** pub any night, *Bulletproof* @ **Carling Academy**... there's a lot more if you search around!

'For the rock/metal crowd: *Krash* @ **Venue** on Thursdays, *Stone Love* @ **Digital** on Thursdays, **Trillians** any night, **Legends**, *Red Room* @ Northumbria, Uni. **The Hancock** pub upstairs any night, *Where Angels Play* @ **Carling Academy**.. . Again, look around, keep your eyes and ears open for gigs and nights.

'For general drinking nights out: **Tiger Tiger**. **Sam Jacks** is always a laugh too, anywhere in **The Gate**, **Liquid**, **Flares** (a disco theme club), **The Goose**, *Solution* @ Newcastle Uni on Fridays, *Wiggle* @ Northumbria. **Blu Bambu** is ok, too.

'What does it cost? Night out anywhere from £10 to £50! I personally never spend more than about £15, but that's because I go to cheaper places and don't drink expensive things. Proper night out to "real clubs", anything around £30 or more. But I'd rather go to a pub, bar or gig, which are always cheaper. Entrance to clubs, anything from £3 to £12, although on average £4 is normal for the places I go to.'

SPORT

The whole city revolves around the fortunes of Newcastle United, so get informed. St James's Park is the most imposing landmark on the city skyline and the second largest stadium in the Premiership. Getting tickets can be a problem, however, despite the 52,000 capacity, but well worth trying for.

Elsewhere, Johnny Wilkinson (occasionally) and the rest of the Newcastle Falcons offer a student friendly environment for rugby fans, while the Newcastle Eagles do the same for basketball followers. Wherever you go, don't mention any allegiance to Northeast rivals Sunderland or Manchester United or you are liable to end up in a bit of bother.

CINEMA

The Odeon is the most central cinema and with its brand new multiplex having recently opened in **The Gate** on Newgate Street, you can enjoy all the top films at student prices right on your doorstep. Also in the city centre is a 12-screen **Warner Village**, while a short drive will take you to **UCI Silverlink** or **Metro Centre**.

For the more artistic, the **Tyneside Cinema** on Pilgrim Street is one of the best independent cinemas in the country.

THEATRE AND COMEDY

Newcastle is one of the Royal Shakespeare Company's second homes. In the autumn, it doth take over most of the city's stages for a month of highbrow entertainment. The major venue is the **Theatre Royal**, the poshest of Newcastle's theatres.

Try the maller, cheaper **Live Theatre**.

If it's a more relaxed, studenty atmosphere you're after you can't beat the **Playhouse** and **Gulbenkian Studio** to get the best in up and coming talent. Both theatres are housed in the same building at the edge of Newcastle University's campus, and are home to the more cutting-edge Northern Stage company.

For comedy look no further than the fantastic **Hyena Café**, open 12 months of the year, and the annual Newcastle Comedy Festival, which plays a number of venues across the city for a two-week spell. **Newcastle Student Union** also puts on a comedy night every Monday during term-time, in it's **Global Café** venue.

SHOPPING

The only major studenty shop is **Period Clothing**, with some fantastic stuff in store. Otherwise Newcastle blends high street stores with smaller designer boutiques well. On Northumberland Street you can check out all the high-street brands such as **H&M**, **Zara** and **Warehouse**, whilst **Eldon Square Shopping Centre**, just off Northumberland Street is home to **Top Shop**, **USC**, **Oasis** and all the major department stores. Grainger Town is where you'll find the 'trendier' and more expensive shops as well as some quality boutiques.

Check out **Mint**, just off Grey Street, it's a truly awesome shopping experience. A short journey will take you to the Gateshead **MetroCentre** and the major stores/labels. For music, **Steel Wheels**, **RPM** and **Flying Records** offer good independent options.

• •

UNIVERSITY OF NEWCASTLE

The University of Newcastle upon Tyne
King's Gate,
Newcastle upon Tyne NE1 7RU

TEL 0191 208 3333
FAX 0191 222 8685
EMAIL Go online - www.ncl.ac.uk/enquiries
WEB www.ncl.ac.uk/undergraduate

The Newcastle University Union Society
Kings Walk
Newcastle upon Tyne NE1 8QB

TEL 0191 239 3900
FAX 0191 222 1876
EMAIL president.union@ncl.ac.uk
WEB www.unionsociety.co.uk

VIRGIN VIEW

*A*cademically, Newcastle is good right across the board. 'Those who live in the north perhaps understand how good it is better than those from the south,' said one Yorkshire-based school careers teacher, adding with weight, 'It is very popular

among students who go there.'

Where Newcastle scores over London and, yes, over Manchester, is in its packing an incredible array of cultural, artistic and hedonistic power centres into a very small space (and at relatively low cost), with the university wholly involved in the middle of it all. So much is going on, and all of it so *concentrated, that the buzz on the street at night is ten times what you will feel in the greater, but more dispersed metropolis.*

In the Higher Education Funding Council's National Student Survey, 87% of Newcastle's students gave it the thumbs-up, and there's barely a 4% drop-out. Newcastle's undergraduates have a real and vibrant city to discover, but their loyalty is down to what goes on in the Students' Union. What you notice on campus is people doing... things happening... students in control of themselves and what they are about. 'We actually own the whole set-up,' they say. They do - union building and all.

Open Days, 2011: 1 and 2 July, and 1 October. Go there and see.

CAMPUS

Newcastle is a campus university situated right in the heart of this compact and compelling city, within walking distance of theatres, cinemas, shops, bars, pubs, restaurants, but equally only a short way from the eye-catching north-east coast.

FEES, BURSARIES

UK & EU Fees, 2011-2012: £3,375 p.a. There's a bursary on a sliding scale between £600 and £1,200 for those whose household income is £32,284 or below. You may also be eligible for an academic achievement bursary of up to £500 if you get three or more A grades at A Level (or equivalent). There are also sport scholarships up to £1,500.

STUDENT PROFILE

The student profile reveals a high proportion of public school entrants: 'The pink pashmina and boat shoe brigade do seem to claim the majority,' as a student put it, 'but people tend to separate into their own different groups according to individual taste. There is enough to do to keep all parties happy. Freshers Week tends to be the only time when you have to put up with people who aren't necessarily your kind of people.'

Writes Katie Ashworth: 'There is something that we call 'Rahs' in the halls where I live... they wear tracksuit bottoms and UGG boots, fake tans and all shout at each other in the halls. "Chavs with too much money" is a good description. They're all from down south. Apparently some duke's daughter came here a few years ago, so there's been an influx of the more posh crowd. However, in the rest of the accommodations, there has been more "normal people"; it's just the big self-catering hall that I'm in tends to attract the more sheltered types! I'm in the rock and indie societies, as well as music; there's a lot of music-obsessed people here, and also some people who would be "alternative". Apart from a few exceptions, I've got on with pretty much everyone I've met here. No one cares about what kind of person you are, as long as you're easy to talk to and friendly, everyone gets on.'

Writes Jack Lewis: 'No type dominates. Such is the emphasis on group work in the first year that I have made friends both in halls and on my course, who are from various backgrounds. Everyone gets along well and I have grown up and matured because of it.'

ACADEMIA & JOBS

'The general ethos seems to be work hard, play hard,' writes Geraldine England. 'The standard of teaching is generally high, some lecturers being able to communicate with their students better than others.'

In fact, the 2010 *Times Higher Education*'s Student Experience Survey found students giving high praise generally to Newcastle's lecturers for interest in their them.

Katie Ashworth is doing English Language and Literature: 'The second semester is better in terms of content for me, as the first was full of funda-

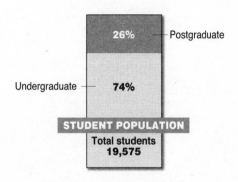

26% — Postgraduate

Undergraduate — 74%

STUDENT POPULATION
Total students
19,575

TEACHING SURVEY AT A GLANCE

Avg. UCAS points accepted	**390**
Acceptance rate	**16%**
Overall satisfaction rate	**87%**
Helpful/interested staff	★★★★★
Small tuition groups	★★★
Students into graduate jobs	**79%**

Teaching most popular with undergraduates:
Accounting, Agriculture, Anatomy, Physiology & Pathology, Archaeology, Aural and Oral Sciences, Biology & related sciences, Business, Chemical, Process & Energy Engineering, Chemistry, Classics, Computer, Creative Arts & Design, Dentistry, Economics, Electronic & Electrical Engineering, English, Finance, Fine Art, French Studies, History, Human & Social Geography, Law, Linguistics, Maritime Technology, Maths & Statistics, Mechanical Engineering, Medicine, Molecular Biology, Music, Subjects allied to Medicine, Pharmacy, Philosophy, Physical Geography & Environmental Science, Physical Science, Politics, Sociology, Technology.

both are well resourced, well staffed and fully computerised, but be prepared for a massive demand on books when it comes to exam time. Don't think that you will be able to pop into the library a day before the holidays and find all the books you need, because you won't. The geeks will have got there first.

'Computing facilities at Newcastle are excellent, each department having a number of its own computer clusters, all linked to the net, in addition to those available in the libraries. There is even a large 24-hour access cluster, a godsend because,

mental language concepts that were pretty hard to grasp. Syntax could have been taught better, and my seminar leader assumed that we all were at the same starting level. Not true, as some people had done A-level Eng Lang., but I hadn't!

'Tutorials are vital. They give you a chance to ask questions and share ideas. I always go to my seminars, even ones that I don't really have to go to. I think it's important that we all meet as a group every week. Seminars for me have a social side. A few of my tutors are postgraduates, so we sometimes have general chats before we start the academic side. I have met some of my best friends through my tutor groups!

Geraldine continues: 'There are two main libraries, the Robinson library and Medical library,

RESEARCH EXCELLENCE

% of Newcastle's research that is
4* *(World-class) or* **3*** *(Internationally rated):*

	4*	3*
Cancer Studies	**15%**	**75%**
Hospital Clinical	**15%**	**50%**
Laboratory Clinical	**15%**	**55%**
Epidemiology	**0%**	**40%**
Health Services	**10%**	**40%**
Clinical Psychology	**5%**	**35%**
Dentistry	**15%**	**45%**
Biological Sciences	**15%**	**45%**
Agriculture	**5%**	**40%**
Environmental Sciences	**15%**	**50%**
Chemistry	**5%**	**40%**
Pure Mathematics	**5%**	**30%**
Applied Mathematics	**15%**	**45%**
Statistics	**10%**	**45%**
Computer Science	**20%**	**50%**
Electrical/Electronic Eng.	**15%**	**45%**
Chemical Engineering	**10%**	**50%**
Civil Engineering	**20%**	**70%**
Mechanical, Aero., & Manufac. Engineering	**15%**	**50%**
Architecture	**25%**	**35%**
Town/Country Planning	**25%**	**40%**
Geography Environment	**10%**	**45%**
Archaeology	**15%**	**35%**
Business/Management	**10%**	**40%**
Law	**0%**	**40%**
Politics	**15%**	**25%**
Sociology	**15%**	**35%**
Psychology	**10%**	**30%**
Education	**10%**	**40%**
French	**15%**	**35%**
German	**20%**	**25%**
Iberian	**15%**	**35%**
English	**25%**	**45%**
Linguistics	**15%**	**25%**
Classics	**10%**	**35%**
History	**15%**	**25%**
Art and Design	**25%**	**60%**
Music	**35%**	**45%**

SUBJECT AREAS (%)

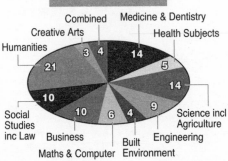

- Combined — 4
- Creative Arts — 3
- Humanities — 21
- Medicine & Dentistry — 14
- Health Subjects — 5
- Science incl Agriculture — 14
- Engineering — 9
- Built Environment — 4
- Maths & Computer — 6
- Business — 10
- Social Studies inc Law — 10

though you might find it difficult to imagine now, you may well have to work through the night.'

Newcastle's research provision places them in the top 20 research institutions in the UK. The best of many world-class (4 star) and internationally excellent (3 star) results were Medicine (Cancer), Civil Engineering, Computing, English, Art & Design, and Music - 70% to 90% of the work in these was 4-star or 3-star.

In Medicine, besides the 6-year MB BS (with pre-med year for students without the necessary science background), there's a 4-year accelerated MB BS designed for graduates, and a 5-year MB BS, Phase 1 of which can be undertaken here or at Durham Uni's Stockton Campus (south down the A1 on the outskirts of Middlesbrough); all come together at Newcastle for Phase II training in cahoots with the NHS.

Clinical relevance is emphasised throughout. You will need Chemistry and/or Biology at AS or A level. If only one of Biology and/or Chemistry is offered at A or AS level, the other should be offered at GCSE grade A (or Dual Award Science grade A). Neither General Studies nor Critical Thinking counts as an A level qualification. You will need UKCAT too.

Fifteen per cent of all Newcastle graduates get jobs in hospitals, most via a degree in Medicine. Then, it's the civil service, fed by graduates in Architecture, Languages, Social Studies, and Historical and Philosophical Studies; accounting largely from dedicated Accountancy degrees; architectural consultancy - again by the dedicated degree; and personnel recruitment: Social Studies and Languages.

> '*Such is the emphasis on group work in the first year that I have made friends both in halls and on my course, from various backgrounds, and I have grown up and matured because of it.*'

In 2006, the university sought the views of hundreds of organisations to determine what skills they required of graduates. From this feedback, a skills framework was developed which is now used to embed skills development within the curriculum and throughout extracurricular activities.

The ncl+ initiative directs students to develop employability skills through activities outside their degree, such as working as a student ambassador or writing for the University newspaper. A Career Development module enables students to count their work experience, volunteering activities or part-time employment towards academic credit for most courses.

An Enterprise Centre turns ideas into action by creating new business, using experts as mentors for students, brokering industry expertise in curriculum development and inviting entrepreneurs and other professionals to lecture to students.

The culture enabled student companies from Newcastle to win four awards in the national final of the Graduate Enterprise Programme in Leicester last year.

Alongside the usual contact with employers and milk round, etc, 'Graduate Connections' is an online database of over 600 Newcastle graduates now employed in a wide range of jobs and professions. They give individual advice, information and insight about the work they do and how to get into a profession.

Newcastle is one of only six universities which take part in the Defence Technical Undergraduate Scheme (DTUS), a scheme sponsored by the Ministry of Defence (MoD) for students who want to pursue a career in the armed forces.

SOCIAL SCENE

STUDENTS' UNION The Student Union building is undergoing an £8m redesign due to be completed by September 2011. Planned in consultation with students it includes a 200-seater computer room and learning areas with 24-hour access, a large multi-purpose space for gigs and events, new bars and cafes, and a bigger and better union shop.

By night the Union is transformed into one of Newcastle's premier scenes with an ents menu that's included world-class names, such as Lily Allen, Paul Oakenfold, Snow Patrol, The Killers, Coldplay, Arctic Monkeys, DJ Tiesto, Razorlight, Goldfrapp, and The Darkness. For main gigs it's The **Basement** and **Basement 2**, with 1,200 capacity. While for small sets it's the **Global Café** on the top floor, often opened out into the adjacent **Union Lounge** and **MLK Lounge**.

The **Mens Bar** - great pub atmosphere - is Union central, with nearby **Cochrane Lounge**. It gets its name from the Union's Latin motto, 'Men Agitat Molem', meaning, 'Mind Over Matter'. Mondays is *Home made Jam* in the Cochrane Lounge, and Big Screen Live Sport in Men's Bar; Tuesdays - *Union Quiz & Rock n Roll Bingo*; Wednesdays - *Get Your Kit Off*, the official post-sports £1-a-drink session from 6pm; Thursdays are *4 Play* - the official town pub crawl pre-bar, live DJ, £1-a-drink from 6.

Friday nights may be *2 Many Rooms*: Basement - Ben Yates (*Born in the 80's*), Basement 2 - Sully

(*Inertia*), Green Room - NSR LIVE /RocSoc, Blue Room - *What's in the Box?* On a Friday in April we saw Bombay Bicycle Club. Then there's legendary once-a-month *Brighton Beach night*. Room 1 guitar-based rock & roll and soul classics, Room 2, a heady cocktail of 60's soul, northern soul, jazz, psyche and freakbeat, and new Room 3, the newest cutting edge indie tracks, some obscure classics and a smattering of local talent to boot.

There's a great student music scene, large studios in a New Music Building, band rehearsal facilities and flexible studio spaces. It's available for use 24 hours a day.'

Writes Katie: 'Newcastle is MASSIVE! Although the SU night is alright, I'm very into music, so I'd prefer to go to a gig or something. I go to about 2/3 a week. Me and my friends went to a play last semester at the theatre, which is gorgeous, and directly opposite the Union. Nice restaurant, too.'

Once a term they have *Arcane* - all the proceeds fund a student from some underprivileged area of the dark continent. Arcane lasts from about 8pm until 6am. As well as the two main dance floors (Basement, Global), there are specialist drum 'n' bass areas and chill out rooms.

'With all these great nights out, some extra cash is bound to come in handy,' writes Geraldine. 'The SU provides a job shop, advertising all kinds of part-time vacancies with accredited employers. It also offers welfare and advisory services in addition to supporting over 100 different societies and more than sixty sports clubs.'

Much is done in the context of the real world outside. Student drama producers, for example, have to survive in real terms, are dependent on public audiences, arrange sponsorship and all the rest. Two or three student-produced plays appear each year either at **Northern Stage Theatre** in the centre of campus, or at **The Gulbenkian**, a small, experimental studio-type place. There might be a production at **Live**, the theatre on the Quayside.

The *Courier* office (student newspaper) was a crammed galley of a room, space enough for the award-winning weekly to be committed to Quark, but is probably now about to find its own bigger space. There's the award-winning radio station, NSR, too.

Writes Katie: 'There's a MASSIVE range of student societies. I'm in English society, indie soc, rock soc and radio society. I participate mostly in radio society, as I interview bands, review gigs and cd's and go to meetings every Tuesday. I go to rock soc socials a lot, some indie and barely any English socs, as I see the English crowd every day anyway.'

SPORT The University Sports Centre incorporates a double-court sports hall together with a state-of-the-art 120-station Health and Fitness Suite, three large multipurpose activity halls, four squash courts and a dance studio. Pitches and courts for outdoor games including rugby, hockey, soccer, cricket, tennis and lacrosse are played at Cochrane Park, Heaton and Longbenton, all within 15 minutes by bus. The boat house is on the Tyne at Newburn. An 18-hole golf course lies about 10 miles west of the city with preferential rates.

There's a Talented Athlete Sports Scholarship (TASS) scheme and 57 sports clubs on offer. The uni came 11th nationally last year.

PILLOW TALK

All University accommodation is within a 3-mile radius of the campus and around half is a 10-minute walk away. Newest block at Castle Leazes opened in December 2009: 7 floors, each with two flats,7 en-suite beds per flat. A multi-million pound teaching and accommodation complex for interna-

WHAT IT'S REALLY LIKE

UNIVERSITY:	
Social Life	★★★★★
Societies	★★★★
Student Union services	★★★
Politics	**Active, mainly student issues**
Sport	**Big nationally**
National team position	**11th**
Sport facilities	★★★★
Arts opportunities	**Drama excellent; rest good**
Student magazine	**Pulp**
Student newspaper	**The Courier**
Student radio	**NSR**
Nightclubs	**Global, Beats, Bassment**
Bars	**Mens Bar, Green Room, Cochrane**
Union ents	**Chart, dance, Indie, d'n b, live, & Arcane**
Union societies	**100**
Most popular societies	**NUTS (theatre), Cheerleading, Jazz**
Parking	**Adequate**
CITY:	
Entertainment	★★★★★
Scene	**Vibrant, fun**
Town/gown relations	**OK**
Risk of violence	**Low**
Cost of living	**Low**
Student concessions	**Good**
Survival + 2 nights out	**£70 pw**
Part-time work campus/town	**Average/excellent**

tional students is due for completion by Autumn 2012 - 540 bedrooms and social areas.

Castle Leazes Halls and Henderson Hall are catered. Self-catered flats include: Richardson Road, Marris House, St Mary's College, Windsor Terrace, Leazes Parade, and Bowsden Court Shared Flats. There's also couple and family accommodation, and places adapted for students with disabilities. Magnet Court opened recently, 3 and 4-bedroomed flats with en-suite shower rooms, situated in city-centre, just 5 mins walk from campus.

Some accommodation sites have free parking, at others it's limited. See www.ncl.ac.uk/accommodation/students/accommodation/.

Says Jack Lewis: 'Uni was my first real experience of living away from home. I chose self-catered accommodation and found fending for myself a lot easier than expected. Cost of living in Newcastle is low. Around £25 is enough for a night out. There is some work available. Some friends work in Primark and other stores.'

ACCOMMODATION

Student rating	★★★★
Guarantee to freshers	**100%**
Style	**Halls, flats**
Security guard	**Team on rota**
Shared rooms	**None**
Internet access	**All**
Self-catered	**Some halls, all flats**
En suite	**Some**
Approx price range pw	**£70-£123.48**
City rent pw	**£50-£100**

GETTING THERE

☛ By road: A1, A167/A696; A167 exit.
☛ By rail: Edinburgh, 1:30; Leeds, 1:45; London King's Cross, 3:00; Manchester Piccadilly, 3:00; Birmingham New Street, 4:00.
☛ By air: Newcastle International Airport.
☛ By coach: London, 6:05; Birmingham, 4:25.

UNIVERSITY OF WALES, NEWPORT

University of Wales, Newport
Caerleon Campus
PO Box 101
Newport NP18 1YH

TEL 01633 432030, 432432
FAX 01633 432850
EMAIL admissions@newport.ac.uk
WEB www.newport.ac.uk

Newport Students' Union
College Crescent
Caerleon
Newport NP18 3YG

TEL 01633 432076
FAX 01633 432688
WEB www.newportunion.com

VIRGIN VIEW

University of Wales, Newport, came out of Gwent College of Higher Education. It became a University College in 1996 and a fully fledged university in 2003. During this period we watched it achieve huge success in a particular area, oblivious to Government assessment that most of its courses were merely 'Satisfactory'. While the wheels of bureaucracy ground it down, Hollywood beckoned, and its students were nominated for Oscars and won BAFTA awards.

Finally, in 2001, the Establishment had to take notice, and awarded its Art, Media & Design provision a top rating for research, recognising its international importance. Seven years on, the most recent assessment found

UNIVERSITY/STUDENT PROFILE

University since	**2003**
Situation/style	**Campus**
Student population	**9300**
Total undergraduates	**7360**
Mature	**64%**
International	**9%**
Male/female ratio	**42:58**
Equality of opportunity:	
state school intake	**99.5%**
social class 4-7 intake	**45%**
drop-out rate	**11%**

that 60% of its research provision is either world-class or internationally excellent. Engineering has even got a bit of world-class clout too.

Overall, 72% of students like what's going down at Newport, and said so in the recent National Student Survey, but 11% drop out before they complete their courses.

CAMPUS

Newport, Gwent, lies half way between Bristol and Cardiff; it is the first town of any size you come to travelling west along the M4 from England. Activities are split between two campus sites: Newport itself and, 10 mins to the north, Caerleon - 'City of Legions and Court of King Arthur,' according to Geoffrey of Monmouth. Caerleon is where all the real stuff goes on.

The village of Caerleon, supposed site of Camelot, takes us back into the mists of time. There are still Roman baths and a fortress to be seen, but the area is a tourist draw as much for its beauty. To the east lies the Wye Valley and the Usk, on whose banks lie the ruins of Tintern Abbey, which inspired Wordsworth to write one of his most important poems. To the west are the Welsh valleys, industrial heartland of South Wales.

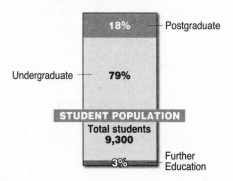

It is a safe and friendly campus, and typically a guy from Gloucestershire reading documentary photography said he had been won over by the green fields as much as the course.

Then there was Allt-yr-yn, campus home to the Newport Business School, to computing, engineering and the School of Health and Social Sciences. It had none of the mystery of Caerleon, but seemed to be enjoying Newport's rise just as much, until this year when it closed and a new campus - the New City Campus opened, first phase of an intended £50m development of Newport City Centre.

It opened its doors in March 2011. Situated on the banks of the Usk, it is attended by 2,700 students from the Business School and design, film and media elements of the School of Art, Media & Design. With it, Newport is looking to double its population within a year.

FEES, BURSARIES

UK & EU Fees for 2011-12, £3,375. Welsh entrants are eligible for a grant. There are scholarships available to students who have represented their country or region in sport.

STUDENT PROFILE

As many as 58% of undergraduates are part-timers, and 64% are mature. The Caerleon profile is not easy to run to ground. You've got arty types and rugger buggers and mysterious geeks with hobbit-style goatees left to run wild. They are broadly a new-university crew, 45% working class and quite a cut from that nebulous 'low-participation' neighbourhood we hear so much about. Gender-wise it's a healthy 59% female.

ACADEMIA & JOBS

The faculty or school that is causing all the fuss is the Newport School of Art Media and Design. It offers courses under the banners, Art & Photography, Film and Animation, Performing Arts, and Design.

Film is a big deal here. There are some of the best art and design facilities in Europe, whose students are taking the world of film animation by storm, with one film, *Famous Fred*, being nominated for a Hollywood Oscar, others, such as *Human Traffic* and *Waking Ned* enjoying great commercial success, and *The Gogs* winning its student makers a clutch of BAFTA awards. Not only could the uni boast 60 of its graduates on the credit list of the massive hit, *Chicken Run*, but also *Women in Love* director Ken Russell has been working closely with the department of film and video.

Camelot has become the International Film School, Wales, with BA (Hons) Animation, Cinema

Studies & Scriptwriting, Computer Games Design, Documentary Film & Television, Film & Video, Performing Arts, MA Animation, and MA Film, BA Creative Sound & Music, Documentary Photography (BA and MA), Fine Art, Photographic Art, Photography for Advertising & Fashion, New Media Publishing, and MA Art.

If this is your bent, go for it, not least because they are among the top graduate providers to the film industry. Eight years ago, we wrote: 'What comes across is that Newport provides an imaginative environment. Subtlety, humour and creative thinking are to the fore.' We can find no reason to change that view.

Meanwhile, there's the Newport Business School, the School of Health & Social Sciences, the Centre for Community and Lifelong Learning, and Education - Primary Initial teacher training at the uni was designated as 'Excellent' by the Higher Education Funding Council for Wales in 2000.

Foundation courses leading to direct entry into the uni are available in Science, Technology, Info Technology (Computing, Business Studies, Statistics), Humanities (English, History, Media Studies), Labour Studies, Business Studies, Social Studies, Youth & Community Work and Politics.

SOCIAL SCENE

STUDENTS' UNION For ents, Caerleon is the centre of things, and students from Allt-r-yn flock to it. Halloween Ball in **Main Hall** (now 1,000 capacity) is the big deal. Otherwise, it's pretty limp, with 'Film Sundays', where two classic films are shown back to back, live music from up and coming indie acts, comedy nights, quiz nights, karaoke, bowling trips and *Bar FTSE* - beat the bar for the cheapest drinks before your Wednesday night in town, see

RESEARCH EXCELLENCE		
% of Newport's research that is 4* (World-class) or 3* (Internationally rated):		
	4*	3*
Mechanical, Aero. & Manufacturing Eng.	10%	15%
Social Work	5%	40%
Education	0%	0%
History	0%	20%
Art and Design	10%	60%

> *'I wanted something else, something more to walk away with in my experience of University. When I was offered the role of manager for NTV, I knew this was the something.'*

Student Cardiff. Saturdays are *Nebula*, which is basically a re-branding of the main venue into a nightclub scene.

Meanwhile, the Rathwell building is student central, and drawing big audiences among the student throng is live music in the **Clarence Bar**. There is also a refectory and café bar. We tried the vegetable curry, £2.30, at the café. The refectory meals looked better, but the rice was a well-advised solid base for a night's drinking at the Clarence, equipped outside front with one of those cash machines that charges you for use, a dirty touch. The bar hosts karaoke, Chris Tarrant-inspired 'Who wants to win a crate of beer?' and other quizzes. Also figuring large in students' lives is Newport's own **TJ's** - bar, disco and music venue.

As for student societies, up until recently Rugby was the deal, and maybe it still is, but there have been some dramatic changes in the society calendar, instigated by the founding of News Port, Radio Noize, and NTV, the online, on-demand TV station entertainment and information service which just won the 2009 RTS TV Awards. *News Port* is a bi-weekly newspaper.

Jennifer Moran, who runs NTV, captured perfectly the real point of student societies: 'I realised this last year, that I wanted more. Not just more of what I was already doing. I wanted something else, something more to walk away with in my experience of University. When I was offered the role of manager for NTV, I knew this was the something. Of course I knew it would be challenging, it would be hard work from my spare time and definitely stressful at times. It was worth it without a doubt. I know this because when I look back at my time here, and imagine not having had this experience I

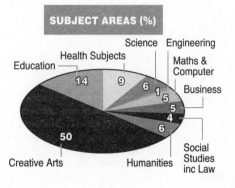

SUBJECT AREAS (%)

Science — Engineering
Health Subjects
Education
Maths & Computer
14
9
6
1
5
Business
5
4
6
50
Social Studies inc Law
Creative Arts
Humanities

WHAT IT'S REALLY LIKE

UNIVERSITY:

Social Life	★★
Societies	★★
Student Union services	★★★
Politics	**Active**
Sport	**Relaxed**
National team position	**108th**
Sport facilities	★★★★
Arts opportunities	**Good**
Student radio	**Radio Noize**
Student newspaper	**News Port**
Student online TV	**NTV**
Venue	**Main Hall**
Bar	**The Clarence**
Union ents	**Chees and live; good May Ball**
Union societies	**23**
Most popular society	**Rugby**
Parking	**Adequate**

TOWN:

Entertainment	★★
Scene	**Pubs, clubs**
Town/gown relations	**OK**
Risk of violence	**Low**
Cost of living	**Average**
Student concessions	**Good**
Survival + 2 nights out	**£70 pw**
Part-time work campus/town	**Good**

It is all a surprisingly eclectic and energetic mix, with regular art exhibitions vying with sporting nights, e-culture (**Cyber Café**) and student concern (a student development officer is *in place*).

SPORT There are 15 clubs, from Surf to Skiing, Rugby to Mountain Sports, boosted on Caerleon with a Sports Centre, hall, gym, fitness suite; also a rugby pitch and 2 floodlit tennis (there's a popular Tennis Academy) and netball courts. There is a need for more sports fields, and the athletic union eye one particular car park with degrees of envy and bitterness, as it was once a hockey pitch. There's no squash or swimming. For these it's off to public facilities in Newport. They get involved with the Welsh Rugby Union and Cricket Association, and run coaching courses. Within easy reach are facilities for sailing and windsurfing, dry-slope skiing, caving, canoeing, mountain biking, rock climbing, orienteering and hill walking.

PILLOW TALK

447 en-suite rooms are located in a student village, arranged into flats of 5 single study bedrooms. The rent is £89.50 p.w. Alternatively, 196 standard rooms are available in four traditional halls, Abergavenny, Blaenavon, Camelot and Dolaucothi. Rent between £77.50.

GETTING THERE

☛ By road: M4/J25. If approaching Caerleon from Cardiff, there is no direct exit from the J25. Either exit at J26, or take J24 and U-turn at r/about to approach Junction 25 from the East.
☛ By rail: London Paddington, 1:50; Birmingham New Street, 2:00; Cardiff, 40 mins; Bristol Parkway, 25 mins.
☛ By coach: London, 2:45; Manchester, 5:15.
☛ By air: Direct coach from Heathrow, Gatwick.

feel like I have lost something. At the end of the day there were fun times, and its been a stepping stone in my self development.'

The Union is also active on student awareness campaigns, which have included breast cancer, access & equality, anonymous marking, sexual health and drug awareness. There is also a focus on theatre, dance, etc, through the Performing Arts department, and Newport's **Riverfront Arts Theatre** figures strongly.

UNIVERSITY OF NORTHAMPTON

The University of Northampton
Boughton Green Road
Moulton Park
Northampton NN2 7AL

TEL 0800 358 2232; 01604 735 500
FAX 01604 713083
EMAIL admissions@northampton.ac.uk
WEB www.northampton.ac.uk

Northampton Students' Union
Boughton Green Road
Moulton Park
Northampton NN2 7AL

TEL 01604 892818
FAX 01604 719454
EMAIL [firstname.surname]@ucnu.org
WEB www.northamptonunion.com

VIRGIN VIEW

*U*niversity College Northampton became *Northampton University in October 2005.*

In the Higher Education Funding Council's National Student Survey, 82% of students approved of what's going down here. The drop-out rate is nudging 11%, which is fair.

CAMPUS

The main Park campus, an 80-acre estate on the edge of town, has been well designed. What strikes the visitor immediately is the careful architectural integration of facilities and services, none of which limit or indeed offend the eye. Halls are in among lecture theatres, sports centre by the nightclub, eaterie and bar; a rugby pitch in the centre of things gives a welcome sense of space and a reminder that rugby is a religion both here and in town, which has one of the best teams in the Premier League.

Close by is the Leather Conservation Centre - (Northampton is the centre of the shoe industry; the football ground is called The Cobblers). Some buildings are named after villages in the county, the halls after notable people of the area, including the tragic Northamptonshire poet John Clare, whose parents were illiterate, but who achieved national renown in his day by imbibing the spirit of this place before going insane.

Artistically, the focus is at UCN's Avenue campus in town, however. This 24-acre site - 20 mins away from Park and linked by a free bus service - houses Art, Design, Technology and Performance Arts. In particular there's quite a tradition for theatre.

FEES, BURSARIES

UK & EU Fees, 2010-11: £3,375 p.a. Deal directly with the university about bursaries and scholarships.

STUDENT PROFILE

Most undergraduates are local; 60% are mature and 35% part-timers.

ACADEMIA & JOBS

There are three faculties. The Faculty of Applied Sciences includes schools of Leather Technology, Built Environment, Engineering & Technology, Environmental Science, Health & Life Sciences, and Nursing & Midwifery. Medical sciences have links with the General Hospital in Northampton and with Milton Keynes, 'Nursing courses are always over-subscribed,' I was told.

The Faculty of Arts & Social Sciences includes

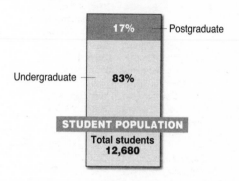

Art & Design, Behavioural Studies (including a BSc in Psychology), Cultural Studies (such as a cross-cultural degree in Performance Studies - Drama, Dance, Music), Education (BA Hons QTS Primary), and Social Studies (American Studies, History, Sociology).

The Faculty of Management & Business includes the schools of Business, Information Systems, Law & International Business, Professional Studies (Finance and Accounting) and Management (MMB, MSc Management Studies).

RESEARCH EXCELLENCE

% of Northampton's research that is
4* *(World-class) or* **3*** *(Internationally rated):*

	4*	3*
Health Professions	**5%**	**5%**
Metallurgy and Materials	**0%**	**20%**
Business/Management	**5%**	**10%**
Education	**5%**	**10%**
Asian Studies	**0%**	**10%**
English	**0%**	**15%**
History	**5%**	**35%**
Art and Design	**0%**	**5%**
Performing Arts	**0%**	**25%**

UNIVERSITY:	
Social Life	★
Societies	★
2010 NSDF (Drama) Awards	**Set design, lighting**
Student Union services	★
Politics	**None**
Sport	**21 clubs**
National team position	**95th**
Sport facilities	★
Student newspaper	**The Squirrel**
Venue	**NN2**
Bar	**Central Park**
Union ents	**Pop, indie, electro**
Union societies	**20**
Parking	**Limited permits**
TOWN:	
Entertainment	★★
Scene	**Pubs, clubs**
Town/gown relations	**OK**
Risk of violence	**Low**
Cost of living	**Average**
Student concessions	**Good**
Survival + 2 nights out	**£70 pw**
Part-time work campus/town	**Good**

A first last year was a degree in accounting, a foundation degree developed with the NHS and directed specifically at the Service's perennial problem of balancing its budgets.

Career strength in the health sector comes out of the occupational therapy and podiatry degrees. Countrywide, Salford and Northampton probably offer the best value - entry requirements to job satisfaction. There are strong links with the General Hospital in Northampton and Milton Keynes, a top notch teaching assessment result and a low entry requirement as well as the strong employment reputation makes it attractive.

Furniture design and manufacture is another niche employment strength. Northampton is in the heart of the leather industry, and furniture was probably always on the agenda for Product Design students. There is also a fast employment flow into these industries out of the Management & Business faculty up at Park (design being at Avenue Campus).

Graphic artists are particularly employable through BA Graphic Communication, and designers and sculptors also register with relatively strong prospects in the employment league.

In the business sector personnel officers/managers are particularly well served, the rush of graduates into the sector coming from a range of courses featuring Human Resource Management, like the 4-year sandwich BA Hons degree, Human Resource Management.

Most of the Education provision finds expression in primary school teaching. You'll be at Park.

SOCIAL SCENE

STUDENTS' UNION There's little going on by way of student activities, with student union wallahs trying desperately to find out what they should be doing by visiting other universities. However, in the recent National Student Drama Festival three graduates in Drama at the university (a well designed practice-led course) made it to the finals and were awarded two gongs, one for lighting, the other for set design, which shows just what might be possible if Northampton Union got its act together. The troupe now operates as Electric Shadows.

Ents are none too inspiring either, with **NN2**, the nightclub, offering *Blast Tuesdays* (retro party), monthly indie and electro club night *fiDget*, and good old *Flirt!* for Fridays.

Perhaps we shouldn't be surprised, most undergraduates are local, and many are part-timers. **Central Park** is the main bar. **Pavilion**, with views over games pitches and Sky TV, is now the university's and not the union's to run.

At **George's**, the hub of Avenue Union, you get *Bazinga!* Thurdays (pop, indie, electro), as well as Xbox, pool, etc and plenty of karaoke and open mic nights.

PILLOW TALK

Uni accommodation is guaranteed to 'first and firm choices' in halls or flats (some 67% are en suite).

ACCOMMODATION

Student rating	★
Guarantee to freshers	**100%**
Style	**Halls, flats**
Security guard	**All**
Shared rooms	**Some**
Internet access	**All**
Self-catered	**All**
En suite	**Most**
Approx price range pw	**£43-£97.70**
City rent pw	**£45**

GETTING THERE

☛ By road: M1/J15/15a/16; easy access to M5/6/25/40, A1 and A45.
☛ By rail: London and Birmingham, 1:00.
☛ By coach: London, 2:00; Birmingham, 1:35.

UNIVERSITY OF NORTHUMBRIA

University of Northumbria
Northumberland Road
Newcastle upon Tyne NE1 8ST

TEL 0191 243 7420
FAX 0191 227 4561
EMAIL er.admissions@northumbria.ac.uk
WEB www.northumbria.ac.uk

Northumbria Students' Union
2 Sandyford Road
Newcastle Upon Tyne NE1 8SB

TEL 0191 227 4757
FAX 0191 227 3760
EMAIL su.enquiries@unn.ac.uk
WEB www.mynsu.co.uk

VIRGIN VIEW

*T*he two universities in the city of Newcastle are situated within walking distance of one another. 'I think what is important about being a student in Newcastle is that the poly [as Northumbria is known] and the uni mix very well. There is little snobbery, rather a healthy rivalry, especially when it comes to sport. Very often students find themselves living in a house with both uni and poly students, which is unheard of in places like Oxford. The poly has a far greater mix of people (the uni being overrun by people from public school). But don't be put off by this - Newcastle, as a city, caters for every taste and every person, and I have not heard of anyone who has not enjoyed it.'

So said Susannah Bell. Over the years the poly (Northumbria is not beleaguered by the distinction, any more than is King's College London, when taunted with it by UCL) has held its own with Newcastle, often enough beaten it in sport, though last year Newcastle came 11th and Northumbria 20th in the overall national team positions. Sure there is an essential difference, Northumbria has 25% part-timers, Newcastle none, which

UNIVERSITY/STUDENT PROFILE	
University since	**1992**
Situation/style	**Civic**
Student population	**32665**
Total undergraduates	**25090**
Mature	**49%**
International	**18%**
Male/female ratio	**43:57**
Equality of opportunity:	
state school intake	**92%**
social class 4-7 intake	**35%**
drop-out rate	**8%**

places it firmly in the more local category, and while Northumbria's mature undergraduate population is 49%, Newcastle's is just 23%, and there is no contest when it comes to research - Newcastle stands at 27th in the country, Northumbria at 81st, though no subject submitted by Northumbria achieved less than 60% of its research rated at international level, and interestingly Northumbria rose 18 places last time, and Newcastle only 5.

Some of our ex-polys have not taken on board the significance of the student culture in student development. Northumbria did, and took big strides. Then it seemed to lose its head of steam. Now it's back on top again with more than 50 student societies and a £7 million makeover of its Students' Union. In the National Student Survey, undertaken by the Higher Education Funding Council, which is answerable to the Government, Newcastle showed 87% student satisfaction and Northumbria 82%, and when it came to getting real graduate jobs within six months after graduation, Northumbria, with 80% graduates employed, pipped Newcastle with 79%.

All said, Northumbria is a powerhouse

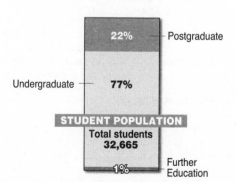

Postgraduate **22%**

Undergraduate **77%**

STUDENT POPULATION
Total students
32,665

1% Further Education

of a university, taking higher education into areas Newcastle University doesn't reach.

The very nub of Northumbria's value is in its dedication to graduate employment. More than 550 employers sponsor the undergraduate programmes and 47 professional bodies accredit various aspects of it curriculum. Enterprise Campus provides advice and support for students wanting to start or develop their own business. 70+ businesses have benefitted in the last two years. And there are some interesting academic niches (see Academia below).

Open Days, 2011: 1 July and 8 October.

CAMPUSES

CITY CAMPUS (address above) Student Union, library, sports centre, language laboratories, art gallery.

COACH LANE CAMPUS Coach Lane, Benton, Newcastle upon Tyne NE7 7XA. Tel: 0191 215 6000. Recent beneficiary of a £40-million development. Health, Social Work & Education are here. Coach Lane also has a Union, library and computing facilities, a sports hall, fitness suite, activity studio and all-weather hockey pitch.

FEES, BURSARIES

UK & EU Fees, 2011-12: £3,375 p.a. If you are a new 'Home' full-time undergraduate student who pays tuition fees and achieves a minimum of 360 UCAS tariff points (from a maximum of three A2 awards or their equivalent) you will automatically be awarded a Northumbria Scholarship of £1,000 in the first year of your course.

STUDENT PROFILE

Around a third of undergraduates are part-timers and half are mature; meanwhile 92% are from state school or college, 35% come from the lower socioeconomic orders, and 18% from overseas. Northumnbria knows its market and educates it well. 'Best thing,' said Jack Ford when he alighted there for the first time, 'was the relaxed atmosphere that enables students to bond and make lots of new friends.'

ACADEMIA & JOBS

Writes Susannah Bell: 'Newcastle probably has the

TEACHING SURVEY AT A GLANCE	
Avg. UCAS points accepted	**290**
Acceptance rate	**22%**
Overall satisfaction rate	**82%**
Helpful/interested staff	★★★
Small tuition groups	★★
Students into graduate jobs	**80%**

Teaching most popular with undergraduates:
Architecture, Film & Photography, European Languages & Area Studies, French Studies, Geographical Studies, Iberian Studies (100%), Teacher Training, Law, Maths, Mechanical, Production & Manufacturing Engineering, Nursing, Physical Geography & Environmental Science, Physical Science, Psychology, Social Work, Sociology, Social Policy & Anthropology.

Teaching least popular with undergraduates:
Dance (45%).

best night life in the country, but there is plenty of potential for Northumbria students to do well on the academic side.' Health is a crucial provision just as it is for the other uni. While Newcastle Uni has Medicine, Northumbria has Nursing (although they will not be offering the Advanced Diploma of Higher Education Nursing next year as the profession is moving to all graduate), Midwifery, Physiotherapy, and Occupational Therapy.

There are excellent Social Science degrees too, including a unique Law degree. MLaw offers the choice of studying for four years to achieve either a Solicitors Exempting or Barristers Exempting award. There is also a new Solicitors Full Qualification route over five years including placements which incorporates all stages of education and training. Graduates will be qualified to enter practice as solicitors. Students are given the opportunity to advise real clients in the School's Student Law Office, gaining hands-on experience and the skills required to work in an increasingly competitive environment.

Business (not accountancy and human resource management) is of course a dominant force at Northumbria, producing 16% of all jobs on graduateion Here you will find another unique jewel, the new BA (Hons) Corporate Management. Corporate Management takes a fresh approach to

> *'Some ex-polys did not take on board the significance of the student culture in student development. Northumbria did, and took big strides, but the very nub of Northumbria's value is in its dedication to graduate employment.'*

business education by combining study with salaried employment enabling students to graduate with two years hands-on business experience. The degree is aimed at high achieving, motivated students who are looking for a prestigious degree.

Art & Design is another part of the curriculum which showed up well in the research assessment. A defining mark of Northumbria is its fashion department. They have even opened a School of Design in London, in Islington, offering fashion courses. There are niche degrees like Apparel Design & Retail Merchandising, hardwired to employment, and there is Furniture Design, and Computer-aided Product Design.

Contact with industry in the North East region is facilitated by all sorts of strategies. Placements are varied and thorough, with training sessions and tutorials at the beginning, middle and end of the semester to develop skills, the rest of the time given to placement.

Property developers, architects, construction managers, quantity surveyors and estate agents pour out of Northumbria too.

SOCIAL SCENE

At City Campus they recently opened a £2-million

RESEARCH EXCELLENCE

% of Northumbria's research that is
4* *(World-class)* or **3*** *(Internationally rated):*

	4*	3*
Nursing/Midwifery	15%	35%
Health Professions	5%	25%
General Engineering	5%	45%
Built Environment	5%	45%
Business/Management	0%	20%
Social Work	5%	30%
Psychology	0%	25%
Sports	5%	15%
English	5%	20%
History	0%	20%
Art and Design	15%	30%
History of Art	15%	15%

WHAT IT'S REALLY LIKE

UNIVERSITY:	
Social Life	★★★★
Societies	★★
Student Union services	★★★
Politics	**Average**
Sport	**Key**
National team position	**20th**
Sport facilities	★★★
Arts opportunities	**Drama, music, film good; dance, art average**
Student magazine	**Nu:Life**
Student TV	**NU:TV**
Nightclubs	**Habita, Stage 2**
Bars	**Reds**
Union ents	**Big club nights and live gigs**
Union societies	**53**
Parking	**Difficult**
CITY:	
Entertainment	★★★★★
Scene	**Vibrant, fun**
Town/gown relations	**OK**
Risk of violence	**Average**
Cost of living	**Low**
Student concessions	**Good**
Survival + 2 nights out	**£80 pw**
Part-time work campus/town	**Average/excellent**

New Bar, **Habita**, an official warm-up bar for club nights on campus and in town. Then there's **Stage 2** with 'the largest student cinema screen in the country', so they claim. 'When we are not showing films or hosting live comedy, **Stage 2** turns into one of the best music venues in the North.' Amy Winehouse, Maximo Park, and the Racounteurs have done their stuff here. Several bars in one, the venue's capacity is 3,000 and becomes everyone's favourite nightclub. Even so, **Reds Bar** (circular bar, capacity 500) is the main club venue, packed to the rafters all week long. 'We are known as one of the best live music venues in the North East,' they say. 'We have hosted the NME music tour, and had acts such as Jamie T, Babyshambles, The Ting Tings, Jack Penate, Klaxons, Sonique, and Kaiser Chiefs to name a few.

Monday might be *NU: Unplugged Mic Night* in Habita. Tuesday it's *Get 'Y' Skates On* (punk, ska, hip hop, drum 'n' bass) in Reds, 10pm to 2 am; Wednesday is *Team Northumbria Warm Up* in Reds. Saturday could be *Curves* (drum 'n' breaks/beats 'n' breaks) or *Brighton Beach* in Reds. And so on, karaoke, *Big Fat Quizz of the Week*, etc.

'We promote our own DJs in Reds.' There are also good opportunities for DJs to make the transition to city clubs. 'One of our DJs, who does Saturday night *Wiggle*, was a student here, and now he's working six nights a week in bars and nightclubs in town.'

There's also a decent drama society - 3 or 4 productions a year, a new magazine called Nu:Life, looking for contributors, and a new TV station.

SPORT September 2010 saw the launch of a £30m sports centre, engagingly called Sport Central, incorporating a 3,000 seat arena, 25m swimming poll, sports hall, training hall, 12m climbing hall, fitness suite, aerobics studio, squash courts, and strength and conditioning area.. Otherwise, there are options to do anything from scuba diving to rugby. They have some very high-class teams and regularly trounce Newcastle Uni - good hockey, football and tennis. They run an Elite Athlete Programme - Team Northumbria - which offers practical and financial support to students with particular potential. Maybe too high class, one student complained that there's only 3 uni football teams and it's hard to get a trial date.

PILLOW TALK

They can house most new UK undergraduates from outside the local area and new overseas students who apply in good time. Priority is given to non-locals. First-year accommodation consists of halls and flats. There are catered and self-catered halls, none en suite, no car parking, none with a security guard, but all on or pretty close to campus. Claude Gibb is the most popular hall, being in crawling distance of town and lectures - 'more of a public school crowd here,' said one. Lovaine, also on campus, is handy but poky.

Of the flats a student recommended Glenamara and Stephenson, both with the advantage of a central location. SThe flats do look more likely, some are en suite, all are self-catering, most have internet access, and some even have car parking and security. Ask the right questions of the Accommodation

ACCOMMODATION	
Student rating	★★
Guarantee to freshers	**Most not all**
Style	**Halls, flats**
Security guard	**Not halls, but some flats**
Shared rooms	**None**
Internet access	**Most**
Self-catered	**Some halls, most flats**
En suite	**Not halls, some flats**
Approx price range pw	**£80.50-£140**
City rent pw	**£60-£97**

office as soon as possible.

Two new halls will open in September 2011.

GETTING THERE

☞ By road to Newcastle: A1(M) from the south and north; A19 from York; A69 from the west; M6 from the southwest.

☞ By road to Carlisle: A7 from the north; M6 from the south; A69 from Newcastle (the east).

☞ By rail to Newcastle: Edinburgh, 1:30; Leeds, 1:45; London King's Cross, 3:00; Manchester Piccadilly, 3:00; Birmingham New Street, 4:00.

☞ By air: Newcastle International airport.

☞ By coach: London, 6:05; Birmingham, 4:25.

STUDENT NOTTINGHAM - THE CITY

Nottingham is without doubt, the best city in the country for a student. Situated in the Midlands, it's never too far UK students to get home, and being in the middle of the country, you get a really good mix of both southern and northern students along with the grounded Nottingham locals themselves.

There are two universities and eight further education colleges in Nottingham, a bustling city that has come into its own, it almost seems, in the very process of catering for the huge number of students it attracts.

LIVE MUSIC

For its sheer size and the big names it attracts, the best venue for live music has to be the **Ice Centre**, situated in the **Lace Market**. The Strokes, Kelly Clarkson and the Little Britain Tour have all been there recently. The drinks are extortionately priced, but if you want to see the big names it generally does mean big bucks.

A venue for live music acts with more *cred.* is the less-commercial **Rock City**. City centre situated, and a lot more edgy, **Rock City** has hosted such as The Killers and Oasis in this small but very atmospheric club. With student club nights throughout the week, this is a *must* if you want to dodge the cheese and get heavily into eyeliner.

If its un-discovered talent you're after, then look no further than the **Rescue Rooms**, which is just round the corner and almost a pint-sized version of **Rock City**.

Live music is really taking off in Nottingham and even Trent's Student Union is jumping on the bandwagon, hosting its very own live music night with some great up-coming bands every second Friday.

CLUBBING

Nottingham is now seen as a bar city, not first and foremost club orientated. Yet, with the mix of clubs it has, catering for all wants and tastes, you will be hard pushed to find better elsewhere. The newlish **Oceana** is very popular with students – 5 rooms filled with different atmospheres and music – but again be prepared to spend a penny or two. The city also has **Mode** nightclub and **Lost Weekend**, both with great student nights, cheap drinks and cheesy tunes.

But the clubs of all clubs remains the mighty **Ocean** nightclub. Not to be confused with **Oceana**, it has just become solely a student night-club every day of the week, with both universities holding nights. You're guaranteed a good night out, if drunken sportsmen, scantily clad ladies and cheap drinks and cheese is your cup of tea.

For an alternative night, try **Stealth**, **The Cookie Club** and **The Bomb**. The venues are slightly more intimate, a lot smaller, but by no less lively.

DRINKING

Nottingham Trent Students Union offers a fantastic place to drink with its **Glo** bar being well equipped for both chilling out and dancing, and its **Sub** bar to kick back and play some pool. **The Ark** at Nottingham Uni's Students Union is no way near as big, but still offers the usual guarantee of cheap drinks and cheese.

In the city centre, **The Horn in Hand**, **Varsity**, **Templars**, **Up and Down Under** and **Walkabout** are very student populated, give student discounts and offer a relaxed atmosphere. Each has a new deal each week.

For more sophistication, try Hockley and the Lace Market, where most of the following are situated – **Revolution** (over 100 different vodka shots can be tried and consumed), **Tantra** (you can hire out beds for the evening), **Quilted Lama** (with its enormous fish bowls), and the sometime church come bar, **Pitcher and Piano**. But be warned, it won't come cheap.

The Waterfront takes it home at the other side of town, and has 7 bars spread across 7 floors. In summer time, the canal-side terrace is packed.

SHOPPING

Prepare to spend, spend, spend when you come to Nottingham and hit the shops. It is worryingly easy to blow your student loan on the incredible shopping experience that Nottingham offers. There are all the chain stores, many cool trendy shops and it's rife with factory shops. Go to the **Victoria Centre** for day-to-day student favourites, the brand new **Topshop**, **La Senza**, **Republic**, and such as HMV, Boots... Along with its market, department store and supermarket, it caters for everyone. **The Broadmarsh** is at the other end of town and is again a shopping complex, but offers fair-priced **H&M**, **TK Max** and **New Look**. The **Broadmarsh** is very handy for fancy dress outfits at a cut rate, too.

If you want to spend that bit more, then walk down Bridlesmith Gate to **Flannels**, **Diesel** and **Kurt Geiger**. You really can get your heart desire, from retro gear at **Ice Nine** and **Wild Clothing** to everyday fashions at **Warehouse** and Zara.

EATING

Whether you are looking for quality (somewhere to drag your parents), quantity (eat all you want), or somewhere to bring your own wine, Nottingham does not disappoint. The **Corner House** in the city centre offers an array of different cuisine from Flaming Dragon, the Chinese buffet, to Bella Italia, a very fair priced and tasty Italian. American style diners proliferate around the city centre, including **Hard Rock Café** and **Frankie and Benny's**, while Hockley has **Fresh**, a great place to eat and very healthy, and some great bars that offer good, extravagant bar meals, like **Browns** and the **Hog's Head**.

For daytime snacking, it's **Subways**, the individual outlets scattered across the city, and you'll find a favourite dive among a whole host of small, reasonably priced city café's.

Whatever you're in the mood for, whatever your needs and requirements, Nottingham really does have something for everyone.

Annabel Woollen

UNIVERSITY OF NOTTINGHAM

The University of Nottingham
University Park
Nottingham NG7 2RD

TEL 0115 951 5559
FAX 0115 846 8062
EMAIL undergraduate-enquiries@nottingham.ac.uk
WEB www.nottingham.ac.uk

Nottingham Students' Union
University Park
Nottingham NG7 2RD

TEL 0115 846 8800
EMAIL studentsunion@nottingham.ac.uk
WEB www.su.nottingham.ac.uk

VIRGIN VIEW

*N*ottingham *is a top university with an 87% satisfaction rate and an 81% chance of getting a top graduate job within six months of leaving.*

It is one of the most employer-friendly universities in the world, and students are happy here, only 4% don't last the course, which is low.

They hold great store by the beauty of their various campuses, but think about opportunity in global terms, operating links with 320 partner universities in over 40 countries (including their own campuses in Malaysia and China).

According to UCAS they are the third most popular university in the UK, so what do they do about selection?

Besides grades and points, they are looking for 'engagement and understanding of the subject area, relevant work experience and/or independent reading outside of the school curriculum, and an awareness of the qualities and skills required to undertake a degree.'

Open Days, 2011: 24 and 25 June; 9 and 10 September.

CAMPUSES

The 300-acre University Park, home to 3,000 students, workplace to a further 26,000 students and staff, and located just a short bus or bike ride from Nottingham city centre, is the main campus - huge lake, views over Trent valley, rolling Downs that sweep away into the distance, all a neat ten minutes by bus from town.

There is a 16-hectare satellite campus at Sutton Bonington, 10 miles distant, for the School of Biological Sciences, and now the new Vet

UNIVERSITY/STUDENT PROFILE	
University since	**1948**
Situation/style	**Campus**
Student population	**32925**
Total undergraduates	**24510**
Mature	**31%**
International	**24%**
Male/female ratio	**43:57**
Equality of opportunity:	
state school intake	**72%**
social class 4-7 intake	**19%**
drop-out rate	**4%**

School. Besides teaching and research facilities, the James Cameron-Gifford Library and student residences, there's a sports centre, bank and bookshop. A free shuttle-bus service runs between it and University Park during the day.

The Jubilee Campus, on a site close to University Park, houses the Schools of Education, Computer Science and Information Technology, as well as The Business School. The site is also the home of The National College for School Leadership. Green in concept and design, an important feature is the series of lakes which, as well as being home to wildlife, provide cooling for the buildings in the summer and receive all surface water. Less visible - but equally important to this model of a sustainable campus - are the roofs which are, quite literally, green. A carpet of low-growing alpine plants helps maintain steady temperatures within the buildings throughout the year and is more effective than traditional insulation. Buildings also feature a super-efficient mechanical ventilation system, lighting sensors to reduce energy consumption, and photovoltaic cells integrated into the atrium roofs. The environmentally-friendly nature of the campus and its buildings have been a big factor in the awards that it has received, including the Millennium Marque Award for Environmental Excellence, the British Construction Industry Building Project of the Year, the RIBA Journal Sustainability Award and the Civic Trust Award for Sustainability.

'When I first visited the university, all fresh-faced and eager,' recalls Mark Tew, 'I couldn't help but be struck by the sheer size of the place. It's BIG.' Writes Phil Barnett: 'Walking through, with the river on one side and incredible architecture on the other, is an experience never to grow tired of. But, when the need arises, living away from main campus does mean a 20-minute walk or a free bus, which is supposed to leave every 15 minutes but always seems to be leaving as the bus stop is approached. The facilities are fantastic and all

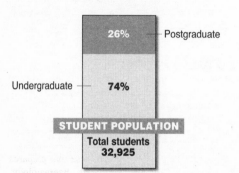

26% — Postgraduate

Undergraduate — 74%

STUDENT POPULATION
Total students
32,925

day to day necessities are available. It has its own shop and a sports centre with good facilities, but no gym: a visit to main campus is necessary.

'Accommodation is all en-suite, fully catered, and the food is more than satisfactory, with a choice of two cafés or the main hall.

'A lot of Jubilee students study business, of course, and can leave hall less than a minute before lectures begin. If you are one of these, living at Jubilee does means that a lot of your course friends are also the people you live with. However, a fair few Jubilee students do in fact study on the main campus, so there must be advantages in this. If you are visiting Nottingham, I'd advise you take a look around. New work to enhance the campus further began in February this year.'

FEES, BURSARIES

UK & EU Fees, 2011-12: £3,375 p.a. There are means-tested bursaries for students with a residual household income of up to £46,700; also dependants bursaries and care leavers bursaries. 'First in the Family' and Kevin B Malone Scholarships are open to students from the local area who also meet certain other criteria. See www.nottingham. ac.uk/financialsupport.

There are also departmental scholarships and others for overseas students. See www.nottingham.ac.uk/internationaloffice/prospective-students/scholarships/index.aspx There is also a sports bursary scheme for athletes competing at a high level. See www.nottingham.ac.uk/sport

STUDENT PROFILE

The uni has one of the lower intakes from the state sector and from so-called non-traditional uni heartlands (lower socio-economic groups and neighbourhoods). But they claim a rigorous step-by-step system to check whether circumstances may affect achievement levels at application, an analysis not only of what you can afford, but whether your school or college is performing below the national average. Then they turn to your personal statement.

'I was told to expect a lot of bitter and twisted Oxbridge rejects with a big fat chip on the shoulder, but this hasn't been the case,' Mark recalls. 'The "rah-rah, sooo drunk!" toff brigade, however, is definitely out in full force! Being from up t' North, it was a culture shock to say the least. But it's well worth being here if just to take the piss. "Another bottle of champers Roger?"'

ACADEMIA & JOBS

The great thing at Nottingham is the interest shown in students by the lecturers, hence the 4-star rating in the Student Experience Survey.

They are particularly strong in medicine and are one of only a few medical schools that offers students the opportunity to participate in full-body dissection. They also offer a course that prepares students for careers in areas haematology,

> *'The "rah-rah, sooo drunk!" toff brigade is definitely out in force! But it's well worth being here if just to take the piss. "Another bottle of champers Roger?"'*

TEACHING SURVEY AT A GLANCE	
Avg. UCAS points accepted	**410**
Acceptance rate	**14%**
Overall satisfaction rate	**87%**
Helpful/interested staff	★★★★
Small tuition groups	★★
Students into graduate jobs	**81%**

Teaching most popular with undergraduates:
Agriculture, Anatomy, Physiology & Pathology, Animal Science, Archaeology, Architecture, Biology & related science, Chemistry, Film & Photography, Civil Engineering, Classics, Computer, Economics, Food Studies, Genetics, German & Scandanavian Studies, History, Human & Social Geography, Maths, Mechanical Eng., Medicine, Music, Nutrition, Pharmacology, Toxicology & Pharmacy, Philosophy, Physical Science, Physics & Astronomy, Subjects Allied to Medicine, Social Policy, Social Studies, Technology, Theology, Zoology.

Teaching least popular with undergraduates:
Asian Studies (58%).

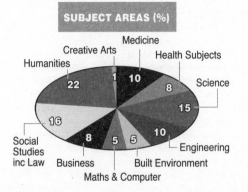

SUBJECT AREAS (%)

Medicine 10
Creative Arts 1
Health Subjects 8
Humanities 22
Science 15
Social Studies inc Law 16
Business 8
Maths & Computer 5
Built Environment 5
Engineering 10

RESEARCH EXCELLENCE

% of Nottingham's research that is
4* *(World-class)* or **3*** *(Internationally rated):*

	4*	3*
Infection/ Immunology	0%	25%
Hospital Clinical	5%	30%
Laboratory Clinical	5%	20%
Epidemiology	5%	35%
Primary Care	30%	40%
Clinical Psychology	5%	30%
Nursing/Midwifery	20%	35%
Health Professions	10%	30%
Pharmacy	35%	45%
Biological Sciences	10%	40%
Human Biol. Sciences	5%	35%
Agriculture, Veterinary	15%	45%
Chemistry	30%	55%
Physics	25%	40%
Pure Mathematics	15%	35%
Applied Mathematics	20%	45%
Statistics	20%	50%
Computer Science	30%	50%
Electrical/Electronic Eng.	10%	55%
General Engineering	25%	50%
Civil Engineering	25%	60%
Mechanical, Aero. & Manufacturing Eng.	25%	50%
Architecture	10%	30%
Environmental Studies	20%	40%
Archaeology	20%	40%
Economics	30%	55%
Business/Management	20%	50%
Law	30%	35%
Politics	15%	35%
Social Work	10%	40%
Sociology	15%	30%
Psychology	10%	50%
Education	20%	25%
American Studiess	25%	20%
Asian Studies	10%	20%
Russian	20%	40%
French	20%	35%
German	10%	30%
Iberian	30%	45%
English	35%	35%
Classics	10%	45%
Philosophy	25%	35%
Theology	20%	40%
History	15%	35%
History of Ar	20%	55%
Media Studies	5%	35%
Music	25%	60%

immunology, genetics, microbiology, embryology and tissue banking. A Foundation Year is designed to widen access to this.

2011 sees the first graduates from their School of Veterinary Medicine and Science, which opened in 2006, the first new school of its kind to open in Britain for 50 years.

Over at Jubilee campus, the medical degree, BMBS, is rigorous - 3 years to BMedSci, then 2 increasingly clinical years. They require Biology and Chemistry at A level, plus a third subject excluding General Studies and Critical Thinking. UKCAT too.

Last year saw a swathe of interest in China., after the University opened up shop there. The School of Contemporary Chinese Studies offer: MSci Contemporary Chinese Studies (previously only BA Contemporary Chinese Studies); MSci Business and Economy of Contemporary China; MSci Global Issues and Contemporary Chinese Studies.

When the Nottingham Law degree was assessed by the LPC Board, it was among the very few to be rated Excellent. The latest national Research Assessment found 65% of Nottingham's Law submission either world-class or internationally excellent. All applicants to Law here must sit the National Admissions Test (LNAT).

Finance, Accounting & Management degrees and Economics & Econometrics and the like prime graduates for one of the strongest areas of graduate employment from Nottingham - accountancy, tax consultancy, banking. And the joint hons. Programme has BSc Maths & Economics, Maths & Management Studies, and BC Economics and Philosophy. Economics & Econometrics scored 85% world-class and internationally significant in the recent research assessment. Applied Maths and Philosophy scored 60% and 65% respectively

Blue-chip companies that maintain ongoing research relationships include Powergen, Boots and GlaxoSmithKline. The Ford Motor Company and Astra Zeneca have both been involved with the uni for over 30 years, and its relationship with Rolls-Royce includes hosting two Technology Centres in the areas of gas turbine transmission systems and manufacturing technology.

Such contacts with industry lead to initiatives that include the Nottingham Advantage Award, developed to recognise and reward students' extracurricular activities and demonstrate to employers the value of the skills they imparted.

The EnterpriseLab, on Jubilee Campus, is open to all and offers advice on starting up a business, workshops on business-related topics, etc.

Finally, Nottingham's top-rated BSc Psychology leads graduates into market research, publicity and PR, choice too of many graduates in languages, social studies, business and humanities.

SOCIAL SCENE

STUDENTS' UNION This is housed in the Portland Building, which overlooks the lake, with SU shop, banks, Blackwells and Boots outlets, and a revolving door that spews students with armfuls of books out onto the steps.

The bar and nightclub are **Mooch**, which serves a range of food throughout the day and has an outdoor terrace, and **The Venue**, an 800-capacity nightclub which hosts regular club nights and comedy nights.

In addition, the **D H Lawrence** bar can be found in the Lakeside Pavilion, where exhibitions and stage productions run as prolifically as in the **New Theatre**, which is elsewhere, tucked up behind Portland and as old as the hills.

There are also bars in the 14 halls of residence, and no difficulty in seeing how the drinking binge known as *Campus 14* became so popular. First-year social life spins off halls, off societies, off departments and off sport, rather more than off the Union: 'It still amazes me how such fine, upstanding, intelligent people, who clearly had the "right stuff" to get into Nottingham University, all seem mystically drawn to the Union on a Friday night,' writes Mark. 'Why? It's a dive! Maybe that's harsh. It's actually really nice during the day, its only real crime may be overcrowding on the weekend.'

Nottingham student radio URN is huge. The students have won more national awards than any other university, they won nine at the Student Radio Awards in 2010, including the coveted Kevin Greening Creativity Award. The magazine, also award-winning, is Impact. NUTS is the relatively new TV station.

But the society with the most successes last year was Dance, attracting 300 members and offering weekly sessions in tap, ballet, street, jazz, and lyrical at beginner and advanced levels. The University has now developed the Nottingham Advantage Award, which recognises and rewards students' participation in extracurricular activities.

Nottingham has also long had an enterprising drama society. The New Theatre, which once exuded all the spit-and-sawdust appeal of true fringe theatre, now more suits its name. They write, produce and direct up to twenty plays a year and invariably take a production or two to Edinburgh. Theatre has always been big in this city, the

> *The New Theatre, which once exuded all the spit-and-sawdust appeal of true fringe theatre, now more suits its name. They write, produce and direct up to 20 plays a year there.*

WHAT IT'S REALLY LIKE	
UNIVERSITY:	
Social Life	★★★★
Societies	★★★★
Student Union services	★★★★
Politics	**Available**
Sport	**Key nationally & v. active inter-hall. 67 clubs.**
National team position	**7th**
Sport facilities	★★★★
Arts opportunities	**Drama excellent; music, art good; dance, film great**
Student magazine	**Impact**
Student radio	**URN**
2010 National Radio Awards	**5 gold, 1 silver, 2 bronze**
Student television	**NUTS TV**
Venue	**Venue**
Bars	**Mooch, DHL**
Union ents	**Vibrant**
Union societies	**207**
Most popular society	**Dance Society**
Parking	**Adequate**
CITY:	
Entertainment	★★★★★
Scene	**Serious nightlife, good arts**
Town/gown relations	**OK**
Risk of violence	**High**
Cost of living	**Average**
Student concessions	**Good**
Survival + 2 nights out	**£90 pw**
Part-time work campus/town	**Good/excellent**

Playhouse's deep-rooted reputation to the fore, and **Malt Cross Music Hall** offers an eerie alternative with drama, music hall, comedy, jazz and folk, poltergeists in attendance and spooky goings-on that no one seems able to explain. Then there's the **Theatre Royal** of course (Gilbert & Sullivan, *Rocky Horror*, Arthur Miller, *My Fair Lady*, etc.), and music and dance at the **Palace Theatre**, Mansfield.

On campus, music societies proliferate, such as Blow Soc (wind, to be sure), and for music and art there's the **Arts Centre** - a superb art gallery (with artist in residence) and recital hall next door.

Students may come from comfortable back-

ACCOMMODATION

Student rating	**★★★★**
Guarantee to freshers	**100%**
Style	**Halls, flats**
Security guard	**Porters**
Shared rooms	**Some**
Internet access	**All**
Self-catered	**All flats**
En suite	**Some**
Approx price range pw	**£85.50-£183**
City rent pw	**£50-£140**

talking fully catered halls & self-catering flats. About a third are en suite. There's lots of other accommodation in flats, but catered halls it probably will be, unless you're at Sutton Bonington. Basic pantry facilities are available, but so is breakfast and dinner, and lunch on a flexible scheme which allows you to eat at any catering outlet on University Park or Jubilee campuses. There's not only internet access in all halls, but students can unsubscribe and will be refunded, if they wish. Porters and central site security is basic

There are 14 halls in total, home to approximately 4,000 students, across two sites - Jubilee Campus and University Park. Each hall offers great amenities - coin-operated laundry facilities, pantries to make snacks, chill-out areas like a bar, Junior Common Room, TV and games room, plus a mini library and computer suite.

Writes Mark: 'To be fair, all the halls are pretty nice. Being a former Lincolnite, my totally unbiased opinion is that it is by far the best hall in the world. Small, yet cosy bar, good food, big rooms, our very own library and even cheese and wine nights in the SCR! What more could you want? Ok, so Hugh Stu has the best bar, Derby has the best women and Sherwood has a slide shaped as a dragon. So what!'

If you have a disability and need accessible accommodation, you'll be guaranteed a suitable room. Email: disabilityadviser@nottingham.ac.uk

GETTING THERE

☛ By road: Nottingham, M1/J 25, A52. Sutton Bonington, M1/J24, A6, then left turn.
☛ By rail: London St Pancras, 1:50; Edinburgh, 4:30; Exeter, 4:00; Birmingham New Street, 1:30.
☛ By air: East Midlands Airport. ☛ By coach: London, 2:55; Birmingham, 1:30; Newcastle, 5:00; Exeter, 6:30.

grounds and rarely set the firmament alight with radical political action any more, but they have a caring nature apparently, expressed in the extraordinary agenda of Community Action: some 2,000 student volunteers getting involved in arts projects (drama, music), welfare projects (including prison visiting), health, education, housing, sport, environmental projects.

SPORT Nottingham teams came 7th nationally last year and claims the largest and most comprehensive inter-hall league. There is opportunity to participate at all levels in as many as 67 clubs. Facilities include three sports halls - a new sports centre was opened on the Sutton Bonington Campus in 2008, so there's now one on each of the three residential campuses. A second floodlit artificial pitch has been created at University Park. Boating (with boathouse) is undertaken on the tidal Trent. Bursaries are available.

PILLOW TALK

Freshers are guaranteed a place in halls if they receive your Preference Form by August 1. You're

NOTTINGHAM TRENT UNIVERSITY

The Nottingham Trent University
Burton Street
Nottingham NG1 4BU

TEL 0115 848 4200
FAX 0115 848 8869
EMAIL ask.ntu@ntu.ac.uk
WEB www.ntu.ac.uk

Nottingham Trent Students Union
Byron House
Nottingham NG1 4GH

TEL 0115 848 6200
FAX 0115 848 6201
EMAIL yourunion@su.ntu.ac.uk
WEB www.trentstudents.org/

*C*entred on the building in Shakespeare Street where, in 1887, the foundation stone was laid by Gladstone for University College

Nottingham, the institution later to become Nottingham University, this, the second uni in town began life as Trent Poly in 1970.

Writes Thomas Bell: 'As you may know, Trent is a former poly, now referred to as a "Modern Uni". We are often compared to the older, and by repute, better universities. This is not true across the board. For instance, my Law school runs some of the best courses around, and even Oxbridge postgrads are drawn to the department. Again, fashion and textiles courses are considered to be very good at Trent.

'We have a charity Varsity sports series with Nottingham University each year, which attracts large crowds from both universities, and whatever happens nationally [Nottingham 7th; Trent 27th last year], we usually prevail, if not so regularly in rowing, where, for a number of reasons, we get our bums paddled. Despite this, in true "Trent" style, we still go out and celebrate like good underdogs should!'

Open Days, 2011: 13 July, 17 September, 15 October. Visit Virtual Open Day at ww.ntu.ac.uk/virtualtour.

CAMPUS SITES

CITY CAMPUS Burton Street is the location of the central admin building, 'front' for a whole load of buildings in neighbouring streets, 2 mins from the action. Writes Thomas: 'The city site is by far the most exciting campus, as its right in the centre of Nottingham. A brand new tram line runs through 'Studentville', past the uni and into the town centre, terminating at the train station.'

The Students' Union HQ, with Byron Sports Hall, are here, along with the £13-million Boots Library, student residences and five of the uni's academic schools: Art & Design, Business, Law, Built Environment, and Social Sciences.

A £70 million regeneration of two buildings at City campus will be completed this year.

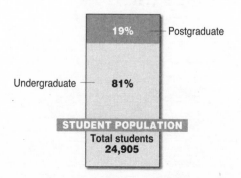

UNIVERSITY/STUDENT PROFILE	
University since	**1992**
Situation/style	**Campus in the city**
Student population	**24905**
Total undergraduates	**20245**
Mature	**33%**
International	**10%**
Male/female ratio	**46:54**
Equality of opportunity:	
state school intake	**93%**
social class 4-7 intake	**36%**
drop-out rate	**6%**

CLIFTON CAMPUS Clifton Lane, Nottingham NG11 8NS. This is a spacious, green field campus some 4 miles southwest of the city centre along the A453. It is wholly self-contained with its own SU, sports grounds and student village, and is home to Arts & Humanities, Education, Biomedical & Natural Sciences, and Computing & Informatics.

'Clifton is the smaller of the two campuses with around 5,000 students,' writes Daniel Ashley, 'and still thrives on the community atmosphere. Probably not a bad thing, as the Clifton locals are not famed for their tolerance of us.'

The Student Village has a bar and diner, supermarket, bank, refectory and bookshop. The Student Union has an active programme here and as Clifton is home to NTU's sports department, there's a pro sports hall, all-weather floodlit sports pitch, a cricket pitch, and well-equipped gym

Clifton Hall, Clifton Village, is a Georgian manor house a few minutes walk from Clifton campus and includes lecture halls for use by the faculty of Education, a resource centre, dance studio and refectory.

BRACKENHURST COLLEGE is NTU's Department of Land-based Studies near the historic town of Southwell, 10 miles north east of Nottingham, which for years has offered NTU degrees and comes with a 200-hectare farm. There's a whole Student Union set-up here, bar, sports, ents, etc and special things with clubs in town.

FEES, BURSARIES

UK & EU Fees, 2011-12: £3,375 p.a. Bursaries ranging from £540 to £1,125 are available for UK students from lower income households. There are also awards available to talented and elite athletes studying at NTU (www.ntu.ac.uk/sport). For scholarships to international (non-EU) students, see www.ntu.ac.uk/fees.

STUDENT PROFILE

There are in fact fewer part-time undergraduates at the old poly than at Nottingham University, and far fewer international students, even though Thomas writes: 'NTU is a very diverse university, with a large Asian community. There is currently a banner outside our Student Union, which reads: "Proud to be diverse".'

The two universities have about the same number of mature students. But the public school intake is more definitive: Nottingham takes 28%, NTU 7%, and NTU's take from the lower socio-economic brackets, at 36%, is far in excess of Nottingham's at 19%.

They would seem to share equally in enthusiasm and focus on what they are about, however. We had the impression that students make the most of their time here.

'The socio-economic backgrounds of a large amount of our students differs from that of a university like Nottingham,' confirms Thomas. 'If you don't achieve your full potential at A-Level, coming to NTU may well be the best thing that's happened to you. 'The one downside in my opinion is the lack of tradition and formality. Our annual Sports Excellence Ball, for example, seems to be simply an expensive lash-up, without any sort of real occasion - we gather at a hotel to eat and watch the award ceremony, perhaps throw some food about, then go on to the student union to do something you can do any other Saturday.'

ACADEMIA & JOBS

As rivals Nottingham gets into Veterinary Medicine, so a new Veterinary Nursing centre is completed by NTU on the university's Brackenhurst campus, where their land-based courses are based. The unit will offer an Integrated Veterinary Nursing Foundation Degree course.

At NTU they more students on sandwich courses than most students experiencing the real world of work as part of their courses. Courses are informed by business, industry and professional people. They have commercial partnerships with over 6,000 companies. A year 2 framework across business degrees gives students a choice to take time overseas with a partner university, complete an internship or undertake an enterprise or community project. In many cases students benefit directly from associate membership to professional institutes upon graduation. The Hive is NTU's purpose-built enterprise development centre. In the summer of 2010, 70 entrepreneurial students went straight from their final year studies into a summer school to shape plans for setting up their own businesses.

> *'Here you will meet and mix with many students from different walks of life, form a well-shaped outlook on the world, and develop skills and an understanding of people you would not get elsewhere.'*

In particular, graduates from the School of Property and Construction attract some of the highest starting salaries in the country. An architectural input brings social, political, economic, environmental features to the fore in otherwise out-and-out technological degrees.

Their European Studies, Global Politics, Politics, Political Economy, and International Studies degrees harvest graduate jobs in government administration local, regional, central.

In teaching, there's a primary school speciality,

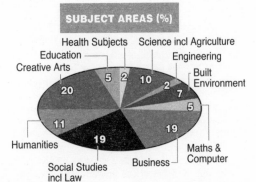

SUBJECT AREAS (%)

Health Subjects — 5
Science incl Agriculture — 2
Education — 20
Creative Arts — 10
Engineering — 2
Built Environment — 7
Humanities — 11
Social Studies incl Law — 19
Business — 19
Maths & Computer — 5

RESEARCH EXCELLENCE

% of Nottingham Trent's research that is
4* (World-class) or **3*** (Internationally rated):

	4*	3*
Health Professions	**20%**	**30%**
Environmental Sciences	**0%**	**5%**
Computer Science	**0%**	**30%**
General Engineering	**15%**	**40%**
Built Environment	**0%**	**30%**
Archaeology	**5%**	**25%**
Business/Management	**5%**	**25%**
Law	**0%**	**10%**
Social Work	**15%**	**45%**
Psychology	**0%**	**15%**
Sports	**0%**	**0%**
French	**0%**	**30%**
English	**10%**	**45%**
History	**5%**	**25%**
Art and Design	**5%**	**30%**
Media Studies	**25%**	**45%**

also advanced early years, and Design & Technology (secondary), while graduates to further education tend to come mostly from Biological Sciences and Creative Arts, then Social Sciences.

For would-be bankers from the Business School, Barclays is sponsoring the country's first retail banking degree. The BA (Hons) Business Management (Retail Banking) places employability and workplace performance at the centre of its course design. The bank and the Business School also run a BA (Hons) in Leadership. Computer Sciences is another popular route into banking.

Countrywide, law students have a choice of eight institutions where the Bar Vocational Course may be undertaken, NTU's Law School is one of them. The course is followed by a year's pupilage.

Their Art & Design Faculty is renowned for its fashion and textile courses. It also leads many into advertising, Design for Television a particular niche.

For radio and TV broadcasting, NTU's Centre for Broadcasting & Journalism is housed in the old BBC studios in Nottingham, making it the only student training centre in the UK to have access to authentic broadcasting facilities. And student media benefits from this. *Platform* is the weekly paper, which the *Nottingham Evening Post* prints for them. 'They have nothing to do with editorial, well... they sort of peruse it, nick some of our stories.' It has won many awards. The NTU student radio station is Fly FM. In 2009 they picked up 1 Gold and 2 Silvers at the Student Radio Awards and got Broadcast Journalist of the Year, an award

sponsored by Sky.

Finally, their sports provision produces more physical training instructors than any uni outside of Brighton.

SOCIAL SCENE

The Students' Union at City has a continental café bar and late-night (2 am at weekends) drinking spot, **Glo** bar, in addition to **Sub** bar, recently refurbished. At Clifton campus there's the **Point** bar and at Brackenhurst, the **Museum** bar.

'In the first week freshers rapidly form social groups. Freshers week is very well organised and provides an action-packed induction course in how to exploit the vibrant nightlife of Nottingham. The key to surviving the first term is eating well and sleeping, neither of which I did much of. My most memorable times were with the rowing team. Our weekly socials were well structured and action packed, if occasionally dangerous (beware "the post-box challenge" - bones have been broken!). These socials end up at **Ocean** nightclub with all the other sports clubs.

WHAT IT'S REALLY LIKE

UNIVERSITY:	
Social Life	★★★★
Societies	★★★
Student Union services	★★★★
Politics	**Interest low**
Sport	**42 clubs**
National team position	**27th**
Sport facilities	★★★
Arts opportunities	**Drama, art, music, good; dance avg; film poor**
Student magazine	**Platform**
Student radio	**Fly FM**
2010 National Radio Awards	**Bronze Award**
2010 *Guardian* Media	**Journalist of Year**
Student television	**Trent TV**
Venue/bars	**Glo, Sub, Point, Museum**
Union ents	**Wild**
Union societies	**76**
Parking	**Clifton good; City poor**
CITY:	
Entertainment	★★★★★
Scene	**Clubby, pubby, good arts**
Town/gown relations	**OK**
Risk of violence	**High**
Cost of living	**Average**
Student concessions	**Good**
Survival + 2 nights out	**£90 pw**
Part-time work campus/town	**Good/excellent**

ACCOMMODATION	
Student rating	★★★
Guarantee to freshers	**If pay by 30.7**
Style	**Halls, flats**
Security guard	**Some**
Shared rooms	**Some**
Internet access	**Most**
Self-catered	**All**
En suite	**Some**
Approx price range pw	**£70-£136**
City rent pw	**£50-£140**

Ocean itself is pretty nondescript, but what really matters is who you're with.'

Explains Annabel Wollen: 'Once a month we have a legendary fancy dress night called Kinki at Ocean nightclub in town, each month with a different theme. It is somewhat infamous (a bit of a religion at NTU). Also at Ocean we have a Wednesday sports and societies night called Campus. Then there's a Thursday night called DV8 at **Walkabout**. Both these mid-week nights play mainly commercial music and a big dollop of cheese is always on offer. On Fridays we hold *Flirt!* at Clifton campus and alternate between *Assault* (a rock night) and *The Tone* club (live) at City, Sub bar being transformed into a late bar, chilled out and relaxed. Finishing the week is Saturday night - *Climax* - where our City site venue is transformed into a nightclub holding 2500 people. Music policy is cheese and golden oldies downstairs with a mix of r&b and garage upstairs. All our nights are NUS only, and packed to the rafters, but on a Saturday we do allow our members to sign townies in as guests.

The Students' Union is also proving that what it has long been doing for student entertainment it can do equally well for more serious pursuits: a Community Action Group was set up, an Employment Store has grown from one small office to two massive departments that together will deal with upwards of 9,000 placements in part-time employment this year, and the SU employment skills training programme, Stride, has broken all expectations, with every programme either full or over-subscribed.

Town The city is very popular with students - see Student Nottingham. Writes Thomas: 'Nottingham is regarded as a dangerous and unfriendly place to live. This, you will find, is not entirely fair. Every city can be dangerous, and part of being 'street aware' is learning to avoid the dodgy places, read and avoid potential situations when you're out. If you don't feel so sure, there's a number of bars and clubs that only let students in during the week.'

Sport Their teams came overall 27th nationally last year. They have many TASS athletes and also a handful who represent the country - in hockey, archery and canoe. The campus already had a sports hall, fitness gym, all-weather floodlit pitches and cricket, rugby and football grass pitches, and now a development - the new Clifton Sports Centre - adds a 50+ station fitness suite, weights and stretching areas, and an innovative human performance laboratory, sports therapy clinic and athlete training kitchen.

PILLOW TALK

They accommodate qround 70% of first years; 25% live in flats and shared houses in the private sector. Not sure where the residual 5% end up. All halls are self-catered, approximately 65% of rooms are en suite.

'City site freshers are likely to find themselves in one of the many halls scattered within a mile or so,' writes Daniel, 'so it is possible to get to college both on foot or by bike. Early enthusiasm for this does tend to wane as it gets a bit colder. However, the parking facilities in City are not brilliant, and a permit must be applied for. Do this as soon as you arrive.'

At some residences limited parking is available but you will require a permit which is available from the Residence Manager. For 2010/11 the charge for UPP residences will be £200 for the year. Look out for the special parking icon.

At Clifton, the student village has 720 en-suite bedrooms with broadband access.

City site: no parking. Clifton campus: limited on campus. Permits are available to qualifying students with access issues, cost in 2010/11 was £25.

On Brackenhurst campus parking is available.

GETTING THERE
☞ By road: M1/J25/6. Good coach service.
☞ By rail: London St Pancras, 1:50; Edinburgh, 4:30; Exeter, 4:00; Birmingham New Street, 1:30.
☞ By air: East Midlands Airport 12 miles away.
☞ By coach: London, 2:55; Birmingham, 1:30.

UNIVERSITY OF OXFORD

The University of Oxford
Undergraduate Admissions Office,
Wellington Square
Oxford OX1 2JD

TEL 01865 288000
FAX 01865 270708
EMAIL undergraduate.admissions@admin.ox.ac.uk
WEB www.ox.ac.uk

OUSU
28 Little Clarendon Street
Oxford OX1 2HU

TEL 01865 270777
FAX 01865 270776
EMAIL info@ousu.org.uk
WEB www.ousu.org

VIRGIN VIEW

*O*xford is consistently in the top rankings for teaching, research and resources, and has a world-class reputation for academic excellence. Their superiority over many other universities can be seen in the collegiate system, in the tutorial teaching, and in the Oxford graduate's employability.

College life is one of the University's greatest assets. The relatively small number of students at each college allows for close and supportive personal attention to be given to a student's induction, academic development and welfare.

Oxford is one of the few universities in the world that bases its teaching on the tutorial system. Tutorials are very small group teaching, maybe one, two or three students plus a tutor. These will take place at least once a week for an hour in each subject studied, an incredible amount of individual attention and teaching from international experts in your chosen field, and you will be expected to respond. You will face rigorous challenges on a weekly basis, encouraging and facilitating your learning in a way that just isn't possible at most other universities.

Oxford claims that surveys of employers show that he college and tutorial system makes their students 'better or much better' than the average UK student at key skills, such as problem solving, leadership, and communication. 'The tutorial system will enable you to research, summarise, present and defend an argument with some of the best scholars in your subject. Under the direction of an experienced researcher, you will extend your skills and experiences through

UNIVERSITY/STUDENT PROFILE	
University since	**1096**
Situation/style	**City**
	Collegiate
Student population	**23760**
Total undergraduates	**15905**
Mature	**37%**
International	**26%**
Male/female ratio	**52:48**
Equality of opportunity:	
state school intake	**55%**
social class 4-7 intake	**12%**
drop-out rate	**1%**

practical or project work, placements or fieldwork, writing extended essays or dissertations.'

Trouble is that a lot of very bright sixth-formers want to go there, and given that they all line up with top grades, how does Oxford make its mind up who to take?

They are quite open about this. What they are looking for in applicants beyond grades are three things:

'1. Evidence that you are able to think independently; 2. Self-motivation and enthusiasm for your subject; 3. Willingness to engage with new ideas, beyond the scope of your school or college syllabus, and that you are committed to your subjects.'

So, that's done then.

Mobile Oxford (m.ox.ac.uk) provides access to information about Oxford using a web browser on your mobile phone. But you should also go along to an open day. Open Days, 2011: 6 and 7 July, 16 September.

FEES, BURSARIES

UK & EU Fees, 2011-12: £3,375 p.a. For those in

receipt of the HE Maintenance Grant, there is a bursary on a sliding scale (from £200 to £3,225) up to an income of £49,999, and a first-year 'start-up' bursary worth £875. See www.oxfordopportunity.com for full details. In addition, Oxford colleges offer various financial awards and funds to their students, including scholarships and exhibitions, awarded after the first year for excellent academic achievement, etc.

RESEARCH EXCELLENCE

4* *(World-class)* or **3*** *(Internationally rated):*

	4*	3*
Cardiovascular Medicine	45%	40%
Cancer Studies	25%	50%
Infection/Immunology	45%	40%
Hospital Clinical	35%	35%
Laboratory Clinical	40%	35%
Epidemiology	40%	25%
Health Services	20%	45%
Community Clinical	45%	40%
Clinical Psychology	15%	45%
Plant Sciences	25%	40%
Zoology	15%	45%
Biochemistry	35%	40%
Human Biol. Sciences	30%	50%
Environmental Sciences	35%	50%
Chemistry	30%	45%
Physics	20%	35%
Pure Mathematics	35%	40%
Applied Mathematics	30%	45%
Statistics	40%	50%
Computer Science	35%	45%
General Engineering	25%	60%
Metallurgy and Materials	25%	55%
Environmental Studies	30%	40%
Archaeology	35%	30%
Economics	40%	55%
Business/Management	30%	40%
Law	35%	35%
Politics	35%	25%
Social Work	20%	50%
Sociology	25%	30%
Anthropology	25%	30%
Development Studies	35%	30%
Psychology	35%	45%
Education	30%	35%
Middle EasternAfrican	40%	30%
Asian Studies	25%	30%
Russian	35%	35%
French	30%	35%
German	25%	30%
Italian	30%	30%
Iberian	15%	45%
English	40%	25%
Linguistics	10%	30%
Classics	40%	30%
Philosophy	35%	30%
Theology	30%	35%
History	35%	35%
Art and Design	30%	35%
Media Studies	20%	35%
Music	50%	25%

STUDENT PROFILE

'Oxford as a vanguard of elitism and discrimination has made the headlines countless times in the past few years. Personally, I haven't experienced any discrimination,' writes history undergraduate Rachel Cocker, 'but as a white, middle-class girl from an independent school in the North West I am not exactly a member of a minority group here.'

Rachel will tell us more, but perhaps Christabel Ashby, from a different background, may have a different story: 'I'm Christabel Ashby, I'm from London. I went to a state school, and I'm a final-year student at Keble, studying Theology. I'm not going to lie; my first few days in Oxford were terrifying. In Freshers week we were inundated with information and events. There were both the university and the college fresher fairs [presentations to freshers by sports clubs and societies], and we were forced into going out and getting drunk by well meaning second-year students. Despite this it was really easy to make friends, and after two weeks I felt as at-home and confident as if I'd been there for years.

'The nice thing about the Oxford student scene is that it is so inclusive. Whatever you're into, you are bound to find people to hang out with. You will probably meet a few people who are a bit elitist or arrogant, but I suspect that is true of any university.'

ACADEMIA & JOBS

'The myth that Oxford students have no time for a social life is false, but that we have a very heavy workload is, however, perfectly true,' continues Rachel. 'Eight weeks is a short period for a term and a lot of work is packed into it. Scientists, medics and lawyers have by far the most to do. Historians get off relatively lightly. Still, it's hard when you hear your mates at other unis talk of two-month deadlines when you're going through the weekly essay grind. It is stressful, but none of my friends have, as yet, launched themselves off Magdalen Bridge. Tutors are generally willing to give more guidance and leeway than you might imagine. At the end of every term you will be given a feedback form, and although for some this may be simply a faculty-prescribed exercise, for others students' comments have shifted the focus and structure of the course they teach.'

'All colleges have computer facilities where

TEACHING SURVEY AT A GLANCE

Avg. UCAS points accepted	**530**
Acceptance rate	**18%**
Overall satisfaction rate	**93%**
Helpful/interested staff	★★★★★
Small tuition groups	★★★★★
Students into graduate jobs	**86%**

Teaching most popular with undergraduates:
Anthropology, Biology, Computer, Creative Arts &
Design, Economics, European Languages, French
Studies, Geology, German & Scandinavian
Studies, History, Archaeology, Human & Social
Geography, Iberian Studies, Law, Medicine,
Molecular Biology, Music, Pjilosophy, Physical
Geography & Environmental Science, Physical
Science, Physics & Astronomy, Politics,
Psychology, Sociology,
Social Policy & Anthropology, Theology.

you can type up your work or check your e-mail, an Oxford e-mail address is provided for everyone upon arrival.

Oxford has some of the best libraries in the world, the state of your college library depends on its personal wealth but as the Bodleian has a copy of every book ever written, or something like it, you don't have much of an excuse for not reading that "essential" item on the reading list.'

The uni is developing a rich diversity of online resources and course materials - full details can be found at http://www.online.ox.ac.uk/. There are also little known welfare resources - a disability service, for example, even grants available from such as the Dyslexia Fund. Again, the Oxford University Resources for the Blind provide tape recordings for students with a print impairment, including dyslexia sufferers. Note-takers or readers are also available.

Oxford believes that employers recognise that their rigorous academic courses and tutorial system give graduates many transferable skills useful in employment. But they also run the Oxford Student Consultancy and International Internships that offer hands-on experience and employability skills, and work with outside organisations, from large corporations to local charities, arts and cultural organisations. For more information visit www.careers.ox.ac.uk.

Language graduates, interestingly, get more jobs than any other part of the Oxford graduate body. Mainly they go into education, publishing, TV and broadcasting, film, the civil service, public relations, advertising, social work, artistic creation, religion or politics. Languages and humanities of all sorts dominate the picture, history and philosophy graduates coming next and finding work in similar areas, though perhaps a little more in business and management.

To become a doctor at Oxford you will need the 4 or 6-year BM BCh. Oxford now stipulate that all candidates applying to read Medicine will sit the Biomedical Admissions Test (BMAT). The test is being used to assess scientific aptitude, not fitness to practise medicine (which will continue to be assessed in other ways, including interview) and focuses on scientific abilities relevant to the study of medicine. Of the three A levels you'll need Chemistry + 1 from Maths, Biology or Physics. Humanities subject welcomed.

For the degree they have retained a 3-year pre-clinical course with small group tutorial teaching (often pairs). There are regular GP visits, too, and clinical experience.

The Law Faculty has a European specialism. Non-Law graduates may opt for a 2-year Senior Status Law Degree. All candidates must sit the National Admissions Test for Law (LNAT).

SOCIAL SCENE

STUDENTS' UNION Once you've made your new-found friends, there is a reasonable social life to be had with them. A lot of it is college based; most have weekly bops. One thing Oxford seriously lacks is a central student venue, but once you venture outside the walls of your cosy college environment there are plenty of university-wide activities in which to get involved. Theatre, journalism, music, student politics and Anglo Saxon re-enactment (apparently) are all strong. *Cherwell* and *ISIS*, famous Oxford student magazines are not in fact published by the Union. *The Oxford Student* is the student newspaper, Oxide, the student radio station. Every year the Oxford University drama festival, 'Cuppers', sees around 30 productions performed, directed and often written by freshers. Hacks tend to gravitate towards the famed Oxford Union, where they can fine tune their debating and back-stabbing skills, and it is possible to infiltrate or avoid their number at will.

SPORT... 'is a big deal from football to ultimate frisbee. There are college leagues for every sport you can think of; even pool. Most colleges have their own sports ground and of course there are the university facilities down Iffley Road, the 25-metre, eight-lane Rosenblatt swimming pool has now opened.

The pool is part of the training facilities for the OU Swimming and Water Polo Clubs, but it's available for recreational use too. Most people try their hand at rowing at some point during their university career and many, many join the ranks of "boaties", consigning themselves to years of early morning outings and gruelling weights sessions. All very rewarding, especially for all who get to cheer them to victory during Eights Week, while getting pissed on Pimms.

TOWN 'There are some great pubs; the most studenty of which are the **Kings Arms** and **The Turf**, both rammed to the rafters after exams. The city is also a haven for cocktail bars, and the **Duke of Cambridge** is immensely popular for its very happy "happy hour", which lasts from 5 till 8.30pm every single day of the week. Oxford also boasts some fantastic restaurants, although some of these are so fantastically priced you might have to wait until your real Mummy and Daddy come to take you home before sampling them.

'Oxford Brookes' Union hosts live touring bands and probably the best student nights to be had in the city on Fridays and Saturdays. College balls also feature largely in Oxford life and for an average non-dining ticket you are looking at around £50. The larger balls, such as Merton in the winter and Magdalen, New, Trinity and Worcester in the summer can set you back up to £110 per person. Luckily, these only take place once every three years so a lot of people attend but one during their time here. Once you get in there, of course, everything is free.

'*Cost of living*: if you take into account that the average student here goes out at least twice a week (most people's workloads make it hard to manage more) then I would say someone with stronger self-discipline than myself might survive on £70.'

If you're a home/EU publicly-funded first-yea, you may be eligible for a bursary. Go to www.admissions.ox.ac.uk/finance/bursaries/index.shtml

'*Safety*: everything being just down the road encourages a feeling of safety, but there have been several attacks on students since I've been here. You do still need to be on your guard. Town/gown relations don't seem to be anywhere near as bad as in Durham, but there are a few unofficially designated townie pubs and clubs, which students avoid, though not through fear for their lives.'

PILLOW TALK

Colleges are responsible for providing accommodation. All will provide first year students with accommodation, most can accommodate you for at least one other year, and some can accommodate you for the duration of your course.

For freshers, most college rooms are single study-bedrooms, some of which have their own bathroom. Some colleges have 'sets', where two students share a study-living room but have their own bedrooms. All rooms are furnished; some have telephone and internet points. Exact facilities vary between colleges.

Car parking is not provided. Exact facilities vary between colleges but include a library, bar, common room, laundry facilities, computer room, sports ground and dining room, where three meals are offered every day.

Costs vary from college to college. For freshers, most college rooms are single study-bedrooms, some of which have their own bathroom.

Some colleges have 'sets', where two students share a study-living room, but have their own bedrooms. All rooms are furnished; some have telephone and internet points. Exact facilities vary between colleges, as do costs. If you were to take three meals a day in college, it might cost you £400 or more a term.

ACCOMMODATION

Student rating	★★★★★
Guarantee to freshers	100%
Style	College
Security guard	Porters
Shared rooms	Some
Internet access	Most
Self-catered	Both facilities
En suite	Some
Approx price range pw	Contact Colls
City rent pw	£85-£115

COLLEGE CAMEOS
by Caroline Rowe & Sacha Delmotte

BALLIOL
Broad Street, Oxford OX1 3BJ
TEL 01865 277777
WEB www.balliol.ac.uk
Founded in 1263, Balliol has a claim to be the oldest Oxford college and is situated right in the centre of town, so access and convenience are optimum. Balliol has very high academic standards, and is proud to boast its 'effortless superiority'. Today its main strengths lie in Classics, PPE, Physics and Philosophy. The college used to be very left-wing, which is still evident today in one of the most active JCRs in the university, and the bar being entirely student-run (only Hertford does this as well). There is also a notable absence of Balls or even formal hall.

Balliol has, however, always been very liberal, and was the first college to admit international students (today it has the highest percentage of overseas students of all colleges), and the first to allow women into Oxford academia. There is a fairly high proportion of state-school students, and social elitism is not rife, despite the existence of the Annandale Society (a pretentious, all public school gentlemen's club of sorts).

Balliol provides a JCR Pantry, which is open all day, serving breakfast until 11:30, and provides colossal portions. College ents are of high standard, rent is second lowest in Oxford and the bar is small but relaxed. There is a long-standing feud between Balliol and Trinity, orchestrated by a (rather rude) song, the 'Gordouli'. College gossip is assured instantaneous propagation via the *John de Balliol* bogsheet.

BRASENOSE
Radcliff Square, Oxford OX1 4AJ
TEL 01865 277510
WEB www.bnc.ox.ac.uk
Founded in 1509, BNC, as it is known, is renowned for its tourist-friendly location and its sporting exploits rather than for academic excellence. Rugby is very big and indeed sports in general tend to be edified, though to be fair it does have a good reputation for PPE and Law. The main social focus of the college is the infamous Gertie's Tea Bar, and it has a medium-size May Ball every summer term. BNC has a fairly low profile within the university, but is interestingly named after the brass doorknocker in hall.

CHRIST CHURCH ('The House')
St Allgates, Oxford OX1 1DP
TEL 01865 276150
WEB www.chch.ox.ac.uk
Founded in 1546, Christ Church is the biggest college (both in number of undergrads and in area), and still to this day has an (entirely undeserved) reputation of being a haven for rich Etonians and other public-school types. Typically, Christ Church students are fairly good at sport,and have the best kept and most central sports ground. The college does well academically and has a strong reputation for law with a specially dedicated library. Christ Church is also the second richest college after St John's and thus welfare and accommodation provisions are excellent, with rooms available for all your time in Oxford. The college is extremely beautiful, with extensive meadows, Oxford's mediaeval cathedral and an art gallery containing works by Leonardo da Vinci and Michelangelo. It holds a yearly impressive ball. Pembroke as its rival, not surprising as it technically owns the college. Film wise, while Magdalen has *Shadowlands*, Ch Ch can boast being the location for much of the new Harry Potter film!

CORPUS CHRISTI
Merton Street, Oxford OX1 4JF
TEL 01865 276693
WEB www.ccc.ox.ac.uk
Founded 1517, Corpus is tiny, really tiny, both in land area and in student number. This feature gives it a sense of intimacy that other colleges cannot claim, and accommodation is guaranteed for all students. Corpus excels academically and is quiet as a result of all the hard work. Recently it has introduced a new tradition, the Tortoise Race, where the Corpus reptile races against the demon

speed-machine from Balliol. Corpus puts on a small-scale Summer Event (advertised as the cheapest Oxford Ball) at the beginning of every Trinity term, but on the whole it has a low profile in the university.

EXETER

Turl Street, Oxford OX1 3DP
TEL 01865 279660
WEB www.exeter.ox.ac.uk
Founded 1314, Exeter is a compact college and is so close to the Bodleian Library it may as well be part of it. Public perception is that it contains rowdy, sport-playing types. This certainly appears to be the case as the bar is very active, with lots of cool, outgoing people, and intimate ents – the JCR is famously apathetic, and one rarely hears of political activism from within Exeter's walls. The college has a long-standing rivalry with its neighbour, Jesus, also on Turl Street.

HARRIS-MANCHESTER

Mansfield Road, Oxford OX1 3TD
TEL 01865 271009
WEB www.hmc.ox.ac.uk
Founded in 1786, there is very little to be said about this college since it only admits mature students, mostly to read an Arts degree. The college was founded in Manchester to provide education for non-Anglican students, who at the time were not allowed into Oxbridge. Following a move to Oxford, it was granted Permanent Private Hall status, and only recently (1996) become a full college. Currently the college faces long-term financial and governance problems. In 2003 they asked Derek Wood QC to review resources, particularly for history, PPE and related subjects. The upshot was to ditch history. Pleasant Gothic Revival buildings.

HERTFORD

Catte Street, Oxford OX1 3BW
TEL 01865 279400
WEB www.bertford.ox.ac.uk
Founded in 1740, Hertford has had a tumultuous past with various changes of name, owner and status over its 250-year history; it used to be a subdivision of Magdalen. Hertford is very central and opposite the ever-popular **King's Arms** pub. Hertford students really know how to party (their bar is rumoured to have the highest fiscal turnover in the university). Whether this is explained by its large population of state-school students, and the distinct Northern flavour of the undergrad body in particular, would not be PC to enquire. Altogether it is a progressive establishment and was one of the first all-male colleges to admit women and the first

to make the entrance exam optional. Students enjoy full accommodation, an excellent atmospheric JCR bar, which is entirely student run and concocts brilliant, toxic cocktails.

JESUS

Turl Street, Oxford OX1 3DW
TEL 01865 279720
WEB www.jesus.ox.ac.uk
Founded in 1571, Jesus is small, beautiful and wealthy, and has a reputation for being the 'Welsh College', which is perfectly fair since a not insignificant proportion of students come from Wales. The college bogsheet is *The Sheepshagger*. The college is quite insular and politically unmotivated. Jesubites have it easy: accommodation is excellent and hall food is cheap. Recently Jesus is feared in rugby circles, and does well in other sports too. It has a feud with Exeter.

KEBLE

Parks Road, Oxford OX1 3PG
TEL 01865 272711
WEB www.keble.ox.ac.uk
Founded 1870. Writes Christabel Ashby: 'Keble College is notable for being the only redbrick, Victorian college. It is ideally placed for town and most university facilities, and is right opposite the University parks. College facilities are good; we have phone and internet lines in every room, and all the rooms are nicely furnished. The college guarantees you two years accommodation.

'Keble is also rather traditional, there is formal hall every night, which means you wear your gown to dinner, which has waiter service. On the social side, there's a mixed bag. It has one of the largest undergraduate populations of Oxford colleges, which means there are lots of people with whom to make friends, but also means you will never know everyone, and seeing people you don't recognise all over the place can be a little disconcerting.

'Keble is sporty, there are lots of teams and clubs, and the bar is also fairly popular. Ents are predictable however, usually consisting of a live band or karaoke nights. These events happen once or twice a term. The JCR is well stocked with electronic games, pinball, table-footy and pool, and also has sky TV. Unlike some of the other colleges, however, there is no JCR shop.

'There is a strong sense of equality at Keble, both in terms of women's and men's rights and in gay/lesbian rights. The environment is welcoming and friendly to anyone and everyone, but at the same time its size means you are able to retain a degree of anonymity not possible in many of the other colleges.'

LADY MARGARET HALL

Norham Gdns, Oxford OX2 6QA

TEL 01865 274300

WEB www.lmh.ox.ac.uk

Founded 1878. LMH was the first college founded solely for women in the university. Since there was no vacant land in the centre of town, LMH is fairly far out of town, but this has resulted in the luxury of extensive gardens. The college began admitting men in the '70s, and since that day and age LMH has achieved an unparalleled male/female ratio of 1:1 at levels of college hierarchy. LMH is socially self-sufficient and has a low profile in the university. It is neither renowned for scholastic or sporting brilliance, and has no great political aspirations. Its sole reputation is for producing Thespians, who tend to hang out in cliques with other college actors (read 'actoars'). Otherwise unpretentious and not intimidating.

LINCOLN

Turl Street, Oxford OX1 3DR

TEL 01865 279800

WEB www.linc.ox.ac.uk

Founded in 1427, Lincoln is the smallest of the three colleges on Turl Street, but beautiful. The college is a rather wealthy one, which is evident from the extensive facilities provided to students: good accommodation, excellent sporting facilities, and allegedly the best hall food in the university. This comfort of college life means that very few Lincolnites emerge from their cushy environment to participate in university-wide activities, and thus charges of insularity are fair and merited. Overall, the college is a rather 'shy' one on the university scene, and is not really noted for spectacular achievement in any academic, political or sporting field. Tradition has it that on Ascension Day, Lincoln undergrads stroll around town in subfusc (formal wear) with the vicar of St Michael's in the Northgate and a gang of choristers 'beating the bounds', or thrashing at the town limits with canes. Then the students drink lots of ivy beer and toss hot pennies at the choirboys.

MAGDALEN

High Street, Oxford OX1 4AU

TEL 01865 276063

WEB www.magd.ox.ac.uk

Founded in 1458, Magdalen (read 'Maudlin') is a gorgeous college in every respect. It is one of the oldest, richest and most beautiful. Its buildings, extensive grounds (including the famous Deer Park), beautiful cloisters, and Magdalen Tower, and location on the banks of the River Cherwell are stunning, breathtaking. On May Day the choir sings from the top of Magdalen Tower and the tradition is to jump off the bridge into the river, although the police keep deciding to cordon it off. The film *Shadowlands* was shot there, and the money earned was spent on renovating certain college rooms. Accommodation facilities are second to none (everyone can live in throughout their whole student career), and some of the sets offered are simply amazing (bedroom, living room, and bathroom!). The college has a huge and lively bar, and puts on very good ents events, but is pretty insular (the **Lower Oscar Wilde Room** is often the site of debauched and drunken student carnage). Magdalen, like Christ Church, owns its own punt. It is academically successful and socially intense, but rather uninterested in political and JCR issues.

MANSFIELD

Mansfield Road, Oxford OX1 3TF

TEL 01865 270970

WEB www.mansfield.ox.ac.uk

Founded in 1886, Mansfield only obtained its college status in 1995; prior to that it was a Permanent Private Hall. It is among the smallest of colleges, only admitting about sixty undergrads every year. This leads to a very close-knit yet appreciably claustrophobic community. Due to the small size of the college many students explore extra-curricular opportunities in the university, and the college is famous for drama. The college is very poor and thus room rents are relatively high. Mansfield has a reputation for tolerance and is sometimes known as the LGB (Lesbian Gay Bisexual) college. Ents are diverse, with bops, karaokes, trips to the theatre, Laserquesting, and there is a triennial Venetian Masked Ball held in the seventh week of Michaelmas term.

MERTON

Merton Street, Oxford OX1 4JD

TEL 01865 276329

WEB www.merton.ox.ac.uk

Founded in 1264, Merton, along with Balliol and University, has a claim to be the oldest Oxford college, and is very rich and beautiful, containing the oldest surviving Oxford quad (Mob quad). The college has an undisputed reputation for being a centre of academic excellence, fuelled by SCR encouragement and a competitive spirit among the student population. Socially Merton appears to be fairly insular, and one rarely meets Mertonites around the university; in fact it would seem that Mertonites are quite dull. Nonetheless every year Merton puts on the only Christmas Ball in Oxford, on the last day of Michaelmas term, which is usually a roaring success. It is particularly popular with Freshers who are able to finish their first term at Oxford with style and panache (and a random snog perhaps!). Merton's tradition, the Time Ceremony, has existed for barely fifteen years, but is now firmly implanted in the college calendar, and for a day lifts the veil of seriousness which rests upon the college. It involves students walking backwards around Merton's Mob Quad while continuously downing port, on a particular day of each year.

NEW COLLEGE

Holywell Street, Oxford OX1 3BN
TEL 01865 279590
WEB www.new.ox.ac.uk

Founded in 1379, here's another beautiful college, and very inappropriately named too! New is one of the oldest, largest and most impressive colleges in Oxford and takes in part of the city walls, as well as a few ancient plague-heaps. Widely accepted as having the best and most beautiful student bar, New puts on great ents: the bops are legendary, and the Long Room is as much a site of drunken mayhem as the Lower Oscar Wilde Room at Magdalen, with many different societies hiring the room to throw crazy parties. New also puts on a gargantuan Commemoration Ball every three summers, described by many as the best ball in Oxford. Scenes from the Bond film *Tomorrow Never Dies* were filmed at New College, and the college has a fair share of Bond-girl lookalikes. New is particularly accomplished in musical matters: the college choir is one of the best in Oxford. New has been described as 'one of Oxford's least stressful places to live'.

ORIEL

Oriel Square, Oxford OX1 4EW
TEL 01865 276555
WEB www.oriel.ox.ac.uk

Founded in 1326, Oriel is mostly famous for its monotonous and undeniable domination of the river: it's a boatie's college. Apparently Oriel brings in students from America especially for their rowing prowess, regardless of their academic (in)abilities, and provides them with the best en-suite rooms in college and lavish free meals. Every extra year that sees Oriel come out victorious of the Summer Eights rowing race, another of its old boats is religiously burnt in the middle of their quad (that's Oxford tradition for you!). Architecturally the college is something of a rabbit warren. The distinctive front quad sees a Shakespeare production every summer, and the college is strong musically, with its own orchestra and choir. Academically very relaxed, the college reveres sport: those who can participate, do, and those who can't, support from one of the best boat houses on the river.

PEMBROKE

St Aldates, Oxford OX1 1DW
TEL 01865 276412
WEB www.pmb.ox.ac.uk

Founded in 1624, Pembroke is one of the poorest colleges in Oxford, and allegedly the college Boat Club Trust Fund is richer than the rest of the college put together! This astonishing fact holds its currency in donations from rich alumni rowers. Thus Pembroke is very strong at rowing, and the only plausible pretender to Oriel's rowing crown. In fact in the fifteen or so years of Oriel dominance on the river, Pembroke has been the only college capable of beating them once, several years ago; now the college is regularly second behind Oriel. Socially Pembroke is rather insular, has a low profile in the university, and academically it is laid back. A college rivalry exists with Christ Church.

QUEEN'S

High Street, Oxford OX1 4AW
TEL 01865 279167
WEB www.queens.ox.ac.uk

Founded 1624. Despite having a very high-profile location, right in the middle of the High, the college has a very low profile in the University; one rarely meets students from Queen's. It has some of the most obviously dramatic architecture in Oxford, ranging from the classical cupola to the UFO-like Florey building off St Clement's. Queen's is very rich and is one of the cheapest colleges to attend, offering full accommodation for all your Oxford years. There is also a particularly good library. Excluded are undergrads wanting to read Single Hons English, however, a fact unconnected with the college being a home from home to Northerners. Quirkily, Queen's has an annual dinner to celebrate the survival of an undergraduate who in 1935 was viciously attacked by a boar and defended himself by driving a tome of Aristotle into the boar's mouth.

ST ANNE'S

Woodstock Rd, Oxford OX2 6HS
TEL 01865 274825
WEB www.stannes.ox.ac.uk

Founded 1879. St Anne's, very far away from the city centre, is atypical – laid back and unpretentious and lacking in the pomp and archaic traditions of older colleges. Isolation breeds self-sufficiency, and the college has a low profile in the university. A large proportion of the undergraduate community come from a state-school background, and the college is now one of the largest in terms of undergraduate numbers. Despite being a poor college, the library has around 100,000 volumes for current use, and is one of the two largest undergraduate college libraries in Oxford. The architecture is modern and unusual for Oxford, and the gardens are pleasant in the summer.

ST CATHERINE'S (St Catz)
Manor Road, Oxford OX1 3UJ
TEL 01865 271703
WEB www.stcatz.ox.ac.uk
Founded in 1963, St Catz possesses some breathtaking architecture, much of which is Grade 1 listed. Designed by Arne Jacobsen, the famous Danish architect, a spirit of openness infuses the place, with quads having no enclosing ends. It is located just outside the tourist-infested city centre, lending it some peace and tranquillity, but is still within a convenient distance of all central facilities. St Catz has exceptional resources, including the largest student theatre in Oxford, an extensive JCR building, and a moat. It is the youngest college, and, though obviously lacking traditions, has a very friendly atmosphere. Every summer St Catz has a Summer Ball which is a big success, and good bops are laid on regularly.

ST EDMUND HALL (Teddy Hall)
Queen's Lane, Oxford OX1 4AR
TEL 01865 279008
WEB www.seh.ox.ac.uk
Founded 1278. Teddy Hall, as it is informally known, is a very poor college, and rumours abound that it has been financially helped by its close neighbour Queen's. Its main reputation across the university is for being very good at sports: men excel at rugby in particular. Despite not being one of the highest profile colleges, Teddy Hall students still manage to get involved at most levels of university life, and are particularly good at drama and music. Teddy Hall is known for being the party college, where academia is not taken too seriously, and it puts on good ents.

ST HILDA'S
Cowley Place, Oxford OX4 1DY
TEL 01865 276816
WEB www.sthildas.ox.ac.uk
St Hilda's, all-female since its foundation in 1893, voted in June 2006 to accept male students. Up until then, the college was home to the notorious, roaming 'Hildabeasts', among the most active members of the university, getting involved in many sports, societies and other extra-curricular pursuits. College buildings are bland but pleasant, and the site is on the banks of the Cherwell, with beautiful gardens adding a colourful touch to the landscape. The college is fairly poor, and facilities are limited. St Hilda's is strong at rowing. Lots of ents are put on, with something to keep the lasses happy every weekend. The bar is unexciting, despite being the cheapest in Oxford. Being next to the river, the college owns its own punts, which are free for use by St Hilda's students and their guests. The college is seldom visited by tourists, which is a good thing.

ST HUGH'S
St Margaret's Rd, Oxford OX2 6LE
TEL 01865 274910
WEB www.st-hughs.ox.ac.uk
Founded in 1886 St Hugh's is so far out (geographically) it may as well be part of another university, and the walk into the centre of town can be long and laborious, although buses are very frequent. This is both an affliction and an attraction: St Hugh's has huge grounds (including croquet lawns and tennis courts) and there is (unfortunately small and ugly) on-site space to accommodate all students. College facilities are good and social life is tumultuous and intense. Ents are good, with a large-scale bop including a bouncy castle and barbecue organised during the summer. Despite being so far out of town, St Hugh's students are reasonably involved across the university activities, especially in art and drama.

ST JOHN'S
St Giles, Oxford OX1 3JP
TEL 01865 277317
WEB www.sjc.ox.ac.uk
Founded 1555. This is the richest college in Oxford. St John's provides excellent facilities: there are financial rewards for the academically strong (1st, Norrington Table 1999): on-site accommodation (including luxurious sets and the strange honeycomb structures for Freshers) is guaranteed for everyone, there is a modern conference centre, and beautiful gardens adorn the quads. St John's is academically very strong and there is considerable pressure on students to work hard.

The college performs well in sports as well, at rugby and rowing in particular. On the social front St John's doesn't deliver quite as well: students tend to be quite dull, a fact reflected by the college bar which is very nice and spacious, but rarely alive and kickin'.

ST PETER'S
New Inn Hall Street, OX1 2DL
TEL 01865 278892
WEB www.spc.ox.ac.uk
Founded in 1929, St Peter's is a relatively new college in Oxford history, and covers very small grounds in the centre of town. Priorities here are much higher on social issues than on academic matters, and St Peter's doesn't excel at sports

either. Nevertheless students seem fairly involved around the university, and the JCR is very active. St Peter's is very poor, which is obvious from the blatant lack or inadequacy of certain facilities. The college has a reasonable bar and puts on good ents events. Every year a middle-size Summer Ball is organised.

SOMERVILLE
Woodstock Road, Oxford OX2 6HD
TEL 01865 270629
WEB www.some.ox.ac.uk
Founded in 1929, Somerville is the most recent of colleges to have gone mixed (1994) and is located just beyond the reach of annoying tourists, yet close enough to the city centre for convenience. The generally left-wing college [with some notable exceptions – this was Margaret Thatcher's college] has always been politically very active and JCR members voice their opinions loudly. Indeed, Somervillians are active in every respect of university life, and the college has a fairly high profile amongst university students. College atmosphere is easygoing though the number of political hacks and activists can sometimes be distressing. Somerville has good ents although the college bar is dull and bare.

TRINITY
Broad Street, Oxford OX1 3BH
Tel 01865 279910
web www.trinity.ox.ac.uk
Founded in 1554, Trinity is centrally located, next door to its arch-rival Balliol. The college has spacious and attractive grounds (which it leases from Balliol!) and elegant buildings. The undergraduate body is fairly small which lends to an intimate college atmosphere. Trinity used to be dominated by public-school types, but this has now changed. Accommodation provisions are good, and the college flats on Woodstock Road are regarded as among the best and poshest in Oxford. Trinity students have a high profile in the university, and are popular and involved in many activities. A Commemoration Ball is organised every three years in the summer and, on a more day-to-day basis, ents is good with fun bops, and Trinity men and women enjoy a lively and atmospheric bar.

UNIVERSITY
High Street, Oxford OX1 4BH
TEL 01865 276602
WEB www.univ.ox.ac.uk

Founded 1249. University is one of the colleges Oxford students hear the least about: it has an extremely low profile and is very quiet. This is despite the fact it is one of the oldest colleges (holding a claim, with Balliol and Merton, to being the oldest, although there is evidence that the college forged some deeds in 1381 to prove that it was founded in advance of Merton). The college is undeniably ancient, however, and very beautiful. Like St John's, it has a reputation for being full of bookworms who take life far too seriously and are unaware of the existence of the words 'fun' and 'enjoyment'.

College life is said to be a little slow, although the alleged existence of bops and a good bar do redeem it a little.

WADHAM
Parks Road, Oxford OX1 3PN
TEL 01865 277946
WEB www.wadham.ox.ac.uk
Founded in 1610, Wadham is a bastion of the left, with an even greater lefty image than Balliol. Getting involved in JCR and student affairs is a great springboard into the political limelight. It has always been liberal, and is very involved in LGB affairs: it hosts Queer Week, which culminates in an S&M and Fetishes Bop (where you get to see some quite outlandish costumes...). The college is also strong in music and drama (helped by the fact that Wadham has one of the university's only reasonably sized theatres), and the Saturday night bops are legendary.

WORCESTER
Worcester Street, Oxford OX1 2HB
TEL 01865 278391
WEB www.worcester.ox.ac.uk
Founded 1714. Worcester possesses huge and beautiful grounds, including tennis courts, sports grounds and a lake. Beautiful gardens decorate the college and provide a suitable backdrop to the medieval cottages and classic colonnade. All students are accommodated on the main college site. The college is presently enjoying some success at rowing and rugby, but is not known for any academic excellence. Lord Sainsbury was a Worcester student, thus hall food is very cheap and also very good. Every three years the college hosts a huge Commemoration Ball in the summer. Worcester is lively, fairly rich and somewhat self-contained.

OXFORD BROOKES UNIVERSITY

Oxford Brookes University
Gipsy Lane Campus
Headington
Oxford OX3 0BP

TEL 01865 483040
FAX 01865 483983
EMAIL admissions@brookes.ac.uk
WEB www.brookes.ac.uk

Oxford Brookes Students' Union
Helena Kennedy Student Centre
London Road
Headington
Oxford OX3 0BP

TEL 01865 484715
FAX 01865 484799
EMAIL obsu.president@brookes.ac.uk
WEB www.theSU.com

VIRGIN VIEW

*O*xford Brookes became the darling of the *'new university' league tables, and being based in 'that sweet city with her dreaming spires' soon found itself with a reputation and student clientele that defied placing it in the ex-poly category. If you are looking for a university still not overly demanding at entry, which offers a host of well-conceived modular courses in some interesting niche areas, and which enjoys the atmosphere of one of the world's great student cities, then Brookes might well be for you.*

A stomping 85% of its students cheered for it in the National Student Survey; its support system is such that only 7% of them will not finish the course; and 74% will find themselves with a proper graduate level job within six months of leaving.

UNIVERSITY/STUDENT PROFILE	
University since	**1992**
Situation/style	**Campus**
Student population	**18615**
Total undergraduates	**13985**
Mature	**48%**
International	**18%**
Male/female ratio	**41:59**
Equality of opportunity:	
state school intake	**74%**
social class 4-7 intake	**44%**
drop-out rate	**7%**

CAMPUS

Brookes has three sites on their Headington Campus, Marston Road, Headington Hill and Gipsy Lane and an additional two campuses, one based in Harcourt and the other in Wheatley.

The Helena Kennedy Student Centre (HKSC), the main Students' Union, is housed with teaching facilities and accommodation across the road from Gipsy Lane on the Headington Hill site, formerly the house of beleaguered tycoon Robert Maxwell, who called it the largest council house in England, which indeed it was. He never owned it.

FEES, BURSARIES

UK & EU Fees, 2011-12: £3,375 p.a. If in receipt of the HE Maintenance grant there's a sliding scale bursary according to household earnings. See www.brookes.ac.uk/studying/finance/support/ug_home. The Brookes Academic Excellence scholarship is awarded to students attaining three A-grade A levels or equivalent and is worth £2,000 p.a. See www.brookes.ac.uk/studying/finance/support/academic_scholarships.

Community Scholarships of £1,000 p.a. are available to students of partner state schools and colleges.

STUDENT PROFILE

Oxford Brookes is uncharacteristic of most recently founded universities because of its high independent school intake (26% of undergraduates). This statistical lurch towards the middle class, unusual for an ex-poly, serves to prompt the stereotypical image of the uni as a hang-out for air-

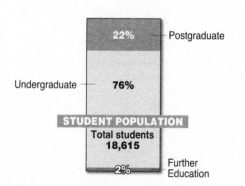

Undergraduate — **76%**

22% — Postgraduate

STUDENT POPULATION
Total students
18,615

2% — Further Education

TEACHING SURVEY AT A GLANCE

Avg. UCAS points accepted	**310**
Acceptance rate	**18%**
Overall satisfaction rate	**85%**
Helpful/interested staff	★★★
Small tuition groups	★
Students into graduate jobs	**74%**

Teaching most popular with undergraduates:
Accounting, Anatomy, Physiology & Pathology, Architecture, Biology & related sciences, Communications & Information Studies, Computer, Economics (98%), English Studies, History, Teacher Training, Law, Management, Molecular Biology, Biophysics & Biochemistry (100%), Nursing, Other Subjects allied to Medicine, Philosophy, Theology, Physical Geography & Environmental Science, Politics, Psychology, Publishing, Social Work, Tourism.

Teaching least popular with undergraduates:
Electronic & Electrical Engineering (48%).

'Brookes has an unusually varied cross section of students, which gives it a cosmopolitan outlook in everything it does. Among the more prominent groups, public-school student types are not as dominant as people suggest, although there probably is a larger public school contingent than at any other of the 1992 universities. Most ignore their fraternising and get on with doing their own thing. Whether you are from an independent school or from a state school you will undoubtedly find "your type".

'There is also a large proportion of foreign students from a huge range of countries. Ethnic minorities from the UK are also very well represented and play a large part in the overall feel of the place.'

ACADEMIA & JOBS

Writes Ed Bellany, whose brother was at Oxford: 'As Oxford University reputedly offers the best in academic traditional university courses and education, Oxford Brookes is undoubtedly the leader in vocational courses and modern university education. It offers hundreds of courses in literally everything under the sun, including Honours in Brewing and Beer Appreciation (only kidding).'

There are 8 academic schools: Arts & Humanities, Built Environment, Biological & Molecular Sciences, the Business School, the Westminster Institute of Education, the School of Technology, Health & Social Care, Social Sciences & Law.

head Sloanes who couldn't get a place at Durham. However, around 3,000 undergraduates are in fact part-time, 48% of students are mature, 44% come from the lower socio-economic orders, and 6% from the 'low participation' neighbourhood category. There is, too, a large (18%) overseas body of students. All of which prompted Giles Balleny to insist that whatever the statistics indicate re: the public-school brigade, on the ground the perception is of a rich tapestry of life.

> *'There probably is a larger public school contingent than at any other of the 1992 universities, but whether you are from an independent school or from a state school you will undoubtedly find "your type".'*

Modular joint honours degrees characterise the curriculum, and an academic year-structure made up not of terms but semesters. Ground-breaking when first launched, the modular system can be made to work to your advantage, but individuals are left pretty much to design their own courses. The undergraduate programme offers 90 single honours degrees, which may be combined appropriately to form combined honours courses. Students may also add introductory modules.

Emily Waller says: 'All the rules and regulations can be confusing, so get help if you need it. The work load is manageable, but depends on the course that you are taking. Work placements both abroad and in Britain are common.'

On many a course they push study- and work-abroad options in Europe, USA, Canada or Australia, both to widen your take on life and earn credits towards your degree. Work placement programmes and grants are available in 27 EU countries. Language skills are another focus. Classes at all lev-

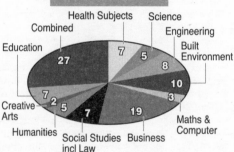

SUBJECT AREAS (%)

Health Subjects — 7
Combined — 27
Education
Science
Engineering — 5
Built Environment — 8
Maths & Computer — 10
Business — 19
Social Studies incl Law — 7
Humanities — 7
Creative Arts — 2, 5
— 3

RESEARCH EXCELLENCE

% of Oxford Brookes' research that is
4* (World-class) or **3* (Internationally rated):**

	4*	3*
Health Professions	10%	20%
Biological Sciences	5%	15%
Applied Mathematics	0%	10%
Computer Science	15%	35%
General Engineering	5%	40%
Town/Country Planning	5%	35%
Business/Management	5%	20%
Law	10%	35%
Politics	0%	20%
Anthropology	5%	30%
Psychology	0%	25%
Education	5%	25%
French	5%	30%
English	5%	35%
Philosophy	0%	0%
History	25%	40%
Art and Design	15%	15%
History of Art	15%	40%
Music	15%	20%

els are available through the Modern Languages Unit. Modules are popular in French, Spanish, Japanese and Mandarin.

'Teaching staff are generally very helpful (if you can find them),' adds Emily. 'Each student is assigned a personal tutor for their years of study.'

They advertise a kind of second-layer support system called Upgrade, a confidential study advice service where you can solicit advice on issues such as planning and writing essays, assignments and dissertations. Upgrade tutors are there to highlight areas for improvement and help you understand what your subject tutors are looking for. Students can book a tutorial at advertised times. See www.brookes.ac.uk/services/upgrade/a-z.html.

Despite all this, in the *Times Higher Education*'s Student Experience Survey Brookes students suggest the actuality is not quite as amazing as it sounds. Brookes came out around middle table for helpful/interested staff and far less well for small-group tuition. We give them 3 stars and 1 out of 5.

Continues Emily: 'There are three libraries, well stocked with up-to-date and ancient texts and an easy-to-use computerised catalogue; friendly individual subject librarians are always willing to help. The main library has over 1,000 private study desks and some group study rooms (great for catching up on gossip, if not for study!). It is open until 10.00 pm weekdays. Every student has free Internet and e-mail access, and computers are accessible 24/7.

Computer Services - in particular the help desk - are invaluable, as the network has an annoying habit of crashing (normally about five minutes before an assignment is due in!).'

They also advertise a Student Disability Service that assists with sensory and mobility impairments, dyslexia and other specific learning difficulties, mental health problems and medical conditions. A Support Worker Scheme can cover such as note-taking in lectures, reading onto tape and mobility support on campus. And there are specialist staff for deaf students. There's also extra time for exams, etc.

More than a quarter of graduates go into the health field. They educate a large number of graduate nurses, the majority SEN. There are BA and BSc degrees in Midwifery, and popular courses in Biomedical Science, Occupational therapy and Physiotherapy. Sixteen per cent of all Brookes graduates get jobs in hospitals. Public Health Nutrition, Environmental Biology, Environmental Science, and Public Health Nutrition are other degrees that take graduates into the public sector health area.

There's also a large primary teaching provision - BA Primary (Work-based) and BA Initial Teacher Training - which accounts for 9% of the graduate workforce.

In Engineering, their graduates are among the most popular with the automobile industry, and there's a particular niche in motor sport.

They are also renowned for a series of degrees in Publishing, having produced the prototype.

Estate agent/managers proliferate out of Brookes. Look at BSc Real Estate Management, also BA Business of Real Estate. Planning is big here, too: see BA Cities - Environment, Design & Development or BA City & Regional Planning. There are jobs aplenty in the construction industry from Brookes degrees. And they are management leaders in the catering and hotel trade, with such as the 4-year sandwich BSc Hotel & Restaurant Management and the two International Hospitality/Tourism Management, again 4-year sandwich BSc.

SOCIAL SCENE

STUDENTS' UNION There's an active ents programme with regular clubnights, film nights, comedy nights and termly balls. Wednesday is *Playground* (new themes and promos each week); Friday is Pleasuredome (9 pm-2 am) - 'the best sound system, lighting and dance tunes in Oxford', a mixture of styles at the main SU **Venue**, which has a capacity of over 1,200.

The main union bars based around the university are the **Harts** lounge bar, **Morals Bar** and the **Mezzanine**. Morals Bar is the home of Blitz (9 till 2 pop tunes), Chalk & Cheese (from live jazz to

WHAT IT'S REALLY LIKE

UNIVERSITY:

Social Life	★★★
Societies	★★
Student Union services	★
Politics	**Average**
Sport	**Competitive**
National team position	**38th**
Sport facilities	★★★
Arts opportunities	**Drama, music, art excellent; film good; dance avg**
Student newspaper	**OBScene**
Student TV	**Brookes TV**
Nightclub	**The Venue**
Bars	**Morals, Harts, Mez**
Union ents	**Pleasuredome, pop, jazz, comedy**
Union societies	**60**
Most popular society	**Cocktail**
Parking	**Poor**

CITY:

Entertainment	★★★
Scene	**Small, good pubs, OK clubs**
Town/gown relations	**Average**
Risk of violence	**Average**
Cost of living	**High**
Student concessions	**Good**
Survival + 2 nights out	**£70 pw**
Part-time work campus/town	**Good**

TOWN 'The night life in Oxford, always busy and full of tourists and students, is varied but expensive, even with the student discount that most clubs, pubs, bars and restaurants offer.

There is a great music and theatre scene with lots of theatres, gig venues and cinemas, but the clubbing scene is definitely mediocre (unless you are a big cheesy '60s to '80s fan). Travel around the city is regular and simple, and for women the Students' Union runs a special Safety Bus from campus to doorstep. As long as 'home' is within the Oxford Ring Road, this is a free service. Coaches run every ten minutes to London, Gatwick, Heathrow and Cambridge. Student discounts are available.

PILLOW TALK

There are nine halls of residence, all with easy

ACCOMMODATION

Student rating	★★
Guarantee to freshers	**97%**
Style	**Halls, flats**
Security guard	**All**
Shared rooms	**None**
Internet access	**All**
Self-catered	**Most**
En suite	**Most**
Approx price range pw	**£94-£137.86**
City rent pw	**£85-£115**

comedy) and the SU's rock and indie night Feedback - the best grunge, rock, metal, punk, alternative with resident DJs Sht Chaos and Hell. High above **The Venue**, the **Mez Bar** is the home of the Sunday Session.

'A free and confidential advice and counselling service is on offer, as is representation for all students on academic, personal and financial issues. Over sixty clubs and societies ensure that there really is something for everyone. Currently the most popular society is Cocktail.'

There's a monthly student paper and a TV stationthat just won two Batiobal TV Awards.

SPORT Facilities are excellent and include Astroturf, squash courts, health suite, heavy weights gym, tennis courts, rugby, football, cricket and hockey pitches, fitness trails, two boat houses and a multi-purpose sports hall for aerobics, martial arts, women's boxing, circuit training, etc. The Centre for Sport is open from 7.30 am to 11.00 pm. The university teams came 41st overall last year.

access to the university, and many, but not all, with an internet facility available in each room. Clive Booth Hall was opened last autumn, and Cheney Student Village in the spring. Although in practice most freshers live in halls, priority is given to those living farthest distant from Oxford. Facilities generally accommodate both sexes, although single sex accommodation is available on request. With the exception of two halls, it's a condition of residency not to keep a car. Seventy new en-suite self-catered rooms opened this year.

GETTING THERE

☞ By road: from north, A423 or A34 or A43; London, M40; south, M4/J13, A34. Wheatley campus, M40/J8, A418. Good coach service.

☞ By rail: London Paddington, 1:00; Birmingham, 1:30; Bristol, 1:45; Sheffield, 3:30.

☞ By air: Heathrow/Gatwick; coaches/buses will stop outside Gipsy Lane campus on request.

☞ By coach: London, 1:40; Birmingham, 1:30; Leeds, 5:30; Bristol, 4:30.

UNIVERSITY OF PLYMOUTH

The University of Plymouth
Drake Circus
Plymouth
Devon PL4 8AA

TEL 01752 585858
FAX 01752 588001
EMAIL prospectus@plymouth.ac.uk
WEB www.plymouth.ac.uk

Plymouth Students' Union
Drake Circus
Plymouth PL4 8AA

TEL 01752 238500
FAX 01752 251669
EMAIL presply-
mouth@su.plymouth.ac.uk
WEB www.upsu.com

VIRGIN VIEW

*V*alue added at Plymouth is graduate employability, supported by 12,500 industry placements each year - that is undergraduates in work
as part of their degree course, and the launch of
what they call the Plymouth Award, a 'degree plus'
accolade that attaches to your degree when you get
it and tells employers that you haven't been wasting
your time outside the lecture hall either, you've been
grooming yourself into just the kind of person graduate recruiters are after.

Of course you won't get the award if you're
that Aussie hunk, idling amidst sand, sea and
surf, the type we were once been led to believe
Plymouth specialised in (they come to study
that Surf Science & Technology degree).

Employability is the same sense of 'value
added' that you'll get at most universities these
days, but Plymouth gilds it with something a
bit different. They have just been voted number
one green university by People and Planet, and
now they say they have embedded 'sustainability'
not just in the campus facilities, but also within the curriculum. Awareness of such is what
makes you recognisably a Plymouth student
today.

This, together with the principle of a flexible

UNIVERSITY/STUDENT PROFILE

University since	**1992**
Situation/style	**Campus**
Student population	**30930**
Total undergraduates	**26840**
Mature	**50%**
International	**8%**
Male/female ratio	**40:60**
Equality of opportunity:	
state school intake	**95%**
social class 4-7 intake	**38%**
drop-out rate	**8%**

learning environment - they have 10,000
degree students enrolled at partner colleges
across Cornwall, Devon and Somerset - is
what you are buying into at Plymouth.

If it sounds attractive, they won't keep
you waiting. Their new application system
promises a decision within 14 days of receipt
by UCAS.

Students love it here - 79% of them gave
the uni their blessing in the National Student
Survey, and a mere 9% don't last the course
(2% below their Government benchmark).

Open Days: 22 June and 15 October 2011,
27 June and 20 October, 2012.

FEES, BURSARIES

UK & EU Fees, 2011-12: £3,375 p.a. There's a sliding scale bursary scheme for those eligible for the
HE Maintenance Grant. There are also sports
scholarships, and academic ones and awards for
students reading Chemistry, Civil Engineering,
Theatre and Performance, and Modern Languages.
There are also mature student and fieldwork bursaries available, and bursaries for students from
university 'compact' schools/colleges, and anyone
from the South West Peninsula region. See
www.plymouth.ac.uk/money for details. those
from the South West Peninsula region.

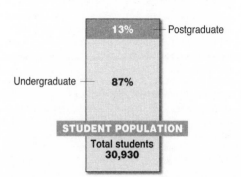

Postgraduate **13%**

Undergraduate **87%**

STUDENT POPULATION
Total students
30,930

TEACHING SURVEY AT A GLANCE

Avg. UCAS points accepted	**270**
Acceptance rate	**33%**
Overall satisfaction rate	**79%**
Helpful/interested staff	★★★★
Small tuition groups	★★
Students into graduate jobs	**71%**

Teaching most popular with undergraduates:
Accounting, Agriculture, American and Australasian studies, Anatomy, Physiology & Pathology, Biology & related sciences, Building, Civil Engineering, Economics, Electronic & Electrical Engineering, English, Geology, History, Archaeology, Human & Social Geography, Law, Marketing, Mechanical, Production & Manufacturing Engineering, Medical Science & Pharmacy, Ocean Sciences, Physical Geography & Environmental Science, Physical Science, Politics, Psychology, Sports Science.

Teaching least popular with undergraduates:
Film & Photography (52%), Fine Art (54%), Management (58%), Social Work (44%).

STUDENT PROFILE

Applicants from the UK tend to be drawn from below a line drawn south of the Midlands through Wales, Bristol and London. Many are local, mature, and more than a third are part-timers. Thirty-eight per cent come from the lower socio-economic orders and only 5% from public schools. The recruitment effort is directed to another area. There's a concerted international draw from 100 countries, including the surf cities of the world, and recently they established the Plymouth Devon International College, with a range of one- or two-year, pre-university courses designed to prepare overseas students for direct entry to courses at both undergraduate and masters level.

CAMPUSES

Plymouth looks south, out across Drake's Island and the Sound to the English Channel. It is the last big place before you tip across the Tamar into Cornwall. South Devon is rich and creamy like its cows, quite distinct from angst-ridden North Devon, up beyond Dartmoor, with its leaner stock. It is an enviable position in which to spend three or four years, what with the city too, its shops, cafés and Union Street bars and clubs. But in the end it is Devon's 600 miles of coastline, the uni's proximity to some of the country's most stunning beaches and countryside, that make it such an ideal environment for study and leisure.

ACADEMIA & JOBS

What's especially promising is the students' commendation in the *Times Higher Education*'s Student Experience Survey of their lecturers as helpful and interested. They're on a par with Bristol in this.

Lecturers are hot on study skills support programmes. There are disability services, support for dyslexia, specialist assessment for students applying for the Disabled Student Allowance, and training in the use of specialist technical equipment. They boast a higher percentage of disabled students than any other university.

Areas of curriculum strength include Nursing, Marine Sciences, Mathematics & Statistics, Health Studies, Human Biosciences, Marketing, Digital Art and Technology & Business Studies.

There is all sorts of marine interest (the Nautical School, the original fount of this uni, was established in 1862, and marine courses account for almost a quarter of Plymouth's undergraduate programme - Aquaculture, Marine Biology, Marine Navigation, Applied Marine Sport Science, Nautical Studies and Ocean Science, Civil & Coastal Engineering, Geography or Geology with Ocean Science, Ocean Exploration. Now degrees in Marine Studies appear with options to specialise in Ocean Yachting, Merchant Shipping or Navigation. And a new £20m marine facility is in prospect. What's more, the Marine Institute just took delivery of a 13-metre catamaran, and a £300,000 remote operated vehicle to boost off-shore research capabilities.

There's also a trio of Maritime Business degrees, and they have a BSc in Cruise Management, with support from Princes Cruises (hospitality, marine studies, business plus a year on a cruise liner!), directing our interest into their hospitality and tourism programme: Business & Tourism, Hospitality & Tourism, International Tourism Mgt, etc. Plymouth takes up the challenge

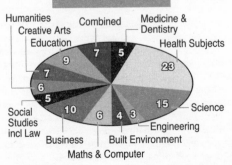

SUBJECT AREAS (%)

Humanities, Creative Arts, Education: 9, 7, 6, 5; Combined: 7; Medicine & Dentistry / Health Subjects: 5, 23; Science: 15; Engineering: 3; Built Environment: 4; Maths & Computer: 6; Business: 10; Social Studies incl Law

RESEARCH EXCELLENCE

% of Plymouth's research that is
4* *(World-class) or* **3*** *(Internationally rated):*

	4*	3*
Hospital Clinical	5%	60%
Epidemiology	5%	20%
Health Services	5%	45%
Nursing/Midwifery	10%	20%
Health Professions	0%	10%
Biological Sciences	0%	25%
Agriculture	0%	10%
Environmental Sciences	5%	45%
Applied Mathematics	0%	25%
Statistics	0%	30%
Computer Science	25%	50%
Electrical/Electronic Eng.	5%	15%
Civil Engineering	15%	30%
Mechanical, Aero., & Manufac. Eng.	0%	25%
Geography Environment	10%	40%
Business/Management	5%	25%
Social Work	5%	50%
Sociology	5%	30%
Psychology	5%	25%
Education	10%	20%
English	10%	20%
History	0%	25%
Art and Design	10%	45%
History of Art	5%	50%
Performing Arts	5%	15%

from the Devon Riviera, excellent International and European Business degrees, plenty of sea air and extra-curricular encouragement.

In preparation for the world of work, besides the work placements and the Plymouth Award mentioned above (the latter designed to recognise and celebrate student achievements outside the curriculum), students benefit from internships, award-winning volunteering schemes, international exchange programmes, dedicated career development advice and extensive cultural, sports and leisure programmes.

The Peninsula College of Medicine & Dentistry is a collaboration with Exeter University and the NHS in Devon and Cornwall, the NHS hand ensuring a strong clinical element in course design. The BM, BS Medicine degree focuses on the biological mechanisms that produce disease and its social impact. It looks very hands-on.

First undergraduate intake occurred in 2002, half in Exeter, half in Plymouth. Both unis already had successful postgraduate medical schools. One of the key points about the College is that it binds the University tighter into the regional community. Students work initially with patients in Plymouth and Exeter, then in Truro in Cornwall, finally up with the hillbillies beyond Dartmoor.

The Dentistry course is a Graduate Entry Hon BDS(4 years). The programme is designed for those with a good honours degree in a biomedical or health care professional subject, or with relevant experience of working as a health professional. The Graduate Medical Schools Admissions Test (GAMSAT) will also be required.

Plymouth also has degrees in Adult Nursing, Community Health Care, Mental Health, Midwifery, Physiotherapy and Podiatry, Dietetics, and Occupational Therapy.

Again, clinical psychologists abound from their BSc Psychology. The psychology and mental health provisions lead to an employment track record in psychotherapy.

Meanwhile, graduates in BSc combinations with their Criminal Justice Studies, Psychology, Social Policy, Social Research, Law, Sociology, Statistics, etc, find a variety of jobs, often probation officers.

The Faculty of Agriculture covers the whole gamut of courses, from Management to Nutrition, from Agriculture to Estate Management, and there's a Wildlife Conservation option too. A recent popular development has been the Veterinary Nursing & Management degree. Foresters also find jobs in quantity from Plymouth, and aspiring environmental officers enjoy a strong niche.

Cartography is another niche, which reminds us too of their popular Geography, Illustration, and Graphics courses. Meanwhile, Computer Science, which was adjudged either world-class or internationally excellent in 75% of its research provision at the 2008 nationwide assessment, accounts for about 7% of the university's graduate employment.

SOCIAL SCENE

STUDENTS' UNION The Plymouth Students' Union has undergone a refurbishment and now boasts leather sofas, Sky TV and new games machines. A new DJ bar has met expectations.

They have a dynamic ents manager, digging out new local bands, and as a result Plymouth is featured in many a uni tour. The May ball, we are told, 'attracted 3,500 to a field', actually Newnham Park, the classical Georgian manor between the outskirts of Plymouth and the foothills of Dartmoor National Park.

Friday night's *Burn* sets the scene for the weekend on the main campus - two dance rooms, 1,450 capacity - cheese and party in **Ignition**; indie to rock, ska to punk in **Illusion**. Saturday is regulation SU fare: *Flirt!* in Ignition. Comedy nights

(*Laughing Goldfish*) are especially popular, as are *Spin What You Bring* and *Open Mic Night*. *S.I.N.* is the official sports & societies DJ night, then it's on to C103 in town for more, where Wednesday is *Boogie Nights* (chart & cheese; Friday is *Total Rock* (Room 1: rock; Room 2: heavy metal).

They say the superclubs are closing down in Plymouth and students are going more for the pub music scene. The union still team up with clubs for student nights - **C103** in Union Street is the present choice, and the Plymouth **Walkabout** does good business with them.

When not clubbing and surfing, there are society activities, notably *Fly* magazine and SCAP, Community Action, which has BIG ideas, last year an international project in Thika, a small town in Kenya no less.

Now, in line with Plymouth's bid to become a 'European City of the Sea', they are planning to develop a 'cultural quarter'. The idea came simultaneously to Newcastle, and it's a good one - a conglomeration of galleries, cinemas, exhibition areas theatre space, and a café. The first building, due to open in 2007, will be a base for the Faculty of Arts and a new home for the Plymouth Arts Centre.

SPORT What is this degree in surfing? 'This is the first academically rigorous surf science course in the world,' boasts Dr Malcolm Findlay of the Institute of Marine Studies. The first year dwells on oceanography, surfing materials and business studies. The second moves uncontroversially into areas like human biology and human performance, but in the third year you develop your own specialism.' Head for the beach presumably. Course code is C6J6.

Back on campus £850,000 has been invested in a fitness complex with squash courts and resistance and cardiovascular training equipment, and over £70,000 has gone into new boats and dinghies for the University's own Diving & Sailing Centre.

There's national/world-class water-sport - sailing, diving, surfing, windsurfing, power-boating, wakeboarding, canoeing and waterski. A fleet of dinghies and yachts provide sailing opportunities. Plymouth is the only UK uni to have its own diving and sailing centre. Students can learn to dive professionally as part of their course (selected disciplines only) or take a recreational diving course, which is open to all students.

There's also the usual land-based team stuff, including a partnership with Plymouth Albion

> '*Among the Frequently Asked Questions on the accommodation web site, is, "I have lots of surfing equipment - where can I store it?"*'

Rugby Club, professional training, facilities and work placements available. Teams overall came 45th nationally last year - most popular club is soccer, though it was their American football squad that was named 'Team of the Year' by the British Collegiate American Football League last year.

TOWN Plymouth - destroyed during the war and rebuilt at a low point in British architecture - has been designated second poorest ward in Europe, but you wouldn't know it since it has won huge EU investment. There's a surfeit of accommodation which costs upwards of £40 per week, you can walk anywhere, it is a safe, friendly, smiley place. When the sun shines it is unbeatable, the beach is 10 minutes away, and when it doesn't shine, maybe the snow on the nearby moors is not so bad an option.

Like nearby Exeter, think huge shopping centre and **Barbican**. The Barbican is waterside, the olde worlde bit of town - boats, fish and tourists, but more to the point, pubs, clubs and restaurants. Arts-wise, there's the **Theatre Royal**, which had the Royal Shakespeare Company in residence

WHAT IT'S REALLY LIKE	
UNIVERSITY:	
Social Life	★★★★
Societies	★★★
Student Union services	★★★★
Politics	**Interest low**
Sport	**47 clubs**
National team position	**45th**
Sport facilities	★★
Arts opportunities	**Drama, dance, music, art avg; film poor**
Student magazine	**Fly!**
Nightclub/bars	**Ignition, Illusion**
Union ents	**Party, cheese, indie**
Union societies	**78**
Most popular society	**Football**
Parking	**Non-existent**
CITY:	
Entertainment	★★★★
Scene	**Clubs, pubs OK**
Town/gown relations	**Poor**
Risk of violence	**Average**
Cost of living	**Below average**
Student concessions	**Average**
Survival + 2 nights out	**£70 pw**
Part-time work campus/town	**OK**

ACCOMMODATION

Student rating	★★★
Guarantee to freshers	**50%**
Style	**Halls, flats**
Security guard	**None**
Shared rooms	**None**
Internet access	**All**
Self-catered	**All**
En suite	**Most**
Approx price range pw	**£78.59-£127**
City rent pw	**£55-£95**

lawyers, personally...and get in quick! Note, all medical students are guaranteed an offer of a place in halls for their first year of study. There are mixed-sex halls, flats and houses, all self-catering.

Mary Newman hall, with 157 en-suite rooms, opened four years ago. In addition, 350 en-suite rooms are now available on campus in the new Faculty of Education development. Francis Drake Hall opened on campus in 2008, but it's not for exclusive use by freshers.

Car parking for freshers: none in halls. Parking permits for approved accommodation (shared houses) through city council.

when we were there, and the alternative Drum Theatre for more progressive fare.

If you're seriously into painting, go west, down to St Ives, to the 'Tate of the South West' .

PILLOW TALK

You are guaranteed a room in halls if you come more than 25 miles away from the campus at which you'll be studying, provided it's your first choice uni and your application for a halls place is received before July 9. In fact, there are even more ifs and buts, so you'd better speak to them, or their

GETTING THERE

☛ By road: M5, A38 Exeter, Plymouth; Newton Abbot, A38, A383; Exmouth M5/J30, A376. Good coach services to Exeter and Plymouth.

☛ By coach to Plymouth: London, 4:40; Bristol, 2:30; Exeter, 1:05. Exeter: London, 4:00.

☛ By rail to Plymouth: London Paddington, 3:30; Bristol Parkway, 3:00; Southampton, 4:00; Birmingham New Street, 4:00. Exeter from London Paddington, 2:30; Bristol Parkway, 1:30; Birmingham New Street, 3:00.

☛ By air: Exeter or Plymouth City Airports.

UNIVERSITY OF PORTSMOUTH

The University of Portsmouth
University House
Winston Churchill Avenue
Portsmouth PO1 2UP

TEL 02392 848484
FAX 02392 843082
EMAIL info.centre@port.ac.uk
WEB www.port.ac.uk

Portsmouth Students' Union
Cambridge Road
Portsmouth PO1 2ET

TEL 02392 843640
FAX 02392843667
EMAIL student-union@port.ac.uk
WEB www.upsu.net

VIRGIN VIEW

Portsea behaves like an island, it has its own microclimate, slightly warmer than nearby Brighton or Bournemouth, as it sits snugly behind the Isle of Wight. For centuries, because of its strategic position, it was an important naval base, but now the focus is moving away from the military, the old naval dockyard giving itself to a pleasure zone of shops, nightclubs, bars, called Gun Wharf.

What once we detected as a military ethic in the university's 'Code of Student

UNIVERSITY/STUDENT PROFILE

University since	**1992**
Situation/style	**City campus**
Student population	**21605**
Total undergraduates	**17265**
Mature	**36%**
International	**15%**
Male/female ratio	**54:46**
Equality of opportunity:	
state school intake	**95%**
social class 4-7 intake	**33%**
drop-out rate	**8%**

TEACHING SURVEY AT A GLANCE

Avg. UCAS points accepted **270**
Acceptance rate **19%**
Overall satisfaction rate **85%**
Helpful/interested staff **★★★★**
Small tuition groups **★★★**
Students into graduate jobs **62%**

Teaching most popular with undergraduates:
Accounting, American & Australasian Studies, Biology & related sciences, Business, Civil Eng.,.Chemical Eng., Economics, Electronic & Electrical Engineering, English Studies, European Languages, Finance, Geology, History, Human & Social Geography, Law, Marketing, Maths & Statistics, Medical Science, Medical Technology, Pharmacology, Toxicology & Pharmacy, Physical Geography & Environmental Science, Physical Science, Politics, Sociology, Social Policy & Anthropology, Sports Science, Tourism.

Teaching least popular with undergraduates:
Social Work (55%), Fine Art (51%).

Discipline' seems like a distant memory now - though there remains an active OTC (Officer Training Corps), and a high input of graduates into the defence arena from a variety of departments. Today, however, military-style disciplines have been sublimated in a caring ethos, modern, civilian, and maybe a slip laden with PR.

For Portsmouth added value lies in 3 principles: 1. Students first - They put the teaching and development of undergraduate students first, and feedback consistently indicates the students appreciate the friendliness and approachability of their lecturers and the support offered by people across the university. Portsmouth was equal with

Nottingham, Edinburgh, Liverpool and Sussex in the *Times Higher Student Experience Survey on this count.*

2. *Professional learning - Half of their students are on courses which lead to professional accreditation. Many more take ones that involve practical work. The uni serves up vocational fare true to its roots, which lead us back to 1869, foundation year of Portsmouth & Gosport School of Science & Art. It was 100 years later that the college became Portsmouth Polytechnic, before receiving its Royal Charter as a university in 1992.*

3. The Student-friendly waterfront City - *Portsmouth is a compact city, modern, urban, historical, with green spaces and a beach, and there's a genuine community feel. No need for a car - just as well, for they aspire to being a green university too.*

How to get in? Portsmouth recognises that 'student potential is not always to be seen within formal academic qualifications. We take a range of factors into account from predicated grades to personal statements to help us with considering candidates.

Eighty-five per cent of students affirmed their devotion in the National Student Survey last year and this; around 8% drop out.

Open Days, 2011: 6 and 9 July, 7 September, 12 and 22 October.

CAMPUS

The main **Guildhall Campus**, dotted around the city centre, has undergone extensive redevelopment and the establishment of a University Quarter, which has a European, café-style feel to it. There are so many students marauding about that it seems not so much town as university precinct.

FEES, BURSARIES

UK & EU Fees, 2011-12: £3,375 p.a. Students whose family residual income is £25,000 or below receive a bursary of £900; £600 if between £25,001 and £32,000; £300 (non means tested) is payable to students who attended one of their local colleges or sixth forms. Care Leavers Bursary - £1,500 per year. Foyer Residents Bursary - £1,500 per year. Global Outreach: Access to Learning (GOAL) is a new bursary scheme for 2011 entry: 10% reduction for students studying on a full-time course with annual fees of £9,600 or more - see www.port. ac.uk/international.

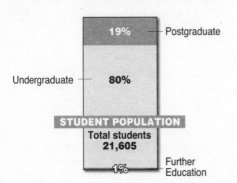

Postgraduate 19%
Undergraduate 80%

STUDENT POPULATION
Total students
21,605

Further Education 1%

STUDENT PROFILE

There's a part-timer body equal to 24% of the student pop.; 37% are mature and it has always been a predominantly male corpus - currently the gender split is 54-46. They tend to recruit from the south of England. For many, Portsmouth is the local university. There is a high state-school intake, and 31% of the undergraduate population come from sections of society new to university. Given the unpractised element, their drop-out rate of 8% should suggest there's something to stay for.

Support for the new uni intake is as good as they claim. 'There's a full-time counselling service,' a student tells me. Why? 'Students find it hard at this...at university, money problems, pressures. People think being at university is easy. It is not. I am the only child of five in my family to have gone to university. It wasn't part of the culture of my family. I have struggled here, had to get jobs. People have this concept of university, students getting drunk all the time, having a good time...I have heard about that, but never experienced it.'

ACADEMIA & JOBS

Faculties are Humanities and Social Sciences; Science; Technology; Environment; and Business.

Says the uni: 'We are known for Science, particularly Sports Science, Biomedical Science, Psychology and Maths.'

The Faculty of Creative & Cultural Industries has particular strengths in Architecture; Animation; Film and Media; Business; Management and Law; Criminology and Forensics.

A £9m dental outreach building opened in 2011 to train dentists, dental technicians & dental nurses together as part of a team. Dentists in

RESEARCH EXCELLENCE		
% of Portsmouth's research that is **4*** *(World-class) or* **3*** *(Internationally rated):*		
	4*	3*
Health Professions	15%	40%
Environmental Sciences	5%	40%
Applied Mathematics	15%	60%
Computer Science	5%	20%
Mechanical, Aero., & Manufac. Eng.	5%	40%
Geography Environment	5%	25%
Business\Management	5%	30%
Psychology	0%	25%
European Studies	15%	30%
Art and Design	0%	10%

their final year at King's College London are involved. There is an ever-increasing focus on health. In the last research assessments, 55% of Portsmouth's research provision was in the area of Allied Health Professions and adjudged either world-class (4 stars) or internationally excellent (3 stars). A £4.5million ExPERT Centre opened recently, manned by computerised mannequins, which breathe oxygen, drool, secrete fluids, blink, bleed and even react to drugs injected into their bodies. The centre trains students in biomedical sciences and healthcare professionals and has two simulation suites (operating theatre and hospital ward).

> *'It was a really nice summer's day and I saw the cafés lining the streets. It looked beautiful. I love it here. I came here shy and now I am going into PR!'*

As with dentistry, there's a tie-up with Southampton University to train student nurses to work alongside trainee pharmacists and trainee radiographers, and so on. Health subjects, such as nursing and radiography are highly rated. The School of Pharmacy & Biomedical Sciences is recommended by both teaching assessments and employment data. There are degrees in Pharmacy, Pharmaceutical Science, and Pharmacology.

Clinical and educational psychologists also find jobs in number from here. The BSc Psychology is accredited by the British Psychological Soc., and if you get at least a second class degree you've taken the first step to becoming a chartered psychologist. There's also BSc Psychol. with Criminology. Many graduates find careers with the police and the probation service. One little gem is the Institute of Criminal Justice Studies,

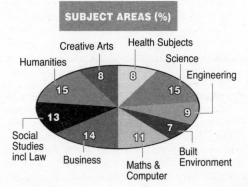

SUBJECT AREAS (%)

Creative Arts 8
Health Subjects 8
Humanities 15
Science 15
Engineering 9
Social Studies incl Law 13
Business 14
Maths & Computer 11
Built Environment 7

whose work on counter-fraud, benefits fraud and so on, has brought it links with TV's *Crimewatch*. Crime author PD James opened a library extension in January 2007 and a 'mock courtroom' opened recently in the new School of Law.

They are commercial & business law specialists. The single honours degree is a 3-year or 4-year (sandwich) LLB with various possible adjuncts: Criminology, European Studies, International Relations, Business, and there are two BA degrees with Languages or Business English.

Generally, top recruiters from Portsmouth are the NHS, central and local government, National Probation Service, IBM (Applied Maths scored highest in the research assessments and their computing degrees are very strong, they are massive in software engineering and systems analysis).

Now the uni has Purple Door Recruitment, an agency working in collaboration with local and national business, which offers work experience and career opportunities.

Languages are another particular strength, useful in finding employment - 45% of research in European Studies was either 4-star or 3-star at the recent assessment; they shine at Russian/Slavonic/East European languages. One student in five takes a language course and around 1,000 go abroad for part of their course. French achieved a near perfect teaching score.

The Business School has moved into a £12m building on campus. Accountants do well here. There's a range of BA degrees with Business, e-Business, and Business Law. Then there's Accountancy Studies or Accountancy & Financial Management for students with sufficient experience or qualifications to miss out on Year 1 of a regular accountancy degree.

A recent addition to the degree portfolio is faculty of Creative and Cultural Industries, working out of refurbished facilities for media studies and art and design. There's even a facsimile newsroom to service a the Journalism degrees.

Graduates get jobs as designers, illustrators, set-designers and film/video producers from here. There are Photography, Video Production and various Film Studies degrees, and facilities include broadcast TV studios and a digital development laboratory.

They produce a number of architects, too. Causing a stir is the BA Hons Architecture which comprises 50% design projects and 50% taught courses. It earns exemption from Part 1 RIBA. Likewise, property and construction employment markets like employing Protsmout quantity surveyors in particular. A dedicated degree has been replaced by BSc Property Development with Quantity Surveying. There's also a good employ-

WHAT IT'S REALLY LIKE	
UNIVERSITY:	
Social Life	★★★★
Societies	★★★
Student Union services	★★
Politics	**Average**
Sport	**40 clubs**
National team position	**24th**
Sport facilities	★★★
Arts opportunities	**Plenty dance, music, film**
Student magazine	**Pugwash**
2010 *Guardian* Awards	**Runner-up Writer of the Year**
Student radio	**PURE FM**
Student TV	**UPSU TV**
Nightclub	**LUX**
Bars	**Waterhole, CO2, Embassy**
Union ents	**Rock, cheese, r&b, comedy**
Most active societies	**People & planet**
Parking	**Poor**
TOWN:	
Entertainment	★★★
Scene	**Good: pubs, clubs**
Town/gown relations	**Good**
Risk of violence	**Low**
Cost of living	**Average**
Student concessions	**Excellent**
Survival + 2 nights out	**£70 pw**
Part-time work campus/town	**Average**

ment record for civil engineers and construction engineer/managers. The B/MEng Civil Engineering is accredited by the appropriate Institute.

There's a traditional tie-up with the navy, excellent career prospects with the army and a good number of jobs, too, for defence operatives and equipment engineers. The Institute of Maritime Heritage Studies preserves the tradition, it's based in an old boathouse in the naval dockyards area. Portsmouth is of course famous for being the site where the Mary Rose is docked.

Finally, there are BSc degrees in Sports Development, Sports Science, Water Sports Science.

STUDENT SCENE

STUDENTS' UNION The SU building once gave them a 2,500 capacity. The nightclub, **LUX**, alone could take in 1,100 and chill-out bar **CO2** a further 500. But they just closed these down in favour of a social learning space. Never mind, there's the **Waterhole** (500) still, and enough clubs in Portsmouth to make amends. Regular ents are

Purple Wednesdays, *Skint* (Saturdays) and *Let's Get Quizzical* on Sundays.

Top of the ents menu are their mammoth balls - including Presentation Ball for Purples (full/half colour awards: sport is big here), various societies' balls, Graduation, and so on.

Media-wise, students are active with monthly magazine, *Pugwash* - they picked up the runner-up gong for Writer of the Year at the *Guardian* Awards in 2010, and Pure Radio has been enjoying its most popular year with daily Internet broadcasts. Now, too, UPSU TV is up and running online.

SPORT Men's sports teams are consistently high in the BUCS league. Geographical position gives them special potential - sailing (larks and lasers), windsurfing and canoeing. Applications for scholarships in hockey, rugby, swimming, water sports, gymnastics and netball are encouraged. Over 40 clubs support a recreational intramural programme offering opportunities to play fun competitive sport within friendship groups.

TOWN The new 170m Spinnaker Tower is already a major British landmark, looming over the buzzing **Gunwharf Quays** designer shopping area with its numerous restaurants, bars and nightclubs. The Historic Dockyard is one of the top 10 heritage attractions in Britain, while the city centre will soon be transformed by a £350m project to confirm its position as the south coast shopping and leisure choice.

Student and singer Genna Hellier says the nightlife was part of the reason she opted for Portsmouth: 'Also, it was a really nice summer's day and I saw the cafés lining the streets. It looked beautiful. I love it here. I came here shy and now I am going into PR! I never did any sport and now I work out every day. This union here provides amazing sporting opportunities.

'Gun Wharf is really nice,' Genna went on, 'all the London-based clubs are here. There is no rivalry between locals and students. It is a very safe place to live. Music is especially good here. The local theatre is the **Theatre Royal**, nice little theatre in the **Guildhall**, often used for student pro-

ductions. The uni also built **Wiltshire Studios**, where a lot of student productions are done.'

There's a bountiful supply of clubs, cafés and wine bars in the Guildhall area. Popular too are **Liquid & Envy** on Stanhope Road (was the Territorial Army Drill Hall before it took a £5-million facelift). It has hosted some big acts - from Tinie Tempah to Calvin Harris. Other student hang-outs, such as **Tiger, Tiger** (Vodka Island on Mondays), **Walkabout** (£1.50 drinks on Tuesday) and **V Bar** (£1 shots all day every day), hit the spot. The club scene ranges from cheesy handbag to razor-tuned, techno beats.

PILLOW TALK

Only around two-thirds of fresher UK and EU undergraduates get beds, so get in early. If you don't get a place with them, then the uni will sort you out: 'It is our philosophy to care all the way through.' Campus is wireless and all halls have free broadband. A web-based e-intro programme will help you 'hit the ground running', they say. Plans are afoot for a new 600-room hall for 2013. Meanwhile, the private rental market is good.

GETTING THERE
☞ By road: A3(M), 2 hours from London.
☞ By rail: London Waterloo, 1:30; Bristol Parkway, 2:15; Birmingham New Street, 3:30; Sheffield, 4:45.
☞ By coach: London, 2:30; Exeter, 6:45.☞ By air: Southampton Airport.

ACCOMMODATION

Student rating	★★★★
Guarantee to freshers	**66%**
Style	**Halls, flats**
Security guard	**24-hr security**
Shared rooms	**Some**
Internet access	**All**
Self-catered	**Most**
En suite	**Most**
Approx price range pw	**£75-£119**
City rent pw	**£70-£80**

QUEEN MARGARET UNIVERSITY

Queen Margaret University
University Drive
Edinburgh EH21 6UU

TEL 0131 474 0000
FAX 0131 474 0001
EMAIL admissions@qmu.ac.uk
WEB www.qmu.ac.uk

Queen Margaret University Students' Union
Musselburgh
Lothian EH21 6UU

TEL 0131 317 3400
FAX 0131 317 3402
EMAIL union@qmu.ac.uk
WEB www.qmusu.org.uk/

VIRGIN VIEW

*Q*ueen Margaret University set out in 1875 as the Edinburgh School of Cookery, when any sort of further education for women was unusual. The original lectures took place before huge audiences in the Royal Museum in Chambers Street, but it was in fact peripatetic in nature, teaching staff in those days went out with mobile gas and paraffin cooking equipment to give programmes of public lectures and demonstrations all over Britain, literally from the Shetlands to the Channel Islands.

In 1930 a new name, The Edinburgh College of Domestic Science, gave it authenticity as a seat of academic learning . In 1972, following the introduction of a range of new courses, came the big break and it changed its name again, this time to Queen Margaret University College, the QM part a deliberate attempt to take it away from its image as a college of domestic science.

Soon it was located at four sites in Edinburgh. The main Corstorphine campus, out near Edinburgh Airport in the grounds of a former stately home, was home to Applied Consumer Studies, Communication & Information Studies, Hospitality & Tourism Management, Management & Social Sciences, Dietetics & Nutrition, Health & Nursing, and Speech & Language Sciences, which just shows how one thing can lead to another.

The second site lay to the northeast of the city centre, just off Leith Walk, in one of the most characterful parts of the city, to the northeast of the centre, just off Leith Walk, where, as a boy, Robert Louis Stevenson

UNIVERSITY/STUDENT PROFILE	
University since	**2007**
Situation/style	**Campus**
Student population	**5045**
Total undergraduates	**3870**
Mature	**52%**
International	**18%**
Male/female ratio	**23:77**
Equality of opportunity:	
state school intake	**95%**
social class 4-7 intake	**37%**
drop-out rate	**14%**

stood and stared at the great ships in the Western Harbour, listening to the sailors as they pulled on their ropes, his imagination fired with thoughts that would later produce the novels Kidnapped and Treasure Island. Queen Margaret even had a hall of residence named after him, possibly because one of the college's founders was one Louisa Stevenson, who may have been a relation. The Leith site was home to another academic dimension of the college, Occupational Therapy, Physiotherapy, Podiatry, and Radiography.

There was also a site near Edinburgh's Haymarket Station, a Business Development Centre, which provided a training and consultancy service to the business community, and the Gateway Theatre, actually on Leith Walk, once a repertory theatre and more recently the Edinburgh base for Scottish Television. This was to be its base for a degree in Drama, which looked at first like something of a tangent to an otherwise distinctive organic development, but drama is one of those interests which can also benefit students and impart personal skills that would be useful whatever a student's course. It was certainly a popular move: 'The opportunities for drama are excellent,' a student told us, 'now that we have our own Drama Department, theatre and studio.' It is still on the curriculum today.

In the late 1990s when we came upon Queen Margaret for the first time, sixth-form careers teachers said to us: 'People who choose QM mostly do so with a specific career in mind.' It was a vocational college, but with a wide range of subjects. Everyone was interested enough to wonder where next

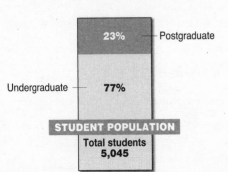

STUDENT POPULATION
Total students
5,045

23% — Postgraduate
Undergraduate — 77%

TEACHING SURVEY AT A GLANCE

Avg. UCAS points accepted	**312**
Acceptance rate	**14%**
Overall satisfaction rate	**68%**
Helpful/interested staff	★★★
Small tuition groups	★★
Students into graduate jobs	**68%**

it would go: 'Queen Margaret is making a big push towards Media and Business Studies,' said another; 'also the professions supplementary to Medicine, Physiotherapy and so on...'

Everything they did seemed to be done with purpose. The Business Development Centre now offered an ideal link to the industry for Business degree development and graduate employment. And that house of drama in Leith Walk had by this time become a major venue for the International Edinburgh Festival: a better shop window for QM would have been hard to find.

Thus did Queen Margaret, 132 years after its inception, come to the latest and most notable of its many transformations. In January 2007, it was granted full university title, and it changed its name to 'Queen Margaret University'.

CAMPUS

This latest transformation occasioned another, that of a 35-acre site at Craighall, East Lothian, from low grade farm land into landscaped parkland. QM has uprooted from Edinburgh. The new Musselburgh campus opened in Autumn 2007 and is located on the east side of the city, by Musselburgh. The site is bordered by the main east coast rail line to London and the A1. It also neighbours the city by-pass.

Campus is environmentally friendly and will leave less of a carbon footprint than Peter Pan. With its learning resource at its centre, it includes student residences, a Student Union building (social spaces, a café, an events area and a games room), indoor sports facilities and all weather surfaces, a variety of catering outlets, a shop and landscaped gardens.

It is a 15-min. walk to Musselburgh, which has a racecourse, a theatre, shops, bars and cafés. Also nearby is the Fort Kinnaird shopping complex, with a cinema and entertainment complex. Edinburgh is but 6 minutes away by train.

The relocation provoked a negative reaction after there was a delay in completion of the building of the campus and Drama students were stranded at the already sold Gateway Theatre for several months.

Students who studied at the Edinburgh college sites could be forgiven for feeling sad to uproot. The new campus, however friendly, has hardly had time to bed in. It is exceptionally well served by bus and rail from the city, but students are perched on farmland really nowhere, and the last train is at 11.15 p.m.

Still these ruffles are as nothing surely to what has been endured and overcome to get thus far.

FEES, BURSARIES

Fees for English, Welsh, Northern Irish: £1,820 p.a. Local nationals go Scot free.

STUDENT PROFILE

'Fifty-two per cent are mature students, 78% are female, and 38% are part-time.

ACADEMIA & JOBS

What is on offer is what its history has been preparing it for: 'At Queen Margaret University,' they say, 'we offer a wide range of undergraduate and postgraduate courses in the areas of healthcare; drama and the creative industries; media, communication and sociology; and business and enterprise. We also have a number of continuing professional development (CPD) courses, which will be of interest to anyone who is wishing to update their current professional skills.'

Naturally the library is not extensive yet, more of a resource that will find books for you. But Edinburgh is at hand.

SOCIAL SCENE

It is all wonderfully new, the SU, its café a 'flexible venue', with a capacity of between 150 and 250 tops, but they have license problems: nothing later than 1 a.m. will be allowed. Freshers live in halls

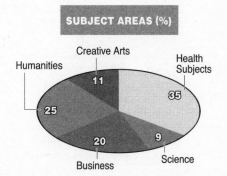

SUBJECT AREAS (%)

Creative Arts 11
Humanities 25
Health Subjects 35
Business 20
Science 9

RESEARCH EXCELLENCE

*% of Queen Margaret's research that is
4* (World-class) or 3* (Internationally rated):*

	4*	3*
Health Professions	**0%**	**5%**
Business/Management	**0%**	**5%**
Linguistics	**10%**	**30%**
Drama	**0%**	**0%**
Media Studies	**10%**	**30%**

on campus, so there are people around, but no great ents yet, but there is work space for campaigns, sports, societies and welfare volunteers, once things get going.

A bar and the café are open Monday to Wednesday 11-11, Thursday to Friday 11am to 1am. Saturday and Sunday the bar is closed.

So what goes on of an evening? They say it's the usual pub quiz, themed events, live music, karoke, open mic nights, and big balls: Halloween, Christmas and the end of term Grand Ball.

SPORT Alongside the SU is a multi-purpose sports hall, a fitness suite, an aerobic studio and an outdoor all-weather sports pitch. In addition, a trim track runs around the site.

PILLOW TALK

800 brand new single study en-suite bedrooms in self contained flats for three to six students.

Parking is not available for students staying in on-campus accommodation.

GETTING THERE

☞ By road: cars can access the campus via a slip road off the A1 southbound, between the exit for Newcraighall/Craigmillar and the Old Craighall Roundabout.

☞ By bus: the No. 30 Lothian bus goes directly from Princes Street into the campus and runs approximately every 10 minutes.

ACCOMMODATION

Student rating	★★★
Guarantee to freshers	**100%**
Style	**Halls, flats**
Security guard	**All**
Shared rooms	**Some**
Internet access	**All**
Self-catered	**All**
En suite	**All**
Approx price range pw	**£97.50-£103**
City rent pw	**£58-£86**

☞ By train: the new campus is located right beside Musselburgh rail station. From Waverley Station to Musselburgh Station takes 6 minutes. Trains from West Lothian and Stirlingshire call at Newcraighall Station, which is 15/20 minutes walk from campus. For details, see www.firstgroup.com/scotrail/content/timetables/index.

• •

QUEEN MARY, UNIVERSITY OF LONDON

Queen Mary, University of London
327 Mile End Road
London E1 4NS

TEL 0207 882 5555
FAX 0207 882 5588
EMAIL admissions@qmul.ac.uk
WEB www.qmul.ac.uk

Queen Mary College
Students' Union
432 Bancroft Road
London E1 8031

TEL 020 7882 5390
EMAIL president@qmsu.org
WEB www.qmsu.org

VIRGIN VIEW

*Q*ueen Mary, a constituent college of the *federal University of London, and once known as Queen Mary & Westfield, arose out of the merger (in 1989) of two colleges: Westfield College, a 19th-century pioneer in higher education for women, and Queen*

Mary College, founded in 1885 and located at the People's Palace in Mile End Road, ideally situated for its essential purpose, namely to educate the East End poor. It is situated still in Mile End Road today. A later, medical foundation arose out of a merger in 1995 between the Royal London School of Medicine & Dentistry in Whitechapel and St

Bartholomew's Hospital Medical School at Chrterhouse Square EC1, between Barbican and St Paul's, now QMW's Medical School. Medical students undergo their clinical training at the Royal London in Whitechapel and Barts in West Smithfield.

True to its working class roots, in June 2010 Queen Mary agreed a new Widening Participation Strategy for 2010-15, focused on raising less advantaged students' aspirations and attainment through mentoring schemes, master classes, evening revision sessions, and a programme of non-residential summer schools. It became co-sponsor (with the Drapers' Company) of the Drapers' Academy School in Havering, and lead educational partner of the St Paul's Way Trust School in Tower Hamlets. It also support the Centre of the Cell, a bioscience education centre in the medical school, a resource for schools to stimulate awareness and understanding of bioscience and the careers to which it can lead.

What they look for in applicants to the University beyond grades is a 'commitment to the subject, research of the subject beyond the curriculum, and suitable work experience'. And you will need these along with high grades, because outside the charitable work this is a major player in higher education. Queen Mary graduates are in the top ten for the highest starting salaries in the UK.

FEES, BURSARIES

UK & EU Fees, 2011-12: £3,375 p.a. There's a bursay of £1,129 for those in receipt of the full Maintenance Grant and £901 if in receipt of the par-

UNIVERSITY/STUDENT PROFILE	
University since	**1915**
Situation/style	**Ciampus**
Student population	**14025**
Total undergraduates	**10950**
Mature	**28%**
International	**23%**
Male/female ratio	**49:51**
Equality of opportunity:	
state school intake	**86%**
social class 4-7 intake	**37%**
drop-out rate	**10%**

tial Grant. There are a number of college-wide and department-based awards usually given at the end of an academic year through the recommendation of the head of department. See www.qmul.ac.uk/undergraduate/financialsupport.

STUDENT PROFILE

'Integration between medical students and the rest of the college leaves a lot to be desired,' writes Kieran Alger, 'the two groups preferring to indulge in separate activities, the medical students enjoying their own bar, for example, and playing for separate sports teams while the main body of students mixes well, regardless of subject.'

As at other medical schools, the medical students sharply increase the public school quota and give QMW a state/public school ratio akin to Reading's or Southampton's, Warwick's or York's. The Mile End Road student population is another story. 'Queen Mary proper is a cultural melting pot,' agrees Kieran - 'a fascinating blend of overseas students, a large ethnic contingent and UK residents,' and a 37% draw last year from the lower social classes, 4 to 7. There's also a large overseas student contingent - they draw from some 100 countries worldwide, reflecting the multi-cultural character of the area as it is today. Central to this strategy is a Study Abroad programme. Languages are to the fore throughout the curriculum, and are rated highly.

CAMPUS

'QM, with its modern architecture, is one of the few universities to combine the class of the well established with the youth, vigour and dynamism of an ex-polytechnic set in the heart of the multi-cultural hotchpotch which forms the East End, home of imports, the cloth trade, Phil, Grant and the Kray twins,' continues Kieran. 'From jellied eels at Spitalfield's Market to chicken balti in one of Brick Lane's curry houses, this area caters for a huge range of tastes. The combination of Canary

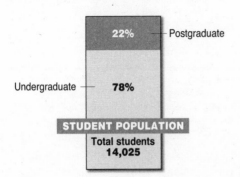

Postgraduate 22%

Undergraduate 78%

STUDENT POPULATION
Total students
14,025

Wharf Tower dominating on one side and the trendification of the E1, E2, and E3 postal areas is causing a surge in social and cultural activity. The East End, with its fashionable gangster land history and eerie Jack the Ripper connections, is the place London's affluent young professionals want to live.'

The **Mile End Camps** in Mile End Road, an extension east of Whitechapel Road, is the £100m hub: cafés, bars, Student Union, and canal-side student village.

The **Whitechapel Campus** is for the Barts & London School of Medicine and Dentistry, ranked top in London and tucked behind the Royal London Hospital opposite Whitechapel tube. The Queen Mary BioEnterprise Innovation Centre opened here in 2010, so there is a growing network of world-class clinical, teaching and research resources.

The Charterhouse Square campus is 5 mins walk from Barts (the hospital), which is itself home to the Genome Centre

There's also a postgrad Law Centre at Lincoln's Inn Fields.

ACADEMIA & JOBS

The top areas of employment for graduates of Queen Mary are hospitals and other human health activities, banking, dental practice, specialist retail (could be anything from old books to pharmacy), publishing, recruitment and personnel, the civil service, accountancy, higher education, community & counselling activities, general retail, some sort of financial activities, hotels & restaurants, and telecommunications. Software consultancy and supply, radio and TV, and engineering design consultancy lurk not far behind. But really these do well delineate the Queen Mary graduate.

Mostly it's about health - 38% of all graduate

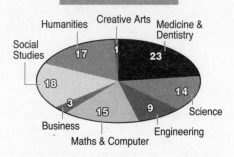

SUBJECT AREAS (%)

Humanities 1, Creative Arts, Medicine & Dentistry 23, Science 14, Engineering 9, Maths & Computer 15, Business 3, Social Studies 17, Humanities 18

jobs here come out of the Medicine and Dentistry degrees. The Medicine degree, a 5-year BM BS (Medicine, Surgery), stresses clinical method and communication skills and the experience of the patient in the community, and there's a significant element of problem-based learning (small-group explorations of particular scenarios). First 2 years at the Mile End campus, final three at the Royal London Hospital, Whitechapel Campus. There's a 4-year graduate entry, too. To get in you will need Chemistry and Biology at AS and one or other of them at A level. Two science A levels (out of Chemistry, Biology, Physics and Maths) required. One of them must be Chemistry or Biology. The third may be a non-science (General Studies and Critical Thinking excluded). The AS and A levels must be taken within a two-year period. If you can understand that lot you deserve to get in. UKCAT will also be needed.

The dental degree is a 5-year BDS plus a B/MEng Dental Materials. Like Medicine, it made a fine showing in the research assessments - 75% of the work was adjudged world-class or internationally significant.

After health it doesn't much matter whether you are looking at Economics, Business, Maths, or even Physical or Biological Sciences, destinations seem to be in banking, accountancy, and financial activities of some sort.

The Computer provision finds graduates jobs in telecommunications and various programming activities, and the Design & Innovation degrees make their mark on the design front.

Publishing is interesting because there is no dedicated publishing degree at its root but it has been a popular destination. Mostly this is the preserve of Language graduates.

Languages, history, politics and literature crop up time and again in joint honours degrees. For example, history may be studied as a single hons of course, but then they offer you History &

TEACHING SURVEY AT A GLANCE

Avg. UCAS points accepted	**340**
Acceptance rate	**13%**
Overall satisfaction rate	**86%**
Helpful/interested staff	★★★
Small tuition groups	★★
Students into graduate jobs	**72%**

Teaching most popular with undergraduates:
Biology, Chemistry, Computer, Drama, Economics, Electronic & Electrical Engineering, English Studies, Finance, Germand & Scandinavian Studies, History, Human & Social Geography, Iberian Studies, Law, Linguistics, Communications, Mechanical Engineering, Media Studies (97%), Other Languages & Area Studies, Physical Science, Physics & Astronomy, Politics.

RESEARCH EXCELLENCE

% of Queen Mary's research that is
4* (World-class) or 3* (Internationally rated):

	4*	3*
Cancer Studies	15%	70%
Hospital Clinical	15%	65%
Epidemiology	30%	50%
Health Services	30%	35%
Psychiatry	10%	30%
Dentistry	25%	50%
Biological Sciences	5%	35%
Human Biol. Sciences	20%	45%
Physics	15%	35%
Pure Mathematics	10%	50%
Applied Mathematics	10%	40%
Statistics	10%	30%
Computer Science	25%	50%
Electrical/Electronic Eng.	15%	35%
General Engineeringg	10%	35%
Metallurgy and Materials	15%	40%
Geography Environment	25%	50%
Economics	30%	55%
Business/Management	15%	40%
Law	20%	40%
Politics	5%	40%
Russian	20%	20%
French	10%	45%
German	5%	35%
Iberian	25%	35%
English	40%	30%
Linguistics	25%	55%
History	30%	30%
Performing Arts	50%	40%

Comparative Literature, History & German Literature, History & German Language, History & Politics. Again, instead of Media Studies you have Journalism & Contemporary History degree, and Languages and History.

They are offering you an opportunity to explore inter-faculty connections and interactions within humanities and cultural traditions. The QM curriculum is a rich cultural resource, well suited, for example, to serious publishing or indeed to investment banking, where a wide-ranging take on the world pays dividends.

Politics and history get together beyond the curriculum in the Mile End Group (MEG), whose emphasis is on the worlds of Westminster and Whitehall, past and present. Contributions from individuals with inside knowledge of the workings of government has informed a seminar series attracting increasingly high profile speakers.

It took the last national assessment of Britain's research provision to make us aware of what all this meant to QM's standing in the world of higher education. Suddenly, from 48th position, Queen Mary rose to 13th nationwide, with 60%, 70%, 80%, even 90% of the subjects submitted by her adjudged world class and internationally excellent.

Drama illustrates the point well: 50% of their research into Drama is also world-class and 40% international standard and it is a result of this rich inter-faculty cultural approach: 'Drama at Queen Mary provides a study of performance in a variety of cultures and historical periods...[it] offers a practical and theoretical investigation into the ways in which drama can be used in different settings - art galleries, schools, prisons, warehouses and museums, as well as theatres, across the UK and internationally. Through a grounded exploration of the act of performance, you are encouraged to become a scholar-artist with your own interests and expertise.'

At QM 'vocational' doesn't just refer to getting a job. It has a more profound ring to it than at all our new universities, which bandy the word around so. QM, it seems, is an education for life.

SOCIAL SCENE

The medics have their own union - BLSA (Barts & the London Students' Association), with activity centred on a new bar/nightclub at Whitechapel campus. There's also **Bart's Bar**, close to Bart's Hospital in Charterhouse Square (where there is also a swimming pool, squash, tennis and badminton courts). Regular high jinks are the Association Dinner, the Christmas Show, Burn's Night and the sporting cup finals. There's a flourishing drama society - plays, a Christmas Show, a production for the Edinburgh Fringe - a Gilbert & Sullivan Society, a choir and orchestra, and of course Rag. Otherwise, they bounce around at Toga nights, Star Wars night, Austin Powers Night, and Mummies and Daddies Night. I guess Doctors & Nurses Night is simply 'too day-time' to compete.

At main non-medical Mile End Road campus there's **Drapers Bar** and club, Drapers a stunning style bar in the evenings, stacked with state of the art sound and lighting system. *Friday Night Drapers* - *FND* - is the hottest night of the week in the club, with different themes each time playing the best in chart classics, commercial r'n'b and club bangers to get you into the mood.

Otherwise, it's QM's sponsored *Jailbreak 2011*, which is as popular as it is in 40 other universities. You have 24 hours to get as far away from QM as possible without money. Blag your way onto cars, trains, boats, planes to - Amsterdam? Jamaica? China?

No stranger to student media awards, *CUB*, was

WHAT IT'S REALLY LIKE

UNIVERSITY:

Social Life	★★
Societies	★★★
Student Union services	★★★
Politics	**Apolitical**
Sport	**19 clubs**
National team position	**86th**
Sport facilities	★★★
Arts opportunities	**Drama excellent**
Student magazine	**Cub**
Student newspaper	**QMessenger**
Student television	**QM TV**
Nightclub	**Drapers Club**
Bars	**Drapers Bar**
Union ents	**FND**
Union societies	**52**
Most active siocieties	**Islamic Soc**
Parking	**None**
CITY:	
Entertainment	★★★★★
Scene	**Wild, expensive**
Town/gown relations	**Average-good**
Risk of violence	**London**
Cost of living	**High**
Student concessions	**Good**
Survival + 2 nights out	**£100 pw**
Part-time work campus/town	**Excellent**

SPORT Sports fields are at Chislehurst. 'Sports are abundant,' Kieran writes, 'from rock climbing, netball and fencing, to the somewhat more comfortable pastimes of rowing and rugby. The football club is of a particularly high standard, as is the women's football team. Collegiate London Uni delivers many an opportunity for battle.'

PILLOW TALK

There are currently 2,500 bedroom places in mixed sex self-catering residences on or near the Mile End Campus, at the Whitechapel Campus (Floyer House) and at the Charterhouse Square Campus (Dawson Hall). With the completion of the award-winning Westfield Student Village, the main

ACCOMMODATION

Student rating	★★★
Guarantee to freshers	**100%**
Style	**Halls, flats**
Security guard	**Secure**
Shared rooms	**Some**
Internet access	**Most**
Self-catered	**All**
En suite	**Some**
Approx price range pw	**£92-£202**
City rent pw	**£100+**

founded in 1947, and only recently transformed into a glossy 64-page monthly magazine. Brilliant design, interesting content. Then there's *QMessenger*, the fortnightly 16-page newspaper. Not to mention *The Paper*, the organ responsible for the *DIY Guide to Shop;lifting* that caused such a furore in the press last February. The newspaper was put together with money from the Centre for Ethics and Politics at the college's School of Business and Management. Claimed variously as 'satirical', 'irresponsible', and 'Marxist propaganda', the offending item actually included thieving tips and came a cropper.

There's a clubs and societies resource centre that pulls such things together.

College is now the largest self-contained student campus in London. The Village has a restaurant, launderette, central reception and 24 hour security on one site, creating a really lively community. No parking, apart from moving in and out days. Special arrangements for students displaying an authorised blue disabled sticker.

GETTING THERE

☛ By Underground: QMW, Stepney Green (District, Hammersmith & City) or Mile End (+Central line). The Royal London, Whitechapel tube (East London, District, Hammersmith & City lines); nearest Bart's is Barbican. St Paul's (Central).

THE QUEEN'S UNIVERSITY, BELFAST

The Queen's University of Belfast
University Road
Belfast BT7 1NN

TEL 00 44 (0) 28 9097 3838
FAX 00 44 (0) 28 9097 5151
EMAIL admissions@qub.ac.uk
WEB www.qub.ac.uk

Queen's University Students' Union
University Road
Belfast BT7 1PE

TEL 028 9097 3106
FAX 028 9097 1375
EMAIL studentsunion@qub.ac.uk
WEB www.qubsu.org

VIRGIN VIEW

*T*he Queen's University Belfast, Northern Ireland's leading educational institution, has its origins in the Queen's College, Belfast, founded in 1845. There is a traditional Oxbridge-style reputation, with good lines into the professions, medicine, dentistry, the City and law.

A model of enterprise. Queen's were the Times Higher Education's *Entrepreneurial University of the Year* in 2009, having pioneered a model of entrepreneurship education embedded in the curriculum.

Jewels in the crown include the 1.2 million volume McClay Library, which opened in 2009 in superb surroundings. Also a facility for its international students, the £1.3 million International and Postgraduate Student Centre, opened last year, a space for study, group work and socialising, and the Seamus Heaney Centre for Poetry, a living breathing tribute to our greatest living poet.

Students are a happy crew, 85% raised their hats to the university at the latest National Student Survey. But don't expect an easy ride in. Mature students returning to study after a significant break may meet with modified entrance targets, but, say Queen's, 'these would not apply to applicants who have studied A-level or equivalent qualifications continuously since leaving school.'

Indeed more than grades will be required. 'In all cases evidence of independent study skills are important and for vocational courses evidence of motivation and commitment together with a knowledge of what the chosen career entails, should be demonstrated.'

Open Days, 2011: 8 and 9 September.

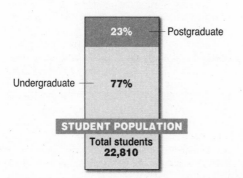

Undergraduate	**77%**
	23% — Postgraduate

STUDENT POPULATION

Total students
22,810

CAMPUS

Set a few kilometres from the city centre in a so-called 'safe' area of Belfast, the campus encompasses the Botanic Gardens and Ulster Museum. Areas around Queen's University, Stranmillis and Botanic Avenue are now busier than ever and spilling over into the once isolated city centre.

Writes Laura Cattell: 'The big red buses that pass by Queen's every few minutes are packed with camera-happy tourists snapping a shot of the redbrick Lanyon hall. The impressive building (apparently modelled on Oxford University's Magdalen College), is at the heart of the city campus and though few actual lectures take place in the building it's the focus for academic and ceremonial life at Queen's. Set in the southern and leafier part of Belfast, most of the departmental buildings are housed in the Georgian terraces along University Square, opposite Lanyon hall or in the larger more modern Ashby Hall further along Stranmillis Road. As a student, most of your social life will be based in this area - from Eglantine to Botanic Avenue. The Student Union is located opposite the Lanyon buildings and as with most 1960s university structures it's not architecturally stunning, but it has everything you need - from banks, second-hand bookshops, convenience stores and a laundry, to cafés, bars, toilets and a nightclub. Although much of Belfast has been affected by the troubles in recent years this part of the city remains largely untouched by sectarianism.'

FEES, BURSARIES

UK & EU Fees, 2011-12: £3,375 p.a. There are £1,100 bursaries for those with household income up to £19,203 and £550 for those earning £19,204 to £24,203. The Experience Bursary Award provides £110 up to £34,203 earnings. £1,000 STEM scholarships are awarded to students gaining 3 As at A-level (or equivalent) and studying science, technology, engineering or maths. There's a range of other scholarships too, including travel scholarships for students from outside Northern Ireland. www.qub.ac.uk/directorates/AcademicStudentAffairs/AcademicAffairs/ScholarshipsAwards/

STUDENT PROFILE

Queen's claims to be one of the most socially inclusive universities in the United Kingdom. It consistently out-performs national benchmarks in attracting students from poorer backgrounds. Perhaps they should do more for the beleaguered English public school boy and girl who find themselves victims of discrimination too. Certainly there are some opportunities for them here. For example, Queen's Uni's medical school is one of the best in the world, and the application acceptance rate has a history of accommodation.

Otherwise, most of the student population is local, and 29% are part-timers. Almost all that come here had a state school education.

ACADEMIA & JOBS

The 2008 Research Assessment Exercise identified areas of world-class research in all disciplines at Queen's, including engineering, medicine and the humanities, from creative writing and poetry to the design of new catalysts for cars; from conflict resolution and peace studies to vascular biology and its implications for vision science; from cognition and culture to renewable energy; and from

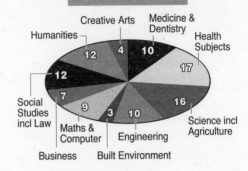

SUBJECT AREAS (%)

Humanities — Creative Arts — Medicine & Dentistry — Health Subjects — 12 — 4 — 10 — 17 — Social Studies incl Law — 12 — 7 — 9 — 3 — 10 — 16 — Maths & Computer — Engineering — Science incl Agriculture — Business — Built Environment

drug design and synthesis to green chemistry.

Their Institute for Electronics, Communications and Information Technology (ECIT) has been demarcated as the UK Innovation Knowledge Centre for Secure Information Technologies (CSIT). Their Centre for Cancer Research and Cell Biology (CCRCB) has been designated a Centre of Excellence by the Cancer Research UK and the National Cancer Institute in the USA.

'Academically,' Laura says, 'Queen's is Northern Ireland's best university and lies in the top three of Ireland's higher education institutions. It is still overlooked by many students in mainland Britain not only because of its location, but also because of its lowly ranking alongside U.K institutions. It is let down by a few weak departments, but this is counteracted by other world-class departments: Medicine, Engineering, English and Politics.

'There is a thriving literary scene, enlivened by the excellent teaching and research record of the English department. The School of English has some of the best academics in their field and is of course well-known for being the *alma mater* of Northern Ireland's most celebrated poets: Seamus Heaney and Paul Muldoon.'

Queen's is an artistic hub, home to Belfast's International Festival and to Northern Ireland's sole arthouse cinema in the Queen's Film Theatre, and to the region's newest museum, the Naughton Gallery. The University runs a host of musical events, including an annual international festival of Contemporary Music. Courses in drama and film studies underpin its cultural contribution and the Seamus Heaney Centre for Poetry reinforces the university's reputation as a world literary force.

'Famous-Seamus has also given his name to several buildings around campus and is an occa-

---

TEACHING SURVEY AT A GLANCE

Avg. UCAS points accepted	**370**
Acceptance rate	**17%**
Overall satisfaction rate	**85%**
Helpful/interested staff	**★★**
Small tuition groups	**★**
Students into graduate jobs	**70%**

Teaching most popular with undergraduates:
Aerospace Engineering, Anatomy, Physiology & Pathology, Anthropology, Archaeology, Biology & related sciences, Business, Chemical Process & Energy Engineering (100%), Chemistry (100%), Computer, Dentistry (96%), Drama, Economics, English, Food Studies, Geographical Studies, History. Languages, Management, Maths & Statistics, Mechanical, Production & Manufacturing Eng., Medicine, Nursing, Pharmacology, Toxicology & Pharmacy, Physical Geography & Environmental Science, Physics & Astronomy, Politics, Psychology, Subjects Allied to Medicine, Theology.

Teaching least popular with undergraduates:
Music (61%), Philosophy (59%).

sional visitor at the university,' writes Laura. 'The Heaney Centre, found at the back of the School of English, organises regular literary events - most of which are free and usually boast free wine as an incentive (if you need one!). Recent guests to the centre have been Jackie Kaye, Nick Laird, Ali Smith, Paul Durcan and Terry Eagleton. There's also a lively English Society and several reading and writing groups.'

The academic framework consists of 21 large schools within 3 faculties: Arts, Humanities & Social Sciences; Engineering & Physical Sciences; and Medicine, Health & Life Sciences. It is too early to say how successful the reorganisation will be, though there have been criticisms about the organisational sense of the reshuffling of some schools into super-schools.

In 2010 students were anything but complementary about the helpfulness of staff and their interest in them. They expressed their view in the *Times Higher Magazine's* Student Experience Survey. They actually came last, with City University and the University of Westminster. It was a sharp reverse from the previous year, and possibly a blip, though overall it dropped 40 places in the national poll.

There are niche areas in abundance in the curriculum. For example, their post-conflict degrees, MA in Violence, Terrorism and Security, MA in Comparative Ethnic Conflict, BA in International Politics and Conflict Studies. Then there are the courses which explore the history, language and politics of Ireland, for example Irish Politics, Irish History, Irish Studies, Irish and Celtic Studies, Irish Translation Studies, English-Irish Writing, Postcolonial Studies in Context. Queen's offered the first undergraduate degree in PPE (Politics, Philosophy and Economics) in Ireland, and they are known too for their specialist BSc in Actuarial Science and Risk Management, MSc in Risk Management and Financial Regulation, MSc in Business Economics

In addition, the School of Psychology offers an inspired MSc in Political Psychology, a growing sub-field on the borders of psychology and political science, and the School of History & Anthropology offers courses in Ethnomusicology, which explores the social and cultural dimensions of world music. The School of Geography, Archaeology & Palaeoecology meanwhile offers an MSc in Heritage Science and an MSc in Dating and Chronology, and Queen's School of Law teams up with the National University of Ireland Galway to offer a unique 'cross-border' perspective: LLM in Human Rights (Cross Border), and LLM in Human Rights and Criminal Justice

RESEARCH EXCELLENCE

% of Queen's Belfast's research that is
4* *(World-class)* or **3*** *(Internationally rated):*

	4*	3*
Cancer Studies	10%	40%
Hospital Clinical	10%	35%
Laboratory Clinical	5%	25%
Epidemiology	5%	35%
Dentistry	5%	60%
Nursing/Midwifery	10%	30%
Health Professions	15%	45%
Pharmacy	15%	40%
Biological Sciences	5%	25%
Agriculture	5%	25%
Chemistry	5%	40%
Physics	10%	40%
Pure Mathematics	5%	40%
Computer Science	15%	45%
Electrical/Electronic Eng.	20%	40%
Civil Engineering	20%	55%
Mechanical, Aero. & Manufacturing Eng.	15%	50%
Town/Country Planning	10%	20%
Geography/Environment	10%	40%
Archaeology	25%	30%
Business/Management	15%	40%
Law	25%	35%
Politics	10%	40%
Social Work	20%	35%
Sociology	20%	35%
Anthropology	35%	20%
Psychology	5%	25%
Education	10%	40%
French	5%	45%
German	5%	10%
Iberian	15%	40%
Celtic Studies	10%	20%
English	35%	30%
Classics, Ancient History	20%	10%
Philosophy	5%	60%
History	15%	45%
Performing Arts	15%	40%
Music	35%	35%

(Cross Border).

Students across the curriculum are encouraged to develop entrepreneurial skills. Their Careers, Employability and Skills Unit (CES) was ranked 7th in the UK Top 30 universities for student engagement by the 2010 High Fliers Research. Career management programmes are embedded within the academic curriculum and, where appropriate, integrated with Personal Development Planning (PDP) and the Personal Tutor System. The Degree Plus Award gives

WHAT IT'S REALLY LIKE

UNIVERSITY:

Social Life	★★★
Societies	★★★
Student Union services	★★★★
Politics	**Yes**
Sport	**Competitive**
National team position	**93rd**
Sport facilities	★★★
Arts opportunities	**Cinema excellent; theatre poor**
Student newspaper	**The Gown**
Venue/bars	**Speakeasy, Bunatee, Bar Sub, etc.**
Union ents	**Shine**
Live venue capacity	**1,000**
Union societies	**100**
Parking	**Adequate**

CITY:

Entertainment	★★★
City scene	**Clubs, pubs, arts**
Town/gown relations	**Generally OK**
Risk of violence	**Average-high**
Cost of living	**Low**
Student concessions	**Good**
Survival + 2 nights out	**£65 pw**
Part-time work campus/town	**Average**

official recognition of employment friendly skills and experiences gained in the course of extra-curricular experience, skills such as teamwork, leadership, communication and commercial awareness. In 2010 some 400 Queen's students graduated with Degree Plus.

SOCIAL SCENE

STUDENTS' UNION The Students' Union has had a £9 million refurbishment. There are various SU pleasure zones - the plush **Speakeasy Bar** with big screen sport, pub quizzes, Playstation challenge and hedonistic nights on the pull, the subterranean **Bunatee Bar** and intimate venue, **Bar Sub**, **Mandela Hall** (capacity: 1,000, one of the best live venues in Belfast, home to the *Underground* and the Comedy Network) and **Varsity** (just round the corner from the Union buidings).

Writes Laura: 'The Union is a hub of activity during term time and the long opening hours mean you can always pop in to grab something to eat or drink or even to buy some paper to print those essays on... Every night there is something going on.'

A typical offering at the Speak is Wednesday's *Franchise* (electro, funk, rock and roll: drinks £1.80), Thursday's *RADAR* gigs (local bands and talent - see www.qubsu-ents.com), and Friday's *Good Friday*, with DJs from the Friends of Jesus Sound System.

Every so often the big Saturday night is *Shine* - infamous house night. Also watch website for gig listings. Altogether the union building can take 2,500 for entertainments.

The Snooker Room, relic of the original 1967 Union, is something else, and Queen's are often British University Pool Champions. Once a favourite haunt of 'a young hustler named Alex 'Hurricane' Higgins, and exhibition venue of Jimmy White, Joe Swail and Peter Ebdon

Students are highly politicised, with a strong focus on Northern Ireland politics, and on student issues. The Union is generally characterised as nationalist and left of centre.

Student media has risen phoenix-like from the ashes in recent times. *SU Magazine* is a colourful freebie, four per year, 2,500 print, 5,000 downloads. It was judged 'Best Magazine of the Year' and 'Best Design and Layout' at the Irish National Student Awards in Dublin 2008. Queen's Radio is the only student radio station currently operating in Northern Ireland and broadcasts 24/7 over 1134 MW (AM) and online at www.queensradio.org.

Students have a range of 150 clubs and societies to choose from, with everything from Athletics to Amnesty International, Canoeing to Chess, Gaelic games to Rugby and much more. Enterprise SU

ACCOMMODATION

Student rating	★★★
Guarantee to freshers	**100%**
Style	**Halls, flats**
Security guard	**All**
Shared rooms	**None**
Internet access	**All halls, most flats**
Self-catered	**All**
En suite	**Most halls, some flats**
Approx price range pw	**£67.77-£96.61**
City rent pw	**£51-£68**

supports students who have ideas for business, social enterprise and voluntary or charitable projects, through its Student Business Clinic. The unit also hosts a number of events and activities such as the Headstart Enterprise Programme, Money + workshops, CV sessions, guest speakers, creativity workshops, competitions and much more.

SPORT Underway is the Physical Education Centre

(PEC), a £13 million project to enhance Queen's outdoor sporting facilities. Ptherwise, they have two swimming pools (diving, subaqua, water polo and canoeing facilities), conditioning rooms, squash courts, badminton, basketball, tennis courts, volleyball, handball, hockey, netball courts, two judo squares, cricket nets, a purpose-built mountain wall and facilities for gymnastics, athletics, fencing, golf, karate, bowls, yoga and archery, seventeen pitches for rugby, soccer, Gaelic, hockey, hurling, camogie and cricket, net-ball and tennis courts, a floodlit training area and an athletics arena where the Mary Peters Track is situated.

Opportunities for golf at Malone Golf Club (3 miles away), sailing at Belfast Lough and Lough Neagh, waterskiing at Craigavon, gliding and para-chuting at Magilligan, mountaineering in the Mourne mountains, caving in Fermanagh and rowing on the nearby River Lagan.

PILLOW TALK

Queen's has recently invested £45 million to develop new self-catering accommodation in Elms Student Village, a 10-minute walk from the main campus. The Treehouse is at the heart of Elms Village, with a shop, bar, **The Lounge**, laundry and ATM. There is a Student Support reception attended by Community Youth Workers.

ays Laura: 'All the room facilities such as internet connections and en-suite bathrooms are excellent. If you're lucky enough to get a place in any of the university-owned houses then Mount Charles just off Botanic Avenue or Guthrie house on Fitzwilliam Street are the best of the bunch.

'In general, though, living in privately-owned accommodation is much cheaper so most students move out once they finish the first year. Most live in South Belfast, along or off the Lisburn or Ormeau Road and rent per month is around £200 a month or less. Stranmillis, just a ten minute walk from the campus, is the most sought-after area, though naturally as a result it's a bit pricier - all to be expected if you want a BT9 postcode.'

GETTING THERE

☛ An hour by air from London, with at least 24 flights a day each way.

STUDENT BELFAST – THE CITY

TENSIONS

Town/gown relations are good and local businesses tend to recruit heavily from the university. Recent tension in the Holylands between students and res-idents has meant that the university comes down very hard on any students thought to be displaying 'anti-social behaviour'. Good community relations are very important and as such there are many local volunteering and work experience opportuni-ties on offer at the uni careers service.

Belfast is one of those places that is stereotyped over and over again – descriptions such as 'divided', 'troubled', 'industrial' and 'the wettest place on earth' all come to mind. There are re-occurring sets of binaries that fracture the city: politically, socially and religiously. And whether you are from Northern Ireland or not, these fractures cannot be ignored, but this doesn't mean the city can't over-come such problems and enjoy itself.

Despite the tensions and occasional setbacks (the riots and fires of last October caused blockades and chaos around the city for several days), Belfast is a lively and great place to live. It's a small and compact city so you'll soon find your way around. The new bus system is cheap and efficient and as such you'll rarely find it necessary to get a train anywhere – they're far too pricey anyway. Unless you have a car already, don't get one to live in Belfast – driving around the city can be a night-mare.

Central and South Belfast is the focus for most of student life. Botanic gardens are a haven away from the busy city; the green is packed in the sum-mer and there's often a brass band playing on the bandstand by the rose garden. Inside the gardens you'll find the pretty **Palm House** and also the **Ulster Museum**, which tends to show interesting contemporary art and houses the permanent 'Ireland in Conflict' exhibition. Botanic Avenue and Dublin Road lead the way from the city to the University area – a mere 15-minute walk.

Apart from the stunning white marble **City Hall** and several redbrick Victorian buildings (**The Linen Hall** and **Marks & Spencer**), the rest of the centre is fairly unspectacular. The waterside is still being developed although the **Waterfront Hall** and the **Odyssey Complex** are already good music and entertainment venues, and along and near Royal Avenue there are the usual High Street stores, lots of secondhand bookshops, plus, off Queen's Street, some pricier boutiques. But if you want to do any serious shopping, take the 2-hour train journey to

Dublin. It is well worth it.

CRAIC

As a newcomer to Belfast you'll soon learn the true meaning of the famous 'craic'. People really know how to go out and have a great time here. Bars and pubs are plentiful (though very smoky!) – from trendy 'sit-in-and-be-seen' cocktail bars, such as **The Apartment**, to traditional taverns such as **Whites**. In the city centre the Cathedral quarter contains the lovely **John Hewitt** pub (with an excellent choice of ales & beers) and **The Spaniard** – a great bar with quirky décor and fantastic music – serves tapas and light meals. **The Kitchen Bar** in the nearby **Cornmarket** is very classy and holds a jazz night every Monday. Going away from the city centre and leading towards the uni area, **Katie Daly's** and the **Limelight** are well known for their student-orientated theme nights. Closer to Queen's there's always a good atmosphere in **Auntie Annies** while **The Bot** and **The Egg** (off Eglantine Avenue) are convenient and cheap student dives (**The Egg** does a £5 Sunday roast). Though the variety of nightclubs doesn't really rival that of pubs, there are a couple worth checking out – **Milk** and **The Pothouse** being the best of the bunch. Although there isn't much of a gay/lesbian scene in Belfast there are a couple of sympathetic clubs in the cathedral quarter: **The Cremlin** and **The Nest**.

ART

Belfast is full of poets and musicians and as such there's always a poetry reading or a band playing in a pub nearby. All music events are listed in the free pamphlet – *The List*, or you can find full entertainment listings in the *Belfast Telegraph* on a Friday. Traditional music sessions can usually be heard at **Whites**, **The John Hewitt** or **Kelly's Tavern**, while folk or rock bands often play in **Katie Daly's**, **The Empire** or **Auntie Annies**. **The Limelight**, **The Ulster Hall** and **The King's Hall** all host bigger bands – such as The Magic Numbers, K.T. Tunstall and Gabriel y Rodrigo.

Spring and autumn see lots of festivals in Belfast – such as the big Belfast Festival (all over the city), Between the Lines (literature & music – at **The Crescent Arts Centre**), Belfast Film Festival, the Cathedral Quarter Arts Festival and the new Holylands Arts Festival. Throughout the summer there are Irish festivals or fleadh held in West Belfast, and the **An Cultural Ann** (Culture Centre) on the Falls road has a lovely café and an Irish language book shop, where you can often hear local musicians.

Laura Cattell

UNIVERSITY OF READING

The University of Reading
Whiteknights
PO Box 217
Reading RG6 6AH

TEL 0118 378 8619
FAX 0118 378 8924
EMAIL student_recruitment@reading.ac.uk
WEB www.reading.ac.uk

Reading University Students' Union
PO Box 230
Reading RG6 2AZ

TEL 0118 378 4100
FAX 0118 975 5283
EMAIL b.p.elger@reading.ac.uk
WEB www.rusu.co.uk

VIRGIN VIEW

*T*he University of Reading is consistently one of the most popular higher education choices in the UK. They receive, on average, seven applications for every undergraduate place.

Value added consists in an unusual diversity of degree provision, a careful monitoring of teaching staff with a reward system for excellence and innovation, an emphasis on learning resources and graduate employability, cultural diversity, campus environment, and good sport.

Students are happy at Reading - a huge 88% gave their approval in the 2010 National Student Survey, organised by the Higher Education Funding Council for England, and less than 6% fail to last the course.

What they look for in applicants beyond grades are 1. Awareness of the relevance of the work experience you do to your degree, indicating how focused you are on the course and your future; 2. Self-motivation, enthusi-asm, good inter-personal skills and tenacity; 3. An ability to collaborate with others in solving problems.

CAMPUS

Reading has two of the most beautiful university campuses in the UK, based at Whiteknights in Reading and Greenlands in Henley.

Writes Laura Cattell: 'Set in the leafy Whiteknights grounds on the outskirts of the town, Reading maintains a close campus atmosphere while being only 45 miles from the bright lights of London.'

One and a half miles from Reading town centre, Whiteknichts just underwent a £30m development making a new home for the University's Institute of Education, which is the largest trainer of teachers for the region (hitherto out at smaller campus Bulmershe, a further mile out).

Now, the Film, Theatre and Television department also moves from the abandoned Bulmurshe, to an £11m centre at Whiteknights, with three fully-equipped performance spaces, screening room, editing suites and a sound studio.

Whiteknichts, 130 hectares of parkland, is the centre of university life. The riverside campus on the outskirts of Henley-on-Thames is home to the MBA, DBA and executive education programmes run by Henley Business School.

There is a regular bus service to Whiteknights campus from the train station.

FEES, BURSARIES

UK & EU Fees, 2011-12: £3,375 p.a. There are bursaries of £1,400 for UK students whose family income is up to £25k; then bursaries tapering down to nil where family income is £45k. Other bursaries e.g. of up to £1,000 may be awarded to students from specified Berkshire schools. Academic scholarships of £1000 are offered in all subjects for the highest-achieving students, see www.reading.ac.uk/studentfinance.

Special help is available for those with children (especially single parents), and those with caring responsibilities, or with disabilities, for mature students and for self-financing international students. There are sports scholarships of up to £2000, scholarships for IB students who are classed as international students, music scholarships of up to £800.

STUDENT PROFILE

'There's no denying the middle-class, white, home counties feel at Reading,' writes Laura, 'and the "agrics" and "rugger-buggers" with their rugby shirt

UNIVERSITY/STUDENT PROFILE	
University since	**1926**
Situation/style	**Campus**
Student population	**15955**
Total undergraduates	**10860**
Mature	**41%**
International	**19%**
Male/female ratio	**46:54**
Equality of opportunity:	
state school intake	**82%**
social class 4-7 intake	**26%**
drop-out rate	**6%**

collars turned up are never far away, but there is also a large take from overseas (19%).' And an increasing take (26%) from the lower classes. The first international student arrived at Reading in 1904 from Kenya. Since then their international student population has grown to some 3,000 students from 125 countries worldwide. 'Nevertheless,' says Laura, 'the uni still retains an upper to middle class/middle England feel.'

ACADEMIA & JOBS

There is an unusually broad portfolio of degrees covering the arts, humanities, sciences and social sciences, and flexibility within courses to take a module into your degree from another department, take on a free language class for example, or to transfer from one programme to another.

Defining the provision are niche courses which few other universities provide, degrees such as agriculture, construction management, horticulture, cybernetics, meteorology, real estate and typography.

Besides many of their lecturers being at the forefront of research - Environmental Sciences, Architecture & Built Environment, Town & Country Planning, Archaeology and Philosophy all produce research adjudged between 50% and 75%

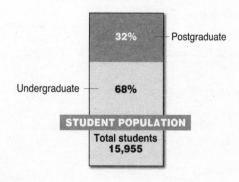

world-class or internationally excellent - Reading is resolutely a teaching establishment, their lecturers voted by students in the 2011 *Times Higher* Student Experience Survey 10th in the country for helpfulness and interest. They have even founded a Centre for the Development of Teaching and Learning to keep abreast of new techniques and technologies, and throughout the year the University rewards excellence, leadership and innovation with staff awards.

Learning resources include a library of over one million volumes, 8,750 e-books, some 21,500 e-journals, multimedia material, and a restricted loan Course Collection holds high demand texts. There are in addition computing and communications facilities, electronic media and communication tools at the Student Access to Independent Learning suite, and online study resources via 'Blackboard', the virtual learning environment.

All undergraduates are matched with a personal tutor, a constant for the duration. This can work well as long as you attend some lectures and meet with him/her when you're meant to.

They tackle graduate jobs in part by including a Career Management Skills module in all undergraduate courses, designed to develop job-hunting strategies, help students to focus on a suitable career, find job opportunities (they provide over 1,500 employment-related web links), complete applications and perform effec-

> *'There's still no denying the middle-class feel at Reading, but it is now a very active community, demanding more from the student experience, as in student media.'*

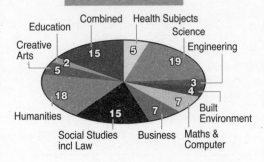

SUBJECT AREAS (%)

Education — 15
Combined — 5
Health Subjects Science — 19
Engineering
Creative Arts — 5, 2
— 3
— 4
Humanities — 18
— 7
Built Environment
Social Studies incl Law — 15
Business — 7
Maths & Computer

tively at interviews.

Students may also take other interactive modules in entrepreneurship, or in museum, archive and library work (another niche strength in the curriculum), or tutoring pupils in local schools. There are opportunities, too, to command an additional language through the Institute Wide Language Programme, which offers Arabic, Chinese (Mandarin), French, German, Italian, Japanese and Spanish.

Finally, the Reading Experience and Development (RED) Award gives formal recognition on a student's degree transcript for volunteer work undertaken during their time at Reading.

They are big providers of graduates into accountancy - three degrees, two with Economics (one BSc), the other with Management, and there is great employment strength in both finance and business management. Recently Reading merged with the Henley Business College to create 'The Henley Business School at the University of Reading'. Henley is the world's third largest supplier of MBA education and one of a few to be triple accredited by the major UK, US and European accreditation bodies (AMBA, EQUIS, AACSB). It becomes a faculty of the university.

From the important research areas of Built Environment and Planning come BSc in Building Construction & Management and a degree in Construction Management & Surveying that gives you the entire construction process, from brief to architect through design, planning and project completion. The Chartered Institute of Building (CIOB) grants membership after two years experience. There's also BSc Building Surveying.

TEACHING SURVEY AT A GLANCE

Avg. UCAS points accepted	**350**
Acceptance rate	**15%**
Overall satisfaction rate	**88%**
Helpful/interested staff	**★★★★**
Small tuition groups	**★★**
Students into graduate jobs	**71%**

Teaching most popular with undergraduates:
Agriculture & related sciences, Anatomy, Physiology & Pathology, Archaeology, Biology & related sciences, Chemistry, Classics, Electronic & Electrical Engineering, English, Finance, French Studies, Food and Beverage Studies, German & Scandinavian Studies, History, Human & Social Geography, Teacher Training, Italian Studies, Law, Maths & Statistics, Pharmacology, Philosophy, Physical Geography & Environmental Science, Physical Science, Politics, Psychology, Subjects allied to Medicine, Zoology.

The third big employment area is health, fed by Reading's degrees in subjects allied to Medicine, like Biochemistry, Biomedical Engineering, Primary Care Nursing (Public Health Nursing is also available) - and Biological Sciences.

Farmers know Reading as the top-rated research establishment, and very strong on Agricultural Business Management, but also other sorts of management - Rural Resource, Landscape, Habitat & Soil. Also very big in Food Science, with Business or as Food Technology.

Geography, Rural Environmental Science, Rural Resource Mgt, Land Mgt also define Reading. This is a big area in research and a useful employment niche comes with the BSc Meteorology, which sits alongside one with a year in Oklahoma, and there's a Foundation year opportunity.

Cybernetics is another defining influence on the curriculum, as is Educational Studies (primary level, a massive contributor to the graduate employment figures). Language graduates also find jobs as lecturers in further education, as do many graduates from the famous Faculty of Letters & Social Sciences with its unique set of arts and social science mixes. Humanities pack graduates into libraries and museums as curators, librarians, archivists. Archaeologists also abound (a dedicated degree leaving few hungry), and publishing is a very popular destination from Reading.

SOCIAL SCENE

STUDENTS' UNION 'The RUSU houses a student advice centre, large shop, off-licence, insurance outlet, student travel agency and three entertainment venues,' writes Laura. 'There are plenty of eateries and cafés open to grab a cheap lunch while by night the impressive Union offers up **Mojos**, **Café Mondial** and **3sixty** as watering holes/dance floors.'

They have curry nights, sometimes a quiz, karaoke or comedy, but Wednesday (currently *Wednesday Union*) and Saturday club nights at **3sixty** are the biggest.

The Union also occasionally attracts big bands. Feeder, Ash, NDubz, The Automatic, Pendulum, Biffy Clyro, The King Blues, The Twang, Wiley, Taio Cruz have all graced the 3sixty stage.

'Also, the music department organises regular choir recitals and concerts. RUMS (Reading University Music Society) has a Choral Society, Gospel Choir and the also the more relaxed University Singers. There's also an orchestra, concert and jazz band, and it's home to the infamous *Reading Rock Festival* and the *WOMAD* world music festival, which liven up the town in the summer and offer up volunteer opportunities if you want a chance to see your favourite band for free.'

The HUB, within the Students Union is the central resource for students seeking any kind of advice or information, or backing/facilities for sports clubs and societies, the most active of which is Campaigns Forum. They also support around 1,500 volunteer groups of students working on projects within the local community. Despite Reading being a university focused on elite sportsmen and women at the expense of participation, students from around the campus have gained notable success in a wide range of activities from arts and music to firmly being at the heart of the student movement nationally.

Reading is now a very active community, demanding more from the student experience, as in student media. The student newspaper - *Spark* - has been around in one form or another for 75 years. Junction 11 is the student radio station, out of

WHAT IT'S REALLY LIKE

UNIVERSITY:

Social Life	★★★
Societies	★★★
Student Union services	★★★★
Politics	**Strong internal**
Sport	**52 clubs**
National team position	**28th**
Sport facilities	★★★★
Arts opportunities	**Good, esp. drama**
Student newspaper	**Spark**
Student radio station	**Junction 11**
Student TV & film	**RU:ON**
Nightclub	**3sixty**
Bars	**Mojo's, Breeze, Café Mondial,**
Union ents	**Good**
Union societies	**48**
Most active societies	**Campaigns Forum**
Parking	**Limited in halls**

TOWN:

Entertainment	★★★
Scene	**Pubs, clubs OK**
Town/gown relations	**Average**
Risk of violence	**Average**
Cost of living	**High**
Student concessions	**Good**
Survival + 2 nights out	**£90 pw**
Part-time work campus/town	**Excellent**

are never far away if you fancy a walk along the river. Reading has bowed to the fashion for making every British town centre look exactly the same. There is the standard riverside development, known as the Oracle, full of chain restaurants and High Street stores. Look beyond the main High Street - to places like the Chinese supermarket or the Global café. In town, pubs and clubs-wise there's plenty of choice. And of course London and Oxford are only a short train ride away.'

PILLOW TALK

New halls Stenton and Mackinder opened in September 2010, en-suite bedrooms arranged in flats of 8-10 people, with a shared self-catering kitchen. In addition, there's to be a catering and

ACCOMMODATION

Student rating	★★★★
Guarantee to freshers	**95%**
Style	**Halls, flats**
Security guard	**All**
Shared rooms	**None**
Internet access	**All**
Self-catered	**Some**
En suite	**Some**
Approx price range pw	**£72-£170**
City rent pw	**£70-£80**

which just came RU:ON, a small group of dedicated film and TV students recently rewarded for their enthusiasm with new broadcast equipment. If you are interested in media, the way is open at Reading.

SPORT 'Sport is an integral part of life on campus. The sports facilities are excellent and most of the playing fields are on campus so whenever there's a big match there's a great atmosphere and everyone goes along to watch. The Wolfenden Sports Centre has a flashy gym and there are squash courts and several halls where most of the fitness classes and clubs/societies take place. Well over a hundred quid for six months may seem a bit steep at the beginning of term, but it does entitle you to use all facilities in the centre at any time you like and you don't have to pay another penny after that.'

Generally, team standards are pretty high, especially for women's netball and hockey. Overall the teams came 28th nationally last year.

TOWN 'Reading is set in picturesque countryside and pretty villages such as Sonning or Pangbourne

bar facility for Stenton, Mackinder and Windsor Hall.

Sixty to 70% of first years are allocated catered hall accommodation, and if you want to make lectures in your first year, it's no bad idea. The best has to be Whiteknights, but equally fun and popular halls are Wantage, an Oxbridge-style building just off campus, but very close, St Patricks, and, for friendliness, Bridges. A redevelopment of St Georges Hall recently opened - 426 bedrooms, majority en-suite.'

Limited parking is available at most halls; however students need to gain permission from the Hall in advance if they wish to bring their car with them.

GETTING THERE

☛ By road: M4/J11, A33. An express bus service to London leaves from outside the university.
☛ By rail: London Paddington, 0:30; Birmingham, 2:15; Oxford, 0:40; Bristol Parkway, 1:00.
☛ By air: Heathrow and Gatwick. ☛ By coach: London, 1:20; Brighton, 3:45; Exeter, 3-5:00; Leicester, 5:00.

THE ROBERT GORDON UNIVERSITY

The Robert Gordon University
Aberdeen AB10 1FR

TEL 01224 262728
FAX 01224 262147
EMAIL admissions@rgu.ac.uk
WEB www.rgu.ac.uk

Robert Gordon Students' Association
Aberdeen AB10 1JQ

TEL 01224 262294
FAX 01224 262268
EMAIL rgusa@rgu.ac.uk
WEB www.rgunion.co.uk/

VIRGIN VIEW

The University developed from a hospital founded from the estate of philanthropist Robert Gordon in 1750. It is the beneficiary of another Aberdeen entrepreneur too, an architect by name of Tom Scott Sutherland, who presented them with the grounds and mansion where the Scott Sutherland School of Architecture was based, a beautiful site overlooking the River Dee. Another of RGU's constituent parts is the Gray's School of Art, named after Aberdeen engineer John Gray; it was founded in 1885.

Now, they are investing £115 million over ten years to create four 'academic precincts' for art, business, health and technology - what they call 'the best riverside campus in Europe'.

In 2010 Robert Gordon was voted by its students in the Times Higher Education's *Student Experience Survey providers of the best student experience of any 'new' (i.e. 1992 founded) university in the UK. Two years earlier, the national Research Assessment declared it the best modern university in Scotland for research, with 70% of its provision of international quality.*

It consistently appears in the top 5 UK universities for graduate employment, alongside such as Imperial College, Oxford and Cambridge.

Now, this year Robert Gordon is the well-deserved Sunday Times *Scottish University of the Year, described as 'the model modern university producing dynamic graduates capable of making an immediate contribution to life, work and wider society'. But how many applicants south of the border know what Robert Gordon is?*

UNIVERSITY/STUDENT PROFILE

University since	**1992**
Situation/style	**Civic**
Student population	**13625**
Total undergraduates	**9435**
Mature	**54%**
International	**22%**
Male/female ratio	**40:60**
Equality of opportunity:	
state school intake	**93%**
social class 4-7 intake	**35%**
drop-out rate	**9%**

CAMPUS

While the Students' Association and uni are based at the Schoolhill site in Aberdeen, 75% of RGU students are now taught at the Garthdee Campus on the south side of the city on the banks of the Dee, which includes the mighty impressive Aberdeen Business School, the Faculty of Health & Social Care, and two schools - the Scott Sutherland School and the Gray's School of Art - of the Faculty of Design and Technology. Over £60 million has been invested in the development of this campus in the last four years.

The Schoolhill site encompasses the Schools of Engineering and Pharmacy and the Student Association. The St Andrew Street building is located near Schoolhill and is home to the Schools of Computing and Life Sciences, and a library that

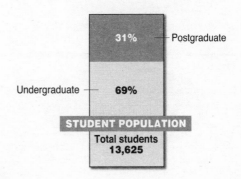

31% — Postgraduate

Undergraduate — 69%

STUDENT POPULATION
Total students
13,625

TEACHING SURVEY AT A GLANCE

Avg. UCAS points accepted	**324**
Acceptance rate	**23%**
Overall satisfaction rate	**84%**
Helpful/interested staff	★★★★
Small tuition groups	★★★
Students into graduate jobs	**83%**

Teaching most popular with undergraduates:
Accounting, Anatomy, Physiology & Pathology, Business, Communications & Information Studies, Computer, Electronic & Electrical Engineering, Engineering & Technology, Law, Communications, Mechanical, Production & Manufacturing Engineering (97%), Medical Technology, Subjects allied to Medicine (97%), Pharmacology, Toxicology & Pharmacy, Publicity, Publishing, Social Work (100%), Social Studies, Sociology.

Teaching least popular with undergraduates:
Design Studies (58%), Sports Science (43%).

serves all the schools at the Schoolhill campus.

FEES, BURSARIES

UK & EU Fees, 2011-12. For students domiciled in England, Wales or Northern Ireland fees in 2011/12 are £1,820. Fees for a placement year are £910. Tuition fees loans may be available - students should contact the appropriate Student Finance for details. The Sports Scholarship Programme supports promising sports men and women and is currently supporting London Olympic swimming hopeful, Hannah Miley, as she trains for the 2012 Olympics. See www.rgu.ac.uk/sports-scholarships. Academic scholarships in a range of academic disciplines are also available: www.rgu.ac.uk/scholarships.

STUDENT PROFILE

There is a large undergraduate intake from the

state sector, 54% are mature, many are local. and 33% are part-timers. But last year over 1,000 international students enrolled, 10% of the student population, from more than 50 countries. The culture - local, national and international - provides a rich experience for both staff and students.

RGU's admissions policy is clear: 'We will look for evidence of academic achievement as well as personal and professional experiences.' They want evidence of an enthusiasm and understanding of the course you've applied for and an ability to communicate this in your personal statement. 'For courses that require an interview/selection visit as part of the application process you may have to demonstrate your contribution to a team, display an understanding of the role of the professional or have some relevant work experience.'

RESEARCH EXCELLENCE

% of Robert Gordon's research that is
4* *(World-class)* or **3*** *(Internationally rated):*

	4*	3*
Health Professions	**5%**	**15%**
Computer Science	**5%**	**40%**
General Engineering	**5%**	**15%**
Architecture	**10%**	**20%**
Accounting and Finance	**5%**	**15%**
Business/Management	**5%**	**35%**
Information Management	**15%**	**45%**
Law	**0%**	**5%**
Politics	**0%**	**25%**
Sociology	**0%**	**15%**
Art and Design	**5%**	**40%**

ACADEMIA & JOBS

Research-wise they are focused on Health and Welfare; the Digital Economy; Design, Energy & Sustainability; and Management, Governance & Information. They offer degree programmes in Nursing, Business, Law, Engineering, Science, Computing, Art, Design, Architecture, Pharmacy and Health Sciences.

Particular niche areas are legendary: they are the largest provider of social work in Scotland; they have one of the oldest pharmacy schools in the UK (1898); their Design for Industry programme has some cracking Product Design degrees; they have close connections to the energy sector, including placement opportunities, scholarships and tailored programmes such as Mechanical Engineering with Offshore Engineering. Ninety per cent of undergraduate programmes have a work placement as

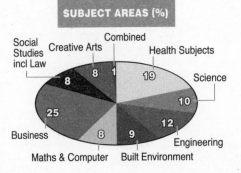

SUBJECT AREAS (%)

Social Studies incl Law — 8
Creative Arts — 8
Combined — 1
Health Subjects — 19
Science — 10
Engineering — 12
Built Environment — 9
Maths & Computer — 8
Business — 25

WHAT IT'S REALLY LIKE

UNIVERSITY:

Social Life	★★★★
Societies	★★★
Student Union services	★★★★
Politics	**Interest low**
Sport	**9 clubs**
National team position	**59th**
Sport facilities	★★★★
Arts opportunities	**Drama, dance, music good; film, art average**
Student magazine	**Cogno**
Nightclub/bars	**U-bar, Blue Iguana**
Union ents	**7 nights a week**
Union societies	**30**
Most active society	**Cogno**
Parking	**Limited. Permits**

CITY:

Entertainment	★★★★
Scene	**Intoxicating**
Town/gown relations	**Good**
Risk of violence	**Low**
Cost of living	**Average**
Student concessions	**Average**
Survival + 2 nights out	**£70 pw**
Part-time work campus/town	**Good/excellent**

part of the course.

SOCIAL SCENE

STUDENTS' ASSOCIATION RGUnion has two bars at Schoolhill, which provide a wide range of entertainment 7 nights a week. Regular nights include: Open Mic, *Karaoke Idol*, r&b hip hop, *The Master Chill*, and everyone's disco favourite, *Thursday Night Fever*. The downstairs bar is available for private functions on Tuesdays and Sundays; students have recently used these nights for events such as speed dating and games like *Play Your Cards Right*.

The Union actively encourages students to get involved in university life by awarding recognised certificates for their volunteering efforts. A new Marketing and Communications Centre opened in January 2006, with up to date software that'll be used to develop the re-vamped student magazine, which goes by the name of Cogno.

SPORT A Sports Science degree is backed by a multi-million pound sports and leisure centre at its Garthdee Campus, providing a centre of excellence for the region in hockey, as well as a 25-metre swimming pool, and a huge sports hall for hockey, five-a-side football, badminton, tennis, basketball, volleyball and trampolining.

PILLOW TALK

Accommodation is thin on the ground, and students' advice is to get in quick. It consists of self contained, self-catering flats, six to eight sharing,

ACCOMMODATION

Student rating	★★
Guarantee to freshers	**98%**
Style	**Flats**
Security guard	**Some**
Internet access	**All**
Self-catered	**Most**
En suite	**Some**
Approx price range pw	**£85-£103**
City rent pw	**£88-£110**

all with own bedroom, 20% en suite. A permit to park at Garthdee costs £135 p.a.

GETTING THERE

☞ By road: from south, A92, thence ring road for signs; from north, A96 or A92.
☞ By coach: London, 11.30; Newcastle, 7.35.
☞ By rail: London King's Cross, 7:00; Glasgow, 2:45; Edinburgh, 2:30; Newcastle, 4:30.
☞ By air: Aberdeen International Airport.

ROEHAMPTON UNIVERSITY

Roehampton University
Erasmus House
Roehampton Lane
London SW15 5PU

TEL 020 8392 3232
EMAIL enquiries@roehampton.ac.uk
WEB www.roehampton.ac.uk

Roehampton Students' Union
Froebel College
Roehampton Lane
London SW15 5PJ

TEL 020 8392 3221
EMAIL info@roehamptonstudent.com
WEB www.roehamptonstudent.com

VIRGIN VIEW

Roehampton University, in south-west London, offers vocational courses in the Arts, Education, Social Sciences, Sciences and Sports areas, but with a rather attractive, artistic and caring ethos, which is part and parcel of the place.

Of its four constituent colleges, Digby Stuart College (Arts & Humanities) has a Roman Catholic foundation; Froebel College (Education) follows the teachings of Friedrich Froebel, the caring chappie who invented kindergartens; Southlands College (Social Sciences) has a Methodist base; and Whitelands College (Science) has a Church of England base.

They are not, however, in the business of shoving this down your throat. Now, with university status, they have fathered their sometime scattered colleges into one campus in south west London, and things are looking bright. In the latest National Student Survey, 79% said they were satisfied; 12% drop out.

CAMPUS

The uni's four colleges are cosily set together on the edge of Richmond deer park. Writes Becky Neaum: 'Roehampton University is situated in an affluent area of south west London, and within a 20-minute train ride of the central of the capital city. It is set within lush green grounds and only a few minutes from Richmond Park; a 9-mile deer park. So, if you are torn between choosing country and city, and if you love the bright lights of the city, but also the peaceful landscape of the country, then this University really is ideally located.'

'Roehampton combines the best aspects of living in London,' agrees Gina Wright. 'I cannot imag-

UNIVERSITY/STUDENT PROFILE	
University since	**1992**
Situation/style	**City campus**
Student population	**8910**
Total undergraduates	**6560**
Mature	**43%**
International	**10%**
Male/female ratio	**25:75**
Equality of opportunity:	
state school intake	**97%**
social class 4-7 intake	**42%**
drop-out rate	**12%**

ine a more perfect site - a peaceful green campus set in landscaped grounds with lakes and trees, yet near enough to buses and tubes to make the journey into central London in about half an hour.'

Digby College has the Belfry Bar, a Learning Resource Centre, self-catering flats and a warm, welcoming atmosphere. Froebel College is dominated by the imposing, Georgian Grove House, its period feel making it popular with students and TV productions such as Inspector Morse. It also has the music venue, Montefiore Hall.

Southlands, relocated from Wimbledon in 1997, is clean, modern and the musical pulse of the uni, with studios, a Steinway concert grand and a double-manual French harpsichord.

Whitelands founds its way here in 2004, and occupies an 18th-century Palladian mansion, Parkstead House, at the heart of campus.

FEES, BURSARIES

UK & EU Fees, 2011-12: £3,375 p.a. If in receipt of the Higher Education Maintenance grant, there's a bursary, and there are academic achievement scholarships.

STUDENT PROFILE

More than a third of undergraduates come from the lowest four socio-economic classes, and 5% from so-called 'low participation' neighbourhoods, for whom university is a new experience. Only about 4% come from the independent school sector.

ACADEMIA

Continues Becky: 'It being a small university, the lecturers have time for the students, and it's true that you feel a name, not a number here. Lecture and seminar groups are relatively small, which allows for more interaction and discussion.' This was confirmed by last year's Higher Education Funding Council's National Student Survey.

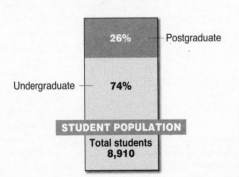

Undergraduate — **74%**

26% — Postgraduate

STUDENT POPULATION
Total students
8,910

Roehampton lecturers are helpful and interested, and in the fields of Anthropology, Dance and Drama it has notched up some impressive recent research successes.

Students say the teaching is best in Business, Classics, Communications, Dance, European Languages, Management, Media Studies, Philosophy, Sports Science, Theology & Religious Studies, and least popular in Film & Photography.

In the last Research Assessment Exercise, work in the Anthropology department was adjudged to be 15% world-class (4-star) and 65% internationally excellent (3-star), though it is the second worst taught, according to students this year.

Meanwhile, Dance scored 55%-30%, an amazing result, which made them first in the country for Dance and second among all the universities providing any kind of Performing Arts. Drama wasn't far behind, with 15% 4-star, 45% 3-star.

'Workloads are not immense,' continues Becky. 'Pressure does build up towards the deadlines, but you are given plenty of time to do the work in.

There is 24/7 Internet access in the library and in most halls.'

When it comes to graduate supply to primary teaching, Roehampton mounts a very strong case. Output is almost totally Primary. They are renowned for their Drama and QTS courses in particular.

The religious background to the constituent colleges comes through in courses for the caring professions, such as healthcare and therapeutic work (and teaching too, under their particular educational regime). Look at the foundation course, Childcare and Early Years Education, and BSc

RESEARCH EXCELLENCE

% of Roehampton's research that is
4* (World-class) or **3* (Internationally rated):**

	4*	3*
Health Professions	**0%**	**20%**
Biological Sciences	**0%**	**5%**
Sociology	**5%**	**25%**
Anthropology	**15%**	**65%**
Psychology	**0%**	**20%**
Education	**5%**	**25%**
Sports	**0%**	**0%**
French	**0%**	**5%**
Iberian	**5%**	**25%**
English	**10%**	**25%**
Theology	**5%**	**15%**
History	**10%**	**25%**
Drama	**15%**	**45%**
Dance	**55%**	**30%**
Media Studies	**5%**	**30%**

Integrative Counselling, Counselling, Psychology & Counselling, Psychology, Psychology & Health, BA Early Childhood Studies, BSc Health & Social Care, Health Studies, and BA Human Rights.

They are also among the leaders in getting jobs for graduates in sport - as players or sport officials. The BSc Sport & Exercise Science is the prototype, a good balance of Physiology, Biomechanics and Psychology.

SOCIAL SCENE

'Unlike other universities in the London area, Roehampton has its own, very beautiful campus, and campus life is brilliant,' writes Becky. 'It is a small uni, but sizeable enough for footy games, summer sports day and an amazing annual Summer Ball. It is friendly as well, with a huge mix of people from all walks of life and of all ages. This is one of the first things that attracted me.

SUBJECT AREAS (%)

Health Subjects — 1
Combined — 35
Maths & Computer Science — 12
Business — 3
Social Studies incl Law — 6
4
5
Humanities — 15
Creative Arts
Education — 19

Upper Richmond Road in nearby Putney. Of the balls, the infamous, extravagant Summer Ball is best. Froebel boasts the second largest ball after Oxford and Cambridge.

Societies tend to be transient. Large and long-standing socs are RIACAS, which promotes Afro-Caribbean and Asian culture, and top soc. Open Mic. There's a monthly newspaper, *Fresh*, and other societies spin off undergraduate courses.

Says Gina: 'The football battles between the Digby Lions and their "natural prey", the Froebel Zebras, are legendary!'

PILLOW TALK

'Accommodation at Roehampton ranges from typi-

'Freshers Week was a fantastic experience here, although daunting at times. It was packed with things to do, day and night. Now the social scene off campus is rich and varied; with many student nights at local nightclubs. Putney is our local pub haunt.'

Each of the four campuses has its own bar. Ents are OK. In the week this is being written, Thursday is Bands Night, featuring, for example, Last Gang In Town, Blue Mojo, Dancing Bears at Belfry Bar, Digby. Friday, at Froebel, is invariably *The Bop: Heaven or Hell*, or *Vicars and Tarts*, or some other theme. Monday might be comedy at the **Lounge**. Wednesday, Sports Night, is held at **Fez Club**,

cal halls, with up to 25 or so people sharing a floor, and all facilities, to flats of 6 to 10 with private facilities,' Becky writes.

All Colleges cater for vegetarians. There are some en-suite ground floor rooms for students with disabilities. They allocate rooms on a 'first come, first served basis', so get onto it fast. The £63 per week price, above, is for a twin.

GETTING THERE

☛ US Roehampton, Barnes British Rail station or No. 72 bus from Hammersmith Underground; No. 265 runs from Putney Bridge.

ROYAL HOLLOWAY, LONDON UNIVERSITY

Royal Holloway College
Egham
Surrey TW20 0EX

TEL 01784 434455
FAX 01784 473520
EMAIL liaison-office@rhul.ac.uk
WEB www.rhul.ac.uk

Royal Holloway Students' Union
Egham
Egham TW20 0EX

TEL 01784 486300
FAX 01784 486312
EMAIL reception@su.rhul.ac.uk
WEB www.su.rhul.ac.uk

VIRGIN VIEW

*R*oyal Holloway, a college of London
University, is situated on a 120-acre
campus at Egham in Surrey, far enough to
the south west of London's bright lights to
favour a well-focused regime. Students
almost uniformly mention the workload, and
it is clear that campus life can be a bit dull,
one student suggesting that 'the best thing
about Royal Holloway is that you are 35
minutes away from central London, with a
great train connection.'

The University on the other hand lists
the campus first among features that add
value to the student experience, describing it
as 'friendly... a living environment set in 135
acres of beautiful landscaped and wooded
grounds'.

Friendly it certainly is and situated
amongst pictureque greenery and forest
walks. But it is quiet. Nearby Egham is even
quieter. 'The campus is Egham life,' said one.

Nonetheless, the university enjoys high
scores for student satisfaction, achieving an
overall satisfaction of 86% in the 2010
national student survey (and 100% from the
Language Department). There are high ratings all round for helpful and interested lecturers, and for small tuition groups.

CAMPUS

'Holloway, isn't that a women's prison?' says Sarah
Toms with a sigh which suggests she has heard the
jibe many times before. 'It is of course, but not
here, it's in South London! You'll get used to that
question. This is Royal Holloway, University of
London - yes, the one with THAT building
(Founders Hall). Located a train ride from central
London - forty minutes on a good day, barring

UNIVERSITY/STUDENT PROFILE	
University since	**1800**
Situation/style	**Campus**
Student population	**8760**
Total undergraduates	**6955**
Mature	**23%**
International	**30%**
Male/female ratio	**42:58**
Equality of opportunity:	
state school intake	**78%**
social class 4-7 intake	**25%**
drop-out rate	**5%**

leaves on the line or the wrong kind of snow.'

It has been called 'London's Country Campus',
and it is certainly a beautiful spot, made distinctive
by Founder's Building, a copy of the Chateau de
Chambourd in the Loire built by Thomas
Holloway, who in 1886 founded a college for
women there. Nearly a century later it merged
with another all-female foundation, Bedford
College, creating Royal Holloway and Bedford New
College. It is a close, rather private situation far
from the bustle.

FEES, BURSARIES

UK & EU Fees, 2011-12: £3,375 p.a. There's a bur-
sary for those eligible for a HE Maintenance Grant,
also the Founder's Scholarship and Bedford
Scholarships. Other awards are made through the
Lyell Bursaries in Geology, the Bioscience Entrance
Scholarships and Physics Bursaries for freshers.
There are also choral and organ scholarships, and
instrumental scholarships/RCM exhibitions.
Finally, they offer computer science scholarships,
and sports persons are looked after through the
Talented Athlete Recognition Scheme. See
www.rhul.ac.uk/prospective-student/finance/
ug.bursaries.

STUDENT PROFILE

The student body is small, little more than a third
the size of King's College or University College,
London, and largely female (58%). 'Holloway has a
massive imbalance of girls to boys, especially in
Drama, where boys make up roughly 10% of the
students. Apart from that I think all different personality types and interests interact well together,'
writes Alisdair Hinton. Public school intake is high,
as it is from overseas (30%). The African-Caribbean
society became an instant success. The LGBT (les-
bian-gay) society is also popular, it runs sex health
workshops, trips to Thorpe Park and nights out at
Popstarz in Soho and **Heaven** in Charing Cross.

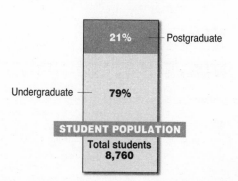

Postgraduate 21%

Undergraduate 79%

STUDENT POPULATION

**Total students
8,760**

411

TEACHING SURVEY AT A GLANCE

Avg. UCAS points accepted	**360**
Acceptance rate	**17%**
Overall satisfaction rate	**86%**
Helpful/interested staff	★★★★
Small tuition groups	★★★
Students into graduate jobs	**63%**

Teaching most popular with undergraduates:
Biology & related sciences, Film & Photography,
Classics, Geology, History, Human & Social
Geography, Maths & Statistics, Media Studies,
<olecular Biology, Biophysics & Biochemistry,
European Languages & Area Studies (100%),
Physical Geography & Environmental Science,
Physics & Astronomy, Politics, Psychology.

Teaching least popular with undergraduates:
Social Work (50%).

ACADEMIA & JOBS

University of London degrees are offered through three faculties: Arts, History & Social Sciences, and Science. They are ranked 16th in the UK for the proportion of research in the top 4* category. The Department of Music is the top department for research in the UK; there's a link with the Royal College of Music. A further eight departments are ranked in the top ten - Biological Sciences, Drama, Earth Sciences, Economics, Geography, German, Media Arts and Psychology.

> *'The best thing about Royal Holloway is that you are 35 minutes away from central London. The worst thing: the town of Egham is worse than sleepy. Campus IS Egham life.'*

There is an international reputation in many areas, including Information Security, Holocaust Studies, Genetic vaccines, Quaternary Science and Musicology.

They have developed a method of study that allows a flexible approach to major/minor combos and course units can be drawn from across 18 departments, with plenty of scope for interdisciplinary study and research. Latin is offered as a BA single hons, but also with English (a tantalising prospect for students of syntax and etymology).

The Creative Writing course has benefited from the attentions of poet laureate Andrew Motion, Holloway's Professor of Creative Writing, and some of his students have achieved publication.

Those taking Languages actually take most of the graduate jobs - often in publishing, recruitment and personnel, business, community and counselling, banking, radio and TV. The International Building incorporates the English, French, German, Hispanic and Italian departments, a dedicated Japanese Studies section (including the Noh theatre - donated by the Japanese government), and a stylish café. Languages and European Studies, Literature, Culture are frequent course elements.

Principally at Royal Holloway students find jobs in banking, specialist retail stores, personnel and recruitment, civil service and government administration, social work, community and counselling, accounting, publishing, higher education and radio & TV.

The Careers Service is part of The Careers Group, University of London, the largest and most comprehensive careers service in Europe. Royal Holloway Entrepreneurs is a highly popular initiative run by students with College backing (Patron Sir Alex Reed CBE). It runs weekly events relevant to the workplace and there have been numerous successful business start ups and awards in regional and national business competitions.

Alisdair, reading Drama and Theatre Studies, wrote in his first year: 'So far, the teaching has been mostly excellent, the weakest coming from less capable PhD students, only allowed to teach first years. Tutorials are excellent, small intimate groups and lively discussion. The course is very interesting so far, with many and varied aspects of Drama and Theatre being taught.'

Science is a big way forward here, with interesting developments in biological science - a degree in Molecular Biology & Genetics recently. In September 2010, Royal Holloway was awarded a Bronze Athena SWAN Charter to recognise their commitment to the career progression of women in science, engineering and technology.

SOCIAL SCENE

STUDENTS' UNION Every night is an ents night of some description, ranging from the usual pub quizzes on quiet Sundays to the late bars and DJs which dominate weekends and have a significant foothold in the working week as well.

There's a late licence five nights a week, main hall functions two to three times a week, bar ents every other night. How many unions boast two resident DJs poached from the brighter lights of London? Both Brandon Block and DJ Swing are employed to keep the body student moving, and the latter has been known to hurl the crispest of currency into the crowd too, enhancing popularity and drinks consumption in equal measure. Imported additions include Ministry of Sound, A1, Trevor Nelson, Apollo 440.

Tommy's is the newest bar in the union, and the most popular haunt of the socialites. Only Tuesday and Sunday see it shut before midnight, so the quiet beer with a friend at nine has a sneaky habit of turning into eight loud beers with a roomful of pissheads by kicking out time.

The **Dive Bar,** attached to Tommy's, isn't as seedy as it sounds, and offers a cosier venue. The **Union Bar** is a pretty standard affair, and it is these three which combine to hold 1,200 for the big function nights - it has its own in-house technical crew.

Also on campus is the **Stumble Inn** ('Stumble Out' would surely have been more appropriate), a pub to all intents and a popular one at that, ideal for those nights when aggravating your tinnitus shies you from Tommy's.

Holloway's Bar houses sixteen pool tables, dart boards and a host of ever-changing video games, a free Playstation for the deprived, and live sports courtesy of the ubiquitous Sky TV.

There is also the coffee bar, **TW20's,** a food and caffeine establishment that, according to some, is lamentable, but being dirt cheap and on campus attracts students like flies around the proverbial.

Every June they run a Summer Ball in the quads of Founders: 2,000 tickets are sold in exchange for big name acts, cocktail bar, champagne bar, Glastonbury stage, dance tent, fairground rides, hog roast - it runs from 7 until 7 all through the night.

Media, drama and entertainments in general, are of a high standard. The Musical Theatre Society goes to the Edinburgh Fringe. The radio station, 1287 Insanity and the student mag Orbital are award winners. Politics is less of a preoccupation.

Sport The college has a reputation as the best sporting college in London University, and it does well in inter-LU leagues. They recently partnered with the World Academy of Sport to deliver several new programmes, including a Sports Management postgraduate course

A new sports complex has lifted it above its neighbours. Cricket, women's football have bossed the London indoor leagues for a few years, and men's rugby supplies players to senior sides, such as Harlequins and London Welsh.

Town 'Sadly, the surrounding area, quaint little Egham, with as many useful shops as you are likely to see students at a nine o'clock lecture, fails to happen,' Sarah Toms reports, 'though it does have three

RESEARCH EXCELLENCE		
% of Royal Holloway's research that is **4*** *(World-class) or* **3*** *(Internationally rated):*		
	4*	**3***
Biological Sciences	**15%**	**55%**
Environmental Sciences	**20%**	**50%**
Physics	**10%**	**45%**
Pure Mathematics	**0%**	**25%**
Computer Science	**25%**	**40%**
Geography Environment	**20%**	**45%**
Economics	**20%**	**60%**
Business/Management	**15%**	**40%**
Politics	**5%**	**25%**
Social Work	**10%**	**35%**
Psychology	**15%**	**55%**
French	**15%**	**30%**
German	**20%**	**35%**
Italian	**5%**	**35%**
Iberian	**15%**	**30%**
English	**30%**	**35%**
Classics	**10%**	**25%**
History	**20%**	**40%**
Performing Arts	**35%**	**40%**
Media Studies	**20%**	**55%**
Music	**60%**	**30%**

supermarkets, a covey of takeaways, a bevy of student-friendly pubs, and The Staines Massive, which boasts not only a cinema, but wait for it... a nightclub! Those for whom the excitement proves too much, worry not. Royal Holloway is positioned a train ride away from the capital - deliberately, strategically even, to enable you to enjoy London life without paying a high price.

'Sure, the prices locally are higher than average, but not too damaging, and there is the advantage of the London loan rate and that both campus and surrounding area are fairly safe.

PILLOW TALK

All undergraduate students who firmly accept a conditional or unconditional offer of a place at Royal Holloway through UCAS and apply for Student Housing by the deadline of 3rd June 2011 are guaranteed a place in halls for their first year.

'On the one hand, there is Founders Hall,' writes Sarah. 'Its rooms are fairly large and filled with an odd assortment of furniture from across the centuries. On the other, we have New Halls, built in the 1950s by an architect who won a prize for designing a Swedish prison! Affectionately known as Cell Block H, the rooms are, let us say, cosy...'

New-ish halls Athlone, Cameron and Williamson - are catered and come with common

WHAT IT'S REALLY LIKE

UNIVERSITY:

Social Life	★★
Societies	★★★
Student Union services	★★
Politics	**Big right now**
Sport	**36 clubs**
National team position	**52nd**
Sport facilities	★★★
Arts opportunities	**Drama excellent; music, film good; dance, art avg**
Student magazine	**The Orbital**
Student radio	**1287 Insanity**
2008 National Awards	**Silver award**
Nightclub	**Union +Tommy's**
Bars	**Union, Tommy's, Stumble Inn, Holloway's, Dive**
Union ents	**Cheese, Spaced, Orgasmatron, etc**
Union societies	**99**
Most popular society	**James Bond Appreciation Soc**
Smoking policy	**No smoking**
Parking	**None on campus.**
CITY:	
London	★★★★★
Local scene	**Good pubs, but London beckons**
Town/gown relations	**Good**
Risk of violence	**Low**
Cost of living	**High**
Student concessions	**Average**
Survival + 2 nights out	**£40 pw**
Part-time work campus/town	**Good/poor**

ACCOMMODATION

Student rating	★★★★★
Guarantee to freshers	**100%**
Style	**Halls**
Security guard	**All**
Shared rooms	**Some**
Internet access	**Most**
Self-catered	**Some**
En suite	**Some**
Approx price range pw	**£90-£168**
City rent pw	**£50-£150**

Founder's comes with common rooms, TV rooms, bar/snack bar (Crossland Suite); it's hard to get a room here. Reid Hall, near New Halls, is catered with en-suite rooms. Runnymede is self-catered, flat-style around a central kitchen/social area, en-suite. The latest housing development (Tuke, Butler, & Williamson) opened in September 2007 - en-suite accommodation in self-catering flats.

Three halls - Beeches, Chestnuts, Elm Lodge - are converted Victorian houses, catered but with small kitchen/pantries and laundries. Kingswood is catered, off campus (but less than a mile away and with a free bus service to campus during the day) and has rooms and flatlets on a hillside overlooking the Thames at Runnymede with squash and tennis courts, TV/common room, tapas bar and dining room.

Students living on campus cannot bring a car.

GETTING THERE
☛ By road: M25/J13, A30.
☛ By rail: London Waterloo, 35 mins; Reading, 40.

rooms, bar, snack bar, and a good community spirit.

UNIVERSITY OF ST ANDREWS

The University of St Andrews
Old Union Building
St Andrews
Fife KY16 9AJ

TEL 01334 476161
FAX 01334 462004

EMAIL admissions@st-andrews.ac.uk
WEB www.st-andrews.ac.uk

St Andrews Students' Association
St Mary's Place
St Andrews
Fife KY16 9UZ

TEL 01334 462700/1
FAX 01334 462740

EMAIL pres@st-andrews.ac.uk
WEB www.yourunion.net

VIRGIN VIEW

*T*he University of St Andrews was founded in 1410, which makes it 41 years older than Glasgow, 173 years older than Edinburgh, and the third oldest in the English-speaking world.

It appeals almost as much to the English as to Scots as an alternative to Oxbridge. It is a small, very traditional university set in the far north-east of Scotland, 13 miles south of Dundee and 45 miles north of Edinburgh.

Jargon is as prevalent here as in the great Imperial days of the public school system, whence many of its students come, but some of the practices earmarked as traditions are in fact only a few years old, so the tradition of being traditional is not about to change.

The sojourn here a few years ago of a future King of England as an undergraduate and his recent marriage to a fellow student underlines the much vaunted statistic that more under-graduates of St Andrews marry boy/girlfiends met at uni, than at any other institution.

> '*Discretion is vital. You should not discuss your application, other than with your partner or a close family member.*'

There's a spectacular chance to be happy here. In the recent Higher Education Funding Council's National Student Survey, 93% confessed they were blissfully so, and only 3% of undergraduates fail to stay the course.

However, while the teaching is fine and caring, some get a bit of a jolt after graduation - only 68% of them got real graduate jobs within six months of leaving last time, which is very low.

Help is at hand, however. In a move that really defines the university better than we can, an advertisement appeared recently in the student magazine, The Saint, offering a position in MI5, part of which read: 'Discretion is vital. You should not discuss your application, other than with your partner or a close family member.' It was genuinely placed by the security services. A university spokesman said, 'MI5 comes to St Andrews...because it knows our graduates are highly intelligent, critical thinkers.' Civil liberties campaigner Mike Dailly said: 'St Andrews is a rarefied atmosphere that has little in common with the realities faced by real people. Where are the adverts in campuses like Abertay and Glasgow Caledonian?'

CAMPUS

St Andrews is a long way away from a lot of places, a small, ancient seaside town in north-east Scotland - beautiful, surrounded by open countryside and sea, and with one of the world's greatest golf courses on its doorstep.

FEES, BURSARIES

UK & EU Fees, 2011-12: Non-Scottish domiciled students fees in year 2009-10: £1,820 for all courses except Medicine. If you are a Scottish-domiciled first degree student you are eligible for your tuition fees to be covered by the Scottish Government. Subject-based scholarships are awarded on academic merit and made in the year of entry only. There are Purdie Chemistry Awards and Institute of Physics Bursaries, as well as a whole range of

UNIVERSITY/STUDENT PROFILE	
University since	**1410**
Situation/style	**Campus**
Student population	**9275**
Total undergraduates	**7420**
Mature	**19%**
International	**40%**
Male/female ratio	**43:57**
Equality of opportunity:	
state school intake	**61%**
social class 4-7 intake	**No data**
drop-out rate	**3%**

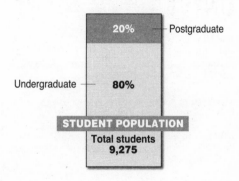

Postgraduate 20%

Undergraduate 80%

STUDENT POPULATION
Total students 9,275

TEACHING SURVEY AT A GLANCE

Avg. UCAS points accepted	**464**
Acceptance rate	**12%**
Overall satisfaction rate	**93%**
Helpful/interested staff	★★★★
Small tuition groups	★★★★
Students into graduate jobs	**68%**

Teaching most popular with undergraduates:
Anthropology, Biology & related sciences, Business, Chemistry, Classics, Computer, Economics, English, European Languages & Area Studies, French Studies, Geology (98%), German & Scandinavian Studies, History, Archaeology, Human & Social Geography, Iberian Studies, Languages, Maths & Statistics, Medicine (97%), Philosophy, Physical Geography & Environmental Science, Physical Science, Physics & Astronomy, Politics, Theology and Religious Studies (100%).

Music and Sports Scholarships.

STUDENT PROFILE

The student body is dominated by public school types, and for a Scottish university there is a surprisingly large percentage of English students. Most students are from the middle and upper classes. They fail hopelessly to make their quota for socio-economic classes 4-7, managing only a 13% take from them last year and there being no data available this. Indeed, it would be a hopelessly one-dimensional scene if it did not have an unexpectedly high (40%) intake from overseas.

It is a friendly community. 'You can almost guarantee that every time you leave your front door, you'll see someone you know,' writes Melanie Hartley, though that has to be said to be true of most small universities. 'When you've just crawled out of bed for a 9am tutorial and you've only had four hours sleep, it's debatable whether that's a good thing or not! But St Andrews is a pretty close-knit society. Indeed, once people get here they don't tend to leave. They'll even tell you that one in three graduates end up marrying other St Andrews graduates!'

ACADEMIA & JOBS

When we look at graduate careers, we find an emphasis on analysis, management science and interpersonal skills, which St Andrew's clearly teaches well in whatever subject form.

But this is a small uni, with nearly a fifth of graduates on humanities degrees and another fifth on combined subject degrees, many of them involving languages and humanities, and one fears that job hunting, for some at least, might be a lottery.

The teaching is very good, the National Student Survey found terrifically helpful and interested lecturers and small tuition groups. It is, at the same time, highly regarded for research (14th nationally in the recent assessment), so they really shouldn't have time for students. But hey, what else is there to do?

However, can subjects like Mediaeval History, Hebrew, Biblical Studies, Classical Studies, Art History and the like find their graduates jobs, however well taught? After six months a tidy number of St Andrews graduates appear in the statistics as secretaries, sales assistants, clerks, bar staff and receptionists. But one has to be careful here, for the curriculum doesn't teach fast-fix vocational. This is a real university in the traditional sense. Like, for example, Queen Mary's in London University, a rich cultural resource, one that most of the brash new universities do not even attempt to emulate, nor could they. It is as if St Andrews is operating in a parallel dimension, one that transcends the Government's shorter-term policy-making. In that context, employment-after-six-months seems a less than appropriate yardstick.

Originally, the more vocational degrees were based in Dundee and became the curriculum of Dundee University, when the split came in the 1960s. Recently, the two have moved closer again with the launch of a joint degree in engineering - Microelectronics & Photonics (there had already been a parlay through their pairing of Art History with Dundee's excellent school of Art & Design). But there is evidence, too, that this very traditional university somehow gets behind the new-uni 'how-to' ethos into a kind of 'can-do', that in their hands the business of university is, as it was originally meant to be, a training of the mind per se, that far from being out-of-date, they are moving forward with insight. They show this not least in their

SUBJECT AREAS (%)

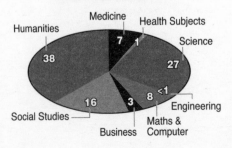

Humanities 38
Medicine 7
Health Subjects 1
Science 27
Social Studies 16
Business 3
Maths & Computer 8
Engineering <1

inspired cross-faculty strategy.

Besides an increasing range of sciences with language degrees, there are some tantalising combinations such as Arabic-International Relations, Classics-Integrated Information Technology, Hebrew-Mathematics, and Economics-Social Anthropology. There is even the ultimate cross-faculty mesh - Integrated Information Technology and Theological Studies, which if not exactly offering a fast-track to the meaning of life, suggests a challenging examination of the traditional tensions between science and humanities.

End result is a sound training for whatever you do, and a good record for jobs that do not require specific training at degree level - journalists and editors abound, for instance.

Elsewhere on the list, education and financial activities are to the fore. Instructors and secondary school teachers come from here in great number, the languages and humanities provision serving them well. For finance, it's the well-rated Economics, Financial Economics and Management degrees, some in combination with Russian (and including a year there), or with International Relations, European Languages, Mathematics, etc.

The medical degree asks AAB, including Chemistry and at least one

other of Biology, Mathematics or Physics at GCE A2 Advanced level. If either Biology or Mathematics is not offered at AS or A2 level, each must normally have been passed at GCSE grade B or better. Dual award

science is not acceptable in lieu of GCSE Biology. UKCAT will also be required. You will get a head start if you happen to attend Perth College, with which a new Pathway to Medicine initiative allows mature students from non-traditional backgrounds achieving an HNC in Applied Sciences to graduate to Medicine at the uni.

Clinical training for medical students takes place at Glasgow, Edinburgh, Aberdeen and Dundee universities. Work commenced in June 2008 on a new £45-million School of Medicine and the Sciences.

There's a good employment reputation for psychologists and care assistants, BSc Psychology providing the harder edge to what is offered in the MA joint hons system, where a good combo may be had with, say, Social Anthropology. Look also at physiology, Neuroscience, Medicinal Science, Medicinal Chemistry.

There is also a fair number of graduates getting jobs as software engineers, IT consultants, computer programmers, which shows that where they do go for a vocational dimension they can get it right. Computer Science comes with languages, Maths, Linguistics, Philosophy, Management,

RESEARCH EXCELLENCE

% of St Andrews' research that is 4* (World-class) or 3* (Internationally rated):

	4*	3*
Laboratory Clinical	15%	25%
Biological Sciences	10%	40%
Chemistry	30%	40%
Physics	25%	40%
Pure Mathematics	5%	30%
Applied Mathematics	25%	45%
Statistics	10%	50%
Computer Science	15%	45%
Geography Environment	20%	40%
Economics	15%	40%
Business\Managements	10%	50%
Politics	10%	35%
Anthropology	25%	30%
Psychology	20%	45%
Russian	0%	20%
French	10%	50%
German	20%	40%
Italian	5%	25%
Iberian	10%	55%
English	35%	35%
Classics	15%	45%
Philosophy	40%	35%
Theology	20%	30%
History	20%	40%
History of Art	15%	60%
Performing Arts	50%	35%

Physics, or Statistics. A new computer building opened in 2004.

Finally there's traditionally a close relationship with the army, and a big take-up in the civil service and defence.

A Learning and Teaching Support Unit (LTSU) works closely with the academic schools to co-ordinate and advise.

SOCIAL SCENE

STUDENTS' ASSOCIATION The student population makes up a large proportion of the town and the social life is created by students. Location denies them any big bands at the union.

Reports Melanie: 'There is no club as such; the union doubles up as a venue (**Venue 1** and **Venue 2**: 1,000 capacity), hosting events all through the week. Every Friday is the bop - a cheesy night [Red Not Bed], very reminiscent of your old school discos, but a particularly revered part of student life. Venue 2 hosts a range of different nights; Rock-soc, Bulletproof (alternative music) and Jazz-soc are regulars.' Saturday clubnights include *Squeeze* ('80s), Explosion (R&B), *Ebenezer* ('90s) or *Retro*.

WHAT'S ITS REALLY LIKE

UNIVERSITY:

Social Life	★★★★
Societies	★★★★★
Student Union services	★★★
Politics	**Student issues; activity high**
Sport	**50 clubs**
National team position	**26th**
Sport facilities	★★★
Arts opportunities	**Drama excellent; performing arts all very popular**
Student magazine	**The Vine**
Student newspaper	**The Saint**
Student radio	**Star FM**
Nightclub	**Venue 1**
Bars	**Main Bar, Venue 2**
Union ents	**Disco dance, retro, live acts massive & refined**
Union societies	**130**
Most popular society	**Breakaway (outdoor pursuits), Debating**
Parking	**Adequate**

TOWN:

Entertainment	★★
Scene	**Pubs, coffee houses**
Town/gown relations	**Average**
Risk of violence	**Low**
Cost of living	**High**
Student concessions	**Average**
Survival + 2 nights out	**£100 pw**
Part-time work campus/town	**Poor**

'Pre-Sessional week - known as Freshers week everywhere else - is non-stop events, including some biggish acts: recent weeks have hosted Space, Toploader and Euphoria. There are lots of 2nd, 3rd and 4th years willing to make friends - (some a bit too willing!) - and to show you around. Some will become your academic parents, a tradition that involves a weekend of parties with them, some time in November, before you get dressed up - many wittily/ridiculously as bottles of wine, Care Bears or condoms - and are frogmarched to the Quad on the Monday morning for a huge shaving foam fight. So fondly do many look back on their Raisin experience that they try to recreate it every year. [It can in fact degenerate into a mass piss-up and/or an excuse to pull: "Remember not to be forced into anything ..." warns the SA's Alternative Prospectus.]

'Student life is very much centred around the pubs. There are reputed to be more pubs per square mile than in any other university town, which means you're never stuck for choice: **Broons** or **Bridges** if you want to hang with the yahs, **Ogstons** or **The Raisin** if you want large and loud, **Drouthy Neebors** or **The Cellar** if you're into Real Ale. Such is the pace of life that by the time you've been here a fortnight, you should have an encyclopaedic knowledge of what's available, and your weekly "happy hour"' schedule will be sorted!

'There are lots of ways in which this is a relatively cheap place to live, not least because it's small, though in fact taxis do a healthy business with flat fares anywhere in the town.

'For entertainment other than pubs, most students look to student societies. Everybody is a member of at least one, and most people more. Options range from academic to music to political. The International Politics society recently had Michael Douglas to talk on behalf of the United Nations. You might prefer the Tunnocks Caramel Wafer Appreciation society or Quaich (whisky appreciation). You could also get involved with The Saint (student newspaper), which often wins awards, or the new radio station: Star FM.'

The Union also has one of the oldest debating societies in the world, and drama is an active aspect of student life. Each year Mermaids, a sub-committee of the Students' Association, gives financial assistance to several productions, some of which go to the Edinburgh Festival.

SPORT Golfers' paradise - the student team is one of the best in Britain. 'If this isn't your thing,' says Melanie, 'you still get to see the likes of Hugh Grant and Samuel L. Jackson strutting their stuff around town at the Dunhill Cup every October.'

In the national team championships they came 26th last year, which is very good for such a small uni. There's a sports centre with sports hall, gym, activities room, weight training room, squash courts, solarium. Extensive playing fields, jogging and trim tracks. Golf bursaries are funded by the Royal and Ancient Golf Club.

PILLOW TALK

Uniquely, nearly two-thirds of students live in University owned accommodation. Each residence has a mixed population of first year and returning students, home and overseas students, as well as students from different faculties.

'Most of the halls are in the centre of town, and are steeped in traditions,' writes Melanie. 'Most first years procure an undergraduate gown soon after arrival - a tasteful red fleece type-thing and a bit pricey. Although it varies from hall to hall, there will be occasions throughout the year when you can wear these - hall dinners, photographs,

ACCOMMODATION

Student rating	★★★
Guarantee to freshers	100%
Style	Halls, flats
Security guard	Some
Shared rooms	Some
Internet access	All
Self-catered	Some halls, all flats
En suite	Some
Approx price range pw	£78-£223
Town rent pw	£50-£130

isn't the word for these flats, but they're cheap.'

Around half St Andrews students live in halls or other uni-owned accommodation Freshers are almost automatically given a place, but you must apply for it by May 31 in the year of entry. From then on there is no guarantee and the hunt for flats, particularly near the centre of town, can begin around the middle of January. Accommodation is quite expensive for such a small town - £80 per week - largely because students make up a high proportion of the population.

chapel. Most of the halls are catered, and the food is pretty reasonable, although you'd be well advised to avoid the universally acclaimed lemon "toilet duck" mousse. Self-catering accommodation can be found in Albany Park and in Fife Park, which provide some of the most economical student accommodation in the country. "Simplistic"

GETTING THERE

☞ By road: Forth Road Bridge, M90/J3, A92 to Kirkcaldy, A915 to St Andrews; or M90/J8, A91.
☞ By rail: Nearest station on main line London (King's Cross) – Edinburgh – Aberdeen line is Leuchars (5 miles). Then bus or taxi.
☞ By air: Edinburgh Airport, airport bus to Edinburgh, thence by rail.

ST GEORGE'S, UNIVERSITY OF LONDON

St George's, University of London
Cranmer Terrace
Tooting
London SW17 0RE

TEL 020 8725 2333
FAX 020 8266 6282
EMAIL enquiries@sgul.ac.uk
WEB www.sgul.ac.uk

St George's is the University of London Medical School in Tooting, a distinguished college of the federal University. Entry requirements are four AS with three subjects continued through to A level: Chemistry and/or Biology at A level and two other subjects. Non-science subjects are encouraged. UKCAT must also be taken. There's a Foundation course available for mature students.

Leisure-wise there's a Friday disco at the Med School Bar (650 capacity) and 42 clubs and societies, Rowing and Film being the most popular. Rootin' Tootin' itself has a colourful culture, plenty of curry houses, and - incomprehensibly to anyone not born of the London property boom - is now classed as a gentrified area.

The sports ground is in Cobham, Surrey - 9 winter pitches and 2 cricket squares, grass and hard tennis courts. They also keep an eight and a four in the London Uni boathouse and have facilities for sailing. Back at the hospital there's the Lowe Sports Centre, 6 squash courts, gym and

COLLEGE PROFILE

Founded	1751
Status	Associate of London Uni
Situation/style	City site
Student population	4420
Full-time undergraduates	3960
ACCOMMODATION:	
Availability to freshers	100%
Style	Halls
Cost pw (no food/food)	£100+
City rent pw	£100+

areas for badminton, basketball, etc.

Horton Hall, is the new hall of residence, 15 minutes' walk away: 332 students in self-catering single study/bedroom units, each unit with its own en-suite facilities. Flats are formed from four or six units grouped together. There are on-site laundry facilities, internet access in all units, and a 24-hour security-manned reception.

GETTING THERE

☞ Tooting Broadway Underground station (Northern Line), Tooting overland.

UNIVERSITY OF SALFORD

TheUniversity of Salford
The Crescent,
Salford,
Greater Manchester M5 4WT

TEL 0161 295 5000
FAX 0161 295 5999
EMAIL course-enquiries@salford.ac.uk
WEB www.salford.ac.uk

Salford Students' Union
University House
Salford,
Greater Manchester M5 4WT

TEL 0161 736 7811
FAX 0161 737 1633
EMAIL students-union@salford.ac.uk
WEB www.salfordstudents.com

VIRGIN VIEW

Salford University is about Enterprise, Entrepreneurship, and Employment for its graduates. These are its 'added value', along with this year's big move: MediaCityUK, located at the heart of Salford Quays with six national BBC departments and loads of independent creative, digital and media organisations, is a unique chance for 1,500 students to choose from 39 courses and work alongside media professionals with a view to a future in the industry.

For years Salford was known for Built Environment, Science, Engineering, Computer and Business. But now it's also into the Arts, Languages and Media.

Salford itself is minutes from the centre of Manchester, and is famous for being the birthplace of L S Lowry. The Lowry Museum and Art Gallery are also to be found at the renovated Salford Quays, the old docks where on Pier 9 at the new Media City, the BBC has taken residence.

There is a relatively low ask at Salford, around 240 points, but 78% of their students said in the 2010 National Survey that they

UNIVERSITY/STUDENT PROFILE	
University since	**1967**
Situation/style	**Campus**
Student population	**20095**
Total undergraduates	**15870**
Mature	**49%**
International	**17%**
Male/female ratio	**48:52**
Equality of opportunity:	
state school intake	**98%**
social class 4-7 intake	**43%**
drop-out rate	**15%**

were satisfied with what goes on, and 70% of them got real graduate jobs within six months of leaving. The drop-out rate (15%) is high, a function perhaps of the number of students from families new to the whole idea of higher education.

CAMPUS

Thirty-nine Courses will be taught at the MediaCityUK base from autumn 2011. 'The main campus, Peel Park, is 2 miles from Manchester City Centre,' reports Shauna Corr.

'So what do you know about Salford? Well, have you ever seen the opening credits of Coronation Street? That's Salford,' informs Lindsay Oakes. 'It's where Corrie is set and filmed. You may also have heard that it's a rough area with a high car crime rate. Sadly, Salford is known more by its bad reputation than for any of its good points. Of course I'd be lying if I told you that there aren't any negative aspects to living here; it's like any suburban city area: if you're not sensible then it could be dangerous. But where better to spend three or four years of your student life than in the student capital of Britain - Manchester? Salford University actually lies closer to the centre of Manchester than Manchester University itself. It is only a fifteen-minute bus ride away, or five minutes in a taxi.'

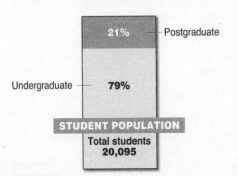

Postgraduate 21%

Undergraduate 79%

STUDENT POPULATION

Total students
20,095

FEES, BURSARIES

UK & EU Fees, 2011-12: £3,375 p.a. Bursary for students in receipt of full HE Maintenance Grant is £338. Other than the International Undergraduate bursary, which is worth up to £2,000, there are the £1,000 Vice-Chancellor's Scholarship and various subject specific, community and placement bursaries, which do not exceed £1,000. See www.isite.salford.ac.uk/money/help/grants/.

STUDENT PROFILE

This is an indelibly 'new university' student body, with 43% from the lowest socio-economic groups, 19% from so-called low-participation neighbourhoods, 49% mature students, and 27% part-timers.

'There are students from all walks of life here,' says Lindsay, 'and from practically every continent. There is a real international feel to Salford because of all the links we have with universities abroad [see Academia, below]. And it may be true of many universities, but there is a real community among Salford students,' in particular among freshers in the student village.

ACADEMIA & JOBS

The University has replaced its four faculties with three colleges to oversee a number of schools. The **College of Arts & Social Sciences**: Art & Design; English, Sociology, Politics & Contemporary History; Languages; Law; Media, Music & Performance: Salford Business School. **College of Health & Social Care**: Health, Sport & Rehabilitation Sciences; Nursing & Midwifery; Social Work, Psychology & Public Health. **College of Science & Technology**: School of the Built Environment; Computing, Science & Engineering; Environment & Life Sciences.

The last Research Assessment Exercise found that 12% of Salford's research is world class (4 star) and 83% of international significance (3 star). Built Environment, Library & Information Management,

TEACHING SURVEY AT A GLANCE

Avg. UCAS points accepted	**240**
Acceptance rate	**21%**
Overall satisfaction rate	**78%**
Helpful/interested staff	★★★
Small tuition groups	★★★
Students into graduate jobs	**70%**

Teaching most popular with undergraduates:
Accounting (100%), Anatomy, Physiology & Pathology, Biology & related sciences, Civil Engineering, Economics, Finance, History, Iberian Studies, Imaginative Writing, Law, Nursing, Other Subjects Allied to Medicine, Physical Science, Physics & Astronomy, Social Policy, Sociology, Sports Science, Zoology (100%).

Teaching least popular with undergraduates:
Journalism (50%).

and Media made the best showing.

This year the BBC will be moving five major departments, including Sport, Children's and Radio Five Live from London to MediaCity UK at Salford Quays, and Salford University's facilities there will include HD TV studios, radio broadcast studios, digital media and performance labs, post-production suites, a lab research facility, meeting rooms with video conferencing.

The University building will be the only one at MediaCityUK with space open for everyone to use. The theory is that this will place students in prime position for digital and media careers. Salford has signed partnership agreements with the BBC. Visiting professors in the media department include Alex Connock of Ten Alps Media, and Panorama producer Steve Hewlett.

And yet, when the *Times Higher Magazine* asked students in 2010 which courses were best taught at the University, media didn't get a look in, only 50% of the class gave one course (journalism) their approval. This despite the fact that The National Council for the Training of Journalists (NCTJ), the training body for the journalism industry, has ranked the (postgraduate) MA Journalism course as one of the top four in the UK.

It seems odd that there is this dislocation with research/post-grad Media at Salford, for there's great hands-on student media - Shock FM and Channel M (TV) are the leisure-time expression. The campus-based TV channel broadcasts to half a million people in the Manchester region with programmes developed and made at Salford's media facilities.

There are degrees in Radio, TV (including Mobile & Internet TV), TV & Radio (theoretical

SUBJECT AREAS (%)

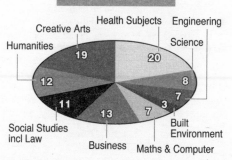

Creative Arts
Humanities
Health Subjects
Engineering
Science
Social Studies incl Law
Business
Built Environment
Maths & Computer

19 / 20 / 12 / 8 / 11 / 7 / 3 / 13 / 7

RESEARCH EXCELLENCE

% of Salford's research that is
4* *(World-class) or* **3*** *(Internationally rated):*

	4*	3*
Nursing/Midwifery	10%	30%
Health Professions	5%	30%
Statistics	0%	35%
Metallurgy and Materials	10%	40%
Built Environment	25%	40%
Geography, Environment	5%	25%
Business/Management	5%	25%
Info. Management	25%	20%
Law	0%	20%
Social Work	5%	45%
European Studies	5%	20%
English	10%	25%
Linguistics	5%	30%
Art and Design	5%	15%
Media Studies	15%	35%
Music	0%	25%

professional strengths - communication skills, leadership, teamwork, career management, organisational skills. 100 graduates have so far found employment through this scheme.

The University was a pioneer of sandwich courses, work placement schemes. Their links with local firms are legendary. 'There are certainly strong links with industry,' says Shauna, 'and opportunity on many courses for industrial sandwich years, home and abroad.'

In the bedrock subjects, aspiring property developers still flock to Salford's world-class School of Construction & Property Management. In the Research Assessment Built Environment was something of a coup - 65% of the research was either 4* or 3*, which gave it lead position in the subject in at least one league table.

Serious employment strengths shore up the business sector, where graduates find jobs quickly in Finance, Marketing, Personnel, Human Resources, Economics, and Business Computing. There's also a niche or two, like Gambling & Leisure Management, with study in North America, and Tourism Management.

elements married to practical modules, such as editing, producing, directing, a new Film degree, Journalism (with Broadcasting and other combinations, including War Studies), Professional Broadcasting, Professional Sound & Video Technology, Digital Broadcast Technology, Media Production and Media Technology (aimed at technical operators and operational engineers), Audio Technology, Audio & Visual Systems, Design for Digital Media... Whether the move to Salford Quays will galvanise this area of the prvision remains to be seen.

If their attitude is anything to go by, it will. A cohort of journalism students from the University are currently helping prisoners at HMP Styal women's prison near Wilmslow to write and produce their own in-house quarterly magazine, *Innit*.

As mentioned above, Salford is all about Enterprise, Entrepreneurship and Employment. A Salford lecturer has just been named University Adviser of the Year at the national Students in Free Enterprise (SIFE) competition for her work to encourage students to think about entrepreneurship as part of their studies. Salford's Origin scheme offers a 12-month place to any Salford student or graduate who has a business idea and submits a proposal. The first three months are rent-free and the remaining nine months are heavily subsidised. Business support is available for tenants as well as mentoring opportunities to help these new businesses to develop. A Graduate Gateway scheme starts with a 5-day programme of intensive training which focuses on each individual's personal and

WHAT IT'S REALLY LIKE

UNIVERSITY:

Social Life	★★
Societies	★★★
Student Union services	★★
Politics	**Interest low, but SWSS & Anti-Nazi League**
Sport	**19 clubs**
National team position	**107th**
Sport facilities	★★★
Arts opportunities	**Excellent**
Student newspaper	**Student Direct**
Student radio	**Shock fm**
Student TV	**Channel M**
Nightclub	**The Pav**
Bars	**Lowry, Sub Club, Wallness Tavern**
Union ents	**Themed**
Union societies	**19**
Most popular societies	**Plastic Surgery**
Parking	**Adequate**
CITY:	
Entertainment	★★★★★
City scene	**Legendary**
Town/gown relations	**Average-poor**
Risk of violence	**High**
Cost of living	**Average**
Student concessions	**Good**
Survival + 2 nights out	**£90 pw**
Part-time work campus/town	**Average/excellent**

The School of Languages is another that is impressive employment-wise. Degrees such as Arabic/English Translation & Interpreting catch the eye. There's also Chinese, Portuguese, Spanish, Italian, French, German... Translators and interpreters come in number out of Salford, and a £1m campus-based Language Resource Centre offers advanced multimedia and language facilities, so many courses have an international dimension.

Would-be health care professionals are equally well served by their courses in Radiography, Midwifery, Occupational Therapy, Physiotherapy, Podiatry, Prosthetics/Orthotics, and Sport Rehab.

Among Biological Sciences, one of the most popular for its teaching is BSc Aquatic Sciences, which covers water resources, hydrology, glaciology, climate change, freshwater, estuarine and marine biology, and fisheries.

Finally, 47 Salford students were the first ever to graduate from the new Law faculty in July 2010. A £10-million building features a Law Society accredited library and mock-up court room.

SOCIAL SCENE

STUDENTS' UNION 'The union runs 4 bars (one being a nightclub-come-bar),' writes Shauna. 'The **Pav** (at Castle Irwell student village) has two main nights: Tuesday and Friday.

> *BBC TV is already involved with Salford's Media courses. This year five BBC departments are moving from London next door to the uni at Salford Quays.*

Tuesday's *Flair*, '60s, '70s and '80's music, is a constant, and whatever they call Friday night when you get there, it won't be retro. The **Lowry** bar on Peel Park is situated in University House, it's a good day-bar. So far this year we have had a Ministry of Sound night, at which Youseff played, and we've had Jason Donovon, Timmy Mallet and Tymes four as well as student bands and DJs. We also have the Wallness Tavern, recently refurbished, open all day. The sub club, Frederick road, is a good day bar for students on site. All bars have games' machines and pool tables. Local pubs are a bit rough and not always safe for students.

'One thing I should point out,' writes Lindsay, 'is that unlike most unis, beer and food at Salford are not subsidised.'

Especially active among numerous societies is the LGB group - lesbian/gay. Salford has been recognised as one of the most gay-friendly universities in the UK by leading lesbian, gay and bisexual charity Stonewall whose website - www.gaybydegree.org.uk/

As for media, '*Student Direct* is our weekly publication,' Shauna continues, 'shared with both Bolton Uni and Manchester University.' The union rates most active societies as Plastic Surgery/Shock fm, both music societies: 'Plastic Surgery is the DJ soc, and Shock fm deals with the student radio station (see *Academia* above).'

Arts and media are part of the lives of the predominantly scienctific student body. Shock radio took a Bronze at the Awards last year. As the Arts provision has grown, so their interest in what is changing around them has galvanised the students, and extra-curricular Arts have become a reality. Recently, the **Robert Powell Theatre** was opened by namesake Salfordian actor, Robert Powell.

Salford Community Action Project (SCAP) is a student project involved with children in the locality, and senior citizens, the disabled, ex-offenders, and in giving English lessons to overseas students and others.

SPORT Writes Suzanne: 'The Union provides a swimming pool, climbing wall, weights room, badminton, tennis and squash courts, five-a-side football pitches, sun beds, sauna and Jacuzzi. There is a large sports hall with just about every indoor pitch marked down, facilities for trampoline, and sports pitches at Castle Irwell for rugby, football, hockey and cricket.' The annual Two Cities Boat race between Salford and Manchester University at Salford Quays is the North's answer to Oxford and Cambridge. There's a partnership with Salford City Reds Rugby League Club and Lancashire County Cricket Club whereby students on sports science and physiotherapy courses gain experience of treating professional athletes. The Salford Reds have also been coaching the University rugby teams and train on the uni's playing fields.

TOWN Cost-wise, as Suzanne Ashton points out, 'Salford has all the advantages of a town - cheap rent, everything close by, a friendly atmosphere - and yet still with the facilities of a city nearby.' Notes Shauna: 'There's part-time work in union bars, in ents, in the library and in Manchester, and a Job shop.'

PILLOW TALK

They guarantee a place in one of the 4,000 study bedrooms to all freshers who have an unconditional offer and whose accommodation application form has been received by 12 noon on the September 1 in the year of admission.

The 3 main campuses (Peel Park, Frederick

Road, Adelphi) are within walking distance of the residences.

'There is a good selection of accommodation ranging from Castle Irwell Student Village to blocks of flats and on-campus catered accommodation,' Shauna reports. Writes Lindsay: 'In the summer, the entire village turns out on to the playing fields to play sports, sunbathe or even have barbecues. In the winter, you'll find yourself having a snowball fight with someone you've never met before.'

Free parking at Castle Irwell, Brammall and Matthias Courts, John Lester and Eddie Colman Courts. A paid-for permit is required for Horlock and Constantine Courts Monthly price tbc

All accommodation sites are visited by a free campus bus.

GETTING THERE
☛ By road: M62 (which connects with the M6, M63)/M602. Coach services good.

ACCOMMODATION	
Student rating	★
Guarantee to freshers	**100%**
Style	**Halls, flats**
Security guard	**All**
Shared rooms	**Family rooms**
Internet access	**All**
Self-catered	**All**
En suite	**Some**
Approx price range pw	**£63-£98**
City rent pw	**£44-£103**

☛ By rail: Salford Crescent station is on-campus; Manchester Oxford Road is a few minutes away; Liverpool, 1:20; Sheffield, 1:30; Birmingham New Street, 2:30; London Euston, 3:30.
☛ By air: Manchester Airport,.
☛ By coach: London, 4:35; Bristol, 5:00.

SCHOOL OF ORIENTAL & AFRICAN STUDIES

School of Oriental & African Studies
Thornhaugh Street
London WC1H 0XG

TEL 020 7898 4034
EMAIL study@soas.ac.uk
WEB www.soas.ac.uk

SOAS Student Union
Thornhaugh Street
London WC1H 0XG

TEL 0207 898 4996
EMAIL pb14@soas.ac.uk
WEB www.soasunion.org/

VIRGIN VIEW

*S*OAS *is unique, the only university in the UK offering programmes in law and social sciences, languages and cultures, arts and humanities focused exclusively on Asia, Africa and the Middle East. It was recently awarded the coveted Queen's Anniversary Prize for Higher Education.*

It is a university of character with an unusual history. A small (only 2,845 undergraduates) specialist college of the federal University of London, it had its beginnings around 1912 as an institution for the training of young men of the British Empire in the skills necessary to run the colonies. Today, women outnumber men (60:40), left wing politics and human rights have taken over from imperialism, and 44% of the student cohort comes from 140 different nations.

SOAS is a small, chilled, international but amazingly cohesive community, a cool, cosmopolitan enclave hidden away on a secluded campus in Bloomsbury, central London, with its own unpretentious bar of legendary status and atmosphere, where

UNIVERSITY/STUDENT PROFILE	
University since	**1916**
Situation/style	**Civic**
Student population	**4895**
Total undergraduates	**2845**
Mature	**40%**
International	**44%**
Male/female ratio	**40:60**
Equality of opportunity:	
state school intake	**76%**
social class 4-7 intake	**28%**
drop-out rate	**8%**

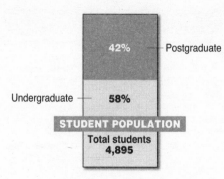

STUDENT POPULATION

42% — Postgraduate

Undergraduate — 58%

Total students
4,895

you are more likely to meet an intellectual adventurer just back from three months in the jungles of South East Asia than Tracey from Essex wondering whether her BA in media studies will get her an internship at Sky TV come summer.

Students in the latest Times Higher Student Experience Survey *rated SOAS for its high-quality, helpful and interested staff, its amazing library, the campus environment, and its community atmosphere.*

How do you become one of them?

When it comes to the crunch, what SOAS wants beyond good grades is evidence of enthusiasm for your subject and interest in Asia and/or Africa, and relevant work experience.

Say SOAS graduates Peter Beveridge and Catherine Wynne, 'Do not think of coming if you haven't dragged a backpack through either a) Thailand or b) India, and claimed to have gained a unique insight into unspoilt and indigenous cultures. If, however, you haven't, lie.'

CAMPUS

You arrive on campus by means of noisy, dusty Russell Square and your attention is at once arrested by the sight of the Brunei Gallery, part of London's 'Museum Mile', which stretches from King's Cross to the River Thames. The modern gallery hosts a changing programme of exhibitions about subjects and regions studied at the School and you will come to know it well, along with its cubbeyhole of a shop on the ground floor, which does a nice and inexpensive line in postcards from the Qing dynasty, Kangx period.

Beyond the Brunei and the main SOAS building opposite, lie University College (UCL) and Birkbeck College, fellow members of London University, whose Student Union is also close by. It is a

precinct of scholarship set apart from the madding crowd, but not at all intimidating. If you are the sort of person to be accepted by SOAS you will feel almost immediately a mutual sense of belonging.

Later, you will discover a second campus at Vernon Square, just a 20 minute walk away, with teaching space, a Learning Resource Centre, an internet café and two purpose-built student residences.

FEES, BURSARIES

UK & EU Fees, 2011-12: £3,375. Overseas: £12,600 p.a. Undergraduate Research Awards, SOAS Bursaries and the Gulkenkian Scholarship in Armenian Studies are available.

STUDENT PROFILE

There is a state school/public school ratio of 76:24, typical of a Russell Group university, although interestingly 28% of these come from social classes 4-7 (the working classes). Forty per cent of the student body is mature, 44% from overseas and 60% female. There appear to be no subsets or dominant groups: it is a small classless student body, politically aware and internationally minded.

ACADEMIA

Their research strengths lie in Anthropology, Middle-Eastern, African and Asian Studies, History, History of Art and especially Music: 80% of Music is either world class or of international importance. But they are teachers too. With more than 300 academic staff dedicated to teaching 300 undergraduate degree combinations there is highly personal, small group teaching, with a student-staff ratio one of the best in the UK.

The Library houses the greatest concentration of scholarly works on Asia, Africa and the Middle East in the world and is one of just five National Research Libraries in the country. It holds over 1.2 million volumes, books, periodicals and audio-visual materials, and the interior is designed by Denys Lasdun, famed for his ziggurats at the University of

TEACHING SURVEY AT A GLANCE	
Avg. UCAS points accepted	390
Acceptance rate	19%
Overall satisfaction rate	85%
Helpful/interested staff	★★★
Small tuition groups	★★★
Students into graduate jobs	78%

Teaching most popular with undergraduates:
Anthropology (97%), Asian Studies, History, Archaeology, Law, Social Studies.

RESEARCH EXCELLENCE

*% of SOAS's research that is
4* (World-class) or 3* (Internationally rated):*

	4*	3*
Business/Management	5%	35%
Law	5%	40%
Politics	15%	45%
Anthropology	30%	40%
Development Studies	10%	30%
Middle Eastern/African	25%	35%
Asian Studies	30%	35%
Linguistics	10%	25%
Theology, Religions	15%	50%
History	30%	30%
History of Art	30%	20%
Music	35%	45%

East Anglia campus. Here, at SOAS, his tiered floor levels reach up around a central space like the hanging gardens of Babylon. The £8m Library Transformation Project is part of a bigger scheme that will transform the School as it approaches its centenary in 2016 and provide a modern environment for its staff, students and users from around the world. IT facilities are available. The first phase is now complete.

Also in support of the teaching provision is a welfare team, a disability adviser, diversity adviser and various academic advisers.

Employers attracted by the unique combination of skills, knowledge and cultural experience acquired from the SOAS study programmes participate in careers events on campus, and many advertise online through the SOAS Careers Service, which organises insight days, presentations and meetings with individuals in all employment sectors. Many graduates go on to further study, but a large proportion build careers as human rights lawyers, politicians, journalists, diplomats, and ambassadors, or take jobs in the civil service, business and finance, or the arts and cultural institutions. Some have been known to take up PR and consultative functions with Medecins Sans Frontieres, Amnesty International, UNESCO, the World Bank and the Aga Khan Trust for Culture, while others have joined the BBC or Al-Arabiya news. SOAS is active in securing highly sought after internships with these, and such as the UN Refugees Agency, the European Union, and Action Against Hunger.

SOAS alumni include Jung Chang (author of *Wild Swans*); Aung San Suu Kyi (leader of opposition to military junta in Burma); Michael Jay (former ambassador to France and head of the Diplomatic Service); Paul Robeson; Professor Fred Halliday (Middle East expert at the LSE); Zeinab Badawi (newsreader); the comedian, Dom Joly; and, of course, Beveridge and Wynne: 'Forget Oxbridge, this is the place to come for experts on Africa and Asia. Law students whine that they are the only people who ever do any work, but generally all students here are highly motivated and courses are demanding. Beware, language courses are very intense. Teachers say that languages should become your life. Be prepared to decorate your bathroom with Vietnamese verbs.'

SOCIAL SCENE

There is a history of political protest and sit-ins at the SOAS Union. It was once a hot-bed of left wing activity. 'But now,' says Peter Beveridge, 'the Student Union fills its days drinking instant coffee out of polystyrene cups, with occasional single-issue activism and petition signing to stop evil, multi-national corporations destroying native cultures, flora and fauna. Most activities are organised by SOAS's student societies. Many are worth getting involved in, and have interesting debates and guest speakers. You could find yourself chatting over wine and nibbles with some chap who could get you a flash job in the UN or World Bank.'

The Union's history is also to be concerned with problems close to home. The 'Great Occupation of 1997' (spoken of in hushed tones

WHAT IT'S REALLY LIKE

UNIVERSITY:

Social Life	★★
Societies	★★
Student Union services	★★★★
Politics	**Global, strong**
Sport	**19 clubs**
National team position	**107th**
Sport facilities	★★★
Arts opportunities	**Excellent**
Student newspaper	**Spirit**
Student radio	**Open Air**
Bars	**The Bar**
Union ents	**Friday live**
Union clubs & societies	**150+**
Parking	**None**

CITY:

Entertainment	★★★★★
City scene	**London**
Town/gown relations	**Average-poor**
Risk of violence	**High**
Cost of living	**Average**
Student concessions	**Good**
Survival + 2 nights out	**£100+ pw**
Part-time work campus/town	**Average/excellent**

even today) was over the School refusing to buy library tickets for students to Senate House Library. It lasted three weeks. This term a decision to allow a 'Miss University' contest resulted in a loud, largely female student protest. 'People here aren't your average,' says a student, 'there's an edge that makes it a really worthwhile place to come. If you're independent, confident, and know your own mind, then come. If you want organised pub crawls and your hand held, go to just about any other uni.'

The Union bar is often crowded and has a great atmosphere, people playing backgammon during the day, a jukebox, a quiz on Wednesday, live music in the JCR on Friday. Otherwise, it's extra-curricular seminars, lectures and concerts rather than mad party pranks. The environs of Bloomsbury are great for pubs, however. Indeed, being in central London, anything is feasible.

The first of a long line of college magazines was published in 1934, entitled inspiringly *The Magazine of the Students* Union. *The Spirit* first drew breath in 1991 and is the student union magazine still today, published twice a term. Open Air Radio was launched in December 2005 and is now known as SOAS Radio. It produces amazing programmes on FM with a focus on Africa, Asia and the Middle East, and their Diasporas of course.

They have their own rugby, football and net-ball teams, but the University of London Union (ULU) across the precinct offers a much wider

ACCOMMODATION	
Student rating	★★
Guarantee to freshers	**100%**
Style	**Halls, flats**
Security guard	**All**
Shared rooms	**None**
Internet access	**Most halls, all flats**
Self-catered	**No halls, all flats**
En suite	**Most halls, all flats**
Approx price range pw	**£120-£314**
City rent pw	**£100+**

range, as well as swimming pool and gym facilities.

PILLOW TALK
SOAS students have exclusive use of three student residences, two located on Pentonville Road, adjacent to the Vernon Square campus, and one in Stoke Newington. There are 769 rooms all told (en-suite, self-catering); 180 in seven intercollegiate residences. No car parking.

GETTING THERE
☛ By tube: Russell Square (Piccadilly line); overland stations (King's Cross, St Pancras and Euston) are all within a short walk.

SCHOOL OF PHARMACY, LONDON UNIVERSITY

School of Pharmacy
29-39 Brunswick Square
London WC1N 1AX

TEL 020 7753 5831
FAX 020 7753 5829
EMAIL registry @ulsop.ac.uk
WEB www.ulsop.ac.uk

The School of Pharmacy is another specialist school of the University of London. In 2008 the Government's research assessments confirmed its national and international reputation, with 25% of its research rated world-class and 40% of international significance. In the same year, in the Higher Education Funding Council's National Student Survey, 88% of its students said they were satisfied and 100% of them got jobs within six months of graduating. The mystery is that the school registered the worst drop in applications of any higher education institution in 2008: 28.1% fewer applicants chose it than in the previous year.

Situated within walking distance of the British Museum, the school has a small amount of its own

accommodation, otherwise it's London University's intercollegiate halls. For sport, the school shares grounds out at Enfield with the Royal Free Hospital Medical School (now part of University College, London); closer to home are facilities for squash, badminton, swimming, etc., and the London University Union is close at hand. There is a union bar, a theme night on Friday, and facilities for table tennis, pool, etc..

GETTING THERE
☛ By tube: Russell Square (Piccadilly line); overland stations (King's Cross, St Pancras and Euston) are all within a short walk.

STUDENT SHEFFIELD - THE CITY

Steely Sheffield is a born-again cosmopolitan city offering pretty much anything you desire. Many students choose to stay after graduation.

CLUBS, BARS AND EATERIES

Writes current undergraduate Rosie Legg: 'The best places to go are **Embrace** on a Monday and **Plug** on a Thursday. These are both really big clubs and always packed. On a Friday, the best is the **O2 Academy** to *Propaganda*. This is an Indie night, but it also has a dance room too. The drinks are quite expensive here, but it's worth going.

'If you fancy just going to a few bars, find your way to West Street. There are loads of places, from a standard **Wetherspoons** to some nice cocktail bars. Some of the best are **Cavendish**, which is a good place to start, **Vodka Revolution**, **Varsity** and **SOYO**. There is also Division Street, with a really nice trendy bar called **Bungalows and Bears**. I recommend the Nachos from here, they're HUGE!

'If your parents ever visit, get them to take you to Leopold Square at the end of West Street, which has a **Zizzis** and a **Strada**. Both do student deals if you print off the vouchers from studentbeans.com. There's also a **Wagamammas** and other posh restaurants.

COST

'Nights out are as cheap as you want them. Most tickets for Union nights are £4/5 and there are always drink offers. The good thing about Sheffield, if you are saving your pennies, is that you can just walk everywhere, if needs be, and trams and buses are cheap (Stagecoach bus company does student travel).'

GALLERIES AND THEATRES

The Crucible and **Lyceum** are Sheffield's 2 major playhouse venues, they have shows running all year round, ranging from pantomime, to ballet to Shakespeare. Both offer discounts for students, who also have their own productions at the **Drama Studio** on Glossop Road.

Among major arthouses, the star attraction is the **Millennium Galleries**. **Graves Art Gallery** has smaller, but still great, exhibitions, a recent highlight the William Blake show from the Tate in London.

SCREENS

Film buffs love the **Showroom** on Paternoster Row, an arty cinema with bar attached; it even does a 'film and meal deal'. Cheap and cheerful in-town cinema is the 10-screen **Odeon**, while out at **Meadowhall** there's a 15-screen multiplex, where a film can be incorporated into a day out shopping. The **UGC, also** outside the city centre, boasts a huge 'Full Monty' screen, perfect for watching the latest blockbuster.

SPORT

Sheffield has Sheffield Wednesday, who play at **Hillsborough**, and Sheffield United at **Bramall Lane**. Whatever you do, don't confuse the two. Also, the Sheffield Steelers glide across the ice at **The Arena,** and the Westfield Sharks shoot the hoop there on non-ice days. Of course, the **Crucible** hosts the Embassy World Snooker Championship. Alternatively, many like a flutter at **Owlerton Greyhound Stadium** on Penistone Road.

STUDENT GHETTOES

As with most cities, students have monopolised a couple of areas. Broomhill, a paradise of pubs, takeaways, a supermarket and the ever popular **Record Collector** – whatever your taste in music, they'll stock it. Convenient for the Sheffield Uni campus – 10 minutes away on foot – it's reasonably cheap and pretty safe. Hallam students, meanwhile, tend to congregate around the Ecclesall Road area, or roads just off the city centre, being just a stone's throw away form their 3 campuses. Again, these areas have everything a student needs – supermarket, pubs and the odd bookshop or two.

VIOLENCE AND TOWN/GOWN

Writes Rosie: 'The whole time I've been at Sheffield I've honestly never felt unsafe, even on nights out. Taxis wait outside the main clubs and also outside the union. There's the odd fight here and there, but security, especially around the union, is first class.

CONSUMERISM

The debt-riddled student gets a lifeline from Broomhill's array of charity shops, also from **Castle Market** – brilliant for cheap veg, fish and meat. Those past caring visit Division Street, where all the latest trendy and alternative gear purveyed in chic boutiques and the **Forum Shopping Centre**. Chapel Walk is full of small shops with large price tags, and although Ecclesall Road is a student area, it, too, has shops generally far too expensive for a student's pocket. Then there is the experience of **Meadowhall** (Meadow 'hell' on a Saturday) .

Ellen Grundy with Rosie Legg

UNIVERSITY OF SHEFFIELD

The University of Sheffield
Western Bank
Sheffield S10 2TN

TEL 0114 222 2000
FAX 0114 222 1234
EMAIL ask@sheffield.ac.uk
WEB www.sheffield.ac.uk

Sheffield University Students Union
Western Bank
Sheffield S10 2TG

TEL 0114 222 2000
FAX 0114 275 2506
EMAIL [firstname.surname]@sheffield.ac.uk
WEB www.sheffieldunion.com

VIRGIN VIEW

Sheffield is a top university across the board. Whichever one of our statistical boxes you care to consult, it excels. And, as the Student Profile shows (below) this is an exceptionally well balanced university.

Rose Wild writes: 'In today's cut-throat world, where new students have to pay just to enter this carnival of hedonistic abandon, and thereafter graduate to a future in which security is not guaranteed, it is probably worth choosing a university which gives you best value for your dosh and which has a reputation that will outshine the competition. That university is Sheffield.'

A resounding 89% of Sheffield student voices agreed with Rose in the last National Student Survey, and 78% will have real graduate jobs within six months of leaving. Up among the Top 100 Universities of the World, it is one of the top few universities in the UK for extra-curricular opportunity, and union was voted number 1 by the The Times Higher's *Student Experience Survey in 2011.*

What do they look for from applicants other than grades? 'Creative thinkers and problem solvers,' they tell us, 'students who like getting involved in communities, people who want to make a difference to the world around them.' That is Sheffield.

CAMPUS

Writes Rosie Legg: 'Sheffield University is pretty much just on the edge of the city centre, within 20 minutes walking distance. Catch a bus or a tram and it will take you 10. Sheffield Union is at the heart of campus, with loads of places to eat, bars, a few shops and computer study areas. It's always lively and busy.

'The building that will stand out to you most is

UNIVERSITY/STUDENT PROFILE	
University since	**1905**
Situation/style	**Civic**
Student population	**24715**
Total undergraduates	**17600**
Mature	**28%**
International	**22%**
Male/female ratio	**48:52**
Equality of opportunity:	
state school intake	**87%**
social class 4-7 intake	**23%**
drop-out rate	**5%**

Firth Court. It's beautiful. With huge windows and turrets, it looks like something out of Hogwarts. This is the building they show most in the prospectus. The others, which are more modern, are nowhere near as nice, and to be frank are quite bleak, just concrete blocks.

'Coming from a small town I was really worried that I would feel overwhelmed, lost, but the city centre is much smaller than I anticipated. You only need to hop on a tram and you'll be near enough anywhere in less than 30 minutes. Buses and trams are really reliable. Some bus companies offer 50p student travel, or an all-day ticket at £3.'

FEES, BURSARIES

UK & EU Fees, 2011-12: £3,375. You could have a bursary of between £275 and £290 depending on

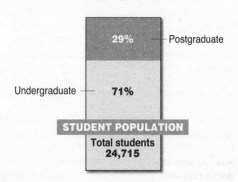

29% — Postgraduate

Undergraduate — 71%

STUDENT POPULATION
Total students
24,715

TEACHING SURVEY AT A GLANCE

Avg. UCAS points accepted	**410**
Acceptance rate	**13%**
Overall satisfaction rate	**89%**
Helpful/interested staff	★★★★
Small tuition groups	★★★
Students into graduate jobs	**78%**

Teaching most popular with undergraduates:
Accounting, Aerospace Engineering (97%), Architecture, Asian Studies, Aural/Oral Sciences, Biology, Business, Chemical Engineering, Chemistry, Civil Engineering, Computer, Dentistry, Economics, Electronic & Electrical Engineering, English, European Languages & Area Studies (100%), Finance, Genetics (100%), History, Archaeology, Human & Social Geography, Journalism, Landscape Design, Materials & Minerals Technology, Maths, Mechanical Engineering, Medicine, Molecular Biology, Music, Ophalmics, Eastern, Asian & African Languages & Area Studies (100%), Performing Arts, Philosophy, Physical Geography & Environmental Science (100%), Physical Science, Physics & Astronomy, Planning, Politics, Subjects Allied to Medicine, Technology, Theology, Zoology.

household income. See www.sheffield.ac.uk/bursaries/. They offer a range of scholarships for international undergraduate students who show exceptional promise - www.sheffield.ac.uk/international. Otherwise, there are Alumni Scholarships (www.sheffield. ac.uk/ssid/finance/alumni.html); Eliahou Dangoor Scholarships for talented students of science, technology, engineering and maths (£1,000), awards for past or present employees of Samuel Osborn & Co Ltd (£150 and £1,000 toward your fees), Choral Scholarships (up to £2000), and the St John's Church Ranmoor Music Scholarships for organists and choristers.

STUDENT PROFILE

There are plenty of bright undergraduates, most of them capable of 410 points at A level. There's a good balance of public and state school types, far healthier than the Bristol-Durham-Edinburgh axis, and a fair number of the lower socio-economic social groups (23%). As for mature students and groups from overseas, Sheffield is taking in 28% and 22% respectively. So, students come from a variety of backgrounds and together they are happy enough to admit to only a 5% drop-out rate.

Writes Rose Wild: 'One of the most striking and pleasing things about the cosy little cocoon of life, which makes this university a very pleasant place to be, is that you will rarely - if ever - come across prejudice of any sort. The union's absolute tolerance of the sizeable gay community is but one reflection of this. Another striking feature is the high visibility of the religious community.'

Says Rosie Legg: 'I've never noticed a dominant social group at Sheffield,. One thing I have noticed is that because the Union is so organised, masses of people get involved in what's going on, and this gives you a real sense of belonging.'

ACADEMIA & JOBS

The research is good, they came 14th nationwide in the Government's last assessment. The teaching is also good, with the *Times Higher Education's* Student Experience Survey finding lecturers with an eye to students' interests and decent sized tuition groups. Meanwhile, masses of subjects attracted 85% plus of the student vote for good teaching in the funding council's nationwide survey.

Library facilities are among the best in the UK. These include the iconic Western Bank Library that has just undergone a £3.4 million facelift, and the award-winning Information Commons.

Information Commons, the £23-million Sheffield campus learning resource has over 500 PCs, wireless networking and IT equipped classrooms; well-equipped spaces for teaching, learning and study, 100,000 of the most in-demand books, and a 70-seat café.

The Sheffield Graduate scheme gives students the opportunity to enhance employability by developing essential workplace skills. The largest single employer of Sheffield graduates is the National Health Service, but significant numbers also join organisations such as Sheffield City Council, PwC, KPMG, The Royal Bank of Scotland, Rolls-Royce, Tesco, Teach First, Atkins, Mott MacDonald, the Army, The British Council, government departments and local government.

Almost a fifth of graduates go into health. There's a £3.1-million Health Centre and £26 million was recently spent on the refurbishment of teaching and research facilities in the Medical School.

In the 5/6-year MB ChB there's an emphasis on self-learning and computer-aided learning packages. Wide clinical experience offered. The 6-year course includes a pre-med year for students with non-scientific backgrounds. Preferred subjects at AS level are Chemistry, Biology, Mathematics or Physics, plus a fourth AS in any subject. At A level, you'll need Chemistry plus another science and any other subject which was also completed at AS, not General Studies.

A £5.5 million extension has recently been

built to the School of Clinical Dentistry, which

offers the BDS/Dent for AAA plus UKCAT, a course the teaching of which achieved a 93% student approval rate at the Higher Education Funding Council's National Student Survey last year.

'I'm studying Dentistry,' writes Rosie Legg, 'and I absolutely love it! I do have a more substantial workload than most other first years, but it doesn't bother me because I really enjoy it. There's always a good atmosphere, which makes it easy to get on and find the balance between work and play, which I think is important. The teaching and lecturers are really good and have a real interest in their subject, but also in you as a dental student. Most of them know your name and take time to chat with you.

'The resources are outstanding, from the dental hospital to the dissection room, and also the libraries. The Information Commons Library is the resource used by all students; this really does have everything you need, six floors, computers, a café, nice views of the city out of the windows, and even showers! It's really modern and very easy to use, but they're very strict on overdue books, and charge a hefty fine.'

Another noticeable strength is BSc Psychology, fully accredited and first step to becoming a Chartered Psychologist. Speech therapists also thrive on the BMedSci Speech Science.

Accountancy is also big at Sheffield. Graduates bound out of here to become tax consultants, and tomorrow's actuaries get happy with their Maths degrees, especially BSc Financial Mathematics.

The University claims to attract more to their School of Architecture than any other. There are a number of courses besides the BA hons Architectural Studies, and various landscape and urban environment degrees, and MEng Structural Engineering & Architecture.

A new £25 million multidisciplinary science and engineering campus has recently been completed. Engineering design consultants find their way from all over the Engineering faculty, but in particular there's Architectural Engineering Design, and such as B/MEng Medical Systems Engineering, Computer Systems Engineering, Systems & Control Engineering. There's also Biomedical Engineering, which gets into design for prosthetics, and a Sports Engineering degree.

The Faculty of Social Sciences mixes social and political studies and reaches into China, Korea and Japan. Aspiring translator/interpreters note the 4-year BA Modern Languages with Interpreting. A new Confucius Institute offers a valuable resource for Chinese-related

WHAT IT'S REALLY LIKE

UNIVERSITY:

Social Life	★★★★★
Societies	★★★★★
Student Union services	★★★★★
Politics	**High level**
Sport	**Key**
National team position	**23rd**
Sport facilities	★★★★★
Arts opportunities	**Film excellent, drama, dance music, art good**
Student magazine	**Stainless**
Student newspaper	**The Steel Press**
Student radio	**Forge Radio**
2010 *Guardian* Awards	**Broadcast Journalist of Year**
Nightclub	**Fusion & Foundry, Octagon**
Bars	**Bar One, Interval + SU pubs in town**
Union ents	**Eclectic**
, Union clubs/societies	**188**
Parking	**Poor**
CITY:	
Entertainment	★★★★★
Scene	**Seriously good**
Town/gown relations	**Good**
Risk of violence	**Low**
Cost of living	**Low-average**
Student concessions	**Good**
Survival + 2 nights out pw	**£80**
Part-time work campus/town	**Good**

studies, in partnership with Beijing Language and Culture University and Nanjing University.

SOCIAL SCENE

STUDENT UNION The Students' Union, voted 1st in the *national* Student Experience Survey (2011), and Students' Union of the Year in the NUS Awards every years since 2008, has had an exciting £5 million rebuild.

'Sheffield University is infamous for the amazing student union,' writes Rosie Legg, 'and I have to say rightly so. Freshers Week was impressive. A couple of weeks before you arrive, they send you a booklet which tells you everything that's going on. Each night there were things organised at the union or clubs in town. Get organised, because nearly every night sells out.

'The best union nights I would say are *Population* on a Monday. Normally this has a theme, for example pirates, chocolate or seasonal, with standard chart music. *ROAR* on a Wednesday is amazing. Normally people dress as

animals. It's the night of sport society socials, and it's quite lairy, but in a good way! Saturday is also a good night, but perhaps not to everyone's taste. It's called *Poptarts*, and the whole night is filled with cheesy pop. There's also a dub-step and drum 'n' bass night on a Tuesday, *Tuesday Club*. I was surprised how good it was, as it's not really my kind of scene at all. The Scratch Perverts were playing. I came home with a few bruises, but it was definitely worth it. People are always travelling up from other unis just to go to this night.'

Not all is ents, however. At the top of the Union building, you'll find the **Gallery**. Heart of sports clubs and societies, it consists of meeting rooms and work areas with telephones and computing facilities that members can use to contact each other, meet and organise events. One floor down is Source, information bank on the Union's 200 societies and sports clubs, and events across Sheffield.

Here, you'll also find a multimedia computer suite, with digital cameras and camcorders available for hire. A recent initiative is the *Give It A Go* programme. The idea is to encourage you to dip in to a whole host of activities - suck it and see before making a long-term commitment to one society or another. In 2005/06 around 12,000 tickets were sold for *Give it a Go* activities.

Behind Source is Sheffield Volunteering, gateway to community projects in and around Sheffield.

Societies cover almost everything, as Rose discovered: 'Whether you're one of the rare few who actually come here to learn, or you're one of the many who come to play rugby, edit a newspaper, watch bands, worship God, fight injustice, walk up big hills, practise politics, become an actor or do any number of diverse and often bizarre activities, you can not only do them here, but you can meet a load of people who'll do them with you.'

Sheffield is politically active, with strong representation from across the political spectrum. Union Elections receive the highest turnout of any Union in the country and are hotly contested attracting a large number of high quality candidates for the eight positions. Below this there are a number of Committees and a strong Union Council, and numerous student political interest groups from the classic Socialist Students, through People and Planet to Conservative Future.

The Radio Society, Forge Radio, started as an individual's idea and they're now broadcasting around the union from their own studio. Sheffield Base looks after the Website and the student newspaper, *Steel Press*, has won Newspaper of the Year at the *Guardian* Awards more times than one cares to remember.

The Union is one of only a few to boast its own 400-seat cinema, run by students. The Theatre Company uses the Drama Studio for productions ranging from Shakespearean tragedy to student-written plays and musicals. A 400-seat auditorium, extension to the union, is used by the Film Unit as a cinema four times a week, showing films prior to release on video.

SPORT The sports teams have been more popular and successful in recent years, with men's and women's tennis, football, basketball and rugby teams making themselves known on the circuit (23rd last year). Squash and badminton have recently been added to a portfolio which is strong on martial arts, ranging from Karate to Capoeira, with lessons held regularly in the basement dojo, and the hall in Vernon Square.Writes Rosie Legg:

'The University Gym S10 is really hi-tech and good quality equipment, with personal trainers. There is also a swimming pool. It's quite expensive, but there are flexible packages to suit every budget and time scale.'

TOWN See *Student City Sheffield.*

PILLOW TALK

Brand new accommodation at the Endcliffe Village opened in 2008. Located in leafy suburbs, 15 minutes walk to campus, the apartments have all mod cons. Focal point is **The Edge**, dining room, bar, café, support facilities, 24-hour IT space, WiFi, plasma screens, launderette. Otherwise it's

ACCOMMODATION	
Student rating	★★★★★
Guarantee to freshers	**100%**
Style	**Halls, flats**
Security guard	**Most halls, some flats**
Shared rooms	**Some flats**
Internet access	**Most halls, some flats**
Self-catered	**All flats, some halls**
En suite	**Some**
Approx price range pw	**£74-£125**
City rent pw	**£55-£85**

'Ranmoor Village', which opened in 2009.

Concludes Rosie Legg: 'I may be a little bit bias in saying this, but Endcliffe, where I am, is the best place to stay. It has a lovely feel of a student village, in pretty grounds with modern flats and its own bar, the Edge.

'It's a mini community with different things going on each night and a pub quiz every Sunday, which is always fun.

'The worst accommodation is Tapton, old and dated, and from the outside it looks like a prison.'

GETTING THERE

☛ By road: M1/J33, A630, A57.
☛ By rail: London, 2:30; Liverpool Lime Street, 1:45; Manchester Piccadilly, 1:00; Nottingham 1:00; Leeds, 30 mins.
☛ By air: Manchester Airport.
☛ By coach: London, 3:45; Newcastle, 4:45.

SHEFFIELD HALLAM UNIVERSITY

Sheffield Hallam University
City Campus
Sheffield S1 1WB

TEL 0114 225 5555
FAX: 0114 225 4449
EMAIL: enquiries@shu.ac.uk
WEB www.shu.ac.uk

Sheffield Hallam Union of Students
The HUBS
Paternoster Row
Sheffield, S1 2QQ

TEL 0114 225 4124
FAX 0114 225 4140
EMAIL [initial.name]@shu.ac.uk
WEB www.hallamunion.com

VIRGIN VIEW

*H*allam is big business. With almost 30,000 students, they turn over some £150 million a year. Its work-orientated courses suggest that it is bent on stoking the nation's economy. The courses are indeed worked out with the industries that will employ their graduates, but that is not all. Hallam, while coming out among the top 1992 universities in the recent Government Research Assessment, were also voted by *their own students into 42nd position in the 2011* Times Higher Education *magazine's Student Experience Survey. One of the things that came out of that was that their lecturers show a real interest in the development of their students. This is a different Hallam to the one a student described 13 years ago: 'Your degree will find you a job, but you will need to be self-motivated. If you're after close-knit tutorials with tutors that take a thorough interest in you, you'd be better off at Sheffield University.'*

Overall, 79% of Hallam students are satisfied with the deal on offer here. There's a fair social life and they challenge the other Sheffield university in the BUCS team sport league. Drop-out rate is 8%, well below its Government benchmark.

CAMPUSES

SHU is based around 2 sites, City and Collegiate Crescent. Psalter Lane, with it's school-like corridors and grim exterior, has closed.

'Collegiate campus is really quite good,' writes Chris Gissing. 'It's a traditional, leafy campus, ideally placed on the revelation that is Ecclesall Road. Sheffield's Eccy Road is the hub of student ents, with about 830 bars and 6,000 coffee houses (well, maybe not as many as that, but after the first 5 pubs, who cares?).

'City Campus is excellent too, centrally located and based around 4 or 5 disparate buildings, connected by the stunningly designed Atrium. This glass/steel construction has masses of open space, and is like a cosmopolitan street café with tables and chairs and...well...a café. The Adsetts Centre is based here and offers 24-hour access to computers, Internet, books, photocopying etc. Fortunately, the library staff who seemed to fine me on a weekly basis don't work twenty-four hours.'

FEES, BURSARIES

UK & EU Fees, 2011-12: £3,375 p.a. There are bursaries for students in receipt of the HE Maintenance Grant. See www.shu.ac.uk/guides/ studentfinance/getmoney.html. There is also a limited number of scholarships for first years based on academic achievement.

STUDENT PROFILE

'We have the whole range,' Chris continues, 'from working-class-kid-scraped-through-on-a-BTEC/through-Clearing sort, to Mummy-and-Daddy-paid-for-my-flat-and-course-fees-darling sort. They're all here in this city - 12% of the city's pop-

UNIVERSITY/STUDENT PROFILE	
University since	**1992**
Situation/style	**City campus**
Student population	**33830**
Total undergraduates	**25555**
Mature	**44%**
International	**13%**
Male/female ratio	**45:55**
Equality of opportunity:	
state school intake	**97%**
social class 4-7 intake	**35%**
drop-out rate	**8%**

ulation are students. Sheffield Hallam has more working-class students than Sheffield University does.'

Few come here from public school. They take 35% of their students from the lower socio-economic groups. More than 20% are part-timers and 44% are mature. Quite different to the student body at Sheffield University, but as Chris says, 'We all seem to get along fairly well, and we are of course allowed to use each others' union bars/ women/blokes (delete as appropriate).'

ACADEMIA & JOBS

Students say the best teaching at Sheffield Hallam is in Education, Accounting, Anatomy, Physiology & Pathology, Architecture, English, Finance, Food Studies, Geographical Studies, Human & Social Geography (97% of the class gave it the thumbs-up), Law, Marketing, Mathematical Sciences (100%), Statistics (100%), Medical Technology, Molecular Biology, Nutrition (97%), European Languages, Planning, Psychology, Social Policy, Sports Science.Least popular was Fine Art, which took a meagre 41% of the class vote.

Back-up resources are increasingly good, and Chris Gissing concludes: 'The teaching within my school (Computing & Management Science) was

SUBJECT AREAS (%)

Humanities — 7
Education — 5
Creative Arts — 7
Health Subjects — 10
Science — 17
Engineering — 5
Built Environment — 6
Maths & Computer — 7
Business — 20
Social Studies incl Law — 16

on the whole very good. I cannot fault the department for what they offer in terms of specialist knowledge and resources. On the IT courses there is a strong bias towards industrial placements and business skills, invaluable when going into the real world of work.'

More than 10% of graduates go into education - secondary and primary. Graduates of Computer Science, Health, Business, Social Science, and Creative Arts also march confidently into the higher education sector as lecturers.

Hallam is among the leaders for sheer number of graduates into banking, a 3/4-year sandwich BA in Banking & Finance requires 240 points only. A BSc Business & Finance is a top-up alternative. Hallam is again the place for insurance/pension brokers/underwriters.

They have an Enterprise Centre to imbue the whole uni with an enterprise culture. There are Finance, Human Resources Mgt, Marketing or Financial Services adjuncts and a series of International Business Studies (French, German, Italian, Spanish) and languages with e-Commerce degrees.

Employment figures show success in human resources in particular through such as the 4-year sandwich BA Hons Business & Human Resource Management. Look, too, at transport, where Hallam is out in front for graduate employment. BA Planning & Transport or Geography with Transport are the degrees. For the catering trade (another key graduate employment area) there's BSc Hons Hospitality Business Management with Conference/Events or Culinary Arts possibilities,

---

TEACHING SURVEY AT A GLANCE

Avg. UCAS points accepted	**260**
Acceptance rate	**17%**
Overall satisfaction rate	**79%**
Helpful/interested staff	★★★★
Small tuition groups	★★★
Students into graduate jobs	**73%**

Teaching most popular with undergraduates:
Education, Accounting, Anatomy, Physiology & Pathology, Architecture, English, Finance, Food Studies, Geographical Studies, Human & Social Geography (97%), Law, Marketing, Mathematical Sciences (100%), Statistics (100%), Medical Technology, Molecular Biology, Nutrition (97%), European Languages, Planning, Psychology, Social Policy, Sports Science.

Teaching least popular with undergraduates:
Journalism (39%), Media Studies (51%).

---

or Leisure Events Management with Arts & Entertainments, Outdoor Recreation, or Tourism. They scored full marks at the assessments.

Marketing is another strength and there is a steady flow of graduates into advertising.

Engineering has always been a dimension; jobs from this part of the curriculum are in related engineering and technical consultancy, and in particular in the manufacture of air and space machinery.

Computer science graduates account for about 8% of the graduate jobs.

BSc Pharmaceutical Sciences puts the uni into the Top 10 for finding graduates work in the pharmaceutical manufacturing industry. Meanwhile, health subjects make a huge impact on their employment figures - degrees in Physiotherapy, Occupational Therapy, Radiotherapy, Oncology, Nursing... They have opted for areas where the other Sheffield university doesn't tread, and they dropped only one point at the assessments. The Diagnostic Radiography and Radiography & Oncology BSc degrees corner well over 4% of the national employment market in this sector at a low asking rate.

They're among the leading providers, too, for social workers/counsellors. The BA Social Work Studies hits the spot, but see, too, Social Policy, Social, Cultural and Psychology mixes.

See also the BSc Psychology, fully accredited by the British Psychological Society and first step to becoming a Chartered Psychologist.

Stats show, too, that BSc Architectural Technology or Architecture & Environmental Design are both solid lines into a career. Look also

---

RESEARCH EXCELLENCE

% of Sheffield Hallam's research that is
4* *(World-class)* or **3*** *(Internationally rated):*

	4*	3*
Nursing/Midwifery	10%	25%
Health Professions	0%	25%
Metallurgy and Materials	5%	30%
Built Environment	5%	40%
Town/Country Planning	20%	30%
Business/Management	5%	20%
Information Management	5%	20%
Law	0%	5%
Psychology	0%	10%
Education	5%	20%
Sports	10%	25%
English	5%	25%
History	10%	20%
Art and Design	20%	30%
Media Studies	5%	35%

WHAT IT'S REALLY LIKE

UNIVERSITY:

Social Life	★★★★
Societies	★★★
Student Union services	★★★★
Sport	35 clubs
National team position	29th
Sport facilities	★★★
Arts opportunities	Few
Student magazine	SHU-Life
Student radio	SHU Radio
Nightclub/bars	Bar Phoenix
Union ents	Cheese, indie
Union societies	65
Parking	Poor

CITY:

Entertainment	★★★★★
Scene	Seriously good
Town/gown relations	Good
Risk of violence	Average
Cost of living	Average
Student concessions	Good
Survival + 2 nights out	£80 pw
Part-time work campus/town	Good/excellent

SOCIAL SCENE

STUDENTS' UNION The stunning silver drums of the new Union Building (HUBs) beat a fanfare to what the uni describes as 'a unique and unrivalled welfare and social facility for 28,000 students'. It cost them £5 million, so we should allow them that.

There's a student advice centre and volunteering team, a shop, social space and activities area, plus 3 multi-functional entertainment rooms and a café/bar. **Bar Phoenix** is the focal point, downstairs from the club nights. Ents come on weekday nights in the shape of *Pounded - Total Request*. DJ Dave 'the hitman' Hunter plays an anthemic mix of chart

ACCOMMODATION

Student rating	★★★
Guarantee to freshers	95%
Style	Halls, flats
Security guard	24/7
Shared rooms	Some
Internet access	All
Self-catered	Most
En suite	Some
Approx price range pw	£66-£121
City rent pw	£55-£85

at Construction Management, Construction Commercial Management and Building Surveying. There is employment strength in-depth at Hallam for jobs in the construction industry and BSc Quantity Surveying is no exception. There's a track record, too, in property - look at BSc Property Studies.

Law also has a good reputation. Note the LLB /Maitrise En Droit (Francaise) - 2 years in Paris - and the joint degrees with Criminology, Business, Psychology. It is not difficult to see why more probation officers come out of Hallam than anywhere. You can study BA Criminology and Psychology/Sociology, Social Work Studies, Society & Cities, Social Policy, Social Policy & Sociology.

The Law is also a recognised pathway into Civil Service administration from here, while local and regional government administration call on Hallam graduates in such as Social Policy, Society & Cities, Urban Regeneration, Education, Architecture, Building & Planning, and Business & Administration. BA Business & Public Policy is clearly useful. Note also their BSc Public Health Nutrition, and the Planning & Transport BA.

Finally, they are employment leaders in sport, a fact which knits academia together with student leisure - they came 29th in the national sporting league last year. The department was among the few nationwide to score 24 points (full marks) in the teaching assessments.

toons from classic party anthems to current chart bangers. *Sheff One* needs no further mention (more floor filling chart anthems), and *Last Laugh Comedy Club*. Regular fancy dress themes add to the fun, like *Baywatch Party - Love the Hoff, 90s Rave Special*, or *Smirnoff Moulin Rouge Party* (free top hats and feather boas). Saturday night at Hallam is, and always has been, a night for the discerning clubber: *Sheff One* is the chart and dance favourite choice of this city.

There are 30 student societies, Media = the weekly *HUGE* - Hallam Union Guide to Events, also SHU-Life their magazine, and SHU Radio, 'with a brand new look and a brand new attitude!' There are 35 sports societies and thoroughly professional facilities are available.

SPORT The sports facilities have recently been refurbished, with a £2-million gym and sports conditioning suite spanning 600 square metres. It has more than 70 fitness stations, an array of the latest equipment, and an advanced weights and training area. The changing facilities are fully equipped for the disabled, and there's also 'a sunbed, assessment rooms and full audio and satellite TV system' - they call that exercise? There's another suite on Collegiate Campus.

PILLOW TALK

Catered halls and self-catered purpose-built complexes are available. Some catered - about 10%. The

Trigon is a newly developed site offering 361 en-suite rooms, CCTV, security patrols, on site office, laundry facilities.

GETTING THERE
☞ By road: M1/J33, A630, A57.

☞ By rail: London, 2:30; Liverpool Lime Street, 1:45; Manchester Piccadilly, 1:00; Nottingham 1:00; Leeds, 30 mins.
☞ By air: Manchester Airport.
☞ By coach: London, 3:45; Newcastle, 4:45.

STUDENT SOUTHAMPTON – THE CITY

Southampton is situated on the South Coast of England, with good communications in all directions. Bournemouth is only a 30-minute drive away, with its fantastic beaches and nightlife. London is 70 miles distant. Open countryside and the coast are within easy reach.

If the city was human it would be described as dynamic, but modest, always willing to welcome new people.

During the day it is student dominated (c. 40,000), and a shopaholic's paradise. Since the war, when it was badly bombed, the city has developed into a modern, pedestrian-friendly location with a wide variety of entertainment and activities on offer, still a few glimpses of its architectural heritage.

CLUBS
There are clubs suited to everyone's taste, such as the renowned **Jester's**, dubbed 'The Palace of Dreams,' where you are guaranteed to have a very cheap, alcohol fuelled night. It is the only club with a beer garden, lounge area and dance floor all-in-one. **Sobar**, located a few doors down, is very similar to Jester's, but marginally more expensive. **Bliss** is a very cool, sleek club in the heart of the city. There are two dance floors, each playing different genres of music, great if you fancy dancing all night and are prepared to wait a long time for drinks. **Oceana**, located down by the docks, is one of the largest clubs in England with a capacity of 4,000. It is also the one place, over two storeys, where you can travel the world within a night from the cool ice bar to the island of Hawaii. By the end of the journey you are ready to hit the huge dance floor. **Orange Rooms** and **Revolution** are two contemporary up-beat bars, the latter with a great choice of cocktails, albeit quite expensive. **Whitehouse**, **Junk** and **Rhino** all play the latest urban, drum 'n' bass music, often hosted by guest DJs.

PUBS
There are some great pubs, the **Hobbit** a popular student choice for its beer garden, one of the largest in the UK. It also serves great authentic Caribbean food, courtesy of Chef Bernie, and a

favourite flavoured cocktail, the Fellowship, one of a variety relating to Lord of the Rings characters. **The Cowherds**, located next to the Common, is a great place to enjoy a pint and some good, heart-warming, food after either playing sport or simply relaxing on the 326 acres of grass. Two other pubs I would recommend are the **Gordon Arms**, where you can sample a selection of local ales, and the **Shooting Star**, which apart from serving good food and beer, is a venue for live music.

CINEMAS, GALLERIES, THEATRES
Of the two cinemas in Southampton, the **Odeon** offers a 13 screens in the city centre, whilst down in Ocean Village, **Cineworld** offers five. For those who like the theatre, the **Mayflower** is the largest in Southern England, whilst on Highfield campus students can watch plays performed by the University's drama societies in the **Nuffield Theatre**. For art, the **City Art Gallery** contains over 3,500 works from over six centuries. There is also the **Bargate Monument Gallery** and the University's **John Hansard Gallery**, which has a special photographic collection.

MUSIC
Of many music venues around the city, the **Guildhall** has played host to Pendulum, Calvin Harris and Rufus Wainwright. For those who prefer classical, jazz and chamber music, the renowned **Turner Sims Concert Hall** is located on campus. Pubs such as the **Brook** and **Joiners Arms** are great for hearing the latest unsigned bands. Annual highlight is *Bestival*, which takes place on the Isle of Wight in early June and features some of the top bands around.

SHOPPING
Southampton is a haven for those who love to shop. **The Mall** and **West Quay** are two huge complexes which contain the latest designer clothes, jewellery and gadget shops. There is a large **Primark**, and a massive **Ikea** located below West Quay.

EATING
West Quay and Ocean Village offer great places to

eat for students, cheaper at West Quay. Most mainstream eateries offer a student discount. I would also recommend **Banana Wharf**, a fantastic bar and restaurant down by the marina.

STUDENT GHETTOS

Portswood and Highfield are the two residential areas dominated by students. Portswood is a 15-minute walk from campus and a 15-minute bus journey from the city centre.

Portswood High Street contains a good range of shops and banks. Rental prices are surprisingly competitive in such a popular area. It is friendly, safe and a 5 minute walk from Jesters, Sobar, and the Hobbit.

Highfield is about a 10-minute walk from campus and a 20-minute bus journey from the city centre. It is not far from Portswood High Street, but a better neighbourhood and the rents are slightly higher.

VIOLENCE

I would rate Southampton University and the city 8/10 for how safe I feel living here. The two main areas to avoid in the city after dark are the Flowers Estate, Bassett, very close to Highfield Campus, and Shirley. There is no reason for students to go to either of them.

Will Gastrell

UNIVERSITY OF SOUTHAMPTON

The University of Southampton
University Road
Southampton SO17 1BJ

TEL: 023 8059 5000
FAX: 023 8059 3939
EMAIL: admissns@southampton.ac.uk
WEB SITE: www.soton.ac.uk

Southampton Students' Union
Highfield
Southampton SO17 1BJ

TEL 023 8059 5201
FAX 023 8059 5252
EMAIL susu@soton.ac.uk
WEB www.soton.ac.uk/~susu/

VIRGIN VIEW

Southampton was ranked in the top 100 universities in the world by two rankings guides published in September 2010: in the Times Higher Education *World University Rankings, Southampton is one of only 14 UK universities in the top 100, and the 2010 QS World University League Rankings placed Southampton at number 81. At the same time, students praised their lecturers in the Government's national student survey for their help and interest in them, this positive response following hot on the heels of the Government's Research Assessment, which tied Southampton with Durham, St Andrews, Sheffield, Leeds, and Bristol in 14th place nationally, and labelled more than 25 % of their research world-class.*

It's an all-round deal on which few are foolish enough to turn their backs. Only 4% did by dropping out last time. That's very low.

Besides grades, what they look for in

applicants is evidence of enthusiasm for and of reading around a subject, evidence of how related work experience made an impression on you, an awareness of how your course delivers the subject and fits with your own long-term aims, teachability - a readiness and keenness to learn, an ability to communicate in the personal statement or interview. Plus 'our programmes are designed to challenge you and change the way you think. We'll expect you to challenge what you are

UNIVERSITY/STUDENT PROFILE	
University since	**1952**
Situation/style	**Campus**
Student population	**22680**
Total undergraduates	**16800**
Mature	**33%**
International	**20%**
Male/female ratio	**44:56**
Equality of opportunity:	
state school intake	**85%**
social class 4-7 intake	**23%**
low-participation area intake	**4%**

taught. *Critical thinking and independent learning are essential to you becoming a future leader and decision maker.'*

This year they launched a new i-phone application for applicants to discover some of what it is like to become a student here: http://itunes.apple.com/gb/app/university-southampton-undergraduate/id385729235? mt=8

Open Days, 2011: 8 and 9 July, 2 and 3 September.

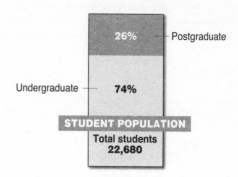

CAMPUS

HIGHFIELD CAMPUS From east or west you rattle along the M27 until you hit Junction 5, whereupon you dive down south, following the uni signs, and suddenly, 2 miles from the centre of the city, there you are in it. You don't *enter* the main Highfield campus as you might Sussex campus or Nottingham. It is a campus split by University Road, a public road with uni buildings off to the left and right, so that you're not sure whether the city has wandered onto the campus or the campus has not yet quite commandeered its piece of the city.

Will Gastrell, a first year Geography student from North Yorkshire, writes: 'Southampton is situated on the South Coast of England, with good communications in all directions.

'The University comprises six campuses: Highfield, Avenue, Boldrewood, General Hospital, National Oceanographic Centre, and, 35minutes away, Winchester School of Art.

'Highfield is the main campus and is a 20-minute bus journey from the city centre. It has large expanses of grass and streams, perfect for relaxing or studying.

'The majority of buildings are modern, with a few of 1960s vintage. The library, where you will spend numerous nights stressing over essays and dissertations, is the most prominent building on site. The main student concourse contains a well stocked shop, salon, travel agents and the Cube entertainment venue. Around the campus lie seven cheap restaurants and two pubs.

'Unilink buses provide a fast, efficient service around Southampton, and a bus pass is the best investment a student can make. Bicycles are a quick and healthy alternative. Those who commute to Winchester take the train. A small number of students bring their cars, but there is no parking on campus until second year.'

FEES, BURSARIES

UK & EU Fees, 2011-12: £3,375 p.a. There's a bursary for students in receipt of the HE Maintenance Grant. They offer a variety of scholarships to the most talented students across their subject areas, plus a generous range of support to help UK undergraduates in most financial need. See www.southampton.ac.uk/study/feesandfunding/index.shtml.

STUDENT PROFILE

The tradition is that, apart from a small scattering of minority groups and locals, Southampton students are thoroughly middle-class. However, the public school kid intake is in fact more similar to that of Reading than it is to Durham, Bristol or Exeter, who still take many fewer from the state schools. In a survey of student drug-taking habits by the Adam Smith Institute, Southampton came out 'most abstemious'. The survey was undertaken before the opening of the new on-campus pleasure dome, the **Cube**, when there was a good deal less to do on campus.

Will Gaskell found only a welcoming community. 'There are no dominant social groups at Southampton, although those who enjoy the water love the city, as it boasts some of the best water sports facilities in the UK. A number of students live relatively locally and go home regularly.

'I was incredibly nervous when I first arrived, coming from the North, being on my own and not knowing anyone.

'In fact, every student is welcomed by second year students and given a fresher's pack and T-shirt. The T-shirt, with introductory facts about yourself (filled in by every fresher), was a great ice breaker. Within a couple of hours I realised that settling in would be no problem. The next two Freshers' weeks were a blur.'

ACADEMIA & JOBS

In the last Government Research Assessment, Engineering (Civil and Environmental Engineering in particular) scored especially well, as did Medicine, with primary care ranked 3rd in the country, and other community-based clinical subjects and cancer studies scoring particularly highly. Nursing and Midwifery, European Studies, Computer Science, Earth systems and Environmental Sciences, Applied Mathematics, and Statistics also scored highly, as did Music, Archaeology and History. Their multidisciplinary approach attracts researchers from across the University to address global challenges such as climate change, global health, hi-tech crime and our ageing population, crossing the boundaries that traditionally separate subject areas.

Research is not teaching of course, but they are following a similar interdisciplinary pathway at Southampton: from September 2012, undergraduates will have the opportunity to personalise their degrees by choosing modules from other disciplines, giving them greater choice and opportunity to prepare them for life-changing careers in the 21st century.

Southampton students rallied behind their lecturers this year in the national survey, voting them among the most interested/helpful in the country.

Overall, 86% of students said that they were satisfied with the quality of their course, and voted the University 10th overall nationally.

The 5-floor Hartley Library on the main Highfield campus has recently undergone a massive refit, making it one of the most advanced university libraries in Britain. Access to resources has been improved and personal study areas have been restyled to allow more privacy.

The Medical Faculty offers a 5-year BM with integrated course structure and clinical contact from first year. A 4th-year 8-week period of clinical experience may be had in subject and place of your choice (many opt to go abroad). It's more competitive than most to get in here, but subjects with overlap of material, such as Biology/Sports Studies, Maths/Further Maths, may not be considered in combination at A level; General Studies cannot be accepted. UKCAT is required.

They are looking for the committed, well-rounded applicant capable of approaching problems with a certain flair, not confined by speciality. Coursework is geared towards problem-solving; patient contact is made in the first term in order to develop communication skills.

If you look at another area in which the uni is renowned - Geography - you see a similar sort of picture. Analytical skills, problem-solving and written and oral expression are to the fore - it's

TEACHING SURVEY AT A GLANCE	
Avg. UCAS points accepted	**400**
Acceptance rate	**14%**
Overall satisfaction rate	**86%**
Helpful/interested staff	★★★★
Small tuition groups	★★★
Students into graduate jobs	**71%**

Teaching most popular with undergraduates:
Aerospace Engineering, Archaeology, Aural/Oral Sciences, Biology (100%), Business, Chemistry, Complementary Medicine, Computer, Electronic & Electrical Engineering, English, Finance, French Studies (100%), Geology, German & Scandinavian Studies, History, Archaeology, Iberian Studies, Law, Management, Maritime Technology, Mechanical Engineering, Media Studies, Molecular Biology, Music, Nursing, Ocean Sciences, Philosophy, Physical Geography & Environmental Science, Physics & Astronomy, Politics, Physical Science, Psychology, Sociology, Social Policy & Anthropology, Sports Science.

Teaching least popular with undergraduates:
Design Studies (59%), Fine Art (52%).

an approach to which employers relate.

'I am a first year Geography student' writes Will Gastrell, 'hoping to focus my degree in Human Geography. I have definitely made the correct decision with my course. I have found the majority of lectures interesting and most of the lecturers good communicators, although the odd one or two are not. Before each lecture there is an option to download the lecture slides, which saves scribbling notes rather than concentrating on what the lecturer is saying.

'Student to tutor ratio is 7:1. The tutors are good at discussing any issues you may have and you can go to Student Services to seek any additional help. Books, journals and a lot of background reading are crucial to obtaining a good degree pass. The library has an efficient system for searching, loaning and returning books. When books are on loan the waiting time is very short! Work pressure is constant throughout the year, even without actual essay deadlines and exams. There is always the need for extra reading. This is the same for my friends studying subjects ranging from Medicine to Sports Science. The feeling is that the pressure

'Work pressure is constant throughout the year, There is always the need for extra reading. This is the same for my friends. The feeling is that the pressure motivates them to work.'

RESEARCH EXCELLENCE

% of Southampton's research that is
4* *(World-class)* or **3*** *(Internationally rated):*

	4*	3*
Cancer Studies	15%	60%
Hospital Clinical	10%	50%
Community Clinical	25%	60%
Nursing and Midwifery	45%	40%
Health Professions	0%	25%
Biological Sciences	10%	40%
Environmental Sciences	20%	50%
Chemistry	10%	50%
Physics	15%	40%
Pure Mathematics	5%	45%
Applied Mathematics	15%	55%
Statistics	15%	50%
Computer Science	35%	50%
Electrical/Electronic Eng.	25%	40%
Civil Engineering	25%	55%
Mechanical, Aero. & Manufacturing Eng.	15%	45%
Geography Environment	20%	35%
Archaeology	25%	35%
Economics	20%	60%
Business/ Management	15%	40%
Law	5%	45%
Politics	5%	25%
Sociology/Social Policy	35%	35%
Social Work Studies	0%	35%
Psychology	15%	45%
Education	10%	25%
European Studies	30%	25%
English	25%	40%
Philosophy	5%	35%
History	30%	40%
Art and Design	5%	20%
History of Art	15%	35%
Music	50%	30%

enrolled with the Student Entrepreneurs Club. SETsquared is a dedicated support and mentoring facility for entrepreneurs and fledgling enterprises.

In the Oceanography Centre at Southampton's Dockside, Marine Science students again have access to exceptional analytical and research facilities. Ellen MacArthur's stunning performance in Kingfisher, in the Vendee Global Challenge, carried with it tank and wind-tunnel research work done by the university. The yachtswoman was closely involved in the design and testing processes.

Defence is clearly a priority. Like Portsmouth along the coast, Southampton has an active OTC. There's a University Air Squadron and Royal Naval Unit.

Writes Will: 'I am a serving member in the Royal Naval Unit, which has been the best decision I have ever made and there is no commitment to joining the Navy afterwards. The Unit has its own ship HMS Blazer which we regularly go out on to various ports along the South Coast. During Easter and summer holidays, 'Blazer' ventures further afield and this summer we will sail to the Baltic. The RAF equivalent is the University Air Squadron; for the Army it is the Officer Training Corps. The units pay you for your service to them, which is great in helping with your student finances.'

Many Southampton graduates bound for the Defence industry come through the Faculty of Engineering & Applied Science, which gained world-class ratings in the research assessments. They regard themselves to be 'a golden triangle of Engineering research excellence' with Imperial College and Cambridge.

The Marine aspect is of course marked. Boat/ship designers/surveyors/brokers are all served well. Southampton satisfies through design, construction and operation. See in particular the B/MEng Ship Science, the MEng comes in various orientations: Yacht & Small Craft, Naval Architecture, Inter-Disciplinary, and the 4-year

motivates them to work. The internet is crucial for researching journals, checking emails, and accessing lecture notes and assignments.'

After health, which also includes Physiotherapy, Occupational Therapy and Podiatry degrees, Nursing (Adult, Child, Learning Disability, Mental) and Midwifery, the City claims most of Southampton's graduates. Accounting & Economics or Finance ensure good employment figures, and there's a leaning to careers for tax expert/consultants and actuaries. For the latter, look at Economics with Actuarial Studies and Mathematics with Actuarial Studies.

Southampton are hot on student enterprise. 'Spin out' companies have raised more than £20 million of private funds. More than 60 students

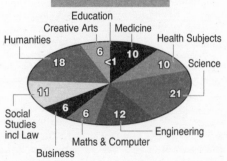

SUBJECT AREAS (%)

Education 6
Creative Arts <1
Medicine 10
Humanities 18
Health Subjects 10
Science 21
Social Studies incl Law 6
Business 6
Maths & Computer 12
Engineering 11

WHAT IT'S REALLY LIKE

UNIVERSITY:	
Social Life	★★★★
Societies	★★★★
Student Union services	★★★★
Politics	**Tory heartland**
Sport	**70 clubs**
National team position	**19th**
Sport facilities	★★★★★
Arts opportunities	**Drama, film excellent**
Student newspaper	**Wessex Scene**
Student radio	**Surge**
Student TV	**SUTV**
Nightclub	**The Cube**
Bars	**Bridge Bar, Stag's Head**
Union ents	**Kinki**
Union societies	**160+**
Most active society	**Theatre Group**
Parking	**No first years**
CITY:	
Entertainment	★★★
Scene	**Pubs, clubs, water**
Town/gown relations	**Average-poor**
Risk of violence	**Average**
Cost of living	**Average**
Student concessions	**OK**
Survival + 2 nights out	**£80 pw**
Part-time work campus/town	**Good/excellent**

Advanced Materials.

Computer programmers and software engineers also proliferate. They offer BSc Computer Science and various orientations - with AI, Distributed Systems & Network, Image & Multimedia Systems, Software Eng. There are also two MEng degrees: Software Engineering and the 4-year Computer Engineering, and a facility, too, to study Computer Science for a BEng with Foundation year.

For would-be sound recordists Southampton leads the employment field with B/MEng Acoustical Engineering. Look at course links between their Institute of Sound & Vibration and the Dept of Music: BSc Acoustics and/with Music and the Acoustical Engineering Foundation course.

Meanwhile, their Sports Management & Leadership and Sport Studies degrees put them in the Top 10 for athletes, sportsmen, players and officials.

Career Destinations offers interactive sessions (application writing, assessment centres, interviews and getting the most out of your CV) with leading graduate recruiters and careers advisors, plus an extensive programme of work placements and internships.

An initiative known as 'Graduate Passport' adds a personal development element to a student's academic employment profile.

SOCIAL SCENE

STUDENTS' UNION There's a Student Services Centre, site for SUSU's Advice & Information Centre, a cinema cum nightclub with three bars collectively known as **The Cube**. At the Friday night *Kinki* event - low drinks prices and music across three floors (from cheese, to dance, to indie) - it's heaving.

The Cube is open until 2 am, three nights a week. **The Stag's Head** is a pub-style bar with license until midnight, and runs events such as Karaoke and the Sunday Quiz.

There is also the **Bridge bar**, located at the top of the Union building and with a view of campus and stream below. The Bridge hosts the *Jazz Lounge*, the *Laughter Lounge*, and the chill-out **Living Room** events.

Writes Will Gastrell: 'The main feature of the Union is the **Cube**, which is transformed from a cinema into a nightclub. *Kinki* is the main on-campus clubbing event, which takes place every Friday night. As **Cube** is at Highfield, most students can stagger back to their nearby halls, whilst those who live further away may take the 'Safety Bus', which is extremely cheap and will deliver you directly to your door!

They have also had *Fat Poppadaddys* on Saturday (funk, 60s, hip hop, reggae, drum 'n' bass) and on Thursday *Generator* - their indie and rock night, which has featured live bands, like Arab Strap. There have also been big name DJs such as Dave Pearce, Carl Cox and Judge Jules. But all said, many students prefer the deals in town, which is why this year we are happy to entertain the first Southampton Student City article (page 439), which would barely have been a workable proposition only a few years ago.

Will seems to manage to keep an incredibly tight rein on expenses. 'I am currently living in Hall with catered accommodation. I spend £10-£15 each week on lunches and weekend eating. Those who are self-catered spend a lot more. Travel only costs after late nights out. On average, I go out two or three times a week and budget £10-£15 each night for entertainment. Total average spend, £40 weekly.' Previous quotes from students have been double that.

Societies have always been strong. *Wessex Scene*, the student paper, and Surge Radio remain a feature, the latter, which has recently benefited from a new £20k studio, taking a Bronze in the 2009 Radio Awards. Wessex Scene has won

Guardian Media Awards. Now, they have SUSU TV, and have indeed hosted the National Student TV Awards to show that they had truly arrived.

There are three internationally celebrated arts venues on campus, the **Turner Sims** concert hall, the **John Hansard Gallery**, and the **Nuffield Theatre**, where the Drama Society do their stuff, and there's a thriving Film Society, too, with a 320-seat cinema which shows second-release films through Dolby surround sound. There's also a tradition of student bands.

SPORT Sport is huge at Southampton. There's a newish sports centre on campus, complete with Olympic swimming pool, gym, 8-badminton court sports hall and 140-station fitness suite. A few years ago the Wide Lane Sports Complex was opened by John Inverdale. This £4.3m complex boasts 76 acres of pitches (including 2 floodlit synthetic pitches), 24 changing rooms, meeting rooms and a fully-licensed bar. There's also a boatyard for watersporters. The sailors have won the BUSA championship more times than Portsmouth care to recall.

Writes Will: 'The Jubilee Sports Centre and 76-acre complex, Wide Lane, are "state of the art". Sportrec membership is a substantial, but essential if you want to play for a team and a good investment. Be aware that your team kit and club membership is not included in the Sportrec membership.

'Being by the sea the University is particularly renowned for its water sports. The coaching is first class, with many Olympians having started their careers here.'

PILLOW TALK

University accommodation (halls and flats) is guaranteed to all first year undergraduates who meet the terms of their offers, and name Southampton as their firm choice.

Some halls have sports facilities, all have launderettes and many have shops and bars. Every room has a phone. Students say avoid Bencraft and Stoneham halls. Bencraft is miles from anywhere and Stoneham is Southampton's answer to the walled city of Kowloon apparently.

Writes Will: 'Connaught Halls, where I am, is part

ACCOMMODATION	
Student rating	★★★★★
Guarantee to freshers	**100%**
Style	**Halls**
Security guard	**All**
Shared rooms	**Some**
Internet access	**All**
Self-catered	**Most**
En suite	**Some**
Approx price range pw	**£71.40-£148**
City rent pw	**£65-£75**

of Wessex Lane Halls. It is small, catered, and in my opinion the best hall, because of its very close-knit community. Students here are entitled to two meals a day during the week and one meal a day during the weekend. Facilities include a gym, snooker room, huge lounge area and bar, with space outside in the quads to lie out on the grass.

'The rooms are a good size in Old Quad but do not have en-suite washing facilities. The rooms in New Quad are generally smaller but the majority have en-suite washbasins.

'Montefiore is the other part of Wessex Lane complex. It is the largest self-catered hall of residence in Europe, very modern, and like Connaught in a good location for transport links to the City and sports facilities. This would be my choice if I decided to go self -catered. Other halls include Archer's Road, Highfield and Glen Eyre.'

First year undergraduate students may not bring a car onto the halls site (unless there are exceptional circumstances). They encourage students to travel by public transport; an annual uni-link bus pass is included within the halls fee, providing unlimited access to the bus service whilst staying in halls. A uni-link bus service connects the teaching campuses, all hall sites and the city centre, airport, rail and coach services.

GETTING THERE
☛ By road to Southampton: M3/J 14, A33.
☛ By coach to Southampton: London, 2:30; Bristol, 2:45; Birmingham, 3:40.
☛ By rail to Southampton: London Waterloo, 1:40; Birmingham, 3:30; Sheffield, 4:45.
☛ By air: Southampton International Airport.

SOUTHAMPTON SOLENT UNIVERSITY

Southampton Solent University
Southampton SO14 OYN

TEL 023 8031 9000
FAX 023 8022 2259
EMAIL ask@solent.ac.uk
WEB www.solent.ac.uk/

Solent Students' Union
Southampton SO14 OYN

TEL 023 8031 9571
FAX 023 8023 5248
EMAIL su.feedback@solent.ac.uk
WEB www.solentsu.co.uk/

VIRGIN VIEW

Southampton Solent University, out of Southampton's College of Art and College of Higher Education and the College of Nautical Studies at Warwash, offers an apparently innovative vocational portfolio, has an enviable record of excellence in teaching assessments, a lively student scene, and is not too demanding at entry.

Their mission is clear, 'accessibility and teaching strongly underpinned by research and community engagement. We will continue to offer and develop innovative courses with an emphasis on preparing students for work.'

Accessible they certainly are. On average you need only 230 points to get in. At this stage the research is fairly patchy, but 76% of those who were asked in the Student National Experience Survey said they were satisfied with the teaching, and the Times Higher's *Student Experience Survey 2011 shows that Solent's lecturers display interest in their students.*

Yet they are bleeding badly, the latest published figures show a near 12% drop-out rate, which is a little above the Government benchmark. Also, only 52% are found real graduate jobs within six months of leaving

UNIVERSITY/STUDENT PROFILE	
University since	**2005**
Situation/style	**Civic**
Student population	**19255**
Total undergraduates	**11010**
Mature undergraduates	**34%**
International undergrads	**16%**
Male/female ratio	**59:41**
Equality of opportunity:	
state school intake	**96%**
social class 4-7 intake	**39%**
drop-out rate	**12%**

last time, which is low.

FEES, BURSARIES

UK & EU Fees, 2011-12: £3,375 p.a. There are bursaries for students in receipt of the HE Maintenance Grant on a sliding scale, according to parental income. Sports scholarships are available, as are the Lisa Wilson scholarship and Toft Scholarship for students 'who have overcome adversity or can demonstrate why he/she needs extra financial help with his/her studies'.

STUDENT PROFILE

Statistics show a student body made up 96% of state educated students, 39% from the lower socio-economic orders and 13% from the so-called 'low-participation' neighbourhoods. Writes Tanver Hussain. 'The blokes all look like fugitives from just about any boy band and the girls could form All Saints 100 times over. This excludes Art students and the rugby team, as you will find that they are in worlds of their own.'

ACADEMIA & JOBS

The faculties are: Business; Media, Arts and Society; and Technology. Besides Maritime (including yacht and powercraft design), departments include Design (Fashion, Fine Art, Graphic Design, Interior, etc); Built Environment (big strength in Architectural Technology degrees, Construction Management, etc); Business (Tourism

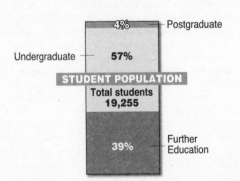

Postgraduate 4%

Undergraduate 57%

STUDENT POPULATION
Total students
19,255

Further Education 39%

Management is new with options like Cruise and Travel Operations); Law (Commercial Law degrees); Media Arts (Film, Fiction, Journalism, Advertising); Social Science (Community Studies, Psychology, Criminology, Politics); Systems Engineering (masses of computer courses and a tasty specialist degree in Media Technology for the broadcast, film & entertainment industries).

Students say that the best teaching is in Accounting, Engineering & Technology, Finance, Mechanically-based Engineering, Naval Architecture, Creative Arts & Design, Technology, Publicity, Sociology, Sports Science, Teacher Training.

Clothes retail and 'beverage serving activities' (presumably bars and pubs) and restaurants are an immediately popular work destination after gaduation - the Fashion degrees, other facets of Arts & Design, tbusiness courses (tourism degrees) and communications (PR) degrees account for this.

Thereafter it's banks and financial institutions off the business and finance degrees, then social work (community studies and psychology degrees) and advertising agencies (dedicated advertising degrees).

Then it's public administration, other sorts of retail, computer programming (computer games degrees) and work in employment agencies and secondary education. specialised design (the maritime derees), and construction - again there are dedicated degrees.

In the past there has been good investment in music, media and broadcasting courses, upgrading studios, creating digital radio facilities and setting up a centre for professional development in broadcasting and multimedia production in collaboration with ITV Meridian, the local media set-up. Among the smaller student populations Solent, like Edinburgh Napier make a good fist at getting graduates into publishing. Solent mounts its strategy not only through Journalism through Media Cultural Studies, Media Communication, and through its Graphics, Design Studies, Product

Design with Marketing degrees. Its general Marketing, Management and Communications degrees are also a gateway.

It also claims a world first in its Comedy Writing and Performance BA, devised and run by academic and stand-up comic Chris Ritchie. Other institutions do run modules in comedy, often as part of drama courses. Kent is one.

In Advertising the emphasis is on developing the creative faculties by means of idea generation exercises and creative thinking workshops. Budding art directors or copywriters will also get genned up on campaign planning, media buying, targeting and brand positioning. Conversely, if you want to play a strategic role as account planner, handler, media buyer or brand manager, you get a chance to produce campaign concepts for a creative portfolio of work. There's a twinning with a London ad agency, and hands-on experience available from tutors.

There's constantly new things going on in art and design - a whole host of new fashion, fashion photography, interiors degrees last year - and recently Muti-media Design and Digital Imaging degrees have led to a big increase in jobs. BA Illustration with Animation also scores high in the world of computer games design.

BSc Mobile Web Technology was new recently, and Electronic Engineering is another strength. Many come through the HND or Foundation years, their destination almost exclusively telecommunications. Employment figures are good.

Finally, boat/ship designer/surveyor/brokers find their way to courses dedicated to their interests - such as Maritime Business, Marine Operations, Yacht Manufacturing & Surveying and Yacht & Powercraft Design. Foundation years are

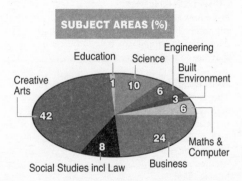

SUBJECT AREAS (%)

Education — 1
Science — 10
Engineering
Built Environment — 6
— 3
— 6
Creative Arts — 42
Maths & Computer — 24
Social Studies incl Law — 8
Business

WHAT IT'S REALLY LIKE

UNIVERSITY:

Social Life	★★★
Societies	★★
Student Union services	★★
Politics	**Not much**
Sport	**25 clubs**
National team position	**55th**
Sport facilities	★★
Arts opportunities	**Available**
Student magazine	**Sonar**
Student radio station	**Sonar Radio**
National Radio Awards	**Gold, 2010**
Student television	**Sonar TV**
Nightclub	**In-town clubs**
Bars	**Top Bar, Bottom Bar**
Union ents	**Skint**
Union societies	**10**
Parking	**Some**

CITY:

Entertainment	★★★
Scene	**Pubs, clubs, water**
Town/gown relations	**Average-poor**
Risk of violence	**Average**
Cost of living	**Average**
Student concessions	**OK**
Survival + 2 nights out	**£80 pw**
Part-time work campus/town	**Good/excellent**

ACCOMMODATION

Student rating	★★★
Guarantee to freshers	**90%**
Style	**Halls, flats**
Security guard	**All**
Shared rooms	**Some**
Internet access	**All**
Self-catered	**All**
En suite	**Some**
Approx price range pw	**£86.80-£110**
City rent pw	**£65-£75**

invariably available, if necessary.

SOCIAL SCENE

STUDENTS' UNION The union has two bars, renovated within the not so distant past, the imaginatively named **Bottom Bar** (downstairs) opens during the week, 11am-11pm in concert with **Top Bar** aka **The Venue**, which has staged such as Rolf Harris, Jools Holland, Dave Benson Phillips, etc, etc. Wednesday is Full House, official night for sports and societies (Radio Sonar djs). Saturday is *Skint* (electro/nu-disco/indie remixes/bass).

Media-wise there's the aforementioned Radio Sonar, which was awarded a Gold medal at the 2010 National Student Radio Awards, and *Sonar*, the student magazine. There are apparently only 10 societies in operation.

SPORT They have 25 sports clubs, from Capoeira to roller hockey, and triathlon to taekwon do, as well as rugby, rowing, American Football, and, as expected, water plays a key part. Sailing is the strongest sport - they've been national champions three times in the past four years (came second the other time) and three times in the top three in the world. Students come to the university because of its reputation in this sport. Sports scholarships were introduced to attract top performers in all sports. Ground-based sports facilities include a sports hall and fitness suite, sauna and solarium. Playing fields are 4 miles from the city. There's a licensed pavilion, the **Budweiser Sports Bar**.

PILLOW TALK

Cream of the halls crop would have to be Lucia Foster Welch, not only is it the biggest, but it has the advantage of having Ocean Village on its doorstep. The downside is that you are 15 minutes away from the main campus and there is no common room. The other halls all have their plus points, Kimber and its spangly new kitchens or Deanery, one of the newest. All have their own laundry, and all have recently been wired for intranet and intranet access, giving students 24-hour on-line access to the university's managed learning environment and email and internet. You can't choose where you live, but you can choose to have an en-suite bathroom or not.

GETTING THERE

☛ By road: M3/J 14, A33. Warsash: M27/J8, A27.
☛ By coach to Southampton: London, 2:30; Bristol, 2:45; Birmingham, 3:40.
☛ By rail: London Waterloo, 1:40; Bristol Parkway, 2:15; Birmingham, 3:30; Sheffield, 4:45.
☛ By air: Southampton International Airport.

STAFFORDSHIRE UNIVERSITY

Staffordshire University
College Road
Stoke-on-Trent ST4 2DE

TEL 01782 294400
    01782 292752 (prospectus)
FAX 01782 292740
EMAIL enquiries@staffs.ac.uk
WEB www.staffs.ac.uk

Staffordshire Students' Union
College Road
Stoke-on-Trent
Staffs ST4 2DE

TEL 01782 294629
FAX 01782 295736
EMAIL theunion@staffs.ac.uk
WEB www.staffsunion.com

VIRGIN VIEW

The sometime Staffordshire Polytechnic has expanded enormously and has the necessary contacts with industry to sustain a strong vocational curriculum. There's also good sport, a strong local ents scene and plenty of student activities to widen your perspective on life.

CAMPUSES

There are sites in Stoke and Stafford, 12 miles to the south, opposite the railway station. This is an area known as the Potteries, a borough incorporated in 1907 to include Stoke-on-Trent, Hanley, Burslem, Tinstall, Longton and Fenton. Its most famous son, Arnold Bennett (author of Clayhanger, Anne of the Five Towns – he preferred the sound of five, so left out Fenton) couldn't get away fast enough, but that had nothing to do with the university, which only gained its status in 1992.

FEES, BURSARIES

UK & EU Fees, 2011-12: £3,375 p.a. Bursaries of between £500 and £1,000 p.a. are available if your family income is lower than £30,810.

STUDENT PROFILE

The student profile is as you would expect. There's a sizable mature population and a sizable local intake. All but 2% of entrants are from state schools, 42% from social groups 4 to 7, while around a fifth come from neighbourhoods new to the idea of university. The uni appeals to the region with a priority application scheme for locals, bringing close links with industry, commerce, public sector and professions to the party.

ACADEMIA & JOBS

The faculties are Arts, Media & Design; Business & Law; Computing, Engineering & Technology; Health & Sciences; the Staffordshire University Business School; and the Staffordshire Law School. At Stoke there's Art & Design, Business, Law, Humanities & Social Sciences and Sciences. At

UNIVERSITY/STUDENT PROFILE	
University since	**1992**
Situation/style	**Civic**
Student population	**16990**
Total undergraduates	**13385**
Mature	**51%**
International	**12%**
Male/female ratio	**47:53**
Equality of opportunity:	
state school intake	**98%**
social class 4-7 intake	**42%**
drop-out rate	**10%**

Stafford, Computing, Engineering & Advanced Technology and Health. But what's novel is the HE-FE federation being developed with Tamworth & Lichfield College and other further education colleges. There is a Lichfield Campus for the purpose and a whole range of courses, degrees and HNDs with links to what's going on at the mother house.

There are top teaching assessments in Economics, Psychology, Philosophy, Art & Design, Physics, Sport, Biosciences, Nursing and other subjects allied to Medicine – the latter featuring midwifery and the nursing (adult, child and mental health). There is a healthcare facility at the Stafford campus to provide NHS care to students, staff and the community, including doctors' consulting rooms, a practice nurse physiotherapy service and

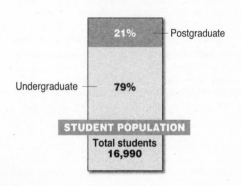

Postgraduate — 21%

Undergraduate — 79%

STUDENT POPULATION
Total students
16,990

TEACHING SURVEY AT A GLANCE

Avg. UCAS points accepted	**220**
Acceptance rate	**22%**
Overall satisfaction rate	**81%**
Helpful/interested staff	★★★★
Small tuition groups	★★★
Students into graduate jobs	**76%**

Teaching most popular with undergraduates:
Biology & related sciences, Drama, English,
Forensic & Archaeological Science, Geographical
Studies, Historical & Philosophical Studies,
Languages, Nursing (100%), Performing Arts,
Physical Geography & Environmental Science,
Psychology, Sports Scoience,
Subjects Allied to Medicine (100%).

a retail pharmacy.

Meanwhile, Staffs' IT & Computing faculty is brimming with opportunity: Graphics/Imaging /Visualisation, Science, Systems, Applicable Maths, Internet Technology, Intelligent Systems, Software Engineering, Forensic, Mobile, computer Design, Games Design, Network Engineering... Aspiring computer programmers and IT consultants (they lead the employment field nationally) should go through it with a toothcomb, Staffordshire Uni is the top graduate supplier to this sector. Resources in computing are especially good – two IT centres, the £5-million Octagon centre being a central focus with 800+ workstations.

Graduates acquire accounting knowledge with computer-based analytical, management and design skills. The single honsBA Accounting is joined by combos with Business, Economics and Law. A fast track provision offers 2-year degrees in such as Law, Business Management, Accounting and Finance, Computing Science and English.

There's a £1.25-million incubation business project at the Stafford Business Village, with 'high specification incubation' for 40 businesses. Marketing is one highly successful employment area at the Business School, which also explores management and entrepreneurship in areas such as personnel, travel and tourism, as well as having a clutch of degrees in business, computing and IT.

Staffordshire's Applied Social Studies top-ups, Sport degrees and Social Psychology, or the Psychology degrees, which can be done alone or with Criminology or Sport & Excercise all put large numbers of graduates to work in the community, as does the BA Social Work. The Sport & Leisure Department is up there employment-wise with the big boys at Brighton and Nottingham Trent.

The Law Society has awarded the University's LPC course an 'Excellent' rating, the highest acco-

lade it can bestow. Staffordshire is one of only five to share this status. See their recent additions to the curriculum: LLB Sports Law/Human Resources Management/Human Rights/Business Law. A Crime Scene House provides simulated scenes for forensic students to develop detection skills. BSc Forensic Science can be studied alone or with Criminology or Psychology.

For niche employment areas, media is also to the fore. The BA degrees come in Journalism, Film, TV, Broadcast Journalism, Music Broadcasting, Sports Journalism, TV & Radio Documentary. While in Media & Entertainment Technology are the BSc degrees in technology in areas such as film, music, computer games design, 3D animation,, simulation, etc, etc.

Art & Design melds media with art – Animation, Media Production, Photography, for example, and BA CGI Animation & Special Effects..

SOCIAL SCENE

STUDENTS' UNION Students' Union There are three bars – two at the Stoke campus, **Leek Road Venue** (**LRV** – 1800 capacity) and College Road's refur-

WHAT IT'S REALLY LIKE

UNIVERSITY:	
Social Life	★★
Societies	★★
Student Union services	★★★
Politics	**Activity low**
Sport	**Busy**
National team position	**82nd**
Sport facilities	★★
Arts opportunities	**Good**
Student newspaper	**One Media**
Student radio	**One Media Radio**
Student TV	**One Media TV**
Nightclub	**Legends**
Bars	**LRV, Ember Lounge**
Union ents	**Serious clubnights & live**
Union societies	**23**
Most active society	**Drama**
Parking	**Plentiful**
TOWN:	
Entertainment	★★★
Town scene	**Pubs, clubs**
Town/gown relations	**Average**
Risk of violence	**Average**
Cost of living	**Average**
Student concessions	**Good**
Survival + 2 nights out	**£60 pw**
Part-time work campus/town	**Good**

bished **Ember Lounge** (500) and one at Stafford, **Legends**, which goes forth as Sleepers during the day.

LRV stages some of the biggest student nights in the Midlands. There are two resident DJs and guest appearances by the famous (DJs and bands). There's also Comedy Club on Saturday. It's a busy, well-worked scene. 'We're not on the main gig circuit,' they admit, 'but the DJs and their agents now ring us!' There are also three balls a year, May in March, Summer in June and Graduation in November. May Ball's the biggest.

It isn't all music. There are in fact twenty-three societies at Stoke, and the most active is Drama – there's a good Drama & Theatre Arts degree; at Stafford there are a further ten. The uni newspaper was GK (Get Knotted - the paper has received awards from the *Guardian* and the *Daily Telegraph*) and the student radio station, GK Radio. But now it's all One Media - online news, radio and TV.

SPORT Academic influence brings good facilities for all and fame for some. They have 41 clubs and came 82nd nationally in the team ratings last year. Hockey is their sport. Cross country and badminton teams are also strong, and they have had their top-ranked swimmers, too.

Facilities include a sports centre, sports halls, squash courts, floodlit synthetic and grass pitches for football or rugby, fitness suites, gym with multi-gym, weights and fitness machines. There's also a dance and aerobics studio at the Sir Stanley Matthews Sports Centre in Leek Road.

TOWN Contrary to expectation Hanley, not Stoke, is the main man down among the potteries. There are pubs and clubs in both, however, to which you will soon feel like is home. Just outside Hanley is Festival Park - multi-screen cinema, Quasar, Water World, Super Bowl, etc. Stoke has a dry ski slope. Theatres include the New Victoria at nearby

ACCOMMODATION	
Student rating	★★★
Guarantee to freshers	**100%**
Style	**Halls, flats**
Security guard	**Most halls, all flats**
Shared rooms	**All halls, some flats**
Internet access	**All**
Self-catered	**All**
En suite	**Halls none, flats most**
Approx price range pw	**£58-£100**
City rent Stoke pw	**£50**
City rent Stafford pw	**£60**

Newcastle-under-Lyme, the Rep Theatre (Stoke) and Theatre Royal (Hanley). Sundays and Wednesdays are film nights at Legends in Stafford; the Drama Soc. is forty strong and puts on four plays a year, including panto.

PILLOW TALK
Stoke: 6 on-campus halls of residence, 8 off campus. Student houses: 36-bedroom houses on Leek Road. Student Flats: blocks of flats, two thirds sharing, within two miles of Leek Road. Stafford: Stafford Court includes 249 en-suite rooms; an additional 307 rooms will be open by the time you get there and Yarlet House with fifty-one. Parking available outside halls.

GETTING THERE
* By road: Stafford – M6/J14, A513. Stoke – M6 (J15 from south; J16 from north), A500.
* By coach: London, 4:00.
* By rail: Birmingham New Street, 40 mins; Manchester Piccadilly, 1:20; London Euston, 1:45; Nottingham, 2:00; Sheffield, 2:15.

UNIVERSITY OF STIRLING

The University of Stirling
Stirling FK9 4LA

TEL 01786 467046
FAX 01786 466800
EMAIL recruitment@stir.ac.uk
WEB www.stir.ac.uk/students

Stirling University Students' Association
University of Stirling FK9 4LA

TEL 01786 467166
FAX 01786 467190
EMAIL susa@stir.ac.uk
WEB www.susaonline.org.uk/

VIRGIN VIEW

*T*he University of Stirling is a premier-league university with a reputation *for leading the way. It is a classic example of a campus university - typical 60s breeze-block buildings, but set in beautiful surroundings with a small loch in the centre,* hills in the background, and more than enough ducks, rabbits, and squirrels to keep a nature lover happy. Situated a mile or so outside the city, it is so completely self-sufficient that you could, if you so desired, spend the whole semester there without leaving once.

Value added for Stirling has to include the city itself, gateway to the Highlands, if only because it was judged as inducing the best student living experience in the UK (National Student Housing Survey, 2010 awards). Given that the latest Times Higher Education Student Experience Survey rates the campus environment as best, location scores high.

So do its sports facilities. Stirling is Scotland's University for Sporting Excellence, and a proven springboard for careers in golf, swimming, tennis and football.

The University also likes to point out its diverse, multi-cultural student population. It may be farflung, but students from over 80 nationalities seek it out.

Open Days, 2011: 24 September and 15 October (10 a.m. - 3 p.m.)

> 'It's a classic example of a campus university. Typical '60s breeze-block buildings, but set in beautiful surroundings with a small loch in the centre, hills in the background, and more than enough ducks, rabbits and squirrels. By the second year it can become slightly claustrophobic.'

UNIVERSITY/STUDENT PROFILE	
University since	**1967**
Situation/style	**Campus**
Student population	**10125**
Total undergraduates	**7550**
Mature	**42%**
International	**18%**
Male/female ratio	**37:63**
Equality of opportunity:	
state school intake	**93%**
social class 4-7 intake	**35%**
drop-out rate	**10%**

in March. Think of Stirling as the apex of a triangle north-east of Glasgow, north-west of Edinburgh. It's an hour from either, give or take. Commonly, students hire a minibus for a night out in these cities. You need to escape occasionally from campus, for beautiful as it is, Stirling is also a bubble apart from the world.

The loch is the centrepiece of campus, with the Wallace Monument towering over it. You look out over the water from the halls of residence, enjoy summer and even Christmas barbecues beside it, and criss-cross it by bridge daily on the way to the Robbins Centre, Atrium and MacRobert Arts Centre in the Union facility, or for lectures in the Cottrell or Pathfoot buildings. The loch gives itself to canoeing and fishing and to academic experiment in Aquaculture and Marine Biology.

It has suited various writers (Iain Banks among them) and many golfers too, for Airthrey Golf Course is close. Some find it pleasantly secure, others slightly claustrophobic, but the spirit of the place espouses a student-centred ethos. One told us that he felt that Stirling had given him the kind of individual teaching and personal treatment that he imagined he might have enjoyed as a sixth former had he gone to a public school.

New facilities at a satellite campus in Inverness (Stirling's Highland Campus) offer up-to-the-minute training for student nurses.

CAMPUS

The 310-acre campus is was once part of the grounds of Airthrey Castle, base camp for the Highlands. As you approach, you see the Ochil hills in the distance, snow capped when we went

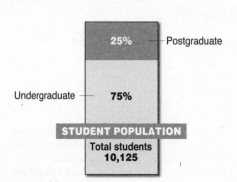

25% — Postgraduate

Undergraduate — 75%

STUDENT POPULATION
Total students
10,125

FEES, BURSARIES

UK & EU Fees, 2011-12: non-Scottish domiciled students pay £1,820. If you are a Scottish-domiciled first degree student you are eligible for your tuition fees to be covered by the Scottish

Government. Stirling offers no bursary to students eligible for the HE Maintenance Grant, but a hardship fund is available. There are scholarships in golf, swimming, disability swimming, tennis, triathlon, men's football, women's football), and the main academic award is the Carnegie Trust Scholarship.

STUDENT PROFILE

Ninety-three per cent of Stirling undergraduates are in fact state school educated, 35% of its undergraduates come from the lower socio-economic groups, and they take a fair few from the so-called 'low-participation' neighbourhoods. There is a keen focus on international recruitment too. Already there are over 80 nationalities represented on campus, and its policy is to attract more. To that end, English language support is provided to help international applicants meet entry requirements, arrangements are made to meet students on arrival at the airport, and long before they arrive they will have corresponded with the International Society and taken a virtual tour of campus by means of a video available in Polish, Spanish, Russian, Japanese, Hindi, and Chinese. A story goes the rounds that when finally they reach campus, they have been known to greet the student stars of the video like long-lost friends, which gives a charming sense of the adventure they are on.

The small size of the student body (there are

TEACHING SURVEY AT A GLANCE	
Avg. UCAS points accepted	**324**
Acceptance rate	**15%**
Overall satisfaction rate	**89%**
Helpful/interested staff	★★★★
Small tuition groups	★★★
Students into graduate jobs	**70%**

Teaching most popular with undergraduates:
Accounting, Biological Sciences, Business, Computer, English, Finance & Accounting, History, Initial Teacher Training, Journalism, Languages, Law, Marketing (98%), Maths & Statistics (100%), Media Studies, Physical Geography & Environmental Science, Politics, Psychology, Sociology, Social Policy & Anthropology, Tourism.

barely 10,000 in all) and the seclusion of Stirling, dictate student experience. People get to know one another quickly across the years. As a fresher it won't be long before you know every second person. If this is what you like, you'll like Stirling. It certainly isn't an intimidating place: 'integration' is the administration's No. 1 buzz word.

ACADEMIA & JOBS

At Stirling, your degree is built up of credits, accumulated through taking modules on a semester-by-semester basis, rather than at the end of the academic year. The key benefit of modular study is flexibility. It is possible to start on one degree programme and graduate in something entirely different. In fact, around half of Stirling students change the focus of their degree in some way. It is perhaps their flexibility that leads to their claim that they can fast-track aspiring school teachers in a year less than other universites.

In the *Times Higher Education Magazine's* Student Experience Survey, Stirling undergraduates rated highly the helpful and interested nature of their lecturers and the relatively small-size tuition groups.

Students say the best teaching is in Accounting, Biological Sciences, Business, Computer, English, Finance & Accounting, History, Initial Teacher Training, Journalism, Languages, Law, Marketing (98% voted OK), Maths & Statistics (100%), Media Studies, Physical Geography & Environmental Science, Politics, Psychology, Sociology, Social Policy & Anthropology, and Tourism.

The Stirling Management School has four divisions: Accounting & Finance, Business & Organisation, Marketing and Economics. The latter is an area of particular expertise. Fifteen per cent of their research in this area is world class (4-

RESEARCH EXCELLENCE		
% of Stirling's research that is		
4* (World-class) or 3* (Internationally rated):		
	4*	**3***
Nursing/Midwifery	**20%**	**30%**
Aquaculture	**5%**	**45%**
Environmental Sciences	**5%**	**35%**
Computer Science	**5%**	**40%**
Economics	**15%**	**45%**
Accounting/Finance	**0%**	**45%**
Business/Management	**10%**	**30%**
Law	**5%**	**35%**
Politics	**5%**	**10%**
Social Work	**10%**	**45%**
Psychology	**5%**	**10%**
Education	**15%**	**40%**
Sports	**15%**	**25%**
European Studies	**5%**	**25%**
Englishe	**10%**	**45%**
Philosophy	**25%**	**45%**
History	**15%**	**35%**
Film & Media	**10%**	**60%**

star), 45% internationally excellent (3-star).

Another subject that did well in the research assessment was Nursing and Midwifery, which achieved 20% 4-star and 30% 3-star. Seventeen per cent of all graduates jobs at Stirling involve employment in hospitals. Stirling trains nurses and midwives on three campuses, in Stirling, Inverness and the Western Isles, but an interesting development is a return-to-nursing-practice scheme after a period of absence - online learning, a dissertation and clinical practice.

Film and Media is another area worth highlighting. In the research assessment 70% of research was found to be either world class or internationally excellent. Out of this rich culture comes a series of film and media degrees, and some convincing sounding Journalism joint degree courses. A few years ago a news room became part of the teaching resources. The Student Union is known for its award-winning media and has launched its own TV station.

In the wake of the uni's fortieth anniversary the library was redeveloped and recently reopened its doors on an £11.4m refurbishment, a stunning modern learning environment,

SOCIAL SCENE

STUDENTS' ASSOCIATION To sustain life far from the city, SUSA puts on a fairly cheesy show from its base in the **Robbins Centre**, but no-one seems to mind. In fact, the SA won *Best Bar None* in 2005, 2006 and 2007 (for excellence in 'corporate social responsibility'). There are 3 bars: **Studio** is open from 9.30am for breakfast, and on into the small hours. Although it has its own programme of ents (pub quizzes, NFL Sundays), its main function in the evening is as pre-club for the nightclub downstairs, with capacity for up to 750. There are weekly live music nights, as well as frequent live comedy nights.

On campus too are the usual sports clubs and societies - 'SUDS, the Drama Society, aims to put on at least a couple of productions each semester,' writes Suzanne Bush, 'and there's a ready supply of theatre, cinema and music in the form of the MacRobert Arts Centre.'

The **MacRobert** is a multi-arts centre situated in the heart of campus, with a cinema, café bar restaurant, 468-seater auditorium, children's theatre, and arts crÊche. The complex also has rehearsal studio and gallery space. A mix of modern, arthouse and mainstream films are shown daily, and a mixed live programme in the main theatre. See www.macrobert.org.

Among non-sporting societies you can opt for anything from Chocolate Appreciation Society to Debating, Politics, or the award-winning media -

WHAT IT'S REALLY LIKE	
UNIVERSITY:	
Social Life	★★★
Societies	★★★★
Student Union services	★★★
Politics	**Student issues**
Sport	**Very competitive, 37 clubs**
National team position	**22nd**
Sport facilities	★★★★★
Arts opportunities	**Excellent**
Student newspaper	**BRIG**
Student radio	**Air 3**
Student TV	**Air TV**
Nightclub	**The Nightclub**
Bars	**Studio, Nightclub, Long Bar**
Union ents	**Hip hop, cheese, retro**
Union societies	**40**
Parking	**No to freshers**
CITY:	
Entertainment	★★
Scene	**Pubs, 3 clubs**
Town/gown relations	**Average**
Risk of violence	**Low**
Cost of living	**Low**
Student concessions	**Some**
Survival + 2 nights out	**£60**
Part-time work campus/town	**Fair**

Brig (the student newspaper), Air3 radio or Air TV.

Continues Suzanne: 'The student Musical Society works towards at least one big production every year. The University Choir brings together students and people from the community and puts on a big concert every December in Dunblane Cathedral. Politics is not a big issue until a big issue finds its way onto campus, namely Car Parking! Some time ago the barriers went up and parking permits were required.'

SPORT Stirling has invested heavily in sport in recent years and has now been formally designated by the Scottish Government as Scotland's University for Sporting Excellence, not just in terms of high-performing students, but in research, education and sports science. Facilities include a sports hall, squash courts, a state-of-the-art fitness suite, and a 400m running track.

The National Swimming Academy, with its 50 metre pool, is a designated Intensive Training Centre for the Olympics and Paralympics. It can be split into two and one of the 25 metre pools has a moveable floor, changing the water depth from 0 metres to 2 metres. There's a conditioning room next to the pool, as well as an Omega timing system and a full range of water polo fittings and equipment.

Next door, the National Tennis Centre recently expanded and has six indoor courts with more outside.

The MP Jackson Fitness Centre houses 3 sports science laboratories: athlete assessment laboratory, research laboratory, analytical laboratory, a fitness suite with 50+ pieces of cardiovascular and resistance equipment, and there's a strength and conditioning 'super centre' with 5 lifting platforms.

There are 23 acres of playing fields for football, rugby, athletics and hockey, with 2 all-weather pitches as well. Then there's the loch for angling, sailing and canoeing. Finally, there's a Golf Centre with a short game practice area, three target greens and a nine-hole golf course. Jogging routes are situated around campus.

PILLOW TALK

All freshers continue to be guaranteed university accommodation, though not necessarily on campus. In Alexander Court there is self-catered, flat accommodation where kitchen and bathroom facilities are shared by 7 students. In Geddes Court

ACCOMMODATION	
Student rating	★★
Guarantee to freshers	**100%**
Style	**Halls, flats**
Security guard	**All**
Shared rooms	**None**
Internet access	**£15 extra**
Self-catered	**All**
En suite	**Some**
Approx price range pw	**£67-£106**
Town rent pw	**£70-£110**

and A K Davidson, the accommodation has communal bathroom facilities. In Andrew Stewart hall, the accommodation is en suite, and is probably the best for freshers. A K Davidson has also just been refurbished. Murray Hall has just undergone a refit.

GETTING THERE
☛ By road: M9/J11, A9 or A91, A907, A9.
☛ By coach: London, 9:00; Edinburgh, 2:20.
☛ By rail: Glasgow/Edinburgh, 55 mins; Aberdeen, 2:30; London King's Cross, 6:00.

UNIVERSITY OF STRATHCLYDE

The University of Strathclyde
Graham Hills Building
50 George Street
Glasgow G1 1XQ

TEL 0141 548 2814
FAX 0141 552 5860
EMAIL scls@mis.strath.ac.uk
WEB www.strath.ac.uk

Strathclyde Students' Association
90 John Street
Glasgow G1 1JH

TEL 0141 567 5000
FAX 0141 567 5050
EMAIL theunion@strath.ac.uk
WEB www.strathstudents.ac.uk

VIRGIN VIEW

Strathclyde had its beginnings in 1796 as Anderson's Institution, an equal-opportunity, science and technology college. John Anderson had been Professor of Natural Philosophy at Glasgow University and the institution that bore his name was founded under the terms of his will. University status came in 1964 following the merger of the Royal College of Science and the Scottish College of Commerce, which fact alerts us to Strathclyde's second largest faculty after Engineering, the Strathclyde Business School. In 1993, Glasgow's Jordanhill College joined the fold and became Strath's third largest faculty, Education.

Value added are its close links with industry, commerce, the public sector and professions; tutors with industry expertise and vocational facilities to match; courses that relate to the real world of work; and living costs lower than many other univesities. Some students are accepted at Strathclyde on the strength of skills or experience relevant to their subject area of interest.

UNIVERSITY/STUDENT PROFILE	
University since	**1964**
Situation/style	**City campus**
Student population	**21300**
Total undergraduates	**14610**
Mature	**43%**
International	**12%**
Male/female ratio	**46:54**
Equality of opportunity:	
state school intake	**93%**
social class 4-7 intake	**28%**
drop-out rate	**11%**

CAMPUS

Today Strathclyde University occupies the same site as Anderson's Institution in the heart of Glasgow, just behind George Square and a walk from either Central or Queen Street stations. The concentration of students in the immediate vicinity is extraordinary: Strathclyde and Caledonian universities, the College of Building and Printing, the College of Food & Technology, and the College of Commerce. The Jordanhill campus is in the west end of the city, close to Glasgow University. Jordanhill will close in 2010 and the Education Faculty move to a new building in the city centre.

> *'Glasgow Uni looks down on Strathclyde as being John Street Poly. Strathclyde looks down on Caledonian as being the old Glasgow Technical College, lowest of the low.'*

FEES, BURSARIES

UK & EU Fees, 2011-12: Non-Scottish-based UK residents pay £1,820 p.a. for all courses at Scottish universities, except Medicine. Bursaries of between £500 and £1,000 p.a. are available if your family income is lower than £30,810.

STUDENT PROFILE

Strathclyde is one of three unis in the city. 'Vibe

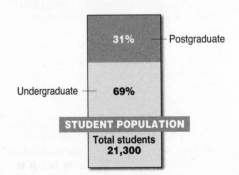

31% — Postgraduate

Undergraduate — 69%

STUDENT POPULATION
Total students
21,300

wise, it has a more relaxed atmosphere in comparison with Glasgow University, which tends to have a more academic outlook,' said a student of Glasgow Uni. Peter Mann, a student at Strathclyde, suggested differences run deeper: 'Caledonian and Strathclyde have a similar kind of population. Glasgow is quite different and generally disliked because it is full of English people. There is not a tremendous amount of mixing.' A student of Caledonian offered this Pythonesque picture of the pecking order: 'Glasgow University looks down on Strathclyde as being John Street Poly, although it's been a university since 1964. And Strathclyde looks down on us as being the old Glasgow Technical College, the lowest of the low.'

There's a 93% state school population and a 28% take from the working classes, which is not particularly high. Unlike Caledonian, Strathclyde carries none of the poly cultural baggage, for it was the Royal College; Caledonian was the Poly. But a lot of the students are local. 'There's one guy in student radio,' said Peter, 'who's from Surrey, and he sticks out like a sore thumb.'

ACADEMIA & JOBS

Best research work is in Business, Engineering, Law and Science. Students say best teaching is in Accounting, Biological Sciences, Biology, Business, Chemical Process & Energy Engineering, Chemistry (100% of the class gave the thumbs-up), Economics, Electronic & Electrical Engineering, Finance, Forensic and Archaeological Science, French Studies, Geographical Studies, History, Human Resource Management, Human & Social Geography, Management, Marketing, Mechanical, Production & Manufacturing Eng., Microbiology, Music, Pharmacology, Physical Science, Physics & Astronomy, Politics, Psychology, Social Work, Sociology, Tourism & Transport.

A fast track provision offers 2-year degrees in such as Law, Business Management, Accounting and Finance, Computing Science and English.

The biggest cohort of Strathclyde graduates go for acounting, then primary school teaching, which occupies around 9% of the total, then banking and finance, engineering, community work, engineering design consultancy, specialist retail (pharmacy, etc), public admin., and higher education. Many go on to further training in the Law.

Key to the social and community work are degrees in such as Community Arts, Community

Education, Outdoor Education in the Community, Social Work, Sport in the Community, but also Speech and Language Pathology, which may find its application in hospitals (for example with accident and stroke victims) and school, nurseries and special centres.

There is a fine academic reputation. Students gave the lecturers are high rating for interest and helpfulness. The key thing is the way they teach: audio-visual, video, visual materials, computer-assisted learning programmes are all to the fore. Very close links with industry and commerce ensure a real-world, highly practical emphasis. They have a Learning Resources Base which, among other things, is there to help you in adjusting to study methods, curriculum design etc. Every student is assigned a personal tutor, and there's a built-in early-warning system to prevent any first year getting lost along the way.

The uni's Careers Service has received the National Charter Mark for excellence in customer service on more than one occasion.

Mechanical Engineering is another major

TEACHING SURVEY AT A GLANCE

Avg. UCAS points accepted	**404**
Acceptance rate	**18%**
Overall satisfaction rate	**86%**
Helpful/interested staff	★★★★
Small tuition groups	★★★
Students into graduate jobs	**79%**

Teaching most popular with undergraduates:
Accounting, Biological Sciences, Biology, Business, Chemical Process & Energy Engineering, Chemistry (100%), Economics, Electronic & Electrical Engineering, Finance, Forensic and Archaeological Science, French Studies, Geographical Studies, History, Human Resource Management, Human & Social Geography, Management, Marketing, Mechanical, Production & Manufacturing Eng., Microbiology, Music, Pharmacology, Physical Science, Physics & Astronomy, Politics, Psychology, Social Work, Sociology, Tourism & Transport.

Teaching least popular with undergraduates:
Architecture (45%), Journalism (36%).

RESEARCH EXCELLENCE

% of Strathclyde's research that is
4* (World-class) or **3*** (Internationally rated):

	4*	3*
Health Professions	**15%**	**45%**
Pharmacy	**15%**	**40%**
Chemistry	**10%**	**60%**
Physics	**5%**	**35%**
Applied Mathematics	**10%**	**40%**
Statistics	**10%**	**30%**
Computer Science	**15%**	**35%**
Electrical/Electronic Eng.	**15%**	**35%**
General Engineering	**15%**	**45%**
Chemical Engineering	**5%**	**35%**
Civil Engineering	**5%**	**35%**
Mechanical Engineering	**15%**	**35%**
Naval Architecture & Marine Eng.	**10%**	**45%**
Built Environment	**5%**	**35%**
Business/Management	**25%**	**40%**
Law	**20%**	**40%**
Politics	**0%**	**30%**
Social Work	**5%**	**35%**
Sociology	**0%**	**20%**
Psychology	**0%**	**30%**
Education	**5%**	**25%**
European Studies	**10%**	**10%**
Italian	**0%**	**20%**
Iberian	**0%**	**20%**
English	**15%**	**30%**
History	**5%**	**35%**

focus for Strathclyde. The faculty has expanded in a highly successful collaboration with Glasgow Uni over Naval Architecture degrees. Besides the naval architecture degrees, there's the traditional 4-year BSc Architectural Studies (with European Studies); also BEng Architectural Engineering.

They are also leaders in forensic science (Forensic & Analytical Chemistry, Forensic Biology). The Forensic Science Society (www.forensic-science-society.org.uk) take many of their members from Strathclyde.

A new Centre for Forensic Science - the first of its kind in the UK - has built on the University's international reputation and provides a comprehensive range of educational, research and consultancy services to laboratories, police forces and other agencies.

Finally, there's a strong reputation for law - they are commercial & business and European law specialists, and have an LLB based on Scots Law too.

SOCIAL SCENE

Strathclyde is Glaswegian not only because of the number of Glaswegians who attend, but in the very Glaswegian way students here go about having a good time. 'Their ents are marvelled at by other unions for their ability to bring in droves of students from rival unis, and give them just what they want – an excellent hangover for those on a budget!' reports Rachel Richardson. In fact, it is hard to assimilate the energy that is devoted to exciting pleasure in the students at Strathclyde. Whatever the legal capacity for the big night, it is not uncommon to find between 2,000 and 2,500 students here totally out of their heads. The legendary pleasure zone itself is 10 floors high, yet it is not the skyscraper you expect because in some extraordinary Alice-in-Wonderland fashion they have conspired to fit its ten floors, mezzanine-style, into the space of six or seven, leading this first-time visitor into utter confusion.

So, now the fun elements of the world-famous 10-floored Union are – Level 2: **Barony Bar** (main bar/club which is home to most of the regular nights); Level 3: **Gameszone** (Scotland's largest pool hall with 26 tables); Level 4: **The Scene** (eats); Level 5: **The Lounge** place to chill, relax; can consult support group Ask here too); Level 6: **The Priory** (relaxed café bar); Level 8: **Vertigo** (the larger gig space, where Girls Aloud, Fratellis, The View, and Vengaboys have played).

Ents include *12-hour Tuesdays*: 3pm-3am, all

drinks 99p (**Barony**); *TFI Friday* is hosted by legendary, acerbic DJ Phil. This night has been running for 12 years and is the most successful student night in Glasgow. Cheap drinks and crazy antics, *TFI* is not for the faint hearted; Wednesday is touted as 'the only university gay night in Glasgow', every Wednesday comes with cocktails, and tunes from DJ Ricci.

Besides the live acts, guests DJs play here. Edith Bowman has graced the decks at Barony, and survived.

But it isn't all booze and sweat at Strath. There are 70 or more clubs and societies. Sport is excellent (see below) and media-wise they have a cracking set-up. 'It was a few years ago radio station SUR had its first restricted licence,' Peter Mann told me. 'It was funded from our *alumni* fund. Now we have more DJ talent than we could possibly use. Then we've got the *Strathclyde Telegraph*. Basically, I started up Fusion, took this sabbatical year to get it off the ground. When I leave here I am going for a job connected with the Internet.' You'd better believe it.

For drama, they have two theatres – the **Ramshorn** at John Anderson, the **Crawfurd** at Jordanhill; both offer courses in all aspects of theatre and there's plenty of opportunity, too, just to be involved in student productions. The Strathclyde Theatre Group puts on ten major productions a year. The **Collins Gallery**, also on campus, runs year-round exhibitions and workshops, and there's also a concert hall for the many musical productions. Choirs, bands, a symphony orchestra, ensembles, etc go to make up the Music Society, which presents weekly lunchtime recitals by visiting artists as well as by students in the National Trust for Scotland's **Hutchesons' Hall**.

See also Student Glasgow.

SPORT They came 47th in the national league last time. Successes: Rugby Men won British Unis' Plate; Football Men won British Unis' Vase. Badminton, Volleyball, Rugby, Hockey and Football all won their respective Scottish Leagues.

At John Anderson campus there are indoor facilities for basketball, netball, archery, volleyball, tennis, badminton, handball, martial arts, fencing, table tennis, gymnastics, circuit training, yoga, indoor training facilities for track & field, cricket, golf and hockey, a weight training & conditioning room, squash courts and swimming pool. Beyond campus there are grass pitches, artificial floodlit pitches, and a pavilion – team games include hockey, rugby, American football and soccer. Jordanhill has a similar range of indoor and outdoor facilities on campus. Proximity to river, sea and mountains enables a whole range of other sports – from mountaineering to sailing, from row-

WHAT IT'S REALLY LIKE	
UNIVERSITY:	
Social Life	★★★★★
Societies	★★★
Student Union services	★★★★★
Politics	**Student issues**
Sport	**38 clubs**
National team position	**47th**
Sport facilities	★★★
Arts opportunities	**Drama, music, film, art good; dance poor**
Student newspaper	**Strathclyde Telegraph**
Student radio	**SUR**
Nightclub	**Vertigo**
Bars	**Barony, Darkroom, Lounge, Priory**
Union ents	**Club nights, cheese, live bands**
Union societies	**35-40**
Most active society	**SUPSA, SUDS**
Parking	**Poor/non-existent**
CITY:	
Entertainment	★★★★★
Scene	**Very cool**
Town/gown relations	**Good**
Risk of violence	**Average**
Cost of living	**Average**
Student concessions	**Poor**
Survival + 2 nights out	**£80 pw**
Part-time work campus/town	**Good/excellent**

ACCOMMODATION

Student rating	★★★
Guarantee to freshers	**100%**
Style	**Halls, flats**
Security guard	**All**
Shared rooms	**Some**
Internet access	**All**
Self-catered	**All**
En suite	**Some**
Approx price range pw	**£66-£102**
City rent pw	**£85-£110**

group. There is an on-site management team in the Village Office and a Nightporter to take care of emergencies through the night. A 'watched' CCTV system beamed back to University Security Control provides an extra level of security. Two off-campus halls, 10 mins walk away. There are a limited number of car parking places available for these residences at a small cost, which are allocated on a 'first come first served' basis.

ing to skiing. There are eight bursaries for low handicap golfers from The Royal and Ancient.

PILLOW TALK

All the accommodation in the Campus Village is self catered. Single sex flats, except for second year students, who can choose to live in a mixed sex

GETTING THERE
☛ By road: The John Anderson campus – M74, M8/J15 or A82, M8/J15 or M8/J15. Jordanhill – M74, M8/J19 or A82, M8/J19 or M8/J19.
☛ By rail: Edinburgh, 0:50; Newcastle, 2:30; Aberdeen, 2:45; Birmingham New Street, 5:30; London King's Cross, 6:00.
☛ By air: Glasgow Airport, 15-20 minutes' drive.
☛ By coach: Edinburgh, 1:10; London, 8:20; Birmingham, 6:20; Newcastle, 4:20.

UNIVERSITY OF SUNDERLAND

The University of Sunderland
Student Recruitment & Admissions
Edinburgh Building
Chester Road
Sunderland SR1 3SD

TEL: 0191 515 3154
FAX: 0191 515 3155
EMAIL: admissions@sunderland.ac.uk
WEB www.sunderland.ac.uk

Sunderland Students' Union
Wearmouth Hall
Chester Road
Sunderland SR1 3SD

TEL 0191 514 5512
FAX 0191 515 2441
EMAIL su.president@sunderland.ac.uk
WEB www.sunderlandsu.co.uk

VIRGIN VIEW

Sunderland was an area robbed of its core industries a few decades ago, but has since been reborn and its uni with it. The poly became a university in 1992, the very year that Sunderland became a city. Since then they have been engaged in expansion.

Their niche areas are Media, Design, Law, Education, Business, Psychology, Pharmacy, Computing and Social Work.

This is a 'new university' student body. Undergraduates have a good time, 82% of them said in the National Student Survey that they were satisfied with what is on offer. But only 62% of them got real graduate jobs last time within six months of leaving. And the drop-out rate is 14%, which is above their Government benchmark.

CAMPUS SITES

The Chester Road **City Campus** is in easy reach of the town centre, while the newer, award-winning **Tom Cowie Campus** at St Peter's is but a stone's throw out, at the mouth of the River Wear. They had been going to pull out of the city centre and bring everyone to St Peter's, but instead they built a multi-million pound 'Gateway' there, 'a one stop shop' for student services and information, and a Sports Science Centre with a range and quality of hi-tech equipment. Now they plan to develop it further, making provision for a 6-court sports hall, spectator gallery, fitness suite, catering and retail outlets, climbing wall, multi-purpose room, sports injuries service, and a large social space. They call the £12-million project City Space. Also at City is the Murray Library and the science complex, a modern range of laboratories for Science students.†

UNIVERSITY/STUDENT PROFILE	
University since	**1992**
Situation/style	**Campus**
Student population	**20150**
Total undergraduates	**17160**
Mature	**58%**
International	**23%**
Male/female ratio	**45:55**
Equality of opportunity:	
state school intake	**98%**
social class 4-7 intake	**45%**
drop-out rate	**14%**

Tom Cowie at St Peter's fits unobtrusively into the landscape, as the ground falls away to the river. Wearmouth's iron bridge arches splendidly across the water like a young relation of Stephenson's famous iron bridge at nearby Newcastle; cranes complete the backdrop of the area's industrial past, against which the campus is heralded as an expression of the re-born character of the region. Jutting roofs and walkways on campus (a modern version of Oxbridge cloisters) keep students dry as they criss-cross University Square, to and from the Prospect Building. Rainwater plunges down huge chrome pipes from roofs topped with strange deckchair-shaped receivers, scanning the northern skies. Impressive, but the design never quite recovers from the creams and browns that make St Peter's look old before its time.

Business, Law and Psychology are here, as is the David Goldman Informatics Centre (Computing) and the David Putnam Media Centre, with studios, edit suites and a 200-seat cinema.

The uni is also associated with a £300-million film academy and studios at Seaham, a coastal town 10 minutes drive away. The plan is for a film studio complex, student campus, educational buildings, parkland, hotels and leisure facilities.

FEES, BURSARIES

UK & EU Fees, 2011-12: £3,375 p.a. For students in receipt of the HE Maintenance Grant, Sunderland's support package is £525 p.a. if you're earning less than £39,305 p.a. There is also a Success Scholarship, worth up to £965, and a scholarship of £525 p.a. for Foundation degree students. Finally, there is a £1,500 Bursary for Care Experienced Students.

STUDENT PROFILE

Sunderland are leaders in what is known as 'widening participation in higher education': 98% are from state schools, 45% are from the lower socio-economic orders, 24% from 'low-participation'

neighbourhoods, and 58% are mature students. International students are also attracted in increasing number.

ACADEMIA & JOBS

The University has four academic faculties: Applied Sciences; Arts, Design & Media; Education & Society; Business & Law. But when it comes to jobs, Education accounts for some 17% of graduate futures: 75% of school-teacher output is into secondary, which is the largest single graduate employment provision. The primary provision is also strong and there's a well-trod path into further education lecturing, particularly via the media and communications degrees and biological sciences, which scored full marks at the assessments.

Next most popular occupation is in pharmacy, which accounts for around 8% of graduates. There are foundation courses for both Chemical & Pharmaceutical Science and Pharmacology degrees. They do all in their power to wean you onto a course. The university has a strong Disability Support Team, offering a range of advice, including an outstanding learning support programme for dyslexic students.

Computing is another popular and successful employment pathway - AI, Business Computing, Forensic Computing, Intelligent Robotics, Network Computing and a strong Computer Studies presence on the joint honours scheme (a defining factor of the curriculum at Sunderland; most subjects figure). Graduates get jobs as IT consultants and software engineers in particular, as well as programmers and computer operators.

Graphic artists and designers also proliferate and a look into the art and design provision brings us unerringly to another defining aspect, the Glass,

TEACHING SURVEY AT A GLANCE	
Avg. UCAS points accepted	**220**
Acceptance rate	**19%**
Overall satisfaction rate	**82%**
Helpful/interested staff	★★★
Small tuition groups	★★★
Students into graduate jobs	**62%**

Teaching most popular with undergraduates:
Biological Sciences, Education, English Studies, History, Languages, Law, Media, Pharmacy, Pharmacology & Toxicology, Psychology, Publicity, Sports Science, Subjects allied to Medicine.

Teaching least popular with undergraduates:
Drama, Mechanical, Production & Manufacturing Engineering (58%), Engineering & Technology (55%)..

WHAT IT'S REALLY LIKE

UNIVERSITY:	
Social Life	★★
Societies	★★★
Student Union services	★★
Politics	**Student issues Activity low**
Sport	**32 clubs.**
National sporting position	**102nd**
Sport facilities	★★★★
Arts opportunities	**Film good; rest 'average'**
Student magazine	**Degrees North**
Student radio	**Spark FM**
New Student TV	**Sunderland TV**
Nightclub	**Campus**
Bars	**Wearmouth, Bonded**
Union ents	**Volume, Live**
Union societies	**51**
Parking	**Adequate**
CITY	
Entertainment	★★★
Scene	**Cheap fun**
Town/gown relations	**Poor**
Risk of violence	**Average**
Cost of living	**Low**
Student concessions	**Average**
Survival + 2 nights out	**£65 pw**
Part-time work campus/town	**Excellent**

Architectural Glass & Ceramics degree. But see also the more modern dimension: the Photography, Video & Digital Imaging degree and those in Animation and Advertising & Design.

Business is always quoted as a big strength at Sunderland, and around 16% of students do leave with a business degree. There's Business & Administration/Human resource Mgt/Marketing/Enterprise/etc There's a Law degree with Business Studies, and indeed Sunderland are commercial and business law specialists.

On another tack, there is, too, a very strong showing in welfare and community care, and in nursing, where they dropped only one point at the assessments.

SOCIAL SCENE

STUDENTS' UNION The main student haunts are the **Wearmouth Bar** at City Campus, **Campus** nightclub at St Peter's and **Bonded**, a bar across the river from St Peter's at Panns Bank.

An early 19th-century marine store and smithy, Bonded has a shop and bar downstairs and right across the first floor is this large, beamed bar with snooker table and big screen. Initial custom

was 'a slow but steady stream,' then they started a series of comedy nights, which won them a decent audience. Now, with the halls up the road it is never quiet.

The main nightspot remains Campus, however. The club incorporates **Roker Bar** and operates as a daytime watering hole, food bar, pool and games room. For footie nights et al it boasts 'the biggest screen in Sunderland'. With no residents in the near neighbourhood the 3 am chuck-out time on Mondays, Tuesdays and Thursdays causes no grief. The club is cool, with good size stage, balcony and bar.

Tuesday is Rock Night; Wednesday, *Juicy*; Friday, *Route 69* (dance and r&b); Saturday, *Volume indie* or *Bands Night*. Recent acts include Dead 60's, Arctic Monkeys, Golden Virgins, The Stranglers, The Subways. There's a Sunday Quiz in Wearmouth Bar, and a Karaoke Night on Friday in Bonded.

Besides all this, throughout the year, poets and musicians (roots, jazz, classical) are invited to perform on campus.

The Royal Shakespeare Company, Northern Playwrights and Ballet Rambert have done workshops with the drama and dance elements of the Faculty of Arts, Design & Communication. Also on campus is the uni's Screen on the River, based in the 400-seater Tom Cowie Theatre, a focus for weekend film festivals, and sister cinema to Newcastle's little Tyneside Cinema, renowned for its arthouse fare.

There are 19 societies and as many as 32 sports clubs, the most popular being Football, Netball, Rugby and CCSA. The student radio station has won awards in its time, and a new TV station took Best Documentary at the 2008 *Guardian* Media Awards. The magazine is *Degrees North*.

SPORT The fitness suite within CitySpace features a range of cardio, resistance, and yoga equipment, provided by Technogym and comes with a customer management interface system which allows users to have specific programs tailored to their needs and requirements. There's also a 25-metre swimming pool with canoeing facilities, and a sports hall for badminton, football and basketball.

TOWN Masses of pubs around Chester Road and city clubs keep students happy. Cost of living is low. Every university wants to play down hassle in town, but Sunderland cannot be classed as the safest of the cities we visit, though uni properties seem to be well protected.

PILLOW TALK

First years get single study-bedrooms in one of three University-managed halls of residence: The

ACCOMMODATION

Student rating	★★
Guarantee to freshers	**100%**
Style	**Flats**
Security guard	**All**
Shared rooms	**Some**
Internet access	**All**
Self-catered	**All**
En suite	**Some**
Approx price range pw	**£48 - £90**
City rent pw	**£45**

tutors is on call during the evenings, throughout the night and at weekends to offer advice and support. 80% of the accommodation is designed and built post 1994. They also manage a range of private properties throughout the city, available to let. Halls are situated on both sides of the river, with the newest, Panns Bank and Scotia Quay, being close to the Bonded Warehouse. Work begins this year on a new 552-bedroom student village.

GETTING THERE

☛ By road: A1(M), A690 or A19, A690.
☛ By rail: Newcastle, 0:25; Leeds, 2:15; Edinburgh, 2:30, Manchester, 3:30, London King's Cross, 3:45.
☛ By air: Newcastle International Airport.
☛ By coach: London, 6:20; Bristol, 6:25.

Precinct, Clanny House, Panns Bank or the privately managed The Forge. A Domestic Services Manager and a team of domestic staff manage the halls, all of which have 24-hour security. A team of resident

UNIVERSITY OF SURREY

The University of Surrey
Guildford GU2 7XH

TEL 01483 689305
FAX 01483 689388
EMAIL admissions@surrey.ac.uk
WEB www.surrey.ac.uk

Surrey Students' Union
Guildford GU2 7XH

TEL 01483 689223
FAX 01483 534749
EMAIL ussu.president@surrey.ac.uk
WEB www.ussu.co.uk

VIRGIN VIEW

*T*he University of Surrey has roots in Battersea Poly. Its rise is a triumph of the career orientation of its courses and its very good teaching. It is many students' first choice.

In 2006 the Times Higher Education *Student Experience Survey revealed at least one of its secrets, namely a body of lecturers who have the students' interests at heart, at least as much as they do their research work.*

Since receiving a Royal Charter in 1966, Surrey has gone its own way, done its own thing, making the business of higher education seem almost clinically straightforward. Most recently, in the past few years, it has seen a huge increase in applications, a reflection partly on its expansion in such as English, Accounting and Financial Management, Film, and Criminology.

UNIVERSITY/STUDENT PROFILE

University since	**1966**
Situation/style	**Campus**
Student population	**15755**
Total undergraduates	**10280**
Mature	**45%**
International	**27%**
Male/female ratio	**42:58**
Equality of opportunity:	
state school intake	**93%**
social class 4-7 intake	**30%**
drop-out rate	**10%**

In the Higher Education Funding Council's *National Student Survey, 82% of Surrey's students applauded what they do, and almost as many, 80% of them will get real graduate jobs within six months of leaving.*

CAMPUS

Surrey's self-contained, concrete, in-fill, landscaped campus lies just off the A3 in the ancient city of Guildford, adjacent to the cathedral, 15 minutes walk from the city centre. writes Madeleine Merchant: 'The campus contains most first-year residences, all the teaching buildings, lecture theatres, library, computer labs, a sports centre, a shop, a health centre, a counselling service, a post office, a Nat West bank, many cafés, restaurants, and bars, the Students' Union building, picnic areas and a lake. It is in an attractive setting with many trees and shrubs, on a hill in the shadow of Guildford Cathedral. Many students complain of being woken up on Sunday mornings by the cathedral bells! A train line runs around a third of the perimeter, and the trains can also be heard in some of the residences.'

Much of the area is covered by CCTV cameras, and it is generally well-lit and perfectly safe, but three years ago, the Student Council debated whether more cameras should be put in for greater safety in off-campus paths nearby, which were deemed not so safe, even if the cameras might overlook some student residences. The Students' Union reported that the university had assumed responsibility of up-keep and maintenance from the council for some of these paths, and improved safety.

FEES, BURSARIES

UK & EU Fees, 2011-12: £3,375 p.a. If in receipt of the HE Maintenance grant there's a sliding scale according to household earnings. There are also academic scholarships and awards for sport.

STUDENT PROFILE

'The University of Surrey may be a depressing collection of ugly concrete monstrosities,' writes Alistair Gerard, 'but it's not the buildings that make a university, it's the people, and I wouldn't have chosen to be anywhere else. Campus is a cosmopolitan enclave in the whole middle-class Caucasian experiment that is Guildford. Besides the obvious lean towards science and engineering bods at Surrey, around a fifth of undergraduates are from overseas, nearly a quarter are mature students, and the state/independent ratio is well balanced. Students are saved from the male dominance that can affect science unis by the nursing provision and Human Studies. Everyone is happy.'

ACADEMIA & JOBS

Characteristically, Surrey graduates get jobs for which they have been educated - they enter

> *'Campus is a cosmopolitan enclave in the whole middle-class Caucasian experiment that is Guildford.'*

TEACHING SURVEY AT A GLANCE

Avg. UCAS points accepted	**360**
Acceptance rate	**18%**
Overall satisfaction rate	**82%**
Helpful/interested staff	★★★
Small tuition groups	★
Students into graduate jobs	**80%**

Teaching most popular with undergraduates: Aerospace Engineering, Biology & related sciences, Chemical Engineering (100%), Civil Engineering, Economics, Electronic & Electrical Engineering, Maths & Statistics, Mechanical, Production & Manufacturing Engineering, Molecular Biology, Music, Nursing, Nutrition, Psychology, Sociology, Subjects allied to Medicine, Technology, Tourism.

Teaching least popular with undergraduates: Media Studies (60%).

employment not only at graduate level but in occupations directly related to their degrees. This is not typical through the length and breadth of the nation.

'In the third year, most students work for companies in placements, and earn lots of money,' Madeleine reports, 'and from what I've heard, most of these come back in the fourth year with clear ideas about whether they really want to continue working in that field, and many have definite job offers for when they graduate.'

Surrey leads the nation in producing computer programmers. See BSc Computer Modelling & Simulation and various alternative applications - Engineering, Communications, Info Technology. All are 4-5 years, depending on whether you take

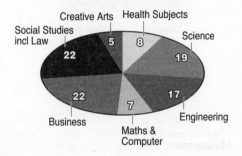

SUBJECT AREAS (%)

- Creative Arts
- Health Subjects
- Social Studies incl Law — 22
- Science — 19
- Engineering — 17
- Maths & Computer — 7
- Business — 22
- 5
- 8

one of these professional years out, after which you are eligible to Associate Membership of the Uni. Look, too, at their BEng Electronics & Computer Eng, and the BSc/MPhys Physics with Computer Modelling.

Most students at Surrey graduate in business and engineering subjects, and the manufacturing industry benefits by taking around a fifth of all those graduating from the uni.

Computer Science, Engineering and Business are the main routes into electrical and electronic manufacturing, with the occasional input from Surrey's sound recording courses. Note the 4-year BMus Music & Sound Recording (Tonmeister) for the performance spin.

Civil engineers are the next most in demand in the engineering sector. They mix with Computing in the 3/4/5-year B/MEng programmes, or you can of course take the single hons. Again, there's an Associateship of the University in the offing.

Then there's mechanical, process & production, electronic and software engineers, all well serviced with dedicated degrees and interesting combo options relevant to these job sectors.

Note also the B/MEng Space Technology & Planetary Exploration degrees, remembering that both Physics and engineering achieved near full marks in the assessments.

WHAT IT'S REALLY LIKE

UNIVERSITY:

Social Life	★★
Societies	★★★
Student Union services	★★★
Politics	**Low interest**
Sport	**40 clubs**
National team position	**75th**
Sport facilities	★★★★
Arts opportunities	**Dance, music OK**
Student newspaper	**The Stag**
Student radio	**GU2**
Radio Awards 2008, 2009	**Bronze, Silver**
Radio Awards 2010	**Gold**
Student televiaion	**MADTV**
Nightclub	**Rubix**
Bars	**Chancellors Bar**
Union ents	**Cheese, r&b, dance**
Union societies	**100 +**
Parking	**Non-existent**
TOWN:	
Entertainment	★★
Scene	**Rich man's clubs/pubs**
Town/gown relations	**OK-good**
Risk of violence	**Low**
Cost of living	**Very high**
Student concessions	**Good**
Survival + 2 nights out	**£90+ pw**
Part-time work campus/town	**Excellent/good**

RESEARCH EXCELLENCE

% of Surrey's research that is
4* *(World-class)* or **3*** *(Internationally rated):*

	4*	3*
Health Services	0%	5%
Health Professions	20%	40%
Physics	10%	45%
Applied Mathematics	15%	55%
Computer Science	10%	40%
Electrical/Electronic Eng.	30%	40%
General Engineering	15%	60%
Economics	15%	50%
Business/Management	10%	40%
Sociology	30%	25%
Psychology	10%	30%
European Studies	5%	25%
Performing Arts	20%	40%
Music	15%	60%

The health provision is next most productive, and is served by the European Institute of Health & Medical Sciences (Nursing, Midwifery, etc. A degree in Veterinary Biosciences is currently up for validation.In the business sector the Retail Management degree is singly the most productive at point of employment, and the International Hospitality degrees lead unerringly to careers in the field of hotel management. Throughout the faculty, sales managers, marketing managers and management consultants are produced in quantity.

Graduates of Financial Mathematics and Business Economics degrees find their way, in number, into accountancy, and economists also proliferate.

A new Learning Resource Centre will be started this year and is due for completion in 2011.

SOCIAL SCENE

STUDENTS' UNION **Chancellors** bar, one of 5, can be found under Union House and opens as restaurant from 8.30am, transforming itself into a venue in the evening for Cocktail Nights, Chancellors Comedy, Pre *Citrus* and *Flirt* Drinks, Open Mic Night and Live Sky Footy on Saturdays. Nightclub is **Rubix**, with a capacity of 1600. Regular ents are *Flirt!* with Duncan Wilson – 'the cult of chav is with us, homage to world of Burberry, Elizabeth Duke & the Citroen Saxo' – and *Citrus* with Leroy Wilson. Then there are sell-out specials, which go under the name of *UNIFIED*, with such as 'Nicholas from

X Factor, Master Stepz, Da Jump Off Ent, to mention a few', across 2 rooms.

Music and dance departments evolve their own series of concerts and the uni choir, orchestra, chamber orchestra and student Drama Society regularly perform.

There's a special relationship with nearby **Guildford School of Acting**. The uni validates its degrees in Acting and Stage Management. And an award-winning student radio station, GU2 (it took a Bronze in the *Radio* Awards in 2008, a Silver in 2009, and in 2010 a Gold), newspaper *The Stag, and TV station - MADTV - make for a seriously amusing media mix.* There is also a film unit and many other societies in a Student Activities Centre, cultural, religious, political, course/interest-based. Lesbian/Gay is active, but generally, due to student apathy in this direction, political activity is low.

SPORT Surrey Sports Park opened in April this year. With its 50m swimming pool, 700sqm, 120-station health and fitness centre, 12m high climbing centre, sports arenas, squash courts, floodlit tennis courts, floodlit artificial and grass pitches, and over 100 classes and courses each week in dance, exercise and sport, there is something for everyone. A month earlier they agreed a deal with Harlequins which will see the new sports facility become the Guinness Premiership rugby union club's main training base.

The Campusport Centre is the sports hall. The Varsity Centre is for field, squash and tennis, and pitches. Uni teams came 75th nationally last year.

Writes Madeleine: 'Everyone gets Wednesday afternoons free of lectures as these are set aside for BUSA matches. If you aren't interested in sports, the university offers free language courses. As in sport, all levels are catered for.'

TOWN Writes Alistair. 'London is only 35 minutes away by train. Ergo, Guildford is very expensive. With the introduction of tuition fees, this must now be a consideration. There are sociological implications, too. It's a notoriously blue pocket of middle-class conservatism. Guildford shuts at 11 pm, with the exception of its nightclubs, where prices reflect

ACCOMMODATION	
Student rating	★★★★
Guarantee to freshers	**100%**
Style	**Halls, flats**
Security guard	**All halls, most flats**
Shared rooms	**Some halls**
Internet access	**All**
Self-catered	**All**
En suite	**Some halls, most flats**
Approx price range pw	**£60-£155**
Town rent pw	**£75-£90**

this. The people who live in Guildford have done their partying; they have moved to a gilt-edged ghetto to live in peace and tranquillity.'

Writes Madeleine: 'There is a mixture of the usual high street shops with student discounts, and the more expensive variety such as French Connection, Gap, House of Fraser etc, two theatres and a large Odeon, two or three nightclubs and many pubs and bars.

'For temporary ways to earn money, Guildford shops and businesses usually have positions available, and the university runs a Job Shop. The Union also employs many casual staff. Student nurses supplement their income by working at the local hospital as "bank" health care assistants, and for agencies.'

PILLOW TALK

Accommodation is in flats arranged in residential courts on campus. Many are en-suite. All freshers are guaranteed accommodation in these. None is catered, all have access to the internet. To keep pace with the uni's dramatic expansion, new fresher accommodation is to be made available this year and in September 2010, 568 rooms and 260 rooms respectively. Rent in town is anything from £75.00.

GETTING THERE
- ☛ Surrey Uni by road: A3, signs to University.
- ☛ By coach: London, 1:00; Birmingham, 4:30.
- ☛ By rail: London Waterloo, 30 mins.
- ☛ By air: Gatwick and Heathrow.

UNIVERSITY OF SUSSEX

University of Sussex
Brighton BN1 9RH

TEL 01273 678416
FAX 01273 678545
EMAIL enquiries@sussex.ac.uk
WEB www.sussex.ac.uk

Sussex Students' Union
Brighton BN1 9QF

TEL 01273 678555
FAX 01273 678875
EMAIL info@ussu.sussex.ac.uk
WEB www.ussu.info/

VIRGIN VIEW

*A*s Sussex celebrates its 50th anniversary, it is ranked 8th in the UK, 16th in Europe, and 79th in the world by the Times Higher Education Magazine. *Value added is a superb campus location on the Downs above Brighton, beautiful countryside and only minutes from a tireless student-friendly city scene. Then there's a famously stimulating learning environment, which encourages independent thought rather than box ticking to get a job with whatever industry designed the course.*

Finally, their international diversity gives them a truly global perspective when looking at applications, Sussex assesses 'the complete student'. Admissions tutors take into account academic performance certainly, but alongside other factors, such as interest in the subject, wider reading, relevant work experience, life skills and other contextual data.

They are looking for students who can demonstrate their interest in, commitment to, and understanding of, their chosen discipline; as well providing evidence that they have the ability to cope with the academic demands of that programme.

Open Days in 2011 are to be held on 11 June, 8 October.

> **'There is something about this liberal, free-thinking campus that favours the generation and development of artistic ideas.'**

CAMPUS

The Sussex campus is entirely surrounded by the newly established South Downs National Park, 5

UNIVERSITY/STUDENT PROFILE	
University since	**1961**
Situation/style	**Campus**
Student population	**12365**
Total undergraduates	**9635**
Mature undergraduates	**39%**
International undergrads	**18%**
Male/female ratio	**41:59**
Equality of opportunity:	
state school intake	**88%**
social class 4-7 intake	**25%**
drop-out rate	**4%**

miles above Brighton. As at UEA, so here: 'At times being on campus can feel a bit isolated and claustrophobic,' writes Keren Rosen, 'but it is fifteen minutes to Brighton by bus and you are never more than ten minutes walk from the fields of the South Downs. Escape is always possible.'

FEES, BURSARIES

UK & EU Fees, 2011-12: £3,375 p.a. If in receipt of full HE Maintenance grant there's a bursary. And academic and sporting scholarships are available, as well as bursaries for applicants living in certain postcodes, and for ethnic minorities. Check out www.sussex.ac.uk/ study/funding/ug.

STUDENT PROFILE

'Owing to its strong international links, a large part of the student population comes from foreign parts and although the rest tend to come from London and the south of England, in general there is quite a nice mix of backgrounds,' observes Keren. 'There is also a large number of mature studentsand although socially it is quite divided they definitely add a different perspective to study.'

ACADEMIA & JOBS

Sussex get feedback from employers that they like the fact that their students are taught in seminars and are used to getting up and giving presentations and are articulate and confident, that they think on their feet, are analytical.

Two-thirds graduate in social studies, languages, humanities and biological sciences. More than a third enter the professions: health, education, finance and business management. There are also strong pockets of jobs in computing, media, publishing, drama and music, and there is something

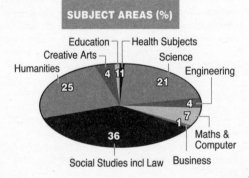

SUBJECT AREAS (%)

Education — Health Subjects
Creative Arts —
Humanities — Science
4 11 — Engineering
25 — 21
— 4
— 7
36 — Maths & Computer
Social Studies incl Law — Business

about this liberal, free-thinking campus that favours the generation and development of artistic ideas. They produce writers, and Sussex's student media is very active - newspaper *Badger*, magazine Pulse, radio station URF win awards frquently, most recently a Gold in the 2009 Radio Awards. Courses may not all be overtly vocational, but, 'We have an Innovation Centre, where a number of outfits are student-started. It is an incubation centre rather than a money-making business park.' Again, the newish Sussex Plus initiative encourages students to take part in extra-curricular activities and documents their skills in an online webfolio for employers to access.

Sussex constantly reassesses the curriculum, always has done. For its 50th birthday it restructured its academic units, creating 12 specialist schools of studies, which will improve students' access to support, and expanding its degree programmes in popular areas such as biomedical science, business and management, digital media, international security, and science and enterprise.

TEACHING SURVEY AT A GLANCE

Avg. UCAS points accepted	**360**
Acceptance rate	**18%**
Overall satisfaction rate	**91%**
Helpful/interested staff	★★★★
Small tuition groups	★★
Students into graduate jobs	**77%**

Teaching most popular with undergraduates:
Anatomy, Physiology & Pathology, Biology & related Sciences, Chemistry, Computer, Drama, Economics, Engineering & Technology, English, History, Archaeology, Human & Social Geography, Law, Linguistics, Maths, Mechanical, Production & Manufacturing Engineering, Molecular Biology, Music, Languages, Philosophy, Physical Science, Physics & Astronomy, Politics, Psychology, Sociology, Social Work.

RESEARCH EXCELLENCE

% of Sussex's research that is
4* *(World-class)* or **3*** *(Internationally rated):*

	4*	3*
Hospital Clinical	**5%**	**30%**
Biological Sciences	**5%**	**30%**
Human Biol. Sciences	**20%**	**35%**
Chemistry	**10%**	**40%**
Physics	**15%**	**45%**
Applied Mathematics	**10%**	**40%**
Computer Science	**20%**	**50%**
General Engineering	**10%**	**50%**
Environmental Studies	**15%**	**50%**
Economics	**10%**	**50%**
Law	**5%**	**50%**
Policy Research	**20%**	**30%**
International Relations	**15%**	**40%**
Social Work	**15%**	**45%**
Sociology	**25%**	**30%**
Anthropology	**25%**	**30%**
Psychology	**15%**	**45%**
Education	**20%**	**35%**
American Studiess	**30%**	**30%**
European Studies	**15%**	**45%**
English	**20%**	**35%**
Linguistics	**0%**	**30%**
Philosophy	**10%**	**50%**
History	**25%**	**40%**
History of Art	**45%**	**25%**
Culture and Media	**15%**	**60%**
Music	**20%**	**45%**

Computing was shown to be one of its great strengths in the last Research Assessment: 20% of its work was ajudged world-class and 50% internationally excellent. Software publishing, IT Consultants and computer programmers come out of a fine range of degrees, including Computer Systems Engineering, AI, Robotics, Cybernetics & Process Automation, etc.

For biosciences they have a similarly fine track record for degrees and jobs. The BSc Psychology (with American Studies, Cognitive Science or Neuroscience) looks particularly attractive.

Now that the Brighton & Sussex Medical School has lift-off, the 5-year BMBS is no different from the rest of the Sussex provision: they are looking for personal qualities, commitment, compassion in their applicants. Chemistry and Biology is required at AS and at least one of these at GCE A level. Three A levels, ideally both Chemistry and Biology are among them. If either is only taken to AS level, grade B additionally is required. The UK Clinical Aptitude (UKCAT) test is also required.

In Social Studies, Humanities and Languages their strategy is to provide subject combinations that are more than the sum of their parts. The curriculum is planned with flair.

The civil service is one significant employment destination for Sussex graduates in Social, Economic & Political Studies, Languages and Biological sciences, and there's a significant flow from these areas of the curriculum also into adult education, and as one would expect, into social work and counselling.

Graduates entering the niche employment areas at which Sussex excel, such as publishing, radio/TV, journalism, came not in the old daysfrom departments dedicated to Media Studies and the like, but from across the scholastic board, students calling on their own extra-curricular interest. There may be Media Practice and Studies degrees now but the interest in extra-curricular activities continues to flow.

Sussex is a small university, but it has more extra-curricular societies (around 150) than many much larger. There is a vigorous student culture, even if the Union itself doesn't get the students' vote, and employers like to pick the fruits of that.

STUDENT SCENE

STUDENTS' UNION The focus is **East Slope Bar**: 'Live music, football, barbeques, but above all a great place to meet friends any night of the week,' says Tom Harle, 'and a great place to watch out for your next bus into town if the weather's not so good. Then there's Park Village Lounge: sea, sun, sand, well no, but a huge range of well-priced cocktails, wines and beers and a great place for a quiet evening chill-out. Get a free cocktail if it's your birthday! **Falmer Bar** is the place for a lunch time

coffee, or your usual tipple on the way home, a (veggie) burger or nachos to share. Meanwhile, The Hothouse is packed out every weekend, a great place to hide from over-priced central Brighton clubs.'

What of student politics in the midst of all this middle-class reverie? I ask. In its first decade it was home to '60s radicalism, fighter of causes. 'Politics are as important today as they were in the late '60s,' they say. Student politics at Sussex is 'doing the right thing', removing Coca Cola from all Union outlets, presenting a motion of no-confidence in the University Council, campaigning on housing issues for first year students, campaigning about the Falmer (football) stadium project, on widening participation, encouraging a wider social mix among Sussex's privileged student clientele. They were just having a Green Week when we went to press. For the last two years they have won a 'Green Impact' award. But none of this seems to warm the Union to students who voted them down radically in the last Student Experience Survey - part of the reason why Sussex plummeted from 26th nationally to 63rd. Maybe they just don't like polls. Can't blame them.

Student media is *The Pulse* (magazine), *The Badger* (newspaper) and URF, University Radio Falmer, which took a Bronze in the National Student Awards in 2008. The campus Attenborough Centre for the Creative Arts, is being refurbished for 2012. It will have theatre and performance

spaces, and will host regular performances, screenings, displays of photography and art work, digital media installations.

SPORT It's sport-for-all at Sussex, not too keenly competitive, yet they came 51st in the national team ratings last year. There are two large sports halls, a fitness room with multi-gym and training facilities, four glass-backed squash courts, sauna, solarium, café and bar. Elsewhere on campus are the pitches, tennis courts, and more squash courts.

Town See Student Brighton for more.

PILLOW TALK

Standard of accommodation is pretty high, all self-catering and varies between flats and rooms on corridors. In particular, check out 250 en-suite rooms in newly-built Swanborough residence (self-contained flats in the centre of campus), and 463 en-suite rooms, plus 11 studio flats, in newly-built Stanmer Court, also on campus. Northfield student residences open this year, 777 study-bedrooms and a social centre.

GETTING THERE

☛ By road: M23, A23, A27.
☛ By coach: London, 1:50.
☛ By rail: London Bridge/Victoria, 1:10; Portsmouth, 1:30; Birmingham New Street, 3:45; Leeds, 4:15; Manchester Piccadilly, 5:00.
☛ By air: Gatwick and Heathrow Airports.

• •

UNIVERSITY OF WALES, SWANSEA

University of Wales, Swansea
Swansea SA2 8PP

TEL 01792 205678
FAX 01792 295157
EMAIL admissions@swansea.ac.uk
WEB www.swansea.ac.uk

Swansea Students' Union
Swansea SA2 8PP

TEL 01792 295466
FAX 01792 206029
EMAIL president@swansea-union.co.uk
WEB www.swansea-union.co.uk

VIRGIN VIEW

*V*alue added at Swansea is a solid academic reputation and an excellent track record of graduate employment. Then there is the sport and the positioning of the whole thing on the Gower peninsula, one of the loveliest stretches of sea coast in the whole of Britain.

'You can come here and never leave it,' a student said to us. 'It's a bit like a black hole. It's all so easy, see? Everything's in walking distance. Students come to Swansea for that alone,' he said, pointing to the surf.

On campus there's a friendly air, more noticeably Welsh than Cardiff, people are chatty, the scene tighter than in some more cosmopolitan universities. Students - 84% of them - gave it their absolute thumbs-up in the Student Experience Survey. So, what do they want from you?

Beyond grades they want candidates who will seize the opportunity to gain new skills and knowledge and who have the potential and drive to succeed. They want to read in the personal statement why you have applied for a specific course and how it relates to your previous experience and studies. They want evidence of motivation and commitment.

Open Days, 2011: 2 July, 8 October.

UNIVERSITY/STUDENT PROFILE	
University since	**1920**
Situation/style	**Campus**
Student population	**18935**
Total undergraduates	**11890**
Mature	**38%**
International	**12%**
Male/female ratio	**43:57**
Equality of opportunity:	
state school intake	**95%**
social class 4-7 intake	**32%**
drop-out rate	**7%**

CAMPUS

Singleton Campus is set in a glorious position with wide open Swansea Bay stretched out in front and parkland behind, just a couple of miles west of the town. Further west along the coast you come to the old fishing village of Mumbles (birthplace of Catherine Zeta Jones), its pubs, fish & chip and Indian restaurants a favourite trawl for students, and the Gower Peninsula, described by Dylan Thomas as 'one of the loveliest sea-coast stretches in the whole of Britain.' On a sunny day I didn't disagree, nor do Swansea's surfer dudes. 'It's all so easy, see; everything's in walking distance,' the same student opined. 'Students come to Swansea for that alone.' He was pointing at the surf.

Writes Maxine French: 'The Gower is a stretch

of coastline incorporating bays such as Caswell, Port Eynon and Langland, the last a favourite spot for surfers and host recently to the Welsh leg of some mad, never-ending surf competition. During the summer term its almost compulsory to go to Caswell when the Geography Society holds its annual beach party. For those whose lives are not ruled by tide tables, the coast means the Mumbles, renowned for the "Mile", strictly non-athletic, a pub crawl to end all pub crawls, something Dylan Thomas might have liked too.'

He did. In 'Who Do You Wish Was With Us?' he wrote - 'Why don't we live here always? Always and always. Build a bloody house and live like bloody kings!'

They are about to build a new Bay Science and Innovation Campus within the Swansea Bay and the Western Valleys region.

FEES, BURSARIES
UK & EU Fees, 2011-12: £3,375 p.a. Welsh students get a grant from the Welsh Assembly Government. See www.swansea.ac.uk/scholarships.

STUDENT PROFILE
There is a well-balanced demography. Campus is a friendly place. 'There's a fantastic, multi-cultural community feeling at Swansea,' said one student.

> *Students come for the surf alone. 'Why don't we live here always? Always and always. Build a bloody house and live like bloody kings!'*

'Students here are generally very laid back, and not just the surfers.'

ACADEMIA & JOBS
In the last assessment of their research capability, out of 31 subject areas submitted, Swansea came first within Wales in 17 areas and first or second in 24 areas. Strong disciplines are Engineering, Medicine and Computer Science, also Geography, Economics, Welsh, History, Social Work and Social Policy, and English.

One of the most important developments has been the opening of the College of Medicine and the subsequent development of a full four-year graduate entry medical degree, launched in 2009. The degree is linked to a new NHS University Health Board and the £50-million Institute of Life Science. Multidisciplinary and collaborative research at Swansea University has resulted in major medical breakthroughs including the development of an artificial lung and a breath test for cancer and diabetes.

There are eight Schools: Arts & Humanities; Business & Economics; Engineering; Environment & Society; Human & Health Sciences; Law; Medicine; Physical Sciences.

Entry requirements are not overly taxing, and because Swansea is thought of as a bit off the beaten track the emphasis is more how on earth you'll ever get out. 'Once they are here, people do well,' a student said, adding rather languidly as he nursed a Sunday morning hangover, 'but I guess it comes down to nothing else to do but work.'

Engineering is an enduring strength in graduate employment. Computing is highly productive. Languages (Celtic Studies included) are an important element too, and every area of the curriculum benefits from them. In sport, extra-curricular interest is enormous, and employment stats for Sports Science graduates are good. But hospitals now claim the lion's share of Swansea graduates, the Nursing degrees, Clinical Physiology, Audiology, Midwifery, all contributing strongly .

Finally, Law comes with a host of possible combinations, and an intercalary year in the US with Law & American Studies.

SOCIAL SCENE
STUDENTS' UNION There are 2 bars: **Idols** at Hendrefoelan student village - cosy atmosphere with karaoke every Tuesday, and **JC's**, on campus

WHAT IT'S REALLY LIKE	
UNIVERSITY:	
Social Life	★★★★★
Societies	★★★★
Student Union services	★★★★
Politics	**NUS and national issues**
Sport	**70+ clubs**
National team position	**25th**
Sport facilities	★★★★
Arts opportunities	**All good**
Student newspaper	**Waterfront**
Student radio	**X-treme**
National Radio Awards	**Silver, 2009 & 2010**
Nightclubs/bars	**Divas, Idols, JC's**
Union ents	**Flirt! + in town**
Union societies	**50+**
Parking	**Some**
TOWN:	
Entertainment	★★★
Scene	**Clubs, pubs, sea**
Town/gown relations	**Good**
Risk of violence	**Low**
Cost of living	**Low**
Student concessions	**Good**
Survival + 2 nights out	**£60 pw**
Part-time work campus/town	**Good**

- great pub with big screen for all sporting events, friendly and popular venue. **Divas** is the union nightclub - extremely popular, with a wide range of nights to cater for all tastes.

Time and Envy in the city centre hand over their club to the union on Mondays and Wednesdays - Monday is Student Night, and Wednesday is AU Night (Athletic Union). Besides karaoke at Idols every Tuesday, there's a pub quiz at JC's each Sunday, and in Diva's *Flirt!* on a Friday and *Live and Wired* (basically like an open Mike night) on Sunday.

There are 70+ sports clubs and 50+ societies up and running, RAG and Dance being the most active right now, though politics is a perennial interest, 'all parties represented, Lib Dem and Socialist and Respect,' they say. And the Tories? main issues this year have been about changes to the university, campaign against the arms trade, and student safety. *Waterfront* is the newspaper; X-treme Radio won a Silver at both the 2009 and 2010 National Radio Awards.

There's an international Swansea Arts Festival every autumn. The Glynn Vivian Gallery in town, The Swansea Arts Workshop in the Maritime Quarter (the former docklands) and **The Taliesin Arts Centre** on campus, deliver year-round exhibitions and events, a constantly unfolding pro-

gramme (for and by students and outsiders) of drama, dance, film and concerts from classical through jazz and rock. The building has a bar and a bookshop. For Swansea-based opera and comedy there's the **Pontardawe Arts Centre**; for comedy, rock, classical and musicals there's the **Penyrheol Theatre**, while **The Grand** delivers Welsh National Opera, Lily Savage, *The Pirates of Penzance*, Paul Merton and the *South Wales Evening Post* Fashion Show in quick succession.

SPORT Swansea University has helped launch a number of inspiring international careers in sport. Each year the University offers 10 undergraduate entrance scholarships for students with outstanding sporting talent. Each scholarship is worth £1,000 a year and is renewable for three years. The University's £20-million Sports Village includes a 50-metre pool and warm-up pool. The swimming pool is the Wales National Pool and is one of only five facilities in the UK to be awarded Intensive Training Centre status. Facilities attract top performers and include: sports hall, climbing wall, fitness centre, tsquash courts; tennis courts, pitches, eight-lane athletics track; indoor athletics training area, two artificial hockey pitches. Ideally location for watersports.

PILLOW TALK

Swansea provides accommodation on campus in the Singleton Halls, off-campus in Hendrefoelan Student Village (approx 2 miles from the campus), and also runs a Managed Property Scheme of high quality housing in the surrounding areas of Uplands and Brynmill. Car parking for freshers is available adjacent to campus.

GETTING THERE

- ☛ By road: M4/J42B.
- ☛ By coach: Cardiff, 1:10.
- ☛ By rail: London Paddington, 2:50; Bristol, 2:00; Cardiff, 0:50; Birmingham, 3:15; Manchester, 4:30.
- ☛ By air: Cardiff Airport.

ACCOMMODATION	
Student rating	★★★
Guarantee to freshers	**98%**
Style	**Halls, flats**
Security guard	**Some**
Shared rooms	**None**
Internet access	**All**
Self-catered	**Some**
En suite	**No halls, all flats**
Approx price range pw	**£73-£109**
City rent pw	**£56-£68**

TEESSIDE UNIVERSITY

Teesside University
Middlesbrough
Tees Valley TS1 3BA

TEL 01642 218121
FAX 01642 342067
EMAIL enquiries@tees.ac.uk
WEB www.tees.ac.uk

Teesside University Students' Union
Borough Road
Middlesbrough TS1 3BA

TEL 01642 342234
FAX 01642 342241
EMAIL enquiries@utsu.org.uk
WEB www.utsu.org.uk

VIRGIN VIEW

*T*eesside University was named University of the Year by the Times Higher Education Magazine in 2009, the first modern university ever to receive this honour, and in 2010 became England's top new university for student experience winning the title in the same magazine's annual Student Experience Survey.

Teesside, who see their purpose as 'inspiring success', sit high in the league table of those that have widened access to higher education among the working classes.

What this means is that points requirements are not demanding, that they welcome applications from students studying for the new 14-19 diploma, which offers hands-on experience as well as classroom learning, and that skills gained from work experience, volunteering and vocational training are given due consideration.

Teesside is particularly strong in computer games design and animation, design, digital media, sport and exercise, forensic science and health-related courses, such as physiotherapy and radiography.

Tens of millions have been spent on two new developments on campus - the Institute of Digital Innovation and the Centre for Creative Technologies. Both opened in 2007 and enhance Teesside's reputation as a leading university for digital innovation and design.

Value added are its industry-recognised

UNIVERSITY/STUDENT PROFILE	
University since	**1970**
Situation/style	**Campus**
Student population	**27505**
Total undergraduates	**23395**
Mature	**71%**
International	**10%**
Male/female ratio	**43:57**
Equality of opportunity:	
state school intake	**99%**
social class 4-7 intake	**50%**
drop-out rate	**16%**

and accredited courses, and a campus learning environment boosted by a £130m investment in digital innovation, a well resourced library, a £6.5m centre for sport, forensic facilities and the new Sport and Health Sciences building.

They welcome applications from people on Access courses recognised by the Quality Assurance Agency (www.qaa.ac.uk/). Open Days, 2011: 22 June, 19 and 29 October.

CAMPUS

The campus is located within a few minutes walk of the centre of Middlesbrough, on the south bank of the River Tees, a short hop from the North Yorks Moors and Redcar and Saltburn beaches.

Students using the union building run a gauntlet of pubs on Southfield Road: The Dickens' Inn, licensed till midnight, The Star & Garter, offering '£1-a-pint, £2-for-2' and The Fly & Firkin. The architecture of the union and adjacent, £11-million, 5-storey Learning Resources Centre stuns - these

13% — Postgraduate

Undergraduate — 85%

STUDENT POPULATION
Total students
27,505

Further
Education
2%

TEACHING SURVEY AT A GLANCE

Avg. UCAS points accepted	**240**
Acceptance rate	**28%**
Overall satisfaction rate	**82%**
Helpful/interested staff	★★★★
Small tuition groups	★★★
Students into graduate jobs	**75%**

Teaching most popular with undergraduates:
Anatomy, Physiology & Pathology (100%),
Biological Sciences, History, Law, Media Studies,
Medical Technology, Nursing, Others in subjects
allied to Medicine, Sports Science.

delicately ribbed, green-tinted glass buildings glistening with seductive appeal.

FEES, BURSARIES

UK & EU Fees, 2011-12: £3,375 p.a. The Teesside University Bursary is £500 per year and is paid to any home or EU student paying the full tuition fee whose household income is less than £31,000 per year. An international student scholarship of £1,500 is paid to all full fee paying students not sponsored by their employer of government. There's a Care Leavers Bursary of £1,075 and up to £1,000 worth of support for elite athletes. See www.tees.ac.uk/ug/funding.

STUDENT PROFILE

There's a large mature student intake (71%) and many come from non-traditional uni heartlands close by. Students here have a job-seeker's attitude to academia and are seriously motivated, but many too have an appetite for the hedonistic pleasures that Student Union and town afford.

ACADEMIA

Teesside's two largest academic schools are Health & Social Care and Computing. Both have increased dramatically in size over the last five years. Together they account for half undergraduates.

They are highly regarded for specialist provision in animation and computer games design, crime scene and forensic science, criminology, engineering, health, police training, sport and exercise, and across the curriculum with a fine eye for niche courses to meet specific employer needs.

Extensive use is made of a Virtual Learning Environment - E@T (Elearning@Tees). Each subject has its own support site and a range of online learning tools, resources and links. The sites are accessible both on and off campus 24/7.

By far the most of students wqho enter the health sector on graduation become senior hospital nurses (SRN, RGN), then it's physiotherapists, community & youth workers, non-hospital nurses, occupational therapists, medical radiographers, social workers and midwives.

New courses in dental health and therapy and dental nurse practice have been designed to address the skills shortage in dental services in the region and are proving extremely popular. Centuria South is a new £17m dental education practice facility and sports therapy complex with hydrotherapy pool. The sports therapy facilities include laboratories and biomechanic and hydrotherapy facilities. The dental suite has 20 dental chairs and practice 'phantom heads'.

In the area of commmunity welfare they lead with BSc (Hons) Youth Studies and Youth Work, and the various Youth Studies combinations with Sociology, Criminology or Psychology, BSc degrees in Social Work, and Psychology, which comes on its own or with Counselling or Criminology.

In the Government's Research Assessment, Teesside's work in Computer Science was found to be 10% world-class and 45% internationally excellent. A significant niche area in undergraduate degrees lies in computer games design.

Business-wise there's a strong lean towards information management and marketing. Their graduate enterprise scheme has helped create 175 companies and 308 jobs. The Phoenix Building is the hub for new and established business ventures. 'Entrepreneurs at Tees' is a network for students, staff and alumni to exchange ideas and experience and gain entrepreneurial skills. Collaboration with local and regional industry is the nub of their academic and employment strategy in business.

Note, too, that they are specialists in European and commercial law. There's a tie-up with Criminology, and links with Cleveland and Durham constabularies underwrite the pioneering BSc in Criminology. They claim their Crime House Lab, where forensic science students put their

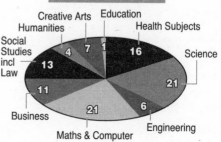

SUBJECT AREAS (%)

WHAT IT'S REALLY LIKE

UNIVERSITY:

Social Life	★★★
Campus scene	★★★
Student Union services	★★★★
Politics	**Activity low**
Sport	**Keen**
National team position	**76th**
Sport facilities	★★★★
Arts opportunities	**Dance, music excellent, rest OK**
Student magazine	**The Tease**
Student radio	**Click**
National Radio Awards	**Silver, 2009 & 2010**
Nightclub	**Hub**
Bars	**Terrace Bar**
Union ents	**Chart, r&b, Indie, retro, disco**
Union societies	**60 (40 sport)**
Parking	**Poor**

TOWN:

Entertainment	★★★★
Scene	**Pubs, big-time clubs**
Town/gown relations	**Average**
Risk of violence	**Average**
Cost of living	**Low**
Student concessions	**Good**
Survival + 2 nights out	**£50-£60 pw**
Part-time work campus/town	**Excellent/good**

ACCOMMODATION

Student rating	★★★
Guarantee to freshers	**100%**
Style	**Halls, flats**
Security guard	**Campus**
Shared rooms	**Some halls, no flats**
Internet access	**All**
Self-catered	**All**
En suite	**Some**
Approx price range pw	**£52.50-£90**
City rent pw	**£40-£70**

investigative skills into practice, is the most elaborate facility of its kind in any UK university, and have just opened a Vehicle Examination Centre for forensic and crime scene science students to practise their skills.

A significant graduate population find work as graphic designers, set and interior designers, and there are interesting interior design and advertising specialities. There's synergy, too, with Cleveland's TV & Film production degree. Web: www.ccad.ac.uk. The Northern Region Film & Television Archive is housed on campus, providing a resource for students of history and media.

Finally, Teesside are among the top unis for turning out sports players and officials through their Coaching and Applied Sports Science/Exercise Science degrees.

SOCIAL SCENE

There's **The Terrace Bar**, and the new second floor venue, **The Hub**, split level with 4 big screens and many plasma screens, a cool open space to relax through the day and let go on a Saturday night if SU put something on. The theory is that **Room 2 @ The Hub** works as a bookable meeting/training room during the day and in the evening as a second DJ room. There's a clubnight in one or other every Friday and Saturday, the first being current chart and r&b, and Saturday rotates with indie, retro, school disco and current chart.

On a good night the buzz is tangible. 'I've lived down south,' said Michelle, 'and I am not being biased, but the scene up here is great, one of the best in the North East. We've got far too many bars, people are just competing with each other, so it's great for students.'

Nor is it all night-time reverie. There are 20 societies and 40 sports clubs. Most popular is the International Students Society with about 100 members. Then there are things like the Dilated Pupil Society, Dance Music Society, and Drama did a series of satirical sketches last Christmas. Said a Union wallah: 'Our Law society is very successful in the courtroom battles with high profile unis in the North East, Durham, Newcastle.'

In January 2009, the University of Teesside Radio Network (UTRN) was launched via the internet. Now, Radio Station Click has won a Silver at the national Student Radio Awards in successive years. Student media also includes a magazine, *The Tease*.

SPORT They have a £6.5 million Olympia Building with squash courts, floodlit artificial pitch and large sports hall, plus a range of up to the minute teaching facilities and the latest climate simulation facility - designed to test sporting performance in a range of temperatures. But they are languishing far down the national student team league (at 76th).

> *'I've lived down south, and I am not being biased, but the scene up here is great, one of the best in the North East.'*

PILLOW TALK

Campus residences are exclusively for first years. Allocations are made on a first come first served basis, so apply early. There are houses, halls, flats and managed housing off campus. Five mixed halls of residence all have self-catering facilities; 34% of campus accommodation is en suite.

GETTING THERE

☛ By road: A19, or A1/M, A66.
☛ By rail: Newcastle, 1:15; Leeds, 1:45; Manchester Piccadilly, 2:45; Liverpool, 3:45.
☛ By air: Teesside International Airport.
☛ By coach: Birmingham, 3:15; York, 1:15.

UNIVERSITY OF ULSTER

University of Ulster
University House
Cromore Road
Coleraine
Co. Londonderry BT52 1SA

TEL 08 700 400 700
FAX 028 7032 4908
EMAIL online@ulster.ac.uk
STUDENT UNION TEL 028 7032 4319
WEB www.ulster.ac.uk

VIRGIN VIEW

*U*lster is the largest of the 9 universities in Ireland. Spread across four sites (between seventy and eighty miles apart) it is an enormous place in terms of students, 80% of whom are local.

The uni came out of a merger in 1984 between Ulster Poly (now the Jordanstown campus) and the New University of Ulster (which was the old university, if you follow). Sites are at Belfast (art college), at Newtownabbey, in the hills above Belfast (the Jordanstown campus), at Coleraine (this is HQ, far northwest of Belfast, near the Giant's Causeway), and in Londonderry (Magee College campus, founded in 1865), yet further west.

To solve communications problems they have formed a wireless microwave network capable of transmitting data of Encyclopaedia Britannica proportions in a second. The Centre for Communications Engineering links them to Queen's Uni and Nortel Networks, and is a feature of their strategy for close working with industry.

There are plans afoot for massive improvements and expansion.

STUDENT PROFILE

There's a high mature undergrad percentage and an unusually high number of part-timers among the predominantly local student body; university strategy ensures that many, too, come from social groups with no great tradition of higher education. Together with this comes a high drop-out rate - 13%

UNIVERSITY/STUDENT PROFILE	
University since	**1964**
Situation/style	**Campus sites**
Student population	**23160**
Total undergraduates	**18415**
Mature	**41%**
International	**13%**
Male/female ratio	**41:59**
Equality of opportunity:	
state school intake	**100%**
social class 4-7 intake	**49%**
drop-out rate	**13%**

among non-mature entrants.

CAMPUS

BELFAST York Street, Belfast BT15 1ED. **Location:** close to city centre, part of the city's up and coming Cathedral Quarter, is traditionally considered the home of the School of Art and Design, though other disciplines are increasingly being taught there. **Faculty HQs:** Art & Design (including Interior Design and Textile & Fashion Design). Also American Studies, Architecture, Irish Literature, Chinese, English. **Accommodation:** none, but small number of Belfast students may use Jordanstown. A £30-million redevelopment of this campus was completed in 2008 and established a creative hub in the heart of Belfast City Centre. **Ents facilities:** Conor Hall (400-capacity venue). **Sports facilities:** 'What's sport?' said a student when asked. Arts facilities: foyer exhibition area, art shop, artist (writer, artist or musician) in residence. **Arts opportunities:** 'Second to none, vibrant, innovative, love it!' said our student contact. **Media:** monthly magazine, Ufouria.

Teaching most popular with undergraduates:
Accounting, Architecture, Aural & Oral Sciences, Biological Sciences, Celtic Studies, Civil Eng., Communications, English, European Languages, Finance, Food Studies, Human Resource Management, Law, Marketing, Nursing, Nutrition, Ophthalmics, Other subjectes related to Medicine, Performing Arts, Physical Geography & Environmental Science, Politics, Psychology, Sociology (100%), Tourism, Transport & Travel.

Teaching least popular with undergraduates:
Anatomy, Physiology & Pathology, Medical Science & Pharmacy (50%).

JORDANSTOWN Newtownabbey BT37 OQB. **Location:** seven miles north of Belfast on the shore of Belfast Lough; largest site. **Faculty HQs:** Business & Management (including Government, Law, Marketing), Engineering (including Biomedical Eng), Informatics, Social (economics, accounting, politics, social policy, sociology, counselling) & Health Sciences (nursing, physiotherapy, podiatry, speech & language therapy). Also architecture and construction, languages library management, sport. **Accommodation:** new high quality Dalriada Student Village opened in Summer 2009. **Ents facilities:** Students' Union Bar (700 capacity), split level, two stages, tiered seating/standing; regular disco night is Monday. **Sports facilities:** two large sports halls, gym, fitness suite, six squash courts, eight-lane swimming pool and hydrotherapy pool, playing fields, synthetic training pitch,

ACCOMMODATION

Student rating	★
Guarantee to freshers	**40%**
Style	**Flats**
Security guard	**Most**
Shared rooms	**Most**
Internet access	**Most**
Self-catered	**Most**
En suite	**Most**
Approx price range pw	**£70-£90**
Belfast	**None**

local water sports facility and River Lagan. **Arts facilities:** recital rooms, concert hall. Low key. **Media:** Naked is student newspaper.

COLERAINE (address with entry title) **Location:** market town close to north coast, 35 miles from Derry. The original uni, admin HQ and home to the Centre for Molecular Sciences. Biosciences, health (nursing, optometry), pharmacology, environmental science, dietetics, social sciences (psychology,), humanities (history, geography) languages and Euro studies, media (film, journalism, publishing), business, computer. **Accommodation:** residential blocks and student houses. Most students prefer to live out in coastal resort towns Portrush and Portstewart. **Ents facilities:** Biko Hall (venue) and recently rebuilt Uni-Bar; 550 capacity. Regular disco night is Monday. **Sports facilities:** Biko Hall is sports hall by day, five squash courts, fitness suite, solarium and steam room, playing fields, floodlit football pitch, pavilion, tennis courts, water sports centre on River Bann. **Arts facilities:** the Octagon (500-seat recital room), the Diamond (1,200-seat concert hall, prestigious Riverside Theatre, third largest pro theatre in Ireland, venue for drama, rock and classical concerts, ballet, opera, etc.

MAGEE COLLEGE Northland Road, Londonderry BT48 7JL. **Location:** residential quarter of Derry, Ireland's second largest city. A mixture of historical and new buildings and modern and traditional facilities, a small and tightly knit student population. New moves bring drama, music, dance and computing to the bedrock business, humanities, social sciences (psychology, law, politics, social policy, community youth work, sociology) & nursing. Languages are also to the fore, and Irish Studies. It is home to the Institute for Legal & Professional Studies. **Accommodation:** three halls of residence and student village (modern houses). **Ents facilities:** two bars, The Terrapin (known as 'the wee bar') and The Bunker (bar/nightclub, 400 capacity). **Ents:** bands and discos (Thursday); Derry wild with pubs. **Sports facilities:** sports hall, fitness suite and solarium; recent additions include sports pavilion, sand-carpet soccer pitch, synthetic training pitch; sailing at Fahan, rowing and canoeing on the Foyle. **Arts facilities:** the Great Hall.

GETTING THERE

☛ An hour by air from London, with at least 24 flights a day each way.
☛ Ulsterbus operates a fast and frequent service across Northern Ireland.

UNIVERSITY COLLEGE, LONDON

University College, London
Gower Street
London WC1E 6BT

TEL 020 7679 3000
FAX 020 7679 3001
EMAIL study@ucl.ac.uk
WEB www.ucl.ac.uk/

UCL Students' Union
25 Gordon Street
London WC1H 0AH

TEL 020 7387 3611
EMAIL mc.officer@ucl.ac.uk
WEB www.uclu.org

VIRGIN VIEW

The college was the original University of London, the first in England after Oxford and Cambridge, inspired by the first principle of Utilitarianism, 'the greatest happiness of the greatest number' and the movement's founder, Jeremy Bentham. It was a pioneering move by a group of thinkers, John Stuart Mill among them, for an alternative approach to higher education, which, in 1826, meant the privileged education dished out by Oxford and Cambridge.

The idea was to open the doors of education to the rising middle-classes and to free the educational establishment from the doctrinal prejudices of the Anglican Church. Roman Catholics, Jews and Nonconformists were barred from an Oxbridge education in those days. To ensure freedom from dogma, it was decided not to have subjects appertaining to religion taught at UCL.

Value added at UCL today is a staff to student ratio of 1:9, small-group teaching, good interaction between tutors and students, high-quality academic and pastoral support.

Then, of course, there's London. UCL's central London location provides access to a wealth of academic resources, as well as the cultural and social benefits of a thriving and vibrant capital city. Many major businesses have their headquarters here, and strong links facilitate visits by guest speakers and the opportunity to look at the real-world application of your studies.

Finally, UCL's Global Citizenship Agenda focuses on the development of students as people, not merely as job fodder - intellectual growth and personal and social development are to the fore.

What do they look for in applicants,

UNIVERSITY/STUDENT PROFILE	
College of London Uni since	**1826**
Situation/style	**City campus**
Student population	**21210**
Total undergraduates	**12415**
Mature	**32%**
International	**34%**
Male/female ratio	**48:52**
Equality of opportunity:	
state school intake	**64%**
social class 4-7 intake	**21%**
drop-out rate	**3%**

beyond grades? 'In general, evidence of commitment to and enthusiasm for the chosen degree programme through investigation and activity beyond the school curriculum.'

Open Days, 2011: 30 June.

CAMPUS

The location of UCL's main site, just to the north of London's West End and hard by the University of London Students' Union building, provides an amazing resource opportunity, and most halls of residence are within walking distance.

FEES, BURSARIES

UK & EU Fees, 2011-12: £3,375 p.a. If in receipt of the Maintenance Grant, bursaries up to £2,835 are available, depending on household income; see

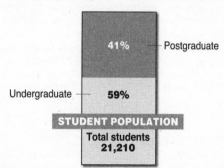

TEACHING SURVEY AT A GLANCE

Avg. UCAS points accepted	**460**
Acceptance rate	**12%**
Overall satisfaction rate	**87%**
Helpful/interested staff	★★★
Small tuition groups	★★
Students into graduate jobs	**83%**

Teaching most popular with undergraduates:
Anatomy, Physiology & Pathology, Aural & Oral Sciences, Biology & related sciences, Business, Chemistry, Classics, English, Forensic and Archaeological Science (100%), French, Others in European Languages & Area Studies, History, Archaeology, Human & Social Geography, Iberian Studies, Italian Studies, Law, Maths, Medicine, Pharmacology, Toxicology & Pharmacy, Philosophy, Physical Science, Physics & Astronomy, Psychology.

www.ucl.ac.uk/current-students/money/loans/bursary_policy. Details of all scholarships can be accessed from www.ucl.ac.uk/scholarships.

STUDENT PROFILE

Writes Oli Burbage-Hall, 'One need look no further than the students themselves for an idea of how the college maintains its strong identity. Intercollegiate rivalry has always existed in London, especially between UCL and its counterpart, 'the Strand Poly', King's College. Throughout its history, this rivalry has centred around the stealing of mascots - Reggie at King's and Phineas at UCL. While modern policing methods have put a damper on these activities, students still manage the odd attack, one of the most embarrassing in recent memory occurring against UCL. The real, preserved head of Jeremy Bentham, an atheist behind the Utilitarian concept on which UCL was founded [hence the epithet 'Godless scum', used by King's students about those at UCL], whose preserved body sits in a case outside the Provost's office and was stolen and suffered considerable damage at the hands, or one should say feet, of King's students. Nowadays a wax replica of the head sits on the body, while the real head resides in the college safe.'

'Intercollegiate rivalry has always existed in London, especially between UCL, known as "Godless scum", and its counterpart King's College, "the Strand Poly"...'

ACADEMIA & JOBS

UCL's research record is formidable and they manage to combine this with helpful, interested teaching, a point made by its own undergraduates in the National Student Experience Survey, where 87% were satisfied. They place great importance on their tutorial system. All students are allocated a personal tutor for consultation on academic or personal matters. Further support is offered by departmental and faculty tutors and two advisers specialising in women students. There's also a professional counselling service and a Students' Union Rights & Advice Centre to see you through any problems academic, financial or emotional. Also, a special educational needs IT suite was opened in December 2001, offering computers and related software and equipment. An IT trainer and a disabilities co-ordinator are at your disposal.

UCL is 4th amng UK universities in the *Times Higher's* 2010 World Top 200 Universities, and remains one of our foremost seats of learning. Its Slade School of Fine Art is reckoned to be the best in the country. Its School of Slavonic & East European Studies – SSEES (pronounced Cease) is an enigmatic institution specialising in the study of Eastern Europe, and 'holds the academically acknowledged best lecturers in their fields,' according to Gideon Dewhurst.

But UCL's chief thing is to give its students a higher education for life, an education that assumes you will get a good graduate job - last time out, 83% of graduates got one within 6 months of leaving - but is not obseessed with that first run of the ladder at the expense of a well-rounded, in-depth education.

Partly with that in mind, for 2012 entry, UCL is launching a new Bachelor of Arts and Sciences BASc degree. This has been developed to respond

SUBJECT AREAS (%)

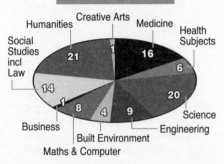

- Humanities — 21
- Creative Arts
- Medicine — 16
- Health Subjects — 6
- Social Studies incl Law — 14
- Business — 1
- Maths & Computer — 8
- Built Environment — 4
- Engineering — 9
- Science — 20

to the need for outstanding graduates with cross-

RESEARCH EXCELLENCE		
% of UCL's research that is **4*** *(World-class) or* **3*** *(Internationally rated):*		
	4*	*3**
Cancer Studies	**25%**	**50%**
Infection/mmunology	**20%**	**60%**
Hospital Clinical	**40%**	**30%**
Epidemiology	**25%**	**35%**
Health Services	**5%**	**25%**
Community Clinical	**10%**	**40%**
Psychiatry	**15%**	**55%**
Dentistry	**15%**	**45%**
Nursing/Midwifery	**5%**	**40%**
Health Professions	**25%**	**35%**
Biological Sciences	**15%**	**40%**
Human Biol. Sciences	**35%**	**35%**
Environmental Sciences	**25%**	**55%**
Chemistry	**15%**	**50%**
Physics	**20%**	**40%**
Pure Mathematics	**20%**	**40%**
Applied Mathematics	**10%**	**40%**
Statistics	**10%**	**40%**
Computer Science	**35%**	**45%**
Electrical/Electronic Eng.	**25%**	**35%**
Chemical Engineering	**15%**	**60%**
Civil Engineering	**15%**	**40%**
Mechanical, Aero. & Manufacturing Eng.	**20%**	**35%**
Architecture	**35%**	**40%**
Town/Country Planning	**20%**	**40%**
Geography Environment	**25%**	**40%**
Archaeology	**30%**	**30%**
Economics	**55%**	**40%**
Information Management	**30%**	**25%**
Law	**35%**	**40%**
Politics	**20%**	**45%**
Social Workn	**15%**	**60%**
Anthropology	**30%**	**30%**
Psychology	**30%**	**45%**
Russian	**10%**	**35%**
French	**10%**	**45%**
Dutch	**5%**	**35%**
German	**25%**	**30%**
Scandinavian Studies	**10%**	**45%**
Italian	**20%**	**25%**
Iberian	**10%**	**35%**
English	**30%**	**35%**
Linguistics	**20%**	**30%**
Classics	**30%**	**35%**
Philosophy	**45%**	**30%**
Theology	**30%**	**40%**
History	**40%**	**25%**
Art and Design	**35%**	**35%**
History of Art	**30%**	**50%**

disciplinary knowledge and experience. Along with discipline-based options, combining arts and sciences, students will undertake core courses covering the basis of knowledge, quantitative methods, research methods, and foreign language study; they will also undertake an internship.

UCL's Education for Global Citizenship agenda coupled with high quality research-led education ensures students have the skills and experiences to be highly employable when they graduate.

Every academic department has a specialist careers adviser who works with the department to develop and run a bespoke programme of activities supported by the Association of Graduate Recruiters. Many degree programmes are accredited by professional bodies or qualify graduates for professional accreditation. Programme based placements, work shadowing and mentoring opportunities, an Enterprise Bootcamp and participation in volunteering activities also provide students with insight and skills relevant to future employment. Students monitor their skill development through a Key Skills Programme.

The Royal Free & University College Medical School is the result of merger between the Royal Free Hospital Medical School and UCL a decade or more ago. To become a doctor here, you'll need to be accepted onto the 4/5-year MB BS. The approach of the MB BS is lectures, tutorial and lab classes in Phase 1, with a lot of computer-assisted learning and problem-solving exercises. Only in Phase 2 do you go out in small teams of consultants and doctors. Phase 3 offers intensive clinical experience. Three A levels and BMAT are required. Also, four AS levels in first year sixth form, including Biology and Chemistry. Three subjects then to be taken on to A level must include Chemistry and not General Studies. If candidates take two Maths A levels, only one will count towards achieving an offer.

After Medicine, Languages (21 are offered), and Physical and Social Sciences degrees are the most popular. A language GCSE, or similar, is now a compulsory qualification for acceptance at UCL. With the takeover of the School of Slavonic & Eastern European Studies in 1999, the Language options here increased dramatically. New language teaching facilities were opened in February 2007 as part of the Centre for Excellence in Teaching and Learning - Languages of the Wider World. This is run in cahoots with the School of Oriental and African Studies across the precinct (see entry).

They actively encourage you to add an international dimension to your degree programme. A growing number of courses now include a year abroad, for example as part of a Socrates exchange. A newly established Study Abroad Office advises

WHAT IT'S REALLY LIKE

UNIVERSITY:	
Social Life	★★★
Societies	★★★
Student Union services	★★★
Politics	**Activity average.**
Sport	**54 clubs**
National team position	**40th**
Sport facilities	★★
Arts opportunities	**Excellent**
Student magazine	**Pi Magazine**
Student radio	**Rare FM**
Student TV	**BTV**
Nightclub	**Windeyer**
Bars	**Easy J's. Gordons, 2econd Floor, Huntley, Phineas**
Union ents	**SportsNite, 2Phat**
Union societies	**90**
Most active society	**Indian Society**
Parking	**None**
CITY:	
Entertainment	★★★★★
Scene	**Wild, expensive**
Town/gown relations	**Average-good**
Risk of violence	**Average**
Cost of living	**High**
Student concessions	**Abundant**
Survival + 2 nights out	**£100 pw**
Part-time work campus/town	**Good/excellent**

students on the opportunities open to them, ensures that students going abroad are fully briefed, and also works to expand further UCL's links with overseas organisations.

SOCIAL SCENE

STUDENTS' UNION Phineas is the hub. The mascot watches over students from an alarm glass case in the bar that bears his name. The largest venue is the comfortable **Windeyer**, with a capacity of 550, large dance floor and a variety of catering. Wednesday attracts *SportsNite* to the **2econd Floor** bar. Thursday's *2Phat* runs across **Phineas** and **Windeyer**.

The union oversees more than 144 clubs and societies, based, for the most part, in a specially created, open plan area with computers, phones, photocopy and TV/video facilities. The union's many arts societies fill a gap in UCL's academic curriculum. Drama Soc performs to professional level at UCL's **Bloomsbury Theatre, where** the New London Orchestra is a kind of orchestra-in-residence, and there's a smaller experimental **Garage Theatre** and a stage in Huntley Street.

Student media is active with *Pi Magazine,* the student radio station, Rare fm, and student TV – Bloomsbury Television (BTV).

Popular out-of-hours lectures (unusual speakers, boundary-breaking, often controversial) are generally free, but necessarily ticket events.

SPORT There are 54 active sports clubs, and UCL came 40th nationally last year. Facilities include two large grounds (with bars), a gym, fitness centre (with multi-gyms, squash courts, Dojo, aerobics/dance hall, sun beds & sauna) and a large sports hall. There is access to the University of London Union pool, next door.

PILLOW TALK

Apply for accommodation by the deadline (May 31 of year of entry), and be sure you hold a firm offer and have not previously been living in London as a degree student.

There are two types of accommodation on offer: halls of residence (catered/breakfast and evening meal) and student houses (self-catering accommodation, some purpose built, others converted private houses). UCL has a rolling programme of upgrading its accommodation; a 100 bed extension at Ramsay Hall is due to be completed in 2008. Newer residences have en-suite facilities and computer points networked to the UCL system. Frances Gardner House is newly built – 215 single en-suite rooms, just 20 mins' walk from campus.

ACCOMMODATION

Student rating	★★★
Guarantee to freshers	**100%**
Style	**Halls, flats**
Security guard	**Wardens**
Shared rooms	**Some**
Internet access	**All**
Self-catered	**Most halls, some flats**
En suite	**Some**
Approx price range pw	**£90-£189**
City rent pw	**£130**

GETTING THERE

☛ UCL: Euston Square (Metropolitan, Circle, Hammersmith & City lines), Warren Street (Victoria, Northern), Euston (Victoria, Northern). Royal Free: Belsize Park Underground (Northern line) or overland railway, Hampstead Heath.

UNIVERSITY OF THE ARTS, LONDON

University of the Arts
65 Davies Street
London W1Y 5DA

TEL 020 7514 6000
FAX 020 7514 8179
EMAIL info@arts.ac.uk
WEB www.arts.ac.uk

VIRGIN VIEW

Granted University title in 2003 and re-named the following year, this is the old London Institute, Europe's largest university for art, design, fashion, communication and the performing arts, and one of the biggest arts institutions in the world. It showed a healthy 7.8 % increase in applications last year - fourth highest countrywide.

Described by Newsweek as 'the epicentre of London style', their glittering alumni include some of the most celebrated artists and designers of the past century, including Gilbert and George (artists); Alexander McQueen (fashion designer); Chris Ofili (artist); Rebekah Wade (newspaper editor); Mike Leigh OBE (director); Simon Callow (actor), Rankin (photographer); Sir Terence Conran (design entrepreneur), Stella McCartney and John Galliano (fashion designers), and Alan Fletcher (designer).

UA offers a distinctive education in Art, Design, Communication and Performance in a range of distinct and distinguished Colleges across London, with roots that run as deep as 1842.

As elsewhere in the country students here live their interests as much outside class as in. Last year UA took the Design of the Year and was runner-up Photographer of the Year at the Nation Student Awards, for its work on the student magazine, Less Common More Sense. See www.suarts.org/lesscommon.

In class, learning is practice-based, creative and strongly linked with industry. Half the teaching is undertaken by Associate Lecturers, who combine teaching with their own practice and up-to-the-minute industry experience.

COLLEGE SITES
Camberwell College of Arts
TEL:†+44 (0)20 7514 6302
FAX: +44 (0)20 7514 6310
EMAIL: enquiries@camberwell.arts.ac.uk†

UNIVERSITY/STUDENT PROFILE	
University since	**2003**
Situation/style	**Collegiate**
Student population	**28790**
Total undergraduates	**12915**
Mature	**41%**
International	**37%**
Male/female ratio	**28:72**
Equality of opportunity:	
state school intake	**91%**
social class 4-7 intake	**31%**
drop-out rate	**8%**

WEB: www.camberwell.arts.ac.uk/
Camberwell College of Arts has an international reputation in the field of art and heritage conservation, with graduates working in some of the most important museums and galleries in the world. The undergraduate and postgraduate courses provide exceptional teaching in conservation practice, science, history and museology.

Each College has its own gallery space and this year Camberwell gets a new one, the Peckham Pier.

Central Saint Martins College of Art and Design
TEL: +44 (0)20 7514 7022
FAX: +44 (0)20 7514 7254
EMAIL: info@csm.arts.ac.uk†
WEB: www.csm.arts.ac.uk/
Work has begun on its new multi-million pound home in the heart of King's Cross. The move, which is due to take place in 2011, will see Central Saint Martins focus its world leading expertise in art, design, communication and performance on one site, forming a powerhouse of creative energy in the heart of London.Courses range from foundation to PhD. Fashion and Textiles, Media Arts, Fine Art, Graphic Design, Theatre and Performance, 3D Design, Interdisciplinary.

Drama Centre, part of Central Saint Martins, is one of only two drama schools to operate in Central London.

Chelsea College of Art and Design
TEL: +44 (0)20 7514 7751
FAX: +44 (0)20 7514 7778
EMAIL: enquiries@chelsea.arts.ac.uk
WEB: www.chelsea.arts.ac.uk/

TEACHING SURVEY AT A GLANCE

Avg. UCAS points accepted	**270**
Acceptance rate	**13%**
Overall satisfaction rate	**62%**
Helpful/interested staff	★★
Small tuition groups	★
Students into graduate jobs	**66%**

Teaching most popular with undergraduates:
Creative Arts & Design (88%)..

Teaching least popular with undergraduates:
Film & Photography (56%), Communications,
Journalism (50%), Business Studies (41%).

In 2004, Chelsea moved to a single campus on Millbank by the River Thames, next to Tate Britain. Courses: Art and Design, Communication, Digital Arts and Media, Drawing, Film and Video, F i n e Art, Furniture, Graphic Design, Interactive Multimedia, Interior Design, Knitwear, Model Making, New Media, Painting, Photography, Printmaking, Printed Textiles, Screenprinting, Sculpture, Stitch/embroidery, Textile Design, Visual Design and Display.

LONDON COLLEGE OF FASHION
TEL: +44 (0)20 7514 7407
FAX: +44 (0)20 7514 7484
EMAIL: enquiries@fashion.arts.ac.uk
WEB: www.fashion.arts.ac.uk/
Courses: Accessories, Beauty Science and Beauty Therapy, Business and Management, Buying and Merchandising, Culture and Communication, Cosmetic Science, Costume, Curation, Design and Technology, Fashion Design, Footwear, Journalism, Make up and Hair Styling, Marketing, Media, Menswear, Millinery, Photography, Promotion, Styling, Tailoring and Garment Production, Technical Effects, Textiles for Fashion, Womenswear. Specialist facilities include a 3D body scanner, and the Archive of Mary Quant.

When Cordwainers College, a name in footwear, saddler and leathercraft since 1887, joined the University in 2000, it brought with it an expertise in footwear and accessories, two of the fastest growing areas in the fashion industry, and contact with the very roots of footwear craft skills.

LONDON COLLEGE OF COMMUNICATION
TEL: +44 (0)20 7514 6569
FAX: +44 (0)20 7514 6535
EMAIL: info@lcc.arts.ac.uk
WEB: www.lcc.arts.ac.uk/
Courses: Book Arts & Crafts, Film & Video, Interior Design, Photography, Print Media, Sound Arts, Surface Design, Graphic & Media Design, Advertising, Digital Media Production, Journalism, Magazine Publishing, Marketing & Advertising, Public Relations, etc, and foundation degrees in some of these and such as sports journalism and print and production.

Their specialist Printing and Publishing School is founded on 100 years of expertise and recently launched a unique MA course in Print Media Management, run in partnership with Heidelberg Print Media Academy in Germany. Students spend two intensive weeks at the Print Media Academy - the training centre for Heidelberg Druckmaschinen AG, in Heidelberg, Germany.

Specialist facilities include radio, TV and film broadcast studios, sonic arts studios, and a facsimile of a newsroom. They won the 2009 RTS Student TV Awards. Finally, the college is home to the extensive Archive of the Stanley Kubrick.

WIMBLEDON COLLEGE OF ART
TEL: +44 (0)20 7514 9641
FAX: +44 (0)20 7514 9642
EMAIL: info@wimbledon.ac.uk
WEB: www.wimbledon.arts.ac.uk
Wimbledon School of Art joined the uni as its sixth college in 2006. The merger saw it renamed Wimbledon College of Art. It enjoys a reputation for excellence in theatre design, boasting the UK's largest School of Theatre, home to the largest theatre centre in the UK offering undergraduate and postgraduate degrees in design and related studies for stage, screen, costume and special effects.

Drawing is also a key focus - the distinguished Jerwood Drawing Prize is offered here. The College has produced many of the greatest names in theatre design and the arts, including triple Oscar winning costume designer James Acheson, production designer Sarah Greenwood, fashion designers Georgina Chapman and Phoebe Philo, guitarist Jeff Beck, and Turner Prize winner Tony Cragg.

FEES, BURSARIES
UK & EU fees 2011-12: £3,375 p.a. From September 2009, students in receipt of the full Government Maintenance Grant of £2,906 p.a. will receive a bursary of £319 p.a. All students who receive a proportion of the Maintenance Grant will be eligible to apply for an Access Bursary of £1,000 p.a. In addition, scholarship provision is a priority. There is a £1-million-plus scholarship programme at London College of Fashion, established by fashion entrepreneur Harold Tillman. The Tillman scholarships are awarded annually to ten MA fashion students unable to finance an MA course; ensuring young talented designers are not lost through lack

of support. London College of Communication has recently launched a Penguin Scholarship for MA Publishing students. Successful applicants receive a £3,000 scholarship funded by Penguin Books.

SOCIAL SCENE

There are student bars at the various colleges, of course, and quite frankly you are as much a part of London as you are of a college. Still, last year saw the uni trying to centralise things a bit, by opening the Student Hub at their headquarters in Davies Street, Mayfair, the heart of the West End of London.

It's a focus for student services and the idea is that it provides a central place for students to come together to work, learn, exchange ideas, be inspired, relax and socialise as part of a community. Besides the offices, there's an Arts Gallery which shows work by graduates and is open to the public, a café bar, an activities studio, computing facilities and the Learning Zone, with 'key library texts', PCs and Macs, laptops for use in the area, WIFI interactive and standard whiteboards, projectors, photocopiers and printers, spray mount booth, cutting tables and mats, trimmers, and light-box facilities.

PILLOW TALK

There are halls on 13 sites throughout north, south,

ACCOMMODATION	
Student rating	★
Guarantee to freshers	**65%**
Style	**Halls, flats**
Security guard	**Some**
Shared rooms	**Some**
Internet access	**Most**
Self-catered	**All**
En suite	**Most**
Approx price range pw	**£83-£180**
City rent pw	**£110+**

southeast and east London, varying from small independent houses to large more traditional halls of residence. Approximately 65% of freshers who want to live in University accommodation are successful in securing a place. Disabled students and students under 18 at the start of their course are guaranteed accommodation. Priority is given to students who come from outside London. Accommodation includes self-catering halls, flats and self-contained studio rooms. New build residence Will Wyatt Court opened in September 2008 in the heart of London's Hoxton and close to Old Street tube station.

UNIVERSITY OF WALES

*T*he University of Wales Trinity Saint David was formed in 2010 from the merger of Wales' two oldest higher education institutions, the University of Wales Lampeter and Trinity University College.

Now, in a radical move, two more universities are set to join the fold. As we go to press, University of Wales Institute Cardiff (UWIC) and Swansea Metropolitan are, together with Trinity St David's, to be known as The University of Wales, not to be confused with the federal University of Wales to which other universities in Wales belong...

Investment from the Welsh Assembly Government and HEFCW means 'significant redevelopment of all campuses to create an environment benefiting twenty-first century learning, teaching, research and scholarship,' we hear.

Lampeter was adamant there would be no campus closures. Swansea meanwhile stressed that they will continue to operate as 'an independent entity within the University

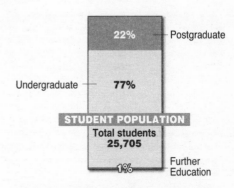

Undergraduate — **77%**
22% — Postgraduate

STUDENT POPULATION
Total students
25,705

1% — Further Education

of Wales regardless...and [the move] will not affect the students who study or apply to us'.

The union may take time to adhere; each element has its own well-honed character.

CARMARTHEN CAMPUS

College Road, Carmarthen, SA38 3EP.
TEL 01267 676767
EMAIL admissions@trinitysaintdavid.ac.uk
WEB www.trinitysaintdavid.ac.uk

Set on a hill overlooking Carmarthen, the campus

was once upon a time Trinity College, a teacher training establishment that spread its wings and moved into degrees in all sort of subjects, such as Acting, Theatre Design & Production, Business, Management, Computing, Tourism, Creative Writing, Film, Fine Art and other Media, and Sport, and took leave to call themselves Trinity University College.

Deep in their past they had a reputation for being quite a handful. A peculiar college trinity of religion, rugby and raucousness seemed to cut a sliver off the backside of Welsh culture and must have had the inhabitants of Carmarthen looking nervously up the hill as they listened to their reveries, like a permanent exhibition of mooning.

But in the end, nerves gave way to native Welsh friendliness, and news reached the *Guide* of some 60 pubs, 4 nightclubs, a cinema and a Bingo hall bringing town, a mere 15,000 population, and campus together.

Said student Robin Rowlands: 'Trinity, or Drindad as we all like to call it, is very friendly and compact... The town itself is a 10 to 15 minute walk down the hill. Night life can be a bit rough, but the pubs are good and busy and the nightclubs are always packed full of Celtic tribes out on the hunt.'

FACULTIES

Faculty of Arts and Social Studies: Schools of Art, Film & Media; Business; Sport, Health & Outdoor Education; Theatr Cerdd a'r Cyfryngau/ Theatre & Performance. **Faculty of Education & Training**: Schools of Early Childhood; Initial Teacher Education & Training;Social Justice and Inclusion; Welsh & Bilingual Studies Associate Faculty.

Open Days, 2011: 8 July, 20 and 21 October.

SOCIAL SCENE

There are alcohol awarness campaigns these days, but a healthy disregard also on a 6-day ents calendar in **Attic Bar** and **Unity** (the venue): Sunday is *Quiz Night*; Monday, *Manic Mondays*; Tuesday, *Chill Out*; Wednesday, *Flirt!*; Thursday, the latin-crazed dance party *Zumba*; Friday, *Back 2 Basics* (different genre each week).

PILLOW TALK

Single study bedrooms, £80 (self-catered), £105 (catered). Parking £150 p.a. or £1 per day.

LAMPETER CAMPUS

Lampeter, Ceredigion SA48 7ED
TEL 01570 422351
FAX 01570 423423
EMAIL apply@lamp.ac.uk

There is a logic to Carmarthen's marriage to Lampeter, for Trinity College was established 150 years ago by the Anglican Church, and years ago Lampeter was a Theological college, the gradual change into a university spurred in the 1940s and 1950s when distinguished Anglican Canon Henry Archdall, a Fellow of Trinity Cambridge, was Principal. Its courses included Theology and Religious Studies, alongside such as Ancient History, Latin, Classical Studies, and Archaeology.

This last is apt, for Lampeter is situated in a beautiful, ancient and inspirational place, littered with burial mounds and cromlechs redolent of civilisations long past, and not far from the Preseli Mountains where the gigantic stones of the innermost sacred circle of pre-historic Stonehenge - once Britain's national necropolis - are supposed to have been cut.

This is mythic Wales, celebrated in the oldest story in the *Mabinogion*, a magical collection of eleven stories sustained orally since earliest times and written down in the 14th century. The story which comes from this area (Pwyll, Lord of Dyved [Dyfed]) is probably the oldest of all, maybe as old as the second millennium BC.

Writes Rachel Extance: 'Don't be surprised if you have only just heard of the place, it is set in the heart of mid-west Wales and its train station was removed by Beeching in the 1960s.

'Clearly its isolation will be a consideration. Looking at a map, you may note the distance between Lampeter and the nearest towns with more than ten houses, a post office and possibly a branch of Spar, but be advised that it is quite easy to get out if you know exactly when the two-hourly bus service runs.

'The theoretical advantage of being away from the shops is that your money will last longer. In practice you may spend as much as your friends in the city because Lampeter contains 14 pubs within a mile radius, with a cash point next to each of them practically.'

Lampeter is a close-knit community, a small, cosy university. You will enjoy your time here if, as Rachel writes, 'your idea of the perfect university looks like an Oxbridge college, is peaceful, friendly, tucked away in the country, and a little bit out of the ordinary.'

With the millennium a new Lampeter became evident in its course programme. Not only did Islamic Studies join the Christian curriculum, which many of the old guard would have found an exciting opportunity, but Business, Film and Media, and Information Technology was chalked up too.

It cannot have been easy to make the passage

into the 21st century, and it is significant that in the Higher Education Funding Council's National Student Survey, it was the old Lampeter that the students applauded. Similarly, when it came to the research assessment of our universities, nationally, Lampeter was found to be doing world-class research in Ancient History and Classics, in Theology, Divinity, and Religious Studies, and especially in Archaeology. The modern additions to the curriculum were not even submitted.

Now, as one campus of the University of Wales, it is old Lampeter, traditional Lampeter, that has survived:

FACULTIES

Faculty of Humanities: Schools of Archaeology, History & Anthropology; Classics; Cultural Studies (Chinese Studies, Creative Writing, English, Philosophy); Theology, Religious Studies & Islamic Studies; and the Confucius Institute.

Open Days, 2011: 6 July, 28 October.

SOCIAL SCENE

At the hub, **Old Bar** is the warm and friendly watering hole, host to Band in the Bar on Tuesdays and occasionally to karaoke nights. **The Extension** is the club venue, holds the latest licence in Ceredigion on a Saturday night; scene of discos on Wednesdays, Fridays and Saturdays, also big bands, comedy, games and more.

PILLOW TALK

Two mainly first-year halls are on campus. Living out in the second year and third year, you can get a nice place for around £50 a week, and you don't have to pay for the summer holidays. The size of the town means you're never living too far away. Halls £65-£85 (self-catered). Parking free.

CARDIFF CAMPUS

Western Avenue, Cardiff CF5 2SG
TEL 029 2041 6070
EMAIL uwicinfo@uwic.ac.uk
WEB www.uwic.ac.uk

UWIC, the old University of Wales Institute Cardiff is the Cardiff dimension of the new collegiate. One aspect of UWIC goes back to a school of art which opened in St Mary Street in 1865 and moved to what is now its Howard Gardens campus in 1965; another recalls a College of Food Technology and Commerce which opened in 1940 or thereabouts in Crwys Street and in 1966 took itself to what is the college's Colchester Avenue Campus today; then, in 1950 Cardiff Training College opened its doors

for the first time at Heath Park, and in 1962 moved to new buildings in what is now the Cyncoed Campus; finally its roots are in Llandaff Technical College which began life in 1954 at Western Avenue, the college's Llandaff campus today. It took degree awarding powers in 1993 and became a College of the University of Wales in 1996.

Like Carmarthen, it has a reputation as a place where students have a ribald time. 'Social life here, combined with Cardiff city life make an amazing combination,' says Jon Ruch, 'guaranteed to turn your three years studying here into an experience you will never forget.' 'When a Cyncoed student hits the bar, anything goes,' nods Rob Blunt sagely, and again there is a strong rugby culture. They are big on sport altogether and put more graduates than most into the industry. **Taffy's Bar, the** main Student Union ents venue is next to the Sports Hall at Cyncoed Campus.

Thoughts of academic work may often flow out on a river of beer from Taffy's Bar, but in fact they have also been adjudged world class in research, in both Art & Design and Management as well as Sport Science. And the students themselves have voted the teaching of all three as great too, though it must be said that that Food and Beverage Studies got the higher approval, with 93% of the Cardiff class giving it the thumbs up.

Teaching the Ruchs and Blunts of this world may not fit into every world-class academic's idea of a higher education vocation, but it should be said that these subjects form part of a curriculum the teaching of which is at a very high standard and meets, on average, with 82% student satisfaction, which is good.

There are four campuses, each with its own schools. Parking for students is limited but the university provides a dedicated bus service between campuses and the city centre.

FACULTIES

Cyncoed Campus, Cyncoed Road, Cardiff CF2 6XD, is central. Schools: Education and Sport. The Wales Sports Centre for the Disabled is also here, so they've got some of the best resistance-training equipment available anywhere.

Colchester Avenue Campus, Colchester Avenue, Cardiff CF3 7XR. Schools: Business, Leisure and Food.

Howard Gardens Campus, Howard Gardens, Cardiff CF2 1SP. School: Art & Design.

Llandaff Campus, Western Avenue, Cardiff CF5 2YB. Schools: Management, Art & Design (also),

Health Science. The School of Management has just relocated here from Colchester Avenue to a £20m facility.

Open days, see *uwic.ac.uk/opendays*.

SOCIAL SCENE
Taffy's Bar at Cyncoed, with £15,000 sound and light system, is a venue awash with cheesy disco nights, stand-up comedy, live team socials, pool, darts, etc. **Tommy's Bar** is the focus at Howard Gardens; eclectic ents. Ents at Llandaff occur in **The Loft**; Thursday and Saturday are disco nights.

PILLOW TALK
Halls and flats, but not enough for all freshers: £76.50-£121 approx. weekly. City is cheap, £54 p.w.

SWANSEA CAMPUS
Mount Pleasant , Swansea SA1 6ED
TEL 01792 481010
EMAIL enquiries@smu.ac.uk

Swansea Metropolitan has its roots in local colleges of Technology, Art, and Teacher Training over 150 years ago, and was until recently Swansea Institute of Higher Education, achieving university status in 2008. Most of the students are local not only to Wales but to Swansea. A third are part-timers and 53% mature.

But Swansea is not shooting above its station. It has a reputation for finding among areas of society unused to university, students with the motivation, potential and knowledge to benefit from a degree course.

The guiding principle for admission is that the applicant must have a reasonable expectation that s/he will be able to complete the course requirements, fulfill the objectives of the programme and achieve the standard required for the final award. Teachers are vocationally minded and translate this motivation into real graduate jobs - 93.2 % of their students are in work or further study within six months of graduating, 71% of them in real graduate jobs.

Employability and entrepreneurship are embedded in the curriculum. They rank as the best in Wales for producing successful graduate start-up businesses. They claim that '26% of all thriving Welsh graduate start-ups, which have survived three years or more, began life at our University'. As a result, they were the only institution to get an increase in government funding last time round.

FACULTIES
Faculty of Applied Design & Engineering: Welsh School of Architectural Glass; schools of Automotive Engineering; Built & Natural Environment; Applied Computing; Digital Media; Industrial Design; Logistics & Manufacturing Engineering: 21% of Swansea Met's real graduate jobs out of here. **Faculty Art, Design & Media**:: Fine Art, Design for Advertising, Illustration, Graphic Design, Photography, Photojournalism, Surface Pattern Design, Video: 31% of Swansea Met's graduate jobs come out of here. **Faculty of Humanities**: Performance & Literature, Psychology & Counselling: 4% of Swansea Met's graduate jobs come out of here. **Faculty of Business & Management**: 17% of Swansea Met's graduate jobs out of here.

Open days: visit www.smu.ac.uk.

SOCIAL SCENE
This is mainly a week-day university, but the Student Union is active and they've always had ents, either at the **Metro Bar** or at a nightclub in town.

PILLOW TALK
There's a bed for whoever wants one, 265 rooms in three halls, Gwyr Hall (en-suite shower cubicles, mixed accommodation toilets nearby), Dyfed Hall (mixed accommodation), Cenydd Hall (mixed; one flatlet for disabled use with en-suite facilities). Then at Mount Pleasant (Business Faculty) there are 6 twin and 37 single study units all with en-suite toilet/shower. Price: £59 - £71. City: £45 - £80. Parking is available for a fee.

UNIVERSITY OF WARWICK

The University of Warwick
Senate House
Coventry CV4 7AL

TEL 024 7652 3523
FAX 024 7652 4649
EMAIL student.recruitment@warwick.ac.uk
WEB www.warwick.ac.uk

University of Warwick Students' Union
Gibbet Hill Road
Coventry CV4 7AL

TEL 02476 572777
FAX 02476 572759
EMAIL enquiries@warwicksu.com
WEB www.warwicksu.com

VIRGIN VIEW

*W*arwick has exploded upon the university scene and there can be few who wouldn't want to have it on their UCAS list. 'I knew from the first time that I visited that it was the place for me,' writes Emma Burhouse. 'As far as I could see, it had the ideal balance of a good reputation, a sound education and excellent social life.'

Emma night have added that the extra-curricular scene here is also one of the best in the country, with student drama, media and even sport these days figuring strongly at national level. They came 1st in the country for clubs and society strength in the Times Higher *Student Experience Survey* this year, where they came 11th overall.

89% of students give the teaching their approval in the Government's National Student Survey last year, and 82% found themselves with real graduate-type jobs within six months of leaving. Unsurprisingly, the drop-out rate is a mere 4%.

CAMPUS

Warwick, lovely little market town, big castle... And not a university within ten miles of the place. Don't be fooled, the University of Warwick is not in Warwick, it's in Coventry. The reason it's called Warwick is that it was part-funded by Warwickshire County Council.

'Campus architecture is entirely uninspiring,' reports Simon McGee, 'but the greyness of the endless car parks and square buildings is fortunately balanced by hundreds of acres of surrounding grassland and forest.'

Writes Andrew Losowsky: 'If you're not paying attention, campus can feel like a Doctor Seuss cartoon - you are surrounded by pointy concrete and

UNIVERSITY/STUDENT PROFILE	
University since	**1964**
Situation/style	**Campus**
Student population	**28435**
Total undergraduates	**19235**
Mature	**50%**
International	**25%**
Male/female ratio	**48:52**
Equality of opportunity:	
state school intake	**77%**
social class 4-7 intake	**19%**
drop-out rate	**4%**

sculptures straight off the set of Blake Seven. Some people take to campus life, and others quite frankly don't.'

Write Ben Jones and Chris Wilding: 'Warwick is a self-contained pit of riotous hedonism. It's ace, eventful and memorable. Don't let things that surprise you in the first week be a yardstick. If shit happens, it happens. If not, why not?'

FEES, BURSARIES

UK & EU Fees, 2011-12: £3,375 p.a. If in receipt of the HE Maintenance Grant there's a sliding-scale bursary dependent on household earnings.

STUDENT PROFILE

'You get the usual independent school boys and girls, for whom going to a university is the first time they haven't had to wear a uniform,' and, as Andrew points out, 'an unusually high mix of international students, meaning that, although most of the British students are from a middle-class background, there is still plenty of variety propping up the bar with you. The English - there are few Scots and Welsh - generally have the bland accentless tone of the home counties. Regional individuality may be gently mocked, but is in fact both envied and welcomed. Students on the whole are genuinely friendly here, and if you can't make any friends then you probably don't deserve to.'

ACADEMIA & JOBS

Warwick came 9th in the country in the recent Government Research Assessment, with powerful results in subjects such as Economics, where 40% of the work was rated world-class (4 star), and 55% internationally excellent (3 star). Business, Engineering, and History all fared well too, but it was Film & Tv Studies (60% 4* and 30% 3*) and Theatre, Performance & Cultural Studies (30 4*, 55% 3*) that made a special mark.

Accounting, American & Australasian Studies, Biology, Business, Chemistry, Classics, Comparative

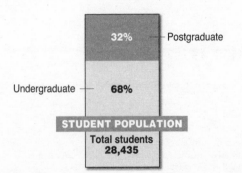

32% — Postgraduate

Undergraduate — 68%

STUDENT POPULATION

Total students
28,435

TEACHING SURVEY AT A GLANCE

Avg. UCAS points accepted	**460**
Acceptance rate	**12%**
Overall satisfaction rate	**89%**
Helpful/interested staff	**★★★★**
Small tuition groups	**★★★**
Students into graduate jobs	**82%**

Teaching most popular with undergraduates:
Accounting, American & Australasian Studies, Biology, Business, Chemistry, Classics, Comparative Library Studies, Drama, Electronic & Electrical Engineering, English, Languages & Area Studies, Finance, French Studies, German & Scandinavian Studies, History, Archaeology, Imaginative Writing, Law, Management, Maths, Mechanical, Production & Manufacturing Engineering, Media, Medicine, Molecular Biology, Operational Research, Physics & Astronomy, Politics, Psychology, Sociology, Social Policy & Anthropology, Subjects Allied to Medicine.

Teaching least popular with undergraduates:
Academic Studies in Education (53%).

Library Studies, Drama, Electronic & Electrical Engineering, English, Languages & Area Studies, Finance, French Studies, German & Scandinavian Studies, History, Archaeology, Imaginative Writing, Law, Management, Maths, Mechanical, Production & Manufacturing Engineering, Media, Medicine, Molecular Biology, Operational Research, Physics & Astronomy, Politics, Psychology, Sociology, Social Policy & Anthropology, and subjects allied to Medicine.

With Birmingham and Nottingham they recently founded the Midlands Physics Alliance, a joint School of Physics, with £3.9 million backing from the Government, delivering a subject to a new generation of students at a time when other universities are taking it off the curriculum.

Then there's the Leicester Warwick Medical School collaboration, an accelerated 4-year MB ChB for graduates of biological and health sciences. At the last count the application acceptance rate was 21, so there's a good chance of getting in.

The uni is heavily targeted by employers. Over 100 visit campus each autumn to give presentations and skills training sessions; many conduct first interviews with undergraduates on site. Five major recruitment fairs are held here each year.

In the matter of accountancy, there is nothing between Nottingham, Durham and Warwick. In the latest figures Warwick lies second to Nottingham and ahead of Durham in the matter of producing accountants. Together they are responsible for around 12% of graduates into the sector.

Education and finance dominate the graduate employment picture. After accountants it's investment analysts. Warwick's programmes stress business skills and enterprise 'working in interdisciplinary terms, just as they would in a corporate setting.' Tax experts and consultants also proliferate, as do actuaries. Three universities are head and shoulders above the rest in equating degree success with employment in actuarial science, namely Heriot-Watt, Warwick and Oxford. Warwick has BSc Maths-Operational Research-Statistics-Economics (Actuarial and Financial Mathematics). Together, the big three account for more than 20% of jobs in the sector.

Thirteen per cent of graduates go into education, most as teachers, primary, secondary and tertiary - full marks in the assessments.

Warwick's Business School certificate in Applied Management is designed to develop the management skills of professional footballers who are in, or who want to take on, football management roles. Students include England players Les Ferdinand, Paul Ince and Steve Hodge.

There's also a strong English/creative writing scene - a whole raft of fascinating degrees that combine English with Theatre Studies, languages, American, even Latin, literature. And a useful employment niche in theatre. They have the national teaching centre with the Royal Shakespeare Company.

Finally, they are European law specialists, 2-4 years, including a year abroad.

STUDENTS' UNION

STUDENTS' UNION The two-phase Union rebuild is simply the biggest thing to happen on campus since anyone can remember. The stylish new glass-fronted, copper-roofed building is opening in two stages. By the time you get there it should all be complete. Central is the massive new first-floor **Terrace Bar,**

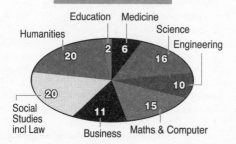

SUBJECT AREAS (%)

Humanities 20
Education 2
Medicine 6
Science 16
Engineering 10
Maths & Computer 15
Business 11
Social Studies incl Law 20

which looks out from one whole side of the building over the entrance Piazza and has the **Island Bar** within. Behind it and below it is the Atrium, a light and airy covered space which runs right through the heart of the new Union, and takes in the cosy laid-back **Piazza café**. **The Graduate** pub remains, but has been extended and re-designed. The real jewel in the Union's new crown is the **Venue**, a split-level 3-floor space that provides a brilliantly equipped performance area and crowd space for 1,400, leading to the **Upstairs Club** (an additional 600 capacity; sound proofed it can be made separate or part of the Venue), and the **Venue Bar**, which runs the whole triple-staged height of the building.

Regular clubnights include *Top Banana*, party music; *Score*, Wednesday's after sports entertainment; Coalition, hip hop; *Pressure*, drum 'n' bass; *Heat*, international music; *Latin Night*, salsa rhythms; *School Dayz*, relive the best days of your life; *Vapour*, our very own house night; *Crash*, one of the biggest alternative nights in the Midlands; *Pure*, r&b; *Time Tunnel*, 60s, 70s and 80s music; *Metropolis*, the union gets turned into a major city for the night; and live music. Recent acts include: The Streets and Camera Obscura. Recently, too, they've been taking *Score* and *Top Banana* on the road, to clubs in the neighbourhood.

Strong in the student scene are not only ents but clubs & societies - there's an amazing 249 (74-odd sport), which must be a record, and they don't sustain them if interest flags. Encouraging them each year are their own society awards.

Media is especially strong - magazine (*The Word*), newspaper (*The Boar*), student radio (RaW), and WTV, the student television station. Last year RaW won 4 Golds and 2 Silvers; in 2010 1 Gold and 1 Bronze.

Strong, too, are arts activities - the **Warwick Arts Centre** is the second largest in the country, and has recently been refurbished thanks to a £33 million lottery grant. There is a concert hall, theatre, cinema, and art gallery. Student theatrical societies do well at the Edinburgh Festival and regularly get gongs at the National Student Drama Festival, where last year they took The Striker and won the Timothy West Award and two commendations for Acting and Direction. RAG and Community Action (13 projects in Coventry and Leamington Spa) are popular and the non-party political union works hard on ethical, human rights and environmental campaigns, though recently effort has been focused on anti-war and education funding.

'As a first year, the mere mention of a night out in Coventry may fill you with dread and terror. However, should you choose to dodge the bullets of the bright lights, it is possible to find satisfactory entertainment and lubrication.'

SPORT Facilities are excellent - athletics track, games fields, artificial pitch and a recently completed £1-million sports pavilion. The Sports Centre, which also hosts Bear Rock, a rather vicious looking climbing wall for eager lemmings to try and scale, is free for students. Teams came 21st last year in the national teams league. There's a new indoor tennis Centre.

TOWN 'Cov has a reputation for being dangerous,' writes Andrew, and as Jones and Wilding point out,

	RESEARCH EXCELLENCE	
% of Warwick's research that is **4*** (World-class) or **3*** (Internationally rated):		
	4*	3*
Hospital Clinical	5%	35%
Health Services	10%	55%
Biological Sciences	10%	40%
Food Science	20%	40%
Chemistry	15%	60%
Physics	15%	35%
Pure Mathematics	35%	45%
Applied Mathematics	30%	30%
Statistics	25%	45%
Computer Science	15%	50%
General Engineering	20%	50%
Economics	40%	55%
Business/Management	25%	50%
Law	10%	35%
Politics	20%	40%
Social Work	10%	50%
Sociology	30%	25%
Psychology	5%	60%
Education	20%	40%
French	20%	45%
German	15%	30%
Italian	30%	30%
English	35%	30%
Classics	25%	40%
Philosophy	15%	40%
History	30%	45%
History of Art	15%	55%
Film & TV Studies	60%	30%
Theatre/Cultural Policy	30%	55%

WHAT IT'S REALLY LIKE

UNIVERSITY:	
Social Life	★★★
Societies	★★★★★
Student Union services	★★★★
Politics	**Activity high, whole spectrum**
Sport	**74 clubs**
National team position	**21st**
Sport facilities	★★★★★
Arts opportunities	**Drama, music, film, art excellent; dance good**
NSDF Drama Awards	**5 in 2010**
Student magazine	**The Word**
Student newspaper	**Warwick Boar**
Student radio	**RaW**
2010 Radio Awards	**1 Gold; 1 Bronze**
Student TV	**WTV**
Nightclub	**Venue**
Bars	**Terrace, Island, Graduate**
Union ents	**Top Banana, Score**
Union societies	**175**
Most popular society	**Cinema**
Parking	**None**
TOWN/CITY:	
Entertainment	★★★
Scene	**Local homely**
Town/gown relations	**Average**
Risk of violence	**Average**
Cost of living	**Average**
Student concessions	**Average**
Survival + 2 nights out	**£60 pw**
Part-time work campus/town	**Excellent/good**

'As a first year, the mere mention of a night out in Coventry may fill you with dread and terror. However, should you choose to dodge the bullets of the bright lights, it is possible to find satisfactory entertainment and lubrication, and so long as you don't run multi-million narcotic rings, spill pints of lager over shaven-headed locals called Bubba or start talking about astrophysics in Canley Working Men's Club, then there is every possibility that trouble will have a hard time locating you.'

PILLOW TALK

From top quality en-suite halls to basic single rooms, all study bedrooms have unmetered high-bandwidth connection to ISP services. Everyone

ACCOMMODATION

Student rating	★★★★★
Guarantee to freshers	**100%**
Style	**Halls, flats**
Security guard	**All**
Shared rooms	**Some halls**
Internet access	**All**
Self-catered	**All**
En suite	**Some**
Approx price range pw	**£76-£145**
City rent pw	**£70**

gets thrown out in their second year to live in Leamington Spa or Coventry. Leam is cheap, Cov even more so. If you can't handle a 20-minute bus ride each day, then Leam is not an option.

Write Jones and Wilding: 'Despite being a daunting 8 miles from the University, Leamington Spa is the more popular choice for students when cruelly hurled off campus in the second year. The main reason for this is, quite simply, that it isn't Coventry. A smallish town in Warwickshire it boasts a vast selection of pubs, fast food outlets and dirt cheap curry houses that more than make up for its distance from the Union. What more could you ask for? Free shuttle between town and Uni? Proper club scene? Lottery win? Now you're just being greedy.'

GETTING THERE

☞ By road: M1/J21, M69, A46; or M1/J17, M45, A45, or M40/J15, A46; or M5/J4a, M42/J6, A45.
☞ By rail: Birmingham New Street, 30 mins; Manchester Piccadilly, 2:30; Nottingham, 1:45; Bristol, 2:30; London Euston, 1:20.
☞ By air: Birmingham International Airport.
☞ By coach: London, 1:20; Leeds, 4:00.

UNIVERSITY OF WEST LONDON

The University of West London
St Mary's Road
London W5 5RF

TEL 020 8579 5000
FAX 020 8231 1353
EMAIL learning.advice@uwl.ac.uk
WEB www.uwl.ac.uk

West London Student Union
St Mary's Road
London W5 5RF

TEL 020 8231 2276
FAX 020 8231 2569
WEB www.westlondonsu.com

UNIVERSITY/STUDENT PROFILE	
University since	**1992**
Situation/style	**Civic**
Student population	**17110**
Total undergraduates	**15035**
Mature	**76%**
International	**17%**
Male/female ratio	**36:64**
Equality of opportunity:	
state school intake	**99%**
social class 4-7 intake	**49%**
drop-out rate	**17%**

VIRGIN VIEW

*T*he University of West London (the new name for Thames Valley University) received the highest increase of UCAS applications for any higher education institution in 2011. Formerly West London Poly and incorporating the Ealing School of Art, where Pete Townshend (the Who), Ronnie Wood (the Stones) and Freddie Mercury (Queen)... erm...studied, West London works with local colleges on access programmes, allowing successful completion of an access course as an alternative to usual entry requirements.

The University reaches out to all ages and backgrounds, so there is a large and welcoming student body, with many mature, part-time and ethnic minority students. They aim to be among the foremost universities in the UK for employer engagement.

Among current undergraduates, 67% are satisfeid with the teaching, and 72% will get a graduate-level job within six months of leaving.

CAMPUS

The main campus with Student Union in Ealing, West London, sits close to landscaped parks with restaurants, pubs and shops, and central London is but a short tube ride away. A new halls development, called Paragon, is located 1.5 miles south of the St Mary's Road campus in Ealing.

As Thames Valley University, West London was based on sites in Ealing and Slough, and at Reading and Brentford. Both Slough and Reading sites are set to close at the end of the 2010-11 academic year. However, a new teaching hub will then be opening close by the old Reading campus to enable the University to continue delivering its Nursing, Midwifery and Healthcare programmes, and some professional business qualifications will continue to be taught in Slough at The Centre on Farnham Road. Make of that what you will. It isn't clear what the nursing provision at Reading will mean to the Brentford campus, hitherto West London's Faculty of Health and Human Sciences, with its many nursing and midwifery students. This. the largest healthcare faculty in the UK, has 849 study bedrooms, 221 key worker flats and 12,000 sq.m of teaching/office accommodation.

FEES, BURSARIES

UK & EU Fees, 2011-12: £3,375 p.a. If your household income is assessed as below £40,000, you may be eligible for a TVU bursary of £530 or £1,060. Other educational support linked to subject areas may be available.

STUDENT PROFILE

'The most positive point to be made about West London concerns the diversity,' writes student Ian Draysey. 'Students of all ages come from all over the world, and studying there has given me the opportunity to meet people I never would have otherwise. The majority of universities make similar claims, but in this case it's true, honest!'

The student body is anything but like a traditional university. For a start most of the undergraduate population is part-time, 76% of it is mature and 17% come from overseas. Almost all are educated in the state system and some 49% come from the lowest socio-economic orders.

ACADEMIA & JOBS

There are three faculties: **Professional Studies**, (Business School, Law School, London School of Hospitality & Tourism, and the School of Computing & Technology); **Health & Human Sciences** (Psychology, Social Care & Human

TEACHING SURVEY AT A GLANCE	
Avg. UCAS points accepted	**180**
Acceptance rate	**21%**
Overall satisfaction rate	**67%**
Helpful/interested staff	**No data**
Small tuition groups	**No data**
Students into graduate jobs	**72%**

Teaching most popular with undergraduates:
Biological Sciences (88%).

Teaching least popular with undergraduates:
Drama (58%), Design Studies, Art & Design (57%),
Media Studies (48%), Film & Photography (38%).

Sciences, Nursing, Midwifery & Healthcare); and **The Arts** (London College of Music, School of Art & Design).

Business degrees include finance and accounting, business studies, and management, which ranges across airport management, hospitality and tourism, event management, international business management, and music management.

The nursing and healthcare provision is huge and includes mental health and midwifery and interesting degrees like Operating Department Practice. They sit within the same faculty as the very good psychology and social work degrees.

Built environment is another mainstay, as is engineering of course, and computing, which specialises in animation and games development.

There is also commercial law, criminology and foensic science.

Then you come to the media, communications and arts provision, public relations, journalism, broadcasting, web design, advertising, film, photography and digital media production. And among the arts there is acting, dance, fashion and textiles, music, musical theatre and theatre production.

This last comes out of a collaboration with the local Questors Theatre in Ealing, which has produced a number of new theatre courses, besides Theatre Production (Design and Management),

Music Management, Ballet Education, Music Performance and Recording, Popular Music Performance and Recording. There may be more.

The only feedback we can find from students about the teaching is that one area of the curriculum only achieved 85% or more of their approval for its teaching in the Government's national student survey 2010: Biological Sciences, which preumably includes psychology. They offer little else which traditionally falls under this umbrella. The latest Government research assessment rates the research element of their nursing and midwifery provision very highly: 40% of their work is either world class or of international significance.

Career planning and management, they say, is a high priority supported by means of the Career Management Skills module embedded in the curriculum, by job search workshops, employer led presentations and access to excellent and easily accessible careers information, advice and guidance. Graduates may avail themselves of this support for up to three years after graduation.

The graduate employment picture may be lowish - 65% get real graduate jobs within six months of leaving - but they are often feeding quite difficult areas.

After the nurses have flocked to the hospitals, West London's chief graduate output is in creative, arts and entertainment activities, and not far down the list sound recording, music publishing, film, TV and broadcasting. There also place plenty of teachers across primary, secondary and higher education (both psychology and the creative arts are suppliers here).

All this beside the hotel and hospitality jobs, achitectural and engineering jobs, social work placements which you would expect from their dedicated degree courses. Even air transport is a provider of jobs, which suggests that the Airline & Airport Management degree is well conceived and sourced and taught.

SOCIAL SCENE

STUDENTS' UNION **Freddies Bar** at Ealing opens

Monday to Friday, 12 am to 12 pm: a traditional pool table and juke-box scenario is supplemented by Bhangra music and Hindi films. Ents include live bands, karaoke, DJs and drinking competitions. The London College of Music hosts a dynamic programme of free events, including gigs and musical theatre shows, throughout the year for all students. Tube Radio, ambitiously aimed not just at students but at the wider community around Ealing, bene-fits from LCM's hardware. The magazine is now called *Edify* and it looks good. New societies this year include Women's Rugby Appreciation and Bollyarobics. Stalwarts are Art & Anima, Afro-Caribbean, and Badminton.

GETTING THERE
☛ Ealing: Ealing Broadway Underground (Central and District Lines).

UNIVERSITY OF WEST OF SCOTLAND

The University of West of Scotland
Paisley Campus
Paisley, PA1 2BE

TEL 0141 848 3000
or course enquiries 0800 027 1000
EMAIL uni-direct@uws.ac.uk
WEB www.uws.ac.uk

West of Scotland Students' Union
Paisley
Strathclyde PA1 2HB

TEL 0141 849 4157
FAX 020 7911 4158
EMAIL info@sauws.org.uk
WEB www.sauws.org.uk

VIRGIN VIEW

*O*n 1st August 2007, the University of Paisley and Bell College merged to create Scotland's biggest modern university with campuses in Ayr, Dumfries, Hamilton and Paisley.

Paisley University came out of Paisley Technical College, founded in 1897. In the same year as it became a fully fledged university (1995) it began its development into Nursing and Midwifery, a faculty largely to be found at its campus to the south, in Ayr - Robbie Burns country. The main university campus is in Paisley itself, the largest town in Scotland and just a mile or so from Glasgow airport. Only a few years old is a third campus, a joint venture with Glasgow Uni and Dumfries & Galloway College, on an 80-acre parkland site half a mile from the centre of Dumfries, which is many miles to the south, close to the Solway Firth.

Bell College in Hamilton was founded in 1972, its degrees validated by Strathclyde University in Glasgow up until now. It lies 11 miles south east of Glasgow.

West of Scotland is an international student community with strong links to business, industry and the public sector. The University encourages applications from under-represented groups, and as for selection criteria is 'keen to identify additional measurements of potential', additional to exam results that is.

Open Days, 2011: Ayr Campus, 1 November; Paisley Campus, 25 October; Hamilton Campus, 11 October; Dumfries Campus, TBC.

UNIVERSITY/STUDENT PROFILE	
University since	**2007**
Situation/style	**Campuses**
Student population	**17895**
Total undergraduates	**16145**
Mature	**68%**
International	**5%**
Male/female ratio	**36:64**
Equality of opportunity:	
state school intake	**99%**
social class 4-7 intake	**39%**
drop-out rate	**21%**

CAMPUS
PAISLEY CAMPUS takes getting to know: 'It would be really easy for a fresher, such as yourself, to mistake the main campus for a hospital wing in need of a cosmetic facelift,' writes Nausheen Rai. 'The "traditional" building has a blend of lino-type tiled floors, a supposed up-to-date glass "hamster" tunnel walkway (for fashion purposes darling), a surgical hospital smell that leaves one feeling oddly confused, and a brand new, £6-million, out-of-sync library with glass lift, plush pink carpets, novelty

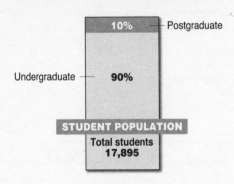

Postgraduate **10%**

Undergraduate — **90%**

STUDENT POPULATION

Total students
17,895

chairs and lots of space.'

AYR CAMPUS Tel 01292 886000. A new £70 million campus at Ayr is scheduled to open in September.

DUMFRIES CAMPUS Tel 01387 702060. It is situated beside the Crichton Business Park in eighty-five acres of parkland and gardens. A £1.8-million grant from the Scottish Funding Council is underwriting the development, which builds on franchise links which Paisley has had with Dumfries & Galloway College since 1994. The campus is an element in their open-access strategy, an attempt 'to widen the provision of higher education in the south west of Scotland.' It's worked.

HAMILTON CAMPUS Tel 01698 283100. This is the old Bell College, its higher education portfolio including business, accounting, law, journalism, sport (management, coaching, etc), social sciences, environmental sciences, engineering, product design, biosciences and computing. There is also a thriving further education provision.

FEES, BURSARIES
Fees for English, Welsh, Northern Irish: £1,820 p.a. For scholarships/bursaries, visit uws.ac.uk/finance. International students, see www.uws.ac.uk/international/scholarships.asp.

STUDENT PROFILE
Many students are local, mature and/or part-timers and almost exclusively come to West of Scotland from the state sector, flooding in from neighbourhoods which haven't traditionally supplied universities.

ACADEMIA & JOBS
UWS achieved 4* world-class research ratings in six academic areas in the 2008 Research Assessment Exercise - Allied Health Professions, Accounting &

Finance, Business & Management Studies, Social Work, Education, and Communications & Media - and an 'international excellence' in seven others, notably Metallurgy & Materials, Computer Science, Physics and Library & Information Management.

The taught Faculties are Education, Health and Social Sciences; Science and Technology; and Business and Creative Industries.

The University offers a wealth of programmes spanning the areas of Business; Creative Industries; Education; Social Sciences; Health, Nursing & Midwifery; Computing; Engineering; and Science.

All degree courses are designed with input from industry and commerce. Languages, IT training and work placements are key. IBM, M&S, BBC, Volkswagen, Standard Life and BAe all take Paisley undergrads on annual placements.

Guest lectures, workshops and seminars help students gain added insight into their degrees and future careers - serial entrepreneur Chris Gorman, of Channel 4's *Make Me A Million*, is an Honorary Professor of the University and has provided numerous workshops and seminars for students.

Students in media have benefited from insight from some of Scotland's stage and screen stars, including actor and director Peter Mullan. Also, representatives from Sony Computer Entertainment Europe have participated in student seminars, while motorsport students at the Hamilton campus have enjoyed workshops with rally and autosport experts.

The aim is to equip students with real-world skills through placement in industry. UWS students have worked with BT, Rolls-Royce, BBC, Channel, and IBM.

West of Scotland was the first UK university to gain accreditation with Cisco, Microsoft and Macromedia and became the first CIW-approved authorised training partner outside the US.

The University's Computer Games Technology degree is one of only two in the UK with full

TEACHING SURVEY AT A GLANCE

Avg. UCAS points accepted	**280**
Acceptance rate	**43%**
Overall satisfaction rate	**No data**
Helpful/interested staff	★★★
Small tuition groups	★★
Students into graduate jobs	**74%**

Teaching most popular with undergraduates:
No data.

Teaching least popular with undergraduates:
No data.

accreditation from Skillset, the industry standards body.

Their £1m cross-campus Employability Link offers advice on part-time and summer vacancies, voluntary work, graduate careers, work-based learning and placement.

Another boost to the degree portfolio recently has been the offer of a BSc Sports Studies, with its dedicated option routes. It's designed for students building on HNDs to degree level. Special focus areas are sports therapy, exercise, health and fitness, sports development, outdoor recreation administration.

Far and away the most jobs go to UWS students who graduate in health subjects, nursing, midwifery, etc. Then it's business, then biological sciences - the Applied Science degrees, Psychology, Sport BSc degrees, etc. These sectors are followed by Engineering (chemical, civil, mechanical, product design and technology), Computer (computer games, animation, etc.) and Social Studies (social work, etc.). Education turns out well of course too; almost all find their way into primary schools. Few from their many media course find it easy to get the wok they would like, but some do.

STUDENTS' UNION

STUDENTS' ASSOCIATION UPSA have been campaigning for a proper union building since 1971. Now, following a new SU at Ayr - café-style, chrome tables, Chesterfield sofas, very slick - they have one, a £5-million town centre HQ.

Hitherto they have held comedy and home-grown theme nights, karaoke, quizzes and talent contests.

Now they do much the same, but with **Big Bar** the venue - a massive hanger of a place - and *Salamander* returns with resident DJs Brad and Anthony as the official Friday night extravaganza. Monday is pub quiz, *Universally Challenged*; Tuesday is Karaoke; Wednesday is Games Nights. A trip the six miles into the centre of Glasgow is a regular alternative.

At Craigie there are two or three discos, a Saturday party, quizzes, karaoke, etc, and a popular live act Acoustic Night. In town there's the **Wulf & Whistle** and **O'Briens,** virtually union property by adoption, and three cheesy nightclubs with weekly student nights.

Hamilton entertains with a few pubs and clubs, a wide range of sports facilities, and cinemas, theatres and museums are available locally. At the Students' Union there's ents throughout the year; clubs and societies range from sport to political and cultural groups.

SPORT The Robertson Trust Sports Centre is located in the student village in Paisley and has had a £1.5-million facelift. Some 1,500 students are members. Recent improvements include turf pitches for rugby and soccer and floodlit synthetic pitches. There are also facilities for squash, multi-gym workouts, badminton, hockey, netball, tennis, basketball, volleyball and table tennis.

There's not much sport in Ayr. At Hamilton there's a fitness studio and Sportsbarn.

PILLOW TALK

In Ayr, halls of residence are on campus and accommodate 100 students. In Hamilton, all first year students are guaranteed a place. Purpose-built flats, next to the campus, accommodate 156.

Thornly Park, 2 miles from Paisley campus, accommodates 235 students, and a £13.6m student residences complex will be ready for September 2012. Underwood Residence accommodates 168 five minutes walk away. There are flats close to campus for 225.

ACCOMMODATION	
Student rating	★
Guarantee to freshers	**100%**
Style	**Halls, flats**
Security guard	**No**
Internet access	**Some**
Self-catered	**All**
En suite	**Some**
Approx price range pw	**£70**
City rent pw	**£45**

GETTING THERE

☞ By road to Paisley: M8 - M74, A726, A737. For Ayr, M77/A77. For Dumfries, A76 or A701 from the north; A75 from the south.
For Hamilton, M74/J6.
☞ By rail to Paisley: Ayr, 45 mins; Glasgow Central, 15 mins. Glasgow to London, 6:00. For Dumfries: Glasgow, 2:00; Ayr, 1:50. For Hamilton: London, 5:27; Edinburgh, 2:04.
☞ By air: Birmingham International Airport

UNIVERSITY OF WESTMINSTER

The University of Westminster
309 Regent Street
London W1B 2UW

TEL 020 7911 5000
FAX 020 7911 5788
EMAIL admissions@wmin.ac.uk
WEB www.westminster.ac.uk

Westminster Students' Union
32-38 Wells Street
London W1T 3UW

TEL 020 7911 5000 x 5454
FAX 020 7911 5793
EMAIL gensec@wmin.ac.uk
WEB www.uwsu.com

VIRGIN VIEW

*T*he *uni comes out of The Royal Polytechnic Institution, established in 1838 by (among others) Sir George Cayley, the North Yorkshire squire who invented the first man-powered flying machine, inveigling his unwilling butler to fly it solo down Brompton Dale, near Scarborough.*

Westminster suffers all sorts of drawbacks characteristic of a new university in the metropolis - split sites, low entry requirements/high non-traditional student intake/high drop-out rate. Their showing in the most recent Student Experience Survey was dire. They came last. Neither the teaching nor the social life cut the mustard.

In recent years they have been beautifing their London campuses, and there are clear pockets of energy (like in the student media, where once again they were national award winners), but people who come here have a plan and they want some good teaching. Nevertheless, when all is said, it is a fact that 70% of Westminster's graduates got real graduate jobs within 6 months of leaving last time, which is a telling statistic.

UNIVERSITY/STUDENT PROFILE	
University since	**1992**
Situation/style	**Campus & city sites**
Student population	**23160**
Total undergraduates	**16430**
Mature	**49%**
International	**24%**
Male/female ratio	**43:57**
Equality of opportunity:	
state school intake	**96%**
social class 4-7 intake	**44%**
drop-out rate	**12%**

CAMPUSES

REGENT CAMPUS (address above). **Faculties** on four neighbouring sites: *Regent Street* (Social & Behavioural Sciences, including Psychology, some Business courses), *Little Titchfield Street, Euston Centre* and *Wells Street* (Law and Languages). **Academic resources:** Self-Access Language Centre, libraries, IT suites. **Leisure facilities:** Sport and Fitness Centre with cardiovascular and resistance equipment, saunas, solaria and indoor games hall; **Deep End Café** (Regent Street). The gym is on the way out and a bigger social space is in the making.

CAVENDISH CAMPUS 115 New Cavendish Street, London W1M 6UW (use main phone number above). The campus is undergoing a £25-million development, the first phase of which is due for completion this summer. **Courses:** Biosciences, Computing, Health. **Academic resources:** computer suites, science labs, library. **Leisure facilities:** bar and refectory. Soon to be the home of The Hub, see *Social Scene*, below.

MARYLEBONE CAMPUS 35 Marylebone Road, London NW1 5LS (use main tel. above). **Faculties:** Westminster Business School, School of Architecture and the Built Environment. **Academic resources:** library and laboratory. **Leisure facilities:** bar and **Café West**. A new venue is the big new gift to students. See *Social Scene* below.

HARROW CAMPUS Watford Road, Northwick Park, Harrow HA1 3TP. Tel: 020 7911 5936; Fax: 020 7911 5943. **Style:** well-designed, self-contained campus, close to horrendous looking hospital. **Faculties:** Harrow Business School, Computer Science, Media, Arts & Design. **Academic resources:** Information Resources Centre, including library, computers (1,000+ campus-wide), AV aids for presentations; also TV, radio, photography and music studios. **Leisure facilities:** venue (**Area 51**), open-air performance court, **The Undercroft Bar**, sports hall, fitness suite and playing fields close by.

FEES, BURSARIES

UK & EU Fees, 2011-12: £3,375 p.a. If in receipt of a HE Maintenance Grant there's a bursary of £400. In addition, Westminster has a wide range of scholarships for both undergraduate and postgraduate students, for both UK/EU and international students.

STUDENT PROFILE

In its student clientele, Westminster mirrors many other ex-polys. There's a sizeable mature, part-time, local and overseas population – they received a Queen's Award for Enterprise for their success in International Markets, and were the first post-1992 uni to have been so rewarded.

There's also a significant non-degree student population, and many students are the first in their families to experience university – 44% are from new-to-uni social groups.

ACADEMIA & JOBS

In their vocational, modular course planning they have taken advice from the professions and industry, and translated it into a strategy underpinned by an expert language provision. Their School of Professional Language Studies lays claim to one of the widest range of language teaching in the UK - they are particularly strong on Asian Studies. Russian, Arabic and Chinese also feature.

There's a reputation for finding students work

TEACHING SURVEY AT A GLANCE

Avg. UCAS points accepted	**240**
Acceptance rate	**22%**
Overall satisfaction rate	**73%**
Helpful/interested staff	★★
Small tuition groups	★★
Students into graduate jobs	**70%**

Teaching most popular with undergraduates:
History, Tourism, Transport & Travel.

Teaching least popular with undergraduates:
Iberian Studies (63%), Management Studies (62%), Marketing (62%).

in those most difficult areas of art, design and media. Though it would be wrong to suggest that these jobs come in a flood, relative to most other unis they are areas in which Westminster enjoy success and have some very good courses.

In Art & Design they have graphic design, illustration, photography, animation, mixed media fine art and ceramics. In Communication/Design & Media they cover digital and photographic imaging, film and TV production, journalism, public relations, radio production, music informatics, and commercial music. The latter, for aspiring music industry managers, concerns music production, but also the business side, including the law. Strong industry links, good reputation in business management. You'll be based at the Harrow Campus. In the 2008 Research Assessment they had a spectacular result in media: 60% internationally significant, and 30% world class..

The majority of undergraduates read for degrees in business, many of them destined for jobs as accounts and wages clerks - at least in the first instance. Retail is a strength, as is marketing; there are dedicated degrees. See also their human resource business degrees, e-business, commercial law, etc, and the International degrees, making use of their excellent language provision. There are degrees in business at both central London and Harrow campuses, so be sure you know where you are destined.

In Law, they are commercial, business and European specialists, but with an interesting range of courses.

The computing provision is also strong and directs graduates along the clearest employment pathways: IT consultants, systems analysts, software engineers, analyst/programmers, etc.

There's enormous strength in architecture, town planning, and the building industry. The Architecture degrees are mostly technology, engineering, and there are BA degrees in Interior

RESEARCH EXCELLENCE

% of Westminster's research that is
4* (World-class) or 3* (Internationally rated):

	4*	3*
Community Clinical	10%	15%
Health Professions	10%	25%
Environmental Sciences	5%	30%
Computer Science	5%	20%
Electrical/Electronic Eng,	0%	15%
Built Environment	20%	40%
Town/Country Planning	5%	20%
Geography/Environment	10%	40%
Business/Management	5%	25%
Law	0%	35%
Politics	5%	15%
Psychology	0%	15%
Asian Studies	10%	20%
French	0%	25%
English	0%	20%
Linguistics	5%	5%
History	0%	15%
Art and Design	20%	55%
Media Studies	60%	30%
Music	10%	15%

WHAT IT'S REALLY LIKE

UNIVERSITY:	
Social Life	★
Societies	★
Student Union services	★
Politics	**Interest low**
Sport	**15 clubs**
National sporting position	**138th**
Sport facilities	★
Arts opportunities	**Drama excellent; film, music good; dance, art poor**
Student magazine	**The Smoke**
Radio Station	**Smoke Radio**
2010 Radio Awards	**Bronze**
TV station	**Smokescreen TV**
Nightclub	**Inter:Mission, Area 51**
Bars	**Dragon Bar, Undercroft**
Union ents	**r&b, bhangra, indie**
Union societies	**20**
Most popular society	**Law Soc, Dram Soc**
Parking	**Adequate**
CITY:	
Entertainment	★★★★★
City scene	**Wild, expensive**
Town/gown relations	**Average-good**
Risk of violence	**Average**
Cost of living	**Very high**
Student concessions	**Good**
Survival + 2 nights out	**£120 pw**
Part-time work campus/town	**Poor/excellent**

Design and Urban Design. See, too, the Construction, Surveying and Property degrees, Urban Estate Management.

Then there is the health provision, with a full-marks teaching assessment score for BSc Psychology with Neuroscience. Note there is a foundation course into this, and a sound reputation for employment. There are nutrition and health degrees, physiology and pharmacology, sport and exercise, and complementary medicine degrees - they were one of the first to offer these and have made them a success. Westminster also award the degrees of The British College of Osteopathic Medicine.

SOCIAL SCENE

The Uni has revamped its central London campuses. They've opened up a new venue, **Inter:Mission**, at the Marylebone campus (that's the one opposite Madame Tussauds) which is, well, white leather, mood lights, BOSE sound... alcoholic and alcohol-free sections, giant movable plasma screens and little TVs in every table.

This campus is envisaged as a major centre for the creative arts in London. **P3** is a vast new underground exhibition space. A 3-year programme of events, Ambika at P3, is bringing together artists, architects and creative practitioners from across the capital.

The gym at Regent Street has been replaced by a new social space there too. Meanwhile, at New Cavendish Street, they are creating **The Hub**, a kind of central social space for West End students.

Out at Harrow, the self-contained campus close to the station, students already have their infamous nightclub, **Area 51**, and a cosy little bar, The Undercroft, as well as their typical Student Union dive-in central, the Dragon Bar.

Typical ents are *Happy Mondays* at **Undercroft**, *Candy Floss* on Thursday at Inter:Mission, and *Baby Shake*, a pre-party for *Milkshake* at **Ministry of Sound** on Tuesday. Says Rob: 'We've got a pretty full schedule of events at all these bars and clubs, including club nights and live music nights. We cater for most tastes, with the hugely successful FONO playing indie. The Freshers and May Balls bring in some of the best performers in the country. But because we cater for so many international and non-drinking students, we also provide activities around London.

'We're battling against student apathy, because many students in our central campuses live at home and don't get involved. We've a huge number of different nationalities and races here, and we have to try and cater for so many different interests, it's a big job.'

Some of the best society activity comes out of course disciplines (media, music), and you can't help wondering whether, if they really got this aspect of student life together, they might whittle down the drop-out rate. Clearly, with all these new social spaces in the West End, that's what's in the mind of the uni, too.

The student media is excellent. Student newspaper *Smoke* has been up there at the national media awards in recent times, and in 2008 Smoke Radio won three Silvers and a Bronze, while in 2009 it took 2 Golds, and this year a Bronze award, while student station Smokescreen TV was nominated at the RTS Awards.

SPORT The uni is not known nationally for its sporting prowess, but their football and cricket teams are amongst the best in the local leagues, and the Ju-Jitsu team wins tournaments apparently.

PILLOW TALK

There are halls on Harrow and Marylebone campus and at some choice sites in London. Beaumont Court is 10 mins from Camden Town (standard en suite). Harrow Hall has self-contained units with own front door, lobby and en-suite facilities - standard or 'premium' shared en suite and double studio. Marylebone Hall has standard, recently refurbished (2008) rooms and 14 larger ones, all en suite. Alexander Fleming House in groovy Hoxton has 3 separate purpose-built low rise modern blocks offering good quality self-contained units with their own front door and lobby. International Hall is a 10-storey collection of 92 large and small rooms in Lambeth Road, close to tourist London (Houses of Parliament, London Eye, Tate Modern). Wigram House, a Victorian mansion block Ashley Gardens, Thirleby Road, near Victoria Station. Rooms surrounded by pods of bathrooms, showers and WCs, with kitchen on each floor.

ACCOMMODATION	
Student rating	★
Guarantee to freshers	**60%**
Style	**Halls, flats**
Security guard	**All**
Shared rooms	**Some**
Internet access	**All**
Self-catered	**All**
En suite	**No halls, all flats**
Approx price range pw	**£71.10-£188.70**
City rent pw	**£100+**

GETTING THERE

By Underground:
- ☛ Regent Campus: Oxford Circus station.
- ☛ Cavendish Campus: Warren Street station.
- ☛ Marylebone Campus: Baker Street station.
- ☛ Harrow Campus: Northwick Park station.

UNIVERSITY OF WINCHESTER

The University of Winchester
Winchester
Hampshire SO22 4NR

TEL 01962 827234
FAX 01962 827288
EMAIL course.enquiries@winchester.ac.uk
WEB www.winchester.ac.uk

Winchester University Students' Union
Winchester
Hampshire SO22 4NR

TEL 01962 827418
FAX 01962 827419
EMAIL SU_Pres@winchester.ac.uk
WEB www.winchesterstudents.co.uk/

VIRGIN VIEW

*F*ounded as a Diocesan teacher training establishment, and until recently King Alfred's College, a university sector college with a range of Southampton University degrees and a speciality in producing primary school teachers, they are now, since 2005, a university.

They always had ambitions to be something other than what they were, and tried various things to hasten the process. In 1994, for example, they took over the Basingstoke and Winchester School of Nursing and Midwifery and began developing all sorts of multi-disciplinary courses in Health Care. But you'll not find a student nurse or midwife closer than Southampton today. Then, in September 2003, a 'new' Basingstoke campus opened with 'new earn-

UNIVERSITY/STUDENT PROFILE	
University since	**2005**
Situation/style	**Campus**
Student population	**5905**
Total undergraduates	**4670**
Mature	**37%**
International	**5%**
Male/female ratio	**29:71**
Equality of opportunity:	
state school intake	**95%**
social class 4-7 intake	**35%**
drop-out rate	**8%**

while-you-learn Foundation Degrees', a feeder site for a future university, the perfect thing to satisfy the widening participation requirement of all universities.

Meanwhile, one or two unusual specialities were emerging, a course in

TEACHING SURVEY AT A GLANCE

Avg. UCAS points accepted	**260**
Acceptance rate	**19%**
Overall satisfaction rate	**79%**
Helpful/interested staff	★★★★
Small tuition groups	★★
Students into graduate jobs	**57%**

Teaching most popular with undergraduates:
Academic Studies in Education, American &
Australasian Studies, Archaeology, Dance,
English Studies, History, Imaginative Writing,
Social Work, Social Studies, Sports Sciencel.

Teaching least popular with undergraduates:
Media Studies (55%), Tourism, Transport
& Travel (42%).

Biopsychology, another in Archaeology
(taught by people actively involved on site
work), an East Asian Studies course with
Business Studies and BA hons combos with
Japanese. All but Archaeology disappeared
as magically as the nursing provision, but
teaching assessments, after years of scoring
18-21 points at best, suddenly returned
results of full marks for Archaeology and
Education, and 23 out of 24 for bedrock
Theology, and 22 points for Business and
Sport.

After all, that was the way to go, and,
following a swift baptism as University
College Winchester, Alfie moved with all
speed to achieve university status.

In 2008 Winchester climbed from 99th to
78th place in the Government's Research
Assessment, with 5% of its research, including 15% of its History research, getting the
highest, world-class, rating. At the same time
86% of its students told the National Student
Survey that they were satisfied with the
teaching, and in the Times Higher's Student
Experience Survey lecturers here were
praised for their helpful and interested
approach and for the size of their tuition
groups.

That is still the case. They came 26th in
the country in 2010, and although the overall
satisfaction rate has dipped to 79% in the
annual Government sponsored national student survey and the graduate job rate 6
months after leaving has slipped to 57%, this
is still the refrain.

Value added at Winchester is perceived
in terms of student experience (which did
take them to 38th position nationally in the
Times Higher Magazine's survey), in the
superb location of the campus grounds and
Winchester itself, and in the extra-curricular
student life (sports and societies).

They are looking for passion in their
applicants, passion for their subject and an
understanding of what studying at degree
level entails. Open Days: 7 May, 8, 15 and
22 October 2011, and 12 May 2012.

STUDENT PROFILE

There is a fair proportion of mature students
(37%), and the student body is overwhelmingly
female (71%), as you would expect from a uni
where many are studying to be primary school
teachers. There are also many part-timers and
locals. There is a kind of innocent cheery fun
about the place, but big fish may find it something of a small pond.

FEES, BURSARIES

UK & EU Fees, 2011-12: £3,375 p.a. There are bursaries for those eligible for the Government
Maintenance Grant, and ll UK domicile students
are eligible to receive the Winchester Scholarship, a
package of financial support specially designed to
put money in your pocket during your study here
at Winchester. All 4th-year BA Education undergraduates get a scholarship in recognition of the
extra costs compared with the three year and PGCE
qualified teacher status routes. There are also
Winchester Partner Colleges Scholarships, and the
King Alfred Scholarship for students under 25 at
entry who have been 'looked after' for at least 13
weeks since the age of 14 and who have left care.

CAMPUS

This is a campus university overlooking the historic

SUBJECT AREAS (%)

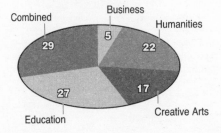

Combined 29
Business 5
Humanities 22
Creative Arts 17
Education 27

cathedral city of Winchester in Hampshire, 15 miles north of Southampton. It has its own theatre and dance studio, Student Union and student accommodation. It is quiet, picturesque and may prove to be a bit dull for some people

ACADEMIA

Today Winchester offers undergraduate courses in American Studies, Archaeology, English, Creative Writing, Dance, Drama, Education, Film, Heritage, History, Horticulture, Journalism, Leisure, Management, Marketing, Media, Performing Arts, Psychology, Religious Studies, Social Care, Sport, Teaching, Tourism. There is a feeder site in Basingstoke, where you can get on degrees via foundation courses.

History at Winchester performs particularly strongly. Fifteen per cent of research undertaken in this area is reckoned to be world class, 40% of international standing. Students are firmly behind the university's teaching. They rank Choreography and Dance top in the UK in the Government's National Student Survey; Education Studies comes second in the country; History, Sports Studies and Creative Writing are ranked in the top 10; and Business Management and English appear in the Top 20 nationally for student satisfaction.

Media and film courses at Winchester benefit from a link-up with the Asian Academy of Film and TV in the Bollywood city of Noida, near Delhi.

SOCIAL SCENE

STUDENT UNION The Union provides three bars - **Bar 22**, **The Lounge** and **C2H** (Close to Home). Ents include club nights (*Timewarp* or *Club Tropicana*), bar quizzes, comedy evenings, live music, promotions, multi-venue events and theme nights, plus society nights, like *Indie Three Sixty* recently from *BFLP* Magazine. Bigger occasions are the Winton Reunion Weekend (sporty), and the Freshers, Christmas, Summer and Graduation Balls which traditionally play host to top name acts in the **Guildhall**, 'a great venue, with a main hall and lots of smaller rooms with jazz, karaoke, live music and a casino.'

The Stripe Theatre is the performing arts space and film studio on campus, hosting live productions by students and visiting professionals. In town, it's the **Town Arts Centre** and **Theatre Royal** for everything from stand-up comedy to children's theatre, music and dance to plays.

There's a year-round welfare-themed campaign called Play Mates, various societies, from Alternative Music to Ultimate Frisbee, and a media group that is causing something of a stir with *Big Fish Little Pond* magazine and Voice Radio.

ACCOMMODATION	
Student rating	★★★★
Guarantee to freshers	**98%**
Style	**Halls, flats**
Security guard	**All**
Shared rooms	**Some halls**
Internet access	**All**
Self-catered	**Most**
En suite	**Some**
Approx price range pw	**£96-£140**
City rent pw	**£80-£100**

SPORT They play in the national student leagues, but are happier in the Southern England Student Sports Association (SESSA), and in SUSC, a collection of local universities. There are a rugby pitch and 2 football pitches a mile away; also a New Club House with bar. A sports hall hosts 5-a-side football, badminton, netball, hockey, volleyball, cricket, and is the home of the Knights and Angels Basketball teams. There are also 2 tennis courts (next to Alwyn Halls on campus), a squash court and fitness suite.

CITY There are nightclubs in nearby Eastleigh and Woodmancote, and 15 miles away in Southampton. Winchester itself is fairly barren, except for pubs, but watch out for squaddies from the barracks. In general, they don't appreciate students, 'unless served on a plate with chips,' writes Stephanie Kirk. 'I followed Drama, Theatre and Television Studies, and a small group of us worked with a day centre. Most of the people were homeless, or on a very low budget, some are ex-offenders, some drug addicts. None of them wanted anything to do with drama! It took us ten weeks to get a workshop up and running, but the course was so satisfying in the end.'

Winchester Passport is an optional, non-credit bearing certificate designed to recognise and reward students for carrying out extra-curricular activities that enhance employability skills.

PILLOW TALK

There are catered and self-catered halls on campus. Priority is given to students who live more than 25 miles away. West Downs Student Village is a few hundred metres away. On campus accommodation costs £3,556.00 - £5,042.10 on varying contracts of 40, 37, or 28 weeks. Queens Road Halls opened September 2010, 400 en-suite study rooms, arranged in flats with shared kitchen facilities. There is parking available on campus but limited spaces; permit required.

GETTING THERE

☛ By road: M3/J10; northwest, A272, B3041; southwest, A3090.
☛ By rail: London, 1:00; Bristol Parkway, 2:15;

Birmingham, 3:15; Southampton, 20 mins.
☛ By air: Gatwick, Heathrow, Southampton.
☛ By coach: London, 2:00; Birmingham, 5:30.

UNIVERSITY OF WOLVERHAMPTON

The University of Wolverhampton
Wolverhampton WV1 1LY

TEL 0800 953 3222 (course enquiries)
01902 321000 (general enquiries)
FAX 01902 32 2517
EMAIL enquiries@wlv.ac.uk
WEB www.wlv.ac.uk

Wolverhampton Students' Union
Wolverhampton WV1 1LY

TEL 01902 322021
FAX 01902 322020
EMAIL president@wlv.ac.uk
WEB www.wolvesunion.org

VIRGIN VIEW

The University of Wolverhampton was spawned by the Wolverhampton Poly following a merger with three teacher training colleges and West Midlands College of Higher Education. Operating on campus sites in and around Wolverhampton and in Shropshire, they have recruiting associations with dozens of colleges, and were the first to attract entrants via a high street shop.

Their students praise the good library, the helpful and interested staff, and the high-quality of the teaching, and they will be pleased to benefit from £700,000 which has just been spent on new IT resources. The University won an international platinum award for its 'high impact' use of technology in teaching at the IMS Learning Impact Awards.

There's 'outstanding' student support at Wolverhampton, according to the Government's Quality Assurance Agency, and graduate level employment comes to 72% of their students within 6 months of leaving.

UNIVERSITY/STUDENT PROFILE	
University since	**1992**
Situation/style	**Campus and city sites**
Student population	**21770**
Total undergraduates	**17915**
Mature	**52%**
International	**15%**
Male/female ratio	**40:60**
Equality of opportunity:	
state school intake	**99%**
social class 4-7 intake	**54%**
drop-out rate	**13%**

west of main campus. **Courses:** Business Admin, Info Management, some Human Resourcing, Marketing, some Computing.

WALSALL CAMPUS Gorway Road, Walsall WS1 3BD. **Location:** six miles east of town centre. **Campus scene: known as** 'the concrete jungle', but strong community spirit. **Courses:** Education (incl. Sports Studies). New this year 350 study bedrooms, all en-suite. A £7.1 million Sports and Judo Centre includes a full fitness suite, coffee bar and crËche, new tracks and all-weather pitches and the surrounding community will also have access to the facilities.

CAMPUSES

CITY CAMPUS Location: a few minutes walk from Wolverhampton rail and bus stations. **Campus scene:** the busy centre of it all. **Courses:** Applied Sciences, Art & Design, Computing, Construction, Engineering, Health Sciences, Languages, Humanities and Social Sciences, including Law.

COMPTON PARK CAMPUS Compton Road West, Wolverhampton WV3 9DY. **Location:** mile or so

SHROPSHIRE (TELFORD) CAMPUS Priorslee Hall, Shifnal Road Telford TF2 9NT. **Location:** 12 miles northwest of town. **Campus scene:** the International Students' Association thrives. **Courses:** Business, Computer-aided Product Design.

FEES, BURSARIES

UK & EU Fees, 2011-12: £3,375 p.a. There's a 'Start Right' bursary if eligible for HE Maintenance Grant.

See www.wlv.ac.uk/moneymatters or www.wlv.ac.uk/feechanges2012

STUDENT PROFILE

As many as 54% are from the lowest 4 social groups and many from families who have previously not considered uni an option. Perhaps that explains the persistently cheerful student scene at Wolverhampton, which was voted the friendliest university in the West Midlands via the Friends Reunited website.

More than 52% of its undergraduate intake is mature, a great number are part-timers, and the SU tells us that there is a high percentage of disabled students, too. There are certainly a number of very good special needs degree courses.

They are in that sense a modern university, playing an ambitious game. 'If there is any university with ambition, giving clear signs that it wants to play with academia's big boys, then Wolverhampton surely is the one,' said Mark Wilson. 'It may take a few years, but there is no doubt that it will get there. We are fortunate to have a 23,000-strong melting pot of cultures, skills, talents - sectors, like Lesbian, Gay & Bisexual (LGB), mature students or ethnic minorities, get people together and entertain them. It may take time to shake the wally poly stereotype, but the future is looking blinding from where I stand.'

> *'The best thing may be that they teach subjects that lead to jobs.'*

ACADEMIA & JOBS

'The teaching is particularly good for the vocational courses on which we focus,' says Mark. 'Lectures and seminars, but also film screenings, guest speakers, hands-on activities and group work with assessments. The best thing may be that they teach subjects which lead to jobs.'

SUBJECT AREAS (%)

Combined 6
Health Subjects 7
Creative Arts 17
Humanities 2
Engineering Science 12
3
1
8
Social Studies incl Law 32
Business 12
Maths & Computer
Built Environment

TEACHING SURVEY AT A GLANCE

Avg. UCAS points accepted	**180**
Acceptance rate	**23%**
Overall satisfaction rate	**78%**
Helpful/interested staff	★★★
Small tuition groups	★
Students into graduate jobs	**72%**

Teaching most popular with undergraduates:
Academic Studies in Education, Dance, English, Fine Art, Maths & Statistics, Music, Pharmacology, Toxicology & Pharmacy, Tourism, Transport & Travel.

Teaching least popular with undergraduates:
Architecture (61%), Film & Photography (60%).

The University recently reviewed all its undergraduate courses. The new structure includes the interesting but oddly named School of World & Sign Languages, which in fact includes Deaf Studies, English for International Business Communication, Interpreting, Linguistics, and Teaching English to Speakers of Other Languages. There has always been a niche in British Sign Language Interpreting at Wolverhampton.

The other schools are:

Applied Sciences: Biological sciences, Biomedical Science & Physiology; Pharmacy; Forensic science; Psychology. Education.

Law, Social Sciences & Communications: Criminology; English, Writing & Philosophy; History, Politics & War Studies; Law; Media & Film Studies; Social Sciences & Social Policy; World & Sign Languages.

Technology: Architecture; Computing; Construction; Engineering; Information Systems; Maths; Product Design; Technology.

Art & Design: Design & Applied Art; Digital Media; Fine Art; Photography & Visual Communication.

Health & Wellbeing: Nursing; Midwifery; Social Work; Other Health & Social Care Subjects.

Sport, Performing Arts & Leisure: Sport; Music; Drama & Dance; Leisure, Tourism & Hospitality.

The University continues to focus on graduate employment, with business links, collaborative working, and a specialist recruitment agency called

RESEARCH EXCELLENCE

% of Wolverhampton's research that is
4* (World-class) or 3* (Internationally rated):

	4*	3*
Health Professions	5%	15%
Mechanical, Aero. & Manufac. Eng.	5%	25%
Built Environment	10%	40%
Business/Management	0%	20%
Information Management	25%	40%
Law	0%	25%
Education	5%	15%
European Studies	0%	25%
Linguistics	15%	40%
History	5%	25%
Art and Design	10%	25%

The Workplace, which has a database of over 9,000 companies and where vacancies are advertised. Local, national and international positions covering all careers are on offer.

Wolverhampton also took the relationship between academia and industry to a new level by insisting that its teaching staff take part-time jobs in local industry under the aegis of 'staff development'. The deputy vice-chancellor said: 'Our staff already work in partner organisations. We have people working one day a week in the health service or people on secondments. We are now looking at joint appointments as well.'

Many courses are devised in consultation with businesses and the uni is committed to increasing the number of courses which offer accreditation or a licence to practice alongside a degree.

They have a £4.5-million Learning Centre - 967 study spaces, 130 IT spaces, 200,000 library volumes - following the opening of a similar centre in Shropshire.

A close association with industry in this high density industrial area, as well as commerce and the professions, gives confidence, and their employment record is good - 72% got graduate style jobs within 6 months of leaving last time.

Twenty per cent of graduates find their way into education, about as many primary as secondary teachers, and a number into higher education. Next most popular employments sector is health and social work (nursing degrees, health and social care, and social work). This is a big part of what Wolverhampton is about. Then it's the designers, business, law and other graduates into thriving local Midlands industry. But in fact, there is employment strength right through the curriculum, through biological sciences, engineering and

technology, computer science, construction, media.

Finally, there's a good reputation for Law. Non-Law graduates may opt for a 2-year full-time or 3-year part-time Senior Status Law Degree. Many law graduates from Wolverhampton find work immediately in the motor industry, public administration or in financial and insurance institutions.

SOCIAL SCENE

STUDENTS' UNION The Ambika Paul Student Union Centre has just opened at the Wolverhampton City Campus. It's got a cosy coffee bar area with plasma screens, a study zone with computers, meeting rooms and offices for the Student Union sabbatical officers.

For leisure it's **Fat Micks** (dance floor, food, pool tables, widescreen TV, 1,200 capacity, licensed till midnight and till 2 am Wednesday, Friday and Saturday), the **Poly Bar** (a pre-club comedy or light entertainment venue) and now they also have **Zone 34** (**The Zone**, as it's known), replacement for the JL nightclub, which is now the Student

WHAT IT'S REALLY LIKE

UNIVERSITY:

Social Life	★★
Societies	★
Student Union services	★
Politics	**Student issues**
Sport	**20+**
National team position	**88th**
Sport facilities	★★
Arts opportunities	**Music, art excellent; drama, dance good; film average**
Student magazine	**Cry Wolf**
Nightclub	**Zone 34**
Bars	**Fat Mick's, Poly Bar, Bertie's, Auntie Rita's**
Union ents	**Chart and cheese**
Union societies	**50**
Most popular societies	**Qur'an & Sunnah, Christian Union**
Parking	**Limited but free**

TOWN:

Entertainment	★★★
Scene	**Pubs, diverse studenty clubs**
Town/gown relations	**OK-ish**
Risk of violence	**Average**
Cost of living	**Low**
Student concessions	**Good**
Survival + 2 nights out	**£70 pw**
Part-time work campus/town	**Good**

Activities Hub. Yet, Tuesdays is student night in **Walkabout**, the new club in town - indie classics and alternative in main room, old skool in surfers paradise upstairs. Not until Wednesday does it warm up in the SU, when in parallel, at Fat Mick's and The Zone respectively, there's *Cut Loose* - indie, alternative, hip hop, soul, funk, and *BassSick* - RnB, hip hop, soul. Then Friday it's good old *Flirt!* - the student cliché that wows a nation - and Saturday, *FHUK* funky house.

There's much else besides, both in and out of the bars and clubs. Wolves has a strategy for developing an on-going programme of these to help students develop the skills they'll need. If you flip onto their web site you'll see the kind of helpful community this union is striving to create, whether it's revision classes, welfare or just plain fun.

At Telford, it's **Auntie Rita's** (capacity 250), licensed to 11 pm – 12 on Wednesday and Friday. **Berties Bar** (capacity 300) is on the third floor of Walsall Campus. Ents are theme nights, quizzes, movie nights, barbecues.

SPORT There are sports hall, squash courts, fitness centre at Wolverhampton; sports hall, playing fields, running track, swimming pool, dance studio, tennis courts at Walsall, where judo hopefuls for the 2012 Olympic Games are using the uni's National Judo Centre of Excellence. This is also home to the town's basketball national league team, and at Telford, there's a new sports centre.

TOWN Wolverhampton can be unnerving, but the SU supplies advice, information, attack alarms. Clubland is good. Cinemas include **The Light**

ACCOMMODATION	
Student rating	★★
Guarantee to freshers	**70%**
Style	**Halls**
Security guard	**All**
Shared rooms	**Some**
Internet access	**All**
Self-catered	**All**
En suite	**Some**
Approx price range pw	**£64-£95**
City rent pw	**£50**

House (mainstream/foreign); **Wolverhampton Art Gallery** for British and American Pop Art; the uni's own **Arena Theatre** for alternative, touring, student drama and music; the city's **Grand Theatre** for London shows.

PILLOW TALK

Allocation is on a first come first served basis. The average is approx 70% 1st years, 30% returners. There are around 2,000 places in halls, on or close to all campuses, more than half en suite. There's been no new accommodation since Walsall Student Village, which opened in 2005-6 Academic Year.

Car parking is provided free of charge at all sites, but there's a limited amount.

GETTING THERE
☛ By train: London Euston less than two hours;
☛ By road: M6/J10, M54/J2, M5/J2
☛ By coach: London, 4:00.

UNIVERSITY OF WORCESTER

The University of Worcester
Henwick Grove
Worcester WR2 6AJ

TEL 01905 855111
    01905 855141 (prospectus request)
FAX 01905 855377
EMAIL admissions@worc.ac.uk
WEB www.worcester.ac.uk

Worcester Student Union
Henwick Grove
Worcester WR2 6AJ

TEL 01905 543210
EMAIL studentsunion@worc.ac.uk
WEB www.worcsu.com/

VIRGIN VIEW

Worcester began as a teacher training college in 1946. In the '70s it became a college of higher education. In 1995 it merged with a college of nursing and mid-wifery, and in 2002 it was granted university college status, platform for their bid for full university status, which was secured in 2005.

Worcester University is the only Higher Education Institution in Herefordshire and Worcestershire, and has a largely female student body (71%), owing to the primary

UNIVERSITY/STUDENT PROFILE	
University since	**2005**
Situation/style	**Campus**
Student population	**8320**
Total undergraduates	**6665**
Mature	**56%**
International	**5%**
Male/female ratio	**29:71**
Equality of opportunity:	
state school intake	**97%**
social class 4-7 intake	**41%**
drop-out rate	**12%**

teacher training and nursing courses. It is not a place for the faint hearted. University of Worcester graduates, Joanne Yapp and Mel Berry, were rival rugby captains a few years back in the England and Wales Women's Six Nations clash. Sport is another of this uni's major preoccupations.

CAMPUS

Headquarters is a parkland campus within walking distance of the centre of this Cathedral city. On campus there's a new Digital Arts Centre, a Drama Studio, Sports Centre and Students' Union. Now, flush with a £10-million grant from the Government they have created an additional campus on a 5-acre site in the city, which will include a new library and Learning Centre, teaching and residential accommodation.

FEES, BURSARIES

UK & EU Fees, 2011-12: £3,375 p.a. Eligibility for the HE Maintenance Grant confers a bursary. Up to 50 academic achievement scholarships of £1,000 are available after the first year of study. The uni also works in partnership with Worcestershire County Cricket Club and the Worcester Wolves Basketball Club to award sports scholarships.

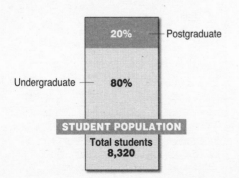

STUDENT POPULATION

Postgraduate — 20%

Undergraduate — 80%

Total students
8,320

STUDENT PROFILE

Many of the mainly female undergraduates are local and 56% are mature; a fair proportion (41%) are from the working classes and new to the idea of going to university

They have partnerships with colleges in the region, in order, they say, to widen participation further, though widening into the upper socio-economic and overseas groups might seem to be more the challenge.

ACADEMIA & JOBS

There' is a modular course structure and 6 academic departments: Applied Sciences, Geography & Archaeology; Arts, Humanities & Social Sciences; the Worcester Business School; Education; Health & Social Care; Sport & Exercise Science.

A large educational, nursing and sporting provision (their teams came 57th in the national BUCS

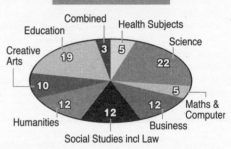

SUBJECT AREAS (%)

Combined 3 — Health Subjects 5
Education 19
Creative Arts
Science 22
10
5
12
12 — Maths & Computer
Humanities
12
Social Studies incl Law
Business

league last year, which is amazing for so small a university; there are a number of PE, coaching and sports science degrees), together with degrees in drama and social welfare, make for an employment record of use to the health and welfare of the community they serve.

For many years the teaching inspections picked out Education, then Sport and Nursing, Sociology, Art & Design, Business, Biosciences and Psychology for special praise. There is a BSc Psychology accredited by the British Psychological Society, first step to becoming a chartered psychologist.

In the Government's 2010 National Student Survey, 85% or more of the class said that the best teaching at Worcester is in English Studies, Geographical Studies, Human & Social Geography, Teacher Training, Nursing (96%), Social Studies, Sociology, Social Policy & Anthropology.

But only 68% of graduates found real graduate jobs within six months of leaving, which is not high

TEACHING SURVEY AT A GLANCE

Avg. UCAS points accepted	**240**
Acceptance rate	**22%**
Overall satisfaction rate	**77%**
Helpful/interested staff	★★★
Small tuition groups	★★
Students into graduate jobs	**68%**

Teaching most popular with undergraduates:
English Studies, Geographical Studies, Human &
Social Geography, Teacher Training,Nursing
(96%), Social Studies, Sociology,
Social Policy & Anthropology.

Teaching least popular with undergraduates:
Art & Design (55%).

where there is so strong a vocational line. Primary school teachers in particular, plus nursery, secondary and other teachers account for 30% of the graduate emplyment; then come the nurses from adult, child or mental health nursing degrees. The sport provision leads to some jobs in secondary education and other activities, physical training instructors, police, etc. Thos reading social studies find jobs in secondary and higher education, in various services to the community, or they work for the council and quite a number in shops. Given the number of business degrees, there is a poor showing in commerce. Graduates are scattered across a number of sectors, mostly retail.

Among their regional network of partner colleges, the following feed the uni with students on foundation degrees and HNDs: Evesham & Malvern Hills College, Halesowen College, Herefordshire College of Technology, Josiah Mason College, Kidderminster College, Pershore Group of Colleges, Stourbridge College, and Worcester College of Technology. Foundation degrees include Business in the Electronic Age, Commercial Web Development, Food Safety & Quality Management, Learning Support, and Adventure Tourism.

Writes Emma Aves. 'Worcester gains greatly from the sense of intimacy which its size brings, you feel truly part of the institution, one that supports you throughout your course. The onus is on you to balance your interests and ensure academic requirements are fulfilled, but a personal tutor system is available to all and helps to compensate for the formal nature of lectures.' They also have a Student Advice and Employment Bureau, and are active in work-related skills training of undergrads.

SOCIAL SCENE

STUDENTS' UNION There are decent ents in the Dive Bar, cheesy fare but also live and an active Alternative Music Society, which keeps people on their toes into the small hours. Birmingham is 45 mins to an hour away by train, with all its nighttime distractions.

'Activities such as RAG and Student Community Action are enthusiastically attended in order to establish that we are here for more than personal gain,' Emma continues. Indeed, English Student Sophie Nixon runs Kids Club in Dines Green, a local estate, and was recently presented with the Millennium Volunteer of the Year award for the West Midlands. With 15 other student volunteers, Sophie raised drama productions, discos, music lessons, arts & craft sessions, and organises trips out.

There are 33 clubs and societies at Worcester this year, from mountain boarding to the new dance soc. and Loco Show Co., the tried and tested musical theatre society. *The Voice* is the student newspaper, issued twice a semester.

SPORT There is a multi-million pound Sports Centre on campus and huge interest in sport, both through the sports courses and competitively across the board. They have all the traditional sports, and on, right through to Y'ai Chi. Worcester County Cricket Ground overlooks the River Severn – they list a Men's Cricket club only, odd that the women aren't interested. Worcester Rugby offers

WHAT IT'S REALLY LIKE

COLLEGE:	
Social Life	★★
Societies	★★
Student Union	★★
Sport	**Competitive**
National team position	**57th**
Sports facilities	★★★
Arts opportunities	**Excellent**
Student magazine	**The Voice**
Nightclub/bar	**The Dive Bar**
Union ents	**Cheese, live + balls**
Union clubs/societies	**33**
Parking	**Adequate**
CITY:	
Entertainment	★★
Scene	**Cathedral, arts, cricket, rugby, pubs**
Risk of violence	**Low**
Cost of living	**Average**
Student concessions	**Excellent**
Survival + 2 nights out	**£560 pw**
Part-time work campus/town	**Excellent**

ACCOMMODATION

Student rating	★★★
Guarantee to freshers	**100%**
Style	**Halls, flats**
Security guard	**Secure**
Shared rooms	**Some**
Internet access	**All**
Self-catered	**All**
En suite	**Some**
Approx price range pw	**£75-£127**
City rent pw	**£65**

premiership rugby, its ground at Sixways a Centre of Excellence. The uni's close association with the club provides exceptional facilities and expertise. TOWN Pubs and cheesy clubs predominate. Royal Worcester (porcelain) is their heritage, but the **Edward Elgar Birthplace Museum** points to another distinguishing mark, England's greatest composer. **The Swan Theatre** (for drama, comedy, dance) and **Huntingdon Hall** (seriously lively venue for jazz, folk, blues and classical), the **Odeon Film Centre**, the **Vue Cinema** complex, the **Worcester Arts Workshop**, and the recently reconstructed **Festival Theatre** at nearby Malvern complete the arts picture.

PILLOW TALK

Elizabeth Barrett Browning and A E Housman Halls were built on campus in 2009: up to £127 p.w. Avon and Ledbury halls are the economy alternative at £95 p.w., with Chandler at the bottom of the pile for £75.

Alternatively, there are two brand new halls 20 mins away in the city centre, Bishop Bosel and Chancellor Halls at £127 p.w. Sansome, opened September 2008, at £112. All en suite.

GETTING THERE

☛ By road: M5/J7.
☛ By rail: Birmingham, 60 mins; Cheltenham, 24 mins; Hereford, 40 mins.

UNIVERSITY OF YORK

The University of York
Heslington
York YO10 5DD

TEL 01904 324000
FAX 01904 433538
EMAIL ug-admissions@york.ac.uk
WEB www.york.ac.uk

Student Union
University of York
Heslington
York YO10 5DD

TEL 01904 433724
EMAIL few1@yusu.org
WEB www.yusu.org/

VIRGIN VIEW

Founded in 1963, York University is relatively small with a huge reputation for its teaching and is among the top Universities worldwide. British students are drawn fairly evenly from the Southeast, from the North and elsewhere.

The University was named University of the Year at the Times Higher Education *Awards 2011. It is also ranked 9th among UK universities in the magazine's Top 200 Universities in the World.*

Its academic strengths span a wide disciplinary range within the arts, social sciences and sciences, and attract students with high career ambitions.

It rose from 18th to 10th place nationally in the latest Government Research Assessment, and it came top in English Language and Literature, and in Health and Sociology it improved dramatically.

Whilst York offers perhaps fewer vocational programmes than some other universities, its graduates are highly sought after by employers. What's more, the university is

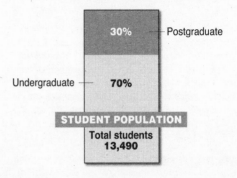

30% Postgraduate

Undergraduate — 70%

STUDENT POPULATION
Total students
13,490

very popular with its students, who are bright, fun-loving and notably unpretentious.

In the National Student Survey 86% said they were satisfied with the teaching, and in the Times Higher's *Student Experience Survey* their lecturers came out very well as helpful and interested in their students. Said a school careers adviser: 'York requires a lot from their students, but provides more for them in terms of contact than Warwick.'

Now they are expanding onto a new site - Heslington East - close to the

> **'York requires a lot from their students, but provides more for them in terms of contact than Warwick.'**

current campus on the outskirts of York. The oldest surviving human brain in Britain has been unearthed during excavations. A good omen.

They consider a wide range of qualifications for entry, and welcome applications from students with disabilities and non-tradi-

UNIVERSITY/STUDENT PROFILE	
University since	**1962**
Situation/style	**Campus**
Student population	**13490**
Total undergraduates	**9400**
Mature	**29%**
International	**22%**
Male/female ratio	**44:56**
Equality of opportunity:	
state school intake	**80%**
social class 4-7 intake	**22%**
drop-out rate	**3%**

tional or overseas qualifications. Their Access Scheme actively seeks out applicants who have faced social, personal or educational challenges which affected their performance in education.

Beyond grades, they say they are looking for 'well-rounded students, with a good academic background and willingness to make the most of their higher education experience'.

Applicants must demonstrate 'enthusiasm for reading around their subject' if they are to be successful. They want evidence of how any related work experience made an impression. They want to see that you are aware of

how the course you've chosen delivers the subject and fits with your own long-term aims. They want also to see a readiness and keenness to learn, and an ability to communicate all this in the personal statement or interview.

Open Days, 2011: 6 July, 1 October.

CAMPUS

It's a purpose-built campus at Heslington, on the south-east edge of the city: 'Very suburban, not at all monumental. It could get on the garden register,' mused Elaine Harwood of English Heritage. Student Gemma Thomas disagrees, 'Overall, the campus is a very pleasant place to live and along with York itself, one of the safest places. Heslington Hall, a gorgeous manor house on the edge of campus, provides an antidote to some of the bleaker aspects. It possesses extensive gardens, part of which, the Quiet Place, a collection of gigantic topiary knobs, is perfect for late-night games of hide-and-seek, or whatever else springs to mind.' The York Quakers, who were among those responsible for raising £70,000 for the Georgian gazebo and garden known as the Quiet Place will no doubt be pleased it is being put to such imaginative use. But, warns Gemma, 'Do NOT come here if you are anything less than tolerant of ducks. They are everywhere. On the lake, crossing paths, dive-bombing students wending their way to early morning lectures (or not).'

The university is a safe campus. Each college has a porter's lodge which is staffed 24/7. In the interests of ensuring a safe and secure environment, Security provide campus-wide patrols both on foot and in vehicles on a 24-hour basis.

Since the millennium, the University has added 20 buildings to the campus, and embarked on an ambitious £500m expansion on Heslington East. The first college, Goodricke College, moved there in 2009 - accommodation and social space for 640 students. The Departments of Computer Science, and Theatre, Film and Television, along with the York Law and Management Schools followed. Langwith College will be relocating in 2012.

FEES, BURSARIES

UK & EU fees, 2011-12: £3,375 p.a. There is a sliding-scale bursary for those in receipt of HE Maintenance Grant, according to parental income. Also available to some students on low income families is the York Annual Fund for students from

Yorkshire (£700). For students of Mathematics there is a £2,000 award. The Nigel Thompson Memorial Scholarships are for two students studying Economics (£3,000). There are scholarships too for high achieving Electronics students and sponsorship for students of chemistry. www.york.ac.uk/admin/uao/ugrad/money/bursaries.htm.

STUDENT PROFILE

'After ducks, students form the most numerous campus species,' Gemma continues. 'No one type dominates, the balance between state and private sectors a surprise bonus in a university with this much prestige. York is a small, friendly, unpretentious university, which makes it incredibly easy to settle in.'

ACADEMIA & JOBS

York places equal emphasis on research and teaching. Ranked in the top ten for research in the Governmen's Assessment Exercise, they excel too as teachers. In the 2011 *Times Higher* Student Experience Survey, students voted York fifth in the country for helpfulness and interest.

Some 30 departments teach a range of subjects in the arts, social sciences, sciences and technology. The University also offers a degree in Medicine through the Hull York Medical School.

The launch of the Hull York Medical School in 2003 has been a great success. They offer a 5-year BMBS (Bachelor of Medicine, Bachelor of Surgery). You may be based at either Hull University campus (see entry) or York; all follow the same curriculum. Hull has a decade's experience in Medicine through its Postgraduate Medical School, while York's Biosciences and Health departments are top rated for teaching and research. There is now also a Mother and Infant Research Unit at York.

An equal emphasis on physical, psychological and social aspects marks the Medicine syllabus. You will need A Level Biology and Chemistry, and they don't accept General Studies at A2 or AS, or Critical Thinking at A-Level. The UKCAT test is also required, and caring experience and interpersonal skills are significant.

Students say that the best teaching generally is in Academic Studies in Education, Archaeology, Biology & related sciences, Chemistry, Computer, Electronic & Electrical Engineeering, Engineering & Technology, English, European Languages & Area Studies, History, Linguistics, Maths, Molecular Biology, Philosophy, Physics & Astronomy, Psychology, Sociology, Social Policy & Anthropology. They recorded no bad teaching at all.

A wide range of employers visit the campus recruiting York graduates, and the University encourages students to equip themselves with the skills to be successful in future life and work through such as the York Award, which gives

RESEARCH EXCELLENCE

% of York's research that is
4* *(World-class)* or **3*** *(Internationally rated)*:

	4*	3*
Epidemiology	**0%**	**30%**
Health Services	**35%**	**40%**
Nursing/Midwifery	**35%**	**35%**
Biological Sciences	**25%**	**35%**
Environmental Sciences	**10%**	**50%**
Chemistry	**15%**	**60%**
Physics	**15%**	**40%**
Pure Mathematics	**10%**	**35%**
Applied Mathematics	**10%**	**40%**
Computer Science	**25%**	**50%**
Electrical/Electronic Eng.	**10%**	**45%**
Archaeology	**25%**	**35%**
Economics	**15%**	**45%**
Business/Management	**10%**	**40%**
Politics	**15%**	**30%**
Social Work	**25%**	**40%**
Sociology	**30%**	**30%**
Psychology	**20%**	**45%**
Education	**15%**	**45%**
English	**45%**	**30%**
Linguistics	**20%**	**45%**
Philosophy	**15%**	**40%**
History	**25%**	**30%**
History of Art	**45%**	**25%**
Music	**50%**	**25%**

recognition for extra-curricular activities, voluntary work and experiential learning.

SOCIAL SCENE

There are eight Colleges, seven for undergraduates and one for graduates. Each has its own Junior Common Room (JCR) Committee, who coordinate weekly and two or three big annual events. The Student Union organises up to 5 large-scale club nights or other events per term.

Although students give the union only 1 star, the point about York is the interest and activity levels beyond mere ents. 'Students get involved,' said Helen Woolnough. They do it themselves. 'The university has an excellent academic reputation, but its students don't work themselves into the ground twenty-four hours a day and they certainly don't take themselves too seriously.'

Student media: University Radio York (URY), launched by John Peel thirty years ago and now with fm licence, York Television (YSTV), and two fortnightly newspapers, *Nouse* (pronounced 'Nooze' after the River Ouse, which flows through York, and of course 'news', which is what it dispenses) and *York Vision*. Other publications appear occasionally - *Point Shirley*, a literary arts magazine; *PS...*, an arts review; *Havoc*, a miscellany of creative writing; *Matrix*, a women's issue paper; Christis, a Christian magazine, and Mad Alice, an on-line features magazine.

They win awards by the basket-full, but recently for a while it seemed they were picking up only runners-up awards. Then the real stuff came through: Feature Writer of the Year, Best Live TV, and for URY a Gold and two Bronze awards, and a Creativity Award. In 2009 they won Website of the Year, and URY took 2 Golds and a Bronze. In 2010 they picked up 2 Silvers for the radio station.

At the National Student Drama Festival in 2009, awards came just as thick and fast for the Drama Society's production of Metamorphosis: Stage Director of the Year, Best Actor, Lighting, Ensemble, and for Promoting Student Theatre.

Among some 90 societies there are 8 active drama societies with three venues, the intimate Drama Barn, the large and versatile Wentworth College Audio Visual Studio and the aforementioned Central Hall, which is huge.

There is a tradition too of political activity and a left-wing stance.

SPORT For such a small uni they do well at sport, and recently have leapt up the BUCS teams league table to 44th position. Plans for a new Sports Village have now been approved, which will see a competition-standard eight lane 25 metre pool,

learner pool, 100 station gym, full size 3G astroturf pitch and three further five-a-side pitches, opening in July 2012.

The Boat Club goes to Henley Royal Regatta, the Lacrosse team to the world championships, basketball is a bit a speciality and they have the best parachutists in the country apparently. There are forty acres of playing fields – rugby, football, hockey, cricket – floodlit artificial hockey pitch, all-weather (three floodlit) tennis courts, squash courts, a sports centre for archery, badminton (seven courts), basketball, climbing, cricket (five nets), fencing, five-a-side soccer, judo, karate, netball, sauna, table-tennis, tennis, trampoline, volleyball, a 400-metre, seven-lane athletics track.

Rowing and sailing are on the Ouse about a mile from the University, golf at Fulford Golf Club, swimming at the Barbican Centre half a mile from

WHAT IT'S REALLY LIKE	
UNIVERSITY:	
Social Life	★★★★
Societies	★★★★
Student Union services	★★
Politics	**Activity high Student and world issues**
Sport	**50 clubs**
National team position	**44th**
Sport facilities	★★
Arts opportunities	**Drama, film excellent; dance, music, art avg**
Student newspapers	**Nouse, York Vision**
Guardian Awards 2009	**Website award**
Student radio station	**URY**
Radio Awards 2009	**2 Golds; Bronze**
Radio Awards 2010	**2 Silver**
Student TV	**YSTV**
Nightclub	**College-based only**
Bars	**1 in every college**
Union ents	**Club D, House Trained, Cooker, Dust**
Union societies	**140**
Most popular societies	**Media, Drama**
Smoking policy	**Bars, halls OK**
Parking	**Non-existent**
CITY:	
Entertainment	★★★
City scene	**Tourist haven**
Town/gown relations	**Good**
Risk of violence	**Low**
Cost of living	**Average**
Student concessions	**Good**
Survival + 2 nights out	**£70 pw**
Part-time work campus/town	**Excellent/good**

ACCOMMODATION

Student rating	★★★★
Guarantee to freshers	**100%**
Style	**Halls**
Security guard	**Porters, patrols**
Shared rooms	**Some**
Internet access	**All**
Self-catered	**Can choose**
En suite	**Some**
Approx price range pw	**£81-£112**
City rent pw	**£75-£80**

Whop-Ma-Gate, and in the snickleways which offer those in the know an alternative way to scuttle about. Then there are the waters of the Ouse, lapping over green-field banks or warehouse walls, redolent of the city's merchant past.

It is, however, far from being the clubbing capital of the North. If you are a hardened clubber, take a 20-minute ride to Leeds.

For theatre, there's the **Arts Centre** and the **Theatre Royal** (good rep), and the **Grand Opera** has a full programme of touring companies. There's a multi-screen **Warner's** cinema out at Clifton Moor Estate (on the north side of the city), **Odeon** and independent **City Screen** in York, as well as **York Student Cinema** on campus.

PILLOW TALK
None of the Colleges is a teaching college. they are all really glorified halls.

GETTING THERE
☞ By road: A1237 ring road; Heslington is on the southeast side, 10 miles from A1/M1; 20 from M62.
☞ By coach: London, 4:30; Edinburgh, 5:15.
☞ By rail: Leeds, 20 mins; Sheffield, 1:15; Manchester, 1:30; London King's Cross, 2:00.
☞ By air: Nearest airport is Leeds Bradford.

campus. Gliding, hang-gliding, riding and other facilities also found locally.

Highlight of the year - both socially and sportswise is The Rose, when the white rose of York meets the red rose of Lancaster in sporting competition and two days of wild socialising that takes over the entire campus in May.

Town York itself is one of our most beautiful cathedral cities, a magnet for tourists from all over the world owing to the wealth of Viking and Roman remains, as well as its mediaeval resonances in the Minster, in streets like the Shambles (where buildings lean inwards and over you as if out of a fairytale), in street names like Whip-Ma-

YORK ST JOHN UNIVERSITY

York St John University College
Lord Mayor's Walk
York YO31 7EX

TEL 01904 624624
FAX 01904 612512
EMAIL admissions@yorksj.ac.uk
WEB www.yorksj.ac.uk

York St John Students' Union
Cordukes Building
York YO31 7EX

TEL 01904 629816
FAX 01904 620559
EMAIL su@yorksj.ac.uk
WEB www.ysjsu.com/

VIRGIN VIEW

*F*ounded by the Anglican Church in 1841 as a teacher training college, York St John now offers very much more.

In February, 2006, it was granted University College status and the power to award its own degrees, and on October 1 that year, full university status.

It is lucky to have Dr John Sentamu, Archbishop of York and the most acute mind in the Church of England, as its first

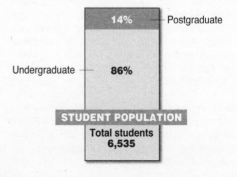

Postgraduate — 14%

Undergraduate — 86%

STUDENT POPULATION
Total students
6,535

Chancellor.

It is appropriate that a university that has risen to prominence partly on a reputation for pastoral care should have made the invitation.

York St John have grasped their new status with both hands. There is a freshness and a buzz about the place. Major investments in recent years includes a library and sports facilities, a Design Centre and a Creative Arts Centre. The new £15-million De Grey Court is for Occupational Therapy and Physiotherapy.

CAMPUS

UNIVERSITY/STUDENT PROFILE	
University since	**2006**
Situation/style	**Campus**
Student population	**6535**
Total undergraduates	**5590**
Mature	**40%**
International	**3%**
Male/female ratio	**31:69**
Equality of opportunity:	
state school intake	**94%**
social class 4-7 intake	**33%**
drop-out rate	**8%**

The college is situated close to York Minster on a very attractive, newly re-vamped campus on this ancient site. The only worry is that there is nowhere for it to expand, as expand it surely must, in its present city-tight location.

FEES, BURSARIES

UK & EU Fees, 2011-12: £3,375 There is a bursary: £540-£1,610 on a sliding scale according to household income, plus scholarships of £500 a year principally to alleviate financial hardship.

STUDENT PROFILE

This is a small, largely feminine student body, some 6,000 students, of which 69% are female. Some 20% are mature students, and a quarter of undergraduates are part-timers. Some 94% are recruited from the state sector, 3% more than demanded of them by the government, and 33% come from socio-economic backgrounds not traditionally drawn to university. In comparison, York University is positively rah: only 80% from state schools and 22% from the working classes.

TEACHING SURVEY AT A GLANCE	
Avg. UCAS points accepted	**270**
Acceptance rate	**18%**
Overall satisfaction rate	**81%**
Helpful/interested staff	★★★★
Small tuition groups	★★★
Students into graduate jobs	**61%**

Teaching most popular with undergraduates:
Anatomy, Physiology & Pathology (95%), Dance, English Studies, History, Initial Teacher Training, Management Studies, Subjects allied to Medicine, Psychology, Sports Science, Theology.

Teaching least popular with undergraduates:
Film & Photography (57%), Communications, Fine Art (56%), Design (55%), Media (52%).

ACADEMIA & JOBS

There are four faculties. Arts incorporates performance, film and television, literature, media, history, American studies and art and design. They are known for film. In February 2007 at City Screen two films by York St John student crews took the first BAFTA North event by storm, though this year and last the Gocernment's National Student Survey found only 56% of the class approved the teaching of film, which is quite a drubbing.

Nevertheless, 'Performing arts, the therapies, Counselling Studies, and Linguistics I have heard very good reports about,' said one careers teacher. 'We had someone with straight A grades, could have gone anywhere, but chose York St John.'

In the Faculty of Education & Theology there's Teacher Education, Education Studies, Theology and Religious Studies, Theology and Ministry and Evangelism Studies. It is tempting to say that this is what attracted Sentamu, but he is as relaxed in the company of businessmen as he is clerics, which brings us to the third faculty: Business and Communication, which reflects the balance of the Archbishop with counselling and languages as well as business management and communication.

Finally, in Health & Life Sciences they have Professional Health Studies and Sports Science and Psychology. If you want a career in personal training, exercise instruction and referral, new in Sport Science is Exercise Practitioner BSc (Hons), endorsed by the British Association for Sport and Exercise Sciences. Health degrees include Occupational Therapy BHSc and Physiotherapy BHSc. The BSc Psychology Specialist programme is the first step towards registration as a Chartered Psychologist.

In December 2008 the uni opened its new £15-

UNIVERSITY:	
Social Life	★★
Societies	★★★
Student Union services	★★
Politics	**Aware**
Sport	**18 clubs**
National team position	**91st**
Sport facilities	★★
Arts opportunities	**Plenty**
Student magazine	**Messenger**
Bar	**Archies**
Union ents	**Theme nights**
Union societies	**18**
Most popular societies	**Big Band**
Parking	**Limited. Patrolled**
CITY:	
Entertainment	★★★
City scene	**Tourist haven**
Town/gown relations	**Good**
Risk of violence	**Low**
Cost of living	**Average**
Student concessions	**Good**
Survival + 2 nights out	**£70 pw**
Part-time work campus/town	**Excellent/good**

They have a newspaper, *The Messenger*, and a growing number of good societies, from Drama to Dance and Big Band. With degrees in counselling, welfare is to the fore and the Education & Welfare Committee is one of the strongest in the union.

Just how even-handed are the students round here that when a controversy over the girlie Netball Calendar raged early in 2007 following a complaint to the Union's Women's Officer and then to the *Saint*, the complainant was invited to present her case to the Union Council, as well as representatives from the Netball Club. After the council had heard both sides of the story, a compromise was decided upon that advertising of the calendar would be text-only, limiting viewing of the photos to those who want to see it. Both parties exited content and the point of the calendar - to raise money for (appropriately) Breast Cancer Research - was achieved.

PILLOW TALK

Accommodation is on campus and on other city sites. Broadly, you can choose between catered, self-catered and en-suite halls and flats. Ninety-three per cent of freshers can be accommodated.

Percy's Lane opened in 2008: self-catered, en-suite accommodation for 272 students. Gray's

million De Grey Court building, situated on the corner of Lord Mayor's Walk and Clarence Street, and housing new facilities for Physiotherapy and Occupational Therapy.

A new degree, Children, Young People & Families BA (Hons) aims to meet the needs of students aiming to work in the fast developing field of child welfare.

The Student Counselling Network employs a team of qualified and experienced counsellors for student use. It is just one example of healthy cross-fertilisation between academia and the real world.

Every undergraduate programme has employment skills integrated into it.

SOCIAL SCENE

There is a bar with conservatory within the main hub of the Students' Union, and a programme of discos, live music, balls in summer and at Christmas. Also a coffee bar, a shop and The Crunch Bar, which is uni owned. Doesn't sound much, but this is a lively enough scene.

Happy Hours, pound a pint nights, Bar Footsie nights, live premiership matches, quiz machines, pool tables, table football, themed nights, quiz nights, acoustic nights are *de rigueur*. Saturdays you can get slewed all day for £1 pint and doubles-for-singles.

ACCOMMODATION	
Student rating	★★
Guarantee to freshers	**93%**
Style	**Halls, flats**
Security guard	**Most halls, all flats patrol**
Shared rooms	**None**
Internet access	**All**
Self-catered	**Most**
En suite	**Some**
Approx price range pw	**£74.50-£129**
City rent pw	**£75-£80**

Wharf will open in September 2010: 235 bedrooms. Internet access is available from all bedrooms. A high level of security is provided by controlled access to all entrances and CCTV cameras linked to a 24-hour security office at Lord Mayor's Walk. The accommodation is situated inside the city's historic walls, 15 minutes walk to York St John's main campus and 5 minutes from the city centre.

GETTING THERE

☛ By Road A1 into central York. Otherwise, see York University information.